# A Checklist of Canadian Literature and Background Materials 1628-1960

A CHECKLIST OF

# Canadian Literature

AND BACKGROUND MATERIALS

1628-1960

In two parts: first, a comprehensive list of the books which constitute Canadian literature written in English; and second, a selective list of other books by Canadian authors which reveal the backgrounds of that literature

Second edition, revised and enlarged

REGINALD EYRE WATTERS
The Royal Military College of Canada

UNIVERSITY OF TORONTO PRESS

First edition 1959

Reprinted 1960, 1966
Second edition 1972

Reprinted in 2018
Toronto and Buffalo

Printed in Canada

ISBN 0-8020-1866-1
ISBN 978-1-4875-7307-2 (paper)
Microfiche ISBN 0-8020-0197-1
LC 72-80713

To the memory of
Professor A.S.P. Woodhouse
1895-1964
Teacher, colleague, friend

# FOREWORD TO THE FIRST EDITION

When the Humanities Research Council of Canada received its first grant from the Rockefeller Foundation, it determined to put a part of its funds into an effort to foster comparative studies of culture and letters in Canada and other members of the British Commonwealth, and first of Australia, in the belief that a comparison of what happened to the British tradition when set down on two such different frontiers could hardly fail to yield interesting results. It was soon discovered, however, that while Australia had Edmund Miller's bibliography, *Australian Literature,* Canada lacked a comparable instrument of research altogether; and the Council decided that before any effective work could be done a checklist of English-Canadian writings must be provided. Accordingly, it invited Dr. R.E. Watters of the University of British Columbia to undertake the task. Though the Council was able to promise no more than the defraying of actual expenses, and could not even guarantee publication of his results, he heroically undertook the task, which he has now brought to completion. As Dr. Watters explains in his preface, he has conformed to the desires of the Council and has produced a work differing in scope and character from Miller's *Australian Literature* in two respects. It casts a wider net by going beyond belles-lettres to include a selection of writings illustrating historical and social background. It makes no attempt to record full bibliographical detail, but is frankly a checklist of Canadian writings in English from the beginning to 1950, designed to furnish a starting point for, and to give practical aid to, further research.

It was the hope of the Council that the study of Canadian culture and letters would itself benefit greatly from the plan of comparative examination; and even from this preliminary effort the benefit to Canadian studies will be immense: for Dr. Watters' work is the indispensable instrument for further exploration in the Canadian field, and for the writing of the literary history of Canada now being planned.

On behalf of the Humanities Research Council, I would express gratitude to Dr. Watters for his devoted labours, to the Rockfeller Foundation for the support that has made these labours possible, and to the University of Toronto Press for its very generous grant in aid of publication.

A.S.P. WOODHOUSE
*Chairman, Humanities Research Council of Canada*

*University College*
*Toronto*
*9 October 1958*

# PREFACE

This revised and enlarged *Checklist of Canadian Literature* attempts to provide as complete a record as possible of the separately published works that constitute the literature of English-speaking Canada up to 1960. Its purpose is to stimulate interest and suggest research in our literary culture, to reveal individual figures and areas of investigation rich in published material, and to facilitate the finding of the books concerned. Background materials are included because the cultural soil must be known if a nation's belles-lettres are to be adequately studied or fully appreciated.

Part I of the *Checklist* attempts to record all known titles in the recognized forms of poetry, fiction, and drama that were produced by English-speaking Canadians.[1] The titles and accompanying information had to be obtained from the entries of the various library catalogues searched, and not from actual examination of the books themselves. Therefore, no attempt whatever was made to apply any qualitative evaluation of these writings. The *Checklist* is simply an inventory of what Canadians are known to have published, together with some locations where the publications can be found. Separation of the bad from the excellent, the trivial from the important, can come only from those who carefully examine and appraise the books listed here. It is to be hoped that among the thousands of forgotten or overlooked books many more of significant worth may be found to exist than Canadians at present may expect.

Part II of the *Checklist* does not aim at the same completeness. It is a more or less selective listing of books by Canadians which seem likely to be of value to anyone studying the literature or culture of Canada. Here are included books in such categories as biography, literary criticism, scholarship, local history, religion, and so forth. Books in more general categories with less immediate relationship to literature – such as military, economic, or constitutional history, and writings in law, commerce, or the sciences – have been omitted.

The inadequacies of Part II, in both the original (1959) edition and this revision, are readily acknowledged. I had hoped – too optimistically, it is true – that during the dozen years following the first appearance of the *Checklist* properly qualified persons would have produced checklists or bibliographies in the various categories of Part II, and thereby rendered unnecessary the entire section. Although this has not yet happened, excellent beginnings have been made. Raymond Tanghe's *Bibliography of Canadian Bibliographies* (1960), together with its *Supplements* and the second edition edited by Douglas Lochhead (1972) – not to mention *On Canadian Literature 1806–1960* (1966), co-authored by the present compiler and Inglis Freeman Bell – make unnecessary the retention of a "Bibliography" section in

[1] The title of earliest date is *Quodlibets Lately Come Over from New Britaniola, Old NewFound-Land. ...* This is a collection of epigrams and verses by Robert Hayman, printed in London in 1628.

this revision. Similarly, the "Education" section has been dropped because of the appearance of such works as *A Bibliography of Higher Education in Canada* (1960) by Robin Harris and Arthur Tremblay, with its supplements (1965, 1971). Eventually, if not quite yet, the multiplication of such works as Bruce Peel's *A Bibliography of the Prairie Provinces to 1953* (1956), *Supplement* (1963), William F.E. Morley's *The Atlantic Provinces* (1967), and André Beaulieu's *La Province de Québec* (1971), written in collaboration with Benoit Bernier and Agathe Garon – the first three volumes of a projected series of bibliographies of Canadian local histories – may also render superfluous the "Local History" section of the present *Checklist.* Meanwhile, literary scholars awaiting more of such specialized compilations may perhaps still find useful the material provided here in Part II. (The "Miscellaneous" section of the original edition has also been eliminated. Enough information was found about each title to permit it to be either re-classified or dropped as irrelevant to the intention of the *Checklist*.)

To the best of my knowledge, all of the approximately 16,000 books[2] listed in both parts of the *Checklist* are by Canadian authors, some 7,000 of whom are represented here. The definition of "Canadian author" was, however, deliberately left very broad. In dealing with thousands of authors it seemed wiser to include persons whose claims might be rather weak than to attempt an impracticable strictness. Decisions based on place of birth, length of residence in Canada, whether certain books were written in or out of Canada, or reflected early Canadian environment, and so on, may be very appealing in theory, but their application poses staggering problems. The extreme difficulty of discovering enough biographical or other information – even dates of birth or death – about authors of limited production or small reputation to make such decisions possible can be appreciated only when it is experienced. Of course, the great majority of the authors listed could, if required, conform to stringent definitions. However, it should be understood that Canadian birth alone was not considered a sufficient claim for persons who left Canada in early childhood and apparently never returned. On the other hand, persons who came to Canada in maturity to reside here and then commenced or continued as authors are normally included, whether or not in later life they left the country. Authors who might be termed tourists or visitors (whether in private or official capacity) are excluded. To be sure, exceptions exist to all working principles and must remain until much more information about our authors becomes generally available. Definitions that can be applied only to well-known persons are obviously useless to screen others whose lives might be parallel but about whom almost nothing can be found. To exclude the known and include the unknown solves no problems, even though in practice this result may have been inadvertently achieved all too often. In previous compilations of a

[2]This revised and expanded edition includes up to 4,000 more titles than the original edition. Between twenty and twenty-five per cent of these are titles published before 1951; the rest have dates up to 1960.

somewhat similar nature but different purpose (e.g., *The Canadian Catalogue of Books ... with Imprint 1921–1949,* the *Check List of Canadian Imprints 1900–1925,* and the National Library's *Canadiana*), books by Canadians, about Canada, or printed in Canada were combined, sometimes without national identification of the authors. A great many names and titles found in these lists do not appear in this *Checklist* simply because investigation revealed them not to be Canadian even by loose definition. No doubt the decisions made about various individual authors will often be considered arbitrary, but in the absence of wider agreement the contrary decisions would have been regarded by other critics as no less arbitrary.

Separate publication was a requirement for each work listed. A minimum of 8 or 9 pages was also required, although some items of fewer pages, mostly poetry, were included for reasons that seemed sufficient to override this principle of minimum length. Offprints of periodical articles, even when separately bound or catalogued in libraries, were excluded. Consequently, the "Transactions" and similar publications of the numerous societies are not listed.[3] Sometimes, of course, material that first appeared in a periodical was also published independently under the same or a different title. These items were listed if they met the requirement of minimum length.

Canadian bibliography is complicated by facts of publication which are relatively unusual elsewhere. For instance, a novel by a Canadian may appear with a New York imprint or a London imprint or a Canadian imprint, or with two or even all three different imprints. The copy bearing the Canadian imprint may actually have been printed in England by the English publisher, and may therefore have the same pagination as the English imprint, whereas the American imprint may have 15 or 30 more or fewer pages. Or the Canadian and American imprints may have the same pagination, with the English imprint being different. Sometimes all three imprints have slightly different pagination, and occasionally different copyright dates. Whenever it seemed clear that the same work was involved, the existence of these variant imprints was not normally indicated in this *Checklist*, since for nearly all purposes it would make little or no difference to a reader whether he reads an American edition of 198 pages or an English or Canadian edition of 204 pages. The imprint with earliest copyright date, when located in a library, is regularly preferred in almost all circumstances – and when a change of title is known the change is also recorded. Canadian imprints were regarded without prejudice either for or against. However, because of the availability and up-to-date excellence of the printed catalogues of the British Museum Library and the Library of Congress, the *Checklist* undoubtedly contains a high proportion of British and American imprints of Canadian books, and thereby probably creates a misleading impression about Canadian publishing quite unwarranted by the actual facts.

[3]A very useful project for some future bibliographer would be a combined index of all the papers and reports printed in the Transactions and Proceedings of Canada's many historical and literary societies.

Another result of the disregarding of different imprints should also be stated. Out of five library locations which follow a title, all but one library may have copies with a different imprint and pagination, or a later date. To connect each library with its specific holding would have demanded labour and apparatus incommensurate with the immediate purpose of the *Checklist.*

For the works published between 1950 and 1960 the various cumulative volumes of *Canadiana* were the usual source of the bibliographical data given here. For the vast majority of the pre-1950 titles the information was obtained from library catalogue entries, either as filmed by the National Library or filed as print-outs, photo-copies, etc., in the Union Catalogue in Ottawa. Libraries are by no means uniform about the information provided on their catalogue cards. For instance, pagination and the names of printers or publishers are sometimes omitted. Direct inquiry would almost always elicit the desired information, but the burden of correspondence was too great to remedy all such incompleteness. Minor differences in pagination as recorded from library to library were disregarded, because the main purpose in supplying pagination – to distinguish between slight pamphlets and substantial volumes – was not affected.

The towns or cities given as places of publication are in Canada unless otherwise indicated – except for well-known cities in Great Britain and the United States; "London, Ont." is so identified. Unless confusion was probable between towns of the same name in different provinces, no provincial designation was considered necessary. For clarity and practical convenience, and in accord with the official preference of the Post Office, "Saint John" is the form used for the New Brunswick city as a place of publication, regardless of whether or not the form "St. John" was employed by the printers. If the form "St. John" appeared in the *title* of the book, however, the *Checklist* also uses "St. John" in recording the title, while adhering to "Saint John" for place of publication. The Newfoundland capital is always given as "St. John's," while the third city of this trio is given as "St. John, Que."

Most of the location symbols used to indicate libraries are those created by the bibliographic staff of the National Library for use in the Union Catalogue of Canadian Libraries.[4] Other symbols, also explained in the list of abbreviations, were

[4]Since the original compilation of this *Checklist* some important library changes have occurred which are, from my point of view, rather unfortunate. Many of the titles with the location-symbol OOP (Library of Parliament) have been transferred to the National Library, which uses OONL as symbol. The same kind of transfer has recently occurred in Toronto, with many, if not most, of the Toronto Public Library (OTP) holdings being taken over by the Metropolitan Toronto Library Board, whose symbol is OTMCL. Finally, the symbol NSHPL is now being used not to indicate just a holding by the Nova Scotia Provincial Library itself, but rather a listing in the Nova Scotia Union Catalogue maintained there to record the holdings of some forty libraries in the province. Entries in the Union Catalogue in Ottawa do not yet record these transfers and changes. For me or my assistants to recheck in person all titles with OOP, OTP, or NSHPL locations was simply impossible - and not really necessary. Persons wishing to examine at first hand any particular book associated here with one of these location symbols will surely be given all possible help by the reference staffs of the libraries concerned.

required for titles not located in any of the libraries searched. For nearly every such title the source was a book-seller's catalogue or a bibliography or reference book, such as Tod and Cordingley's *A Check-List of Canadian Imprints 1900–1925* or Morgan's *Canadian Men and Women of the Time.* Non-biographical compilations of more general character, such as the *English Catalogue, American Catalogue,* or *Cumulative Book Index,* although frequently consulted were not systematically checked, because the main effort had to be expended on discovering information sufficient to determine Canadian authorship and on titles that could be located in libraries. Otherwise it would have been all too easy to group together titles by two authors of the same name, only one of whom was a Canadian. The unlocated titles included here are offered in the hope that their being listed may lead to acquisition of the actual books by libraries or collectors. Any compiler of a checklist who includes unlocated titles incurs the risk of offering possibly "phantom" titles of non-existent books. However, to me, the risk has seemed somewhat vindicated by the fact that a great many titles unlocated in the original edition have subsequently been located for this revised edition. Another fact may also be mentioned: the vast improvement in the Canadiana holdings of our major libraries during the past decade or so can readily be verified by the greatly increased number of locations recorded in this revision.

However, users of the *Checklist* are asked to remember that only rarely is more than one sample location given for each of four areas in Canada: the Maritimes, Quebec, Ontario, the west. A book might be owned by every major library in Ontario, for instance, but have its title associated here with only one library in that province. Location symbols, therefore, are no reliable indication of the prevalence or scarcity of any book.

No locations at all are provided for titles published between 1951 and 1960 inclusive. The simple reason is that all or nearly all of these are held by the National Library and can probably also be found in those university libraries which have consistently and energetically been adding steadily to their Canadiana collections during the past twenty years.

The classification of titles into the various categories will, it is hoped, be recognized for the tentative effort it is. Despite the risks of making grotesque errors when the books themselves could not be examined, the attempt seemed well worth while. Library call-numbers were, of course, the principal source of information - but disagreement was not infrequently found, with a title classified as fiction in one library, biography in another, and travel and description in a third. In such an event, the practice in the *Checklist* was to follow the decision of the majority of the libraries holding the book or the more authoritative of two. When possible, such books were of course examined. No perfect solution, however, could be discovered for border-line cases, such as the character sketches and familiar essays and fictional satires of writers like Stephen Leacock, or books of miscellaneous prose generally, even though the makeshift category of "Poetry and Prose" might serve for combinations of these two forms. The Author Index is designed to enable any reader to compile for himself the complete canon of any author's publications which come within the scope of the *Checklist.* By subsequently examining the books themselves, he can achieve more precise classifications. Plans for considerably more extensive classifications within this *Checklist* were eventually abandoned with reluctance simply because they could not be achieved by available methods. For instance, the complete separation of juvenile from adult fiction would have been a desirable accomplishment, and grouping local history by region or community, and biography by subject, would be more useful than arranging simply by author - but such divisions would be possible only by actual examination of the books, since not all library catalogue entries attempt to give the information which would be needed.

The Index of Anonymous Titles is partly intended to lead a reader with the actual book in hand to discover the name of the author if that is known, just as the inclusion of initials and pseudonyms in the Author Index, with cross-references to the real name when it is known, is intended to serve a similar purpose. Sometimes the anonymity or pseudonymity was broken by the compiler or his assistants through examination of biographical books; more often, perhaps, the real author was uncovered by finding that one or two libraries attributed the title to him, even though in other libraries the real authorship apparently remained unknown. In this way the *Checklist* should serve as a kind of clearing-house for such information. If a descriptive term such as "Backwoodsman" or "A Manitoba Lady" was used on a title-page instead of a proper name, the work was considered to be pseudonymous rather than anonymous and is to be found by looking under "Backwoodsman" or "Manitoba Lady" in the Author Index. Books published with initials instead of names may also be found through the Author Index, with the last initial regarded as the name. Thus, a book whose author designated himself "A.B.C." would be found under "C., A.B."

In the world of bibliography perfect accuracy and total inclusiveness, however ardently desired and pursued, have apparently seldom if ever been achieved. Users of this book, therefore, are cordially urged to send corrections and additions to the compiler or to the University of Toronto Press.

I welcome the present opportunity of here recording manifold acknowledgements:

The project of compiling *A Checklist of Canadian Literature...* was originally conceived by a committee of the Humanities Research Council of Canada headed by the late Professor A.S.P. Woodhouse.[5] To him I shall always remain deeply indebted on many counts.

My preface to the original edition mentioned the names of some of the scores of persons who contibuted advice, information, and effort, or assisted in other ways

[5]The foreword written by Professor Woodhouse for the original edition is reprinted on a previous page.

towards its preparation. I would here like to reiterate my most sincere thanks to them and to those left unnamed, for only upon the foundation which they helped to build could this revised and enlarged edition be constructed.

Although perhaps fewer persons were directly involved in preparing this revision, their assistance was equally indispensable. Again I received encouragement and generous help from librarians across the country, whose answers to my letters enabled me to re-classify correctly titles about which I had enquired and complete entries in which some bibliographical data were missing. Again I was provided with working facilities and staff assistance by Miss Martha Shepard of the National Library while working with the Union Catalogue in Ottawa. Other librarians whose contributions were especially valuable included Mr. Inglis F. Bell, Associate Librarian, University of British Columbia; Miss N.V. Gregg, Head of the Reference Department, Harriet Irving Library, University of New Brunswick; and Dr. Douglas Lochhead, Librarian of Massey College, Toronto. Each of these, by making available to me the results of a search of their library's card catalogue for titles given in the original *Checklist,* has saved me countless hours in my attempt to provide an increased number of present locations. Similar help was afforded me by the staff of the Library of the University of Western Ontario.

My colleague, Dr. George Parker, not only searched the new series of British Museum printed catalogues for locations and additional titles and transcribed for me the results of his previous search of the catalogues of the University of Toronto libraries, but also solved some puzzles by direct investigation at Toronto and at the British Museum. Also to be thanked is Elizabeth McGaw, whose accurate typing in recording some thousands of new entries was indispensable. Thanks to the support of a grant to the Royal Military College by the Defence Research Board, I was able to enlist the help of Mrs. Molly McClung (now Dr. McClung) in the summer of 1971, when I was incorporating and consolidating the added material with that of the original edition, filling gaps in entries, checking and rechecking, and preparing the final master-copy. Because of her interest and efficiency the work proceeded more expeditiously than I had dared to hope. Credit is also due to my wife Beth, who has lived with the *Checklist* since its inception, has transcribed data from film and cards, has read proof, has stood for what must have seemed interminable hours before the long lines of Union Catalogue drawers in the National Library extracting information, and is still cheerful, as I write this, about the proofreading of this revised edition yet to come.

Finally, among individuals whose correspondence or conversation has been especially helpful, I wish to thank, however inadequately, the following: Dr. Fred Cogswell, Mr. T.B. Higginson, Mr. R.D. Hilton Smith, Dr. Carl F. Klinck, Mr. William F.E. Morley, Mr. Edward Phelps, and Dr. Gordon Roper.

To the Canada Council I am particularly indebted for the award of a Senior Fellowship for 1967-68, which enabled me to devote a full year to planning this revised edition and accomplishing a major part of the task. I wish also to express my appreciation to the Royal Military College of Canada, which granted me leave of absence for that year and has since provided me with essential secretarial and other facilities.

To the staff of the University of Toronto Press, and in particular to Miss Jean Jamieson and Miss Jean Wilson, who provided editorial supervision and readied the master-copy for the printers, I am deeply obligated. Their unstinted professional assistance has been invaluable in reducing the number of inconsistencies and errors.

Perhaps my heaviest obligations, nevertheless, are still to those predecessors, known and unknown, upon whose earlier work this *Checklist* is built. Such pioneers in Canadian biography and bibliography as Henry J. Morgan, C.C. James, W. Stewart Wallace, Marie Tremaine, and many others are here saluted. I wish also to express my indebtedness to Dr. Jean Lunn and her assistants for their invaluable compilation, the National Library's *Canadiana* volumes. The host of anonymous cataloguers responsible for the cards in all the library collections searched, including those compiling the Union Catalogue at the National Library in Ottawa, and especially those who produced the monumental printed catalogues of the British Museum and the Library of Congress, are here being collectively thanked once again. Without their careful skills and prodigious labours the *Checklist of Canadian Literature* simply could not have existed. My sincere hope is that the work done here will, in turn, be of use to them or their successors, as well as to readers and students of Canadian literature and its backgrounds.

This book has been published with the help of a grant from the Humanities Research Council of Canada, using funds provided by the Canada Council.

R.E.W.

*Kingston, Ontario*
*15 September 1971*

# SYMBOLS AND ABBREVIATIONS

(A symbol used to indicate a library location, but which is not included in this list, may be found in *Symbols of Canadian Libraries,* 4th ed., 1968, National Library of Canada.)

| | |
|---|---|
| AC | Alberta: Calgary Public Library |
| ACG | Alberta: Glenbow Foundation, Calgary |
| ACU | Alberta: University of Calgary |
| Adelphi | Divers catalogues issued by The Adelphi Book Shop, Victoria, B.C. |
| AE | Alberta: Edmonton Public Library |
| AEP | Alberta: Provincial Library, Edmonton |
| AEU | Alberta: University of Alberta, Edmonton |
| Allibone: Supp | *A Critical Dictionary of English Literature and British and American Authors.* ... By S. Austin Allibone. With Supplement in 2v by John Foster Kirk. (Philadelphia, Lippincott, 1891) |
| AmCat | *American Catalogue of Books,* 1861–1910; also its predecessor Roorbach's *Bibliotheca Americana,* 1820–1861 |
| Amtmann | Divers Canadiana catalogues issued by Bernard Amtmann, Bookseller, Montreal |
| BCF | *A Bibliography of Canadian Fiction* (English). By Lewis E. Horning and Lawrence J. Burpee. (Toronto, Briggs, 1904) |
| BibC | *Bibliotheca Canadensis; or, A Manual of Canadian Literature.* By Henry J. Morgan. (Ottawa, Desbarats, 1867) |
| BKO | British Columbia: Okanagan Regional Library, Kelowna |
| BM | British Museum, London. Printed Catalogues, 1881–1900; 1900–1905; 1959–1966 |
| Brown U | Harris Poetry Collection, Brown University, Providence, R.I. |
| BVa | British Columbia: Vancouver Public Library |
| BVaS | British Columbia: Simon Fraser University, Burnaby |
| BVaU | British Columbia: University of British Columbia, Vancouver |

BVi British Columbia: Victoria Public Library

BViP British Columbia: Provincial Library, Victoria

BViPA British Columbia: Provincial Archives, Victoria

BViV British Columbia: University of Victoria

CAAE Canadian Association for Adult Education, Commission for Continuous Learning. "A Selective Bibliography of Canadian Plays" (1957)

CanLit *Canadian Literature,* ed. by George Woodcock, 1959–. [a continuing serial]

CAR *The Canadian Annual Review of Public Affairs,* 1901–1938. Ed. by J. Castell Hopkins [*et al.*]. (Toronto, Canadian Review Co., 1903–)

CBI *Cumulative Book Index,* 1928– [a continuing serial]; also its predecessor *The United States Catalogue,* 1912–1928

CC *Canadian Catalogue of Books Published in Canada, about Canada, as well as Those Written by Canadians* [with Imprints 1921–1949]. (Toronto, Public Libraries, 1923–1950)

CCJ *A Bibliography of Canadian Poetry (English).* By Charles C. James. (Toronto, Briggs, 1899)

CT *Canadian Novelists 1920–1945.* By Clara Thomas. (Toronto, Longmans, 1946)

CWW *The Canadian Who's Who.* Ed. by Charles G.D. Roberts and Arthur L. Tunnell [*et al.*]. (Toronto, Trans-Canada Press, 1936–). [A continuing serial. Figures following the letters abbreviate the year of issue of the volume referred to.]

DCB *The Dictionary of Canadian Biography.* By W. Stewart Wallace. 2nd ed. in 2v. (Toronto, Macmillan, 1945)

Dionne *Inventaire chronologique,* 4v, by Narcisse E. Dionne. Quebec, 1905–1909

Dora Hood Divers Canadiana catalogues issued by the Dora Hood Bookstore, Toronto

EngCat *The English Catalogue of Books,* 1801–. [a continuing serial]

Haight *Canadian Catalogue of Books* [1791–1895]. By W.R. Haight. (Toronto, Haight, 1896). Also the Supplements covering 1896–1897 and 1898–1904

LC Library of Congress, Washington, D.C. Printed Catalogues with supplements

Matthews *Canadian Diaries and Autobiographies,* by William Matthews. Berkeley, U. of California Press, 1950

MBC Manitoba: Brandon University

MOR *The Canadian Men and Women of the Time. A Handbook of Canadian Biography.* By Henry J. Morgan. (Toronto, Briggs, 1898). Rev. and enl. ed.: Toronto, Briggs, 1912. [Figures following the letters abbreviate the date of the 1898 or 1912 edition.]

MW Manitoba: Winnipeg Public Library

MWP Manitoba: Provincial Library, Winnipeg

MWU Manitoba: University of Manitoba, Winnipeg

MWUC Manitoba: University of Winnipeg (formerly United College)

NBB *New Brunswick Bibliography. ...* By William G. McFarlane. (Saint John, Sun Print., 1895)

NBFL New Brunswick: Legislative Library, Fredericton

NBFU New Brunswick: University of New Brunswick, Fredericton

NBS New Brunswick: Saint John Regional Library

NBSaM New Brunswick: Mount Allison University, Sackville

NBSM New Brunswick: New Brunswick Museum, Saint John

NBSU New Brunswick: University of New Brunswick in Saint John

NfSA Newfoundland: Provincial Archives, St. John's

NfSG Newfoundland: Gosling Memorial Library, St. John's

NfSL Newfoundland: Legislative Library, St. John's

NfSM Newfoundland: Memorial University, St. John's

NSH Nova Scotia: Halifax Memorial Library

NSHA Nova Scotia: Canada Fisheries Research Board, Halifax

NSHD Nova Scotia: Dalhousie University, Halifax

NSHK Nova Scotia: University of King's College, Halifax

NSHL Nova Scotia: Legislative Library, Halifax

NSHP Nova Scotia: Public Archives, Halifax

NSHPL* Nova Scotia Public Library, Halifax

NSWA Nova Scotia: Acadia University, Wolfville

OH Ontario: Hamilton Provincial Library

OHM Ontario: McMaster University, Hamilton

OKQ Ontario: Queen's University, Kingston

OKR Ontario: Royal Military College of Canada, Kingston

* See footnote 4 on page xii.

| | |
|---|---|
| OL | Ontario: London Public Library |
| OLU | Ontario: University of Western Ontario, London |
| OOA | Ontario: Public Archives Library, Ottawa |
| OOC | Ontario: Ottawa Public Library |
| OOCC | Ontario: Carleton College [now Carleton University], Ottawa |
| OODF | Ontario: Library, Department of Forestry and Rural Development, Ottawa |
| OOGB | Ontario: Geographical Bureau Library, Ottawa |
| OOL | Ontario: Department of Labour, Ottawa |
| OOND | Department of National Defence, Administration Branch, Interservice Reference Library, Ottawa |
| OONL | Ontario: National Library of Canada, Ottawa |
| OONM | Ontario: National Museum, Ottawa |
| OOP* | Ontario: Library of Parliament, Ottawa |
| OORD | Ontario: Department of Indian Affairs and Northern Development Library, Ottawa |
| OOS | Ontario: Dominion Bureau of Statistics, Ottawa |
| OOSJ | Ontario: Scolasticat St.-Joseph, Ottawa |
| OOSU | Ontario: St. Paul University, Ottawa |
| OOT | Ontario: Department of Transport |
| OOU | Ontario: University of Ottawa, Ottawa |
| OPAL | Ontario: Lakehead University, Port Arthur |
| OSu | Ontario: Laurentian University, Sudbury |
| OTAr | Ontario: Ontario Archives, Toronto |
| OTK | Ontario: Knox College Library, University of Toronto |
| OTL | Ontario: Legislative Library, Toronto |
| OTMC | Ontario: Massey College, University of Toronto |
| OTP* | Ontario: Toronto Public Library |
| OTTC | Ontario: University of Trinity College, Toronto |
| OTU | Ontario: University of Toronto, Toronto |
| OTUV | Ontario: Victoria University, Toronto |
| OTW | Ontario: Wycliffe College, Toronto |
| OTY | Ontario: York University, Toronto |
| OWA | Ontario: University of Windsor (formerly Assumption University) |

* See footnote 4 on page xii.

OWtL Ontario: Waterloo Lutheran University

OWtU Ontario: University of Waterloo

Patrick cat Divers catalogues issued by Joseph Patrick, book dealer, Toronto

PC Prince Edward Island: Prince Edward Island Libraries, Charlottetown

PCL Prince Edward Island: Legislative and Public Library, Charlottetown

Peel *A Bibliography of the Prairie Provinces to 1953.* Comp. by Bruce Braden Peel. (Toronto, University of Toronto Press, 1956.) [Supplement, 1963.]

Phelps *A Bibliography of Lambton County and the City of Sarnia, Ontario,* by Edward Phelps. University of Western Ontario Library Bulletin Series, No. 8 (March 1970)

QMBM Quebec: Bibliothèque de la Ville de Montréal

QMG Quebec: Sir George Williams University, Montreal

QMJ Quebec: Jewish Public Library, Montreal

QML Quebec: Loyola College, Montreal

QMM Quebec: McGill University, Montreal

QMSS Quebec: Bibliothèque nationale du Québec (formerly Bibliothèque Saint-Sulpice), Montreal

QMU Quebec: Université de Montréal

QQ Quebec: Bibliothèque municipale, Quebec

QQL Quebec: Législature de la Province de Québec, Quebec

QSherU Quebec: Université de Sherbrooke

RES Royal Empire Society, London. Subject Catalogue of the library, vol. 3: Canada, etc. (London, the Society, 1932)

Rhod *Canadian Literature in English,* by Vernon Blair Rhodenizer. Montreal, Quality Press, 1965. Also the *Index* compiled by Lois Mary Thierman. Edmonton, La Survivance Print., [1968?]

Ryerson Impt *The Ryerson Imprint.* By W. Stewart Wallace. (Toronto, Ryerson, 1954)

S&T *A Bibliography of Canadiana.* ... Ed. by Frances M. Staton and Marie Tremaine. (Toronto, Public Library, 1934). [Also Supplement, 1959.]

SR Saskatchewan: Regina Public Library

SRL Saskatchewan: Legislative Library, Regina

SRP Saskatchewan: Saskatchewan Provincial Library, Regina

SS Saskatchewan: Saskatoon Public Library

SSU Saskatchewan: University of Saskatchewan, Saskatoon

T&C *A Check-List of Canadian Imprints 1900–1925.* By Dorothea D. Tod and Audrey M. Cordingley. (Ottawa, King's Printer, 1952)

Tremaine *A Bibliography of Canadian Imprints, 1751–1800.* Comp. by Marie Tremaine. (Toronto, University of Toronto Press, 1952)

UTQ *University of Toronto Quarterly,* "Letters in Canada" issues, 1936–. [An annual survey which began with the year 1935; included a checklist.]

# CONTENTS

## INDEXES

# PART I

# POETRY

## Chapbooks, individual works, collections, anthologies

**Abbott, F.W.**
VAGRANT VERSES FROM A BLUENOSE PEN. [Liverpool, N.S.?], n.p., [1914]. 8p [NSWA

**Abbott, Frederick**
BOY TALKS TO GOD. A Serious Fantasy. Boston, Humphries, 1940. 51p [LC
LIFE'S AN OPPORTUNITY, AND OTHER INSPIRATIONAL VERSE. Boston, Humphries, 1943. 63p [LC
LOLLYPOP TREE, AND OTHER CHILD VERSE. Boston, Humphries, 1940. 85p [CBI
SOME LEGENDS, AND OTHER VERSE. New York, Harrison, 1938. 127p [LC

**Abell, Walter Halsey, 1897–1956**
ETERNAL SPRINGTIME. A Love Cycle. Yellow Springs, Kahoe & Spieth, 1927. 75p [LC

**Abraham, Dorothy E., 1894–**
BOOK OF REMEMBRANCE. Victoria, Author, [1941?]. 31p [BVi

**Acadia University**
SONGS OF ACADIA COLLEGE. Wolfville, 1907. 91p [NSWA

**Acorn, Milton, 1923–**
THE BRAIN'S THE TARGET. Toronto, Ryerson, 1960. 16p
IN LOVE AND ANGER. Montreal, Author, 1956. 20p

**Acklom, George Morebye, 1870–**
MARGARET. An Idyll. Portland, Smith & Sale, 1898. 104p [NSHD OTUV
WINTER VIGIL. New York, Vinal, 1928. 30p [LC NSHD

**Acland, Peregrine Palmer, 1892–1963**
THE REVEILLE OF ROMANCE. N.p., 1914. 4p [OTU

**Adams, Levi –1832**
THE CHARIVARI; OR, CANADIAN POETICS. A Tale after the manner of Beppo. [Anon] Montreal, 1824. 48p [Attributed to Adams by C.F. Klinck in *Dalhousie Review*, V.40] [BVaU NSHPL OTP QMU
JEAN BAPTISTE. A Poetic Olio in II Cantos. Montreal, 1825. 34p [OLU
TALES OF CHIVALRY AND ROMANCE. [Anon] Edinburgh, Robertson; London, Baldwin, Cradock & Joy, 1826. 306p [Attributed to Adams by C.F. Klinck in *Dalhousie Review,* V.40] [BM

**Adams, Mary Electa, 1823–1898**

FROM DISTANT SHORES. Poems. [Toronto, 1898?] 23p [OTP

**Adams, Myrtle (Reynolds), 1889–**

MORNING ON MY STREET. Toronto, Ryerson, 1958. 12p

REMEMBER TOGETHER. Toronto, Ryerson, 1955. 12p

TO ANY SPRING. Toronto, Ryerson, 1960. 12p

**Adams, Norman Edgar, 1904–**

BANFF NATIONAL PARK. A Poem. Calgary, Author, 1960. 4p

CALGARY. A Poem. Forest Lawn, Alta., Author, 1958. 8p

CALGARY'S GREAT STAMPEDE SHOW. A Poem. Forest Lawn, Alta., Author, 1959. 4p

**Adams, R.F.**

POEMS OF THE CANADIAN WEST. Vancouver, Evans & Hastings, 1919. 86p [BM BVaU OTP

**Adams, Robert Chamblet, 1839–**

THE HISTORY OF ENGLAND IN RHYME. Boston, Lothrop, 1880. 30p [An illustrated ed. pub. 1889. 78p] [LC OLU OOU

THE HISTORY OF THE UNITED STATES IN RHYME. Boston, Lothrop, 1884. 72p [Later pub. as ILLUSTRATED HISTORY OF THE UNION IN RHYME, rev. by Herbert Heywood. Boston, Thayer, 1891. 156p] [Brown U LC OLU

ON BOARD THE "ROCKET." Boston, Lothrop, 1879. 335p [Contains sailors' songs with music.] [BVaU LC

**Ager, Paul R.**

LIFE THOUGHTS. Toronto, Briggs, 1912. 36p [BVaU NSHPL OTP

SOME THOUGHTS IN VERSE. London, Stockwell, 1921. 16p [BM

**Aikins, Charles Carroll Colby, 1888–**

POEMS. Boston, Sherman French, 1917. 36p [BVaU LC NBFU OKQ

**Aimsfeld [pseud]**

THE HOWLS OF A DINGO. Australian Bush Rhymes. Victoria, Diggon-Hibben, 1919. 48p [BVaU

**Aitken, Melita**

THE MAPLE GROVE AND OTHER POEMS. Toronto, Warwick & Rutter, 1920. 61p [NBFU OTP

**Aldwinckle, Eric, 1909–**

TWO FABLES. Toronto, Toronto Theosophical Society, 1950. 27p [OONL

**Alexander, Bertha M.**

THE HIGHWAY AND OTHER POEMS. 2nd ed. St. John's Nfld., Evening Telegram, [1952?]. 31p [1st ed.: Vancouver, [1950?].]

**Alexander, Rev. James Lynne, 1800–1879**

A DAY AT NIAGARA IN THE YEAR 1825. Revived, Revised, and Annotated by his great-grandson, Richard Lonton Denison. Toronto, 1952. 28p [mimeographed]

ONTARIO'S OLDEST POEM: A DAY AT NIAGARA IN THE YEAR 1825. By the Rev. James Lynne Alexander. Revived, Revised and Annotated by his Great-Grandson, Richard Lonton Denison. Toronto, 1952. 15p [A reprint of the following title.]

WONDERS OF THE WEST; or, A Day at the Falls of Niagara, in 1825. A Poem. By a Canadian [pseud]. York, Fothergill, 1825. 46p [OTP

**Alexander-Armstrong, J.**

SONGS OF THE NEW WORLD. Toronto, Imrie, 1896. 74p [BM OTUV

**Allan, Mrs. Ethel Stilwell, 1883–**

TO YOU. By Ethel Stilwell [pseud]. Toronto, Author, 1926. [OKQ

**Allan, Eva Valentine**

VERSES. ... Ottawa, 1904. 26p [Brown U

**Allan, Mrs. Marguerite Buller**

THE RHYME GARDEN. London, Lane, 1917. 64p [BM LC

**Allan, Peter John, 1825–1848**

THE POETICAL REMAINS OF PETER JOHN ALLAN, ESQ., LATE OF FREDERICTON, NEW BRUNSWICK. Ed. by Rev. Henry Christmas. London, Smith Elder, 1853. xxiv + 171p [BM BVaU NBFU OLU

**Allen, Egbert Chesley, 1882–1947**

OUR NORTHERN YEAR. Stories and Songs of the Canadian Seasons. ... Toronto, Ryerson, 1937. 119p [NBFU OTU

POEMS. ... N.p., Author, 1945. 36p [NSHPL

**Allen, Favia Gordon**

ECHOES FROM LOVE'S MONUMENT. Epic Poem. Yarmouth, Davis, 1912. 18p [NSHPL

AN IDYLL REVERIE, MY PARADISE I'LL SEEK AND OTHER POEMS. 1912. [Rhod p872

**Allen, Grant, 1848–1899**

THE LOWER SLOPES. Reminiscences of Excursions Round the Base of Helicon. London, Mathews & Lane, 1894. 79p [BM LC NBFU OTU

**Allen, Jacob D.**

THE MUSINGS OF UNCLE JAKE. London, Ont., 1866. 208p [OLU

POEMS. London, Ont., Advertiser, 1869. 240p [Brown U OTU

**Allen, James A.**

MAPLE LEAVES. A Collection of Verse. London, Stockwell, 1938. 79p [BM BVaU OOP

**Allen, Rev. John Slater, 1841–1923**

FROM APOLLYONVILLE TO THE HOLY CITY. A Poem. Halifax, Wesleyan Office, 1880. 302p [LC NSHD OKQ

**Allen, Joseph Antisell, 1814–1900**

THE CHURCH OF THE POPE, AND PRIMITIVE CHRISTIANITY. Kingston, British Whig, [1891]. 103p [OTUV

DAY-DREAMS BY A BUTTERFLY. In Nine Parts. Kingston, Creighton, 1854. 156p [BM BVaU LC OTP

THE LAMBDA-NU TERCENTENARY POEM ON SHAKESPEARE. Stratford-upon-Avon, Morgan, 1864. 46p [BM OTUV

**Alline, Rev. Henry, 1748–1784**

HYMNS AND SPIRITUAL SONGS. Stonington-Port, Conn., Turnbull, 1802. 281p [Same title pub. at Boston in 1784 and at Dover, N.H., in 1795 and 1798.] [BM NBFU

**Allison, Dorothea**

A FAIRY'S GARLAND OF B.C. FLOWERS. Vernon, B.C., Vernon News, n.d. 31p [BViPA

**Allison, Mary Gertrude (Mother Agatha)**

AN OLD SONG IN NEW METERS. By M.G.A. Toronto, Longmans, 1923. [T&C

**Allison, William Talbot, 1874–1941**

THE AMBER ARMY, AND OTHER POEMS. Toronto, Briggs, 1909. 85p [BM BVaU NBFU OKQ

**Alpha Arts and Letters Society, Hamilton**

THE GOOD SHIP "FUN." Hamilton, Davis-Lisson, 1935. 32p [CC

**Amoss, Harry [Harold Edwin], 1880–**

CHURCHILL AND OTHER POEMS. Toronto, Ryerson, 1957. 34p

PRAYER OF THE GOOD TROUPER, AND OTHER POEMS. Toronto, Ryerson, 1933. 88p [BVaU LC OTU

SUNDAY-MONDAY. Selected Poems. Toronto, Ryerson, 1947. 56p [BVaU NBFU OKQ

**Anderson, Agnes Nicholson**

FROM TOWERING HEIGHTS. 4th ed. Victoria, Diggon-Hibben, 1952. 33p

**Anderson, Alvah John**

A BOOK OF POEMS. [Saskatoon, 1939?]. 93p [SSU

**Anderson, Annie M.**

A CHAPBOOK. [Poems by six students and one graduate of the University of British Columbia.] By Abbie M. Anderson, Geoffrey Bruun, Geoffrey Coope, Sallee Murphy, Alfred Rive, Lionel Stevenson, Dorothy H. Walsh. Vancouver, priv. print., 1922. 28p [BVaU OTP

**Anderson, Rev. David**
POEMS. Toronto, Author, 1930. 24p [Brown U

**Anderson, Rev. Duncan, 1828–1903**
LAYS OF CANADA, AND OTHER POEMS. Montreal, Lovell, 1890. 115p [BVaU LC NSHD OKQ

**Anderson, Mrs. Helen B., 1865–**
UNDER COUNTRY SKIES. Toronto, Writers' Studio, 1933. 32p [Brown U

**Anderson, James, 1838?–1923**
SAWNEY'S LETTERS; or Cariboo Rhymes. Barkerville, B.C., Cariboo Sentinel, 1868. 4p [Enlarged ed., Barkerville, Cariboo Sentinel, 1869. Also, under title SAWNEY'S LETTERS AND CARIBOO RHYMES, Toronto, Johnston, 1895. 49p. Repub. in 1950 and 1962.] [BVaU BViPA NBFU OTU

**Anderson, Patrick, 1915–**
THE COLOUR AS NAKED. Toronto, McClelland, 1953. 93p
A TENT FOR APRIL. Montreal, First Statement, 1945. 28p [BVaU LC OTU
THE WHITE CENTRE. Toronto, Ryerson, 1946. 72p [BVaU LC MWU NSHD OKQ QMM

**Anderson, Robert Stuart Guthrie**
THE YOUNG MINISTER AND OTHER POEMS. By R.S.G.A. [pseud]. Toronto, Westminster, n.d. 10p [Cover title: "KIRK FOLK"] [BVaS NBFU OTU

**Anderson, Robert Thompson, 1880–**
CANADIAN BORN AND OTHER WESTERN VERSE. Edmonton, Esdaile, 1913. 100p [BM BVaU
THE OLD TIMER, AND OTHER POEMS. Edmonton, Edmonton Print., 1909. 103p [BM BVaU OTU
TROOPERS IN FRANCE. Edmonton, Coles Print., 1932. 122p [BViPA

**Anderson, Mrs. Violet Louise, 1906–**
THE LEDGE. Toronto, Emblem Books, 1957. 15p

**Andress, Clara E.**
COMMONPLACE SKETCHES. Sudbury, Author, 1938. 25p [Brown U OTU

**Andrews, Frederick**
VALOUR AND FAITH. Ilfracombe, Devon, Stockwell, 1958. 80p

**Andrews, William Darling, 1853–1903**
THE LIFEBOAT AND OTHER POEMS. Toronto, Briggs, [1888]. 64p [Same title: Toronto, Briggs, n.d. (1887?). 32p] [BVaU LC NBFU OKQ QMSS

**Angus, Frances Ramsay**
AS WE ARE. Boston, Humphries, 1940. 107p [LC NSHD OKQ QMM

**Angus, Marion Isabel (Hand), 1902–1951**

FRAGRANT WISDOM. Vancouver, Vancouver Bindery, 1931. 63p [BVaU NBFU OTP

SEA MIST AND OTHER POEMS. N.p., [1926?]. 24p [BViPA OKQ

**Angus, Mary**

CHRISTMAS GREETINGS TO THE CHILDREN YOUNG AND OLD FROM THE FISH, INSECTS AND BIRDS. N.p., 1946. 13p [QMU

**Anonymous**

AN ADDRESS TO THE LIEGE MEN OF EVERY BRITISH COLONY. Kingston, Herald, 1822. 13p [OTU QMSS

CANADA. A Satire. By One of her Sons. N.p., [18–?]. 24p [OTU

CANADIAN CANTICLES [A Collection of 127 Poems]. Toronto, Musson, [1912?]. 114p [BVaU NBFU OTUV

THE CANADIAN TEMPERANCE MINSTREL. Being a Collection of Hymns, Songs, and Poetry, Selected and Original. Montreal, Campbell, 1842. 108p [OOP

THE CARLETON ELECTION; or, The Tale of a Bytown Ram. An Epic Poem. In Ten Cantos. [Ottawa?], Author, 1832. 38p [OOA

CURIOUS FACTS. Toronto, 1895. 124p [CCJ

A FEW HYMNS. N.p., 1906. 24p [QMU

GEMS FROM CANADIAN AUTHORS. Toronto, Bryce, 1888. 12p [OONL

A GLIMPSE AT TORONTO IN THE 20TH CENTURY, WITH A RETROSPECTIVE GLANCE. Toronto, 1875. 14p [OTUV

HUNTING ADVENTURES IN UTOPIA. Toronto, 1880. 30p [CCJ

HYMNS FOR SPECIAL SERVICES. Ottawa, Hunter Rose, 1868. 16p [QMU

JOHNNY CRAPAUD. A Legend of Bygone Days. After the late Thomas Ingoldsby, Esq. Toronto, Sylvester Blowhole, 1851. 12p [NSHP

LINES COMMEMORATIVE OF THE AWFUL CONFLAGRATION OF ST. ROCH'S. Quebec, 1845. 11p [QMU

"LOVE, A LA MODE": A SLIGHT SLAP AT THE NEAT LITTLE ELOPEMENT AT TORONTO. A Very Moral Dissertation. London, Ont., n.p., 1863. 39p [OTU

THE MAPLE LEAF; or, Canadian Annual. A Literary Souvenir. ... Toronto, Rowsell, 1847–1849. 3v [BVaU OOP OTP

THE NEW-BRUNSWICK TEMPERANCE SONGSTER. A Collection of Songs and Hymns Original and Selected. Respectfully Dedicated to the Several Total Abstinence Societies throughout the British Provinces. By a member of the "Saint John Temperance Association Choir." Saint John, McMillan, 1848. 180p [OTP

NO SECT IN HEAVEN. Saint John, 1868. [LHC, p118

POESIE'S DREAM. Part 1st and 2nd. Rose Glen and other Poems. Halifax, J. Howe, 1835. 72p [NSHPL

POETS FOR PEACE. A Collection of Poems, by British Columbia Poets, intended to express a Position of Non-neutrality on the Matter of the Testing of Thermonuclear Weapons and the Preservation of Peace. Vancouver, 1960. 33p [mimeographed]

PRO AND CON. A Satirico-Political Dialogue in Familiar Rhyme. Quebec, 1828. 12p [OTP QMSS

THE PROVOST'S KINDERGARTEN. Being the Dinner of the Year of One-ty Four at the St. Charles Grill. ... 1910. Toronto, n.d. 12p [Adelphi cat. no. 58

RAISE THE FLAG, AND OTHER PATRIOTIC CANADIAN SONGS AND POEMS. Toronto, Rose, 1891. 63p [BM Brown U NSHD OTU

THROUGH THE YEAR WITH CANADIAN POETS. Gananoque, Ont., Hilda M. Ridley, 1960. 29p (Carillon Poetry Chap-Books)

WAIFS FROM THE HEDGES AND HIGHWAYS. V. 1 [Montreal], Anon. Pub. Co., 1903. 98p [OTP

**Appleton, Lydia Ann**

MISCELLANEOUS POEMS, MORAL AND RELIGIOUS. Written on Various Occasions. Toronto, "Watchman," 1850. 92p [OTUV

**Apps-Brown, Minnie (Poole), 1866–1948**

THAT WORLD OF MY OWN. Paris, Ont., Pickell, 1949. 36p

**Archibald, Alexander Kent, 1803–**

POEMS. Boston, Wiley, 1848. 200p [BM BVaU LC NSHD

**Archibald, Ernest**

THOUGHTS OF A RAMBLING MUSE. Halifax, Imperial, 1948. 181p [Brown U

**Arion (pseud)**

ALPHONZO STILLETTO'S POETIZATION OF THE INCIPIENT STAGE OF THE GREAT PACIFIC SCANDAL AND OF THE CELEBRATED SPEECH OF LORD DUFFERIN IN REPLY TO A HEALTH TOAST AT A DINNER GIVEN BY THE HALIFAX CLUB. By Arion [pseud]. Montreal, "Witness" Print., 1874. 29p [Brown U BVaU OTU

**Armour, Edward Douglas, 1851–1922**

ECHOES FROM HORACE IN ENGLISH VERSE. Toronto, U. of Toronto Press, 1922. 100p [BM OTU

LAW LYRICS. Toronto, Canada Law Book, 1918. 39p [BM BVaU LC NBFU OTU QMM

**Armstrong, Clara**

MY ROSARY OF FRIENDSHIPS AND OTHER POEMS. Montreal, Witness Press, 1936. 31p [OTU

STARS OF HAPPINESS. Abbey, Sask., Author, 1938. 23p [CC

**Armstrong, Joseph H., 1867–1891**

LYRICS, IDYLS AND FRAGMENTS. Ed. by Norman De Lagutry. New York, Publishers' Print. Co., 1892. 111p [LC NSHPL OTP

SONGS OF A PAGAN. 1889 [Rhod p897

**Ascher, Isidore Gordon, 1835–1914**

COLLECTED POEMS. London, Elliot Stock, 1929. 300p [BM

ONE HUNDRED AND FIVE SONNETS. Oxford, Blackwell, 1912. 117p [BM LC

VOICES FROM THE HEARTH. A Collection of Verses. By "Isidore." Isidore G. Ascher. Montreal, Lovell, 1863. 168p [BVaU LC NBFU OKQ QMU

**Ashmead, Henry A.**

POEMS FROM THE PRESS. Patriotic, Descriptive, Sentimental and Humorous. Toronto, Hunter Rose, 1916. 179p [Brown U BVaU NBFU OOP

**Athena (pseud)**

IN MY CORNER. By Athena [pseud]. London, Stockwell, 1926. 15p [BM

**Atkin, Grace Murray, 1891–**

FLOWERS OF THE WIND. New York, Kennerley, 1919. 58p [BVaU LC

**Attfield, Mrs. Hilda Mary, 1900–**

ECHOES OF WAR AND OTHER VERSE. Ilfracombe, Devon, Stockwell, 1944. 46p [BM LC OTP

**Austin, Rev. Benjamin Fish, 1850–1932**

THE DAWN OF A NEW ERA. The Ideal State in the Light of Mental Science. By Hedwig S. Albarus [pseud]. Toronto, Austin, 1903. 23p [OPAL

**Austin, Lilian Edna**

ETCHINGS OF FENELON FALLS. Boston, Meador, 1931. 64p [LC OTU

**Avison, Margaret Kirkland, 1918–**

WINTER SUN. Toronto, U. of Toronto Press, 1960. 89p

**Awde, Robert**

CANADA: PRESENT AND FUTURE. A Patriotic Poem. ... Toronto, 1889. 3p [OTU

JUBILEE, PATRIOTIC, AND OTHER POEMS. Toronto, Briggs, 1887. 50p [BVaU NBFU OKQ

WAITING AT TABLE. Poems and Songs. London, Author, 1865. 143p [BM OTU

**Ayscough, Florence (Wheelock), 1878–1942**

FIR-FLOWER TABLETS. Poems. Translated from the Chinese by Florence Ayscough. ... English Versions by Amy Lowell. Boston, Houghton, 1921. xcv + 227p [BM BVaU OTU QMM

**B., P.**

SONGS FROM A CANADIAN HOMESTEAD. Morland, Amersham, Bucks., 1923. 28p [BViPA

**B., P.J.**

PENCILLINGS BY THE WAY, during a Vacation Visit in Chebucto. By a Student who is a Native of Halifax. P.J.B. Montreal, Lovell, 1868. 24p [Brown U NSHD OTU

**Bagg, Stanley Clark, 1820–**

LEISURE MOMENTS. A Few Poems. By Stella [pseud]. Montreal, Rose, 1871 24p [QMM

**Bailey, Alfred Goldsworthy, 1905–**

BORDER RIVER. Toronto, McClelland, 1952. 61p [BVaU NBFU OTP

SONGS OF THE SAGUENAY AND OTHER POEMS. Quebec, Chronicle-Telegraph, 1927. 34p [BVaU NBFU OKQ QMM

TÂO. Toronto, Ryerson, 1930. 8p [BVaU NBSaM OTU QMM

**Bailey, George Taylor, 1887–**

POEMS OF LIFE. Toronto, Warwick Bros., 1925. 128p [BVaU NSHD OTU QMBM

**Baillie, Oliver E.**

ON ACTIVE SERVICE. N.p., [1915?]. 7p [Same title, with different estimated dates, and pagination given as "19", "[24]", and "2 v. in 1".] [Amtmann cat. 149 BVaU OONL OTP

**Bain, Ebenezer, 1838?–**

RAMBLINGS IN RHYMELAND. War Poems, Songs and Other Verse, Sentimental, Humorous, Philosophical. Montreal, Author, 1918. 101p [BM BVaU NSHD OTU QMM

**Bainbridge, Edith**

POEMS. Toronto, Author, 1943. 16p [OTU

**Baker, Henry**

TRANSLATIONS AND CHOICE PIECES FROM SOME OF THE BEST FRENCH AND GERMAN AUTHORS. Montreal, Lovell, 1867. 286p [OTP

**Baker, Ida Emma (Fitch), 1858–1948**

AT EVENTIDE. Toronto, Presbyterian Pub., 1943. 48p [BVaU LC OTU

BY LAMPLIGHT. Toronto, Author, 1936. 50p [BVaU NBFU OTU

GLEAMS OF IMMORTALITY. Toronto, Ross Press, n.d. 16p [OTU

NAME ABOVE EVERY NAME. Toronto, Author, 1941. [CC

SELECTED POEMS. With an intro. by Ray Palmer Baker. Toronto, Ryerson, 1951. 82p

**Baker, Maude E.**

PEN SYMPHONIES. Halifax, Allen, n.d. 27p [OTUV

**Baker, Ray Palmer, 1883–**

CROYNAN HALL, THE MAID OF THE MASK, A TALE OF ROTHENBURG. Toronto, Briggs, 1908. 100p [BVaU NBFU OKQ QMM

A TALE OF ROTHENBURG AND OTHER POEMS. Toronto, Haynes, 1906. 24p [BVaU NBFU OTP

**Baker, William King**

COLLECTED SHORTER POEMS. London, Routledge, 1927. 300p [BM NSHD OTU QMM

A FOREST IDYLL AND OTHER POEMS. London, Baker, 1916. 107p [BM

GABRIEL LAJEUNESSE. ... London, Routledge, 1923. 52p [BM NSHD OTU QMSS

THE LOYALISTS. London, Routledge, 1921. 149p [BM LC NBFU

PENN, THE STATESMAN AND GULIELMA. A Quaker Idyll. Edinburgh, Oliphants, [1918]. 327p [BM LC OLU

A QUAKER APOSTLE: IN MEMORIAM, JOHN T. DORLAND. London, Baker, 1916. [BM

**Baldwin, Harry, 1883–1953**

WHICH CODE? Ottawa, Author, 1949. 100p [AEU OOP

**Baldwyn, Augusta, 1821?–1884**

POEMS. Montreal, Lovell, 1859. 163p [BVaU OKQ QMM

**Ball, Mrs. Helen**

THE MOMENT SNARED. Toronto, Author, 1952. 32p

THESE THINGS LINGER. Toronto, Author, 1946. 23p [BVaU OTP

**Ball, Nellie (Martin), 1882–1950**

SELECTED POEMS OF NELLIE BALL. With an intro. by Luella Carlyle Thomson. Toronto, Crucible Press, 1951. 16p

**Ballantyne, Lereine (Hoffman), 1891–1962**

FIRELIGHT FANCIES. Toronto, McClelland, 1926. 40p [BVaU NSHD OTP

**Bannatyne, William**

POEMS AND SONGS ON VARIOUS SUBJECTS. Toronto, Campbell, 1875. 198p [BVaU OTU

**Bannerman, Frances (Jones), 1855–**

MILESTONES. A Collection of Verses. London, Richards, 1899. 197p [BM

**Bannon, Richard Valentine, 1900–**

EASTLAND ECHOES. Toronto, Macmillan, 1937. 44p [Brown U BVaU OTUV

**Barbeau, Charles Marius, 1883–1969**

COME A-SINGING! Canadian Folk-songs. By Marius Barbeau, Arthur Lismer, [and] Arthur Bourinot. Ottawa, King's Printer, 1947. 59p [BVaU LC NSHD OKQ QMM

FOLK-SONGS OF FRENCH CANADA. Ed. by ——. Trans. by Edward Sapir. New Haven, Yale U. Press, 1925. 216p [BM BVaU LC NBFU OTU QMM

FOLK SONGS OF OLD QUEBEC. Trans. by Regina Lenore Shoolman. Ottawa, National Museum, 1935. 72p [BM BVaU LC NSWA OKQ QMM

**Barclay, Charles A.**

DAWN, EAST AND WEST. A Canadian Political Sketch. Toronto, Sovereign, 1914. 63p [BVaU NBFU OTU

**Barnard, Sylvia, 1937–**
THE TIMELESS FOREST. Toronto, Contact Press, 1959. 45p

**Barnes, F.H.**
POEMS. By F.H.B. Toronto, Briggs, 1912. 88p [BM OKQ

**Barrett, Ena Constance, 1894–1967**
LILTS OF NEWFOUNDLAND. 2nd ed., with Additional Lilts. Curling, Nfld., Western Star Press, 1931. 39p [NfSM
MAYFLOWERS AND ROSES. A Bouquet of Verse. Curling, Nfld., Barrett's Print. Shop, 1946. 119p [NfSM OTP
RAINBOW LYRICS. London, Erskine MacDonald, n.d. 104p [NBSaM

**Barrington, Gwenyth, 1901–**
WAR, WORDS, AND THE WASTEBASKET. N.p., [1942?]. 19p [LC

**Bartole, Genevieve**
FIGURE IN THE RAIN. Toronto, Ryerson, 1948. 7p [BVaU NBSaM OKQ

**Barton, J. King**
NOTHING TO YOU; or, Mind Your Own Business. In Answer to "Nothings" in General and "Nothing to Wear" [by William Allen Butler] in Particular. By Knot-Rab [pseud]. New York, Wiley, 1857. 68p [BM LC OLU

**Bate, Fanny**
GEMS OF HOPE. In Memory of the Faithful Departed. Selected and Arranged by ——. Toronto, Briggs, 1896. 280p [BM OLU

**Bates, Ronald Gordon Nudell, 1924–**
THE WANDERING WORLD. Toronto, Macmillan, 1959. 60p

**Battersby, Mrs. H.S. –1887?**
HOME LYRICS. A Book of Poems. V. II. Toronto, Hunter Rose, 1887. 143p [HOME LYRICS, V. I is stated to have been published in 1876. Nothing else discovered about it.] [Brown U BVaU OLU

**Baubie, William Edward**
FRENCH-CANADIAN VERSE. Written and Illus. by ——. Chicago, Lakeside Press, 1917. 74p [BVaU LC OTP

**Bayer, Mary Elizabeth**
FACES OF LOVE. Toronto, Ryerson, 1959. 12p
OF DIVERSE THINGS. Toronto, Ryerson, 1957. 12p
THE SILVER SWAN. An Epithalamion. Toronto, Ryerson, 1960. 8p

**Bayley, Cornwall, 1784–1807**
CANADA. A Descriptive Poem. Written at Quebec, 1805. With Satires – Imitations – and Sonnets. [Anon] [Quebec], John Neilson, [1806]. 52p [OTP

**Bayley, Robert Charleton, 1913–**

A BAKER'S DOZEN. A Sheaf of Thirteen Occasional Poems. Moncton, priv. print., n.d. 16p [BVaU NBFU OTU

SEVEN SONGS IN THE MAJOR AND MINOR. Moncton, Imprimerie Acadienne, [1949?]. 10p [NBFU OKQ

VISIONS FUGITIVE. ... Fredericton, Ubsdell Print., 1946. 16p [BM BVaU NBFU OKQ

**Baylis, Samuel Mathewson, 1854–1941**

ECHOES OF THE GREAT WAR 1914–1918. Montreal, Witness Press, 1919. 32p [BM LC NSHD OTU QMM

**Baynes, O'Hara**

A CLOSE CALL. N.p., [1918?]. 9p [NSWA OTUV

**Beattie, Jessie Louise, 1896–**

BLOWN LEAVES. Toronto, Ryerson, 1929. 24p [BVaU NBFU

SHIFTING SAILS. Toronto, Ryerson, 1931. 24p [OKQ

**Beattie, John McNab, 1916–**

POEMS AND BALLADS OF THE OTTAWA VALLEY. By Mac Beattie [pseud]. Arnprior, Ont., Arnprior Press, 1960. 59p

**Beattie, Kim, 1900–**

"AND YOU!" Toronto, Macmillan, 1929. 91p [BVaU OTP

**Beattie, William**

ODES OF APPRECIATION OF ROBERT BURNS. N.p., n.d. 32p [Odes dated 1909–1916.] [OTK QMU

**Beck, George Fairley**

DAYBREAK. A Poem. Toronto, 1873. 13p [OTP

**Beck, Roland Stanley**

THE FLASK OF LOVE AND OTHER POEMS. By Roland St. Anbeck [pseud]. Vancouver, Sun Pub., 1926. 61p [BVaU

**Bedell, Laura Amelia (Whitemarsh), 1875–1971**

ALWAYS THE TIDES. Picton, Picton Gazette, 1964. 131p

BLUE HARBOUR. Picton, Author, 1947. 80p [BVaU NBSaM OTU

FROM DAWN TO DUSK. Bloomfield, Ont., Author, 1944. 71p [OTP

SPUN LACE. Toronto, Writers' Studio, 1933. 30p [AEU Brown U OTP

**Bedford-Jones, Henry James O'Brien, 1887–1949**

THE MISSION AND THE MAN. The Story of San Juan Capistrano. Pasadena, San Pasqual Press, 1939. 40p [LC

**Beeman, Herbert, –1931**

FOR OUR BUREAU. Being the Bureau Ballads contributed to Volumes One and

Two of "Via Vancouver," the Journal of the Foreign Trade Bureau of the Vancouver Board of Trade. Vancouver, Cowan Brookhouse, 1924. 63p [BVaU OTU QMU

VANCOUVER, THE HALFWAY HOUSE OF THE EMPIRE. Vancouver, Pacific Printers, 1929. 12p [BViPA

SOME ADVENTURES OF MR. SURELOCK KEYS, HITHERTO UNRECORDED. ... Point Grey, B.C., Kerrisdale Kronickle, 1913. 15p [BVaU

**Belcher, Alexander Emerson, 1844–1926**

POEMS AND PATRIOTIC VERSES. N.p., n.d. [1916]. 8p [QMU

**Belcher, Antoine L.**

WOODLAND GNOMES. Vancouver, Evergreen Press, 1957. 32p

**Belcher, Beaufort**

RADICAL RICIDULE. Toronto, Macdonald Galleries, 1935. 78p [BVaU OTP

**Bell, John Allison**

CHEBUCTO AND OTHER POEMS. ... Halifax, Bowes, 1890. 53p [NSHD

**Bell, William Aitchison, 1847–1915**

POEMS ON VARIOUS OCCASIONS. With a Biographical Sketch. Toronto, Best, 1927. 59p [BVaU OKQ

**Bellmore, Euphemia**

BOOK OF POEMS. 8th ed. Toronto, Dudley & Burns, 1874. 27p [Brown U BVaU OTUV

**Benedict, Charles Julius Ernest Leslie, 1868–**

CRUELTY. Montreal, Author, 1930. 16p [BVaU

LIFE AND THE LAND WE LOVE. Montreal, Author, 1932. 104p [BM BVaU

THE RETURN. Montreal, Author, 1932. 7p [BM BVaU

SEMPER EADEM. Montreal, Author, 1932. 4p [BVaU

WESTMOUNT IN SONG AND STORY. Westmount, Westmount News, 1933. 99p [BVaU QMM

**Bengough, John Wilson, 1851–1923**

IN MANY KEYS. A Book of Verse. Toronto, Briggs, 1902. 237p [BM BVaU NBFU OKQ QMM

MOTLEY. Verses Grave and Gay. Toronto, Briggs, 1895. 172p [BVaU LC NSHD OKQ QMM

**Bennett, Dorothy R.**

SPRINGTIME AND OTHER POEMS. London, Stockwell, 1933. 15p [BM

**Bennett, Ethel Hume (Patterson), 1881–**

NEW HARVESTING. Contemporary Canadian Poetry, 1918–1938. Chosen by ——. Toronto, Macmillan, 1938. 198p [BM BVaU LC NSHD OKQ QMM

**Bennett, Rev. James, 1817–1901**

SONG OF THE FLOWERING GIRLS. THE LARK AND THE REAPERS. AN ELEGY ON THAT PIOUS DOG HECTOR. CONSCIENCE. Saint John, 1900. 8p [OTP

**Bennett, Owen J.**

CLOTH OF GOLD AND OTHER POEMS. Vancouver, Wrigley Print., 1950. 11 + 57p [BVaU

**Benson, Mrs. Irene Chapman**

JOURNEY INTO YESTERDAY. Toronto, Ryerson, 1943. 10p [BVaU LC NBFU OKQ QMM

**Benson, Mary Josephine (Trotter), 1887–**

MY POCKET BERYL. Toronto, McClelland, 1921. 127p [BM BVaU NSHD OKQ

**Benson, Nathaniel Anketell Michael, 1903–1966**

DOLLARD. A Tale in Verse. Toronto, Nelson, 1933. 44p [BVaU LC NBFU OKQ QMM

THE GLOWING YEARS. Toronto, Nelson, 1937. 137p [BVaU NSHD OKQ

MODERN CANADIAN POETRY. Ed. by ——. Ottawa, Graphic, 1930. 227p [BM BVaU LC NSHD OTU QMM

ODE ON THE DEATH OF GEORGE V. Toronto, Ryerson, 1936. 4p [BM LC NSHD OKQ

POEMS. Toronto, Robertson, 1927. 43p [BVaU NBFU OKQ QMM

TWENTY AND AFTER. Toronto, Ryerson, 1927. 20p [BVaU NBSaM OKQ QMM

THE WANDERER, A NARRATIVE POEM ... AND OTHER POEMS. Toronto, Ryerson, 1930. 31p [Sequel to TWENTY AND AFTER.] [BVaU NBSaM OKQ QMM

**Bentley, E.**

EPISTLES AND POEMS. [Toronto? 1896?]. 31p [OTUV

**Bentley, Eliza**

PRECIOUS STONES FOR ZION'S WALLS. A Record of Personal Experience in Things connected with the Kingdom of God on Earth. Toronto, Briggs, 1897. 440p [BM Brown U OTU

**Bentley, Mrs. Verna Bessie, 1904–**

IN HER MIND CARRYING. By Verna Loveday Harden [pseud]. Toronto, Ryerson, 1959. 12p

POSTLUDE TO AN ERA. By Verna Loveday Harden [pseud]. Toronto, Crucible Press, 1940. 26p [LC

WHEN THIS TIDE EBBS. By Verna Loveday Harden [pseud]. Toronto, Ryerson, 1946. 8p [LC MWU NBSaM OKQ

**Bernhardt, Clara Mae, 1911–**

FAR HORIZON. Preston, Ont., Author, 1941. 32p [AEU LC OONL

HIDDEN MUSIC. Galt, Galt Print., 1948. 38p [NBFU

NIN NAUNANIMIN: A Sonnet Sequence, by Clara Bernhardt; KYNDILL, by Lillian Collier Gray; DRUID'S DREAM, by Wallace Havelock Robb; MEADOW-LONG DAY, by Dorothy Murray Sliter; BLUE INK, by Gertrude Bowen Webster. Belleville, Intelligencer, 1939. 47p [Brown U NBFU

SILENT RHYTHM. Preston, Ont., Author, 1938. 40p [Brown U MW

**Berridge, Amelia**

THOUGHTS IN ST. MARK'S AND OTHER POEMS. Ilfracombe, Devon, Stockwell, [1954]. 46p

**Berry, Mrs. Nora, 1907–**

A BOUQUET OF VERSES. By Jane Cadmore [pseud]. Kingston, 1954. 70p [Another ed., noted as "Slightly Revised," same date, same pagination.]

**Bertram, W.E.**

SELECTED POEMS. N.p., 1930. 32p [QMU

**Betts, Craven Langstroth, 1853–1941**

A GARLAND OF SONNETS ... in Praise of the Poets. ... New York, Mansfield & Wessels, 1899. 7 + xxxiiip [BVaU LC NBFU OTU

THE PERFUME-HOLDER. A Persian Love Poem. New York, Saalfield & Fitch, 1891. 49p [BVaU LC NBFU OTU

SELECTED POEMS OF CRAVEN LANGSTROTH BETTS. New York, Associated Authors & Compilers, 1916. 353p [LC NBFU

SONGS FROM BERANGER. Trans. in the Original Metres. New York, Stokes, 1888. 253p [BM LC

THE TWO CAPTAINS: AT LONGWOOD, AT TRAFALGAR. New York, Watts, 1921. 16p [BM LC NBFU OKQ

**Betts, Mary**

DREAMS. N.p., n.d. 33p [UTQ'37

**Bevan, Molly**

"CHRISTMAS AGAIN" AND OTHER POEMS. Montreal, 1923. 18p [QMSS

GIFTS OF THE YEAR AND OTHER POEMS. Toronto, Macmillan, 1927. 67p [BVaU NBFU OTU QMM

**Bevans, Mrs. Florence Edith**

ROGUE'S GALLERY OF PUPS. By Jemima Remington [pseud]. London, Stockwell, 1938. 43p [BM

WHERE PUSSYWILLOWS DIP AND OTHER POEMS. By Jemima Remington [pseud]. Toronto, Author, 1936. 32p [BVaU OTU

**Bevis, Henry**

CANADIAN AUTUMN AND OTHER POEMS. [Gloucester, Minchin & Gibbs, 1925]. 37p [BM OTP

**Bezanger, Gilbert**

OUTLAW LYRICS. Montreal, Pelletier, n.d. 62p [BVaU OKQ

**Biggs, Alfred**

SONGS OF LIMEHOUSE AND OTHER VERSE. Gardenvale, Que., Garden City Press, 1939. 52p [OTU

**Bigney, Mark Frederick, 1817–1886**

THE FOREST PILGRIM AND OTHER POEMS. New Orleans, Gresham, 1867. 258p [LC

**Bigsby, Bernard**

COLLECTED VERSE. Poems of Personal and Family Interest. New York, Rowland & Ives, 1916. 166p [LC

MINNOWS FROM BRENCHLEY BROOK. Ed. by ——. London, Barrett, 1861. 24p [BM OTMC

**Bird, Ashmore H.**

WRITTEN THOUGHTS. Victoria, Colonist, 1925. 38p [AEU BVaU

**Birney, Earle, 1904–**

DAVID AND OTHER POEMS. Toronto, Ryerson, 1942. 40p [BVaU LC NSHD OKQ QMM

NOW IS TIME. Poems. Toronto, Ryerson, 1945. 56p [BVaU LC NBFU OKQ QMM

THE STRAIT OF ANIAN. Selected Poems. Toronto, Ryerson, 1948. 84p [BVaU LC NSHD MWU OTU

TRIAL OF A CITY AND OTHER VERSE. Toronto, Ryerson, 1952. 71p

20TH CENTURY CANADIAN POETRY. An Anthology with Intro. and Notes. Ed. by ——. Toronto, Ryerson, 1953. 169p

**Bishop, Mrs. Celia Maria Colpitts, 1879–**

MEMORIES IN RHYMES DOWN IN THE MARITIMES. Moncton, Author, 1952. 82p

**Bishop, M. Blanche, 1864–1917**

TIDAL YEARS AND OTHER POEMS. Memorial Edition. Wolfville, N.S., Kentville Pub. Co., 1929. 66p [Brown U NSHD

**Bishop, Mary (Davidson), 1905–1957**

IN HEAVEN'S VIEW. A Selection of the Verse of ——. Hounslow, Middlesex, Cedar Press, 1958. xiv + 46p

**Bishop, Mrs. Vivien Oonah de Blois, 1889–**

VARIED VERSE. By V.O. de B. [pseud]. Victoria, Author, 1957. 46p [mimeographed]

**Bjarnason, Paul**

ODES AND ECHOES. Vancouver, Author, 1954. 186p

**Black, Hibbert Crane**

ANONYMOUS POEMS. [Anon] Amherst, N.S., Gazette Power Print., 1889. 54p [NSWA

RANDOM POEMS. Sackville, Tribune Press, 1909. 85p [OTU NBSaM

**Black, Vera**

POEMS. Ste Agathe des Monts, Que., Author, 1939. 47p [OTU

**Blackadder, Edward, 1869–1922**

FANCIES OF BOYHOOD. A Series of Poems, Original and Translated. Halifax, Nova Scotia Print., 1890. 73p [BVaU OTP

POEMS: SONNETS, LYRICS, AND MISCELLANEOUS. Halifax, Nova Scotia Print., 1895. 34p [OTUV

**Black-Myers, Mrs. Mabel**

SONGS FROM NOVA SCOTIA. N.p., 1957. 48p (Carillon Poetry Chap-Books)

**Blair, Duncan Black, 1815–1891**

THE PSALMS OF THE APOCALYPSE. New Glasgow, Mackenzie, 1893. 14p [NSWA

**Blair, John Jr.**

COLLECTION OF RHYMES &c. [Parkhill, Ont., Gazette Print., 18—?] 157p [Various paging.] [OH

POEMS SERIOUS, SENTIMENTAL, PATRIOTIC, AND HUMOROUS. St. Catharines, Ont., Meek, 1875. 132p [BVaU NBFU OKQ

**Blake, Samuel Verschoyle, 1868–**

HER SOLDIER DEAD, AND OTHER VERSE. ... Toronto, [1914?]. 16p [Brown U BVaU OTU

**Blennerhasset, Margaret (Agnew), 1778?–1842**

THE WIDOW OF THE ROCK AND OTHER POEMS. By a Lady [pseud]. Montreal, Sparhawk, 1824. 192p [BM LC NSHD OTP QMM

**Blewett, Jean (McKishnie), 1862–1934**

THE CORNFLOWER AND OTHER POEMS. Toronto, Briggs, 1906. 256p [BM BVaU NSHD OKQ QMM

HEART SONGS. Toronto, Morang, 1897. 264p [BM BVaU OTP

JEAN BLEWETT'S POEMS. Toronto, McClelland, 1922. 259p [BM BVaU NSHD OKQ

**Bliss, William Blowers, 1795–1874**

TRANSLATIONS FROM CATULLUS, HORACE, ETC. Halifax, Author, 1872. 70p [NSHD

**Blomfield, Mary Diamond**

A LOYALIST SEQUENCE. A Book of Verse on Loyalist and Patriotic Themes. Toronto, Ontario Press, 1924. 31p [OTP

**Boa, Myrtle J., 1891–**

IDYLLS OF OUR ISLAND. Montreal, Witness Press, [1923]. 28p [BM BVaU QMM

RAINBOW RHYMES OF THE TIMES. Westmount, Que., Westmount News, 1933. 63p [Brown U

**Boag, John H.**

VICTORY VERSE. London, Lutterworth Press, 1941. 54p [BM BVaU LC

**Boak, Ethel Lawson**

ESCAPE. Victoria, Diggon-Hibben, n.d. 15p [AEU NSWA

**Bolton, B. Frank**

THE ROUT OF THE MUSES. A Political Poem. N.p., n.d. 24p [BVaU NBFU OPAL QMU

**Bolton, Margaret**

A ROBIN CALLS AND OTHER POEMS. Toronto, Wilson Press, 1946. 32p [BVaU

**Bonis, Rev. Robert Raynes, 1906–**

OUT IN THE WILDERNESS AND OTHER POEMS. Minden, Ont., Echo Press, 1933. 41p [Brown U OTU

**Boone, W.T.**

D'ARCY DUNN, OR THE HAUNTED CHURCH; AND OTHER POEMS. Windsor, N.S., New Book Pub. Library, 1867. 106p [NSHD NSWA

**Boreham, Margaret Bossance**

LITTLE WHITE BOATS. London, Stockwell, [1935?]. 72p [Brown U NBSaM

NEW SONGS. N.p., n.d. 12p [AEU NBSaM OPAL QMU

SONGS OF THE ROAD. N.p., n.d. 10p [NBSaM

**Borrett, William Coates, 1894–**

TALES TOLD IN RHYME, "THE FUSILIER" AND OTHERS. ... Halifax, Imperial Pub. Co., 1950. 138p [NSHD

**Borthwick, Rev. John Douglas, 1832–1912**

THE HARP OF CANAAN; or, Selections from the Best Poets on Biblical Subjects. Ed. by ——. Montreal, Worthington, 1866. 269p [Also: Montreal, Desbarats, 1871. 192p] [BVaU NBFU OTUV

POEMS AND SONGS ON THE SOUTH AFRICAN WAR. An Anthology from England, Africa, Australia, United States, but Chiefly Canada. Collected by ——. Montreal, [Gazette Pub. Co.], 1901. 215p [BVaU LC NSHD OTU

**Boswell, R.**

NORA. A Romance of the Great War. London, Stockwell, [1933?]. 64p [AEU

**Boultbee, Horatio Clarence**

LONGER POEMS. Toronto, T.H. Best, 1953. 149p

THE OXFORD LISTS AND OTHER POEMS. Toronto, Oxford U. Press, 1931. 44p [BM BVaU NBFU OTP

**Bourinot, Arthur Stanley, 1893–1969**

CANADA AT DIEPPE. Toronto, Ryerson, 1942. 16p [LC NBFU OTP

THE COLLECTED POEMS. ... Toronto, Ryerson, 1947. 222p [BVaU LC MWU NSHD OTP

DISCOVERY. Toronto, Ryerson, 1940. 11p [BVaU LC NBSaM OTU QMM

ELEVEN POEMS. Ottawa, Author, 1937. 9p [BM BVaU NSHD OTP

EVERYTHING ON EARTH MUST DIE. Ottawa, Author, 1955. 3p

FIVE POEMS. Toronto, Ryerson, 1943. 8p [LC NSHD OTP

A GATHERING. Poems. Ottawa, Author, 1958. 14p

LA SALLE. Written on ... the 250th Anniversary. ... Ottawa, Author, 1937. 4p [Rev. version later pub. in RHYMES OF THE FRENCH REGIME.] [BM NSHD OKQ QMM

LAURENTIAN LYRICS AND OTHER POEMS. Toronto, Copp Clark, 1915. 30p [BM BVaU NSHD OTU QMM

LINES FROM DEEPWOOD. Toronto, Heaton Print., 1946. 8p [OTP

LYRICS FROM THE HILLS. Ottawa, Hope, 1923. 40p [BM BVaU LC NSHD OKQ QMM

MORE LINES FROM DEEPWOOD. [Toronto, Shepard Print., 1949]. 16p [BVaU NBFU OKQ

NINE POEMS. Toronto, Ryerson, 1944. 12p [NSHD OTP

OTTAWA LYRICS, AND VERSES FOR CHILDREN. Ottawa, Graphic, 1929. 71p [BVaU NSHD OTU QMM

PATTERING FEET. A Book of Childhood Verses. Ottawa, Graphic, 1925. 77p [BM BVaU LC NBFU OKQ

POEMS. Toronto, Best, 1921. 47p [BM BVaU LC NSHD OKQ QMM

RHYMES OF THE FRENCH REGIME. Toronto, Nelson, 1937. 44p [BVaU LC NSHD OKQ QMM

SELECTED POEMS (1915–1935). With a Note by Sir Andrew Macphail. Toronto, Macmillan, 1935. 90p [BVaU LC NSHD OKQ QMM

SONNETS IN MEMORY OF MY MOTHER. Ottawa, Hope, [1931]. 18p [OTP NSHD

TEN NARRATIVE POEMS. Ottawa, Author, 1955. 32p

THIS GREEN EARTH. Gananoque, Ont., 1953. 52p

THE TREASURERS OF THE SNOW. Toronto, Ryerson, 1950. 16p [NBSaM OTP

TOM THOMSON AND OTHER POEMS. Toronto, Ryerson, 1954. 10p

TRUE HARVEST. Poems. Toronto, Ryerson, 1945. 56p [BVaU LC NSHD OTU QM

UNDER THE SUN. Poems. Toronto, Macmillan, 1939. 69p [BVaU LC MWU NSHD OKQ QMM

WHAT FAR KINGDOM. Poems. Toronto, Ryerson, 1941. 66p [BVaU LC NSHD OTU QMM

**Bourke, David Dominick, 1845–1921**
THE NARROW DELL. A Story in Verse, and Other Poems. Ed. and completed by his daughter, Julia Bourke. New York, Exposition Press. 1955. 190p

**Boutilier, Daniel William, 1897–1957**
ROCKIN' CHAIR RHYMES. [Amherst, N.S.?], Author, [1954?]. 48p

**Bowden, Ernest J.**
OUR DESTINY AND OTHER POEMS. Toronto, Briggs, 1911. 111p [BM BVaU OKQ

**Bowen, Minnie Hallowell**
ADORATION. Poems. Sherbrooke, Que., n.d. 16p [Brown U
THE CANADIAN NAVY. [Anon] N.p., n.d. 7p [OONL
INNKEEPER OF BETHLEHEM. Sherbrooke, Que., Page-Sangster Print., 1937. 15p [OTU
RED FLOWER OF LIFE. Poems. Sherbrooke, Que., Page Print., [193–?]. 17p [Brown U
THE STORY OF THE LONE PINE. Sherbrooke, Que., Page Print., 1921. 7p [BM OTP

**Bowen, Mrs. Minnie Henrietta Bethune, 1861–**
WINNOWAIA. By M.H. Bowen. With a Foreword by Frank Oliver Call. Sherbrooke, Que., Page-Sangster Print., 1935. 39p [OKQ QMU

**Bowes, Carleton Frederick, –1962**
IDYLLS OF ACADIE AND OTHER POEMS. [Halifax?], 1924. 24p [Brown U NSHPL
MISCELLANEOUS VERSE. Halifax, Author, 1921. 30p [BVaU NSWA

**Bowles, Walter**
VERSE AND VERSE. Toronto, Ryerson, 1956. 56p

**Bowman, Anne**
RHYMES FROM THE SHADOWS. Guelph, n.d. 15p [Adelphi cat. 58

**Bowman, Ariel**
HOURS OF CHILDHOOD, AND OTHER POEMS. [Anon] Montreal, A. Bowman, 1820. 94p [OTUV QMSS

**Bowman, Louise (Morey), 1882–1944**
CHARACTERS IN CADENCE. Toronto, Macmillan, 1938. 91p [BM BVaU NBFU OTUV QMM
DREAM TAPESTRIES. Toronto, Macmillan, 1924. 91p [BM BVaU LC NBFU OKQ QMM
MOONLIGHT AND COMMON DAY. Toronto, Macmillan, 1922. 63p [BM BVaU NBFU OLU QMM

**Box, William McNab**

FORTY POEMS. London, Chester & Lang, 1944. 49p [BM LC

NATURE'S BYWAYS. Toronto, Crucible Press, 1941. 10p [LC OTP

**Boyd, Adam**

FRASER CANYON AND OTHER POEMS. Victoria, Diggon-Hibben, 1946. 20p [BViPA

**Boyd, Ann**

SPRING MAGIC. Toronto, Ryerson, 1931. 16p [OKQ

**Boyd, Edna Alice**

SCRIBBLINGS. Toronto, Author, [1933?]. 39p [OTU

**Boyd, John, 1864–1933**

THE DEATH OF DOLLARD AND OTHER POEMS. Montreal, Author, 1914. 64p [BVaU OOP QMM

**Boyle, Charles Frederick, 1911–1966**

EXCUSE FOR FUTILITY. Toronto, Ryerson, 1939. 8p [BVaU NBSaM OKQ QMM

PRAYERS AT A HIGH ALTAR. Toronto, Ryerson, 1942. 14p [NBFU

STARS BEFORE THE WIND. Toronto, Ryerson, 1937. 8p [BVaU NBSaM OKQ QMM

**Boyle, David, 1842–1911**

UNCLE JIM'S CANADIAN NURSERY RHYMES. For Family and Kindergarten Use. [Anon] Toronto, Musson, 1908. 83p [OTP

**Boyne, Edward**

[POEMS] COMPOSED BY BLIND POET BOYNE. Toronto, [1896?]. 47p [OKQ

**Bradford, John Locke**

THE BLIND SOLDIER AND OTHER POEMS. Halifax, Imperial Pub., 1921. 32p [Brown U

DAD AND THE LONG TREK. Wolfville, N.S., Davidson, 1943. 40p [NSHD

**Brack, Jessie (Wanless), 1826–**

"DREAMS OF HOME" AND OTHER POEMS. Toronto, 1911. 32p [OTP

**Bradbury, Fred G.R.**

LIGHTS AND SHADOWS OF LANDSCAPE AND LIFE. Songs, Poems, and Rhymes. N.p., Author, 1932. 95p [AEU OOP

PEN PICTURES FROM NATURE'S ART GALLERIES. N.p., n.d. 79p [AEU

**Bradshaw, B. Maude**

POETRY FOR EVERY MONTH. Toronto, Educational Book, 1930. 128p [CC

**Bradshaw, Thecla Jean (Robbins)**

MOBILES. Toronto, Ryerson, 1955. 16p

**Bramley-Moore, Alfred Arthur, 1881–**

POEMS ON THE GOSPEL. Montreal, Chapman, 1923. 94p [BM Brown U BVaU NBFU OOP

**Brannen, Sterling, 1888–1953**

SNACKS. A Collection of Original Verse, Epigrams, Paragraphs. Fredericton, Author, [1947?]. [BVaU NBFU

**Breakenridge, John, 1820–1854**

THE CRUSADES AND OTHER POEMS. Kingston, Rowlands, 1846. 327p [BM BVaU LC OTP

**Breckenridge, Rev. James, –1879**

POEMS. Toronto, Dredge, 1860. 256p [OTP

**Breeze, James T.**

THE ASSASSINATION OF PRESIDENT LINCOLN. A Poem. Belleville, Bell, 1865. 8p [Bound with MEMORIES OF MY YOUTH. ... See below.]

THE BEAUTIES OF BELLEVILLE. [Anon] Belleville, 1864. 20p [OKQ

CANADIAN POEMS. Port Hope, "British Canadian" Office, 1866. 16p [OKQ

THE DOMINION OF CANADA. The Great Institution of Our Country. A Poem on the Grand Trunk Railway. Montreal, 1867. 24p [OTP QMSS

THE FENIAN RAID!! THE QUEEN'S OWN! Poems on the Events of the Hour. Napanee, "Weekly Express," 1866. 6p [QMSS

THE GLORY OF THE AGE, THE ATLANTIC CABLE. A Poem on the Wondrous Achievements of Science. Ottawa, Citizen, 1866. 16p [NSWA

THE GREAT THEME OF THE AGE. A Poem on the Confederation of the British American Provinces. Ottawa, "Daily Citizen," 1866. 23p [QMBM

THE MARTYRED PRESIDENT. 3rd ed. Montreal, 1867. 8p [CCJ

MEMORIES OF MY YOUTH. A Collection of Poems. Napanee, Kennedy, 1865. 32p [OTP

ORIGINAL CANADIAN LITERATURE. The Miscellaneous Works of the Canadian Poet, J.T. Breeze. Brockville, O'Brien, 1868. 16p [OTP

A POEM OF WELCOME TO HER ROYAL HIGHNESS THE PRINCESS LOUISE ... with A POEM ON THE WRECK OF THE STEAMER "WAUBUNO". ... Collingwood, "Bulletin," 1879. 8p [OTP

THE POET'S GLANCE OF KINGSTON SCENES. Picton, 1864. 24p [CCJ

THE POET'S MEMENTO OF PICTON. A Poem on the Scenery, Institutions, Ministers, Literary and Public Men of the Town. Picton, "North American," 1865. 24p [OTUV

THE POET'S RAMBLES THROUGH TORONTO. ... Toronto, Guardian, 1864. 24p [OTP

TO MY BROTHER IN HEAVEN. THE BETHANY FAMILY. ABRAHAM LINCOLN IN HEAVEN. N.p., [18–?]. 16p [OTP

**Bresnahan, Mrs. Jessie M.**
POEMS OF THE PEACE RIVER COUNTRY AND OTHERS. Ilfracombe, Devon, Stockwell, 1960. 71p

**Brewer, Alice**
SPRING IN SAVARY. Toronto, Ryerson, 1926. 16p [BVaU NBSaM OKQ

**Brewster, Elizabeth Winnifred, 1922–**
EAST COAST. Toronto, Ryerson, 1951. 8p
LILLOOET. Toronto, Ryerson, 1954. 28p
ROADS AND OTHER POEMS. Toronto, Ryerson, 1957. 12p

**Breyfogle, W.R.**
AUTUMN LEAVES AND OTHER VERSE. Peterborough, Ont., Author, 1936. 58p [NSHPL
DRIFTWOOD AND OTHER VERSE. Peterborough, Ont., Author, 1938. 42p [NSWA
IN LILAC TIME AND OTHER RHYME. Peterborough, Author, 1934. 56p [BVaU NSWA OPeT

**Brichan, Wellington, 1812–1880?**
THE WIFE, OR THE WUDDY, AND OTHER POEMS AND SONGS. Sarnia, Observer Steam Job Press, 1876. 106p [Phelps p89

**Brindle, Walter, 1869?–**
FRANCE AND FLANDERS. Four Years Experience Told in Poem & Story. By Sapper W. Brindle. Saint John, Smith, 1919. 84p [Brown U NBFU

**British Columbia, University of. Student Publications Board**
CHAPBOOK. Vancouver, Boyd, 1931. 22p [BVaU

**Broadfoot, Samuel Rupert**
CANADA, THE LAND OF PROMISE, AND OTHER POEMS. Woodstock, Sentinel-Review Press, 1916. 51p [2nd ed.: Same publisher, s.d. 101p] [BM BVaU NBFU OTP QMSS
HOLIDAYING IN CANADA ON THE OTTAWA RIVER. Ottawa, Author, 1941. 203p [NBFU OOA

**Brooke, Frances (Moore), 1724–1789**
VIRGINIA. A Tragedy. With Odes, Pastorals, and Translations. London, Author, 1756. 159p [BM

**Brooke, John**
POEMS. Toronto, Hunter Rose, 1882. 84p [BVaU NBFU OTU QMM

**Brooks, Anne Sutherland**
BLUE DUSK AND OTHER POEMS. By Anne Sutherland. [Toronto], Livingstone, [1934]. 63p [AEU Brown U OTP
I MET SOME LITTLE PEOPLE. Toronto, Ryerson, 1941. 55p [BVaU NSHD OTP

LITTLE SONGS FOR SALE. By Anne Sutherland. Toronto, Ryerson, 1928. 24p [NBFU OKQ

A RIBBAND OF BLUE. By Anne Sutherland. Guelph, Author, 1929. 31p [AEU OTU

THE SUNNE-BEAM STAIRE. Guelph, Author, 1930. 38p [AEU

WITHIN A WICKET GATE. 2nd ed. By Anne Sutherland. Toronto, Ryerson, 1927. 24p [NBFU OKQ

**Brooks, Lillie A. (Macmillan), 1874–**

THE BAND OF PURPLE. A Collection of Canadian Poems. Ed. by ——. Toronto, Oxford U. Press, 1915. 19p [BM BVaU NBFU OTU

CHRISTMAS SONGS. N.p., n.d. 8p [OKQ

THE FORTY-EIGHTH HIGHLANDERS. [1915]. [BM

THE LAND OF THE NORTHERN MEN. Toronto, Ryerson, 1924. 55p [BVaU NBFU OKQ QMBM

**Brown, Audrey Alexandra, 1904–**

ALL FOOLS DAY. Toronto, Ryerson, 1948. 56p [Brown U BVaU LC NBFU OTP

CHALLENGE TO TIME AND DEATH. Toronto, Macmillan, 1943. 55p [BVaU LC NSHD OTP

A DRYAD IN NANAIMO. Toronto, Macmillan, 1931. 70p [New ed., together with eleven new poems: Toronto, Macmillan, 1934. 120p] [BM BVaU LC NSHD OTU QMM

THE TREE OF RESURRECTION AND OTHER POEMS. Toronto, Macmillan, 1937. 151p [BM BVaU LC NSHD OKQ QMM

V-E DAY. Toronto, Ryerson, 1947. 5p [BVaU LC NBSaM OKQ

**Brown, Edward Killoran, 1905–1951**

SELECTED POEMS OF DUNCAN CAMPBELL SCOTT. With a memoir by ——. Toronto, Ryerson, 1951. 176p

**Brown, Frank S., –1915**

CONTINGENT DITTIES AND OTHER SOLDIER SONGS OF THE GREAT WAR. By Frank S. Brown, Sergeant, P.P.C.L.I. (The Pats). Ed. by Holbrook Jackson. London, Low Marston, 1915. 79p [BM Brown U BVaU LC NBFU

**Brown, J.**

RIVULET. A Collection of Hymns and Temperance Songs, for Bands of Hope and Temperance Meetings. Comp. by ——. Halifax, Messenger Print., [1876]. 8p [NSHD

**Brown, James N.J.**

PROSPECTOR'S TRAIL. [Vancouver?], Author, 1941. 64p [BVaU

**Brown, Jessie Findlay**

UP CAME THE MOON. Oshawa, Ont., Mundy-Goodfellow, 1936. 79p [Brown U BVaU NBFU OTU

**Brown, John Henry, 1859–1946**

POEMS. Lyrical and Dramatic. Ottawa, Durie, 1892. 204p [BM BVaU LC NSHD OTU QMM

**Brown, Margaret H., 1887–**

THE AWAKENING. Shanghai, Author, 1933. 29p [AEU OTUV QMG

**Browne, H.F.**

THE STRANGE ADVENTURES OF A CARP. By "Norroy" [pseud]. London, Dean, 1884. 19p [BM

A TALE OF A WHALE. Written and Illus. by "Norroy" [pseud]. London, Dean, 1884. 19p [BM LC

**Browne, Thaddeus A.**

THE BELGIAN MOTHER AND BALLADS OF BATTLE TIME. Toronto, Macmillan, 1917. 105p [BM Brown U BVaU NBFU OTU

A TRIBUTE TO SIR WILFRID LAURIER, PREMIER OF CANADA, 1896–1911. IN MEMORIAM. [A Poem. With Portraits.] Ottawa, Modern Press, 1919. 39p [BM NBSaM OTP QQL

THE WHITE PLAGUE, AND OTHER POEMS. Toronto, Briggs, 1909. 75p [BM Brown U BVaU NSHD OTU

**Browning, Samuel**

POEMS. V. I. London, Green, 1846. 320p [V. II, THE HISTORY OF JOSEPH AND OTHER POEMS, not published (?); *cf.* Announcement Prefixed.] [BM LC QMSS

**Brownlow, Edward Burrough, 1857–1895**

ORPHEUS AND OTHER POEMS. Montreal, Pen and Pencil Club, 1896. 96p [BM BVaU MWU NBFU OTU QMM

**Bruce, Charles Tory, 1906–1971**

THE FLOWING SUMMER. Toronto, Ryerson, 1947. 31p [BVaU LC NSHD OTP

GREY SHIP MOVING. Toronto, Ryerson, 1945. 34p [BM BVaU LC MWU NSHD OTU QMM

THE MULGRAVE ROAD. Toronto, Macmillan, 1951. 39p

PERSONAL NOTE. Toronto, Ryerson, 1941. 8p [BVaU NBFU OTU QMM

TOMORROW'S TIDE. Toronto, Macmillan, 1932. 28p [BVaU NBFU OOCC

WILD APPLES. Sackville, N.B., Tribune Press, 1927. 23p [NSHD OKQ

**Bruce, Mary**

MAN IS A CREATOR. N.p., Author, 1940. 34p [OTU QMU

**Brundle, John, 1882–**

ACROSS THE ARCTIC SEAS. From the pen of John, a Suffolk Herd Boy [pseud]. Roche's Point, Ont., Author, 1951. 79p

BROMESWELL, MY SUFFOLK HOME. A Pastoral of My Child and Boyhood. From the pen of John, a Suffolk Herd Boy [pseud]. Roche's Point, Ont., Author, 1952. 31p

CULLED SELECTIONS OF THE MIND. From the pen of John, a Suffolk Herd Boy [pseud]. Roche's Point, Ont., Author, 1957. 24p

THE FORSAKEN PLOT IN THE LITTLE CHURCHYARD. From the pen of John, a Suffolk Herd Boy [pseud]. Roche's Point, Ont., Author, 1950. 32p [Brown U BVaU OTU

THE GINK. Roche's Point, Ont., Author, 1954. 3p

THE GIRL WHO DIED OF A BROKEN HEART. From the pen of John, a Suffolk Herd Boy [pseud]. Roche's Point, Ont., Author, 1941. 33p [Brown U LC OTU

THE GREAT ANTARTIC [*sic*] CALL. From the pen of John, a Suffolk Herd Boy [pseud]. Roche's Point, Ont., Author, 1954. 32p

LAURA, THE HEROINE OF BEAVER DAM, JUNE 24TH 1813. From the pen of John, a Suffolk Herd Boy [pseud]. Roche's Point, Ont., Author, 1949. 40p [Brown U BVaU OTU

THE LITTLE ROSEBUD. From the pen of John, a Suffolk Herd Boy [pseud]. Roche's Point, Ont., Author, 1958. 14p

OFF BOSTON LIGHT, JUNE 1, 1813. From the pen of John, a Suffolk Herd Boy [pseud]. Roche's Point, Ont., Author, 1945. 20p [BVaU OTP

THE SIX PIECES. Words and Music. Roche's Point, Ont., Author, 1946. 16p [BVaU OTU

SONGS, SPIRITUAL AND OTHERWISE. Words and Music. Roche's Point, Ont., Author, 1941. 19p [Brown U BVaU OTU

SUNDAY PICKINGS OF THE MIND. From the pen of John, a Suffolk Herd Boy [pseud]. Roche's Point, Ont., Author, 1941. 22p [Brown U OTU

TWO CAROLS. Roche's Point, Ont., Author, 1954. 4p

THE UNNAMED MAID OF LYME. From the pen of John, a Suffolk Herd Boy [pseud]. Toronto, McLean, 1939. 20p [Brown U BVaU LC OTU

THE WOMAN OF THE UNBEATEN TRAIL, NANCY HANKS, 1782–1818. Roche's Point, Ont., Author, 1940. 8p [Brown U OTU

YE SAILORS OF THE ISLAND RACE. ... Roche's Point, Ont., Author, 1956. 10p [Refers to Admiral Robert Blake and Admiral Lord Nelson.]

**Bruun, Arthur Geoffrey, 1898–**

MAGIC CASEMENTS AND OTHER VERSES. Vancouver, Author, 1922. 9p [BVaU

**Brymner, Douglas, 1823–1902**

THE TWO MONGRELS. A Modern Eclogue. By Tumas Treddles [pseud]. Toronto, Hunter Rose, 1876. 7p [OTP

**Bucham, Mary A.**

MEMORIES, AND OTHER POEMS. Toronto, Briggs, 1905. 87p [BM BVaU OKQ

**Buchanan, Mrs. Mary**

COUNTRY BREEZES FROM BREEZY BRAE. Thornbury, Ont., Beaver Valley Pub., n.d. 174p [OTUV

**Buck, Alanson L.**

THE OUTLAW AND OTHER POEMS. Toronto, Briggs, 1913. 161p [BM Brown U NBFU OLU SSU

**Buck, Annie Lucinda (Myers), 1865–**

MY LOVE'S GARDEN AND OTHER POEMS. London, Stockwell, [1922?]. 19p [OONL

POETICAL PAMPHLETS. N.p., n.d. [Contains autobiography.] [OLU

**Buck, James A.**

THE SAVIOUR'S SECOND COMING. The Great Mystery of Babylon Unravelled. The Great Judgement Day at Hand. ... [Anon] Belleville, 1884. 27p [Brown U

**Buckley, Beatrice Barron**

SONGS OF WEENY GOPHER. Toronto, Macmillan, 1941. 61p [OONL OTP

**Buckley, Joan**

BLUE STEEPLES. Vancouver, Clarke & Stuart, 1942. 21p [BVaU NBFU OKQ

GREEN FLAME. Toronto, Crucible Press, 1940. 22p [BVaU LC NBFU OTP

SPRING AFTER WAR. Langley Prairie, B.C., Advance Press, 1946. 24p [Brown U BVaU

WESTERN SUNFLOWERS. An Anthology of British Columbian Verse. Langley Prairie, B.C., Author, 1946. 33p [BVaU OKQ

**Bullen, John Ravener, 1886–1927**

WHITE FIRE. Athol, Mass., Recluse Press, 1927. 86p [LC

**Bullock, Rev. William, 1797–1874**

SONGS OF THE CHURCH. Halifax, Clapp, 1854. 235p [Also: London, 1855.] [BM NSHD OTP

**Bunner, Freda Helen (Newton), 1904–**

ORPHAN AND OTHER POEMS. Toronto, Ryerson, 1956. 8p

**Burchell, M. Edith**

RHYMES AND CHIMES. N.p., [1927?]. 14p [NSHP OONL QMU

**Burns, Elizabeth Rollit**

LITTLE CANADIANS. ... [Montreal], Desbarats, [1899]. 40p [BM BViP OTUV

**Burns, Malcolm, 1887–**

GOLDEN GLEAMS. Vancouver, Rose, Cowan & Latta, 1936. 93p [BVaU OLU

**Burpee, Lawrence Johnstone, 1873–1946**

A CENTURY OF CANADIAN SONNETS. An Anthology. Ed. by ——. Toronto, Musson, 1910. 112p [BVaU NBFU OTU QMM

FLOWERS FROM A CANADIAN GARDEN. Selected and ed. by ——. Toronto, Musson, [1909?]. 112p [BVaU NBFU OKQ QMM

SONGS OF FRENCH CANADA. Trans., selected, and arranged by ——. Toronto, Musson, 1909. 88p [BVaU OKQ QMM

**Burr, Everett Harold, 1894–1931**

RICH MAN, POOR MAN. Toronto, Ryerson, 1932. 8p [BVaU NBSaM OTU QMM

**Burtis, William Richard M., 1818–1882**

THE NEW DOMINION. A Poem. Saint John, McMillan, 1867. 16p [Brown U NBFU

**Burton, Violet, 1894–**

NO STONE TO THROW, AND OTHER POEMS. London, Stockwell, 1935. 12p [CC

**Burwell, Rev. Adam Hood, 1790–1849**

SUMMER EVENING CONTEMPLATIONS. Montreal, Lovell, 1849. 12p [BM

**Buschlen, John Preston, 1888–**

THE WORLD WAR. Poems. Toronto, Hollingsworth & Buschlen, [1914]. 19p [ACU BM BVaU OTU

**Butchart, Reuben, 1863–1963**

THE LYRIC FLUTE, AND OTHER POEMS. Toronto, Macmillan, 1928. 78p [Brown U BVaU LC NBFU OTU

**Butcher, Albert Edward Valentine**

POEMS. Ilfracombe, Devon, Stockwell, 1959. 17p

THE SAGA OF THE NANCY, AND OTHER POEMS. Ilfracombe, Devon, Stockwell, 1960. 32p

**Butcher, John H., 1879?–**

THE FARMER POET. A Book of Homespun Poetry. N.p., 1953. 88p

**Butler, Ethel H.**

LITTLE THUNDER'S WOOING. A Legend of the Blomidon and Glooscap Country. Port Royal, N.S., Abanaki Press, 1950. 16p [Brown U BVaU

**Butler, J. Edward P., 1902–**

THE HOUND OF EARTH. A Selection of Poems. Newcastle, N.B., Union Advocate, 1937. 16p [NBFU

RECOLLECTED IN TRANQUILLITY. A Selection of Poems. Chatham, N.B., priv. print., 1956. 40p

**Butler, Martin, 1857–**

MAPLE LEAVES AND HEMLOCK BRANCHES. A Collection of Poems. Fredericton, "Gleaner," 1889. 60p [146p?] [NBFU OTP QMM

PATRIOTIC AND PERSONAL POEMS. Fredericton, Journal Office, 1898. 146p [NBFU OTU

**Byrnes, John Maclay**

THE PATHS TO YESTERDAY. Memories of Old St. John's, Newfoundland. Including a number of typical Newfoundland Poems, each from the gifted pen of a Terra Novian. Boston, Meador, 1931. 235p [BVaU LC OTU

**C., A.P.**

EXTRACTS AND HYMNS. Brockville, Merrill, n.d. [187–?] 16p [Amtmann cat. 140

**Cain, Sydney C.**

PRAIRIE FAIRIES AND OTHER VERSES. Regina, Leader, n.d. 30p [BViPA

**Calder, Robert McLean**

A BERWICKSHIRE BARD. The Songs and Poems of Robert McLean Calder. Edited, with Introductory Memoir by W.S. Crockett. Paisley, J. & R. Parlane, 1897. 306p [BM

HAME SANGS. London, King, 1887. 140p [OTUV

**Caldwell, James Ernest, 1862–1954**

THE CASTLE ON THE HILL. Ottawa, Thorburn, 1899. 30p [OTUV

SONGS OF THE PINES. Toronto, Briggs, 1895. 142p [BVaU LC NSHD OTUV QMM

**Call, Frank Oliver, 1878–1956**

ACANTHUS AND WILD GRAPE. Toronto, McClelland, [1920]. 80p [BM BVaU LC NSHD OKQ QMM

BLUE HOMESPUN. Toronto, Ryerson, 1924. 43p [BM BVaU LC NSHD OTU

IN A BELGIAN GARDEN, AND OTHER POEMS. London, MacDonald, 1917. 45p [BM BVaU NBFU OKQ

SIMPLES, CURTAINS, BURNED FORESTS, THE CATHEDRAL BUILDERS. N.p., n.d. 4p [OONL

SONNETS FOR YOUTH. Toronto, Ryerson, 1944. 8p [BVaU LC NSHD OTP

**Callaghan, Francis, 1902?–**

THE REED AND THE CROSS. Toronto, Ryerson, 1923. 51p [BM BVaU LC NSHD OKQ QMM

**Callan, Richard**

CHAINS OF HARMONY. Atlanta, Ga., Banner Press, Emory University, 1939. 67p [BVaU LC OTUV

**Calvert, William Dobree**

YPNOS. Toronto, Crucible Press, 1941. 56p [V.1] [BVaU LC OKQ

YPNOS. [North Vancouver], Author, 1942–44. [V.2–4] [BViPA

**Cameron, Rev. Charles Innes, 1837–1879**

POEMS AND HYMNS. Geelong, Australia, Purdie, 1870. 119p [Also: Toronto, Robinson, 1879. 60p] [BVaU LC NSHD OTP QMM

**Cameron, Elizabeth**

SONGS THAT THE WIND HAS SUNG. Lakefield, Ont., The News, [1926?]. 26p [Brown U OTU

**Cameron, Fred J.**

THE HERMIT OF CHOKECHERRY CREEK, AND OTHER POEMS. Edmonton, Institute of Applied Arts, 1950. 113p [AEU Brown U

**Cameron, George Frederick, 1854–1885**

LYRICS ON FREEDOM, LOVE AND DEATH. Ed. by his brother Charles J. Cameron. Boston, Moore; Kingston, Shannon, 1887. 296p [BM BVaU LC NSHD OKQ QMM

**Cameron, Hugh Duncan, 1833–**

THE GARLAND. A Collection of Songs and Lyrics, Original and Selected, for Schools and Colleges. Goderich, 1865. 120p [CCJ Rhod.

**Cameron, Jean**

CHAPBOOK. [Poems by members of the Letters Club of the University of British Columbia. ...] By Jean Cameron, Carol Coates, Roy Daniells, James Dunn, Ronald Grantham, Lionel Haweis, Jeanne Lakeman-Shaw, Frances Lucas, Betty Moore, R.A. Pilkington, Vernon van Sickle, Frank Wilson. Vancouver, priv. print., 1931. 24p [BVaU

**Cameron, William Bleasdell, 1862–1951**

THE YARN OF THE HOWLING GALE. (An Alberta Barque with a Bad Bight). [Anon] Athabasca, Alta., Cameron Shipyards, 1938. 12p [A satire aimed at the Social Credit party. Attributed to William Bleasdell Cameron.] [AEU

**Campbell, Amy E.**

HEART FORGET-ME-NOTS. Toronto, Briggs, 1910. 80p [BM BVaU NBFU OTU

**Campbell, Arthur**

SONGS OF THE PINEWOODS. London, Cox, 1894. 90p [BM OTUV QMM

**Campbell, Austin, 1884–**

... THEY SHALL BUILD ANEW. Toronto, Ryerson, 1944. 7p [BVaU LC NBFU OTU

**Campbell, Charles**

CANADA. A Metrical Story. Toronto, Briggs, 1897. 32p [BM BVaU LC NSHD OTUV

**Campbell, H.**

CHRIST'S COMING DAY. A Rhapsody on the Apocalypse. New York, Our Hope Pub. Co., 1938. 68p [CC

**Campbell, John Lorne, 1906–**

A COLLECTION OF FOLK-SONGS AND MUSIC MADE IN NOVA SCOTIA. [Dublin?], 1947. 59p [LC

HIGHLAND SONGS OF THE FORTY-FIVE. Ed. and Trans. ... by ——. Edinburgh, Grant, 1933. xxxvi+327p [LC OTU QMM

**Campbell, John Robert Lamont, –1959**

THE GARDEN OF THOUGHTS. Charlottetown, Author, n.d. 20p [QMU

GOLDEN MOMENTS COINED IN THE MINT OF TIME. By John of the Lilacs [pseud]. Sackville, N.B., Tribune Press, 1947. 322p [OOP OTU

**Campbell, [Miss] M.A.**

POSTHUMOUS POEMS. Woodstock, Ont., 1865. 26p [OOP

**Campbell, Marjorie (Freeman), 1896–**

HIGH ON A HILL. Toronto, Ryerson, 1949. 16p [BVaU NBSaM OTP

MERRY-GO-ROUND. Toronto, Ryerson, 1946. 16p [BVaU LC NBSaM OKQ

PORTS OF CALL. Toronto, Ryerson, 1960. 56p

**Campbell, Ralph J., 1904–1936**

LOCAL LYRICS. Halifax, Allen, [192–?]. 35p [Brown U

**Campbell, Wilfred, 1858–1918**

ATLANTEAN LYRICS. [Two Poems.] N.p., Author, [1913?]. 3p [NSWA OTP

BEYOND THE HILLS OF DREAM. Boston, Houghton, 1899. 137p [BM BVaU LC NSHD OTU QMM

THE COLLECTED POEMS OF WILFRED CAMPBELL. New York, Revell, 1905. 354p. [Also: Toronto, Briggs, 1905, under title of THE POEMS OF WILFRED CAMPBELL (*q.v.*).] [BM LC NBFU OTU

DECEMBER LYRICS. Ottawa, 1913. 2p [OTU

DEPARTURE. Ottawa, 1899. 2p [NBFU OTU

THE DISCOVERERS. A Poem ... issued for the New Year, 1905. [Ottawa, 1904?] 3p [NBFU OTP QMU

THE DREAD VOYAGE. Poems. Toronto, Briggs, 1893. 190p [BVaU NSHD OTU QMM

LAKE LYRICS AND OTHER POEMS. Saint John, McMillan, 1889. 160p [BVaU LC NSHD OKQ QMM

LANGEMARCK, AND OTHER WAR POEMS. With intro. by Rev. Dr. Herridge. Ottawa, St. Andrew's Church, [1917]. 14p [NBFU

THE LYRE DEGENERATE. A Poem ... issued for the New Year, 1904. [Ottawa, 1903?]. 3p [NBFU OLU QMG

LYRICS OF IRON AND MIST. Ottawa, Author, 1916. 4p [NBFU

LYRICS OF THE DREAD REDOUBT. Ottawa, Author, 1917. 3p [NBFU

NIGHT. THE HOUSE OF DREAMS. Two Poems. ... Issued Privately to ... Friends for the New Year, 1903. N.p., 1903. 3p [OKQ

THE OXFORD BOOK OF CANADIAN VERSE. Chosen by ——. Toronto, Oxford U. Press, 1913. 343p [BM BVaU LC NSHD

POEMS OF LOYALTY BY BRITISH AND CANADIAN AUTHORS. Selected by ——. London, Nelson, 1913. 99p [BM BVaU NBFU OTU

THE POEMS OF WILFRED CAMPBELL. Toronto, Briggs, 1905. 354p [BM BVaU NBFU OKQ QMM

THE POETICAL WORKS OF WILFRED CAMPBELL. Ed. with a Memoir by W.J. Sykes. London, Hodder, 1923. xxii + 363p [BM BVaU LC NSHD OTU QMM

REQUIEM. EDWARD THE PEACE MAKER. [Ottawa, Author, 1910]. 3p [BVaU NBFU OTU

SAGAS OF VASTER BRITAIN. Poems of the Race, the Empire and the Divinity of Man. Toronto, Musson, 1914. 163p [BM BVaU NSHD OTP

A SHEAF OF WINTER LYRICS. Ottawa, Author, [1906]. 4p [BVaU OTU QMM

SNOWFLAKES AND SUNBEAMS. St. Stephen, St. Croix Courier, 1888. 36p [OTP

THE VANGUARD. A Poem ... issued Privately to his Friends for the New Year, 1901. Ottawa, Author, [1900?]. 4p [AEU NBFU OLU QMU

WAR LYRICS. Ottawa, Author, 1915. 4p [NBFU

**Campbell, William M.**

ZORRA. Boston, Sherman, 1915. 74p [BM OTL

**Campbell, Zola Isabell (Campbell), 1880–1967**

A TALE OF THE EARLY YEARS. Edmonton, n.d. 16p [Describes early days of South Edmonton (Strathcona).] [BViPA Peel

**Canadian Authors' Association. Calgary Branch**

CANADIAN POEMS. Calgary, the Branch, 1937. 46p [AEU Brown U OTU

COLLECTED POEMS. Calgary, McAra, 1934. 39p [BVa

**Canadian Authors' Association. Edmonton Branch**

ALBERTA POETRY YEAR BOOK, 1930. Edmonton, the Branch, 1931. [Also issued in subsequent years.] [OTU QMM

ALBERTA POETRY YEAR BOOK [21st]. [Edmonton], Edmonton Branch, Canadian Authors Association, [1950]. 62p [OONL

**Canadian Authors' Association. Manitoba Branch**

MANITOBA POETRY CHAPBOOK, 1933. Winnipeg, Israelite Press, 1933. 32p [BViP OKQ OTP

**Canadian Authors' Association. Montreal Branch**

MONTREAL IN VERSE. An Anthology of English Poetry by Montreal Poets. Ed. by Leo Cox. Montreal, Poetry Group of the Montreal Branch, 1942. 48p [LC NBFU OKQ QMM

POETRY YEAR-BOOK, 1925. Montreal, the Branch, 1925. [Also issued in subsequent years.] [BVaU LC NBFU OTU QMM

**Canadian Authors' Association. Nova Scotia Branch**

AN ACADIAN SHEAF. Selections from Current Nova Scotian Poetry. Halifax, Macnab, 1934–35. 2v [NSHD OTU QMM

**Canadian Authors' Association. Ottawa Branch**

PROFILE. A Chapbook of Canadian Verse. Ottawa, the Branch, 1946. 47p [BVaU OTP

**Canadian Authors' Association. Saskatchewan Branch**

SASKATCHEWAN. Her Infinite Variety. [Regina, Leader Pub. Co., 1924]. 88p [BVaU LC OKQ

SASKATCHEWAN POETRY YEAR-BOOK, 1935. Regina, Western, 1935. 38p [Also issued in subsequent years. Title varies.] [BM Brown U LC OTU

**Canadian Authors' Association. Toronto Branch**

VOICES OF VICTORY. Representative Poetry of Canada in War-time. Toronto, Macmillan, 1941. 97p [BVaU OTP

**Canadian Authors' Association. Victoria and Islands Branch**

VICTORIA POETRY CHAPBOOK. A Year Book. Victoria, Clarke Print., 1935. 26p [Also issued in subsequent years–5 vols. to 1942.] [BViPA OTU

VICTORIA POETRY CHAP-BOOK, 1935–42. Victoria, the Branch, 1942. 26p [Brown U BVaU LC NSHD

**Canadian Authors' Association. Windsor Branch**

BORDER VOICES. Ed. by Carl Eayrs. Windsor, Ont., the Branch, 1946. 48p [OOP

**Canadian Expeditionary Force**

O CANADA! A Medley of Stories, Verse, Pictures and Music Contributed by Members of the Canadian Expeditionary Force. London, Simpkin; Hamilton, Kent, [1916]. 95p [BM NSHD OKQ

**Canadian Soldier-Poets**

RHYME AND REASON. A Souvenir Volume of Verse by Canadian Soldier-Poets. With Compliments of the *Maple Leaf,* Italy. Foreword by C.W. Gilchrist. Rome, 1945. 63p [NBFU

**Card, Dorothy Edith**

PRAIRIE HARVEST AND OTHER POEMS. New York, Vantage Press, 1954. 48p

**Carlon, J.**

THE CRUCIFIX. Poems and Songs. [Peterborough?], n.p., n.d. 29p [OTP

**Carman, Bliss, 1861–1929**

"AN OPEN LETTER" FROM BLISS CARMAN. Boston, Small Maynard, [1920]. 17p [BVaU LC NBFU OKQ

APRIL AIRS. Toronto, McClelland, 1922. [Publisher's dummy copy made up of miscellaneous unconsecutive pages.] [OONL

APRIL AIRS. A Book of New England Lyrics. Boston, Small Maynard, 1916. 77p [BM BVaU LC NSHD OTP

AT MICHAELMAS. A Lyric. Wolfville, Acadian Press, 1895. 11p [NSHD OKQ

BALLADS AND LYRICS. London, Bullen, 1902. 79p [A different selection from the following title.] [BM NBFU OKQ

BALLADS AND LYRICS. Toronto, McClelland, 1923. 293p [A different selection from the one pub. under same title in 1902.] [BM BVaU NSHD OKQ QMM

BALLADS OF LOST HAVEN. A Book of the Sea. Boston, Lamson Wolffe, 1897. 117p [BM BVaU LC MWU NSHD OKQ

BEHIND THE ARRAS. A Book of the Unseen. Boston, Lamson Wolffe, 1895. 102p [BVaU LC MWU NSHD OTU QMM

BLISS CARMAN'S POEMS. Toronto, McClelland, 1931. 546p [BM BVaU LC NBFU OTU QMBM

BY THE AURELIAN WALL, AND OTHER ELEGIES. Boston, Lamson Wolffe, 1898. 132p [BM BVaU LC NSHD OKQ

CHRISTMAS EVE AT S. KAVIN'S. New York, Kimball, 1901. 15p [BVaU LC NBFU OKQ

CORONATION ODE. Boston, Page, 1902. 12p [BM LC NBFU OKQ

CORYDON. A Trilogy in Commemoration of Matthew Arnold. ... Fredericton, MacNutt, 1898. 15p [NBFU

ECHOES FROM VAGABONDIA. Boston, Small Maynard, 1912. 65p [BM BVaU LC NBFU OKQ

ECHOES FROM VAGABONDIA. Toronto, McClelland, [1922]. [Publisher's dummy copy made up of miscellaneous unconsecutive pages.] [BM OONL

FAR HORIZONS. Boston, Small Maynard, 1925. 85p [BM BVaU LC NSHD OTU QMM

FLOWER OF THE ROSE. By Louis Norman [pseud]. Cambridge, Mass., 1938. 4p [First pub. under pseud. of Louis Norman. New York, Primrose Bindery, 1892.] [NSHD OTU

FOUR SONNETS. Boston, Small Maynard, 1916. 4p [BVaU NBFU OKQ

... FROM THE GREEN BOOK OF THE BARDS. Boston, Page, 1903. 137p [BVaU LC NSHD OKQ

... FROM THE BOOK OF MYTHS. Boston, Page, 1902. 88p [BVaU LC NBFU OTU

... FROM THE BOOK OF VALENTINES. Boston, Page, 1905. 103p [BVaU LC NBFU OTU

THE GATE OF PEACE. A Poem. New York, Village Press, 1907. 14p [NBFU OKQ

THE GIRL IN THE POSTER. For a Design by Miss Ethel Reed. [Springfield, Mass.], Wayside Press, 1897. 9p [LC NSHD OKQ

THE GREEN BOOK OF THE BARDS. Cambridge, Mass., University Press, 1898. 12p [NBFU OKQ

LAST SONGS FROM VAGABONDIA. Toronto, McClelland, [1922]. [Publisher's dummy copy made up of miscellaneous unconsecutive pages.] [BM OONL

LAST SONGS FROM VAGABONDIA. By Bliss Carman and Richard Hovey. Boston, Small Maynard, 1901. 79p [BM BVaU LC NBFU OKQ

LATER POEMS. With an Appreciation by R.H. Hathaway. Toronto, McClelland, [1921]. xxix + 203p [BM BVaU LC NBFU OKQ QMM

LOW TIDE ON GRAND PRE. By Bliss Carmen [*sic*]. Toronto, Copp Clark, [1899].

13 leaves (Canadian Series of Booklets) [Unauthorized publication] [BVaU LC NSHD OKQ

LOW TIDE ON GRAND PRE. A Book of Lyrics. New York, Webster, 1893. 120p [Numerous later editions.] [BM BVaU LC NBFU OTU QMM

THE MAN OF THE MARNE, AND OTHER POEMS. By B.C. and M.P.K. New Canaan, Conn., Ponus Press, 1918. 26p [LC NBFU OKQ

MORE SONGS FROM VAGABONDIA. Toronto, McClelland, [1922]. [Publisher's dummy made up of miscellaneous unconsecutive pages] [BM OONL

MORE SONGS FROM VAGABONDIA. By Bliss Carman and Richard Hovey. Boston, Copeland & Day, 1896. 72p [BM BVaU LC NSHD OKQ

THE MUSIC OF EARTH. With foreword and notes by Lorne Pierce. Toronto, Ryerson, 1931. 45p [BM BVaU LC NBSaM OTP QMM

ODE ON THE CORONATION OF KING EDWARD. Boston, Page, 1902. 34p [BVaU LC NSHD OTU QMM

OUR CANADIAN LITERATURE. Representative Verse (English). Chosen by Bliss Carman and Lorne Pierce. Toronto, Ryerson, 1925. 361p [Rev. ed., 1935, with French poems added. Rev. and enl. ed., with V.B. Rhodenizer: CANADIAN POETRY IN ENGLISH. Toronto, Ryerson, 1954. xxxvi + 456p] [BVaU LC NBFU OTU QMM

THE PATH TO SANKOTY. [Siasconset, Mass.], The Gift Shop, 1908. 4p [LC OKQ

A PAINTER'S HOLIDAY, AND OTHER POEMS. New York, F.F. Sherman, 1911. 43p [BVaU LC NBFU OKQ

PIPES OF PAN. Containing "From the Book of Myths," "From the Green Book of the Bards," "Songs of the Sea Children," "Songs from a Northern Garden," "From the Book of Valentines." Boston, Page, 1902–1905. 5v [The volumes were later bound as one and so published. Numerous editions. First Canadian ed.: Toronto, Ryerson, 1942.] [BM BVaU LC NBFU OKQ

POEMS. New York, Scott-Thaw; London, Murray, 1904. 2v [BM BVaU LC NBFU OKQ

THE PRINCESS OF THE TOWER; THE WISE MEN FROM THE EAST; TO THE WINGED VICTORY. New York, Village Press, 1906. 18p [LC NBFU OKQ

THE ROUGH RIDER, AND OTHER POEMS. New York, Kennerley, 1909. 78p [BM BVaU LC NBFU OKQ

SAINT KAVIN. A Ballad. [Cambridge, Mass., Author], 1894. 9p [NBFU OKQ

SANCTUARY, SUNSHINE HOUSE SONNETS. New York, Dodd Mead, 1929. 55p [BVaU LC NSHD OKQ

A SEAMARK. A Threnody for Robert Louis Stevenson. Boston, Copeland & Day, 1895. 10p [BVaU LC NSHD OTU QMM

SELECTED POEMS. Ed. and with an intro. by Lorne Pierce. Toronto, McClelland, 1954. 119p

... SONGS FROM A NORTHERN GARDEN. Boston, Page, 1904. 121p [BM BVaU LC OTU QMM

SONGS FROM VAGABONDIA. Toronto, McClelland, [1922]. [Publisher's dummy made up of miscellaneous consecutive pages] [BM OONL

SONGS FROM VAGABONDIA. By Bliss Carman and Richard Hovey. Boston, Copeland & Day, 1894. 54p [1st ed.] [BM BVaU LC NSHD OKQ

SONGS FROM VAGABONDIA; MORE SONGS FROM VAGABONDIA; LAST SONGS FROM VAGABONDIA. By Bliss Carman and Richard Hovey. Boston, Small Maynard, [1911]. 3v in 1. [LC OLU QMSS

... SONGS OF THE SEA CHILDREN. Boston, Page, 1904. 182p [BM BVaU LC NBFU OKQ

SAPPHO. Lyrics. With Excerpts from a Literal Rendering by H.T. Wharton. [N.p., Author, 1902]. 8p [NBFU OKQ

SAPPHO. One Hundred Lyrics. With an intro. by Charles G.D. Roberts. Boston, Page, 1904. 130p [Numerous later editions.] [BM BVaU LC NBFU OTU QMM

TO A CHICKADEE. (Sierra Madre Mountains, California). Palo Alto, Calif., Yerba Buena Press, 1933. 7p [NBFU OKQ

THE VENGEANCE OF NOEL BRASSARD. A Tale of the Acadian Expulsion. Cambridge, Mass., Bradley, 1899 [mis-dated MDCCCCXIX]. 23p [BVaU NBFU OKQ QMM

A VISION OF SAPPHO. [New York], Author, 1903. 7p [NBFU OKQ

A WINTER HOLIDAY [AND OTHER POEMS]. Boston, Small Maynard, 1899. 43p [BVaU LC NBFU OKQ

WILD GARDEN. New York, Dodd Mead, 1929. 76p [BM BVaU LC NSHD OTU QMM

THE WORD AT ST. KAVIN'S. Nelson, N.H., Monadnock Press, 1903. 28p [BM BVaU LC NSHD OKQ

YOUTH IN THE AIR. A Poem. Palo Alto, Calif., Yerba Buena Press, 1932. 4p [LC NBFU OKQ

**Carnochan, Janet, 1839–1926**

FORT GEORGE'S LONELY SYCAMORE. A Reminiscence of Niagara. N.p., n.d. 4p [QMU

**Carpenter, Edmund Snow, 1922–**

ANERCA. [Eskimo Poems.] Ed. by ——. Toronto, Dent, 1959. 45p

**Carsley, Sara Elizabeth (Keatley), 1887–**

ALCHEMY AND OTHER POEMS. Toronto, Macmillan, 1935. 61p [BVaU NBFU OKQ

THE ARTISAN. Toronto, Ryerson, 1941. 8p [BVaU LC NBSaM OTU QMM

**Carter, Eldon**

RHYMES OF A CANADIAN IN FRANCE. London, Stockwell, [1938]. 24p [BM Brown U

**Carter, Ross L.**
RAMBLING RHYMES. Edmonton, Douglas Print., n.d. [Peel Supp

**Cartwright, Rev. Conway Edward, 1837–1920**
LENA. A Legend of Niagara and Other Poems. Dublin, McGee, 1860. 72p [BVaU OOP

**Cartwright, George, 1739–1819**
LABRADOR. A Poetical Epistle. [1792]. St. John's, Nfld.,Withers, 1882. 18p [A reprint.] [NSHP OTP

**Cary, Thomas, 1751–1823**
ABRAM'S PLAINS. A Poem. ... Quebec, Author, 1789. 20p [QMBM

**Casey, Rev. David A., 1886–**
AT THE GATE OF THE TEMPLE. Toronto, Briggs, 1914. 72p [BM Brown U OTUV
LEAVES ON THE WIND. Toronto, McClelland, 1919. 91p [BM BVaU OTP

**Casey, Michael Thomas, 1900–1938**
... SONNETS AND SEQUENCE. Toronto, Ryerson, 1938. 11p [BVaU LC NBSaM OTP

**Caswell, Edward Samuel, 1861–1938**
CANADIAN SINGERS AND THEIR SONGS. A Collection of Portraits and Autograph Poems. Toronto, Briggs, 1902. 45p [Later editions much enlarged, *e.g.*, Toronto, McClelland, 1925. 268p] [BM BVaU LC NSHD OTU QMBM

**Catley, Elaine Maud (Clark), 1889–**
CANADA CALLING. Calgary, Author, 1938. 31p [AEU NBSaM
ECSTASY AND OTHER POEMS. Toronto, Ryerson, 1927. 8p [BVaU NBSaM OTP QMM
LIGHT AND OTHER POEMS. Calgary, Author, 1960. 32p
STAR DUST AND OTHER POEMS. Calgary, Author, [1927]. 30p [ACG OKQ QMM

**Cattapani, Henrietta (Gardner)**
SONGS OF SENTIMENT. N.p., 1909. 154p [BM BVaU OKQ

**Caustick, Christopher (pseud)**
THE OUTLINES OF A SPEECH TO BE DELIVERED ON THE HUSTINGS, AT THE NEXT GENERAL ELECTION FOR THE PROVINCE OF NOVA SCOTIA. By Christopher Caustick, Esq. Saint John, G.W. Day, 1853. 32p [NSWA OTP

**Cawdell, James Martin, 1781?–1842**
THE WANDERING RHYMER. A Fragment, with Other Poetical Trifles. [Anon] York, Gazette, 1826. 22p [OTP

**Cawthorpe. Margaret A.**
LYRICS FROM THE WESTLAND. Toronto, Briggs, 1912. 90p [BM BVaU NBFU OKQ

**Chalmers, Monica Roberts**
AND IN THE TIME OF HARVEST. Toronto, Ryerson, 1945. 12p [BVaU NBSaM OTP

**Chamberlain, Alexander Francis, 1865–1914**
AN ODE ON THE QUEEN'S BIRTHDAY. Toronto, 1891. 12p [OTP
POEMS. Boston, Badger, 1904. 77p [AEU LC

**Chambers, Catherine (Mintie) Wilkinson, 1881–**
POTLUCK POEMS. By Kay Wilkinson. [Vancouver, 1951.] 32p [Mimeographed. Also pub. with slip mounted on cover changing title to TRINKET & TREASURE. Poems.]

**Chandler, Amos Henry, 1837–**
LYRICS, SONGS AND SONNETS. By Amos Chandler and Charles Pelham Mulvany. Toronto, Hunter Rose, 1880. 232p [BVaU LC MWU NBFU OKQ

**Chandler, Mrs. Mary Rena**
NEIGHBOUR LORE. Wolfville, Davidson, 1931. 54p [Brown U BVaU

**Chant, Joseph Horatio, 1837–1928**
GLEAMS OF SUNSHINE. Optimistic Poems. Toronto, Briggs, 1915. 189p [BM BVaU Brown U OTP

**Chaplein, R.A.**
POETRY OF THE HEART; or, Thoughts from the Soul. Together with Verses on various Subjects. Saint John, McMillan, 1872. 130p [AEU NBFU OTP

**Chapman, Edward John, 1821–1904**
A DRAMA OF TWO LIVES; THE SNAKE-WITCH; A CANADIAN SUMMER-NIGHT; AND OTHER POEMS. London, Kegan Paul, 1899. 97p [A DRAMA OF TWO LIVES also privately printed at Toronto, earlier.] [BM BVaU LC NBFU OKQ
EAST AND WEST. A Summer's Idleness. By E.J.C. Toronto, Trout, 1887. 18p [OTU
A MEMORY. By E.J.C. Toronto, Lovell, 1874. 7p [OONL QMU
A SEQUEL TO "CHRISTABEL." By "L" [pseud]. N.p., 1899. 23p [Pseudonymous review of his own poem, "The Snake-Witch."] [OTU
A SONG OF CHARITY. By E.J.C. Toronto, Armour, 1857. 80p [Also: London, Pickering, 1858. 98p] [BM BVaU LC NBFU OKQ

**Cherrington, Joseph Henry, 1895–**
PORTRAITS IN RHYME. New York, Vantage Press, 1959. 73p

**Chestnut, Robert Henry, 1884–**

RAMBLING RHYMES OF THE SEA, THE FOREST, THE COAST, THE MISSIONS. ... Pertaining to the British Columbia Coast. Vancouver, Clarke & Stuart, 1933. 76p [BVaU NBFU

**Chicanot, Eugene Louis**

HOMESTEAD RHYMES. N.p., n.d. 77p [QMU

RHYMES OF THE MINER. An Anthology of Canadian Mining Verse. Comp. and Ed. by ——. Gardenvale, Federal Publications, 1937. 222p [BM BVaU NBFU OTU QMM

**Child, Philip, 1898–**

THE VICTORIAN HOUSE AND OTHER POEMS. Toronto, Ryerson, 1951. 54p [BVaU NBFU OTP

**Chilton, Robert S.**

POEMS. Goderich, McGillicuddy, 1885. 70p [OTUV

**Chilton, Mrs. Vina Bruce**

A FEW MORE DAWNS. Toronto, Copp Clark, 1952. 50p

**Chipman, Hamilton Borradaile, 1885–**

MERI-KA-CHAK–HIS MESSAGE. Winnipeg, Manitoba Co-operative Conference, [1930?]. 77p [QMU

**Chipman, Warwick Fielding, 1880–1967**

THE AMBER VALLEY. Poems. Toronto, Gundy, [1915]. 93p [BM BVaU OTUV

BEYOND THE ROAD'S END. Toronto, Dent, [1929]. 40p [BM BVaU QMM

**Chisholm, Thomas, 1842–**

DIALOGUES ON ENGLISH HISTORY, AND THE HISTORY OF ENGLAND IN ONE HUNDRED LINES. Toronto, Briggs, 1903. 67 + 3p [BM Brown U OTU

**Christie, E. Copeland**

IN MANY MOODS. N.p., n.d. 13p [OTUV

**Churchill, Asa Gildersleeve**

A DIRECTORY OF THE BUSINESS MEN OF SUNDRIDGE. Huntsville, Forester Office, 1885. 13p [Brown U

POETICAL DIRECTORY OF THE TOWN OF LINDSAY AND BUSINESS MEN OF THE SURROUNDING COUNTRY. Lindsay, Canadian Post, 1873. 30p [OTUV

**Churchill, Lavern**

POINTS ON THE COMPAS. Volume A. Toronto, McClelland, 1922. 59p [BM BVaU NBFU OOP QMM

**Clark, Daniel, 1835–1912**

SELECTIONS FROM SCOTTISH CANADIAN POETS. ... With an intro. by ——.

Toronto, Imrie, Graham, 1900. 314p ["Vol. I" stamped on spine, but apparently no further volumes were published.] [BM BVaU OKQ

**Clark, Jeremiah Simpson, 1872–1950**

THE ACADIAN EXILE, AND SEA SHELL ESSAYS. Charlottetown, Irwin, 1902. 59p [BM OLU QMM

**Clark, Mary Elizabeth**

WARTIME AND OTHER POEMS. N.p., n.d. 24p [NSWA

**Clarke, George Frederick, 1883–**

... THE SAINT JOHN AND OTHER POEMS. Toronto, Ryerson, 1933. 14p [BVaU NBSaM OKQ

**Clarke, George Herbert, 1873–1953**

AT THE SHRINE, AND OTHER POEMS. Cincinnati, Stewart & Kidd, 1914. 146p [LC NBFU OKQ

HALT AND PARLEY AND OTHER POEMS. Toronto, Macmillan, 1934. 30p [BM BVaU LC NBFU OTU

THE HASTING DAY. Poems. Toronto, Dent, 1930. 99p [Same title: Toronto, Ryerson, 1933. 100p] [BM BVaU NBFU OTU QMM

HYMN TO THE SPIRIT ETERNAL. Toronto, Macmillan, 1937. 4p [BVaU NSHD OKQ

McMASTER UNIVERSITY, 1890 – 1940. Commemoration Ode. Toronto, Macmillan, 1940. 4p [OKQ

THE NEW TREASURY OF WAR POETRY. Poems of the Second World War. ... Ed. with intro. and notes by ——. Boston, Houghton, 1943. 285p [BM BVaU LC NBFU OTU QMM

ODE ON THE BURIAL OF KING GEORGE THE FIFTH. Toronto, Macmillan, 1935. [OTU

ODE ON THE ROYAL VISIT TO CANADA. Toronto, Macmillan, 1939. 4p [BVaU NSHD OTU

SELECTED POEMS. Ed. by George Whalley. Toronto, Ryerson, 1954. xxvi + 54p

THREE LYRIC SONGS. London, Harris, 1937. 11p [UTQ'38

A TREASURY OF WAR POETRY. British and American Poems of the World War, 1914–1917. Ed. with intro. and notes by ——. Boston, Houghton, 1917. xxx + 280p [BM LC NBFU OTU QMM

A TREASURY OF WAR POETRY. British and American Poems of the World War, 1914–1919. 2nd series. Ed. with intro. and notes by ——. Boston, Houghton, 1919. xxxvii + 361p [BViP LC OKQ

WARFARINGS. Chicago, Windsor & Kenfield, 1901. 94p [LC NBFU OKQ

**Clarke, Henriette (Burchell)**

LITTLE TOWNS. Philadelphia, Poetry Publishers, 1934. 40p [BVaU LC OTU

UNSEEN BLOSSOMS, AND OTHER POEMS. New York, Exposition Press, 1951. 62p

**Clarke, J.**

POEMS. Vancouver, Clarke, 1922. 19p [BVaU

**Clarke, James Paton, 1807?–1877**

CANADIAN CHURCH PSALMODY. Consisting of Psalm Tunes, Chants, Anthems, with Introductory Lessons and Exercises in Sacred Music. Ed. by ——. Toronto, Rowsell, 1845. 108p [OTU QMBM

LAYS OF THE MAPLE LEAF; or, Songs of Canada. The Poetry from the Canadian Annual, the Music composed by ——. Toronto, Author, n.d. 30p [OTP

**Clarke, Katherine A.**

GLEANINGS FROM MY PORTFOLIO. Original Poems. Toronto, 1894. 75p [Brown U BVaU OTU

LYRICAL ECHOES. Toronto, Briggs, 1899. 157p [BM BVaU OTUV

**Clarke, Mrs. Phyllis Comyn**

FROM THE CANADIAN PRAIRIES AND OTHER SONNETS. London, Cranton, 1940. 29p [BM BVaU LC OTP

**Clarke, Violet Alice**

THE VISION OF DEMOCRACY AND OTHER POEMS. Toronto, Ryerson, 1919. 180p [BM BVaU NBFU OKQ

**Clarke, Mrs. W.N.**

THE NEW SONG, AND OTHER POEMS. Toronto, 1883. [CCJ

**Clarkin, Mrs. Lucy Gertrude**

POEMS. Charlottetown, Irwin Print., 1947. 120p [Brown U

WAY O' DREAMS. Charlottetown, Dillon & Coyle, [1922?]. 78p [NBFU

**Clement, Claude**

THOUGHTS IN VERSE. By Claude Clement and Others, Who saw the Doings at Y—— ville. [Toronto?], 1855. 12p [Brown U

**Cleveland, Rev. Edward, 1804–1886**

BIBLE SKETCHES (A CONNECTED SERIES); or, The Stream of Time. A Poem. Boston, Mudge, 1875. 300p [LC QMM

**Clinch, Rev. Joseph Hart, –1884**

EPISTOLA POETICA AD FAMILIARUM. ... Olicanae, Bowes, 1864. 17p [NSHK

THE CAPTIVITY IN BABYLON AND OTHER POEMS. Boston, Burns, 1840. 115p [LC NSHK

**Coates, Carol**

FANCY FREE. Toronto, Ryerson, 1939. 15p [BVaU NBSaM OKQ

INVITATION TO MOOD. Toronto, Ryerson, 1949. 54p [BVaU LC NBFU OTUV

THE RETURN AND SELECTED POEMS. Toronto, Caronell Press, 1941. 34p [Brown U BVaU

**Coburn, Rev. David E., 1870–**

AGAPE. The Story of Jesus as Portrayed in the New Testament. London, Stockwell, 1936. 206p [BVa LC NBFU

ALWAYS REJOICING. Meditation. N.p., priv. print., 1946. 80p [NBSaM

BALLADS OF YESTERDAY AND TODAY. N.p., priv. print., 1937. 24p [NBSaM

BEULAH LAND. N.p., priv. print., 1949. 40p [NBSaM

THE BIRTH OF CANADA. N.p., priv. print., 1949. 62p [NBSaM

THE BOOK OF BOOKS. The Bible. N.p., priv. print., 1950. 39p [NBSaM

THE CENTURIES. N.p., priv. print., 1949. 105p [NBSaM OONL

THE CHRISTIAN. N.p., priv. print., 1949. 24p [NBSaM

A CHRISTMAS PAGEANT. [Poems]. N.p., priv. print., n.d. 10p [Bound with SONGS OF THE SIMPLE LIFE and LET THERE BE LIGHT.] [NBSaM

THE CHURCH. N.p., priv. print., 1948. 100p [NBSaM

EASTER SONGS. N.p., priv. print., 1948. 7p [NBSaM

THE GOLD SEEKERS. N.p., priv. print., 1937. 22p [NBSaM

THE HARP OF ISRAEL ON ENGLISH STRINGS. ["An attempt to express the Psalms in English verse."] N.p., priv. print., 1937. 219p [NBSaM

IN ACADIE. N.p., Author, n.d. 40p [NBFU

IN 1880 A.D. N.p., n.d. [Contains "We can't Have Everything," 24p, and "Keswick Ridge in 1880," 46p] [OONL

IN FAITH'S BRIGHT GLOW. Long Reach, N.B., Author, 1958. 80p [NBFU

THE ISLE OF SAINTS. N.p., priv. print., 1949. 16p [NBSaM

LET THERE BE LIGHT. ... Books 1-3. N.p., priv. print., n.d. [Bound with A CHRISTMAS PAGEANT and SONGS OF THE SIMPLE LIFE.] [NBSaM

LIFE SONGS. N.p., n.d. 16p [NSWA

LOOKING UPWARDS. Meditations. N.p., priv. print., 1947. 80p [NBSaM

MAH ENOSH AND OTHER POEMS. N.p., priv. print., 1937. 56p [NBSaM

MEDITATIONS. N.p., priv. print., 1948. 80p [NBSaM

MEDITATIONS. Man and his Needs. N.p., priv. print., 1948. 32p [NBSaM

MEDITATIONS 1950. N.p., priv. print., 1950. 120p [NBSaM

MID THINGS INVISIBLE. N.p., priv. print., 1948. unpaged. [NBSaM

A MISSION TO THE NATION, AND OTHER POEMS. Long Reach, N.B., Author, 1957. 1v (various paging) [NBFU

THE OUTLOOK, 1950. N.p., priv. print., 1950. 24p [NBSaM

A PILGRIM'S SONGS. N.p., priv. print., 1949. 2v [NBSaM

PSALMS OF LIFE. Long Reach, N.B., Author, 1958. 40p [NBFU

REVERIES OF A COMMON FELLOW. N.p., priv. print., 1948. 56p [NBSaM

THE SHADOW OF DEATH. N.p., priv. print., 1940–1945. 6v [NBSaM OONL

THE SHINING WAY. N.p., n.d. 16p [NBSaM

SONGS FROM CANADA. N.p., priv. print., 1948. 40p [NBSaM OONL

SONGS OF THE SIMPLE LIFE. N.p., priv. print., n.d. 19p [Bound with A CHRISTMAS PAGEANT and LET THERE BE LIGHT.] [NBSaM

THE UNFOLDING MYSTERY. Long Reach, N.B., Author, n.d. 8p [NBFU
THE VIRGIN MARY. N.p., n.d. 6p [NBSaM
WAYSIDE SONGS. N.p., priv. print., 1949. 24p [NBSaM OONL
WE CAN'T HAVE EVERYTHING. N.p., Author, n.d. 46p [NBFU OONL
WILD FLOWERS. Long Reach., N.B., Author, 1958. 16p [NBFU
"WITH PSALMS AND HYMNS AND SPIRITUAL SONGS." N.p., priv. print., 1945. 78p [NBSaM
WOLFE AND MONTCALM, AND OTHER POEMS. N.p., Author, n.d. 61p [NBFU OONL
YESTERDAY AND TODAY BALLADS. N.p., n.d. 211p [OONL

**Cochrane, E.G.**
EBLANA; or, Dublin Doings. A Poem in Twelve Cantos. Quebec, 1846. 124p [CCJ

**Cochrane, Hugh**
IDEAL, AND OTHER POEMS. Montreal, Waters, 1890. 12p [OTUV QMBM
RHYME AND ROUNDELAY. Montreal, Drysdale, [18–?]. 18p [OTP
ROUNDELS. Montreal, 1891. 12p [QMBM

**Cockin, Hereward Kirby, 1854–1917**
THE HAPPY FAMILY; or, Deacon Brown's Dream; and, THE LORD MAYOR OF YORK AND HIS BROTHER NED. By Hereward [pseud]. Toronto, Clougher, n.d. 16p [BVaU OTUV
GENTLEMAN DICK O' THE GREYS, AND OTHER POEMS. Toronto, Robinson, 1889. 119p [3rd ed.: Toronto, Robinson, [1889]. 126p] [BVaU NSHD OTP

**Cockings, George, –1802**
THE AMERICAN WAR. A Poem in Six Books. In which the Names of the Officers who have Distinguished Themselves, during the War, are Introduced. London, Richardson, 1781. 181p [BM LC
ARTS, MANUFACTURES, AND COMMERCE: A Poem. London, Author, 1769. 36p [BM
BENEVOLENCE AND GRATITUDE: A Poem. London, Author, 1772. 44p [BM
POEMS ON SEVERAL SUBJECTS. London, Author, 1772. 42p [BM
WAR. An Heroic Poem. From the Taking of Minorca by the French, to the Raising of the Siege of Quebec, by General Murray. London Printed; Portsmouth, N.H., Reprinted and Sold by Daniel Fowle, 1762. 26p [LC
WAR. An Heroic Poem, from the Taking of Minorca by the French, to the Reduction of Havannah by the Earl of Albemarle, Sir George Pocock. ... The 2nd ed. to the Raising the Siege of Quebec. With large Amendments and Additions by the Author. Boston, Adams, 1762. 190 + 46p ["Britannia's Call to her Brave Troops and Hardy Tars" and other poems. 46p at end.] [BM BVaU LC

**Cody, Hiram Alfred, 1872–1948**

SONGS OF A BLUENOSE. Toronto, McClelland, 1925. 111p [BVaU NSHD OOP

**Coghill, Linnie Allen**

REVERIES. Kingsville, Ont., Author, 1937. 38p [UTQ'38

**Cogswell, Charles**

AMBITION'S DREAM. In two fyttes. New & rev. ed. London, Griffith & Farren, 1878. 92p [NSHD

**Cogswell, Frederick William, 1917–**

DESCENT FROM EDEN. Toronto, Ryerson, 1959. ix + 38p

THE HALOED TREE. Toronto, Ryerson, 1956. 16p

LOST DIMENSION. Dulwich Village, Eng., Outposts Publications, 1960. 12p

THE STUNTED STRONG. Fredericton, U. of New Brunswick, 1954. 16p

THE TESTAMENT OF CRESSEID. By Robert Henryson [1430?–1506?] Trans. by ——. Toronto, Ryerson, 1957. 24p

**Cohen, Leonard Norman, 1934–**

LET US COMPARE MYTHOLOGIES. Toronto, Contact Press, 1956. 79p

**Cole, Harriet, 1841–1882**

SONGS FROM THE VALLEY; or The Valley of Vision and Other Poems. Halifax, Messenger Print., 1879. [NSHD gives pagination as 19p, NSWA as 94p] [NSHD NSWA

**Coleman, H. Bromley**

O DELILAH! A Chap Book of "Silhouettes." London, Giraffe Press, 1928. [BM

VAGABOND THOUGHTS IN RHYTHM. Vancouver, Boyd, 1923. 56p [BVaU OKQ

**Coleman, Helena Jane, 1860–1953**

MARCHING MEN–WAR VERSES. Toronto, Dent, 1917. 40p [BM BVaU NSHD OKQ

SONGS. Being a Selection of Earlier Sonnets and Lyrics. Toronto, Ryerson, 1937. 24p [NBSaM OKQ QMM

SONGS AND SONNETS. Toronto, Briggs, 1906. 158p [BM BVaU NBFU OTP

**Coleman, Herbert Thomas John, 1872–**

COCKLE-SHELL AND SANDAL-SHOON. Toronto, Ryerson, 1927. 24p [BVaU NBSaM OKQ

THE FAR HILLS AND OTHER POEMS. Toronto, Ryerson, 1958. 48p

PATRICIA ANN. The Story of a Doll. Toronto, Dent, 1936. 63p [QMSS

THE POET CONFIDES. Toronto, Ryerson, 1928. 24p [BVaU NBSaM OTP

A RHYME FOR A PENNY. Toronto, Macmillan, 1929. 49p [BVaU LC OTU

**Coleman, Mary Garland (King)**

TAPESTRY. Sidney, B.C., The Review, 1949. 12p [BViP

**Coleman, Rev. Oliver, 1875–**

FOR XMAS AND THE NEW YEAR. London, Stockwell, 1938. 16p [BM BVaU

**Colgan, John C.**

THE POEMS OF JOHN C. COLGAN. Toronto, Hunter Rose, 1873. 197p [BVaU OKQ

**Collie, Michael John, 1929–**

POEMS. Toronto, Ryerson, 1959. 20p
SKIRMISH WITH FACT. Toronto, Ryerson, 1960. 24p

**Collin, William Edwin, 1893–**

MONSERRAT AND OTHER POEMS. Toronto, Ryerson, 1930. 11p [BVaU NBFU OKQ

**Collins, Alice Helen (Roger), –1955**

FRIENDS AND OTHER VERSES. N.p., n.p., [192–?]. 20p [BVaU OTP
GREEN SHUTTERS AND OTHER THOUGHTS. [Walkerton], Gazette, 1935. 47p [OTP
THE HILL OF JOY AND OTHER VERSES. [Elora, Express, 1929?]. 12p [AEU NBFU QMSS
THE KEY OF GOLD AND OTHER THOUGHTS. Walkerton, Telescope, n.d. 72p [OKQ QMSS
LOOK UP! Walkerton, Herald-Times, 1939. 16p [OTU
REALLY TRUE AND OTHER VERSES. Tavistock, Ont., Gazette, 1924. 22p [BVaU QMSS
THE STAR. N.p., n.d. 12p [NBFU OONL QMSS
THIS TINY BOOK. Silhouettes by Helen A. Roger Collins; Verses by Alice H. Roger Collins. Elora, Express, 1928. 23p [Brown U
THOUGHTS. [Toronto, Hunter Rose], 1920. 30p [BVaU OTP
WINGED WORDS. Walkerton, Herald-Times, 1938. 36p [NBFU

**Collins, Burton L., 1880–**

BIRDS UNCAGED AND OTHER POEMS. New York, Abbey Press, 1901. 143p [AEU OTU QMU

**Collins, Herbert Eugene**

PETALS FROM THE FLOWER OF SONG. Campbell, Calif., Keesling Press, 1934. 95p [Also: same title, without place or publisher, dated 1916. 26p] [BM BVaU LC OTU

**Colman, Mary Elizabeth, 1895–**

FOR THIS FREEDOM TOO. Toronto, Ryerson, 1942. 16p [BVaU LC NBSaM OTU
THE IMMIGRANTS. Toronto, Ryerson, 1929. 8p [BVaU NBSaM OKQ

**Colombo, John Robert, 1936–**

FIRE ESCAPES, FIRE ESC, FIRE. Toronto, Hawkshead Press, 1959. 4p (Bagatelle series, no. 2)

FRAGMENTS. Kitchener, priv. print., 1957. 11p
THE IMPRESSION OF BEAUTY. Toronto, Hawkshead Press, 1959. 1p (Bagatelle no. 4)
IN THE STREETS. By Ruta Ginsberg [pseud]. Kitchener, Hawkshead Press, [1959?] 2p
POEMS AND OTHER POEMS. Toronto, Hawkshead Press, 1959. 8p (Bagatelle no. 6)
POEMS TO BE SOLD FOR BREAD. Toronto, Hawkshead Press, 1959. 4p (Bagatelle no. 3)
RUBATO. New Poems by Young Canadian Poets. Ed. by ——. Toronto, Purple Partridge Press, 1958. 28p [Poems by 10 students of the University of Toronto.]
TEN POEMS. By —— and Others. Ed. by ——. Toronto, Editor, 1959. 10p
THIS CITADEL IN TIME. Kitchener, Hawkshead Press, 1958. 12p
THIS IS THE WORK ENTITLED CANADA. Toronto, Purple Partridge Press, 1959. 4p
THIS STUDIED SELF. Kitchener, Hawkshead Press, 1958. 16p
TWO POEMS. Toronto, Hawkshead Press, 1959. 4p (Bagatelle no. 1)
VARIATIONS. Kitchener, Hawkshead Press, 1958. 18p
THE VARSITY CHAPBOOK. Ed. by——. Toronto, Ryerson, 1959. 28p

**Colquhoun, Kathryn E.**

THE BATTLE OF ST. JULIEN, AND OTHER POEMS. Toronto, Ryerson, 1928. 8p [BVaU NBSaM OTP
THE NET OF DREAMS. New York, Harrison, 1942. 31p [BVaU NSHD OTU

**Commander, Kingsmill**

VIKINGS OF THE STARS. New York, Vinal, 1928. 97p [LC OKQ

**Commercial Traveller, A**

"THAT MOST PERSISTENT BEGGAR." With Apologies to Mr. Rudyard Kipling. By a Commercial Traveller [pseud]. St. Catharines, Ont., Pacard, 1900. 10p [NBFU OOP

**Complin, Margaret (Robertson), –1951**

FOR REMEMBRANCE. Regina, Author, 1944. 21p [OTP
WINGED MOCCASINS TO WINGED WORDS. Regina, Author, [1937?]. 23p [BViPA OTP

**Conklin, William J., 1906–**

FOR THE INFINITE. Toronto, Ryerson, 1960. 8p
WIND-BLOWN LEAVES. N.p., 1951. 18p (Carillon Poetry Chap-Books)

**Connor, Fredric Jarrett, 1920–**

GALARIAN. By Fredric Jarrett [pseud]. Montreal, Hart Severance, 1953. 128p
LYRICS CANADIENNES. Pt. I. By Fredric Jarrett [pseud]. Shawbridge, Que., Hart Severance, 1947. 20p [BVaU Brown U NSHD OTP

**Conron, Joy Linton**
SHADOWS ON THE WALL. Poems. Toronto, Author, 1950. 20p [OONL

**Contact Press**
POETS 56. Ten Younger English Canadians. Toronto, Contact Press, 1956. 51p [mimeographed]

**Conybeare, Charles Frederick Pringle, 1860–1927**
LYRICS FROM THE WEST. Toronto, Briggs, 1907. 77p [BM BVaU OTP
VAHNFRIED. London, Kegan Paul, 1902. 196p [AEU BM OLU

**Cook, Evelyn M., 1918–**
FRAGMENT. Islington, Ont., Author, n.d. 12p [CC
HARVEST. Islington, Ont., Author, n.d. 12p [CC
SOLILOQUY. Islington, Ont., Author, n.d. 12p [CC

**Cook, Merrill H.**
SHORE LINES AND SAND SONGS. Toronto, Beacon Press, 1937. 19p [OLU
THE STUMPS AND OTHER MUSINGS. Toronto, Author, 1940. 21p [AEU
WEEDS AND CREEDS. Toronto, Author, 1938. 19p [SRU

**Coombs, William Gordon, 1884–**
POEMS TRUE TO LIFE. Worcester, Eng., Littlebury, 1958. 109p

**Copeland, John Morison, 1878–**
SIR TOBY'S LAMPOONS AND LAMENTS. Toronto, Sovereign Press, 1933. 112 p [Brown U BVaU OTP

**Copway, George, 1818–1863**
THE OJIBWAY CONQUEST. A Tale of the Northwest. By Kah-ge-ga-gah-bowh. New York, Author, 1850. 91p [BM OTP

**Cormack, Barbara (Villy), 1903–**
RUTH. A Tale of New Beginnings. Edmonton, Author, 1948. 23p [ BVaU
SEEDTIME AND HARVEST. Toronto, Ryerson, 1942. 7p [AEU BVaU NBSaM OKQ QMM

**Cosens, Abner**
WAR RHYMES. By Wayfarer [pseud]. Wingham, Ont., Advance Print., [1919?]. 92p [Brown U

**Couch, Ankrem**
JUVENILE POEMS. Toronto, Bell & Co., 1877. 56p [OLU
POEMS. Brooklyn, Webb & Phelps, 1884. 52p [OTP
ROGUES' HOLLOW. A Satire. Toronto, Author, 1879. 29p [OTP

**Coughlin, Dennis**
VILLAGE SCENES. A Canadian Poem. Ottawa, Woodburn, 1889. 22p [OONL

**Coulby, Margaret Evelyn, 1924–**

THE BITTER FRUIT, AND OTHER POEMS. Toronto, Ryerson, 1948. 8p [BVaU NBSaM OKQ

**Coulter, John William, 1888–**

THE BLOSSOMING THORN. Toronto, Ryerson, 1946. 54p [BVaU MWU NSHD OKQ QMM

**Cowan, Annie Ironside (Simpson), 1859–**

VANCOUVER ISLAND AND OTHER POEMS. N.p., Author, n.d. 15p [BViPA

**Cowan, Thomas Goudie, 1896–**

TOMMY ONE AND TOMMY TWO. Vancouver, priv. print., 1951. 71p

**Cowdell, Thomas Daniel**

THE NOVA SCOTIA MINSTREL. 3rd ed. Dublin, Dugdale, Keene, and Cutler, 1817. 150p [Rev. and enl. ed. of work first published under title: A POETICAL JOURNAL OF A TOUR FROM BRITISH NORTH AMERICA TO ENGLAND, WALES AND IRELAND. ... Dublin, Wilkinson & Courtney, 1809. 76p] [BM LC NSHD OTP

A POETICAL ACCOUNT OF THE AMERICAN CAMPAIGNS OF 1812 and 1813. By an Acadian [pseud]. Dedicated to the People of Canada, by the publisher. Halifax, Howe, 1815. 139p [NSHD OTU

**Cowherd, Thomas**

THE EMIGRANT MECHANIC, AND OTHER TALES IN VERSE. Together with Numerous Songs upon Canadian Subjects by the Brantford Tinsmith Rhymer. Jackson, Mich., Daily Citizen Book & Job Print., 1884. 319p [Also: Brantford, Author, 1884. 319p] [BVaU OTP QMM

**Cowles, Nellie Campbell**

VERSES BY THE WAYSIDE. Toronto, Musson, 1910. 128p [BM Brown U

**Cox, Edward**

THOUGHTS BY THE WAY. Toronto, Robinson, 1886. 63p [OKQ

**Cox, Geoffrey Warburton**

WHAT-NOTS. Toronto, Ryerson, 1927. 20p [BVaU NBSaM OKQ

**Cox, Leonard (Leo), 1898–**

NORTH STAR. Toronto, Macmillan, 1941. 56p [BVaU LC NSHD OTUV QMM

RIVER WITHOUT END. Toronto, Ryerson, 1937. 16p [BVaU NBSaM OKQ

SHEEP-FOLD. Toronto, Ryerson, 1926. 8p [BVaU NBSaM OKQ

THE WIND IN THE FIELD. Toronto, Ryerson, 1932. 32p [BVaU NBSaM OKQ

**Craig, Martha**

LEGENDS OF THE NORTH LAND. N.p., [19–?]. 23p [OTP

**Crawford, Alexander Wellington, 1866–1933**

POEMS OF YESTERDAY. Toronto, Ryerson, 1924. 54p [BVaU NSHD OTP

**Crawford, George Johnson Adair, 1858–1915**
LOCAL AND OTHER RHYMES. Petrolia, Ont., Advertiser Pub. House, 1908. 39p [OLU

**Crawford, Isabell C.**
THE REDMAN'S PRAYER AND OTHER POEMS. Kamloops, B.C., Sentinel, 1929. 48p [BVaU QMBM

**Crawford, Isabella Valancy, 1850–1887**
THE COLLECTED POEMS. Ed. by J.W. Garvin. Toronto, Briggs, 1905. 309p [BM BVaU LC NSHD OKQ
OLD SPOOKSES' PASS, MALCOLM'S KATIE, AND OTHER POEMS. Toronto, Bain, 1884. 224p [BM BVaU MWU NBFU OKQ QMM

**Crawford, Mrs. John**
SONGS OF ALL SEASONS, CLIMES, AND TIMES. A Motley Jingle of Jumbled Rhymes. Toronto, Rose, 1890. 117p [BVaU NBFU OKQ

**Creed, Gavin L.**
BARDS IN BATTLE DRESS. Ed. by ——. 1944. [Rhod p958
FOR FREEDOM. Toronto, Dent, 1942. 60p [BM BVaU LC OTU

**Creighton, Alan B., 1903–**
CROSS-COUNTRY. Toronto, Macmillan, 1939. 68p [NBFU OLU QMM
EARTH CALL. A Book of Poems. Toronto, Macmillan, 1936. 67p [BVaU NBFU OKQ QMM
A NEW CANADIAN ANTHOLOGY. Ed. by Alan Creighton. Assisted by Hilda M. Ridley. Toronto, Crucible Press, 1938. 236p [BVaU LC OKQ

**Creighton, Helen, 1899–**
SONGS AND BALLADS FROM NOVA SCOTIA. Collected by ——. Toronto, Dent. 1932. 333p [BM BVaU NBFU OTU
TRADITIONAL SONGS FROM NOVA SCOTIA. Collected by Helen Creighton and Doreen H. Senior. Toronto, Ryerson, 1950. 284p [Includes music] [BVaU NSHD OTU
TWELVE FOLK SONGS FROM NOVA SCOTIA. Collected by Helen Creighton and D.H. Senior. London, Novello, 1940. 41p [OTU

**Crofton, Arthur M.**
RAGNAROK. A Vision of the Last Great Day. Sydney, N.S., Author, 1919. 37p [BM BVaU

**Crofton, Francis Blake, 1841–1912**
SOMBRE TINTS. Halifax, Imperial Pub., 1904. 18p [BM BVaU NSHD OKQ

**Cumberland, Robert William, 1895–**
VERSE AND TRANSLATION. Kingston, Jackson Press, 1925. 50p [NSHD OTU

**Cuming, Thomas Grant Austin, 1890–**

SPECKLED THOUGHTS AND OTHER THINKING. By Tag-a-long, Thomas G.A. Cuming. Smith's Cove, N.S., Author, 1959. 67p

**Cumming, Robert Dalziel, 1871–**

PAUL PERO. Toronto, Ryerson, 1928. 30p [BVaU NBSaM OKQ QMM

SONGS OF A SICK TUM TUM. By Skookum Chuck [pseud]. New York, Totem, 1912. 105p [BVaU

**Cummings, Virginia (MacDonald)**

THE MIRACLE OF DOGWOOD, AND OTHER POEMS. Vancouver, Author, 1946. 16p [BVaU OTP

**Cumpston, William Henry**

GLIMMERINGS OF TRUTH; Being a Collection of Poems. Hull, H. Brown; London, Simpkin Marshall, 1887. 107p [BM

POEMS FOR THE TIME. Montreal, Howard Print., 1915. 27p [BM Brown U BVaU NBFU

**Cunningham, Willis W., 1867–**

ANVIL WHISPERS. N.p., n.d. 91p [BVaU NBFU OTP

**Currie, George Graham, 1867–1926**

EPITAPHS, EPIGRAMS, AND OTHER EPHEMERA. Jacksonville, Fla., Drew Press, 1912. 244p [LC

HOW I ONCE FELT. Songs of Love and Travel. Montreal, Lovell, 1893. 142p [BVaU NBFU OKQ QMU

IN THE OTHER MAN'S PLACE. Some Latter Day Tragedies in Verse. Jacksonville, Fla., Drew Press, 1911. 194p [LC

SONGS OF FLORIDA AND OTHER VERSE. New York, J.T. White, 1922. 298p [LC

SONNETS AND LOVE SONGS. Jacksonville, Fla., Drew Press, 1911. 200p [LC

**Currie, John Allister, 1868–1931**

A QUARTETTE OF LOVERS. Toronto, Williamson, 1892. 65p [NBFU OTP

**Currie, Margaret (Gill), 1843–**

GABRIEL WEST AND OTHER POEMS. Fredericton, Cropley, 1866. 127p [BVaU NBFU OTUV

JOHN SAINT JOHN AND ANNA GREY. A Romance of Old New Brunswick. Toronto, Briggs, 1897. 128p [BM BVaU NBFU OTU QMM

**Curzon, Mrs. Sarah Anne, 1833–1898**

LAURA SECORD, THE HEROINE OF 1812. A Drama; And Other Poems. Toronto, Robinson, 1887. 215p [BM BVaU LC MWU NSHD OTU QMM

**Cuthbertson, Ethel Imrie**

MISCELLANEOUS POEMS. Vancouver, Ward, Ellwood, & Pound, 1914. 14p [BVaU

POEMS OF PROGRESS OR PROHIBITION. Vancouver, Ward, Ellwood, & Pound, n.d. 12p [BVaU

**Dagger, Gordon, 1888–**

THE PROSPECTOR AND OTHER POEMS. New York, Harrison, 1942. 61p [BVaU OKQ

**Dakin, Laurence B., 1904–**

THE DREAM OF ABARIS, AND OTHER POEMS. Paris, Obelisk Press, 1933. 78p [BM

THE HOUSE OF ORSEOLI. [A Poem.] Manchester, N.H., Falmouth Press, 1952. 98p

POEMS. Paris, Obelisk Press, 1932. 55p [BM LC

SONNETS AND LYRICS. Paris, Obelisk Press, 1935. 59p [BM

SORROWS OF THE HOPEFUL ["A Prose Poem"]. London, 1936. 15p [BM

THE TOWER OF LIFE. Portland, Me., Falmouth Book House, 1946. 101p [BM NSHD

**Dalton, Annie Charlotte (Armitage), 1865–1938**

THE AMBER-RIDERS. Toronto, Ryerson, 1929. 109p [BVaU NBFU OKQ

THE CALL OF THE CARILLON. Vancouver, Wrigley, [193-?] 16p [BVaU NBFU OKQ

A CHRISTMAS CAROL FOR ALL GOOD SOLDIERS AND SAILORS. Vancouver, Clarke & Stuart, 1914. 7p [BVaU OKQ

THE EAR TRUMPET. Toronto, Ryerson, 1926. 8p [BVaU NBFU OKQ

FLAME AND ADVENTURE. Toronto, Macmillan, 1924. 73p [BVaU LC NSHD OKQ

LILLIES AND LEOPARDS. Toronto, Ryerson, 1935. 68p [BVaU NSHD OOP

THE MARRIAGE OF MUSIC. Vancouver, Evans & Hastings, 1910. 71p [2nd ed., with additional poems. London, E. Macdonald, 1915. 92p] [BM BVaU NBFU OKQ

THE NEIGHING NORTH. Toronto, Ryerson, 1931. 80p [BVaU NBFU OKQ

THE SILENT ZONE. [Vancouver, Cowan & Brookhouse, 1926]. 111p [BVaU NBFU OOP

SONGS AND CAROLS. Vancouver, priv. print., 1925, 16p [BVaU NBFU OKQ

A SOUVENIR OF VANCOUVER. Vancouver, priv. print., 1906 12p [BM OKQ

**Daniel, Charles T.**

WILLIAM AND ANNE; or, A Tale of Love and War. Guelph, The Herald, 1864. 112p [OLU

**Daniells, Roy, 1902–**

DEEPER INTO THE FOREST. Toronto, McClelland, 1948. 76p [BVaU OKQ

**Darby, Ray**

THE ADVENTURES OF GLEN ALAN. Regina, School Aids, n.d. 1v [unpaged] [AEU

OOMAH. With Pictures by John Phillips. Winnipeg, Contemporary Pub., 1945. 39p [ACG

PETER SMITH AND THE SKY-PEOPLE. Regina, School Aids, 1944. 1v [unpaged] [AEU

**Darling, Elizabeth**

SPARE MOMENTS. A Little Book of Poems. [Kingston, Whig Steam Presses], n.d. 25p [OTU

**Darling, Rev. William Stewart, 1818–1886**

THE EMIGRANTS. A Tale of the Backwoods of Canada. Toronto, Lovell & Gibson, 1863. 40p [LC

**Darnell, Rev. Henry Faulkner, 1831–1915**

KINDESLIEBE. A Romance of Fatherland. Philadelphia, MacCall, 1891. 188p [NSHD OTU

SONGS BY THE WAY. A Collection of original Poems for the Comfort and Encouragement of Christian Pilgrims. Montreal, Lovell, 1862. 185p [BVaU LC NBFU OKQ

SONGS OF THE SEASONS. Avon, N.Y., 1886. 57p [Patrick cat. 30

VERSES IN MEMORY OF THE RIGHT REV. G.J. MOUNTAIN. St. John's, Que., 1863. 7p [CCJ

**Date, Henry Harrington, –1905**

SONG OF THE U.E. LOYALIST AND YORK PIONEER. N.p., 1895. 16p [BVaU OTUV

**David, Joan Eira**

IN HOLLY TIME. [Toronto? 1937?]. 30p [Brown U

**Davidson, Fisher, 1912–**

DOMINION AND OTHER POEMS. Toronto, Author, 1948. 45p [BVaU LC NBFU OKQ

MISTS OF QUEBEC. Ten Poems. Montreal, Quality Press, 1960. 11p

TWO SONNETS FOR A CENTENARY: William Lyon Mackenzie, 1838–1938; Durham, 1839–1939. Welland, Ont., Author, 1939. 4p [OTU

**Davidson, Frederick**

CAPTURED FANCIES. Toronto, [Printer's Guild], 1942. 122p [LC

**Davidson, Judson France**

THE ANACREONTEA, AND PRINCIPAL REMAINS OF ANACREON OF TAOS, in English Verse. With an Essay, Notes, and Additional Poems by ——. Ed. by Frederick J.A. Davidson. Toronto, Dent, 1915. 212p [BM OTU

A LAPFUL OF LYRICS AND MERRY MUSE-WHANGS. By Judson France [pseud]. Toronto, Imrie & Graham, 1885. 32p [Brown U OOP

R.R.R. MUSE WHANGS. Poems Amorous, Bacchanalian, Political, Memorial, Humorous, and Miscellaneous. By Judson France [pseud]. Toronto, Sign o' the Will-o'-the Wisp, 1887. 104p [BVa OTUV QMM

**Davidson, Kathleen**

SEVEN SHEAVES. By Kathleen Davidson, Amy Downey, Kathleen Dupuis, Borgny Eileraas, Lois Borland, Myra Smith, Jean Sibbald. Saskatoon, 1945.

38p ["Dedicated to The Sheaf" – the Univ. of Sask. campus newspaper.] [SSU

**Davidson, True, 1901–**

MUSES OF THE MODERN DAY AND OTHER DAYS. Toronto, Dent, 1931. 131p [BVaU NBFU OTU QMU

**Davies, Hilda A.**

OVERGROWN TRAILS AND OTHER POEMS. By Tanis [pseud]. Calgary, Dichmont, 1932. 18p [ACG

**Davin, Nicholas Flood, 1843–1901**

ALBUM VERSES AND OTHER POEMS. Ottawa, MacLean Roger, 1882. 32p [BM LC OTUV

EOS: AN EPIC OF THE DAWN, AND OTHER POEMS. Regina, Leader Co., 1889. 141p [BM BVaU LC NSHD OKQ SSU

EOS: A PRAIRIE DREAM, AND OTHER POEMS. Ottawa, Citizen Print., 1884. 36p [BM OTU

**Davis, Alastair Jeffreys**

THE CHILDREN'S HOUR. Eton, Spottiswoode, 1938. 63p [BM

**Davis, Allan Ross, 1858–1933**

CANADA'S POLITICAL STRUGGLES. Toronto, 1925. 4p [Amtmann cat. 151

**Davis, Ella M.**

GIFT BOOK OF SONNETS AND BIRTHSTONE RONDOLETTES. Regina, Author, 1946. 12p [BVaU OTU

**Davis, Stuart, 1921–**

SONGS BY "STU" DAVIS. A Collection of Original Western and Folk Songs Composed and Sung by "Canada's Cowboy Troubador." Folio no. 3. Toronto, Canadian Music Sales Corp., 1953. 40p

**Davison, Leslie Loring, 1871–1889**

STRAY LEAVES FROM THE "BOOK OF WONDERS." Ed. by Ben Zeene [pseud]. Wolfville, Davison, 1890. 72p [NSHD OTUV

**Davison, R.E.**

A ROMANCE OF THE WEST. A Tale of the Iroquois and Delaware Indians. Winnipeg, Winnipeg Print., n.d. 27p [BVaU MWP QMU

**Dawson, Rev. Aeneas MacDonell, 1810–1894**

DOMINION DAY, CARACTACUS, MALCOLM & MARGARET. Poems. Ottawa, Mitchell, 1886. 62p [LC NSHD OTU QMM

LAMENT FOR THE RIGHT REVEREND JAMES GILLIS, D.D., BISHOP OF EDINBURGH ... and Other Poems. Ottawa, Bell & Woodburn, 1864. 57p [Brown U OTUV

THE LAST DEFENDER OF JERUSALEM. ... Ottawa, Free Press, 1882. 16p [BM BVaU NSHD OTP

LINES ON THE MASSACRE OF OSZMINIA (LITHUANIA). Glasgow, 1844. [OOP

[THREE POEMS, WRITTEN DURING 1866. Ottawa?, n.p., 1866?. 11p] [No cover, no t.p.] [NSHP

ZENOBIA, QUEEN OF PALMYRA. A Poem. Ottawa, Mitchell, 1883. 108p [BM BVaU LC NSHD OTUV

**Dawson, Cristall**

POEMS. Toronto, 1924. 29p [OOP

**Dawson, Julia**

THE CHANGING YEAR, AND OTHER POEMS. Toronto, Mundy-Goodfellow Print., 1937. 68p [AEU Brown U OTUV

**Dawson, Samuel Edward, 1833–1916**

CHAMPLAIN. Montreal, Author, 1890. 8p [OTUV

**Day, Alfred Ernest, 1875–**

THE KINGDOM SONG. A Group of Little Poems with Airs. Made by Evan Reay [pseud]. Toronto, Ryerson, 1931. 16p [BVaU LC OKQ

**Dean, Louis Mitchell**

DRIFTED LEAVES. Aylmer, Ont., Express, 1946. 48p [UTQ'48

**Dean, T.C.**

T.C. DEAN'S POEMS. Being a Collection from the Magazines with some that will first see the Light in this Volume. Trenton, Ont., Courier Book Office, 1879. 16p [Patrick cat. 30

**Dear, Allan**

CANADIAN SONG LYRICS. Comp. by ——. Winnipeg, Canada Pub. Co., 1940. 61p [CC

**Delafosse, Frederick Montague, 1860–1950**

A DREAM AND AN ALLEGORY. N.p., n.p. 1944. 27p [OTU

VERSES GRAVE AND GAY. Peterborough, Author, 1937. 70p [OKQ

**De Mille, James, 1833–1880**

BEHIND THE VEIL. A Poem. Halifax, Allen, 1893. 30p [BVaU NSHD OKQ

**Dermot, Walter H.**

THE AUTUMN WREATH. A Poem. Ottawa, Hunter Rose, 1869. 14p [NBFU OTU QMSS

**Des Brisay, Margaret Elizabeth**

MEMORIALS OF MARGARET ELIZABETH, ONLY DAUGHTER OF REV. ALBERT DES BRISAY, of the Province of New Brunswick. By a friend. ... New York, Carlton & Phillips, 1856. 236p [Brown U

**Devine, Frederick**

THEY TURNED HER OUT IN THE STREET AND OTHER POEMS. Saint John, N.B. Globe Pub., 1914. 62p [NBFU QMBM

**Devine, Thomas Godfrey, 1875–**

MADAWASKA. Boston, Badger, 1912. 55p [LC OTU

**Dewart, Rev. Edward Hartley, 1828–1903**

ADDITIONAL POEMS. N.p., [1892?]. pp257-268. (cover title) [paged to follow text of SONGS OF LIFE] [OKQ

SELECTIONS FROM CANADIAN POETS. With Occasional Critical and Biographical Notes. Ed. by ——. Montreal, Lovell, 1864. 304p [BM BVaU LC MWU NSHD OKQ

SONGS OF LIFE. A Collection of Poems. Toronto, Dudley & Burns, 1869. 256p [BVaU LC MWU NBFU OTU QMM

**Dewing, Winifred F.**

POEMS. N.p., n.d. 24p [OKQ

**DeWolfe, Cecil Edgar**

A LITTLE BOOK OF LYRIC VERSE. Windsor, N.S., [1916?]. [Rhod p879

**Dick, Alexander**

SPLORES OF A HALLOWEEN TWENTY YEARS AGO. Woodstock, Warwick, 1867. 22p [OTP

**Dickie, Charles Herbert, 1859–**

RHYME ... AND REASON. West Vancouver, Author, 1945. 47p [BVaU

**Dickie, Donalda James, 1883–**

THE CANADIAN POETRY BOOK. A Book of Modern Verse. Comp. by ——. Toronto, Dent, [1924]. 111p [BViP OPAL QMU

**Dickson, Stephen, 1761?–**

THE UNION OF TASTE AND SCIENCE. A Poem. To which are subjoined a few Elucidating Notes. Quebec, Neilson, 1799. 17p [Facsimile reprint: Toronto, Bibliog. Soc. of Canada, 1952.] [NBFU OTU QMBM

**Diespecker, Richard E. Alan, 1907–**

BETWEEN TWO FURIOUS OCEANS, AND OTHER POEMS. Toronto, Oxford U. Press, 1944. 91p [BVaU LC NBFU OTP

PRAYER FOR VICTORY. Post-War Thoughts by a Soldier [pseud]. Montreal, Woodward Press, 1943. 8p [Brown U

THREE WINDOWS WEST. Toronto, Dent, 1956. xv + 160p

**Dingwall, M.M.**

NOW THAT I'M FIFTY. Edmonton, Author, 1949. 19p [UTQ'51

**Dixon, Benjamin Homer, 1819–1899?**

GOLDEN MOMENTS. Comp. by B.H.D. Toronto, Chewett, 1865. 153p [The 2nd ed. of his SELECTED HYMNS] [NBFU OTP

SELECTED HYMNS. Comp. by B.H.D. Toronto, Chewett, 1863. 114p [OTUV

**Dixon, George**

THE BARD OF WAR. A Poetical Series in which the Author proposes to treat of the Russian, Persian and China Wars. Also the Rebellion of British India and the Civil War in America from 1861 to 1865, to conclude with the true Fenian Episode and Fall of Republics. Saint John, Chubb, 1868. [CCJ NBB

**Dobell, Curzon**

LOVE LYRICS AND REBEL RHYMES. New York, Exposition Press, 1954. 96p

**Dole, William Peters, 1825–**

CARMEN ACADIUM. Ode for the Jubilee Year of the Reign of Queen Victoria. Saint John, 1887. 11p [CCJ

OUR COUNTRY. By W.P. Dole, James Hannay, and H.L. Spencer, Saint John, 1889. [CCJ

**Dollard, Rev. James Bernard, 1872–1946**

THE BELLS OF OLD QUEBEC, AND OTHER POEMS OF NEW FRANCE. Toronto, Extension Print., 1920. 59p [Brown U OTU

IRISH LYRICS AND BALLADS. New York, Kenedy, 1917. 131p [BVaU LC NBFU OTU QMM

IRISH MIST & SUNSHINE. A Book of Ballads. Toronto, Blake, 1901. 89p [Another ed.: Toronto, Blake, 1902. 144p] [BVaU LC NBFU OTU

POEMS. Toronto, Catholic Church Extension Society, 1910. 148p [BM BVaU OTP

**Donald, Rev. Andrew, 1806–**

POEMS. Campbell Settlement, Sussex, N.B., Printed by L.M. Donald, 1876. 20p [Brown U NBFU

**Dorey, Mrs. Alice Ann**

LIGHT AND SHADOW. Toronto, Ryerson, 1949. 25p [Brown U BVaU OTU

**Dorland, Ella Wilson, 1878–**

GLEN ECHOES. By E. Dee [pseud]. St. Catharines, Ont., Author, 1941. 59p [UTQ'42

GLEN IDYLLS. St. Catharines, Ont., Author, 1938. 47p [OTU

**Dorman, Robert, 1883–**

THOUGHTS OF A RESTLESS MIND. Ottawa, Author, 1956. 40p

**Dorsey, J. Leo M.**

STAIR BUILDING. Poems. N.p., [1943?]. 32p [OTP

**Doucet, Rev. Stanislaus J., 1847–1925?**

EMMANUEL THE LIVING BREAD. A Religious Poem. By Monsignor Doucet. Chatham, N.B., 1922. 16p [Amtmann cat. 221

THE SOUL. A Philosophic Poem. Saint John, McMillan, 1917. 23p [2nd ed.: Chatham, N.B., 1923. 32p] [Brown U NBFU OTU

**Dougall, Lily, 1858–1923**

ARCADES AMBO. Verses by Lily Dougall ... and Gilbert Sheldon. Oxford, Blackwell, 1919. 63p [LC QMM

**Doughty, Arthur George, 1860–1936**

HELEN AND APHRODITE. [Priv. printed]. [CCJ

NUGAE CANORAE. By A.G.D. Portland, Smith & Sale, 1897. 69p [OTUV

ROSE LEAVES. A Collection of Simple Verses Written on Various Occasions. London, Moring, 1894. 80p [BM BVaU OTUV QMM

THE SONG STORY OF A FRANCESCO AND BEATRICE. [Priv. printed, 1896?]. [CCJ

**Douglas, Gilean**

NOW THE GREEN WORD. Mill Valley, Calif., Wings Press, 1952. 56p

THE PATTERN SET. Montreal, priv. print., 1958. 20p

POETIC PLUSH. Dallas, Tex., Story Book Press, 1953. 40p

**Douglas, Robert W., –1931**

LOVE SONGS OF SCOTLAND; JEWELS OF THE TENDER PASSION. ... Selected and Ed. by ——. New York, New Amsterdam Book Co., 1901. 214p [BVaU LC OTUV

**Dowhan, Stanley J., 1917–**

THE LEAVES ARE SCATTERED. Ed. by M.F. Liddell. London, British Authors' Press, 1944. 39p [BM LC OKQ

**Downes, Gwladys Violet**

LOST DIVER. Fredericton, U. of New Brunswick, 1955. 16p

**Dowsett, Frank Martin, 1897–**

SONNETS OF A SEEKER. Toronto, Author, 1954. 18p

**Dowson, Eric Arthur**

COUNTRY PLACES AND OTHER POEMS. Ilfracombe, Devon, Stockwell, 1957. 64p

**Doyle, Gerald Stanley, 1892–1956**

OLD TIME POETRY AND SONGS OF NEWFOUNDLAND. St. John's, Author, 1940. 80p [NFSM OONL

OLD TIME SONGS OF NEWFOUNDLAND. St. John's, Nfld., Manning & Rabbitts, 1927. 71p [3rd ed., 1955. 88p] [BViP LC NSHD OTU

**Drayton, Geoffrey, 1924–**

THREE MERIDIANS. Toronto, Ryerson, 1950. 8p [BVaU NBSaM OTU

**Drew, Mabel Ellen**

TIME IS THE MEASURE. Toronto, Crucible Press, 1950. 26p [Brown U OONL

**Drummond, Frank S., 1873–**

POEMS. N.p., 1931. 83p [OTP

THE "ROYAL SAUVAGE" AND OTHER SKETCHES. Toronto, Gilchrist-Wright, 1930. 8p [OTP

SKETCHES. Toronto, Hunter Rose, 1929. 19p [OTP

**Drummond, William Henry, 1854–1907**

COMPLETE POEMS. With an intro. by Louis Fréchette and an appreciation by Neil Munro. Toronto, McClelland, 1926. 34 + 450p [BM BVi OTU QMM

THE GREAT FIGHT. Poems and Sketches. With a Biographical Sketch. ... New York & London, Putnam, 1908. 158p [BVaU LC NSHD OTU QMM

THE HABITANT, AND OTHER FRENCH-CANADIAN POEMS. New York, Putnam, 1897. 137p [BVaU LC NSHD OTU QMM

HABITANT POEMS. Intro. by Arthur L. Phelps. Toronto, McClelland, 1959. 111p [New Canadian Library, no. 11]

JOHNNIE COURTEAU, AND OTHER POEMS. New York, Putnam, 1901. 161p [BM BVaU LC NSHD OTU QMM

PHIL-O-RUM'S CANOE, AND MADELEINE VERCHERES. Two Poems. New York, Putnam, 1898. 12p [BVaU MWU NSHD OKQ QMM

THE POETICAL WORKS OF WILLIAM HENRY DRUMMOND. With an intro. by Louis Fréchette. New York, Putnam, 1912. 449p [BVaU LC NSHD OTUV

THE VOYAGEUR AND OTHER POEMS. New York, Putnam, 1905. 142p [BM BVaU LC NSHD OTU QMM

**Drury, Susie**

MAPLE LEAVES. By Susie D. [pseud]. London, Ont., Daily Free Press, 1871. 200p [BVaU NBFU OKQ

**Duddridge, Hugh, 1872–**

SEEN FROM MY SEEDER STEP. A Volunteer Crop of Verse from a Saskatchewan Farm. Prince Albert, Sask., Author, 1950. 73p [OONL SSU

**Dudek, Louis, 1918–**

CANADIAN POEMS, 1850–1952. Ed. by Louis Dudek and Irving Layton. 2nd ed. Toronto, Contact Press, 1952. 127p [Also: 2nd ed., rev., 160p]

CERBERUS. Poems by Louis Dudek, Irving Layton, Raymond Souster. Toronto, Contact Press, [1952]. 98p

EAST OF THE CITY. Poems. Toronto, Ryerson, 1946. 51p [BVaU LC MWU NBFU OKQ

EN MEXICO. Toronto, Contact Press, 1958. 78p

EUROPE. Toronto, Laocoön (Contact) Press, 1954. 139p

LAUGHING STALKS. Toronto, Contact Press, 1958. 113p

THE SEARCHING IMAGE. Toronto, Ryerson, 1952. 12p

THE TRANSPARENT SEA. Toronto, Contact Press, 1956. 114p

TWENTY-FOUR POEMS. Toronto, Contact Press, 1952. 24p

UNIT OF FIVE. Poems by Louis Dudek, Ronald Hambleton, P.K. Page, Raymond Souster, James Wreford. Ed. by Ronald Hambleton. Toronto, Ryerson, 1944. 87p [BVaU LC MWU NSHD OTU QMM

**Dumbrille, Dorothy, 1898–**

LAST LEAVE, AND OTHER POEMS. Toronto, Ryerson, 1942. 16p [BVaU LC NBFU

STAIRWAY TO THE STARS. Toronto, Allen, 1946. 72p [BVaU NBFU OKQ QMM

WATCH THE SUN RISE! A Collection of Poems. Alexandria, Ont., Author, 1943. 47p [BVaU LC NBFU OTP

WE COME! WE COME! Toronto, Crucible Press, 1941. 46p [LC OKQ

**Duncan, Eric, 1858–1944**

THE RICH FISHERMAN, AND OTHER SKETCHES. Toronto, Macmillan, 1932. 113p [BVaU NBFU OTU

THE RICH FISHERMAN, AND OTHER TALES. London, Century, 1910. 99p [BM BVaU

RURAL RHYMES, AND THE SHEEP THIEF. Toronto, Briggs, 1896. 64p [BM BVaU OTUV QMM

**Duncan, Nora M. (Dann), 1881–**

DOWN TO THE SEA. North Vancouver, North Shore Press, 1936. 35p [BVaU

THE HEROINE OF MOODYVILLE. An Epic of Burrard Inlet. N.p., n.d. 4p [BViPA

RAINBOW REVERIES. North Vancouver, North Shore Press, 1934. 85p [BVaU OOP

**Dunlap, Louie Spencer**

REMEMBRANCE. Toronto, [Noble Scott Ltd?], 1924. 68p [QMU

**Dunn, Mrs. C.A.**

FUGITIVE PIECES. Woodstock, Ont., Author, 1867. 94p [BVaU OTP

**Dunn, Marcia (Christoforides), 1910–**

THE BALLAD OF A BATHURST BOY, 1874–1956. Fredericton, University Press of N.B., 1956. 21p [About Sir James Dunn.]

**Dunning, Elsa**

HERITAGE. Toronto, Crucible Press, 1941. 24p (Carillon Poetry Chap-Books) [AEU NBSaM OTP

UNREAPED CORNERS. N.p., n.d. 31p [QMU

**Dunsmore, J.M.**

SONGS OF DISCOVERY AND EXPLORATION. Toronto, 1938. 29p [Adelphi cat. 41A

**Durand, Evelyn, 1870–1900**

ELISE LE BEAU, A Dramatic Idyll; and Lyrics and Sonnets. ... Ed. with a memoir by Laura B. Durand. Toronto, U. of Toronto Press, 1921. 27 + 168p [BM BVaU NBFU OTP

**Durie, Mrs. Anna**

WOLFE AND OTHER POEMS. Toronto, College Print., 1929. 10p [NBFU OTU

OUR ABSENT HERO. Poems in Loving Memory of Captain William Arthur Peel Durie, 58th Battalion, C.E.F. Toronto, Ryerson, 1920. 113p [BM BVaU OTUV QMM

**Durkin, Douglas Leader, 1884–1968**

THE FIGHTING MEN OF CANADA. Toronto, McClelland, 1918. 85p [BM BVaU LC NSHD OKQ

**Durrant, Louisa**

TWELVE TIMES SEVEN AND OTHER POEMS. Ilfracombe, Devon, Stockwell, 1957. 79p

**Duvar, John Hunter-, 1830–1899**

JOHN A' VAR. His Lays. [Priv. print.] [CCJ

**Dyas de Lom, Elizabeth English, –1912**

POEMS. Toronto, 1911. 42p [Brown U BVaU

**Dyde, Samuel Walters, 1862–1947**

FROM MY GALLERY. Kingston, Author, n.d. 31p [OKQ

THE HIGHWAY. Kingston, Jackson Press, 1928. 15p [OKQ

WAR VERSES. Kingston, Jackson Press, 1924. 25p [LC OKQ

A YEAR. Kingston, Jackson Press, 1927. 8p [OKQ

**Dyer, Mary Sparks**

SPIRES ALOFT. Galt, Galt Printers, [1938?]. 39p [Brown U NBFU

**Dyer, W.E.**

ECHOES FROM A SUNDAY-SCHOOL. Toronto, Briggs, 1890. 120p [OONL

**Dynes, Violet E.**

AGATES IN THE SAND. Vancouver, Sun, 1944. 64p [AEU BVaS

**Dysart, Arthur L.**

POEMS AND LYRICS. Fredericton, Clark, 1909. 83p [NBFU OTL

**Earle, Kathleen**

SPINDRIFT. Toronto, Crucible Press, 1941. 22p [NBSaM OTP

**Eassie, Robert M.**

ODES TO TRIFLES, AND OTHER RHYMES. London, Lane, 1917. 118p [BM BVaU LC OTU

**Easton, C.T.**

SONGS OF FOREST AND STREAM. N.p., Rod and Gun Press, 1912. 38p [PCL

**Eaton, Arthur Wentworth Hamilton, 1849–1937**

ACADIAN BALLADS AND DE SOTO'S LAST DREAM. New York, Whittaker, 1905. 107p [BM BVaU LC NSHD OTU

ACADIAN BALLADS AND LYRICS IN MANY MOODS. Collected Poems. Toronto, McClelland, 1930. 240p [BVaU LC NSHD OLU

ACADIAN LEGENDS AND LYRICS. London, White & Allen, 1889. 148p [BVaU LC NSHD OKQ

THE LOTUS OF THE NILE, AND OTHER POEMS. New York, Whittaker, 1907. 110p [BM BVaU LC NSHD OTU

POEMS OF THE CHRISTIAN YEAR. New York, Whittaker, 1905. 97p [BM LC NSHD OTP

**Eaton, Evelyn Sybil Mary, 1902–**

BIRDS BEFORE DAWN. Toronto, Ryerson, 1942. 12p [BVaU LC NSHD OTU QMM

THE HOURS OF ISIS. London, Barkerville, 1928. 89p [BM

THE INTERPRETER. [Poems.] London, Selwyn & Blount, 1925. 61p [BM

STOLEN HOURS. London, Selwyn & Blount, 1923. 43p [BM OONL

**Eaton, Oliver Mowat**

SYNCHRONISMS OF AN HOUR, AND OTHER POEMS. N.p., 1895. 107p [Also: Brockville, 1897] [OTUV

**Eayrs, Carl**

BORDER VOICES. A Collection of Poems. Ed. by ——. Windsor, Ont., Canadian Authors Assoc., 1946. 48p [OOP

**Ebbs-Canavan, Frances A. (Sweeney)**

HARVEST OF DREAMS. Toronto, Ryerson, 1935. 12p [BVaU NBSaM OKQ

THE TALE OF A BELGIAN HARE. By Frances Ebbs-Canavan and Lillian Clarke Sweeney. Victoria, Diggon-Hibben, 1945. 7p [BM BVaU

**Eby, Oscar S.**

RED CHALK TALKS. Kitchener, 1922. 32p [Brown U BVaU

**Edelstein, Hyman, 1889–1957**

ALL QUIET IN CANADA – AND WHY. "Cpl. Ray's" pen-and-camera Pictures of the War (1939–44), with Verse Comment and Later Poems. Ottawa, Tower Books, 1944. 42p [LC OKQ

CANADIAN LYRICS AND OTHER POEMS. Toronto, Briggs, 1916. 63p [Enl. ed.: Montreal, Belles Lettres Pub., 1921. 64p] [BM BVaU NSHD OTU QMM

FROM JUDEAN VINEYARDS. Poems. Montreal, 1914. 60p [OTU

"HE SHALL ROLL THEIR STONES AWAY." Including "Invocation" from an Epic Poem on the R.C.M.P. Ottawa, Tower Books, 1957. 12p

LAST MATHEMATICIAN. Toronto, Ryerson, 1949. 11p [BVaU NBSaM OTP

LATTER ROSE. Poems. Ottawa, Belles Lettres Pub., 1924. 59p [BVaU NSHD OTU QMM

PINE AND PALM. Poems. Montreal, Capitol Print., 1927. 26p [BVaU QMM

POEMS. 3rd ed. Montreal, Belles Lettres Pub., 1922. 64p [QMM

SELECTED POEMS. Ottawa, Overbrook, 1931. 158p [BVaU OOP QMM

SPIRIT OF ISRAEL. Toronto, Ryerson, 1942. 8p [BVaU LC NBSaM OTP QMM

SPIRIT OF ISRAEL AND OTHER POEMS. Toronto, Ryerson, 1950. 67p [BVaU NBFU OTP

**Edgar, Florence Hester (Hayes), 1874?–1944**

A LEGACY OF LYRICS. Toronto, U. of Toronto Press, 1946. 111p [BVaU LC OTUV QMM

OUT OF THE INFINITE. By Florence H. Edgar and William Wilkie Edgar. N.p., n.d. 12p [OKQ

**Edgar, James David, 1841–1899**

THIS CANADA OF OURS, AND OTHER POEMS. Toronto, Briggs, 1893. 64p [BM BVaU LC MWU NSHD OKQ

THE WHITE STONE CANOE. A Legend of the Ottawas. Toronto, Toronto News, 1885. 27p [BVaU NBFU OTU QMM

**Edgar, Mary Susanne, 1889–**

WOOD-FIRE AND CANDLE-LIGHT. Toronto, Macmillan, 1945. 121p [AEU LC NBFU OTP

**Edgar, Oscar Pelham, 1871–1948**

POEMS. N.p., n.d. 32p [OOP

**Edgar, William Wilkie**

DUETS IN VERSE, FRENCH AND ENGLISH. [French] by Marie Sylvia and [trans. into English] by W.W. Edgar. Ottawa, Graphic, 1929. 81p [BVaU OTU QMM

**Edwards, George**

POEMS. Clarence, Ont., 1867. 50p [CCJ

**Edwards, Henry Arthur, 1905–**

STAR SHINE AND MOON LIGHT. Vancouver, Author, 1947. 20p [BVaU OKQ

"WHITE MAGIC" AND OTHER POEMS. Vancouver, Author, 1948. 20p [OKQ

**Edwards, Lydia Agnes**
HOW CANADIANS MOURNED FOR THEIR QUEEN. Tributes of Loyalty and Love in Memory of Queen Victoria. Comp. by ——. Truro, N.S., News Pub. Co., 1901 51p [NSHD OTP

**Edwards, Mary Frances, 1913–**
AFTER DUSK. Toronto, Author, 1942. 31p [LC

**Eggleston, Wilfrid, 1901–**
PRAIRIE MOONLIGHT AND OTHER LYRICS. Toronto, Author, 1927. 23p [OKQ SSU

**Elder, Robert**
THE BRAVIES. Boston, Meador, 1933. 61p [LC

**Ellenbogen, George, 1934–**
WINDS OF UNREASON. Toronto, Contact Press, 1957. 87p

**Ellice, Edward, 1781–1863**
THE BOOK-KEEPER; and A Translation from the German of Schiller. By Mercator [pseud]. Montreal, Dawson, 1868. 61p [OTL

**Elliott, Albert E.**
POEMS OF COMFORT. Out of the Shadows and Into the Sunshine. By Albert E. Eliott [*sic*]. Toronto, McClelland, 1948. 63 + 58p [BVaU OTP QMU

**Elliott, James** (See p217.)

**Elliott, Robert, 1858–1902**
POEMS. Ed. by John Dearness and Frank Lawson. Published under the Auspices of the Baconian Club, London. London, Ont., Lawson & Jones, 1904. 105p [BM Brown U BVaU OTU

**Ellis, W.A.**
WAR WARBLINGS OF A BRITISH TAR. Vancouver, Terminal City Press, n.d. 33p [BVaU QMU

**Ellis, William Hodgson, 1845–1921**
WAYSIDE WEEDS. Toronto, Dent, 1914. 70p [BVaU LC NBFU OTU

**Ells, Willard W.**
ORIGINAL POEMS. Kentville, N.S., "New Star," 1890. 24p [BVaU

**Ellwood, Thomas**
NIGHT OF DOOM. Halifax, Howe & Sons, 1865. 28p [NSHD

**Elmore, Blanche**
POEMS. Detroit, Wilson-Smith, [18–?]. 20p [OTP
POEMS. [1st Ser.?] Toronto, 1894. 22p [BVaU OTU
POEMS. Toronto, Ellis, 1895. 22p [BVaU OTV QMU

POEMS. [2nd Ser.?] Toronto, Ellis, 1896. 23p [OTP
POEMS. 3rd Series. Toronto, Ellis, 1897. 23p [BVaU OKQ
POEMS. [4th Ser.] Toronto, Imrie Graham, 1898. 23p [BVaU OTUV
POEMS. [5th Ser.] Toronto, Douglas Bros., 1899. 22p [OTP

**Elsom, Albin Edmund, 1889–**
JUBILEE RHYMES. Moose Jaw, Sask., Author, 1955. 32p

**Elsom, Margaret**
PLEASANT PATHS. Toronto, Crucible Press, 1946. 18p [BVaU NBSaM
THIS HOUR. Woodstock, Ont., Author, 1945. 13p [CC

**Elson, John Mebourne, 1880–**
RIDERS OF THE DAWN. Toronto, Macmillan, 1934. 33p [BVaU LC NBFU OKQ

**Emberson, Frederick C., –1913**
GOLD AND SILVER. The Best Twenty Poems and Thoughts Extant. Selected with some Approach to Analytical Certainty. By F.C. Emberson and Maud Ogilvy. Montreal, Drysdale, n.d. 94p [QMM

**Emerson, Nan (MacPherson)**
WIND SONG AND OTHER VERSE. Winnipeg, Author, 1957. 128p

**Ernst, Howard Sheldon**
"LOOKING UP." Weston, Ont., Author, 1940. 22p [OTU

**Errol, Constance**
BY LOST LAGOON. [Vancouver, 1927?], 23p [BVaU NBFU

**Este, C.H. Douglas**
LOWLY SONGS. Montreal, Witness, 1916. 35p [BM
LYRICS OF AN OPTIMIST. Montreal, 1917. 62p [BM

**Evans, Allen Roy, 1885–**
BITTER SWEET. Vancouver, Wrigley, 1933. 71p [BVaU

**Evans, Rev. Richard C., 1861–**
THE SONGS, POEMS, NOTES AND CORRESPONDENCE OF BISHOP R.C. EVANS, and Some Addresses Presented to him from many Parts of the World. London, Ont., 1918. 208p [Brown U BVaU OLU

**Evans, Robert**
TABOR MELODIES. Toronto, Rose, 1878. 125p [BVaU NBFU OKQ QMM

**Evans, Walter Norton, 1836–1896**
CARTIER AND HOCHELAGA. MAISONNEUVE AND VILLE-MARIE. Two Poems of Montreal. Montreal, Drysdale, 1895. 28p [BM LC OLU QMM
MOUNT ROYAL. Montreal, Robinson, 1886. 27p [Same title: Illus. by Elizabeth Warren and A.B. Clarkson. Montreal, 1893. 66p] [BVaU NSHD OTP QMM

**Everson, Ronald Gilmour, 1903–**

A LATTICE FOR MOMOS. Toronto, Contact Press, 1958. 58p

THREE DOZEN POEMS. Montreal, Cambridge Press, 1957. 51p

**Ewach, Honoré, 1900–**

UKRAINIAN SONGS AND LYRICS. A Short Anthology of Ukrainian Poetry. Trans. and ed. by ——. Winnipeg, Ukrainian Pub. Co., 1933. 77p [BM BVaU OTU

**Ezra, Isaac Ben, 1896–**

THE GOLDEN KERNEL AND OTHER POEMS. Toronto, Derby Pub. Co., 1951. xiii + 115p

THE LEGEND OF THE FOUR AND OTHER POEMS. Philadelphia, Dorrance, 1954. 136p

**F., T.D.J.**

CHRIST ENTERING JERUSALEM. Winnipeg, 1911. 11p [Amtmann cat. 151

**Fairbairn, Helen, 1864–**

FROM DAWN TO DUSK. Verses. Toronto, U. of Toronto Press, 1945. 50p [BM BVa OTU QMM

**Fairbanks, Cassie**

THE LONE HOUSE. A Poem Partly Founded on Fact. Halifax, Bowes, 1859. 16p [NSHD OTP

**Fairweather, George Edwin**

ROTHESAY, AND OTHER VERSES. N.p., 1896. 12p [OTUV

THE STONE CHURCH BELL, AND OTHER POEMS. Saint John, Barnes, 1895. 60p [BVaU NBFU OTP

**Farley, Judith Julia**

AN HISTORICAL POEM, THE SAINT LAWRENCE RIVER. Quebec, Daily Telegraph Print., 1906. 11p [OTU QMSS

**Farley, Tom, 1917–**

IT WAS A PLANE. Toronto, Ryerson, 1952. 12p

**Farmer, Broadus Baxter**

SONGS OF THE ISLAND, AND OTHER POEMS. N.p., n.d. 7p [OTU

**Farmer, Thomas Devey Jermyn**

SHRINES OLD AND NEW, AND OTHER POEMS. Toronto, Briggs, 1913. 258p [BM BVaU OTU

WHERE THE RIVERS MEET. A Retrospect and a Contrast. Winnipeg, 1911. 23p [ACG OH

**Farrill, Mrs. Caroline Grant**

SOME MORNING SOON. Toronto, Crucible Press, 1941. 20p [LC

**Faulkner, Rhoda Ann (Page), 1826–1863**

WILD NOTES FROM THE BACK WOODS. By R.A.P. [Ed. with intro. by Edwin C. Guillet, 12 April 1942, unpub.] Cobourg, "Star," 1850. 62p [OTP

**Faulkner, Sarah E. (Sherwood), 1853–**

SEA MURMURS AND WOODLAND SONGS. Toronto, Briggs, 1903. 111p [BM BVaU NBFU OKQ

**Fenerty, Charles**

BETULA NIGRA. A Poem. By Charles Fennerty [*sic*]. Halifax, Cunnabell, 1855. 12p [NSHD

ESSAY ON PROGRESS. Halifax, Bowes, 1866. 12p [NSHD

HID TREASURE; or, The Labours of a Deacon, and Other Poems. Manuscript. 81p [NSHD

**Fenton, Frederick B.**

POEMS OF PEACE AND WAR. London, Heath Cranton, 1916. 27p [BM OTU

**Ferguson, Rose**

MAPLE LEAVES AND SNOWFLAKES. Toronto, Briggs, 1913. 72p [BM OKQ

**Ferne, Doris Maud (Napper), 1896–**

EBB TIDE. Toronto, Ryerson, 1941. 8p [BVaU NBSaM OTU QMM

PASCHAL LAMB, AND OTHER POEMS. Toronto, Macmillan, 1946. 39p [BM BVaU LC NBFU OKQ

**Fewster, Ernest Philip, 1868–1947**

THE IMMORTAL DWELLER. Vancouver, Murphy & Chapman, 1938. 66p [BVaU NSHD OKQ

LITANY BEFORE THE DAWN OF FIRE. Toronto, Ryerson, 1942. 10p [BVaU LC NBSaM OTU QMM

REJOICE, O MY HEART. Vancouver, Grace Fewster, 1949. 68p [BVaU NBFU OKQ QMM

WHITE DESIRE. Ottawa, Overbrook, 1930. 54p [BVaU NSHD OKQ

THE WIND AND THE SEA. Poems. Vancouver, Poetry Soc., 1946. 113p [BVaU OKQ

**Fiamengo, Marya Ekaterina, 1926–**

THE QUALITY OF HALVES AND OTHER POEMS. Vancouver, Klanak Press, 1958. 41p

**Field, George Blackstone, 1883–1952**

ECHOES FROM YPRES. New Westminster, B.C., priv. print., 1954. 45p

RHYMES OF THE SURVEY AND FRONTIER. Toronto, Briggs, 1911. 77p [AEU BM BVaU NBFU OKQ

**Finch, Robert Duer Claydon, 1900–**

ACIS IN OXFORD, AND OTHER POEMS. Toronto, U. of Toronto Press, 1961. 46p [Earlier ed. priv. print. at New Bodleian, Oxford, 1959.]

NEW PROVINCES. Poems of Several Authors. [Ed. by F.R. Scott.] Toronto, Macmillan, 1936. 77p [Contains poems by Finch and Others.] [BVaU NBFU OKQ QMM

POEMS. Toronto, Oxford, 1946. 51p [BM BVaU LC MWU NBFU OTU QMM

THE STRENGTH OF THE HILLS. Toronto, McClelland, 1948. 132p [BVaU MWU NBFU OKQ

**Finnigan, Joan, 1925–**

THROUGH THE GLASS, DARKLY. Toronto, Ryerson, 1957. 12p

**Firth, Mrs. Rose Lyle, 1893–**

STRANGE ROADS. Vancouver, Author, 1940. 56p [BVaU OKQ

STRANGE ROADS. II. Vancouver, Author, 1955. 55p

**Fischer, William Joseph, 1879–1921**

SONGS OF THE WAYSIDE. Boston, Badger, 1903. 85p [OTUV

THE TOILER AND OTHER POEMS. Toronto, Briggs, 1907. 167p [BM BVaU NBFU OKQ

**Fisher, Peter, 1782–1848**

THE LAY OF THE WILDERNESS. A Poem in Five Cantos. By a Native of New Brunswick [pseud]. Saint John, Chubb, 1833. 165p [NSHP

**Fishpool, John Foster, 1885–**

SPARKS FROM THE ANVIL. St. Thomas, Ont., Municipal World, 1935. 47p [Brown U

**Fitzgerald, Desmond, 1915–**

THE SYMPHONY OF THE STARS. By Daryl Gerald [pseud]. London, Ont., Crucible Press, 1939. 11p [OTP

**Fleck, Widow [Mrs. John Fleming?]**

POEMS ON VARIOUS SUBJECTS. By Widow Fleck. Montreal, 1833. 12p [CCJ

**Fleming, Ann (Cuthbert) (Knight), –1860**

HOME. A Poem. By Ann Cuthbert Knight. Edinburgh, 1815. 98p [CCJ

A YEAR IN CANADA, AND OTHER POEMS. By Ann Cuthbert Knight. Edinburgh, Doig & Stirling, 1816. 126p [BM OTP QMSS

**Fleming, Rev. Everett Samuel James, 1895–**

BIBLE STORY POEMS. Old Friends in New Attire. Sidney, B.C., 1949. 28p [BVaU OTUV

THE FORBIDDEN PLATEAU; OR, THE GREAT BETRAYAL. A Legend of Vancouver Island. Campbell River, B.C., Author, 1959. 8p

THE GREAT WHITE ROCK. A Legend of Semiahmoo Bay. Sidney, B.C., Author, 1950. 5p [OONL

THE JERICHO ROAD AND OTHER BIBLE STORY POEMS. Sidney, B.C., Author, 1949. 28p [QMU

LOGS FOR THE FIRE. Campbell River, B.C., Author, 1959. 49p

MY NURSE AND OTHER POEMS. Sidney, B.C., Author, 1951. 24p

A POCKETFUL OF LAUGHING GAS AND OTHER POEMS FOR FUN. New Westminster, B.C., Author, 1945. 33p [BVaU OTUV

SOURDOUGH AND GOLD DUST. New Westminster, B.C., Author, 1954. 15p

WHITHER AND WHY. Sidney, B.C., Author, 1949. 22p [BVaU OTU

**Fletcher, Edward Taylor, 1816?–1897**

THE LOST ISLAND (Atlantis). A Poem. Ottawa, Bureau, 1889. 24p [BM BVaU LC NSHP OKQ

NESTORIUS. A Phantasy. By E.T.F. Ottawa, Bureau, 1892. 23p [BM OTU QMM

**Fletcher, Mrs. Elizabeth, 1879–**

POEMS. Guelph, Author, [1933?]. 28p [OKQ

**Fletcher, Mary E., 1874–1929**

CRUSTULA JURIS. Being a Collection of Leading Cases on Contract Done into Verse. By Mary E. Fletcher and Bernard Wallace Russell. Toronto, Carswell, [1913]. 62p [BVaU NBFU OTU

**Fletcher, Olive H.**

SONGS OF OUR EMPIRE'S WAR AND PRAISEWORTHY ALLIES. Schumacher, Ont., Author, 1944. 96p [OOP

**Flint, Annie Johnson, 1866–1932**

BY THE WAY.... [Verses.] Toronto, Evangelical Pub., 1920. 48p [BM

FLINT'S BEST-LOVED POEMS. Toronto, Evangelical Pub., 1948. 141p [Adelphi cat. 68

OUT OF DOORS. Nature Songs. Toronto, Evangelical Pub., 1920. 56p [BM OTU QMU

POEMS. Vol. I. Toronto, Evangelical Pub., 1944. 142p [AEP

POEMS. Vol. II. Toronto, Evangelical Pub., 1948. 141p [BM

SONGS OF FAITH AND COMFORT. Toronto, Evangelical Pub., 1919. 56p [BM

SONGS OF THE BLESSED HOPE. Toronto, Evangelical Pub., n.d. 47p [QMU

**Flood, John N., 1893–**

THE SAGA OF THE CARIBBEAN CRUISE OF M.V. AROSA SUN, FEBRUARY 1956. Saint John, Author, n.d. 8p [A diary in rhyme, addressed to the author's daughter.]

**Flood, Robert William, 1877–**

BITS O'RHYME TO PASS THE TIME. Vancouver, Wrigley Print Co., 1954. 26p

ROUGH TIMES AND OTHER RHYMES. Vancouver, Murphy Chapman, 1941. 31p [BVaU

**Foran, Ethel Ursula**

POEMS. A Few Blossoms from the Garden of my Dreams. Montreal, Beauchemin, 1922. 128p [BM BVaU NSHD OOP QMM

**Foran, Joseph Kearney, 1857–1931**

POEMS AND CANADIAN LYRICS. Montreal, Sadlier, 1895. 244p [BVaU LC NBFU OTU QMM

**Foran, Michael McKeon, 1898–**

NIGHT FLIGHT ... AND OTHER POEMS. London, Ont., Young Press, 1945. 46p [BVaU OTU

THIS IS MY WORST. A Collection of Humorous Verse. Toronto, Author, 1955. 54p

**Ford, Robert Arthur Douglas, 1915–**

A WINDOW ON THE NORTH. Toronto, Ryerson, 1956. 48p

**Forsyth, William Langdon**

ZEBUNISA, AND OTHER POEMS. By Sauda [pseud]. Montreal, 1873. 99p [BVa LC OTUV

**Fortner, Dora Pearl, 1894–**

DAYDREAMS. N.p., 1957. 20p (Carillon Poetry Chap-Books)

FLIGHTS OF FANCY. Poems. N.p., 1955. 20p (Carillon Poetry Chap-Books)

**Found, Lillian (Redmond), 1878–**

BANNER IN THE SKY, AND OTHER POEMS. Ottawa, Author, 1945. 38p [Brown U

WHAT MATTER WHAT WAY. Ottawa, Le Droit, 1950. 36p [OONL

**Fowke, Edith Margaret (Fulton)**

CANADA'S STORY IN SONG. By Edith Fowke and Alan Mills [pseud of Albert Miller.] Piano accompaniments by Helmut Blume. Toronto, Gage, 1960. x + 230p

FOLKSONGS OF CANADA. Ed. by ——. Waterloo, Ont., Waterloo Music Co., 1954. 198p

SONGS OF WORK AND FREEDOM. By Edith Fowke and Joe Glazer. Music arrangements: Kenneth Bray. Chicago, Roosevelt University, Labor Education Division, 1960. 208p

**Fox, Annie Marion**

QUESTING AND OTHER POEMS. Toronto, Author, 1935. 16p [OTU

WINGED WORDS. Toronto, Livingstone, 1930. 32p [BVaU OTP

**Fox, Marion Wathen, 1871–1956**

SILHOUETTES OF THE FOREST. Saint John, Barnes Hopkins, [194–?]. 21p [NBFL

**Fox, William Sherwood, 1878–1967**

ON FRIENDSHIP. Toronto, Ryerson, 1953. 17p

**Frame, Margaret Fulton**

PHANTOM CARAVAN. Selected and Arranged by Charles Clay. Ottawa, Tower Books, 1947. 48p [BVaU NBFU OLU

**Fraser, Alexander Louis, 1870–1954**

AFTERMATH. Saint John, Globe, 1919. 55p [BVaU NBFU OKQ

AT LIFE'S WINDOWS. Saint John, Globe, 1910. 67p [NBFU OKQ

BY COBEQUID BAY. Toronto, Ryerson, 1927. 12p [BVaU NBSaM OKQ QMM

BY EASTERN WINDOWS. Saint John, Globe, 1933. 109p [NBFU OTU

THE DRAINED CUP AND OTHER POEMS. Saint John, Globe, 1925. 46p [BVaU NBFU OKQ

FOR THINKING HEARTS. Toronto, H.M. Ridley, 1954. 20p (Carillon Poetry Chap-Books)

FUGITIVES. Saint John, Globe, 1912. 79p [NBFU QMM

GOD'S WEALTH, AND OTHER POEMS. Saint John, Globe, 1922. 42p [NBFU OKQ

HALIFAX, 1749–1949. Halifax, MacCurdy, 1949. 16p [Brown U NBFU

THE INDIAN BRIDE. A War Legend. Saint John, Globe, 1915. 16p [NBFU OKQ

MOOSE RIVER MINES, AND OTHER POEMS. Toronto, Crucible Press, 1949. 20p [NBFU OTUV

PEOPLE OF THE STREET AND OTHER POEMS. Saint John, Globe, 1929. 85p [NSHD OKQ

RUTH AND OTHER POEMS. Toronto, Crucible Press, 1946. 22p [BVaU NSHD OTP QMM

SONNETS AND OTHER VERSES. Saint John, Globe, 1909. 62p [BVaU LC NSHD OTUV QMM

**Fraser, Dawn**

SONGS OF SIBERIA AND RHYMES OF THE ROAD. Glace Bay, N.S., Eastern Pub., [1919?]. 229p [BM OLU

**Fraser, Donald Andrew, 1875–1948**

CENTENARY. A Collection of Verses arranged in Celebration of the One Hundredth Birthday of the City of Victoria, B.C., 1843–1943. Victoria, Diggon-Hibben, 1943. 39p [BVaU OKQ

MY NUGGET-POKE. A Selection of Sonnets and Other Short Poems. Victoria, Author, n.d. 108p [BVaU OKQ

PEBBLES AND SHELLS. A Book of Verses. Toronto, Briggs, 1909. 172p [BM BVaU NSHD OLU

THE THREE KINGS, AND OTHER VERSES FOR CHILDREN. Victoria, Cusack, 1922. 64p [BVaU OKQ

**Fraser, Hermia (Harris), 1902–**

THE ARROW-MAKER'S DAUGHTER AND OTHER HAIDA CHANTS. Toronto, Ryerson, 1957. 16p

SONGS OF THE WESTERN ISLANDS. Toronto, Ryerson, 1945. 10p [BVaU NBSaM OTU

**Fraser, James MacDonell, 1882–**

SEASONAL SONGS INCLUDING "WE SHALL REMEMBER THEM." Comp. by ——. Picton, Ont., Gazette, 1935. 16p [NSHD OTU

**Fraser, John, 1820–1899**

A TALE OF THE SEA, AND OTHER POEMS. Montreal, Dawson, 1870. 87p [BVaU NSHD OKQ QMM

**Freebairn, Adam L., 1881–**

KOOTENAI BROWN AND OTHER WESTERN POEMS. Pincher Creek, Alta., Author, [194–?]. 32p [AEU OTU

THE MOUNTAIN HEIGHTS AND OTHER POEMS. [Pincher Creek, Alta.], n.d. 24p [ACG OTU

MY SON AND OTHER POEMS. Pincher Creek, Alta., Author, [194–?]. 30p [ACG

RHYMES FROM THE FOOTHILLS. [Pincher Creek, Alta.], n.d. 31p [ACG OTU

**French, Jane E.L.**

POEMS AND LYRICS. Victoria, Victoria Print., [1923]. 96p [BM BVaU OOP

**Freund, Philip, 1909–**

PRIVATE SPEECH. London, Allen, 1950. 358p [BM LC

**Frisch, Anthony John, 1921–**

THE HOUSE. New Poems, in English, French, German. Hull, Que., Ivy Pub. Co., 1950. 32p [BVaU NBFU OLU QMM

POEMS. Toronto, Ryerson, 1954. 22p

THIRD POEMS. Hull, Que., Ivy Pub. Co., 1951. 28p

THOUGH I SPEAK. Poems. Montreal, Ivy Pub. Co., 1949. 31p [BVaU NBFU OKQ

**Frost, George**

MAN AND NATURE; or, Evening Thoughts in Poetry. Saint John, Barnes, 1874. 75p [Brown U OTU

**Fry, Alice**

THE RUBY BOOK OF REMEMBRANCE. Toronto, Crucible Press, 1947. 23p [Brown U

**Fuller, Ada Elizabeth**

A ROMANCE OF DREAM VALLEY. [A Poem.] Canada, 1921. [BM

SUNSHINE AND SHADOW. Poems. Niagara Falls, Ont., 1919. 64p [BM Brown U OTU

**Fuller, William Henry**
YE BALLAD OF LYTTEL JOHN A. [MOR'98

**Fulton, S.O.**
RED TARN; or, The Vision of the Lake. A Thrilling Temperance Poem in Fourteen Cantos. Amherst, N.S., Gazette, 1873. 156p [NSHD

**Fulton, Sadie E.**
POEMS. Montreal, 1890. 10p [Brown U OLU

**Funk, I.J.**
THE ROCK CALLED HADES. London, Stockwell, [194–?]. 79p [OOP

**Fyles, Thomas W., 1832–**
POEMS. Toronto, Briggs, 1907. 111p [BM BVaU NBFU OTUV

**Gahan, James Joseph, 1851–**
CANADA. Quebec, Delisle, 1877. 21p [OTP
THE IMMACULATE MARY, AND OTHER POEMS. Quebec, Barrow, n.d. 24p [QMSS
VIVIAN. A Tale of Chateau Richer. Toronto, Boyle, 1880. 24p [NSHD OTP

**Galloway, Andrew Strome Ayees, 1915–**
THE YEW TREE BALLAD, AND OTHER POEMS. Aylmer, Ont., Barnecott & Monteith, 1936. 48p [Brown U

**Galloway, Christian F.J.**
PEACE RIVER, AND OTHER VERSE. London, Mitre Press, 1953. 59p

**Garbutt, Mrs. Elizabeth, 1887–**
MT. EISENHOWER AND OTHER POEMS. Calgary, Dominion Text Book Co., 1946. 40p [ACU NBSaM

**Gardiner, Lue (Gillmor)**
RHYMES FROM RANGES. Edmonton, Author, 1942. 30p [CC
RHYMES FROM THE NORTHWEST. Edmonton, Author, 1940. 39p [ACG OONL

**Gardner-Smith, E.**
THE CALL OF THE WEST AND OTHER POEMS. Calgary, Burnand, [1928?]. 32p [ACG OKQ

**Garrett, Mrs. Florence Pearl, 1883–**
LIFE'S GLEANINGS. Winnipeg, Wallingford, 1937. 36p [Brown U BVaU
MEMORIES. Winnipeg, Author, 1936. 28p [CC
THE WHISPERING LEAVES. Winnipeg, Author, 1936. 32p [CC

**Garrett, Rev. John C.**
THE CENTENNIAL. A Poem Written on the Centenary of St. Mark's Church, Niagara, Ont., (1792–1892). N.p., 1892. 24p [OTU

**Garvey, Michael**

VOTIVE LIGHTS, INCENSE AND MELODY. Toronto, Author, 1926. 61p [OTP

**Garvin, John William, 1859–1935**

CANADIAN POEMS OF THE GREAT WAR. Chosen and ed. by ——. Toronto, McClelland, 1918. 256p [BVaU LC NSHD OKQ

CANADIAN POETS. Ed. by ——. Toronto, McClelland, 1916. 471p [Rev. ed.: Toronto, McClelland, 1926. 536p [BM BVaU LC NBFU OTU QMM

CANADIAN POETS AND POETRY. Chosen and ed. by ——. Toronto, McClelland, 1916. 471p. [BVaU LC OTUV QMM

CANADIAN VERSE FOR BOYS AND GIRLS. Ed. by ——. Toronto, Nelson, 1930. 215p [BVaU NBFU OTUV QMM

CAP AND BELLS. An Anthology of Light Verse by Canadian Poets. Chosen by ——. Toronto, Ryerson, 1936. 105p [BM BVaU LC NBFU OTU

**Gay, James, 1810–1891**

CANADA'S POET; YOURS ALWAY JAMES GAY. Poet Laureate of Canada and Master of All Poets, this Day. ... London, Field & Tuer, 1884. 87 + 15p [BM BVaU LC NSHD OKQ

POEMS BY JAMES GAY, POET LAUREATE OF CANADA, MASTER OF ALL POETS. Written while Crossing the Sea in 1882. Guelph, Author, 1883. 18p [W.A. Deacon, THE FOUR JAMESES, *q.v.*

**Gerrard, George**

THE CONSOLATION. A Poem. Toronto, Hunter Rose, 1881. 64p [BVaU NBFU OTU QMM

**Ghent, Percy Parker, 1888–1952**

VAGRANT RHYMES. Sundridge Village, Ont., Harper, 1935. 21p [OTP

**Gibbon, John Murray, 1875–1952**

BALLADS OF B.C. Toronto, Thompson, n.d. 19p [BViPA

CANADA IN SONG. With Musical Arrangements by L.R. Bell. Toronto, Thompson, 1941. 27p [CC

CANADIAN CADENCES. Toronto, Ryerson, 1947. 16p [BVaU NSHD OLU

A CANADIAN CALENDAR. Ste Anne de Bellevue, Que., Canadian Bookman, 1919. 15p [BM BVaU OKQ

CANADIAN FOLKSONGS (OLD AND NEW). Selected and trans. by ——. Toronto, Dent, 1927. 105p [Rev. and enl. ed.: Toronto, Dent, 1949. 114p] [BVaU NSWA OTU

FRENCH CANADIAN FOLK SONGS; FRENCH AND ENGLISH TEXTS. English translation by J. Murray Gibbon. Arranged for chorus of men's voices by Ernest MacMillan. Boston, Boston Music Co., 1928. 4v [NSHD

NEW WORLD BALLADS. Toronto, Ryerson, 1939. 177p [BVaU LC NBFU OTP QMM

NORTHLAND SONGS. Toronto, Thompson, 1936. 4v [BVa LC OTP

PIONEER SONGS OF CANADA. Musical Arrangements by Irvin Cooper. Toronto, Thompson, 1941. 28p [BVaU

PRINCE CHARLIE AND FLORA. A Scottish Ballad Opera. Libretto by ——. Toronto, Dent, 1929. [32p [OTU

**Gibson, George Herbert Rae, 1881–1932**

IRONBARK CHIPS AND STOCKWHIP CRACKS. Melbourne, Australia, [1893]. 219p [QMM

IRONBARK SPLINTERS FROM THE AUSTRALIAN BUSH. 2nd ed. London, Werner Laurie, [191–?]. 167p [BVi OTP

SOUTHERLY BUSTERS. In Verse. By Ironbark [pseud]. Sydney, Australia, J. Sands, n.d. 15 + 210p [BM

**Gibson, J.E.**

YOU'LL HATE ME FOR THIS. A Book of Impromptu Verse. Vancouver, Wrigley, 1946. 92p [BVaU OONL

**Gill, Frank P.**

RHAPSODY. Songs and Lyrics. Calgary, Star Print., [1928?]. 46p [BVaU OTU

**Gillespie, George W.**

MISCELLANEOUS POEMS. Toronto, Author, 1843. 152p [OTP

**Gillespy, William, 1824–1886**

FUGITIVE POETRY. Hamilton, 1846. 100p [CCJ

**Gillies, Rev. Archibald C., 1834–1887**

DAILY MEDITATIONS. A Collection of Poems. Kingston, 1860. 96p [CCJ

**Gillis, James Donald, 1870–**

THE GREAT ELECTION. [Cape Breton], North Sydney Herald, [1915?]. 43p [NSHD OTUV

**Gillmore, E.T.B.**

MAPLE LEAVES IN KHAKI–The Blooding of the Whelps, and Other Verses. Ottawa, Taylor & Clarke, [1901?]. 16p [NSHD OTP

**Gilmour, Lucy C.**

SCRAPS OF VERSE. From a Shut-In. Charlottetown, Maritime Stationers, 1912. 35p [OONL

**Gilpin, Lois A. (Hunter), 1876–**

THE ARBUTUS TREE. Vancouver, Clarke & Stuart, [1955?]. 40p

EASTER SUNDAY, EARLY, AND OTHER POEMS. Vancouver, Vancouver Stationers, 1935. 18p [Brown U BVaU

**Girling, T.A.**

THE SALIENT AND OTHER POEMS. London, Palmer & Hayward, 1918. 51p [2nd ed., 1918. 65p] [BVaU LC

**Glassco, John, 1909–**

THE DEFICIT MADE FLESH. Toronto, McClelland, 1958. 64p

**Gleave, Thomas Barwell**

BECKONING HILLS. Toronto, Kirkby, 1949. 47p [Brown U

BEYOND OUR WALLS. Toronto, Kirkby, 1946. 48p [OTP

COME REST AWHILE. Toronto, Kirkby, 1948. 47p [Brown U BVaU OTU

ENCHANTED BY-WAYS. Toronto, Kirkby, 1947. 55p [Brown U OTUV

HERE'S TO HAPPINESS. Toronto, Kirkby, 1945. 48p [Brown U OTU

THE MYSTIC CAVE. Twelve Original Fairy Tales in Verse. Montreal, Richardson etc., n.d. 40p [OTU

VISTAS GRAVE AND GAY. Toronto, Kirkby, 1944. 48p [BVaU OTP

**Glendinning, Alexander**

RHYMES. ... V. I London, Ont., Free Press Print., 1871. 240p [BVaU NBFU OKQ

**Goddard, Evelyn**

POEMS ON THE DOGWOOD, B.C.'S FLORAL EMBLEM. By Cowichan poets. Selected by ——. Duncan, B.C., Cowichan Leader, 1958. 12p

**Godfrey, Mrs. Norah, –1948?**

CAVALCADE. Toronto, Ryerson, 1946. 16p [BVaU LC MWU NBSaM OTP

**Goldberg, Nathan Ralph, 1919–**

COFFEE AND BITTERS. By Nathan Ralph [pseud]. Toronto, Macmillan, 1947. 37p [BM BVaU LC NBFU OTP

TWELVE POEMS. By Nathan Ralph [pseud]. Toronto, Ryerson, 1941. 8p [BVaU LC NBSaM OTP QMM

**Goldsmith, Oliver, 1794–1861**

THE MANUSCRIPT BOOK OF OLIVER GOLDSMITH. ... Description and comment by E. Cockburn Kyte. Toronto, Bibliographical Society of Canada, 1950. 4 + 9p [OONL

THE RISING VILLAGE. A Poem. London, Sharpe, 1825. 48p [BM NSHD

THE RISING VILLAGE, with Other Poems. By Oliver Goldsmith, a Descendant of the Author of "The Deserted Village." Saint John, M'Millan, 1834. 144p [BM BVaU LC MWU NSHD OKQ

**Goodchild, Roland**

THISTLEDOWN. Occasional Verses. London, Stockwell, 1917. 48p [BM

**Gooderham, Grace A.**

FRIENDLY FEET. N.p., Author, [192–?]. 16p [Brown U

**Gooderham, Mary W.**

COMPANION BOOK TO A CHRISTMAS GARLAND. Being Hymns for Christmas, Eighteen Hundred and Ninety-nine to Christmas, Nineteen Hundred and Ten. Toronto, [1910?]. 11p [Brown U BVaU

**Goodley, Margaret**
SIFTING STARDUST. Oshawa, Author, 1939. 44p [UTQ'40

**Gordon, Alexander McGregor Rose, 1846–1898**
HOCH DER KAISER. Myself and God. By A. McGregor Rose (A.M.R. Gordon). Pictures by Jessie A. Walker. New York, Abbey Press, 1900. 31p [Brown U LC OTU
POEMS. By A. McGregor Rose [pseud]. Collected and Ed. with a Life of the Author by Robert Dey. Manchester, Heywood, n.d. 168p [OTUV
SIR WILFRID'S PROGRESS THROUGH ENGLAND AND FRANCE IN THE JUBILEE YEAR. Montreal, Sterling, 1897. 19p [OTUV

**Gordon, Alfred, 1888–**
DANDELION. A Tale for Children. N.p., priv. print., n.d. 4p [NBFU
IN PROPHESY (A RECESSIONAL), AND SONNETS OF THE EUROPEAN WAR. Montreal, Author, 1914. 16p [BM Brown U BVaU NBFU OTU
POEMS. Toronto, Musson, 1915. 120p [BM BVaU NBFU OTU
VIMY RIDGE AND NEW POEMS. Toronto, Dent, 1918. 64p [BVaU NSHD OTU

**Gordon, Huntly K., 1895–1949**
VERSES AND SKETCHES. Toronto, U. of Toronto Press, 1952. 33p

**Gordon, John R., 1889–**
RHYMES OF THE RANGE. Calgary, Author, 1952. 11p

**Gordon, Robert Kay, 1887–**
A CANADIAN CHILD'S A B C. Toronto, Dent, 1931. 56p [Brown U BVaU OTUV

**Gould, Alice Kathryn**
BY THE RIDEAU. A Tale of Smiths Falls in Song and Story. [Smith Falls], Record-News, 1935. 32p [OTU

**Gould, Mona Helen (McTavish), 1908–**
GOSSIP! Verse. Toronto, Gossip, 1949. 48p [UTQ'50
I RUN WITH THE FOX. Toronto, Macmillan, 1946. 30p [BVaU NBFU OTP
TASTING THE EARTH. Toronto, Macmillan, 1943. 44p [BVaU LC NBFU OTP

**Gowman, Henry**
PICKLE CROW AND OTHER POEMS. Toronto, Hilda M. Ridley, 1951. 18p (Carillon Poetry Chap-Books)

**Grace, Edith Jayne**
GEMS OF WISDOM. Ilfracombe, Devon, Stockwell, 1957. 16p

**Graham, Alexander, fl. 1840–1873**
LEISURE HOUR MUSINGS. Peterborough, 1873. 256p [OTUV

**Graham, Hannah Isabel**
BE OF GOOD CHEER. Toronto, Allen, 1939. 106p [BM BVaU OTP

BEN ONA AND THE CHRISTMAS CAROL. Toronto, Ryerson, 1931. 16p [BVaU OTP

SAINT IGNACE AND OTHER POEMS. Toronto, Ryerson, 1934. 15p [BVaU OTU

A SONG OF DECEMBER AND OTHER POEMS. Toronto, Briggs, 1904. 19p [BM BVaU OTP

**Graham, Janet (Pollock), 1880–**

FROM HILL AND DELL. Little Nature Sketches of the Ottawa Valley. Lachute, Que., Watchman, 1940. 56p [LC OTU QMM

**Grant, Francis Wylie, 1904–**

SPINDRIFT. A Booklet of Maritime Rhymes. [Wallace, N.S.?] Author, 1957. 60p

**Grant, Mrs. J.P.**

STRAY LEAVES. A Collection of Poems. Montreal, Lovell, 1865. 166p [BVaU LC NBFU OTU QMM

**Grant, James Miller, 1853–1940**

CANADA, MY HOME. N.p., Author, 1901. 5p [BM NSHD OTUV

CANADA, MY HOME, AND OTHER POEMS. By Grant Balfour [pseud]. Toronto, Musson, 1910. 88p [Another ed., 1925] [BVaU NBFU OTU QMM

CANADA THE FREE. [A Poem]. By Grant Balfour [pseud]. N.p., 1908. s. sh. folio [BM

MY MOTHERLAND. By Grant Balfour [psued]. N.p., 1904 13p [BM OTP

ON STRIKE TILL THREE. By Grant Balfour [pseud]. Toronto, Briggs, 1913. 15p [BM BVaU NBFU OKQ

**Grant, William Ewart**

LEAVES OF EMPIRE. Toronto, Ryerson, 1919. 58p [BVaU OKQ

**Grantham, Ronald, 1910–**

NEW EARTH. Vancouver, Boyd, 1931. 22p [BVaU NBFU OTP

**Gray, Alice Rowan**

KENILWORTH AND OTHER POEMS. Winnipeg, Peerless, 1934. 44p [BViV MWP

**Gray, Rev. Archibald**

SHADES OF THE HAMLET, AND OTHER POEMS. Woburn, Mass., Fowle, 1852. 57p [NSHD

**Gray, Francis William, 1877–1958**

CHRISTMAS REMEMBRANCES, 1953. Victoria, Author, 1953. 24p

MUSINGS OF A MARITIME MINER, IN WAR AND PEACE. ... Sydney, N.S., Author, 1940. 26p [BVaU NSHD

**Gray, J.H. Gresham**

JINGLES OF A JESTER. By Gresham Gray. 1st ed. [Victoria], 1951 [c1950]. 160p

RHYMES WITHOUT REASON. By Gresham Gray. [Victoria], J.H. Gray, [1951]. 216p

**Gray, James Martin, 1930–**
POEMS. Edinburgh, Serif Books, 1958. 46p

**Gray, Mrs. Lillian Collier**
GRAY ACRES. Toronto, Crucible Press, 1944. 32p [OTP

**Gray, Nelson Cockburn**
NEW PATRIOTIC POEMS. Montreal, Nova Co., 1908. 12p [NSWA OPAL

**Grayson, Ethel Kirk, 1890–**
BEGGAR'S VELVET. Toronto, Ryerson, 1948. 42p [BVaU MWU NBFU OTP QMBM

**Greaves, Arthur**
BUBBLES FROM THE DEEP. Sonnets and Other Poems, Dramatic and Personal. Philadelphia, Author, 1873. 194p [LC OTP

**Green, E.**
DEVIL'S DRIFT. Winnipeg, Author, 1932. 30p [CC

**Green, James Albert**
VERSES OF THE CANADIAN NORTHLAND. [Cincinnati, 1920.] 22p [OWA

**Greene, Charles Johnson**
CANADA-LAND. ... Lyrics of a Group of Ten Original Songs. Vancouver, Campbell, [1948?]. 10p [BVaU

**Gregory, Alice**
PARK HILL. An Historical Poem. Toronto, 1928. 8p [Amtmann cat. 152

**Grier, Eldon, 1917–**
A MORNING FROM SCRAPS. Montreal, n.d. 22p
THE RING OF ICE. Poems. Montreal, Cambridge Press, 1957. 101p

**Grier, Rose J.E., 1832–1920**
ALLEVIATIONS. Toronto, Brown Searle, 1905. 60p [BM NBFU OTUV

**Griffin, Edith May**
RAMBLING WITH EDITH GRIFFIN. Sarnia, priv. print., [1946?]. 42p [Phelps

**Griffin, Frederick, 1798–1879**
THE DESTINY OF MAN, THE STORM KING, AND OTHER POEMS. 2nd ed. London, Trübner, 1883. 103p [1st ed.: London, 1872.] [BM
THE WORLD UNDER GLASS. London, 1879. [BM

**Griffiths, Thomas George, 1888–**
THE DREAMER AND OTHER POEMS. Toronto, United Church Pub. House, 1932. 8p [OKQ

**Grigg, B.W.A.**
THE LILIES AND OTHER POEMS. N.p., n.d. 15p [NSWA

**Grigg, Richard**
INGERSOLL RHYMINGS. Ingersoll, Oxford Tribune, 1894. 106p [OTUV

**Grigsby, Joan S., 1909–**
LANTERNS BY THE LAKE. London, Kegan Paul, 1929. 136p [BM OKQ
THE ORCHID DOOR, ANCIENT KOREAN POEMS. Collected and Done into English Verse. Kobe, Thompson, 1935. 105p [BVa LC

**Groom, I. Sutherland**
QUEENS AND OTHERS. Toronto, Ryerson, 1955. 16p

**Grote, George Whitfield**
ODE ON THE CORONATION OF KING EDWARD VII, 1902. Toronto, Author, 1902. 23p [BM OKQ

**Groves, Edith (Lelean), 1870–1931**
EVERYDAY CHILDREN, A BOOK OF POEMS. With ... a Biographical Sketch of the Author by Helen Macmurchy. ... Toronto, Committee in Charge ... Groves Memorial Fund, 1932. 155p [Brown U BVaU OLU
THE KINGDOM OF CHILDHOOD. Toronto, Warwick & Rutter, 1925. 106p [Brown U BVaU OTU
WE ARE SEVEN. ... Songs for Children and Grown-Ups. Music by B.L. Tamblyn. Toronto, 1927. 20p [Adelphi cat. 55A

**Guerin, Mrs. Agnes Carter, 1850–**
WOVEN THOUGHTS. By Mrs. R.C. Guerin. Toronto, Briggs, 1904. 101p [BM BVaU OTU

**Guise, Mary Ellen**
PENNIES ON MY PALM. Toronto, Ryerson, 1931. 8p [BVaU NBFU OKQ

**Gunn, Garrioch**
WHITE LAURUSTINE. Poems. Toronto, Macmillan, 1914. 132p [BVaU OKQ

**Gunn, John M.**
A CHRISTMAS MESSAGE, AND SOME BITS OF VERSE. London, Ont., Talbot, 1923. 23p [OTP

**Gunne, A. Evelyn**
THE SILVER TRAIL. Poems. Boston, Badger, 1906. 110p [BViPA LC NBFU
THE SPIRIT OF THE NORTH, AND OTHER POEMS. Toronto, Imrie, 1900. 41p [BM OTUV

**Gunter, Lillian Forbes**
LOVING MEMORIES, AND OTHER POEMS. Regina Leader Pub. Co., 1922. 45p [BM QMU

**Gurney, F.C.**

SOUL SO DARK, AND OTHER POEMS. Didsbury, Alta., 1942. 86p [OONL

**Gustafson, Ralph Barker, 1909–**

ANTHOLOGY OF CANADIAN POETRY (English). Comp. by ——. Harmondsworth, Middlesex, Eng., Penguin Books, 1942. 123p [BM BVaU LC NSHD OLU

EPITHALAMIUM IN TIME OF WAR. New York, Author, 1941. 11p [BVaU NBFU OKQ

FLIGHT INTO DARKNESS. Poems. New York, Pantheon, 1946. 96p [Earlier ed., 1944.] [BVaU LC NBFU OTU QMM

THE GOLDEN CHALICE. London, Nicholson & Watson, 1935. 105p [BM NSHD OTU QMM

A LITTLE ANTHOLOGY OF CANADIAN POETS. Ed. by ——. Norfolk, Conn., New Directions, 1943. 26p [BVaU LC MWU OTP

LYRICS UNROMANTIC. New York, 1942. 19p [BVaU NBFU OKQ

THE PENGUIN BOOK OF CANADIAN VERSE. Ed. with an intro. and notes by ——. Harmondsworth, Middlesex, Penguin Books, 1958. 255p

RIVER AMONG ROCKS. Toronto, McClelland, 1960. 1v [unpaged].

ROCKY MOUNTAIN POEMS. Vancouver, Klanak Press, 1960. 36p

**Guthrie, James C., 1898–**

FOOTSTEPS ON THE WATER. Toronto, Hunter Rose, 1930. 164p [Brown U

**Guthrie, Norman Gregor, 1877–1929**

FLAKE AND PETAL. Toronto, Musson, 1928. 83p [BVaU NSHD OTP

FLOWER AND FLAME. By John Crichton [pseud]. Toronto, Ryerson, 1924. 74p [BVaU NBFU OTP QMM

PILLAR OF SMOKE. By John Crichton [pseud]. Toronto, Musson, 1925. 90p [BVaU NBFU OTP

A VISTA. Poems. By John Crichton [pseud]. Montreal, Chapman, 1921. 85p [BM BVaU NBFU QMM

**Gutteridge, Donald George, 1937–**

THE BROODING SKY. Poems. London, Ont., Author, 1960. 20p

**Gwilt, Fanny G.**

CONSTANCE. A Lay of the Olden Time. By Maple Leaf [pseud]. Montreal, Lovell, 1874. 50p [BVaU LC NBFU OTP QMM

**H., A.L.O.**

GREETINGS FROM MAYFLOWER LAND. Halifax, [1896?]. [unpaged] [NSWA

**Hackett, John A.**

RHYMES OF THE NORTH, AND OTHER RHYMES. Victoria, Diggon, 1924. 66p [BVaU

**Hagarty, John Hawkins, 1816–1900**

A LEGEND OF MARATHON. By an Ontario Judge [pseud]. [Toronto, Author, 1888]. 36p [OTUV QMM

POEMS. N.p., priv. print., 1902. 77p [BVaU NBFU OTU

**Hagerman, Jessie Sills**

EUGENIA RECITES. Recitations from Canadian Verse. Ed. by ——. Toronto, Crucible Press, 1940. 60p [LC OKQ

**Haliburton, Ida Mae (Siddall), 1879–**

SHINING HOURS. Toronto, Ryerson, 1958. xii + 83p

**Haliburton, Robert Grant, 1831–1901**

VOICES FROM THE STREET. A Series of Poems. Halifax, priv. print., n.d. 20p [CCJ

**Hall, Charles Frederick**

POEMS. Truro, N.S., Cosmocrat Press, 1890. 41p [NSHPL NSWA

**Hall, Emma L.**

THE GESTE OF JANUS THE JONGLEUR. By Yvonne St. Claire [pseud]. N.p., n.d. 4p [OKQ]

THE OCEAN'S ORATORIO. By Yvonne St. Claire [pseud]. Toronto, Author, n.d. 4p [Reprinted and enl.: Toronto, Author, 1937.] [NSHD OKQ

THE SCENTED GARDEN. By Yvonne St. Claire [pseud]. Toronto, Author, 1936. 24p [NBFU OKQ

SONGS OF A YOUNG COUNTRY. By Yvonne St. Claire [pseud]. Toronto, Author, 1935. 15p [BVaU NBFU OKQ

THE SOUL'S INQUIRY. By Yvonne St. Claire [pseud]. Toronto, Author, 1939. 4p [OTUV

**Hallett, M.E.**

SUNSHINE & SHADOW. Victoria, Diggons, 1924. 28p [QMU

**Halliburton, Brenton, 1775–1860**

REFLECTIONS ON PASSING EVENTS. Written prior to the Termination of the late War with Russia. [With notes.] By an Octogenarian [pseud]. Halifax, Bowes, 1856. 24p [NSHD

**Halpin, Barney**

PULPIT POUNDING BILL. Black Diamond, Alta., [1938?]. [Peel Supp

**Hambleton, Ronald, 1917–**

OBJECT AND EVENT. Toronto, Ryerson, 1953. 38p

UNIT OF FIVE. Poems by Louis Dudek, Ronald Hambleton, P.K. Page, Raymond Souster, James Wreford. Ed. by ——. Toronto, Ryerson, 1944. 87p [BVaU LC MWU NBFU OTU QMM

**Hamilton, Hans Patrick, 1889–**

CANDLESTICKS. The Golden Candlesticks and Light. London, The Art Store, 1926. 47p [LC

CARMEL. ... London, The Art Store, 1926. 22p [LC

THE GOLDEN CANDLESTICKS, AND OTHER POEMS. Guelph, Gummer Press, 1926. 48p [Also pub. under the title CANDLESTICKS.] [LC

THINGS THAT MIGHT HAVE BEEN. London, The Art Store, 1926. 23p [BVaU LC

WAVES FROM THE SEA. London, The Art Store, 1926. 23p [LC

**Hamilton, Margaret Mildred, 1905–**

RHYTHMIC REVERIES ROUND THE YEAR. Fredericton, Brunswick Press, 1956. 45p

**Hamilton, Pierce Stevens, 1826–1893**

THE FEAST OF ST. ANNE, AND OTHER POEMS. Halifax, Burgoyne, 1878. 151p [2nd ed.: Montreal, Lovell, 1890. 165p] [BVaU NSHD OTP

**Hamlyn, Harvey**

ONE HUNDRED FAMOUS LOVE LYRICS. Collected by ——. New York, Sully & Co., 1926. xiv + 142p [LC NBSaM

TO MY PAL. Comp. by ——. Toronto, Ryerson, 1927. 95p [OTP

**Hammond, George Arthur**

EIGHTEEN BASIC QUESTIONS. Also "An Inquiry." Kingsclear, N.B., Lahstok Pub., 1900–1905. 12 + 36p [NSWA

FINAL [VARIOUS POEMS]. Kingsclear, N.B. Author, 1908. [Various pagings] [NSWA

THE HARP. York County, N.B., Author, 1869. 300p [OTUV

AN INQUIRY. "In a Moment–in the Twinkling of an Eye." Kingsclear, N.B., Lahstok Rustic Press, 1900. 36p [NSHPL

THE PILLAR OF WITNESS. Kingsclear, N.B., Lahstok Pub., 1899. 52p [OTUV

QUEEN VICTORIA'S OLIVE TREE, AND OTHER POEMS. London, Robert Banks, n.d. 82p [OTUV

RAYON. An Idyllic Vagary. Kingsclear, N.B., Lahstok Pub., 1901. 34p [NSWA OTUV

THE RECLUSE, AND OTHER POEMS. Kingsclear, N.B., Lahstok Pub., 1893. 10p [NSWA OTUV

A SERENADE. Lahstok, N.B., Rural Press, 1888. 102p [OTP

THE STORK, FLYING EASTWARD. [Kingsclear, N.B.] Rural Press, 1887. 56p [NSWA OTUV

A TRIAD. Lahstok, N.B., Rural Press, 1887. 3 parts in one. [Pt. 1: The Lake of Tears, an Allegory; Various Poems. Pt. 2: On the Strand, a Fable; Golden Circle Dirges. Pt. 3: Knud Iverson, a Dramatic Sketch; Twilight Cimmerian; Autumnal Musings; The Loiterer, a Fragment.] [OTP

**Hannay, James, 1842–1910**

BALLADS OF ACADIA. Saint John, Bowes, 1909. 47p [BVaU NBFU OTU

THE MAIDEN'S SACRIFICE. Saint John, 1909. 7p [Brown U BVaU NBFU OTU

**Hansberger, Clara**

LIGHTED LANTERNS. By Clara Hansberger, Evangeline Chapman, Alma Golling Barker [and others]. Moose Jaw, Mrs. G.C. Barker, [1943?]. 22p [Brown U OTU

**Hardy, Edwin Austin, 1867–1952**

SELECTIONS FROM THE CANADIAN POETS. Ed. by ——. Toronto, Morang, 1906. 128p [Another ed.: Toronto, Macmillan, 1920. 128p] [BM BVaU NSHD OTP

**Hargadon, Michael A., 1888–**

AMONG THE MOUNTAINS. Montreal, Southam Press, 1925. 31p [OTP

IRISH AND CANADIAN POEMS. Montreal, Modern Print., 1921. 74p [BM BVaU OTP

A LOVELY HOME. [Verses.] Dublin & London, Maunsel, 1915. 75p [BM

**Harlton, W.D.**

A POEM ON GEOGRAPHY. Toronto, n.p., 1891. 16p [OTU

**Harper, Alice, 1883–1935**

COLOURED SAND. Vancouver, Mrs. E.E. Harper, [1938?]. 31p [BVaU

**Harper, Constance Ward**

THE MOON-MAN AND THE FAIRIES. Vancouver, Sun Pub. Co., n.d. 32p [BVaU

PATRIOTIC AND OTHER POEMS. Vancouver, Thomson, 1916. 64p [BM BVaU OTUV

**Harper, John Murdoch, 1845–1919**

THE ANNALS OF THE WAR. Illus. by a Selection of Historical Ballads. Toronto, Musson, 1913. 268p [BVaU LC NSHD OLU

THE BATTLE OF THE PLAINS. Quebec, 1895. 46p [BVaU NSWA OTUV

SACRAMENT SUNDAY. Montreal, 1894. 15p [CCJ

TRANSLATIONS IN VERSE FROM HOMER AND VIRGIL. Montreal, Dawson Bros., 1888. [Patrick cat. 30

WOLFE AND MONTCALM. Toronto, Copp Clark, n.d. 20p [NSHD OTUV

**Harrington, Dorothy**

LITTLE THINGS. Kitchener, Author, n.d. 22p [UTQ'46

**Harrington, Michael Francis, 1916–**

NEWFOUNDLAND TAPESTRY. Dallas, Tex., Kaleidograph Press, 1943. 80p [LC

POEMS OF NEWFOUNDLAND. This Volume Contains The Prize-Winning Poems in The O'Leary Newfoundland Poetry Award 1944–1952. Ed. by ——. St. John's, F.M. O'Leary, 1953. xix + 118p

THE SEA IS OUR DOORWAY. Toronto, Ryerson, 1947. 8p [BVaU NBFU OKQ

**Harris, Lawren Stewart, 1885–1970**

CONTRASTS. A Book of Verse. Toronto, McClelland, 1922. 125p [BM BVaU NSHD OKQ

**Harris, Robert, 1849–1919**

VERSES BY THE WAY. From an Artist's Sketch Book. Charlottetown, 1920. 89p [BVaU NBFU QMM

**Harris, William Critchlow**

OCCASIONAL POEMS. EARLY AND LATE. Charlottetown, Examiner, 1915. 69p [BVaU

**Harrison, Edna Kent**

THE LAMP, AND OTHER VERSE. London, Stockwell, [1929?]. 16p [Brown U NSHD OTU

**Harrison, Elizabeth**

A WHIP FOR TIME. Toronto, Macmillan, 1947. 28p [BVaU LC MWU OTP

**Harrison, Stanley Gordon, 1889–**

GENTLEMEN, –THE HORSE! Lexington, Ky., Thoroughbred Press, 1951. 88p

OMAR OF THE TURF. Lexington, Ky., Thoroughbred Press, 1950. 6p [OONL

SONGS OF THE PRAIRIE AND THE C.E.F. London, Macdonald, 1919. 72p [BM BVaU OTL

**Harrison, Susie Frances (Riley), 1859–1935**

THE CANADIAN BIRTHDAY BOOK. Comp. by Seranus [pseud]. Toronto, Blackett Robinson, 1887. 415p [BVaU NBFU OTP

FOUR BALLADS AND A PLAY. By Seranus [pseud]. N.p., 1933. 18p [OTP

IN NORTHERN SKIES, AND OTHER POEMS. By Seranus [pseud]. [Toronto? 1912?] 20p [OKQ

LATER POEMS AND NEW VILLANELLES. Toronto, Ryerson, 1928. 16p [BVaU NBSaM OTP

PENELOPE AND OTHER POEMS. By Seranus [pseud]. N.p., [19–?] 16p [OTP

PINE, ROSE AND FLEUR DE LIS. Toronto, Hart, 1891. 208p [BVaU LC NSHD OTP

SONG OF WELCOME IN HONOUR OF HIS EXCELLENCY, THE MARQUIS OF LANSDOWNE, GOVERNOR-GENERAL OF CANADA. Written and Composed by Seranus [pseud]. Ottawa, Free Press, 1883. 8p [Brown U

SONGS OF LOVE AND LABOR. By Seranus [pseud]. Toronto, Author, [1925?]. 20p [BVaU NBFU OTP

**Harshaw, Augusta F.**

LAYS OF THE FIRESIDE. A Collection of Poems. Toronto, Musson, 1905. 90p [BVaU OTUV

**Harvey, Emeline Daggett**
MOODS AND TENSES. Chicago, priv. print., 1923. 53p [LC

**Harvey, Peggy, 1884–**
A WHIMSICAL VANCOUVERITE. N.p., n.p., [1936?]. 32p [BVaU

**Harvey, William Earl, 1898–**
BALLADS OF BATTLE. Vancouver, Roedde, 1941. 83p [BVaU LC OOP
BALLADS OF THE WEST. Vancouver, Pacific Print., 1920. 94p [BM BVaU OTU
SONGS OF AMERICA. Portland, Ore., Ryder, 1928. 66p [LC
SONGS OF THE WEST. St. Paul, Minn., Author, 1927. 68p [BVa LC

**Haskins, James, 1805–1845**
THE POETICAL WORKS OF JAMES HASKINS. Ed. by Henry Baldwin. Hartford, Parsons, 1848. 320p [BVaU OTP

**Hatheway, Warren Franklin, 1850–1923**
GOD AND THE DOUBTER. Saint John, Ellis Robertson, n.d. 19p [NBFU

**Hatt, Daniel Elisha, 1869–1942**
THE ALL SEASON RECITER. With Selections for Special Church Occasions. Toronto, Musson, 1924. 79p [AEU OTP
DIGBY CHICKENS.... By D.E.H. [pseud]. Digby, N.S., Courier Print., n.d. 18p [NBSaM
OKANAGAN. N.p., Vernon Press, n.d. 20p [BVaU NBSaM
OUTDOOR VERSE. ... Seattle, Teller Pub. Co., n.d. 64p [AEU BViPA
RANDOM RHYMES. Being a Collection of Dialect and Other Pieces. Summerland, B.C., Review, 1915. 39p [BM BVaU NSHPL
RELIGIOUS LYRICS. Vancouver, Wilson Bible & Tract Depot, n.d. 29p [BViPA NBFU OPAL QMU
SITKA SPRUCE. Songs of Queen Charlotte Islands. Thurston Harbour, B.C., Latta Co., 1918. 51p [BM BVaU NBFU OTUV

**Hatzan, Alexander Leon, 1864–**
MAM'SELLE L'ANGE VOX[!]; or, The Lady with the Angel Voice. A Poem Story of Love, Travel and Adventure. Niagara Falls, Mohawk Book, 1932. 177p [BM BVaU LC QMSS

**Haughton, William**
SILVICOLA; or, Songs from the Backwoods. Viroqua, Casson, 1878. 100p [OTUV

**Haultain, Theodore Arnold, 1857–1941**
VERSICULI. Toronto, Author, 1893. 32p [BVaU OTP

**Haverson, James Percival, 1880–**
SOUR SONNETS OF A SOREHEAD, AND OTHER SONGS OF THE STREET. Toronto, McLeod Allen, 1908. 62p [BM BVaU LC OTU QMSS

**Haweis, Lionel Thomas Joy, 1870–1942**

LITTLE LANTERNS. ... [Series 1]. Vancouver, Citizen Print., 1918. [64p] [Printed on one side of page only.] [BVaU

LITTLE LANTERNS. ... [Series 2]. Vancouver, Citizen Print., 1924. [63p] [Printed on one side of page only.] [BVaU NBFU

TSOQALEM. A Weird Indian Tale of the Cowichan Monster. A Ballad. Vancouver, Citizen Print., 1918. 66p [BVaU NBFU OTP

**Hawley, William Fitz, 1804–1855**

QUEBEC, THE HARP, AND OTHER POEMS. Montreal, Herald and New Gazette, 1829. 172p [BVaU LC OTU QMM

THE UNKNOWN; or, Lays of the Forest. Montreal, Hoisington, 1831. 240p [BM BVaU LC OKQ

**Hayes, Catherine E. (Simpson), 1852–1943**

DERBY DAY IN THE YUKON, AND OTHER POEMS OF THE NORTHLAND. By Yukon Bill [pseud]. Toronto, Musson, 1910. 128p [BVaU OKQ QMM

**Hayman, Robert, 1579?–1631?**

QUODLIBETS LATELY COME OVER FROM NEW BRITANIOLA, OLD NEWFOUND-LAND. EPIGRAMS, AND OTHER SMALL PARCELS, BOTH MORALL AND DIVINE. ... By R.H., Sometimes Governour of the Plantation. ... London, Mitchell, 1628. 64p [BM LC NBFU

**Haynes, James**

POEMS. Quebec, Hunter Rose, 1864. 152p [BVaU LC NSHD OLU QMBM

**Haynes, Laura E. (Nixon), 1876–**

COMING MY WAY? Ed. and Selected by Carl Eayrs. Ottawa, Tower Books, 1948. 99p [OOP

LANTERNS IN THE DUSK. St. Catharines, Falcon Print., 1944. 22p [OTP

PIONEERS. St. Catharines, Print. Shop, 1938. 48p [OTP

WHEN YOU AND I REMEMBER. N.p., n.d. 20p [OTP

**Hayward, Mrs. Caroline**

THE BATTLES OF THE CRIMEA, WITH OTHER POEMS. By Mrs. Alfred Hayward. Port Hope, Ansley, 1855. 67p [BM BVaU OTP

**Hazel, Emily, 1882–1955**

THE BEAUTY OF THE EARTH AND OTHER POEMS. Ottawa, Author, 1952. 12p

FROM A HOSPITAL WINDOW. Ottawa, Author, 1950. 12p [OONL

HAPPY THOUGHTS AND OTHER POEMS. With A Children's Section. Ottawa, Author, 1954. 18p

LOVELY BLOSSOMS AND OTHER POEMS. With a Children's Section. Ottawa, Author, 1954. 24p

SIMPLE JOYS AND OTHER POEMS. Ottawa, Author, 1951. 12p

**Hazelton, Mrs. Ruth Cleaves**
MINT AND WILLOW.... Toronto, Ryerson, 1952. 12p

**Hazlemere, Robert**
"GLORY AND LOVELINESS HAVE PASSED AWAY." A Choric Ode. Vancouver, 1928. 2p [OKQ
STARRY EARTH. A Book of Poems and Lyrics. Toronto, McClelland, 1929. 80p [BVaU NSHD QMBM

**Hazlewood, Hetty**
A GARLAND GATHERED AT MORN. A Collection of Short Poems. Toronto, Hunter, 1871. 79p [BVaU OKQ

**Heath, John, 1917–1951**
APHRODITE. Toronto, Ryerson, 1958. 24p

**Heaton, Hugh**
THE STORY OF ALBERT THE CAMEL'S SON. Toronto, Heaton, 1936. 39p [BM
THE STORY OF MADAM HEN AND LITTLE HORACE. Toronto, Heaton, 1935. 37p [BM BVaU LC NBFU OONL

**Heavysege, Charles, 1816–1876**
THE DARK HUNTSMAN (A Dream). Montreal, Witness Press, 1864. 8p [A poem with same title pub. in *The Canadian Monthly & National Review,* 10:134-135 (Aug. 1876).] [OONL
JEPHTHAH'S DAUGHTER [and Twenty Sonnets]. Montreal, Dawson, 1865. 74p [BM BVaU MWU NSHD OKQ
THE OWL. Montreal, 1864. 4p [CCJ
THE REVOLT OF TARTARUS. A Poem. [Anon] Liverpool, Hamilton, 1852. [Also: Montreal, 1853.] [BM BVaU
SONNETS. By the Author of THE REVOLT OF TARTARUS. Montreal, Rose, 1855. 61p [OLU

**Hedges, Doris (Ryde), 1900–**
CRISIS. Toronto, Ryerson, 1947. 8p [BVaU MWU NBFU OKQ
THE DREAM IS CERTAIN. Boston, Christopher Pub. Hse., 1954. 32p
THE FLOWER IN THE DUSK. Toronto, Ryerson, 1946. 8p [BVaU LC MWU NBSaM OKQ
WORDS ON A PAGE, AND OTHER POEMS. Toronto, Ryerson, 1949. 42p [BVaU LC OTP

**Heffernan, W.E.**
NOVA SCOTIA: WARBLINGS OF THE WILDWOOD. Springhill, N.S., Jones, 1906. 218p [BVaU

**Hemsley, Stuart Davidson, 1905–**
BEASTLY BALLADS. By Stuart Davidson Hemsley and James Simpkins. Toronto, Burns & MacEachern, 1954. 61p

**Henderson, Christine Margaret (Lighthall), 1868–1968**

THE BLUE JAY'S MESSAGE, AND OTHER POEMS. Montreal, Author, 1934. 8p [BVaU

OUR VOLUNTEERS, AND OTHER POEMS. Montreal, Author, 1940. 8p [CC

SHIP'S WAKE AND ROAD'S LURE. Montreal, Lovell, 1937. 102p [BVaU NBFU OTU QMM

THOUGHTFUL PETIE'S ADVENTURES, AND OTHER POEMS. New York, Banner, 1939. 42p [OTU

THE UNWELCOME GUEST, AND OTHER POEMS. Montreal, Author, [1931?]. 8p [CC

**Henderson, Edith Beatrice**

OUTWARD BOUND. Toronto, Ryerson, 1930. 8p [BVaU NBSaM OKQ

**Henderson, W.R., 1876–**

HENDY'S NORTHERN SPASMS. Flin Flon, Man., Flin Flon Miner, 1931. 25p [MWP

**Henry, Eileen Cameron, 1908?–**

SEA-WOMAN AND OTHER POEMS. Toronto, Ryerson, 1945. 8p [BVaU LC NBSaM OTP

**Henry, James**

SONGS BY THE WAY. Montreal, "Witness," 1892. 159p [BVaU NSHD

**Henry, Marion Kathleen (Waddell), 1893–**

CENTAURS OF THE WIND. Toronto, Ryerson, 1956. 12p

**Henry, Mrs. P.A.**

SELECTIONS FROM THE WRITINGS OF MRS. P.A. HENRY. Bowmanville, n.d. 13p [OTUV

**Hensley, Sophia Margaret (Almon), 1866–**

THE HEART OF A WOMAN [Poems]. By Almon Hensley. London, Putman, 1906. 175p [BM LC

POEMS. (For Private Circulation). By Sophie M. Almon. Windsor, N.S., Anslow, 1889. 18p [BVaU NSHD OTU

THE WAY OF A WOMAN, AND OTHER POEMS. By Sophia Margeretta Hensley. San Diego, Canterbury Co., 1928. 112p [LC NSHPL

A WOMAN'S LOVE LETTERS [Poems]. By Sophie M. Almon-Hensley. New York, Tait, 1895. 82p [LC NSHPL OTUV QMM

**Herbert, George**

MISCELLANEOUS POEMS AND SONGS. [Fredericton?], Author, 1885. 32p [OTUV

**Herbert, Sarah, 1824–1844**

THE AEOLIAN HARP; or, Miscellaneous Poems. By Sarah Herbert and Mary E. Herbert. Halifax, Fuller, 1857. 237p [BM BVaU NSHD OTP

**Herbin, John Frederic, 1860–1923**

CANADA AND OTHER POEMS. Windsor, N.S., Anslow, 1891. 12p [BVaU NSHD OTP

THE MARSHLANDS. A Souvenir in Song of the Land of Evangeline. Windsor, N.S., Anslow, 1893. 33p [BVaU NSHD OTUV

THE MARSHLANDS, AND THE TRAIL OF THE TIDE. Toronto, Briggs, 1899. 99p [3rd ed.: Toronto, Briggs, 1909. 124p] [BM BVaU NSHD OKQ

**Herriman, Dorothy Choate, 1901–**

MATER SILVA. With Decorations by the Author. Toronto, McClelland, 1929. 72p [BVaU NBFU OTUV

**Herron, David Henry**

HABITANT NUGGETS. Cobalt, Daily Nugget Print., 1910. 64p [NBFU

HABITANT NUGGETS. Cobalt, Dailly Nugget Print., [192–?]. 33p [BM Brown U OOP

**Hezzelwood, Oliver, 1861–1933**

IN THE ESTUARY, AND OTHER POEMS. Toronto, Davis, 1933. 79p [BVaU OTP

POEMS. And a Play: "The Invisible Urge." Toronto, Ontario Press, 1926. 168p [BVaU OKQ QMM

**Hibbert, William, 1901?–**

OUT OF THE PIT. Drumheller, Alta., Drumheller Mail, 1948. 116p [AC

**Hickson, A. Beatrice**

POEMS, 1916. By A.B.H. N.p., 1916. 18p [BM Brown U NSHD

**Higginson, Thomas, 1794–1884**

POETICAL WORKS. Vankleek Hill, Ont., Otto, 1888. [Bound with writings of Thomas H. Higginson (Persolus) entitled THE LITERARY WORKS OF T.H. HIGGINSON] 2v in 1. [BVaU NSWA OTU QMM

**Higginson, Thomas Boyd, 1912–**

JUVENILIA. London, Mitre Press, [1960?]. 31p

**Higinbotham, John David, 1864–1961**

FOOTHILL AND PRAIRIE MEMORIES. A Group of Poems. N.p., n.d. 32p [ACG OKQ

**Hill, Thomas, –1860**

THE CONSTITUTIONAL LYRIST. Fredericton, "Loyalist" Office, 1845. 240p [CCJ NBB

**Hiltz, W.W.**

MORE VERSES. Toronto, [Regal Stationery], 1931. 45p [BVaU OTU QMU

VERSES OF A CONVALESCENT. Toronto, 1929. 45p [Brown U BVaU NBFU OTUV

**Hindley, Rev. John Ingham, 1842–**

INDIAN LEGENDS: Nanabush, the Objibbeway Saviour; Moosh-kuh-ung, or The Flood. [Barrie? Ont.], 1885. 22p [BVaU LC OLU

**Hine, William Daryl, 1936–**

THE CARNAL AND THE CRANE. Toronto, Contact Press, 1957. 50p

THE DEVIL'S PICTURE BOOK. Poems. New York, Abelard-Schuman, 1960. 31p

FIVE POEMS, 1954. Toronto, 1954. 13p (Emblem Books)

**Hodgins, James Cobourg, 1866–1953**

FUGITIVES. Toronto, Rose, 1891. 16p [OTUV

A SHEAF OF SONNETS. Philadelphia, Franklin Print., 1896. 22p [BVaU LC

**Hodgson, Alice Muriel (Neve)**

SOME GOLDEN MEMORIES. Lachute, Watchman Print., 1944. 71p [AEU QMU

**Hoey, Willa**

A BOOK OF VERSES. Toronto, Garden City Press, 1931. 15p [OTU

**Hogan, Anastasia**

SELECTION OF POEMS. St. John's, Nfld., Milligan, n.d. 146p [NSfG OTP

**Hogarth, Thomas William**

BULL TERRIER DOGGEREL. Galashiels, Scot., Walker, 1937. 30p [BM LC

**Hogg, James, 1800–1866**

POEMS. Religious, Moral and Sentimental. Saint John, Chubb, 1825. 228p [NBFU OTP

**Holland, Norah Mary, 1876–1925**

SPUN-YARN AND SPINDRIFT. Toronto, Dent, 1918. 96p [BM BVaU NBFU OKQ QMM

WHEN HALF GODS GO, AND OTHER POEMS. Toronto, Macmillan, 1924. 124p [BVaU LC NSHD OKQ QMM

**Holman, Carrie Ellen, 1877–**

IN THE DAY OF BATTLE. Poems of the Great War. Comp. by ——. Toronto, Briggs, 1916. 166p [3rd ed.: 1918. 224p (Contains first pub. of McCrae's "In Flanders Fields").] [LC NBFU OTU

**Holmes, Vincent, 1929–**

QUIET ENTRY. Victoria, B.C., Author, 1956. 7p

**Honohan, Laura M.**

POEMS. N.p., n.d. [c1945?]. 244p [Adelphi cat. 68

**Hood, Robert Allison, 1880–1958**

BALLADS OF THE PACIFIC NORTH-WEST. Toronto, Ryerson, 1946. 170p [BVaU LC NBFU OKQ QMM

BY SHORE AND TRAIL IN STANLEY PARK. ... Toronto, McClelland, 1929. 156p [BVaU NSHD OTP

VIGNETTES OF VANCOUVER. Vancouver, Education Services, 1954. ix + 84p

**Hooke, Alfred John, 1905–**

A TRIBUTE TO HON. E.C. MANNING ON THE OCCASION OF HIS 50TH BIRTHDAY PARTY, SEPTEMBER 30TH, 1958. ... Edmonton, Alberta Social Credit League, 1958. 4p

**Hooker, Rev. LeRoy, 1840–1906**

STANLEY. A Christmas Ballad by Jason and Boaz. Toronto, 1882. 14p [CCJ

**Hoople, Carrie (Munson)**

ALONG THE WAY WITH PEN AND PENCIL. New York, Grafton Press, 1909. 213p [LC OTUV

**Hope, M.L.**

FRAGMENTS. Toronto, Briggs, 1911. 32p [BM BVaU

INDIAN AND OTHER TALES. Toronto, Briggs, 1911. 21p [BM BVaU OKQ

**Hopkins, Elizabeth Nuttall**

THOUGHTS IN VERSE. With a preface by Professor William Clark. Toronto, Briggs, 1906. 54p [BM Brown U BVaU OTP

**Hopper, Clara**

THE EMIGRANT'S STONE, AND OTHER POEMS. Toronto, Ryerson, 1932. 8p [BVaU NBSaM OKQ QMM

**Horan, John William, 1908–**

SONGS OF THE NORTH. Stories in Verse of Life Down under the Midnight Sun of North Western Canada. Edmonton, Nor'West Miner, 1940. 40p [2nd ed.: Edmonton, Sterling, 1942. 54p] [OKQ QMM

YELLOWKNIFE; " 'Til the Ice-Worms Nest Again." With Selected Poems taken from "Songs of the North." Edmonton, Northgate Books, 1947. 47p [BVaU OTU QMBM

**Horne, Winnifred Alice**

POEMS. Ottawa, 1960. 23p

**Hornsell, William**

THE ICE-BOUND SHIP, and THE DREAM. By W.H. [pseud]. Montreal, Rose, 1860. 48p [OTP

**Hornyansky, Michael Sands, 1927–**

THE QUEEN OF SHEBA. The Newdigate Prize Poem, 1951. Oxford, Blackwell, 1951. 13p

**Hosie, John, 1880–1934**

THE ARBUTUS TREE, AND OTHER POEMS. Toronto, Ryerson, 1929. 8p [BVaU NBSaM OKQ QMM

**Houghton, Frank Llewellyn, 1897–**

QUARTERDECK DITTIES. By Deadlight [pseud]. Printed for Private Circulation only. Ottawa, Author, 1948. 30p [OONL

**Houghton, Levi**

MY TRIP THROUGH THE ROCKIES. [verses and illustrations.] Victoria, 1917. n.p. [BM

VERSES ON EVERYDAY LIFE. Written Chiefly by Request, in the Calgary General Hospital. By a Calgary Old-Timer. ... N.p., n. pub., [1916?]. 20p [Enlarged ed., Victoria, 1918. 31p] [AEU BM BVaU

VICTORIA THE BEAUTIFUL. [verses and illustrations.] Victoria, 1917. n.p. [BM BViPA

**Houliston, George B.**

POEMS. ... Three Rivers, Que., [1889?]. 12p [Brown U

**Howard, Blanche Muirhead**

REACH FOR A STAR. Toronto, Ryerson, 1951. 10p

**Howard, Dorothy**

AS THE RIVER RUNS. Toronto, Ryerson, 1947. 8p [BVaU NBFU OTU

A CHILD CAME LAUGHING. N.p., [194–?]. 20p [OKQ

WHEN I TURN HOME. Toronto, Ryerson, 1945. 8p [BVaU LC OTP

**Howard, Hilda (Glynn), 1887–**

ALONG THE ROAD TO HAZELTON. By H. Glynn-Ward [pseud]. London, Mitre Press, 1960. 56p

THE PIONEERS AND OTHER POEMS. By H. Glynn-Ward [pseud]. Toronto, Ryerson, 1940. 12p [BVaU LC NBSaM OTP QMM

**Howe, Joseph, 1804–1873**

THE MAY-FLOWER OF NOVA SCOTIA. Halifax, June 8, 1840. Halifax, Nova Scotia Philanthropic Soc., 1840. 1p [NSHD

A POEM ON THE SAME SUBJECT. [Sable Island]. Halifax, Wesleyan Conference Steam Press, 1858. [Bound with SABLE ISLAND (pp.31-34), by John Bernard Gilpin, *q.v.*] [BM LC NSWA OTP QMM

**Howey, William, 1883–**

CALIFORNIA CAROLS. Toronto, 1927. 111p [Brown U BVaU OTU

CANADIAN CAROLS. Toronto, Ryerson, 1926. 117p [BVaU OTP

CAROLS AND CAMEOS. ... Toronto, Ryerson, 1927. 124p [BVaU LC NBFU OKQ

A VISIT TO FAIRYLAND, AND LEGENDS OF NATURE. Toronto, Ryerson, 1928. 125p [BVaU OTU

**Howley, Rev. Michael Francis, 1843–1914**

POEMS AND OTHER VERSES. New York, Fisher, 1903. 122p [OOSU QMM

**Howse, Beulah Virginia, 1905–**

POEM PICTURES OF CANADA. Ilfracombe, Devon, Stockwell, 1956. 46p

**Howson, George J.**

A COLLECTION OF ORIGINAL ACROSTICS ON LADIES' CHRISTIAN NAMES. Toronto, Hunter Rose, 1888. [OONL

**Hudson, Dunbar Hibbard**

SONGS OF A CHEERFUL WAYFARER. Toronto, Author, 1926. 124p [BVaU

**Hudson, Reba Marguerite**

BRIEF FOR BEAUTY. Toronto, Macmillan, 1946. 28p [BM BVaU LC OTP

**Hughes, Aubrey Dean**

ARGOSIES AT DAWN. Toronto, Ryerson, 1931. 8p [BVaU NBSaM OKQ

**Hughes, James Laughlin, 1846–1935**

CHESTER HUGHES. N.p., n.d. 15p [Poems by J.L. Hughes in memory of his son.] [OTU

THE CHILD'S PARADISE. Stories and Musings for Parents and Teachers. Toronto, Ryerson, 1919. 127p [BM BVaU NBFU OTU

GOD MADE THEM GOOD. True Stories of the So-called "Bad." Toronto, Allen, 1922. 127p [OKQ QMU

IN NATURE'S TEMPLE SHRINES. Toronto, Allen, 1921. 127p [BVaU NSHD OTP QMBM

LIFE'S GLORIES. Toronto, Gundy, 1926. 292p [Also: Boston, Stratford, 1929. 365p] [BVaU LC OTP

LOVE MEMORIES. Toronto, Warwick, 1919. 127p [BVaU

MY SUNSHINE BOOK. Toronto, Allen, 1923. 127p [BVaU OKQ QMM

NEW SONGS OF GLADNESS. N.p., 1916. 64p [BVaU OTP QMM

RAINBOWS ON WAR CLOUDS. Syracuse, Bradeen, 1919. 112p [BVaU LC NBFU OKQ

SONGS OF GLADNESS. N.p., 1914. 32p [Also: same title, dated 1915, unpaged.] [AEU OTP QMU

SONGS OF GLADNESS AND GROWTH. Toronto, Briggs, 1916. 247p [BM BVaU NSHD OKQ

SONGS OF LIFE AND GROWTH. N.p., 1912. 32p [BVaU OTU

STORIES AND MUSINGS. Toronto, Briggs, 1917. 99p [BM BVaU LC OKQ

**Hughes, Robert, 1882–**

RHYMES–FOR THE TIMES–AND OTHER TIMES. Toronto, Author, [195–?]. 76p

**Humphrey, Mrs. Muriel Miller**

TWENTY SONNETS. Toronto, Ryerson, 1932. 11p [BVaU NSHD OKQ QMM

**Hunt, Anna Rebecca (Gale)**

IN BOHEMIA AND OTHER STUDIES FOR POEMS. By Mrs. T. Sterry Hunt ("Canadienne"). Toronto, Briggs, 1900. 189p [Rev. ed.: 1905. 173p] [BM BVaU OKQ QMM

STUDIES FOR POEMS. By Claude Berwick [pseud]. Boston, Marvin, n.d. 146p [BVaU QMSS

**Hunter, Alexander Jardine, 1868–1940**

THE KOBZAR OF THE UKRAINE. Being Select Poems of Taras Shevchenko done into English Verse with Biographical Fragments by Alexander Jardine Hunter. Teulon, Man., Hunter, 1922. 144p [BM Brown U BVaU

**Hunter, D.J.**

HELLO, FELLOWS! HAVE YOU READ MY RHYMES? ... They're Different. "A Tussle" with the Bulls and Bears in the Stock Market Arena rippled into Raw, Rough and Ripping Rhymes, specially rhythm'd for Unsophisticated and Hardboiled Male and Female Speculators. ... Toronto, Hunter-Rose, 1933. 57p [BVaU OTU

**Husband, Mrs. S. Berthe, 1891–**

ALTAR FLOWERS. London, Ont., Author, 1936. 32p [OLU

**Hutchinson, Rev. Daniel Falloon**

SATISFACTION OF JUSTICE. A Poem. Kingston, 1851. 50p [CCJ

**Hutchison, Thomas**

MASONIC AND MISCELLANEOUS POEMS. North Vancouver, Author, 1932. 46p [BVaU

**Huxtable, Horace L.**

THE FOUNTAIN. A Dramatic Fantasy. Toronto, Ryerson, 1929. 12p [BVaU NBSaM OKQ QMM

**Hynes, Marie J. McGee**

THE BARD'S MINSTRELSY. Toronto, Mission Press, 1951. 24p

**Imrie, John, 1846–1902**

A BOUQUET OF SONNETS FOR THOUGHTFUL MOMENTS. Toronto, Imrie & Graham, [18—?]. 32p [OTP

NEW POEMS. Toronto, 1900. 100p [T&C

SACRED SONGS, SONNETS AND MISCELLANEOUS POEMS. Toronto, Imrie & Graham, 1886. 210p [Several later editions.] [BVaU MWU NSHD OKQ

A SELECTION OF READINGS AND SONGS FROM THE WORKS OF JOHN IMRIE. 4th ed. Toronto, Imrie & Graham, 1899. 96p [BM Brown U OTUV

SONGS AND MISCELLANEOUS POEMS. Toronto, Imrie & Graham, 1891. 348p [5th ed.: Toronto, 1906.] [BM BVaU LC OTP

**Ingersoll, William Ernest**

THE AIR VOYAGER. Boston, Badger, 1902. [AmCat

**Ingraham, Mary (Kinley), 1874–1949**

A MONTH OF DREAMS. Wolfville, N.S., Author, 1932. [unpaged] [NSWA

**Innes, John, 1864–1941**

TRAGEDY OF THE SWAY-BACKED PINTO. Vancouver, Paton, 1920. 24p [BM BVaU OKQ

**Inness, Capt. W.A.**

RHYMES OF THE R.N.C.V.R., AND OTHER VERSES. Halifax, Weeks, 1919. 63p [BM OOP

**Isard, Mrs. Elizabeth Anne**

WAYSIDE SONGS. Newmarket, Ont., Era, 1896. 224p [BM BVaU OKQ

**Isles-Brown, Mrs. Esme**

TWELVE POEMS. Toronto, Ryerson, 1927. 8p [BVaU NBSaM OKQ

**Ivey, John F.**

THE FIELDS OF YESTERDAY. Cobourg, 1935. 76p [Brown U OTU

**Jack, Annie L. (Hayr), 1839–1912**

BELATED VIOLETS. N.p., n.d. 4p [OTUV

RHYME-THOUGHTS FOR A CANADIAN YEAR. Toronto, Briggs, 1904. 12p [BM BVaU OTP

**Jackson, Isa Grindlay**

BALLADES AND BITS. Toronto, Ryerson, 1937. 54p [BVaU OTP

**Jackson, Katherine H. (McDonald)**

SUMMER SONGS IN IDLENESSE. Toronto, Briggs, 1903. 71p [BVaU NBFU OTUV

**Jacobs, Rev. Peter, 1808–1858**

A COLLECTION OF OJIBWAY HYMNS. Trans. by ——. Ed. by the Rev. John Jacobs. Sarnia, Sarnia Canadian, 1886. 191p [BVaU NSWA OTP

**Jacombe, Grace M.**

CHALK DUST. Ottawa, Tower Books, 1950. 40p [OONL

**Jakeway, Charles Edwin, 1847–1906**

THE LION AND THE LILIES, A TALE OF THE CONQUEST, AND OTHER POEMS. Toronto, Briggs, 1897. 278p [BM BVaU NBFU OTU QMM

**James, William T., 1861–**

RHYMES AFLOAT AND AFIELD. Toronto, James, 1891. 144p [BVaU NBFU OKQ

**Jameson, Edward A.**

POEMS. Toronto, Hilda M. Ridley, 1951. 18p (Carillon Poetry Chap-Books)

**Janes, Lemuel Willey, 1889–**

ADVENTURES IN VERSE. N.p., 1932. 52p [OTU
SEA MOODS AND OTHER POEMS. [Montreal? 1936?]. 15p [Brown U
WHEN SHADOWS FALL. [Montreal?], Author, 1937. 16p [Brown U OONL
WHISPERING WINDS. N.p., [193–?]. 12p [MWU OONL

**Jaques, Edna, 1891–**

AUNT HATTIE'S PLACE. Toronto, Allen, 1941. 80p [BM BVaU LC NBFU OTU
BACKDOOR NEIGHBORS. Toronto, Allen, 1946. 80p [BVaU OTP
BESIDE STILL WATERS. Toronto, Allen, 1939. 88p [BVaU LC OTP
BRITONS AWAKE. Toronto, Allen, 1940. 19p [BM BVaU NBFU OTU
DREAMS IN YOUR HEART. Toronto, Allen, 1937. 78p [BM BVaU NBFU OTP
DRIFTING SOIL. Moose Jaw, "Times," 1935. 19p [Earlier ed., 1934.] [Brown U
FIRESIDE POEMS. Toronto, Allen, 1950. 88p [BVaU OTP
THE GOLDEN ROAD. Toronto, Allen, 1953. 86p
HILLS OF HOME. Toronto, Allen, 1948. 80p [BVaU OTP
MY KITCHEN WINDOW. Toronto, Allen, 1935. 83p [BM BVaU LC NBFU OTU
ROSES IN DECEMBER. Toronto, Allen, 1944. 86p [BVaU LC OTP
WIDE HORIZONS. Moose Jaw, "Times," 1935. 20p [Earlier ed., 1934.] [BVaU

**Jardine (pseud)**

THOUGHTS OF HAPPY BOYHOOD. Saint John, McMillan, 1902. 121p [NBFU

**Jarvis, Charlotte (Beaumont), 1803–1875**

LEAVES FROM ROSEDALE. Toronto, Briggs, 1905. 132p [BM BVaU NBFU OTP

**Jefferson, Marie Neilson**

WILD WATERS AND PINE. Sketches in Verse of the St. Maurice Valley. Three Rivers, 1938. 34p [Brown U OTU

**Jefferson, Robert, 1856–**

SASKATCHEWAN VERSE. Battleford, Sask., Battleford Press, [1930?]. 108p [BVaU OKQ SSU

**Jenkins, Mariel**

BEAUTY FOR ASHES. Toronto, Crucible Press, 1943. 40p [LC OTP
LAKE ON THE MOUNTAIN. Toronto, Author, 1937. 20p [OKQ

**Jenkins, Robert Smith, 1870–1931**

CANADIAN POEMS. The Poetical Works of ——. Ed. by Mrs. R.S. Jenkins. Toronto, McClelland, 1939. 285p [BM BVaU LC NBFU OTP

POEMS OF THE NEW CENTURY. First Series. Minor Lyric and Narrative Poems. Toronto, Briggs, 1903. 173p [BM BVaU LC NSHD OTP QMM

**Jennings, Clotilda, –1895**

LINDEN RHYMES. By Maude [pseud]. Halifax, Fuller, 1854. 152p [BVaU NSHD OTP

NORTH MOUNTAIN, NEAR GRAND-PRE. By Mileta [pseud]. [N.p.?], 1883. [CCJ

**Jenns, Eustace Alvenley**

EVENING TO MORNING, AND OTHER POEMS. Victoria, Hibben, 1880. 33p [BVaU

ORPHEUS AND EURYDICE, AND OTHER POEMS. Vancouver, News-Advertiser, 1910. 110p [Brown U BVaU

**Jerdon, Gertrude**

FLOWERING THORNS. London, Nisbet, 1886. 63p [BM BVaU OTUV

**Jerningham, Rosa (Bell) and John**

MRS. JERNINGHAM'S JOURNAL; AND JOHN JERNINGHAM'S JOURNAL. Toronto, Canadian News, 1871. 192p [NSWA OWtU

**Johnson, Albert Edward, 1902?–**

THE CROWN AND THE LAUREL. Oxford, G. Ronald, 1953. 34p

IN A SUMMER SEASON. Syracuse, Syracuse U. Bookstore, 1927. 47p [BVaU LC OKQ

POEMS. Syracuse, Syracuse U. Bookstore, 1925. 48p [BVaU LC OKQ

POEMS. New York, Syracuse U. Bookstore, 1925. 4p [OKQ

WHEN THOU HAST SHUT THE DOOR. Portland, Falmouth, 1939. 49p [LC

A WINNIPEG CHAPBOOK. Winnipeg, Veteran Press, 1923. 13p [BVaU NBFU OKQ

**Johnson, Charles H.**

THE STORY THAT NEVER GROWS OLD. Wolfville, N.S., Davidson, 1944. 76p [OTP

**Johnson, Charles Nelson, 1860–**

POEMS OF THE FARM AND OTHER POEMS. Chicago, Daniels, 1901. 75p [LC

**Johnson, Emily Pauline, 1862–1913**

"AND HE SAID, 'FIGHT ON'." Toronto, Musson, 1913. 6p [OONL

CANADIAN BORN. Toronto, Morang, 1903. 67p [BM BVaU NBFU OTP

FLINT AND FEATHER. With short Biographical Sketch. ... Toronto, Musson, [1912]. 156p [Various later eds.] [BVaU NSHD OKQ QMM

FLINT AND FEATHER. Complete Poems. With Intro. by Theordore Watts-Dunton and a Biographical Sketch of the Author. Toronto, Musson, [1924]. 176p [BVaU NSHD OTP QMM

IN THE SHADOWS. Gouverneur, N.Y., priv. print., 1898. 4p [NBFU

LEGEND OF SIWASH ROCK. Vancouver, Vancouver Business & Professional Women's Club, 1952. 8p

OJISTOH. Illustrated Indian Woman Monologue. New York, Werner, 1911. 39p [LC

"WHEN GEORGE WAS KING," AND OTHER POEMS. Brockville, "Times," 1908. 11p [BVaU NSHD OTP

THE WHITE WAMPUM. London, Lane, 1895. 88p [BVaU LC NBFU OKQ QMM

**Johnson, Frank**

LASHED TO THE MIZZEN; or, A Night off the Cape. Montreal, Lovell, 1872. 19p [First pub. in 1867?–*cf.* BCF. London ed., 1877.] [BM BVaU QMSS

**Johnson, Garland**

FROM CHILDHOOD TO WOMANHOOD IN ONTARIO. Toronto, Best Print., 1936. 27p [AEU OTUV QMU

**Johnson, George Washington, 1839–1917**

MAPLE LEAVES. Hamilton, Author, 1864. 202p [BVaU OTP

SUMMARY OF CANADIAN HISTORY IN RHYME. Toronto, Educational Pub. Co., 1908. 15p [Brown U BVaU OONL

**Johnson, Helen Mar, 1834–1863**

POEMS. Boston, Himes, 1855. 249p [OONL

**Johnson, Mrs. Herrick**

THE SHADOW OF THE ROCK AND THE VOICE IN THE TWILIGHT. [Two Poems.] Toronto, Hart & Rawlinson, n.d. 14p [QMU

**Johnston, Albert Richard, 1917–**

FOLK SONGS OF CANADA. Arr. by Richard Johnston. Ed. by Gordon Hallett. [Piano solo ed.] Waterloo, Ont., Waterloo Music. Co., 1957. 24p

**Johnston, George Benson, 1913–**

THE CRUISING AUK. Toronto, Oxford U. Press, 1959. 72p

**Johnston, Katherine Leila**

OVER THE THRESHOLD AND OTHER POEMS. ... Toronto, Ryerson, 1922. 53p [BM BVaU NBFU OTP

**Johnston, Rev. Minton C.**

THE STILL SMALL VOICE. Montreal, Author, 1938. 16p [OTU

**Johnston, Thomas**

CANADIAN AND SCOTTISH SONGS AND POEMS. Calgary, Author, 1920. 149p [BViPA

**Johnston, William, 1840–1917**

CANADIAN MELODIES AND MISCELLANEOUS POEMS. Stratford, Ont., Beacon, 1909. 212p [Brown U BVaU OTU

**Johnston-Smith, Frederick James**
THE UNION JACK. What It is and What It Means. With Twelve Lyrics. Toronto, n.d. 38p [Brown U

**Johnstone, Rev. John**
A VISION OF IMMANUEL. Toronto, Briggs, 1906. 65p [BVaU NSHD OTUV

**Jones, Douglas Gordon, 1929–**
FROST ON THE SUN. Toronto, Contact Press, 1957. 46p

**Jones, Ellen Lavinia (Clutterbuck), 1888–**
CAROLS OLD AND NEW. [Calgary?], 1939. [Rhod p926

**Jones, James Edmund, 1866–1939**
CAMP-FIRE CHORUSES. Songs Old and New that Everyone can Sing. Comp. by ——. Toronto, Oxford, 1916. 133p [BM BVaU NBFU OTU
THE LAST SUPPER AND GETHSEMANE. In Two Parts. Toronto, My Friends' Book & Gift Shop, 1927. 67p [OLU

**Jones, K.L.**
MEETING OF THE WATERS. Kingston, n.d. [Rhod p868

**Jones, Lily Edwards**
WOODLAND SONGS. Hamilton, Hamilton Typesetting, 1936. 96p [BVaU OH

**Jones, William Griffith, 1914–**
JINGLES FROM THE JONESES. Ponoka, Alta., Herald, 1952. 52p

**Joseph, Alexander Callow, 1886–1958**
BANG. Explosions in Verse. By Al Pat [pseud]. With Reprints from his Last Book RHYMES OF AN OLD WAR HORSE. Trenton, Ont., Author, 1944. 64p [OTP
RHYMES OF AN OLD WAR HORSE. By Al Pat [pseud]. 1938 Canadian Corps Reunion ed. Toronto, Author, 1938. 31p [2nd ed., Toronto, Southam, 1955. 40p] [OTUV
ROGER. ... A Collection of Verse & Yarns from "The Troops." By Al Pat [pseud]. Toronto, Author, 1946–1947. 2 parts. [OTP

**Joussaye, Marie**
SELECTIONS FROM ANGLO-SAXON SONGS. Dawson, Dawson News. Pub., [1920?]. 56p [NSWA OONL
THE SONGS THAT QUINTE SANG. Belleville, Sun, 1895. 91p [BVaU NBFU OTP QMM

**Joy, G.F.**
PRAIRIE CHICKENS. In Memoriam G.E.S. By Chanticleer [pseud]. London, Stockwell, 1908. 32p [OONL

**Joynes, Agnes**
THE SHEPHERD OF THE HILLS. Toronto, Ryerson, 1926. 8p [BM BVaU NBSaM OTP QMM

**Judge, May Edith Perceval**

THE BLUE-WALLED VALLEY. Toronto, Ryerson, 1929. 8p [BVaU NBFU OKQ QMM

KINDREDSHIP AND OTHER POEMS. Vancouver, Clarke & Stuart, 1944. 30 p [BVaU OKQ

THE WAY TO FAIRYLAND, AND OTHER RHYMES. Toronto, Ryerson, 1931. 16p [BVaU NBFU OKQ QMM

**Julien, Henri Octave, 1852–1908**

SONGS OF THE BY-TOWN COONS. [Anon] Montreal, Montreal Star, [1899?]. 26p [OTU

**Kaye, Leslie Lonker, 1936–**

THE McGILL CHAPBOOK. Ed. by ——. Toronto, Ryerson, 1959. 28p

**Kearney, W.D.**

AN EPIC POEM ENTITLED "THE OPEN HAND." An Indian Tale of Maine and New Brunswick, Founded on Historical Facts and Sustained by Tradition. Presque Isle, Me., Gilman, 1864. 58p [Reprinted under title: THE OPEN HAND. An Epic Poem dealing with the Early Settlement of Maine and New Brunswick. ... Hartland, N.B., Stevens, 1920. 58p [BVaU LC NBFU OTP

**Kearns, Rose Anne (or, Anne Rose)**

LYRICS, GRAVE AND GAY. Little Poems for Many Moods. N.p., Seagers Press, 1943. 36p [OKQ

LYRICS OF LOVE AND LAUGHTER. Toronto, 1933. 30p [Brown U OTUV

**Keating, James W.**

AN EPIC POEM: THE NORTON HOUSE. St. Catharines, March 3rd, 1886. St. Catharines, Sherwood, 1886. 14p [AEU

**Kelland, Otto Paul, 1904–**

ANCHOR WATCH. Newfoundland Stories in Verse. St. John's, 1960. 123p

**Kelley, Frank Mortimore, 1875–**

FIREWEED. With the Season's Greetings. N.p., Author, [1945?]. 12p [AEU OPAL

**Kemp, Ernest Arthur, 1888–**

FROM SEA TO SEA. Poems. Ilfracombe, Devon, Stockwell, 1959. 47p

**Kennedy, A. Allison**

WISPS. Lyrics and other Verse. Toronto, Burns & MacEachern, 1956. 70p

**Kennedy, Leo, 1907–**

NEW PROVINCES. Poems of Several Authors. [Ed. by F.R. Scott.] Toronto Macmillan, 1936. 77p [Contains poems by Kennedy and others.] [BVaU NBFU OKQ

THE SHROUDING. Poems. Toronto, Macmillan, 1933. 59p [BM BVaU LC OKQ QMM

**Kent, Thomas**

THE HARP OF PROPHECY. London, Ont., Author, 1910. 39p [OTP QMU

**Kenvyn, Ronald**

WATERFRONT WAILS, AND OTHER VERSES. Vancouver, Cowan & Brookhouse, 1918. 44p [BM BVaU

**Keogh, W.O.**

POEMS OF A CANADIAN PIONEER FAMILY [by Mary Nolan (Brown) Keogh (Mrs. T.A.), Alice B. Keogh, and Lucius R. Keogh]. Comp. by ——. [Anon] N.p., [1921?]. 120p [BM BVaU OKQ

**Keough, Walter James, 1881–**

THE GREAT WHITE BANNER. Saint John, Barnes, 1913. 100p [BM Brown U LC NBFU

**Kern, Julia Ann (Pegg)**

GLOWING EMBERS. ... Vancouver, Wrigley, [1935?]. 16p [BViPA

**Kernighan, Robert Kirkland, 1857–1926**

THE KHAN'S BOOK OF VERSE. [Anon] Toronto, Evening Telegram, 1925. 197p [BVaU OKQ

THE KHAN'S KANTICLES. Hamilton, Spectator, 1896. 240p [BM BVaU NBFU OKQ QMM

THE MEN OF THE NORTHERN ZONE. Hamilton, Duncan, n.d. 10p [NBFU

WAR POEMS. By The Khan [pseud]. Dundas, R. W. Karch, 1916. 31p [BM BVaU OTU QMU

**Kerr, Estelle Muriel, 1879–1971**

THE ISLAND. Rhymes and Sketches. Toronto, Print Craft, [19—?]. 22p [OTP QMU

LITTLE SAM IN VOLENDAM. Rhymes and Pictures. New York, Moffat Yard, 1908. 32p [LC

**Kerr, J. George**

"SINGING FOR JESUS" AND OTHER POEMS. Woodstock, Ont., 1891. 51p [Adelphi cat. 64

**Kerr, William Henry Corrie, –1891**

EDWARD HANLAN. A Lay of Young Canada. Toronto, Belfords Clarke, 1879. 29p [Commemorates Hanlan's winning of sculling championship in 1879.] [OTP

**Kerrigan, Hilda Mary, 1911–**

ENCHANTMENT. Poems. Author, 1950. 12p [OONL

FAIR WINDS. Ottawa, Author, 1953. 10p
PLEASANT PATHWAYS. Ottawa, Author, 1958. 18p [Also: 1959, 22p]

**Kerry, Esther Wilson**
HE IS A CANADIAN, AND OTHER VERSE. Montreal, Regal Press, 1919. 31p [BM BVaU LC OTP

**Kester, Mary Sparks**
ROAD O'DREAMS. Poems. Elmira, Ont., Elmira Print., 1922. 31p [BVaU OLU

**Ketchum, William Quintard, 1898–**
REQUIESCANT AND OTHER POEMS. Toronto, 1919. 35p [BM BVaU OOP

**Kidd, Adam, 1802–1831**
THE HURON CHIEF, AND OTHER POEMS. Montreal, Herald & New Gazette, 1830. 216p [BM BVaU LC OKQ QMM

**Kidd, Thomas, 1846–1930**
HISTORY OF LULU ISLAND, AND OCCASIONAL POEMS. Vancouver, Wrigley Print., 1927. 247p [On cover: HISTORY OF RICHMOND MUNICIPALITY.] [BVaU

**Killingsworth, J. Alexander**
ROSES AND THORNS. St. Thomas, Author, 1921. 62p [BM
SPARKS AND CINDERS. St. Thomas, Journal Press, 1913. 146p [BM BVaU OTU

**King, Amabel (Reeves), 1899–**
THE NEW CRUSADERS AND OTHER POEMS. Toronto, Macmillan, 1943. 66p [BVaU LC OTP
VOICES OF VICTORY. Representative Poetry of Canada in Wartime. Comp. by — Toronto, Macmillan, 1942. xii + 97p [BVaU NSHPL

**King, Benjamin Franklin, 1857–1894**
BEN KING'S VERSE. Toronto, McClelland, 1923. 238p [BM BVaU NBFU

**King, Rev. John Harry**
THE HERO OF THE DRAMA OF GENESIS. An Epic of Sacred Story. Halifax, Nova Scotia Print., 1895. 72p [BVaU NSHD OOP

**King, William James, 1879–**
FOR YOU, MY DEAR. "Life's Varied Moods." Montreal, Author, 1938. 78p [OLU QMM
ROMANCE THRO' MORE THAN FORTY YEARS. Montreal, Author, 1944. 51p [OTP

**Kingsley, Mary**
HOMELY POEMS OF HUMBLE FORM. N.p., n.d. 30p [OPAL QMU

**Kingsley, Roland Edward, 1882–**
RHYMES OF BREVITY FOR TIMES OF LEVITY. Montreal, Author, 1937. 48p [OTU

**Kingsmill, Col. William, 1794–1876**

A STORY OF THE OLD MARINE. Guelph, 1869. 24p [Story of Cordingley, survivor of the Battles of the Nile and Trafalgar, living near Toronto, aged 106.] [BVaU OTU

**Kingston, George Allen, 1870–1943**

CHAMPLAIN AND D'ARONTAL. A Story in Verse. Toronto, Author, 1932. 11p [OTU

FROM LAND TO LINDBERGH. A Tale of Revolutionary Times with a 1932 Sequel. Toronto, Author, 1932. 12p [AEU OH

LEGENDARY LYRICS. Picton, Gazette, 1938. 117p [BVaU NBFU OTP

ON TO THE BAY. Toronto, Author, 1932. 7p [CC

RT. HON. SIR GILBERT PARKER, BART., DECEASED. A Tribute in Blank Verse. Toronto, Author, 1932. [CBI

**Kinnear, Caroline A.**

THE HOME TRAIL AND OTHER VERSES. Kamloops, Sentinel, 1938. 22p [BViPA OTU

**Kinney, Edwin Enoch**

WESTWARD AND OTHER POEMS. Vancouver, Chalmers, 1923. 75p [BVaU

**Kirby, William, 1817–1906**

CANADIAN IDYLLS. 2nd ed. Welland, 1894. 175p [1st ed., limited to 200 copies: Welland, 1884.] [BVaU LC NBFU OKQ

CANADIAN IDYLLS ... Interlude Second: The Harvest Moon. ... Toronto, Hunter Rose, 1883. 24p [Included in CANADIAN IDYLLS (1894).] [OTP

CANADIAN IDYLLS. Pontiac and Bushy Run. Niagara, Author, 1887. 44p [Included in CANADIAN IDYLLS (1894).] [OTP

CANADIAN IDYLLS. The Queen's Birthday. Toronto, Hunter Rose, 1881. 16p [Included in CANADIAN IDYLLS (1894).] [OTP

CANADIAN IDYLLS. ... The Queen's Birthday; Interlude First: The Bells of Kirby Wiske, and the Lord's Supper in the Wilderness. Toronto, Rose Belford, 1882. 22p [OTP

CANADIAN IDYLLS. Number IV: Spring, Stony Creek. Toronto, Briggs, 1880. 30p [Included in CANADIAN IDYLLS (1894).] [OOP

THE HUNGRY YEAR. Toronto, Methodist Book, 1878. 15p [Reprinted as "Autumn Poem" in CANADIAN IDYLLS (1894).] [OTP

THE U.E. A Tale of Upper Canada in XII Cantos. [Anon] Niagara, "Mail," 1859. 178p [BM BVaU NBFU OKQ

**Kirkconnell, Watson, 1895–**

CANADA TO ICELAND. ... Lindsay, Warder Press, 1930. 7p [Brown U

CANADIAN OVERTONES. An Anthology of Canadian Poetry written originally in Icelandic, Swedish, Hungarian, Italian, Greek, and Ukrainian, and now Translated. ... Winnipeg, Columbia Press, 1935. 104p [LC MWU NBFU OTU QMM

THE ETERNAL QUEST. Winnipeg, Columbia Press, 1934. 135p [BVaU NBFU OTP QMM

EUROPEAN ELEGIES. One Hundred Poems Chosen and Translated from European Literature in Fifty Languages. Ottawa, Graphic, 1928. 166p [BVaU NSHD OKQ QMM

THE FLYING BULL AND OTHER TALES. London, Oxford U. Press, 1940. 189p [Also: Toronto, Clarke Irwin, 1956.] [BVaU LC MWU NSHD OTP

A GOLDEN TREASURY OF POLISH LYRICS. Selected and Rendered into English. Winnipeg, Polish Press, 1936. 109p [BM BVaU OKQ QMM

A LITTLE TREASURY OF HUNGARIAN VERSE. Ed. and Trans. by ——. Washington, D.C., American Hungarian Federation, 1947. 55p [BM BVaU OTU QMM

LYRA SACRA. Four Occasional Hymns. Winnipeg, Author, 1939. 7p [CC

THE MAGYAR MUSE. An Anthology of Hungarian Poetry, 1400–1932. Ed. and Trans. by ——. Winnipeg, Kanadai Magyar Ujság Press, 1933. 222p [BM BVaU LC NSHD OTU QMM

MANITOBA SYMPHONY. N.p. [1937?]. 9p [OKQ

THE NORTH AMERICAN BOOK OF ICELANDIC VERSE. New York, Carrier & Isles, 1930. 228p [BM BVaU LC NSHD OKQ QMM

THE PATH OF DEMOS. [Winnipeg], n.d. 5p [NSHPL

THE QUEBEC TRADITION. An Anthology of French-Canadian Prose and Verse. Selected by Séraphin Marion and Translated into English by ——. Montreal, Les Editions Lumen, 1946. 245p [French and English on opposite pages.] [NBFU OTU

THE TIDE OF LIFE AND OTHER POEMS. Ottawa, Ariston Publishers, 1930. 79p [BVaU NSHD OTU QMM

WESTERN IDYLL. Hamilton, Author, 1940. 10p [OTU

**Kirkpatrick, Mrs. Helen, 1877–**

BOOK OF POEMS. By Gemmill [pseud]. Winnipeg, Evans Print., 1937. 31p [AEU

RAMBLINGS IN VERSE. By Gemmill [pseud]. Winnipeg, Evans Print., 1949. 59p [Brown U

**Kirkwood, Kenneth Porter, 1899–**

ABSTRACTIONS. ["Prose Poems."] Tokyo, Meiji Press, 1937. 93p [OTU

IN GARDENS OF PROSERPINE. Tokyo, Taiheiyosha Press, 1930. 27p [BM LC

LYRICS AND SONNETS. Tokyo, Author, 1934. 165p [BM OTP

POEMS. Tokyo, Author, [1930–32]. 76p [Contents: In Gardens of Proserpine; Travel Dust; Song in my Heart.] [QMM

SONG IN MY HEART. Tokyo, Author, 1932. 76 p [BM LC OTU

TIME'S TAVERN. Tokyo, Meiji Press, 1937. 158p [QMM

TRAVEL DUST. Tokyo, Author, 1932. 90p [BM LC OTU

**Klein, Abraham Moses, 1909–**

HATH NOT A JEW. New York, Behrman's Jewish Book House, 1940. 116p [BVaU LC MWU NSHD OTU QMM

THE HITLERIAD. New York, New Directions, 1944. 30p [BVaU LC MWU NSHD OTU QMM

HUIT POEMS CANADIENS (EN ANGLAIS). Montreal, Author, 1948. 16p [OKQ QMBM

NEW PROVINCES. Poems of Several Authors. [Ed. by F.R. Scott.] Toronto, Macmillan, 1936. 77p [Contains poems by Klein and others.] [BVaU NBFU OKQ

POEMS. Philadelphia, Jewish Pub. Soc., 1944. 82p [BVaU NBFU OTU

THE ROCKING CHAIR AND OTHER POEMS. Toronto, Ryerson, 1948. 56p [BVaU LC MWU NSHD OTU QMM

SEVEN POEMS. Montreal, Author, 1947. 8p [OTU QMBM

**Kmietowicz, Frank Andrews, 1912–**

REJOICE WE CONQUER. By Frank Andrews [pseud]. Toronto, New Line Fraternity, 1960. 59p

**Knapp, M. Emma**

LYRICS OF THE PAST, AND OTHER POEMS. ... Saint John, McMillan, 1872. 160p [Brown U NSHD

**Knatchbull-Hugessen, Kenneth Wyndham, 1925–1942**

JEUNESSE, AND OTHER POEMS. With an Introductory Memoir by his Father. Montreal, Southam Press, 1944. 47p [BVaU NBFU OTUV

**Knight, Dorothy W., 1881–**

OTHER VERSES (1893). N.p., n.d. 29p [Also bound with VERSES, below.] [NSWA

VERSES. By Dorothy Knight, Eleven Years Old. With a Preface by her Father. Brockville, priv. print., 1892. 41p [Cover title: ECHOES FROM THE THOUSAND ISLANDS.] [BVaU NSWA OKQ

THE VISION OF THE SEASONS AND OTHER VERSES. Montreal, Drysdale, 1898. 68p [BM BVaU NSHPL OKQ QMM

**Knight, Fulton Stanley, 1883–**

HORS D'OEUVRES. A Little Offering to whet the Appetite, a Tid-bit to roll under the Tongue and, as a Connoisseur, to titillate pleasurably the Senses. V. 1; Christmas 1960. Meaford, Ont., Knight Press, [1960?]. 28p

**Knight, George**

JOY OF LIVING, AND OTHER VERSES. Toronto, Dent, 1948. 66p [OTU QMM

**Knight, Rev. Matthew Richey, 1854–**

POEMS OF TEN YEARS, 1877–1887. Halifax, Macgregor & Knight, 1887. 143p [BVaU NSHD OTP

**Knister, Raymond, 1900–1932**

COLLECTED POEMS OF RAYMOND KNISTER. Ed. with a memoir by Dorothy Livesay. Toronto, Ryerson, 1949. 45p [BVaU NBFU OTP

**Korn, Rachel H.**

BASHERTKEIT (KISMET) POEMS 1928–1948. Montreal, Canadian Jewish Congress, 1949. 116p [Brown U

**Laborde, Margaret Faith, 1897–**

POEMS FOR CHILDREN. Brantford, Author, 1933. 47p [CC

**Lacey, Gladys Margaret**

ON REEDS FROM NISO'S STREAM. Boston, Humphries, 1947. 88p [LC OTP

**Lady, A (pseud)**

A POEM ON THE THREE-FOLD ESSENCE OF GOD. By a Lady [pseud]. Montreal, Starke, [18—?]. 16p [OTP

**Laidlaw, Thomas, 1825–1902**

IN THE LONG AGO; or, The Days of the Cattle Bell. N.p., [18—?]. 7p [OTP

THE OLD CONCESSION ROAD. Guelph, Mercury Press, 1892. 54p [Same title: Guelph, Turnbull, 1899. 69p] [OTP

SPRIGS O' HEATHER FOR SCOTTISH GATHERINGS. Guelph, Mercury Press, [18—?]. 28p [OTP

**Lamb, Elkin**

EXCEPT IT DIE. Toronto, Rous & Mann, 1945. 45p [OTP

THINGS NEW AND OLD. [Anon] Toronto, Rous & Mann, 1945. 22p [Brown U

**Lambert, Gertrude M.**

RHYMES AT RANDOM. Vancouver, Ernest Church, 1939. 16p [OTU

**Lambie, Alexander, 1870–**

WHEN POLLY WENT AWAY. A Book of Rhyme for Sleepy Time. Vancouver, Williamson, 1917. 26p [BVaU

**Lampman, Archibald, 1861–1899**

ALCYONE. Ottawa, Ogilvy, 1899. 110p [NBFU OKQ

AMONG THE MILLET, AND OTHER POEMS. Ottawa, Durie, 1888. 151p [BM BVaU LC MWU NSHD OKQ QMM

AT THE LONG SAULT AND OTHER NEW POEMS. Foreword by Duncan Campbell Scott, introduction by E.K. Brown. Toronto, Ryerson, 1943. 45p [BVaU NSHD OKQ

HAPPINESS. A Preachment ... carrying to you the Best Wishes of the Ryerson Press, Christmas, 1925. Toronto, Ryerson, 1925. 15p [BVaU NBFU OTP

LITTLE BOOK, THY PAGES STIR. An Autograph Poem. [facsim.] Toronto, Ryerson, 1923. 3p [BVaU LC NBFU OTP

LYRICS OF EARTH. Boston, Copeland & Day, 1895. 56p [BVaU LC NSHD OKQ

LYRICS OF EARTH. Sonnets and Ballads. With an intro. by D.C. Scott. Toronto, Musson, 1925. 276p [BVaU NSHD OKQ QMM

THE POEMS OF ARCHIBALD LAMPMAN. Ed. with a memoir by Duncan Campbell Scott. Toronto, Morang, 1900. 473p [BM BVaU LC NSHD OKQ QMM

SELECTED POEMS OF ARCHIBALD LAMPMAN. Chosen with a memoir by Duncan Campbell Scott. Toronto, Ryerson, 1947. 176p [LC MWU NBFU OTP QMM

THESE POEMS. By Archibald Lampman and Duncan Campbell Scott. N.p., 1897. 6p [NBFU OKQ

TWO POEMS. By Archibald Lampman and Duncan Campbell Scott ... issued to their Friends at Christmastide, 1896. N.p., 1896. 3p [NBFU OKQ

**Lancaster, William**

THE CHRIST. A Poem. Toronto, Guardian, 1873. 30p [OTUV

**Lande, Lawrence Montague, 1906–**

BABBLINGS AND RANDOM VERSE. Montreal, priv. print., 1952. 51p

EXPENDABLE, AND OTHER POEMS. Montreal, priv. print., 1960. 33p

RESPONSE TO PRECIOUS MOMENTS. Montreal, Author, 1959. 53p

RESPONSE. With an intro. by Edgar A. Collard. Enl. ed. Montreal, Author, 1960. 89p

**Lane, Wilmot Burkmar, 1872–**

THE CLOSED BOOK (An Epic of the Soul's Quest). Toronto, Macmillan, 1943. 42p [BVaU LC NSHD OTP

QUINTE SONGS AND SONNETS. Toronto, Ryerson, 1925. 91p [BVaU NBFU OTP

**Lang, Christopher D.**

RHYMES OF A PROPER ROUGHNECK. Winnipeg, Jackson Trade Pub. Co., 1935. 47p [UTQ

**Lang, Sidney Edward, 1864–**

THE STORY OF PHILOSOPHY IN VERSE. A Handbook for Amateurs. Toronto, Macmillan, 1934. 101p [BVaU LC

**Langford, Dorothy J.**

HEAVENLY TREASURE. Toronto, Evangelical Pub., 1948. 40p [AEU NSHP

**Langford, Walter Frederick, 1898–**

NORTHERN MEDLEY. An Anthology of Canadian Verse. Ed. by ——. Toronto, Longmans, [1954]. 95p

**Langlands, Katharine Louise, 1913–**

MEMORIES. Huntsville, Ont., Author, 1937. 28p [OTU

**Lanigan, George Thomas, 1846–1886**

NATIONAL BALLADS OF CANADA. Imitated and Trans. from the Originals by "Allid" [pseud]. Montreal, Lovell, 1865. 15p [BM OTP

SOME EARLY TRANSLATIONS OF GEO. T. LANIGAN. N.p., [1922?]. 12p [OTP

**Lanigan, John Alphonsus, 1854–1919**

LEISURE HOURS. A Selection of Short Poems and Miscellaneous Scraps. 2nd ed. Buffalo, Author, 1870. 108p [1st ed., 1869.] [BVaU LC NSHD QMM

WOODLAND RAMBLES. Poems. Buffalo, Peter Paul Book Co., 1894. 153p [LC NSHD

**Larkin, Sarah Elizabeth, 1896–**

RADISSON. Trois-Rivières, Les Editions du Bien Public, 1938. 147p [LC OTU QMBM

THREE RIVERS. A Tale of New France. New York, Putnam, 1934. 93p [BM BVaU LC NBFU OTP QMBM

THE TREVALS. A Tale of Quebec. Montreal, Renouf, 1936. 147p [BVaU LC OLU QMBM

**Larsen, Thorleif, 1887–1960**

SOME UNDERGRADUATE POEMS. [Anon] [An Anthology ed. and copyrighted by Thorleif Larsen.] Toronto, Briggs, 1905. 72p [BVaU OTU

**Laskey, John K.**

LEISURE HOURS. A Collection of Original Poems. Saint John, Durant, 1838. 71p [NBSaM

MARS HILL AND OTHER POEMS. Saint John, 1838. 70p [CCJ NBB

**Laurence, Frances Elsie (Fry), 1893–**

THE BAND PLAYS A MARCH, AND OTHER POEMS. [Edson, Alta.], Author, 1936. 66p [BVaU OKQ

REARGUARD AND OTHER POEMS. Toronto, Ryerson, 1944. 10p [BVaU LC NSHD OTP

XII POEMS. Toronto, Ryerson, 1929. 8p [BVaU NBSaM OKQ QMM

**Lauriston, Victor, 1881–**

MAPLE LAND. 1905. [MOR'12

**Lauzon, Edythe Morahan-de**

ANGEL'S SONGS FROM THE GOLDEN CITY OF THE BLESSED. Montreal, Urquhart, 1918. 311p [BVaU LC OTP

**Lawson, Francis Edgar, 1861–1911**

SONGS OF FRANK LAWSON. Toronto, Briggs, 1912. 90p [AEU NBFU OLU QMU

**Lawson, James Reid, 1820–1891**

SONGS OF ZION. Saint John, n.d. 32p [CCJ

**Lawson, Jessie (Kerr), 1838–1917**

LAYS AND LYRICS. Toronto, Briggs, 1913. 123p [BM BVaU NBFU OTP QMU

**Lawson, Mary Jane (Katzmann), 1828–1890**

FRANKINCENSE AND MYRRH. Selections from the Poems of the late Mrs. William Lawson (M.J.K.L.). Selected and ed. by Harry Piers and Constance Fairbanks. Halifax, Morton, 1893. 152p [BVaU NSHD OLU

**Lawson, Thomas**

THE POETICAL WORKS OF THOMAS LAWSON. Halifax, Holloway, 1888. 44p [NSHD OTUV

**Layton, Irving, 1912–**

THE BLACK HUNTSMEN. Montreal, First Statement Press, 1951. 56p

THE BLUE PROPELLER. Montreal, Contact Press, 1955. 50p

THE BULL CALF AND OTHER POEMS. Toronto, Contact Press, 1956. 49p

CERBERUS. Poems by Louis Dudek, Irving Layton, Raymond Souster. Toronto, Contact Press, [1952]. 98p

THE COLD GREEN ELEMENT. Toronto, Contact Press, 1955. 56p

HERE AND NOW. Montreal, First Statement Press, 1945. 44p [BVaU MWU NBFU OKQ QMM

THE IMPROVED BINOCULARS. Selected Poems. Highlands, N.C., J. Williams, 1956. 106p [2nd ed., 1957. 139p]

IN THE MIDST OF MY FEVER. Palma de Mallorca, Spain, Divers Press, 1954. 39p

A LAUGHTER IN THE MIND. Highlands, N.C., J. Williams, 1958. 54p

A LAUGHTER IN THE MIND. 2nd print., with 20 additional poems. Montreal, Editions d'Orphée, 1959. 97p [1st ed.: Highlands, N.C., J. Williams, 1958.]

THE LONG PEA SHOOTER. Montreal, Laocoön Press, 1954. 68p

LOVE THE CONQUEROR WORM. Toronto, Contact Press, 1953. 49p

MUSIC ON A KAZOO. Toronto, Contact Press, 1956. 59p

A RED CARPET FOR THE SUN. Toronto, McClelland, 1959. 240p

**Lazechko-Haas, Myra**

VIEWPOINT. Toronto, Ryerson, 1952. 12p

**Leacock, Stephen Butler, 1869–1944**

HELLEMENTS OF HICKONOMICS, IN HICCOUGHS OF VERSE DONE IN OUR SOCIAL PLANNING MILL. New York, Dodd Mead, 1936. 84p [BM BVaU LC NSHD OTU

THE MARIONETTE'S CALENDAR, 1916. Rhymes by Stephen Leacock; drawings by A.H. Fish. London, Lane, 1915. 14p [BM BVaU OTU

**Leaver, Harold R.**

THE MYSTERY OF JOHN JASPER. Edmonton, Capital City Press, 1925. 76p [An attempted completion of Dickens' *The Mystery of Edwin Drood.*] [BVaU NSHD OKQ

**LeClaire, Gordon, 1905–**

CARPENTER'S APPRENTICE AND OTHER POEMS. Toronto, Ryerson, 1957. 24p

DUST INTO FLAME. 1943. [Rhod. p938-9

INTIMATE MOMENTS. Random Runinations Expressed in Verse. Chicago, André, 1934. 19p [LC

SONNETS TO THE STARS, AND OTHER POEMS. Boston, Meador, 1936. 76p [OTU

STAR-HAUNTED. New York, Harrison, 1937. 95p [LC OTU QMM

THOUGH QUICK SOULS BLEED. New York, Banner Press, 1939. 122p [BVaU LC OTU QMM

**Ledingham, Mary**

SUCH THORNS AS PIERCE MY HEART. New York, Fortuny's, [1939?]. 62p [BVa OTUV

**Lee, Joseph, 1876–**

BALLADS OF BATTLE. Toronto, Gundy, 1916. 101p [BVaU NSHD OTP

**Lee, Sophia Victoria (Gilbert)**

WAYSIDE ECHOES. Poems. Toronto, Briggs, 1894. 179p [LC OKQ

**Lefevre, Lily Alice (Cooke), –1938**

A GARDEN BY THE SEA, AND OTHER POEMS. London, Humphreys, 1921. 128p [BVaU NSHD OKQ

THE LIONS' GATE AND OTHER VERSES. Victoria, Province Pub. Co., 1895. 95p [BVaU NBFU OKQ QMM

THE LIONS' GATE AND THE BEAVER AND THE EMPRESS. N.p., 1903. 9p [Same title: Vancouver, Thomson, 1933. 17p] [BVaU OTP

**Leggett, William Martin, 1813–1863**

THE FOREST WREATH. A Collection of Lyrics. Saint John, Durant & Sancton, 1833. 191p [NSHD OTP

**Lehigh, M. Stanley**

TRAIL OF THE SERPENT, RHYMES, AND MADRIGALS. Brockville, Recorder Print., 1905. 73p [BM

VICTOR AND OTHER POEMS. Brockville, Recorder Print., 1901. 69p [BM OTUV QMM

YOUTHFUL FANCIES, AND IONE. Brockville, Recorder Print., 1897. 95p [AEU OTUV

**Leichliter, G.A.**

SONGS TO MEN AND NATURE. Toronto, Standard Pub., n.d. 30p [NBSaM

**Leland, S.P.**

POEMS. Montreal, Dawson Bros., [1865]. [Priv. info.

**LeMoine, James MacPherson, 1825–1912**

THE LEGENDARY LORE OF THE LOWER ST. LAWRENCE. Quebec, Mercury Office, 1862. 33p [BM NSHP OTUV

**Leonard, Mrs. Carrie**

GEMS FOR THE HOME CIRCLE. Original Poems. London, Ont., Cameron, 1869. 150p [OTP

**Lepage, John, –1885**

THE ISLAND MINSTREL. A Collection of the Poetical Writings of John LePage. Charlottetown, Haszard, 1860. 242p [OLU QMBM

THE ISLAND MINSTREL. A Collection of Some of the Poetical Writings of John LePage. Vol. II. Charlottetown, Bremner, 1867. 219p [BVaU NSHD OOP QMM

**Le Pan, Douglas Valentine, 1914–**

THE WOUNDED PRINCE AND OTHER POEMS. London, Chatto & Windus, 1948. 39p [BM BVaU LC MWU NBFU OTP

THE NET AND THE SWORD. London, Chatto & Windus, 1953. 56p

**Leprohon, Rosanna Eleanor (Mullins), 1829–1879**

THE POETICAL WORKS OF MRS. LEPROHON (Miss R.E. Mullins). Montreal, Lovell, 1881. 228p [BVaU LC NBFU OKQ

**Le Scrivinir, Robert**

DO FLOWERS BLOOM FOR LOVE, AND OTHER POEMS. Toronto, Print-craft Ltd., [193–?] 21p [Brown U

**Leslie, Kenneth, 1892–**

BY STUBBORN STARS, AND OTHER POEMS. Toronto, Ryerson, 1938. 64p [BVaU LC NBFU OTP QMM

LOWLANDS LOW. Poems. [Halifax, McCurdy, 1935.] 47p [BVaU QMM

SUCH A DIN! Poems. Halifax, n.d. 45p [BVaU QMM

WINDWARD ROCK. Poems. New York, Macmillan, 1934. 61p [BM LC NBFU QMM

**Leslie, Mary, 1842–1920**

HISTORICAL SKETCHES OF SCOTLAND IN PROSE AND VERSE. ... Being an Account of the Kings and Queens of Scotland from the Reign of Fergus the First to Victoria. ... Toronto, Bryant, [1905?]. 174p [BM BVaU OTP

RHYMES OF THE KINGS AND QUEENS OF ENGLAND. Being an Account of the Rulers of England from the Norman Conquest to the Reign of Victoria. Toronto, Briggs, 1896. 177p [BM BVaU OTP

**Leveridge, Lilian, 1879–1953**

THE BLOSSOM TRAIL. Toronto, Ryerson, 1932. 30p [BVaU NBSaM OTP QMM

A BREATH OF THE WOODS. Toronto, Ryerson, 1926. 24p [BVaU NBSaM OKQ QMM

THE HERO SONGS OF CANADA. Toronto, Canadian Magazine, 1927. 23p [BVaU NBFU OKQ

LYRICS AND SONNETS. Toronto, Ryerson, 1939. 32p [BVaU NSHD OKQ

OVER THE HILLS OF HOME, AND OTHER POEMS. New York, Dutton, 1918. 89p [Same title: Toronto, McClelland, 1918. 64p] [BM BVaU LC NSHD OKQ QMM

**Levine, Albert Norman, 1923–**

MYSSIUM. Toronto, Ryerson, 1948. 8p [BVaU NBSaM OKQ

THE TIGHT-ROPE WALKER. London, Totem Press, 1950. 30p [BM BVaU OTP

**Lewis, Charles Edward**

BRIAR-WREATHES [*sic*]. London, Eyre & Spottiswoode, 1899. 22p [BM LC

**Lewis, Fred**

IMMORTALITY. Winnipeg, Author, 1944. 28p [OTP

**Lewis, Lydia T.**

LOVE SONGS AND OTHER LYRICS. By Lesbia [pseud]. Ottawa, Hope, 1922. 40p [BM BVaU OOP

ROSES FOR LOVE. A Miscellany in Verse. London, Stockwell, 1933. 94p [BM

**Lewis, Ray**

THE CUP OF CIVILIZATION. From "Songs of the Universe." Ed. by Isadore Bernstein. Flushing, N.Y., McConnell, n.d. 8p [OKQ

SONGS OF EARTH. New York, Boni, 1917. 121p [AEU NBFU OTP

**Lewis, Richard G.**

VERSE AND REVERSE. Hamilton, Luday Studios, 1936. 50p [OPAL

**Lewis, Susan Victoire**

COLLECTED VERSE OF SUSAN VICTOIRE LEWIS. Ottawa, Ru-Mi-Lou Books, 1929. 96p [BVaU NBFU OKQ

**Lighthall, William Douw, 1857–1954**

CANADIAN POEMS AND LAYS. Selections of Native Verse. ... Arranged and Ed. by ——. London, Scott, 1893. xxxii + 276p [BM BVaU LC NBFU OKQ QMM

CANADIAN POEMS AND SONGS. See SONGS OF THE GREAT DOMINION.

CANADIAN POETS OF THE GREAT WAR. Ottawa, Royal Society, n.d. 24p [OTP QMM

THE LAND OF MANITOU. Montreal, Desbarats, 1916. 18p [BM BVaU LC NSHD OTU QMM

OLD MEASURES. Collected Verse. Montreal, Chapman, 1922. 140p [BVaU NBFU OTP QMM

SONGS OF THE GREAT DOMINION. Voices from the Forests and Waters, the Settlements and Cities of Canada. Selected and ed. by ——. London, Scott, 1889. xxxvii + 465p [Also pub. under title: CANADIAN SONGS AND POEMS. London, Scott, 1892. 465p [BM BVaU LC NSHD OKQ

THOUGHTS, MOODS AND IDEALS. Crimes of Leisure. With Appendix. Montreal, Witness, 1887. 24p [Also a supplement in 1895.] [BVaU NSHD OTP QMM

**Lindsell, Gerald Charles Huntingdon, 1883–**

THE GREY GEESE. Toronto, Apted, 1931. 18p [OTP

**Linnell, John Stainforth**

YOUTH AND OTHER POEMS. Toronto, Macmillan, 1929. 76p [BM Brown U BVaU OOU

**Liston, James Knox, fl. 1843–1868**

NIAGARA FALLS. A Poem in Three Cantos. Toronto, Lawrence, 1843. 100p [BM BVaU LC OTP QMBM

POETRY FOR THE DOMINION OF CANADA. Consisting of Songs of the Canadian Winter, Songs of the Morning Stars, Shouts of the Sons of God, The Antemundane State. Toronto, Adam Stevenson, 1868. 96p [BVaU LC NBFU OTP QMM

**Litster, Thomas Harkness, 1859–1943**

SONGS IN YOUR HEART AND MINE. Toronto, McClelland, 1917. 142p [BM BVaU NBFU OKQ

**Little, David Fleming, –1881**

POEMS. Halifax, Nova Scotia Print., 1881. 101p [BVaU NSHD OTP

**Little, Jean**

"IT'S A WONDERFUL WORLD." Guelph, Author, 1947. 30p [Adelphi cat. 55

**Little, Robert D., 1888–**

RHYME AND REASON. Richmond Hill, Ont., Author, 1946. 58p [OTU

**Lively, Gerald J.**

THE PLEA OF THE WEST AND OTHER POEMS. London, Stewart, 1913. 24p [AEU QMSS

**Livesay, Dorothy, 1909–**

CALL MY PEOPLE HOME. Toronto, Ryerson, 1950. 24p [BVaU NBFU OTP

DAY AND NIGHT. Poems. Toronto, Ryerson, 1944. 48p [BVa MWU NBFU OTP QMM

GREEN PITCHER. Toronto, Macmillan, 1928. 16p [BVaU NBFU OTP

NEW POEMS. Toronto, Emblem Books, 1955. 15p

POEMS FOR PEOPLE. Toronto, Ryerson, 1947. 40p [BM BVaU NBFU OTP

SELECTED POEMS, 1926-1956. With an intro. by Desmond Pacey. Toronto, Ryerson, 1957. xxii + 82p

SIGNPOST. Toronto, Macmillan, 1932. 61p [BM BVaU LC NBFU OTP

**Livesay, Florence Hamilton (Randal), 1874–1953**

SHEPHERD'S PURSE. Toronto, Macmillan, 1923. 67p [BM BVaU NSHD OTP QMM

SONGS OF UKRAINIA. With Ruthenian Poems. Trans. by ——. London, Dent, 1916. 175p [BM BVaU LC NBFU OTP QMM

**Livingston, Irvin Stanley, 1909–**

FLAX AFIRE. New York, Pageant Press, 1953. 69p

**Livingston, Kay**

ACA NADA. Toronto, Copp Clark, n.d. 16p [NSWA OONL

**Livingston, Stuart, 1865–1923**

IN VARIOUS MOODS. Poems. Toronto, Briggs, 1894. 100p [BVaU LC NBFU OTP

**Lloyd, Cecil Richard Francis, 1884–1938**

LANDFALL. The Collected Poems of Cecil Francis Lloyd. Toronto, Ryerson, 1935. 47p [BVaU NBFU OTP QMM

LEAVES OF THE SYBIL. [Winnipeg, Author], 1927. 45p [Also: Toronto, Hunter Rose, 1928. 47p] [BM LC NSHD OKQ QMM

ROSEMARY AND RUE. Winnipeg, Stovel, 1929. 16p [BM OKQ QMM

VESPER BELLS. Toronto, Hunter Rose, 1929. 19p [BVaU OTP

**Lloyd, Rev. William, 1884–**

MORN MIST AND OTHER POEMS. Ilfracombe, Devon, Stockwell, 1960. 38p

**Llwyd, Rev. John Plummer Derwent, 1861–1933**

POEMS OF NATURE, CHILDHOOD, AND RELIGION. Toronto, Macmillan, 1928. 64p [NSHD

**Lobb, Roy Leonard, 1888–**

PLAIN-FOLKS. A Book of Friendly Verse. Beatty, Sask., Author, 1949. 146p [Brown U OTU

WHERE ARE YOU GOING? Spiritual poems. New York, Greenwich Book Pub., 1959. 64p

**Lochhead, Douglas Grant, 1922–**

THE HEART IS FIRE. Toronto, Ryerson, 1959. 12p

IT IS ALL AROUND. Toronto, Ryerson, 1960. 24p

AN OLD WOMAN LOOKS OUT ON GABARUS BAY REMEMBERING HISTORY, JUNE 8, 1958. Halifax, Three Fathom Press, 1959. 4p

**Lockerby, Elizabeth N.**

OAK LEAVES. ... Halifax, Macnab, 1869. 57p [NSHD

THE WILD BRIER; or, Lays by an Untaught Minstrel. ... By E.N.L. Charlottetown, Bremner, 1866. 196p [BVaU NSHP OTP

**Lockhart, Rev. Arthur John, 1850–1926**

BESIDE THE NARRAGUAGUS, AND OTHER POEMS. Buffalo, Peter Paul Book Co., 1895. 112p [BVaU LC OKQ QMM

THE BIRDS OF THE CROSS, AND OTHER POEMS. Winterport, Longee, 1909. 239p [LC OKQ

THE HARP OF ACADIA. An Anthology ... of [Maritime] Authors. Ed by ——. N.p., 1923. 2v [NSWA

THE MASQUE OF MINSTRELS AND OTHER PIECES. Chiefly in Verse. By Two Brothers. Bangor, Burr, 1887. 361p [Pub. jointly with his brother Burton Wellesley Lockhart.] [LC NBFU OKQ QMM

**Lockhart, Olive Octavia (Moores), 1900–**

ST. AIDAN'S AND OTHER POEMS. Victoria, B.C., St. Aidan's United Church, 1956. 24p

**Logan, John Daniel, 1869–1929**

CHRISTOBEL. A Trifoliate Coronal of Sonnets to the Ideal Incarnate. By Aloysius Novicius [pseud]. [Priv. print.], [19—?]. 4p [NBFU OTP

CONFESSIO AMANTIS. An Epistle in Verse to Welcome Rt. Rev. Monsignor William Foley. ... Halifax, Author, 1926. 8p [NBFU

FROM THE SOUL'S OBSERVATORY; or, Songs of the Spirit at Vesper-rise. ... Five Poems. ... Halifax, Author, 1921. 8p [BVaU NBFU OTP

INSULTERS OF DEATH, AND OTHER POEMS OF THE GREAT DEPARTURE. With a Prose Preachment entitled "The Fatal Paradox and Sin of Sorrow for the Dead." Halifax, Davidson, 1916. 37p [NBFU OTP

THE LITTLE BLUE GHOST. An Easter Madrigal. With the Lost Love Letters of a Florian Apostate. ... Halifax, Allen, 1922. 23p [BVaU NBFU OOP

LUX IGNATIANA. An Inaugural Ode composed for ... the Inauguration of the Rev. William M. Magee, S.J., as President of Marquette University. ... Milwaukee, Marquette U. Press, 1928. 12p [NBFU

MATER CORONATA. An Ode with Lyrical Interlude. ... Halifax, Dalhousie Alumni Assoc., 1924. 11p [NBFU OKQ

MORE TINY TOWN TALES. ... Poems for Tiny Tots. Halifax, Author, 1924. 10p [NBFU

THE NEW APOCALYPSE, AND OTHER POEMS OF DAYS AND DEEDS IN FRANCE. With an essay ... "The New Atonement of the Living Dead." Halifax, Allen, 1919. 39p [BVaU NBFU OTU

PICTOU POETS. A Treasury of Verse in Gaelic and English. Selected ... by ——. With an intro. by ... George Geddie Patterson. Pictou, N.S., Advocate Press, 1923. 48p [OOP

PRELUDES, SONNETS AND OTHER VERSES. With an Epistle in Criticism and an Essay entitled "The Rhythmical Dummy; a Recipe for Verse-makers." Toronto, Briggs, 1906. 68p [BM BVaU NSHD OTP

A ROSARY OF RENUNCIATION. Six Sestets. With a Little Prose Homily on Mystical Union with the Ideal Beauty. Halifax, Author, 1925. 7p [NBFU

THE SINGING SILENCE. An Elegy in Memory of the late Monsignor William Foley. [Milwaukee], Author, 1927. 4p [NBFU

SONGS OF THE MAKERS OF CANADA AND OTHER HOMELAND LYRICS. Toronto, Briggs, 1911. 64p [BVaU NBFU OTP

TINY TOWN TALES. Three Poems. Halifax, Author, 1923. 6p [NBFU

TWILIGHT LITANIES, AND OTHER POEMS FROM THE IVORY TOWER. Halifax, Allen, 1920. 92p [BM BVaU NBFU OOP

TWO POEMS. ... Halifax, Author, 1921. 4p [NBFU OKQ

**Logan, John Edward, 1852–1915**

A CRY FROM THE SASKATCHEWAN. [Anon] Montreal, Robinson, 1885. 13p [BVaU

VERSES. Montreal, Pen and Pencil Club. 1916. 129p [BM BVaU NSHD OTP

**London, Ont. Writers' Club, Poetry Group**

LONDON POETRY GROUP OFFERS A SELECTION OF POEMS. London, Ont., 1953. 43p [A continuing series.]

**Lorimer, John G., 1807–1897**

THE RECLUSE OF NEW BRUNSWICK; or, The Hermit of Point Lepreaux. Saint John, Shives, 1842. 24p [CCJ NBB

**Lort, Ross Anthony, 1889–**

ALL CREATURES GREAT AND SMALL. Vancouver, Bradbury, 1931. 255p [BVaU

**Loucks, Vera Agnes (Morden), 1904–**

ESSENCE OF LIVING. Fort St. John, B.C., Alaska Highway News, 1956. 22p

**Love, Mrs. Georgina A.**

HILLS AND HIGHWAYS. Poetry of Life. Toronto, Merchants Press, [1948?]. 40p [CC OPAL

**Lovell, Kathleen Frances (Ramsay), 1926–**

MY THOUGHTS. Ilfracombe, Devon, Stockwell, 1957. 56p

**Lovell, R.G.**

DREAMS IN LAMPLIGHT. London, Ont., Hunter, 1940. 33p [OLU

PEACE AND WAR. Foleyet, Ont., Crucible Press, 1950. 28p [UTQ'51

TWISTED GOLD. Toronto, Crucible Press, 1944. 20p [Brown U NBSaM OLU

**Lover of Truth, A (pseud)**

ALLAN GRAY AND HIS DOUBTS; or, Rhyme and Reason for the Young. ... Halifax, Nova Scotia Print., 1881. 112p [BVaU NSHD

THE POEM: NO SECT IN HEAVEN! And a Reply to the Same in Poetry. Saint John, "News" Office, 1868. 16p [NBFU

**Loverove, A.G.**

POEMS BY A DOUKHOBOR. N.p., [193–?]. 16p [SSU

**Low, May (Austin), 1863–**

CONFESSION, AND OTHER VERSES. Boston, Sherman French, 1909. 47p [LC NSHD OTU QMU

**Low, Mildred, –1963**
IF I FORGET THEE. ... Souvenir of the Centenary of Ottawa, Capital of Canada, 1826–1926. Ottawa, 1926. 16p [Brown U
VICTORY OR DEATH AND OTHER POEMS. London, Robert Scott, 1916. 20p [BM

**Lowrey, David**
FLORENCE. Toronto, 1904. 29p [Brown U BVaU
IN HADES. Toronto, Author, 1906. 16p [BM BVaU OTUV

**Lowry-Calder, Sarah Isabell**
POEMS. Ottawa, Ru-Mi-Lou Books, 1928. 202p [OONL QMU

**Lowther, Armstrong John, 1880–1948**
POEMS. By Laird [pseud]. Vancouver, Clarke & Stuart, [1946?]. 91p [BVaU

**Lund, Charles Edward, 1850–**
MISCELLANEOUS VERSE. Readings, Recitations, Songs and Hymns. (Enl. ed.) Toronto, Best, 1926. 126p [1st ed., 1912.] [BM NBFU OTUV

**Luxton, Mary Clendinning O'Donnell (Martin), 1879–**
VIGNETTES. Poems. Victoria, Author, 1954. 35p
VIGNETTES IN VERSE. Victoria, Diggon, 1952. 16p

**Lynch, Norman C.**
THE SUNSET TRAIL AND OTHER POEMS. Montreal, Regnault, 1928. 51p [QMSS

**Lytle, Mrs. W.J.A.**
IN STORM AND SUNSHINE. By Beryl Berney [pseud]. London, Stockwell, 1936. 19p [BM

**M., A.**
NIAGARA. A Poem. By A.M. New York, Seymour, 1822. 24p [OTP

**M., F.**
ASTRAY. By F.M. Toronto, Chewett & Co., n.d. 8p [NSWA

**McArthur, Peter, 1866–1924**
FIVE SONNETS. New York, American Lithograph, 1899. 8p [LC
LINES. New York, priv. print., 1901. 28p [NBFU OTU
THE PRODIGAL, AND OTHER POEMS. New York, Kennerley, 1907. 64p [BVaU LC NBFU OKQ

**MacBride, Morrison Mann, 1877–1938**
SELECTED POEMS FROM THE PEN OF THE HONOURABLE MORRISON MANN MACBRIDE. V. I. Brantford, Mercantile Press, 1938. 149p [Brown U BVaU OTL

**McBride, Robert**
THE CANADIAN ORANGE MINSTREL FOR 1860. Contains Nine New and Original

Songs, Mostly all of them Showing some Wrong that affects the Order or the True Course of Protestant Loyalty to the British Crown. London, Ont., Free Press Print., 1860. 13p [OTP

THE CANADIAN ORANGE MINSTREL FOR 1870. Written for the Purpose of Keeping in Rememberance the Dark Doings and Designs of Popery in this Country. An Antidote for Pamphile Lemay's Songs, &c. Toronto, Stewart, 1870. 13p [OTP

POEMS SATIRICAL AND SENTIMENTAL ON MANY SUBJECTS CONNECTED WITH CANADA. London, Ont., Dawson, 1869. 302p [Earlier ed.: London, Author, 1858. 78p [BVaU OTP QMM

**McCaig, Donald, 1832–1905**

MILESTONE MOODS AND MEMORIES. Poems and Songs. Toronto, Hunter Rose, 1894. 132p [BVaU NBFU OTP

**McCall, Oswald Walter Samuel, 1885–**

IN SUCH A NIGHT AS THIS. Toronto, Musson, 1947. 204p [BM BVa LC

**McCallum, John**

PATRIOTIC ODES. Kingston, n.d. 16p [OLU

**McCarroll, James, 1815–1896**

MADELINE, AND OTHER POEMS. Intro. by Charles Lotin Hildreth. Chicago, Belford Clarke, 1889. 325p [BVaU LC OTUV

**McCausland, Margaret**

POSIES FOR FOLLY. Child Verse. St. Thomas, Ont., "Municipal World," 1910. [BM

**McCawley, Stuart**

A BOOK OF SONGS AND "COME-ALL-YE'S" OF CAPE BRETON AND NEWFOUNDLAND. Collected by ——. Glace Bay, N.S., Brodie, 1929. 64p [BVa NSHPL OKQ

RHYMES OF A ROUGHNECK. Glace Bay, N.S., Brodie Print., n.d. 24p [NSHK

**McClelland, Lily Coulter**

GEMS OF PRAISE. Saskatoon, 1950. 47p [SSU

**McColl, Carrie Wetmore**

APPLE BLOSSOMS. ... Toronto, Ryerson, 1920. 73p [BM NSHD OOP

**MacColl, Evan, 1808–1898**

THE ENGLISH POETICAL WORKS OF EVAN MACCOLL. ... With a Biographical Sketch of the Author by A. MacKenzie. ... Toronto, Hunter Rose, 1883. 360p [Other editions, with some variation in contents: "Second Canadian Edition," Toronto, Hunter Rose, 1885. 351p; Montreal, Drysdale, 1887. 338p; "Fourth Canadian Edition," Kingston, British Whig, 1888. 332p] [BVaU LC NSHD OTP QMSS

THE MOUNTAIN MINSTREL; or, Poems and Songs in English. 2nd ed., enl. Edinburgh, M'Lachlan & Stewart, 1838. 232p [BM OTP

**McColl, Hugh**

THE DAY OF JUDGMENT AND OTHER POEMS. Translated from the Gaelic of Dugald Buchanan and Peter Grant. To which is Prefixed a Sketch of the Life of Dugald Buchanan. ... Strathroy, Ont., Age Book & Job Office, 1870. 72p [OTU

**MacColl, Mary Jemima, 1847–**

BIDE A WEE, AND OTHER POEMS. Buffalo, Peter Paul, 1880. 103p [Also: Toronto, Rose Pub., 1882. 113p] [BVaU NBFU OTP

**McCollum, Alma Frances, 1879–1906**

FLOWER LEGENDS AND OTHER POEMS. Toronto, Briggs, 1902. 116p [BM BVaU LC NBFU OTP

**McComb, James**

POEMS OF FAITH, HOPE & LOVE. Vancouver, Clarke & Stuart, 1936. 16p [CC

**MacConnell, H.B.**

WHERE DUTY LEADS. Toronto, Briggs, 1916. 71p [BM BVaU OKQ

**MacCormack, Franklyn**

WHY I LOVE YOU, AND OTHER POEMS, FROM MY OLD BOOK OF MEMORIES. Toronto, Winston, 1948. 245p [BM

**McCoy, Charlotte**

SING A SONG OF CANADA. By Charlotte McCoy and Anne S. Brooks. With Music by Ada T. Kent. Toronto, Nelson, 1937. 32p [UTQ

**McCrae, John, 1872–1918**

IN FLANDERS FIELDS AND OTHER POEMS. With an Essay in Character by Sir Andrew Macphail. Toronto, Briggs, 1919. 141p [BM BVaU LC NBFU OTP

**McCrossan, Charles Wesley**

CANADIAN HEART SONGS. Toronto, Briggs, 1912. 163p [BM BVaU NBFU OKQ

**McCuaig, William Wilberforce**

SONGS OF A SHANTY-MAN, AND OTHER "DIALECT" POEMS OF FRENCH-CANADIAN LIFE. Toronto, Musson, [1913]. 91p [BVaU OTP QMSS

**McCulloch, Mercy Emma (Powell)**

RHYMING THROUGH THE YEARS. Toronto, Ryerson, 1951. 125p

**McCullough, Mary Eleanor, 1915–1942**

THE SKY WAS MY FRIEND. Songs of the Ottawa Valley. Ottawa, Le Droit, 1942. 48p [BVaU NSHD OTP

**McCully, Laura Elizabeth, 1886–1924**

BIRDS OF DAWN, AND OTHER LYRICS. [Toronto], 1919. 28p [BM BVaU NBFU

MARY MAGDALENE AND OTHER POEMS. Toronto, Macmillan, 1914. 99p [BM BVaU NBFU OTP

**McDavitt, Alice Pyne**

HOMESTEADER AND OTHER POEMS. New York, Cosmopolitan, 1913. 80p [OTL

**Macdonald, Agnes (Foley)**

ONCE AND AGAIN. Port Royal, N.S., Abanaki Press, 1951. 25p

**MacDonald, Ann Celestine (Rock), 1876–1960**

CARILLON PEACE TOWER, OTTAWA AND OTHER POEMS. Ottawa, Flora Printers, 1955. 36p

**McDonald, D.A.**

THOUGHTS OF A CONVICT. By Ex-Convict No. 1999, Kingston Penitentiary [pseud]. N.p., [1934?]. 32p [Brown U

**McDonald, Rev. Donald, 1783–1867**

SPIRITUAL HYMNS. Charlottetown, 1835. [Another ed., 1840.] [DCB

**Macdonald, Rev. Donald**

HYMNS FOR PRACTICE. Not to be Used in the Solemn Worship of the Sanctuary. By Rev. Donald Macdonald and Elders. Charlottetown, Haszard & Moore, 1894. 238p [Brown U OLU

**McDonald, Donald**

MONEY TALKS. Letters to the Sarnia Canadian Observer on Hard Times and Their Cure. Camlachie, Ont., Author, 1931. 32p [New ed., 1932. 68p] [BVaU

**MacDonald, Goodridge, 1897–**

ARMAGEDDON AND OTHER POEMS. N.p., Author, [1917?]. 8p [NBFU

BEGGAR MAKES MUSIC. Toronto, Ryerson, 1950. 11p [BVaU NBFU OTP

COMPASS READING AND OTHERS. Toronto, Ryerson, 1955. 11p

THE DYING GENERAL, AND OTHER POEMS. Toronto, Ryerson, 1946. 8p [BVaU LC NBSaM OTP

RECENT POEMS. Toronto, Ryerson, 1957. 12p

TWENTY-FOUR POEMS. London, Poets' and Painters' Press, 1958. 31p

**Macdonald, James Edward Hervey, 1874–1932**

VILLAGE & FIELDS. A Few Country Poems. Thornhill, Ont., Woodchuck Press, 1933. 13p [OTP

MY HIGH HORSE. A Mountain Memory. Thornhill, Woodchuck Press, [193–?]. 6p [BVaU OTP

WEST BY EAST AND OTHER POEMS. Toronto, Ryerson, 1933. 37p [BVaU LC NBFU OTP QMM

A WORD TO US ALL. Being a Message for Canadians. ... Toronto, Ryerson, 1945. 8p [NBFU OTP

**MacDonald, Jane Elizabeth Gostwycke (Roberts), 1864–1922**

DREAM VERSES, AND OTHERS. Toronto, Copp Clark, 1906. 122p [BVaU LC NBFU OTUV

POEMS. Fredericton, Author, 1885. 16p [BVaU NBFU OOP

**Macdonald, John James, 1849–**

AN IDEAL COURTSHIP. By James MacRae [pseud]. Toronto, Ryerson, 1923. 43p [BM OKQ

POEMS. Written by John J. Macdonald, a Native of County Glengarry. N.p., [1877?]. 64p [QMSS

**Macdonald, M.C.**

NO TAX ON THE PERICRANIUM. Toronto, Smithers & Bonelli, 1938. 48p [OLU

**McDonald, Ruth M. (Gulley), 1912–**

PRAIRIE SILHOUETTES. A Chap-Book of Verse. Edmonton, Author, 1960. 12p

**MacDonald, Robert Gear, 1874–1943**

FROM THE ISLE OF AVALON. London, Morland, 1908. 53p [BM

**MacDonald, Wilson Pugsley, 1880–1967**

ARMAND DUSSAULT, AND OTHER POEMS. Buffalo, Broadway Press, 1946. 46p 4th ed. [First ed. published in Toronto in 1933 with title: PAUL MARCHAND AND OTHER POEMS, *q.v.* Second ed. rev. and third ed. pub. in Toronto by S.J.R. Saunders, 1935, 1940, with title QUINTRAINS OF "CALLANDER" AND OTHER POEMS, *q.v.* 5th and 6th printings, 1948 and 1958, had title: ARMAND DUSSAULT. ...] [BM BVaU NBFU OKQ QMG

CAW-CAW BALLADS. Toronto, MacDonald, 1930. 44p [Also: Buffalo, N.Y., Broadway Press, 1958 (8th printing). 47p] [BVaU LC NBFU OKQ

COMBER COVE. Toronto, Saunders, 1937. 91p [BVaU LC NBFU OTP

A FLAGON OF BEAUTY. Toronto, Pine Tree Pub. Co., 1931. 217p [Also: Buffalo, N.Y., Broadway Press, 1958 (6th printing). 233p] [BM BVaU LC NBFU OTP

THE GIRL BEHIND THE MAN BEHIND THE GUN. [Verses.] Victoria, Lane & Son, [1915]. 1p [BM BViPA

GREATER POEMS OF THE BIBLE. Metrical Versions, Biblical Forms, and Original Poems. Toronto, Macmillan, 1943. 277p [BVaU NBFU OKQ

THE LYRIC YEAR. Poems and Pen-work by ——. Toronto, Ryerson, 1952. 53p [BVaU NBFU OTP

THE MIRACLE SONGS OF JESUS. Toronto, Author, 1921. 12p [Not the same book as the following title.] [BVa NBFU OONL QMG

THE MIRACLE SONGS OF JESUS. Toronto, Ryerson, 1921. 26p [BM BVaU LC NBFU OTP QMBM

AN ODE ON THE DIAMOND JUBILEE OF CONFEDERATION. Toronto, Warwick, [1927]. 14p [BVaU NBFU OTP

OLD SAMUEL CASHSWIGGER. Willowdale, Ont., Author, 1958. 3p

OUT OF THE WILDERNESS. Ottawa, Graphic, 1926. 209p [9th printing: Toronto, Ryerson, 1957.] [BVaU LC NBFU

PAUL MARCHAND, AND OTHER POEMS. Toronto, Pine Tree Pub. Co., 1933. 46p BVaU LC NBFU OKQ

PUGWASH. Toronto, Pine Tree Pub. Co., 1957. 15p

QUINTRAINS OF "CALLANDER" AND OTHER POEMS. Toronto, Saunders, 1935. 46p [Includes PAUL MARCHAND, first pub. in 1933.] [BVaU NBFU

SONG OF THE PRAIRIE LAND, AND OTHER POEMS. Toronto, McClelland, 1918. 144p [Same title: Toronto, Ryerson, [1923]. 155p] [BM BVaU LC NBFU OKQ

THE SONG OF THE UNDERTOW AND OTHER POEMS. Toronto, Saunders, 1935. 175p [Also: Buffalo, Broadway Press, 1935. 175p] [BVaU LC NBFU OTP

**McDonnell, William, 1814–1900**

CLEOPA. Lindsay, "Watchman," [18—?]. 17p [OTP

FATHER AMBROSE. Lindsay, "Watchman," [18—?]. 12p [OTUV

MANITA. A Poem. ... Being an Indian Legend of Sturgeon Point, Ontario. ... [Lindsay?], [18—?]. 29p [BVaU OTP

**McDougald, Annie (Bethune)**

CANADA'S CORONATION CAVALCADE, 1910–1937. Westmount, Que., Author, 1937. 27p [QMBM

SONGS OF OUR MAPLE SAPLINGS. Toronto, Musson, 1917. 13p [BM NBFU OTP QMSS

**Macdougall, Beatrice**

LIFT UP YOUR HEARTS. Montreal, Author, 1931. 47p [OTP

**McDougall, Joseph Easton, 1901–**

BLIND FIDDLER. Toronto, Ryerson, 1936. 17p [NBSaM OTU QMM

IF YOU KNOW WHAT I MEAN. Toronto, Macmillan, 1929. 91p [BVaU LC OTU

**McDougall, Margaret (Dixon), 1826–1898**

VERSES AND RHYMES BY THE WAY. By Nora Pembroke [pseud]. Pembroke, Mitchell, 1880. 180p [BVaU OTP QMM

**McElheran, Irene Beatrice (Brock), 1879–1955**

MESSAGES. Toronto, Nelson, 1932. 12p [OONL

**McElhinney, Mark Gamble, 1867–**

MORNING IN THE MARSH. Poems for Lovers of the Great Outdoors. Ottawa, Graphic, 1927. 61p [BVaU NBFU OTP QMM

**McEown, Frank**

VANCOUVER. Words and Melody. Vancouver, 1925. 4p [Adelphi cat. 45

**McEvoy, Bernard, 1842–1932**

AWAY FROM NEWSPAPERDOM, AND OTHER POEMS. Toronto, Morang, 1897. 144p [BM BVaU NBFU OTP QMSS

ELVIRA AND FERNANDO, AND OTHER SELECTIONS. Toronto, Oxford U. Press, 1927. 150p [BVaU NBFU OKQ

THE FEAST OF THE DEAD. Toronto, Brown-Searle, 1899. 8p [BVaU NBFU OTP

THE RHYME OF THE STREET CAR. Vancouver, Author, 1926. 7p [BVaU

VERSES FOR MY FRIENDS. Vancouver, Cowan Brookhouse, 1923. 209p [Reprints most of the verses in AWAY FROM NEWSPAPERDOM.] [BM BVaU LC OTP

**McFadden, Mrs. Isobel**

LIGHT UPON THE HILLS. Toronto, Author, 1948. 26p [Brown U BVaU OTUV

REWARD AND OTHER POEMS. Toronto, Ryerson, 1939. 8p [BVaU NBSaM OTP

**Macfarlane, John, 1857–1914**

THE CORONATION ODE. 1902. [MOR'12

THE HARP OF THE SCOTTISH COVENANT. Poems, Songs and Ballads. Ed. by ——. Paisley, 1895. 341p [BM OTU QMM

HEATHER AND HAREBELL. Songs and Lyrics. Montreal, Drysdale, 1891. 62p [BVaU OTP QMSS

SONGS OF THE THISTLE AND MAPLE. Toronto, Briggs, 1913. 103p [BM BVaU OTP QMM

WITHIN THE NIGHT, AND OTHER LYRICS. Toronto, Hart, 1892. [CCJ

**Macfie, Archibald**

THE FARMER AND HIS SON. A Dialogue. Chatham, Planet Print., 1888. 28p [OTP

**McGaffey, Ernest, 1861–**

WAR LYRICS FROM BRITISH COLUMBIA. ... In Aid of the Red Cross Society. [Victoria?], 1915. 8p [BVaU NSWA OPAL QMU

**McGee, Mrs. Rosa Bateman**

SONGS FOR SIGHS. ... Peterborough, Dawe's Print., [194–?]. 22p [Brown U

**McGee, Thomas D'Arcy, 1825–1868**

CANADIAN BALLADS, AND OCCASIONAL VERSES. Montreal, Lovell, 1858. 124p [BM BVaU LC NBFU OTP QMSS

THE POEMS OF THOMAS D'ARCY MCGEE. With copious notes ... and biographical sketch by Mrs. J. Sadlier. New York, Sadlier & Co., 1869. 612p [BM BVaU LC NSHD OTP QMSS

**MacGeorge, David, 1845–**

BUBBLES FROM THE BOILER ROOM. Galt, Reformer Press, 1910. 197p [BVaU OTU

ORIGINAL POEMS. Galt, Reformer Press, 1904. 145p [BM BVaU OTP QMBM

**MacGeorge, Rev. Robert Jackson, 1811?–1884**

THE CANADIAN CHRISTIAN OFFERING. Ed. by ——. Toronto, Trinity Church Office, 1848. 102p [NSHD OTP QMM

**McGillicuddy, Owen Ernest, 1887–1954**

THE LITTLE MARSHAL AND OTHER POEMS. Toronto, Goodchild, 1918. 48p [BVaU OTP QMSS

**MacGowan, James Alexander**

MAPLE UNDERWOOD, RUDELY CUT BY A YOUTHFUL BEAVER. A Collection of Infant Verse. Toronto, Hunter Rose, 1884. 61p [Brown U

**MacGregor, R. Aldine**

PATRICIA HERALD VERSE. Sioux Lookout, Ont., Patricia Herald, n.d. [c1927]. 17p [OTU

**Machar, Agnes Maule, 1837–1927**

"THE CLIFF" TO "THE ISLANDS". ... Gananoque, 1891. 9p [NSHD

EASTER POEMS: Easter Lilies, by Agnes Maule Machar; An Easter Poem, by Mrs. L.C. Whiton. Boston, Lothrop, 1889. 11p [LC

LAYS OF THE "TRUE NORTH," AND OTHER CANADIAN POEMS. London, Elliot Stock, 1899. 243p [2nd and enl. ed.: London, Elliot Stock, 1902. 260p] [BM BVaU LC NBFU OTP QMM

THE THOUSAND ISLANDS. Toronto, Ryerson, 1935. 16p [A posthumous pub.] [BVaU NBSaM OTP

**MacInnes, Thomas Robert Edward, 1867–1951**

COMPLETE POEMS OF TOM MACINNES. Toronto, Ryerson, 1923. 298p [BM BVaU NSHD OTP

THE FOOL OF JOY. Toronto, McClelland, 1918. 83p [BM BVaU NBFU OTP

FOR THE CROWNING OF THE KING, JUNE 26TH, 1902. An Ode. N.p., [1902]. 10p [BViPA OTP

HIGH LOW ALONG. A Didactic Poem. Vancouver, Clarke & Stuart, 1934. 68p [BVaU LC NBFU OKQ

IN AMBER LANDS. Poems. New York, Broadway Pub., 1910. 202p [BVaU LC NBFU OKQ

IN THE OLD OF MY AGE. A New Book of Rhymes. Toronto, Ryerson, 1947. 55p [BVaU LC MWU NSHD OTP QMBM

LONESOME BAR, A ROMANCE OF THE LOST, AND OTHER POEMS. Montreal, Desbarats, 1909. 205p [2nd ed. of A ROMANCE OF THE LOST, *q.v.*] [BVaU NSHD OKQ

RHYMES OF A ROUNDER. New York, Broadway Pub., 1913. 79p [Same title: Vancouver, Sasamat Pub. Co., 1935. 136p] [BVaU LC NBFU OTP

A ROMANCE OF THE LOST. Montreal, Desbarats, 1908. 175p [BM BVaU NSHD OTP

ROUNDABOUT RHYMES. ... A Foreword by Charles G.D. Roberts. Toronto, Ryerson, 1923. 80p [BM BVaU NBFU OTP

**McInnis, Edgar Wardell, 1899–**

BYRON. [Newdigate Prize Poem, 1925.] Oxford, Blackwell, 1925. 15p [NBFU OKQ

POEMS WRITTEN AT "THE FRONT." Charlottetown, Irwin, 1918. 17p [BM NBFU OTP

THE ROAD TO ARRAS. Charlottetown, Irwin, 1920. 31p [NBFU

**MacIntosh, Claire (Harris), 1882–**

ATTUNE WITH SPRING IN ACADIE. New York, Putnam, 1931. 106p [BM LC NSHD OTP

PHANTOM PIRATES. Halifax, Imperial Pub. Co., 1941. 47p [LC NBFU OTP

THE SPIRIT OF THE BLUENOSE, AND OTHER POEMS. Halifax, Imperial Press, 1951. 43p

**McIntosh, Duncan**

THE TRAVELLER'S COMPANION. [Glasgow, Pickering & Inglis], 1924. 342p [BVaU NBFU OTP QMU

VERSES FROM MY DIARY. ... Glasgow, McIntyre, 1907. 160p [OLU

**McIntyre, James, 1827–1906**

MUSINGS ON THE BANKS OF CANADIAN THAMES. Including Poems on Local, Canadian and British Subjects, and Lines on the Great Poets of England, Ireland, Scotland and America, with a Glance at the Wars in Victoria's Reign. Ingersoll, Ont., Rowland, 1884. 128p [BVaU OTP QMM

POEMS OF JAMES MCINTYRE. ... Ingersoll, Ont., Chronicle, 1889. 198p [BVaU LC OTP QMM

**MacIntyre, John Horton, 1863–**

ACORNS AND AGATES. By Mack [pseud]. London, Ont., 1931. 57p [OOP

LOWLY LIVES, WITH LOFTY LONGINGS AND OTHER POEMS. London, Ont., Hunter, 1935. 165p [BVaU OLU

FOREGLEAMS OF THE DAWNING. By Mack [pseud]. London, Ont., Author, 1940. 73p [Brown U

MAPLE LEAVES AND SPRIGS O' HEATHER. By Mack [pseud]. Toronto, Ryerson, 1925. 170p [BVaU OTP QMM

ODES AT EVENTIDE. London, Ont., Author, 1939. 149p [AEU OL

**MacIver, Iver Donald, 1910–**

THE VACANT HOUSE AND OTHER VERSE. Wolfville, N.S., Davidson, 1937. 16p [NSHD OKQ

**Mackay, Angus, 1865–1923**

BY TRENCH AND TRAIL IN SONG AND STORY. By Angus Mackay (Oscar Dhu). ... Seattle and Vancouver, Mackay Print., 1918. 144p [BViPA LC

DONALD MORRISON, THE CANADIAN OUTLAW. A Tale of the Scottish Pioneers. By Oscar Dhu [pseud]. N.p., 1892. 118p [AEU NSWA OTP QMU

**MacKay, Isabel Ecclestone (Macpherson), 1875–1928**

BETWEEN THE LIGHTS. Toronto, Briggs, 1904. 65p [BM BVaU NBFU OTP

THE COMPLETE POEMS OF ISABEL ECCLESTONE MACKAY. Toronto, McClelland, 1930. 345p [BM BVaU LC NBFU OTP

FIRES OF DRIFTWOOD. Toronto, McClelland, 1922. 139p [BM BVaU NBFU OTP

PANSIES FOR THOUGHTS. N.p., n.d. 16p [BVaU

THE SHINING SHIP AND OTHER VERSE FOR CHILDREN. Toronto, McClelland, 1918. 82p [New and enl. ed.: Toronto, McClelland, 1929. 174p] [BVaU NBFU OTP

**Mackay, J.**

QUEBEC HILL; or, Canadian Scenery. A Poem in Two Parts. London, Blackader, 1797. 34p [BM LC OTP

**Mackay, Mrs. Jean C.**

THE REDMAN'S SHRINE. Toronto, Crucible Press, 1941. 32p [LC

**McKay, John George, 1886–1923**

APRES LA GUERRE. Ed., with a Memoir ... by Neilson Campbell Hannay. ... Boston, Fort Hill Press, 1925. 100p [BM BVaU LC NSHD OTUV QMM

**MacKay, Louis Alexander, 1901–**

THE ILL-TEMPERED LOVER, AND OTHER POEMS. Toronto, Macmillan, 1948. 72p [BVaU LC NBFU OTP QMM

VIPER'S BUGLOSS. By John Smalacombe [pseud]. Toronto, Ryerson, 1938. 7p [BVa NBSaM OKQ QMM

**McKellar, Duncan**

POEMS. Toronto, Allen, 1922. 63p [NBFU OKQ

**MacKenzie, D.E.**

RHYMES FROM THE ROCKS. Halifax, Mission Press, 1946. 37p [NBSaM

**McKenzie, Ethel (O'Neil)**

SECRET SNOW. Philadelphia, Swain, 1932. 178p [LC NBFU OOP QMM

**Mackenzie, George Allan**

"IN THAT NEW WORLD WHICH IS THE OLD." Poems of the New Life. Toronto, Musson, [1914?]. 95p [BVaU NBFU OKQ

MALCOLM. A Story of the Day-Spring. Toronto, Rowsell & Hutchison, 1887. 39p [AEU LC OTP

MALCOLM AND OTHER POEMS. Toronto, Haynes Press, 1912. 41p [BVaU OTUV QMSS

SIX LYRICS OF THE HIGHER LIFE. Toronto, [Haynes?], 1913. 6p [BVaU OTU

SONG OFFERINGS FROM INDIA. Selections from the Poems of Rabindranath Tagore of Bengal, rendered into English. Toronto, Author, 1913. 6p [NBFU OTU

SONGS IN THE NIGHT WATCHES. N.p., 1926. 13p [BViP NSWA QMU

SONGS OF THE INNER LIFE. [Anon] Toronto, Author, 1900. 24p [NSWA OTP

VIA CRUCIS. N.p., 1924. 15p [QMU

**Mackenzie, James Bovell, 1851–1919**

ALFRED THE GREAT AND OTHER POEMS. Toronto, Imrie, 1902. 95p [BVaU NBFU OTP

CLIVE, BARON PLASSEY. A Lay of Empire; and Other Poems. Toronto, Rous & Mann, 1912. 63p [BVaU OTP

**McKenzie, Marjorie**

GRAPHITE AND GALENA. Kingston, Jackson Press, 1927. 27p [BVaU

**McKenzie, Rev. William Patrick, 1861–1942**

THE AULD FOWK. Some Verses in Scots. Toronto, Ryerson, 1930. 16p [BVaU NBFU OTP

BITS O' VERSE IN SCOTS. Toronto, Ryerson, 1927. 16p [BVaU NBFU OKQ

FIELDS OF BLOOM. Cambridge, Mass., Cambridge Tribune, 1930. 44p [BVaU LC

FOWLS O' THE AIR AND OTHER VERSES IN SCOTS. Toronto, Ryerson, 1928. 16p [BVaU NBSaM OKQ

HEARTSEASE HYMNS, AND OTHER VERSES. Toronto, Tyrrell, 1896. 44p [CCJ lists an earlier ed.: Toronto, 1895. 44p; later editions: Cambridge, 1901. 53p; Chicago, 1938. 44p] [BM BVaU LC NSHD OTP QMM

PRELUDE POEMS FOR THE NEW DAY. By W.P.M. Chicago, Associated Authors, 1942. 63p [LC OKQ

A SONG OF TRUST AND OTHER THOUGHTS IN VERSE. Toronto, Hart, 1887. 42p [LC

SONGS OF THE HUMAN. Toronto, Hart, 1892. 132p [BVaU OTP

THE SOWER, AND OTHER POEMS. Cambridge, Mass., Author, 1903. 56p [Later ed.: Cambridge, Tribune Press, 1928. 44p] [LC OKQ

VOICES AND UNDERTONES IN SONG AND POEM. Toronto, Hart, 1889. 156p [BVaU LC OOC QMM

**Mackenzie, William Roy, 1882–1957**

BALLADS AND SEA SONGS FROM NOVA SCOTIA. Ed. by ——. Cambridge, Mass., Harvard U. Press, 1928. 421p [AEU NBFU OLU

THE QUEST OF THE BALLAD. Princeton, N.J., Princeton U. Press, 1919. 247p [BVi NBFU OTP QMG

**MacKeracher, Rev. William Mackay, 1871–1913**

CANADA, MY LAND, AND OTHER COMPOSITIONS IN VERSE. Toronto, Briggs, 1908. 66p [BM BVaU NBFU OTP

JEAN BATEESE AT THE CARNIVAL. Toronto, Briggs, 1909. 15p [BM OTP

SONGS OF A SOPHOMORE. By W.M.M. Montreal, 1892. 24p [CCJ

SONNETS AND OTHER VERSE. Toronto, Briggs, 1909. 80p [BM NBFU OTP QMM

VACATION VERSE. By W.M.M. Montreal, Witness, 1891. 23p [OTU

VERSES OF FEELING AND FANCY. Montreal, Drysdale, 1890. 96p [BVaU OTP QMBM

**McKibbin, Isabel Reid**

CHRISTMAS CRACKERS, AND OTHER RHYMES. London, Stockwell, 1933. 46p [BM

**Mackie, Mrs. Delia Elizabeth**

MY SHIPS COME A-SAILING. Ottawa, Legge Press, 1954. 26p

**McKillop, Archibald**

THE FLOOD OF DEATH; or, The Malt that Lay in the House that Jack Built. Toronto, Dudley & Burns, 1875. 24p [OTP

TEMPERANCE ODES, AND MISCELLANEOUS POEMS. Quebec, Thomson, 1860. 96p [BVaU OTP

**McKinnell, Mrs. George**

COUCHICHING CAROLS. [Anon] Orillia, 1889. 51p [Brown U BVaU OTUV

**MacKinnon, Cecilia**

FOUNTAINS OF ORDUNNA. Boston, Brimmer Press. 1923. 72p [AEU NBSaM OOP

**MacKinnon, Rev. Murdoch Charles, 1889–1956**

CHRIST IN KHAKI AND SACRED SONG. [Perth, Ont., Author, 1930?] [8]p [OTUV

FROM THE WINEPRESS. Toronto, Ryerson, 1933. 20p [BVaU NBSaM OTP

**MacKinnon, Mrs. Una H. Morris**

TIDES OF THE MISSIQUASH. ... Halifax, Weeks Print. Co., [192–?]. 32p [NSHD

**McKinnon, Rev. William Charles, –1862**

BATTLE OF THE NILE. A Poem in Four Cantos. ... [Contains also "The Steep of Fame," a poem; its sequel "Life"; and "An Elegy to the shade of Thomas Campbell. ..."] Sydney, N.S., Kuhn, 1844. 75p [NSHD

**MacKnight, Samuel John**

ATAVAR OF PEACE AND OTHER POEMS. Boston, Shawmut Steam Print., 1896. 16p [NSHD

LYRIC AND OTHER POEMS. Halifax, Bowes, 1892. 28p [BVaU NSHD OTP QMBM

**MacLachlan, Alan**

RHYMES OF A MONTREALER. Montreal, Author, 1942. 60p [NBFU OTU QMU

**McLachlan, Alexander, 1818–1896**

THE EMIGRANT, AND OTHER POEMS. Toronto, Rollo & Adam, 1861. 236p [BM BVaU NBFU OTP

LYRICS. Toronto, Armour, 1858. 151p [BVaU MWU NBFU OTP QMBM

POEMS. [Chiefly in the Scottish Dialect.] Toronto, Geikie, 1856. 192p [BVaU NBFU OTP

POEMS AND SONGS. Toronto, Hunter Rose, 1874. 223p [BM BVaU LC MWU NBFU OTP QMSS

THE POETICAL WORKS OF ALEXANDER MCLACHLAN. ... Toronto, Briggs, 1900. 424p [BVaU NBFU OTP

THE SPIRIT OF LOVE, AND OTHER POEMS. Toronto, Cleland, 1846. 36p [OTP

**McLachlan, James**

INHUMANITY. A Poem in Three Parts. Montreal, Lovell, 1868. 40p [NSHD OTP QMSS

**McLaren, Mrs. Floris Clark, 1904–**

FROZEN FIRE. Toronto, Macmillan, 1937. 39p [BVaU NBFU OTU QMM

**MacLaren, Ian**

A RESENTMENT IN RELIEF. Ilfracombe, Devon, Stockwell, 1957. 31p

**McLaughlin, Angus**

POEMS THAT WILL INTEREST EVERYBODY. N.p., Author, 1912. 30p [NSWA OONL

SELECTED POEMS. N.p., n.d. 78p [BVaU OONL QMSS

TITANIC. N.p., Author, [1912?]. 44p [QMU

**McLean, Adele Peters**

POEMS, LEGENDS AND LETTERS. Toronto, Musson, [19—?]. 128p [BM BVaU OTP QMBM

**MacLean, Alexander Henry, 1916–**

POEMS. ["ca 1939"] [Rhod p947

**Maclean, B.C.**

SONNETS. Montreal, 1900. 8p [OTP QMSS

**MacLean, Rev. D.**

POEMS AND HYMNS. Charlottetown, Haszard & Moore, 1902. 172p [QMM

**MacLean, Kate (Seymour)**

ADVENT DAYS AND POEMS OF REMEMBRANCE. Kingston, Jackson Press, 1902. 28p [Brown U BVaU

THE COMING OF THE PRINCESS, AND OTHER POEMS. Toronto, Hunter Rose, 1881. 175p [BVaU OTP QMM

FROM THE BALCONY, AND OTHER POEMS. Kingston, Jackson Press, 1904. 32p [Brown U OLU

**McLeish, John Alexander Buchanan, 1892–**

NOT WITHOUT BEAUTY. Montreal, Lovell, 1940. 7p [Same title: Toronto, Ryerson, 1948. 8p] [BVaU MWU NBFU OTP

ODE IN A WINTER EVENING, AND OTHER POEMS. Montreal, Lovell, 1938. 40p [OTU QMM

**McLennan, William, 1856–1904**

SONGS OF OLD CANADA. Trans. by ——. Montreal, Dawson, 1886. 83p [BM BVaU LC NSHD OKQ

**MacLeod, Audrey**

FAGGOTS FOR THE FIRE. Toronto, Nelson, 1933. 114p [OKQ

**MacLeod, Calum Iain Nicholson, 1913–**

AN t-EILTHIREACH. Original Gaelic Poems and Melodies. Sydney, N.S., Author, 1952. 43p

**McLeod, Carroll W.**

DAT H'AMPIRE H'AIR TRAIN PLAN. Toronto, Heaton Print., 1943. 85p [BVa LC OTP QMM

THE PATH OF THE "PROP." Quebec, Le Soleil, 1935. 61p [OWtL QMG

**MacLeod, Elizabeth Susan (MacQueen), 1842–1939**

CAROLS OF CANADA. ... Charlottetown, Coombs, 1893. 198p [2nd ed., 1899. 230p] [BVaU LC NBFU OTP

FOR THE FLAG; or, Lays and Incidents of the South African War. Charlottetown, Irwin, 1901. 185p [BM BVa OTP

**MacLeod, Euphemia**

MY ROSE AND OTHER POEMS. Boston, The Four Seas Co., 1919. 100p [BVi LC NSHPL OONL

SEANCES WITH CARLYLE. Boston, The Four Seas Co., 1919. 88p [LC NSHPL OH

**MacLeod, Margaret (Arnett), 1877–1966**

SONGS OF OLD MANITOBA. With Airs, French and English Words, and Introductions. Toronto, Ryerson, 1959. x + 93p

**McMartin, L.E.**

A BOOK OF VERSES, GAY AND SOMBRE. By Pendragon [pseud]. Toronto, Sovereign Press, 1936. 66p [BVaU OTL

**McMaster, Bryce**

COLLECTED POEMS. Oxford, Blackwell, 1947. 122p [BM LC

SHORT POEMS. By Clansman [pseud]. London, Kegan Paul, 1908. 47p [BM

THE STRANGER, AND OTHER POEMS. London, Arnold, 1923. 79p [BM OKQ

A TRIBUTE. [In verse]. By Clansman [pseud]. 1911. [BM

**McMaster University, Members and Associates of**

THE TOWER. An Anthology of Poems. [A continuing publication.] Hamilton, McMaster University, 1952–.

**McMaster University Monthly**

POEMS SELECTED FROM "THE McMASTER UNIVERSITY MONTHLY." Toronto, Briggs, 1894. 76p [OKQ

**MacMechan, Archibald McKellar, 1862–1933**

LATE HARVEST. Toronto, Ryerson, 1934. 54p [BVaU NSHD OKQ QMM

THREE SEA SONGS. (Nova Scotia Chapbook). Halifax, Marshall, 1919. 10p [BVaU NBFU OKQ

**McMeekan, John Murray**
A RHYME OF ROUYN. Rouyn, Que., Author, 1941. [CC

**Macmillan, Lachlan, 1878–**
"VERSES FROM A SURGEON'S DIARY." Vancouver, Author, 1956. 2v

**McMillan, Sophia Louise**
MANITOBA'S VISION AND OTHER POEMS. [Winnipeg?], n.d. 58p [MWP OONL

**Macmurray, Rev. Thomas James, 1852–**
THE LEGEND OF DELAWARE VALLEY AND OTHER POEMS. Toronto, Briggs, 1887. 132p [BVaU NSHD OTU

**McMurray, William**
[TWO POEMS: LABRADOR; ADVICE TO A MARRIED LADY.] Quebec, Moore, 1790. 16p [Title supplied by Tremaine. No copy known to exist now.] [Tremaine Cdn Imprints

**McNab, B.A.**
CONFISCATION. Being the Tale of a "Kicker" and a Calf. [Anon] Malagash, N.S., Author, 1920. 4p [NSWA

**McNair, Rev. John**
THE SONGS OF HEBREW HISTORY. [N.p., 1902?] 94p [NSWA OTU

**McNaughton, Harry P.**
SHADOW LIGHTS OF SHAMSHUIPO. A Rhyming Picture of the Yesteryears. Winnipeg, Author, 1944. 74p [OONL

**Macnaughton, Isabel Christie**
WOOD FIRES. New Ed., containing Three Additional Poems, also a Fantasy. Oliver, B.C., Chronicle, 1948. 34p [First pub. in 1942.] [BVaU OTUV

**MacNeill, A.D., –1895?**
WOODLANDS AND OTHER RHYMES. Orangedale, N.S., Author, [1898?]. 40p [NSHD OKQ

**McNeill, Kate**
POEMS. Vancouver, Evans & Hastings, 1918. 128p [BM BVaU NBFU OOP

**McNeilly, Jean**
POEMS FROM THE PRAIRIES. London, Stockwell, 1939. 24p [BM BViPA

**McNichol, Vera Luella (Ernst), 1910–**
BIBLE STORIES IN VERSE. [Kitchener, Dixon Press, 1957.] 2v
SUNSHINE AND AFTERGLOW. [Toronto, Livingstone Press, 1956.] 96p

**MacNiven, Mrs. C., 1823–1865**

AILEEN. A Poem. Ingersoll, 1865. 52p [BibC CCJ

**MacNiven, Hope**

THE BARD OF CLUTHA AND OTHER POEMS. Ingersoll, Gurnett, 1875. 82p [BVaU OTP QMBM

**Macphail, Andrew, 1864–1938**

THE BOOK OF SORROW. Ed. by ——. London, Oxford U. Press, 1916. 500p [BM BVaU LC NSHD OTU QMM

**Macpherson, (Jean) Jay, 1931–**

THE BOATMAN. Toronto, Oxford U. Press, 1957. x + 70p

A DRY LIGHT & THE DARK AIR. Toronto, Hawkshead Press, 1959. 4p

NINETEEN POEMS. Deya, Mallorca, Spain, Robert Graves Seizin Press, 1952. 9p

O EARTH RETURN. Toronto, 1954. 9p (Emblem Books)

**McPherson, John, 1817–1845**

POEMS, DESCRIPTIVE AND MORAL. With an introductory memoir by J.S. Thompson. Halifax, Chamberlain, 1862. 46 + 252p [BVaU NBFU OTP

THE PRAISE OF WATER. A Prize Poem. Halifax, Croskill, 1843. 16p [NSHP

**McQuarrie, Nora**

RAINBOW OF VERSE. Powell River, B.C., Town Crier, 1945. 74p [UTQ'46

**MacQueen, Thomas, 1803–1861**

THE EXILE. A Poem. Glasgow, Duncan, 1836. 166p [BM OTP

MY GLOAMING AMUSEMENTS. A Variety of Poems on Several Serious and Entertaining Subjects. Beith, Scotland, 1831. [BM

THE MOORLAND MINSTREL. Glasgow, Muir Gowans & Co., 1841. 214p 2nd ed. [1st ed. in 1840] [BM OLU

**McRobbie, Kenneth Alan, 1929–**

EYES WITHOUT A FACE. Toronto, Gallery Editions, 1960. 58p

**Magaret, Helene**

THE TRUMPETING CRANE. New York, Farrar & Rinehart, 1934. 156p [NBFU

**Main, Robert, 1873–1957**

"HAPPY HOURS" FOR BOYS AND GIRLS. Nelson, B.C., Daily News, 1948. 23p [BVaU

POEMS. Toronto, Heaton, 1944. 57p [BVaU OTU

**Mair, Charles, 1838–1927**

DREAMLAND AND OTHER POEMS. Montreal, Dawson, 1868. 151p [BM BVaU LC NBFU OOC QMBM

TECUMSEH, A DRAMA (2nd ed.) AND CANADIAN POEMS. Toronto, Briggs, 1901. 276p [BM BVaU OTP QMM

**Maitland, Mary A. (Davidson), 1839–1919**
AUTUMN LEAVES. Toronto, Briggs, 1907. 16p [BM OTUV
GOD SPEED THE TRUE. A Little Volume of Cheerful Canadian Verse. Toronto, Hunter Rose, 1919. 87p [Brown U

**Major, J.C.**
THE RED RIVER EXPEDITION. Winnipeg, P.G. Laurie 'News Letter Office,' 1870. 28p [Reprinted in Bibliog. Soc. of Canada's Facsimile Series, no. 3, Toronto, 1953.] [AEU NSHPL OKQ QQLA

**Major, Marie Austen, 1903–**
ROSES WITH THE THRONG. Manchester, Granite State Press, 1937. 90p [LC

**Mandel, Elias Wolf, 1922–**
FUSELI POEMS. Toronto, Contact Press, 1960. 66p
TRIO. First Poems. By Gael Turnbull, Phyllis Webb and E.W. Mandel. Toronto, Contact Press, 1954. 89p

**Manners, Robert Rutland**
PASCO, A CUBAN TALE, AND OTHER POEMS. With an essay on music appended. Cambridge, Mass., Riverside Press, 1877. 170p [Rev. ed. pub. under title: CUBA, AND OTHER VERSE. Toronto, Briggs, 1898. 155p] [BM BVaU OTUV QMBM

**Manning, Frederick Charles, 1895–1917**
POEMS. N.p., priv. print., [1920?]. 35p [BVaU NSHD OTP

**Manning, James Harold, 1897–1924**
COURCELETTE, AND OTHER POEMS. Saint John, McMillan, 1925. 106p [BVaU NBFU OTU QMM

**Marcus, Rev. Moses**
THE TEAR OF SYMPATHY, OR POETIC EFFUSIONS. Hallowell, Ont., Wilson, 1834. 120p [Brown U

**Marham, Rose Etheridge**
FALLEN ROSE LEAVES, GATHERED AND PRESSED. Toronto, Briggs, [1889?] 96p [Another ed., 1907.] [BVaU OTUV QMM

**Marquis, Thomas Guthrie, 1864–1936**
THE CATHEDRAL. A Poem. Toronto, Ryerson, 1924. 10p [NBFU OLU
THE CATHEDRAL AND OTHER POEMS. With a Foreword by Sir Charles G.D. Roberts. Toronto, Musson, 1936. 53p [BVaU NBFU OTP QMSS

**Marriott, Anne, 1913–**
CALLING ADVENTURERS! Toronto, Ryerson, 1941. 8p [BVaU NBFU OTP
SALT MARSH. Toronto, Ryerson, 1942. 16p [BVaU LC NBFU OTP QMM
SANDSTONE, AND OTHER POEMS. Toronto, Ryerson, 1945. 42p [BVaU LC MWU NBFU OTP

THE WIND OUR ENEMY. Toronto, Ryerson, 1939. 8p [BVaU NBSaM OKQ QMBM

**Mars, P.C.**

THE CALL OF TERRA NOVA. Newfoundland, 1924. 83p [Brown U BVaU

**Marsden, Rev. Joshua, 1777–1837**

AMUSEMENTS OF A MISSION; or, Poems, Moral, Religious and Descriptive, Interspersed with Anecdotes. Written during a Residence Abroad. By J.M. 2nd ed. London, Blanchard, 1818. 123p [BM OTP

THE BACKSLIDER. A Descriptive Moral Poem in Four Books. Plymouth-Dock, Johns, 1815. 64p [BM NSHD OTP

LEISURE HOURS; or, Poems, Moral, Religious & Descriptive. New York, Paul & Thomas, 1812. 160p [LC

THE MISSION. A Poem. Plymouth-Dock, Johns, 1816. 39p [BM

POEMS ON METHODISM: Embracing The Conference, or Sketches of Wesleyan Methodism. Philadelphia, Sorin & Ball, 1848. 156p [LC

**Marshall, Emily Marguerite**

IN LOVING MEMORY. Toronto, Best Print., 1938. 44p [OTP

"THE LADY OF MYSTERY" AND OTHER POEMS. Toronto, Beaver Print., [194–?]. 191p [Brown U BVaU QMU

THE LEGEND OF LOVESICK LAKE AND OTHER POEMS. Toronto, Warwick, 1925. 117p [BVaU NBFU OTU QMU

A ROMANCE OF THE MALIBU HILLS. New York, Vantage Press, 1958. 45p [NBFU

**Marshall, John George, 1786–1880**

REFLECTIONS DURING MY VISIT TO MY NATIVE PLACE. Halifax, Wesleyan Office, 1881. 22p [NSHP

**Marshall, William Edward, 1859–1923**

A BOOK OF VERSE. Bridgewater, Cragg, 1908. 126p [NSHD OTU

BROOKFIELD AND OTHER VERSE. Montreal, Lovell, 1919. 201p [BVaU NSHD OTU QMM

A LEGEND OF VENICE. Told in Rhymes. Bridgewater, Bulletin Press, 1907. 30p [NSWA

**Martin, Alfred Tobias John**

MARTIN'S ADDRESS TO MERCURY. Quebec, 1837. 7p [OTP

**Martin, George, 1822–1900**

MARGUERITE, or, The Isle of Demons; and Other Poems. Montreal, Dawson, 1887. 285p [BVaU NSHD OTP QMSS

**Martin, Martha, 1875–**

CAUGHT IN FLIGHT. Poems. New York, Vechten Waring, 1931. 103p [LC QMSS

CHAUTAUQUA GREETS YOU! New York, Gotham Press, 1940. 38p [LC QMSS

COME INTO MY GARDEN. A Collection of Flower and Tree Poems. New York, Beekman Hill Press, 1935. 61p [QMBM

NATURE LYRICS AND OTHER POEMS. Boston, Badger, 1907. 89p [LC QMM

OUT OF THE SHADOWS, AND OTHER POEMS. New York, Beekman Hill Press, 1937. 78p [LC QMSS

POEMS. With The Birth of a Poem. New York, Gotham Press, 1941. 46p [BVaU LC QMSS

POEM – ANECDOTES OF CHILD-MUSICIANS. New York, Beekman Hill Press, 1934. 50p [QMM

POEM-MINIATURES. Montreal, Guertin, 1899. 61p [BM

POETS' PILGRIMAGE. New York, Beekman Hill Press, 1938. 60p [BVaU LC NBFU OTU QMSS

THE WEED'S PHILOSOPHY AND OTHER POEMS. Montreal, 1913. 43p [BVaU NSWA QMM

**Martin, William Henry**

SONGS BY THE WAY. Toronto, Crucible Press, 1941. 30p [Brown U OTUV

**Martley, John**

SONGS OF THE CASCADES. Pt. I. By Erl Viking [pseud]. London, Cox, 1894. 192p [BM BVaU

**Marty, Aletta Elise, 1866–1929**

CREATIVE YOUNG CANADA. Collection of Verse, Drawings, and Musical Compositions, by Young Canadians from Seven to Twenty years of age. Toronto, Dent, 1928. 143p [Brown U BVaU OTUV

**Mary Francis of Jesus, Sister, 1878–**

GREY DAYS AND GOLD. By Miriam [pseud]. Victoria, Sisters of St. Ann, 1933. 149p [Brown U BViPA

**Mason, Rev. George**

LO – THE POOR INDIAN. Prize Poem. Victoria, Rose, 1875. 8p [BViPA

ODE ON THE LOSS OF THE STEAMSHIP "PACIFIC," NOVEMBER 4TH, 1875. Nanaimo, B.C., Free Press, 1875. 4p [BVaU

**Mason, Guy Montague, 1893–1954**

THE CRY OF INSURGENT YOUTH. Toronto, Ryerson, 1927. 16p [BVaU NBFU OTP

SPENDTHRIFTS. Toronto, Ryerson, 1928. 12p [BVaU NBFU OTP

**Mason, Harold Campbell, 1895–**

THREE THINGS ONLY. Toronto, Nelson, [1953?]. 75p

**Massey, Gwendolen May (Merrin), 1907–**

LEGEND AND OTHER POEMS. By Gwendolen Merrin. Toronto, Ryerson, 1944. 12p [BVaU LC NSHD OTU QMM

SYMPHONY AND OTHER POEMS. By Gwendolen M. Merrin. Toronto, Author, 1935. 15p [BVaU NBFU OTP

**Matheson, Charles Winfield, 1878–**
POETICAL WORKS. N.p., n.d. 248 leaves [NSHD

**Matheson, Daniel C.**
POEMS. Hullcar, B.C., 1909. 11p [BM

**Matheson, Duncan M.**
CHEBUCTO, AND OTHER POEMS. ... Halifax, 1917. 125p [2nd ed.: Halifax, 1919. 152p] [Brown U NSHD OTU

**Matheson, Mary Mackenzie (Nasmyth), 1885–**
AUTUMN AFFLUENCE. Toronto, Ryerson, 1960. 8p
DESTINY AND OTHER POEMS. Toronto, Ryerson, 1928. 8p [BVaU NBFU OKQ
THE FRIENDLY HEART AND OTHER POEMS. [Toronto, priv. print., 1955]. 33p
I SEEK MY WAY. Toronto, Ryerson, 1949. 26p [BVaU
JOY AND OTHER POEMS. N.p., n.d. 20p [AEU BViPA QMU
LET'S LAUGH A LITTLE. By Merry Matheson. Vancouver, Halsall Print., [1957?]. 38p
MAGIC HILL AND OTHER POEMS. Toronto, Ryerson, 1929. 18p [BVaU NBFU OTP QMM
"THE MOVING FINGER" AND OTHER POEMS. Vancouver, Clarke & Stuart, 1944. 48p [BVaU OTP
OUT OF THE DUSK. Toronto, Ryerson, 1941. 8p [BVaU LC NSHD OTP QMM
SHINING WINGS. Vancouver, Wrigley, n.d. 36p [BVaU OTUV
SMILING THROUGH. Vancouver, Wrigley, 1934. 16p [OKQ
TO A PRAIRIE ROSE AND OTHER POEMS. Vancouver, Clarke & Stuart, 1933. 28p [BVaU
THE URGE DIVINE, AND OTHER POEMS. Toronto, Ryerson, n.d. 33p [BVa
WORSHIP, AND OTHER POEMS. N.p., n.d. 21p [OKQ

**Mathieson, Hugh**
THE BACKWASH OF HELL, AND FIFTY OTHER POEMS AND SONGS. Montreal, 1928. 62p [Brown U

**Matthews, Richard F., 1832–**
POEMS. London, Ont., Dawson, 1866. 68p [BVaU NSHD OTP

**Maunsell, H. Wakefield**
THESE WALLS. Toronto, Crucible Press, 1945. 22p [BViPA OTU

**Maura, Sister (née Mary Power), 1881–1957**
BREATH OF THE SPIRIT. Toronto, Macmillan, 1937. 35p [Brown U NSHD OOP

INITIATE THE HEART. New York, Macmillan, 1946. 46p [LC
RHYME AND RHYTHM. Toronto, Ryerson, 1932. 11p [BVaU NBFU OTU QMM
RHYTHM POEMS. Toronto, Ryerson, 1944. 8p [BVaU LC NSHD OTP
THE ROSARY IN TERZA RIMA. Toronto, Dent, 1941. 30p [BVaU LC OTU QMM
A SHEAF OF SONGS BY SISTER MAURA. Lower Granville, N.S., Abanaki Press, 1948. 24p [Brown U BVaU NBFU OTU

**Mawle, William Waddy, 1902–**

RANDOM RHYME AND VARIED VERSE. Victoria, Author, 1959. 97p

**Maxwell, Lilian Mary (Beckwith), 1877–1956**

THE RIVER ST. JOHN AND ITS POETS. 2nd printing, enl. Sackville, N.B., Tribune Press, 1947. 85p [1st ed.: Fredericton, Author, 1946. 64p] [BVaU NBFU OTP QMSS

**May, Roberta E.**

SCATTERED SEEDS. Ilfracombe, Devon, Stockwell, 1952. 31p

**May, Sydney**

PRAIRIE FAIRIES AND OTHER VERSES. Calgary, Author, 1932. [CC

**Mayne, Daniel Haydn**

POEMS AND FRAGMENTS. Toronto, Coates, 1838. 126p [OTP

**Meek, Kenneth, 1908–**

A CAROL OF THANKS. Part Song for Female Voices. New York, Gray, 1946. [CC

**Mellor, Violet**

ISLAND LIGHT. From A COLLECTION OF POEMS, by ——. Toronto, Aberdeen Press, 1953. 8p

**Melville, Tom ("Scotty")**

BARBED WIRE BALLADS. Regina, School Aids Pub. Co., 1945. 61p [BVaU OTP

**Menzies, Alfred**

BEAUTY AND HUMILITY. Winnipeg, 1933. 89p [OONL

**Menzies, George, 1796?–1847**

THE POSTHUMOUS WORKS OF THE LATE GEORGE MENZIES. Being a Collection of Poems, Sonnets, &c. &c. Written at Various Times when the Author was connected with the Provincial Press. Woodstock, Ont., Douglass, 1850. 95p [OTP

**Merkel, Andrew Doane, 1884–1954**

THE ORDER OF GOOD CHEER. A Narrative Poem. Halifax, Imperial Pub. Co., 1944. 46p [Same title, with drawings ... by Robert Chambers: Lower Granville, N.S., Abanaki Press, 1946. xix + 102p] [BVaU LC NBFU OTU

TALLAHASSEE. A Ballad of Nova Scotia in the Sixties. Halifax, Imperial Pub. Co., 1945. 103p [BVaU LC NBFU OTP QMM

**Merkley, George E., 1865–1904?**

CANADIAN MELODIES AND POEMS. Toronto, Hart & Riddell, 1893. 104p [BVaU NBFU OTP QMM

**Merner, F.**

TRUE CANADIANISM. An Appeal. 4th ed., rev. and enl. N.p., n.d. 16p [AEU OPAL

**Merrill, Anne**

SONGS OF SHERBROOKE. Sherbrooke, Que., Page-Sangster, 1932. 73p [BVaU OKQ QMM

VERSE. Goffstown, N.H., Gibbs & Brown, 1941. 16p [LC

**Merrill, Helen M.**

SANDPIPERS AND OTHER POEMS. Toronto, priv. print., 1915. 7p [NBFU OTU

**Meyers, Leonard William, 1917–**

WHEN WORDS COLLIDE. San Antonio, Tex., Naylor Co., 1960. 48p

**Michie, A.R.**

LYRICS AND POEMS. ... Toronto, Briggs, 1912. 112p [BM Brown U BVaU OLU

**Middleton, Clara J. (Russell) Jackson, 1872?–1955**

GREEN FIELDS AFAR. Memories of Alberta Days. By Clara and J.E. Middleton. Toronto, Ryerson, 1947. 61p [BVaU NBFU OTP

**Middleton, Helen E.**

DRUMBEATS THROUGH YOUR DREAMS. Saint John, Author, 1945. 40p [Brown U BVaU NBFU

**Middleton, Jesse Edgar, 1872–1960**

SEA DOGS AND MEN AT ARMS. A Canadian Book of Songs. Toronto, McClelland, 1918. 104p [BM BVaU LC NBFU OTP QMM

**Mildmay, Rev. Aubrey Neville St. John, 1865–**

HORAE MEDITERRANEAE. [Selected Passages of English verse, with Greek and Latin Renderings and Some Original Poems by the Author.] London, Baxter, 1947. 71p [BM

IN THE WAITING TIME OF WAR, AND OTHER POEMS. London, Swan Sonnenschein, 1900. 39p [BM BVaU

SEA-ROOM. A Vancouver Empire Song. Toronto, Briggs, 1910. 9p [BM Brown U BVaU OTUV

**Miller, Ewart**

OVER THE WHEEL. Toronto, Author, 1940. 25p [LC OTU

**Miller, Margaret Gertrude (Lang), 1869–**
GLEANINGS ALONG THE HIGHWAYS. A Collection of Poems. Hamilton, Davis-Lisson, 1934. 349p [Brown U OLU

**Miller, P. Florence**
IN CARIBOU LAND. Intro. by E.J. Pratt. Toronto, Ryerson, 1929. 64p [BVaU OKQ QMBM

**Miller, Peter, 1920–**
MEDITATION AT NOON. Toronto, Contact Press, 1958. 101p
SONATA FOR FROG AND MAN. Toronto, Contact Press, 1959. 82p

**Miller, Roscoe R.**
ELIXIR OF MORALE. Toronto, Standard Pub., 1943. 104p [BVaU LC OTP QMM

**Milligan, James Lewis, 1876–**
THE BECKONING SKYLINE AND OTHER POEMS. Toronto, McClelland, 1920. 111p [BM BVaU NBFU OTU QMM
CHRISTMAS. Eight Poems. Toronto, Gothic Press, [1925?]. 10p [BVaU OKQ
A CLOCK IN A BASSINET. A Ballad of Love and Time. Toronto, Ryerson, 1938. 8p [BVaU OTL
SILURIA AND OTHER POEMS. Toronto, Ryerson, 1947. 24p [BVaU OTP
SONGS IN TIME'S DESPITE. London, Griffiths, 1910. 64p [BM BVaU LC OKQ
THEY SHALL RETURN AND OTHER POEMS. Toronto, Forward Pub. Co., 1943. 16p [BVaU OTP

**Milliken, Lorene Frances (Ritz)**
MANITOBA LANDSCAPE. N.p., 1954. 8p (Carillon Poetry Chap-Books)
A MORNING MOOD. Gananoque, Ont., Hilda M. Ridley, 1953. 12p (Carillon Poetry Chap-Books)
MY SOUL SINGS. N.p., 1955. 8p (Carillon Poetry Chap-Books)
PRINCESS OF AUNE. [Winnipeg, Author,] 1956. 10p (Carillon Poetry Chap-Books)
WHITE ORCHIDS. Gananoque, Ont., Hilda M. Ridley, 1952. 12p (Carillon Poetry Chap-Books)

**Mills, David, 1831–1903**
POEMS WRITTEN AT SPARE MOMENTS. Ottawa, Crain, 1901. 79p [BM Brown U OTU

**Mills, Phebe A.**
VESPER CHIMES. Halifax, Macnab, 1872. 122p [BVaU NSHD OOP

**Minto, Charles**
THE HOWES O' BUCHAN, AND FAR AWA', WITH OTHER POEMS. Montreal, priv. print., 1896. 173p [BM OTP QMSS

**Mitchell, John, 1882–1951**

THE WATER-DRINKER. By Patrick Slater [pseud]. Toronto, Allen, 1937. 148p [BVaU OTP

**Mitchell, John Hanlon, 1897–1953**

OTHER SONGS. By John Hanlon [pseud]. Toronto, Ryerson, 1927. 32p [BVaU NBSaM OTP QMM

SONGS. By John Hanlon [pseud]. Toronto, Ryerson, 1927. 24p [BVaU LC NBFU OTU QMM

**Mitchell, Ronald Elwy**

DAN OWEN AND THE ANGEL JOE. ... New York, Harper, 1948. 250p [BM LC

DEEP WATERS. London, Gollancz, 1937. 286p [BM LC

**Mocket, John**

A FEW THOUGHTS JOTTED DOWN IN RHYME TO WHILE AWAY A LITTLE TIME. N.p., n.d. [Amtmann cat. 250

**Moffatt, Gertrude (MacGregor), 1884–1923**

A BOOK OF VERSES. With an intro. by Bernard K. Sandwell. Toronto, Macmillan, 1924. 139p [Reprinted: Toronto, Book Society of Can., 1950. 139p] [BVaU NSHD OTP

**Moffatt, Warneford**

NEW CANADIAN POEMS. Composed at Various Times. ... Toronto, Briggs, 1914. 105p [Brown U

AN ODE ON THE CANADIAN SOLDIERS WHO FELL NEAR YPRES, WITH OTHER POEMS. London, Simpkin, 1916. 31p [BVaU OTU

**Molesworth, Eva Sarah, –1944**

A GARDEN IN ANTRIM. Toronto, Briggs, 1908. 10p [BM OTU

**Monckton, Geoffrey F.**

LOVERS OF ENGLAND. London, Vickery, 1921. 55p [BM

**Monk, Samuel Cornwallis, 1814–1888**

THE SAGUENAY. An Unpublished Poem. [Anon] Montreal, priv. print., 1860. [OOP

THE ROMAN CONQUEST. A Manuscript Poem. [Anon] N.p., priv. print., 1870. 62p [OOA

**Montgomery, Lucy Maud, 1874–1942**

THE WATCHMAN AND OTHER POEMS. Toronto, McClelland, 1916. 159p [BM BVaU LC NBFU OTU QMM

**Montreal, Que. Women's Art Society**

POEMS ON PEACE, From Among Those Submitted in Competition. Montreal, the Society, [1931?]. 6p [CC

**Moodie, Marion Elizabeth, 1867–**

SONGS OF THE WEST. Toronto, Briggs, 1904. 8p [AEU BM OTP QMU

SONGS OF THE WEST AND OTHER POEMS. Toronto, Ryerson, 1934. 23p [BVaU NBSaM OTP QMM

**Moodie, Susanna (Strickland), 1803–1885**

ENTHUSIASM AND OTHER POEMS. London, Smith Elder, 1831. 214p [BM NSHPL OTP QMM

**Moody, Irene Helen (Hawkins), –1958**

ALWAYS THE BUBBLES BREAK. Toronto, Macmillan, 1947. 39p [BVaU LC NBFU OTP

ATTAR OF SONG AND OTHER POEMS. Toronto, Macmillan, 1936. 71p [BM BVaU NBFU OTP QMBM

LAVA. Toronto, Macmillan, 1940. 96p [BVaU LC NBFU OKQ

WRAITHS. Toronto, Macmillan, 1934. 66p [BM BVaU NBFU OTL QMBM

**Mooney, Hugh R., 1914–**

CLIPPED WINGS. Victoria, Quality Printers, 1946. 88p [BVa

**Moore, Charles Ed [Edward?], [Editor?]**

THE POETIC GLOBE. Poems. Toronto, 1887. [OOP

**Moore, Francis, 1870–**

MEDITATIONS IN RHYME OF THINGS MATERIAL, MORAL, AND MYSTIC. By F.R.M. Collingwood, Ont., Enterprise Bulletin, 1942–49. [Four pamphlets bound together.] [QMM

**Moore, Helen, –1941**

HELEN'S POEMS. [Anon] Collected by Anna M. Walker. Stanger, Alta., 1944. 39p [OPAL

**Moore, James Mavor, 1919–**

AND WHAT DO *YOU* DO? A Short Guide to the Trades and Professions. London, Toronto, Dent, 1960. 57p

**Moore, Philip Hooper, 1879–1961**

ROSSIGNOL RHYMES. 1929. White Point Beach, N.S., Rossignol Press, [1930?]. 164p [NSHD OTU

SMOKE SCREEN. Bridgewater, N.S., Bulletin Press, 1944. 78p [OTP

**Moore, S.**

POEMS. Montreal, Lovell, 1887. 315p [BVaU OTP QMSS

**Moore, William Wallace**

RANDOM RHYMES. Toronto, Hunter Rose, 1885. 224p [BVaU OTUV

**Moose Jaw, Sask. Prairie Poetry Club**

THE CRESCENT MOON. A Magazine of Original Verse by Canadian Prairie Writers. ... Moose Jaw, Crescent Press, 1934–35. 2 issues. [UTQ

**Moose Jaw, Sask. Writers' Club**

CHRISTMAS, 1940. Moose Jaw, the Club, 1940. 32p [OTU
CHRISTMAS, 1942. Moose Jaw, the Club, 1942. 24p [SSU
OUR AUTUMN OFFERINGS. [Moose Jaw, the Club, 1944?]. 23p [SSU
PRAIRIE POEMS. Moose Jaw, the Club, 1943. 24p [Brown U SSU
VERSES FOR YOU. Moose Jaw, the Club, 1941. 35p [Brown U

**Morant, Mollie (Wylde)**

THE SINGING GYPSY. Toronto, Ryerson, 1941. 8p [BVaU NBSaM OTP QMM

**Morden, Charles Draper**

UNIVERSUS. ... Ottawa, Author, 1911. 55p [BM Brown U BVaU OTU

**More, Amelia**

GLORY GEMS. Orillia, Gospel Light, 1893. 48p [Amtmann cat. 151

**Morgan, Mary, 1856?–**

ECHOES FROM THE SOLITUDES. London, Allen, 1901. 95p [BM NSWA OTUV QMM
GLIMPSES INTO THE LETTERS OF A WANDERER, including Poems & Translations. London, Mathews, 1914. 66p [BM
HALF-SILENT FELLOWSHIPS. Edinburgh, Foulis, 1909. 104p [BM BVaU OLU QMM
MARGUERITES. London, Haas, 1898. 71p [BM
POEMS AND TRANSLATIONS. Montreal, Robinson, 1887. 195p [*Cf.* WOOD NOTES IN THE GLOAMING, *below*] [BVaU NBFU OTP QMM
SEEDS FROM THE GARDEN OF THE WORLD. Edinburgh, Foulis, 1904. 208p [BM
SONNETS FROM SWITZERLAND. 1896. [MOR'98
TRAUMEREIEN. [MOR'12
WOODNOTES IN THE GLOAMING. Poems and Translations. Boston, Cupples, 1889 [AmCat

**Morgan, Mary Ellen (O'Brien)**

IN OUR HOUSE. By Nana [pseud]. Victoria, B.C. 1958. 54p

**Morgan, Mrs. Seraph A.C.**

SCRAPS OF SONG FROM LA RIVIERE AUX BROCHETS. St. John, Que., Author, n.d. 51p

**Morgan-Powell, Samuel, 1898–**

DOWN THE YEARS. Toronto, Macmillan, 1938. 90p [BVaU NBFU OTP QMM

**Morison, Mrs. J.A.**

MY SOLDIER BOY AND OTHER POEMS. Toronto, Copp Clark, 1916. [CAR

**Morley, Edna Lillian, 1891–**

SONGS OF FREEDOM. Milverton, Ont., Sun, [1940?]. 8p [Brown U OTUV
VERSES. Milverton, Ont., Author, 1938. 42p [OTU
WATCHWORDS OF LIBERTY. Toronto, Crucible Press, 1942. 28p [LC OTU

**Morris, Frank**
A MASTER MIND. "Thou madest him lower than the angels." Port Hope, Ont., Author, 1906. 16p [OTU

**Morris, Maria**
METRICAL MUSINGS. By M. and C.M. Morris [of Halifax]. New York, Craighead, 1856. 188p [NSHD

**Morris, Melba, 1909–**
ON WINGS OF THOUGHT. Owen Sound, Bates Advt. & Print., 1936. 38p [Brown U MWU
THROUGH CASEMENT WINDOWS. Owen Sound, Bates Advt. and Print., 1935. 38p [UTQ

**Morrison, Llewellyn A.**
HEART BELLS. London, Ont., Lawson & Jones, 1899. 303p [BVaU OTP

**Morrison, Sara Moore**
SCENES AND HOURS. Toronto, Crucible Press, 1945. 40p [CC

**Morse, William Inglis, 1874–1952**
ACADIAN LAYS AND OTHER VERSE. Toronto, Briggs, 1908. 65p [BVaU NBFU OTP
THE LADY LATOUR. With Picture Poses Appended for those who Journey. Toronto, Ryerson, 1920. 91p [BM BVaU NBFU OOP QMM
THE NARROWING PATH, 1901–1920. London, priv. print., 1933. 80p [BVaU NBFU OTU QMM

**Morse-Farnum, Mrs. H.I.**
POEMS AND THOUGHTS TERSELY TOLD.... N.p., 1910. 48p [Brown U

**Mortimer, John**
DAY DREAMS OF A PIONEER, AND OTHER POEMS. Toronto, Briggs, 1911. 64p [BM Brown U BVaU OLU

**Morton, Irene (Elder), 1849–1923**
IDYLLS OF THE DANE. Boston, Gorham, 1916. 106p [LC

**Morton, James** [of H.M. Customs, Nova Scotia]
IRELAND: A Poem. Dublin, Milliken, 1846. 95p [BM

**Morton, James** [of Victoria, B.C.], **1870?–1967**
THE CHURCHILL TREE. Songs of War and Peace. Victoria, Diggon-Hibben, 1945. 44p [BVaU OTP
HERESIES AND OTHER POEMS. Victoria, Author, 1937. 64p [BVaU OTU

**Moscovitch, Henry, 1941–**
THE SERPENT INK. Toronto, Contact Press, 1956. 35p

**Mounfield, William M.**

LINES OF A LUNGER. [Hamilton?], n.p. 1917. 21p [NBFU

**Mountain, Mrs. Annie**

THE LEGEND OF ST. HELIER. Jersey, LeFeuvre, 1863. 16p [NSHP

OLD AND NEW SARUM; ADDISON'S BIRTHPLACE AND STONEHENGE. Salisbury, England, Brown & Co., 1862. 26p [Selected from WILTSHIRE BALLADS.] [AEU QMU

"A WREATH OF RUE," FOR LENT, AND THE SACRED LAKE. Toronto, Rowsell & Hutchison, 1873. 49p [BVaU OTP

**Mountain, Rev. George Jehoshaphat, 1789–1863**

SONGS OF THE WILDERNESS. Being a Collection of Poems written in 1844. London, Rivington, 1846. 155p [BM BVaU LC NBFU OTP QMM

**Mountcastle, Clara H., 1837–**

IS MARRIAGE A FAILURE? LOST! AND MANY GEMS OF VERSE. Toronto, Imrie & Graham, 1899. 64p [BM OTP

THE MISSION OF LOVE, LOST, AND OTHER POEMS. With Songs and Valentines. By Caris Sima [pseud]. Toronto, Hunter, 1882. 200p [BVaU LC NBFU OKQ

**Mowat, Grace Helen, 1875–1964**

FUNNY FABLES OF FUNDY. Ottawa, Ru-Mi-Lou Books, 1928. 79p [BVaU NBFU OOP QMBM

**Moyer, W.A.E.**

SOME RHYMING RAMBLINGS. St. Catharines, Author, 1942. 14p [CC

**Moyse, Charles Ebenezer, 1852–1924**

ELLA LEE. Glimpses of Child Life. London, Mathews, 1910. 43p [BM OONL QMM

THE LURE OF EARTH, AND OTHER POEMS. London, 1911. 71p [BM OONL QMM

**Muchall, Mary Elizabeth Jane (Traill), 1841–1892**

STEP BY STEP; or, The Shadow on a Canadian Home. ... A Story in Two Parts: ... "The Beginning" ... "And the End." Toronto, Rowsell & Hutchison, 1876. 59p [BVaU NSHD OTP

THE STOLEN SKATES. A Canadian Tale. By Mrs. Muchall. Toronto, James Campbell, n.d. [187–?]. 45p [Patrick cat. 39

**Mullane, George, 1850–1938**

VICTOR HUGO'S DAUGHTER AND OCCASIONAL VERSE. Halifax, 1923. 32p [OTU

**Mulliss, William, 1876?–1932**

MORE "WORDS, WORDS, WORDS." Montreal, Southam Press, 1931. 13p [OTP

"WORDS, WORDS, WORDS." Montreal, Southam Press, 1927. 26p [BVaU OTP

**Mulock, Edith**

VOICES OF THE DUSK. Toronto, Oxford U. Press, 1934. 32p [LC OTU

**Mulvenna, Robert D.**

HAPPY DAYS. A Salute to Toronto on its 125th Anniversary. Toronto, [1960?]. 14p

THE OLD HOME TOWN. Toronto, Author, [1945?]. 11p [OTUV

**Muncaster, Eric, 1889–**

"GENTLEMEN, THE KING!" AND OTHER THOUGHTS. Montreal, Author, 1934. 60p [Brown U OTUV

**Munday, Albert R.**

LOVER LYRICS, AND OTHERS. Toronto, Briggs, 1916. 51p [BM BVaU OKQ

**Munday, Rupert**

WITHIN THE TAVERN CAUGHT. Foleyet, Ont., Crucible Press, 1950. 40p [BVa

**Munn, George**

PATRIOTIC AND OTHER POEMS. Toronto, Imrie & Graham, 1900. 128p [BM BVaU NSHD OKQ

**Munro, Mrs. Elizabeth V., 1900–**

BRICKS WITHOUT STRAW. Saint John, Wayside Press, 1934. 19p [AEU NBSaM

**Munro, W.D.**

MIRROR AND REFLECTIONS. Victoria, Diggon-Hibben, 1942. 21p [OKQ

**Munro, William**

MANITOULIN ECHOES FROM BLUFF, DALE, LAKE AND STREAM, IN VERSE. Gore Bay, Ont., Recorder Press, [19—?]. 53p [OTP

**Murdoch, Robert, 1836–**

A COMPLETE WORK OF ROBERT MURDOCH. ... Containing his Poems, Songs, Toasts and Epigrams. With a Sketch of the Life of the Poet. Halifax, Macnab, 1890. 149p [BVaU NSHD OTU

**Murdock, William, 1823–1887?**

DISCURSORY RUMINATIONS, A FIRESIDE DRAMA, Etc., Etc. Saint John, Chubb, 1876. 233p [BVaU NBFU OTP QMBM

POEMS AND SONGS. Saint John, Barnes, 1860. 152p [2nd ed., enl. and improved: Saint John, McMillan, 1872. 232p] [BVaU MWU NSHD OTP QMM

**Murphy, J.A.**

SONGS OF THE EVENING. A Volume of Original Verse. Ottawa, Mortimer, 1896. 18p [OTP

**Murphy, James, 1867–1931**

MURPHY'S SEALERS' SONG BOOK. Comp. by —. St. John's, Telegram Print., 1905. 28p [NfSM

CORONATION SONG BOOK OF NEWFOUNDLAND. Comp. by —. St. John's, Murphy, 1911. 12p [NfSG

OLD SONGS OF NEWFOUNDLAND. Comp. by —. St. John's, 1912. 11p [NfSM

SONGS AND BALLADS OF NEWFOUNDLAND, ANCIENT AND MODERN. St. John's, Milligan, 1902. 90p [NBSaM

SONGS OF OUR LAND. "Old Home Week" Souvenir. Comp. by —. St. John's, Telegram Print., 1904. 89p [NfSG

SONGS SUNG BY OLD-TIME SEALERS OF MANY YEARS AGO. Comp. by —. St. John's, 1925. 20p [NfSM

SONGS THEIR FATHERS SUNG. For Fishermen. Old Time Ditties. Comp. by —. St. John's, Murphy, 1923. 17p [NfSM OTUV

**Murphy, Louise**

SWEET CANADA. Twelve Bird Songs and a Round. Toronto, Longmans, 1923. [BVa

**Murray, George, 1830–1910**

HOW CANADA WAS SAVED. ... Toronto, Copp Clark, 1874. 17p [NSHD

MEN AND WOMEN MERELY PLAYERS. Drawings by R.G. Mathews; Verses by George Murray. Montreal, Renaissance Press, 1903. 21p [QMM

POEMS. Ed. with a memoir by John Reade. Montreal, O'Connor, 1912. 236p [BM BVaU NSHD OTP QMM

VERSES & VERSIONS. Montreal, Brown, 1891. 403p [BVaU LC OTP QMM

**Murray, Rev. John Clark, 1836–1917**

EPIMETHEUS [a Poem], to my students. Montreal, 1897. 12p [BVaU OTP QMM

**Mutter, Mrs. Jean**

MUD-PUP. A Sequence in Light Verse. Victoria, Diggon-Hibben, 1944. 30p [BVaU OTP

**Myers-Funnell, Rozelle V.**

A BOOKLET OF VERSE. A Jubilee Offering. Ottawa, Birkett, 1897. 25p [BM OOP

**Nairn, Robert, 1854–1937**

VERSES, HUMOROUS AND PATHETIC. Rat Portage, News Pub. Co., 1900. 47p [OKQ

**Napier, Nina (Marwick), 1900–**

LIBRARY LEVITY. Seattle, McCaffrey, 1946. 38p [2nd ed., enl., 1952. 47p] [BVaU LC OTP

**Nash, Arthur Charles, 1878–**

BUDS AND BLOSSOMS. Vancouver, Clarke & Stuart, 1960. 60p

THE DRAMA OF DUNQUERQUE. Vancouver, Storer, 1941. 38p [BVa LC OTP

LYRICS OF LIFE. Vancouver, Storer, 1941. 64p [BVa LC OTP

MEMORIES IN MELODY. Toronto, Ryerson, 1920. 86p [BM BVaU OTP

AN ODE TO CANADA AND OTHER POEMS. Toronto, Briggs, 1910. 60p [Reprinted: Vancouver, Clarke & Stuart, 1958.] [BM BVaU OOP

REVERIES IN MELODY. New York, Exposition Press, 1957. 63p
RUTH AND OTHER POEMS. Vernon, B.C., News Print., 1910. 33p [BViP
THE SOJOURNER. Vancouver, Storer, 1943. 64p [BVa LC OTP
SONGS OF THE SEASONS. Vancouver, Dunsmuir Print., 1944. 40p [BVaU LC OTP

**Nasir, George**
FIFTEEN POEMS. Winnipeg, Dahl Co., 1948. 15p [NBFU OKQ
NEW POEMS. Winnipeg, Dahl Co., 1949. 8p [OKQ

**Nealis, Jean Elizabeth U. (Wilkenson), 1842–**
DRIFT. Montreal, Sadlier, 1884. 98p [NBFU OTP

**Nease, Lilla Stewart (Dunlap), 1858–**
PASTURES NEW. By Lilla Stewart Nease and Henry Roche. Picton, Times Pub. Co., 1935. 24p [UTQ

**Needler, George Henry, 1866–1962**
THE BATTLEFORD COLUMN. Versified Memories of a Queen's Own Corporal in the Northwest Rebellion, 1885. Montreal, Prov. Pub. Co., 1948. 92p [Also: Montreal, Provincial Pub. Co., 1957.] [BVaU NBFU OTP
THE NIBELUNGLEID. Trans. into Rhymed English Verse in the Metre of the Original. New York, Holt, 1904. 349p [NBFU OTU

**Neilan, William Sydney**
THROUGH WAYSIDE GARDENS. A Collection of Verses. Montreal, Renouf, 1931. 114p [BVaU OTP QMBM

**Nelson, Edwin G.**
RAISE THE FLAG AND OTHER PATRIOTIC CANADIAN SONGS AND POEMS. 1891. [Rhod p858

**Nelson, H.M.**
PROMOTION BALLADS, AND OTHERS ABOUT THE INVINCIBLE NOTHING. Toronto, Briggs, 1914. 74p [2nd ed., rev., 1915. 99p] [BM BVaU OTP

**Nelson, V.H.**
THE NEW BRUNSWICK MINSTREL. Saint John, n.d. [CCJ NBB

**New Frontiers**
THE STONE, THE AXE, THE SWORD, AND OTHER CANADIAN POEMS. Toronto, New Frontiers, 1955. 32p [Selections from the poems of Alexander McLachlan, Isabella Valancy Crawford, Archibald Lampman, and Peter McArthur.]

**Newell, Rev. John Robert, 1853–1912**
POEMS AND SONGS. Boston, Badger, 1904. 136p [BVa LC OTU
THE TIMES, AND OTHER POEMS. Toronto, Hunter, 1881. 151p [BVaU NBFU OKQ

**Newson, William Victor, 1877–1931?**

A VALE IN LUXOR. Intro. note by Nellie L. McClung. Toronto, Ryerson, 1926. 12p [BVaU NBSaM OTP

WAIFS OF THE MIND. Toronto, Ryerson, 1927. 30p [BVaU NBFU OKQ

**Newton, John**

THE EMIGRANT AND OTHER PIECES. Hamilton, Robertson, 1846. 48p [OTP

**Nicholl, M.A.**

LAYS FROM THE WEST. By "Stella"—M.A. Nicholl. Winnipeg, Manitoba Free Press, 1884. 103p [BVaU OTU

**Nichols, J. Arthur**

AROUND HOME. By Art Nichols. Windsor, Curtis, 1937. 48p [AEU OH QMU

FIRE-SIDE FANCIES. Chatham, Planet Press, 1925. 111p [OKQ

**Nichols, Mrs. Ruby**

SONGS FROM THEN AND NOW. Toronto, Ryerson, 1947. 7p [BVaU MWU NBFU OTU

SYMPHONY. Toronto, Ryerson, 1956. 12p

**Nickerson, Moses Hardy, 1846–1943**

CAROLS OF THE COAST. Songs, Ballads, and Legends, Original and Translated. Halifax, Nova Scotia Print., 1892. 288p [BVaU NSHD OTP

SONGS OF SUMMERLAND, AND OTHER POEMS. To which are added "Rhymin' Remarks on Men and Things," by Thomas Cod. Boston, Nickerson, 1927. 212p [LC OTP

**Nicolls, Minnie P.**

IDEALS. Vancouver, Evans & Hastings, 1904. 48p [BVaU

**Nightingale, Winnifred M., 1902–**

HUMBLY YOURS. Guelph, Author, 1935. 24p [OTU

**Niven, Frederick John, 1878–1944**

A LOVER OF THE LAND, AND OTHER POEMS. New York, Boni, 1925. 72p [BM BVaU LC NBFU OKQ

MAPLE LEAF SONGS. London, Sidgwick & Jackson, 1917. 44p [BM BVaU OTP

**Nixon, John Eric, 1897–**

MORRISON'S PLACE AND OTHER POEMS. Regina, Commercial Print., [194–?]. 39p [Peel Adelphi

SELECTED POEMS. Toronto, Crucible Press, 1945. 46p [BVaU OKQ

**Nixon, Marian Essley**

FOUR WISHES, AND OTHER POEMS. London, Stockwell, 1933. 64p [BM

**Nobody Knows Who (pseud)**

POEMS. By Nobody Knows Who [pseud]. Southampton, Forbes & Pittman, 1857. 134p [BVaU

**Noel, Garet (pseud?)**
THE SONG OF NIAGARA. By "Garet Noel." Toronto, Copp Clark, n.d. 12p [NSHD OTUV

**Norcross, Rene**
THE UP AND UP. Vancouver, City Museum, 1949. 8p [BM BVaU NBFU

**Norman, Dorothy, 1905–**
DUALITIES. New York, priv. print., 1933. 114p [LC

**North, John**
TALE OF THE DAYS OF HI YU BILL AND ITS ROYAL COMMISSION. As told by Isaac, the Moosehide Chief. Arranged by John North. Toronto, Moore Print-Shop, 1908. 30p [BM BVaU OKQ

**North, Peter Robert, 1894–**
HARSHLY THE RAIN FELL. Toronto, Author, 1950. 12p [Brown U OONL

**Norton, Mrs. Mary**
THE MINISTRY OF FLOWERS AND OTHER POEMS.By Mrs. Norton. ... Toronto, Briggs, 1890. 110p [BVaU NBFU OTP

**Norwood, Rev. Robert Winkworth, 1874–1932**
BILL BORAM. New York, Doran, 1921. 96p [BVaU LC NSHD OKQ
HIS LADY OF THE SONNETS. Boston, Sherman French, 1915. 85p [BVaU LC NSHD OKQ QMM
ISSA. New York, Scribner, 1931. 95p [BVaU LC NSHD OKQ
THE MODERNISTS. New York, Doran, 1918. 146p [BVaU LC NSHD OKQ
MOTHER AND SON. New York, Doran, 1925. 72p [BVaU LC NSHD OKQ
THE PIPER AND THE REED. New York, Doran, 1917. 119p [BVaU LC NSHD OKQ

**Nott, Edward Vernon, 1878–**
THE BALLAD OF THE SOUL'S DESIRE. London, Greening, 1903. 124p [BM OTUV
CLEOPATRA WITH ANTHONY. London, Greening, 1904. [BM
THE JOURNEY'S END, AND OTHER VERSE. London, Greening, 1904. 98p [BM
SUMMER DAYS AND OTHER VERSES. London, Greening, 1906. 95p [BM

**Nova Scotia. Poetry Society**
NOVA SCOTIA BOOK OF VERSE. Halifax, the Society, [1949–51?]. 2v [NBFU OTP

**Nova-Scotian, A (1827) (pseud)**
HENRY. A Poem in Two Cantos. By a Nova-Scotian [pseud]. Halifax, Cunnabell, 1827. 22p [NSHP

**Nowlan, Alden A., 1933–**
A DARKNESS IN THE EARTH. Eureka, Calif., Hearse Press, [1959?]. 16p
THE ROSE AND THE PURITAN. Fredericton, U. of New Brunswick, 1958. 16p

**Obodiac, Stanlee, 1922–**

THE SOUL SPEAKS. Yorkton, Redeemer's Voice, 1950. 63p [Brown U OONL

**O'Brian, Grace (Williams)**

AT THE TOP OF THE HILL. Toronto, Dent, 1928. 86p [BM OTL

**O'Brien, Rev. Cornelius, 1843–1906**

AMINTA. A Modern Life Drama. New York, Appleton, 1890. 187p [BM BVaU LC NSHD OOU QMM

**O'Byrne, Michael Cyprian**

NYSSIA. An Old World Story. Toronto, Ellis, 1905. 85p [NSWA

**Odell, Jonathan, 1737–1818**

THE AMERICAN TIMES. A Satire in Three Parts. ... By Camillo Querno [pseud], Poet-Laureate to the Congress. London, Richardson, 1780. 40p [Attributed to Odell, but his authorship has been questioned. See *American Literature* 2: 79–82 (March 1930).] [BM BVaU LC OTU

THE LOYAL VERSES OF JOSEPH STANSBURY AND DOCTOR JONATHAN ODELL. ... Ed. by Winthrop Sargent. Albany, N.Y., Munsell, 1860. 199p [BVaU LC NBFU OLU

THE LOYALIST POETRY OF THE REVOLUTION. Ed. by Winthrop Sargent. Philadelphia, Collins, 1857. 218p [Poems by Odell included.] [BVaU LC OTU

**Ogden, H.G.**

BALLADS OF CORNER BROOK. ... St. John's, Nfld., 1925. 47p [Brown U BVaU

**Ogilvy, Maud**

A CHRISTMAS SONG, AND OTHER VERSES. [1913]. 8 leaves. [BVaU

**O'Grady, Standish, fl. 1793–1841**

THE EMIGRANT. A Poem in Four Cantos. Montreal, Lovell, 1841. 204p [BVaU OTP

**O'Hagan, Thomas, 1855–1939**

COLLECTED POEMS. Toronto, McClelland, 1922. 178p [BM BVaU LC NBFU OTP

A GATE OF FLOWERS, AND OTHER POEMS. Toronto, Briggs, 1887. 64p [BVaU LC NBFU OTU QMM

IN DREAMLAND, AND OTHER POEMS. Toronto, Williamson, 1893. 84p [BM BVaU LC NBFU OTP

IN THE HEART OF THE MEADOW AND OTHER POEMS. Toronto, Briggs, 1914. 47p [BM BVaU LC OTP

SONGS OF HEROIC DAYS. Toronto, Briggs, 1916. 44p [BM BVaU NBFU OTU QMSS

SONGS OF THE SETTLEMENT, AND OTHER POEMS. Toronto, Briggs, 1899. 70p [BM BVaU LC OTP

THE TIDE OF LOVE. Toronto, Ryerson, 1928. 8p [BVaU NBFU OTU QMM

**Okanagan Historical Society**
SONGS OF THE OKANAGAN. Vernon, B.C., the Society, 1944. 31p [BViPA OOA

**Old Presbyterian, An**
POETRY BY AN OLD PRESBYTERIAN. [Anon] Glencoe, Transcript Presses, 1902. [Phelps

**Old Resident Of New Brunswick, An**
SOLITUDE AND OTHER POEMS. By an Old Resident of New Brunswick [pseud]. 1842. 24p [OKQ

**Olivers, Thomas**
DESCRIPTIVE AND PLAINTIVE ELEGY ON THE DEATH OF THE LATE REV. JOHN WESLEY. Lunenburg, N.S., Moody, 1837. 12p [NSHD

**O'Malley, Rev. Andrew, 1863–1921**
JOAN OF ARC. Barrie, Author, 1920. 110p [OTU
SONNETS OF A RECLUSE. Toronto, Register Extension Print., 1915. 100p [V. II and V. III were pub. at Barrie by Gazette Print., no dates. Pagination in each was also 100p.] [BVaU QMU
THE WRECK OF THE TITANIC. Toronto, Blake, 1912. 38p [NSWA OTP

**O'Neill, Rev. Arthur Barry, 1858–**
BETWEEN WHILES. Akron, Ohio, McBride, 1899. 189p [LC

**Ontario. Women's Liberal Association**
HEARTS OF GOLD. Being Chronicles of Heroism in Canadian History. Toronto, Globe, 1915. 30p [LC NBFU OTU QMU

**Orford, McLeod**
INVERHURON AND OTHER POEMS. Toronto, Hilda M. Ridley, 1951. 20p (Carillon Poetry Chap-Book)

**Oria (pseud)**
IVY LEAVES FROM THE OLD HOMESTEAD. By Oria [pseud]. Halifax, Bowes, 1854. 154p [NSHP

**Ormsby, Iërne**
EGYPT'S GOLD. [Poems.] Bradford, Beamsley House, 1933. 36p [BM

**Osborn, Edith Margaret (Camp), 1902–**
FROSTY-MOON AND OTHER POEMS. By Margot Osborn. Toronto, Ryerson, 1946. 8p [BVaU LC NBSaM OTP

**Osborne, Marian (Francis), 1871–1931**
FLIGHT COMMANDER STORK, AND OTHER VERSE. Toronto, Macmillan, 1925. 48p [BM BVaU OKQ
POEMS. London, Chiswick Press, 1914. 84p [BM BVaU NBFU OTU QMM
THE SONG OF ISRAFEL AND OTHER POEMS. Toronto, Macmillan, 1923. 67p [BM BVaU NBFU OTP

**Osler, Annie F.**

THOUGHTS IN VERSE. Toronto, Tyrrell, 1911. 69p [OTU QMBM

**Ostenso, Martha, 1900–1963**

IN A FAR LAND. Poems. New York, Dodd Mead, 1942. 70p [Earlier ed.: New York, Seltzer, 1924.] [BVaU LC NBFU OTU QMM

**Outram, Richard Daley, 1930–**

EIGHT POEMS. Toronto, Tortoise Press, 1959. 8p

**P., T.W.**

THE POLITICIAN. Toronto, Rose, 1888. 31p [QMU

**Pacey, Desmond, 1917–**

THE COW WITH THE MUSICAL MOO, AND OTHER VERSES FOR CHILDREN. Fredericton, Brunswick Press, 1952. 26p

HIPPITY HOBO AND THE BEE AND OTHER VERSES FOR CHILDREN. Fredericton, Brunswick Press, 1952. 26p

**Pagdin, Thomas, 1868–**

POEMS. Ilfracombe, Devon, Stockwell, 1958. 62p

**Page, Patricia Kathleen, 1916–**

AS TEN AS TWENTY. Toronto, Ryerson, 1946. 43p [BVaU MWU NBFU OTP

THE METAL AND THE FLOWER. Toronto, McClelland, 1954. 64p

UNIT OF FIVE. Poems by Louis Dudek, Ronald Hambleton, P.K. Page, Raymond Souster, James Wreford. Ed. by Ronald Hambleton. Toronto, Ryerson, 1944. 87p [BVaU LC MWU NSHD OTU QMM

**Painter, Mrs. Ann**

THE WIDOW JUSTIFIED; or, The Age of Wonders. A Satirical Poem. To which is added THE FAIR; or, Waterdown Annual Show; also THE QUEEN OF MAGIC INVENTIONS. A Comic Song. Hamilton, Gillespy-Robertson, 1858. 47p [OTUV

**Palmer, David, 1789–1866**

NEW BRUNSWICK AND OTHER POEMS. Saint John, McMillan, 1869. 171p [BVaU NBFU OTU

**Palmer, Lizzie (Estabrooks)**

SELECTED POEMS. Fredericton, Reporter, 1889. 40p [NBFU

**Parham, Charles J.**

LYRICAL TRANSLATIONS. From the Languages of Oc, Italian, Spanish, Portuguese and Provincial Dialects. ... Ottawa, 1887. 88p [Brown U OOP

**Parke, Shubael**

THE SMUGGLER. A Poem. Hamilton, 1852. 76p [BibC CCJ

**Parker, Gilbert, 1862–1932**

EMBERS. Being a Book of Verses. Plymouth, Brendon, 1908. 197p [Also pub. with A LOVER'S DIARY. 2v in 1. New York, Scribner, 1913.] [BM BVaU NBFU OTP

EMBERS; A LOVER'S DIARY. New York, Scribner, 1913. [2v in 1]. 261p [BVa OKQ

A LOVER'S DIARY. Songs in Sequence. Chicago, Stone & Kimball, 1894. 147p [Also: Toronto, Copp Clark, 1898.] [BVaU LC NBFU OTP QMU

**Parker, Hedley S.V.**

MIRAMICHI POET. Six Poems. Ed. with a memoir and notes by Louise Manny. Saint John, New Brunswick Museum, 1947. 20p [BVaU NBFU

**Parker, Mayne Leonard, 1892–**

SHADOWS LAY NORTH. By Len Parker. Dallas, Texas, Story Book Press, 1955. 74p

**Parker, William Frederick, 1860–1918**

FRONDOLEER. By Spatha [pseud]. [Davenport, Iowa?], Globe, 1878. 38p [LC

NORMEELYON. Florence, Neb., 1883. 27p [LC

POEMS. [Davenport, Iowa?], Globe, 1880. 46p [LC

**Parkinson, Amy, 1859?–1938**

BEST. The Story of the Messenger Hours, with Some of the Thoughts they have Brought. Toronto, Briggs, 1902. 43p [BM BVaU NBFU OTP

IN HIS KEEPING. Words of Sustaining from the Source of All Strength; with Kindred Thoughts in Verse. Toronto, Upper Canada Tract Society, n.d. 33p [BM OPAL

LOVE THROUGH ALL. A VOICE FROM A SICK ROOM. THOUGHTS FOR EACH DAY. Toronto, Endeavor Herald, 1893. 36p [OTP

**Parsons, Richard Augustus, 1893–**

REFLECTIONS. St. John's, Newfoundland Academy of Art, 1954. 52p

REFLECTIONS, BOOKS I & II. Toronto, Pub. for the Author by Ryerson Press, 1958. 117p [Bk. I first pub. by Newfoundland Academy of Art, 1954.]

THE VILLAGE POLITICIANS. St. John's, Newfoundland Academy of Art, 1960. 133p

**Partridge, Thomas Jefferson, 1860–**

ANNAPOLIS ROYAL AND OTHER POEMS. Halifax, [1921?]. 33p [NSWA OTUV

LOUISBURG, AMERICA'S FIRST FIELD. Cambridge, Mass., Powell, 1931. 70p [NSHD

POEMS. Gloucester, Mass., H.C. Lantz, n.d. 71p [OONL

**Pasmore, Malvina (Copp)**

GREEN LEAVES. Montreal, Witness Press, 1937. 45p [Brown U BVaU OLU QMU

SAINT JOAN. London, Burns Oates, 1926. 20p [AEU BM

THIS LIFE OF OURS. London, Werner Laurie, 1925.
YOU AND I. London, Phillimore, 1928. 73p [BM NBSaM

**Paterson, A.O.**
CANADA, STORY IN VERSE. [Victoria, Diggon-Hibben, 1942.] 12p [Also eds. in 1943, 1947.] [BVaU
DREAM OF NOEL. By A.O.P. Victoria, Author, 1945. 12p [BVaU

**Paton, James Morton, 1863–**
LIVING POETRY. Ed. by ——. Toronto, Ryerson, 1942. 122p [BVaU LC OOP

**Patterson, Henry**
SONGS IN TRAVEL. Montreal, Lovell, 1872. 186p [BVaU OTP QMBM

**Payne, Mabel Lucy (Formby), 1886–**
MOON IN THE AFTERNOON, AND OTHER POEMS. Mayne Island, B.C., and Vancouver, the Author, 1955. 31p

**Peace, Mrs. N.S.**
THE CONVICT SHIP, AND OTHER POEMS. Greenock, Baird, 1850. 264p [BM OTUV

**Peacock, Annie Louisa, 1873–1957**
ERE SUNRISE. N.p., 1956. 12p (Carillon Poetry Chap-Books)

**Peacock, Harold**
ROUGH RHYMES OF A CANADIAN SOLDIER. Birmingham, Eng., Allday Ltd., [19—?]. 48p [OTUV

**Pearce, Peggy**
REVERIES. St. Thomas, 1934. 23p [OKQ
WAYSIDE GRASSES. Toronto, Ryerson, 1935. 10p [BVaU NBSaM OTP QMM

**Pearce, S. Moore**
AMERICANADA. Poems. Ilfracombe, Devon, Stockwell, 1960. 79p

**Pearce, Theodocia, 1894–1925?**
LIGHTS FROM LITTLE LANTERNS. New York, Lawren, 1926. 77p [BVa NSHD OTP

**Pearson, J.J.**
POEMS. Toronto, Briggs, 1913. 107p [BM BVaU OKQ

**Peck, Nellie M.**
NIGHT FLOWERING STOCK 1942–1944. Poems. By N.M.P. Montreal, Gazette Print., 1945. 102p [NBSU OTU

**Pecknold, Dorothy Martin, 1893–**
THOUGHTS ... AND BY-GONE MEMORIES. Port Alice, B.C., Author, 1950. 32p [BVaU OONL

**Peddel, Nicholas**
HOME SWEET HOME. Newfoundland Poems. N.p., 1904. 36p [Brown U OLU

**Pegley, Charles Edward**
THE FOUR HORSEMEN, AND OTHER VERSE. Sandwich, Border Cities Star Print., 1923. [BM
SHADOWS AND OTHER POEMS. Windsor, Author, 1926. 48p [AEU

**Pellerin, Mrs. Maude Gage, 1884–**
THE SONGS OF OLD QUEBEC. Lennoxville, Press, 1949. 52p [OONL

**Penman, Rev. Archibald D., 1882–**
MIRACLE MEDITATIONS AND SONG SERVICES FROM SCRIPTURES. Poem. New York, Comet Press, 1957. 83p

**Pennington, Richard, 1904–**
BISCAY BALLADS. By David Peterley [pseud]. Montreal, Redpath Press, 1958. 17p

**Penny, Arthur Guy, 1886–1963**
ECHOING LAUGHTER. Verses Selected From "Penny-A-Liner's" Column, "Lines-O-Type," in the Quebec *Chronicle-Telegraph*. Quebec, Chronicle-Telegraph Print. Co., 1954. 98p
THE KING'S CONSCIENCE AND VARIOUS VERSE. Quebec, Chronicle-Telegraph, 1925. 101p [BVaU NBFU OTU QMSS
"MIXTURE, AS BEFORE." Further Echoes From "Penny-a-Liner's" Column, "Lines-o-type," in the Quebec *Chronicle-Telegraph*. Quebec, Chronicle-Telegraph Print. Co., 1955. 114p
RHYMES FOR CHRISTMAS AND OTHER OCCASIONS, 1904–1954. Quebec, Chronicle-Telegraph Print. Co., 1956. 82p

**Perigoe, Harvey**
THE GENIUS AND NELSON, AND OTHER POEMS. Feversham, Ont., Author, [1902]. 64p [BM OTUV

**Perry, Martha Eugenie**
CANTEEN. Victoria, Clarke, 1944. 20p [BVaU OTP
GREEN TIMBERS AND OTHER POEMS. Toronto, Ryerson, 1955. 57p
HEARING A FAR CALL. Toronto, Ryerson, 1943. 12p [BVaU LC NBSaM OTP QMM
HERO IN ERMINE AND OTHER POEMS. Victoria, Clarke, 1939. 32p [BVaU NBFU QMM
SONG IN THE SILENCE, AND OTHER POEMS. Toronto, Ryerson, 1947. 16p [BVaU LC MWU NBSaM OKQ

**Pettit, Phyllis Adye**
PROMISE. Narrative and Other Poems. Toronto, Crucible Press, 1943. 36p [LC

**Phelps, Arthur Leonard, 1887–1970**

A BOBCAYGEON CHAPBOOK. Lindsay, Ont., Author, 1922. 8p [NBFU OKQ

POEMS. Mount Vernon, Iowa, Cornell College English Club, 1921. 17p [NBFU OKQ

**Philips, Frederic**

JOTTINGS BY THE WAY. 1909. [CAR

VERSE FROM A WESTERN ISLE. Victoria, Cusack, 1909. 49p [BM Brown U BVaU NSHD OTP

**Phillipps-Wolley, Clive Oldnall, 1854–1918**

IN MEMORY OF OUR DEAD AT MODDER RIVER FEB. 21, 1900. Victoria, 1900. 6p [BViPA

OUR TESTAMENT. [Anon] Victoria, 1900. 6p [OTP

SONGS FROM A YOUNG MAN'S LAND. Toronto, Allen, 1917. 160p [A re-issue of SONGS OF AN ENGLISH ESAU, and other verse.] [BM BVaU NSHD OTP QMBM

SONGS OF AN ENGLISH ESAU. Toronto, Morang, 1902. 133p [BM BVaU OTP

**Phillips, Mrs. Adria C.**

SONGS OF THE AVON. Toronto, Crucible Press, 1948. 28p [Brown U

**Phillips, Mrs. Bluebell Stewart, 1904–**

FREEDOM'S HOPE AND OTHER VERSE. Point Claire, Que., 1942. 19p [Brown U

**Phillips, William Rupert**

FAR AWAY FIELDS ARE GREEN. Niagara, Ont., 1941. 28p [Brown U

THE RAINBOW OF NIAGARA FALLS, AND OTHER POEMS. Niagara Falls, Ont., Lindsay Press, 1940. 32p [QMU

**Pickel, Enid M., –1956**

PRAIRIE SKYLINE. By Enid and Vestal Pickel. Regina, priv. print., 1949. 40p [BVaU

**Pickthall, Marjorie Lowry Christie, 1883–1922**

THE COMPLETE POEMS OF MARJORIE PICKTHALL. Toronto, McClelland, 1927. 250p [Several later editions.] [BM BVaU MWU NBFU OKQ QMM

THE DRIFT OF PINIONS. Montreal, University Magazine, 1913. 94p [BM BVaU NBFU OTP QMM

THE LAMP OF POOR SOULS, AND OTHER POEMS. New York, Lane, 1916. 140p [Includes contents of THE DRIFT OF PINIONS.] [BM BVaU LC NBFU OTP QMM

LITTLE SONGS. Toronto, McClelland, 1925. 87p [BM BVaU NBFU OTP QMM

MARY TIRED. London, Stonebridge Press, 1922. 4p [OKQ

THE NAIAD AND FIVE OTHER POEMS. [Anon] Toronto, Ryerson, 1931. 11p [Poems chosen by Lorne Pierce from a hitherto undiscovered MS book, and printed for a few friends. Only 14 copies printed.] [BM NBFU OTP

THE SELECTED POEMS OF MARJORIE PICKTHALL. Ed. and with an intro. by Lorne Pierce. Toronto, McClelland, 1957. 104p

TWO POEMS. [Contents: "Ebb Tide"; "Vision."] Toronto, Ryerson, 1923. 5p [BM OKQ

THE WOODCARVER'S WIFE, AND LATER POEMS. Toronto, McClelland, 1922. 105p [BM BVaU NBFU OTP QMM

**Pierce, H.A.**

POEMS. N.p., Author, 1896. 16p [OTUV

**Pierce, Harriet (Singleton)**

AN EASTERN WINDOW: A BOOK OF DAYS. Collected by Lorne Pierce, and made into a Scrap-Book before his Mother's Death. Toronto, United Church, 1938. 20p [NBFU

**Piers, Constance (Fairbanks), 1866–1939**

CHRISTMAS PIE. Selections from Verses Written for Private Greeting Cards and Calendars. Halifax, 1938. 18p [NSHD

**Pike, Mrs. Annie Margaret**

AN ARAB CHIEF, AND OTHER PLAYTIME VERSES. Vancouver, McBeath Spedding, 1923. 32p [BM BVaU LC

PHELIM THE BLIND AND OTHER VERSES. London, Headley, [1913?]. 31p [BM BVaU

PLAYTIME RHYMES. London, Headley, 1907. 47p [BM BVaU

SILVER BELLS AND COCKLE SHELLS. London, Merton, 1926. 114p [BM BVa

**Pincock, Jenny (O'Hara), 1890–1948**

HIDDEN SPRINGS: A Narrative Poem of Old Upper Canada; and Other Poems. Waterloo, Ont., Mrs. F.J.T. Maines, 1949. 66p [OLU

**Pleiter, Mrs. Derk (Neisje), 1885–1967**

REVERIES IN VERSE. Corunna, Ont., Author, [c1966]. 36p [Earlier ed., London, Ont., n.d. 31p] [Phelps p101

**Poetry Society, England. Nova Scotia Centre**

NOVA SCOTIA BOOK OF VERSE. V. 1. 1949. Halifax, 1949. 61p [A continuing pub. Various pagings]

**Pollard, William Correll, 1878–**

POEMS. London, Stockwell, 1936. 35p [OTP

**Polley, Lucy (Mrs. Alvin Polley)**

AUNT JUDITH'S RHYMES. 1912. [Rhod p877

**Pollock, J.E.**

LORENZO, AND OTHER POEMS. Toronto, Briggs, 1883. 117p [BVaU OTP

**Poole, Thomas Wesley, 1831?–1905**

THE POLITICIAN. By T.W.P. [pseud]. Toronto, Rose Pub. Co., 1888. 31p [Patrick cat. 30

**Pooley, W.J.**

FAIR DEVON AND OTHER POEMS. Merritt, B.C., Author, n.d. 18p [mimeographed]. [Also same title: [Victoria?], 1948. 4th ed. 12p] [BViPA

**Pope, William, fl. 1848**

REMINISCENCES OF PRINCE EDWARD ISLAND, IN AN HISTORICAL AND DESCRIPTIVE POEM. With Explanatory Notes Addressed to the Hon. Joseph Pope. Liverpool, Dunsford, 1848. 38p [BVaU OTUV

**Porter, James**

THE BONFIRE. A Poem. Victoria, Author, 1908. 6p [BViPA

1608: QUEBEC TERCENTENARY: 1908. A Poem. Victoria, Author, 1908. 7p [BViPA

**Porter, John Elmoran**

FURROW IN THE DUNES. By Jacke E. Porter. New York, Harrison, 1942. 63p [LC

A NOVA SCOTIAN SINGS. Yarmouth, N.S., Davis, [1958?]. 20p

THE STOPPER'S OUT. By Jacke E. Porter. Yarmouth, N.S., Davis, 1934. 47p [MWU NSHPL QMU

**Porter, Rev. William Henry, 1840–1928**

CANADIAN SCENES AND OTHER POEMS. Toronto, Briggs, 1907. 112p [BM BVaU NSHD OKQ QMU

GATHERED LILIES. Poems of Sympathy and Comfort for the Bereaved. [Brantford, Expositor, n.d.] 16p [NSHPL

GLIMPSES OF CANADA. Acrostics. N.p., n.d. [1901?]. 38p [Adelphi cat. 41A

OUR LORD'S PRAYER IN GETHSEMANE. N.p., n.d. 32p [NSHPL

THE YEAR ROUND. Original Poems. ... London, Ont., Knowles, 1888. 29p [OLU

**Potter, Frank G.**

ALL CANADIAN POEMS. Original, Patriotic and Spiritual; written in Nova Scotia, Alberta, and British Columbia. Kentville, N.S., Kentville Pub. Co., 1936–38. 47p [NBFU OTP

**Poynter, Mary Augusta (Dickinson)**

ALONG THE WINDING ROAD. New York, Revell, 1925. 98p [LC OTU

**Pratt, Edwin John, 1883–1964**

BEHIND THE LOG. Toronto, Macmillan, 1947. 47p [BM BVaU LC MWU NBFU OTP QMM

BREBEUF AND HIS BRETHREN. Toronto, Macmillan, 1940. 65p [BVaU LC NSHD OTP

COLLECTED POEMS. Toronto, Macmillan, 1944. 314p [BM BVaU LC NSHD OTP QMM

COLLECTED POEMS. 2nd ed. Ed. with an intro. by Northrop Frye. Toronto, Macmillan, 1958. xxviii + 395p

DUNKIRK. Toronto, Macmillan, 1941. 13p [BVaU LC MWU NSHD OTP

THE FABLE OF THE GOAT AND OTHER POEMS. Toronto, Macmillan, 1937. 47p [BVaU LC NBFU OTP QMM

THE IRON DOOR. An Ode. Toronto, Macmillan, 1927. 30p [BM BVaU NBFU OTP QMM

MAGIC IN EVERYTHING. Toronto, Macmillan, 1955. 6p

MANY MOODS. Toronto, Macmillan, 1932. 53p [BM BVaU LC NSHD OTU QMM

NEW PROVINCES. Poems of Several Authors. [Ed. by F.R. Scott.] Toronto, Macmillan, 1936. 77p [Contains poems by Pratt and others.] [BVaU NBFU OKQ

NEWFOUNDLAND VERSE. Toronto, Ryerson, 1923. 140p [BM BVaU NBFU OTP QMM

RACHEL. A Sea Story of Newfoundland in Verse. [Anon] New York, priv. print., 1917. 15p [NfSM OTU

THE ROOSEVELT AND THE ANTINOE. New York, Macmillan, 1930. 44p [BM BVaU LC NBFU OTP QMM

STILL LIFE AND OTHER VERSE. Toronto, Macmillan, 1943. 40p [BVaU LC NBFU OTP QMM

TEN SELECTED POEMS. With Notes. Toronto, Macmillan, 1947. 149p [BVaU OTP

THEY ARE RETURNING. Toronto, Macmillan, 1945. 15p [BVaU LC NBFU OTP QMM

THE TITANIC. Toronto, Macmillan, 1935. 42p [BM BVaU NSHD OTP QMM

TITANS. London, Macmillan, 1926. 67p [BM BVaU LC NBFU OTU QMM

TOWARDS THE LAST SPIKE. A Verse Panorma of the Struggle to Build the First Canadian Transcontinental from the Time of the Proposed Terms of Union with British Columbia (1870) to the Hammering of the Last Spike in the Eagle Pass (1885). Toronto, Macmillan, 1952. 53p

VERSES OF THE SEA. With an intro. by Charles G.D. Roberts. Toronto, Macmillan, 1930. 97p [BVaU NBFU OKQ

THE WITCHES BREW. London, Selwyn & Blount, 1925. 32p [BM BVaU NBFU OTP QMSS

**Pratt, Lenore Alexandra (Tucker), 1901–**

BIRCH LIGHT. Toronto, Ryerson, 1956. 15p

MIDWINTER THAW. Toronto, Ryerson, 1948. 12p [BVaU NBSaM OTP

**Prentice Boy, A**

DERRY HARMONIST. By "A Prentice Boy" [pseud]. Ottawa, 1861. [CCJ

**Prescott, Henrietta, –1875**

POEMS, WRITTEN IN NEWFOUNDLAND. London, Saunders & Otley, 1839. 311p [BM LC NSHD OTP QMSS

**Price, Bertha Maud (Weston), 1872–1955**

LEGENDS OF THE LAKES. A Tribute to the Lakes of the Eastern Townships. Sherbrooke, Que., Author, 1923. 43p [Rev. ed. pub. under title: LEGENDS OF OUR LAKES AND RIVERS. Massawippi, Que., Author, 1937. 58p] [BM BVaU OTP QMM

OUT OF DOORS IN CANADA. Poems. Sherbrooke, Que., Page Print., 1927. 14p [QQL

**Priestley, Norman Flaxman, 1884–1958**

SUMMER FEVER AND OTHER VERSES. Calgary, 1945. 24p [Peel Supp.

**Prince, Sadie O., 1861–1905**

POEMS. Toronto, Briggs; Montreal, Coates, 1890. 179p [BVaU NSHD OOP

**Procter, John James, 1838–1910**

THE BLACK HAWK, STANDARD BEARER, AND OTHER POEMS. St. John, Que., News Print., 1883. 144p [OTP QMSS

VOICES OF THE NIGHT, AND OTHER POEMS. Montreal, Lovell, 1861. 118p [BM BVaU OTP QMSS

**Protestant, A (pseud)**

RHYMES FOR THE TIMES. Original Poems on Popery, Slavery, and Intemperance. By a Protestant [pseud]. Montreal, 1857. 119p [Brown U BVaU OTU

**Prower, Nelson, 1856–**

SONNETS AND OTHER VERSES. Vancouver, Wrigley, 1935. 29p [CC

VARIOUS VERSES. By William Frederick Harvey, M.A., Nelson Prower, M.A., and the Rev. R.C. Fillingham, B.A. London, Hayman, Christy & Lilly, 1893. 88p [BM

**Prowse, Mrs. I.S.**

THE BURNING FOREST. A Tale of New Brunswick. 1830. [Lit Hist p116

POEMS. London, Smith Elder, 1830. 183p [BM NSHD

**Purdy, Alfred Wellington, 1918–**

THE CRAFTE SO LONGE TO LERNE. Toronto, Ryerson, 1959. 23p

EMU, REMEMBER! Fredericton, U. of New Brunswick, 1956. 16p

THE ENCHANTED ECHO. Vancouver, Clarke & Stuart, 1944. 62p [Brown U BVaU NBFU

PRESSED ON SAND. Toronto, Ryerson, 1955. 16p

**Quest, R.E. (pseud)**
WANDERINGS. By R.E. Quest [pseud]. Montreal, Renouf, 1960. 122p

**Raby, Mary C.**
BEAUTY WALKS THE EARTH. Toronto, Crucible Press, 1941. 15p [Brown U OTU

**Ragg, Alban E.**
POEMS BY A BUSINESS MAN, A.E.R. [pseud]. Toronto, Brown-Searle, 1901. 21p [Copyright was issued to "William Tyrrell," *q.v.*] [BM BVaU OKQ

**Ramage, Kate Douglas**
VASHTI, AND OTHER POEMS. Montreal, Lovell, 1884. 90p [OTUV

**Ramsay, Andrew John, 1849?–1907**
THE CANADIAN LYRE. By J.R. Ramsay [pseud]. Hamilton, Donnelley, 1859. 126p [BVaU OTP QMBM
I SHALL NOT TELL [and Other Poems]. By A. Ramsay. New York, [c1880]. [CCJ
MURIEL THE FOUNDLING, AND OTHER ORIGINAL POEMS. By Andrew Ramsay. Toronto, Hovey, 1886. 288p [BVaU NBFU OTP
WIN-ON-AH; or, The Forest Light, and Other Poems. By J.R. Ramsay [pseud]. Toronto, Adam Stevenson, 1869. 98p [BVaU NBFU OTP

**Rand, Rev. Silas Tertius, 1810–1889**
THE DYING INDIAN'S DREAM. A Poem. Halifax, Nova Scotia Print., 1872. 15p [3rd ed. rev. with some additional Latin poems: Windsor, N.S., Knowles, 1881. 28p] [BM BVaU NSHP OTP
HYMNI RECENTES LATINI. Translationes et Originales. Halifax, Selden, 1888. 168p [English and Latin versions on facing pages.] [BVaU NBFU OTP QMU

**Rand, Theodore Harding, 1835–1900**
AT MINAS BASIN, AND OTHER POEMS. Toronto, Briggs; Montreal, Coates, 1897. 173p [2nd ed., 1898. 206p] [BM BVaU NBFU OTP QMM
SONG WAVES. Toronto, Briggs, 1900. 121p [BM BVaU NBFU OTP
A TREASURY OF CANADIAN VERSE. Ed. by ——. Toronto, Briggs, 1900. 412p [Also an ed. in 1924.] [BM BVaU LC NBFU OTP QMM

**Rashley, Richard Ernest, 1909–**
MOON LAKE AND OTHER POEMS. Toronto, Ryerson, 1959. 10p
PORTRAIT, AND OTHER POEMS. Toronto, Ryerson, 1953. 8p
VOYAGEUR, AND OTHER POEMS. Toronto, Ryerson, 1946. 16p [BVaU LC NBSaM OTP

**Ratcliffe, Walter A., 1865–**
LAURIER AND VICTORY! A Souvenir of the Campaign of 1896. Toronto, Ellis, 1896. 17p [OTU

MORNING SONGS IN THE NIGHT. Toronto, Briggs; Montreal, Coates, 1897. 151p [BM BVaU OTU QMM

**Ray, Evan**

THE KINGDOM OF SONG. A Group of Little Poems, with Airs. Toronto, Ryerson, 1931. [Ryerson Impt

**Read, Mrs. Jane B.**

POEMS FOR YOUNG PEOPLE, EMBRACING TEMPERANCE AND RELIGION. Brantford, Stewart & Mathison, 1871. 16p [OTP

POEMS ON MORAL AND RELIGIOUS SUBJECTS. Brantford, Daily Courier, 1872. 16p [OTP

**Reade, Mrs. Frances Lawson**

POEMS FROM ARABESQUE. By Yolande Langworthy [pseud]. New York, Black, 1930. 94p [LC

**Reade, John, 1837–1919**

MADELEINE DE VERCHERES. Toronto, Copp Clark, n.d. 19p [NSHD OTUV

THE PROPHECY OF MERLIN AND OTHER POEMS. Montreal, Dawson, 1870. 237p [BVaU LC NSHD OTP QMM

**Reade, Robert Cyrus, 1884–**

THE '05 STORY. Verses. Toronto, U. of Toronto Press, 1955. 12p [Written for the Jubilee Reunion Dinner of the class of 1905 of University College, U. of Toronto, held May 25, 1955.]

**Reaney, James Crerar, 1926–**

THE RED HEART. Toronto, McClelland, 1949. 73p [MWU NBFU OTP

A SUIT OF NETTLES. Toronto, Macmillan, 1958. x + 54p

**Recoskie, Rose Mary**

ORCHIDS TO LADY MARIA. New York, Pageant Press, 1953. 46p

PETALS OF FLOWERS. Poems. New York, Exposition Press, 1952. 56p

**Redpath, Beatrice Constance (Peterson), –1937**

DRAWN SHUTTERS. London, Lane, 1916. 96p [BM BVaU LC NBFU QMM

WHITE LILAC AND OTHER POEMS. London, Lane, 1922. 80p [BM BVaU NBFU OTP QMM

**Redwing (pseud)**

ELMO, THE STORY OF A CANADIAN GIRL, AND OTHER POEMS. By Redwing [pseud]. N.p., n.d. 12p [OPAL

**Reed, Wilfred Joseph, 1911–**

THE CITY BY THE SEA, AND OTHER IMAGINATIVE STORIES. Vancouver, Wrigley, 1936. 133p [BVaU

THE EMPIRE OF THE NORTH AND OTHER IMAGINATIVE STORIES OF THE PAST AND FUTURE. Vancouver, Wrigley, 1935. 129p [BVaU OTP QMBM

STORIES OF TRAVEL. Vancouver, Wrigley, 1935. 126p [BVaU

**Reeder, Will**

GEMS FROM WILL REEDER'S NOTE BOOK. Vol. 1: Vancouver, 1941; Vol. 3: Vancouver, 1949. [BViPA

**Reid, Lionel Meredith, 1900–**

RHYMES AND FANCIES, BY A BOY. Boston, Badger, 1913. 47p [Written when author was a schoolboy at Campbellford and Toronto.] [OTP

**Reid, Robert, 1850–1922**

KEN YE THE LAND? By Rob Wanlock [pseud]. Outremont, Que., 1894. 2p [Patrick cat. 30

POEMS, SONGS AND SONNETS. Paisley and London, Gardiner, 1894. 264p [BM BVaU LC OTU QMM

A SONG OF CANADA. Montreal, 1896. 3p [Patrick cat. 30

**Reid, Robert Scott, 1924–**

DANDELION BOUQUET. Clarionette Rhymes Collected from the 1959 Issues of the Kindersley *Clarion*. Kindersley, Sask., Clarion, [1960?]. 39p

**Renison, Rev. Robert John, 1875–1957**

A SUMMER ODYSSEY. Toronto, Rous & Mann, 1938. 7p [UTQ

**Rennie, Doris Victoria, 1903–**

DAWN'S AWAKENING. Poems. Ilfracombe, Devon, Stockwell, 1956. 15p

**Reynolds, Ella Julia**

SAMSON IN HADES. Toronto, Ryerson, 1957. 15p

**Rhodenizer, Vernon Blair, 1886–1968**

CANADA FOR MAN AND OTHER POEMS. Montreal, Quality Press, 1958. 16p

**Rhynas, Mrs. Margaret, 1878–**

A BOUQUET OF REMEMBERINGS. N.p., n.d. 15p [NBSaM

LITTLE STARS ON CHRISTMAS SKIES. [Burlington, Ont., Author, 1935.] 20p [NBSaM OPAL

SILVER BELLS OF MEMORY. Burlington, Ont., Author, 1938. 29p [OTU

**Rice, William, 1817–**

POEMS. Toronto, Rowsell & Hutchinson, 1898. 22p [BVaU OTP

**Richan, Sarah (Hopkins), 1871–**

THE UNRESTING SEA. An Anthology comp. by ——. Kentville, N.S., Kentville Pub. Co., 1950. 41p [OONL

**Richardson, John, 1796–1852**

KENSINGTON GARDENS IN 1830. A Satirical Trifle. By the Author of ECARTE. London, Marsh & Miller, 1830. 32p [Reprinted by the Bibliographical Society of Canada, Facsimile Series No. 6, Toronto, 1957.] [BM BVaU NBFU OTU

TECUMSEH; or, The Warrior of the West. A Poem in Four Cantos, with Notes. By an English Officer [pseud]. London, Glynn, 1828. 135p [Republished by Richardson in abridged form in his *New Era*, Brockville, V. 2, 1842. 16p] [BM NBFU OKQ

**Richardson, Martha E.**

SONNET REVERIES. Montreal, Witness Press, 1908. 22p [BM QMU

**Richey, Rev. James Arminius**

FRAGMENTS AND VERSES. Halifax, Bowes & Sons, 1869. 94p [NSHD OLU

MORE HALF-HOURS; or, a Second and Enlarged Edition of FRAGMENTS AND VERSES. Halifax, Author, 1877. 108p [NSWA OLU

POEMS. By J.A.R. Montreal, 1867. [OOP

POEMS, DEVOTIONAL AND MISCELLANEOUS. Halifax, Author, 1886. 180p [2nd ed. of VERSES, DEVOTIONAL AND MISCELLANEOUS.] [BVaU OTP

A SERIES OF POEMS. By J.A.R. Montreal, Wilson, 1857. 46p [BVaU NSHD OTP QMSS

VERSES, DEVOTIONAL AND MISCELLANEOUS. Halifax, Theakston, 1882. 164p [BM NSHD OTP

**Riddehough, Geoffrey Blundell**

THE PROPHET'S MAN. Toronto, Ryerson, 1926. 12p [BVaU NBSaM OTU QMM

**Ridley, Hilda M., –1960**

A NEW CANADIAN ANTHOLOGY. Edited by Alan Creighton ... assisted by Hilda M. Ridley. Toronto, Crucible Press, 1938. 236p [BVaU LC OTU

**Ridley, Laura Adelaide, –1953**

CHRISTMAS EVE AND OTHER POEMS. Toronto, Crucible Press, 1943. 16p [BVaU OTP

**Rigby, Carle Almond**

VICTORY AND OTHER POEMS. Yarmouth, N.S., 1946. 30p [NBSaM OLU QMU

**Ripley, Anne**

EN ROUTE. Nelson, Daily News Print., 1945. 18p [OTP

**Ritchie, Cicero Theodore, 1914–**

SPRIGS OF BALSAM. Upsalquitch, N.B., Author, 1942. 15p [NSHD

**Ritchie, Eliza, 1850–1933**

IN THE GLOAMING. Halifax, Weeks Pub. Co., 1935. 23p [NSHD

SONGS OF THE MARITIMES. An Anthology of the Poetry of the Maritime Provinces of Canada. Toronto, McClelland, 1931. 213p [BM BVaU NSHD OTP QMM

**Robb, Wallace Havelock, 1888–**

AN ABBEY DAWN POEM. Kingston, Author, 1944. 8p [QMU

A DAY AT ABBEY DAWN. By Charles Honce and Wallace Havelock Robb. Mt. Vernon, N.Y., Golden Eagle Press, n.d. 12p [OTU

THE DOOR OF DAWN. New York, Poets' Press, 1937. 96p [LC OTU QMM

ELEGY. Kingston, Author, 1952. 3p

A FAR BELL CALLING. A Selection of Bell Poems in a Pastoral Mood and Morningsong From the Works of Wallace Havelock Robb. 2nd ed. Kingston, Abbey Dawn Press, 1956. 12p

INDIAN CHRISTMAS CAROL. Kingston, Abbey Dawn, 1940. 16p [LC OTU QMM

THE QUILL AND THE CANDLE. Poems of Birdland in Canada. Toronto, Ryerson, 1927. 54p [BVaU OORD QMM

SAID SIR JOHN MACDONALD, "THAT'S THE LAW"; or, Ballad of the High-Stepping Bays (*circa* 1842). Kingston, Author, 1957. 5p

TECUMTHA: SHAWNEE CHIEFTAIN–ASTRAL AVATAR. Kingston, Abbey Dawn Press, 1958. xiii + 223p

**Robbins, Ronald Cynewulf, 1915–**

OUT OF SOLITUDE. London, Linden Press, 1959. 47p

**Roberts, Charles George Douglas, 1860–1943**

AUTOTOCHTHON. Windsor, N.S., Author, 1889. 4p [NBFU OTU

AVE. An Ode for the Centenary of the Birth of P.B. Shelley, 4th August, 1792. Toronto, Williamson, 1892. 27p [BVaU LC NBFU OTU

BE QUIET WIND; UNSAID. [Two Poems.] Toronto, Author, 1929. 2p [BVaU

THE BOOK OF THE NATIVE. Toronto, Copp Clark, 1896. 156p [BM BVaU LC NBFU OTU QMSS

THE BOOK OF THE ROSE. Boston, Page, 1903. 83p [BM BVaU LC NBFU OTU QMM

CANADA SPEAKS OF BRITAIN AND OTHER POEMS OF THE WAR. Toronto, Ryerson, 1941. 15p [LC NSHD OTU QMM

FLYING COLOURS. An Anthology. Ed. by ——. Toronto, Ryerson, 1942. 126p [BVaU LC NBFU OTU

THE ICEBERG AND OTHER POEMS. Toronto, Ryerson, 1934. 31p [BVaU LC NSHD OTU QMBM

IN DIVERS TONES. Boston, Lothrop, 1886. 134p [BM BVaU LC NBFU OTP QMM

LATER POEMS. [Fredericton], Author, 1881. 8p [OTP

LATER POEMS. ... In September; Before the Breath of Storm; Actaeon; A Ballad of Philomela; In the Afternoon; Lotos. [Fredericton], Crockett, [1882]. 13p [OTP

NEW POEMS. London, Constable, 1919. 44p [BM BVaU NBFU OKQ

NEW YORK NOCTURNES AND OTHER POEMS. Boston, Lamson Wolffe, 1898. 84p [BM BVaU LC NSHD OLU QMM

NORTHLAND LYRICS. By William Carman Roberts, Theodore Roberts, and Elizabeth Roberts MacDonald. Selected and arranged by ——. Boston, Small Maynard, 1899. 86p [BM BVaU LC NBFU OKQ

ORION, AND OTHER POEMS. Philadelphia, Lippincott, 1880. 113p [BM BVaU LC NBFU OTU QMM

POEMS. New York, Silver Burdett, 1901. 222p [BM BVaU LC NSHD OTU QMM

POEMS. ... New Complete Edition. Boston, Page, 1907. 257p [BVaU LC NSHD OOU

POEMS OF WILD LIFE. Selected and ed. by ——. London, Scott, 1888. 238p [BM BVaU LC NSHD OTU QMM

SELECTED POEMS. Ed. with an intro. by Desmond Pacey. Toronto, Ryerson, 1956. xxv + 100p

SELECTED POEMS OF SIR CHARLES G.D. ROBERTS. Toronto, Ryerson, 1936. 188p [BM BVaU LC NSHD OTU

SONGS OF THE COMMON DAY, AND AVE: AN ODE FOR THE SHELLEY CENTENARY. Toronto, Briggs, 1893. 126p [BM BVaU NSHD OTP

THE SWEET O' THE YEAR AND OTHER POEMS. Toronto, Ryerson, 1925. 8p [BVaU NBSaM OTU QMM

TWILIGHT OVER SHAUGAMAUK, AND THREE OTHER POEMS. Toronto, Ryerson, 1937. 10p [BVaU NBFU OTP

THE VAGRANT OF TIME. Toronto, Ryerson, 1927. 46p [Another ed. containing "These Three Score Years": Toronto, Ryerson, 1927. 63p] [BVaU NBFU OTP QMM

**Roberts, Dorothy Mary Gostwick, 1906–**

DAZZLE. By Dorothy Roberts. Toronto, Ryerson, 1957. 12p

IN STAR AND STALK. By Dorothy Roberts. Toronto, Emblem Books, 1959. 14p

SONGS FOR SWIFT FEET. By Gostwick Roberts. Toronto, Ryerson, 1927. 8p [BVaU NBFU OTP QMM

**Roberts, Frank Calvin, 1861–**

DAT RIVAAR METABATCHUAN, AND OTHER OUTDOOR VERSE. Philadelphia, Burbank, 1924. 65p [Brown U LC

**Roberts, Lloyd, 1884–1966**

ALONG THE OTTAWA. A Book of Lyrics. Toronto, Dent, 1927. 92p [BM BVaU NBFU OTU QMM

BOOK OF POEMS. Toronto, Goodchild, 1919. [CAR

ENGLAND OVER SEAS. London, Matthews, 1914. 56p [BM LC NBFU OKQ

I SING OF LIFE. Selected Poems. Toronto, Ryerson, 1937. 99p [BVaU LC NBFU OTP

**Roberts, Theodore Goodridge, 1877–1953**

THE LEATHER BOTTLE. Toronto, Ryerson, 1934. 87p [BVaU LC NBFU OTU QMM

THE LOST SHIPMATE. Toronto, Ryerson, 1926. 14p [BVaU NBFU OTP QMM

NORTHLAND LYRICS. By William Carman Roberts, Theodore Roberts, and Elizabeth Roberts MacDonald. Selected and Arranged by Charles G.D. Roberts. Boston, Small Maynard, 1899. 86p [BM BVaU LC OKQ

SEVEN POEMS. Fredericton, Author, 1925. 11p [BVaU

**Roberts, William Carman**

NORTHLAND LYRICS. By William Carman Roberts, Theodore Roberts, and Elizabeth Roberts MacDonald. Selected and Arranged by Charles G.D. Roberts. Boston, Small Maynard, 1899. 86p [BM BVaU LC NBFU OKQ

**Robertson, John**

WARBLINGS AND WAILINGS OF LEISURE HOURS. By Scotus [pseud]. Three Rivers, Que., Author, 1859. 78p [OTP

**Robertson, John Charles, 1864–1956**

LATIN SONGS NEW AND OLD. Selected and written by ——. Toronto, U. of Toronto Press, 1934. 64p [Rev. and enl.: Toronto, 1937.] [LC OTP

**Robertson, John Wilson**

WOOD-NOTES WILD. By John Wilson (Bard O' Glen Eerie) [pseud]. 2nd & enl. ed. Toronto, Briggs, 1912. 200p [First ed.: Fort William, 1903. 24p] [BM BVaU OKQ

**Robeson, Ephraim, 1862–1951**

POETICAL MUSINGS. [3rd ed. rev. and enl.] Athens, Ont., Standard Pub. House, 1947. 46p [OKQ

**Robinson, Mrs. F. Maud**

SONGS FROM SISSIBOO HILL. ... Toronto, Livingstone Press, 1934. 24p [NBFU

**Robinson, Harold.**

PRAIRIE DAYS AND OTHER VERSES. Winnipeg, Hull Print., [1935?]. 67p [BViPA

**Robinson, Hazel Alberta, 1913–1955**

POEMS. N.p. [19—?]. 40p [OKQ

POEMS AND A PLAY. Toronto, Ryerson, 1955. 39p [Radio play, "This Perilous Dream," presented on the CBC, Nov. 11, 1949.]

**Robinson, Helen Templeton Douglas, 1877–1956**

THE CALL OF LIFE. Boston, Humphries, 1957. 60p

SKY WAYS. Boston, Humphries, 1943. 48p [OTP

CANDLE AND CUP. A Collection of some of H.T.D. Robinson's Most Popular Published Lines. Toronto, Crucible Press, 1941. 20p [LC OTP

**Robinson, Jessie M.**

ALPHA AND OMEGA. London, Stockwell, 1932. 46p [BM

CAROLS FOR CHRISTMAS. London, Stockwell, 1926 [BM

THE EMPIRE CALL; or, The Line that Belts the World. Toronto, priv. print., 1901. [Rhod. p869

**Roddick, Amy (Redpath), –1954**

THE ARMISTICE, AND OTHER POEMS. Montreal, Dougall, 1919. 60p [BVaU OTP QMM

THE BIRTH OF MONTREAL (A Chronicle Play), AND OTHER POEMS. Montreal, Dougall, 1921. 174p [BM BVaU NSHD OTP QMM

ENGLAND'S OLDEST COLONY. Montreal, Author, 1940. 4p [OTU

THE FLAG, AND OTHER POEMS. Montreal, Dougall, 1918. 47p [BM BVaU NSHD OTU QMM

FROM MONTREAL ELSEWHERE. Poems. Montreal, Dougall, 1929. 80p [BVaU NSHD OTU QMM

I TRAVEL TO THE POETS' MART. Montreal, Dougall, 1936. 52p [BVaU LC OTP QMM

THE IROQUOIS ENJOY A PERFECT DAY; A CHANCE MEETING; AND OTHER POEMS. Montreal, Dougall, 1939. 64p [BVaU LC OTU QMM

THE ROMANCE OF A PRINCESS; A COMEDY; AND OTHER POEMS. Montreal, Dougall, 1922. 94p [BM BVaU LC OTP QMM

THE TOMAHAWK, A PLAYLET; AND OTHER POEMS. Montreal, Dougall, 1938. 76p [BVaU LC OTU QMM

WAITING'S WEDDING, AND OTHER POEMS. Montreal, Dougall, 1941. 62p [BVaU LC OTU QMM

**Rodgers, Robert Wylie**

DRY BELT JINGLES. Cabin Lake, Alta., [193–?]. 12p [ACG

DRY BELT GINGLES [*sic*]. No. 2. Cabin Lake, Alta., [1948?]. 8p [ACG

**Rody, Margaret Ellen Vance (Strain), 1882–**

BEAUTY AND THOUGHT IN VERSE. Vancouver, Capitol, 1942. 54p [BVaU

GLEANINGS. Kamsack, Sask., Kamsack Times, [1931]. 47p [Same title: New York, Poets' Press, 1942. 32p] [BVaU BViPA CC

**Rogers, Amos Robert, 1927–**

THE WHITE MONUMENT. Toronto, Ryerson, 1955. 13p

**Rogers, Charles Gordon**

BALLADS O' BARLEYCORN. Ottawa, Graphic, 1925. 164p [BVaU OTU QMBM

GOVERNMENT CLERKS. A Book of Ballads. New York, Kellogg, 1902. 39p [BM LC OOP

**Rogers, Thomas George, 1877–1961?**

THOUGHTS IN VERSE. N.p., [1959?]. 18p

**Rogerson, Isabella (Whiteford)**

POEMS. By Isabella Whiteford. Belfast, 1860. 297p [BVaU

THE VICTORIAN TRIUMPH AND OTHER POEMS. Toronto, Briggs, 1898. 232p [OTP

**Rooke, Archibald Gordon, 1885–**

GOLDEN GLEAMS. North Vancouver, Review Press, 1933. 15p [BVaU

PATRIOTIC PARADE AND PARODIES WITH A PUNCH. Mother Goose Up to the Minute. Priv. print., 1941. 17p [BViPA

**Rooker-Clark, May**

LATE BLOSSOMS. London, Stockwell, 1940. 24p [OKQ

**Rorison, Jean (Kilby)**

IN MY GARDEN. Toronto, Ryerson, 1929. 8p [BVaU NBFU OTP QMM

**Rose, George MacLean, 1829–1898**

LIGHT FOR THE TEMPERANCE PLATFORM. A Collection of Readings, Recitations and Dialogues. ... Toronto, Hunter Rose, 1876. Pt. II. 120p [OTP QMU

**Rose, Harry**

RHYMES OF A ROVER. Toronto, Rose, 1933. 22p [OTU

**Ross, Alexander, 1783–1856**

SELMA: A Tale of the Sixth Crusade. By A. Ross. London, 1839. [BM

**Ross, Allan, 1833–**

POEMS. Treherne, Man., Treherne Times, 1907. 182p [BVaU OTP

**Ross, Henry**

NORMAN HAZARD; or, The Fur Trader's Story. Stanbridge East, 1905. 16p [OTP

**Ross, James Alway, 1869–1945**

CANADA FIRST AND OTHER POEMS. Toronto, McClelland, 1920. 111p [BM Brown U BVaU OTU

THE SINGER AND HIS SONG, AND OTHER POEMS. Ottawa, Tower Books, 1950. 79p [BVaU OONL

**Ross, Malcolm Mackenzie, 1911–**

POETS OF THE CONFEDERATION. Charles G.D. Roberts, Bliss Carman, Archibald Lampman, Duncan Campbell Scott. Ed. and with an intro. by ——. Toronto, McClelland, 1960. xiv + 130p [New Canadian Library Original, No. 01]

**Ross, William Wrightson Eustace, 1894–1966**

EXPERIMENT: 1923-29. By W.W.E. Ross. Toronto, Contact Press, 1952. 23p [mimeographed]

LACONICS. By E.R. [pseud]. Ottawa, Overbrook Press, 1930. 92p [BVaU Brown U

SONNETS. By E.R. [pseud]. Toronto, Heaton Pub. Co., 1932. 72p [BVaU OTU

**Rowan, Alice Margaret**

POEMS. With foreword by the Rev. Robert C. Johnstone. Winnipeg, Lasker, 1925. 27p [OTP

**Rowley, William Philip**

A CARAVAN OF THOUGHTS. Toronto, Author, 1940. 24p [mimeographed] [CC

IN SUBJECT MOOD. Trio of Poems. Toronto, Author, 1941. 16p [CC

**Roy, George Ross, 1924–**

THE CITY. A Prose Poem. Strasbourg (France), Imprimerie régionale Strasbourg, 1956. 4p

TWELVE MODERN FRENCH CANADIAN POETS. Translated by G.R. Roy, with French text. Toronto, Ryerson, 1958. xi + 99p

**Roy, Rev. James, 1834–1922**

LET DOWN THE NETS, AND OTHER VERSES. Ottawa, 1902. 43p [OTU Royal Empire Society

**Roy, James Alexander, 1884–**

CHRIST IN THE STRAND AND OTHER POEMS. Kingston, Jackson, 1922. 68p [OTU QMM

**Royal, Charles Elliott**

ROYAL RHYMES AND ROMANCES. Vancouver, International Pub. Co., 1919. 64p [BVaU

THE TRAIL OF A SOURDOUGH. Rhymes and Ballads. Toronto, McClelland, 1919. 168p [BM BVaU QMM

**Ruark, Fletcher, 1880–1952**

JECILA AND OTHER POEMS. Windsor, Ont., Curtis, 1934. 78p [BVaU LC OTP QMM

MOSAIC, AND OTHER POEMS. Windsor, Ont., Curtis, 1948. 157p [OTP QMM

POEMS. Windsor, Ont., Curtis, 1931. 79p [BVaU LC OTU QMM

RED WIND, AND OTHER POEMS. New York, Avon House, 1940. 64p [BVaU LC OTP QMM

THE SOUTHLAND AND OTHER POEMS. 1920.

**Rumsey, John**

CURIAE CANADENSES; or, The Canadian Law Courts. A Poem. By Plinius Secundus [pseud]. Toronto, Rowsell, 1843. 126p [BVaU LC OTP

**Russell, Euphemia**

BOOK OF POEMS. 4th ed. Toronto, Stewart, 1872. 30p [Apparently first pub. as: POETRY. Toronto, 1869. 23p –See CCJ.] [OTP

**Russell, Foster Meharry, 1907–**

BRAIDS OF BEAUTY. Cobourg, Ont., Sentinel-Star, 1960. 149p

**Russell, Margaret (Clarke), 1875–**

HOUSEWORK POEMS. Toronto, My Friends' Little Book Shop, 1923. [BM

THE NAUGHTY SUN AND OTHER VERSE. London, Stockwell, 1931. 32p [BM

THE SILLY MOON AND OTHER VERSE. London, Stockwell, 1935. 48p [BM Brown U
STARS. A Fairy Tale. London, Ont., Players' Craft Press, 1928. 63p [NBFU OLU

**Ruttan, Kate (McIntyre)**
RHYMES, RIGHT OR WRONG, OF RAINY RIVER. I.O.O.F. and Masonic Madrigals by McIntyre [pseud]. Orillia, Times Print., 1926. 182p [Brown U

**Ryan, F.B.**
THE SPIRIT'S LAMENT; or, The Wrongs of Ireland. A Poem. Montreal, 1847. 194p [BVaU

**Ryan, Mary Anne (McIver), 1839–1919**
POEMS. Ottawa, Taylor, 1869. 176p [BVaU NSHD OTP QMBM

**Ryan, William Thomas Carroll, 1839–1910**
OSCAR, AND OTHER POEMS. By Carroll Ryan. Hamilton, Franklin, 1857. 120p [BVaU OTU
PICTURE POEMS. By Carroll Ryan. 1884. [CCJ MOR'98
POEMS, SONGS, BALLADS. By Carroll Ryan. Montreal, Lovell, 1903. 223p [BM BVaU OOP QMM
SONGS OF A WANDERER. By Carroll Ryan. Ottawa, Desbarats, 1867. 289p [BM BVaU NSHD OTU QMM

**S., G.A.**
"PREPARE!" An Appeal to Britons. By G.A.S. [pseud]. Toronto, [1911?]. 22p [Brown U OTU

**Sabiston, M.**
GRENADA AND OTHER POEMS. London, Tinsley, 1876. xxii + 202p [BM OLU

**Sadler, Mrs. Violet T., –1958?**
HARBOUR BELL RECITER. Vancouver, Greetings, n.d. 122p [BVaU
SUNLIGHT AND SHADOWS. Poems. Vancouver, O. Smith Print., 1958. 40p

**Sage, Donalda Margaret (MacKinnon)**
FRAGMENTS OF FANTASY. By Nelda MacKinnon Sage. Toronto, Ryerson, 1928. 8p [BVaU NBFU OKQ QMM
TOP O' THE WORLD. By Nelda MacKinnon Sage. Toronto, Dent. 1929. 94p [BM BVaU OKQ

**Sahagian, Y.S.**
ECHOES PENNED FOR YOUNG LADIES AND YOUNG LADS. Hamilton, Spectator Print., 1914. 27p [OH

**St. Clare, Reginald**
TRANSATLANTIC SKETCHES FROM LIFE. A Satire. Hamilton, Lyght, [18—?]. 46p [OTP

**St. George, V.J.**

TO A SOLDIER OF BRITISH COLUMBIA. ... Victoria, Quality Press, n.d. 11p [BVaU

**St. John, Charles Henry**

CORPORAL DAY. Boston, Badger, 1904. 47p [LC

THE DAWN OF FREEDOM. Boston, Badger, 1904. 156p [LC

POEMS. Boston, 1859. 144p [OOP

**Salter, John**

THE POETICAL WORKS. Comprising Metrical Sketches on the Functions of the Brain, and Other Pieces. Halifax, Cunnabell, 1852. 116p [NSHPL

**Salverson, Laura (Goodman), 1890–1970**

WAYSIDE GLEAMS. Toronto, McClelland, 1925. 97p [BVaU NBFU OTP QMM

**Samson, Solomon, 1885–1957**

A GLIMPSE OF NEWFOUNDLAND (AS IT WAS AND AS IT IS) IN POETRY AND PICTURES. All Edited, Arranged, Illustrated and Set with Pictures appropriate to the Poems, by Robert Saunders. Poole, Eng., J. Looker, 1960. xv + 80p

**Sandercock, W. Clark, –1938**

THE DANCE IN THE BUFFALO SKULL AND OTHER POEMS. Toronto, Saunders, 1935. 156p [BVaU OTU

**Sanders, Robert Walter, 1876–**

HELP FOR MOTHERS AND FOR OTHERS, RHYMES. Greenville, S.C., 1922. 35p [LC

UP INTO THE HILLS AND OTHER POEMS. Niagara Falls, Ont., Slingerland, 1939. 24p [2nd & enl. ed.: St. Catharines, Author, 1958. 60p] [OTP

**Sanderson, Camilla**

GOOD MORNING. Toronto, Briggs, 1918. 53p [BVaU

IF I COULD SING. Toronto, Briggs, 1913. 12p [BM OTU

**Sanderson, Rev. Joseph Edward, 1830–1913**

FORESTS. A Canadian Pastoral. Toronto, Briggs, 1906. 12p [BVaU OTUV

**Sanford, Melissa T.**

ORIGINAL FABLES AND RIDDLES IN RHYME. With Other Poems. By Melissa T. and Edwin L. Sanford. Montreal, Drysdale, 1888. 57p [OTP

**Sangster, Charles, 1822–1893**

HESPERUS, AND OTHER POEMS AND LYRICS. Montreal, Lovell, 1860. 186p [BM BVaU LC MWU NBFU OTP QMM

... OUR NORLAND. ... Toronto, Copp Clark, [1896?]. 14p [Brown U NSHD OOP

THE ST. LAWRENCE AND THE SAGUENAY, AND OTHER POEMS. Kingston, Creighton & Duff, 1856. 262p [BVaU LC NBFU OTP QMM

**Sarson, H. Smalley**

FROM FIELD AND HOSPITAL. London, E. Macdonald, 1916. 24p [BM

**Saskatchewan Poetry Society, Regina**

THE SASKATCHEWAN POETRY BOOK. Regina, the Society, 1952. 44p

**Saskatchewan, University of. Writers' Club.**

STUDENT VERSES. Saskatoon, the Club, 1927–. [Issued from time to time over a decade or more.] [CC

**Saskatchewan. Western Producer.**

AN ANTHOLOGY OF Y.C. VERSE. A Volume of Selections from the Verse contributed by the Young Co-operators and published in the Western Producer from 1932 to 1936. Saskatoon, Western Producer, 1937. 75p [Brown U SSU

**Saturday Night (Toronto)**

POEMS FOR THE INTERIM. A Selection of Twenty-four Poems by Nineteen Canadian Authors. Published during 1945–46 in "Saturday Night." Toronto, Saturday Night, 1946. 24p [BVaU NBFU QMM

**Saunders, Daisy L.**

CHURNINGS FROM A PRAIRIE KITCHEN. Toronto, Hunter Rose, 1926. 83p [Brown U QMM SSU

**Saunders, Thomas A., 1909–**

THE DEVIL AND CAL McCABE; OR, THE TALE OF THE COWMAN'S CORNS. A Story in Verse. Toronto, Ryerson, 1960. 26p

HORIZONTAL WORLD. Toronto, Ryerson, 1951. 41p

SCRUB OAK. Toronto, Ryerson, 1949. 12p [BVaU NBSaM OTP

SOMETHING OF A YOUNG WORLD'S DYING. Toronto, Ryerson, 1958. 20p

**Sauvey, Katherine Isobelle (McKowen), 1863?–1944**

GRIST FOR THE MILL. Toronto, Crucible Press, 1941. 18p [NBSaM OTP

**Savage, Rocke**

PRAIRIE TRAILS. A Book of Verse. London, Stockwell, 1939. 122p [BM OTU

**Sawdon, Mrs. Edna Johnston**

DREAM VALLEY. Winnipeg, Canada Music Pub. Co., 1940. 210p [CC

**Sawtell, Mrs. M. Ethelind**

THE MOURNER'S TRIBUTE; or, Effusions of Melancholy Hours. Montreal, Armour & Ramsay, 1840. 271p [BM BVaU OTP QMM

**Saw-Waw-Goosh, or The Yellow Fox**

A MONTH IN THE MARSH. By Saw-Waw-Goosh, or The Yellow Fox. Chatham, Ont., Thompson, 1860. 32p [OTP

**Scaife, Arthur Hodgkin**

THE SOLILOQUY OF A SHADOW-SHAPE ON A HOLIDAY FROM HADES, etc. [An Imitation of the Rubaiyat of Omar Khayyam]. London, Karslake, 1900. [BM

**Scharfe, Ruth Elva, 1917–**

A SCRAPBOOK OF VERSE. Ottawa, Author, 1960. 20p

**Schofield, Bob**

MARILYN – QUEEN OF THE LAKE. And other Lyrics. Ilfracombe, Devon, Stockwell, 1957. 24p

**Schooley, Mary (Rice)**

SINCERE DESIRES. Vancouver, Wrigley, 1936. 27p [Brown U BVaU

**Schrum, Hazel (Keenan), 1915–**

GOLDEN DAWN VERSES. Sudbury, Author, [1960?]. 16p

**Schull, Joseph, 1910–**

I, JONES, SOLDIER. Toronto, Macmillan, 1944. 62p [BVaU NBFU OTU

THE LEGEND OF GHOST LAGOON. Toronto, Macmillan, 1937. 178p [Brown U BVaU NBFU OOP

**Scott, Archibald**

DESULTORY POEMS. Hampton, N.B., 1880. 60p [NBFU OTP

**Scott, Duncan Campbell, 1862–1947**

AT SCARBORO' BEACH. N.p., priv. print., n.d. 2p [NBFU

BEAUTY AND LIFE. Toronto, McClelland, 1921. 96p [BM BVaU NBFU OTP QMM

BYRON ON WORDSWORTH. Being Discovered Stanzas of Don Juan. N.p., priv. print., [1924?]. 4p [OKQ

THE GREEN CLOISTER. Later Poems. Toronto, McClelland, 1935. 96p [BVaU LC NBFU OTP

LABOR AND THE ANGEL. Boston, Copeland & Day, 1898. 59p [BVaU LC NBFU OTU QMM

LINES IN MEMORY OF EDMUND MORRIS. N.p., 1915. 14p [BM NBFU OTU

LUNDY'S LANE AND OTHER POEMS. New York, Doran, 1916. 194p [BVaU LC NBFU OTP QMM

THE MAGIC HOUSE AND OTHER POEMS. Ottawa, Durie, 1893. 95p [BM BVaU MWU NBFU OTP QMM

NEW WORLD LYRICS AND BALLADS. Toronto, Morang, 1905. 66p [BM BVaU LC NBFU OTP QMM

THE POEMS OF DUNCAN CAMPBELL SCOTT. Toronto, McClelland, 1926. 341p [BM BVaU NBFU OKQ QMM

REALITY. N.p., n.d. 4p [NBFU

SELECTED POEMS OF DUNCAN CAMPBELL SCOTT. With a memoir by E.K. Brown. Toronto, Ryerson, 1951. 176p

TO THE CANADIAN MOTHERS, AND THREE OTHER POEMS. N.p., priv. print., 1917. 14p [BVaU NBFU OKQ

VIA BOREALIS. Toronto, Tyrrell, 1906. 21p [BM BVaU NBFU OTP QMM

**Scott, Elise Aylen, 1904–**

ROSES OF SHADOW. By Elise Aylen [pseud]. With a foreword by Duncan Campbell Scott. Toronto, Macmillan, 1930. 56p [BVaU NBFU OKQ QMM

**Scott, Francis Reginald, 1899–**

THE BLASTED PINE. An Anthology of Satire, Invective and Disrespectful Verse, Chiefly by Canadian Writers. Selected and arr. and with an intro. by F.R. Scott and A.J.M. Smith. Toronto, Macmillan, 1957. xix + 138p

EVENTS AND SIGNALS. Toronto, Ryerson, 1954. 58p

THE EYE OF THE NEEDLE. Satires, Sorties, Sundries. Montreal, Contact Press, 1957. 71p

NEW PROVINCES. Poems of Several Authors. [Ed. by ——.] Toronto, Macmillan, 1936. 77p [Contains poems by Finch, Kennedy, Klein, Pratt, F.R. Scott and A.J.M. Smith.] [BVaU NBFU OKQ

OVERTURE. Poems. Toronto, Ryerson, 1945. 79p [BVaU MWU NBFU OKQ QMM

**Scott, Rev. Frederick George, 1861–1944**

COLLECTED POEMS. Vancouver, Clarke & Stuart, 1934. 199p [BM BVaU LC NSHD OTP QMM

THE GATES OF TIME, AND OTHER POEMS. London, Bagster, 1915. 149p [AEU BM NBFU QMG

A HYMN OF EMPIRE, AND OTHER POEMS. Toronto, Briggs, 1906. 55p [BM BVaU NBFU OTP QMM

IN SUN AND SHADE. A Book of Verse. Quebec, Dussault & Proulx, 1926. 38p [BM BVaU NBFU OKQ QMSS

IN THE BATTLE SILENCES. Poems Written at the Front. London, Constable, 1916. 33p [BM BVaU LC NBFU OTP QMM

MY LATTICE AND OTHER POEMS. Toronto, Briggs, 1894. 108p [BVaU LC MWU NBFU OTP QMM

LIFT UP YOUR HEARTS. Toronto, Ryerson, 1941. 23p [BVaU NBFU OTP

NEW POEMS. Quebec, Lafrance, 1929. 39p [BM BVaU LC OTU QMM

POEMS. London, Constable, 1910. 297p [BM BVaU LC NBFU OTP QMM

POEMS. London, S.P.C.K., 1936. 322p [BM OTU QMM

POEMS OLD AND NEW. Toronto, Briggs, 1900. 154p [BM BVaU LC NBFU OTP QMM

SELECTED POEMS. Quebec, Robitaille, 1933. 118p [BM BVaU NSHD OTP QMM

THE SOUL'S QUEST. A Poem. Market End, Coggeshall, Essex, Edwin Potter, 1886. 11p [Amtmann cat. 248

THE SOUL'S QUEST AND OTHER POEMS. London, Kegan Paul, 1888. 123p [BM BVaU NBFU OTP QMM

THE UNNAMED LAKE AND OTHER POEMS. Toronto, Briggs, 1897. 48p [BM BVaU LC MWU NBFU OTP

**Scott, George**

BALLADS OF DISARMAMENT AND OTHER POEMS. Saint John, Globe Pub., 1923. 60p [NBFU

**Scott, J. Donald**

FIRST BORN. ... Toronto, 1931. 36p [Brown U OTU

**Scott, Leslie (Grant)**

THE LIGHT OF GENIUS, THE MYSTIC, AND OTHER POEMS. Toronto, Briggs, 1912. 38p [BM BVaU OTU

**Scott, Mary Zillah**

POEMS. Vancouver, Author, 1946. 28p [BViPA

**Scribble, Sam (pseud)**

THE KING OF THE BEAVERS. Montreal, 1865. 20p [OOP

ORPHEUS AND EURYDICE. A Classical Extravaganza. Montreal, 1866. 25p [OOP

**Scriven, Joseph Medlicott, 1819–1886**

HYMNS AND OTHER VERSES. Peterborough, Stephens, 1869. 112p [OTU

WHAT A FRIEND WE HAVE IN JESUS, AND OTHER HYMNS. With a Sketch of the Author by James Cleland. Port Hope, Williamson, 1895. 30p [NSWA OTUV

**Sedgewick, Garnett Gladwin, 1882–1949**

THE GRAVEYARD BY THE SEA. Vancouver, Author, 1938. 26p [Text of Paul Valéry's "Le Cimetière Marin"] [OTU

**Sella, Ernestine E.**

PALM ROOM BALLADS. By Ernestine [pseud]. N.p., 1913. 62p [BM Brown U

**Selle, Leonard Saville George, 1910–**

MOMENTS, AND OTHER POEMS. Fraserdale, Ont., Author, 1951. 30p (Carillon Poetry Chap-Books)

ONCE UPON A RHYME. Reflections in Light Verse. North Bay, Ont., Northland Printers, 1955. 52p

**Selwyn, Cecil Edward**

PRAIRIE PATCHWORK; or, Western Poems for Western People. Winnipeg, Stovel, 1910. 96p [BM BVaU OTP

REGIMENTAL DITTIES. ... Winnipeg, Author, 1914. 31p [BM

RHYMING SNAPSHOTS OF AN IDLE FELLOW. Toronto, Ryerson, 1924. 132p [BVaU NBFU OKQ

**Sepass, Khalserten, 1841–1943 [Indian Chief]**

THE SONGS OF Y-AIL-MIHTH. Trans. by Mrs. C.L. Street; ed. by Eloise Street. Vancouver, Indian Time, 1955. 76p

**Service, Robert William, 1874–1958**

BALLADS OF A BOHEMIAN. New York, Barse, 1921. 220p [BM BVaU LC NBFU OTU QMM

BALLADS OF A CHEECHAKO. Toronto, Briggs, 1909. 137p [Many later editions by many publishers.] [BM BVaU NBFU OTP QMM

BAR-ROOM BALLADS. A Book of Verse. New York, Dodd Mead, 1940. 169p [Also: London, Benn, 1940. 206p] [BM BVaU LC NBFU OTU QMM

CAROLS OF AN OLD CODGER. Verse. London, Benn, 1954. 198p

COLLECTED VERSE. London, Benn, 1930. [Various pagings] [BM BVa LC NBFU OTP

THE COMPLETE POEMS. New York, Dodd Mead, 1940. 735p [BVaU NBFU OTU

THE COMPLETE POEMS. New York, Dodd Mead, 1942. [1032p] [Various pagings] [LC NBFU OOU

COMPLETE POETICAL WORKS. New York, Barse, 1921. [855p] [Various pagings] [Reprinted as: COLLECTED VERSE. London, Benn, 1930; and COMPLETE POEMS. New York, Dodd Mead, 1933.] [BM BVa LC NBFU OTP

LYRICS OF A LOW BROW. New York, Dodd Mead, 1951. 182p

MORE COLLECTED VERSE. London, Benn, 1955. 1v [Various pagings]

RHYME AND ROMANCE. A Robert Service Anthology. London, Benn, 1958. 320 + 191 + 336 + 232p [Contents: THE TRAIL OF '98; SONGS OF A SUN-LOVER; THE HOUSE OF FEAR; RHYMES OF A REBEL.]

RHYMES FOR MY RAGS. A Verse Book. London, Benn, 1956. 191p

RHYMES OF A REBEL. New York, Dodd Mead, 1952. 213p [Also: London, Benn, 1952. 232p]

THE RHYMES OF A RED-CROSS MAN. London, Unwin, 1916. 192p [BM BVaU LC NBFU OTP QMM

RHYMES OF A ROLLING STONE. Toronto, Briggs, 1912. 195p [BM BVaU LC NBFU OTP QMM

RHYMES OF A ROUGHNECK. New York, Dodd Mead, 1950. 207p [BM BVaU LC NBFU OTP

SELECTED POEMS BY ROBERT SERVICE. With Some Account of his Life and Experiences. London, Unwin, 1917. 28p [BM BVaU

THE SHOOTING OF DAN McGREW, AND OTHER VERSES. New York, Barse & Hopkins, 1920. [BM

SONGS FOR MY SUPPER. Verse. London, Benn, 1953. 207p

SONGS OF A SOURDOUGH. Toronto, Briggs, 1907. 116p [Many later editions.] [BM BVaU LC NSHD OTP QMM

SONGS OF A SUN-LOVER. London, Benn, 1949. 191p [BM BVaU LC OTP

SONGS OF THE HIGH NORTH. London, Benn, 1958. 126p

THE SPELL OF THE YUKON AND OTHER VERSES. New York, Barse, 1907. 126p [BVaU LC OTU QMM

TWENTY BATH-TUB BALLADS. London, Francis, Day & Hunter, 1939. 48p [LC

**Sewell, (Henry) Fane, –1944**

THE KING, CANADA AND EMPIRE. By Fane Sewell. Toronto, Briggs, 1910. 20p [BM BVaU OTP

**Shackleton, Helen**

SAUCY AGAIN. Verses. Toronto, Macmillan, 1937. 49p [BM LC OOP

SAUCY AND ALL. Verses. Toronto, Macmillan, 1929. 48p [BM OTMC

**Shannon, William**

THE DOMINION ORANGE HARMONIST. ... Toronto, Maclear, 1876. 394p [OLU OTP

THE UNITED EMPIRE MINSTREL. A Selection of the Best National, Constitutional and Loyal Orange Songs and Poems, etc. etc. Toronto, Rowsell, 1852. 292p [OONL

**Sharkey, Hugh Francis Xavier**

AN ANVIL OF THE CROSS. [Vancouver, Author, 1934.] 141p [BVaU OWA

THE LOOM OF THE FAIRIES. N.p., [1929?]. 71p [OWA

**Sharland, Rose E.**

BALLADS OF OLD BRISTOL. Bristol, Arrowsmith, 1914. 69p [BM

EXMOOR LYRICS, AND OTHER VERSES. Bristol, Arrowsmith, 1910. 66p [BM

MAPLE LEAF MEN, AND OTHER WAR GLEANINGS. Toronto, Musson, [1916?]. 88p [BM OTP QMU

VOICES OF DAWN OVER THE HILLS. Bristol, Arrowsmith, 1912. 77p [BM BVaU

**Sharman, Mrs. Lyon, 1872–**

THE SEA WALL, AND OTHER VERSE. Toronto, Macmillan, 1925. 79p [BVaU NBFU OTP QMM

TOWN AND FOREST. Toronto, Macmillan, 1942. 73p [LC NBFU OTU

**Shaw, Mrs. Amanda**

THE WONDROUS HUSH. New York, Revell, 1931. 48p [BVaU LC OTP

**Shaw, Bill**

RHYMES OF THE R.C.A.F. Aylmer, Ont., Author, 1942. [CC

**Sheard, Virna (Stanton), 1865?–1943**

THE BALLAD OF THE QUEST. Toronto, McClelland, 1922. 52p [BVaU LC NBFU OTP

CANDLE-FLAME [and Other Poems]. Toronto, McClelland, 1926. 79p [BVaU NBFU OTP QMM

CARRY ON! Toronto, Warwick & Rutter, 1917. 23p [BM BVaU NBFU OTU

FAIRY DOORS. Toronto, McClelland, 1932. 76p [BVaU OTP

LEAVES IN THE WIND. Toronto, Ryerson, 1938. 55p [BVaU NBFU OTP

THE MIRACLE AND OTHER POEMS. Toronto, Dent, 1913. 111p [BM BVaU NBFU OTU QMSS

**Sheldon-Williams, Ralf Frederic Lardy**
TO FRANCE. N.p., 1917. 8p [Adelphi cat. 92

**Shepard, Fred Scott**
NATURE'S CATHEDRAL AND OTHER POEMS. Toronto, Evangelical Pub., n.d. 14p [OONL

**Shepminster, John**
THE IRON PONY, AND OTHER RHYMES, HUMOROUS AND SATIRICAL. Toronto, Author, 1884. 33p [OTP

**Sherk, Florence Nightingale (Horner), 1859–**
THE WORKSHOPS AND OTHER POEMS. Fort William, Times-Journal, 1919. 65p [BVaU OTP

**Sherman, Francis Joseph, 1871–1926**
A CANADIAN CALENDAR: XII LYRICS. Havana, Author, 1900. 23p [NBFU
THE COMPLETE POEMS OF FRANCIS SHERMAN. Ed. with a memoir by Lorne Pierce. Toronto, Ryerson, 1935. 178p [BVaU NBFU OTP QMM
THE DESERTED CITY. Stray Sonnets by F.S. Rescued for the Few who Love them, by H.D. N.p., priv. print., 1899. 12p [NBFU OONL
IN MEMORABILIS MORTIS. Cambridge, Mass., University Press, Author, 1896. 10p [BVaU NBFU OTP
MATINS. Boston, Copeland & Day, 1896. 58p [BM BVaU NBFU OKQ
A PRELUDE. Fredericton, priv. print., 1897. 10p [NBFU OTP

**Sherwood, Harold**
A WELCOME TO ALBERT, PRINCE OF WALES, AND OTHER POEMS. Toronto, Lovell & Gibson, 1860. 49p [BVaU OTP

**Sherwood, William Albert, 1859–1919**
LAYS, LYRICS AND LEGENDS. Toronto, Hunter Rose, 1914. 152p [BVaU NBFU OTP

**Shiels, Andrew, 1793–1879**
DUPES AND DEMAGOGUES. A Souvenir. By "Albyn" [pseud]. Halifax, n.p., 1879. 40p [NSHD
EYE TO THE ERMINE. A Dream. By "Albyn" [pseud]. Halifax, Bowes, 1871. 20p [NSHD
JOHN WALKER'S COURTSHIP. A Legend of Lauderdale. By Albyn [pseud]. Halifax, Bowes, 1877. 32p [NSHD
THE LATE HONOURABLE SIMON BRADSTREET ROBIE. By Albyn [pseud]. [For the *Halifax Sun,* Jan. 7, 1858.] [Halifax?], 1858. 1p [NSHP
LETTER TO ELIZA. By Albyn [pseud]. Halifax, MacNab, 1869. 43p [NSHD
MY MOTHER. In Memoriam. By Albyn [pseud]. Halifax, Bowes, 1868. 10p [NSHD

THE PREFACE. A Poem of the Period. By Albyn [pseud]. Halifax, Bowes, 1876. 55p [NSHP

RETRIBUTION. A Literary Contribution to the Nova Scotia Department of the Philadelphi Exhibition. By Albyn [pseud]. Halifax, MacNab, 1875. 21p [NSHD

RUSTICATING IN REALITY. A Pierian Paraphrase. By Albyn [pseud]. Halifax, Bowes, 1873. 30p [NSHD

SABBATH IN DARTMOUTH. By Albyn [pseud]. Halifax, Bowes, 1870. 15p [NSHP

THE WATER LILY. A Poem. By Albyn [pseud]. Halifax, Bowes, 1852. 32p [BM NSHP

THE WITCH OF THE WESTCOT. A Tale of Nova Scotia in 3 Cantos. And other Waste Leaves of Literature. Halifax, Howe, 1831. 213p [BVaU NSHP OTP

**Shoolman, Regina Lenore, 1909–**

UNCERTAIN GLORY. Toronto, Ryerson, 1932. 8p [BVaU NBFU OTP QMM

**Shortt, Prescott (pseud)**

SONGS FROM THE SILENCE. Toronto, Crucible Press, 1941. 22p [OTU

**Shute, Evan Vere, 1905–**

ANATOMY CLASS. By Vere Jameson [pseud]. London, Ont., Author, 1953. 59p

BLUEBIRD. By Vere Jameson [pseud]. London, Ont., Author, 1954. 47p

HASTY PUDDING. By Vere Jameson [pseud]. London, Ont., Hunter Print., 1951. 102p

HEIRLOOMS. By Vere Jameson [pseud]. London, Ont., Hunter Print., 1956. 59p

HY–BRASIL. By Vere Jameson [pseud]. London, Ont., Author, 1952. 49p

MOTHS AFTER MIDNIGHT. By Vere Jameson [pseud]. Toronto, Ryerson, 1945. 14p [BVaU LC NBFU OKQ QMU

OMAR FROM NISHAPUR. By Vere Jameson [pseud]. London, Ont., Author, 1948. 36p [BVaU NBFU OKQ

SKY PAINTER. By Vere Jameson [pseud]. London, Ont., Author, 1950. 94p [OTU

THE SULTAN OF JOBAT [and Other Poems]. By Vere Jameson [pseud]. London, Ont., Author, 1947. 50p [BVaU NBFU OKQ

WHERE THE HERON STANDS. By Vere Jameson [pseud]. N.p., Author, 1949. 113p [NSHPL OKQ

**Sigurdson, A.S.**

PENCIL STUB STANZAS. A Book of Light Verse. Vancouver, Author, 1950. 91p [BVa OONL

**Silcox, Ethel Audrey (Smith), –1944**

EARTHBOUND, AND OTHER POEMS. Toronto, Ryerson, 1932. 8p [BVaU NBFU OTP

BEGINNINGS IN SONG. By E.A.S.S. Newport, R.I., Milne, 1918. 10p [LC NBFU

**Silverman, Harold S.**

TWENTY-TWO IMPROVISATIONS. Toronto, Author, 1940. 22p [BVaU

**Simcox, J.P.**
IF HITLER WON, AND OTHER VERSES. Killam, Alta., 1941. 26p [Amtmann

**Simpson, Andrew R.**
MISCELLANEOUS POEMS. London, Ont., Advertiser, 1906. 148p [BM BVaU OTU

**Sims, Frederick L.H.**
DRINK AND DRUDGERY. Two Social Sins. Toronto, Author, 1900. 29p [OKQ

**Simson, Letitia F.**
FLOWERS OF THE YEAR, AND OTHER POEMS. Saint John, McMillan, 1869. 103p [BVaU NBFU OTU QMSS

**Sinclair, Rev. Alexander Maclean, 1840–1924**
CLARSACH NA COILLE. A Collection of Gaelic Poetry. Glasgow, Sinclair, 1881. 345p [NBFU OTU
COMHCHRUINNEACHADH CHLINN-A-BHAIRD. The Glenbard Collection of Gaelic Poetry. Charlottetown, Haszard & Moore, 1890. 434p [OTP
THE GAELIC BARDS FROM 1411 TO 1715. Ed. by ——. Charlottetown, Haszard & Moore, 1890. 216p [NSHD OTP
THE GAELIC BARDS FROM 1715–1765. Ed. by ——. Charlottetown, Haszard & Moore, 1892. 260p [OTU
NA BAIRD LEATHANACH. The Maclean Bards. V. 2. Charlottetown, Haszard & Moore, 1900. 176p [OTU
ORAIN LE IAIN LOM MAC-DHOMHNAILL. Poems by John Lom Macdonald. Ed. by ——. Antigonish, The Casket, 1895. 127p [OTU

**Sinclair, Rev. Lawrence**
ADDITIONAL WRITINGS. Huntsville, Ont., Author, 1929. 12p [NSHK
IMPERIAL AND OTHER POETICAL WRITINGS. London, Stacey, [1925]. 140p [OONL

**Singer, James C.**
POEMS. Toronto, Thompson Bros., 1929. 47p [BVaU OTP

**Sivell, Rhoda (Cosgrave), 1874? –**
VOICES FROM THE RANGE. Toronto, T. Eaton Co., 1911. 43p [Another ed., Toronto, Briggs, 1912. 102p] [BM BVaU OKQ SSU

**Skeats, Wilfred S.**
THE SONG OF THE EXILE. A Canadian Epic. Visions and Miscellaneous Poems. Toronto, Hart & Co., 1891. 160p [BVaU NSHD OTP

**Skelton, Robin, 1925–**
PATMOS AND OTHER POEMS. London, Routledge, [1955]. x + 76p
THIRD DAY LUCKY. Toronto, Oxford U. Press, 1958. 71p

**Skene, James H.**

JUST A FEW THOUGHTS. Poems of Peace, Faith and Hope. Stratford, Ont., B–H Press, 1939. 23p [Amtmann cat. 141

**Skimings, Eloise A.**

GOLDEN LEAVES. Goderich, Signal, 1904. 346p [BVaU OTU

**Skinner, Constance Lindsay, 1879? –1939**

SONGS OF THE COAST DWELLERS. New York, Coward-McCann, 1930. 85p [BVaU LC NBFU OTP

**Slack, Crawford Chelson, 1855–1929**

VILLAGE VERSE STORIES, AND OTHER POEMS. Athens, Ont., "Reporter," n.d. 126p [OTUV

**Slader (*i.e.* Sladen), Arthur**

THE CONFLAGRATIONS. Comprising Two Poems. ... First, The Burning Boat–A Serio-Satiric Poem on the Destruction by Fire of the Steamer "Royal Tar." ... Second, The Burning City–A Descriptive Poem in Commemoration of the Lamentable Fire ... in the City of St. John, N.B. ... 1837. Saint John, Observer Office, 1837. 32p [NSHP OTP

**Sliter, Dorothy Browning (Murray)**

HIGH WIND. Toronto, Crucible Press, 1944. 32p [OTP

**Small, Mercator**

THE BOOKKEEPER and a Metrical Translation of "The Song of the Bell" from the German of Schiller. Montreal, 1868. [OOP

**Small, Watten**

POEMS AND SONNETS. Saint John, Day, 1866. 76p [NBSaM

**Smellie, George, 1811–1896**

THE SEA. Sketches of a Voyage to Hudson's Bay. ... By The Scald [pseud]. London, Hope, 1855. 195p [OTP

**Smillie, J.**

RUSTIC RHYMES. Brussels, Ont., "Post," 1894. 43p [OTUV

**Smith, Anna Beatrice, 1904–1936**

WATER FROM THE ROCK. By Anna Beatrice Smith (Imogen Carroll). Ed. by Dr. Mabel Cartwright. Toronto, Macmillan, 1937. 60p [BM BVaU OKQ QMSS

**Smith, Arthur James Marshall, 1902–**

THE BLASTED PINE. An Anthology of Satire, Invective and Disrespectful Verse, Chiefly by Canadian Writers. Selected and arr. and with an intro. by F.R. Scott and A.J.M. Smith. Toronto, Macmillan, 1957. xix + 138p

THE BOOK OF CANADIAN POETRY. A Critical and Historical Anthology. Ed. with an intro. and notes by ——. Chicago, U. of Chicago Press, 1943. 452p [Rev. and enl. ed.: Toronto, Gage, 1948. 487p; 3rd ed., rev. and enl., 1957. xxv + 532p] [BM BVaU LC NBFU OTP QMM

NEW PROVINCES. Poems of Several Authors. [Ed. by F.R. Scott.] Toronto, Macmillan, 1936. 77p [Contains poems by Smith and others.] [BVaU NBFU OKQ

NEWS OF THE PHOENIX AND OTHER POEMS. Toronto, Ryerson, 1943. 42p [BVaU MWU NBFU OTP QMM

THE OXFORD BOOK OF CANADIAN VERSE IN ENGLISH AND FRENCH. Chosen and with intro. by ——. Toronto, Oxford U. Press, 1960. lvi + 445p

A SORT OF ECSTASY. Poems, New and Selected. East Lansing, Mich., Michigan State College Press; Toronto, Ryerson, 1954. 55p

THE WORLDLY MUSE. An Anthology of Serious Light Verse. Ed. by ——. New York, Abelard Press, 1951. 388p

**Smith, F. Percy**

SONGS OF THE SAGUENAY. Arvida, Que., n.d. 28p [Brown U

**Smith, Goldwin, 1823–1910**

BAY LEAVES. Translations from the Latin Poets. Toronto, Blackett Robinson, 1890. 115p [Also: New York, Macmillan, 1893. 89p] [BM BVaU LC MWU NBFU OTP QMU

**Smith, Gordon Stace, 1886–**

IN THE KOOTENAY AND OTHER VERSES. London, Mitre, 1931. 75p [BM BVaU

POEMS AND A REVERIE. Toronto, Weaver, 1940. 32p [OTP

**Smith, Jennie Nelson**

ISLE OF PAISLEY. New York, Vinal, 1928. 102p [LC NSHD OTP

MOOR-MISTS. Halifax, Royal Print., 1925. 128p [NSHD OTP

**Smith, Kay, 1911–**

FOOTNOTE TO THE LORD'S PRAYER, AND OTHER POEMS. Montreal, First Statement Press, 1951. 36p

**Smith, Lyman Cyrus, 1850–1928**

A BLOSSOM OF THE SEA, AND OTHER POEMS. Wilmington, Ind., New Amstel, 1910. 218p [LC NBFU OTP QMM

MABEL GRAY AND OTHER POEMS. Toronto, Briggs, 1896. 131p [Another ed., 1897. 120p] [BM BVaU LC OTP

WAR POEMS. Kingston, British Whig, 1918. [7]p [OOC

**Smith, Martin F., 1840–**

A BOOK OF CANADIAN AND AMERICAN POEMS. Hamilton, Donnelly & Lawson, 1863. 316p [OTP

**Smith, Mary Barry**

JUBILEE POEM. Saint John, "Globe," 1887. [CCJ

**Smith, Mary Irene (Doherty), 1928–**

SONGS OF THE ATHABASKA. Regina, 1960 [c 1949]. 65p

**Smith, Norma Ethel, –1948**

BELTHOR, THE SHEPHERD OF BETHLEHEM. Halifax, McAlpine, n.d. [12] p [OTUV

THE HILL AND FAR AWAY. Halifax, Imperial Pub. Co., 1948. 60p [NSWA

**Smith, Rev. Oswald Jeffrey, 1889–**

MALCOLM AND MARIE. A Romance of the Russian Revolution. London, Stockwell, 1932. 64p [AEU BM

POEMS OF A LIFETIME. Wheaton, Ill., Van Kampen, [1954]. 192p [Later ed., London, Marshall, Morgan & Scott, 1965. 224p] [AEU OTU

SONGS IN THE NIGHT. Toronto, Alliance Tabernacle, 1922. 95p [Amtmann cat. 151

SONGS OF THE SPIRIT. Toronto, Tabernacle Pubs., 1932. 32p [Amtmann cat. 151

VOICES OF HOPE. Toronto, 1919. 133p [Adelphi cat. 55A

**Smith, Rev. William Wye, 1827–1917**

ALAZON, AND OTHER POEMS. Including many of the Fugitive Pieces of Rusticus [pseud]. Toronto, Scobie, 1850. 125p [BVaU OTP

THE POEMS OF WILLIAM WYE SMITH. Toronto, Dudley Burns, 1888. 265p [BM BVaU LC OTP QMM

THE SELECTED POEMS OF WILLIAM WYE SMITH. Toronto, Briggs, 1908. 230p [BM BVaU NBFU OTP QMM

**Smyth, John, –1852**

SELECT POEMS. Toronto, 1841. 32p [OTP

A SMALL SPECIMEN OF THE GENIUS OF CANADA WEST, AND THE WONDERS OF THE WORLD. Toronto, Coates, 1845. 34p [OTP

**Smythe, Albert Ernest Stafford, 1861–1947**

THE GARDEN OF THE SUN. With an introduction by "A.E." (George Russell). Toronto, Macmillan, 1923. 81p [BM BVaU NBFU OTP QMM

POEMS GRAVE AND GAY. Toronto, Imrie & Graham, 1891. 184p [BM BVaU OTP

THE STORY OF ARMAND VILLIERS. Being Crusts and Crumbs for Christmas, 1916. N.p., [1916]. 14p [NBFU

**Snook, Percy**

RHYMES OF THE TRAIL. By a Canadian Pioneer (Percy Snook). London, Erskine Macdonald, 1923. 63p [BM Brown U

**Snow, Victoria (Langton), 1864–**

SPARKS FROM A KITCHEN FIRE. Toronto, Nelson, 1935. 143p [OTU

**Snyder, Joseph A.**
POEMS. Ilfracombe, Devon, Stockwell, 1956. 64p

**Snyder, Olive Anderson**
LITTLE TOWNS. N.p. [Elora, Ont.?], n.d. 25p [OTP
PICTURES ... AND OTHER POEMS. [Elora, Ont.], Express Print., n.d. 22p [OTUV
SONGS OF THE MONTH, AND OTHER POEMS. [Elora, Ont.], Express Print., n.d. 25p [OTP

**Sollows, Atlanta Sara, 1889–1954**
CLIMB THE RIGGING. Toronto, Crucible Press, 1944. 52p [BVaU NBFU OTP

**Souster, Raymond, 1921–**
CERBERUS. Poems by Louis Dudek, Irving Layton, and Raymond Souster. Toronto, Contact Press, [1952]. 98p
CITY HALL STREET. Toronto, Ryerson, 1951. 8p
CREPE-HANGER'S CARNIVAL. Selected Poems, 1955–58. Toronto, Contact Press, 1958. 65p [mimeographed]
A DREAM THAT IS DYING. Poems. Toronto, Contact Press, n.d. 27p
FOR WHAT TIME SLAYS. Poems. Toronto, Author, 1955. 24p [mimeographed]
GO TO SLEEP, WORLD. Toronto, Ryerson, 1947. 59p [MWU NBFU OTP QMM
SELECTED POEMS. Chosen by Louis Dudek. Toronto, Contact Press, 1956. 135p
SHAKE HANDS WITH THE HANGMAN. Poems 1940–1952. Toronto, Contact Press, 1953. 24p
UNIT OF FIVE. Poems by Louis Dudek, Ronald Hambleton, P.K. Page, Raymond Souster, James Wreford. Ed. by Ronald Hambleton. Toronto, Ryerson, 1944. 87p [BVaU LC MWU NSHD OTU QMM
WALKING DEATH. Poems. Toronto, Contact Press, 1954. 24p
WHEN WE ARE YOUNG. Montreal, First Statement Press, 1946. 28p [BVaU MWU NBFU OTP QMM

**Sparrow, Charles, 1877–**
POEMS OF MEMORY AND ENVIRONMENT. Toronto, Briggs, 1908. 32p [Brown U BVaU OTU

**Spears, Heather, 1934–**
ASYLUM POEMS AND OTHERS. Toronto, Emblem Books, 1958. 15p

**Spedon, Andrew Learmont, 1831–1884**
THE CANADIAN MINSTREL. Montreal, Mitchell & Wilson, 1870. 112p [LC NSHD OTP
THE WOODLAND WARBLER. A Volume of English and Scottish Poems and Songs. Montreal, Becket, 1857. 136p [OTP

**Spence, Francis Stephens, 1850–1917**

CANADA. Toronto, Copp Clark, [1912?]. 27p [Brown U BVaU NSWA OTUV

**Spencer, Agnes**

THE LOGS' LAMENT. N.p., "Dorset Farm," 1898. 14p [OTUV

**Spencer, Hiram Ladd, 1829–1915**

THE FUGITIVES. A Sheaf of Verses. [With an Introductory Sketch of the Author by A.M. Belding.] Saint John, Bowes, 1909. 173p [BM BVaU NBFU OTP QMU

POEMS. Boston, Phillips Sampson, 1850. 95p [BM LC NSWA

A SONG OF THE YEARS, AND A MEMORY OF ACADIA. Saint John, 1889. 19p [LC NSWA OTP

**Spiers, William**

THE FINAL CRISIS. A Poem. [Anon] Toronto, 1882. 23p [Brown U

**Spreckley, R.O.**

"OLD QUEBEC" AND OTHER VERSE. Godalming, Eng., Craddock, 1919. [BM

**Sproule, Dorothy (Corrigan), 1877–1963**

BREAD AND ROSES. Montreal, Woodward Press, 1937. 48p [BVaU OKQ QMM

THE CLOUD AND THE FIRE. Montreal, Author, 1940. 40p [BVaU OTU QMM

EARTH AND STARS. Montreal, Mercury Press, 1935. 46p [OTP

THE GOLD OF DAWN. Poems. New York, Harrison, 1938. 109p [BVaU LC OTU QMM

THE GOLDEN GOAL. Montreal, Mercury Press, 1933. 42p [QMM

THE MYSTIC STAR. Montreal, Mercury Press, 1931. 32p [BVaU OTP

POEMS OF LIFE. ... With an intro. by Lloyd C. Douglas. Montreal, Mercury Press, 1931. 32p [BVaU OTP QMM

THE SILVER CLOUD. Montreal, de la Salle Print., 1942. 35p [BVaU QMM OLU

**Squire, Ada A.**

ACROSS THE SEA. London, Ont., "Advertiser," 1892. 51p [OTUV

**Srzentich, Mirko, 1934–**

HOT ALPHABET. ... By Mike Strong [pseud]. Toronto, Hawkshead Press, 1960. 8p

**Stafford, Rev. Ezra Adams, 1839–1891**

RECREATIONS. Toronto, Briggs, 1883. 96p [BVaU LC OTP

**Stafford, Ezra Hurlburt, 1865–**

A CHRISTMAS CANTICLE, SAINTS' DAY BALLADS, AND SUNDRY OTHER MEASURES. Toronto, Bryant Press, 1895. 20p [OTP

THE DAUGHTER OF THE REPUBLIC. Montego Bay, Jamaica, St. James Press, 1927. 62p [BM OTP

THE ORANGE GROVE AND OTHER POEMS OF THE JAMAICA PEASANTRY. Montego Bay, Jamaica, St. James Press, 1927. 62p [BM OTP

**Stancliff, Isabella Morison, 1891–**

– AND SINCE. By Ella Stancliff. Powell River, B.C., Town Crier Press, 1937. 24p [CC

JUST ONE YEAR. By Ella Stancliff. Powell River, B.C., Town Crier, 1936. 20p [BVaU

**Stanford, Joseph Hunt, 1871–1935**

MIRIAM AND OTHER POEMS. Toronto, Briggs, 1908. 55p [BVaU OKQ

**Stansbury, Joseph, 1740–1809**

THE LOYAL VERSES OF JOSEPH STANSBURY AND DOCTOR JONATHAN ODELL. ... Ed. by Winthrop Sargent. Albany, N.Y., Munsell, 1860. 199p [BVaU LC NBFU OLU

**Stark, James**

DESTINY OF CANADA. Toronto, Imrie & Graham, 1892. 31p [OTP

**Starke, Richard Griffin, 1831–1909**

THE LORD OF LANORAIE. A Canadian Legend. Montreal, Lovell, 1898. 92p [BM BVaU LC NBFU OTP QMM

**Stead, Robert James Campbell, 1880–1959**

THE EMPIRE BUILDERS AND OTHER POEMS. Toronto, Briggs, 1908. 100p [Several later editions.] [BM BVaU NSHD OTP QMM

KITCHENER AND OTHER POEMS. Toronto, Musson, 1917. 161p [BM BVaU LC NBFU OTP QMM

PRAIRIE BORN AND OTHER POEMS. Toronto, Briggs, 1911. 95p [BM BVaU NSHD OLU

SONGS OF THE PRAIRIE. Toronto, Briggs, 1911. 96p [BM BVaU OKQ

WHY DON'T THEY CHEER? Poems. London, Unwin, 1918. 166p [BM BVaU LC LC OTP

**Steele, Harwood Elmes Robert, 1897–**

CLEARED FOR ACTION. By Howard Steele [pseud]. London, Fisher Unwin, 1914. 166p [BM BViP MWU OH

**Steiner, Florence B., 1877–1946**

TOY BALLOONS. Verses for Children. Toronto, Ryerson, 1934. 62p [Brown U BVaU NBFU OOP

TOY SHIPS. Poems for Children. Ottawa, Graphic, 1926. 63p [OKQ

**Stenning, Annie A.**

THE NEVER NEVER ROAD. Montreal, Renouf, 1923. 15p [BM

**Stephen, Alexander Maitland, 1882–1942**

BROWN EARTH AND BUNCH GRASS. Vancouver, Wrigley Print., 1931. 133p [BVaU OKQ QMM

THE GOLDEN TREASURY OF CANADIAN VERSE. Chosen by ——. Toronto, Dent, 1928. 146p [BVaU NBFU OKQ QMM

THE LAND OF SINGING WATERS. London, Dent, 1927. 189p [BM BVaU LC NSHD OTP QMM

LORDS OF THE AIR. Poems of the Present War. Vancouver, Author, 1940. 16p [BVaU LC OKQ

THE ROSARY OF PAN. Toronto, McClelland, 1923. 137p [BM BVaU NBFU OTP QMM

VERENDRYE. A Poem of the New World. Toronto, Dent, 1935. 66p [BVaU LC NBFU OKQ

**Stephens, William A., 1809–1891**

THE CENTENNIAL. An International Poem. Toronto, 1878. 72p [Brown U BVaU

HAMILTON, AND OTHER POEMS. Toronto, Rogers & Thompson, 1840. 180p [2nd ed., 1871. 410p] [BVaU NSHD OTP QMM

A POETICAL GEOGRAPHY, AND RHYMING RULES FOR SPELLING. Toronto, Brewer McPhail, 1848. 36p [OTP

**Stevens, George Roy, 1895–**

TRAVELOGUE. Montreal, Southam Print., 1959. 43p

**Stevens, W.H.**

MOODS AND SEASONS; OR, MULTUM-IN-PARVO. Toronto, Anderson-Kew, 1904. N.p. [OTUV

**Stevens, Winifred Mary (Hird), 1882–1934**

GOLD DUST. New Westminster, B.C., Author, 1930. 32p [BVaU

THE VIKING'S BRIDE. Toronto, Ryerson, 1929. 8p [BVaU NBFU OKQ QMM

**Stevenson, Lionel, 1902–**

A CHAPBOOK. By Lionel Stevenson ... [and Others]. Vancouver, priv. print., 1922. 28p [BVaU NBFU

A POOL OF STARS. Toronto, Ryerson, 1926. 16p [BVaU NBSaM OKQ QMM

THE ROSE OF THE SEA. Toronto, Ryerson, 1932. 12p [BVaU NBSaM OTP QMM

**Stevenson, Orlando John, 1869–1950**

FIFTY-FOUR NARRATIVE POEMS. Ed. by ——. Toronto, Copp Clark, 1933. 241 p [NBSM

A GROUP OF POEMS. Guelph, Author, 1944. 18p [BVaU NBFU OTP

... SEVEN POEMS. ... With Annotations by ——. Toronto, Copp Clark, 1933. 90p [OLU

THE UNCONQUERABLE NORTH, AND OTHER POEMS. Toronto, Macmillan, 1938. 79p [BVaU LC OTP

**Stewart, Alexander Charles, 1867–1944**

THE BEAVER, AND OTHER ODDS AND ENDS. Toronto, Hunter Rose, 1918. 108p [BVaU NSHD OLU QMM

DUST AND ASHES (Chiefly). [Toronto], Author, 1910. 188p [BVaU NSHD OTP QMM

THE PENSIONERS. A Poem. Toronto, Rose Pub. Co., 1890. 16p [OTP

THE POETICAL WORKS OF ALEXANDER CHAS. STEWART. Toronto, Hunter Rose, 1890. 189p [BVaU OTP

THE SHELL, WITH FRAGMENTS AND REVERBERATIONS. Toronto, Briggs, 1917. 69p [BVaU OTUV

**Stewart, Charles**

THE HARP OF STRATHNAVER, A LAY OF THE SCOTTISH HIGHLAND EVICTIONS–AND OTHER POEMS. Buffalo, Peter Paul, [18—?]. 89p [Also: Galt, Ont., 1884. 89p] [CCJ OTP

**Stewart, Thomas Brown Phillips, 1864–1892**

POEMS. By Phillips Stewart. London, Kegan Paul, 1887. 89p [BM NBFU OTP QMM

**Stickle, Charles Harris**

POEMS OF A GREAT RANGE. Toronto, Author, 1901. [T&C

**Stilson, Dorothy Elizabeth**

CHRISTMAS EVERY DAY. San Gabriel, Calif., Willing Pub. Co., 1949. 64p [AEU

**Stitt, James Herbert, 1891–1958**

SONGS FOR REMEMBRANCE. Ottawa, priv. print., 1959. 10p

**Stockton, Noel, 1917–**

FAMILY VERSE AND OTHER SELECTED POEMS. Bracebridge, Ont., Herald-Gazette Office, 1958. 41p

**Stone, Clement R.**

VANCOUVER VISTAS. Vancouver, Author, 1936. 24p [BVa OKQ

**Story, Duncan Albert, 1853–**

WHERE THE TIDES EBB AND FLOW. Montreal, Gazette Print., 1932. 72p [BVaU OLU QMSS

**Strachan, Ada M.**

HEPATICAS IN SPRING. [Toronto?], Author, 1935. 23p [Brown U

**Strachan, Jessie**

POEMS AND SCOTCH PROSE. Bluevale, Ont., Author, 1935. 40p [UTQ'37

**Strachan, Richard**

GLIMPSES OF GLORY; or, Incentives to Holy Living. An Antidote to Weariness in Well-Doing, and Comfort for the Afflicted and Bereaved. Ed. by Zethar [pseud]. Toronto, Briggs, 1890. 138p [Brown U

**Strangways, Britton, 1863–**

THE MORNING GOETH FORTH AND OTHER POEMS. Toronto, Ontario Press, 1924. 95p [BVaU LC OOP

**Straton, Barry, 1854–1901**

THE BUILDING OF THE BRIDGE. An Idyl of the River St. John. Saint John, McMillan, 1887. 19p [NSWA

LAYS OF LOVE, AND MISCELLANEOUS POEMS. Saint John, McMillan, 1884. 80p [BVaU NSHD OTP QMM

**Stringer, Arthur John Arbuthnot, 1874–1950**

DARK SOIL. Indianapolis, Bobbs-Merrill, 1933. 123p [BM BVaU LC OLU

EPIGRAMS. London, Ont., Warren, 1896. 42p [OTP

HEPHAESTUS; PERSEPHONE AT ENNA; AND SAPPHO IN LEUCADIA. Toronto, Methodist Book, 1903. 43p [BM BVaU NBFU OTU

IRISH POEMS. New York, Kennerley, 1911. 110p [Another ed., under title OUT OF ERIN, pub. in 1930.] [BM BVaU LC NBFU OTU

THE KING WHO LOVED OLD CLOTHES, AND OTHER IRISH POEMS. New York, Bobbs-Merrill, 1941. 105p [BM LC MWU OLU

NEW YORK NOCTURNES. Toronto, Ryerson, 1948. 12p [BVaU MWU NBFU OTP

THE OLD WOMAN REMEMBERS, AND OTHER IRISH POEMS. Indianapolis, Bobbs-Merrill, 1938. 57p [BM BVaU LC OLU

OPEN WATER. New York, Lane, 1914. 132p [BM BVaU LC OTU

OUT OF ERIN (SONGS IN EXILE). Indianapolis, Bobbs-Merrill, 1930. 155p [Pub. in 1911 as IRISH POEMS.] [BVaU LC NSHD OLU QMM

PAULINE, AND OTHER POEMS. London, Ont., Warren, 1895. 64p [OTU

SAPPHO IN LEUCADIA. Boston, Little Brown, 1907. 264p [Extract from THE WOMAN IN THE RAIN AND OTHER POEMS.] [LC NBFU

SHADOWED VICTORY. Indianapolis, Bobbs-Merrill, 1943. 78p [BM BVaU LC NBFU OTU

WATCHERS OF TWILIGHT, AND OTHER POEMS. London, Ont., Warren, 1894. 43p [BVaU NBFU OTP

A WOMAN AT DUSK, AND OTHER POEMS. Indianapolis, Bobbs-Merrill, 1928. 154p [BM BVaU LC NSHD OTU QMBM

THE WOMAN IN THE RAIN, AND OTHER POEMS. Boston, Little Brown, 1907. 264p [Also: Toronto, McClelland, 1949. 264p] [BVaU LC NBFU OTU QMM

**Stuart, Mabel L.**

ROSES OF FRANCE AND OTHER POEMS. Toronto, Warwick, 1919. 16p [NSHPL OONL

**Stuart, Mary F.**
WAYSIDE POEMS. By Slinfold [pseud]. Fort William, Author, 1939. 98p [BVaU

**Sturrock, W.**
A MILITARY MITE TO THE MOUNTAIN OF LITERATURE; or, The Rhymes of a Red Coat [pseud]. Quebec, Middleton & Dawson, 1858. 142p [BVaU OTL QMBM

**Sullivan, Alan, 1868–1947**
VENICE AND OTHER VERSE. Toronto, Bryant, 1893. 48p [NSWA OTP
THE WHITE CANOE AND OTHER VERSE. Toronto, Bryant, 1891. 30p [OTP

**Summerss, George, 1834–**
BIRD OF THE BUSH. A Collection of Poems [with Autobiographical Sketch]. Toronto, Hunter Rose, 1908. 240p [BVaU OKQ
POEMS. N.p., [1880?]. 84p [BVaU NSHD OTP

**Sutherland, Alexander Hugh, 1870–1952**
EARLE, AND OTHER POEMS. Victoria, Quality Press, n.d. 28p [BViPA
MANITOBA MEMORIES. Winnipeg, Stovel Co., [1928?]. 35p [A 1912 imprint is listed in BM.] [BM BViPA NBFU OTP
OUR KING AND QUEEN. N.p., n.pub., n.d. 4p [BViPA
THE PASSING OF AEGEUS. A Greek Epic. [Anon] Victoria, Clarke, n.d. 11p [BViPA
STAR-DUST. Astronomical Poems. Victoria, Clarke, 1943. 18p [BVaU

**Sutherland, John, 1919–1956**
OTHER CANADIANS. An Anthology of the New Poetry in Canada, 1940–1946. Ed. by ——. Montreal, First Statement Press, 1947. 113p [BVaU LC NSHD OTP QMM

**Swaan, William**
SONGS OF THE SOUTH SEAS. Winnipeg, Hull Print., 1949. 52p [UTQ'50

**Swanson, Robert E.**
BUNKHOUSE BALLADS. Book 3. Toronto, Allen, 1945. 58p [BVaU LC
RHYMES OF A HAYWIRE HOOKER. By Robert E. Swanson and Seattle Red [pseud]. Vancouver, Lumberman Print., 1953. 68p
RHYMES OF A LUMBERJACK. A Second Book of Verse. Toronto, Allen, 1943. 94p [BVaU LC OTP QMSS
RHYMES OF A WESTERN LOGGER. Vancouver, Lumberman Print., 1942. 56p [Other later editions.] [BVaU LC NBFU
RHYMES OF A WESTERN RAMBLER. Vancouver, Author, 1942. 48p [mimeographed] [Adelphi cat. 64

**Swanson, William J., 1862–**
NORTH COUNTRY RHYMES. Desbarats, Ont., 1938. 41p [Brown U OTU

**Swart, George G.**

THE BOOK OF LIFE EVERLASTING EXPLAINING THE CHART, THE ETERNAL WHEEL OF LIFE EVERLASTING. ... Kitchener, Ont., n.d. 32p [Adelphi cat. 55A

**Swart, Morley Lewis, 1879–**

WAR-TIME MELODIES, AND OTHER SONGS. London, Ont., Advertiser, 1904. 91p [OLU

**Swayze, James Frederick, 1907–1967**

AND SEE PENELOPE PLAIN. Toronto, Ryerson, 1958. 16p

IN THE EGYPTIAN GALLERY. Toronto, Ryerson, 1960. 12p

**Sweeney, John, 1864–**

SONGS AND VERSES OF A PEACE RIVER PIONEER. Peace River, Record-Gazette, [194–?]. 36p [AEU

**Sweeny, Robert, –1840**

ODDS AND ENDS: ORIGINAL AND TRANSLATED. New York, Magarey, 1826. 156p [Same title: Montreal, Starke, 1836. 188p] [LC OTP

REMNANTS. By the Author of "Odds and Ends" [pseud]. Montreal, Starke, 1835. 64p [OTP

**Swift, Sherman Charles, 1879–1947**

"TREASURE TROVE" AND OTHER POEMS. Toronto, U. of Toronto Press, 1911. 53p [BM BVaU OTP

**Swire, Frederick**

SHORT POEMS AND OTHER WRITINGS. London, Ont., Vivian, 1877. 109p [OTP

**Sykes, Mrs. Eileen**

THE GAY GARLAND. New York, Pageant Press, 1954. 53p

**Symons, Frank Stewart, 1887–**

POEMS. [Montreal?], 1948. 46p [OONL QMU

WORLD SO FULL. Montreal, Gazette Print., 1952. 112p

**Tait, Robert Holland**

"THE TRAIL OF THE CARIBOU." The Royal Newfoundland Regiment, 1914–1918. Boston, Newfoundland Pub. Co., 1933. 65p [A verse history.] [Brown U OTU

**Talbot, Thomas (fl. 1844–82)**

THE ENCHIRIDION OF EPICTETUS, AND THE GOLDEN VERSES OF PYTHAGORAS, TRANSLATED. ... Together with some Original Poems. London, Sampson, 1881. 244p [An earlier ed.: Montreal, 1872.] [BM

THE EXILE, AND OTHER VERSES. Together with Translations from some of the Greek and Latin Poets. London, Low Marston, 1879. 246p [BM OLU

**Tamblyn, Bertha Louise**

HOLLY TIME SONGS. Fifteen Original Christmas Songs for Children and Grown-ups ... music by Bertha Louise Tamblyn. Toronto, Thompson, 1938. 32p [OTP

**Taylor, Alastair MacDonald**

FIRE-MIST. Los Angeles, O.D.S. Print. Co., 1936. 31p [BM LC OOP

**Taylor, Archibald M'Alpine**

BOYHOOD HOURS. A Collection of Simple Poems, Songs and Odes. Toronto, Hunter Rose, 1881. 178p [BVaU LC NBFU OKQ

**Taylor, Frances Beatrice, 1891–**

THE SONG OF KORTHAN. New York, Revell, 1923. 30p [LC

WHITE WINDS OF DAWN. Toronto, McClelland, 1924. 128p [BVaU NBFU OTU QMM

**Taylor, Gertrude Emilie (Bartlett), 1876–**

THE WHITE BIRD AND OTHER POEMS. Toronto, Macmillan, 1932. 57p [BVaU NBFU OTP

**Taylor, Helen B.**

VANCOUVER AND OTHER POEMS. Vancouver, Author, [1944?]. 26p [BViPA

**Taylor, Lilian (Fortier), 1889–**

MAGIC WINDOWS. [Hollyburn, B.C.], Author, [1946]. 34p [BViPA

WHITE MISTS OF ACADIE. Wolfville, Acadian Print., 1934. [2nd ed.: Kentville, Kentville Press, 1935. 20p] [Brown U NSHD

**Taylor, Mabel Cecilia (Ryan)**

MY CHRISTMAS TREE. Moose Jaw, Author, 1944. 68p [OTP

**Taylor, Phena Catherine**

"THE GATEWAY OF THE NORTH." Vancouver, Capitol Print., n.d. 55p [BViPA

**Taylor, Wardlaw**

FRUSTA. St. Andrews, N.B., Beacon, n.d. 18p [NBS

**Taylor, William Henry**

CANADIAN SEASONS. ... With a Medley of Reveries in Verse and Prose and Other Curios. Toronto, Miln-Bingham Printers, 1913. 150p [BM BVaU OKQ

**Tebbs, Rev. George William, 1873–**

SUNNY MEMORIES. By Old Man Sunshine [pseud]. [Hamilton?], Author, 1934–35. 86p [OPAL

**Telford, William, 1828–1895**

THE POEMS OF WILLIAM TELFORD ... Bard of Peterborough St. Andrew's Society. Peterborough, Stratton, 1887. 156p [BVaU OTP QMM NBFU

**Tener, John Frost**

CALLING ALL FREE MEN. Vancouver, Murphy & Chapman, 1941. 34p [BVaU LC

**Tenny, W.H.F.**

COMPANIONSHIP AND THE CROWD AND OTHER POEMS. Toronto, Ryerson, 1925. 8p [BVaU NBSaM OTU QMM

SONGS OF THE NORTH, AND OTHER POEMS. Toronto, Ryerson, 1923. 143p [2nd ed., enl., 1924.] [BM BVaU NBFU OTU QMM

**Thayers, M.J. (Shaw)**

BUDS AND BLOSSOMS. Toronto, McLean, 1894. 192p [BVaU NBFU OKQ

A WREATH OF WILD FLOWERS. Toronto, Morton, 1877. 79p [OTP

**Thomas, A. Vernon, 1876–1950**

MAIN STREET. Manitoba's Historic Highway. A Panorama of Buffalo, Indians, Explorers ... Portrayed in Verse. ... [Winnipeg?], n.p., [193–?]. 15p [MWP

**Thomas, Edgar James, 1881–**

THREE POEMS. [Jubilee Ode, Christmas Carol, New Year Wassail]. [? Winnipeg, 193–] 7p [Adelphi cat. 33-A

A WREATH OF PRAIRIE FLOWERS FOR A QUEEN. Winnipeg, Author, 1953. 8p

**Thomas, Hartley Munro, 1896–**

SONGS OF AN AIRMAN, AND OTHER POEMS. With an introduction by S.W. Dyde, Principal of Queen's Theological College, Kingston, Ont. Toronto, McClelland, 1918. 101p [BM BVaU LC NSHD OKQ

**Thomas, Mrs. L. Burns**

STRAY LEAVES. Vancouver, n.p., [1916?]. 48p [BVaU OTP

**Thompson, Andrew Thorburn, 1870–1938?**

THE CANADIAN KNIGHTS ENTERTAINMENT. N.p., 1918. 11p [BM OTU

THE ODYSSEY OF THE GENTLEMEN ADVENTURERS TRAVELLING INTO THE BRAZILS. ... Ottawa, priv. print., 1928. 46p [BVaU OOU QMU

**Thompson, Blanche Jennings, 1887–**

A GLIMPSE INTO MY GARDEN. Short Poems by Thornapple [pseud]. Thorold, Ont., Thorold Post Print., 1903. 100p [BM Brown U BVaU OTUV

**Thompson, Claude Willett**

VAGRANT VERSES. Quebec, Telegraph Pub. Co., 1926. 35p [NBFU

**Thompson, Dorothy (Burr), 1900–**

SWANS AND AMBER. Some Early Greek Lyrics, Freely Translated and Adapted. Toronto, U. of Toronto Press, 1948. xii + 193p [BVaU OTU NBSaM MWU

**Thompson, Ida Isabella Margaret (Clarke), 1881–**
OUT OF THE NORTH WITH DRUMS AND OTHER POEMS. N.p., n.d. 3p [QMU
PRAIRIE JUNE AND OTHER POEMS. N.p., n.d. 41p [BVaU

**Thompson, John Sparrow**
SCRIPTURE SKETCHES. Halifax, Cunnabell, 1829. 280p [NSHD

**Thomson, Mrs. Annie Laurence, 1837?–1926**
A LITTLE BOOK OF VERSE. Bexhill-on-Sea, Parsons, 1914. 73p [BVaU NSHD

**Thomson, Edward William, 1849–1924**
THE MANY-MANSIONED HOUSE, AND OTHER POEMS. Toronto, Briggs, 1909. 151p [BM BVaU NBFU OTU QMM
PETER OTTAWA. Toronto, 1905. 16p [NBFU OKQ
THIS IS OF AUCASSIN AND NICOLETTE. ... Verse Translation. Boston, Copeland, 1896. 78p [BM LC
WHEN LINCOLN DIED, AND OTHER POEMS. Boston, Houghton, 1909. 146p [According to QMM, this is another ed. of THE MANY-MANSIONED HOUSE. ...] [BM LC NBFU OLU QMM

**Thomson, John Stuart, 1869–1950**
A DAY'S SONG. Toronto, Briggs, 1900. 124p [BM BVaU NBFU OKQ QMM
ESTABELLE AND OTHER VERSE. Toronto, Briggs, 1897. 113p [BM BVaU OTP QMM
EULALINE. New York, 1899. 9p [Brown U

**Thomson, Robert Burns, 1847–1922**
THE POEMS OF ROBERT BURNS THOMSON. Winnipeg, Wallingford, 1936. 387p [BM LC OOP

**Thomson, Theresa Emily (Meeres)**
MYTH AND MONUMENT. By Theresa E. & Don W. Thomson. Toronto, Ryerson, 1957. 16p
RIVER & REALM. By Theresa E. & Don W. Thomson. Toronto, Ryerson, 1959. 14p
SILVER LIGHT. By Theresa E. and Don W. Thomson. Toronto, Ryerson, 1955. 13p
SILVER SHADOWS. Toronto, Ryerson, 1951. 8p

**Thomson, Wilson**
THE SHIFTBOSS, AND OTHER POEMS. Timmins, Ont., Author, [1943?]. 23p [LC

**Thow, William, 1896–**
A CAST OF REVERIES. Montreal, 1956. 71p
MORE ODD MEASURES. Toronto, Ryerson, 1937. 12p [BVaU NSHD OTP QMM
ODD MEASURES. Toronto, Ryerson, 1936. 11p [Same title: Montreal, Author, 1959. 46p] [BVaU NBSaM OTU QMM
POET AND SALESMAN. Toronto, Ryerson, 1939. 16p [BVaU NSHD OTP QMM

A SORT OF SENTIMENT. Montreal, 1953. 75p
TALES OF A SONGSMITH. Montreal, 1951. 130p [Reprinted 1961.]
VERSES OF A VAGRANT. Toronto, Best, 1929. 173p [BVaU OTU QMSS

**Tilden, Vera Willis**
LINES BY VERA WILLIS TILDEN. ... [London, Ont.?], Author, [1946?]. 65p [LC
NOSEGAY OF SONG. Blenheim, Ont., News Tribune, 1946. 31p [LC OTP

**Tobin, Anastasia Bertille, 1888–**
AUTUMN IN KING'S COVE AND OTHER POEMS. King's Cove, Bonavista Bay, Nfld., Author, 1951. 50p

**Todd, Maude Pepper**
IN A GARDEN OF YESTERDAY. Toronto, Ryerson, 1925. 12p [OKQ

**Todd, Robert Henry, 1877–**
CHEER-UP VERSES AND RANDOM RHYMES. Brampton, Charters, 1931. 191p [OTU

**Tolchard, John T.**
A WEB OF DREAMS. Toronto, Ryerson, 1933. 32p [OPAL

**Tolcher, H.**
POEMS. Calgary, Gibson, 1896–98. 3v [43, 90, 29p]. [OTUV

**Tolkien, J. Kenneth**
THE INN OF GAHNOBWAY. Montreal, Benallack Litho. Co., 1903. 177p [BVaU OTUV QMSS

**Toll, Ellsworth R.**
SELECTED POEMS. N.p., n.p., 1943. 76p [OTUV

**Tolmie, Margaret (Duncan), 1886–**
"DEAR CANADA WE SING TO THEE" AND OTHER POEMS. Sarnia, Frontier Print., 1946. 32p [BVaU OKQ

**Tooth, Arthur, 1914–1942**
FLIGHT'S END. ... New York, Exposition Press, 1947. 45p [Brown U LC

**Toots (pseud)**
THE TWO ELDERS, AND THE SEQUEL, THE MEAL CLUB PLOT. By Toots [pseud]. Toronto, Citizen Office, 1856. 15p [BVaU OTP

**Toronto, Ont. Danforth Technical School**
ZEPHYRS. A Collection of Poetry and Art, the Work of Students of Danforth Technical School. Toronto, Tech Tatler Pub., 1936. 44p [UTQ'37

**Toronto, Ont. Jarvis Collegiate Institute. Poetry Club**

CARAVAN. A Book of Verse. Toronto, College Press, 1930. 30p [Also in 1931. 31p] [CC

**Toronto Tandem Club**

PROCEEDINGS OF THE TORONTO TANDEM CLUB, 1839, 1840, 1841. [Anon] Toronto, Rowsell, 1841. 66p [BM BVaU

**Toronto Women's Press Club**

VERSE AND REVERSE. By Members of the Toronto Women's Press Club. Toronto, Goodchild, 1921, 1922. 47p [BVaU NBFU OKQ

CANADIAN DAYS. Selections for Every Day in the Year from the Works of Canadian Authors. Toronto, Musson, [1911]. 168p [BVaU LC NBFU OTU

**Torville, Charles Hollis, 1888–**

POEMS. [Vancouver?], Author, n.d. 24p [BVaU

**Tovell, Rev. Isaac, 1845–**

GOLDEN WEDDING DAY; or, Semi-Centennial Pulpit and Pew of Richmond St. Methodist Church, Toronto. Toronto, Briggs, 1884. 48p [OTP

THE OLD FRAME CHURCH, AND THE FRIENDS OF YORE. St. Catharines, Author, 1890. n.p. [OTUV

**Towriss, Mrs. Louise Yates, 1877–1942**

CHORDS AND ECHOES. Athens, Ont., Author, 1940. 24p [CC

A HOUSE OF MEMORIES. Athens, Ont., Athens Reporter Presses, 1935. 39p [OKQ

**Tracy, Neil, 1905–**

THE RAIN IT RAINETH. Sherbrooke, Que., La Tribune, 1938. 30p [NBFU

**Tranter, Mrs. Gladdis Joy, 1902–**

A SOLDIER'S LEGACY. Toronto, Ambassador Books, 1944. 85p [BVaU LC OTP QMM

WINGED WORDS. Winnipeg, Wallingford Press, 1935. 20p [MWP

**Treleaven, A.E.L.**

GUELPH'S 50TH ANNIVERSARY. A Poem. Guelph, Herald Steam Print., 1877. 4p [Brown U

**Trott, James Charles**

A COLLECTION OF POEMS AND SONGS. Halifax, "Guardian," 1895. 196p [BM BVaU

**Trotter, Bernard Freeman, 1890–1917**

A CANADIAN TWILIGHT, AND OTHER POEMS OF WAR AND OF PEACE. Toronto, McClelland, 1917. 127p [BM BVaU LC NSHD OTU QMM

**Tuck, Clyde Edwin**

VOICES IN THE WIND. Boston, Christopher Pub. House, 1950. 94p [LC

**Tucker, James Alexander, 1872–1903**

POEMS. With a prefatory memoir by Arthur Stringer. Toronto, Briggs, 1904. 133p [BM BVaU LC NBFU OTU QMM

**Tucker, Norman**

NARRATIVE POEMS. Vernon, B.C., News Print., 1927. 111p [BVaU OTU

**Tucker, Rev. William Bowman, 1859–1934**

LAURENTIAN TALES. Montreal, Southam, 1922. 275p [BM BVaU NBFU OTU QMM

SONGS OF THE WAYSIDE. Montreal, Lovell, 1918. 192p [BM BVaU NBFU OTU QMM

THE SPRINGS OF THE PISGAH HILLS AND OTHER POEMS. [MOR'12

**Tudor-Hart, Edith**

SONGS OF THE SHADOWS. London, Fowler Wright, 1927. 128p [BM BVaU

VISTAS OF OUR LADY.... London, Fowler Wright, n.d. 57p [BM

**Tunstall, C.A.**

COLLECTED POEMS OF C.A. TUNSTALL, M.D., Class Poet, McGill Medical Faculty, 1891.... Montreal, 1891. 6p [Brown U

**Tupper, Charles Andrew**

THE GLEAMING EDGE. With a Foreword by Theodore Goodridge Roberts. Tweed, Ont., Valley Press, 1947. 39p [OTP

PRELUDE TO SONG. Toronto, Crucible Press, 1941. 20p [LC OTP QMM

**Tupper, Kathryn (Munro)**

FORFEIT AND OTHER POEMS. By Kathryn Munro. Toronto, Ryerson, 1926. 8p [BVaU NBFU OTP

NEW MOON. By Kathryn Munro. Toronto, Nelson, 1938. 125p [BVaU NBFU OTP

TANAGER FEATHER. By Kathryn Munro. Toronto, Ryerson, 1950. 12p [BVaU NBFU OTP

UNDER THE MAPLE. By Kathryn Munro. Toronto, Ryerson, 1930. 23p [BVaU NBFU OTP

**Tuque-Rouge (pseud)**

"MAMMA'S JOY" AND "PAPA'S PEARL"; or, Canada's Winter Carnival. By Tuque Rouge [pseud]. [Montreal, 1885?]. 12p + 12p [QMSS

**Turnbull, Gael, 1928–**

TRIO. First Poems. By Gael Turnbull, Phyllis Webb and E.W. Mandel. Toronto, Contact Press, 1954. 89p

BJARNI SPIKE-HELGI'S SON, AND OTHER POEMS. Ashland, Mass., Origin Press, 1956. 32p

**Turner, Jack**

BUDDY'S BLIGHTY AND OTHER VERSES FROM THE TRENCHES. Halifax, Imperial Pub., 1917. 29p [Another ed., Boston, Small Maynard, 1918. 106p] [BM OOP

**Tweedale, Bernard**

SOME VERSES AND DRAMATIC PIECES. Vancouver, 1914. 35p [BVaU

**Twomlow-Britt, Joseph, 1914–**

ACTION STATIONS! New York, Harrison, 1946. 45p [LC OTP

THE SONG OF THE SEA. Dallas, Kaleidograph Press, 1939. 39p [LC

**Tyndall, W.J.**

DE LUCKY GARCON AND OTHER FRENCH CANADIAN POEMS. Ottawa, Author, [1922?]. 94p [BM BVaU OTP

**Tyrrell, William, 1816–1904**

POEMS BY A BUSINESS MAN. Toronto, 1901. [Possibly same as item listed for Alban E. Ragg, *q.v.*] [T&C

**Uncle Albert (pseud)**

POEMS. Commemorating construction of the Alaska Highway. N.p., ("printed in Canada"), n.d. 61p [Adelphi cat. 41A

**Uren, Alfred Ernest, 1881–**

BOB AND BILL SEE CANADA. A Travel Story in Rhyme for Boys and Girls. Toronto, Musson, 1919. 94p [Another ed., 1926.] [BM BVa OTU

**Urquhart, William T.**

POEMS. Montreal, 1868. 36p [CCJ

**Urwick, Hilary**

21 POEMS. London, Fortune Press, 1944. 29p [BM LC

**Vance, S.C.**

RURAL RHYMES. Truro, Daily News Print., [18—?]. 36p [NSHD OTP

**Vancouver Poetry Society**

A BOOK OF DAYS, 1916–46. Toronto, Ryerson, 1946. 93p [BVaU OTP

FULL TIDE. A Magazine of Poetry. [A 12-page mimeographed pamphlet issued annually, 1936–50.] [BVaU OKQ

THE V.P.S. CHAPBOOK. Vancouver, Sign of the Raven, 1925. 22p [Poems by Ernest Fewster, A.M. Stephen, and H. Bromley Coleman.] [BVaU NBFU

**Vancouver Poetry Writers' Group**

POEMS. West Vancouver, Mrs. Lewis, 1938. 36p [BVa OKQ
POEMS ... 1929–30. Vancouver, priv. print., 1930. 28p [BVaU OTP
POEMS ... 1931–1933. Vancouver, the Group, 1933. 38p [BVaU OTP
POEMS ... 1933–34. Vancouver, Commonwealth Press, 1934. 39p [BVaU OTP
VERSES ... 1928–1929. Vancouver, Mrs. Moody, 1929. 29p [OTP

**Veazey, Mary Emma, 1871–**

THE MARITIMER AND OTHER POEMS. Toronto, Crucible Press, 1941. 24p [LC NBFU OTU
MY SHIPS OF YESTERDAY AND OTHER POEMS. Toronto, Ryerson, 1935. 12p [Brown U NBFU
PATRIOTIC POEMS. 1916.

**Vidal, James Henry, 1864–1960**

ROMANCE OF AMBITION. White Rock, B.C., Author, 1945. 14p [Phelps p105
WORLD WAR I EPIC. A Story in Verse. White Rock, B.C., Author, n.d. 20p [AEU

**Viets, Rev. Roger, 1738–1811**

ANNAPOLIS-ROYAL. [A Poem]. [Anon] Halifax, Henry, 1788. 7p [Attributed to Roger Viets.] [Tremaine: Cdn Imprints NBFU

**W., R.**

BUD O' THE BUSH; or, The Beauty of Mysteries. N.p., 1924. 36p [OKQ

**W., W.W.**

A POEM ON THE TIMES, SHOWING FORTH THE VIRTUES OF LINCOLN, MCCLELLAN, AND FREMONT. By W.W.W. Toronto, "Merchants" Press, [1864?]. 40p [OTP

**Waddell, Jean (Percival), 1867–**

CANDLED BY STARS. Toronto, Ryerson, 1944. 52p [BVaU LC NSHD OTP QMM
DOWN AISLES OF CALM. Toronto, Ryerson, 1934. 71p [BVaU OTP QMM
A HARP IN THE WIND. Toronto, Ryerson, 1938. 65p [BVaU OTP QMM

**Waddington, John Frushard**

CANADA AND OTHER POEMS. London, Heath, [1918?]. 100p [BM OKQ

**Waddington, Miriam (Dworkin), 1917–**

GREEN WORLD. Montreal, First Statement, 1945. 28p [BVaU MWU NBFU OTP QMM
THE SEASON'S LOVERS. Toronto, Ryerson, 1958. 56p
THE SECOND SILENCE. Toronto, Ryerson, 1955. 57p

**Wade, H. Gerald, 1875–**
AN ACADIAN SINGER, FRANCIS SHERMAN. 2nd ed. Winnipeg, Stovel, 1930. 20p [1st ed., same year.] [NSHD OTP QMM

**Waight, Quentin, 1894–**
PRELUDE TO GLORY. [Poems and a Play.] Seattle, Superior Pub. Co., 1951. xiv + 166p [Includes a one-act play.]

**Wain, Walter Everard, 1904–**
MURMURINGS OF A SOJOURNER. Vancouver, Author, 1959. 59p [mimeographed]

**Wales, Julia Grace, 1881–**
ARGENTEIUL LYRICS. By Julia Grace Wales, Anna Letitia Wales, Emma Theodosia Wales. Lachute, Que., Watchman, 1935. 41p [Brown U

**Walker, (Sergeant) Alexander, fl. 1848–1867**
THE KNAPSACK. A Collection of Fugitive Poems. By a Soldier [pseud]. Kingston, Creighton, 1853. 132p [OTP

**Walker, Annie Louisa (Mrs Henry Coghill), 1836–1907**
LEAVES FROM THE BACKWOODS. [Anon] Montreal, Lovell, 1861. 174p [2nd ed., 1862.] [BM BVaU OKQ QMM
OAK AND MAPLE. English and Canadian Verses. By Mrs. Harry Coghill. London, Paul, 1890. 114p [BM OOP

**Wallace, Horatio, 1866–**
POEMS AND SONGS OF LIFE. London, Wright & Brown, 1935. 96p [Brown U BVaU OLU
THE SONG OF THE MADNESS OF THE CHILDREN OF ODIN, AND OTHER POEMS, 1914–1917. Winnipeg, Columbia Press, 1917. 30p [BM OKQ

**Wallace, Joseph S., 1890–**
THE GOLDEN LEGEND. Moscow, Foreign Languages Pub. House, 1958. 98p [Compiler's intro., commentary, and notes in Russian by I.L. Armand.]
HI, SISTER, HI, BROTHER! Toronto, New Frontiers, 1956. 36p
NIGHT IS ENDED. Thoughts in Lyric. Winnipeg, Contemporary Publishers, 1942. [BVa LC MWP NBFU OTP

**Wallace, Rev. Michael A., –1892**
HYMNS OF THE CHURCH, THE NATIVITY, AND OTHER POEMS. Portland, Me., Sanborn & Carter, 1853. 321p [LC NSHD OTP

**Wallis, Katherine Elizabeth, 1861–1957**
CHIPS FROM THE BLOCK. Poems. New York, Exposition Press, 1955. 56p

**Walsh, Lillian Crewe, 1883–**
WELCOME TO CAPE BRETON, THE HIGHLANDS OF CANADA. A Collection of Verse. Glace Bay, N.S., priv. print., 1955. 16p

**Walsh, Marie**

SMILE. Poems. Ilfracombe, Devon, Stockwell, 1957. 12p

**Walters, Annie Godfrey (Lewis), 1898–**

THIS IS ANNIE. Woodstock, Ont., Author, 1959. 64p

**Walton, George, 1897–**

THE WAYWARD QUEEN. Toronto, Contact Press, 1959. 64p

**Wanklyne, Hazel**

THE FLOWER WITHIN. Montreal, priv. print., 1936. 16p [OTP

**Wanless, Andrew, 1824–1898**

POEMS AND SONGS, MAISTLY SCOTCH. Detroit, Wanless, 1873. 192p ["2nd. ed. to which is Added a Number of New Pieces never before Published"; 1st ed., 1872.] [BVaU LC NBFU OLU QMM

SCOTCH AND CANADIAN RHYMES AND SONGS. Toronto, Thompson, 1857. 84p [BVaU OTP

**Ward, Burnett A.**

VEREY LIGHTS FROM THE LISTENING POST. By Flare-Pistol Pete [B.A. Ward]. Vancouver, Commonwealth Press, 1935. 64p [BVaU

**Ward, J.G.**

THE SPRING OF LIFE. A Didactic Poem in Four Books. Montreal, Author, 1834. 228p [BVaU OTP

**Ward, James Edward, 1883–1958**

INDIAN SUMMER AND OTHER POEMS. Toronto, Macmillan, 1933. 79p [BVaU NBFU OKQ

... THIS ENGLAND. Toronto, Longmans, 1942. 48p [BVaU LC NBFU OTP QMM

**Warman, Cy, 1855–1914**

DAYS REMEMBERED. ... New Glasgow, Mackenzie, 1899. 14p [NSHD

MOUNTAIN MELODIES. Denver, Colo., 1892. 63p [LC

OL' QUEBEC. Toronto, McLeod & Allen, 1908. 15p [BVaU QMSS

SONGS OF CY WARMAN. Boston, Rand Avery, 1911. 177p [BM BVaU LC OLU QMM

**Warmington, Mrs. M.**

MISCELLANEOUS POEMS. Drayton, [Ont.?], n.d. 52p [OTUV

**Warner, Ernest Albert, 1884–1957**

CRUMBLES. Being a Collection of Verses, Written at Various Times and Upon Different Themes. Burks Falls, Ont., [Arrow, 1928]. [24p] [Priv. info.

**Warnock, Amelia Beers (Mrs. John Garvin), 1878–1956**

THE FLUTE AND OTHER POEMS. By Katherine Hale [pseud]. Toronto, Ryerson, 1950. 16p [BVaU NBSaM OKQ

GREY KNITTING AND OTHER POEMS. By Katherine Hale [pseud]. Toronto, Briggs, 1914. 15p [BM BVaU NSHD OKQ

THE ISLAND, AND OTHER POEMS. By Katherine Hale [pseud]. Toronto, Author, 1934. 96p [NBFU OKQ QMM

MORNING IN THE WEST. A Book of Verse. By Katherine Hale [pseud]. Toronto, Ryerson, 1923. 68p [BM BVaU NSHD OTUV QMM

THE NEW JOAN AND OTHER POEMS. By Katherine Hale [pseud]. Toronto, McClelland, 1917. 19p [BM BVaU NBFU OKQ

THE WHITE COMRADE AND OTHER POEMS. By Katherine Hale [pseud]. Toronto, McClelland, 1916. 23p [BM BVaU NBFU OKQ

**Warr, Bertram Howard, 1883–**

IN QUEST OF BEAUTY. Selected Poems. Foleyet, Ont., Crucible Press, 1950. 40p [OONL

**Warr, Bertram J., 1917–1943**

YET A LITTLE ONWARDS. Resurgam Younger Poets No. 3. London, Favil Press, [1941?]. 5p [BM

**Warren, G.B.**

FOR THE SCEPTRE OF THE SEA. London, John Long, 1916. 62p [BM BVaU OH

THE LAST WEST AND PAOLO'S VIRGINIA. Vancouver, Evans & Hastings, 1919. 45p [BM Brown U BVaU OOP

**Warren, Hugh L.**

RHYMES OF A NORTHLAND. Toronto, Goodchild, 1920. 63p [BVaU NSHD OOP

**Warren, Mrs. Sara Evangeline Matheson**

PRAIRIE PANELS. Vauxhall, Alta., Author, 1950. 22p [OONL

SONGS OF THE ISLAND. Vauxhall, Alta., Author, 1951. 24p

**Waterman, Guy Victor, 1902–1944**

WORK UNFINISHED. Biographical Note by Angeline Waterman. Collected Work. Ottawa, Tower, 1947. 36p [OONL

**Waters, Francis Lealy Dominick, 1857–**

EIGHT BELLS. Sailor's Snug Harbor Yarns and Ballads. By Frank Waters. New York, Appleton, 1927. 151p [BM LC

THE MUSICIAN. A Legend of the Hartz Mountains. By Frank Waters. Boston, Badger, 1903. 88p [LC NSHD

THE WATER LILY. An Oriental Fairy Tale. By Frank Waters. Ottawa, Durie, 1888. 87p [BM BVaU NBFU OTP QMM

**Watson, Albert Durrant, 1859–1926**

THE DREAM OF GOD. A Poem. Toronto, Author, 1922. 42p [BM BVaU OKQ

HEART OF THE HILLS. Toronto, McClelland, 1917. 117p [BM BVaU OTU QMM

LOVE AND THE UNIVERSE, THE IMMORTALS AND OTHER POEMS. Toronto, Macmillan, 1913. 191p [BM BVaU NSHD OTU QMM

THE POETICAL WORKS OF ALBERT DURRANT WATSON. Toronto, Ryerson, 1924. 342p [BVaU NBFU OTP

THE WING OF THE WILD BIRD, AND OTHER POEMS. Toronto, Briggs, 1908. 125p [BVaU NBFU OTU QMM

WOMAN. A Poem. Toronto, Ryerson, 1923. 64p [BM BVaU NBFU OTP

**Watson, Elizabeth C.**

THE METROPOLITAN MOTHER GOOSE. Ottawa, Metropolitan Insurance Co., n.d. 10p [Amtmann cat. 141

**Watson, Isabella B.**

WAR TIME POEMS AND HEART SONGS. Toronto, Briggs, 1918. 123p [BM BVaU OOP

**Watson, James Wreford, 1915–**

OF TIME AND THE LOVER. By James Wreford [pseud]. Toronto, McClelland, 1950. 92p [BVaU NBFU OTP

UNIT OF FIVE. Poems by Louis Dudek, Ronald Hambleton, P.K. Page, Raymond Souster, James Wreford [pseud]. Ed. by Ronald Hambleton. Toronto, Ryerson, 1944. 87p [BVaU LC MWU NBFU OTU QMM

**Watson, John L.**

OCCUPANTS OF THE OLD GRAVEYARD; and Miscellaneous Poems and Songs. Brampton, Conservator Print., 1918. 131p [OTU

**Watson, Robert, 1882–1948**

CANADA'S FUR-BEARERS [Little Nature Studies in Verse]. Ottawa, Graphic, 1925. 48p [Same title: Winnipeg, Author, 1925. 32p] [BVaU OTP QMM

DREAMS OF FORT GARRY. An Epic Poem on the Life and Times of the Early Settlers of Western Canada. With Woodcuts. ... Winnipeg, Stovel, 1931. 63p [BVaU QMM

THE MAD MINSTREL. Toronto, Ryerson, 1923. 128p [BM BVaU LC OTP QMM

**Watson, Samuel James, 1837–1881**

THE LEGEND OF THE ROSES–A POEM; RAVLAN–A DRAMA. Toronto, Hunter Rose, 1876. 228p [BVaU NBFU OTU QMM

**Watson, Thomas, 1857–1937**

CANADIAN CRYSTALS. Poems. Toronto, Briggs, 1901. 160p [BM BVaU NBFU OKQ

LOVING HEARTS AND HAPPY HOMES. Toronto, Standard, n.d. 27p [OONL

**Watson, Wilfred, 1911–**

FRIDAY'S CHILD. London, Faber & Faber, 1955. 56p

**Watt, Alexander, 1890–**
BLESSED BE HE. A Tribute to Alexander Watt. Kitchener, Hawkshead Press, 1958. 4 + 6p

**Watt, David H.**
POEMS ON THE MANITOBA SCHOOL QUESTION. Toronto, Stewart Pub. Co., 1895. 23p [BM MWP OTP

**Watt, (Ernest) Frederick Balmer, 1901–**
BOY BLUE'S VERSES. Edmonton, Author, 1918. 16p [BVaU OKQ
LANDFALL. Toronto, Macmillan, 1946. 59p [BM Brown U BVaU OTU
VAGRANT. Toronto, Ryerson, 1927. 20p [BVaU NBSaM OKQ QMM
WHO DARE TO LIVE. Toronto, Macmillan, 1943. 68p [BM BVaU OTP QMM

**Weaver, R.A.**
REFLECTIONS. A Collection of Poems. Cranberry Lake, B.C., Author, 1945. 36p [UTQ'47

**Webb, Phyllis, 1927–**
EVEN YOUR RIGHT EYE. Toronto, McClelland, 1956. 64p
TRIO. First Poems. By Gael Turnbull, Phyllis Webb and E.W. Mandel. Toronto, Contact Press, 1954. 89p

**Webber, George**
THE LAST OF THE ABORIGINES. A Poem in Four Cantos. St. John's. [BibC

**Webber, William Lester, 1882–**
SKOOKUM WA-WA. "Good Talk." Vancouver, Lumberman Print., 1945. 94p [BVaU

**Weber, Manasseh, 1872–1957**
SUCH WAS LIFE. Calgary, 1956. 72p [Rhymed history of Didsbury, Alta.]

**Webling, Peggy**
VERSES TO MEN. London, Author, 1920. 46p [BM

**Webling, Walter Hastings, 1866–**
FORE! Brantford, Ont., Author, 1907. 9p [OTUV
FORE! "A Few More Golf Shots." Brantford, Ont., Author, 1908. [BM
FORE: THE CALL OF THE LINKS. New York, Caldwell, 1909. 73p [AEU
GOLF, IN VERSE AND REVERSE. Brantford, Harley Print., 1924. [20] p [AEU OONL
LOCKER-ROOM BALLADS. Toronto, Gundy, 1925. 95p [BM BVaU LC NBFU OTU
"ON AND OFF THE LINKS." Hamilton, Davis Print., 1921. 20p [NBSaM

**Webster, Joseph H.**
THE ACADIAN MINSTREL. Comp. by ——. Halifax, MacKinlay, 1860. 114p [NSWA

**Wees, Frances Shelley (Johnson), 1902–**

POEMS. Poems. Printed for her Friends. [Toronto?], 1936. 16p [BVaU OSUL

**Weir, Arthur, 1864–1902**

FLEUR DE LYS AND OTHER POEMS. Montreal, Renouf, 1887. 147p [BVaU OLU QMM

THE ROMANCE OF SIR RICHARD, SONNETS AND OTHER POEMS. Montreal, Drysdale, 1890. 121p [BVaU OLU QMM

THE SNOWFLAKE, AND OTHER POEMS. Montreal, Lovell, 1897. 144p [BM BVaU LC NBFU OLU QMM

**Weir, Robert Stanley, 1856–1926**

AFTER YPRES, AND OTHER VERSE. Toronto, Musson, 1917. 47p [BM BVaU LC OTU QMSS

POEMS, EARLY AND LATE. Toronto, Oxford U. Press, 1922. 63p [BVaU OTU QMM

**Wellband, Florence, 1907–1933**

SCENTED PETALS. Vancouver, Clarke & Stuart, 1933. 40p [Brown U BVaU

**Wensley, Amelia**

AT SUMMER'S END. Toronto, Ryerson, 1941. 8p [BVaU NBSaM OTP

**Wesleyan Minister, A**

SACRED POETRY. By a Wesleyan Minister. N.B., Sentinel Office, 1840. 24p [NSHD

**West, Gilbert Ashton, 1883–**

KOOTENAY KUTS. Including "The Cherry Picker" and Other Jingles. A Small Collection Of Rhymes and Reasonings Of A Rambling Rancher. 2nd ed. Nelson, B.C., Nelson Daily News, 1953. 28p

KOOTENAY KUTS AND OTHER JINGLES. By Kap-o-Kaslo [pseud]. Kaslo, B.C., Author, 1929. 24p [BVaU

**West, Paul Noden, 1930–**

THE SPELLBOUND HORSES. Toronto, Ryerson, 1960. 16p

**Westacott, Florence Elizabeth**

"THE CITY DWELLER" AND OTHER POEMS. ... Toronto, Sovereign Press, 1935. 40p [BVaU NBFU OTP

**Westaway, John**

THE JOHN WESTAWAY SOCIETY SONGS. Vancouver, n.d. 65p [Adelphi cat. 61

**Wetherald, Agnes Ethelwyn, 1857–1940**

THE GARDEN OF THE HEART. A Garland of Verses. By Ethelwyn Wetherald and Others. Boston, Badger, 1903. 16p [NBFU

THE HOUSE OF THE TREES AND OTHER POEMS. Boston, Lamson Wolfe, 1895. 94p [BVaU LC NBFU OTP

THE LAST ROBIN. Lyrics and Sonnets. Toronto, Briggs, 1907. 193p [BM BVaU OKQ

LYRICS AND SONNETS. Toronto, Nelson, 1931. 304p [BM BVaU NBFU OKQ

POEMS, LYRICS, AND SONNETS. Toronto, Musson, n.d. 193p [BVaU OTUV

THE RADIANT ROAD [and Other Poems]. Boston, Badger, 1904. 43p [BVaU LC OTP

TANGLED IN STARS. Poems. Boston, Badger, 1902. 45p [LC NBFU OTP

TREE-TOP MORNINGS. Boston, Cornhill, 1921. 65p [BVaU LC NBFU OKQ

**Wetherell, James Elgin, 1851–1940**

AESOP IN VERSE. Toronto, Macmillan, 1926. xvi + 199p [BVaU OLU

LATER CANADIAN POEMS. Ed. by ——. Toronto, Copp Clark, 1893. 187p [BVaU NSHD OTU QMM

LATER ENGLISH POEMS, 1901–1922. Ed. by ——. Toronto, McClelland, 1922. 208p [NSHD OTU

POEMS OF THE LOVE OF COUNTRY. Selected and ed. by ——. Toronto, Morang, 1905. 144p [BVaU NBFU OTU

**Whalley, George, 1915–**

NO MAN AN ISLAND. Toronto, Clarke Irwin, 1948. 72p [BVaU LC NBFU OTP QMM

POEMS 1939–1944. Toronto, Ryerson, 1946. 16p [BVaU NBSaM OKQ

**Wharton, Lewis, 1885–**

SONGS OF CARTHAGE AND OTHER POEMS. Ottawa, Overbrook Press, 1930. 61p [BM BVaU LC OTP

**Wheeler, Julia A.**

WAYS OF PLEASANTNESS. Knowlton, Que., Smith, 1942. 55p [OTP QMM

**Whelan, Michael**

THE CALL OF CHRIST, AND OTHER POEMS. Chatham, N.B., "Gazette" Office, 1922. 24p [NBFU OTUV

THE GREAT MIRAMICHI FIRE OF 1825 IN STORY AND SONG. With Other Poems. [Chatham, N.B.], 1925. 24p [NBFU OTUV

THE PIONEERS, AND OTHER POEMS. Newcastle, N.B., "Union Advocate," 1917. 16p [OTUV

QUEEN OF THE NORTH, AND OTHER SONGS AND SONNETS. Newcastle, N.B., 1914. 36p [NBFU OTUV

THE SACRED SILENCE, AND OTHER POEMS. Chatham, N.B., Gazette Press, [1925?]. 8p [Brown U NBFU

**White, Isaac S.**

FIVE WAR POEMS. A Memento of this Great, Most Cruel and Atrocious War. Winnipeg, Author, 1915. 23p [BM MWP

MANITOBA MUSES; or, Gentle Joseph and Other Poems. Toronto, Bryant, 1912. 327p [BM BVaU OOP

**White, Samuel Alexander, 1885–1956**

THE DAUGHTERS OF CONTENT, AND OTHER POEMS. London, Stockwell, 1921. 16p [BM

**White, Vine B.**

SONGS FOR YOU. Toronto, McClelland, 1917. 93p [BM Brown U OTU

**White, William Thomas, 1866–1955**

THE BATTLE OF BRITAIN, AND OTHER POEMS. Montreal, Author, 1945. 60p [BVaU LC NSHD OOP QMM

ESSAYS OF FRANCIS BACON, LORD VERULAM, PARAPHRASED IN BLANK VERSE. Montreal, Author, 1945. 54p [BVaU NBFU OTUV

**Whitehouse, Francis Cecil, 1879–**

CANADIAN AND OTHER POEMS. Toronto, Ryerson, 1934. 122p [BM BVaU OTP QMM

THE COQUIHALLA WRECK AND OTHER POEMS. Toronto, Ryerson, 1932. 18p [BVaU NBSaM OTP QMM

THE DREAMERS. N.p., Author, 1936. 19p [A supplement to CANADIAN AND OTHER POEMS.] [BM BVaU OTU

REBELS AND OTHER LOVE POEMS. By Ramon Francisco [pseud]. Ottawa, Graphic, 1929. 93p [BM BVaU OTP

SONGS OF THE SERVICE. [Toronto?], 1916. 16p [BM

**Whitell, Evelyn**

HEALING POEMS. Vancouver, Caxton Press, 19—. 16p [BViPA

LIFE'S GREATEST ADVENTURE. Vancouver, Caxton Press, n.d. 8p [BViPA

**Whiting, Lilian B.**

CANADIAN WILD FLOWERS. [Ottawa?], 1952. 33p

NORTH OF THE BORDER UP CANADA WAY. [Ottawa?], 1951. 41p

**Whitman, Howard Murray**

COME WALK WITH ME–AND OTHER VERSE. Philadelphia, Dorrance, 1938. 54p [LC OTP

**Whitman, James, fl. 1858–1885**

CANADA. A Ballad in Three Parts. Halifax, Smith, 1885. 23p [NSHD OTP

**Whitnall, Samuel Ernest, 1876–**

JOKINGS APART. With a Poem of Farewell to the Author, by Stephen Leacock. Oxford, Alden Press, 1950 [c1951]. 143p [OONL

**Whylock, R.M.**

COSMIC ORATORY. By Regis [pseud]. Toronto, Ryerson, 1929. 8p [BVaU NBSaM OTU QMM

**Whyte, James C.**
A MEDLEY OF POEMS, HYMNS AND SONGS. Hanover, Ont., Post Print., n.d. 116p [BVaU OOP

**Whyte, Thomas Henry**
POETICAL INSPIRATION. ... Toronto, Rowen Press, 1934. 40p [Brown U

**Whyte-Edgar, Mrs. C.M., 1869–1948**
A WREATH OF CANADIAN SONG. Containing Biographical Sketches and Numerous Selections from Deceased Canadian Poets. Toronto, Briggs, 1910. 284p [BM BVaU NBFU OTU

**Wickenden, Alfred Ahier, 1886–**
UP TRAIL. Philadelphia, Poetry Publishers, 1937. 78p [LC QMM

**Wickenden, Helen (Slack), 1887–**
A QUEBEC BOUQUET. Boston, Stratford, 1930. 35p [BVaU LC

**Wicksteed, Gustavus William, 1799–1898**
THE EXCOMMUNICATED. An Episode in the History of Canada and the British Flag. N.p., n.d. 10p [Parallel text in French by Louis Frechette] [QMU
WAIFS IN VERSE. Montreal, Lovell, 1878. 137p [2nd ed., Ottawa, Bureau, 1887. 165p] [BM BVaU LC NSHD OKQ

**Wigle, Rev. Hamilton A., 1858–1934**
LEAVES, ORIGINAL POEMS. Halifax, Book Room, [1915?]. 16p [Brown U
POETRY FOR PULPIT AND PLATFORM. Toronto, Briggs, 1911. 160p [BM BVaU
THE VETERAN AND OTHER POEMS. Toronto, Briggs, 1910. 88p [BM BVaU OTP

**Wilbee, (Sergeant) Arthur Frank, 1894–**
GEMS FROM THE GARDEN. White Rock, B.C., White Rock Printers, 1959. 44p
SOUVENIRS. Vancouver, Author, 1941. 48p [BVaU OKQ

**Wilcox, Noel H.**
THE PIPER OF DREAMS. [Halifax?], Author, 1927. 31p [NSHD OKQ
SILVER ARROWS. ... Halifax, Weeks Print., 1930. 30p [NSHD

**Wilkins, Caroline M.**
POEMS. N.p., Author, 1926. 95p [BVaU OPAL QMU

**Wilkins, Harriet Annie, 1829–1888**
THE ACACIA. By Harriet Annie [pseud]. Hamilton, "Spectator," 1863. 200p [1st ed.: Hamilton, 1860. 120p–OLU.] [BVaU NSHD OKQ
AUTUMN LEAVES. By Harriet Annie [pseud]. Hamilton, "Spectator," 1869. 87p [BVaU OTP QMM
THE HOLLY BRANCH. By Harriet Annie [pseud]. Hamilton, "Spectator," 1851. 140p [BVaU OTP

VICTOR ROY. A Masonic Poem. Hamilton, "Spectator," 1882. 128p [BVaU OKQ
WAYSIDE FLOWERS. Toronto, Hunter Rose, 1876. 255p [BVaU LC OTP QMM

**Wilkinson, Anne Cochran (Boyd), 1910–1961**
COUNTERPOINT TO SLEEP. Montreal, First Statement Press, 1951. 36p
THE HANGMAN TIES THE HOLLY. Toronto, Macmillan, 1955. 57p

**Wilkinson, Caroline Eleanor (Carter), –1949**
POEMS THAT APPEAL. Niagara Falls, Ont., Leslie, 1928. 100p [Brown U BVaU

**Wilkinson, John Richardson, –1908**
CANADIAN BATTLEFIELDS AND OTHER POEMS. Toronto, Briggs, 1899. 292p [2nd ed., rev. and enl., 1901. 309p] [BM BVaU LC OKQ

**Willerton, Irene**
SO LITTLE MAKES ME GLAD. Victoria, [1938?]. 28p [BVaU

**Willey, Christina**
POEMS OF CHRISTINA WILLEY. Toronto, Weaver, 1928. 22p [OKQ

**Williamson, Alexander Johnston, 1796?–1870**
DEVOTIONAL POEMS. Toronto, Rogers & Thompson, 1840. 24p [OTP
ORIGINAL POEMS ON VARIOUS SUBJECTS. ... Toronto, Coates, 1836. 151p [OTP
THERE IS A GOD. With Other Poems. Toronto, Lawrence, 1839. 24p [OTUV

**Williamson, Lydia (Buckland), 1860–1952**
DUET FOR CELLO AND DRUM. By Richard Scrace [pseud] and O.T.G. Williamson. Toronto, Southam Press, 1947. 45p [OTP

**Wills, Percy Edward, 1898–**
RAMBLING RHYMES FROM THE GRAVEYARD. Port Alberni, B.C., West Coast Printers, 1933. 32p [BVaU

**Willsher, E. Ann**
STANLEY PARK, VANCOUVER, B.C.: Spring, Summer, Autumn, Winter. Four Poems. Vancouver, Clarke & Stuart, 1944. 18p [BViPA OTP

**Willson, David, 1778?–1866**
HYMNS AND PRAYERS FOR THE CHILDREN OF SHARON. Newmarket, 1846. 108p [Another ed., 1849. 207p] [CCJ OLU
HYMNS OF PRAISE. Containing Doctrine and Prayer. ... Newmarket, Porter, 1853. 320p [OTP

**Willson, (Henry) Beckles, 1869–1942**
HEARTACHE IN CANAAN, AND OTHER POEMS. Oxford, Shakespeare Head Press, 1938. 93p [BM Brown U BVaU OTU

**Wilson, Alice Elizabeth, 1897–1934**
MY SANCTUARY GARDEN. ... Toronto, McClelland, 1937. 96p [Brown U BVaU OLU

**Wilson, Anne Elizabeth, 1901–1946**
EAGER FOOTSTEPS. Toronto, Musson, 1924. 47p [BM BVaU OKQ

**Wilson, Daniel, 1816–1892**
ANE AULD PROPHECIE. London, Jack, 1849. 12p [OTU
THE QUEEN'S CHOIR. A Revery in Roslin Woods. By D.W. [pseud]. Edinburgh, priv. print. [Thomas Nelson], 1853. 24p [BM OTU
SPRING WILD FLOWERS. London, Nelson, 1875. 243p [Original ed. pub. earlier under pseud. of Wil. D'Leina, Esq.] [BM OTUV

**Wilson, Estelle Hollister**
ROSEMARY AND RUE. Montreal, Renouf, 1914. 91p [BVaU NSHD

**Wilson, Mrs. Mabel May, 1899–**
IN FRIENDSHIP'S NAME. Moose Jaw, Author, 1952. 31p

**Wilson, Milton Thomas, 1923–**
RECENT CANADIAN VERSE. Selected and ed. by ——. Kingston, Jackson Press, 1959. 44p

**Wilson, William Shire**
SELECT PATHETIC AND THRILLING POEMS. Pamphlet Form. Hamilton, Author, 1914. 8p [BM OKQ

**Wilton, Margaret Harvey, 1902–**
PAGEANTRY OF DAYS. Toronto, Author, 1940. 15p [NBFU OKQ
WITH THE BEAUTY OF THAT HOUR. Toronto, Author, 1950. 24p [OKQ

**Windross, T.B.**
GATES OF GLORY AND OTHER POEMS. Ottawa, Tower Books, 1949. 42p [BVaU

**Wingfield, Alexander Hamilton, 1828–1896**
THE CENTENNIAL. An International Poem. Toronto, 1878. 310p [OONL
POEMS AND SONGS, IN SCOTCH AND ENGLISH. Hamilton, "Times," 1873. 255p [BVaU MWU OKQ

**Winkel, William C.**
PETALS FROM FLORAVALE. N.p., 1944. 18p [Adelphi Cat. 33A

**Winkler, George E.**
LONELY TRAILS. By the Prospector [pseud]. Victoria, Victoria Print., [1935]. 170p [BVaU
SONGS UNBIDDEN. Victoria, Victoria Print., [1920]. 170p [BVaU

**Winlow, Alice Maud (Dudley), 1885–**
POEMS OF ARMAGEDDON. By A.M.W. and E.P.F. [Ernest Philip Fewster?] Vancouver, Sun Pub. Co., 1914. 24p [BVaU

**Winnipeg, Man. Poetry Society**

PRIZE POEMS. 1942 Competition. [Winnipeg, the Society, 1942.] 14p [BVaU MWU OTU

**Winspear, Alban Dewes, 1899–**

THE ROMAN POET OF SCIENCE. Lucretius. De rerum natura. Set in English verse by ——. New York, Harbor Press, 1956. xx + 299p

**Wise, William H., –1949**

OF FOUR AND FORTY YEARS. Toronto, Author, 1935. 59p [OTU

**Withrow, Oswald Charles Joseph, 1878–1946**

POEMS FROM PRISON. Toronto, Author, 1937. 48p [BVaU OTP

**Wood, Mrs. Alexandrina Gertrude, 1881–**

A HANDFUL OF LILACS AND OTHER POEMS. By Gertrude Wood. N.p., 1946. 32p [SSU

THROUGH THE YEAR WITH GERTRUDE WOOD. Aneroid, Sask., News Magnet Press, 1950. 27p [Brown U OONL SSU

**Wood, Harold Samuel, 1903–**

CHUCKLES FROM HOME. Toronto, Reliance, 1930. 69p [BVaU LC OTP

WHY SHOULD WE FIGHT FOR ENGLAND? Toronto, McClelland, 1941. 12p [UTQ'42

YOUR HOME AND MINE. Toronto, Musson, 1932. 95p [BVaU OTP NBFU QMM

**Woodcock, George, 1912–**

THE CENTRE CANNOT HOLD. London, Routledge, 1943. 44p [BM LC

IMAGINE THE SOUTH. Pasadena, Cal., priv. print., 1947. 40p [BVaU LC

THE WHITE ISLAND. London, Fortune, 1940. 39p [BM LC OTU

**Woodley, Elsie Caroline, 1909–**

BITTERSWEET. Toronto, Ryerson, 1930. 8p [BVaU NBSaM OTU QMM

**Woodman, Mary A.L., 1880–**

PEN PICTURES OF NOVA SCOTIA, BERMUDA, JAMAICA. Wolfville, N.S., Author, 1959. 30p

PEN PICTURES OF OUR VALLEY. Published in Honour of Twenty-Fifth Anniversary of Apple Blossom Festival, Also for Benefit of Those Unable to Visit Our Valley. Wolfville, N.S., Author, 1957. 21p

**Woodrow, Constance (Davies), 1899–1937**

CAPTIVE AND OTHER POEMS. Toronto, Author, 1930. 4p [Adelphi cat. 41A

THE CAPTIVE GYPSY. Introductory note by Charles G.D. Roberts. Toronto, Ryerson, 1926. 20p [Also: Toronto, Balk-Preston, 1928. 34p] [BVaU NBSaM OTP QMM

THE CELTIC HEART. Toronto, Ryerson, 1929. 69p [BVaU LC NBFU OKQ

IMMORTALITY. Toronto, Balk-Preston, 1928. Broadside. [NBFU OKQ

PIERRETTE TO PIERROT. A Group of Love Lyrics. Toronto, Tower Print., 1929. 4p [BViPA NBFU OKQ

SELECTIONS FROM "SONNETS TO GABRIEL." Toronto, Author, 1931. 4p [NBFU OTU

**Wordon, Harry, 1935? –**

A BARD IN EXILE. Poems. Ottawa, Clementson Co., 1960 [c1959]. 52p

**Worfolk, Estelle Jean**

WAYSIDE REVERIES. Montreal, Menu Print. Service, 1939. 60p [BVaU

**Wraith, W.J.**

THE WANDERING JEW AND OTHER POEMS. By Walter Alexander [pseud]. Lucknow, Ont., Sentinel Presses, 1917. 100p [Brown U BVaU OTU

**Wrigglesworth, Lewis John, 1882–1956**

POETICAL WRITINGS OF LEW WRIGGLESWORTH. [Calgary?], n.d. 32p [ACG

**Wright, Alice E.**

COMFORT AND OTHER POEMS. Toronto, Goodchild, 1924. 63p [Brown U BVaU

**Wright, Arthur Walker, 1855–1944**

VERSES, VERSIONS, AND VERSICLES. Mount Forest, Author, 1907. 52p [Adelphi cat. 33A

**Wright, Daisy (McLeod)**

LITTLE JOHN BULL. Boston, Gorham, 1915. 60p [LC

**Wright, Evelyn Rose (Foster), 1897–**

RHYMES FOR A RAINY DAY. Fredericton, Brunswick Press, 1955. 25p

**Wright, Frederick, 1810–1878**

LAYS OF A PILGRIM. Brockville, Wylie, 1864. xii + 142p [OTP

WAY-SIDE PENCILLINGS. Ogdensburg, N.Y., Hitchcock, Tillotson & Haddock, 1855. 200p [OTP

**Wright, George A.**

LIFE LINES. Brockville, Recorder Print., 1944. 32p [OTL

**Wright, Geraldine**

THE SKATER, AND OTHER POEMS. Vancouver, Author, 1948. 10p [BVaU

**Wright, Mrs. Grace Armstrong, 1901–**

THE BIRTH OF SCOUTING, AND OTHER POEMS. N.p., 1958. 46p (Carillon Poetry Chap-Books)

**Wright, Laura Moore, 1892–**

VICTORY VERSES. ... Shaunavan, Sask., Author, 1942. 36p [Brown U BVaU OTU

**Wright, Robert Walter, 1852–1938**

AMONG THE IMMORTALS. Songs and Sonnets from the Hebrew. Toronto, Briggs, 1906. 238p [BVaU OKQ

THE DREAM OF COLUMBUS. A Poem. Toronto, Briggs, 1894. 64p [BVaU OTUV

**Writers' Craft Club, Carillon Group**

A SHEAF OF VERSE. By Members of the Carillon Group of the Writers' Craft Club. Toronto, Ryerson, 1929. 20p [BVaU NBFU QMM

**Wrong, Harold Verschoyle, 1891–1916**

VERSES. Oxford, [Blackwell?], 1922. 31p [OPAL

**Wyle, Florence, 1881–1968**

POEMS. Toronto, Ryerson, 1959. 16p

**Wylie, David, 1811–1891**

METRICAL WAIFS FROM THE THOUSAND ISLANDS. Brockville, "Recorder," 1869. 62p [BVaU OKQ

**Wyllie, Evelyn**

TWILIGHT MUSINGS. Victoria, Diggon's, 1928. 31p [BViPA

**Yarker, Margaret G.**

ECHOES OF EMPIRE. Toronto, Briggs, 1900. 32p [BVaU OTUV

**Yeoman, Eric McKay, 1885–1909**

POEMS. Toronto, 1910. 22p [QMM

**Yorke, W. Milton**

TALES OF THE PORCUPINE TRAILS. Toronto, Musson, 1911. 108p [BM BVaU OKQ

**Young, Rev. Egerton Ryerson, 1869–**

THE BELLS OF CHRISTMAS. Toronto, Briggs, n.d. 14p [OKQ

**Young, Flornie (Baxter)**

SONGS FROM KAWARTHA. New York, Vantage Press, 1959. 221p

**Young, Thomas Frederick, –1940**

CANADA, AND OTHER POEMS. Toronto, Hunter Rose, 1887. 117p [BVaU NBFU OTP

**Yule, Pamelia S. (Vining), 1825? –1897**

THE NAMES OF JESUS. A Poem. By Pamelia S. Vining. N.p., 1866. 11p [OTP

POEMS OF THE HEART AND HOME. By Mrs. J.C. Yule. Toronto, Bengough & Moore, 1881. 220p [BVaU NBFU OKQ QMM

**Zemke, Paul H.**

PRIVATE REFLECTIONS. With Cartoons by Len Norris. Toronto, Classic, 1946. 44p [CC

**Elliott, James**

ORIGINAL LYRICS. By a Canadian Rhymer [pseud]. Toronto, Author, 1856. 66p [OTP OTUV

OUR TRAVELLER WITH THE VALISE. Toronto, Bengough, Moore & Bengough, 1882. 22p [OTP

PENCIL SKETCHES? CITY OF GOSHEN? INDIANA. By Pat Prodpen [pseud]. N.p., n.d. 42p [OTP

THE PEREGRINATIONS OF PAT PRODPEN, THE POET POEM PEDDLER OF PARRY SOUND [pseud]. Being Part Second of OUR TRAVELLER WITH THE VALISE. Toronto, 1882. 32p [OTP

POEMS AND PEN PICTURES. By Pat Prodpen [pseud]. N.p., n.d. [c1883]. 29p [Brown U BVaU OTP

POEMS AND PEN PICTURES. V. 2. By Pat Prodpen [pseud]. N.p., n.d. [1884]. 47p [OTP

# POETRY AND PROSE

## Mixed anthologies and collections, and books in which both forms are employed by the same author

**Allen, Egbert Chesley, 1882–1947**

OUR NORTHERN YEAR. Stories and Songs of the Canadian Seasons. Toronto, Ryerson, 1937. 119p [AEU NBFU OTU

**Anonymous**

LESSONS ON BIRD PROTECTION. Ottawa, Dominion Parks Branch, Dept. of the Interior, 1922. 15p [QMU

THE PILGRIM'S ANNUAL. A Book of Folly and Wisdom Compiled by an Average Man. Cranbrook, B.C., 1916. 52p [Preface signed "W.H.B."] [BVaU

REMINISCENCES OF A SOLDIER. Consisting of Poems, Fragments, and Short Prose Pieces. Toronto, Rogers Thompson, 1843. 120p [BVaU NSWA OTP

THE VARSITY BOOK, PROSE AND POETRY. Toronto, Varsity Pub. Co., 1885. 200p [An assortment of pieces by such persons as W.H. Blake, W.W. Campbell, T.A. Haultain, M. Hutton, F.H. Sykes, A. MacMechan, and others.] [BVaU OKQ

**Armstrong, Janet M.**

RHYMES AND RAMBLES. Guelph, Guelph Pub., 1935. 31p [MWU OONL

**Audette, Adalard**

A FEW VERSES AND A BRIEF HISTORY OF THE CANADIANS ON THE SOMME AND VIMY RIDGE IN THE 1914 – WORLD WAR – 1918. London [Ont.?], Talbot & Co., 1919. 32p [OPAL

VERSES AND HISTORY OF THE GREAT WAR 1914. [Ottawa, Le Courrier Fédéral], 1919. 32p [OTP

VERSES WRITTEN IN THE TRENCHES. N.p., n.d. 21p [NSWA QMU

**Austin, Rev. Benjamin Fish, 1850–1932**

THE MISSION OF SPIRITUALISM AND ORIGINAL POEMS. Toronto, Austin Pub. Co., [1902?]. 32p [NBFU OPAL QMU

**Avery, Mrs. Geneva**

GARNERED GRAIN. [Toronto?], Colonist Print. & Pub., [1944?]. 69p [Phelps p88

**Baker, Henry**

LE SOUVENIR: TRANSLATIONS AND CHOICE PIECES FROM SOME OF THE BEST

FRENCH AND GERMAN AUTHORS. Ed. by ——. Montreal, Lovell, 1867. 288p [OTP

**Ball, John Bernard, 1911–**

AHOY FOR ETERNITY AND NATIONAL CREDIT. Regina, Ball Pub., 1956. 113p

OUR ISLAND UNIVERSE AND POETRY SELECTIONS. Regina, Author, 1955. 96p

**Baulch, S. Fred**

THE BRAUNDS OF BUCKS. Containing some Account of the Lives saved during a Series of Years by Means of a small Boat only in Bideford Bay. With a Copy of Verses. Toronto, Sovereign Press, 1889. 8p [NSWA QMU

**Baylis, Samuel Mathewson, 1854–1941**

AT THE SIGN OF THE BEAVER. Northland Stories and Stanzas. Toronto, Briggs, 1897. 225p [Also: Toronto, Briggs, 1907.] [BM BVaU NSHD OKQ QMM

CAMP AND LAMP. Rambles in Realms of Sport, Story, Song. Montreal, Drysdale, 1897. 316p [BM BVaU NBFU OTU QMM

**Belding, Albert Martin, 1859–1937?**

A HEART-BROKEN CORONER, AND OTHER WONDERS. By A.M. Belding and H.A. Woodworth. Saint John, Sun Print., 1895. 80p [BVaU NSHD OLU

**Bird, William Richard, 1891–**

ATLANTIC ANTHOLOGY. Ed. by —— and Alec Lucas. Toronto, McClelland, 1959. 310p

**Birney, Earle, 1904–**

NEW VOICES. Canadian University Writing of 1956. Comp. by ——. Toronto, Dent, 1956. 184p

**Broadus, Edmund Kemper, 1876–1936**

A BOOK OF CANADIAN PROSE AND VERSE. Comp. and ed. by —— and Eleanor Hammond Broadus. Toronto, Macmillan, 1923. 390p [New and completely rev. with additions: Toronto, Macmillan, 1934. 415p] [BM BVaU LC MWU NSHD OKQ QMM

**Brooker, Bertram, 1888–1955**

YEARBOOK OF THE ARTS IN CANADA, 1936. Ed. by ——. Toronto, Macmillan, 1936. 256p [BM BVi NBFU OKQ

**Brundle, John, 1882–**

THE RAPE OF SNAKE ISLAND INDIAN RESERVE BY THE DEPARTMENT OF INDIAN AFFAIRS, OTTAWA, AND THE TOWNSHIP OF NORTH GWILLIMBURY, ONTARIO. Roche's Point, Ont., Author, 1952. 44p

**Burns, David**

RANDOM WRITINGS. Brooklin, Author, 1916. 96p [QMU

**Burpee, Lawrence Johnstone, 1873–1946**

HUMOUR OF THE NORTH. Selected and arranged by ——. Toronto, Musson, 1912. 104p [BVaU LC NSHD OTP

**Burr, Rev. W.K.**

LEAVES FROM MY PORTFOLIO. Belleville, Daily Ontario, 1880. 255p [OTUV

**Byrne, Peter, 1929–**

ONCE AND SOME WORDS BETWEEN THE MINUTES. Montreal, Editions Quartz, 1960. 1v [unpaged]

**Canadian Expeditionary Force**

O CANADA! A Medley of Stories, Verse, Pictures and Music Contributed by Members of the Canadian Expeditionary Force. London, Simpkin; Hamilton, Kent, [1916]. 95p [BM BVaU NSHD OKQ

**Canadian Grenadier Guards**

A BRIEF OUTLINE OF THE STORY OF THE CANADIAN GRENADIER GUARDS. ... Told in an Anthology of Verse and Prose. Comp. by an Officer of the Guards. Montreal, for private circ'n, 1926. 76p [NSHPL

**Cawdell, James Martin, 1781?–1842**

THE ROSEHARP; for Beauty, Loyalty and Song. [Toronto, 1835]. 8p [Purports to be the introductory number of the organ of the Roseharp Patriotic Academy, but appears to have been written entirely by Cawdell.] [OTP

**Chandler, E.**

A FEW THINGS IN VERSE AND PROSE. Montreal, Lovell, 1877. 124p [BVaU QMU

**Chapman, Edmar**

BATCHAWANA ECHOES. Tales of the Trails, in Verse and Prose. N.p., Author, n.d. 41p [OKQ

**Charland, Gustave-Marquis**

FACTS AND FANCIES. By Gustave-Marquis Charland and Dorothy Lovell Charland. Sherbrooke, Tribune, 1943. 404p [Bk. I (Travels) ... by G.M.C. Bk. II (Poetry and Prose) by D.L.C.] [BVaU LC OTU QMM

**Coates, George Reed, 1876–1898**

SONNETS, POEMS, SKETCHES. [Toronto, n.p., 1898] [76p] [BVaU NBFU OLU

**Coleman, Edmund T.**

PRIZE ESSAY AND POEM OF THE LITERARY INSTITUTE, VICTORIA, V.I. On the Beauties of the Scenery as Surveyed from Beacon Hill. [Poem by W.H. Parsons.] Victoria, McMillan, 1868. 15p [BViPA

**Cook, Merrill H.**
MARGARET OF THE MOHAWKS. Story and Verse. Toronto, Beacon Press, n.d. 25p [NBSaM OTU

**Cross, Ethelbert F.H., 1872–**
FIRE AND FROST. Stories, Dialogues, Satires, Essays, Poems. ... Toronto, Bryant, 1898. 239p [BM BVaU MWU NBFU OTU QMM

**Currie, George Graham, 1867–1926**
SONNETS AND LOVE SONGS, AND IRENE, A MEMOIR. West Palm Beach, Fla., Dean Pub. Co., 1901. 263p [LC

**Davidson, Rev. G.F.**
NEPTUNE'S CAVE. A Fish Story in Three Slices. Toronto, Oxford Press, 1901. 38p [AEU NBSaM

**Dawson, Rev. Aeneas MacDonell, 1810–1894**
OUR STRENGTH AND THEIR STRENGTH. The North West Territory and other papers chiefly relating to the Dominion of Canada. Ottawa, Times Office, 1870. 326p [Also contains 80p of poems and lectures on the poets of Canada.] [BM BVaU LC NSWA OTU SSU

**Dewart, Rev. Edward Hartley, 1828–1903**
THE CANADIAN SPEAKER AND ELOCUTIONARY READER. Comprising a Choice Selection of Orations, Dialogues and Poetry. ... Ed. and comp. by ——. Toronto, Miller, 1868. 326p [BVaU LC OKQ

**Diespecker, Richard E. Alan, 1907–**
WHISPERS FROM THE WILD. [Victoria? 1924?] 31p [BVaU

**Douglas, Mia Farquharson (Mrs. D.H.)**
MIGNONETTE. Priv. print., 1939. 30p [QMU

**Duncan, Jessie**
BYWAYS OF LIFE. Being Travel Talks, Poems, and a Biblical Drama, "Athaliah." N.p., n.d. 165p [NBFU

**Dunlap, David Alexander, 1863–1924**
SHAHWANDAHGOOZE DAYS. N.p., Author, 1917. 76p [BVa OTU QMU

**Edgar, Mary Susanne, 1889–**
UNDER OPEN SKIES. Toronto, Clarke Irwin, 1955. xiv + 167p

**Edmonton, Alta. Words Unlimited Writers Group**
ALBERTA SPEAKS. Edmonton, the Group, 1957. 48p [A continuing serial. Various pagings.]

**Edwards, William, 1810–1881**

CORRESPONDENCE AND PAPERS ON VARIOUS SUBJECTS. ... Together with a sketch of his life, compiled and arranged by his brother, James Edwards. Peterborough, Examiner Steam Press, 1882. 170p [OLU OTP

**Ells, Sidney Clarke, 1878–**

NORTHLAND TRAILS. Toronto, Garden City Press, 1938. 189p [New and rev. ed.: Toronto, Burns & MacEachern, 1956. 229p] [BM BVaU OTP

**Emberson, Frederick C., –1913**

HASH (Wholesale to Boarding Houses). Montreal, Drysdale, n.d. 61p [OOP

THE YARN OF THE LOVE-SICK JAP. Montreal, Drysdale, n.d. 126p [BVaU OOP QMSS

YARN OF THE LOVE SICK PARSEE. Montreal, Drysdale, [1897?]. 126p [BVaU OTU QMM

**Fairbairn, Mrs. Christabel**

VERSES AND PROSE. N.p., F.P. Fairbairn, 1939. 25p [QMU

**Fairley, Margaret Adele (Keeling), 1885–1968**

SPIRIT OF CANADIAN DEMOCRACY. A Collection of Canadian Writings from the Beginnings to the Present Day. Toronto, Progress Books, 1945. 319p [BVaU LC MWU NBFU OKQ

**Farmer, Thomas Devey Jermyn**

THE GREAT POETS OF ITALY, in Prose and Verse. ... Toronto, Briggs, 1916. 283p [BM BVaU NBFU OTU

**Fletcher, Beatrice Ellen**

UPS AND DOWNS. Prose and Verse. Ilfracombe, Devon, Stockwell, 1952. 80p

**Fletcher, Mary E., 1874–1929**

POETRY AND PROSE. With an intro. by Archibald MacMechan. Toronto, Ryerson, 1930. 46p [BVaU NSHD OKQ

**Foran, Ethel Ursula**

SPRINGTIME FANCIES. Montreal, Gazette, 1935. 159p [BVaU LC NSHD OLU QMM

**Foran, Joseph Kearney, 1857–1931**

A GARLAND. Lectures and Poems. 1857–1931. Montreal, Gazette, 1931. 251p [BVaU LC NBFU OTU QMM

**Frame, Elizabeth, 1820–1913**

DESCRIPTIVE SKETCHES OF NOVA SCOTIA. In Prose and Verse. By a Nova Scotian [pseud]. Halifax, MacKinlay, 1864. 242p [BVaU NSWA OTP QMM

**French, Donald Graham, 1873–1945**

STANDARD CANADIAN RECITER. A Book of the Best Readings and Recitations from Canadian Literature. Comp by ——. Toronto, McClelland, 1918. 348p [BVa NSHD OTP

**Frisch, Anthony John, 1921–**

FIRST FLOWERING. A Selection of Prose and Poetry by the Youth of Canada. Ed. by ——. Toronto, Kingswood House, 1956. 210p

**Garvie, Alexander Rae, 1839–1875**

THISTLEDOWN. Miscellanies in Prose and Verse. With an intro. by G. Stewart. Toronto, Hunter Rose, 1875. 274p [BVaU NBFU OTU

**Gibson, Mary Stewart (Durie), 1875–1911**

STORIES AND VERSES. By Mary Stewart Durie. Toronto, Briggs, 1912. 168p [BM BVaU OTU

**Gill, Robert**

VERSES WITH A SKETCH IN DRAMATIC FORM, Written for his Family and Friends; and Addresses delivered on Various Occasions. Toronto, priv. print., 1927. 83p [Brown U OTU

**Gillis, James Donald, 1870–**

A MARITIMES LIFE. N.p., n.d. 126p [NSHD OTU

THE PIE SOCIAL. A Modern Romance. N.p., n.d. 74p [AEU NSHD OTU

**Goulding, Dorothy Jane, 1923–**

DOROTHY JANE'S BOOK. Songs and Stories from Kindergarten of the Air. Toronto, Dent, 1949. 90p [AEU MWU OH

**Graham, Janet (Pollock), 1880–**

AUNT JEAN'S CHRISTMAS PROGRAMME. Lachute, Que., Watchman, 1933. 30p [Contains poems as well as "dialogues" and plays.] [NSHPL

**Gustafson, Ralph Barker, 1909–**

CANADIAN ACCENT. A Collection of Stories and Poems. Ed. by ——. Harmondsworth, Middlesex, Eng., Penguin Books, 1944. 144p [BVaU LC MWU OTP

**Halldorsson, Albert Laurence, 1925–**

WINGS OF THE WIND. A Selection of Poems and Essays in Continuous Form. Winnipeg, Columbia Press, 1948. 80p [BViPA OTP

**Halliburton, Brenton, 1775–1860**

JOHN BULL AND HIS CALVES. Reflections on Passing Events. [Halifax?], priv. print., [1864?]. 47p [Separate issue of the appendix to G.W. Hill's MEMOIR OF SIR BRENTON HALLIBURTON, *q.v.*] [NSHD OTP QMSS

**Hardy, William George, 1896–**

THE ALBERTA GOLDEN JUBILEE ANTHOLOGY. Ed. by ——. Toronto, McClelland, 1955. 471p

**Harper, John Murdoch, 1845–1919**

SACRAMENT SUNDAY, AND BELLS OF KARTDALE. Toronto, Musson, n.d. 101p [BVaU NBFU OONL

**Hatheway, Warren Franklin, 1850–1923**

WHY FRANCE LOST CANADA, AND OTHER ESSAYS AND POEMS. Toronto, Briggs, 1915. 210p [BVaU LC NBFU OTP

**Hayes, Catherine E. (Simpson), 1852–1943**

PRAIRIE POT-POURRI. By Mary Markwell [pseud]. Winnipeg, Stovel, 1895. 186p [BM OTP QMM SSU

**Heighington, Wilfrid, 1897–1945**

WHEREAS AND WHATNOT. Toronto, Macmillan, 1934. 152p [BVaU LC OTP

**Henderson, Christine Margaret (Lighthall), 1868–1968**

ENGLAND REMEMBERED. Montreal, Lovell, 1944. 47p [BVaU NSWA OTP QMM

**Henderson, J. Duff**

ALVIRA alias ORCA. The Nineteenth Century Story. [Also some Poems and some Dramas.] Toronto, Hunter Rose, 1899. 279p [BCF OTP

**Herbert, Mary E.**

FLOWERS BY THE WAYSIDE. A Miscellany of Prose and Verse. ... Halifax, Citizen Office, 1865. 78p [NSHD

**Higginson, Thomas H., 1829–1868**

THE LITERARY WORKS OF T.H. HIGGINSON (Persolus). Vankleek Hill, Ont., Otto, 1888. [Bound with separately titled POETICAL WORKS, by Thomas Higginson.] 2v in 1 [BVaU OTU QMM

**Hopper, Alfred E., 1870–**

COMPOSITE CARGO. A Unique Collection of Poems and Prose Pieces. Ottawa, Tower Books, 1948. 43p [BViPA

**Howe, Joseph, 1804–1873**

POEMS AND ESSAYS. Montreal, Lovell, 1874. 341p [BVaU LC MWU NBFU OTU QMM

**Hunt, William Edward**

POEMS AND PASTELS. Toronto, Briggs, 1896. 137p [BM BVaU NBFU OKQ QMM

**Jamieson, Nina (Moore), 1885–1932**
THE CATTLE IN THE STALL. Sketches and Poems. ... Toronto, Garden City Press, 1932. 194p [BVaU LC NBFU OTU QMBM

**Jennings, Clotilda, –1895**
THE WHITE ROSE IN ACADIA, and AUTUMN IN NOVA SCOTIA. A Prize Tale and Poems. By Maude [pseud]. Halifax, Bowes, 1855. 36p [NSHD

**Johnson, Frank**
THE VILLAGE OF MERROW. Its Past and Present. Montreal, Lovell, 1876. 208p [BM BVaU LC NBFU OTP QMM

**Johnson, Helen Mar, 1834–1863**
CANADIAN WILD FLOWERS. Selections from the Writings of Miss Helen M. Johnson, of Magog, P.Q., Canada. With a Sketch of her Life by Rev. J.M. Orrock. ... Boston, Orrock, 1884. 200p [BVaU LC OTP

**Johnston, Mabel Annesley (Sullivan), 1870–1945**
A CANADIAN BOOK OF MONTHS, VERSE AND PROSE. By Susanne Marny [pseud]. Toronto, Briggs, 1908. 96p [BM BVaU OTP

**Joseph, Alexander Callow, 1886–1958**
THE ROVIN' PIGEON. With Verse, Yarns, Humor, Short Stories, etc. from D.V.A. Hospital Patients across Canada. By Al Pat [pseud]. Toronto, 1948–54. Pts. 1–7. [Unbound. Pagination and cover titles vary.] [OTP

**Kendrick, William K.F.**
CANADIAN STORIES IN PROSE AND VERSE. Toronto, Clarke Irwin, 1932. 130p [Rev. ed., 1936.] [OOP OTU

**Kidner, Frank, 1853–1924**
"PI." A Compilation of Odds and Ends Relating to Workers in Sanctum and Newsroom, culled from the Scrapbook of a Compositor. [Anon] Hamilton, Griffin & Kidner, 1890. 216p [BVa OKQ QMU

**King, Carlyle Albert, 1907–**
SASKATCHEWAN HARVEST. A Golden Jubilee Selection of Song and Story. Ed. by ——. Toronto, McClelland, 1955. 224p

**Klinck, Carl Frederick, 1908–**
CANADIAN ANTHOLOGY. Ed. by —— and R.E. Watters. Toronto, Gage, 1955. xvi + 558p

**Layton, Irving, 1912–**
NOW IS THE PLACE. Stories and Poems. Montreal, First Statement Press, 1948. 57p [BVaU LC NBFU OKQ QMM

**Leckie, Rev. Neil MacMillan**

ANY WELL THAT SPRINGS. Toronto, Ryerson, 1956. 89p

**Leitch, Patrick Joseph, 1847–1905**

POEMS AND LECTURES. Montreal, Pelletier, 1901. 116p [BM BVaU OTU QMSS

**Lockhart, Rev. Arthur John, 1850–1926**

THE PAPERS OF PASTOR FELIX (Arthur John Lockhart). Toronto, Briggs, 1903. 386p [BVaU LC NSHD OKQ QMSS

**MacCulloh, Lewis Luke**

THE SCRIBBLER. A Series of Essays published in Montreal on Literary, Critical, Satirical, Moral, and Local Subjects. Interspersed with Pieces of Poetry. Montreal, Lane, 1822. 8v [NSWA QMSS

**Macdonald, John James, 1849–**

POEMS AND ESSAYS. Ottawa, Ru-Mi-Lou Books, 1928. 132p [BVaU OOP QMM

**Macdonald, William Livingstone**

GLIMPSES OF LIFE. Poems and Prose of Inspiration and Education. Toronto, Ontario Pub. Co., 1936. 139p [OODF

**MacGeorge, Rev. Robert Jackson, 1811?–1884**

TALES, SKETCHES AND LYRICS. Toronto, Armour, 1858. 269p [BVaU NBFU OTP QMM

**MacGowan, James Alexander**

THROUGH THE TWILIGHT. Poems and Essays. Toronto, Rowsell, 1893. 59p [OTUV

**McGregor, J. Herrick**

THE WISDOM OF WALOOPI. Letchworth, Herts., Garden City, [1913?]. 250p [Reprintings from the Victoria "Times" and "Colonist."] [BM BVaU LC OLU

**MacKenzie, Evan James, 1869?–**

A VETERAN OF THE FIRST WORLD WAR TELLS HIS STORY. Victoria, [1954?]. 46p

**MacLennan, Catherine Mae**

RAMBLING ROUND STANLEY PARK. Vancouver, Wrigley, 1935. 47p [BVaU OTU

**McLeod, Murdoch**

LIFE ON THE ALGOMA FARM. [Vancouver, Author, 1954.] 82p [mimeographed]

POEMS AND STORIES FROM RAMBLES AROUND BRITISH COLUMBIA, FOR B.C. CENTENNIAL YEAR 1958. [Vancouver, Author, 1958?] 82p [mimeographed]

TALES OF THE B.C. TRAILS, 1959. [Vancouver, Author, 1959?] 82p [mimeographed]

**Mair, Charles, 1838–1927**

TECUMSEH, A DRAMA AND CANADIAN POEMS; DREAMLAND AND OTHER POEMS;

THE AMERICAN BISON; MEMOIRS AND REMINISCENCES. With intro. by Robert Norwood. Toronto, Radisson Society, 1926. 72 + 470p [BM BVaU NBFU OTP QMM

**Marsden, Rev. Joshua, 1777–1837**

THE NARRATIVE OF A MISSION to Nova Scotia, New Brunswick, and the Somers Islands; with a Tour to Lake Ontario. To which is added, THE MISSION, An Original Poem. ... Plymouth-dock, Johns, 1816. 289p [2nd ed., 1827.] [BM BVaU LC NSWA OTP QMSS

**Mason, Harold Campbell, 1895–**

BITS O' BRONZE. Toronto, Allen, 1921. 119p [BM BVaU NSHD OOP

**Merrill, Helen M.**

PICTURESQUE PRINCE EDWARD COUNTY. Picton, Ont., Gazette, 1892. 128p [BVaU OTP QMSS

**Mildmay, Rev. Aubrey Neville St. John, 1865–**

VIGNETTES. [In Verse and Prose.] London, Elliot Stock, 1894. 89p [BM

**Milliken, Lorene Frances (Ritz)**

NEW POEMS AND PROSE PIECES. Winnipeg, Author, 1960 [c 1958]. 68p

**Moore, Frederick William Louis**

MUSIC——EVERYWHERE. A Message over the Air to Young Canada. ... Victoria, Diggon-Hibben, [1934?]. 35p [BViPA NBFU

**Morrison, Dorothy, 1909–**

THE PRAIRIE LILY. Regina, School Aids, 1948. 40p [OH SRL

**Morse, Charles, 1860–1945**

APICES JURIS, and Other Legal Essays in Prose and Verse. Toronto, Canada Law Book Co., 1906. 356p [BM BVaU LC OTP

**Munro, Bruce Weston, 1860–1900?**

GROANS AND GRINS OF ONE WHO SURVIVED. Toronto, Warwick, 1889. 385p [BVaU LC NSHD OTMC

**Murdoch, Beamish, 1800–1876**

CELEBRATION OF THE CENTENERY [*sic*] ANNIVERSARY OF THE SETTLEMENT OF THE CITY OF HALIFAX. Oration by Beamish Murdoch; Poem by Joseph Howe. Halifax, 1849. 12p [NSWA

**Nairn, Robert, 1854–1937**

POEMS AND ADDRESSES. Toronto, Briggs, 1912. 80p [BM OTUV

**Nelson, George Edmondson, 1902–**

CAVALCADE OF THE NORTH. An Entertaining Collection of Distinguished Writing by Canadian Authors. Ed. by ——. Garden City, N.Y., Doubleday, 1958. 640p

**Nobile, Achilles Alexander, 1833–**

GEMS OF FOREIGN POETRY ... TRANSLATED INTO ENGLISH PROSE. New York, 1888. 32p [French, Italian, and Spanish.] [LC

MISCELLANEOUS POEMS, TRANSLATED INTO ENGLISH PROSE. Toronto, Williams, 1883. 116p [Earlier ed.: Paris, 1881. 62p] [BVaU LC NSHD QMM

MISCELLANEOUS WORKS OF SIGNOR A.A. NOBILE. Novels, Translations, Lectures. San Francisco, Patterson, 1894. 160p [On cover: v.1.] [No more published?] [LC

**Orrock, Rev. J.M., 1830–**

THE ARMY OF THE GREAT KING. Short Sermons on Short Texts; Miscellaneous Pieces, and Poetic Musings. Boston, Himes, 1855. 224p [LC

**Oxley, James Macdonald, 1855–1907**

A CHRISTMAS PORTFOLIO. Contributed to by Canadian Authors and Artists. [Ed. by ——.] London, Ont., Y.W.C.A., [1903]. 110p [BM NBFU OTP

**Palmer, George**

"STAND TO." By 2571 [pseud]. Calgary, Hynd, 1919. 76p [BM BVaU NBFU OTP

**Parker, Gilbert, 1862–1932**

THE WORKS OF GILBERT PARKER. Imperial ed. New York, Scribner, 1912–23. 23v [BM BVaU LC NBFU OTU QMM

**Pendle, Walter Henry, 1889–**

POEMS, SHORT TALES, PHANTASIES. Vancouver, 1951. 97p

**Penman, Rev. Archibald D., 1882–**

THE COMINGS OF CHRIST, PAST AND FUTURE (POEMS, SONGS AND TRIBUTES). Ilfracombe, Devon, Stockwell, 1956. 139p

**Peterson, Flora (Culp)**

LIFE AND SHE. Boston, Christopher Pub. House, 1960. 166p

**Phillips, John Arthur, 1842–1907**

THOMPSON'S TURKEY, AND OTHER CHRISTMAS TALES, POEMS. Montreal, Lovell, 1873. 256p [BVaU OTP QMSS

**Porter, Rev. William Henry, 1840–1928**

CONVERSE WITH THE KING. [Brantford, Expositor, 1892.] 240p [NSHPL OTUV

**Ramsay, Andrew John, 1849?–1907**

ONE QUIET DAY. A Book of Prose and Poetry. By J.R. Ramsay [pseud]. Hamilton, Lancefield, 1873. 191p [BVaU MWU NSHD OTP

**Regina College Writers' Club**

TUESDAY NIGHT, 1935. Regina, Western Printers, 1935. 32p [CC

**Richardson, Bond & Wright Limited**

ONE HUNDRED CHIN LIFTERS ON OUR 100TH YEAR, 1853–1953. Montreal, the Company, 1953. ix + 132p

**Rickard, Thomas Arthur, 1864–1953**

AUTUMN LEAVES. Vancouver, Wrigley, 1948. 194p [BViPA OTU

**Ridley, Hilda M., –1960**

CANADIAN BIRTHDAY BOOK. Ed. by ——. London, Davis, 1934. 99p [BM

**Robins, John Daniel, 1884–1952**

A POCKETFUL OF CANADA. Ed. by ——. Toronto, Collins, 1946. 430p [BVaU LC NBFU OTP QMM

**Rogers, Thomas George, 1877–1961?**

THE LIFE BEYOND. Thoughts by a Layman, in Prose and Verse, Concerning the Life to Come. Toronto, Author, 1960. 71p

**Rorke, Louise Richardson, –1949**

SOME CANADIAN CHRISTMASES IN PROSE AND VERSE. N.p., n.d. 6p [NBS

**Ross, George William, 1841–1914**

PATRIOTIC RECITATIONS AND ARBOR DAY EXERCISES. Comp. by ——. Toronto, Warwick, 1893. 374p [Poems, Speeches, etc., principally by Canadian authors.] [BVaU NSHD OTP QMM

**Rutherford, John**

CHARLIE CHATTERTON. A Montreal Story. With Canadian and Other Poems. Montreal, Lovell, 1868. 144p [BVaU NBFU OTP QMM

**Ryan, Norman J.**

"RED" RYAN'S RHYMES AND EPISODES. Hamilton, n.d. 92p [Brown U OOP

**Scott, Duncan Campbell, 1862–1947**

THE CIRCLE OF AFFECTION, and Other Pieces in Prose and Verse. Toronto, McClelland, 1947. 237p [BVaU NBFU OTP

**Seymour, Rev. James Cooke, 1839–1902**

HUMOR, PITH AND PATHOS. Readings and Recitations. Toronto, Briggs, 1887. [Ryerson Impt.

**Sheldrake, Sparham, 1851–1903**

CURIOUS FACTS. Prose and Verse. By Sparham Sheldrake ("Sigma"). Toronto, Williamson, 1895. 123p [OTP

**Shute, Evan Vere, 1905–**

WHERE THE HERON STANDS. By Vere Jameson [pseud]. [London, Ont.?], Author, 1949. 113p [OKQ

**Simpson, John, 1807–1878**

THE CANADIAN FORGET ME NOT FOR MDCCCXXXVII. Ed. by ——. Niagara, Sewell, 1837. 157p [BVaU LC OTP

**Smyth, John, –1852**

A SMALL SPECIMEN OF THE GENIUS OF CANADA WEST. ... Toronto, Coates, 1845. 34p [OTP

**Snell, Miss M.S., 1841–**

ESSAYS, SHORT STORIES AND POEMS. Including a Sketch of the Author's Life. Chatham, Ont., Banner Steam Print., 1881. 162p [BVaU OLU

**Snider, John H.**

SCRIBBLINGS OF A SCRIBE. By Taylor C. Knight [pseud]. Dryden, Ont., Observer, 1946. 74p [BVaU OKQ

**Stead, Robert James Campbell, 1880–1959**

THE MAPLE'S PRAISE OF FRANKLIN DELANO ROOSEVELT 1882–1945. Ed. by ——. Ottawa, Tower Books, 1945. 18p [OTU QMU

**Stephen, Alexander Maitland, 1882–1942**

THE VOICE OF CANADA. Canadian Prose and Poetry. Selected by ——. Toronto, Dent, 1926. 144p [BM BVaU LC NSHD OTP

**Stephens, William A., 1809–1891**

HAMILTON AND OTHER POEMS AND LECTURES. 2nd ed. Toronto, Lovell, 1871. 410p [BVa MWU OKQ

**Stevenson, Orlando John, 1869–1950.**

REMINISCENCES. Guelph, n.p., 1951. 32p

**Stewart, George, 1848–1906**

STEWART'S LITERARY QUARTERLY MAGAZINE. Devoted to Light and Entertaining Literature. Ed. by ——. Saint John, n.p., 1867–72. 5v [NSWA

**Stone, Phil**

"GOLD IN THE BRASS." A Collection. Toronto, Author, 1938. 35p [OTU

**Strong, William**

THE NEW HEAVEN. Letters, Editorials, and Poems. London, Friars Print. Assoc., 1902. 110p [Brown U BVaU OTUV

**Sutherland, Alexander Hugh, 1870–1952**

THE SELKIRK SETTLEMENT ON THE RED RIVER. Victoria, Author, 1938. 61p [Brown U BViPA

VICTORIA, B.C. Victoria, Clarke Print. Co., n.d. 30p [BViV NBFU

**Swift, Sherman Charles, 1879–1947**

THE VOYAGES OF JACQUES CARTIER IN PROSE AND VERSE. Sonnets by S.C. Swift, Prose Sketches by T.G. Marquis. Toronto, Allen, 1934. 79p [BM BVaU LC OKQ QMM

**Tennyson, Bertram, –1903?**

THE LAND OF NAPIOA and Other Essays in Prose and Verse. Moosomin, N.W.T., Spectator Print., 1896. 163p [BM BVaU OOP

**Toronto, University of**

VARSITY BOOK, PROSE AND POETRY. Toronto, Varsity Pub., 1885. 200p [OTU

**Toronto Art Students' League**

A CALENDAR FOR 1895–1896. With some Selections from Canadian Writers. Toronto, the League, 1895–6. 2v [NBFU

**Waid, J.B., 1804–**

VARIETY, POETRY AND PROSE. By the Bard of Niagara [pseud]. Montreal, Lovell, 1872. 254p [BVaU LC NBFU OKQ QMM

**Walters, Harry Macdonald**

CIVIL SERVICE JINGLES, AND OTHER THINGS. Ottawa, Lowe-Martin, 1911. 71p [BVaU OOP

**Wanless, Andrew, 1824–1898**

SKETCHES AND ANECDOTES. Detroit, Author, 1891. 300p [BVaU LC OLU

**Warman, Cy, 1855–1914**

TALES OF AN ENGINEER, with Rhymes of the Rail. New York, 1895. 242p [BVaU LC OLU

**Watson, Albert Durrant, 1859–1926**

OUR CANADIAN LITERATURE. Representative Prose and Verse. Chosen by Albert Durrant Watson and Lorne Albert Pierce. Toronto, Ryerson, 1922. 309p [Also: Toronto, Ryerson, 1923. 443p] [BVaU NSHD OTP QMM

**Watters, Reginald Eyre, 1912–**

BRITISH COLUMBIA. A Centennial Anthology. Toronto, McClelland, 1958. xvi + 576p

CANADIAN ANTHOLOGY. Ed. by C.F. Klinck and R.E. Watters. Toronto, Gage, 1955. xvi + 558p

**Weber, Ephraim, 1870–1956**

MUSINGS BY THE WAY. N.p., n.d. 33p

**Webling, Lucy**

POEMS AND STORIES. By Lucy Webling and Peggy Webling. Toronto, McLean, [18—?]. 150p [BVaU NBFU

**Wetherell, James Elgin, 1851–1940**

THE GREAT WAR IN VERSE AND PROSE. Selected and ed. by ——. Toronto, Wilgress, 1919. 160p [BM BVaU OTU

**Wicksteed, Gustavus William, 1799–1898**

WAIFS IN VERSE AND PROSE. Ottawa, Bureau, 1891. 260p [Another ed., 1891; also an 1894 ed. with addenda paged 261-328.] [BVaU LC OLU QMM

**Wigmore, Annie**

DREAMS OF THE FIRST AND TWENTIETH CENTURY. Toronto, Hunter Rose, 1898. 94p [OTP QMU

**Willis, John Howard**

SCRAPS AND SKETCHES; or, The Album of a Literary Lounger [pseud]. Montreal, Cunningham, 1831. 246p [OTP QMSS

**Woodrow, Constance (Davies), 1899–1937**

THE CHILDREN'S CARAVAN. Toronto, Balk-Preston, 1928. 40p [NBFU OTU

**Wootton, Wilfrid Shakespeare, 1910–**

THE SINGING WATERS OF BRITISH COLUMBIA. Vancouver, Author, 1953. 31p

**Wylie, David, 1811–1891**

RECOLLECTIONS OF A CONVICT, and Miscellaneous Pieces. By Y-łe [pseud]. Montreal, Chalmers, 1847. 197p [BVaU OTU QMSS

# FICTION

## Novels, collected short stories, anthologies (juvenile fiction included)

**Abbott, Rev. Joseph, 1789–1863**

PHILIP MUSGRAVE; or, Memoirs of a Church of England Missionary in the North American Colonies. Ed. by ——. London, Murray, 1846. 158p [Fictional presentation of MEMORANDA material; *q.v.* below, p. 949.] [BM BVaU NSWA OTP

**Acklom, Rauff de Ryther Daun, 1900–**

CONVENIENT SEASON. By David J. Manners [pseud]. New York, Dutton, 1941. 281p [LC NBFU OTMC

UNDER RUNNING LAUGHTER. By David J. Manners [pseud]. New York, Dutton, 1943. 315p [LC NBFU OTU

**Acland, Baldwyn John Dyke, 1883–**

FILIBUSTER. A Novel of Adventure. By B. Dyke Acland. London, Hodder, 1929. 320p [BM LC NBFU OTMC

PEREGRINE. A Novel. By B. Dyke Acland. London, Hodder, 1930. 320p [BM BVaU LC NBFU

STICKY FINGERS. London, Hodder, 1932. 316p [BM

SUNDOWN. By Dyke Acland. London, Hodder, 1931. 320p [Pub. in the U.S. as GRAND OLD MAN. New York, McBride, 1931. 277p] [BM BVaU LC OTMC

THE THIRTY THIEVES. By B. Dyke Acland. London, Hodder, 1930. 310p [BM LC NBFU

**Acland, Eric**

DRUMS OF NIAGARA. An Adventure Story of Early Canada. Toronto, Nelson, 1953. 226p

**Acland, Peregrine Palmer, 1892–1963**

ALL ELSE IS FOLLY. Toronto, McClelland, 1929. 345p [English ed., subtitled "A Tale of War and Passion. ... With a ... Foreword by Ford Madox Ford." London, Constable, 1929. 273p] [BM BVaU NBFU OTMC QMM

**Adam, Graeme Mercer, 1839–1912**

AN ALGONQUIN MAIDEN. A Romance of the Early Days of Upper Canada. By G. Mercer Adam and A. Ethelwyn Wetherald. Montreal, Lovell, 1887. 240p [BM BVaU LC NBFU OTP QMM

**Adams, Isabel**

THE DUMB MAN. New York, Appleton, 1933. 279p [BM BVaU LC OOP

HEART OF THE WOODS. A Story of Life among the Habitants in the Laurentian Foot-hills. New York, Century, 1928. 365p [BM BVaU LC NBFU OTMC QMM

**Adams, Percy Miller, 1894–**

LIFE ON THE HEAD END. New York, Vantage Press, 1956. 192p

**Adshead, Herbert Bealey, 1862–1932**

PIONEER TALES AND OTHER HUMAN STORIES. Calgary, Alberta Job Press, 1929. 70p [AC OTMC

**Algie, James, 1857–1928**

BERGEN WORTH. By Wallace Lloyd [pseud]. London, Fisher Unwin, 1901. 276p [BM BVaU

HOUSES OF GLASS. A Philosophical Romance. By Wallace Lloyd [pseud]. New York, Dillingham, 1898. 398p [BM LC OTU

THE SWORD OF GLENVOHR. By Wallace Lloyd [pseud]. Toronto, [19—?]. [T&C

**Allen, Barney, 1902–**

THE GYNECOLOGIST. Toronto, Rock Pub., 1949. 58p [LC

THEY HAVE BODIES. A Realistic Novel in Eleven Chapters and Three Acts. New York, Macaulay, 1929. 279p [LC NBFU

TORONTO DOCTOR. Toronto, Rock Pub., 1949. 390p [BVaU LC NBFU OKQ

**Allen, Grant, 1848–1899**

AN AFRICAN MILLIONAIRE. London, Richards, 1897. 317p [BM BVaU OTU

AN ARMY DOCTOR'S ROMANCE. New York, Tuck, 1893. 93p [BM LC

AT MARKET VALUE. Chicago, Neely, 1894. 329p [BM BVaU LC OTU

BABYLON. By Cecil Power [pseud]. New York, Munro, 1885. 310p [BM BVaU LC NBFU OTU

THE BACKSLIDER. New York, Lewis Scribner, 1901. 380p [10 stories] [LC

THE BECKONING HAND AND OTHER STORIES. London, Chatto, 1887. 341p [BM OTU

BLOOD ROYAL. New York, Cassell, 1892. 276p [BM BVaU LC OTU

A BRIDE FROM THE DESERT. New York, Fenno, 1896. 192p [3 stories] [LC OTMC

THE BRITISH BARBARIANS. New York, Putnam, 1895. 281p [BM BVaU LC OTU

THE CRUISE OF THE ALBATROSS; or When was Wednesday the Tenth? A Story of the South Pacific. Boston, Lothrop, 1898. 121p [AEU LC NBFU OTU

THE DEVIL'S DIE. London, Chatto, 1888. 3v [BM OTU

DR. PALLISER'S PATIENT. London, Mullen, 1889. 152p [BM

THE DUCHESS OF POWYSLAND. London, Chatto, 1892. 3v [BM OTU

DUMARESQ'S DAUGHTER. New York, Harper, 1891. 297p [BM BVaU LC NBFU OTU

FOR MAMIE'S SAKE. A Tale of Love and Dynamite. New York, Munro, 1886. 295p [BM LC OTMC

THE GREAT TABOO. London, Chatto, 1890. 280p [BM LC OTMC

HILDA WADE. New York, Putnam, 1900. 383p [BM BVaU LC OTU

IN ALL SHADES. London, Chatto, 1886. 3v [BM BVaU OTU

THE INCIDENTAL BISHOP. New York, Appleton, 1898. 306p [BM LC OTU

IVAN GREET'S MASTERPIECE. London, Chatto, 1893. 330p [BM OTU

THE JAWS OF DEATH. London, Simpkin, 1889. 110p [BM OTU

KALEE'S SHRINE. By Grant Allen ... and May Coates. Bristol, Arrowsmith, 1886. 196p [LC OTU

LINNET. London, Richards, 1898. 394p [BM LC OTU

MICHAEL'S CRAG. Chicago, Rand McNally, 1893. 242p [BM BVaU LC NBFU OTU

MISS CAYLEY'S ADVENTURES. New York, Putnam, 1899. 344p [BM BVaU LC NBFU OTU

MOORLAND IDYLLS. London, Chatto, 1896. 257p [BM

PHILISTIA. ... By Cecil Power [pseud]. New York, Munro, 1884. 254p [BM LC OTMC

RECALLED TO LIFE. New York, Holt, 1891. 230p [BM LC

ROSALBA. The Story of Her Development. By Olive Pratt Rayner [pseud]. New York, Putnam, 1899. 396p [BM LC

THE SCALLYWAG. New York, Cassell, 1893. 437p [BM LC OTU

SIR THEODORE'S GUEST, AND OTHER STORIES. Bristol, Arrowsmith, 1902. 316p [BM

A SPLENDID SIN. London, White, 1896. 228p [BM LC

STRANGE STORIES. London, Chatto, 1884. 356p [BM BVaU OTU

THE TENTS OF SHEM. A Novel. London, Chatto, 1889. 3v [BM BVaU LC OTU

A TERRIBLE INHERITANCE. New York, Crowell, [18—?]. 57p [LC OTU

THIS MORTAL COIL. A Novel. London, Chatto, 1888. 3v [BM NBFU OTU

TOM, UNLIMITED. A Story for Children. By Martin Leach Warborough [pseud]. London, Richards, 1897. 250p [BM

TWELVE TALES. London, Richards, 1899. 351p [BM BVaU LC OTMC

THE TYPEWRITER GIRL. By Olive Pratt Rayner [pseud]. London, Pearson, 1897. 261p [Same title: By Grant Allen. New York, Street & Smith, 1900.] [BM LC OTU

UNDER SEALED ORDERS. In Two Parts. ... New York, Collier, 1894. 470p [BM LC OTU

WEDNESDAY THE TENTH. A Tale of the South Pacific. Boston, Lothrop, 1890. 131p [Same as THE CRUISE OF THE ALBATROSS, *q.v.*] [BVaU NSHD OONL

WHAT'S BRED IN THE BONE. £1000 prize novel. London, "Tit-Bits," 1891. 414p [BM BVaU LC NBFU OTMC

THE WHITE MAN'S FOOT. ... London, Hatchards, 1888. 216p [BM OTU
THE WOMAN WHO DID. Boston, Roberts, 1895. 223p [Repub. with intro. by Ernest Boyd. Boston, Little Brown, 1926. xv + 223p] [BM BVaU LC NBFU OTU

**Allen, Joseph**

THE MAKING OF A CANADIAN. Newark, N.J., Allen Pub., 1918. 383p [LC BVaU OTP

**Allen, Ralph, 1913–1966**

THE CHARTERED LIBERTINE. Toronto, Macmillan, 1954. 270p
HOME MADE BANNERS. Toronto, Longmans, 1946. 256p [BVaU LC NBFU OTU
PEACE RIVER COUNTRY. London, Hodder, 1958. 191p

**Allison, Dorothea**

MERRY BELLS; or, Tales of the Okanagan Fairies. Comp. by ——. Vernon, B.C., Vernon News, 1945. 25p [BKO

**Alloway, Mary H. (Wilson), 1848–1919**

CROSSED SWORDS. A Canadian-American Tale of Love and Valor. By Mrs. Clement Alloway. Toronto, Briggs, 1912. 391p [BM BVaU NBFU OTMC QMM

**Amy, William Lacey, –1962**

THE BEAST. By Luke Allan [pseud]. Boston, Small Maynard, 1924. 335p [BM BVaU LC OTMC
BEHIND THE WIRE FENCE. By Luke Allan [pseud]. London, Arrowsmith, 1935. 287p [BM OONL
BEYOND THE LOCKED DOOR. By Luke Allan [pseud]. London, Jenkins, 1938. 286p [BM
THE BLACK OPAL. By Luke Allan [pseud]. London, Arrowsmith, 1935. 288p [BM OONL
BLUE PETE AND THE KID. By Luke Allan [pseud]. London, Jenkins, 1953. 190p
BLUE PETE AND THE PINTO. By Luke Allan [pseud]. London, Jenkins, 1948. 192p [BM
BLUE PETE AT BAY. By Luke Allan [pseud]. London, Jenkins, 1951 [1952]. 190p
BLUE PETE BREAKS THE RULES. By Luke Allan [pseud]. London, Jenkins, 1943. 187p [ACU
BLUE PETE: DETECTIVE. By Luke Allan [pseud]. London, Jenkins, 1928. 312p [BM LC OTUV SRL
BLUE PETE: HALF BREED. By Luke Allan [pseud]. London, Jenkins, 1921. 256p [BM BVaU LC OTMC
BLUE PETE, HORSE THIEF. A Mounted Police Story. By Luke Allan [pseud]. London, Jenkins, 1938. 283p [AEU BM
BLUE PETE IN THE BADLANDS. By Luke Allan [pseud]. London, Jenkins, 1954. 173p

BLUE PETE, INDIAN SCOUT. By Luke Allan [pseud]. London, Jenkins, 1950. 221p [BM OONL

BLUE PETE, OUTLAW. By Luke Allan [pseud]. London, Jenkins, 1944. 192p [BM

BLUE PETE PAYS A DEBT. By Luke Allan [pseud]. Toronto, Longmans, 1942. 288p [ACU BM

BLUE PETE: REBEL. By Luke Allan [pseud]. London, Jenkins, 1940. 286p [ACU BM OTU

BLUE PETE RIDES THE FOOTHILLS. By Luke Allan [pseud]. London, Jenkins, 1953. 188p

BLUE PETE TO THE RESCUE. By Luke Allan [pseud]. London, Jenkins, 1947. 196p [BM

BLUE PETE, UNOFFICIALLY. By Luke Allan [pseud]. London, Jenkins, 1949. 224p [BM

BLUE PETE WORKS ALONE. By Luke Allan [pseud]. London, Jenkins, 1948. 240p [BM

BLUE PETE'S DILEMMA. By Luke Allan [pseud]. London, Jenkins, 1945. 190p [BM

BLUE PETE'S VENDETTA. By Luke Allan [pseud]. London, Jenkins, 1947. 186p [BM

THE BLUE WOLF. A Tale of the Cypress Hills. London, Hodder, 1913. 311p [ACU BM OTP

CASE OF THE OPEN DRAWER. By Luke Allan [pseud]. London, Arrowsmith, 1936. 288p [BM

THE DARK SPOT. By Luke Allan [pseud]. London, Arrowsmith, 1932. 295p [BM

THE END OF THE TRAIL. By Luke Allan [pseud]. London, Arrowsmith, 1931. 311p [BM OONL

FIVE FOR ONE. By Luke Allan [pseud]. Bristol, Arrowsmith, [1934]. 288p [BM NBFU OONL

THE FOURTH DAGGER. London, Arrowsmith, 1932. 287p [BM NBFU OTMC

THE GHOST MURDER. By Luke Allan [pseud]. London, Jenkins, 1937. 316p [BM OTU

JUNGLE CRIME. By Luke Allan [pseud]. London, Arrowsmith, 1931. 318p [BM

THE LONE TRAIL. By Luke Allan [pseud]. London, Jenkins, 1921. 312p [BM OTUV

THE MAN ON THE TWENTY-FOURTH FLOOR. By Luke Allan [pseud]. London, Jenkins, 1937. 312p [BM OTU

THE MANY-COLOURED THREAD. By Lacey Amy. Toronto, Longmans, 1932. 311p [BM NBFU OTUV

THE MASKED STRANGER. By Luke Allan [pseud]. London, Arrowsmith, 1930. 287p [BM

MURDER AT MIDNIGHT. By Luke Allan [pseud]. London, Arrowsmith, 1930. 288p [BM LC

MURDER AT THE CLUB. By Luke Allan [pseud]. Bristol, Arrowsmith, 1933. 288p [BM OONL

THE PACE. By Luke Allan [pseud]. London, Hutchinson, 1926. 282p [BM LC

THE RETURN OF BLUE PETE. By Luke Allan [pseud]. London, Jenkins, 1922. 312p [BM BVaU LC NBFU OTMC

SCOTLAND YARD TAKES A HOLIDAY. London, Arrowsmith, 1937. 288p [BM

THE SIRE. By Luke Allan [pseud]. London, Hutchinson, 1927. 288p [BM BVaU LC OPAL

THE TENDERFOOT. By Luke Allan [pseud]. London, Jenkins, 1939. 286p [BM NBFU OTU

THE VENGEANCE OF BLUE PETE. A Mounted Police Story. By Luke Allan [pseud]. London, Jenkins, 1939. 284p [BM OTU

THE TRAITOR. London, Arrowsmith, 1933. 288p [BM

THE WESTERNER. By Luke Allan [pseud]. London, Jenkins, 1923. 304p [BM NBFU

THE WHITE CAMEL. By Lacey Amy. London, Jarrolds, 1926. 318p [BM LC

**Anderson, Clara (Rothwell), –1958**

JOHN MATHESON. A Wholesome Human Story of Canadian Rural Life. Toronto, Ryerson, 1923. 346p [BM NBFU OKQ QMM

**Anderson, Margaret Pauline, 1870–**

LEONA CLINCH; or, Lord Kendale's Repentance. Saint John, Barnes, 1907. 338p [BM

**Annett, Ronald Ross, 1895–**

ESPECIALLY BABE. Toronto, Ryerson, 1942. 263p [LC NBFU OTU

**Anonymous**

THE ADOPTED DAUGHTER; or, The Trials of Sabra. A Tale of Real Life. Ogdensburgh, N.Y., Hitchcock, 1858. 199p [3rd ed., rev.: Montreal, Lovell, 1863. 196p. Also a 4th ed., 1873.] [BVaU NSHPL OHM OTP QMU

ELLEN MASON. Or, Principle and Prejudice. Toronto, James Campbell, n.d. [Also: Edinburgh, Gall & Inglis; London, Houlston & Wright, [1862]. 111p [OTP

ELSPETH SUTHERLAND; or, The Effects of Faith. Toronto, n.d. 48p [BCF

HOUSE OF THE GALLERY, 2d Session, 3d Parliament. Official Correspondence between the Hon. the First Minister of Duffy, and His Exalted Majesty Night Blooming Ceres, Monarch of the Moon ... relative to the Construction of the Imperial, Lunar, Grand, Mid-air, Lunatic Governmental Railway. ... Ottawa, Citizen, 1875. 14p [NSHP OTU

THE HUNTED OUTLAW; or, Donald Morrison the Canadian Rob Roy. Montreal, Montreal News, 1889. 98p [OTP

NEWS FROM THE INVISIBLE WORLD; or, Interesting Anecdotes of the Dead. Halifax, Nicholson, 1840. 627p [OTP

"OUR SWELL." Chatham, Ont., Planet Steam Print., 1881. 36p [NSHP OTP

THE PRINCE AND THE PROTEGE. A Tale of the Early History of Nova Scotia. Halifax, Croskill, 1844. [Prize story, "Morning Post" competition.] 15p [NSHP

SIR PETER PETTYSHAM. A Satirical Story of Canadian Life. Montreal, Canadian Railway News Co., 1882. 42p [NSWA QMSS

TRUE CANADIAN DETECTIVE STORIES. Toronto, Howard Pub., 1944. 127p [NBFU

WARS OF THE GULLS. An Historical Romance in Three Chapters. New York, Dramatic Repertory, Shakespeare Gallery, 1812. 36p [Reprinted for C.L. Woodward, New York, 1880.] [LC OOND

THE YOUNG CANADIAN. A True Story. London, J. Groom, [1855?]. 32p [BM

**Appleby, M.**

TOLD BY THE INNKEEPER. Ed. by ——. London, Old Royalty Book Pubs., n.d. 143p [BVaU

**Archibald, Edith Jessie (Mortimer), 1854–1938**

GUFSHATHI AND HERRIAMAN. A Missionary Story. Saint John, n.d. 82p [NSWA

THE TOKEN. A Tale of Cape Breton Island. ... Toronto, Ryerson, 1930. 315p [BM BVaU NSHD OKQ QMM

**Ardagh, Alice Maud, 1866–1936**

FOR ME TO LIVE. Chicago, Bible Institute Colportage Assoc., 1936. 208p [LC

TANGLED ENDS. By "Espérance" [pseud]. Toronto, Briggs, 1888. 148p [OTU

**Armbrest, Duncan**

THE BEECH WOODS. How the Neighbours Learned the Many Secrets of a Canadian Wood. Toronto, Briggs, 1916. 120p [BM OTU

**Armitage, John, 1885?–**

WING PO. A Romance of Modern China. By Hin Me Geong [pseud]. Toronto, Macmillan, 1929. 323p [BVaU NBFU OTMC

**Armour, Agatha, –1891 (Mrs. John G. Thompson)**

LADY ROSAMOND'S SECRET. A Romance of Fredericton. Saint John, Telegraph, 1878. 146p [NBFU OTU

MARGUERITE VERNE; or, Scenes from Canadian Life. Saint John, Telegraph, 1886. 324p [NSHD

MARION WILBURN. Saint John, Telegraph, n.d. [NBB

SYLVIA LEIGH; or, The Heiress of Glenmarle. Saint John, Telegraph, 1880. [BCF

**Armsmith, Catherine**

FAIRY TALES OF KOOTENAY. London, Stockwell, 1929. 80p [BM BVaU OTMC

**Armstrong, Matt**

TURTLE RIVER FILLY. Garden City, N.Y., Doubleday, 1950. 213p [OONL

**Armstrong, Rinaldo William**

RIVERS RUN TO THE SEA. Toronto, Ryerson, 1936. 288p [BM BVaU LC NBFU OTMC

**Arnold, Gertrude**

SISTER ANNE! SISTER ANNE! Toronto, McClelland, 1920. 235p [BM BVaU NBFU

**Arthur, Sidney**

A MAN'S WORTH. A Canadian College Romance. Toronto, Hunter Rose, 1926. 294p [AEU OH QQL

**Ascher, Isidore Gordon, 1835–1914**

THE DOOM OF DESTINY. London, Diprose & Bateman, 1895. 174p [BM

AN ODD MAN'S STORY. London, Elliot Stock, 1889. 207p [BM NSWA OONL

A SOCIAL UPHEAVAL. London, Greening, 1898. 304p [BM

**Ashtalcovitch, Michael K.**

WHAT IS FEAR? Toronto, Author, 1945. 403p [CC

**Ashworth, Edward Montague**

LA ROUX. By Johnston Abbott [pseud]. Toronto, Macmillan, 1924. 348p [BVaU LC NBFU OTMC

THE SEIGNEURS OF LA SAULAYE. Gentlemen Adventurers of New France. ... By Johnston Abbott [pseud]. Toronto, Macmillan, 1928. 379p [BVaU LC NBFU OTP

**Atkin, Grace Murray, 1891–**

THE CAPTIVE HERD. Toronto, McClelland, 1922. 311p [BM BVaU LC OTMC

THE NEW WORLD. Toronto, McClelland, 1921. 285p [BVaU LC OTMC QMM

A SHADOW FALLS. Toronto, Ryerson, 1954. 186p

THAT WHICH IS PASSED. New York, Crowell, 1923. 334p [LC NBFU OTMC

**Atlee, Benge, 1890–**

BLACK FEATHER. New York, Scribner, 1939. 345p [LC NBFU OTMC

**Austin, Rev. Benjamin Fish, 1850–1932**

CHRIST OR BARABBAS. A Psychic Novel. Los Angeles, Austin Print., 1921. 142p [LC OLU

THE MYSTERY OF ASHTON HALL. By Benjamin Nitsua [pseud]. Rochester, New York, Austin, 1910. 321p [BM LC OTMC

**Austin, Lilian Edna**

SHUDDERS. Boston, Meador, 1931. 61p [LC

**Ayscough, Florence (Wheelock), 1878–1942**

THE AUTOBIOGRAPHY OF A CHINESE DOG. Ed. by his Missuss. ... Boston, Houghton, 1926. 105p [BM LC QMM

**B., H.H.**

THE LAST OF THE ERIES; or, A Tale of Canada. By H.H.B. Simcoe, Author, 1849. 224p [NSWA OLU

**Babcock, John Pease, 1855–1936**

PEACE RIVER JOE. The Prize Winning Story of the I.O.D.E. 1924 Competition. Victoria, B.C., Litchfield's, 1924. 24p [BVaU OTMC

**Bacchus, Noel, 1888–**

YOU'VE GOT TO SHOW ME, AND OTHER STORIES. New York, Pageant, 1953. 117p

**Baird, Mrs. C.A.**

A FRAGMENT OF ONTARIO'S SCOTT ACT; or, A Ruined Life. By a "W.C.T.U." [Mrs. Dewolf of Hamilton, Ont.]. LAWYER ROBERT STREIGHTON'S DISCOVERY AT A MINERAL SPRING. By Carleton [pseud–Mrs. C.A. Baird]. Boston, Barta, 1893. 85p [OH

**Baird, Rev. Frank, 1870–1951**

PARSON JOHN OF THE LABRADOR. London, R.T.S., 1924. 246p [BM NBFU

ROB MACNAB. A Story of Old Pictou. ... Halifax, Royal Print., 1923. 250p [BVaU NSHD OTMC

ROGER DAVIS, LOYALIST. London, R.T.S., 1907. 191p [BM NBFU OTMC

**Baird, Irene**

HE RIDES THE SKY. Toronto, Macmillan, 1941. 241p [BVaU NSHD OTMC QMM

JOHN. Philadelphia, Lippincott, 1937. 235p [BM BVaU LC NBFU OTMC QMM

WASTE HERITAGE. Toronto, Macmillan, 1939. 329p [BVaU LC NBFU OTMC QMM

**Baker, Ida Emma (Fitch), 1858–1948**

PRESSED DOWN AND RUNNING OVER. Toronto, Author, 1939. 26p [OTU

**Baldwin, Harold, 1888–**

PELICANS IN THE SKY. A Novel. London, Murray, 1934. 311p [BM

**Ball, Augustus Harry, 1873–**

ROVERS OF THE VALLEY. Toronto, Dent, 1928. 248p [BM OTMC

**Ball, Derrick**

THE BURLESQUE VOYAGE. London, Davies, 1953. 281p

**Ballantyne, Lereine (Hoffman), 1891–1962**

SPIRIT FIRE. A Story of the Petun Indians. New York, Revell, 1932. 188p [LC NBFU OTMC

**Bambrick, Winifred**

CONTINENTAL REVUE. London, Faber, 1946. 352p [BM BVaU LC NBFU OTMC QMM

**Banks, William, 185-?–1920**

WILLIAM ADOLPHUS TURNPIKE. Toronto, Dent, 1913. 260p [BM BVaU OTMC

**Banwell, Selwyn, 1880–**

THE LOYALIST. Toronto, Rous & Mann, 1934. 31p [BVaU NBFU OKQ QMBM

**Barbeau, Charles Marius, 1883–1969**

THE DOWNFALL OF TEMLAHAM. Toronto, Macmillan, 1928. 253p [BM BVaU LC NBFU OTMC QMM

THE GOLDEN PHOENIX AND OTHER FRENCH-CANADIAN FAIRY TALES. By Marius Barbeau, retold by Michael Hornyansky. Toronto, Oxford U. Press, 1958. 144p

THE INDIAN SPEAKS. By Marius Barbeau and Grace Melvin. Toronto, Macmillan, 1943. 117p [BVaU LC NSHD OKQ

MOUNTAIN CLOUD. Toronto, Macmillan, 1944. 300p [BM BVaU LC NSHD OKQ QMM

THE TREE OF DREAMS. Toronto, Oxford U. Press, 1955. ix + 112p [Legends and sketches of folk personalities.]

**Barnard, Leslie Gordon, 1890–1961**

THE IMMORTAL CHILD. A Christmas Letter to an Unknown Friend. Montreal, Author, 1941. 24p [BVaU NBFU OTMC QMM

JANCIS. Toronto, Macmillan, 1935. 245p [Also: London, Dickson, 1936. 245p] [BM BVaU NBFU OTU QMM

ONE GENERATION AWAY. Montreal, Dodd-Simpson, 1931. 438p [BVaU LC NBFU OTMC QMM

SO NEAR IS GRANDEUR. Toronto, Macmillan, 1945. 207p [BVaU NBFU OTMC QMM

**Barrington, Gwenyth, 1901–**

WOMEN WITHOUT MONEY. Woman's Private Life with the Dollar. Toronto, Longmans, 1947. 156p [AEP OOP PC

**Barry, Lily Emily Frances, 1863?–1955**

IN THE PATHS OF PEACE. Montreal, Canada Engraving, 1901. 310p [BM OTMC QMM

**Bartley, E.T.**

LILIAN'S RETROSPECT. Toronto, Hunter Rose, 1877. 142p [BVaU OTMC

**Barton, J. King**

IO. A Tale of the Ancient Fane. By K. Barton. New York, Appleton, 1851. 251p [BM LC

**Batson, Alfred, 1900–**

AFRICAN INTRIGUE. New York, Garden City Pub. Co., 1933. 307p [AEP BVa LC NSHPL

**Baubie, William Edward**

THE MAN CONDEMNED. Written and illus. by ——. Boston, Stratford, 1936. 350p [LC QMSS

**Baxter, Arthur Beverley, 1891–1964**

THE BLOWER OF BUBBLES. London, Chalmers, 1919. 262p [BM BVaU LC NBFU OTMC QMM

THE PARTS MEN PLAY. New York, Appleton, 1920. 330p [BM BVaU LC NBFU OTMC QMM

**Bayley, Mrs. Diana**

EMPLOYMENT THE TRUE SOURCE OF HAPPINESS; or, The Good Uncle and Aunt. London, Harris, 1825. 147p [BM

IMPROVEMENT; or, A Visit to Grandmama. London, Arnold, 1832. viii + 172p [Adelphi

SCENES AT HOME AND ABROAD. By Mrs. Henry Bayley. London, Stokes, 1827. 115p [BM

TALES OF THE HEATH. ... London, Harris, 1825. 228p [BM

**Beames, John, 1889–**

AN ARMY WITHOUT BANNERS. Toronto, McClelland, 1930. 301p [BM BVaU LC NBFU OTP

DUKE. London, Benn, 1933. 287p [BM OTP

GATEWAY. London, Benn, 1932. 253p [BM NBFU OTP

**Beardsley, Charles E.**

THE VICTIMS OF TYRANNY. A Tale. Buffalo, 1847. 2v [OONL OTP

**Beaton, Maude Pettit (Hill), 1877–**

KEEP YOUR QUILT, MARY ANN. New York, Margent Press, 1944. 249p [NBFU OTMC QMSS

RING IN THE GRASS. New York, Margent Press, 1946. 202p [LC OTU

**Beattie, Earle James, 1916–**

THE DAY SLIPPERY RAN AWAY. Toronto, McClelland, 1959. 32p

**Beattie, Jeann, 1922–**

BEHOLD THE HOUR. Toronto, Ryerson, 1959, [c1957]. 309p

BLAZE OF NOON. Toronto, Ryerson, 1950. 353p [BVaU NBFU OTMC

**Beattie, Jessie Louise, 1896–**

HILL-TOP. A Tale of Ontario Rural Life. Toronto, Macmillan, 1935. 276p [LC NBFU OTMC

THE SPLIT IN THE SKY. Toronto, Ryerson, 1960. xii + 214p

THREE MEASURES. Toronto, Macmillan, 1938. 295p [NBFU OTMC

**Beaugrand, Honoré, 1849–1906**

LA CHASSE-GALERIE, AND OTHER CANADIAN STORIES. Montreal, Pelletier, 1900. 101p [BVaU LC OTU

**Beavan, John**

LITTLE INDIAN CAMEOS. Stories of Canadian Indians. Ilfracombe, Devon, Stockwell, 1942. 208p [BM

**Beavon, Eric A., 1898–**

SINDIGA THE SAVAGE. A Tale of the Wilds. New York, Harper, 1931. 292p [BM LC

**Bech, Birger**

FIVE YEARS IN A SAILOR'S LIFE. Toronto, Queen City Pub., 1886. 72p [BVaU OTP

THE UNKNOWN. Toronto, Queen City Pub., 1887. 92p [OTP

**Beck, Lily Adams (Moresby), –1931**

ANNE BOLEYN. By E. Barrington [pseud]. Garden City, Doubleday, 1932. 396p [BM BVaU LC NBFU OTMC QMM

CAPTAIN JAVA. By Louis Moresby [pseud]. Garden City, Doubleday, 1928. 368p [BM BVaU LC NBFU OTMC

THE CHASTE DIANA. By E. Barrington [pseud]. New York, Dodd Mead, 1923. 325p [BM BVaU LC NBFU OTMC

THE CROWNED LOVERS. The True Romance of Charles the First and his Queen. By E. Barrington [pseud]. London, Cassell, 1935. 191p [BM LC

THE DIVINE LADY. A Romance of Nelson and Emma Hamilton. By E. Barrington [pseud]. New York, Dodd Mead, 1924. 417p [BM BVaU LC NBFU OTMC

DREAM TEA. London, Benn, 1934. 285p [BM LC NBFU OOP

DREAMS AND DELIGHTS. New York, Dodd Mead, 1926. 317p [BM BVaU LC NBFU OTMC

THE DUEL OF THE QUEENS. A Romance of Mary, Queen of Scotland. By E. Barrington [pseud]. Garden City, Doubleday, 1930. 387p [BM BVaU LC NBFU OTMC QMM

THE EMPRESS OF HEARTS. By E. Barrington [pseud]. New York, Dodd Mead, 1928. 300p [BM BVaU LC NBFU OTMC QMM

THE EXQUISITE PERDITA. By E. Barrington [pseud]. New York, Dodd Mead, 1926. 377p [BM BVaU LC NBFU OTMC QMM

THE GALLANTS. By E. Barrington [pseud]. Boston, Atlantic Monthly, 1924. 308p [BM BVaU LC NBFU OTMC QMM

THE GARDEN OF VISION. New York, Cosmopolitan Book, 1929. 421p [BM LC NBFU OTMC QMM

GLORIOUS APOLLO. By E. Barrington [pseud]. New York, Dodd Mead, 1925. 371p [BM BVaU LC NSHD OTMC

THE GLORY OF EGYPT. ... By L. Moresby [pseud]. London, Nelson, 1926. 281p [BM LC NBFU OTMC

THE GRACES. London, Cassell, 1934. 308p [BM NBFU

THE GREAT ROMANTIC. Being an Interpretation of Mr. Sam. Pepys and Elizabeth his Wife. By E. Barrington [pseud]. Garden City, Doubleday, 1933. 339p [BM BVaU LC NBFU OTMC

THE HOUSE OF FULFILMENT. ... New York, Cosmopolitan Book, 1927. 342p [BM BVaU LC NBFU OTMC

THE IRISH BEAUTIES. By E. Barrington [pseud]. Garden City, Doubleday, 1931. 310p [BM BVaU LC NBFU OTMC QMM

THE JOYOUS STORY OF ASTRID. New York, Cosmopolitan Book, 1931. 283p [LC NBFU

THE KEY OF DREAMS. New York, Dodd Mead, 1922. 351p [BM BVaU LC NBFU QMM

"THE LADIES!" A Shining Constellation of Wit and Beauty. By E. Barrington [pseud]. Boston, Atlantic Monthly, 1922. 286p [BM BVaU LC NBFU OTMC QMM

THE LAUGHING QUEEN. By E. Barrington [pseud]. New York, Dodd Mead, 1929. 307p [BM BVaU LC NSHD OTMC QMM

THE NINTH VIBRATION, AND OTHER STORIES. New York, Dodd Mead, 1922. 313p [BM BVaU LC NSHD OTMC QMM

THE OPENERS OF THE GATE. Stories of the Occult. New York, Cosmopolitan Book, 1930. 368p [BVaU LC NBFU OLU QMM

THE PERFUME OF THE RAINBOW, AND OTHER STORIES. New York, Dodd Mead, 1923. 324p [BM BVaU LC NBFU OTMC

RUBIES. By Louis Moresby [pseud]. New York, Doran, 1927. 287p [BM BViP LC NBFU

THE THUNDERER. A Romance of Napoleon and Josephine. By E. Barrington [pseud]. New York, Dodd Mead, 1927. 333p [BM BVaU LC NBFU OTMC QMM

THE TREASURE OF HO. New York, Dodd Mead, 1924. 303p [BM BVaU LC NSHD QMM

THE WAY OF STARS. A Romance of Reincarnation. New York, Dodd Mead, 1925. 408p [BM BVaU LC NSHD OTMC

THE WOOING OF THE QUEENS. By E. Barrington [pseud]. London, Cassell, 1934. 279p [BM OTMC

**Bedford-Jones, Henry James O'Brien, 1887–1949**

AGAINST THE TIDE. By John Wycliffe [pseud]. New York, Dodd Mead, 1924. 279p [LC NBFU

THE BLACK BULL. New York, Putnam, 1926. 344p [LC NBFU OTMC

THE BREEZE IN THE MOONLIGHT. The Second Book of Genius. By Hao Ch'iu Chuan. Translated ... by George Soulié de Morant, and done into English by H. Bedford-Jones. New York, Putnam, 1926. 371p [BM LC

THE CALIFORNIA TRAIL. New York, Phoenix Press, 1948. 255p [LC

THE CONQUEST. New York, Cook, 1914. 95p [BVaU LC

THE CROSS AND THE HAMMER. A Tale of the Days of the Vikings. Elgin, Ill., Cook, 1912. 95p [LC NSHPL

CYRANO. New York, Putnam, 1930. 344p [LC NBFU OTP

D'ARTAGNAN. The Sequel to *The Three Musketeers*. ... Augmenting and Incorporating a Fragmentary Manuscript by Alexander Dumas. New York, Covici Friede, 1928. 311p [LC NBFU OTMC

D'ARTAGNAN'S LETTER. By M.&H. Bedford-Jones. New York, Covici Friede, 1931. 244p [LC NBFU

DRUMS OF DAMBALA. New York, Covici Friede, 1932. 295p [BM LC NBFU OTMC

FAR HORIZONS. London, Hurst & Blackett, 1925. 287p [BM OTP

FLAMEHAIR THE SKALD. A Tale of the Days of Hardrede. Chicago, McClurg, 1913. 310p [LC

THE HAZARDS OF SMITH. London, Hurst & Blackett, 1924. 306p [BM OTP

JOHN BARRY. By Donald F. Bedford [jt. pseud. for Donald Friede, Kenneth Fearing, and Henry Bedford-Jones]. New York, Creative Age, 1947. 418p [BVa LC PC

THE KING'S PARDON. New York, Covici Friede, 1933. 281p [LC NBFU

THE KING'S PASSPORT. New York, Putnam, 1928. 336p [BM LC NBFU OTMC

MALAY GOLD. Toronto, Harlequin Books, 1953. 128p

THE MARDI GRAS MYSTERY. Garden City, Doubleday, 1921. 313p [LC NBFU

THE MESA TRAIL. Garden City, Doubleday, 1920. 244p [BM LC NBFU OTMC

RODOMONT. A Romance of Mont St. Michel in the Days of Louis XIV. New York, Putnam, 1926. 335p [BM LC NBFU OTMC

SAINT MICHAEL'S GOLD. New York, Putnam, 1926. 314p [BM LC NBFU

THE SHADOW. New York, Fiction League, 1930. 322p [BM BVaU LC NBFU OTMC

THE STAR WOMAN. New York, Dodd Mead, 1924. 293p [BM LC NBFU OTMC

THE TRAIL OF THE SHADOW. London, Hurst & Blackett, 1924. 286p [BM OTP

**Begg, Alexander, 1839–1897**

"DOT IT DOWN." A Story of Life in the Northwest. Toronto, Hunter Rose, 1871. 381p [BVaU LC NSHD OTMC QMM

WRECKS IN THE SEA OF LIFE. New York, Lovell, 1884. 348p [LC

**Belaney, George Stansfeld, 1888–1938**

THE ADVENTURES OF SAJO AND HER BEAVER PEOPLE. By Grey Owl [pseud]. Toronto, Macmillan, 1935. 256p [*Cf.* also: SAJO AND THE BEAVER PEOPLE. ... New York, Scribner, 1936. 187p] [BM BVaU LC NBFU OTMC

BEAVERS. Pages from the Writings of Grey Owl. Edited by E.E. Reynolds. Cambridge, University Press, 1940. 127p [BM

THE TREE. By Wa-sha-quon-asin (Grey Owl) [pseud]. Toronto, Macmillan, 1937. 62p [BM NBFU OTMC

**Belcher, Edward, 1799–1877**

HORATIO HOWARD BRENTON. A Naval Novel. London, Hurst & Blackett, 1856. 3v [BM

**Bell, Frederick McKelvey, 1878–1931**

A ROMANCE OF THE HALIFAX DISASTER. Halifax, Royal Print., 1918. 76p [NBFU OTU

**Bell, Jessie Mary Eleanor (Roberts), 1901–**

THE BLACK TOTEM. Toronto, Ryerson, 1960. 180p

**Bemister, Margaret, 1877–**

INDIAN LEGENDS. Stories of America before Columbus. New York, Macmillan, 1914. 187p [LC

STORIES FROM PRAIRIE AND MOUNTAIN. Toronto, Copp Clark, 1909. 114p [BM

THIRTY INDIAN LEGENDS. Toronto, Macmillan, 1912. 182p [BM OTMC

**Bending, Frederick J., 1883–1954**

THE SHADOW'S EDGE. Toronto, Hodder, 1922. 288p [BM OOP

**Bennett, Ethel Hume (Patterson), 1881–**

CAMP CONQUEROR. Boston, Houghton, 1928. 281p [BVa LC

CAMP KEN-JOCKETY. Boston, Houghton, 1923. 311p [BVa LC OTMC

JUDY OF YORK HILL. By Ethel Hume. Boston, Houghton, 1922. 281p [LC

JUDY'S PERFECT YEAR. Boston, Houghton, 1925. 288p [BM BVa LC

A TREASURE SHIP OF OLD QUEBEC. New York, Dodd Mead, 1936. 266p [BM BVaU LC OTMC

**Bennett, Ethel Mary (Granger)**

LAND FOR THEIR INHERITANCE. Toronto, Ryerson, 1955. 317p

SHORT OF THE GLORY. Toronto, Ryerson, 1960. 333p

A STRAW IN THE WIND. Toronto, Ryerson, 1958. 281p

**Beresford-Howe, Constance Elizabeth, 1922–**

THE INVISIBLE GATE. New York, Dodd Mead, 1949. 241p [BM LC NBFU

MY LADY GREENSLEEVES. New York, Ballantine Books, 1955. 217p

OF THIS DAY'S JOURNEY. New York, Dodd Mead, 1947. 240p [BM LC NBFU OTMC QMBM

THE UNREASONING HEART. New York, Dodd Mead, 1946. 236p [BM BVaU NBFU OTMC QMBM

**Bernhardt, Clara Mae, 1911–**

OPEN WINDOWS. Grand Rapids, Mich., Eerdmans Pub. Co., 1947. 167p [LC OTU

SONG OF ZION. Grand Rapids, Mich., Eerdmans Pub. Co., 1944. 185p [LC OTU

**Bevans, Mrs. Florence Edith**

PERCIVAL PLAIN DOG. By Jemima Remington [pseud]. Toronto, "The Humane Pleader," 1924. 68p [QMSS

**Beynon, Frances Marion**

ALETA DEY. A Novel. London, Daniel, 1919. 255p [BM OTMC

**Beynon, Marie Edith**

SAINTS, SINNERS AND QUEER PEOPLE. Novelettes and Short Stories. New York, Weed, 1897. 341p [LC

**Bhatia, Jamuna (Huband), 1919–**

ALIEN THERE IS NONE. By J. Rana [pseud]. London, Hodder, 1959. 256p

**Bice, Clare, 1909–**

ACROSS CANADA. Stories of Canadian Children. New York, Macmillan, 1949. 119p [BVaU LC NBFU OTMC

THE GREAT ISLAND. A Story of Mystery In Newfoundland. Toronto, Macmillan, 1954. 103p

JORY'S COVE. A Story of Nova Scotia. New York, Macmillan, 1941. 104p [BVaU LC OLU

**Bigman, Sidney, 1919–**

SECOND SIGHT. A Novel. New York, McKay Co., 1959. 219p

WITHIN THESE BOUNDARIES. A Novel. London, Secker & Warburg, 1959. 219p

**Bigsby, Bernard**

"THAT BOWL OF PUNCH!" What It Did, and How It Did It. Six Christmas Stories. ... Toronto, Hunter Rose, 1872. 51p [BVaU OTP

**Billett, Mrs. Mabel Broughton, 1892–**

CALAMITY HOUSE. A Mystery Novel. London, Hutchinson, 1927. 288p [BM

THE ROBOT DETECTIVE. London, Hutchinson, 1932. 288p [BM LC NBFU OTP

THE SHADOW OF THE STEPPE. London, Hutchinson, 1930. 288p [BM LC OTP

THE SMOOTH SILENCE. Toronto, Ryerson, 1936. [CC

**Bilsky, Eva, –1952**

TUCK-A-BED TALES. By Aunt Eva [pseud]. Montreal, Mercury, 1945. 38p [OONL

WHAT HAPPENED AFTER? Some Familiar Fairy Tales Continued. By Aunt Eva [pseud]. Montreal, Mercury, 1941. 63p [OONL

**Bird, William Richard, 1891–**

HERE STAYS GOOD YORKSHIRE. Toronto, Ryerson, 1945. 332p [BVaU LC NBFU OKQ QMM

JUDGMENT GLEN. Toronto, Ryerson, 1947. 315p [BVaU NBFU OTMC

MAID OF THE MARSHES. Amherst, N.S., Author, 1935. 198p [NSHD OTMC QMBM

THE PASSIONATE PILGRIM. Toronto, Ryerson, 1949. 324p [BVaU NBFU OTMC QMM

PRIVATE TIMOTHY FERGUS CLANCY. Ottawa, Graphic, 1930. 325p [BVaU OTU

THE SHY YORKSHIREMAN. A Novel. Toronto, Ryerson, 1955. 253p

SO MUCH TO RECORD. Toronto, Ryerson, 1951. 317p

SUNRISE FOR PETER, AND OTHER STORIES. Toronto, Ryerson, 1946. 224p [BVaU LC NSHD OTU

TO LOVE AND TO CHERISH. Toronto, Ryerson, 1953. 309p

TRISTRAM'S SALVATION. A Novel. Toronto, Ryerson, 1957. 254p

**Birney, Earle, 1904–**

DOWN THE LONG TABLE. Toronto, McClelland, 1955. 298p

THE KOOTENAY HIGHLANDER. London, Landsborough Publications, 1960 [c1958]. 253p [Same as TURVEY, *q.v.*]

TURVEY. A Military Picaresque. Toronto, McClelland, 1949. 288p [BVaU LC NBFU OKQ QMM

**Bishop, Leslie Gurney, 1908–**

PAPER KINGDOM. London, Heinemann, 1936. 278p [BM LC

**Bjarnason, Bogi**

ANDROCLES, JUNIOR. Treherne, Man., The Times, 1930. 26p [CC

CIRCUMSTANTIAL EVIDENCE. N.p., n.d. 48p [MWP

SANS THE GRANDE PASSION. Treherne, Man., The Times, 1935. 122p [MWP

**Blachford, Lt. Col.**

THE ULTIMATUM. A Short Tale with a Long Moral. London, Ont., 1867. 32p [OLU

**Black, Edith Ferguson, 1857–**

ALLAN RUTHVEN, KNIGHT. London, R.T.S., 1907. 304p [BM

A BEAUTIFUL POSSIBILITY. Philadelphia, Union Press, 1904. 330p [BM LC

A PRINCESS IN CALICO. London, R.T.S., 1903. 140p [BM

**Black, Martha Louise (Munger), 1866–1957**

A KLONDIKE CHRISTMAS TALE. Whitehorse, Author, n.d. 11p [OTU

**Blackburn, Kathleen**

THE DAGMAR WHO LOVED. New York, Broadway Pub. Co., 1904. 212p [LC

**Blackburn, Victoria Grace, –1928**

THE MAN CHILD. By Fan-Fan [pseud]. Ottawa, Graphic, 1930. 274p [BVaU OTMC QMM

**Blake, Cameron**

ONLY MEN ON BOARD. London, Hodder, 1933. 316p [BM

SET STORMY. London, Hodder, 1931. 314p [BM NBFU

**Blanchard, Henry Percy, 1862–**

AFTER THE CATACLYSM. A Romance of the Age to Come. New York, Cochrane, 1909. 136p [LC

**Blewett, Jean (McKishnie), 1862–1934**

HEART STORIES. Toronto, Warwick & Rutter, 1919. 29p [BVaU OLU

**Blondal, Patricia (Jenkins), 1927?–1959**

A CANDLE TO LIGHT THE SUN. A Novel. Toronto, McClelland, 1960. 316p

**Bloomfield, Leonard, 1887–**

SACRED STORIES OF THE SWEET GRASS CREE. Ottawa, (Nat. Museum of Canada, Bull. 60), 1930. 346p [In Cree and English.] [BVaU NSHPL OLU QMU

**Boag, Mrs. Isabel**

CHIMNEYS. London, Heath Cranton, 1934. 291p [BM OTP

**Bodsworth, Fred, 1918–**

LAST OF THE CURLEWS. New York, Dodd Mead, 1955. 128p

THE STRANGE ONE. New York, Dodd Mead, 1959. 400p

**Boggs, Helen**

ACORN LEAVES. A Series of Canadian Tales. By Nell Gwynne [pseud]. Toronto, Copp Clark, 1873. 215p [BVaU OTMC QMM

WHEN THE SHADOWS FLEE AWAY. A Story of Canadian Society. By Bernard [pseud]. Montreal, Lovell, 1891. 272p [OTU

**Boniface, Father, 1880–**

THE UNKNOWN HERO OF VERLEBURG. An Historical Novel. Quebec, Franciscan Missionary Press, 1923. 253p [OONL

**Bonner, Margerie**

HORSE IN THE SKY. New York, Scribner, 1947. 189p [BVaU LC NBFU OTMC

THE LAST TWIST OF THE KNIFE. New York, Scribner, 1946. 190p [LC

THE SHAPES THAT CREEP. New York, Scribner, 1945. 216p [BVaU LC OTMC

**Bonner, Mary Graham, 1890–**

RAINBOW AT NIGHT. New York, Furman, 1936. 319p [LC OLU PC

**Boothe, Stella, and Carter, Olive I.**

MARY GAY STORIES. Toronto, Educational Book Co., 1930. 119p [BM

**Borneman, Ernst Wilhelm Julius, 1915–**

THE FACE ON THE CUTTING-ROOM FLOOR. By Cameron MacCabe [pseud]. London, Gollancz, 1937. 320p [BM LC

LOVE STORY. London, Jarrolds, 1941. 192p [BM OTMC

TOMORROW IS NOW. The Adventures of Welfare Willy in Search of a Soul. London, Spearman, 1959. 205p

TREMOLO. New York, Harper, 1948. 224p [BM LC NBFU OTU

**Borrett, William Coates, 1894–**

DOWN EAST. Another Cargo of Tales Told under the Old Town Clock. Halifax, Imperial Pub. Co., 1945. 232p [BVaU LC NSHD OTMC

DOWN TO THE SEA AGAIN, WITH TALES TOLD UNDER THE OLD TOWN CLOCK. Halifax, Imperial Pub. Co., 1947. 221p [AEU NSWA OONL QQL

EAST COAST PORT, and Other Tales Told under the Old Town Clock. Halifax, Imperial Pub. Co., 1944. 237p [BVaU LC NBFU OTMC

HISTORIC HALIFAX. Tales Told under the Old Town Clock. Toronto, Ryerson, 1948. 234p [BVaU OTU QMM

MORE TALES TOLD UNDER THE OLD TOWN CLOCK. Halifax, Imperial Pub. Co., 1943. 233p [BVaU LC OTU QMM

TALES RETOLD UNDER THE OLD TOWN CLOCK. Toronto, Reryson, 1957. xii + 212p

TALES TOLD UNDER THE OLD TOWN CLOCK. Halifax, Imperial Pub. Co., 1942. 196p [BVaU LC NBFU OTMC QMM

**Bossin, Hye**

A TATTLER'S TALES OF TORONTO. Toronto, Handy Library, 1940. 64p [OTU

**Boswell, R.**

MERCY'S HERO. London, Stockwell, 1933. 79p [BM OTP

**Bottomley, Kate Madeline (Barry), 1865–**

THE DOCTOR'S DAUGHTER. By "Vera" [pseud]. Ottawa, Woodburn, 1885. 242p [NBFU assigns this book to WALTER, William Wilfred (Vera, pseud), 1869–] [NBFU OTMC

HONOR EDGEWORTH; or, Ottawa's Present Tense. By "Vera" [pseud]. Ottawa, Woodburn, 1882. 337p [BVaU NSHD OTMC

**Bourinot, John George, 1837–1902**

SEA, FOREST, AND PRAIRIE. ... Montreal, 1893. 323p [RES

**Boyle, David, 1842–1911**

THE UPS AND DOWNS OF NO. 7 REXVILLE. Being a Full, True and Correct Account of what Happened in the said School Section during a period of Twelve Months. ... By an Old Maid. N.p., n.d. 106p [BVaU OTP

**Boyle, Joyce, 1901–**

MUSKOKA HOLIDAY. Toronto, Macmillan, 1953. 216p

THE STONE COTTAGE MYSTERY. Toronto, Macmillan, 1958. 151p

**Brandon, Captain (?Roy Victor?)**

A RIVER OF GOLD. Tales of the Rocky Mountains. By Captain Brandon. Plymouth, W. Brendon, 1927. 155p [BM BVaU OTP

**Bridle, Augustus, 1869–1952**

HANSEN. A Novel of Canadianization. Toronto, Macmillan, 1924. 368p [BM BVaU NSHD OTMC QMM

**Brillant, J. Maurice**

VISION OF MURDER. New York, Comet Press, 1954. 136p

**Brockie, William (pseud)**

TALES OF THE MOUNTED. By William Brockie [pseud]. Toronto, Ryerson, 1949. 182p [OTU

**Brodie, Alfred E.**

THE FRONT MAN. Toronto, Maclean, 1935. 154p [NBFU OTMC QMM

**Brodie, Ethel Mary**

THE ROSE-COLORED WORLD, AND OTHER FANTASIES. New York, Metropolitan Press, 1910. 279p [LC

**Brooke, Frances (Moore), 1724–1789**

THE EXCURSION. London, Cadell, 1777. 2v [BM OTU

THE HISTORY OF EMILY MONTAGUE. By the Author of "Lady Julia Mandeville." London, Dodsley, 1769. 4v [Several later editions. Canadian ed.: With intro. and notes by Lawrence J. Burpee, and appendix by F.P. Grove. Ottawa, Graphic, 1931. 333p] [BM BVaU NSHD OKQ QMM

THE HISTORY OF LADY JULIA MANDEVILLE. By the translator of "Lady Catesby's Letters" [pseud]. 7th ed. ... London, Dodsley, 1782. 2v [First pub. 1763.] [BM BVaU OKQ QMM

**Brooker, Bertram, 1888–1955**

THE ROBBER. A Tale of the Time of the Herods. New York, Duell Sloan, 1949. 307p [BVaU LC NBFU OTMC

THE TANGLED MIRACLE. A Mortimer Hood Mystery. By Huxley Herne [pseud]. Toronto, Nelson, 1936. 300p [BM

THINK OF THE EARTH. Toronto, Nelson, 1936. 288p [BM BVaU LC NBFU OTU

**Brooks, Mrs. Annie Elston**

THE HEIRESS OF MYRTLE GROVE. An English Tale. By a Montreal Lady, A.E.B. [pseud]. Montreal, Lovell, 1870. 200p [BVaU NBFU OTU

**Brown, Mrs. Ellen V., 1900–**

SEDGEWICK MANOR. New York, Pageant Press, 1951. 200p

**Brown, Margaret Adeline (Porter), 1867–**

MY LADY OF THE SNOWS. Toronto, Briggs, 1908. 518p [BM BVaU NSHD OTMC

**Brown, W.H.**

SHE MIGHT HAVE DONE BETTER. A Novel. St. Johns, Que., The News, 1877. 2v [BVaU OKQ

**Brown, William McEvery, –1935**
THE QUEEN'S BUSH. A Tale of the Early Days of Bruce County. London, Bale & Danielsson, 1932. 295p [BM BVaU NBFU OTP

**Browne, Marion, 1912–**
GREATER LOVE. Ilfracombe, Devon, Stockwell, 1957. 416p

**Bruce, Charles Tory, 1906–1971**
THE CHANNEL SHORE. Toronto, Macmillan, 1954. 398p
THE TOWNSHIP OF TIME. A Chronicle. Toronto, Macmillan, 1959. 234p

**Bruce, Eva**
CALL HER ROSIE. New York, Ives Washburn, 1942. 300p [BM BVaU OTMC

**Bruce, Muriel**
MUKARA. A Novel. New York, Henkle, 1930. 278p [LC NBFU OTMC

**Brundle, John, 1882–**
THE FORSAKEN PLOT IN THE LITTLE CHURCHYARD. From the Pen of John, A Suffolk Herd Boy. Roche's Point, Ont., Author, 1950. 32p [OONL

**Buchan, John Stuart, 1852–**
A BIT OF ATLANTIS. By Douglas Erskine [pseud]. Montreal, Chapman, 1900. 197p [BM BVaU OTMC QMBM

**Buckler, Ernest, 1908–**
THE MOUNTAIN AND THE VALLEY. New York, Holt, 1952. 373p

**Buell, John Edward, 1927–**
THE PYX. A Novel. New York, Farrar Straus, 1959. 174p

**Burch, E.T.**
"SO, I SAID TO THE COLONEL." Toronto, Ryerson, 1941. 72p [AEP OTMC OTUV

**Burkholder, Mabel Grace (Clare), 1881–**
BEFORE THE WHITE MAN CAME. Indian Legends and Stories. Toronto, McClelland, 1923. 318p [BM BVaU NBFU OTMC QMM
THE COURSE OF IMPATIENCE CARNINGHAM. Toronto, Musson, 1911. 327p [AEU LC NBFU OTMC
THE SHIELD OF HONOR. Elgin, Ill., Cook, 1929. 76p [LC

**Burnham, John Hampden, 1860–1940**
ADELINE GRAY. A Tale. New York, Wynkoop & Hollenbeck, 1894. 155p [LC
JACK RALSTON; or, The Outbreak of the Nauscopees. A Tale of Life in the Far North-East of Canada. Edinburgh, Nelson, 1901. 448p [BM BVaU OTMC
MARCELLE. An Historical Novel. Toronto, Briggs, 1905. 409p [BM BVaU OTMC

**Burton, Alice Elizabeth, 1908–**

CLING TO HER, WAITING. London, Dakers, 1939. 269p [BM LC

FORTNIGHT IN FRASCATI. By Susan Alice Kerby [pseud]. London, Dakers, 1940. 285p [BM LC

FORTUNE'S GIFT. By Susan Kerby [pseud]. New York, Dodd Mead, 1947. 372p [Same as MANY STRANGE BIRDS, *q.v.*] [BVaU QMM

GONE TO GRASS. By Susan Alice Kerby [pseud]. London, Hutchinson, 1948. 224p [BM

MISS CARTER AND THE IFRIT. By Susan Alice Kerby [pseud]. London, Hutchinson, 1945. 160p [BM LC

MR. KRONION. A Novel. By Susan Alice Kerby [pseud]. London, Laurie, 1949. 223p [BM OLU QMM

MANY STANGE BIRDS. By Susan Alice Kerby [pseud]. London, Hutchinson, 1947. 223p [Same as FORTUNE'S GIFT, *q.v.*] [BM QMM

THE ROARING DOVE. By Susan Kerby [pseud]. New York, Dodd Mead, 1948. 260p [BVaU LC QMM

**Buschlen, John Preston, 1888–**

BEHIND THE WICKET. Short Stories Relating to Life in the Canadian Banks. Toronto, Briggs, 1914. 264p [BM BVaU NBFU OTMC

A CANADIAN BANKCLERK. Toronto, Briggs, 1913. 366p [BM BVaU NBFU OTMC

CURTAIN OF LIFE. By Jack Preston [pseud] and Jesse Lasky, Jr. New York, Macaulay, 1934. 244p [LC

THE DRUMMER. Toronto, Ansell Pub. Co., 1915. 330p [BM BVaU LC NBFU OTMC

FINDING HIS BALANCE; or, The Bank Clerk Who Came Back. By Jack Preston [pseud]. Toronto, Stevenson & Hevey, 1915. 366p [OTMC QMM

HEIL! HOLLYWOOD. By Jack Preston [pseud]. Chicago, Reilly & Lee, 1939. 344p [BVaU LC

NOT ASHAMED. A Romance of the Tropics. By Jack Preston [pseud]. New York, Sears, 1934. 319p [BM LC

PETER BOSTEN. A Story about Realities. By John Preston [pseud]. Lamoni, Ia., Herald, 1915. 352p [LC

SCREEN STAR. By Jack Preston [pseud]. Garden City, Doubleday, 1932. 308p [BM LC

**Butcher, Margaret**

COMET'S HAIR. London, Skeffington, 1939. 256p [BM

DESTINY ON DEMAND. London, Skeffington, 1938. 288p [BM

HOGDOWN FARM MYSTERY. London, Skeffington, 1950. 221p [BM OTMC

VACANT POSSESION. A Novel. London, Skeffington, 1940. 256p [BM OTMC

**Butler, Suzanne, 1919–**

MY PRIDE, MY FOLLY. Boston, Little Brown, 1953. 311p

PORTRAIT OF PETER WEST. Boston, Little Brown, 1958. 291p
VALE OF TYRANNY. Boston, Little Brown, 1954. 266p

**Butler, William Francis, 1838–1910**
RED CLOUD. A Tale of the Great Prairie. ... London, Low & Marston, 1882. 327p [Also new ed.: Toronto, Musson, 1927. 332p] [BM BVaU LC NBFU OTMC QMM

**Byerly, Alpheus Edward, 1894–1960**
JANET CAMPBELL. A Tale of Upper Canada. Guelph, Guelph Pub. Co., 1935. 21p [BVaU OTU

**Byers, Donald A., 1925–**
FOREVER GREEN. New Toronto, Goodyear Tire, 1957. 19p

**C., W.A.**
MICK TRACY, THE IRISH SCRIPTURE READER; or, The Martyred Convert and the Priest. A Tale of Facts. By W.A.C. [pseud]. London, Frome, 1863. [Other eds.: London, Book Society, 1862. 355p; Philadelphia, 1867; and London, Partridge, 1870.] [BM EngCat OTMC
TIM DOOLAN, THE IRISH EMIGRANT. Being a Full and Particular Account of his Reasons for Emigrating–his Passage across the Atlantic–his Arrival in New York–his Brief Sojourn in the United States, and his Further Emigration to Canada. By the Author of MICK TRACY [pseud]. London, Partridge, [1869]. 362p [At the end of prefatory note author locates himself in "Canada West."] [Another ed.: London, Partridge, 1879.] [BVaU EngCat OTMC

**Caden, José-Jean-Marie-Désiré, 1910–**
A MOTHER CHEATS ALTARS. A Novel. New York, Greenwich Book Publishers, 1959. 168p

**Cahill, James**
THE BLACK PIRATE. London, Lutterworth, 1946. 128p [BM
FLYING WITH THE MOUNTIES. London, Black, 1937. 248p [BM BVaU NBFU OTMC
M'BONGA'S TREK. London, Lutterworth, 1947. 127p [BM OHM
THE PILOT OF INDIAN LEAP. London, Oxford U. Press, 1939. 288p [BM NBFU

**Callaghan, Morley Edward, 1903–**
A BROKEN JOURNEY. New York, Scribner, 1932. 270p [BVaU LC NBFU OTMC QMM
IT'S NEVER OVER. New York, Scribner, 1930. 225p [BVaU LC NBFU OTMC QMM
THE LOVED AND THE LOST. A Novel. Toronto, Macmillan, 1951. 234p
LUKE BALDWIN'S VOW. Philadelphia, Winston, [1948]. 187p [BM BVaU LC NBFU OTU QMM

THE MANY COLOURED COAT. Toronto, Macmillan, 1960. 318p

MORE JOY IN HEAVEN. New York, Random House, 1937. 278p [Also, with intro. by Hugo McPherson: Toronto, McClelland, 1960. x + 159p] [BVaU LC NBFU OTMC

A NATIVE ARGOSY. New York, Scribner, 1929. 371p [BM BVaU LC NBFU OTMC QMM

NO MAN'S MEAT. Paris [France], E.W. Titus, 1931. 42p [AEU OLU OTU

NOW THAT APRIL'S HERE, AND OTHER STORIES. New York, Random House, 1936. 316p [BVaU LC NBFU OTMC QMM

STORIES. Toronto, Macmillan, 1959. xi + 364p

STRANGE FUGITIVE. New York, Scribner, 1928. 264p [BM BVaU LC NBFU OTMC QMM

SUCH IS MY BELOVED. New York, Scribner, 1934. 288p [Also, with intro. by Malcolm Ross: Toronto, McClelland, 1957. xiii + 144p] [BM BVaU LC NBFU OTU QMM

THEY SHALL INHERIT THE EARTH. Toronto, Macmillan, 1935. 337p [BM BVaU LC NBFU OTMC QMM

THE VARSITY STORY. Toronto, Macmillan, 1948. 172p [BVaU NBFU OTMC QMM

**Cameron, Rev. Charles J.**

SEA, FOREST, AND PRAIRIE. Being Stories of Life and Adventure in Canada Past and Present. By Boys and Girls in Canada's Schools. [Ed. by ——.] Montreal, Dougall, 1893. 323p [OTMC QMSS

**Cameron, Daniel George, 1856–**

TWIGS FROM THE OAK, AND OTHER TREES. Regina, Commercial Print., 1933. 283p [BVaU OTMC

**Cameron, Edward Robert, 1857–1931**

MEMOIRS OF RALPH VANSITTART, A MEMBER OF THE PARLIAMENT OF CANADA, 1861–1867. Toronto, Musson, 1902. 229p [Another ed.: Toronto, Musson, 1924.] [BM BVaU LC NSWA OTMC

**Cameron, John Alexander Hugh, 1878–**

A COLONEL FROM WYOMING. New York, Christian Press, 1907. 364p [BM BVaU LC OOP

THE WOMAN HATER. New York, Christian Press, 1912. 297p [BM BVaU LC OTMC

**Campbell, Arthur**

THE COMBAT. A Tragedy of the Countryside. London, Long, 1908. 388p [BM OOP

THE MYSTERY OF MARTHA WARNE. A Tale of Montreal. Montreal, Robinson, 1888. 151p [OOP

A RIDE IN MOROCCO, AND OTHER SKETCHES. Toronto, Briggs, 1897. 305p [BM LC NSHD

**Campbell, Austin, 1884–**

THE ROCK OF BABYLON. Ottawa, Graphic, 1931. 354p [BVaU NBFU OTMC QMM

**Campbell, Basil Berridge, 1889–**

TONY. A Truly, Truly Story, or Something of that Sort. Toronto, Ryerson, 1934. 113p [OKQ

**Campbell, Mrs. Dorothy de Brissac**

THE BRAVE LITTLE PEOPLE. Toronto, Ryerson, 1933. 141p [OTMC

**Campbell, Grace MacLennan (Grant), 1895–1963**

FRESH WIND BLOWING. Toronto, Collins, 1947. 233p [BVaU LC NBFU OTMC QMM

THE HIGHER HILL. Toronto, Collins, 1944. 319p [BVaU LC NBFU OTMC QMM

THORN-APPLE TREE. Toronto, Collins, 1942. 230p [BVaU LC NBFU OTMC QMM

TORBEG. Toronto, Collins, 1953. 311p

THE TOWER AND THE TOWN. Toronto, Collins, 1950. 342p [BVaU LC NBFU OTMC

**Campbell, Mrs. Isabella, 1830–1887**

THE INNER LIFE. By Mrs. Campbell. Quebec, Hunter Rose, 1862. 32p [QMSS

**Campbell, Rev. John, 1840–1904**

TWO KNAPSACKS. A Novel of Canadian Summer Life. By J. Cawdor Bell [pseud]. Toronto, Williamson, [1892]. 419p [BVaU OKQ

**Campbell, Margaret Elizabeth (Baird), 1912–**

DEATH AND LILACS. By Fred Bayard [pseud–*i.e.*, Margaret Elizabeth Campbell and Johanna Frederika Jansen]. New York, Phoenix, [1948]. 256p [BM LC

**Campbell, Mrs. Mary Helen**

SUNDAYS IN YOHO. Twelve Stories for Children and their Friends. Ed. by ——. Montreal, Drysdale, 1884. 272p [OTU

**Campbell, Wilfred, 1858–1918**

A BEAUTIFUL REBEL. A Romance of Upper Canada in Eighteen Hundred and Twelve. Toronto, Westminster, 1909. 317p [BM BVaU LC OTMC

IAN OF THE ORCADES; or, The Armourer of Girnigoe. London, Oliphant, 1906. 320p [BM BVaU LC NBFU OTMC

**Canadian Great War Veteran (pseud)**

THE PRINCE. A Canadian Great War Veteran's Stories, chiefly concerning his

Alberta Range Horse, as related to his Grandson, Christmas Day, 1950. Edmonton, Imperial Pub., 1950. 63p [ACG

**Canadian Magazine, Toronto**

SELECTED SHORT STORIES. A Collection of Notable Short Stories by Canadian Writers First Published in the *Canadian Magazine.* Toronto, MacLean, 1936. 246p [Another collection pub. under same title, 1937. Also 246p] [BVaU NBFU OTP QMBM

SEVEN SEA STORIES. From the *Canadian Magazine.* Toronto, Excelsior Pub. Co., 1935. 127p [OTMC

STORIES IN MANY MOODS. A Collection of Notable Short Stories by Canadian Writers First Published in the *Canadian Magazine.* Toronto, MacLean, 1935. 126p [BVaU NBFU OTU

**Carey, Douglas**

THE RAVEN'S FEATHERS. Ottawa, Graphic, 1930. 322p [NBFU OTP QMM

THE SCORPION. A Limehouse Mystery. Ottawa, Graphic, 1931. 312p [BVaU NBFU OTMC

**Carleton, Veros (pseud)**

THE HOUSE OF TEMPTATION. Ottawa, Graphic, 1931. 354p [BVaU NBFU OTMC

**Carman, Albert Richardson, 1865–1939**

THE PENSIONNAIRES. The Story of an American Girl who took a Voice to Europe and Found–Many Things. Boston, Turner, 1903. 314p [BM BVaU LC OTMC

THE PREPARATION OF RYERSON EMBURY. A Purpose. London, Unwin, 1900. 248p [BM BVaU OTMC

**Carmichael, Alfred**

INDIAN LEGENDS OF VANCOUVER ISLAND. Text by ——. Toronto, Musson, 1922. 97p [BM BVaU LC NSWA OTMC QMM

**Caron, Maurice B.**

THE CURE OF ST. MICHAEL. London, Hodder, 1925. 284p [BM QMM

**Carr, Amy**

THE SWINGING PENDULUM. Ottawa, Ru-Mi-Lou Books, 1928. 188p [BVaU OLU

**Carr, Kate**

CUPID AND THE CANDIDATE. Toronto, Briggs, 1906. 243p [BM

**Carroll, Rev. John, 1809–1884**

THE SCHOOL OF THE PROPHETS; or, Father McRorey's Class and Squire Firstman's Kitchen Fire. A Fiction founded on Facts. First Series. Toronto, Burrage & Magurn, 1876. 264p ["Second Series," apparently also in 1876; 264p] [BVaU LC NBFU OTMC QMM

**Carruthers, Janet Anne, 1890–1957**
THE FOREST IS MY KINGDOM. London, Oxford U. Press, 1952. 231p

**Carter, Dyson, 1910–**
FATHERLESS SONS. A Novel. Toronto, Progress Books, 1955. 480p
NIGHT OF FLAME. Toronto, McLeod, 1942. 337p [Reprinted, under pseudonym of Warren Desmond: New York, New Am. Library, 1949. 192p] [BM LC NBFU OTMC
TOMORROW IS WITH US. A Novel. Toronto, Progress Books, [1950]. 235p [BVaU

**Casey, Roy S.**
THE HAPPY FAMILY. Vancouver, Wrigley, n.d. 269p [BVaU OTMC

**Caswell, H.S.**
STORIES AND SKETCHES. Montreal, Lovell, 1872. 179p [BVaU QMSS

**Catley, Harry**
GATE AND GAITERS. A Book of Naval Humour and Anecdotes. By Chief Petty Officer Harry Catley, Gunner's Mate. Toronto, Author, 1949. 322p [OTP

**Cautley, Helen**
THE PUSSIOS AND THE PURR. New York, Carrier, 1929. 80p [CBI

**Chalmers, Audrey (McEvers), 1899–**
HIGH SMOKE. New York, Viking Press, 1950. 224p [OONL

**Chambers, Mrs. Ada Pierce**
IN AN ANATOLIAN VALLEY. Toronto, Ryerson, 1955. 251p

**Chapin, Gardner B.**
TALES OF THE ST. LAWRENCE. Montreal, Lovell, 1873. 382p [BVaU OTU

**Chapman, Ethel M.**
GOD'S GREEN COUNTRY. A Novel of Canadian Rural Life. Toronto, Ryerson, 1922. 287p [BM NBFU OTMC
THE HOMESTEADERS. Toronto, Ryerson, 1936. 252p [BM NBFU OTMC
WITH FLAME OF FREEDOM. Toronto, Allen, 1938. 243p [BVaU NBFU OTMC

**Charach, Paul**
POWER OF A WOMAN. Winnipeg, Author, 1949. 104p [OTP

**Charlton, Margaret Ridley, 1858–1931**
IN THE DAYS OF SIR WALTER RALEIGH. Montreal, 1900. [BCF
WITH PRINTLESS FOOT. By Margaret Ridley Charlton and C.A. Frazer. Montreal, Sabiston, 1894. 82p [NSWA OLU
A WONDER WEB OF STORIES. By Margaret Ridley Charlton and C.A. Frazer. Montreal, Grafton & Sons, 1892. 187p [OTMC

**Cheetham, William**

LIGHTS AND SHADOWS OF CLERICAL LIFE. Montreal, Lovell, 1879. 310p [BVaU OTU

**Cheney, Harriet Vaughan (Foster), 1815–**

A PEEP AT THE PILGRIMS IN SIXTEEN HUNDRED THIRTY SIX. A Tale of Olden Times. By the Author of Divers Unfinished Manuscripts, &c. [pseud]. Boston, Wells & Lilly, 1824. 2v [Another ed.: Boston, Phillips Sampson, 1850. 463p] [BM LC

THE RIVALS OF ACADIA. An Old Story of the New World. [Anon] Boston, Wells & Lilly, 1827. 271p [LC

**Chetwynd, Ralph, 1899–1957**

HEIFER DUST INN. By R. Chetwynd and N. Burris. Lillooet, B.C., Lillooet Pub., 1941. 99p [OTU

**Child, Philip, 1898–**

BLOW WIND–COME WRACK. London, Jarrolds, 1945. 192p [Announced as by John Wentworth (pseud).] [BM CBI

DAY OF WRATH. Toronto, Ryerson, 1945. 274p [BVaU LC NSHD OKQ

GOD'S SPARROWS. London, Butterworth, 1937. 319p [BM LC NBFU OTU

MR. AMES AGAINST TIME. Toronto, Ryerson, 1949. 244p [BVaU LC NSHD OTU

THE VILLAGE OF SOULS. London, Butterworth, 1933. 315p [New ed.: Toronto, Ryerson, 1948. 294p] [BM BVaU LC NSHD OTU

**Chisholm, Arthur Murray, 1872–1960**

BLACK POWDER DAN. London, Hodder, 1925. 319p [BM OTMC

THE BOSS OF WIND RIVER. Garden City, Doubleday, 1911. 340p [LC NBFU OTMC

THE LAND OF BIG RIVERS. A Story of the Northwest. New York, Chelsea House, 1924. 305p [BM BVaU LC NBFU OTMC

THE LAND OF STRONG MEN. New York, Fly, 1919. 432p [LC NBFU OTMC

PRECIOUS WATERS. Garden City, Doubleday, 1913. 422p [BM LC NBFU OTU

PROSPECTIN' FOOLS. London, Hodder, 1927. 320p [BM NBFU OTU

RED. London, Hodder, 1927. 320p [BM

RED BILL. New York, Burt, 1929. 308p [BVaU NBFU OTMC

THE RED-HEADED KIDS. An Adventure Story. New York, Chelsea House, 1925. 320p [BVaU LC NBFU OTMC

THE RED HEADS. London, Hodder, 1926. 312p [BM

WHEN STUART CAME TO SITKUM. A Western Story. New York, Chelsea House, 1924. 320p [LC NBFU OTMC

YELLOW HORSE. A Western Story. London, Hodder, 1926. 311p [BM LC NBFU OTMC

**Choquet, Joseph P.**

UNDER CANADIAN SKIES. A French-Canadian Historical Romance. Providence, R.I., Oxford Press, 1922. 311p [BVaU NBFU OTU

**Christie, Annie Rothwell (Fowler), 1837–1927**

LOVED I NOT HONOUR MORE. By Annie Rothwell [pseud]. Toronto, Hunter Rose, 1887. 150p [OOP

**Christie, Robert Cleland Hamilton, 1917–**

INHERIT THE NIGHT. New York, Farrar, 1949. 409p [BM BVaU OOP

THE TREMBLING LAND. Garden City, N.Y., Doubleday, 1959. 288p

**Chute, Arthur Hunt, 1890–1929**

THE CRESTED SEAS. New York, Sears, 1928. 258p [BM LC NBFU

FAR GOLD. New York, Sears, 1927. 307p [BM BVaU LC NBFU OTMC

THE MUTINY OF THE FLYING SPRAY. New York, Sears, 1927. 308p [BM BVaU LC NBFU OTMC QMM

**Clark, Catherine Anthony (Smith), 1892–**

THE GOLDEN PINE CONE. Toronto, Macmillan, 1950. 181p [NBFU OTMC

THE ONE-WINGED DRAGON. Toronto, Macmillan, 1955. 271p

THE SILVER MAN. Toronto, Macmillan, 1958. 231p

THE SUN HORSE. Toronto, Macmillan, 1951. 209p

**Clark, Daniel, 1835–1912**

JOSIAH GARTH. A Novel Dealing with the Rebellion of 1837. Toronto, n.d. [DCB MOR'12

PEN PHOTOGRAPHS OF CELEBRATED MEN AND NOTED PLACES ... GHOSTS AND THEIR RELATIONS. Tales, Sketches, Essays, etc. Toronto, Flint Morton, 1873. 321p [BVaU OTMC QMSS

**Clarke, George Frederick, 1883–**

THE ADVENTURES OF JIMMY-WHY. Fredericton, Brunswick Press, 1954. 91p

THE BEST ONE THING. London, Mills & Boon, 1926. 255p [BM LC NBFU OTP

CHRIS IN CANADA. London, Blackie, 1925. 224p [BVaU NBFU OTMC

DAVID CAMERON'S ADVENTURES. ... London, Blackie, [1950]. 237p [BM NBFU OONL

THE MAGIC ROAD. London, Mills & Boon, 1925. 272p [BM LC NBFU OKQ

NOEL AND JIMMY-WHY. Fredericton, Brunswick Press, 1959. 97p

RETURN TO ACADIA. An Historical Romance of the Eighteenth Century in What was Later to be New Brunswick. Fredericton, Brunswick Press, 1952. 251p

THETIS SAXON. Toronto, Longmans, 1927. 286p [BM BVaU NBFU OTP QMM

**Clay, Charles, 1906–**

FUR TRADE APPRENTICE. London, Oxford U. Press, 1940. 360p [LC OTMC

MUSKRAT MAN. Toronto, Ryerson, 1946. 283p [BVaU LC NBFU MW OTMC QMM

PHANTOM FUR THIEVES. Toronto, Ryerson, 1944. 248p [BVaU OTMC QMM

SWAMPY CREE LEGENDS. Being Twenty Folk Tales from the Annals of a Primitive, Mysterious, Fast-disappearing Canadian Race. As told to Charles Clay–by Kuskapatchees, the Smokey One. Toronto, Macmillan, 1938. 95p [BM BVaU LC OTU QMM SSU

A TRULY REMARKABLE EXPERIENCE. N.p., 1936. 4p [OTU

YOUNG VOYAGEUR. London, Oxford U. Press, 1938. 409p [BVaU NBFU OLU

**Claxton, Lilian**

IN HIGH SECURITY AND OTHER STORIES. Kingston, Daily News Office, n.d. 68p [OTMC

**Clayton, Rev. F.H.**

SCENES AND INCIDENTS IN IRISH LIFE. By an Irishman [pseud]. Montreal, Lovell, 1884. 340p [BVaU QMBM

**Cleaver, Solomon, 1855–1939**

JEAN VAL JEAN. As told by ——. Toronto, Clarke Irwin, 1935. 119p [OTMC

**Clemo, Ebenezer, 1831?–1860**

CANADIAN HOMES; or, The Mystery Solved. A Christmas Tale. By Maple Knot [pseud]. Montreal, Lovell, 1858. 136p [OTMC QMM

THE LIFE AND ADVENTURES OF SIMON SEEK; or, Canada in all Shapes. By Maple Knot [pseud]. Montreal, Lovell, 1858. 179p [OTP

**Clint, Mabel Brown, 1874–1939**

UNDER THE KING'S BASTION. A Romance of Quebec. By Harold Saxon [pseud]. Quebec, Carrel, [1902?]. 217p [NSHD OTMC QMSS

**Clout, John Allbuary, 1894–**

A CARAVAN TO CAMUL. By John Clou [pseud]. Indianapolis, Bobbs-Merrill, 1954. 383p [Also pub. as: THE GOLDEN BLADE. Abridged ed. Toronto, Graphic Books, 1955. 317p]

**Coates, Carol**

SHANLING; or, The Tale of the Celestial Tea-Pot. A Christmas Fantasy. Oakville, Ont., Barber, 1944. 13p [BM OKQ

**Coates, Taylor, 1903–**

DYSMAS THE THIEF. New York, Vantage Press, 1959. 292p

**Cobb, Humphrey, 1899–**

PATHS OF GLORY. New York, Viking, 1935. 266p [BM BVaU LC NBFU OTU QMM

**Coburn, Kathleen Hazel, 1905–**

THE GRANDMOTHERS. ... Toronto, Oxford U. Press, 1949. 233p [BM BVaU LC NBFU OTMC

**Cockburn, Russell R.**

MALLY. Story of a Dog. Toronto, Macmillan, 1939. 248p [BM BVaU NBFU OTU

**Cody, Hiram Alfred, 1872–1948**

THE CHIEF OF THE RANGES. A Tale of the Yukon. Toronto, Briggs, 1913. 303p [BM BVaU LC NBFU OTMC

THE CRIMSON SIGN. Toronto, McClelland, 1935. 306p [NBFU OTMC

THE FIGHTING-SLOGAN. Toronto, McClelland, 1926. 285p [BM BVaU LC NBFU OTMC

FIGHTING STARS. Toronto, McClelland, 1927. 272p [BM BVaU LC NSHD OTMC

THE FOURTH WATCH. Toronto, Briggs, 1911. 313p [BM BVaU LC NBFU OTMC

THE FRONTIERSMAN. A Tale of the Yukon. Toronto, Briggs, 1910. 342p [BM BVaU LC NBFU OTMC

THE GIRL AT BULLET LAKE. Toronto, McClelland, 1933. 304p [BVaU NBFU OTMC

GLEN OF THE HIGH NORTH. Toronto, McClelland, 1920. 288p [BM BVaU LC NBFU OTMC QMM

IF ANY MAN SIN. Toronto, Briggs, 1915. 309p [BM BVaU LC NBFU OTMC

JESS OF THE REBEL TRAIL. Toronto, McClelland, 1921. 277p [BM BVaU LC NBFU OTMC

THE KING'S ARROW. A Tale of the United Empire Loyalists. Toronto, McClelland, 1922. 280p [BM BVaU LC NBFU OTMC

THE LONG PATROL. A Tale of the Mounted Police. Toronto, Briggs, 1912. 310p [BM BVaU LC NBFU OTMC QMBM

THE MASTER REVENGE. Toronto, McClelland, 1924. 298p [BM BVaU LC NBFU OTMC

THE RED RANGER. Toronto, McClelland, 1931. 293p [BVaU NBFU OTMC

THE RIVER FURY. Toronto, McClelland, 1930. 305p [BVaU NBFU OTMC

ROD OF THE LONE PATROL. Toronto, McClelland, 1916. 348p [BVaU LC NBFU OTMC

STORM KING BANNER. Toronto, McClelland, 1937. 304p [BVaU NBFU OTMC

THE STUMBLING SHEPHERD. Toronto, McClelland, 1929. 301p [BVaU NBFU OTMC

THE TOUCH OF ABNER. Toronto, McClelland, 1919. 310p [BVa LC NSHD OTMC

THE TRAIL OF THE GOLDEN HORN. Toronto, McClelland, 1923. 296p [BM BVaU LC NBFU OTMC

UNDER SEALED ORDERS. Toronto, McClelland, 1917. 318p [BVaU LC NBFU OTMC

THE UNKNOWN WRESTLER. Toronto, McClelland, 1918. 308p [BM BVaU LC NBFU OTMC

**Coleman, Helena Jane, 1860–1953**

SHEILA AND OTHERS. The Simple Annals of an Unromantic Household. By Winifred Cotter [pseud]. Toronto, Dent, 1921. [Also: New York, Dutton, 1920. 196p] [CC LC

**Colfer, Rebecca B.**

STRAY LEAVES FROM THE DRAMA OF EVERYDAY LIFE. ... By "R" [pseud]. Montreal, Lovell, 1878. 193p [BVaU NBFU OTMC QMSS

**Collins, Joseph Edmund, 1855–1892**

ANNETTE THE METIS SPY; A HEROINE OF THE N.W. REBELLION. [Nancy, the Lightkeeper's Daughter]. Toronto, Rose, 1886. 155p [NSHPL OTP QMG SSU

THE FOUR CANADIAN HIGHWAYMEN; or, The Robbers of Markham Swamp. Toronto, Rose, 1886. 158p [OTU

THE STORY OF A GREENLAND GIRL. Toronto, 1884. [BCF NBB

THE STORY OF LOUIS RIEL, THE REBEL CHIEF. Toronto, Rose, 1885. 176p [Also: Toronto, Robertson, [1885]. 192p] [BVaU NBFU OLU SSU

**Collins, Ruth M.**

HORACE, THE HOUND THAT HOWLED. New York, Dodd Mead, 1951. 64p

**Colman, Louis**

LUMBER. Boston, Little Brown, 1931. 296p [BM LC OTP

**Colter, Mrs. Hattie E.**

A GENTLE BENEFACTRESS. By Mrs. J.J. Colter. Boston, Lothrop, 1892. 329p [BM LC

HAROLD BOWDOIN'S INVESTMENT. London, Stockwell, 1904. 171p [BM NBS

IN THE HEART OF THE HILLS; or, The Little Preacher of the Pacific Slope. Edinburgh, Oliphant, 1898. 203p [BM

THE MASTER OF DEEPLAWN. Philadelphia, Am. Baptist Pub. Soc., 1895. 352p [LC NBS

MEDOLINE SELWYN'S WORK. By Mrs. J.J. Colter. Boston, Bradley, 1889. 395p [LC

MILDRED KENT'S HERO. Boston, Bradley, 1889. [BCF MOR'12

ONE QUIET LIFE. By Mrs. J.J. Colter. Boston, Lothrop, 1876. [AmCat

ROBBIE MEREDITH. By Mrs. J.J. Colter. Boston, Lothrop, 1876. [AmCat

**Conger, Janet C.**

A DAUGHTER OF ST. PETER'S. New York, Lovell, 1889. 196p [BVaU LC OTMC

**Conibear, Frank**

DEVIL DOG. New York, Sloane, 1954. 214p

WATER TRIO. By Frank Conibear and J.L. Blundell. London, Davies, 1948. 278p [BViP OTMC

**Conibear, Kenneth, 1907–**

HUSKY. The Story of Cap. By Frank and Kenneth Conibear. London, Davies, 1940. 241p [BM BViPA NBFU OTU

NORTH LAND FOOTPRINTS; or, Lives on Little Bent Tree Lake. London, Dickson, 1936. 339p [BM BVaU NBFU OTMC

NORTHWARD TO EDEN. London, Davies, 1938. 403p [BM LC NBFU OTU QMM

**Cook, Lyn, 1918–**

THE BELLS ON FINLAND STREET. Toronto, Macmillan, 1950. 197p [BVaU NBFU OTMC QMBM

JADY AND THE GENERAL. Toronto, Macmillan, 1955. 242p

THE LITTLE MAGIC FIDDLER. Toronto, Macmillan, 1951. 252p

PEGEEN AND THE PILGRIM. Toronto, Macmillan, 1957. 248p

REBEL ON THE TRAIL. Toronto, Macmillan, 1953. 247p

**Cook, Marjorie Grant**

ANOTHER WAY OF LOVE. London, Heinemann, 1923. 320p [BM NBFU OOP

DEAR EMILY. By Caroline Seaford [pseud]. London, Gollancz, 1938. 304p [BM QMM

GLORY JAM. By Caroline Seaford [pseud]. London, Gollancz, 1934. 328p [BM NBFU OOP QMM

LATCHKEY LADIES. By Marjorie Grant [pseud]. London, Heinemann, 1921. 310p [BM OOP QMM

MORE THAN KIND. By Caroline Seaford [pseud]. London, Gollancz, 1935. 287p [BM OOP QMM

THEY GREW IN BEAUTY. A Novel. By Caroline Seaford [pseud]. London, Cape, 1946. 290p [BM NBFU QMM

VELVET DEER. By Caroline Seaford [pseud]. London, Dickson, 1937. 240p [BM NBFU

**Cooke, Henry Robswood**

ALTURLIE. London, Hodder, 1925. 320p [BM

BUCCANEERS' ISLAND.... London, Long, 1913. 256p [BM

OUTLAWED. A Tale of Culloden. London, Hodder, 1924. 318p [BM BVaU OTMC

**Cooke, Ronald John Victor, 1913–**

ALGONQUIN ADVENTURE. Toronto, Ryerson, 1958. 138p

THE HOUSE ON CRAIG STREET. Winnipeg, Harlequin Books, 1949. 190p [OTMC

THE MAYOR OF COTE ST. PAUL. Toronto, Harlequin Books, 1950. 157p [OTMC

**Coombs, Francis Lovell, 1876–**

THE LOST TRAIN AND OTHER TALES ... OF YOUNG CANADIAN RAILROADERS. V. 1. Ottawa, Mortimer, 1933. [At the head of title: "The Railroad Scouts Series." May be same as following title.] [Amtmann cat. 149

THE RACE FOR YELLOW CREEK. And other Tales of Adventure and Ingenuity of a Group of Young Canadian Railroaders. Ottawa, Mortimer, [1933]. 149p [BVaU

YOUNG CRUSOES OF THE SKY. New York, Century, 1911. 380p [BM LC

THE YOUNG RAILROADERS. Tales of Adventure and Ingenuity. New York, Century, 1910. 380p [BM LC

**Cooney, Percival John, 1871–1932**

THE DONS OF THE OLD PUEBLO. Chicago, Rand McNally, 1914. 439p [BM BVaU LC OTMC

KINSMEN. A Story of the Ottawa Valley. Toronto, Gundy, 1916. 366p [Also: Toronto, McClelland, 1929.] [BVaU NSHD OTMC

**Copland, John A., 1863–**

ESCULAPIUS. Harriston, Ont. [BCF

A METEOR KING. Harriston, Ont., Harriston Tribune, 1899. 122p [BM OTMC

**Corbett, Sidney, 1891–**

THE CRUISE OF THE GULL-FLIGHT. New York, Longmans, 1937. 367p [BM LC NBFU OTMC

THE GULL-FLIGHT SAILS AGAIN. Toronto, Longmans, 1939. 328p [BM LC NBFU OOP

**Coristine, Alwyn**

THE SORRY CAVALIER. London, Stockwell, 1933. 285p [BM OTP

**Cormack, Barbara (Villy), 1903–**

THE HOUSE. Toronto, Ryerson, 1955. 255p

LOCAL RAG. Toronto, Ryerson, 1951. 234p

**Cornell, Beaumont Sandfield, 1892–1958**

LANTERN MARSH. Toronto, Ryerson, 1923. 399p [BM BVaU NBFU OTMC

RENAISSANCE. A Novel. Toronto, Macmillan, 1922. 278p [NSHD OKQ

**Cornell, Hughes**

KENELM'S DESIRE. Toronto, Musson, 1906. 388p [BVaU OTMC

**Cornish, John, 1914–**

OLGA. Toronto, Macmillan, 1959. 174p

THE PROVINCIALS. Toronto, McClelland, 1951. 258p

**Cosier, C.H.T.**

THE MIGHTY MILLSTONE. A Scientific-Religious Novel. London, Stockwell, 1938. 288p [BM

**Costain, Thomas Bertram, 1885–1965**

BELOW THE SALT. A Novel. Garden City, N.Y., Doubleday, 1957. 480p

THE BLACK ROSE. Garden City, Doubleday, 1945. 403p [BM BVaU LC NBFU OTMC

THE DARKNESS AND THE DAWN. A Novel. Garden City, N.Y., Doubleday, 1959. 478p

FOR MY GREAT FOLLY. A Novel. New York, Putnam, 1942. 504p [BM LC OTMC

HIGH TOWERS. Toronto, McClelland, 1949. 403p [BM BVaU LC NBFU OTMC

THE MISSISSIPPI BUBBLE. New York, Random House, 1955. 185p

THE MONEYMAN. New York, Doubleday, 1947. 434p [BM BVaU LC NBFU OTMC

RIDE WITH ME. New York, Doubleday, 1944. 595p [BVaU NBFU OTMC QMM

THE SILVER CHALICE. A Novel. Garden City, Doubleday, 1952. 533p

SON OF A HUNDRED KINGS. A Novel of the Nineties. Garden City, Doubleday, 1950. 465p [BVaU LC NBFU OTMC

STORIES TO REMEMBER. Selected by Thomas B. Costain and John Beecroft. Garden City, N.Y., Doubleday, 1956. 2v

THE TONTINE. A Novel. Garden City, N.Y., Doubleday, 1955. 2v

**Coulter, John William, 1888–**

TURF SMOKE. A Fable of Two Countries. Toronto, Ryerson, 1945. 187p [BVaU NBFU OTMC QMM

**Cousins, Olive Evelyn Joy, 1894–**

THE CORMAC TREASURE. London, Stockwell, 1941. 320p [BM BVa LC QMM

**Covey, Mrs. Elizabeth (Rockfort), 1873–**

COMRADES TWO. [A Tale of the Qu'Appelle Valley]. By Elizabeth Fremantle [pseud]. London, Heinemann, 1907. 254p [Also: Toronto, Musson, [1907?] 254p] [AEU BVaU OTMC

THE ONE, AND I. By Elizabeth Fremantle [pseud]. Philadelphia, Jacobs, [1908]. 319p [Same as COMRADES TWO.] [LC OTMC

**Cowan, Charles L.**

SANDY'S SON. Toronto, Poole, 1931. 288p [BVaU NBFU OTP

**Cowan, Hugh, 1870–1943**

LA CLOCHE. The Story of Hector MacLeod and his Misadventures in the Georgian Bay and the La Cloche Districts. Toronto, Algonquin Hist. Soc., 1928. 327p [BVaU NBFU OTP

**Cox, Corolyn**

STAND BY. New York, Harper, 1925. 351p [BM LC

**Craig, John Ernest, 1921–**

THE LONG RETURN. Toronto, McClelland, 1959. 255p

WAGONS WEST. London, Dent, 1956. 128p [First pub.: Toronto, Dent, 1955.]

**Craig, Hamilton**

A HAZARD AT HANSARD. (The Speech from the Throne, Ottawa, fourth August, 2014). London, Stockwell, 1925. 31p [BM NSHD OTU

**Craig, Mary Coad, 1871–**

THE TWO DECANTERS. Written for his Wife by Duncan Clark, M.D. [pseud] Ed. by ——. Ottawa, Graphic, 1930. 301p [NBFU OTMC QMM

**Crawford, Isabell C.**

THE TAPESTRY OF TIME. Boston, Christopher, 1927. 365p [BViPA LC

**Creal, Margaret**

A LESSON IN LOVE. A Novel. New York, Simon & Schuster, 1957. 281p

**Creighton, Luella Sanders (Bruce), 1901–**

HIGH BRIGHT BUGGY WHEELS. Toronto, McClelland, 1951. 352p

TURN EAST, TURN WEST. New York, Dodd Mead, 1954. 373p

**Crisp, William George, 1904–**

WHITE GOLD IN THE CASSIAR. London, Dent, 1955. 221p

**Crofton, Francis Blake, 1841–1912**

THE BEWILDERED QUERISTS AND OTHER NONSENSE. New York, Putnam, 1875. 127p [LC NSHD OTP

HAIRBREADTH ESCAPES OF MAJOR MENDAX. A Personal Narrative. Philadelphia, Hubbard, 1889. 236p [NSHD OTU

THE MAJOR'S BIG-TALK STORIES. London, Warne, 1881. 152p [BM NSHD

**Cropp, Marjorie Elizabeth, 1903–**

TREMENDOUS ADVENTURE OF THE PEACE FAIRY. Regina, School Aids and Text Book Pub. Co., 1945. [unpaged] [ACU

**Crozier, Rev. Hugh Gibson, 1873–**

DAVID THE THEOLOGUE. Ilfracombe, Devon, Stockwell, 1954. 163p

**Cummins, John S.**

ALTHAM. A Tale of the Sea. London, Saunders & Otley, 1849. 2v [BM OTP

**Cunningham, Louis Arthur, 1900–1954**

AIRMAIL TO EDEN. London, Jenkins, 1954. 188p

DISCORDS OF THE DEEP. London, Quality Press, 1938. 255p [BM OTU

EVERGREEN COTTAGE. New York, Arcadia House, 1949. 256p [LC

FOG OVER FUNDY. Philadelphia, Penn. Pub. Co., 1936. 303p [LC NBFU OTMC

THE FOREST GATE. Hanley, Eng., Locker, 1947. 160p [BM

KEY TO ROMANCE. New York, Arcadia House, 1954. 224p

THE KING'S FOOL. Ottawa, Graphic, 1931. 281p [BVaU LC NBFU OTMC QMM

THE LILY POOL. New York, Arcadia House, 1955. 223p

MARIONETTE. Philadelphia, Penn. Pub. Co., 1941. 303p [LC NBFU OTU

MEG SHANNON. New York, Arcadia House, 1956. 222p

MOON OVER ACADIE. Philadelphia, Penn. Pub. Co., 1937. 310p [LC NBFU OTMC

OF THESE THREE LOVES. Philadelphia, Penn. Pub. Co., 1939. 302p [LC OTU

SHOULD THY LOVE DIE. London, Jenkins, 1954. 192p

THE SIGN OF THE BURNING SHIP. Philadelphia, Penn. Pub. Co., 1940. 290p [LC NBFU OTMC

STARS OVER SEVEN OAKS. New York, Arcadia House, 1957. 220p

A SUNLIT GROVE. New York, Arcadia House, 1959. 220p

SWEET CONSTANCY. London, Jenkins, 1955. 190p

THIS THING CALLED LOVE. New York, Carrier, 1929. 311p [BVaU LC NBFU OTMC QMM

VALLEY OF THE STARS. Philadelphia, Penn. Pub. Co., 1938. 305p [LC NBFU OOP

TIDES OF THE TANTRAMAR. Philadelphia, Penn. Pub. Co., 1935. 313p [BVaU LC NBFU OTMC

THE WANDERING HEART. New York, Gramercy Pub. Co., 1947. 253p [LC OTMC

WHISPER TO THE STARS. New York, Arcadia House, 1958. 222p

YOU ARE THE DREAM. New York, Arcadia House, 1957. 220p

YVON TREMBLAY. An Acadian Idyll. Ottawa, Graphic, 1927. 284p [BVaU NBFU OTMC

**Cunningham, Michael, 1910–**

THE BISHOP FINDS A WAY. New York, Farrar, Straus & Young, 1955. 213p

**Cureton, Stephen**

PERSEVERANCE WINS. The Career of a Travelling Correspondent. Toronto, Clougher, 1880. 269p [OOP

**Curran, James Watson, 1865–1952**

WOLVES DON'T BITE. Sault Ste. Marie, Daily Star, 1940. 225p [OTU

**Cushing, Eliza Lanesford (Foster), 1794–**
SARATOGA. A Tale of the Revolution. [Anon] Boston, Cummings, 1824. 2v [LC
YORKTOWN. An Historical Romance. ... [Anon] Boston, Wells & Lilly, 1826. 2v [LC

**Cushing, Enid Louise**
BLOOD ON MY RUG. New York, Arcadia House, 1956. 223p
THE GIRL WHO BOUGHT A DREAM. By Mabel Louise Dawson [pseud]. New York, Arcadia House, 1957. 220p
MURDER'S NO PICNIC. New York, Arcadia House, 1953. 220p
MURDER WITHOUT REGRET. New York, Arcadia House, 1954. 221p
THE UNEXPECTED CORPSE. New York, Arcadia House, 1957. 223p

**Daem, Mary (Bannerman), 1914–**
LUCKY LURE AT ARROW POINT. London, Abelard-Schuman, 1959. 126p
THE WHISTLING MOUNTAIN. Toronto, Abelard-Schuman, 1960. 154p

**Dale, Mrs. R.J.**
TO THE GREATER GLORY. By V.V. Vinton [pseud]. London, Cape, 1939. 224p [BM OTU QMM

**Dalgarno, Agnes**
THUNDER IN THE SKY. Ilfracombe, Devon, Stockwell, 1958. 34p

**Dalziel, David**
JEWS AND GENTILES; or, Life in Sittsville. Toronto, Author, 1898. 174p [OOP
A PARODY ON PATIENCE. N.p., n.d. 48p [OTP

**Dancey, Stanley Nelson, 1885–**
THE FAITH OF A BELGIAN. A Romance of the Great War. Ottawa, Dadson Merrill, 1916. 325p [BM OONL

**Darnell, Rev. Henry Faulkner, 1831–1915**
THE CRAZE OF CHRISTIAN ENGLEHART. New York, Appleton, 1890. 264p [LC
THE CROSS ROADS. An Allegory. ... Manchester, Eng., Simms, 1856. 40p [OLU
FLOSSY; or, A Child of the People. Buffalo, Darnell, 1889. [Sequel to PHILIP HAZELBROOK. ... ] [AmCat
PHILIP HAZELBROOK; or, The Junior Curate. Buffalo, Sherrill, 1886. [AmCat

**Davidson, Fisher, 1912–**
PRINCIPAL BOY. Boston, Humphries, 1953. 38p

**Davies, Blodwen, 1897–1966**
RUFFLES AND RAPIERS. Toronto, Ryerson, 1930. 124p [BVaU NBFU OTU

**Davies, Robertson, 1913–**
LEAVEN OF MALICE. Toronto, Clarke Irwin, 1954. 312p

A MIXTURE OF FRAILTIES. Toronto, Macmillan, 1958. 379p
TEMPEST-TOST. Toronto, Clarke Irwin, 1951. 376p

**Davis, Allan Ross, 1858–1933**

THE OLD LOYALIST. A Story of United Empire Loyalist Descendants in Canada. Toronto, Briggs, 1908. 367p [BM BVaU NBFU OKQ

**Davis, Harold Lenoir, 1896–**

WINDS OF MORNING. Toronto, McLeod, 1952. 344p

**Davison, Frank Cyril Shaw, 1893–1944?**

HARE AND TORTOISE. By Pierre Coalfleet [pseud]. Toronto, McClelland, 1925. 255p [BM BVaU LC NBFU OTMC
MEANWHILE. By Pierre Coalfleet [pseud]. New York, Duffield, 1927. 360p [BVaU NBFU QMM
SIDONIE. By Pierre Coalfleet [pseud]. London, Collins, [1921]. 273p [BM NBFU
SOLO. By Pierre Coalfleet [pseud]. New York, Putnam, 1924. 351p [BM BVaU LC NBFU OTMC

**Day, Frank Parker, 1881–1950**

JOHN PAUL'S ROCK. New York, Minton Balch, 1932. 242p [LC NBFU OTP
RIVER OF STRANGERS. Garden City, Doubleday, 1926. 237p [BM BVaU LC NSHD OTP
ROCKBOUND. Garden City, Doubleday, 1928. 292p [BM LC NSHD OTP

**Deacon, W.F.**

THE AUTHOR; or, Sketches from Life. Saint John, 1866. 64p [BCF
MURDER WILL OUT; or, Confessions of a Village Apothecary. [BCF

**Deane, Aubrey**

ANNETTE. A Tale. With a Memoir of the Author by T.N. Talfourd. London, Colborn, 1852. 3v [OTMC
THE STREET RIVER TRAGEDY. [BCF

**Deans, Dorothea**

PETALS IN PASSING. Owen Sound, Fleming, 1929. 22p [BVaU OONL

**Delafosse, Frederick Montague, 1860–1950**

ENGLISH BLOODS. By Roger Vardon [pseud]. Ottawa, Graphic, 1930. 227p [BM BVaU OTP QMM

**De La Roche, Mazo, 1879–1961**

BESIDE A NORMAN TOWER. London, Macmillan, 1934. 229p [BM BVaU LC NBFU OTMC QMM
BILL AND COO. Toronto, Macmillan, 1958. 40p
A BOY IN THE HOUSE. London, Macmillan, 1952. 124p
A BOY IN THE HOUSE AND OTHER STORIES. Boston, Little Brown, 1952. 244p
THE BUILDING OF JALNA. Boston, Little Brown, 1944. 366p [BM BVaU LC NBFU OTMC

CENTENARY AT JALNA. Toronto, Macmillan, 1958. 302p

DELIGHT. New York, Macmillan, 1926. 232p [BM BVaU LC NBFU OTMC QMM

EXPLORERS OF THE DAWN. New York, Knopf, 1922. 292p [BM BVaU LC NBFU OTMC

FINCH'S FORTUNE. London, Macmillan, 1931. 399p [BM BVaU LC NBFU OTU QMM

GROWTH OF A MAN. Boston, Little Brown, 1938. 380p [BVaU LC NBFU OTU QMM

JALNA. Boston, Little Brown, 1927. 347p [BVaU LC NSHD OTU

LARK ASCENDING. Boston, Little Brown, 1932. 301p [BM BVaU NBFU OTU QMM

MARY WAKEFIELD. Boston, Little Brown, 1949. 337p [BM BVaU LC NBFU OTU QMM

THE MASTER OF JALNA. Toronto, Macmillan, 1933. 331p [BM BVaU LC NBFU OTU QMM

MORNING AT JALNA. London, Macmillan, 1960. 263p

POSSESSION. New York, Macmillan, 1923. 289p [BM BVaU LC NSHD OTU QMM

RENNY'S DAUGHTER. Boston, Little Brown, 1951. 376p

RETURN TO JALNA. Boston, Little Brown, 1946. 462p [BM BVaU LC NBFU OTMC QMM

THE SACRED BULLOCK, AND OTHER STORIES OF ANIMALS. London, Macmillan, 1939. 221p [BM BVaU LC NBFU OTMC QMM

THE SONG OF LAMBERT. Toronto, Macmillan, 1955. 51p

THE THUNDER OF NEW WINGS. Boston, Little Brown, 1932. 279p [A novel serialized in a magazine and printed in a few copies "that it might be protected from pirating"—letter from author.] [OKQ

THE TWO SAPLINGS. London, Macmillan, 1942. 214p [BM BVaU LC NBFU OTMC QMM

VARIABLE WINDS AT JALNA. Toronto, Macmillan, 1954. 359p

THE VERY HOUSE. London, Macmillan, 1937. 257p [BM BVaU LC NBFU OTMC QMM

WAKEFIELD'S COURSE. Boston, Little Brown, 1941. 406p [BM BVaU LC NSHD OTMC QMM

THE WHITEOAK BROTHERS, JALNA—1923. Toronto, Macmillan, 1953. 307p

WHITEOAK CHRONICLES. [Contains *Young Renny, Jalna, Whiteoaks, Finch's Fortune, The Master of Jalna, Whiteoak Harvest.*] London, Macmillan, 1940. 1390p [BM OTMC

WHITEOAK HARVEST. Boston, Little Brown, 1936. 378p [BM BVaU LC NBFU OTMC QMM

WHITEOAK HERITAGE. Boston, Little Brown, 1940. 325p [BM BVaU LC NBFU OTMC QMM

WHITEOAKS OF JALNA. Boston, Little Brown, 1929. 423p [BM BVaU LC MWU NSHD OTP

YOUNG RENNY. Toronto, Macmillan, 1935. 277p [BM BVaU NBFU OTMC QMM

**De Long, Rev. A.M.**

A WOLF IN SHEEP'S CLOTHING. Toronto, Briggs, 1905. 163p [BM

**De Mille, James, 1833–1880**

Besides titles which follow, the following untraced titles have been attributed to De Mille by either BCF or NBB, or both:

ASHDOD WEBSTER AND HIS STARRING TOUR
THE SOLDIER AND THE SPY [1869? 1865?]
THE ARKANSAS RANGER [1869? 1865?]

(The last two also are mentioned in Allibone Supp.)

THE AMERICAN BARON. New York, Harper, 1872. 132p [BVaU LC NSHD OTMC

AMONG THE BRIGANDS. Boston, Lee & Shepard, 1871. 328p (Young Dodge Club Series) [BVaU NSHD OTMC

ANDY O'HARA; or, The Child of Promise. [Anon] New York, Carlton & Porter, 1861. [AmCat

THE BABES IN THE WOOD. A Tragic Comedy. A Tale of the Italian Revolution of 1848. Boston, Gill, 1875. 142p [BVaU LC NSHD

THE "B.O.W.C." [Brethren of the White Cross]. A Book for Boys. By the author of THE DODGE CLUB, etc. [pseud]. Boston, Lee & Shepard, 1869. 322p [BVaU NSHD OKQ

THE BOYS OF GRAND PRÉ SCHOOL. Boston, Lee & Shepard, 1870. 348p (B.O.W.C. Series) [BVaU NSHD OKQ

A CASTLE IN SPAIN. A Novel. New York, Harper, 1883. 183p [BM BVaU NSHD OTU

A COMEDY OF TERRORS. Boston, Osgood, 1872. 152p [BM BVaU LC OKQ

CORD AND CREESE. A Novel. New York, Harper, 1869. 305p [BM BVaU LC NSHD OKQ

THE CRYPTOGRAM. A Novel. New York, Harper, 1871. 261p [BVaU NSHD OKQ

THE DODGE CLUB; or, Italy in 1859. New York, Harper, 1869. 133p [BVaU NSHD OKQ QMM

THE DODGE CLUB ABROAD. New York, Harper, 1868. [Same as preceding title?]

FIRE IN THE WOODS. Boston, Lee & Shepard, 1872. 323p (B.O.W.C. Series) [BM BVaU NSHD OKQ

HELENA'S HOUSEHOLD. A Tale of Rome in the First Century. [Anon] New York, Carter, 1867. 422p [First pub. in 1858?—see Allibone Supp.] [BM NSHD OKQ

JOHN WHEELER'S TWO UNCLES; or, Launching into Life. [Anon] New York, Carlton & Porter, [1860?]. [AmCat

THE LADY OF THE ICE. A Novel. New York, Appleton, 1870. 146p [BVaU NSHD OTMC

THE LILY AND THE CROSS. A Tale of Acadia. Boston, Lee & Shepard, 1874. 264p [BVaU LC NSHD OTU

THE LIVING LINK. A Novel. New York, Harper, 1874. 171p [BVaU LC NSHD OTMC

LOST IN THE FOG. Boston, Lee & Shepard, [1870]. 316p (B.O.W.C. Series) [BVaU NBFU OTU

THE MARTYR OF THE CATACOMBS. A Tale of Ancient Rome. [Anon] New York, Carlton & Porter, 1865. 202p [First pub. in 1858?–see Allibone Supp.] [AmCat

OLD GARTH. A Story of Sicily. New York, Munro, 1883. 52p [BVaU LC NSWA

AN OPEN QUESTION. A Novel. New York, Appleton, 1873. 233p [BVaU NSHD

PICKED UP ADRIFT. Boston, Lee & Shepard, 1872. 335p (B.O.W.C. Series) [NBFU OKQ

THE SEVEN HILLS. Boston, Lee & Shepard, 1873. 331p (Young Dodge Club Series) [BVaU NSHD

A STRANGE MANUSCRIPT FOUND IN A COPPER CYLINDER. [Anon] New York, Harper, 1888. 291p [Also: Toronto, Macmillan, 1910]. [BM BVaU LC NSHD OKQ

THE TREASURE OF THE SEAS. Boston, Lee & Shepard, 1873. 336p (B.O.W.C. Series) [BM BVaU NSHD OKQ

THE WINGED LION; or, Stories of Venice. New York, Dillingham, 1877. 323p (Young Dodge Club Series) [BVaU LC NSHD OTU

**Denison, Merrill, 1893–**

BOOBS IN THE WOODS. Sixteen Sketches. ... Ottawa, Graphic, 1927. 204p [BVaU NBFU OTMC QMM

**Denison, Muriel (Goggin), –1954**

HAPPY TRAMP. The Story of a Little Girl and her Old English Sheep Dog. New York, Dodd Mead, 1942. 260p [BM BVa LC OOP

SUSANNAH. A Little Girl with the Mounties. New York, Dodd Mead, 1936. 299p [LC NBFU OTMC SRL

SUSANNAH AT BOARDING SCHOOL. New York, Dodd Mead, 1938. 344p [BM LC NBFU OTMC

SUSANNAH OF THE MOUNTIES. A Canadian Story of the Nineties. London, Dent, 1938. 280p [Same as SUSANNAH. A Little Girl. ... ] [BM OTMC

SUSANNAH OF THE YUKON. New York, Dodd Mead, 1937. 343p [BM LC NBFU OTMC

SUSANNAH RIDES AGAIN. New York, Dodd Mead, 1940. 329p [BM NBFU OTMC

**Dennis, June (pseud)**

A MIKE FOR MARION. By June Dennis [pseud]. Toronto, Longmans, 1952. 200p

**Dent, John Charles, 1841–1888**
THE GERRARD STREET MYSTERY, AND OTHER WEIRD TALES. Toronto, Rose, 1888. 206p [BVaU MWU NBFU OTMC QMM

**Dent, Walter Redvers, 1900–**
SHOW ME DEATH! Toronto, Macmillan, 1930. 375p [BM BVaU LC NBFU OTMC

**Deprend, Jeffrey**
EMBERS. Chicago, Wallace, 1919. 340p [BM LC OTMC
THE GOLDEN POPPY. Chicago, Wallace, 1922. 313p [LC NBFU

**Devine, Rev. Edward James, 1860–1927**
THE TRAINING OF SILAS. New York, Benziger, 1906. 322p [LC NSHD OKQ

**Dewdney, Selwyn Harrington, 1909–**
WIND WITHOUT RAIN. Toronto, Copp Clark, 1946. 506p [BVaU NSHD OTMC

**Dickie, Donalda James, 1883–**
THE BOOK OF NEW CANADIANS. Toronto, Dent, 1930. 158p [NBFU
SENT TO COVENTRY. Toronto, Dent, 1929. [BM

**Dickie, Francis Joseph, 1890–**
HUNTERS OF THE WILD. London, Lutterworth, 1937. 125p [BM BVaU
THE MASTER BREED. Toronto, McClelland, 1923. 272p [BVaU LC NBFU OTMC
UMINGMUK OF THE BARRENS. Toronto, Musson, 1927. 278p [BM BVaU NBFU QMM

**Dickson, Mrs. Emma Wells**
MISS DEXIE. A Romance of the Provinces. By Stanford Eveleth [pseud]. Toronto, Briggs, 1895. 426p [OLU

**Dickson, Gordon Rupert, 1923–**
SECRET UNDER THE SEA. New York, Holt Rinehart, 1960. 121p

**Dickson, Lovat, 1902–**
OUT OF THE WEST LAND. Toronto, Collins, 1944. 446p [BM BVaU LC NBFU OTMC

**Diesel, Gladys Cynthia Rebecca (Shope), 1907–**
THE LEGEND OF OWL HOOT HILL. Edmonton, Author, 1957. 8p

**Diespecker, Richard E. Alan, 1907–**
ELIZABETH. Toronto, Dent, 1950. 170p [BVaU NBFU OTMC
REBOUND. Toronto, Harlequin Books, 1953. 224p

**Dix, Maurice Buxton, 1889–**
BEACONS OF DEATH. London, Ward Lock, 1937. 288p [BM LC NBFU OLU

THE DARTMOOR MYSTERY. London, Ward Lock, 1935. 320p [BM
EMILY COULTON DIES. London, Ward Lock, 1936. 286p [BM LC NBFU
THE FIXER. London, Ward Lock, 1936. 318p [BM
THE FLAME OF THE KHAN. London, Ward Lock, 1934. 256p [BM LC OTMC
THE FLEETWOOD MANSIONS MYSTERY. London, Ward Lock, 1934. 317p [BM LC
THE GOLDEN FLUID. London, Ward Lock, 1935. 319p [BM OTMC
THE KIDNAPPED SCIENTIST. An Adventure of the Trio of Mount Street. London, Ward Lock, 1937. 287p [BM LC
LADY RICHLY LEFT. London, Staples, 1951. 264p
THE MASINGLEE MURDERS. London, Hale, 1947. 174p [BM
MURDER AT GRASSMERE ABBEY. London, Ward Lock, [1933]. 320p [BM LC
MURDER STRIKES TWICE. London, Ward Lock, 1939. 285p [BM LC
NIGHT ASSASSIN. London, Hale, 1941. 248p [BM
PROLOGUE TO MURDER. London, Ward Lock, 1938. 303p [BM
THIRD DEGREE. London, Gramol, 1936. 48p [BM
THIS IS MY MURDER. London, Ward Lock, 1938. 288p [BM LC
THE TREASURE OF SCARLAND. London, Ward Lock, 1936. 256p [BM LC
TWISTED EVIDENCE. London, Ward Lock, 1933. 256p [BM LC

**Dobbin, Mrs.**

"THOS." A Simple Canadian Story. By George Graham [pseud]. Montreal, Lovell, 1878. 160p [LC OTMC

**Dolen, G.**

THE DREAMER OF POND LAND AND OTHER STORIES. Toronto, W.M.S. of United Church, n.d. 80p [BVaU

**Dollard, Rev. James Bernard, 1872–1946**

THE GAELS OF MOONDHARRIG; or, The Modern Fianna. Dublin, Sealy, Bryers, 1907. 124p [BM

**Donovan, Edward Joseph, 1904–**

ADVENTURE ON GHOST RIVER. New York, Duell Sloan, 1960. 150p

**Donovan, Peter, 1884–**

LATE SPRING. London, Hodder, 1930. 352p [BM NBFU OTMC

**Dougall, Lily, 1858–1923**

BEGGARS ALL. A Novel. London, Longmans, 1891. 461p [BM LC NBFU OTMC QMM
A DOZEN WAYS OF LOVE. London, Black, 1897. 370p [BM QMM
THE EARTHLY PURGATORY. London, Hutchinson, 1904. 345p [Pub. in the U.S. as THE SUMMIT HOUSE MYSTERY; or, The Earthly Purgatory. New York, Funk & Wagnalls, 1905. 339p] [BM LC OOP QMM
THE MADONNA OF A DAY. New York, Appleton, 1895. 271p [BM BVaU LC OTMC QMM

THE MERMAID. A Love Tale. New York, Appleton, 1895. 290p [BM BVaU OOP QMM

THE MORMON PROPHET. New York, Appleton, 1899. 427p [BM LC QMM

PATHS OF THE RIGHTEOUS. London, Macmillan, 1908. 441p [BM LC NSHD QMM

A QUESTION OF FAITH. Boston, Houghton, 1895. 290p [BM LC OOP QMM

THE SPANISH DOWRY. A Romance. London, Hutchinson, 1906. 312p [BM BVaU OOP QMM

WHAT NECESSITY KNOWS. New York, Longmans, 1893. 445p [BM BVaU NBFU OOP QMM

YOUNG LOVE. London, Black, 1904. 179p [BM QMM

THE ZEIT-GEIST. New York, Appleton, 1895. 184p [BM LC NBFU QMM

**Dow, Lawrence T., –1956**

THE LONESOME DOLL. By Larry Lawrence [pseud]. [Halifax, Patterson-Dow, 1955.] 20p

**Draper, Blanche A., 1893–**

THE GREAT AWAKENING. New York, Vantage Press, 1953. 177p

**Drummond, May Isobel (Harvey)**

THE STORY OF QUAMIN. A Tale of the Tropics. New York, London, Putnam, 1911. 313p [BM LC NSWA

**Duff, Emma Lorne, –1935**

A CARGO OF STORIES FOR CHILDREN. Toronto, McClelland, 1929. 259p [3rd ed., rev. and enl., 1931.] [BViV

**Duff, Louis Blake, 1878–1959**

A SHEPHERD'S CROOK ON THE HILLS OF ST. JOHNS. Welland, Ont., priv. print., 1952. 5p

**Duffield, Dorothy Dean (Tate), 1893–**

ARKADY. By Anne Duffield [pseud]. London, Cassell, 1948. 247p [BM

BELOVED ENEMY. By Anne Duffield [pseud]. London, Cassell, 1950. 223p [BM

A BEVY OF MAIDS. By Anne Duffield [pseud]. London, Cassell, 1941. 254p [BM

BITTER RAPTURE. By Anne Duffield [pseud]. London, Cassell, 1937. 324p [BM LC

BRIEF RAPTURE. By Anne Duffield [pseud]. New York, Arcadia House, 1938. 288p [LC

BUBBLING SPRINGS. By Anne Duffield [pseud]. London, Cassell, 1940. 316p [BM LC

CASTLE IN SPAIN. By Anne Duffield [pseud]. London, Cassell, 1958. 217p

COME BACK MIRANDA. By Anne Duffield [pseud]. London, Cassell, 1955. 215p

DESERT MOON. A Novel. By Anne Duffield [pseud]. London, Cassell, 1939. 298p [BM LC PC

THE DRAGON'S TAIL. By Anne Duffield [pseud]. London, Cassell, 1938. 293p [BM LC

DUSTY DAWN. By Anne Duffield [pseud]. London, Cassell, 1949. 214p [BM

ENCHANTMENT. By Anne Duffield [pseud]. New York, Hillman-Curl, 1937. 320p [LC

FALSE STAR. By Anne Duffield [pseud]. New York, Arcadia House, 1939. 285p [LC

FIAMETTA. By Anne Duffield [pseud]. London, Cassell, 1956. 216p

FLAMING FELICIA. By Anne Duffield [pseud]. London, Cassell, 1934. 336p [BM LC

FLEETING SHADOWS. By Anne Duffield [pseud]. London, Cassell, 1934. 366p [BM LC

FOREVER TOMORROW. By Anne Duffield [pseud]. London, Cassell, 1946. 235p [BM

GAY FIESTA. By Anne Duffield [pseud]. London, Cassell, 1938. 285p [LC

GLITTERING HEIGHTS. By Anne Duffield [pseud]. London, Cassell, 1936. 314p [BM LC

GOLDEN HORIZONS. By Anne Duffield [pseud]. London, Cassell, 1935. 378p [BM LC

THE GOLDEN SUMMER. By Anne Duffield [pseud]. London, Cassell, 1954. 213p

THE GRAND DUCHESS. By Anne Duffield [pseud]. London, Cassell, 1954. 213p

GRECIAN RHAPSODY. By Anne Duffield [pseud]. London, Cassell, 1938. 279p [BM LC OONL

HARBOUR LIGHTS. By Anne Duffield [pseud]. London, Cassell, 1953. 223p

HIGH HEAVEN. By Anne Duffield [pseud]. London, Cassell, 1939. 271p [BM LC NBS

THE HOUSE ON THE NILE. By Anne Duffield [pseud]. London, Cassell, 1937. 363p [BM LC

THE INSCRUTABLE NYMPH. By Anne Duffield [pseud]. London, Cassell, 1942. 268p [BM LC OONL

KAREN'S MEMORY. By Anne Duffield [pseud]. New York, Arcadia House, 1939. 304p [BM LC OONL

THE LACQUER COUCH. By Anne Duffield [pseud]. London, Murray, 1929. 352p [BM NBS

LANTERN-LIGHT. By Anne Duffield [pseud]. London, Cassell, 1933. 367p [BM LC

THE LONELY BRIDE. By Anne Duffield [pseud]. New York, Arcadia House, 1947. 272p [LC

LOVABLE STRANGER. By Anne Duffield [pseud]. Philadelphia, Macrae, 1949. 256p [NBS

LOVE DEFERRED. By Anne Duffield [pseud]. Philadelphia, Macrae, 1951. 253p

LOVE'S MEMORY. By Anne Duffield [pseud]. New York, Arcadia House, 1936. 320p [LC

MISS MAYHEW AND MING YUN. A Story of East and West. By Anne Duffield [pseud]. New York, Stokes, 1928. 311p [LC QMBM
MOON OVER STAMBOUL. By Anne Duffield [pseud]. London, Cassell, 1936. 384p [BM LC
OLD GLORY. By Anne Duffield [pseud]. London, Cassell, 1942. 272p [BM LC
OUT OF THE SHADOWS. By Anne Duffield [pseud]. London, Cassell, 1944. 255p [BM LC
PARADISE. By Anne Duffield [pseud]. London, Cassell, 1936. 378p [BM LC
PASSIONATE INTERLUDE. By Anne Duffield [pseud]. London, Murray, 1931. 331p [BM LC
PHANTASY. By Anne Duffield [pseud]. London, Cassell, 1932. 345p [BM LC
PREDESTINED. By Anne Duffield [pseud]. London, Murray, 1929. 336p [BM
REPENT AT LEISURE. By Anne Duffield [pseud]. London, Cassell, 1945. 267p [BM LC
THE SHADOW OF THE PINES. By Anne Duffield [pseud]. London, Cassell, 1940. 282p [BM LC
SILVER PEAKS. By Anne Duffield [pseud]. London, Cassell, 1941. 312p [BM LC
SONG OF THE MOCKINGBIRD. By Anne Duffield [pseud]. London, Cassell, 1946. 287p [BM NBS
STAMBOUL LOVE. By Anne Duffield [pseud]. New York, Knopf, 1934. 406p [LC
THE STORY OF YUKU. By Dorothy Dean Tate. Toronto, Briggs, 1910. 240p [BM BVaU LC OTMC
SUGAR ISLAND. By Anne Duffield [pseud]. London, Cassell, 1951. 222p
SUNRISE. By Anne Duffield [pseud]. London, Cassell, 1943. 287p [BM LC PC
THE SWEEPING TIDE. By Anne Duffield [pseud]. London, Cassell, 1940. 288p [BM LC PC
TAFFY CAME TO CAIRO. By Anne Duffield [pseud]. London, Cassell, 1944. 171p [BM LC
TOMORROW IS THEIRS. By Anne Duffield [pseud]. London, Cassell, 1951. 232p
TURN TO THE SUN. By Anne Duffield [pseud]. New York, Arcadia House, 1944. 352p [LC
VIOLETTA. By Anne Duffield [pseud]. London, Cassell, 1960. 253p
WILD MEMORY. By Anne Duffield [pseud]. London, Cassell, 1935. 378p [BM LC

**Duley, Margaret, 1896?–1968**

COLD PASTORAL. London, Hutchinson, 1939. 336p [BM OTU
THE EYES OF THE GULL. London, Barker, 1936. 200p [BM OTU
GREEN AFTERNOON. London, Methuen, 1944. 252p [BM
HIGHWAY TO VALOUR. Toronto, Macmillan, 1941. 324p [Also: London, Methuen, 1943.] [BM BVaU NBFU OKQ
NOVELTY ON EARTH. Toronto, Macmillan, 1942. 300p [OTMC

**Dumbrille, Dorothy, 1898–**

ALL THIS DIFFERENCE. Toronto, Progress Books, 1945. 208p [BVaU NBFU OTMC QMM

DEEP DOORWAYS. A Story of Life in Canada between Two Wars. Toronto, Allen, 1947. 277p [BVaU NBFU OTMC QMBM

**Duncan, Norman, 1871–1916**

THE ADVENTURES OF BILLY TOPSAIL. A Story for Boys. New York, Revell, 1906. 331p [BM BVaU LC NBFU OTMC

BATTLES ROYAL DOWN NORTH. New York, Revell, 1918. 269p [BVaU LC OTMC QMM

THE BEST OF A BAD JOB. A Hearty Tale of the Sea. Toronto, Frowde, 1912. 204p [BVaU LC NBFU OKQ

BILLY TOPSAIL AND COMPANY. A Story for Boys. New York, Revell, 1910. 318p [BVaU LC OTMC

BILLY TOPSAIL, M.D. A Tale of Adventure with Doctor Luke of the Labrador. New York, Revell, 1916. 317p [BM BVaU LC NBFU OTMC

THE BIRD STORE MAN. An Old Fashioned Story. New York, Revell, 1914. 136p [BVaU LC NBFU OTMC

CHRISTMAS EVE AT SWAMP'S END. New York, Revell, 1915. 32p [BVaU LC NBFU OKQ

CHRISTMAS EVE AT TOPMAST TICKLE. [A Selection from DOCTOR LUKE OF THE LABRADOR with Additions.] New York, Revell, 1910. 32p [NBFU OKQ

THE CRUISE OF THE SHINING LIGHT. New York, Harper, 1907. 343p [BM BVaU LC NBFU OTMC

DOCTOR LUKE OF THE LABRADOR. New York, Revell, 1904. 327p [BM BVaU LC NBFU OTMC QMM

EVERY MAN FOR HIMSELF. New York, Harper, 1908. 304p [BM BVaU LC NBFU OTMC

FINDING HIS SOUL. New York, Harper, 1913. 61p [BM LC NBFU OTMC

HARBOUR TALES DOWN NORTH. New York, Revell, 1918. 282p [BVaU NSHD OTMC QMM

THE MEASURE OF A MAN. A Tale of the Big Woods. New York, Revell, 1911. 356p [BM BVaU LC NBFU OTMC

THE MOTHER. New York, Revell, 1905. 220p [BM BVaU LC NBFU OTMC

THE SOUL OF THE STREET. Correlated Stories of the New York Syrian Quarter. New York, McClure Phillips, 1900. 168p [BM LC NBFU OLU

THE SUITABLE CHILD. New York, Revell, 1909. 96p [BM BVaU LC NBFU OTMC

THE WAY OF THE SEA. New York, McClure Phillips, 1903. 332p [BM BVaU LC NBFU OKQ

**Duncan, Sara Jeannette (Mrs. Everard Cotes), 1861–1922**

AN AMERICAN GIRL IN LONDON. London, Chatto, 1891. 321p [BM BVaU LC NSHD OTMC

THE BURNT OFFERING. London, Methuen, 1909. 320p [BM BVaU LC NSHD OTU

THE CONSORT. London, Stanley Paul, 1912. 344p [BM MWU OTMC

COUSIN CINDERELLA. A Canadian Girl in London. Toronto, Macmillan, 1908. 365p [BM BVaU LC NBFU OTMC

A DAUGHTER OF TO-DAY. New York, Appleton, 1894. 392p [BM LC NBFU OTMC

THE GOLD CURE. A Novel. London, Hutchinson, 1924. 286p [BM

HILDA. A Story of Calcutta. New York, Stokes, 1898. 317p [Same as THE PATH OF A STAR, *q.v.*] [LC OLU

HIS HONOUR AND A LADY. Toronto, Rose, 1896. 321p [BM BVaU LC NBFU OTMC

HIS ROYAL HAPPINESS. New York, Appleton, 1914. 377p [BM BVaU LC NBFU OTMC

THE IMPERIALIST. Toronto, Copp Clark, 1904. 472p [Also: New York, Appleton, 1904. 476p] [BVaU LC NBFU OTMC

THE PATH OF A STAR. London, Methuen, 1899. 311p [Same as HILDA, *q.v.*] [BM BVaU NBFU OTMC

THE POOL IN THE DESERT. New York, Appleton, 1903. 318p [AEU BM LC OTMC

SET IN AUTHORITY. London, Constable, 1906. 344p [BM BVaU LC NSHD OTMC

THE SIMPLE ADVENTURES OF A MEMSAHIB. New York, Appleton, 1893. 311p [BM BVaU LC NSHD OTMC

THE STORY OF SONNY SAHIB. London, Macmillan, 1894. 114p [BM BVa LC NBFU OTMC OOP

THOSE DELIGHTFUL AMERICANS. New York, Appleton, 1902. 352p [BM BVaU LC NSHD OTU

TITLE CLEAR. A Novel. London, Hutchinson, [1922]. 288p [BM BVaU

VERNON'S AUNT. Being the Oriental Experiences of Miss Lavinia Moffatt. London, Chatto, 1894. 200p [BM LC NBFU OTMC

A VOYAGE OF CONSOLATION. ... A Sequel to ... AN AMERICAN GIRL IN LONDON. London, Methuen, 1898. 318p [BM BVaU LC NBFU OTMC

**Dunham, Bertha Mabel, 1881–1957**

KRISTLI'S TREES. Toronto, McClelland, 1948. 198p [BVaU LC NBFU OLU

TOWARD SODOM. Toronto, Macmillan, 1927. 336p [BVaU LC NSHD OTU

THE TRAIL OF THE CONESTOGA. With a foreword by W.L. Mackenzie King. Toronto, Macmillan, 1924. 341p [Another ed.: Toronto, McClelland, 1942.] [BVaU LC NBFU OTMC

THE TRAIL OF THE KING'S MEN. Toronto, Ryerson, 1931. 314p [BM BVaU NBFU OTMC

**Dunlop, James Donald**

FOREST LILY. A Novel. New York, Neely, 1898. 366p [LC

**Dunlop, William, 1792–1848**

TWO AND TWENTY YEARS AGO. A Tale of the Canadian Rebellion. By a Backwoodsman [pseud]. Toronto, Cleland's Print., 1859. 112p [Attributed to Dunlop by F.S.L. Ford. Reprinted with some changes and expansion by Sarah Anne Curzon as a serial in the *Dominion Illustrated* between Oct. 12, 1889 and Jan. 18, 1890 under the title: "In the Thick of It; a Tale of 'Thirty-Seven.'"] [OKQ

**Durie, Mrs. Anna**

JOHN DANGERFIELD'S STRANGE RE-APPEARANCE. Toronto, Best, 1933. 404p [BVaU NBFU OTP

**Durkin, Douglas Leader, 1884–1968**

THE HEART OF CHERRY MCBAIN. Toronto, Musson, 1919. 325p [BM BVaU NBFU OTMC

THE LOBSTICK TRAIL. Toronto, Musson, 1921. 334p [BM BVaU NSHD OTMC

THE MAGPIE. Toronto, Hodder, 1923. 330p [BM BVaU NBFU OTMC

MR. GRUMBLE SITS UP. New York, Liveright, 1930. 232p [BVaU LC NBFU OOP

**Duvar, John Hunter-, 1830–1899**

ANNALS OF THE COURT OF OBERON. Extracted from the Records. ... London, Digby Long, 1895. 246p [BM

**Dyer, Mary Sparks**

THROUGH THAT BRIGHT WOOD. Galt, Galt Printers, [19—?]. 39p [OLU

**E., J.**

THE OLD AND THE NEW HOME. A Canadian Tale. By J.E. Toronto, Campbell, 1870. 144p [BM OTP

**Earl, Lawrence, 1915–**

THE FROZEN JUNGLE. Toronto, McClelland, 1955. 244p

**Earle, Kathleen.**

LOSTWOOD LODGE. Toronto, Ryerson; Edinburgh, Blackwood, 1954. 352p

**East, Henry Mortimer**

THE LIFE OF "DOC" SHEPPARD; or, The Adventures of a Push-Cart. By Tamen Reysh [pseud]. Toronto, Johnston & Johnston, 1881. 62p [BVaU OTU

**Eaton, Arthur Wentworth Hamilton, 1849–1937**

TALES OF A GARRISON TOWN. By Arthur Wentworth Eaton and Craven Langstroth Betts. New York, Merrill, 1892. 250p [BM BVaU LC OTU

**Eaton, Edith Maud, 1867–1914**

MRS. SPRING FRAGRANCE. By Sui Sin Far (Edith Eaton). Chicago, McClurg, 1912. 347p [LC

**Eaton, Evelyn Sybil Mary, 1902–**

CANADIAN CIRCUS. London, Nelson, 1939. 240p [BM LC NBFU OTU

DESIRE–SPANISH VERSION. London, Chapman & Hall, 1932. 284p [BM LC NBFU

THE ENCIRCLING MIST. London, Selwyn & Blount, 1925. 131p [BM LC

FLIGHT. London, Gollancz, 1954. 207p

GIVE ME YOUR GOLDEN HAND. New York, Farrar Straus, 1951. 309p

HEART IN PILGRIMAGE. By Evelyn Eaton and Edward Roberts Moore. New York, Harper, 1948. 273p [BM LC NBFU OTMC QMM

IN WHAT TORN SHIP. New York, Harper, 1944. 263p [BM LC NBFU OTMC QMM

JOHN–FILM STAR. A Novel for Boys. London, Nelson, 1937. 246p [BM LC

MY MORTAL SIGHT. New York, Random House, 1959. 211p

PRAY TO THE EARTH. Boston, Houghton, 1938. 237p [BM LC NBFU OTMC

QUIETLY MY CAPTAIN WAITS. New York, Harper, 1940. 365p [BM BVaU LC NSHD OKQ

RESTLESS ARE THE SAILS. New York, Harper, 1941. 348p [BM BVaU LC NSHD OTMC QMM

THE SEA IS SO WIDE. New York, Harper, 1943. 281p [BM BVaU LC NBFU OTMC QMM

SUMMER DUST. London, Bles, 1936. 288p [BM LC NBFU

**Eaton, Oliver Mowat**

RODNEY AND FRANCES. A Tale of Divine and Human Love. Kingston, British Whig, 1901. 38p [BM OTL

**Eaton, Sara Lucretia (Sneath), 1928–**

INDIAN PRINCESS. Leeds, E.J. Arnold, 1953. 128p

MOCCASIN AND CROSS. Toronto, Copp Clark, 1959. 181p

**Eayrs, Hugh Smithurst, 1894–1940**

THE AMATEUR DIPLOMAT. By Hugh S. Eayrs and T.B. Costain. London, Hodder, 1917. 313p [BM BVaU

**Edelstein, Hyman, 1889–1957**

CRYING LAUGHING. Montreal, Century Pub., 1939. 126p [BVaU NBFU OKQ

THE HIGHER LOYALTY. By Don Synge [pseud]. Ottawa, Tower Books, 1946. 241p [LC NBFU OKQ

**Edmund, Henry**

BEAVER LODGE. A Story of Frontier Settlement in Northern Saskatchewan. Toronto, United Church, 1930. 75p [OTMC

**Edwards, Charles Austin McNally, 1917–**

SON OF THE MOHAWKS. Toronto, Ryerson, 1954. 188p

**Edwards, Lois (Jennings)**
MY HEART IN HIDING. New York, Morrow, 1951. 248p

**Edwards, Phil**
THE DELINQUENCY OF JOHN MEREDITH. Toronto, 1910. 224p [Adelphi cat. 60

**Edwards, Robert Chambers, 1864–1922**
BOB EDWARDS' SUMMER ANNUAL. Series 1 to 5. Toronto, Musson, 1920–24. [ACG BVaU OKQ

**Eggleston, Magdelana (Raskevich), 1907–**
MOUNTAIN SHADOWS. London, Heinemann; Toronto, British Book Service, 1955. 254p

**Eggleston, Wilfrid, 1901–**
THE HIGH PLAINS. Toronto, Macmillan, 1938. 267p [BVaU OTU QMM SSU

**Eliot, Elinor Marsden**
MY CANADA. Toronto, Hodder, 1915. 269p [BM BVaU OTMC

**Elliott, Andrew Jackson, 1899–**
THE AGING NYMPH. Toronto, Collins, 1948. 252p [BVaU NBFU OTMC QMM

**Elliott, Thomas Rose**
HUGH LAYAL. A Romance of the Up Country. Toronto, Macmillan, 1927. 263p [BVaU LC NBFU OTP QMM

**Elson, John Mebourne, 1880–**
THE SCARLET SASH. A Romance of the Old Niagara Frontier. Toronto, Dent, 1925. 308p [BM BVaU LC NSHD OTP

**Embree, Beatrice Minnie, 1886–**
THE GIRLS OF MISS CLEVELAND'S. Toronto, Musson, 1920. 180p [BM BVaU NBFU OTMC

**English, Anastasia Mary, 1864–1959**
ONLY A FISHERMAN'S DAUGHTER. By Maria [pseud]. St. John's, Manning & Rabbotts, 1899. 209p [NfSM NSHPL
"THE QUEEN OF FAIRY DELL" AND OTHER TALES. By Maria [pseud]. St. John's, Evening Herald Office, 1912. 164p [NfSM

**English, Arthur**
OGYGIA. A Tale of Old Newfoundland. Ottawa, Ru-mi-lou Books, [1930]. 278p [NfSG OTU
THE VANISHED RACE. Montreal, Garand, 1927. 154p [BVaU MWU OOP

**Estey, Emma Louisa (Spurden), 1861–**
THREE LITTLE GIRLS AND THEIR MOTTO. By E.L.S.E. Philadelphia, Am. Baptist Pub. Soc., 1893. 200p [LC

WALTER HARLEY'S CONQUEST. By E.L.S.E. Philadelphia, Am. Baptist Pub. Soc., 1889. 240p [LC

**Eustace, Cecil John, 1903–**

DAMAGED LIVES. [Novel Adaptation from a Columbia Pictures Scenario.] New York, Putnam, 1934. 221p [BM

THE SCARLET GENTLEMAN. Toronto, Macmillan, 1927. 286p [BM LC NBFU

**Evans, Allen Roy, 1885–**

ALL IN A TWILIGHT. Garden City, Doubleday, 1944. 214p [BM BVaU LC NBFU OTU

DREAM OUT OF THE DUST. A Tale of the Canadian Prairies. London, Ward Lock, 1956. 206p

NORTHWARD HO! London, Home & Van Thall, 1947. 220p [BM BVaU NBFU OTMC

REINDEER TREK. New York, Coward-McCann, 1935. 269p [Also pub. as: MEAT: A Tale of the Reindeer Trek (1929–1935). London, Hurst & Blackett, 1935. 288p] [BM BVaU LC NBFU OTMC

**Evans, Hubert Reginald, 1892–**

DERRY, AIREDALE OF THE FRONTIER. New York, Dodd Mead, 1928. 253p [BVa LC OTMC

DERRY, OF TOTEM CREEK. New York, Dodd Mead, 1930. 252p [BVaU LC OTMC

DERRY'S PARTNER. New York, Dodd Mead, 1929. 268p [BVa LC OTMC

FOREST FRIENDS. Stories of Animals, Fish and Birds, West of the Rockies. Philadelphia, Judson, 1926. 218p [BM LC

MIST ON THE RIVER. A Novel. Toronto, Copp Clark, 1954. 282p

MOUNTAIN DOG. Philadelphia, Westminster Press, 1956. 168p

THE NEW FRONT LINE. Toronto, Macmillan, 1927. 291p [BVaU OTMC QMM

THE SILENT CALL. New York, Dodd Mead, 1930. 248p [BVa LC

**F., Miss E.**

NOTHING LIKE BLACK ON WHITE. By Miss E.F. Ottawa, Maclean Roger, 1878. 158p [OTMC

**Fairchild, George Moore, 1854–1912**

THE MAID OF THE MOUNTAIN. Toronto, Rous & Mann, 1932. [BM BVaU NBFU OTMC

A RIDICULOUS COURTING, and Other Stories of French Canada. Chicago, Donnelley, 1900. 261p [BVaU LC NBFU OTMC

**Falkner, Frederick Benjamin, 1902–**

THE AQUALUNG TWINS AND THE 'IRON CRAB.' Toronto, Dent, 1959. 188p

THE AQUALUNG TWINS FIND CHINESE TREASURE. Toronto, Dent, 1956. 167p

**Farran, Roy Alexander St. Thomas Aquinas, 1921–**

THE DAY AFTER TOMORROW. London, Panther Books, 1959. 158p [Earlier ed.: London, Collins, 1956.]

THE SEARCH. London, Collins, 1958. 253p

**Faughnan, Thomas, *fl.* 1835–1883**

THE YOUNG HUSSAR; or, Lady Iris's Adventure. A Story of Love and War. Picton, Ont., Author, 1890. 484p [BVaU NSHD OTP

**Fenety, George Edward, 1812–1899**

THE LADY AND THE DRESSMAKER; or, A Peep at Fashionable Folly. By a Bluenose [pseud]. Halifax, Author, 1842. 24p [Also bound with a continuation added to make a total of 136p] [BVaU NSHP

**Fennell, Irene**

GHOST LIGHT. New York, Pegasus Pub. Co., 1939. 154p [NBFU OTU

**Ferguson, Ida May**

TISAB TING; or, The Electrical Kiss. By Dyjan Fergus [pseud]. Toronto, Hunter Rose, 1896. 300p [BM BVaU NSHD OOP

**Fewster, Edna Lysle.**

LENGTHENING SHADOWS. A Novel. New York, Pageant Press, 1957. 94p

**Field, Bradda, 1904–**

BRIDE OF GLORY. Being the Strange Story of Emy Lyon. New York, Greystone, 1942. 963p [Pub. in England as: MILEDI. Being the Strange Story of Emy Lyon. London, Constable, 1942. 979p] [BM BVaU LC NBFU OTMC

THE EARTHEN LOT. New York, Harcourt, 1928. 400p [BM BVaU LC NBFU

GRAND HARBOUR. London, Constable, 1934. 400p [BM LC NBFU

SMALL TOWN. London, Constable, 1931. 310p [BVaU LC NBFU OTU

**Findlay, David Kilpatrick, 1901–**

SEARCH FOR AMELIA. Philadelphia, Lippincott, 1958. 256p

**Fischer, William Joseph, 1879–1921**

CHILD OF DESTINY. Toronto, Briggs, 1908. 272p [BM OTMC

WINONA AND OTHER STORIES. St. Louis, Mo., Herder, 1906. 219p [OTMC

**Fisher, Olive Margaret, 1889–**

TOTEM, TIPI AND TUMPLINE. Stories of Canadian Indians. By Olive M. Fisher and Clara L. Tyner. Toronto, Dent, 1955. xi + 264p

**Flatt, Mrs. Olive Augusta, 1884–**

GRANDMA'S SHORT STORIES. Hamilton, Davis-Lisson, 1951. 95p

**Flatt, W.D.**

THE MAKING OF A MAN. Toronto, Briggs, 1918. 154p [BM BVaU NBFU OTMC

**Fleet, William Henry**

HOW I CAME TO BE GOVERNOR OF THE ISLAND OF CACONA. By The Hon. Francis Thistleton [pseud]. Montreal, etc., Ramsay, etc., 1852. 220p [BVaU OTP QMM

**Fleming, May Agnes (Early), 1840–1880**

THE ACTRESS' DAUGHTER. New York, Carleton, 1886. 394p [BM LC NBS

THE BARONET'S BRIDE; or, A Woman's Vengeance. Ed. by W.J. Benners, Jr. New York, Munro, 1892. 250p [LC

CARRIED BY STORM. New York, Carleton, 1880. 440p [Also: New York, Dillingham, 1907. 398p] [LC NBFU OTMC

A CHANGED HEART. A Novel. New York, Carleton, 1881. [Later ed.: New York, Dillingham, 1897. 480p] [AmCat OTU

THE DARK SECRET; or, The Mystery of Fontelle Hall. New York, Hurst, 1875. 361p [AEU NBFU

EDITH PERCIVAL. A Novel. New York, Dillingham, 1893. 330p [First pub. in 1860?–BCF] [LC

ERMINIE; or, The Gipsy's Vow. A Tale of Love and Vengeance. New York, Brady, 1863. [Probably same as: GYPSY QUEEN'S VOW. New York, Beadle, 1870.] [AmCat

ESTELLA'S HUSBAND; or, Thrice Lost, Thrice Won. New York, Munro, 1891. 291p [Later pub. under title: THRICE LOST, THRICE WON.] [LC OTU

FATED TO MARRY; [and] A NIGHT OF TERROR; [and] KATHLEEN. New York, Ogilvie, 1881. [AmCat

THE GHOST OF RIVERDALE HAL. New York, Lupton, 1895. 62p [LC

GUY EARLSCOURT'S WIFE. A Novel. New York, Carleton, [1872?]. [Later ed.: New York, Dillingham, 1900. 484p] [LC NBFU

THE GYPSY QUEEN'S VOW. New York, Hurst, 1875. 399p [NBFU

THE HEIR OF CHARLTON; A Story of Shaddeck Light. New York, Dillingham, 1905. 396p [First pub., 1878] [AmCat LC NBFU OKQ

THE HEIRESS OF GLEN GOWER; or, The Hidden Crime. Ed. by W.J. Benners, Jr. New York, Munro, 1892. 251p [LC

KATE DANTON; or, Captain Danton's Daughters. New York, Carleton, 1876. 436p [LC OTMC QMBM

LA MASQUE; or, The Midnight Queen. New York, Brady, 1863. [Later pub. as: THE MIDNIGHT QUEEN. New York, Dillingham, 1888. 396p] [BM LC NSHD OTMC

LADY EVELYN; or, The Lord of Royal Rest. New York, Street & Smith, 1899. 262p [LC

LOST FOR A WOMAN. A Novel. New York, Carleton, 1880. 456p [LC NBFU OTMC

A MAD MARRIAGE. A Novel. New York, Carleton, 1875. 459p [BM LC NBFU

MAGDALEN'S VOW. Ed. by W.J. Benners, Jr. New York, Munro, 1893. 286p [LC OTU

MARRIED FOR MONEY, AND OTHER STORIES. New York, Ogilvie, 1891. 246p [LC

MAUDE PERCY'S SECRET. A Novel. New York, Carleton, 1884. 432p [LC

NORINE'S REVENGE, [and] SIR NOEL'S HEIR. New York, Dillingham, 1888. 402p [First pub. in 1875?–BCF] [LC NBFU

ONE NIGHT'S MYSTERY. New York, Carleton, [1876?]. [Later ed.: New York, Dillingham, 1897. 443p] [AmCat NBFU

PATRICIA KEMBLEY. A Novel. Toronto, Rose Belford, 1882. 479p [OTMC

A PRETTY GOVERNESS, AND OTHER STORIES. New York, Ogilvie, 1891. 218p [LC

PRIDE AND PASSION. A Novel. New York, Carleton, 1882. 416p [LC

THE SECRET SORROW. New York, Ogilvie, 1883. 341p [LC

SHARING HER CRIME. A Novel. New York, Carleton, 1883. 384p [LC

SHE MIGHT HAVE DONE BETTER. A Novel. Toronto, Rose Pub. Co., n.d. 240p [OH

SILENT AND TRUE; or, A Little Queen. New York, Carleton, 1877. 460p [LC NBFU

SIR NOEL'S HEIR. A Novel. New York, Lupton, 1892. 123p [See also under NORINE'S REVENGE.] [LC NBS

THE SISTERS OF TORWOOD. A Novel. New York, Dillingham, 1898. 316p [Earlier ed.: London, Henderson, 1890.] [BM BVaU LC

SYBIL CAMPBELL; or, The Queen of the Isle. New York, Brady, 1863. 151p [Also pub. as: AN AWFUL MYSTERY. New York, Beadle, 1875; and as: THE QUEEN OF THE ISLE. New York, Dillingham, 1886. 400p –LC] [BM LC OTU

A TERRIBLE SECRET. New York, Carleton, [1874?]. [Later ed.: New York, Dillingham, 1897. 410p] [AmCat NBFU

THE THREE COUSINS, [and] ONE SUMMER MONTH. New York, Ogilvie, 1881. [AmCat

THE TWIN SISTERS; or, The Wronged Wife's Hate. New York, Starr, 1869. [Also pub. under title: THE RIVAL BROTHERS; or, The Wronged Wife's Hate. New York, Beadle, 1875. 224p] [AmCat NBFL

UNCLE FRED'S VISIT AND HOW IT ENDED. London, Mowbray, [1888]. 51p [BM

THE UNSEEN BRIDEGROOM; or, Wedded for a Week. Ed. by W.J. Benners, Jr. New York, Munro, 1892. 217p [LC

VICTORIA; or, The Heiress of Castle Cliffe. New York, Brady, 1864. 124p [Later pub. under title: UNMASKED; or, The Heiress of Castle Cliffe. New York, Beadle, 1870.] [BM LC OTU

THE VIRGINIA HEIRESS. New York, Street & Smith, 1888. 239p [LC OTU

WEDDED FOR PIQUE. A Novel. New York, Dillingham, 1897. 302p [LC NBFL

WHO WINS? or, The Secret of Monkswood Waste. New York, Munro, 1895. 225p [LC OTU

A WIFE'S TRAGEDY. A Novel. New York, Carleton, 1881. 431p [Also: Toronto, Rose Belford, 1881. 297p] [LC OTMC

A WONDERFUL WOMAN. A Novel. New York, Dillingham, 1888. [First pub. in 1873? Also: Toronto, J. Ross Robertson, 1881. 109p; and New York, Dillingham, 1901. 544p] [AmCat LC NSHD OTMC

A WRONGED WIFE. New York, Dillingham, 1883. [Same as THE TWIN SISTERS?] [AmCat

**Flewellyn, Julia (Colliton), 1850–**

FORGOTTEN CHILDREN. Anderson, Ind., Gospel Trumpet Co., 1929. 189p [LC

HILL-CREST. Toronto, Cooper, 1894. 269p [Also: Boston, Arena, 1895. 304p] [LC OTMC

**Floroff, Peter C.N.**

THE FAWN. New York, Vantage Press, 1958. 115p

**Foley, Pearl Beatrix, –1953**

THE GIFT OF THE GODS. Toronto, Allen, 1921. 279p [BM LC NBFU OTMC

THE GNOME MINE MYSTERY. A Northern Ontario Mining Story. By Paul de Mar [pseud]. London, Hamilton, 1933. 255p [BM BVaU NBFU

THE OCTAGON CRYSTAL. New York, Carrier, 1929. 265p [BM LC NBFU OTMC

THE YELLOW CIRCLE. Philadelphia, Lippincott, 1937. 315p [BM LC NBFU OTMC

**Fontaine, Robert Louis, 1911–1965**

THE HAPPY TIME. New York, Simon & Schuster, 1945. 269p [BM BVaU NBFU OTU

MY UNCLE LOUIS. New York, Toronto, McGraw-Hill, 1953. 294p

**Footner, Hulbert, 1879–1944**

THE ALMOST PERFECT MURDER. Philadelphia, Lippincott, 1937. 319p [BM LC NBFU OTMC

ANTENNAE. New York, Doran, 1926. 350p [Same as RICH MAN, POOR MAN, *q.v.*] [LC NBFU

ANYBODY'S PEARLS. Garden City, Doubleday, 1930. 325p [BM LC NBFU OTMC

A BACKWOODS PRINCESS. New York, Doran, 1926. 320p [BM BVaU LC NBFU OOP

CAP'N SUE. London, Hodder, 1927. 320p [BM LC NBFU

THE CASUAL MURDERER. Philadelphia, Lippincott, 1937. 337p [BM LC NBFU OTMC

THE CHASE OF THE "LINDA BELLE." London, Hodder, 1925. 320p [BM

COUNTRY LOVE, ETC. London, Hodder, 1922. 319p [BM

DANGEROUS CARGO. New York, Harper, 1934. 339p [BM BVaU LC OTMC

THE DARK SHIPS. New York, Harper, 1937. 384p [BM LC NBFU OTMC

DEAD MAN'S HAT. New York, Harper, 1932. 299p [BM BVaU LC NBFU

THE DEATH OF A CELEBRITY. New York, Harper, 1938. 278p [BM LC OOP

DEATH OF A SABOTEUR. New York, Harper, 1943. 282p [BM LC OTMC
THE DEAVES AFFAIR. Toronto, McClelland, 1922. 319p [BM BVaU LC NBFU OTMC
THE DOCTOR WHO HELD HANDS. A Madame Storey Novel. Garden City, Doubleday, 1929. 310p [BM BVaU LC NBFU OTMC
EASY TO KILL. New York, Harper, 1931. 312p [BM BVaU LC OTMC
THE FOLDED PAPER MYSTERY. London, Collins, 1930. 250p [See THE MYSTERY OF THE FOLDED PAPER, below.] [BM
THE FUGITIVE SLEUTH. London, Hodder, 1918. 268p [BM SSU
THE FUR BRINGERS. A Story of the Canadian Northwest. New York, McCann, 1920. 313p [BM BVaU LC NBFU OTMC
THE HOUSE WITH THE BLUE DOOR. New York, Harper, 1942. 280p [BM NBFU OOP
THE HUNTRESS. New York, McCann, 1922. 312p [BM BVa LC NBFU
ISLAND OF FEAR. London, Cassell, 1936. 287p [BM LC NBFU OOP
JACK CHANTY. A Story of Athabasca. Garden City, Doubleday, 1913. 337p [BVaU LC NBFU OTMC QMM
MADAME STOREY. New York, Doran, 1926. 341p [*Cf.* THE KIDNAPPING OF MADAME STOREY AND OTHER STORIES. London, Collins, 1936. 284p] [BM LC NBFU OTMC
MORE THAN BREAD. Philadelphia, Lippincott, 1938. 365p [BM LC NBFU OTMC
MURDER IN THE SUN. London, Collins, 1938. 252p [BM
THE MURDER OF A BAD MAN. New York, Harper, 1936. 306p [BM LC OOP
MURDER RUNS IN THE FAMILY. New York, Harper, 1934. 258p [BM LC NBFU OOP
THE MURDER THAT HAD EVERYTHING. New York, Harper, 1939. 307p [BM LC OTMC
MURDERER'S VANITY. New York, Harper, 1940. 306p [BM LC NBFU
THE MYSTERY OF THE FOLDED PAPER. New York, Harper, 1930. 350p [BVaU LC NBFU OTU
THE NATION'S MISSING GUEST. New York, Harper, 1939. 270p [BM LC NBFU OOP
A NEW GIRL IN TOWN. London, Hodder, 1927. 327p [BM
THE NEW MADE GRAVE. London, Collins, 1935. 284p [BM LC
ON SWAN RIVER. London, Hodder, 1919. 314p [BM NBFU
THE OBEAH MURDERS. New York, Harper, 1937. 279p [LC
OFFICER! Toronto, McClelland, 1924. 279p [BM LC OTP
ORCHIDS TO MURDER. New York, Harper, 1945. 244p [BM BVaU NBFU OTMC
THE OWL TAXI. New York, Doran, 1921. 309p [BM BVaU LC OTMC
THE QUEEN OF CLUBS. New York, Doran, 1927. 313p [BM BVaU NBFU OTMC
THE RAMSHACKLE HOUSE. New York, Doran, 1922. 311p [BM LC OTP

RICH MAN, POOR MAN. London, Faber, 1928. 286p [Same as ANTENNAE, *q.v.*] [BM

THE RING OF EYES. London, Collins, 1933. 252p [BM LC NBFU

ROGER MANION'S GIRL. New York, Harper, 1935. 303p [BM

SCARRED JUNGLE. New York, Harper, 1935. 303p [BM LC NBFU OTMC

THE SEALED VALLEY. Toronto, Musson, 1914. 356p [BM BViPA LC OTMC

A SELF-MADE THIEF. Garden City, Doubleday, 1929. 285p [LC OTMC

THE SHANTY SLED. New York, Doran, 1926. 294p [BM BVaU LC NBFU OTP

SINFULLY RICH. New York, Harper, 1940. 348p [BM BVaU LC NBFU OTMC

THE SUBSTITUTE MILLIONAIRE. New York, Doran, 1919. 350p [BM LC OTMC

THIEVES WIT. An Everyday Detective Story. New York, Doran, 1918. 345p [BM LC OTMC

TORTUOUS TRAILS. [Detective Stories.] London, Collins, 1937. 283p [BM

TRIAL BY WATER. New York, Farrar & Rinehart, 1931. 321p [BM LC NBFU OOP

TWO ON THE TRAIL. A Story of the Far Northwest. Garden City, Doubleday, 1911. 349p [BM BVaU LC OTMC

THE UNDER DOGS. New York, Doran, 1925. 325p [BM LC NBFU OTP

UNNEUTRAL MURDER. New York, Harper, 1944. 254p [BM LC NBFU OTMC

THE VELVET HAND. New Madame Storey Mysteries. Garden City, Doubleday, 1928. 333p [BM BVaU LC OTMC

THE VIPER. London, Collins, 1930. 245p [BM BVaU OTMC

THE WHIP-POOR-WILL MYSTERY. New York, Harper, 1935. 338p [BM LC OOP

WHO KILLED THE HUSBAND? New York, Harper, 1941. 208p [BM LC OTMC

THE WILD BIRD. New York, Doran, 1923. 282p [BM BVaU LC OTMC

THE WOMAN FROM "OUTSIDE." New York, McCann, 1921. 268p [LC OTMC

**Ford, John David, 1912–**

FEAST OF THE MIDNIGHT SUN. A Story of the Canadian Arctic. New York, Greenwich Book Pub., 1958. 94p

**Forrest, Edmund William, –1880**

NED FORTESCUE; or, Roughing it through Life. A Story founded on Fact. Ottawa, Hunter, 1869. 232p [2nd ed.: Montreal, Author, 1871. 365p] [BVaU NBFU OTMC

VELLENAUX. A Novel. Saint John, "Daily News," 1870. 262p [BVaU NSHD OTMC

**Forster, Agnes J.**

DOORS AWAITING. New York, Ryerson, 1940. 245p [NBFU OTU

**Fortier, Cora B.**

UNKNOWN FAIRIES OF CANADA. Twelve Fairy Stories. By Maxine [pseud]. Toronto, Macmillan, 1926. 90p [NBFU OTU

**Fox, Marion Wathen, 1871–1956**

MIDGET STORIES FOR BUSY PEOPLE. No. 1. Saint John, Barnes Hopkins, 1954. 16p

**Frame, Elizabeth, 1820–1913**

THE TWILIGHT OF FAITH. Toronto, 1872. 128p [Earlier ed.: Boston, 1871.] [BM NSHP

**Frank, Mrs. M.J.**

THE BROCK FAMILY. By A.L.O.M. (A Lady of Manitoba) [pseud]. Toronto, Briggs, 1890. 263p [OTU

**Fraser, Annie Ermatinger, –1930**

THE DRUM OF LANORAYE. A Narrative of the Days of Talon, the Great Intendant. Toronto, Ryerson, 1932. 308p [BVaU NBFU OTMC QMM

**Fraser, Francess Jane (Williams), 1922–**

THE BEAR WHO STOLE THE CHINOOK, AND OTHER STORIES. By Frances Fraser. Toronto, Macmillan, 1959. 72p

**Fraser, Thurlow, 1869–1926**

THE CALL OF THE EAST. A Romance of Far Formosa. Toronto, Briggs, 1914. 351p [BVaU LC OTMC

**Fraser, William Alexander, 1859–1933**

THE BLOOD LILIES. New York, Scribner, 1903. 262p [BM BVaU NBFU OTMC

BRAVE HEARTS. New York, Scribner, 1904. 307p [BM BVaU LC OTMC

BULLDOG CARNEY. Toronto, McClelland, 1919. 306p [BM BVaU LC NBFU OTMC

CASTE. New York, Doran, 1922. 274p [BM BVaU LC NBFU OTMC

DELILAH PLAYS THE PONIES. Toronto, Musson, 1927. 319p [BVaU NBFU OTMC QMM

THE EYE OF A GOD AND OTHER TALES OF EAST AND WEST. New York, Doubleday, 1899. 260p [BVaU LC MWU OTMC QMM

THE LONE FURROW. New York, Appleton, 1907. 354p [BM BVaU LC NBFU OTMC

MOOSWA & OTHERS OF THE BOUNDARIES. New York, Scribner, 1900. 260p [Also later eds.: Toronto, Ryerson.] [BM BVaU LC OKQ

THE OUTCASTS. Toronto, Briggs, 1901. 137p [BVaU LC NSHD OKQ

RED MEEKINS. New York, Doran, 1921. 297p [BVaU LC NBFU OTMC

THE SA'-ZADA TALES. New York, Scribner, 1905. 231p [BM BVaU LC NSHD OTMC

THIRTEEN MEN. New York, Appleton, 1906. 305p [BM LC OTMC QMM

THOROUGHBREDS. New York, McClure, 1902. 405p [BM BVaU LC NBFU OKQ

THE THREE SAPPHIRES. New York, Doran, 1918. 321p [BVaU LC NBFU OTMC

**Fraser, William Ross, 1908–**
A WHITE STONE. A Novel. New York, Philosophical Library, 1955. 188p

**Frazer, Miss C.A.**
ATMA. A Romance. By A.C.F. [pseud]. Montreal, Lovell, 1891. 143p [BVaU LC NBFU OKQ

**Frechette, Annie Thomas (Howells)**
THE FARM'S LITTLE PEOPLE. Sequel to ON GRANDFATHER'S FARM. Philadelphia, Am. Baptist Pub., 1897. 107p [LC OOP
ON GRANDFATHER'S FARM. Philadelphia, Am. Baptist Soc., 1897. 85p [LC OOP
REUBEN DALE. 1873. [BCF

**Freedman, Frank, 1917–**
THIS SIDE OF HOLMAN'S HILL. London, Secker & Warburg, 1957. 197p

**Freeman, John Dolliver, 1864–1943**
KENNEDY'S SECOND BEST. A Story of the Great Northwest. Toronto, McClelland, 1926. 302p [BM BVaU NBFU OTMC

**French, John McLean, 1863–1940**
THE TRAIL OF DESTINY. A Romance of the Canadian Bush. New York, Burt, 1924. 317p [BViV OH

**French, Maida (Parlow)**
ALL THIS TO KEEP. Toronto, Collins, 1947. 354p [BVaU LC NBFU OTMC
BOUGHS BEND OVER. Toronto, McClelland, 1943. 246p [BVaU LC NBFU OKQ QMM

**Freund, Philip, 1909–**
BOOK OF KINGS. A Novel. New York, Pilgrim, 1938. 254p [LC
THE DARK SHORE. A Novel. New York, Ives Washburn, 1941. 296p [BM LC NBFU OTMC
DREAMS OF YOUTH. New York, Pilgrim, 1938. 234p [LC NBFU
EASTER ISLAND. New York, Beechhurst, 1947. 221p [LC NBFU
EDWARD ZOLTAN. New York, Beechhurst, 1946. 200p [BVaU LC OTMC
THE EVENING HERON. New York, Pilgrim, 1937. 218p [BM LC NBFU OTMC
A MAN OF TASTE, AND OTHER STORIES. New York, Beechhurst, 1949. 357p [BVaU LC NBFU
THE MERRY COMMUNIST. New York, Pilgrim, 1934. 116p [LC NBFU
THE SNOW AND OTHER STORIES. New York, Pilgrim, 1935. 226p [LC NBFU
STEPHANIE'S SON. A Novel. New York, Beechhurst, 1947. 373p [LC OTMC
THREE EXOTIC TALES. New York, Pilgrim, 1945. 239p [LC NBFU
THE YOUNG GREEK AND THE CREOLE, AND OTHER STORIES. New York, Pilgrim, 1944. 271p [LC NBFU
THE ZOLTANS. New York, Beechhurst, 1948. 3v [Includes BOOK OF KINGS, EDWARD ZOLTAN, STEPHANIE'S SON.] [BVaU LC NBFU

**Frost, J.W.**

BROKEN SHACKLES. The Story of a Fugitive Slave. By Glenelg [pseud]. Toronto, Briggs, 1889. 304p [BCF OTMC

**Fry, Pamela**

HARSH EVIDENCE. London, Wingate, 1953. 172p

THE WATCHING CAT. London, Davies, 1960. 223p

**Fuller, James William, 1871–**

IZOLDA. A Magyar Romance. New York, Abbey, 1902. 228p [LC OLU

**Furse, Barbara Ross**

CROCODILE TEARS. London, Long, 1935. 287p [BM OTU

**Fytche, Maria Amelia, 1844–1927**

KERCHIEFS TO HUNT SOULS. A Novel. Boston, Arena, 1895. 290p [BM LC

THE RIVAL FORTS; or, The Velvet Siege of Beauséjour. Halifax, A. McNeil, 1907. 369p [NBFU OOP

**G., E.A.**

A SUMMER HOLIDAY. By E.A.G. Toronto, Briggs, 1887. 38p [Haight Pt I

**Gagnieur, Elizabeth**

BACK IN THE FIFTIES; or, Winnings and Weedings. A Tale of Tractarian Times. By Elizabeth Gagnieur (Alba). Montreal, Sadlier, 1907. 437p [OOP

**Galbraith, John**

IN THE NEW CAPITAL; or, The City of Ottawa in 1999. Toronto, Toronto News, 1897. 151p [BM OTU

**Gale, James Scarth, 1863–1937**

KOREAN SKETCHES. Toronto, Revell, 1899. 256p [BM LC NBFU

THE VANGUARD. A Tale of Korea. Toronto, Revell, 1904. 320p [BM LC

**Gallant, Mavis, 1922–**

GREEN WATER, GREEN SKY. Boston, Houghton, 1959. 154p

THE OTHER PARIS. Stories. Boston, Houghton, 1956. 240p

**Galloway, Christian F.J.**

THE EXPLOITS OF LANCELOT. [A Tale.] London, Stockwell, 1924. 35p [BM

**Gamble, Henry Elliot**

D'ARCY. A Romantic Thriller. Toronto, Ryerson, 1947. 131p [OTMC

**Ganong, Joan**

ANGIE AND THE ARAB. Fredericton, Brunswick Press, 1957. 56p

**Gardner, Elizabeth Mary (Vidal), 1857–1932**

CHARACTERISTIC CONVERSATIONS OF CURLY KATE. Toronto, Briggs, 1907. 47p [Phelps p92

**Gardner, Mrs. Elsie Bell**

MAXIE, AN ADORABLE GIRL; or, Her Adventures in the British West Indies. New York, Cupples, 1932. 207p [LC

MAXIE AT BRINKSOME HALL; or, Strange Adventures with her Chums. New York, Cupples, 1934. 212p [LC

MAXIE AND HER ADVENTURES IN SPAIN; or, The Rescue of a Royalist. New York, Cupples, 1936. 205p [LC

MAXIE AND THE GOLDEN BIRD. New York, Cupples, 1939. 210p [LC

MAXIE IN THE JUNGLE; or, The Temple of the Incas. New York, Cupples, 1937. 209p [LC

MAXIE IN VENEZUELA; or, The Clue to the Diamond Mine. New York, Cupples, 1932. 200p [LC

MAXIE SEARCHING FOR HER PARENTS; or, The Mystery in Australian Waters. New York, Cupples, 1932. 204p [LC

**Garner, Hugh, 1913–**

CABBAGETOWN. Toronto, Collins, 1950. 160p [NBFU OLU

PRESENT RECKONING. Toronto, Collins, 1951. 158p

STORM BELOW. Toronto, Collins, 1949. 227p [BVaU NBFU OTMC QMM

WASTE NO TEARS. By Jarvis Warwick [pseud]. New Toronto, Export Pub. Enterprises, 1951. [Priv. info.

THE YELLOW SWEATER, AND OTHER STORIES. Toronto, Collins, 1952. 238p

**Garrioch, Rev. Alfred Campbell, 1848–1934**

THE FAR AND FURRY NORTH. A Story of Love and Travel in the Days of the Hudson's Bay Co. Winnipeg, Douglass McIntyre, 1925. 238p [BVaU NBFU OTMC QMBM SSU

**Genest, Frank Devlin, 1894–1944**

THE LETTERS OF SI WHIFFLETREE, FRESHMAN. With a preface by Stephen Leacock. Montreal, 1921. 69p [BM BVaU NBFU OTMC

**Gibbon, John Murray, 1875–1952**

THE CONQUERING HERO. Toronto, Gundy, 1920. 288p [BM BVaU NSHD OTMC QMM

DRUMS AFAR. An International Romance. London, Lane, 1918. 352p [BM BVaU NBFU OTMC QMM

EYES OF A GYPSY. Toronto, Macmillan, 1926. 255p [BM BVaU NBFU OTMC

HEARTS AND FACES. The Adventure of a Soul. Toronto, Gundy, 1916. 352p [BM BVaU NBFU OTU

PAGAN LOVE. Toronto, McClelland, 1922. 310p [BVaU NBFU OTU QMM

THE TRUE ANNALS OF FAIRYLAND IN THE REIGN OF KING COLE. Ed. by ——. London, Dent, 1909. 338p [BVaU LC NBFU OTMC

**Gibbons, Charles Harrison, 1869–**

A SOURDOUGH SAMARITAN. Toronto, Hodder, 1923. 320p [BVaU NBFU OOP

**Gibbs, Willa, 1917–**

THE DEAN. London, Hodder, 1957. 190p [Same as ALL THE GOLDEN DOORS. New York, Appleton, 1957.]

SIMON OF LEICESTER. London, Hodder, 1960. 313p

THE TWO DOCTORS. A Novel. London, Hodder, 1959. 222p [Pub. in U.S. as THE DEDICATED, New York, Morrow, 1960. 224p]

**Gill, Rev. Edward Anthony Wharton, 1858–1944**

AN IRISHMAN'S LUCK. A Tale of Manitoba. Toronto, Musson, 1914. [Also: London, Hodder, 1914. 310p] [BM OOP

LOVE IN MANITOBA. London, Swift, 1911. 315p [Also: Toronto, Musson, 1912.] [BM BVaU OOP

A MANITOBA CHORE BOY. The Experiences of a Young Emigrant Told from his Letters. London, Religious Tract Soc., 1912. 83p [BM BVaU OTU SSU

**Gill, T.M.**

THE HEART OF LUNENBURG. By Sabattis [pseud]. Levis, Que., Author, 1930. 96p [OTP

THE LURE OF THE CITY. By Sabattis [pseud]. Sackville, N.B., Tribune Press, n.d. 129p [OTU

**Gillen, Mollie (Woolnough)**

A STAR OF DEATH. London, Bles, 1960. 255p

**Gillese, John Patrick, 1926–**

KIRBY'S GANDER. Toronto, Ryerson, 1957. ix + 212p

**Gillis, James Donald, 1870–**

A MARITIMES LIFE. A Romance: The Life of Kalby MacKee. Melrose Hill, Inverness Co., N.S., Author, n.d. 126p [mimeographed]

THE PIE SOCIAL. A Modern Romance. Melrose Hill, Inverness Co., N.S., Author, n.d. 74p [mimeographed]

**Ginsburg, Bere Joseph, 1894–**

GENERATION PASSETH ... GENERATION COMETH. Toronto, Ryerson, 1960. 215p

**Glasier, Alfred A.**

THE IRVING CLUB AMONG THE WHITE HILLS. Saint John, Godard, 1877. 113p [NSWA OONL

**Glassco, John, 1909–**

UNDER THE BIRCH. The Story of an English Governess. By Miles Underwood [pseud]. Paris, France, Ophelia Press, 1965. 187p [First pub. in 1960, with title: THE ENGLISH GOVERNESS.]

**Glay, George Albert, 1905?–**
BEGGARS MIGHT RIDE. New York, Appleton, 1951. 341p
GINA. New York, Pellegrini, 1948. 378p [BM LC

**Glendinning, Margarite**
GERTIE, THE HORSE WHO THOUGHT AND THOUGHT. New York, Whittlesey House, 1951. 88p

**Godfrey, Denis, 1912–**
THE BRIDGE OF FIRE. London, Cape, 1954. 285p
WHEN KINGS ARE ARMING. Toronto, Clarke Irwin, 1951. 224p

**Godfrey, J.J.**
SHAVINGS. A Semi-Legal Medley. Pt. 1. Toronto, Poole, 1907. 46p [BM BVaU LC OTUV

**Gomery, Percy, 1881–1960**
CURVE, GO SLOW. A Romance of the Pacific Coast. Ottawa, Graphic, 1927. 333p [BVaU NBFU OTU QMM
END OF THE CIRCLE. Toronto, Macmillan, 1929. 266p [BVaU NBFU OTMC

**Goosequill (pseud)**
AS OTHERS SEE US. Being the Diary of a Canadian Debutante. By "Goosequill" [pseud]. Toronto, Macmillan, 1915. 299p [BM BVaU NSWA OLU

**Gordon, Charles G. William, 1899–**
GRINGO. Garden City, Doubleday, 1930. 355p [LC NBFU

**Gordon, Rev. Charles William, 1860–1937**
THE ARM OF GOLD. By Ralph Connor [pseud]. New York, Dodd Mead, 1932. 314p [BM BVaU LC NBFU OTMC
BEYOND THE MARSHES. By Ralph Connor [pseud]. Toronto, Westminster, 1898. 19p [BM BVaU LC NSHD OTMC
BLACK ROCK. A Tale of the Selkirks. By Ralph Connor [pseud]. Toronto, Westminster, 1898. 327p [BM BVaU LC NBFU OTMC QMM
BREAKING THE RECORD. By Ralph Connor [pseud]. New York, Revell, 1904. 31p [LC NBFU OKQ
CORPORAL CAMERON OF THE NORTH WEST MOUNTED POLICE. A Tale of the Macleod Trail. By Ralph Connor [pseud]. New York, Hodder, 1912. 454p [BM BVaU LC NSHD OTMC QMM
THE DOCTOR. A Tale of the Rockies. By Ralph Connor [pseud]. Toronto, Westminster, 1906. 399p [Pub. in England under title: THE DOCTOR OF CROW'S NEST. London, Hodder, 1906. 399p] [BM BVaU LC NBFU OTMC QMM

THE FOREIGNER. A Tale of Saskatchewan. By Ralph Connor [pseud]. Toronto, Westminster, 1909. 384p [Also as: THE SETTLER. A Tale of Saskatchewan. London, Hodder. 1909. 307p] [BM BVaU LC NSHD OTMC

THE FRIENDLY FOUR, AND OTHER STORIES. By Ralph Connor [pseud]. New York, Doran, 1926. 275p [BM BVaU LC NBFU OTMC QMM

THE GASPARDS OF PINE CROFT. A Romance of the Windermere. By Ralph Connor [pseud]. Toronto, McClelland, 1923. 318p [BM BVaU LC NBFU OTMC QMM

THE GAY CRUSADER. A Romance of Quebec. By Ralph Connor [pseud]. New York, Dodd Mead, 1936. 376p [BVaU LC NBFU OTMC

THE GIRL FROM GLENGARRY. By Ralph Connor [pseud]. New York, Dodd Mead, 1933. 312p [Also as: THE GLENGARRY GIRL. London, Lane, 1934. 341p [BM BVaU LC NBFU OTMC

GLENGARRY SCHOOL DAYS. A Story of Early Days in Glengarry. By Ralph Connor [pseud]. Chicago, Revell, 1902. 340p [Also as: GLENGARRY DAYS. London, Hodder, 1902. 252p] [BM BVaU LC NBFU OTU QMM

GWEN. An Idyll of the Canyon. By Ralph Connor [pseud]. New York, Revell, 1904. 94p [Reprinting of chapters 9–13 of THE SKY PILOT.] [BM BVaU LC NBFU OTMC

GWEN'S CANYON. By Ralph Connor [pseud]. Toronto, Westminster, 1898. 30p [BM

HE DWELT AMONG US. By Ralph Connor [pseud]. New York, Revell, 1936. 174p [BM BVaU LC NBFU OTMC

THE MAJOR. By Ralph Connor [pseud]. Toronto, McClelland, 1917. 383p [BM BVaU LC NBFU OTMC

THE MAN FROM GLENGARRY. A Tale of the Ottawa. By Ralph Connor [pseud]. Toronto, Westminster, 1901. 473p [Also, with intro. by S.R. Beharriell: Toronto, McClelland, 1960. xiii + 289p] [BM BVaU LC NBFU OTU QMM

MICHAEL McGRATH, POSTMASTER. London, Sharpe, 1900. 42p [BM

THE PATROL OF THE SUN DANCE TRAIL. By Ralph Connor [pseud]. New York, Doran, 1914. 363p [BM BVaU LC NBFU OTU

THE PILOT AT SWAN CREEK [and Other Stories]. London, Hodder, 1905. 184p [BM BVaU NBFU OKQ

THE PROSPECTOR. A Tale of the Crow's Nest Pass. By Ralph Connor [pseud]. New York, Revell, 1904. 401p [BM BVaU LC NBFU OKQ

THE REBEL LOYALIST. By Ralph Connor [pseud]. Toronto, McClelland, 1935. 328p [BM BVaU LC NBFU OTMC

THE ROCK AND THE RIVER. A Romance of Quebec. By Ralph Connor [pseud]. New York, Dodd Mead, 1931. 377p [BM BVaU LC NSHD OKQ

THE RUNNER. A Romance of the Niagaras. By Ralph Connor [pseud]. Garden City, Doubleday, 1929. 481p [BM BVaU LC NBFU OTMC

THE SKY PILOT. A Tale of the Foothills. By Ralph Connor [pseud]. Chicago, Revell, 1899. 300p [BM BVaU LC NBFU OKQ

THE SKY PILOT IN NO MAN'S LAND. By Ralph Connor [pseud]. Toronto, McClelland, 1919. 349p [BM BVaU LC NBFU OTMC QMM

THE SWAN CREEK BLIZZARD. By Ralph Connor [pseud]. New York, Revell, 1904. 29p [*Cf.* THE PILOT AT SWAN CREEK ..., above.] [LC NBFU OTMC

TO HIM THAT HATH. A Novel of the West of Today. By Ralph Connor [pseud]. New York, Doran, 1921. 291p [BM BVaU LC NBFU OTMC

TORCHES THROUGH THE BUSH. A Tale of Glengarry. By Ralph Connor [pseud]. New York, Dodd Mead, 1934. 300p [BM BVaU LC NBFU OTMC QMM

TREADING THE WINEPRESS. By Ralph Connor [pseud]. Toronto, McClelland, 1925. 394p [BM BVaU LC NBFU OTMC QMM

**Gordon, Mrs. Charlotte**

RED GOLD. A True Story of an Englishwoman's Development in the West. Vancouver, McBeath & Campbell, 1928. 265p [BVaU NBFU OTMC

**Gordon, Robert Kay, 1887–**

IN THE GRIP OF THE BARREN LANDS. By Norman Blake [pseud–i.e., R.K. Gordon and Heber Carss Jamieson]. London, Blackie, 1927. 208p [BM NBFU OTU

THREE AGAINST THE GANG. By Norman Blake [pseud–see under previous title]. London, Blackie, 1929. 207p [BM OTP

**Goumois, Maurice-Marc-Albert de, 1896–**

A WORLD GOES BY. A Novel. New York, Pageant Press, 1956. 285p

**Gourlay, John Edgar Reginald, 1854–**

THE NECKLACE OF PANDURA. By Reginald Gourlay. New York, Broadway Pub., 1907. 121p [LC

**Gouzenko, Igor, 1919–**

THE FALL OF A TITAN. A Novel. Trans. from the Russian by Mervyn Black. London, Cassell, 1954. 680p

**Govan, Margaret Kilgour Livingston, 1904–**

ISLAND HIDEAWAY. Toronto, Dent, 1957. 183p

THE TRAIL OF THE BROKEN SNOW-SHOE. London, Toronto, Dent, 1956. 159p

THE TRAIL OF THE RED CANOE. Toronto, Dent, 1954. 179p

**Graham, Angus A., 1867–**

NAPOLEON TREMBLAY. London, Hale, 1939. 336p [BM LC NBFU OTU

**Graham, Charles Ross, 1920–**

THE BODY ON MOUNT ROYAL. By David Montrose [pseud]. Toronto, Harlequin Books, 1953. 189p

THE CRIME ON COTE DES NEIGES. By David Montrose [pseud]. Toronto, Collins, 1951. 160p

**Graham, Gwethalyn, 1913–1965**

EARTH AND HIGH HEAVEN. Philadelphia, Lippincott, 1944. 288p [Also, with intro. by Eli Mandel: Toronto, McClelland, 1960. xi + 254p] [BM BVaU NBFU OTMC QMM

SWISS SONATA. London, Cape, 1938. 383p [BM BVaU LC NBFU OTU

**Graham, Janet (Pollock), 1880–**

THE ENCHANTED WOOD. New York, Pageant Press, 1954. 102p

**Graham, Rosemary Margaret**

MUSTARD AND COMPANY. London, Dent, 1960. 150p

**Grahame, Gordon Hill, 1889?–**

ANTOINE, THE FEARLESS. Toronto, Ryerson, 1935. 288p [BM NBFU OTU

THE BOND TRIUMPHANT. Toronto, Hodder, 1923. 321p [BM BVaU LC NSHD OTU QMM

THE GENTLEMAN. London, Melrose, [1934?]. 288p [BM NBFU OKQ

THE GOLDEN GALLEONS OF CARIBEE. London, Hodder, 1925. 288p [BM BVaU NBFU OTMC

LARRY; or, The Avenging Terrors. Toronto, Musson, 1923. 311p [BM NBFU OTMC

MAPLE LEAF HOLIDAY. Akron, Ohio, Saalfield Pub. Co., 1948. 92p [LC

THE VOODOO STONE. Toronto, Ryerson, 1935. 254p [BM BVa NBFU OTMC

**Grainger, Martin Allerdale, 1874–1941**

WOODSMEN OF THE WEST. Toronto, Musson, 1908. 206p [BM BVaU LC NBFU OTMC

**Grant, Mrs. Hilda Kay, 1910–**

DOVE COTTAGE. By Jan Hilliard [pseud]. London, New York, Abelard-Schuman, 1958. 192p

THE JAMESON GIRLS. By Jan Hilliard [pseud]. Toronto, Nelson, Foster & Scott, 1956. 240p

MIRANDA. A Novel By Jan Hilliard [pseud]. New York, Abelard-Schuman, 1960. 247p

A VIEW OF THE TOWN. By Jan Hilliard [pseud]. New York, Abelard-Schuman, 1954. 269p

**Grant, James Miller, 1853–1940**

THE FAIRY SCHOOL OF CASTLE FRANK. By Grant Balfour [pseud]. Toronto, Poole, 1899. 89p [BM OTP

THE MOTHER OF ST. NICHOLAS (SANTA CLAUS). A Story of Duty and Peril. By Grant Balfour [pseud]. Toronto, Poole, 1899. 91p [BM OTP

ON GOLDEN WINGS THROUGH WONDERLAND. By Grant Balfour [pseud]. Toronto, McClelland, 1927. 269p [LC OTU QMM

**Grant, Minnie Caroline (Robinson), –1923**

SCENES IN HAWAII; or, Life in the Sandwich Islands. By Mrs. W. Forsyth Grant. Toronto, Hart, 1888. 203p [BVaU LC

**Gray, Archie William, 1896–**

THE TOWERS OF ST. ELOI. Rodney, Ont., Gray, 1933. 273p [NBFU OTP

**Gray, John Morgan, 1907–**

ONE-EYED TRAPPER. Toronto, Macmillan, 1941. 256p [BM BVaU NBFU OOP

**Grayson, Ethel Kirk, 1890–**

APPLES OF THE MOON. Toronto, Allen, 1933. 416p [BM NBFU OTU

FIRES IN THE VINE. Toronto, Macmillan, 1942. 497p [BVaU LC NBFU OTU

WILLOW SMOKE. New York, Vinal, 1928. 343p [BVaU LC NBFU OTMC

**Green, Henry Gordon, 1912–**

THE PRAYING MANTIS. A Novel. Fredericton, Brunswick Press, 1953. 309p

**Greene, Harry Irving, 1868–**

BARBARA OF THE SNOWS. New York, Moffatt Yard, 1911. 358p [Also: Toronto, Musson, 1924. 358p] [BM LC OTMC

YOZONDE OF THE WILDERNESS. Toronto, McLeod, 1910. 167p [BVaU LC OTMC

**Greene, Marion, 1900–**

CANAL BOY. Toronto, Macmillan, 1959. 152p

DOWN RIVER LIES THE WORLD. Toronto, Ryerson, 1946. 176p [BM BVaU LC NBFU OTMC QMM

**Greenough, William Parker**

THE CRUISE OF A WOMAN HATER. By G. de Montauban [pseud]. Boston, Ticknor, 1887. 280p [LC

**Greenwood, A.E.**

THE LIGHT AND THE LURE. By Marx Hawthorne [pseud]. Toronto, Carswell, 1897. 104p [BM OTP

**Gregory, Claudius Jabez, 1889–1944**

FORGOTTEN MEN. Hamilton, Davis-Lisson, 1933. 441p [BVaU LC NBFU OTMC

SOLOMON LEVI. New York, Kyle & Hovendon, 1935. 400p [BM LC NBFU OTMC

VALERIE HATHAWAY. Toronto, McClelland, 1933. 415p [BVaU LC NBFU OTMC

**Grenfell, Wilfred Thomason, 1865–1940**

DEEDS OF DARING. Selected from NORTHERN NEIGHBOURS and LABRADOR DAYS. London, Hodder, 1934. 127p [BM NSHPL QMBM

DOWN NORTH ON THE LABRADOR. New York, Revell, 1911. 229p [BM BVaU LC NSWA OTMC QMM

DOWN TO THE SEA. Yarns from Labrador. New York, Revell, 1910. 226p [BM BVaU LC OTMC QMM

THE HARVEST OF THE SEA. A Tale of Both Sides of the Atlantic. New York, Revell, 1905. 162p [BM BVaU LC NSHD OTU QMM

LABRADOR DAYS. Tales of the Sea Toilers. Boston, Houghton, 1919. 230p [BM BVaU LC OTMC

NORTHERN NEIGHBORS. Stories of the Labrador People. Boston, Houghton, 1923. 332p [BM BVaU LC NSHD OTMC

OFF THE ROCKS. Stories of the Deep-Sea Fisherfolk of Labrador. Philadelphia, Sunday School Times, 1906. 203p [BM BVaU LC OTU

TALES OF THE LABRADOR. Boston, Houghton, 1916. 239p [BM BVaU LC NBFU OTMC QMM

THAT CHRISTMAS IN PEACE HAVEN. Boston, Houghton, 1923. 55p [One of the stories in TALES OF THE LABRADOR.] [NfSM

**Grey, Francis William, 1860–1939**

THE CURE OF ST. PHILIPPE. A Story of French-Canadian Politics. London, Ont., Digby Long, 1899. 313p [BM OTP

**Griffin, George H.**

LEGENDS OF THE EVERGREEN COAST. Vancouver, Clarke & Stuart, 1934. 141p [BVaU NBFU

**Griffin, Watson, 1860–1952**

THE GULF OF YEARS. Toronto, Point Publishers, 1927. 407p [BM BVaU NSHD OKQ QMM

TWOK. A Novel. Hamilton, Griffin & Kidner, 1887. 236p [Contains also "Who is Santa Claus?"] [BVaU NSHD OTMC QMM

**Griffith, J.W.**

HELP IN THE DISTANCE. A New Dominion Story. Elora, Ont., Author, 1868. 67p [OTP

**Grodenk (pseud)**

MY OWN STORY. A Canadian Christmas Tale. Toronto, A.S. Irving, 1869. 144p [OONL OTP

**Grove, Frederick Philip, 1879–1948**

CONSIDER HER WAYS. Toronto, Macmillan, 1947. 298p [BVaU LC NSHD OTMC

FRUITS OF THE EARTH. Toronto, Dent, 1933. 335p [BM BVaU LC NSHD OTU QMM

THE MASTER OF THE MILL. Toronto, Macmillan, 1944. 393p [BVaU LC NSHD OTMC QMM

OUR DAILY BREAD. A Novel. New York, Macmillan, 1928. 390p [BM BVaU LC NBFU OKQ

A SEARCH FOR AMERICA. Ottawa, Graphic, 1927. 448p [BVaU LC MWU NSHD OKQ

SETTLERS OF THE MARSH. New York, Doran, 1925. 341p [BVaU LC MWU NSHD OTP QMM

TWO GENERATIONS. A Story of Present-Day Ontario. Toronto, Ryerson, 1939. 261p [BVaU LC NSHD OKQ

THE YOKE OF LIFE. Toronto, Macmillan, 1930. 355p [BVaU LC NSHD OKQ

**Grove, Miss**

LITTLE GRACE; or, Scenes in Nova-Scotia. By Miss Grove. Halifax, Mackenzie, 1846. 178p [OTP

**Grover, Lucius Halen, 1866–**

FIVE SHORT STORIES FOR CHILDREN. By "Uncle Dudley," the Kiddies' Friend. Edmonton, Western Veteran Pub., n.d. 24p [BVaU

THE GOLDEN RULE. ... Sandwich, B.C., Author, 1920. 41p

VIVETTE. Courtenay, B.C., Comox Argus, 1920. 43p [AEU BVaU OTMC

**Guelton, Mrs. Elizabeth**

THE STORY OF PETER, A CANADIAN CAT. A Humane Story. Toronto, Briggs, 1904. 24p [BCF

**Guest, Flora (Bigelow)**

THE JEWELLED BALL. Montreal, Cambridge Corp., 1908. 326p [BVaU NBFU OOP

**Guiton, Helen**

A COUNTRY LOVER. A Canadian Idyll. Toronto, Dent, 1948. 255p [BVaU NBFU OTMC QMM

**Gurd, Mrs. Mabel Hodgson, –1920?**

A BIT OF A DRIFTER, AND OTHER STORIES. Montreal, Chapman, 1921. 191p [BVaU NBFU

**Guttormsson, Ragnhildur (Johnson), 1886–**

IAN OF RED RIVER. Toronto, Ryerson, 1959. 129p

**Hagell, Edward Fredric, 1895–**

WHEN THE GRASS WAS FREE. Toronto, Ryerson, 1954. x + 127p

**Haig-Brown, Roderick Langmere, 1908–**

KI-YU. A Story of Panthers. Boston, Houghton, 1934. 213p [Also pub. under title: PANTHER. London, Cape, 1934. 257p] [BM BVaU LC NBFU OTU QMM

MOUNTED POLICE PATROL. New York, Morrow, 1954. 248p

ON THE HIGHEST HILL. New York, Morrow, 1949. 319p [BM BVaU LC NBFU OTU QMM

PANTHER. See under KI-YU.

SALTWATER SUMMER. New York, Morrow, 1947. 256p [BM BVaU LC NBFU OTU

STARBUCK VALLEY WINTER. New York, Morrow, 1943. 310p [BM BVaU LC NBFU OTU QMM

THE TALL TREES FALL. See under TIMBER.

TIMBER. A Novel of Pacific Coast Loggers. New York, Morrow, 1942. 410p [Also pub. under title: THE TALL TREES FALL. London, Collins, 1943. 288p] [BM BVaU LC NBFU OTUV QMM

**Hailey, Arthur, 1920–**

THE FINAL DIAGNOSIS. A Novel. Garden City, N.Y., Doubleday, 1959. 319p

FLIGHT INTO DANGER. A Novel of Suspense. By John Castle [pseud] & Arthur Hailey. London, Souvenir Press, 1958. 162p [John Castle, pseud. of Ronald Charles Payne and John William Garrod.]

RUNWAY ZERO-EIGHT. Montreal, Bantam Books, 1960. 120p [Same as FLIGHT INTO DANGER, *q.v.*]

**Hale, Charles Maynard, 1889–**

DESTINY ISLAND. London, Cassell, 1939. 280p [BM NBFU

REDEMPTION ISLAND. By Charles M. Hale and Evan John [pseud]. New York, Morrow, 1928. 309p [BM LC NBFU

**Haley, Mildred C. (Rogers), 1890?–**

THE TANGLES AT TALKINGTON. Toronto, Hunter Rose, 1925. [CC

**Haliburton, Thomas Chandler, 1796–1865**

THE ATTACHE; or, Sam Slick in England. By the author of THE CLOCKMAKER; or, Sayings and Doings of Sam Slick [pseud]. [First series.] London, Bentley, 1843. 2v [BM BVaU NSHD OTP

THE ATTACHE; or, Sam Slick in England. By the Author of the THE CLOCKMAKER; or, Sayings and Doings of Sam Slick [pseud]. [Second series.] London, Bentley, 1844. 2v [BM BVaU NSHD OTU QMM

THE BUBBLES OF CANADA. By the Author of THE CLOCKMAKER. ... London, Bentley, 1839. 332p [BM BVaU LC NSWA OKQ

THE CLOCKMAKER; or, The Sayings and Doings of Samuel Slick, of Slickville, [Anon] [First series.] Halifax, Joseph Howe, 1836. 221p [Also: Philadelphia, Cary, Lea & Blanchard, 1837. 218p; and many later editions.] [BVaU LC OKQ

THE CLOCKMAKER; or, The Sayings and Doings of Samuel Slick, of Slickville. [First series.] Intro. by Robert L. McDougall. Toronto, McClelland, 1958. xvi + 156p [New Canadian Library Series, No. 6]

THE CLOCKMAKER; or, The Sayings and Doings of Samuel Slick, of Slickville. [Anon] [First–Third Series.] London, Bentley, 1837–40. 3v [BM BVa LC NSHD OKQ

THE CLOCKMAKER; or, The Sayings and Doings of Samuel Slick, of Slickville. [Anon] Second Series. London, Bentley, 1838. 378p [Many later editions.] [BM BVaU LC NBFU OKQ

THE CLOCKMAKER; or, The Sayings and Doings of Samuel Slick, of Slickville. [Anon] Third series. London, Bentley, 1840. [Also: Philadelphia, Lea, & Blanchard, 1840. 215p; and many later editions.] [BM BVaU LC NBFU OTU

FRAGMENTS FROM SAM SLICK. Selected and arranged by Lawrence J. Burpee. Toronto, Musson, 1909. 91p [BVaU NBFU OTU

JUDGE HALIBURTON'S YANKEE STORIES. Philadelphia, Lindsay & Blakiston, 1846. 2v in 1. [Same as THE CLOCKMAKER, First and Second Series. See Chittick p659.] [BVaU NBFU OTP

THE LETTER BAG OF THE GREAT WESTERN; or, Life in a Steamer. ... By the Author of "The Sayings and Doings of Samuel Slick." London, Bentley, 1840. 323p [Also: Halifax, Howe, 1840. 189p] [BM BVaU LC NSHD OKQ

NATURE AND HUMAN NATURE. By the Author of "Sam Slick the Clockmaker" ... [pseud]. London, Hurst & Blackett, 1855. 2v [BM BVaU LC NSHD OKQ

THE OLD JUDGE; or, Life in a Colony. By the Author of "Sam Slick, the Clockmaker" ... [pseud]. London, Colburn, 1849. 2v [Also: New York, Stringer & Townsend, 1849. 2v in 1. 239p] [BM BVaU NSHD OKQ

SAM SLICK. Ed. with a critical estimate and a bibliography, by Ray Palmer Baker. Toronto, McClelland, 1923. 420p [BM BVaU LC NSHD OTU

SAM SLICK IN SEARCH OF A WIFE. See under SAM SLICK'S WISE SAWS. ...

SAM SLICK THE CLOCKMAKER. His Sayings and Doings. With an intro. by E.A. Baker. London, Routledge, 1904. xvi + 435p [OTMC OTUV [Same title, but with an intro. by T.G. Marquis: Toronto, Musson, n.d. "Centenary Edition" [1936]. xxii + 425p] [OONL OTMC

SAM SLICK'S WISE SAWS AND MODERN INSTANCES; or, What He Said, Did, or Invented. ... London, Hurst & Blackett, 1853. 2v [Also pub. under title: WISE SAWS; or, Sam Slick in Search of a Wife. New York, Dick & Fitzgerald, 1855.] [BM BVaU LC NSHD OTMC

THE SAYINGS AND DOINGS OF SAMUEL SLICK ESQ., TOGETHER WITH HIS OPINION ON MATRIMONY. New York, Dick & Fitzgerald, n.d. 263p [Same as THE CLOCKMAKER, third series?] [BVaU OTMC QMM

THE SEASON TICKET. ... [Anon] London, Bentley, 1860. 376p [BM BVaU LC NSHD OKQ

SELECTIONS FROM SAM SLICK (JUDGE HALIBURTON). Ed. by Paul A.W. Wallace. Toronto, Ryerson, 1923. 150p [BM BVaU OTU QMM

TRAITS OF AMERICAN HUMOR, BY NATIVE AUTHORS. Ed. and adapted by the author of "Sam Slick." London, Colburn, 1852. 3v [BM BVaU LC NSHD OKQ

YANKEE YARNS AND YANKEE LETTERS. Philadelphia, Peterson Bros., [1852?]. 189p [OTU QMSS

**Hall, Emma L.**

THE ASS HE RODE. By Yvonne St. Claire [pseud]. Toronto, Author, 1937. 10p [NBFU OTU

THE ASS HE RODE. THE OCEAN'S ORATORIO. THE SCENTED GARDEN. SONGS OF A YOUNG COUNTRY. By Yvonne St. Claire [pseud]. N.p., n.d. 4v in 1. [QMM

CLAUDIA. A Story of the Early Church. By Yvonne St. Claire [pseud]. N.p., n.d. 11p [OKQ

THE FLIGHT INTO EGYPT. By Yvonne St. Claire [pseud]. N.p., n.d. 8p [OTUV

THE PILLOW. A Story suggested by New Testament Incidents. By Yvonne St. Claire [pseud]. Toronto, Industrial and Educational Pub. Co., n.d. 32p [OTU

SPLENDID DAWN. By Yvonne St. Claire [pseud]. London, Epworth Press, 1949. 141p [OKQ

THE VEIL. A Story of the First Century. By Yvonne St. Claire [pseud]. Toronto, Thorn Press, 1938. 79p [AEU OTMC

**Hall, Ethel May**

SEELING THE NEEDY FOR A PAIR OF SHOES, AND OTHER STORIES. London, Ont., Franks, 1944. 72p [BVaU OLU

**Hallam, Douglas, 1883–1948**

THE SPIDER WEB. The Romance of a Flying Boat. By P.I.X. [pseud]. Edinburgh, Blackwood, 1919. 278p [OTU

**Halldorsson, Albert Laurence, 1925–**

FRUITS OF THE VALLEY. An Historic [*sic*] Novel. Winnipeg, Author, 1950. 128p [MWU OONL

**Ham, George Henry, 1847–1926**

THE FLITTING OF THE GODS. An Authentic Account of the Great Trek from Mount Olympus to the Canadian Rockies. Toronto, Mail Job Print., 1906. 20p [NSWA

**Hambleton, John O. ("Jack"), 1901–1961**

ABITIBI ADVENTURE. Toronto, Longmans, 1950. 173p [BM BVaU NBFU OTMC

CHARTER PILOT. A Bill Hanson Story. Toronto, Longmans, 1952. 216p

CUB REPORTER. Toronto, Longmans, 1951. 231p

FIRE IN THE VALLEY. Toronto, Longmans, 1960. 156p

FOREST RANGER. Toronto, Longmans, 1948. 226p [BM BVaU OOP QMM

TEMAGAMI GUIDE. Toronto, Longmans, 1954. 167p

WINGS OVER LABRADOR. Toronto, Longmans, 1957. 167p

WOLVERINE. Toronto, Longmans, 1954. 184p

YOUNG BUSH PILOT. Toronto, Longmans, 1949. 200p [BVaU NBFU OOP

**Hambleton, Ronald, 1917–**

EVERY MAN IS AN ISLAND. London, Hutchinson, 1959. 245p

**Hamilton, Leslie, 1899–**
CHERCHEZ LA FEMME? Hamilton, Beaver, 1941. 190p [OOP
RENDEZVOUS IN VIENNA. Hamilton, Beaver, 1941. 188p [OTU

**Hango, Mrs. Angéline Rose, 1882–**
TRUTHFULLY YOURS. Toronto, Oxford U. Press, 1948. 144p [BVaU NBFU OTU QMM

**Hanson, Nell**
WINDS OF PITY. London, Murray, 1935. 332p [BM LC

**Hardy, William George, 1896–**
ABRAHAM, PRINCE OF UR. See under FATHER ABRAHAM.
ALL THE TRUMPETS SOUNDED. A Novel based on the Life of Moses. New York, Coward McCann, 1942. 501p [BM BVaU NBFU OTMC
THE CITY OF LIBERTINES. Toronto, McClelland, 1957. 437p
FATHER ABRAHAM. London, Lovat Dickson, 1935. 416p [Pub. in the U.S. under title: ABRAHAM, PRINCE OF UR. New York, Dodd Mead, 1935. 376p] [BM BVaU NBFU OTMC
TURN BACK THE RIVER. New York, Dodd Mead, 1938. 385p [BM BVaU LC NBFU OTU
THE UNFULFILLED. Toronto, McClelland, 1951. 334p

**Harlaw, John**
GLENLYON. A Story of Scotch and Canadian Romance. London, Stockwell, [1936]. 135p [BVaU NBFU OKQ

**Harold, Rev. P.J.**
IRENE OF CORINTH. An Historic Romance of the First Century. Toronto, Hunter Rose, 1884. 298p [LC NSHD OLU

**Harper, John Murdoch, 1845–1919**
THE LITTLE SERGEANT; or, Le Service et les Amours. Quebec, Quebec News Co., [1905?]. 214p [OTMC
OUR JEAMES. [Attributed to Harper in Morgan, *Canadian Men and Women ...* 1912. *Cf.* item listed below under HENDERSON, J. MURDOCH. "Henderson was the maiden name of Harper's mother."]

**Harrington, Evelyn (Davis), 1911–**
OOTOOK, YOUNG ESKIMO GIRL. New York, Abelard-Schuman; Toronto, Nelson, 1956. 127p
STORMY SUMMER. New York, Abelard-Schuman; Toronto, Nelson, 1956. 190p

**Harris, Mrs. Carrie Jenkins, –1903**
CYRIL WHYMAN'S MISTAKE. Toronto, Bryce, 1894. 124p [OONL
FAITH AND FRIENDS. ... Windsor, N.S., Anslow, 1895. 43p [NSHP

A MODERN EVANGELINE. Windsor, N.S., Anslow, 1896. 120p [NSWA QQL
MR. PERKINS OF NOVA SCOTIA; or, The European Adventures of a Would-be Aristocrat. Windsor, N.S., Anslow, 1891. 170p [NBSaM
A ROMANTIC ROMANCE. Windsor, N.S. Anslow, 1893. 153p [NSHP OONL

**Harris, Christie Lucy (Irwin), 1907–**
CARIBOO TRAIL. Toronto, Longmans, 1957. 188p

**Harrison, Charles Yale, 1898–1954**
A CHILD IS BORN. New York, Cape & Smith, 1931. 236p [LC NBFU OTMC
GENERALS DIE IN BED. London, Douglas, 1930. 269p [BM BVaU LC NBFU OTP
MEET ME ON THE BARRICADES. A Novel. New York, Scribner, 1938. 206p [BM LC NBFU OTMC
NOBODY'S FOOL. A Novel. New York, Holt, 1948. 300p [BM BVaU LC NBFU OTMC
THERE ARE VICTORIES. New York, Covici Friede, 1938. 320p [LC NBFU OTMC

**Harrison, Susie Frances (Riley), 1859–1935**
CROWDED OUT AND OTHER SKETCHES. By Seranus [pseud]. Ottawa, Evening Journal, 1886. 165p [BVaU NBFU OTP QMSS
THE FOREST OF BOURG-MARIE. London, Arnold, 1898. 306p [BVaU NBFU OKQ
RINGFIELD. A Novel. By Seranus [pseud]. Toronto, Musson, 1914. 311p [NBFU OKQ

**Hart, Adolphus Mordecai, 1813–1879**
LIFE IN THE FAR WEST; or, The Comical, Quizzical, and Tragical Adventures of a Hoosier. Cincinnati, Pearsons, [1860?]. 131p [LC

**Hart, Julia Catherine (Beckwith), 1796–1867**
ST. URSULA'S CONVENT; or, The Nun of Canada. Containing Scenes from Real Life. Kingston, Thomson, 1824. 2v [BVaU LC NBFU OTP
TONNEWONTE; or, The Adopted Son of America. A Tale, Containing Scenes from Real Life. By an American [pseud]. Watertown, N.Y., Adams, 1825. 2v in 1 (275p) [Also with imprint: Exeter, Meder, 1831. 312p] [BVaU LC OTP

**Hart, Percy William Edward, 1870–**
JASON–NOVA SCOTIA. Founded upon a Romantic Legend of my Native Land. New York, Bibelot Bros., 1903. 238p [BM BVaU LC NSHD OOP
LONG LIFE & HAPPY. A Narratale. New York, Bibelot Bros., 1932. 256p [LC
YARNS. The Ludovic Zam Affair. New York, Bibelot Bros., 1901. 272p [LC NSHD

**Harvey, Emeline Daggett**
GOLD DUST. Chicago, Lotus Pub. Co., 1892. 257p [LC OTMC

**Harvey, William Earl, 1898–**
THE PSYCHOLOGICAL KINGDOM. St. Paul, Minn., Review Pub., 1927. 106p [LC

**Hayes, Catherine E. (Simpson), 1852–1943**
"AWEEMA." An Indian Story of a Christmas Tryst in the Early Days. By Mary Markwell [pseud]. Winnipeg, Hart, 1906. 61p [BVaU OTP SSU

**Hayes, John Francis, 1904–**
BUCKSKIN COLONIST. Toronto, Copp Clark, 1947. 251p [BM BVaU OTU QMBM
BUGLES IN THE HILLS. Toronto, Copp Clark, 1955. 312p
THE DANGEROUS COVE. A Story of Early Days in Newfoundland. Toronto, Copp Clark, 1957. 265p
A LAND DIVIDED. Toronto, Copp Clark, 1951. 285p
QUEST IN THE CARIBOO. Toronto, Copp Clark, 1960. 240p
REBELS RIDE AT NIGHT. Toronto, Copp Clark, 1953. 286p
TREASON AT YORK. Toronto, Copp Clark, 1949. 314p [BVaU OTMC

**Heathcote, Mrs. Edmund**
THE ADMIRAL'S NIECE; or, A Tale of Nova Scotia. London, Newby, 1858. 2v in 1. [BM BVaU QMBM

**Heaton, Hugh**
THE STORY OF PROFESSOR PORKY. Toronto, Heaton, 1937. 34p [BM

**Heavysege, Charles, 1816–1876**
THE ADVOCATE. A Novel. Montreal, Worthington, 1865. 125p [BVaU LC NSHD OTMC QMSS

**Hedges, Doris (Ryde), 1900–**
DUMB SPIRIT. A Novel of Montreal. London, Barker, 1952. 224p
ELIXIR. London, Barker, 1954. 191p
ROBIN. New York, Vantage Press, 1957. 176p

**Heeney, Rev. William Bertal, 1873–1955**
D'ARCY CONYERS. Toronto, Hodder, 1922. 229p [BM NBFU OTMC
PICKANOCK. A Tale. London, Lane, 1912. 288p [BM BVaU NBFU OTMC

**Heighington, Wilfrid, 1897–1945**
THE CANNON'S MOUTH. Toronto, Bryant Press, 1943. 368p [NSHD OTU

**Heming, Arthur Henry Howard, 1870–1940**
THE LIVING FOREST. Toronto, Gundy, 1925. 268p [BM BVaU LC OKQ QMM
THE LIVING FOREST; Two Boys in the Canadian Woods. Garden City, Doubleday, 1935. 268p [LC NBFU OTMC
SPIRIT LAKE. London, Macmillan, 1907. 335p [Also: Toronto, Musson, 1923. 280p] [BM BVaU LC NSHD OKQ

**Henderson, J. Murdoch [pseud?** See note above under Harper, John Murdoch.]
THE CHRONICLES OF KARTDALE. Our Jeames. Ed. by ——. Montreal, Drysdale, 1896. 343p [BM OTP QMM

**Henry, Edwin Arthur, 1866–**

LITTLE FOXES. Stories for Boys and Girls. New York, Fleming Revell, 1922. 160p [BM LC OTMC

**Henry, Vera (Johnson)**

A LUCKY NUMBER. Philadelphia, Lippincott, 1957. 243p

**Henshaw, Julia Wilmotte (Henderson), 1869–1937**

HYPNOTIZED; or, The Experiment of Sir Hugh Galbraith. A Romance. Toronto, Ontario Pub. Co., 1898. 285p [BM OOP

WHY NOT, SWEETHEART? Toronto, Morang, 1901. 246p [BM BVaU NSHD OTMC

**Hensley, Sophia Margaret (Almon), 1866–**

LOVE & COMPANY, LIMITED. By J. Try-Davies [pseud] and Mary Woolson. Montreal, Foster Brown, 1901. 114p [BM NSHPL OTP

A SEMI-DETACHED HOUSE AND OTHER STORIES. By J. Try-Davies [pseud]. Montreal, Lovell, 1900. 164p [BM BVaU NSHPL OTMC QMBM

**Herapath, Theodora, 1889–**

THE MIGHT-HAVE-BEENS. By Anne Capelle [pseud]. London, Melrose, 1936. 288p [BM CC

**Herbert, George**

GERALD FITZGERALD. A Novel. London, Newby, 1858. 3v [BM OLU

**Herbert, Mary E.**

BELINDA DALTON; or, Scenes in the Life of a Halifax Belle. Halifax, 1859. 60p [OONL OLU NSHD

WOMAN AS SHE SHOULD BE; or, Agnes Wiltshire. Halifax, Author, 1861. 145p [BVaU NBFU OTP

A YOUNG MAN'S CHOICE. ... Halifax, Citizen, 1869. 43p [NSHD

**Herbert, Sarah, 1824–1844**

AGNES MAILARD. A Temperance Tale. Halifax, n.d. [BibC

**Herbin, John Frederic, 1860–1923**

THE HEIR TO GRAND-PRE. Toronto, Briggs, 1907. 155p [BM BVaU NSWA OKQ QMBM

JEN OF THE MARSHES. Boston, Cornhill, 1921. 349p [BVaU LC NSHD OTMC

**Herman, Alan, 1916–**

THIS TIME A BETTER EARTH. A Novel. By Ted Allan [pseud]. New York, Morrow, 1939. 279p [BM LC NBFU OOP

**Herring, Frances Elizabeth (Clarke), 1851–1916**

ENA. London, Griffiths, 1913. 187p [BM BVaU LC NBFU

THE GOLD MINERS. A Sequel to ON THE PATHLESS WEST. London, Griffiths, 1914. 120p [BM BVaU LC

NAN AND OTHER PIONEER WOMEN OF THE WEST. London, Griffiths, 1913. 171p [BM BVaU LC

**Hewitt, Foster William 1902–**

ALONG OLYMPIC ROAD. Toronto, Ryerson, 1951. 142p

**Hickey, Rev. David**

WILLIAM AND MARY. A Tale of the Siege of Louisburg, 1745. Toronto, Briggs, 1884. 317p [BVaU NSHD OTP

**Hickman, William Albert, 1875–1957?**

CANADIAN NIGHTS. Toronto, McClelland, 1914. 365p [BVaU LC NBFU OTMC

THE SACRIFICE OF THE SHANNON. Toronto, Briggs, 1903. 323p [BVaU LC NSHD OKQ QMM

AN UNOFFICIAL LOVE-STORY. New York, Century, 1909. 141p [BM BVaU LC NSWA OTMC

**Hiebert, Paul Gerhardt, 1892–**

SARAH BINKS. Toronto, Oxford U. Press, 1947. 182p [BVaU LC NSHD OKQ QMM SSU

**Higgins, David Williams, 1834–1917**

THE MYSTIC SPRING, and Other Tales of Western Life. Toronto, Briggs, 1904. 407p [New and rev. ed.: New York, Broadway Pub., 1908. 312p] [BM BVaU LC NSHD OTP

THE PASSING OF A RACE and More Tales of Western Life. Toronto, Briggs, 1905. 304p [BM BVaU LC OKQ

**Hilts, Rev. Joseph Henry, 1819–1903**

AMONG THE FOREST TREES; or, How the Bushman Family Got their Homes. Toronto, Briggs, 1888. 380p [BM BVaU OTU

CLOTHED WITH THE SUN; or, From Olivet to the Gates of Glory. Toronto, Briggs, 1891. 408p [OTMC

**Hodgins, James Cobourg, 1866–1953**

THE WILDERNESS CAMPERS. Toronto, Musson, 1921. 265p [BM NBFU OOP

**Hodgins, Samuel Raymond Norris, 1895–**

THE PARSLEYS & THE SAGE. Toronto, Ryerson, 1952. 153p

WHY DON'T YOU GET MARRIED. A Hodge-Podge of Sketches, a Few Wise, Many Witty, and all Wholesome. Toronto, McClelland, 1923. 270p [BVaU LC OTMC QMSS

**Hodgson, John C.J., 1892–**

LION AND LILY. A Story of New France. Montreal, Renouf, 1935. 281p [NBFU OKQ QMM

**Holliday, Joseph, 1910–**

DALE OF THE MOUNTED. Toronto, Allen, 1951. 150p

DALE OF THE MOUNTED, ATLANTIC ASSIGNMENT. Toronto, Allen, 1956. 158p
DALE OF THE MOUNTED, ATOMIC PLOT. Toronto, Allen, 1959. 158p
DALE OF THE MOUNTED, DEW LINE DUTY. Toronto, Allen, 1957. 158p
DALE OF THE MOUNTED IN NEWFOUNDLAND. Toronto, Allen, 1955. 160p
DALE OF THE MOUNTED IN THE ARCTIC. Toronto, Allen, 1953. 156p
DALE OF THE MOUNTED ON THE WEST COAST. Toronto, Allen, 1954. 156p
DALE OF THE MOUNTED: PURSUIT ON THE ST. LAWRENCE. Toronto, Allen, 1960. 160p
DALE OF THE MOUNTED: SUB HUNT. Toronto, Allen, 1958. 160p
OIL TRAILS IN HEADLESS VALLEY. Toronto, Longmans, 1954. 157p

**Holmes, Abraham S., 1809–1908**
BELINDA; or, The Rivals. A Tale of Real Life. By A.S.H. Detroit, Bagg & Harmon, 1843. 104p [BVaU NBFU OLU

**Hood, Robert Allison, 1880–1958**
THE CASE OF KINNEAR. Toronto, Macmillan, 1942. 329p [BVaU NBFU OTMC
THE CHIVALRY OF KEITH LEICESTER. A Romance of British Columbia. Toronto, McClelland, 1918. 339p [BVaU LC NBFU OTMC
THE QUEST OF ALISTAIR. Toronto, McClelland, 1921. 328p [BM BVaU LC NBFU OTMC

**Hooke, Hilda Mary, 1898–**
THUNDER IN THE MOUNTAINS. Legends of Canada. Toronto, Oxford U. Press, 1947. 223p [BVaU LC NBFU OTMC QMM

**Hooker, Rev. LeRoy, 1840–1906**
BALDOON. [A Story]. Chicago, Rand McNally, 1899. 278p [BM LC OTU
ENOCH, THE PHILISTINE. A Traditional Romance of Philistia, Egypt, and the Great Pyramid. New York, Rand McNally, 1898. 250p [BM LC
ME AN' TEDDY. By Me. Ed. by ——. Chicago, Conkey, 1906. 87p [BM LC

**Hope, Ethel Penman, –1958**
DR. PAUL. Toronto, McClelland, 1918. 235p [LC OOP
EYES OF THE LAW. Toronto, McClelland, 1920. 236p [BM OTMC
A HILLSIDE CHRISTMAS. The Story of a Smiling Heart. Toronto, McClelland, 1917. 17p [BM OONL
THE WAYS OF THE HEART. Toronto, Musson, 1910. 265p [BM OTMC

**Horn, Harold (pseud)**
MORTIMER'S GOLD. By Harold Horn [pseud]. Toronto, Hodder, 1922. 315p [BM NBFU OOU

**Horner, Leslie**
FAMOUS CANADIAN STORIES RE-TOLD FOR CHILDREN. Ed. by D.G. French. Toronto, McClelland, 1923. 348p [BM BVa NSHD OTMC

**Horsfield, Richard Edward, 1895–**
THE LEASES OF DEATH. By M.B. Gaunt [pseud]. London, Long, 1937. 288p [BM LC

**Hoskin, Mary**
THE LITTLE GREEN GLOVE AND OTHER STORIES. Toronto, Extension Print., 1920. 221p [BVaU OTMC OTUV

**Houghton, Frank Llewellyn, 1897–**
THE BLUE CIRCLE GANG. A Canadian Adventure Story. Toronto, Nelson, 1949. 191p [BViPA NSHPL OTP
THE CAVE AT CORMORANT POINT. A Canadian Navy Adventure. Toronto, Nelson, [1950?]. 169p [NBFU OONL

**Howard, Rev. Allen Leslie, 1875?–**
THE MAGNIFICENT EUGENIC; or, "Give me Joseph." Brampton, Charters, 1933. 283p [NBFU

**Howard, Florence Ruth, 1902–**
GREEN ENTRY. New York, Morrow, 1940. 274p [BM LC
SAILMAKER. A Novel. New York, Morrow, 1948. 222p [BVaU LC
VIEW FROM A WINDOW. A Novel. New York, Morrow, 1942. 341p [BM BVaU LC

**Howard, Hilda (Glynn), 1887–**
THE WRITING ON THE WALL. By H. Glynn-Ward [pseud]. Vancouver, Sun Pub. Co., 1922. 326p [BVaU NBFU OTMC

**Howarth, David**
THE VALLEY OF GOLD. A Tale of the Saskatchewan. New York, Revell, 1921. 272p [BVaU LC NBFU OKQ

**Howe, Joseph, 1804–1873**
THE LORD OF THE BEDCHAMBER. A Political Lampoon. [BCF

**Huddleston, Mrs. George Croft**
BLUEBELL. A Novel. Toronto, Belford, 1875. 315p [Also: London, 1875. 3v] [BM BVaU NBFU OTU
MISS TODD'S DREAM. ... London, Ward & Downey, 1889. 160p [BM

**Hughes, Isabelle Grace (Bragg), 1912–**
LORENA TELFORTH. London, Davies, 1952. 255p [NBFU
SERPENT'S TOOTH. Toronto, Collins, 1947. 342p [BVaU OTU QMM
TIME IN AMBUSH. Toronto, Collins, 1949. 257p [BVaU NBFU OTU
THE WISE BROTHER. Toronto, Ryerson, 1954. 272p

**Hunt, Anna Rebecca (Gale)**
AFTER MANY DAYS. An Anglo-American Romance. By Canadienne [pseud]. London, Kegan Paul, 1914. 404p [BM QMSS

DISTURBERS. By William Henry Williamsonn and "Canadienne" [pseud]. London, Laurie, 1914. 316p [BM

**Hunt, Katherine Chandler, 1909–**

MURDER IS MY SHADOW. New York, Macmillan, 1959. 151p

**Hunter, Alfred Taylour, 1867–**

STORIES TOLD OUT OF LODGE. Toronto, Carswell, 1898. 216p [OTU

**Hunter, Francis James, 1853–1938**

COLONEL GASCOIGNE, V.C. A Story of Travel, Adventure, and Love. [Montreal?], n.p., n.d. 274p [BViPA OTMC QMSS

**Hunter, James Hogg, 1890–**

BANNERS OF BLOOD. Toronto, Evangelical Pub., 1947. 228p [BVaU NBFU OTMC

HOW SLEEP THE BRAVE! A Novel of 17th Century Scotland. Toronto, Evangelical Pub., 1955. 256p

THE MYSTERY OF MAR SABA. Toronto, Evangelical Pub., 1940. 414p [BVaU NBFU OTU

UNCLE JIM'S STORIES FROM NATURE'S WONDERLAND. Grand Rapids, Mich., Zondervan, 1953. 71p [BM LC

**Huntington, Lucius Seth, 1827–1886**

PROFESSOR CONANT. A Story of English and American Social and Political Life. Toronto, Rose, 1884. 291p [BVaU LC NSHD OTU QMM

**Hutchison, Bruce, 1901–**

THE HOLLOW MEN. A Novel. Toronto, Longmans, 1944. 278p [BVaU LC OTMC QMM

**Hutchison, Margaret**

TAMARAC. Toronto, Macmillan, 1957. 282p

**Huyghue, Douglas S.**

ARGIMOU. A Legend of the Micmac. By Eugene [pseud]. Halifax, Courier, 1847. 72p [NSHP

NOMADS OF THE WEST; or, Ellen Clayton. London, Bentley, 1850. 3v [BM LC OTU

**Hyde, Laurence.**

SOUTHERN CROSS. A Novel of the South Seas, Told in Wood Engravings. With a Review of Stories in Pictures from Earliest Times. Intro. by Rockwell Kent. Los Angeles, Ward Ritchie Press, 1951. 255p [Also: Toronto, McClelland, 1951.]

**Iles, George, 1852–1942**
CANADIAN STORIES. Together with Choosing Books ... and Jottings from a Note-book. Montreal, Author, 1918. 184p [BVaU NSHD OTU QMM

**Ingaldson, Violet Paula (Paulson)**
COLD ADVENTURE. Toronto, Copp Clark, 1959. 168p

**Ingersoll, William Ernest**
DAISY HERSELF. Toronto, Musson, 1920. 320p [BM BVaU NBFU OTMC
THE ROAD THAT LED HOME. A Romance of Plow-Land. With some Passages from the Lives of Henry Nicol, Philosopher of Islay; Ernie Bedford, Pedagogue. ... New York, Harper, 1918. 307p [BM BVaU LC NBFU

**Innis, Mary E. (Quayle), 1899–1972**
STAND ON A RAINBOW. Toronto, Collins, 1943. 290p [BVaU LC NBFU OKQ QMM

**Inskipp, M.**
MONSOON MAGIC. London, Unwin, 1927. 288p [BM NBFU QMM

**Irwin, Grace Lillian, 1907–**
ANDREW CONNINGTON. Toronto, McClelland, 1954. 248p
LEAST OF ALL SAINTS. Toronto, McClelland, 1952. 302p
IN LITTLE PLACE. A Novel. Toronto, Ryerson, 1959. 216p

**Israel, Charles Edward, 1920–**
HOW MANY ANGELS. A Novel. Toronto, Macmillan, 1956. 329p

**Jack, Annie L. (Hayr), 1839–1912**
THE LITTLE ORGANIST OF ST. JEROME and Other Stories of Work and Experience. Toronto, Briggs, 1902. 91p [BM BVaU NSHD OTMC QMBM

**Jack, Isaac Allen, 1843–1903**
THE MEMOIRS OF A CANADIAN SECRETARY. A Posthumous Paper. [Anon] Toronto, 1928. 42p [Edited by Ephraim Davis.] [The Toronto imprint and date are fictitious. Actually pub. at Saint John, about 1883. *Cf.* DCB.] [NBFU OTP

**Jacob, Fred, 1882–1926**
DAY BEFORE YESTERDAY. A Novel. Toronto, Macmillan, 1925. 319p [BVaU LC NBFU OTMC
PEEVEE. A Novel. Toronto, Macmillan, 1928. 400p [BVaU LC NBFU OTMC QMM

**James, George Moffat, 1867–**
STANDING BEFORE KINGS. Belleville, James Texts, 1924. 258p [NBFU OTP

**Jamieson, Heber Carss, 1879–1962**

IN THE GRIP OF THE BARREN LANDS. By Norman Blake [pseud–i.e., Robert Kay Gordon and H.C. Jamieson]. London, Blackie, 1927. 208p [BM NBFU OTU

THREE AGAINST THE GANG. By Norman Blake [pseud–see under previous title]. London, Blackie, 1929. 207p [BM OTP

**Jamieson, Nina (Moore), 1885–1932**

THE HICKORY STICK. A Romance of the School in the Cedars. Toronto, McClelland, 1921. 343p [BM NBFU OTMC

**Janes, Lemuel Willey, 1889–**

THE TREASURY OF NEWFOUNDLAND STORIES. Ed. by ——. St. John's, Maple Leaf Mills, n.d. 158p [NfSM OOP

**Janes, Percy**

SO YOUNG AND BEAUTIFUL. Ilfracombe, Devon, Stockwell, 1958. 342p

**Jarvis, Thomas Stinson, 1854–1926**

DR. PERDUE. Chicago, Laird & Lee, 1892. 397p [LC

GEOFFREY HAMPSTEAD. A Novel. New York, Appleton, 1890. 378p [BM LC NBFU OTMC

SHE LIVED IN NEW YORK. A Novel. New York, Judge Pub., 1894. 304p [LC

**Jarvis, William Henry Pope, 1876–1944**

THE GREAT GOLD RUSH. A Tale of the Klondike. Toronto, Macmillan, 1913. 335p [BM BVaU OTU QMBM

THE LETTERS OF A REMITTANCE MAN TO HIS MOTHER. Toronto, Musson, [1909?]. 122p [BM BVaU NSHD OTP SSU

TRAILS AND TALES IN COBALT. Toronto, Briggs, 1908. 157p [BM BVaU OTU

**Jasinskas, Jonas, 1907–**

A KISS IN THE DARK. By J. Jasmin [pseud]. Trans. from the Lithuanian by Milton Stark. Chicago, International Press, 1954. 150p [Previously pub. in Lithuania in 1937.]

**Jenkins, Charles Christopher, 1882–1943**

THE REIGN OF BRASS. A Romance of Two Epochs. Toronto, Ryerson, 1927. 318p [BM NBFU

THE TIMBER PIRATE. New York, Doran, 1922. 318p [BM BVaU LC NBFU OTMC

**Jenkins, Robert Smith, 1870–1931**

THE HEIR FROM NEW YORK. Toronto, Standard Book, 1911. 362p [BM OTU

**Jennings, Clotilda, –1895**

ISABEL LEICESTER. A Romance. By Maude Alma [pseud]. Hamilton, Spectator, 1874. 182p [OH OTP

**Jerdon, Gertrude**

CHANGING PLACES; or, Wilton Fairlegh in Animal Land. London, Partridge, 1886. 144p [BM

KEYHOLE COUNTRY. A Story about Things You would Certainly See if You Went through the Keyhole. London, Sampson Low, 1885. 133p [BM

**Jetna (pseud)**

JOHN ANDERSON, MY JO. Toronto, Poole, n.d. 57p [OTMC

**Johnson, Charles Nelson, 1860–**

THE HERMIT OF THE NONQUON. Chicago, Rand McNally, 1893. 235p [LC

**Johnson, Emily Pauline, 1862–1913**

THE LEGEND OF THE CHUCK OLUK. Abbreviated from LEGENDS OF VANCOUVER. Vancouver, Handicrafts Guild, n.d. 8p [BVaU

LEGENDS OF VANCOUVER. Vancouver, Thompson Stationery Co., 1911. 89p [Various later editions with different paging and place of publication.] [BM BVaU BViPA LC NSHD OTU QMM

THE MOCCASIN MAKER. With introduction by Sir Gilbert Parker, and appreciation by Charles Mair. Toronto, Briggs, 1913. 248p [BM BVaU NBFU OTMC QMM

THE SHAGGANAPPI. With introduction by Ernest Thompson Seton. Toronto, Briggs, 1912. 257p [BM BVaU NSHD OTU QMM

**Johnson, Frank**

GILES AND JANEY; or, The Kindly Gentleman. A Canadian Tale. Montreal, Lovell, 1867. 11p [OTP

**Johnson, George Washington, 1839–1917**

THE BELLE OF BLADEN'S BROOK. A Novel. Cleveland, 1865. 200p [BCF BibC

THE MENTE'S SECRET; or, The Vengeance of Madra. A Novel. Cleveland, 1864. 180p [BCF BibC

**Johnson, Natalie Gordon (Wilson)**

PASSION FRUIT. London, Mitre, 1942. 191p [BM

**Johnson, Walter Seely, 1880–**

PASTOR INVICTUS; or, Rebellion in St. Eustache. A Story of Quebec Province. Montreal, Quality Press, 1931. 78p [BVaU NBFU OTP QMM

**Johnston, Mabel Annesley (Sullivan), 1870–1945**

TALES OF OLD TORONTO. ... By Suzanne Marny [pseud]. Toronto, Briggs, 1909. 166p [BM BVaU OTU QMM

**Johnston, Maysie F.**

BEAUTY NOT COMPLETE. Toronto, Nelson, 1936. 350p [BM

**Jones, Alice, 1853–1933**

BUBBLES WE BUY. Boston, Turner, 1903. 409p [Pub. in England under title:

ISABEL BRODERICK. Bubbles We Buy. London, Lane, 1904. 410p] [BM LC NBFU OOP

FLAME OF FROST. New York, Appleton, 1914. 316p [BM LC NBFU

GABRIEL PRAED'S CASTLE. Boston, Turner, 1904. 380p [BM LC NSHD OOP

MARCUS HOLBEACH'S DAUGHTER. New York, Appleton, 1912. 331p [BM LC OTU

THE NIGHT HAWK. A Romance of the '60's. By Alix John [pseud]. New York, Stokes, 1901. 378p [BM LC

**Jones, Mrs. Nancy, 1890–1959**

THE STARS MAKE ROOM. A Novel. Toronto, Ryerson, 1957. 302p

**Jones, Susan (Morrow), 1864?–1926**

THE CAREER OF MRS. OSBORNE. By Carleton-Milecete [pseud]. New York, Smart Set Pub., 1903. 211p [LC OTMC

A DETACHED PIRATE. The Romance of Gay Vandeleur. By Helen Milecete [pseud]. Boston, Little Brown, 1903. 347p [Also: London, Greening, 1900. 232p] [BM LC OTMC

THE FOREST RUNNER. By S. Carleton [pseud]. London, Melrose, 1925. 268p [BM

A GIRL OF THE NORTH. A Story of London and Canada. By Helen Milecete [pseud]. London, Greening, 1900. 330p [BM OTMC

THE LA CHANCE MINE MYSTERY. By S. Carleton [pseud]. Boston, Little Brown, 1920. 304p [BM LC

THE MICMAC. By S. Carleton [pseud]. New York, Holt, 1904. 234p [BM LC OTMC

OUT OF DROWNING VALLEY. By S. Carleton Jones [pseud]. New York, Holt, 1910. 315p [LC

**Jordan, John, 1920–**

THE YOUNGER ONES. New York, Pageant Press, 1952. 217p

**Jordan, Mary V.**

NOW AND FOREVER. Toronto, Ryerson, 1945. 240p [LC OTMC

**Keirstead, Burton Seely, 1907–**

THE BROWNSVILLE MURDERS. By B.S. Keirstead and D. Frederick Campbell. New York, Macmillan, 1933. 275p [LC NBFU OTMC

**Kelly, Judith Sage, 1908–**

A DIPLOMATIC INCIDENT. Boston, Houghton, 1949. 277p [BM LC OTMC

IT WON'T BE FLOWERS. London, Harper, 1936. 272p [LC OTMC

MARRIAGE IS A PRIVATE AFFAIR. New York, Harper, 1941. 359p [BM LC OTMC

**Kelly, Sidney James, 1892–**

THE END OF BONDAGE. A Novel. Vancouver, Author, 1943. 178p [BVaU

**Kendall, Ralph Selwood, 1878–**

BENTON OF THE ROYAL MOUNTED. A Tale of the Royal Northwest Mounted Police. New York, Lane, 1918. 318p [BM LC NBFU OTMC

THE LUCK OF THE MOUNTED. A Tale of the Royal Northwest Mounted Police. New York, Lane, 1920. 312p [BM BVaU LC NSHD OTMC QMM

**Kendall, Rev. Sidney C.**

AMONG THE LAURENTIANS. A Camping Story. Toronto, Briggs, 1885. 139p [BM BVaU OTU QMM

THE LADY OF MARK. ... New York, Abbey, 1901. 151p [LC

THE SOUNDINGS OF HELL. Los Angeles, 1903. 162p [LC

**Kennedy, Howard Angus, 1861–1938**

THE NEW WORLD FAIRY BOOK. New York, Dutton, 1904. 354p [Also pub. as THE CANADIAN FAIRY BOOK. Toronto, Dent, 1927. 354p] [BM LC OTMC

PROFESSOR BLACKIE, HIS SAYINGS AND DOINGS. London, Clarke, 1895. 344p [BM OTU QMM

THE RED MAN'S WONDER BOOK. [Indian Legends.] New York, Dutton, 1931. 366p [BVaU LC OTMC QMM

UNSOUGHT ADVENTURE. Montreal, Carrier, 1929. 320p [BM BVaU LC NBFU OKQ QMM

**Kennedy, James B.**

AFLOAT FOR ETERNITY; or, A Pilgrim's Progress for the Times. Toronto, Briggs, 1893. 190p [NSHD

**Kennedy, John de Navarre, 1888–**

CRIME IN REVERSE. Toronto, Nelson, 1939. 345p [BM LC NBFU OTMC

IN THE SHADOW OF THE CHEKA. Toronto, Nelson, 1935. 320p [LC NBFU OTMC

THE RAIN OF DEATH. Toronto, Nelson, 1945. 324p [BM BVaU NBFU OTMC

**Kennedy, Roderick Stuart, 1889–1953**

THE ROAD SOUTH. Toronto, Ambassador Books, 1947. 266p [BVaU NBFU OTMC QMM

**Kent, Agnes Scott**

DAVID. A Jewish Lad's Conversion to Christianity. Toronto, Evangelical Pub., 1926. 52p [OTMC

RACHEL. Toronto, Evangelical Pub., 1930. 223p [LC OTMC

ZONYA, DAUGHTER OF ABRAHAM. The Story of her Quest for Light. Toronto, Evangelical Pub., 1938. 314p [LC OTMC AEU

**Kent, Madeleine Fabiola**

THE CORSAIR. A Biographical Novel of Jean Lafitte, Hero of the Battle of New Orleans. Garden City, N.Y., Doubleday, 1955. 299p

**Kerr, Illingworth Holey, 1905–**

GAY DOGS AND DARK HORSES. Toronto, Dent, 1946. 372p [BVaU NBFU OTMC SSU

**Kerr, William Hastings, 1826–1888**

THE ADDRESS OF THE HON. JOHN THORN TO THE FREE AND ENLIGHTENED ELECTORS OF SPLASHVILLE CENTRE, AS ORIGINALLY COMPOSED AND WRITTEN. N.p., n.d. 5p [Amtmann

**Kidd, Henry George, 1878–**

BEN HALLEY'S CREW. A Tale of the Woods and River. Sherbrooke, Page Print., 1923. 404p [BM BVaU LC OOP QMSS

**Kilpatrick, Dorothy Hamilton**

THE ROMANCE OF PRINCE RAMA, AND OTHER INDIAN TALES. Toronto, World Friendship, 1926. 153p [BVaU OTMC

**King, Basil, 1859–1928**

THE BREAK OF DAY. A Novel. London, Harper, 1930. 346p [BVaU LC NBFU OTMC

THE CITY OF COMRADES. New York, Harper, 1919. 405p [BM BVaU LC NSHD OTMC QMM

THE DUST FLOWER. New York, Harper, 1922. 349p [BM BVaU NBFU OTMC QMM

THE EMPTY SACK. New York, Harper, 1921. 445p [BVaU LC NBFU OTMC QMM

THE GIANT'S STRENGTH. New York, Harper, 1907. 341p [BM BVaU LC OTMC

GOING WEST. New York, Harper, 1919. 48p [LC NBFU OTP

GRISELDA. Chicago, Stone, 1900. 333p [LC

THE HAPPY ISLES. New York, Harper, 1923. 485p [BM BVaU LC NSHD OTMC QMM

THE HIGH FORFEIT. A Novel. New York, Harper, 1925. 340p [BM BVaU LC NBFU OTMC QMM

THE HIGH HEART. New York, Grosset & Dunlap, 1917. 419p [BVaU LC NBFU OTMC

IN THE GARDEN OF CHARITY. New York, Harper, 1903. 319p [BM BVaU LC NBFU OTMC

THE INNER SHRINE. A Novel of Today. [Anon] New York, Harper, 1909. 355p [BM BVaU LC NBFU OTMC QMM

LET NOT MAN PUT ASUNDER. A Novel. New York, Harper, 1901. 424p [BM BVaU LC NBFU OTMC

THE LETTER OF THE CONTRACT. New York, Harper, 1914. 209p [BM BVaU LC NBFU OTMC

THE LIFTED VEIL. New York, Harper, 1917. 340p [BM BVaU LC NBFU OTMC QMM

PLUCK. A Novel. New York, Harper, 1928. 323p [BVaU LC NBFU OTMC
SATAN AS LIGHTNING. A Novel. New York, Harper, 1929. 280p [LC NBFU OTMC
THE SIDE OF THE ANGELS. A Novel. New York, Burt, 1916. 394p [BM BVaU LC NBFU OTMC
THE SPREADING DAWN. Stories of the Great Transition. New York, Harper, 1927. 316p [BM BVaU LC NBFU OTMC QMM
THE STEPS OF HONOR. New York, Harper, 1904. 285p [BM BVaU LC NBFU
THE STREET CALLED STRAIGHT. A Novel. By the Author of THE INNER SHRINE [pseud]. London, Harper, 1912. 414p [BM BVaU LC NBFU OTMC QMM
THE THREAD OF FLAME. New York, Harper, 1920. 350p [LC NBFU OTMC QMM
THE WAY HOME. A Novel. New York, Burt, 1913. 546p [BM BVaU LC OTMC QMM
THE WILD OLIVE. A Novel. By the Author of THE INNER SHRINE [pseud]. New York, Harper, 1910. 346p [BM BVaU LC NBFU OTMC

**King, Violet May**

BETTER HARVEST. Toronto, Dent, 1945. 366p [BVaU NBFU OTMC

**Kingsley, Harold**

THE FIFTH GOD. London, Selwyn & Blount, 1928. 301p [BM LC
KONG. New York, Dodd Mead, 1927. 309p [BM LC NBFU QMSS

**Kirby, William, 1817–1906**

THE GOLDEN DOG (LE CHIEN D'OR). A Legend of Quebec. Montreal, Lovell, 1877. 678p [BVaU NSHD OTP QMBM
THE GOLDEN DOG. ... A Romance of the Days of Louis Quinze in Quebec. "Authorized edition." Boston, Page, 1896. 624p [Numerous later editions.] [BM BVaU NSHD OTU QMM
THE GOLDEN DOG (LE CHIEN D'OR). A Romance of Old Quebec. Shortened ed., with an intro. by E.C. Woodley. Toronto, Macmillan, 1931. 227p [BVaU MWU NBSaM OONL

**Kiriak, Illia, 1888–1955**

SONS OF THE SOIL. Toronto, Ryerson, 1959. 303p

**Kirk, Abdier**

THE TWO SPIRITS. A Tale, written in Imitation of the German. Halifax, 1843. 46p [NSHP

**Kirkconnell, Watson, 1895–**

TITUS THE TOAD. London, Oxford U. Press, 1939. 60p [BVa OTU

**Kirkpatrick, Ernest Stanley, 1871–**

TALES OF THE ST. JOHN RIVER AND OTHER STORIES. Toronto, Briggs, 1904. 132p [BM BVaU LC NSHD OTU

**Klanak Press**

KLANAK ISLANDS. A Collection of Short Stories by Henry Kreisel and Others. Vancouver, Klanak Press, 1959. 79p

**Klein, Abraham Moses, 1909–**

THE SECOND SCROLL. New York, Knopf, 1951. 198p

**Knister, Raymond, 1900–1932**

CANADIAN SHORT STORIES. Ed. by ——. Toronto, Macmillan, 1928. 340p [BM BVaU LC NSHD OKQ QMM

MY STAR PREDOMINANT. Toronto, Ryerson, 1934. 319p [BM BVaU NBFU OTU

WHITE NARCISSUS. A Novel. New York, Harcourt, 1929. 250p [BM BVaU LC NBFU OKQ QMM

**Knowles, Robert Edward, 1868–1946**

THE ATTIC GUEST. A Novel. Toronto, Revell, 1909. 402p [BM BVaU LC NBFU OTU QMM

THE DAWN AT SHANTY BAY. Toronto, Revell, 1907. 156p [BM BVaU LC NBFU OTU QMM

THE HANDICAP. A Novel of Pioneer Days. Toronto, Revell, 1910. 386p [BM BVaU LC NBFU OTU QMM

ST. CUTHBERT'S. A Novel. Toronto, Revell, 1905. 339p [Pub. in England as ST. CUTHBERT'S OF THE WEST] [BM BVaU LC NBFU OTU

THE SINGER OF THE KOOTENAY. A Tale of Today. Toronto, Revell, 1911. 368p [BM BVaU LC NBFU OTU

THE UNDERTOW. A Tale of Both Sides of the Sea. Toronto, Revell, 1906. 403p [New ed.: Toronto, McClelland, 1935.] [BM BVaU LC NBFU OTU

THE WEB OF TIME. Toronto, Revell, 1908. 415p [BM BVaU LC OKQ

**Knox, Alexander, 1907–**

BRIDE OF QUIETNESS. Toronto, Macmillan, 1933. 302p [BM LC NBFU OTU

**Knox, Jean**

A MODERN LEGEND. N.p., 1916. 28p [OOP

**Knox, Olive Elsie (Robinson)**

BLACK FALCON. Toronto, Ryerson, 1954. 192p

BY PADDLE AND SADDLE. Toronto, Macmillan, 1943. 270p [BM BVaU LC OTU

RED RIVER SHADOWS. Toronto, Macmillan, 1948. 303p [BM BVaU NBFU OTU

THE YOUNG SURVEYOR. Toronto, Ryerson, 1956. 164p

**Ko-Ko (pseud)**

SOCIETY TYPES. Toronto, Morang, 1899. 108p [OOP

**Kreisel, Henry, 1922–**

THE RICH MAN. A Novel. Toronto, McClelland, 1948. 263p [BM BVaU NBFU OTU QMM

**Kristofferson, Mrs. Kristine Benson**
TANYA. Toronto, Ryerson, 1951. 250p

**Kyle, "Tom" E.**
THE INVESTIGATOR (copyrighted). Founded upon Actual Facts. Toronto, Investigator Pub., 1930. 42p [BVaU

**Lacroix, Henry Olivier, 1826–1897**
THE UN-PACIFIC SCANDAL AT THE CUSTOM-HOUSE OF MONTREAL. ... Montreal, Lacroix, 1873. 16p [NSHD OTU QMSS

**Laing, Nora**
DESERT SHIPS. London, Skeffington, 1936. 288p [BM

**Lambert, Richard Stanton, 1894–**
THE INNOCENCE OF EDMUND GALLEY. London, Newnes, [1936]. 209p [BViP LC MW OTP
NORTH FOR ADVENTURE. [Fictionized account of Samuel Hearne's search for the Coppermine River, 1769–1772.] Toronto, McClelland, 1952. 208p

**Lambie, Alexander, 1870–**
A STRANGER IN OUR MIDST, and Some Western Fables. [Anon] Vancouver, Author, [1934?]. 189p [BM BVaU NBFU OTMC

**Lambkin, Amelia MacMillan**
BUCKSKIN AND ERMINE. Cedar Rapids, Iowa, Torch Press, 1928. 170p [OOP

**L'Ami, Charles E.**
THE GREEN MADONNA. Philadelphia, Westminster Press, 1952. 302p

**Lancefield, Richard Thomas, 1854–1911**
NO LAGGARDS WE. [Anon] Hamilton, Author, n.d. 84p [OTP
TIM AND MRS. TIM. A Story for the "Club" and "Society" Man and the "New Woman." Toronto, Toronto News Co., 1897. 145p [BM LC OTMC

**Lane, Edward**
THE FUGITIVES; or, A Trip to Canada. An Interesting Tale, Chiefly Founded on Facts, Interspersed with Observations on the Manners, Customs, etc., of the Colonists and Indians. London, Effingham Wilson, 1830. 496p [BM BVaU OTP

**Langford, Robert John Spinluff, 1887–**
HOW I WON THE WAR, by Wellington Marlborough Wolseley Smythe. As told to ——. Toronto, Copp Clark, 1940. 96p [OTU

**Lanigan, George Thomas, 1846–1886**
FABLES. By George Washington Aesop [pseud] and Bret Harte. ... London, Hamilton, 1882. 54p [A pirated edition, with three fables by Bret Harte.] [BM LC

FABLES. Taken "Anywhere, anywhere, out of the World." By G. Washington Aesop [pseud]. New York, The World, 1878. 52p [BM LC

**Lanigan, Richard**

THEY TWO; or, Phases of Life in Eastern Canada Fifty Years Ago. Written in 1875 by an Ex-Journalist [pseud]. Montreal, Lovell, 1888. 164p [BVaU NSHD OOP QMBM

**Laskey, John K.**

ALETHES; or, The Roman Exile. Saint John, Shives, 1840. 155p [NBSaM

**Late Physician, A (pseud)**

THE RUINED MERCHANT; GRAVE DOINGS; THE STATESMAN; THE THUNDERSTRUCK; and THE BOXER. By a Late Physician [pseud]. Toronto, Brewer McPhail, 1849. 319p [OTP

**Lauder, Mrs. Maria Elise Turner**

AT LAST. A Novel. Toronto, Briggs, 1893. 310p [BVaU LC OTP

LEGENDS AND TALES OF THE HARZ MOUNTAINS, NORTH GERMANY. By Toofie Lauder [pseud]. London, Hodder, 1881. 259p [BM BVaU LC OTU QMM

**Laurence, Frances Elsie (Fry), 1893–**

HALF A GIPSY. By Christine Field [pseud]. London, Melrose, 1916. 348p [BM LC

**Laurence, Margaret (Wemyss), 1926–**

THIS SIDE JORDAN. Toronto, McClelland, 1960. xi + 281p

**Lauriston, Victor, 1881–**

INGLORIOUS MILTON. An Unconventional Biography. Chatham, Tiny Tree Club, 1934. 408p [BVaU LC NSHD OTMC QMM

THE TWENTY-FIRST BURR. New York, Doran, 1922. 292p [BVaU LC NBFU OTMC

**Laut, Agnes Christina, 1871–1936**

THE FREEBOOTERS OF THE WILDERNESS. Toronto, Musson, 1910. 443p [BM BVaU LC OTMC

HERALDS OF EMPIRE. Being the Story of one Ramsay Stanhope, Lieutenant to Pierre Radisson in the Northwest Fur Trade. Toronto, Briggs, 1902. 372p [BM BVaU LC NSHD OKQ

THE NEW DAWN. New York, Moffat Yard, 1913. 542p [LC NBFU OTMC

LORDS OF THE NORTH. A Romance of the North-west. ... Toronto, Briggs, 1900. 442p [BM BVaU LC NSHD OKQ

THE QUENCHLESS LIGHT. New York, Appleton, 1924. 290p [BM BVaU LC NBFU OTMC

**Lauzon, Edythe Morahan-de**

FROM THE KINGDOM OF THE STARS. The Vision of John Hilary, a Prince of Abyssinia. Montreal, Urquhart, 1922. 410p [LC NBFU OTMC

**Lawrence, W.H.C.**

THE STORM OF '92. A Grandfather's Tale Told in 1932. [Anon] Toronto, Sheppard, 1889. 71p [BVaU OTU

**Lawson, Jessie (Kerr), 1838–1917**

THE CURSE THAT CAME HOME. Edinburgh, Oliphant, 1894. 256p [BM

DOCTOR BRUNO'S WIFE. A Toronto Society Story. London, Simkin Marshall, 1893. 208p [BM OTU

EUPHIE LYN; or, The Fishers of Old Inweerie. Edinburgh, Oliphant, 1893. 256p [BM OTU

A FAIR REBEL. London, Simkin Marshall, 1899. 96p [EngCat

THE HARVEST OF MOLOCH. A Story of Today. Toronto, Poole, 1908. 320p [BM BVaU NSHD OTMC

MISS NERO. London, Simkin Marshall, 1899. 94p [EngCat

A VAIN SACRIFICE. A Novel. Edinburgh, Oliphant, 1892. 221p [BM

WILLIAM MARAH. London, Simkin Marshall, 1900. 94p [EngCat

**Layhew, Mrs. Jane**

$R_x$ FOR MURDER. Philadelphia, Lippincott, 1946. 252p [BM LC OTU

**Leacock, Stephen Butler, 1869–1944**

AFTERNOONS IN UTOPIA. Tales of the New Time. Toronto, Macmillan, 1932. 240p [BM BVaU OTU

ARCADIAN ADVENTURES WITH THE IDLE RICH. London, Lane, 1914. 310p [Also: with an intro. by Ralph L. Curry. Toronto, McClelland, 1959. vii-xi + 157p] [BM BVaU LC NBFU OKQ

BEHIND THE BEYOND, AND OTHER CONTRIBUTIONS TO HUMAN KNOWLEDGE. London, Lane, 1913. 195p [BM BVaU LC NBFU OKQ

THE BEST OF LEACOCK. *See* THE BODLEY HEAD LEACOCK.

THE BODLEY HEAD LEACOCK. Ed. with an intro. by J.B. Priestley. London, Bodley Head, 1957. 464p [Canadian ed., (Toronto, McClelland, 1957), has title: THE BEST OF LEACOCK.]

COLLEGE DAYS. New York, Dodd Mead, 1923. 169p [BM BVaU LC NBFU OTU

THE DRY PICKWICK AND OTHER INCONGRUITES. London, Lane, 1932. 271p [BM BVaU LC NBFU OTU

FRENZIED FICTION. London, Lane, 1918. 240p [BM BVaU LC NSHD OKQ

FUNNY PIECES. A Book of Random Sketches. New York, Dodd Mead, 1936. 292p [BM BVaU LC OTU QMM

FURTHER FOOLISHNESS. Sketches and Satires on the Follies of the Day. London, Lane, 1916. 312p [BM BVaU LC NBFU OKQ

THE GARDEN OF FOLLY. Toronto, Gundy, 1924. 282p [BM BVaU NSHD OKQ

HAPPY STORIES, JUST TO LAUGH AT. New York, Dodd Mead, 1943. 240p [BM BVaU LC NSHD OTU QMM

HERE ARE MY LECTURES AND STORIES. New York, Dodd Mead, 1937. 251p [BM BVa LC OTU QMM

THE HOHENZOLLERNS IN AMERICA. With the Bolsheviks in Berlin and Other Impossibilities. London, Lane, 1919. 269p [BM BVaU LC NSHD OKQ

THE IRON MAN & THE TIN WOMAN. With Other Such Futurities. A Book of Little Sketches of Today and To-morrow. New York, Dodd Mead, 1929. 309p [BM BVaU LC NSHD OTU QMM

LAST LEAVES. Toronto, McClelland, 1945. 213p [BM BVaU LC NSHD OTU

LAUGH PARADE. A New Collection of the Wit and Humor of Stephen Leacock. New York, Dodd Mead, 1940. 326p [BM BVaU LC NBFU OTU QMM

LAUGH WITH LEACOCK. An Anthology of the Best Works of Stephen Leacock. New York, Dodd Mead, 1930. 339p [BVaU LC NBFU OTU

THE LEACOCK BOOK. Being Selections from the Works of Stephen Leacock. Arranged with an intro. by Ben Travers. London, Lane, 1930. 248p [BM BVaU

THE LEACOCK ROUNDABOUT. A Treasury of the Best Works of Stephen Leacock. New York, Dodd Mead, 1946. 422p [BVaU LC OTU QMM

LITERARY LAPSES. A Book of Sketches. Montreal, Gazette Print., 1910. 125p [Many later editions. Also: with an intro. by Robertson Davies. Toronto, McClelland, 1957. xi + 146p] [BM BVaU NBFU OTMC QMM

MEMORIES OF CHRISTMAS. Toronto, Bush, 1943. 29p [Two Christmas essays. ... selected from MY REMARKABLE UNCLE.] [OTP

THE METHODS OF MR. SELLYER. A Book Store Study. New York, Lane, 1914. 37p [Written for Convention of American Booksellers' Assoc., May 14, 1914.] [BVaU NBFU OLU

MODEL MEMOIRS AND OTHER SKETCHES FROM SIMPLE TO SERIOUS. New York, Dodd Mead, 1938. 316p [BM BVaU LC NBFU OKQ QMM

MOONBEAMS FROM THE LARGER LUNACY. New York, Lane, 1915. 282p [BVaU LC NBFU OKQ

MY REMARKABLE UNCLE AND OTHER SKETCHES. New York, Dodd Mead, 1942. 313p [BM BVaU LC NSHD OKQ QMM

NONSENSE NOVELS. London, Lane, 1911. 230p [BM BVaU LC NSHD OKQ

OVER THE FOOTLIGHTS, AND OTHER FANCIES. London, Lane, 1923. 278p [BM BVaU LC NSHD OKQ QMM

THE PERFECT SALESMAN. Ed. by E.V. Knox. New York, McBride, 1934. 151p [Also pub. under title: STEPHEN LEACOCK. London, Methuen, 1934. 151p] [BVa LC NBFU OTU QMM

SHORT CIRCUITS. Toronto, Macmillan, 1928. 336p [BM BVaU LC NBFU OTU QMM

STEPHEN LEACOCK. London, Methuen, 1934. 151p [See THE PERFECT SALESMAN.] [BM

STEPHEN LEACOCK'S LAUGH PARADE. New York, Dodd Mead, 1940. 326p [See LAUGH PARADE.]

SUNSHINE SKETCHES OF A LITTLE TOWN. London, Lane, 1912. 264p [Many later editions. Also: with an intro. by Malcolm Ross. Toronto, McClelland, 1960. iii + 153p] [BVaU LC OKQ QMM

THE UNICORN LEACOCK. Ed. by James Reeves. London, Hutchinson, 1960. 191p

WET WIT AND DRY HUMOUR. Distilled from the Pages of ——. New York, Dodd Mead, 1931. 260p [BVaU LC OTU

WINNOWED WISDOM. A New Book of Humour. New York, Dodd Mead, 1926. 288p [BM BVaU LC NBFU OTU

WINSOME WINNIE, AND OTHER NEW NONSENSE NOVELS. London, Lane, 1920. 243p [BM BVaU LC NBFU OKQ

**Lean, Mary**

JOAN OF GLEN GARLAND. A Canadian Girl Guide Story. Toronto, Upper Canada Tract Soc., 1934. 286p [BM OTP

**Leavitt, Lydia (Brown)**

BOHEMIAN SOCIETY. Brockville, Brockville Times, [1884?]. 65p [BVaU LC OTMC QMM

WISE OR OTHER WISE. By Lydia and Thaddeus Leavitt. Toronto, Wells, 1898. 64p [OTU

**Leavitt, Thaddeus W.H., 1844?–1909**

KAFFIR, KANGAROO, KLONDYKE. Tales of the Gold Fields. Toronto, Browne, 1898. 86p [OTU

THE WITCH OF PLUM HOLLOW. Toronto, Wells, 1892. 254p [LC OTU

**Lemieux, Kenneth**

HICKORY HOUSE. By Kenneth Orvis [pseud]. Toronto, Harlequin Books, 1956. 160p

**LeMoine, James MacPherson, 1825–1912**

THE LEGENDS OF THE ST. LAWRENCE. Told during a Cruise of the Yacht *Hirondelle* from Montreal to Gaspé. Quebec, Holiwell, 1898. 203p [BM BVaU NSWA OTU QMM

**Leonard, Grace Emma (Pettingell)**

THE CANADIAN FAMILY ROBINSON. A Modern Tale of the Shipwreck and Subsequent Adventures of a Family. Toronto, Upper Canada Tract.Soc., 1935. 254p [Also: Fredericton, U. Press of New Brunswick, [1955]. 254p [BM NBFU OTMC

**Leonard, May, 1862–**

TRIXIE'S INHERITANCE; or, Which Shall Win? Saint John, Daily Telegraph, 1886. 50p [OTP

ZOE; or, Some Day. Saint John, Day, 1888. 87p [NSWA

**Leprohon, Rosanna Eleanor (Mullins), 1829–1879**

ANTOINETTE DE MIRECOURT; or, Secret Marrying and Secret Sorrowing. A Canadian Tale. Montreal, Lovell, 1864. 369p [French trans. by J.A. Genand pub. at Montreal in 1865. 342p] [BVaU NBFU OTMC

ARMAND DURAND; or, A Promise Fulfilled. Montreal, Lovell, 1868. 77p [Also pub. in French.] [BM BVaU OTU QMM

CLIVE WESTON'S WEDDING ANNIVERSARY. Montreal, 1872. [BCF DCB

LE MANOIR DE VILLERAI. Un Roman Canadien. Traduit de l'Anglais. Montreal, Beauchemin & Valois, 1884. 383p [The English original appeared in the *Family Herald,* Montreal, 1859. The French translation by E.L. De Bellefeuille first appeared in Montreal, 1861. 405p] [BM BVaU NBFU OTP

The following six novels were pub. only in serial form (see BCF BibC DCB):

CLARENCE FITZ-CLARENCE. 1851.

EVA HUNTINGDON. A Tale. 1850.

EVELEEN O'DONNELL. 1859.

FLORENCE FITZ-HARDINGE. 1849.

IDA BERESFORD. 1848.

MY VISIT TO FAIRVIEW VILLA.

**LeRossignol, James Edward, 1866–**

THE BEAUPORT ROAD. Tales of Old Quebec. Toronto, McClelland, 1928. 291p [BVaU NSHD OTU QMM

THE FLYING CANOE (La Chasse Galerie). Toronto, McClelland, 1929. 302p [BVaU NSHD OTP QMM

THE HABITANT-MERCHANT. Toronto, Macmillan, 1939. 258p [BVaU NSHD OTU QMM

JEAN BAPTISTE. A Story of French Canada. Toronto, Dent, 1915. 269p [BM BVaU LC NSHD OTU QMM

LITTLE STORIES OF QUEBEC. Toronto, Briggs, 1908. 170p [BVaU LC NBFU OTU QMM

**Leslie, Edwin**

KNIGHTS WHO FOUGHT THE DRAGON. Philadelphia, Sunday School Times, 1906. 207p [BM LC OOP

**Leslie, Mary, 1842–1920**

THE CROMABOO MAIL CARRIER. A Canadian Love Story. By James Thomas Jones [pseud]. Guelph, Hacking, 1878. 296p [BVaU LC OTP

**Lesperance, John Talon, 1838–1891**

THE BASTONNAIS. Tale of the American Invasion of Canada in 1775–76. Toronto, Belford, 1877. 359p [Also pub. in French: Montreal, 1896.] [BM BVaU LC NSHP OKQ

TUQUE BLEUE. A Christmas Snowshoe Sketch. Montreal, Dawson, 1882. 35p [BVaU NSHD OTMC QMM

**Levesque, Paul, 1913–**

PLAYING WITH MURDER. By Will U. Lovitt [pseud]. New York, Greenwich Book Publishers, 1960. 69p

**Levine, Albert Norman, 1923–**
THE ANGLED ROAD. Toronto, McClelland, 1952. 158p

**Lewis, Josephine**
AS THE ROWANS GO GAY. Glasgow, Scot., W. MacLellan, 1952. 322p
SANTA CLAUS AND JACK FROST. Story for Children. London, Stockwell, 1935. 80p [CC

**Liddle, Beatrice Boles**
THREE INTERESTING STORIES: ... Glorified Wilderness ...; Path of Earthly Stars ...; Seaward Deluge. ... Calgary, Albertan Job Press, 1946. 54p [LC QMBM

**Lighthall, William Douw, 1857–1954**
THE FALSE CHEVALIER; or, The Lifeguard of Marie Antoinette. Montreal, Grafton, 1898. 328p [BM BVaU NBFU OTU QMM
HIAWATHA THE HOCHELAGAN. An Aboriginal Romance. Montreal, 1906. 200p [T&C
THE MASTER OF LIFE. A Romance of the Five Nations. ... Toronto, Musson, 1908. 262p [BM BVaU LC NSHD OKQ QMM
THE YOUNG SEIGNEUR; or, Nation-Making. A Romance. By Wilfrid Chateauclair [pseud]. Montreal, Drysdale, 1888. 200p [BM BVaU NSHD OTU QMM

**Lindsay, Robert Howard, 1910–**
FOWL MURDER. Mystery of Between the Lines. Boston, Little Brown, 1941. 285p [LC

**Livesay, Florence Hamilton (Randal), 1874–1953**
SAVOUR OF SALT. Toronto, Dent, 1927. 277p [BM BVaU NBFU OTP QMM

**Livingston, Stuart, 1865–1923**
THE HISTORY OF PROFESSOR PAUL. A Novel. Toronto and Hamilton, Hunter & Grant, [1889]. 102p [BVaU

**Lizars, Robina, –1918**
COMMITTED TO HIS CHARGE. A Canadian Chronicle. By R. and K.M. Lizars. Toronto, Morang, 1900. 312p [BM BVaU NBFU OTMC

**Lloyd-Owen, Frances**
THE CALL OF THE COUGAR. London, Harrap, 1941. 256p [BM
THE GNOME'S KITCHEN. A Story of Woodland Animals. London, Harrap, 1937. 254p [BM BVaU
JOE & PINTO. London, Harrap, 1937. 250p [BM BVa

**Logan, Annie Robertson (Macfarlane), –1933**
THE CHILDREN OF THE HEARTH. New York, 1891. [BCF

**Long, Morden Heaton, 1886–**
KNIGHTS ERRANT OF THE WILDERNESS. Toronto, Macmillan, 1925. 223p [BM BVaU LC NBFU OTP

**Loomer, Leslie Oran, 1878–**

THE PROPHET. A Story of the Two Kingdoms of Ancient Palestine. Windsor, N.S. Anslow, 1911. 171p [BM NSHPL OONL

**Louth, Cyril E., 1906?–1956**

BUT FOR THE GRACE OF GOD. New York, Pageant Press, 1956. 112p

**Low, May (Austin), 1863–**

DEVICES AND DESIRES. Montreal, 1892. [MOR'12

**Lowrey, Harold C., 1886–**

INDIAN GOLD. Toronto, Musson, 1929. 244p [BVaU NBFU OTMC

YOUNG CANADA BOYS WITH THE S.O.S. ON THE FRONTIER. Toronto, Allen, 1918. 202p [OONL

**Lowry, Malcolm, 1909–1957**

ULTRAMARINE. London, Cape, 1933. 276p [Rev. ed., Toronto, Clarke Irwin, 1962. 203p] [BM BVaU NBFU OTU

UNDER THE VOLCANO. New York, Reynal, 1947. 375p [BM BVaU LC NBFU OTU QMSS

**Lund, Captain T.**

IN THE SNOW. A Romance of the Canadian Backwoods. Toronto, Musson, n.d. 247p [ACG BM OONL

THE LONE TRAIL OMNIBUS. London, Werner Laurie, 1936. 702p [Contains: "Weston of the Royal North-West Mounted Police," "Up North," and "The Murder of Dave Brandon."] [BM

THE MURDER OF DAVE BRANDON. London, Werner Laurie, 1931. 244p [BM BViPA OONL

ROBBERY AT PORTAGE BEND. A Story of the Royal North-West Mounted Police. London, Werner Laurie, 1933. 252p [BM BViPA OTU

STEELE BEY'S REVENGE. London, Werner Laurie, 1934. 249p [BM

UP NORTH. A Tale from Northern Canada. London, Werner Laurie, 1929. 253p [BM OONL

THE VANISHED PROSPECTOR. A Story from Northern Canada. London, Werner Laurie, 1937. 285p [BM BViPA OONL

WESTON OF THE ROYAL NORTH-WEST MOUNTED POLICE. London, Werner Laurie, 1928. 252p [BM BViPA OOP

**Lyle-Smythe, Alan, 1914–**

ALIEN VIRUS. By Alan Caillou [pseud]. London, Davies, 1957. 249p

THE MINDANAO PEARL. By Alan Caillou [pseud]. London, Davies, 1959. 221p

THE PLOTTERS. By Alan Caillou [pseud]. London, Davies, 1960. 285p

**Lysenko, Vera**

WESTERLY WILD. Toronto, Ryerson, 1956. 284p

YELLOW BOOTS. Toronto, Ryerson, 1954. 314p

**McAlister, Lottie (Plewes), 1865–**
CLIPPED WINGS. Toronto, Briggs, 1899. 186p [BM BVaU NSHD OTU

**McAlpine, Mrs. Jennie**
PAMELA OF ECHO GLEN. New York, Pageant Press, 1954. 118p

**McArthur, Peter, 1866–1924**
THE GHOST AND THE BURGLAR. New York, McArthur & Ryder, 1905. 24p
THE PEACEMAKERS. New York, McArthur & Ryder, 1905. 24p

**Macbeth, Madge Hamilton (Lyons), 1878–1965**
THE GREAT FRIGHT, ONESIPHORE OUR NEIGHBOR. By Madge Macbeth and A.B. Conway [pseud]. New York & Montreal, Carrier, 1929. 326p [Pub. in England as: BEGGAR YOUR NEIGHBOUR. London, Paul & Co., 1929.] [BM BVaU LC NBFU OKQ
THE KINDER BEES. By Gilbert Knox [pseud]. London, Lovat Dickson, 1935. 316p [BM NBFU OTMC
KLEATH. Boston, Small Maynard, 1917. 386p [BM BVaU LC NBFU OOP
THE LAND OF AFTERNOON. A Satire. By Gilbert Knox [pseud]. Ottawa, Graphic, 1924. 352p [BVaU LC NSHD OTU
THE LONG DAY. By W.S. Dill [pseud]. Ottawa, Graphic, 1926. 232p [BVaU NBFU OTU
LOST. A Cavalier. London, Allen, 1947. 242p [BM OOP
THE PATTERSON LIMIT. Toronto, Hodder, 1923. 320p [BM NBFU OTU
SHACKLES. Ottawa, Graphic, 1926. 324p [BVaU LC NBFU OTU
SHREDS OF CIRCUMSTANCE. London, Allen, 1947. 365p [BM NBFU OOP QMBM
WINGS IN THE WEST. London, Hamilton, [1937?]. 320p [BM OTU
THE WINNING GAME. New York, Broadway Pub., 1910. 242p [LC

**McCarroll, James, 1815–1896**
RIDGEWAY. An Historical Romance of the Fenian Invasion of Canada. By Scian Dubh [pseud]. Buffalo, McCarroll, 1868. 262p [BVaU OTP

**McCaughey, Lloyd**
MODERN SHORTS. By Lloyd McCaughey, Yarker Banks, and Leslie Hamilton. Hamilton, Beaver Pubs., 1941. 188p [OTU

**McCawley, Stuart**
CAPE BRETON HUMOR. Glace Bay, N.S., Brodie Print., 1929. 64p [NSHPL

**McClintock, Gray**
ITINERANTS OF THE TIMBER LANDS. New York, Crowell, 1934. 285p [LC NBFU
THE WOLVES ARE RUNNING. A Novel. London, Blackie, 1934. 216p [BM
THE WOLVES AT COOKING LAKE AND OTHER STORIES. Albany, Lyon, 1932. 224p [BViPA LC

**McClung, Nellie Letitia (Mooney), 1873–1951**

ALL WE LIKE SHEEP AND OTHER STORIES. Toronto, Allen, 1926. 261p [BM BVaU NBFU OTMC

BE GOOD TO YOURSELF. A Book of Short Stories. Toronto, Allen, 1930. 179p [BVaU NBFU OTMC

THE BEAUTY OF MARTHA. London, Hutchinson, 1923. 288p [BM

THE BLACK CREEK STOPPING-HOUSE AND OTHER STORIES. Toronto, Briggs, 1912. 224p [BM BVaU NBFU OTP SSU

FLOWERS FOR THE LIVING. A Book of Short Stories. Toronto, Allen, 1931. 212p [BVaU NBFU OTU

LEAVES FROM LANTERN LANE. Toronto, Allen, 1936. 199p [BM BVaU NBFU OTMC

MORE LEAVES FROM LANTERN LANE. Toronto, Allen, 1937. 201p [BVaU NBFU OTU

PAINTED FIRES. New York, Dodd Mead, 1925. 316p [BM BVaU LC NBFU OTU

PURPLE SPRINGS. Toronto, Allen, 1921. 335p [BM BVaU LC NBFU OTU QMSS

THE SECOND CHANCE. New York, Doubleday, 1910. 369p [BM BVaU LC NBFU OKQ

SOWING SEEDS IN DANNY. New York, Doubleday, 1908. 313p [BM BVaU LC NBFU OKQ

WHEN CHRISTMAS CROSSED "THE PEACE." Toronto, Allen, 1923. 149p [BM BVaU NBFU OLU

**McCourt, Edward Alexander, 1907–1972**

THE FLAMING HOUR. Toronto, Ryerson, 1947. 170p [BVaU NBFU OTU QMBM

HOME IS THE STRANGER. Toronto, Macmillan, 1950. 268p [BM BVaU NBFU OTU

MUSIC AT THE CLOSE. Toronto, Ryerson, 1947. 228p [BVaU NBFU OTU

WALK THROUGH THE VALLEY. Toronto, McClelland, 1958. 222p

THE WOODEN SWORD. Toronto, McClelland, 1956. 255p

**McCowan, Daniel, 1882–1956**

HILL-TOP TALES. ... Toronto, Macmillan, 1948. 266p [BVaU LC NBFU OTP

**MacCrimmon, Harriet M.**

THIS IS MY COUNTRY AND OTHER STORIES. Ilfracombe, Devon, Stockwell, 1952. 23p

**McCulloch, John Herries, 1892–**

BACK ROAD TO GLORY. London, Hurst & Blackett, 1944. 168p [BM

DARK ACRES. Edinburgh, Moray Press, 1935. 318p [BM NBFU SSU

THE MEN OF KILDONAN. A Romance of the Selkirk Settlers. Toronto, McClelland, 1926. 276p [BM BVaU LC NSHD OKQ QMM

THE SPLENDID RENEGADE. New York, Coward McCann, 1928. 373p [LC NSHD OOP

TEN DAY TRAIL. Edinburgh, Moray Press, 1936. 301p [BM NBFU OOP

**McCulloch, Rev. Thomas, 1776–1843**

COLONIAL GLEANINGS ... WILLIAM AND MELVILLE. ... Edinburgh, Oliphant, 1826. 144p [Two novels bound together.] [NSHD

LETTERS OF MEPHIBOSHETH STEPSURE [pseud]. Halifax, Blackader, 1860 [actually 1862]. 143p [Reprinted from the *Acadian Recorder* of the years 1821 and 1822.] [NBFU NSHP [Also as THE STEPSURE LETTERS, with an intro. by Northrop Frye. New Canadian Library, Toronto, McClelland, 1960. 143p]

**Macdonald, Flora**

MARY MELVILLE, THE PSYCHIC. Toronto, Austin, 1900. 267p [BM LC OTU

**MacDonald, Jane Elizabeth Gostwycke (Roberts), 1864–1922**

OUR LITTLE CANADIAN COUSIN. 1. The Maritime Provinces. Boston, Page, 1904. 129p [LC NBFU OKQ

**MacDonald, John Arthur, 1912–**

DARKLY THE RIVER FLOWS. A Novel of Family Life. Toronto, Longmans, 1945. 201p [Winner of Longmans Green $1000 prize award.] [BVaU LC NBFU OTP QMM

**MacDonald, John Geddie**

THE CROSS HANGS LOW. New York, Pageant Press, 1952. 185p

**MacDonald, Marianne, 1934–**

BLACK BASS ROCK. Toronto, Macmillan, 1952. 223p

SMUGGLERS COVE. Toronto, Macmillan, 1955. 208p

THE TREASURE OF UR. Toronto, Macmillan, 1958. 222p

**Macdonald, Zillah Katherine, 1885–**

A CAP FOR CORRINE. New York, Messner, 1952. 184p

FIREMAN FOR A DAY. New York, Messner, 1952. 62p

MYSTERY OF THE PIPER'S GHOST. Philadelphia, Winston, 1954. ix + 178p

NURSE FAIRCHILD'S DECISION. Montreal, Bantam Books, 1957. 152p [First pub. New York, Messner, 1952, under title: A CAP FOR CORRINE.]

NURSE TODD'S STRANGE SUMMER. By Zillah K. Macdonald and Vivian J. Ahl. New York, Messner, 1960. 192p

ROSEMARY WINS HER CAP. By Zillah K. Macdonald with Josie Johnston [pseud]. New York, J. Messner, 1955. 192p

ROXANNE, INDUSTRIAL NURSE. By Zillah K. Macdonald with Josie Johnston [pseud]. New York, J. Messner, 1957. 192p

A TUGBOAT TOOTS FOR TERRY. New York, Messner, 1953. 63p

**Macdonell, Blanche Lucile, 1853–1924**

DIANE OF VILLE MARIE. A Romance of French Canada. Toronto, Briggs, 1898. 251p [BM BVaU NBFU OTU QMM

**McDonnell, William, 1814–1900**

EXETER HALL. A Theological Romance. New York, American News Co., 1869. 186p [LC OTMC

FAMILY CREEDS. A Romance. Toronto, Belfords & Clarke, 1879. 468p [LC OTU

THE HEATHENS OF THE HEATH. New York, Bennett, 1874. 498p [BVaU OTU

REMINISCENCES OF A PREACHER. [A Theological Romance.] Boston, Mendum, 1887. 232p [LC

**McDougall, Colin Malcolm, 1917–**

EXECUTION. Toronto, Macmillan, 1958. 227p

**McDougall, E. Jean (Taylor)**

THE LILY OF FORT GARRY. By Jane Rolyat [pseud]. Toronto, Dent, 1930. 287p [BM BVaU NBFU OTP

WILDERNESS WALLS. By Jane Rolyat [pseud]. Toronto, Dent, 1933. 268p [BM BVaU NSHD OTP

**McDougall, Rev. John, 1842–1917**

"WA-PEE MOOS-TOOCH"; or, "White Buffalo." A Tale of Life in Canada's Great West. Calgary, Herald, 1908. 336p [BM BVaU OKQ SSU

**McDougall, Margaret (Dixon), 1826–1898**

THE DAYS OF A LIFE. By Norah [pseud]. Almonte, Ont., Templeman, 1883. 438p [LC OTU

THE LADY OF THE BEACON OF ARAHEERA. A Chronicle of Innishowen. Ed. by Paul Peppergrass [pseud]. Quebec, Corey, 1857. 187p [BCF OTP

**McDowell, Franklin Davey, 1898–1965**

THE CHAMPLAIN ROAD. Toronto, Macmillan, 1939. 421p [Huronian ed.: Toronto, Macmillan, 1949. 338p] [BM BVaU LC NBFU OKQ QMM

FORGES OF FREEDOM. Toronto, Macmillan, 1943. 542p [BM BVaU LC NBFU OKQ

**McEwen, Rev. J.D.**

SANDY McDONALD IN BRAZIL. Sherbrooke, P.Q., Page Print., 1921. 123p [OONL QMSS

**McEwen, Jessie Evelyn, 1911–**

THE BLUE FLY CARAVAN. By Agnes Fisher [pseud]. Toronto, Nelson, 1932. 148p [BVaU OTMC

THE FAIRIES OF THE GLEN. By Agnes Fisher [pseud]. New York, Nelson, 1943. 40p [LC

THE LITTLE YELLOW HOUSE. Toronto, Ryerson, 1953. 249p

ONCE UPON A TIME. By Agnes Fisher [pseud]. New York, Nelson, 1943. 302p [LC

TALTREES. Toronto, Ryerson, 1949. 221p [BVaU NBFU OTMC QMM

**MacFarlan, Allan Andrew, 1899–**

CAMPFIRE ADVENTURE STORIES. New York, Association Press, 1952. 225p

**McFarlane, Arthur Emerson, 1876–1945**

BEHIND THE BOLTED DOOR? New York, Dodd Mead, 1916. 342p [BM BVaU LC

GREAT BEAR ISLAND. A Boy's Story of Adventure and Discovery. Boston, Little Brown, 1911. 290p [LC

REDNEY McGAW. A Story of the Big Show and the Cheerful Spirit. Boston, Little Brown, 1909. 268p [LC OTU

**McFarlane, Leslie, 1902–**

THE MURDER TREE. New York, Dutton, 1931. 275p [BM LC OTMC

STREETS OF SHADOW. New York, Dutton, 1930. 287p [BM LC

**MacGeorge, David, 1845–**

THE DOCTOR'S DAUGHTER. Galt, Jaffray Bros., 1905. 102p [BM BVaU OTP

**MacGillivray, Miss Carrie Holmes, –1949**

THE SHADOW OF TRADITION. A Tale of Old Glengarry. Ottawa, Graphic, 1927. 303p [Later ed.: Toronto, McClelland, 1945. 327p] [BVaU NBFU OTU QMBM

**McGillivray, James**

THE FRONTIER RIDERS. Toronto, Musson, 1925. [Also: London, Hodder, 1925. 320p] [BM

**MacGregor, Mary Esther (Miller), 1876–1961**

AS A WATERED GARDEN. By Marian Keith [pseud]. Toronto, McClelland, 1946. 298p [BVaU NBFU OTMC

THE BELLS OF ST. STEPHEN'S. By Marian Keith [pseud]. New York, Doran, 1922. 336p [BM BVaU LC NBFU OTMC

BOY OF NAZARETH. By Marian Keith [pseud]. New York, Abingdon-Cokesbury, 1950. 158p [LC

DUNCAN POLITE. The Watchman of Glenoro. By Marian Keith [pseud]. New York, Revell, 1905. 306p [BM BVaU LC NBFU OTMC QMM

THE END OF THE RAINBOW. By Marian Keith [pseud]. New York, Hodder, 1913. 352p [BM LC NBFU OTMC

THE FOREST BARRIER. A Novel of Pioneer Days. By Marian Keith [pseud]. Toronto, McClelland, 1930. 308p [NBFU OTP

A GENTLEMAN ADVENTURER. A Story of the Hudson's Bay Company. By Marian Keith [pseud]. New York, Doran, 1924. 301p [BM BVaU LC NBFU OTMC

THE GRAND LADY. By Marian Keith [pseud]. Toronto, McClelland, 1960. 222p

IN ORCHARD GLEN. By Marian Keith [pseud]. Toronto, McClelland, 1918. 274p [BVaU LC OTMC

LILACS IN THE DOORYARD. By Marian Keith [pseud]. Toronto, McClelland, 1952. 256p

LITTLE MISS MELODY. By Marian Keith [pseud]. Toronto, McClelland, 1921. 302p [BM BVaU LC OTMC QMM

'LIZABETH OF THE DALE. By Marian Keith [pseud]. Toronto, Westminster, 1910. 434p [BM BVaU LC NBFU OTMC

THE SILVER MAPLE. A Story of Upper Canada. By Marian Keith [pseud]. New York, Revell, 1906. 357p [BM BVaU LC NBFU OTMC

TREASURE VALLEY. By Marian Keith [pseud]. New York, Doran, 1908. 384p [BM BVaU NBFU OTMC QMM

UNDER THE GREY OLIVES. By Marian Keith [pseud]. Toronto, McClelland, 1927. 175p [BVaU LC NBFU OTMC

YONDER SHINING LIGHT. By Marian Keith [pseud]. Toronto, McClelland, 1948. 278p [Sequel to AS A WATERED GARDEN.] [BVaU NBFU OTMC

**McGuirl, Charles**

"MIKE," THE STRAY DOG. Willowdale, Ont., Author, 1952. 186p [First pub. in 1947 in *Canadian Teacher.*]

**Machar, Agnes Maule, 1837–1927**

DOWN THE RIVER TO THE SEA. New York, Home Book Co., 1894. 279p [BVaU NSHP OTP

FOR KING AND COUNTRY. A Story of 1812. By A.M.M. Toronto, Adam & Stevenson, 1874. 265p [BVaU NBFU OTP QMSS

THE HEIR OF FAIRMOUNT GRANGE. London, Digby Long, [1895?]. 196p [BM NBFU OONL

KATIE JOHNSTONE'S CROSS. A Canadian Tale. By A.M.M. Toronto, Campbell, 1870. 207p [BM BVaU OTP QMSS

LOST AND WON. [No further information found.] [BCF MOR'12

LUCY RAYMOND; or, The Children's Watchword. By the Author of "Katie Johnstone's Cross" [pseud]. Toronto, Campbell, [1902?]. 214p [OONL

MARJORIE'S CANADIAN WINTER. A Story of the Northern Lights. Boston, Lothrop, 1892. 375p [Also: Toronto, Briggs, 1906. 375p] [BVaU NBFU OKQ

THE QUEST OF THE FATAL RIVER. 1904. [No further information found.] [CAR

ROLAND GRAEME, KNIGHT. A Novel of our Times. Montreal, Drysdale, 1892. 285p [Also: Toronto, Briggs, 1906. 285p] [LC NSHD OKQ QMM

**McIlwraith, Jean Newton, 1859–1938**

THE CURIOUS CAREER OF RODERICK CAMPBELL. Boston, Houghton, 1901. 287p [BM BVaU LC NBFU OTU

A DIANA OF QUEBEC. Toronto, Bell & Cockburn, 1912. 316p [BM BVaU NBFU OTU QMSS

KINSMEN AT WAR. Ottawa, Graphic, 1927. 289p [BM BVaU NBFU OTU
THE LITTLE ADMIRAL. Toronto, Hodder, 1924. 288p [NBFU OTMC
THE MAKING OF MARY. By Jean Forsyth [pseud]. New York, Cassell, 1895. 173p [BM LC

**McInnes, Graham Campbell, 1912–**
LOST ISLAND. An Adventure. Toronto, Macmillan, 1954. ix + 229p
SUSHILA. A Novel. New York, Putnam, 1957. 315p

**MacInnes, Thomas Robert Edward, 1867–1951**
CHINOOK DAYS. Vancouver, Sun Co., 1926. 206p [BVaU NBFU OTP

**MacIntyre, Mary**
SKIPPY AND OTHERS. Toronto, Macmillan, 1943. 131p [OOP

**Mack, Elsie Frances (Wilson), 1909–1967**
THE BLUE LOCKET. By Frances Sarah Moore [pseud]. New York, Bouregy & Curl, 1951. 254p
DEBORAH. New York, Bouregy & Curl, 1951. 254p
THE DISPUTED BARRIER. New York, Arcadia House, 1947. 256p [LC
THE ELOPEMENT. New York, Bouregy & Curl, 1952. 256p
THE ENCHANTED HIGHWAY. New York, Bouregy & Curl, 1951. 254p
FAIR IS MY LOVE. By Frances Sarah Moore [pseud]. New York, Avalon Books, 1950. 252p [BM LC OONL
FIREWEED. By Frances Sarah Moore [pseud]. New York, Arcadia House, 1945. 256p [LC
GILDED CHALLENGE. By Frances Sarah Moore [pseud]. New York, Avalon Books, 1950. 256p [BM LC OONL
GROUND MIST. By Frances Sarah Moore [pseud]. New York, Arcadia House, 1946. 272p [LC
THE HEART DIVIDED. By Frances Sarah Moore [pseud]. New York, Arcadia House, 1946. 256p [LC
HIDDEN BOUNDARY. By Frances Sarah Moore [pseud]. New York, Bouregy & Curl, 1952. 254p
LEGACY OF LOVE. By Frances Sarah Moore [pseud]. New York, Avalon Books, 1957. 220p
LOVE SHOULD BE LAUGHTER. By Frances Sarah Moore [pseud]. New York, Curl, 1947. 256p [BM LC
MAGIC IS FRAGILE. New York, Bouregy & Curl, 1952. 256p
MINE TO LOVE. New York, Avalon Books, 1950. 256p [LC OONL
OBBLIGATO. By Frances Sarah Moore [pseud]. New York, Bouregy & Curl, 1952. 253p
OF ALL OUR YESTERDAYS. By Frances Sarah Moore [pseud]. New York, Arcadia House, 1945. 272p [LC

THE QUEST. New York, Bouregy & Curl, 1953. 256p
THE RIGHT GIRL. By Frances Sarah Moore [pseud]. New York, Avalon Books, 1956. 224p
THE STORM. By Frances Sarah Moore [pseud]. New York, Bouregy & Curl, 1951. 256p

**MacKay, Isabel Ecclestone (Macpherson), 1875–1928**
BLENCARROW. A Novel. Toronto, Allen, 1926. 307p [BM BVaU LC NBFU OTMC QMM
THE HOUSE OF WINDOWS. London, Cassell, 1912. 338p [BM BVaU NBFU OTMC
INDIAN NIGHTS. Toronto, McClelland, 1930. 198p [BM BVaU LC NSHD OKQ
MISS WITTERLY'S CHINA. Toronto, Women's Missionary Soc. of the Methodist Church, Canada, n.d. 11p [Short story reprinted from the *Endeavour Herald*, Toronto] [BVaU
MIST OF MORNING. Toronto, McClelland, 1919. 407p [BM BVaU LC NBFU OTMC
UP THE HILL AND OVER. New York, Doran, 1917. 363p [BVaU LC NBFU OTMC
THE WINDOW GAZER. Toronto, McClelland, 1921. 308p [BM BVaU NBFU OKQ

**McKechnie, Neil Kenneth, 1873–1951**
THE HEIR OF ALL THE AGES. The Family Tree of Mr. Smith. Indianapolis, Bobbs-Merrill, 1926. 200p [BM LC NBFU
THE SADDLEROOM MURDER. Philadelphia, 1937. 307p [LC NBFU

**McKelvie, Bruce Alistair, 1889–1960**
THE BLACK CANYON. A Story of '58. London, Dent, 1927. 173p [BVaU NBFU OTMC
HULDOWGET. A Story of the North Pacific Coast. Toronto, Dent, 1926. 221p [BVaU NSHD OTMC
LEGENDS OF STANLEY PARK. N.p., n.pub., [1941?]. 20p [BVaU
PELTS AND POWDER. A Story of the West Coast in the Making. ... Toronto, Dent, 1929. 238p [BVaU NBFU OTMC

**MacKenzie, Donald, 1908–**
DANGEROUS SILENCE. London, Collins, 1960. 192p
THE JURYMAN. London, Elek Books, 1957. 204p
NOWHERE TO GO. London, Elek Books, 1956. 207p [American ed.: Boston, Houghton, 1957. 250p]
THE SCENT OF DANGER. London, Collins, 1958. 192p

**McKibbin, Rev. Archibald, 1863–1925**

THE OLD ORCHARD. By Mack Cloie [pseud]. Toronto, Briggs, 1903. 323p [BM BVaU OTU

THE PANCAKE PREACHER. By Mack Cloie [pseud]. Toronto, Briggs, 1906. 450p [BM OLU

A WEE SCOTCH TOON. [No further information found.] [MOR'12

**McKim, Audrey, 1909–**

ANDY AND THE GOPHER. Boston, Little Brown, 1959. 119p

HERE COMES DIRK. Toronto, Oxford U. Press, 1951. 145p

LEXY O'CONNOR Toronto, McClelland, 1953. 262p

**McKinley, Mabel (Burns)**

THREE BOYS ON THE YANGTSE. House-boating in China. Toronto, McClelland, 1929. 252p [OTP

**MacKinnon, Lilian (Vaux), 1879–**

MIRIAM OF QUEEN'S. Toronto, McClelland, 1921. 310p [BM BVaU LC NBFU OTMC

**McKinnon, Rev. William Charles, –1862**

FRANCES; or, Pirate Cove. A Legend of Cape Breton. Halifax, British North American, 1851. 42p [NSHD

ST. CASTINE. A Legend of Cape Breton. Sydney, N.S., Cape Breton Herald, 1850. 72p [NSHP OOP

ST. GEORGE; or, The Canadian League. A Tale of the Outbreak in 1837. Halifax, Fuller, 1852. 2v [LC NSHP OOP

**McKishnie, Archibald P., 1875–1946**

BIG JOHN WALLACE. A Romance of the Early Canadian Pioneers. Toronto, Massey-Harris Press, 1922. 47p [BVaU NBFU OTP

BRAINS, LIMITED. Toronto, Allen, 1925. 287p [BM NBFU OOP

DWELLERS OF THE MARSH REALM. Chicago, Donohue, 1937. 79p [BVaU LC NBFU OTMC

GAFF LINKUM. A Tale of Talbotville. Toronto, Briggs, 1907. 255p [BM LC NBFU OKQ

LOVE OF THE WILD. Toronto, McLeod & Allen, 1910. 327p [BVaU LC NBFU OTMC QMM

MATES OF THE TANGLE. Toronto, Musson, 1924. 247p [BVaU LC NBFU OTMC

OPENWAY. Toronto, Musson, 1922. 233p [BM BVaU NSHD OTMC

A SON OF COURAGE. Toronto, Allen, 1920. 284p [BM BVaU LC NBFU OTMC

WILLOW, THE WISP. Toronto, Allen, 1918. 308p [BVaU LC NBFU OTMC QMM

**McKnight, J.L.**

VAGRANT. A Landsman's Log Book. Saint John, McMillan, 1888. [BCF NBB

**McKowan, Evah May (Cartwright), 1885–**

GRAYDON OF THE WINDERMERE. Toronto, McClelland, 1920. 310p [BVaU LC NBFU OTMC

JANET OF KOOTENAY. Life, Love and Laughter in an Arcady of the West. Toronto, McClelland, 1919. 279p [BVaU LC NBFU OTMC

**McLaren, Margaret**

CHETIGNE ISLAND. A Novel. West Chezzetcook, N.S., Author, [1916?]. 86p [BVaU NSHD OTU

**MacLean, Annie Marion, –1934**

"CHEERO!" New York, Woman's Press, 1918. 93p [LC

OUR NEIGHBOURS. New York, Macmillan, 1922. 288p [LC NSWA

**Maclean, Charles Sutherland, 1915–**

THE HEAVENS ARE NOT TOO HIGH. London, Kimber, 1957. 282p

**Maclean, Rev. John, 1851–1928**

THE HERO OF THE SASKATCHEWAN. Barrie, Ont., 1891. 49p [OKQ

**MacLennan, Hugh, 1907–**

BAROMETER RISING. New York, Duell Sloan, 1941. 326p [Also, with an intro. by Hugo McPherson. Toronto, McClelland, 1958. xv + 219p] [BM BVaU LC NSHD OTU QMM

EACH MAN'S SON. Toronto, Macmillan, 1951. 244p

THE PRECIPICE. Toronto, Collins, 1948. 372p [BM BVaU LC NBFU OTU QMM

TWO SOLITUDES. New York, Duell Sloan, 1945. 370p [Also: Toronto, Macmillan, 1957.] [BM BVaU LC NBFU OTU

THE WATCH THAT ENDS THE NIGHT. Toronto, Macmillan, 1959. 373p

**McLennan, William, 1856–1904**

AS TOLD TO HIS GRACE, AND OTHER STORIES. Ste. Philomène, 1891. 132p [QMM

IN OLD FRANCE AND NEW. New York, Harper, 1899. 319p [LC NBFU OTU QMM

THE SPAN O' LIFE. A Tale of Louisbourg & Quebec. By William McLennan and J.N. McIlwraith. ... New York, Harper, 1899. 307p [BM BVaU LC NBFU OTU QMM

SPANISH JOHN. Being a Memoir, now First Published in Complete Form, of the Early Life and Adventures of Colonel John McDonnell, known as "Spanish John". ... New York, Harper, 1898. 271p [BM BVaU LC NSHD OTU QMSS

**McLeod, Arthur James, 1836–**

THE NOTARY OF GRAND PRE. A Historic Tale of Acadia. Boston, Author, 1901. 152p [BVaU NBFU OTP QMSS

**MacLeod, Elizabeth Susan (MacQueen), 1842–1939**
DONALDA. A Scottish-Canadian Story. Toronto, Briggs, 1905. 281p [Cover title: DONALDA; or, "Canada's Countess"] [BM NBFU OTU

**McMahon, W.F.**
"PRIZE PAPERS," SATIRICAL. ... Hamilton, McKay Print., [18—?]. 191p [BVaU NSHD OTP

**MacMillan, Anne (Morton), 1893–**
LEVKO. Toronto, Longmans, 1956. 159p
MOUNTIE PATROL. Toronto, Longmans, 1960. 160p
PERKY IN EVER, EVER LAND. By Anne MacMillan and Marion McVeety. Regina, School Aids and Text Book Pub., Co., 1954. 198p
PRINCE OF THE PLAINS. Regina, School Aids and Text Book Pub. Co., 1952. 204p

**Macmillan, Cyrus, 1880–1953**
CANADIAN FAIRY TALES. Toronto, Gundy, 1922. 203p [Same title: London, Lane, 1928. 234p] [BM BVaU LC NBFU OTU QMSS
CANADIAN WONDER TALES. Toronto, Gundy, 1918. 199p [Same title: London, Lane, 1918. 240p] [BM BVaU LC NBFU OTU
GLOOSKAP'S COUNTRY AND OTHER INDIAN TALES. Toronto, Oxford U. Press, 1955. 273p ["The stories in this collection were first published by John Lane, The Bodley Head, Limited in *Canadian Wonder Tales* (1918) and *Canadian Fairy Tales* (1922)."]

**MacMillan, Don A.**
RINK RAT. Toronto, Dent, 1949. 248p [NBFU OLU

**MacMillan, William, 1890–**
ARCTIC ADVENTURE. New York, Mill, 1945. 192p [LC OORD
DARK TREASURE. New York, Mill, 1943. 254p [BM LC
MYSTERY SHIP. New York, Mill, 1944. 185p [LC
NORTHLAND STORIES. Tales of Trapping Life in the Canadian Wilderness. New York, Peltries Pub. Co., 1922. 95p [LC
RED-LEG MORGAN. London, Harrap, 1936. 256p [BM

**McNamee, James**
FLORENCIA BAY. Toronto, McClelland, 1960. 204p

**McNaughton, Rev. Duncan**
THE WIFE OF FAIRBANK ON KIRKS AND MINISTERS. Toronto, Press of the Canada Presbyterian, 1893. 432p [LC OTP

**MacNaughton, Eleanor (Le Sueur), 1846–**
A LITTLE LOVING LIFE. 1892. [MOR'12
THE MEADOWHURST CHILDREN AND OTHER TALES. Franklin, Ohio, Editor Pub. Co., 1898. [AmCat MOR'12

**McNeill, James, 1925–**

THE SUNKEN CITY AND OTHER TALES FROM ROUND THE WORLD. Toronto, Oxford U. Press, 1959. 160p

**McNider, Stanley**

JUAN HALLADO. 1885. [BCF

**Macphail, Andrew, 1864–1938**

THE VINE OF SIBMAH. A Relation of the Puritans. London, Macmillan, 1906. 432p [BM LC OTU

**McPhedran, Marie (Green), 1904–**

DAVID AND THE WHITE CAT.... New York, Aladdin Books, 1950. 47p [BM LC OONL

GOLDEN NORTH. Toronto, Macmillan, 1948. 192p [BVaU LC NBFU OTU QMM

**Macpherson, Charlotte Holt (Gethings), fl. 1828–1890**

TRUE STORIES FOR YOUNG PEOPLE. Montreal, n.d. 28p [OLU QMSS

**Macpherson, Donald (pseud)**

GO HOME, UNICORN. By Donald Macpherson [pseud]. London, Faber, 1935. 271p [BM LC NBFU

MEN ARE LIKE ANIMALS. By Donald Macpherson [pseud]. London, Faber, 1937. 321p [BM LC OTU

**McTavish, R. Lorne**

FOR A BETTER TO-MORROW. Ilfracombe, Devon, Stockwell, 1952. 176p

**Magee, Knox, 1877–1934**

MARK EVERARD. A Romance. New York, Fenno, 1901. 421p [BM LC OLU

WITH RING OF SHIELD. New York, Fenno, 1900. 363p [LC OOP

**Magwood, Millie**

PINE LAKE. A Story of Northern Ontario. Toronto, Briggs, 1901. 198p [BM BVaU OTMC

THE YEAR THAT FOLLOWED. (A Sequel to PINE LAKE.) Toronto, Briggs, 1907. 188p [BM NSHD OTUV

**Mahler, Helen A.**

EMPRESS OF BYZANTIUM. Trans. from the German original by the author with the assistance of Leona Nevler. New York, Coward-McCann, 1952. 376p

**Mainer, R. Henry, 1878–**

NANCY McVEIGH OF THE MONK ROAD. Toronto, Briggs, 1908. 127p [BM BVaU NSHD OTP

**Mallette, Gertrude Ethel, 1887–**

BRIGHT SIDE UP. Garden City, N.Y., Doubleday, 1954. 218p

CALLING DOCTOR MARCIA. New York, Doubleday, 1940. 296p [AEU NBS
CHEE-CHA-KO. New York, Doubleday, 1938. 299p [BM LC
CLEAR TO LAND. Garden City, Doubleday, 1950. 212p [LC
FLYING WING MYSTERY. By Alan Gregg [pseud]. Garden City, Doubleday, 1948. 213p [LC
FOR KEEPS. New York, Doubleday, 1936. 309p [BM LC
HIDDEN WINGS MYSTERY. By Alan Gregg [pseud]. Garden City, Doubleday, 1941. 271p [LC
INSIDE OUT. Garden City, Doubleday, 1942. 278p [BM LC OTU
INTO THE WIND. Garden City, Doubleday, 1942. 295p [NBS OTU
MYSTERY IN BLUE. Garden City, Doubleday, 1945. 217p [BM LC NBS
THE MYSTERY OF BATTY RIDGE. By Alan Gregg [pseud]. Garden City, Doubleday, 1946. 213p [LC
THE MYSTERY OF FLIGHT 24. By Alan Gregg [pseud]. Garden City, Doubleday, 1947. 215p [LC
THE MYSTERY OF THE KING TURTLE. By Alan Gregg [pseud]. Garden City, Doubleday, 1943. 213p [LC
NO VACANCIES. Garden City, Doubleday, 1939. 311p [BM LC OTU
ONCE IS FOREVER. Garden City, Doubleday, 1946. 250p [BVaU LC OTU
PRICELESS MOMENT. Garden City, Doubleday, 1947. 214p [LC
PRIVATE PROPS. Garden City, Doubleday, 1937. 297p [AEU BM OTU
SINGLE STONES. New York, Doubleday, 1940. 296p [BM LC
SKYWINDER MYSTERY. By Alan Gregg [pseud]. Garden City, Doubleday, 1942. 279p [BM LC
UNEXPECTED SUMMER. Garden City, Doubleday, 1949. 212p [BVaU LC
WENDERLEY. Garden City, Doubleday, 1943. 250p [BM LC
WINGED MYSTERY. By Alan Gregg [pseud]. New York, Doubleday, 1940. 302p [BM LC

**Manchee, Carol M. (Cassidy)**

DOWNY WINGS AND SHARP EARS. By Carol Cassidy Cole [pseud]. Toronto, Musson, 1923. 152p [BM BVaU NBFU OTP
LITTLE BIG-EARS AND THE PRINCESS. By Carol Cassidy Cole [pseud]. Toronto, Musson, [c1926, 1944]. 132p [BVaU NBFU OTP
LITTLE WOODEN DUCK. By Carol Cassidy Cole [pseud]. Toronto, Musson, 1945. 140p [OTMC
VELVET PAWS AND SHINY EYES. By Carol Cassidy Cole [pseud]. Toronto, Musson, 1922. 152p [BM BVaU OTP

**Manigault, Gabriel, 1809–1888**

SAINT CECILIA. A Modern Tale from Real Life. [Anon] London, Low Marston, 1871–72. 3v [LC

**Manning, Zella M.**

LORDS OF THE WILDERNESS. Comp. by ——. Toronto, Ryerson, 1934. 188p [BVaU NBFU QMSS

**Mansell, Mrs. C.B.**

THE POWER OF GOLD. By Everett St. Clair [pseud]. Vancouver, Artcraft, 1929. 330p [BVaU NBFU OTMC

**Mantley, John, 1920–**

THE SNOW BIRCH. New York, Dutton, 1958. 316p [Also pub. as WOMAN OBSESSED. Montreal, Permabooks, 1958. 265p]

THE TWENTY-SEVENTH DAY. London, M. Joseph, 1957. 271p [First pub. 1956.]

**Margeson, Mabel (Jones), 1875?–1951**

A TALE OF OLD ACADIA. Saint John, Barnes, 1925. 269p [BVaU NBFU OTU QMSS

**Margolian, Abraham, 1917–**

A PIECE OF BLUE HEAVEN. Fredericton, New Elizabethan Pub. Co., 1956. 240p [A Story of Nazi persecution of the Jews in Amsterdam, 1942–44.]

**Marlyn, John, 1912–**

UNDER THE RIBS OF DEATH. Toronto, McClelland, 1957. 287p

**Marquis, Thomas Guthrie, 1864–1936**

THE KING'S WISH. Toronto, Ryerson, 1924. 164p [BVaU NSHD OTU

MARGUERITE DE ROBERVAL. A Romance of the Days of Jacques Cartier. Toronto, Copp Clark, 1899. 250p [BM NSHD OTP QMSS

**Mars, Alastair, 1915–**

ARCTIC SUBMARINE. London, Elek Books, 1955. 191p

ATOMIC SUBMARINE. A Story of Tomorrow. London, Elek Books, 1957. 192p [Pub. in U.S. as FIRE IN ANGER, New York, Mill Co. & W. Morrow, 1958. 222p]

SUBMARINE AT BAY. London, Elek Books, 1956. 164p

**Marsh, Edith Louise, –1960**

TRILLIUM HILL. New York, Lothrop, Lee & Shepard Co., 1955. 159p

**Marshall, Joyce, 1913–**

LOVERS AND STRANGERS. A Novel. Philadelphia, Lippincott, 1957. 246p

PRESENTLY TOMORROW. Boston, Little Brown, 1946. 310p [BVaU LC NBFU OTU QMM

**Marshall, Robin**

CAMPBELL OF THE MOUNTIES. Toronto, Musson, 1937. 283p [BM OOP

**Mary Rose, Sister, 1903–**

NOT AT SEVENTEEN? By Rena Ray [pseud]. Montreal, Holy Cross Press, 1959. 128p

**Mary St. George, Mother**

ROAD'S END. By Mary Douglas [pseud]. Toronto, Ryerson, 1943. 150p [LC NBFU OTU

**Mason, Mrs. E.M.**

FACES THAT FOLLOW. With illus. by J.W. Bengough. Toronto, Briggs, 1898. 206p [BM BVaU NSHD OTMC

**Max, Felix**

BROKEN BONDS. A Prize Temperance Story. Toronto, 1878. 109p [Bound with SOCIAL HEROISM. A Canadian Prize Temperance Story. By F. Louise Morse. Toronto, 1878. 82p] [Antique cat. 41

**Mayse, Arthur William Caswell, 1912–**

THE DESPERATE SEARCH. New York, Morrow, 1952. 216p

MORGAN'S MOUNTAIN. New York, Morrow, 1960. 211p

PERILOUS PASSAGE. New York, Morrow, 1949. 247p [BM BVaU LC OTMC

**Meade, Edward F., 1912–**

REMEMBER ME. London, Faber, 1946. 318p [BM BVaU LC NSHD OTMC QMM

**Meek, Gladys Clements**

THE DEVIL'S PUNCH BOWL. Edmonton, Inst. of Applied Art, 1946. 221p [OTMC

**Meredith, Wendy A.D.M.**

"TOES UP!" SAID THE BRIGAND, AND OTHER STORIES. Vancouver, 1929. 36p [Written by Wendy Meredith between ages of 10 and 13.] [BVaU

**Merrick, Rev. Earl Chauncey, 1905–**

PACO OF THE HIGH COUNTRY (BOLIVIA). Toronto, Ryerson, 1952. 49p

**Merrill, Marion, 1912–**

SYD OF TAR-PAPER SHACK. Chicago, Wilcox & Follett, 1947. 259p [LC

TREASURE CAVE TRAIL. New York, Morrow, 1943. 158p [LC

THE YOUNG BILLINGS OF BUCKHORN. New York, Morrow, 1942. 71p [LC OTU

**Middleton, Jesse Edgar, 1872–1960**

THE CLEVER ONES. New York, Nelson, 1936. 296p [BM BVaU LC NBFU OTU

GREEN PLUSH. London, Methuen, 1932. 250p [BM NBFU OTU

**Millar, Margaret (Sturm), 1915–**

AN AIR THAT KILLS. New York, Random House, 1957. 247p [English ed. (London, Gollancz, 1957. 222p) has title: THE SOFT TALKERS.]

BEAST IN VIEW. New York, Random House, 1955. 249p

THE CANNIBAL HEART. New York, Random House, 1949. 207p [BM LC OTMC

THE DEVIL LOVES ME. Garden City, Doubleday, 1942. 304p [LC OTMC

DO EVIL IN RETURN. New York, Random House, 1950. 243p [BM LC NBFU OTU

EXPERIMENT IN SPRINGTIME. New York, Random House, 1947. 279p [LC OTMC

FIRE WILL FREEZE. New York, Random House, 1944. 225p [LC OTU

THE INVISIBLE WORM. New York, Doubleday, 1941. 273p [BM LC OTU
THE IRON GATES. New York, Random House, 1945. 241p [LC OTU
IT'S ALL IN THE FAMILY. New York, Random House, 1948. 243p [LC OTU
THE LISTENING WALLS. London, Gollancz, 1959. 236p
ROSE'S LAST SUMMER. New York, Random House, 1952. 245p
A STRANGER IN MY GRAVE. London, Gollancz, 1960. 240p
TASTE OF FEARS. A Psychological Novel. London, Hale, 1950. 224p [BM
VANISH IN AN INSTANT. New York, Random House, 1952. 245p
WALL OF EYES. New York, Random House, 1943. 243p [LC OTU
THE WEAK-EYED BAT. Garden City, Doubleday, 1942. 280p [BM LC OTU
WIVES AND LOVERS. New York, Random House, 1954. 308p

**Miller, Muriel, 1908–**
PETER'S ADVENTURES IN THE OUT-OF-DOORS. ... Toronto, Ryerson, 1940. 218p [AEU

**Millner, George F.**
THE SERGEANT OF FORT TORONTO. Toronto, Copp Clark, 1914. 370p [BM BVaU LC NBFU OTU

**Mirvish, Robert Franklin, 1921–**
DUST ON THE SEA. London, Redmond, 1960. 251p
THE LONG WATCH. New York, Sloane, 1954. 343p
TEXANA. A Novel. New York, Sloane, 1954. 279p
TWO WOMEN, TWO WORLDS. New York, Sloane, 1960. 309p
WOMAN IN A ROOM. London, Redman, 1959. 287p

**Mitchell, John, 1882–1951**
ROBERT HARDING. A Story of Every Day Life. By Patrick Slater [pseud]. Toronto, Allen, 1938. 273p [BVaU NBFU OTMC
THE YELLOW BRIAR. A Story of the Irish on the Canadian Countryside. By Patrick Slater [pseud]. Toronto, Allen, 1933. 253p [Also: Toronto, Macmillan, 1945. 293p] [BM BVaU NBFU OTMC QMM

**Mitchell, Ronald Elwy**
DESIGN FOR NOVEMBER. New York, Harper, 1947. 282p [BM LC

**Mitchell, Sylvia Elizabeth Fisher**
PRAIRIE ADVENTURES. Regina, Author, 1958. 61p

**Mitchell, William Ormond, 1914–**
WHO HAS SEEN THE WIND. Toronto, Macmillan, 1947. 344p [BVaU LC NBFU OTU QMM

**Molnar, Eugene Frank, 1891–**
THE SLAVE OF EA. A Sumerian Legend. Philadelphia, Dorrance, 1934. 299p [LC OKQ

**Monckton, Geoffrey F.**

LOP-EARED DICK. His Book. ... Being a disjointed Account of the Trials of a genial Cowboy in a World of Widows and Wild Animals. London, Ouseley, 1913. 293p [BM

**Monro, Edith**

STORY OF MY LIFE. The Trials and Triumphs of Sandy the Scrapper. As Told by Himself. Vancouver, Saturday Sunset Press, 1914. 58p [BVaU

**Montgomery, Lucy Maud [Mrs. Evan MacDonald], 1874–1942**

ANNE OF AVONLEA. Boston, Page, 1909. 367p [BM BVaU LC NBFU OTU QMBM

ANNE OF GREEN GABLES. Boston, Page, 1908. 396p [Numerous later editions. Also dramatized as a 3-act play by Alice Chadwicke. New York, French, 1937. 139p] [BM BVaU LC NBFU OTU

ANNE OF INGLESIDE. New York, Stokes, 1939. 323p [BM BVa LC NBFU OTU

ANNE OF THE ISLAND. Boston, Page, 1915. 326p [BM BVaU LC NBFU OTU

ANNE OF WINDY POPLARS. New York, Stokes, 1936. 301p [BM BVaU LC OTU

ANNE'S HOUSE OF DREAMS. New York, Stokes, 1917. 346p [BM BVaU LC NBFU OTU

AUNT BECKY BEGAN IT. *See* A TANGLED WEB, below.

THE BLUE CASTLE. A Novel. Toronto, McClelland, 1926. 309p [BM BVaU LC OTU QMM

CHRONICLES OF AVONLEA. In which Anne Shirley of Green Gables and Avonlea plays some part. Boston, Page, 1912. 306p [BM BVaU LC NBFU OTMC

EMILY CLIMBS. New York, Stokes, 1925. 312p [BM BVaU LC NBFU OTU

EMILY OF NEW MOON. New York, Stokes, 1923. 351p [BM BVaU LC NSHD OTU

EMILY'S QUEST. New York, Stokes, 1927. 310p [BM BVaU LC NSHD OTMC

FURTHER CHRONICLES OF AVONLEA. Which have to do with many Personalities and Events in and about Avonlea. ... Boston, Page, 1920. 301p [First Canadian ed.: Toronto, Ryerson, 1953. 301p] [BM BVaU LC OTMC

THE GOLDEN ROAD. Boston, Page 1913. 369p [BM BVaU LC NBFU OTU

JANE OF LANTERN HILL. Toronto, McClelland, 1937. 297p [BM BVaU LC OTU

KILMENY OF THE ORCHARD. Boston, Page, 1910. 256p [BM BVaU LC OTU

MAGIC FOR MARIGOLD. Toronto, McClelland, 1929. 328p [BM BVaU LC NBFU OTMC

MISTRESS PAT. A Novel of Silver Bush. New York, Stokes, 1935. 338p [BM BVa LC OTU

PAT OF SILVER BUSH. New York, Stokes, 1933. 329p [BM BVa LC NBFU OTU

RAINBOW VALLEY. Toronto, McClelland, 1919. 341p [BM BVaU LC NBFU OTU

RILLA OF INGLESIDE. Toronto, McClelland, 1921. 370p [BM BVaU LC NBFU OTU

THE STORY GIRL. Boston, Page, 1911. 365p [BM BVaU LC NBFU OTU

A TANGLED WEB. New York, Stokes, 1931. 324p [Pub. in England under title: AUNT BECKY BEGAN IT. London, Hodder, 1931.] [BM BVaU LC NSHD OTU

**Montreuil, Mrs. Anna B., 1886–**

DUMB-BELL. Boston, Christopher, 1929. 264p [LC OKQ

**Moodie, Marion Elizabeth, 1867–**

LEGEND OF DRYAS. N.p., 1926. 8p [OTMC

**Moodie, Susanna (Strickland), 1803–1885**

DOROTHY CHANCE. 1867. [BCF

FLORA LINDSAY; or, Passages in an Eventful Life. London, Bentley, 1854. 2v [BVaU BM LC OTP

GEOFFREY MONCTON; or, The Faithless Guardian. New York, DeWitt, 1855. 362p [*Cf.* THE MONCKTONS. A Novel. London, 1856. 2v] [BM BVaU LC NSHD OTMC QMM

GEORGE LEATRIM; or, The Mother's Test. Edinburgh, Hamilton, 1875. [Later ed.: Edinburgh, Oliphant, Anderson & Ferrier, 1882. 63p] [BM OH

JOSIAH SHIRLEY, the Little Quaker. [BibC

THE LITTLE BLACK PONY AND OTHER STORIES. Philadelphia, Collins, 1850. [AmCat BibC

THE LITTLE PRISONER; or, Passion and Patience: and, Amendment; or, Charles Grant and his Sister. By the Authors of *Hugh Latimer* [i.e., Susanna Strickland] and *Disobedience* [i.e., Elizabeth Strickland], *etc.* London, 1828. 144p [BM

MARK HURDLESTONE, The Gold Worshipper. London, Bentley, 1853. 2v [Also pub. as: MARK HURDLESTONE; or, The Two Brothers. New York, DeWitt, n.d. 359p] [BM BVaU LC NBFU OKQ

MATRIMONIAL SPECULATIONS. London, Bentley, 1854. 352p [BM LC OONL

THE MONCKTONS. A Novel. London, Bentley, 1856. 2v [BM OTL

PRECEPT AND PRACTICE; or, The Vicar's Tales. [BibC

PROFESSION AND PRINCIPLE. Tales. By S. Strickland. London, Dean, 1833. [EngCat

ROWLAND MASSINGHAM; or, I Will Be my Own Master. By S. Strickland. London, Dean, 1837. 185p [OLU

THE SOLDIER'S ORPHAN; or, Hugh Latimer. (Something more about the Soldier's Orphan, or, the further Adventures of Hugh Latimer.) 2pts London, Dean, 1853. [BM

SPARTACUS. A Roman Story. [Anon] London, Newman, 1822. 131p [Variant title listed in BibC: SPARTACUS; or, The Slave's Struggle for Freedom.] [BM

THE WORLD BEFORE THEM. A Novel. London, Bentley, 1868. 3v [BM

**Moody, Irene Helen (Hawkins), –1958**

DELPHINE OF THE 'EIGHTIES. London, Bale & Danielson, 1931. 252p [BM BVaU NBFU OTMC

**Moore, Arthur W.**

NORMAN STANLEY'S CRUSADE; or, The Dunkin Act in Turnipham. Montreal, Dougall, 1877. 197p [OTP

**Moore, Ida Cecil**

LUCKY ORPHAN. New York, Scribner, 1947. 121p [LC

**Moore, Philip Hooper, 1879–1961**

THE CASTLE BUCK. Hunting and Fishing Adventures with a Nova Scotia Guide. London, Longmans, 1945. 300p [BVaU LC OTMC

SLAG AND GOLD. A Tale of the Porcupine Trail. Toronto, Allen, 1924. 314p [BM BVaU NBFU OTMC

**Moore, William Henry, 1872–1960**

POLLY MASSON. A Political Novel. Toronto, Dent, 1919. 339p [BM BVaU NSHD OTP QMSS

**Moorhouse, Arthur Herbert Joseph, 1882–**

EVERY MAN FOR HIMSELF. By Hopkins Moorhouse [pseud]. Toronto, Musson, 1920. 342p [BM BVaU LC NBFU OTMC

THE GAUNTLET OF ALCESTE. By Hopkins Moorhouse [pseud]. Toronto, Musson, 1921. 311p [BM BVaU LC OTMC

THE GOLDEN SCARAB. By Hopkins Moorhouse [pseud]. Toronto, Musson, 1926. 311p [BM BVaU NBFU OTMC QMM

**Morgan, Grace Jones**

SALVAGE ALL. New York, Croswell, 1928. 337p [BM BViPA LC OTP

TENTS OF SHEM. London, Sampson, Low, 1930. 250p [BM

**Morison, John Archibald, 1867–**

THE WORLD, THE CHURCH, AND THE DEVIL. Boston, Badger, 1916. 198p [LC NSWA

**Morphy, J.**

NED FENTON'S PORTFOLIO. Quebec, Palmer, 1863. 141p [LC OTP QMM

**Morris, Eric Cecil, 1914–**

LE DERNIER VOYAGE. Un Roman de la Gaspésie. French trans. by Martine Hébert-Duguay. Montreal, Chantecler, 1951. 255p [French version of his A VOICE IS CALLING.]

TRESPASS AGAINST NONE. Montreal, Whitcombe & Gilmour, 1950. 317p [NBFU OONL

A VOICE IS CALLING. Montreal, Simpson, 1945. 487p [BVaU OTU QMBM

**Morrison, Dorothy, 1909–**

TALES THE ESKIMOS TELL. Selected and Retold. Regina, School Aids and Text Book Pub. Co., 1944. 60p [OTU

**Morse, F. Louise**

SOCIAL HEROISM. A Canadian Prize Temperance Story. Toronto, 1878. 82p [Bound with BROKEN BONDS. A Prize Temperance Story. By Felix Max.] [Patrick cat. 27

**Morse, Harry Havelock, 1883–1918**

THE ACADIAN HUNTER; or, Jean Breau, the French Brother. An Historical Romance. Ed. by William Inglis Morse. Boston, priv. print. by W.I. Morse, 1927. 462p [LC NSHD

**Morton, Guy Eugene, 1884–1948**

ASHES OF MURDER. London, Skeffington, 1935. 288p [NBFU

BLACK GOLD. Boston, Small Maynard, 1924. 310p [LC NBFU OOP

THE BLACK ROBE. New York, Minton Balch, 1927. 278p [Pub. in England as KING OF THE WORLD, *q.v.*] [LC

BURLEIGH MURDERS. London, Skeffington, 1936. 288p [OTU

THE ENEMY WITHIN. Baltimore, Saulsbury, 1918. 315p [LC

THE FORBIDDEN ROAD. London, Hodder, 1928. 312p [LC OOP

KING OF THE WORLD; or, The Pommeray Case. London, Hodder, 1927. 320p [Pub. in U.S. as THE BLACK ROBE, *q.v.*] [LC NBFU

MURDER. London, Skeffington, 1934. 287p [CBI

MYSTERY AT HARDACRES. London, Skeffington, 1936. 288p [OTU

MYSTERY AT HERMIT'S END. London, Skeffington, 1932. 287p [CBI

PERRIN MURDER CASE. London, Skeffington, 1930. 288p [CBI

THE RAGGED ROBIN MURDERS. New York, Greenberg, [1935?]. 310p [BVaU

RANGY PETE. Boston, Small Maynard, 1922. 409p [AEU LC NBFU OTMC

RED LADY. London, Skeffington, 1930. 288p [CBI

SCARLET THUMB-PRINT. London, Skeffington, 1932. 288p [CBI

SILVER-VOICED MURDER. London, Skeffington, 1933. 288p [CBI

WARDS OF THE AZURE HILLS. London, Hoddard, 1926. 309p [LC NBFU

ZOLA'S THIRTEEN. London, Skeffington, 1929. 288p [BVaU

**Morton, James**

POLSON'S PROBATION. A Story of Manitoba. Toronto, Briggs, 1897. 368p [BM BVaU NSHD OTU

**Morton, James [of Victoria, B.C.], 1870?–1967**

THE SINGULAR TRAVELS OF MEDIUS MIDDLEMAN. Entries from the Journal of his Adventures with Similus Buljo in the Lands of Obesia and Exigua. By Jay Jingle [pseud]. New York, Vantage Press, 1952. 239p

**Mountcastle, Clara H., 1837–**

A MYSTERY. By Caris Sima [pseud]. Toronto, Rose, 1886. 151p [BVaU OTU

**Mowat, Angus McGill, 1892–**

CARRYING PLACE. Toronto, Saunders, 1944. 318p [BVaU NBFU OTU QMBM

THEN I'LL LOOK UP. Toronto, Saunders, 1938. 309p [BM BVaU LC NBFU OTU

**Mowat, Farley McGill, 1921–**
LOST IN THE BARRENS. Boston, Little Brown, 1956. 244p

**Mowat, Grace Helen, 1875–1964**
BROKEN BARRIER. ... A Romance of Staten Island and the Province of New Brunswick. ... Fredericton, University Press, 1951. 182p

**Munday, Albert Henry, 1896–**
CAPTAINS OF THE SKY. The Way of Life of a Military Aviator. Evanston, Ill., Row Peterson, 1942. 64p [LC
NO OTHER GODS. A Novel of Saskatchewan. Boston, Meador, 1934. 271p [LC NBFU OTMC

**Munn, Henry Toke**
HOME IS THE HUNTER. By Henry Toke Munn and Elizabeth Sprigge. Toronto, Macmillan, 1930. 296p [BM BVaU NBS OH

**Munro, Bruce Weston, 1860–1900?**
A BLUNDERING BOY. A Humorous Story. Toronto, Munro, 1887. 395p [BVaU NBFU OTU
SPLINTERS; or, A Grist of Giggles. [Anon] Toronto, Carswell, 1886. 279p [OTU

**Murat, Eugene**
PAPETA. A Story. Abridged and Arranged from the Diary and Private Papers of Mr. Eugene Murat. Saint John, 1867. [BCF NBB

**Murdoch, Rev. Benedict Joseph, 1886–**
THE MENDERS. Francestown, N.H., M. Jones Co., 1953. 259p
SOUVENIR. Lancaster, Wickersham Press, 1926. 198p [LC NBFU OTMC
SPRIGS. Cedar Rapids, Ia., Torch Press, 1927. 210p [LC NBFU

**Murdoch, John A.**
IN THE WOODS AND ON THE WATERS. Winnipeg, Stovel, 1896. 135p [BM BVaU OTP

**Murphy, Emily Gowan (Ferguson), 1868–1933**
OUR LITTLE CANADIAN COUSIN OF THE GREAT NORTHWEST. Boston, Page, 1923. 86p [LC

**Murphy, Rev. William Leo, 1899–**
THE GOLDEN HERITAGE. New York, Kenedy, 1929. 281p [LC OONL
THE HILL OF TRIUMPH. A Story of Jerusalem in the Time of Christ. New York, Kenedy, 1928. 322p [LC NSHD OONL
SILVER GLADE. A Novel. St. Nazianz, Wis., Soc. of the Divine Savior, 1947. 256p [LC
TRAIL'S END. A Tale of the Royal Canadian Mounted Police in the Catholic Land of Evangeline. Ozone Park, N.Y., Catholic Literary Guild, 1941. 208p [LC NBFU
WITHIN THY HEART. Halifax, Mitchell, 1953. 156p

**Murray, Rev. John Clark, 1836–1917**
HE THAT HAD RECEIVED THE FIVE TALENTS. London, Unwin, 1904. 446p [BM OTU

**Murray, Kate**
THE GUIDING ANGEL. Toronto, Wesleyan Book Room, 1871. 136p [OONL

**Murray, Lillian (Marjoram) 1918–**
GINNIE AND THE SNOW GYPSIES. London, Hutchinson, 1958. 191p
IN THE TRACK OF THE HUSKIES. Toronto, McClelland, 1960. 207p

**Murray, William Waldie, 1891–1956**
FIVE NINES AND WHIZZ BANGS. By the Orderly Sergeant [pseud]. Ottawa, Legionary Library, 1937. 244p [BVaU NBFU OTU

**Musgrave, Fanny Wood**
GABRIELLE AMETHYST. Toronto, Briggs, 1908. 246p [BM NSHD OTU
GYPSY. [MOR'12
A RAY OF LIGHT. [MOR'12
TRUE TO THE LAST. [MOR'12

**Nablo, James Benson, 1910–**
THE LONG NOVEMBER. New York, Dutton, 1946. 224p [BVaU LC OTMC

**Nani, Mrs. Kathleen, 1900–**
RAINBOW'S END. Ed. by Albert Nani. New York, Pageant Press, 1953. 162p

**Nasmith, George Gallie, 1877–1965**
SMITHS OF A BETTER QUALITY. Ottawa, National Council of Education, 1925. 138p [Eugenics presented in fictionalized form.] [BM BVaU OTMC

**Naugler, Gertrude Paist, 1912–**
THE WORLD AND JULIE. New York, Scribner, 1955. 286p

**Nease, Lilla Stewart (Dunlap), 1858–**
IN MUSIC'S THRALL. Toronto, Briggs, 1903. 146p [BM NBFU OTMC

**Neil, Stephen, 1877–1947**
ALL THE KING'S MEN. Toronto, Macmillan, 1934. 332p [BVaU NBFU OTP

**Nelson, Frederick**
TORONTO IN 1928 A.D. Toronto, National Business Methods & Pub. Co., 1908. 48p [BM BVaU OTU

**Nelson, George Edmondson, 1902–**
NORTHERN LIGHTS. A New Collection of Distinguished Writing by Canadian Authors. Ed. by ——. Garden City, N.Y., Doubleday, 1960. 736p

**Nelson, John Bertram**

FEATHERS IN THE WIND. New York, Vantage Press, 1959. 127p

**Nil Desperandum (pseud)**

AN EASTER LILY AND OTHER STORIES. By Nil Desperandum [pseud]. Toronto, 1898. [OONL

**Niven, Frederick John, 1878–1944**

ABOVE YOUR HEADS. London, Martin Secker, 1911. 300p [BM OONL

BROTHERS IN ARMS. Being the Account written by James Niven ... of Glasgow, in the 18th Century. ... London, Collins, 1942. 255p [BM LC NBFU OONL

CINDERELLA OF SKOOKUM CREEK. London, Nash, 1916. 319p [BM BVa OONL

DEAD MEN'S BELLS. London, Martin Secker, 1912. 309p [BM BVaU OONL

ELLEN ADAIR. New York, Boni, 1925. 287p [1st ed.: London, Nash, 1913. 320p] [BM BVaU LC NBFU OONL

THE FLYING YEARS. London, Collins, 1935. 284p [BM BVaU LC OONL QMM

HANDS UP! New York, Lane, 1913. 315p [BM BVaU LC NBFU OONL

THE ISLAND PROVIDENCE. New York, Lane, 1910. 310p [BM BVaU LC OONL

JUSTICE OF THE PEACE. New York, Boni, 1923. 453p [Earlier ed.: London, Nash, 1914. 434p] [BM BVaU LC NBFU OONL

THE LADY OF THE CROSSING. Toronto, Hodder, 1919. 317p [BM BVaU LC NBFU OONL

THE LOST CABIN MINE. London, Lane, 1908. 254p [Also: New York, Lane, 1909. 312p] [BM BVaU LC NBFU OONL

MINE INHERITANCE. New York, Macmillan, 1940. 432p [BM BVaU LC NBFU OONL QMSS

MRS. BARRY. New York, Dutton, 1933. 256p [BM BVaU LC NBFU OONL

OLD SOLDIER. A Novel. London, Collins, 1936. 250p [BM BVaU LC NBFU OONL

THE PAISLEY SHAWL. New York, Dodd Mead, 1931. 252p [BM BVaU NBFU OONL

PENNY SCOT'S TREASURE. London, Collins, 1918. 306p [BM NBFU OTMC

THE PORCELAIN LADY. London, Martin Secker, 1913. 354p [BM OONL

QUEER FELLOWS. London, Lane, 1927. 251p [Same as WILD HONEY.] [BM NBFU OONL QMM

THE RICH WIFE. London, Collins, 1932. 256p [BM BVaU LC NBFU

THE S.S. GLORY. London, Heinemann, 1915. 220p [BM BVaU LC NBFU OONL

SAGE-BRUSH STORIES. London, Nash, 1917. 304p [BM OTMC

THE STAFF AT SIMSON'S. A Novel. London, Collins, 1937. 318p [BM BVaU LC NBFU OTMC QMM

THE STORY OF THEIR DAYS. London, Collins, 1939. 444p [BM BVaU LC NBFU OONL QMM

A TALE THAT IS TOLD. Toronto, Collins, 1920. 338p [BM BVaU LC NBFU OONL

THE THREE MARYS. London, Collins, 1930. 284p [BM BVaU LC NBFU OONL
THE TRANSPLANTED. Toronto, Collins, 1944. 310p [BVaU LC NBFU OONL
TREASURE TRAIL. New York, Dodd Mead, 1923. 254p [BVaU LC NBFU OONL
TRIUMPH. New York, Dutton, 1934. 252p [BM BVaU LC NBFU OONL
TWO GENERATIONS. London, Nash, 1916. 358p [BM OTMC QMM
UNDER WHICH KING. London, Collins, 1943. 192p [BM BVaU LC NBFU OONL
WILD HONEY. New York, Dodd Mead, 1927. 251p [Same as QUEER FELLOWS.] [BVaU LC NBFU OONL
A WILDERNESS OF MONKEYS. New York, Lane, 1911. 283p [BM BVaU LC NBFU OONL QMM
THE WOLFER. New York, Dodd Mead, 1923. 314p [BVaU LC NBFU OONL

**Nixon, James Leroy**

A MAID OF ONTARIO. A Story of Buffalo, Toronto, and the Fenian Raid of 1866. Welland, Ont., Yedis Pub. Co., 1905. 348p [BM OTMC

**Nixon, Marian Essley**

MARTHA. A Story. London, Stockwell, [1933?]. 64p [CC

**Nobile, Achilles Alexander, 1833–**

AN ANONYMOUS LETTER. A Novel. Trans. from the Italian. (Fac. page: UNA LETTERA ANONIMA, versione italiana.) Buffalo, Baker, 1885. 217p [OTU

**Noel, Mrs. John Vavasour, 1815–1878**

THE ABBEY OF RATHMORE, AND OTHER TALES. Kingston, Creighton, 1859. 272p [Includes "Madeline Beresford, or The Infidel's Betrothed" and "Grace Raymond, or The Slave's Revenge."] [BVaU OTU
HILDA; or, The Merchant's Secret. [BCF
PASSION AND PRINCIPLE. [BCF

**Nolting, Rev. William Carl, 1907–**

OUR SALLY. A Novel. New York, Vantage Press, 1954. 175p

**Norman, Dorothy, 1905–**

MARJORIE'S ANTIQUE SHOP. New York, Penn, 1942. 261p [LC

**Nota Bene (pseud)**

TO HELL AND BACK. Winnipeg, T.H. Best, 1949. 291p [QMBM

**Nursey, Walter R., 1847–1927**

THE ROMANCE OF THE MERRY MAIDEN; or, How the Farm Mortgage was Lifted by a Jersey Beauty. Lowell, Mass., Hood, 1898. 192p [LC OTU

**Oakes, Christopher**

THE CANADIAN SENATOR; or, A Romance of Love and Politics. Toronto, National Pub. Co., 1890. 179p [BM BVaU LC NBFU OTP

**Obodiac, Stanlee, 1922–**
CASHMIR OF THE R.C.A.F. New York, Pageant Press, 1955. 221p

**O'Brien, Agnes**
WINNOWING. Toronto, Extension Print., 1935. 483p [OTMC

**O'Brien, Rev. Cornelius, 1843–1906**
AFTER WEARY YEARS. A Novel. Baltimore, Murphy, 1885. 433p [LC NSHD OOU

**Odle, E.V.**
THE CLOCKWORK MAN. London, Heinemann, 1923. 213p [BM LC
THE HISTORY OF ALFRED RUDD. A Novel. London, Collins, 1922. 273p [BM

**Ogilvy, Maud**
THE KEEPER OF BIC LIGHT HOUSE. A Canadian Story of To-day. Montreal, Renouf, 1891. 138p [BVaU NBFU OTP
MARIE GOURDON. A Romance of the Lower St. Lawrence. Montreal, Lovell, 1890. 129p [BVaU NSHD OTP

**Ognall, Leopold Horace, 1908–**
ALIBI. By Harry Carmichael [pseud]. London, Collins, 1961. 192p
THE ARMITAGE SECRET. By Hartley Howard [pseud]. London, Collins, 1959. 256p
THE BIG SNATCH. By Hartley Howard [pseud]. London, Collins, 1958. 191p
BOWMAN AT A VENTURE. By Hartley Howard [pseud]. London, Collins, 1954. 192p
BOWMAN STRIKES AGAIN. By Hartley Howard [pseud]. London, Collins, 1958. 192p
THE BOWMAN TOUCH. By Hartley Howard [pseud]. London, Collins, 1956. 192p
THE DEAD OF THE NIGHT. By Harry Carmichael [pseud]. London, Collins, 1956. 192p
DEADLINE. By Hartley Howard [pseud]. London, Collins, 1959. 192p
DEADLY NIGHT-CAP. By Harry Carmichael [pseud]. London, Collins, 1953. 192p
DEATH OF CECILIA. By Hartley Howard [pseud]. London, Collins, 1952. 188p
DEATH COUNTS THREE. By Harry Carmichael [pseud]. London, Collins, 1954. 192p
EMERGENCY EXIT. By Harry Carmichael [pseud]. London, Collins, 1957. 192p
EXTORTION. By Hartley Howard [pseud]. London, Collins, 1960. 192p
FALL GUY. By Hartley Howard [pseud]. London, Collins, 1960. 256p
A HEARSE FOR CINDERELLA. By Hartley Howard [pseud]. London, Collins, 1956. 192p
INTO THIN AIR. By Harry Carmichael [pseud]. New York, Doubleday, 1958. 191p
JAMES KNOWLAND: DECEASED. By Harry Carmichael [pseud]. London, Collins, 1958. 192p
JUSTICE ENOUGH. By Harry Carmichael [pseud]. London, Collins, 1956. 192p

KEY TO THE MORGUE. By Hartley Howard [pseud]. London, Collins, 1957. 192p

THE LAST APPOINTMENT. By Hartley Howard [pseud]. London, Collins, 1951. 256p

THE LAST DECEPTION. By Hartley Howard [pseud]. London, Collins, 1951. 256p

THE LAST VANITY. By Hartley Howard [pseud]. London, Collins, 1951. 252p

THE LONG NIGHT. By Hartley Howard [pseud]. London, Collins, 1957. 192p

MONEY FOR MURDER. By Harry Carmichael [pseud]. London, Collins, [1955]. 192p

NOOSE FOR A LADY. By Harry Carmichael [pseud]. London, Collins, 1955. 192p

NO TARGET FOR BOWMAN. By Hartley Howard [pseud]. London, Collins, 1955. 192p

... OR BE HE DEAD. By Harry Carmichael [pseud]. London, Collins, 1959. 192p

THE OTHER SIDE OF THE DOOR. By Hartley Howard [pseud]. London, Collins, 1953. 188p

PUT OUT THAT STAR. By Harry Carmichael [pseud]. London, Collins, 1957. 192p

A QUESTION OF TIME. By Harry Carmichael [pseud]. London, Collins, 1958. 192p

REQUIEM FOR CHARLES. By Harry Carmichael [pseud]. London, Collins, 1960. 256p

SCHOOL FOR MURDER. By Harry Carmichael [pseud]. London, Collins, 1953. 192p

THE SCREAMING RABBIT. By Harry Carmichael [pseud]. New York, Simon & Schuster, 1955. 277p [First pub. under title: DEATH COUNTS THREE, *q.v.*]

THE SEEDS OF HATE. By Harry Carmichael [pseud]. London, Collins, 1960. 192p

SLEEP FOR THE WICKED. By Hartley Howard [pseud]. London, Collins, 1955. 192p

SLEEP, MY PRETTY ONE. By Hartley Howard [pseud]. London, Collins, 1958. 192p

STRANGLEHOLD. By Harry Carmichael [pseud]. London, Collins, 1959. 192p

THE VANISHING TRICK. By Harry Carmichael [pseud]. London, Collins, 1955. 188p

WHY KILL JOHNNY? By Harry Carmichael [pseud]. London, Collins, 1954. 191p

**O'Hagan, Howard, 1902–**

TAY JOHN. London, Laidlaw, 1939. 264p [Also: New York, Potter, 1960. 264p] [BM BVaU NBFU OTMC

**O'Hara, Mrs. Melita L.**

COAST TO COAST IN A PUDDLE JUMPER, AND OTHER STORIES. Tessier, Sask., Author, 1930. 109p [Also: Philadelphia, Dorrance, 1930.] [BVaU NBFU OONL QMSS

**O'Higgins, Harvey Jerrold, 1876–1929**

THE ADVENTURES OF DETECTIVE BARNEY. New York, Century, 1915. 305p [BM LC

CLARA BARRON. New York, Harper, 1922. 335p [BM BVaU LC OTMC

DON-A-DREAMS. A Story of Love and Youth. New York, Century, 1906. 412p [BM BVaU LC OTMC

FROM THE LIFE. Imaginary Portraits of Some Distinguished Americans. New York, Harper, 1919. 334p [BM LC NBFU OTMC

A GRAND ARMY MAN. New York, Century, 1908. 253p [BM LC OTMC

HIS MOTHER. Toronto, Charles Press, 1909. 24p [OTMC

JULIE CANE. New York, Harper, 1924. 343p [BM BVaU LC OTMC

OLD CLINKERS. A Story of the New York Fire Department. Boston, Small Maynard, 1909. 277p [LC OTU

THE SECRET SPRINGS. New York, Harper, 1920. 242p [BM LC NSHD OTU

SILENT SAM, AND OTHER STORIES OF OUR DAY. New York, Century, 1914. 390p [BM LC OTMC

THE SMOKE-EATERS. The Story of a Fire Crew. New York, Century, 1905. 296p [BM LC

SOME DISTINGUISHED AMERICANS. Imaginary Portraits. London, Harper, 1922. 335p [BM LC NBFU OTMC

**Olson, Oscar, 1908–**

MOUNTIE ON TRIAL. Toronto, Ryerson, 1953. 257p

**Omond, Helen B.**

DILARAM. New York, Fortuny's, 1938. 175p [OTU

**O'Reilly, John A.**

THE LAST SENTINEL OF CASTLE HILL. A Newfoundland Story. London, Stock, 1916. 382p [BVaU NBFU OTP QQLA

**Ormsby, Iërne**

JANE OF THE CROW'S NEST. ... London, Hutchinson, 1936. 256p [BM

WILD WEST SALLY. London, Lutterworth, 1939. 222p [BM OTU

**Osler, Edmund Boyd, 1919–**

LIGHT IN THE WILDERNESS. Toronto, Harlequin Books, 1953. 192p

**Ostenso, Martha, 1900–1963**

THE DARK DAWN. New York, Dodd Mead, 1926. 294p [BM BVaU NBFU OTP

LOVE PASSED THIS WAY. New York, Dodd Mead, 1942. 217p [LC NBFU OTMC

THE MAD CAREWS. New York, Dodd Mead, 1927. 346p [BM BVaU LC NBFU OTMC QMM

A MAN HAD TALL SONS. New York, Dodd Mead, 1958. 365p

THE MANDRAKE ROOT. New York, Dodd Mead, 1938. 304p [LC NBFU OTMC QMM

MILK ROUTE. New York, Dodd Mead, 1948. 250p [BVaU LC NBFU OTMC QMM

O RIVER, REMEMBER! New York, Dodd Mead, 1943. 393p [BM BVaU LC NBFU OTU QMM

THE PASSIONATE FLIGHT. *See* WILD GEESE, below.
PROLOGUE TO LOVE. New York, Dodd Mead, 1932. 265p [BVaU NBFU LC OTMC QMM
THE STONE FIELD. New York, Dodd Mead, 1937. 310p [BVaU LC NBFU OTMC QMM
THE SUNSET TREE. New York, Dodd Mead, 1949. 255p [BM LC NBFU OTMC
THERE'S ALWAYS ANOTHER YEAR. New York, Dodd Mead, 1933. 268p [BVaU LC NBFU OTMC QMM
THE WATERS UNDER THE EARTH. New York, Dodd Mead, 1930. 319p [BM BVaU LC NBFU OTMC QMM
THE WHITE REEF. New York, Dodd Mead, 1934. 288p [BM BVaU LC NBFU OTMC QMM
WILD GEESE. Toronto, McClelland, 1925. 356p [English title: THE PASSIONATE FLIGHT. London, Hodder, 1925. 320p] [BM BVaU LC NBFU OTMC
THE YOUNG MAY MOON. New York, Dodd Mead, 1929. 301p [BM BVaU LC NBFU OTMC QMM

**O'Sullivan, Francis Joseph, 1870–**

THE CHRONICLES OF CROFTON. Toronto, Hunter Rose, 1926. 188p [NBFU OTP

**Owen, John Spencer**

TETE JAUNE CACHE. New York, Pageant Press, 1953. 223p

**Oxley, James Macdonald, 1855–1907**

ARCHIE OF ATHABASCA. Boston, Lothrop, 1893. 262p [Also as: ARCHIE McKENZIE, the Young Nor'-Wester. London, Religious Tract Soc., 1894; and THE YOUNG NOR'-WESTER. London, Religious Tract Soc., 1908. 256p] [BM BVaU OTMC
BAFFLING THE BLOCKADE. London, Nelson, 1896. 375p [BM OONL
BERT LLOYD'S BOYHOOD. A Story of Nova Scotia. Philadelphia, American Baptist Pub. Soc., 1889. 347p [Also: London, Hodder, 1892. 363p] [BM LC NSHD OONL
THE BOY TRAMPS; or, Across Canada. New York, Crowell, 1896. 361p [Also as: TWO BOY TRAMPS. London, Chambers, 1896. 320p] [BM BVaU LC NBFU OTMC
THE CHORE-BOY OF CAMP KIPPEWA. Philadelphia, American Baptist Pub. Soc., 1891. 144p [Also as: THE YOUNG WOODSMAN. London, Nelson, 1894.] [BM LC OONL
DIAMOND ROCK; or, On the Right Track. London, Nelson, 1893. 302p [Same as: THE GOOD SHIP GRYPHON, *q.v.*] [BM OONL
DONALBLANE OF DARIEN. Toronto, Musson, n.d. 126p [Also: London, Partridge, 1902.] [BM OONL
DONALD GRANT'S DEVELOPMENT. Philadelphia, American Baptist Pub. Soc., 1892. 256p [Also as: MAKING HIS WAY. London, Nelson, 1896.] [BM LC NSHD OONL

THE FAMILY ON WHEELS. Adapted from the French. ... New York, Crowell, 1905. 219p [LC

FERGUS MACTAVISH; or, Portage and Prairie. A Story of the Hudson's Bay Co. Philadelphia, American Baptist Pub. Soc., 1892. 344p [BM BVaU LC OONL

FIFE AND DRUM AT LOUISBOURG. Boston, Little Brown, 1899. 307p [BM BVaU LC NSHD OTMC QMSS

FROM RUNG TO RUNG. London, Kelly, 1899. 124p [BM

THE GOOD SHIP GRYPHON. Philadelphia, American Baptist Pub. Soc., 1893. 248p [Same as: DIAMOND ROCK, *q.v.*] [LC OTMC

THE HERO OF START POINT AND OTHER STORIES. Philadelphia, American Baptist Pub. Soc., 1896. 254p [LC

IN PATHS OF PERIL. Boy's Adventure in Nova Scotia. London, Partridge, 1903. 128p [BM BVaU

IN THE SWING OF THE SEA. Philadelphia, American Baptist Pub. Soc., 1898. 268p [BM LC NSHD

IN THE WILDS OF THE WEST COAST. New York, Nelson, 1895. 398p [BM BVaU LC NBFU OTMC

L'HASA AT LAST. Philadelphia, American Baptist Pub. Soc., 1900. 269p [BM BVaU LC OTMC

MY STRANGE RESCUE AND OTHER STORIES. London, Nelson, 1894. 368p [BM OONL

NORMAN'S NUGGET. London, Partridge, 1901. 297p [BM OTMC

NORTH OVERLAND WITH FRANKLIN. London, Religious Tract Soc., 1901. 256p [BM BVaU LC NSHD OTP

ON THE WORLD'S ROOF. Philadelphia, American Baptist Pub. Soc., 1897. 271p [1st ed.: London, Nisbet, 1896. 242p] [BM LC NSHD OTMC

STANDING THE TEST. London, Religious Tract Soc., 1898. 127p [BM

THE SPECIMEN HUNTERS. New ed. London, Religious Tract Soc., 1907. 256p [Earlier ed. at Toronto? –OOP] [BM OONL

TERRY'S TRIALS AND TRIUMPHS. London, Nelson, 1899. 186p [BM OTMC

TI-TI-PU. A Boy of Red River. Toronto, Musson, n.d. 126p [ACG BViPA NSWA OOA

UP AMONG THE ICE-FLOES. Philadelphia, American Baptist Pub. Soc., 1890. 250p [BM LC OONL

WITH ROGERS ON THE FRONTIER. A Story of '56. New York, Wessels, 1902. 253p [LC OONL

WON IN WESTERN CANADA. N.p., 1903. 39p [OTP

THE WRECKERS OF SABLE ISLAND. Philadelphia, American Baptist Pub. Soc., 1891. 108p [Also: London, Nelson, 1904. 121p] [BM BVaU LC NSHD OONL

THE YOUNG NOR'-WESTER. *See* ARCHIE OF ATHABASKA, above.

THE YOUNG WOODSMAN; or, Life in the Forests of Canada. London, Nelson, 1895. 156p [OLU

**Pacey, Desmond, 1917–**

A BOOK OF CANADIAN STORIES. Ed. by ——. Toronto, Ryerson, 1947. 295p [2nd ed., rev. & enl., 1950. 310p. School ed., with intro. and notes by ——, 1952. xxxviii + 312p] [BVaU NSHD OTMC QMBM

THE PICNIC AND OTHER STORIES. Toronto, Ryerson, 1958. xi + 143p

**Packard, Frank Lucius, 1877–1942**

THE ADVENTURES OF JIMMY DALE. Toronto, Copp Clark, 1917. 468p [BM BVaU LC NBFU OTU QMM

THE BELOVED TRAITOR. Toronto, Copp Clark, 1915. 347p [BM BVaU LC NBFU OTMC QMM

THE BIG SHOT. Toronto, Copp Clark, 1929. 286p [BM LC NBFU OTU QMM

BROKEN WATERS. Toronto, Copp Clark, 1925. 294p [BM BVaU LC NBFU OTMC QMM

THE DEVIL'S MANTLE. New York, Doran, 1927. 313p [BM BVaU LC OTU QMM

DOORS OF THE NIGHT. Toronto, Copp Clark, 1922. 298p [BM BVaU LC NBFU OTMC QMM

THE DRAGON'S JAWS. New York, Doran, 1937. 310p [BM LC NBFU OTMC

THE FOUR STRAGGLERS. Toronto, Copp Clark, 1923. 303p [BM BVaU LC NBFU OTMC QMM

FROM NOW ON. Toronto, Copp Clark, 1919. 346p [BM NBFU OTMC QMM

THE FURTHER ADVENTURES OF JIMMY DALE. New York, Burt, 1919. 340p [BM BVaU OTMC

THE GOLD SKULL MURDERS. New York, Doran, 1931. 303p [BM BVaU LC NBFU OTMC

GREATER LOVE HATH NO MAN. Toronto, Copp Clark, 1913. 294p [BM BVaU LC NBFU OTMC QMM

THE HIDDEN DOOR. New York, Doubleday, 1933. 300p [BM BVaU LC NBFU OTMC QMM

JIMMY DALE AND THE BLUE ENVELOPE MURDER. Toronto, Copp Clark, 1930. 290p [BM BVa LC NBFU OTMC QMM

JIMMY DALE AND THE MISSING HOUR. New York, Doubleday, 1935. 310p [BM LC OTMC

JIMMY DALE AND THE PHANTOM CLUE. Toronto, Copp Clark, 1922. 302p [BM BVa LC NBFU OTMC QMM

THE LOCKED BOOK. Toronto, Copp Clark, 1924. 320p [BM BVaU LC NBFU OTMC QMM

THE MIRACLE MAN. Toronto, Copp Clark, 1914. 300p [BM BVaU LC NBFU OTMC QMM

MORE KNAVES THAN ONE. London, Stoughton, 1938. 286p [BM LC OTU

THE NIGHT OPERATOR. Toronto, Copp Clark, 1919. 320p [BM BVaU NBFU OTMC QMM

ON THE IRON AT BIG CLOUD. New York, Crowell, 1911. 343p [BM LC NBFU OTMC

PAWNED. Toronto, Copp Clark, 1921. 288p [BM LC NBFU OTMC
THE PURPLE BALL. New York, Doran, 1933. 310p [BM BVaU LC NBFU OTMC
THE RED LEDGER. New York, Doran, 1926. 318p [BM BVaU LC NBFU OTMC QMM
RUNNING SPECIAL. Toronto, Copp Clark, 1925. 304p [BM BVaU LC NBFU OOP OTMC QMM
SHANGHAI JIM. Garden City, Doubleday, 1928. 374p [BM BVaU LC NBFU OTMC
THE SIN THAT WAS HIS. Toronto, Copp Clark, 1917. 374p [BM BVaU LC NBFU OTMC QMM
THE SLAVE JUNK. London, Hodder, 1927. 312p [AEU BM
TIGER CLAWS. New York, Doran, 1928. 305p [BM BVaU LC NBFU OTMC
TWO STOLEN IDOLS. New York, Burt, 1927. 314p [LC NBFU OTMC QMM
THE WHITE MOLL. Toronto, Copp Clark, 1920. 306p [BM BVaU LC NBFU OTMC QMM
THE WIRE DEVILS. Toronto, Copp Clark, 1918. 318p [BM BVaU LC NBFU OTMC QMM

**Page, Mrs. Elizabeth Merwin, 1889–**
THE TREE OF LIBERTY. New York, Farrar, 1939. 985p [BM BVaU LC NBFU OTU
WILDERNESS ADVENTURE. New York, Rinehart, 1946. 300p [BM LC NBFU

**Page, Patricia Kathleen, 1916–**
THE SUN AND THE MOON. By Judith Cape [pseud]. Toronto, Macmillan, 1944. 200p [BVaU OTU

**Parker, Alice Elizabeth (Foster), 1884–**
BONDS IN A FAMILY. Victoria, Hunter Rose, 1933. 212p [BVaU NBFU OTP

**Parker, Ellanore J.**
THE LAND LAY WAITING.... New York, Pageant Press, 1955. 236p

**Parker, Gilbert, 1862–1932**
AN ADVENTURER OF THE NORTH. Being a Continuation of PIERRE AND HIS PEOPLE. London, Methuen, 1895. 392p [BM BVaU LC NBFU OTMC QMM
THE BATTLE OF THE STRONG. A Romance of Two Kingdoms. London, Methuen, 1898. 432p [BM BVaU LC NBFU OTU QMSS
BORN WITH A GOLDEN SPOON. New York, Doubleday, 1899. 277p [BM LC
CARNAC. Toronto, Copp Clark, 1922. 319p [*Cf.* CARNAC'S FOLLY.] [BM BVaU OTMC QMM
CARNAC'S FOLLY. Philadelphia, Lippincott, 1922. 352p [*Cf.* preceding title.] [LC NBFU OTMC

THE CHIEF FACTOR. A Tale of the Hudson's Bay Company. New York, Trow Directory Co., 1892. 175p [Same title, but also containing "A Ricochet." New York, Home Pub. Co., 1893. 265p] [LC OTMC

THE CHIEF FACTOR. "Good Words" Christmas Story. London, Isbister & Co., 1892. 68p [Probably same as preceding title.] [BVaU QMSS

CUMNER'S SON AND OTHER SOUTH SEA FOLK. London, Heinemann, 1910. 283p [BM BVaU LC NBFU OTMC QMSS

DONOVAN PASHA, AND SOME PEOPLE OF EGYPT. London, Heinemann, 1902. 308p [BM BVaU LC NBFU OTMC QMM

THE GOING OF THE WHITE SWAN. New York, Appleton, 1912. 55p [Reprinted from AN ADVENTURER OF THE NORTH.] [BM BVaU LC NBFU OTMC

THE HILL OF PAINS. Boston, Badger, 1899. 151p [Contains also THE CAVE OF CRYS.] [AmCat has note saying Parker denies authorship "of any book" with this title.] [BVaU LC OTMC

THE JUDGEMENT HOUSE. A Novel. Toronto, Copp Clark, 1913. 470p [BM BVaU LC NBFU OTMC QMM

A LADDER OF SWORDS. A Tale of Love, Laughter, and Tears. London, Heinemann, 1904. 286p [Later pub. under title: MICHEL AND ANGELE. New York, Scribner, 1923. 245p] [BM BVaU LC NBFU OTMC QMSS

THE LANE THAT HAD NO TURNING, and Other Associated Tales concerning the People of Pontiac. New York, Doubleday, 1900. 359p [BM BVaU LC NBFU OTP QMM

THE LIAR. Boston, Brown, 1899. 142p [BVaU LC NBFU OTMC QMM

A LOVER'S DIARY. Songs in Sequence. London, Methuen, 1894. 147p [Also pub. with EMBERS. 2v in 1. New York, Scribner, 1913.] [BM BVaU LC NBFU OTP

THE MARCH OF THE WHITE GUARD. New York, Fenno, 1901. 133p [Reprinted from TAVISTOCK TALES. By Gilbert Parker and Others. London, Isbister, 1893. 254p] [BM BVaU LC NBFU OTMC QMM

THE MONEY MASTER. Being the Curious History of Jean Jacques Barbille, his Labours, his Loves and his Ladies. New York, Harper, 1915. 359p [BM BVaU LC NBFU OTP QMM

MRS. FALCHION. A Novel. London, Methuen, 1893. 2v [New ed.: London, Methuen, 1894. 428p] [BM BVaU LC NBFU OTMC QMSS

NO DEFENCE. Toronto, Copp Clark, 1920. 347p [BM BVaU LC NBFU OTMC QMM

NORTHERN LIGHTS. Toronto, Copp Clark, 1909. 375p [BM BVaU LC NBFU OTP QMM

PIERRE AND HIS PEOPLE. Tales of the Far North. London, Methuen, 1892. 323p [BM BVaU LC NBFU OTMC QMM

THE POMP OF THE LAVILETTES. Boston, Lamson Wolffe, 1896. 191p [BM BVaU LC NBFU OTMC QMM

THE POWER AND THE GLORY. A Romance of the Great La Salle. New York, Harper, 1925. 339p [BM BVaU LC NBFU OTP QMM

THE PROMISED LAND. A Story of David in Israel. London, Cassell, 1928. 325p [BM BVaU LC NBFU OOP OTMC QMM

THE RIGHT OF WAY. Being the Story of Charley Steele, and Another. London, Heinemann, 1901. 368p [BM BVaU LC NBFU OTMC QMM

A ROMANY OF THE SNOWS. Second Series of AN ADVENTURER OF THE NORTH. Being a continuation of PIERRE AND HIS PEOPLE. New York, Stone & Kimball, 1896. 218p [Same title: Toronto, Copp Clark, 1898. 392p] [BM BVaU LC NBFU OTP QMM

THE SEATS OF THE MIGHTY. Being the Memoirs of Captain Robert Moray, Some Time an Officer in the Virginia Regiment, and Afterwards of Amherst's Regiment. London, Methuen, 1896. 376p [BM BVaU LC NBFU OTMC QMSS

TARBOE. The Story of a Life. New York, Harper, 1927. 196p [BM BVaU LC NBFU OTMC QMM

THE TRAIL OF THE SWORD. New York, Appleton, 1894. 277p [BM BVaU LC NBFU OTP

THE TRANSLATION OF A SAVAGE. New York, Appleton, 1893. 184p [BM BVaU LC NBFU OTP QMM

THE TRESPASSER. New York, Appleton, 1893. 275p [BM BVaU LC NBFU OTU QMM

AN UNPARDONABLE LIAR. Chicago, Sergel, 1900. 185p [*Cf.* THE LIAR. Boston, Brown, 1899. 142p] [LC

THE WEAVERS. A Tale of England and Egypt of Fifty Years Ago. New York, Harper, 1907. 531p [BM BVaU LC NBFU OTMC QMM

WHEN VALMOND CAME TO PONTIAC. The Story of a Lost Napoleon. London, Methuen, 1895. 312p [BM BVaU LC NBFU OTMC QMM

WILD YOUTH, AND ANOTHER. [Tale: "Jordan is a Hard Road"]. Philadelphia, Lippincott, 1919. 290p [BM BVaU LC NSHD OTP

THE WORKS OF GILBERT PARKER. Imperial Ed. New York, Scribner, 1912-23. 23v [BM BVaU LC NSHD OTU QMM

THE WORLD FOR SALE. New York, Harper, 1916. 405p [BM BVaU LC NBFU OTU QMM

YOU NEVER KNOW YOUR LUCK. Being the Story of a Matrimonial Deserter. New York, Doran, 1914. 328p [BM BVaU LC NBFU OTMC QMM

**Parker, K.Y.**

BEYOND THE WEST. Truro, N.S., Truro Print., n.d. 145p [OTMC

**Parker, William Wilder McKinley, 1894–**

FLOWING GOLD. Edmonton, Author, 1957. 60p

GREENER PRAIRIE. Edmonton, Author, 1959. 68p

SILVER FORKS. Edmonton, Author, 1955. 66p

**Parks, Georgina**

RUKE ANEHM. By Gabrielle [pseud]. Philadelphia, Dorrance, 1938. 139p [LC OTU

**Parsons, Nell Wilson, 1898–1968**

THE CURLEW CRIED. A Love Story of the Canadian Prairie. Seattle, Frank McCaffrey, 1947. 383p [AEU OTU

**Parsons, Vivian (Lajeunesse)**

LUCIEN. Toronto, McClelland, 1939. 383p [LC OTP QMM

NOT WITHOUT HONOR. New York, Dodd Mead, 1941. 342p [AEU LC QMBM

**Partridge, Basil Gilpin, 1894–**

CHAPLET OF GRACE. Philadelphia, Westminster Press, 1956. 283p

LARRY PENNINGTON. Philadelphia, Westminster Press, 1954. 273p

THE PENNINGTONS. Philadelphia, Westminster Press, 1951. 284p

**Paterson, Isabel M. (Bowler)**

THE FOURTH QUEEN. Toronto, Macmillan, 1926. 315p [BM BVaU LC NBFU

THE GOLDEN VANITY. New York, Morrow, 1934. 372p [BVaU LC NBFU OTMC

IF IT PROVE FAIR WEATHER. New York, Putnam, 1940. 306p [BVaU LC NBFU

THE MAGPIE'S NEST. New York, Lane, 1917. 303p [BM BVaU LC NBFU

NEVER ASK THE END. New York, Morrow, 1933. 332p [BM BVaU LC NBFU OTMC

THE ROAD OF THE GODS. New York, Boni, 1930. 264p [BVaU LC NBFU

THE SHADOW RIDERS. New York, Lane, 1916. 379p [BM BVaU LC NSHD OTMC

THE SINGING SEASON. New York, Boni, 1924. 304p [BM BVaU LC NBFU

**Paterson, Maude Elizabeth, 1867–**

CHILD'S GARDEN OF STORIES. Toronto, Morang, 1911. 155p [2nd rev. ed., Toronto, Macmillan, 1931. 160p] [BM

**Patriarche, Valance St. Just (Berryman), 1875–**

RORY OF WILLOW BEACH. London, Cassell, 1912. 195p [BM OOP

TAG; or, The Chien Boule Dog. Boston, Page, 1909. 138p [BVaU LC NBFU OTMC

**Pearce, Theodocia, 1894–1925?**

THE EVERLASTING BEAUTY. New York, Lawren, 1926. 281p [BVaU NSHD

**Pedley, Rev. Hugh, 1852–1923**

LOOKING FORWARD. The Strange Experience of the Rev. Fergus McCheyne. Toronto, Briggs, 1913. 294p [BM BVaU NSHD OTU QMSS

**Pedro, Dom (pseud)**
SKETCHES. By Dom Pedro [pseud]. Toronto, Rose Pub. Co., 1891. 120p [OTU
SKETCHES. Dedicated to the Veterans of '85. By Dom Pedro [pseud]. Toronto, Hill & Weir, n.d. 32p [AEU NBFU

**Penfield, Wilder Graves, 1891–**
NO OTHER GODS. Boston, Little Brown, 1954. ix + 340p
THE TORCH. Boston, Little Brown, 1960. xiv + 370p

**Pennington, Richard, 1904–**
PETERLEY HARVEST. The Private Diary of David Peterley now for the First Time printed. London, Hutchinson, 1960. 285p

**Pericum, Hic (pseud)**
THE JINX OF THE MINE. A Romance of the Girl Prospector. By Hic Pericum [pseud]. Toronto, Compliments of I.H. Perigoe & Co., Stock Brokers, 1937. 16p [OPAL

**Perrot, Irene**
CATHEDRAL WINDOWS. Montreal, Palm Pub., 1949. 147p [UTQ
TREES GROW TALL. A Novel. Toronto, Ryerson, 1946. 250p [NBS OTU
THE TWAIN TRADITION. New York, Pageant Press, 1952. 169p

**Perry, Alma (Jordan)**
GENTLY SMILING JAWS. New York, Vantage Press, 1959. 118p

**Perry, James Black, 1845–1936**
YON TOON O' MINE. By Logan Weir [pseud]. Toronto, Ryerson, 1924. 220p [BVaU NBFU OTP

**Perry, Martha Eugenie**
THE GIRL IN THE SILK DRESS, AND OTHER STORIES. Victoria, Author, 1931. 144p [BVaU NBFU OTMC

**Peterson, Charles Walter, 1868–1944**
THE FRUITS OF THE EARTH. A Story of the Canadian Prairies. Ottawa, Graphic, 1928. 304p [BViPA NBFU OTP

**Peterson, Len, 1917–**
CHIPMUNK. Toronto, McClelland, 1949. 299p [BVaU NBFU OTMC

**Petitt, Maud**
BETH WOODBURN. A Canadian Tale. Toronto, Briggs, 1897. 158p [BM BVaU OTUV

**Phelan, Josephine, 1905–**
THE BOY WHO RAN AWAY. Toronto, Macmillan, 1954. 152p

**Philip, Alex, 1882–**
THE CRIMSON WEST. Toronto, Allen, 1925. 282p [BM BVaU LC NBFU OTMC

THE PAINTED CLIFF. Ottawa, Graphic, 1927. 213p [BVaU OTMC QMM
WHISPERING LEAVES. Ottawa, Graphic, 1931. 340p [BVaU NBFU OTMC

**Phillipps-Wolley, Clive Oldnall, 1854–1918**

THE CHICAMON STONE. London, Bell, 1900. 295p [BM BVaU OOP
GOLD, GOLD, IN CARIBOO! A Story of Adventure in British Columbia. London, Blackie, 1894. 288p [BM BVaU OTMC
MY SOLDIER'S KEEPER. London, Soc. for Prop. Christian Knowledge, 1888. [EngCat
ONE OF THE BROKEN BRIGADE. London, Smith Elder, 1897. 279p [BM BVaU OTMC
THE QUEENSBERRY CUP. London, Methuen, 1895. 313p [BM
THE REMITTANCE MAN. [BCF
SNAP. A Legend of the Lone Mountain. London, Longmans, 1890. 310p [BM BVaU OTMC

**Phillips, John Arthur, 1842–1907**

FROM BAD TO WORSE; HARD TO BEAT; and A TERRIBLE CHRISTMAS. Three Stories of Montreal Life. Montreal, Lovell, 1877. 277p [OTP
THE GHOST OF A DOG. A Christmas Story in Four Acts, with a Prologue and Epilogue. Ottawa, Woodburn, 1885. 155p [BVaU OTP QMBM
OUT OF THE SNOW, AND OTHER STORIES AND SKETCHES. Ottawa, Free Press, [1886?]. 172p [OTP QMSS

**Pickard, Hannah Maynard (Thompson), 1812–1844**

MEMOIR AND WRITINGS OF MRS. HANNAH MAYNARD PICKARD. ... By Edward Otheman. Boston, Ela, 1845. 311p [NBFU OTP
PROCRASTINATION; or, Maria Louisa Winslow. By a Lady [pseud]. Boston, King, 1840. 115p [Brown U
THE WIDOW'S JEWELS. In Two Stories. By a Lady [pseud]. Boston, Waite Pierce, 1844. 114p [NBB

**Pickford, Mary, 1893–**

THE DEMI-WIDOW. Indianapolis, Bobbs-Merrill, 1935. 272p [BM LC NBFU OTMC
LITTLE LIAR——. New York, O'Brien, 1934. 22p [BM LC
STICKYFINGERS. A Story. London, Allied Artists Corporation, 1927. [BM

**Pickthall, Marjorie Lowry Christie, 1883–1922**

ANGELS' SHOES, AND OTHER STORIES. London, Hodder, 1923. 320p [BM BVaU NBFU OTMC QMM
BILLY'S HERO; or, The Valley of Gold. Toronto, Musson, 1908. 128p [BM BVaU NBFU OKQ
THE BRIDGE. A Story of the Great Lakes. London, Hodder, 1922. 320p [BM BVaU LC NBFU OTP QMM
DICK'S DESERTION. A Boy's Adventures in Canadian Forests. Toronto, Musson, 1905. 128p [BM BVaU NBFU OKQ

LITTLE HEARTS. London, Methuen, 1915. 309p [Other eds., 1922, 1926.] [BM BVaU NBFU OTP QMM

THE STRAIGHT ROAD. Toronto, Musson, [1906?]. 127p [BM BVaU NBFU OKQ

THE WORKER IN SANDALWOOD. New York, Everyland, 1914. 16p [Same title: Toronto, Ryerson, 1934 and 1943.] [BVaU LC NBFU OKQ

**Pimm, Mrs. Ella G.**

HENRY. London, Hodder, 1924. 155p [BM

**Piner, Jack, 1923?–1958**

FEAR NOT MY SON. A Novel. New York, Pageant Press, 1955. 264p

**Pinkerton, Kathrene Sutherland (Gedney), 1887–**

ADVENTURE NORTH. New York, Carrick & Evans, 1940. 268p [BM BVaU LC

A GOOD PARTNER. New York, Harcourt, 1948. 269p [LC

HIDDEN HARBOR. New York, Harcourt, 1951. 278p

THE LONG TRAVERSE. By Kathrene and Robert Pinkerton. New York, Doubleday, 1920. 249p [BM LC NBFU OTMC

PEDDLER'S CREW. New York, Harcourt, 1954. 243p [Pub. in England as ROYAL BROWNE. *q.v.*]

PENITENTIARY POST. By Kathrene and Robert Pinkerton. New York, Doubleday, 1920. 245p [BM BViPA LC OTMC

ROYAL BROWNE. A Novel for Older Girls and Boys. London, Bodley Head, 1955. 192p

THE SILVER STRAIN. New York, Harcourt, 1946. 263p [LC

TOMORROW ISLAND. New York, Harcourt, 1960. 217p

WINDIGO. New York, Harcourt, 1945. 223p [BViPA LC

**Pitts, Herman Henry, 1858–**

OUR JOSHUA AS A REPORTER. By Brother Jonathan [pseud]. Fredericton, "Reporter," 1884. 159p [NBB OONL QMM

**Plenderleith, William Alexander, 1901–**

CONFLICT. Toronto, Ryerson, 1950. 328p [BVaU NBFU OTMC QMBM

**Plummer, Norman M.**

THE GOAD. A Human Story of the Last Great West in the Early Part of the Twentieth Century. London, Stockwell, 1930. 180p [BM BVaU NBFU OTMC

THE LONG ARM. Toronto, Nelson, 1939. 275p [AEU BM NBFU

**Pocklington, Mrs. Kathryn**

THE MORNIN'-GLORY GIRL. By Alice M. Winlow and Kathryn Pocklington. Toronto, McClelland, 1920. 224p [BVaU NBFU

**Pocock, Roger, 1865–1941**

THE ARCTIC NIGHT. London, Chapman, 1896. 180p [EngCat

THE BLACKGUARD. London, Beeman, 1897. 178p [BM NSWA

THE CHARIOT OF THE SUN. A Fantasy. London, Chapman, 1910. 316p [ACG BM

THE CHEERFUL BLACKGUARD. Indianapolis, Bobbs-Merrill, 1915. 400p [Same as THE BLACKGUARD?] [LC

CURLY. A Tale of the Arizona Desert. Boston, Little Brown, 1905. 320p [Pub. in England in 1904.] [BM BVaU LC OTMC

THE DRAGON-SLAYER. London, Chapman, 1896. 414p [Also: New York, Grosset, n.d. 320p] [BM EngCat OTMC

JESSE OF CARIBOO. London, Murray, 1911. 285p [BM BVaU LC

A MAN IN THE OPEN. Indianapolis, Bobbs-Merrill, 1912. 352p [BM BVaU LC

SWORD AND DRAGON. London, Hodder, 1909. 320p [BM

THE SPLENDID BLACKGUARD. London, Murray, 1915. 342p [Same as THE BLACKGUARD (1897)? THE CHEERFUL BLACKGUARD (1915)?] [EngCat BM

THE WOLF TRAIL. Oxford, Blackwell, 1923. 309p [BM BVaU LC OTMC

**Pocock, Wilfred Theodore, 1895–**

THE THREE GIFTS. New York, Pageant Press, 1959. 375p

**Pollock, Francis Lillie, 1876–**

BITTER HONEY. Toronto, Nelson, 1935. 315p [BM BVaU LC NBFU OOP

THE FROZEN FORTUNE. New York, Macaulay, 1910. 322p [LC NBFU

THE GLACIER GATE. An Adventure Story. New York, Chelsea House, 1926. 254p [OTMC

HONEY OF DANGER. New York, Chelsea, 1927. 251p [LC

JUPITER EIGHT. Toronto, Nelson, 1936. 286p [BM BVaU OTU

NORTHERN DIAMONDS. New York, Houghton, 1917. 259p [LC NBFU

RAINBOW LANDING. New York, Chelsea House, 1926. 250p [BVaU

THE TIMBER TREASURE. New York, Century, 1923. 269p [LC NBFU

THE TREASURE TRAIL. Boston, Page, 1906. 367p [LC NBFU

WILDERNESS HONEY. New York, Century, 1917. 325p [LC

THE WOODS-RIDER. New York, Century, 1922. 384p [LC

**Pope, William (fl. 1952)**

PENNILESS DREAMER. New York, Pageant Press, 1952. 186p

**Portlock, Rosa (Elliott), 1839–1928**

THE HEAD KEEPER. Toronto, Briggs, 1898. 227p [OTU

**Potter, Rev. Austin, 1842–1913**

FROM WEALTH TO POVERTY; or, The Tricks of the Traffic. A Story of the Drink Curse. Toronto, Briggs, 1884. 328p [OH

**Pound, Bunny**

LILA AND THE WATERFALL FAIRIES. By Bunny Pound (aged 11 years). Vancouver, Brookhouse, 1922. 14p [BVaU OKQ

**Prentice, James Douglas**

TEDDY'S STORY. Toronto, Macmillan, 1937. 356p [BM NBFU

**Preston, Anna, 1887–**

THE GLORY AND THE DREAM. New York, Huebsch, 1915. 244p [LC

THE RECORD OF A SILENT LIFE. New York, Huebsch, 1912. 327p [BM LC

**Preston, Margaret Mary, 1911–**

AS A WHITE CANDLE. New York, Pageant Press, 1952. 250p

**Preston, Sydney Herman, 1858–1931**

THE ABANDONED FARMER. Toronto, Copp, 1901. 288p [BM QMM

ON COMMON GROUND. New York, Holt, 1906. 316p [BM

**Price, Alfred**

RAIL LIFE. A Book of Yarns. Toronto, Allen, 1925. 285p [BM BVaU NBFU OTMC

**Price, Willard De Mille, 1887–**

SOUTH SEA ADVENTURE. New York, Day, 1952. x + 243p

**Price-Brown, John, 1844–1938**

HICKORY. A Tale of the Lakes. By Eric Bohn [pseud]. Toronto, 1904. [Pub. in *The Farming World,* 1904?] [BCF T&C

HOW HARTMANN WON. A Story of Old Ontario. By Eric Bohn [pseud]. Toronto, Morang, 1903. 269p [BM BVaU OTMC QMM

IN THE VAN; or, The Builders. By Price-Brown [pseud]. Toronto, McLeod, 1906. 352p [BM BVaU NBFU OTMC QMM

LAURA, THE UNDAUNTED. A Canadian Historical Romance. Toronto, Ryerson, 1930. 280p [BVaU OKQ OTMC QMM

THE MAC'S OF '37. A Story of the Canadian Rebellion. By Price-Brown [pseud]. Toronto, McLeod & Allen, 1910. 332p [BM BVaU NSHD OTMC QMM

**Primmer, Phyllis (Griesbach), 1926–**

AT THE RIVER'S TURNING. Grand Rapids, Mich., Zondervan Pub. House, 1960 [c1958]. 120p

**Pringle, Rev. George Charles Fraser, 1873–1949**

TILLICUMS OF THE TRAIL. Being Klondike Yarns Told to Canadian Soldiers Overseas by a Sourdough Padre. Toronto, McClelland, 1922. 253p [BM BVaU NBFU OTMC

**Procter, John James, 1838–1910**

THE PHILOSOPHER IN THE CLEARING. Quebec, Daily Telegraph, 1897. 251p [BM BVaU OTP QMBM

**Prower, Nelson, 1856–**

FREDDY BARTON'S SCHOOLDAYS. London, Ouseley, 1911. 274p [BM

REGGIE ABBOTT; or, The Adventures of a Swedish Officer. London, Rodway, 1890. 314p [BM

**Raddall, Thomas Head, 1903–**

AT THE TIDE'S TURN, AND OTHER STORIES. With intro. by Allan Bevan. Toronto, McClelland, 1959. ix + 178p [New Canadian Library, no. 9]

THE GOVERNOR'S LADY. Garden City, N.Y., Doubleday, 1960. 474p

HIS MAJESTY'S YANKEES. Garden City, Doubleday, 1942. 409p [BM BVaU LC NBFU OTP QMM

A MUSTER OF ARMS AND OTHER STORIES. Toronto, McClelland, 1954. 236p

THE NYMPH AND THE LAMP. A Novel. Boston, Little Brown, 1950. 376p [BM BVaU LC NBFU OTMC QMBM

THE PIED PIPER OF DIPPER CREEK AND OTHER TALES. Edinburgh, Blackwood, 1938. 318p [BM BVaU LC NBFU OTP QMM

PRIDE'S FANCY. Toronto, McClelland, 1946. 308p [BM BVaU LC NBFU OTP QMM

ROGER SUDDEN. Toronto, McClelland, 1944. 358p [BM BVaU LC NBFU OTP QMM

THE ROVER. The Story of a Canadian Privateer. Toronto, Macmillan, 1958. 156p

THE SON OF THE HAWK. Philadelphia, Winston, 1950. 247p [BM BVaU LC NBFU OTMC QMBM

TAMBOUR AND OTHER STORIES. Toronto, McClelland, 1945. 388p [BVaU NBFU OTP QMM

TIDEFALL. A Novel. Toronto, McClelland, 1953. 309p

THE WEDDING GIFT AND OTHER STORIES. Toronto, McClelland, 1947. 325p [BVaU NBFU OTMC QMM

THE WINGS OF NIGHT. New York, Doubleday, 1956. 319p

**Rand, Rev. Silas Tertius, 1810–1889**

LEGENDS OF THE MICMACS. New York, Longmans, 1894. xlvi + 452p [BM BVaU LC NBFU OTP QMM

**Rankin, Rev. Duncan Joseph, 1874–1954**

ON THIS ROCK. ... Ottawa, Overbrook Press, 1930. 198p [NBFU QMSS

OUR AIN FOLK AND OTHERS. Toronto, Macmillan, 1930. 208p [BVa NBFU OTU QMM

**Rankin, George Cameron, 1841–1903**

BORDER CANUCKS. Our Friendly Relations. Detroit, Rankin, 1890. 305p [LC

**Rashleigh, George**

JOHN THE FLUNKY. Designed and written as an Attempt to Assist in Impressing upon Children and Young People Generally the Reform most Necessary for the Future Greatness and Happiness of our Country. Ottawa, Woodburn, 1883. 102p [BVaU OTP

**Ravenhill, Alice, 1859–1954**

FOLKLORE OF THE FAR WEST. With Some Clues to Characteristics and Customs. Ed. by ——. Victoria, 1953. 87p

**Ray, George Raymond, 1869–1935**

KASBA (WHITE PARTRIDGE). A Story of Hudson Bay. Toronto, Briggs, 1915. 259p [BM BVaU LC NBFU OTMC QMM

**Read, Elfreida (Ennock), 1920–**

THE MAGIC OF LIGHT. London, Hutchinson, 1959. 127p

**Reade, Mrs. Frances Lawson**

ARABESQUE. By Yolande Langworthy [pseud]. New York, Lewis Copeland, 1931. 158p [LC OTP

**Ready, William Bernard, 1914–**

THE POOR HATER. A Novel. Chicago, Regnery, 1958. 337p

**Rebbeck, Mrs. Elizabeth**

HOME OF THE DRAGON. A Tonquinese Idyll. By Anna Catherina [pseud]. London, Unwin, 1893. 222p [BM

THE STRAGGLERS. A Tale of Primal Asperities. London, Griffiths, 1910. 178p [BM BVaU

**Reed, Else Clarissa (Porter), 1887–**

A MAN FORBID. New York, Morrow, 1935. 281p [BM LC NBFU OOP

**Reeve, Winifred (Eaton) Babcock, 1879–**

CATTLE. By Onoto Watanna [pseud]. Toronto, Hodder, 1923. 256p [Also: a New York ed., 1924.] [BM BVaU LC NBFU OTMC

DAUGHTERS OF NIJO. A Romance of Japan. By Onoto Watanna [pseud]. New York, Macmillan, 1904. 397p [BM BVaU LC OTMC

THE DIARY OF DELIA. Being a Veracious Chronicle of the Kitchen, with some Sidelights on the Parlour. By Onoto Watanna [pseud]. New York, Doubleday, 1907. 229p [BM LC

THE HEART OF HYACINTH. By Onoto Watanna [pseud]. New York, Harper, 1903. 250p [BM BVaU LC OTMC

HIS ROYAL NIBS. New York, Watt, 1925. 318p [LC OTMC

THE HONORABLE MISS MOONLIGHT. By Onoto Watanna [pseud]. New York, Harper, 1912. 174p [BM LC

A JAPANESE BLOSSOM. By Onoto Watanna [pseud]. New York, Harper, 1906. 263p [BM LC OTMC

A JAPANESE NIGHTINGALE. By Onoto Watanna [pseud]. New York, Harper, 1901. 225p [BM LC OOP

THE LOVE OF AZALEA. By Onoto Watanna [pseud]. New York, Dodd Mead, 1904. 239p [BM LC NBFU OTMC

MARION. The Story of an Artist's Model. By Herself and the Author of ME [pseudonyms for Sara Bosse and Mrs. Reeve]. New York, Watt, 1916. 307p [Written in collaboration with her sister, Mrs. Karl Bosse.] [LC

ME. A Book of Remembrance. [Anon] New York, Century, 1915. 356p [BM LC OOP

MISS NUME OF JAPAN. A Japanese-American Romance. By Onoto Watanna [pseud]. New York, Rand McNally, 1899. 220p [Toronto ed., 1913.] [BVaU LC

SUNNY-SAN. By Onoto Watanna [pseud]. New York, Doran, 1922. 311p [BM BVaU LC OTMC

TAMA. By Onoto Watanna [pseud]. New York, Harper, 1910. 243p [BM LC OTMC

THE WOOING OF WISTARIA. By Onoto Watanna [pseud]. New York, Harper, 1902. 388p [BM BVaU LC OTMC

In addition, three other novels, not located, are listed in *Can. Bookman* for April 1922:

LEND ME YOUR TITLE.

MISS SPRING MORNING.

OTHER PEOPLE'S TROUBLES.

**Regan, John Hugh**

THE END OF THE FURROW. London, Hutchinson, 1927. 288p [BM LC

VALIANT HEART. A Story of a Canadian Ranch. London, Hutchinson, 1926. 312p [BM QMM

**Reid, Leslie Hartley, 1896–**

CAULDRON BUBBLE. London, Gollancz, 1934. 448p [BM

THE RECTOR OF MALISEET. London, Dent, 1925. 272p [BM NBFU OTMC

SALTACRES. London, Dent, [1927?]. 370p [BM BVaU NBFU OOP QMM

TREVY, THE RIVER. London, Dent, 1928. 299p [BM NBFU OTMC QMM

**Reville, Frederick Douglas, 1866–1944**

A REBELLION. A Story of the Red River Uprising. Brantford, Hurley, 1912. 198p [BM BVaU NSHD OTP QMM

**Reynolds, H.T.**

THE UNQUENCHED FLAX. A Story of Western Canada. London, Stockwell, [1931]. 206p [AEU BM OWA

**Reynolds, Helen Mary Greenwood (Campbell) Dickson, 1884–**

ANGRY RIVER. By Dickson Reynolds [pseud]. Toronto, Nelson, 1951. 181p

BIG SHARK. By Dickson Reynolds [pseud]. New York, Nelson, 1948. 159p [BViPA LC

CAPTAIN PEGGY OF THE MAMIE L. By Helen Dickson, New York, Nelson, 1943. 176p [LC OTU

CAROL OF LONG CHANCE MINE. New York, Funk & Wagnalls, 1959. 216p

CHERRIES ARE RIPE. By Dickson Reynolds [pseud]. New York, Nelson, 1950. 191p [LC OTU

DORIS OF SUNSHINE RANCH. By Helen Dickson. London, Nelson, 1948. 184p [BM BViPA

THE FAMILY AT SUNSHINE RANCH. By Helen Dickson. London, Nelson, 1939. 204p [BM OTU

THE FIRE PATROL. By Dickson Reynolds [pseud]. New York, Nelson, 1949. 192p [BViPA LC NBFU OTMC

FORTUNE TRAIL. By Dickson Reynolds [pseud]. New York, Funk & Wagnalls, 1954. 213p

THE FUR BRIGADE. By Dickson Reynolds [pseud]. New York, Funk & Wagnalls, 1953. 207p

GOLD IN MOSQUITO CREEK. By Dickson Reynolds [pseud]. New York, Nelson, 1946. 192p [BM BViPA LC

HE WILL RETURN. By Dickson Reynolds [pseud]. Toronto, Ryerson, 1959. 256p

"KAREN PRESENTS ..." New York, Funk & Wagnalls, 1955. 218p

McBAIN'S BRIER ROSE. By Helen Dickson Reynolds. Toronto, Ryerson, 1957. 191p

MUSIC FOR MELANIE. New York, Funk & Wagnalls, 1958. 220p

MYSTERY OF THE LOGGING CAMP. By Dickson Reynolds [pseud]. New York, Nelson, 1945. 171p [BViPA LC

PERILOUS PRAIRIE. By Dickson Reynolds [pseud]. Toronto, Ryerson, 1956. 189p

PICKUPPIES. By Helen Dickson. London, Stockwell, 1931. 23p [BM

RED BLANKET. By Dickson Reynolds [pseud]. London, Nelson, 1939. 127p [BM BVaU OTU

SUMMER OF SURPRISE. New York, Funk & Wagnalls, 1960. 186p

WE CHASED A RAINBOW. New York, Funk & Wagnalls, 1957. 214p

YOSHIO. Japanese Boy in Canada. By Helen Dickson. London, Nelson, 1937. 111p [BM BVaU OTU

**Richardson, Evelyn May (Fox), 1902–**

DESIRED HAVEN. Toronto, Ryerson, 1953. 286p

NO SMALL TEMPEST. Toronto, Ryerson, 1957. 229p [Sequel to DESIRED HAVEN.]

**Richardson, John, 1796–1852**

THE CANADIAN BROTHERS; or, The Prophecy Fulfilled. A Tale of the Late American War. Montreal, Armour & Ramsay, 1840. 2v [Pub. in the U.S. as: MATILDA MONTGOMERIE. New York, Dewitt & Davenport, 1851. 191p] [BVaU NSHPL OTP QMM

ECARTE; or, The Salons of Paris. [Anon] London, Colburn, 1829. 3v [Republished: New York, Dewitt, 1851. 206p; and New York, Pollard & Moss, 1888.] [BM BVaU LC NBFU OKQ

HARDSCRABBLE; or, The Fall of Chicago. A Tale of Indian Warfare. New York, Dewitt, [1856]. 99p [In *Papers of the Bibliog. Soc. of Canada,* v5, W.F.E. Morley argues that the date of first pub. is either 1850 or 1851. Also seen with imprint: New York, Pollard & Moss, 1888. 113p] [LC NSWA OONL QMSS

MATILDA MONTGOMERIE; or, The Prophecy Fulfilled. ... Being a Sequel to WACOUSTA. New York, Dewitt, 1851. 191p [See under THE CANADIAN BROTHERS.] [BM BVa LC NSHD OTP

THE MONK KNIGHT OF ST. JOHN. A Tale of the Crusades. New York, DeWitt, 1850. 192p [BM NBFU

WACOUSTA; or, The Prophecy. A Tale of the Canadas. By the Author of ECARTE [pseud]. London, Cadell, 1832. 3v [First Am. ed.: Philadelphia, Kay & Biddle, 1833. 2v. First Can. ed.: Montreal, Lovell, 1868. 167p. Several other editions.] [BM BVaU LC NBFU OTP QMM

WAU-NAN-GEE; or, The Massacre at Chicago. A Romance. New York, Long, [1852]. 126p [BM LC NBFU OKQ

WESTBROOK; or, The Outlaw. [Diligent search discovered no copy of this work, whose title has been attributed to Richardson by H.J. Morgan in *Bibliotheca Canadensis* (1867) and, subsequently, by various others.]

**Richardson, Robert Lorne, 1860–1921**

THE CAMERONS OF BRUCE. Toronto, Briggs, 1906. 301p [BM BVaU NBFU OTP

COLIN OF THE NINTH CONCESSION. Toronto, Morang, 1903. 360p [BVaU NBFU OTP

**Richler, Mordecai, 1931–**

THE ACROBATS. A Novel. London, Deutsch, 1954. 204p [Also pub. as WICKED WE LOVE in Popular Library ed.]

THE APPRENTICESHIP OF DUDDY KRAVITZ. Don Mills, Ont., Deutsch, 1959. 319p

SON OF A SMALLER HERO. A Novel. London, Deutsch, 1955. 232p

**Rickerson, Nena C.**

THE BANKER'S GRANDCHILDREN. A Story. Saint John, Day, 1876. 108p [NBB

**Riis, Stella Eugenie (Asling), 1877–**

CROWNED AT ELIM. New York, Smith & Wilkins, 1903. 263p [LC

THE GREAT FRESH SEA. N.p., Author, 1931. 92p [OLU

STAR OVER FLUSHING. Boston, Humphries, 1939. 268p [LC

**Riley, Louise, 1904–1957**

THE MYSTERY HORSE. Oxford, Blackwell, 1957. 188p

ONE HAPPY MOMENT. A Novel. Toronto, Copp Clark, 1951. 212p

A SPELL AT SCOGGIN'S CROSSING. New York, Abelard-Schuman, 1960. 175p

TRAIN FOR TIGER LILY. Toronto, Macmillan, 1954. 186p

**Ringwood, Gwendolyn Margaret (Pharis), 1910–**

YOUNGER BROTHER. Toronto, Longmans, 1959. 213p

**Ritchie, Cicero Theodore, 1914–**

BLACK ANGELS. New York, Abelard-Schuman, 1959. 256p

THE WILLING MAID. London, Abelard-Schuman, 1957. 310p

**Robb, Wallace Havelock, 1888–**

THUNDERBIRD. [Epic of the Mohawks of the Kente.] Kingston, Abbey Dawn, 1949. 242p [BVaU OTP QMM

**Robbins, Ronald Cynewulf, 1915–**

BLOOD FOR BREAKFAST. New York, Pageant Press, 1955. 151p

**Roberts, Charles George Douglas, 1860–1943**

AROUND THE CAMPFIRE. New York, Crowell, 1896. 349p [BM BVaU LC NBFU OTP

BABES OF THE WILD. New York, Cassell, 1912. 243p [Also pub. under title: CHILDREN OF THE WILD. New York, Macmillan, 1913. 300p] [BM LC OTU QMM

THE BACKWOODSMEN. New York, Macmillan, 1909. 269p [BM BVaU LC NBFU OTU QMM

A BALKAN PRINCE. London, Everett, 1913. 248p [BM BVaU NBFU OTU

BARBARA LADD. Boston, Page, 1902. 377p [BM BVaU LC NBFU OKQ

BY THE MARSHES OF MINAS. New York, Silver Burdett, 1900. 285p [BM BVaU LC NSHD OKQ

CHILDREN OF THE WILD. New York, Macmillan, 1913. 300p [Same as BABES OF THE WILD, *q.v.*] [BVaU LC NSHD OTMC QMM

COCK-CROW. New York, Federal Print., 1916. 14p [Also included in THE SECRET TRAILS.] [NBFU

THE CRUISE OF THE YACHT "DIDO." A Tale of the Tide Country. Boston, Page, 1906. 145p [A reprint of REUBE DARE'S SHAD BOAT.] [LC NBFU OTMC

EARTH'S ENIGMAS. A Book of Animal and Nature Life. Boston, Lamson Wolffe, 1896. 290p [New ed., with 3 stories added, 3 dropped: Boston, Page, 1903. 285p] [BM BVaU LC NBFU OTU QMM

EYES OF THE WILDERNESS. New York, Macmillan, 1933. 269p [BM LC NSHD OTMC QMM

THE FEET OF THE FURTIVE. London, Ward Lock, 1912. 277p [BM BVaU LC NBFU OTMC QMM

FOREST FOLK. Chosen and Ed. by Ethel Hume Bennett. Toronto, Ryerson, 1949. 237p [BViP OTMC

THE FORGE IN THE FOREST. Being the Narrative of the Acadian Ranger, Jean de Mer. New York, Lamson Wolffe, 1896. 311p [BM BVaU LC NBFU OTP QMM

FURTHER ANIMAL STORIES. London, Dent, 1935. 128p [BM

THE HAUNTER OF THE PINE GLOOM. Boston, Page, 1905. 61p [Also included in THE KINDRED OF THE WILD.] [BVaU LC OTMC

THE HAUNTERS OF THE SILENCES. A Book of Animal Life. Boston, Page, 1907. 316p [BM BVaU LC NBFU OKQ

THE HEART OF THE ANCIENT WOOD. New York, Silver Burdett, 1900. 276p [BM BVaU LC NBFU OTU QMM

THE HEART THAT KNOWS. Boston, Page, 1906. 378p [BM BVaU NBFU OTU QMM

HOOF AND CLAW. London, Ward Lock, 1913. 267p [BM BVaU LC NSHD OTU QMM

THE HOUSE IN THE WATER. A Book of Animal Life. Boston, Page, 1908. 301p [BM BVaU LC NBFU OKQ

IN THE DEEP OF THE SNOW. New York, Crowell, 1907. 78p [Also in THE BACKWOODSMEN.] [LC NBFU OTU

IN THE MORNING OF TIME. London, Hutchinson, 1919. 319p [BM BVaU NBFU OTU QMM

JIM. The Story of a Backwoods Police Dog [And Other Stories]. New York, Macmillan, 1924. 216p [Same as THE LEDGE ON BALD FACE.] [BVaU LC NBFU OTU QMM

THE KINDRED OF THE WILD. A Book of Animal Life. Boston, Page, 1902. 374p [BM BVaU NBFU OTU QMM

THE KING OF THE MAMOZEKEL. Boston, Page, 1905. 84p [Also included in THE KINDRED OF THE WILD.] [BVaU NBFU

KINGS IN EXILE. London, Ward Lock, 1909. 306p [BM BVaU NBFU OTP

THE LAST BARRIER, AND OTHER STORIES. Intro. by Alec Lucas. Toronto, McClelland, 1958. x + 153p [New Canadian Library, no.7]

THE LEDGE ON BALD FACE. London, Ward Lock, 1918. 255p [Also pub. under title: JIM. The Story of a Backwoods Police Dog. New York, Macmillan, 1924. 216p] [BM BVaU NBFU OKQ

THE LITTLE PEOPLE OF THE SYCAMORE. Boston, Page, 1906. 58p [Also included in THE WATCHERS OF THE TRAILS.] [LC

THE LORD OF THE AIR. Boston, Page, 1905. 59p [Also included in THE KINDRED OF THE WILD.] [BVaU LC OKQ

LOVERS IN ACADIE. London, Dent, 1924. 278p [New ed. of A SISTER TO EVANGELINE, *q.v.*] [BM NBFU OTU QMM

MORE ANIMAL STORIES. London, Dent, 1922. 127p [BM BVaU NBFU OTU

MORE KINDRED OF THE WILD. London, Ward Lock, 1911. 264p [BM BVaU NBFU OKQ

THE MORNING OF THE SILVER FROST. New York, Federal Print., 1916. 8p [Also included in THE SECRET TRAILS.] [NBFU

NEIGHBOURS UNKNOWN. New York, Macmillan, 1911. 266p [BM BVaU LC NSHD OLU QMM

THE PRISONER OF MADEMOISELLE. A Love Story. Boston, Page, 1904. 265p [BM BVaU LC NBFU OKQ

THE RAID FROM BEAUSEJOUR, and HOW THE CARTER BOYS LIFTED THE MORTGAGE. Two Stories of Acadie. New York, Hunt & Eaton, 1894. 230p [First story later pub. under title: THE YOUNG ACADIAN; or, The Raid from Beauséjour. Boston, Page, 1907. 139p] [BVaU LC NBFU OKQ

RED FOX. The Story of his Adventurous Career. ... Boston, Page, 1905. 340p [BM BVaU NSHD OTP QMM

THE RED OXEN OF BONVAL. New York, Dodd Mead, 1908. 71p [Reprinted from: A HOUSE PARTY. An Account of the Stories Told at a Gathering of Famous American Authors. Boston, Small Maynard, 1901. 418p] [NBFU

THE RETURN TO THE TRAILS. Boston, Page, 1906. 50p [Also included in THE WATCHERS OF THE TRAILS.] [LC NBFU

REUBE DARE'S SHAD BOAT. A Tale of the Tide Country. New York, Hunt & Eaton, 1895. 145p [Later reprinted under title: THE CRUISE OF THE YACHT "DIDO." Boston, Page, 1906. 145p] [LC OLU

THE SECRET TRAILS. New York, Macmillan, 1916. 212p [BM BVaU LC NSHD OTU QMM

A SISTER TO EVANGELINE. Being the Story of Yvonne de Lamourie. Boston, Lamson Wolffe, 1898. 289p [New ed. pub. under title: LOVERS IN ACADIE. London, Dent, 1924. 278p] [BM BVaU LC NBFU OKQ

SOME ANIMAL STORIES. London, Dent, [1921]. 128p [BM NBFU

THEY WHO WALK IN THE WILD. New York, Macmillan, 1924. 212p [Pub. in England under title: THEY THAT WALK IN THE WILD. London, Dent, 1924. 290p] [BM BVaU LC NSHD OTU QMM

THIRTEEN BEARS. Chosen and Ed. by Ethel Hume Bennett. Toronto, Ryerson, 1947. 254p [BVaU OTP

THE WATCHERS OF THE CAMP-FIRE. Boston, Page, 1905. 49p [Also included in THE KINDRED OF THE WILD.] [LC OKQ

THE WATCHERS OF THE TRAILS. A Book of Animal Life. Boston, Page, 1904. 361p [BM BVaU LC NBFU OTU QMM

WISDOM OF THE WILDERNESS. Toronto, Dent, 1922. 218p [Also: New York, Macmillan, 1923. 184p] [BM BVaU LC NSHD OKQ QMM

THE YOUNG ACADIAN. Boston, Page, 1907. 139p [Same as THE RAID FROM BEAUSEJOUR.] [BVaU LC OOP QMSS

**Roberts, Leslie, 1896–**

WHEN THE GODS LAUGHED. Toronto, Musson, 1930. 282p [BM LC NBFU OTMC

**Roberts, Theodore Goodridge, 1877–1953**

BLESSINGTON'S FOLLY. London, Long, 1914. 320p [BM BVaU

BROTHERS OF PERIL. A Story of Old Newfoundland. Boston, Page, 1905. 327p [BVaU LC NBFU OKQ

CAPTAIN LOVE. Boston, Page, 1908. 282p [BVaU LC NBFU OTMC

A CAPTAIN OF RALEIGH'S. Boston, Page, 1911. 351p [LC NBFU

A CAVALIER OF VIRGINIA. Boston, Page, 1910. 313p [BVaU LC

COMRADES OF THE TRAILS. Boston, Page, 1910. 308p [BVaU LC

THE EXILED LOVER. London, Long, 1919. 320p [BM BVaU

THE FIGHTING STARKLEYS. Boston, Page, 1922. 250p [BVa LC NBFU

FLYING PLOVER. His Stories. Told him by Squat-by-the-fire. Boston, Page, 1909. 124p [LC OTU

FOREST FUGITIVES. Toronto, McClelland, 1917. 320p [BM BVaU

THE GOLDEN HIGHLANDERS; or, The Romantic Adventures of Alastair MacIver. Boston, Page, 1929. 308p [BM LC NBFU

GREEN TIMBER THOROUGHBREDS. Garden City, Garden City Pub. Co., 1924. 120p [LC

THE HARBOR MASTER. Boston, Page, 1913. 300p [Same as THE TOLL OF THE TIDES. London, Laurie, 1913. 240p] [LC NBFU

HEMMING, THE ADVENTURER. Boston, Page, 1904. 328p [BVaU LC NBFU OTMC

HONEST FOOL. London, Hodder, 1925. 319p [BM

THE HOUSE OF ISSTENS. Boston, Page, 1900. [CT CWW'49

IN THE HIGH WOODS. London, Long, 1916. 320p [BM BVaU LC NBFU

THE ISLANDS OF ADVENTURE. New York, Hodder, 1918. 312p [BM BVaU NBFU

JESS OF THE RIVER. New York, Dillingham, 1914. 329p [BM LC OTMC

LOVE ON SMOKY RIVER. London, Long, 1913. 320p [BM OTMC

THE LURE OF PIPER'S GLEN. New York, Doubleday, 1921. 120p [CWW'49

THE MASTER OF THE MOOSE HORN, and Other Backcountry Stories. London, Hodder, 1919. 315p [BM NBFU

MOONSHINE. London, Hodder, 1920. 317p [BM NBFU

MUSKET HOUSE. New York, Doubleday, 1922. 120p [CWW'49

THE OXBOW WIZARD. Garden City, Garden City Pub. Co., 1924. 121p [BVaU

PRIZE MONEY. Boston, Page, 1926. [CT

RAYTON. A Backwoods Mystery. Boston, Page, 1912. 314p [LC NBFU

THE RED FEATHERS. Boston, Page, 1907. 325p [BVaU LC NBFU OTMC

THE RED PIROGUE. A Tale of Adventure in the Canadian Wilds. Boston, Page, 1924. 272p [BVaU LC NBFU OTMC QMM

SOLDIER OF VALLEY FORGE. [Joint author, with Robert Neilson Stephens.] Boston, Page, 1911. [CBI

THE STRANGER FROM UP-ALONG. Toronto, Gundy, 1924. 188p [BM NBFU

THE TOLL OF THE TIDES. London, Laurie, 1912. 240p [Same as THE HARBOR MASTER.] [BM

TOM AKERLEY. His Adventures in the Tall Timber and at Gaspard's Clearing. Boston, Page, 1923. 283p [BVaU LC OTMC

TWO SHALL BE BORN. New York, Cassell, 1913. 319p [BVaU LC

THE WASP. New York, Dillingham, 1914. 352p [BM BVaU LC

**Robertson, Rev. James, 1801?–1878**

JICKLING'S EXPERIENCES. A Reminiscence of Eton Life. Ed. by J.R. Montreal, Drysdale, 1896. 45p [BM OTMC QMSS

**Robertson, James D.**

THE DREAM OF LIFE (Aisling Na Beatha). London, Williams & Norgate, 1934. 356p [BM LC OTP

**Robertson, Margaret Murray, 1821–1897**

ALLISON BAIN; or, By a Way She Knew Not. London, Hodder, 1891. 482p [See also BY A WAY SHE KNEW NOT, below.]

THE BAIRNS; or, Janet's Love and Service. A Story from Canada. By the Author of "Christie Redfern's Troubles"; "The Orphans of Glen Elder, A Story of Scottish

Life"; etc. [pseud]. London, Hodder, 1870. 581p [Another ed.: 1885.] [BM BVaU OTP

BY A WAY SHE KNEW NOT. Story of Allison Bain. New York, Randolph, 1887. [BM

CHRISTIE REDFERN'S TROUBLES. [Anon] London, Religious Tract Soc., 1866. [New eds., 1886 and 1905] [BM

DAVID FLEMING'S FORGIVENESS. New York, Randolph, 1879. [Also pub. as: By the Author of "The Bairns." London, Hodder, 1891.] [AmCat BM

EUNICE. The Story of Domestic Life in New England. New York, Randolph, 1887. [BM

FREDERICA AND HER GUARDIANS. Boston, Lothrop, 1880. [*See* THE PERILS OF ORPHANHOOD, below.] [AmCat

THE INGLISES; or, How the Way Opened. New York, Randolph, 1872. [BM

JANET'S LOVE AND SERVICE. New York, Randolph, 1869. 581p [Same as THE BAIRNS? *q.v.*] [AmCat NBFU

A LITTLE HOUSE IN THE HOLLOW. By the Author of "Christie Redfern's Troubles" [pseud]. Philadelphia, Am. Sunday School Union, 1868. 237p [LC

LITTLE SERENA IN A STRANGE LAND. By the Author of "Christie Redfern's Troubles," etc. [pseud]. London, Religious Tract Soc., 1870. [BM

THE ORPHANS OF GLEN ELDER. [Anon] London, Religious Tract Soc., 1868. [EngCat

THE PERILS OF ORPHANHOOD; or, Frederica and Her Guardians. By the Author of "The Bairns," "Christie Redfern's Troubles," etc. [pseud]. London, 1874. [BM

SHENAC'S WORK AT HOME. A Story of Canadian Life. By the Author of "Christie Redfern's Troubles" [pseud]. London, Religious Tract Soc., [1868]. 262p [BM BVaU NBFU OTP

STEPHEN GRATTAN'S FAITH. By the Author of "Christie Redfern's Troubles" [pseud]. Philadelphia, Am. Sunday School Union, 1867. 142p [LC OTMC

THE TWO MISS JEAN DAWSONS. New York, Randolph, 1880. 350p [BM NBFU

A YEAR AND A DAY. A Story of Canadian Life. By the Author of "Christie Redfern's Troubles," etc. [pseud]. London, Religious Tract Soc., 1886. [BM

**Robins, John Daniel, 1884–1952**

LOGGING WITH PAUL BUNYAN. Ed. by Edith Fowke. Toronto, Ryerson, 1957. xvii + 97p

**Robinson, Frank Alfred, 1874–**

MASTERED MEN. New York, Doran, 1922. 256p [BVaU LC OTMC

OLD CALEB AND HIS LAST CHRISTMAS. Story from Life in Rural England. Toronto, Livingstone Press, 1941. 46p [OTP

TRAIL TALES OF WESTERN CANADA. London, Marshall, [1914]. 255p [BVaU NBFU OTP

**Rogers, Charles Gordon**

THE SCRAGGVILLE BANDITS; or, The White Caps of Pepper Island, and Other Stories. Ottawa, Woodburn, 1889. 198p [OONL

**Rogers, Frank D.**

FOLK-STORIES OF THE NORTHERN BORDER. Clayton, N.Y., Thousand Islands, 1897. 273p [BM LC

**Rogers, Frederick**

IN THE END. Being the Romance of Two Worlds. New York, Editor Pub. Co., 1903. 229p [LC

NONSENSE. Being Certain Foolish Tales. Detroit, American Pub. Co., 1900. [BM LC OONL

**Rogers, Grace Dean (McLeod), 1865–1958**

THE BREAD OF WICKEDNESS. London, Hurst & Blackett, 1925. 288p [BM

JOAN AT HALFWAY. Toronto, McClelland, 1919. 414p [BM BVaU LC NSHD OTU

RAYMOND'S INHERITANCE. London, Harrap, 1937. 255p [BM

THE SECRET OF VAN ROYEN'S FARM, etc. London, Nelson, 1929. 94p [BM

STORIES OF THE LAND OF EVANGELINE. Boston, Lothrop, 1891. 336p [New ed.: Toronto, McClelland, 1923. 341p] [BM BVaU LC NBFU OTU QMM

**Roper, Edward**

A CLAIM ON KLONDYKE. A Romance of the Arctic ElDorado. Edinburgh, Blackwood, 1899. 312p [BM BViPA LC OTU

FRED SEAGOOD: His Travels and Triumphs, etc. London, Swan Sonnenschein, 1904. 349p [BM OTMC

ICE-BOUND; or, The Anticosti Crusoes. London, Partridge, 1902. 330p [AEU BM NfSM OTUV

**Rorke, Louise Richardson, –1949**

BLACK VIC. Toronto, Nelson, 1949. 176p [BVaU OTMC

LEFTY. The Story of a Boy and a Dog. With a foreword by Marshall Saunders. Toronto, Nelson, 1931. 165p [BVaU NBFU OOP

LEFTY'S ADVENTURE. A Tale for Children. Toronto, Nelson, 1945. 220p [BM BVaU OTMC

SUGAR SHANTY. New York, Nelson, 1941. 314p [LC NBFU OLU

**Ross, Angus, 1860–1929**

MOUNT MORIAH. A Story [of the Lumber Camps]. Founded on Fact. London, Stockwell, [1934]. 128p [OONL

**Ross, Ellen Edith Alice (McGregor), –1892**

A LEGEND OF THE GRAND GORDONS. Ed. by Mrs. Alexander Ross. Montreal, Stevenson, 1873. 647p [BVaU LC NSHD OTP

THE LEGEND OF THE HOLY STONE. Ed. by Mrs. Alexander Ross. Montreal, Stevenson, 1878. 473p [BVaU LC NSHD OTP

VIOLET KEITH; or, Convent Life in Canada. An Autobiography. Montreal, Lovell, 1868. 472p [BVaU LC NBFU OTP QMM

THE WRECK OF THE "WHITE BEAR," EAST INDIAMAN. Montreal, Lovell, 1870. 2v [BVaU LC NSHD OTP QMM

**Ross, (James) Sinclair, 1908–**

AS FOR ME AND MY HOUSE. A Novel. New York, Reynal, 1941. 296p [Also, with intro. by Roy Daniells. Toronto, McClelland, 1957. x + 165p] [BVaU NSHD OTMC

THE WELL. Toronto, Macmillan, 1958. 256p

**Rouleau, Corinne Rocheleau**

LAURENTIAN HERITAGE. Ed. with foreword ... by W.F. Langford. Toronto, Longmans, 1948. 178p [BM BVaU NBFU OTP QMBM

**Rowe, Lizzie**

AN OLD WOMAN'S STORY. Regina, Leader Printing Co., 1886. 15p [BM MWP OOP

**Rowell, Mrs. John H.**

JULIA CAMPBELL; or, The Enlightenment of a Mind. Montreal, Chapleau, 1876. 86p [OOP

**Roy, D. Kinmount**

LINKED LIVES. London, Heath Cranton, 1913. 336p [BM

**Roy, Irene**

JUNETTE; or, Are Women Just to One Another? Edmonton, Douglas, 1919. 292p [BVaU OTMC

**Roy, Katherine (Morris), 1907–**

THE GENTLE FRAUD. Toronto, McClelland, 1959. 183p

LISE. Toronto, McClelland, 1954. 250p

**Royal, Matthew J., –1900**

THE ISLE OF THE VIRGINS. A Romance. Buffalo, Wenborne-Summer, 1899. 328p [LC

**Ruddy, Anna Christian, 1861–**

FROM TENDERFOOT TO SCOUT. New York, Doran, 1911. 297p [LC OTMC

**Running, Arnold, 1918–**

STAY BUT TILL TOMORROW. Toronto, Longmans, 1958. 191p

**Russell, Rev. George Stanley, 1883–1957**

THE MONASTERY BY THE RIVER. New York, Smith, 1930. 107p [BVaU LC NSHD OTP

**Russell, Sheila (MacKay), 1920–**

A LAMP IS HEAVY. Toronto, Longmans, 1950. 257p [BM BVaU NBFU OTU

THE LIVING EARTH. Toronto, Longmans, 1954. 317p

**Ryland, Richard**

THE COINERS OF POMPEII. Toronto, Rowsell, 1845. 136p [OTU

**S., V.M.F.**

PEGGY SINCLAIR'S TRIP ACROSS THE CONTINENT. By V.M.F.S. Montreal, Lovell, 1892. 231p [NSWA OOP QMBM

**Sabiston, Colin A.**

ZOYA. London, Selwyn & Blount, 1933. 288p [BM OTP

**Sadlier, Anna Teresa, 1854–1932**

ARABELLA. St. Louis, Herder, 1907. 177p [LC

COUSIN WILHELMINA. St. Louis, Herder, 1907. 201 p [LC

ETHEL HAMILTON. New York, Sadlier, 1877. 79p [LC

GERALD DE LACEY'S DAUGHTER. New York, Kenedy, 1916. 473p [LC OTMC

HOW FRANK DID IT. THAT WORTHLESS LAD. LITTLE JOHN. Three Stories. New York, Wildermann, 1898. 63p [LC

THE KING'S PAGE. New York, Sadlier, 1877. 51p [LC

THE LOST JEWEL OF THE MORTIMERS. St. Louis, Herder, 1904. 258p [LC

THE MAN FROM NOWHERE. New York, Benziger, 1918. 187p [LC

MARY TRACY'S FORTUNE. New York, Benziger, 1902. 169p [LC

THE MYSTERIOUS DOORWAY. New York, Benziger, 1900. 135p [LC

THE MYSTERY OF HORNBY HALL. New York, Benziger, 1906. 214p [LC

PAULINE ARCHER. New York, Benziger, 1900. 167p [LC

PHILEAS FOX, ATTORNEY. Notre Dame, Ind., Ave Maria, 1909. 349p [LC

THE PILKINGTON HEIR. New York, Benziger, 1903. 212p [LC

THE RED INN OF SAINT LYPHAR. New York, Benziger, 1904. 179p [LC

SEVEN YEARS AND MAIR. New York, Harper, 1878. 184p [LC

SHORT STORIES. Series II. New York, Wildermann, 1900. 3v in 1. [The Catholic Library, v. 38, 48, 58.] [LC

THE SILENCE OF SEBASTIAN. Notre Dame, Ind., Ave Maria, 1913. 405p [LC

STORIES OF THE PROMISES AND OTHER TALES. By Mrs. M.A. Sadlier and her Daughter. Montreal, Sadlier, [1895?]. 247p [OONL QMSS

THE TALISMAN. New York, Benziger, 1903. 186p [LC

THE TRUE STORY OF MASTER GERARD. New York, Benziger, 1900. 321p [LC

WAYWARD WINIFRED. New York, Benziger, 1905. 220p [LC OOU

WHERE THE ROAD LED, AND OTHER STORIES. New York, Benziger, 1905. 209p [LC

WYVERN HALL. TEDDY'S LUCK. A CONTRAST. Three Stories. New York, Wildermann, 1898. 61p [LC

**Sadlier, Mary Anne (Madden), 1820–1903**

ALICE RIORDAN. The Blind Man's Daughter. A Tale for the Young. Boston, Noonan, 1854. 289p [Also: Dublin, Gill, 1884. 294p. An earlier ed.: Boston, Donahoe, 1851.] [BM OOU

AS GOOD AS GOLD. (Wilhelm; or, Christian Forgiveness.) Trans. from the French by ——. Dublin, Gill, 1890. 246p [BM

AUNT HONOR'S KEEPSAKE. A Chapter from Life. New York, Sadlier, 1866. 322p [LC OOU

BENJAMIN. New York, Sadlier, 1885. 249p [A trans. from the French. An earlier ed. in 1852?] [BM LC

BESSY CONWAY; or, The Irish Girl in America. New York, Sadlier, 1862. [AmCat

THE BLAKES AND FLANAGANS. New York, Sadlier, 1858. 391p [An earlier ed., dated 1855—AmCat.] [LC QQL

THE CASTLE OF ROUSSILLON; or, Quercy in the Sixteenth Century. Trans. from the French by ——. Dublin, Gill, 1884. 278p [BM

CON O'REGAN; or, Emigrant Life in the New World. New York, Sadlier, 1864. 405p [BM BVaU LC QMSS

THE CONFEDERATE CHIEFTAINS. A Tale of the Irish Rebellion of 1641. New York, Sadlier, 1868. 461p [An earlier ed. listed in AmCat for 1858–61.] [LC QQL

CONFESSIONS OF AN APOSTATE. New York, Sadlier, 1864. 252p [Also as: SIMON KERRIGAN. The Confessions of an Apostate. London, Washburne, 1889.—EngCat.] [BM LC

THE DAUGHTER OF TYRCONNELL. A Tale of the Reign of James I. New York, Sadlier, 1863. 152p [BM LC

ELINOR PRESTON; or, Scenes at Home and Abroad. New York, Sadlier & Co., 1861. 298p [BVaS

THE EXILE OF TADMOR, AND OTHER TALES. Trans. by ——. New York, Sadlier, 1885. 144p [An earlier ed. 1866—AmCat.] [LC

THE FATE OF FATHER SHEEHY. A Tale of Tipperary Eighty Years Ago. New York, Sadlier, 1863. 132p [LC NfSM OOSJ

THE HEIRESS OF KILORGAN. New York, Sadlier, 1867. 420p [BM LC

THE HERMIT OF THE ROCK. A Tale of Cashel. New York, Sadlier, 1868. 492p [BM LC OOSJ

IDLENESS; or, The Double Lesson, and Other Tales. Trans. from the French by ——. New York Sadlier, 1862. [BM

THE KNOUT. A Tale of Poland. Trans. from the French by ——. Dublin, Gill, 1884. 280p [BM QQL

THE LOST SON. An Episode of the French Revolution. New York, Sadlier, [1885]. 260p [An earlier ed., 1862—AmCat] [OOU

MacCARTHY MORE; or, The Fortunes of an Irish Chief. New York, Sadlier, 1868. [AmCat BM

MAUREEN DHU, THE ADMIRAL'S DAUGHTER. New York, Sadlier, 1870. 391p [BM LC

THE MINISTER'S WIFE, AND OTHER STORIES. New York, Wildermann, 1898. 64p [LC

NEW LIGHTS; or, Life in Galway. New York, Sadlier, 1867. 443p [An earlier ed.: New York, Sadlier, 1853. —Am Cat.] [LC OTMC QMSS

O'BRYNE; or, The Expatriated. New York, Wildermann, 1898. 64p [LC

OLD AND NEW; or, Taste Versus Fashion. New York, Sadlier, 1862. 486p [LC QQL

THE OLD HOUSE BY THE BOYNE; or, Recollections of an Irish Borough. New York, Sadlier, 1865. 375p [Also: Dublin, Gill, 1888. 320p] [BM LC OOU

THE POPE'S NIECE AND OTHER TALES. Trans. from the French by ——. New York, Sadlier, 1862. [BM

THE RED HAND OF ULSTER; or, The Fortunes of Hugh O'Neill. Boston, Donahoe, n.d. 344p [OTL OTMC

SHORT STORIES. Series II. New York, Wildermann, 1900. 3v in 1. [The Catholic Library, v. 32, 42, 52.] [LC

THE SPANISH CAVALIERS. A Tale of the Moorish Wars in Spain. New York, Sadlier, 1861. 203p [OOU

STORIES OF THE PROMISES AND OTHER TALES. By Mrs. M.A. Sadlier and her Daughter. Montreal, Sadlier, [1895?]. 247p [OONL QMSS

TALES AND STORIES. Trans. from the French by ——. New York, Sadlier, 1866. 144p [BM OTMC

TALES OF THE OLDEN TIME. Montreal. [MOR'98

THE VENDETTA AND OTHER TALES. Trans. from the French by ——. New York, Sadlier, 1862. [BM

WILLY BURKE; or, The Irish Orphan in America. Boston, Donahoe, 1850. 298p [LC

THE YOUNG LADIES' READER. New York, Sadlier, [187–?]. [AmCat 1876

**St. George, Mother Mary**

ROAD'S END. By Mary Douglas [pseud]. Toronto, Ryerson, 1943. 150p [NBFU OTP

**Sallans, George Herbert, 1895–1960**

LITTLE MAN. Toronto, Ryerson, 1942. 420p [BVaU LC NBFU OTP QMM

**Salverson, Laura (Goodman), 1890–1970**

BLACK LACE. Toronto, Ryerson, 1938. 255p [BM NBFU OTU

CONFESSIONS OF AN IMMIGRANT'S DAUGHTER. London, Faber, 1939. 523p [BM BVaU LC NBFU OTP QMM

THE DARK WEAVER. Toronto, Ryerson, 1937. 415p [BM BVaU LC NBFU OTU

THE DOVE OF EL-DJEZAIRE.... Toronto, Ryerson, 1933. 287p [BM BVaU NSHD OKQ

IMMORTAL ROCK. The Saga of the Kensington Stone. ... Toronto, Ryerson, 1954. 267p

LORD OF THE SILVER DRAGON. Toronto, McClelland, 1927. 343p [BVaU NBFU OTP QMM

THE VIKING HEART. New York, 1923. 326p [BM BVaU NBFU OTP

WHEN SPARROWS FALL. Toronto, Allen, 1925. 292p [BM BVaU NBFU OTMC QMM

**Sanderson, Douglas, 1922–**

BLONDES ARE MY TROUBLE. A Novel of Suspense. By Martin Brett [pseud]. Toronto, Popular Library, 1955 [i.e., 1956]. 174p [First pub. as THE DARKER TRAFFIC. New York, Dodd Mead, 1954. 213p]

CRY WOLFRAM. A Novel. London, Secker & Warburg, 1959. 190p

DARK PASSIONS SUBDUE. New York, Dodd Mead, 1952. 296p

EXIT IN GREEN. By Martin Brett [pseud]. New York, Dodd Mead, 1953. 256p [Pub. in England as MURDER CAME TUMBLING, London, Hammond, 1959. 221p]

THE FINAL RUN. A Novel. London, Secker & Warburg, 1956. 178p [Paperback ed. (New York, Popular Library, 1957) has title: FLEE FROM TERROR, by Martin Brett (pseud).]

HOT FREEZE. By Martin Brett [pseud]. New York, Dodd Mead, 1954. 246p

NIGHT OF THE HORNS. A Novel. London, Secker & Warburg, 1958. 189p

**Sanderson, Elizabeth**

THE CIRCLE OF THE YEAR. Toronto, Briggs, 1904. 46p [BM OKQ

**Sands, Harold Percy, 1873–**

THE DASHING SALLY DUEL AND OTHER STORIES. New York, Broadway Pub. Co., 1905. 143p [BVaU LC OOP

**Sandwell, Mrs. Helen B.**

THE VALLEY OF COLOR-DAYS. Boston, Little Brown, 1924. 299p [BM LC NBFU OTMC

**Sandys, Edwyn William, 1860–1909**

TRAPPER "JIM." New York, Macmillan, 1903. 441p [BM BVaU LC OTMC

SPORTSMAN "JOE." New York, Macmillan, 1904. 338p [BM LC

**Sanford, Mary Bourchier**

THE HAPPY HARFORDS. London, Collins, 1930. 128p [BM

ISLE OF GLADNESS. London, Religious Tract Soc., 1929. 224p [BM

THE ROMANCE OF A JESUIT MISSION. Toronto, Revell, 1897. 292p [BVa LC OTU

THE TRAIL OF THE IROQUOIS. A Pioneer Romance of Canada. Toronto, Longmans, 1925. 256p [BM BVaU OTP QMM

URANIA'S TRAINING. London, Religious Tract Soc., 1925. 237p [BM

THE WANDERING TWINS. A Story of Labrador. Chicago, McClurg, 1904. 300p [BM BVaU LC NBFU

THE YOUNG GORDONS IN CANADA. London, Religious Tract Soc., 1913. 286p [BM

**Saunders, Margaret Bell, 1894–**

HUBBLE-BUBBLE. By Margaret Bell [pseud]. New York, Dodd Mead, 1927. 337p [LC QMM

**Saunders, Margaret Marshall, 1861–1947**

ALPATOCK. The Story of an Eskimo Dog. Boston, Page, 1906. 51p [LC

BEAUTIFUL JOE. An Autobiography. Philadelphia, American Baptist Pub. Soc., 1894. 304p [Many later editions.] [BM BVaU LC NSHD OKQ QMM

BEAUTIFUL JOE'S PARADISE. Boston, Page, 1902. 365p [BM BVaU LC NBFU OTU

BONNIE PRINCE FETLAR. The Story of a Pony and His Friends. ... Toronto, McClelland, 1920. 352p [LC NSHD OTU

"BOY" THE WANDERING DOG. New York, Grosset, 1916. 363p [BM OTU

CHARLES AND HIS LAMB. Philadelphia, Banes, 1895. 73p [BVaU LC NSHD OTMC

DAISY. A Tale. Philadelphia, Banes, [189–?]. 57p [NSHD

DEFICIENT SAINTS. A Tale of Maine. Boston, Page, 1899. 431p [BM LC NBFU OTMC

ESTHER DE WARREN. The Story of a Mid-Victorian Maiden. New York, Doran, 1927. 305p [LC NSHD OKQ QMM

FOR HIS COUNTRY; and GRANDMOTHER AND THE CROW. ... Boston, Page, 1900. 60p [LC OOP

FOR THE OTHER BOY'S SAKE, AND OTHER STORIES. Philadelphia, Banes, 1896. 374p [LC NBFU OTMC

THE GIRL FROM VERMONT. The Story of a Vacation School Teacher. Boston, Griffith & Rowland, 1910. 248p [BVaU LC OTU

GOLDEN DICKY. The Story of a Canary and his Friends. New York, Stokes, 1919. 280p [BM BVaU LC OKQ QMM

HER SAILOR. A Love Story. Boston, Page, 1900. 321p [An enlarged ed. of MY SPANISH SAILOR.] [LC OTU

THE HOUSE OF ARMOUR. Philadelphia, Rowland, 1897. 543p [LC NSHD OKQ

JIMMY GOLDCOAST; or, The Story of a Monkey and his Friends. Toronto, Hodder, 1923. 319p [BM BVaU LC NSHD OTU

THE KING OF THE PARK. New York, Crowell, 1897. 226p [LC NBFU OTMC

MY SPANISH SAILOR. London, Ward, 1889. 215p [Later rev. and enl. as: HER SAILOR. Boston, Page, 1900. 321p] [BM OOP

NITA. The Story of an Irish Setter. Boston, Page, 1904. 77p [LC

PRINCESS SUKEY. The Story of a Pigeon and her Human Friends. New York, Eaton & Mains, 1905. 336p [BVaU LC OTU

PUSSY BLACK-FACE; or, The Story of a Kitten ... Boston, Page, 1913. 311p [BM LC OOP

ROSE À CHARLITTE. An Acadian Romance. Boston, Page, 1898. 516p [Pub. also under title ROSE OF ACADIA.] [BM BVaU LC NBFU OTP

THE STORY OF AN ESKIMO DOG. London, Hodder, 1906. 63p [Same as ALPATOCK? *q.v.*] [BM

THE STORY OF THE GRAVELEYS. Toronto, Briggs, 1903. 283p [BM BVaU LC NBFU OTU

'TILDA JANE. An Orphan in Search of a Home. Boston, Page, 1901. 287p [BM LC OKQ

'TILDA JANE'S ORPHANS. Boston, Page, 1909. 345p [NSWA SRL

THE WANDERING DOG. Adventures of a Fox-Terrier. New York, Doran, 1916. 363p [BVaU LC NBFU OTMC QMM

**Savage, Mrs. William T.**

MIRAMICHI. 2nd ed. Boston, Loring, 1865. 232p [Later pub. as ADELE DUBOIS. A Story of the Lovely Miramichi Valley in New Brunswick. Boston, Loring, 1865. 232p] [BVaU LC NBFU

**Savigny, Mrs. Annie Gregg, –1901**

DICK NIVEN AND HIS HORSE NOBBY. Lantern Slide Lecture, etc. Toronto, 1898. 20p [BM

A HEART-SONG OF TO-DAY (Disturbed by Fire From the 'Unruly Member'). A Novel. Toronto, Hunter Rose, 1886. 351p [BVaU OTP QMM

LION, THE MASTIFF; From Life. Toronto, Briggs, 1895. 206p [BM BVaU NBFU OTU QMM

A ROMANCE OF TORONTO (Founded on Fact). A Novel. Toronto, Briggs, 1888. 229p [BVaU NSHD OTP

THREE WEDDING RINGS. Toronto, Rose Pub. Co., 1892. 254p [OTMC

**Scaife, Arthur Hodgkin**

AS IT WAS IN THE FIFTIES. By Kim Bilir [pseud]. Victoria, Province Pub. Co., 1895. 287p [BM BVaU

GEMINI AND LESSER LIGHTS. By "Kim Bilir" [pseud]. Victoria, Province Pub. Co., 1895. 187p [BM BVaU

THREE LETTERS OF CREDIT AND OTHER STORIES. By Kim Bilir [pseud]. Victoria, Province Pub. Co., 1894. 123p [OTP

**Scott, Duncan Campbell, 1862–1947**

IN THE VILLAGE OF VIGER. Boston, Copeland Day, 1896. 135p [Also: Toronto Ryerson, 1945. 114p First Can. ed., a complete reprint of the original.] [BVaU LC NBFU OTP QMM

THE WITCHING OF ELSPIE. A Book of Stories. New York, Doran, 1923. 248p [BVaU LC NBFU OTP

**Scott, Rev. Frederick George, 1861–1944**

ELTON HAZELWOOD. A Memoir by his Friend Harry Vane. New York, Whittaker, 1891. 146p [BM BVaU NBFU OTU QMM

**Scott, Margerie (Waite)**

THE DARLING ILLUSION. Toronto, McClelland, 1955. 246p

LIFE BEGINS FOR FATHER. London, Hutchinson, 1939. 255p [BM

MINE OWN CONTENT. Toronto, McClelland, 1952. 248p

**Secretan, James Henry Edward, 1852–1926**

OUT WEST. By Secretan. Ottawa, Esdaile Press, 1910. 206p [BM BVaU LC OTP QMM

**Sellar, Robert, 1841–1919**

GLEANER TALES. [Vol. I.] Huntingdon, Que., Canadian Gleaner Office, 1886. 162p [V.2: Huntingdon, Gleaner Office, 1895. 462p] [BM BVaU NSHD OTP QMM

HEMLOCK. A Tale of the War of 1812. Montreal, Grafton, 1890. 223p (Half-title: Gleaner Tales. 2nd Series.) [Later ed.: Toronto, Britnell, 1918.] [BM BVaU LC NBFU OTP QMM

MORVEN. The Highland United Empire Loyalist. Huntingdon, Que., Gleaner, 1911. 177p [BM BVaU LC NSHD OTP QMM

THE NARRATIVE OF GORDON SELLAR, who Emigrated to Canada in 1825. Huntingdon, Que., Gleaner Book Room, 1915. 185p [Cover-title: THE TRUE MAKERS OF CANADA.] [BM BVaU LC OTP QMM

**Service, Robert William, 1874–1958**

THE HOUSE OF FEAR. New York, Dodd Mead, 1927. 408p [BM BVaU LC NBFU OTU QMM

THE MASTER OF THE MICROBE. New York, Barse, 1926. 424p [BM BVaU LC NBFU OTU

THE POISONED PARADISE. A Romance of Monte Carlo. New York, Dodd Mead, 1922. 412p [BM BVaU LC NBFU OKQ QMM

THE PRETENDER. A Story of the Latin Quarter. New York, Dodd Mead, 1914. 349p [BM BVaU LC NBFU OTU QMM

THE ROUGHNECK. A Tale of Tahiti. New York, Barse, 1923. 448p [BM BVaU LC NBFU OTMC QMM

THE TRAIL OF '98. A Northland Romance. Toronto, Briggs, 1911. 514p [BM BVaU LC NBFU OKQ QMM

**Servos, Launcelot Cressy**

FRONTENAC AND THE MAID OF THE MIST. A Romance of Theala and Frontenac at the Time when Frontenac ruled Canada and Ourouehati dominated over what is now New York State. Toronto, DeGruchy, 1927. 310p [Also: Toronto, Smithers & Bonellie, 1938.] [BVaU LC NSHD OTP QMSS

**Seton, Ernest Thompson, 1860–1946**

ANIMAL HEROES. New York, Scribner, 1905. 362p [BM BVaU LC NBFU OTU

BANNERTAIL. The Story of a Gray Squirrel. New York, Scribner, 1922. 265p [BM BVaU LC NBFU OTU QMM

THE BEST OF ERNEST THOMPSON SETON. Selected by W. Kay Robinson. London, Hodder, 1949. 408p [BM LC

BILLY, AND OTHER STORIES FROM "WILD ANIMAL WAYS." London, Hodder, 1925. 128p [ACG BM NBFU OTMC

THE BIOGRAPHY OF A GRIZZLY. New York, Century, 1900. 167p [BM BVaU LC NBFU OTU QMM

THE BIOGRAPHY OF AN ARCTIC FOX. New York, Appleton-Century, 1937. 126p [LC

THE BIOGRAPHY OF A SILVER FOX. New York, Century, 1909. 209p [BM BVaU LC NBFU OTU QMM

THE BUFFALO WIND. Santa Fé, Seton Village Press, 1938. 12p [LC NBFU

CHINK ... AND OTHER STORIES FROM "LIVES OF THE HUNTED" AND "WILD ANIMALS AT HOME." London, Hodder, 1929. 128p [AEU BM OTMC

THE CUTE COYOTE, AND OTHER ANIMAL STORIES ... TAKEN FROM "WILD ANIMALS AT HOME," "WILD ANIMAL WAYS," "LIVES OF THE HUNTED." London, U. of London Press, 1930. 159p [ACG BM

ERNEST THOMPSON SETON'S TRAIL AND CAMP-FIRE STORIES. Ed. by Julia M. Seton. ... New York, Appleton-Century, 1940. 155p [BM LC

FAMOUS ANIMAL STORIES. ... Myths, Fables, Fairy Tales. Stories of Real Animals. Ed. by ——. New York, Brentano, 1932. 686p [BM LC NSHD

FOAM RAZORBACK ... AND OTHER STORIES FROM "WILD ANIMAL WAYS." London, Hodder, 1929. 128p [BM NBFU OTMC

GREAT HISTORIC ANIMALS: MAINLY ABOUT WOLVES. London, Methuen, 1937. 320p [LC QMM

JOHNNY BEAR, AND OTHER STORIES FROM "LIVES OF THE HUNTED." London, Hodder, 1925. 124p [BM BViV

JOHNNY BEAR, LOBO, AND OTHER STORIES. New York, Scribner, 1935. 162p [LC

KATUG THE SNOW CHILD. Oxford, Blackwell, 1929. 51p [BM

KRAG AND JOHNNY BEAR. New York, Scribner, 1902. 141p [Stories from his LIVES OF THE HUNTED.] [BVaU LC OLU

KRAG, THE KOOTENAY RAM, AND OTHER ANIMAL STORIES. London, U. of London Press, 1929. 176p [ACG BM

LIVES OF THE HUNTED. New York, Scribner, 1901. 360p [BM BVaU LC NBFU OTMC QMM

LOBO, RAG, AND VIXEN. New York, Scribner, 1899. 147p [Stories from WILD ANIMALS I HAVE KNOWN.] [BM LC NBFU OTU

MONARCH, THE BIG BEAR OF TALLAC. New York, Scribner, 1904. 214p [BM BVaU LC NBFU OTU

THE NATURAL HISTORY OF THE TEN COMMANDMENTS. New York, Scribner, 1907. 78p [See below: THE TEN COMMANDMENTS. ...] [BM LC NBFU QMM

OLD SILVER GRIZZLE, THE BADGER, AND OTHER STORIES FROM "WILD ANIMALS AT HOME." London, Hodder, 1925. 128p [BViV BM OTMC

THE PREACHER OF CEDAR MOUNTAIN. A Tale of the Open Country. New York, Doubleday, 1917. 426p [BM BVaU LC NBFU OTMC

RAGGYLUG. Philadelphia, Inst. for the Instruction of the Blind, 1900. 59p [Braille ed.] [LC

RAGGYLUG, AND OTHER STORIES FROM "WILD ANIMALS I HAVE KNOWN." London, Hodder, 1925. 126p [BM OTMC

RAGGYLUG, THE COTTONTAIL RABBIT AND OTHER ANIMAL STORIES. London, Nutt, 1900. 147p [AEU BM

REDRUFF. Philadelphia, Inst. for the Instruction of the Blind, 1900. 65p [Braille ed.] [LC

ROLF IN THE WOODS. New York, Doubleday, 1911. 437p [BM BVaU LC NBFU OTU QMBM

SANTANA, THE HERO DOG OF FRANCE. Los Angeles, Pheonix Press, 1945. 61p [LC

THE SLUM CAT. SNAP. THE WINNIPEG WOLF. [Three stories.] London, Constable, 1915. 135p [OTMC

THE TEN COMMANDMENTS IN THE ANIMAL WORLD. New York, Doubleday, 1923. 78p [First pub. under title: THE NATURAL HISTORY OF THE TEN COMMANDMENTS. 1907.] [BM LC

THE THOMPSON SETON READERS. (Selected Tales from his Works.) London, Constable, 1915. 5 parts [BM

THE TRAIL OF THE SANDHILL STAG. New York, Scribner, 1899. 93p [BM BVaU LC NBFU OTP

TWO LITTLE SAVAGES. Montreal, Montreal News Co., 1903. 552p [BM BVaU LC NSHD OTMC QMM

VIXEN. Philadelphia, Inst. for the Instruction of the Blind, 1900. 45p [Braille ed.] [LC

THE WHITE REINDEER. ARNAUX. THE BOY AND THE LYNX. [Three stories.] London, Constable, 1915. 125p [OTMC

WILD ANIMALS AT HOME. Toronto, Briggs, 1913. 226p [BM BVaU LC NBFU OTU

WILD ANIMALS I HAVE KNOWN. New York, Scribner, 1898. 359p [BM BVaU LC NBFU OTU QMM

WILD ANIMAL WAYS. Garden City, Doubleday, 1916. 247p [Another ed., with 3 fewer chapters: New York, Houghton, 1916. 140p] [BM BVaU LC NBFU OTMC QMM

WOODLAND TALES. New York, Doubleday, 1921. 238p [BM BVaU LC NBFU OTMC

WOODMYTH AND FABLE. Toronto, Briggs, 1905. 181p [BM BVaU LC NBFU OTP

**Seymour, Rev. James Cooke, 1839–1902**

THE TEMPERANCE BATTLE-FIELD AND HOW TO GAIN THE DAY. A Book for the Young of All Ages, full of Humorous and Pathetic Stories. Toronto, Briggs, 1882. 188p [OTP

**Shannon, Mary Jane, –1964**

THE GOLDEN STALLION. By Lytle Shannon [pseud]. New York, Bouregy & Curl, 1952. 252p

**Shapiro, Lionel Sebastian Berk, 1908–1958**

THE SEALED VERDICT. New York, Doubleday, 1947. 278p [BM BVaU LC NBFU OTU QMM

THE SIXTH OF JUNE. Garden City, N.Y., Doubleday, 1955. 351p

TORCH FOR A DARK JOURNEY. Garden City, Doubleday, 1950. 273p [BM BVaU NBFU OTU

**Sharman, Mrs. Lyon, 1872–**

BAMBOO. Tales of the Orient-born. San Francisco, Elder, 1914. 81p [BM LC

THE HORSE THAT EDUCATED THE CHILDREN. A Christmas Story of the Canadian Prairie. Winnipeg, Franklin Press, 1912. [BM

**Sharp, Edith Lambert**

NKWALA. Boston, Little Brown, 1958. 125p

**Shaw, Campbell**

A ROMANCE OF THE ROCKIES. Toronto, Bryce, [1888]. 102p [BViPA OOP

**Shaw, Marlow Alexander, 1867–1929**

THE HAPPY ISLANDS. Stories and Sketches of the Georgian Bay. Toronto, McClelland, 1926. 254p [BVaU LC NBFU OTP QMM

**Sheard, Virna (Stanton), 1865? –1943**

BELOW THE SALT. Toronto, Ryerson, 1936. 316p [BM OTP

BY THE QUEEN'S GRACE. New York, Stokes, 1904. 316p [BM BVaU LC NBFU OKQ

FORTUNE TURNS HER WHEEL. Toronto, McClelland, 1929. 351p [NBFU OTU

THE GOLDEN APPLE TREE. Toronto, McClelland, 1920. 218p [LC NBFU OTMC

A MAID OF MANY MOODS. Toronto, Copp Clark , 1902. 177p [BVa LC OTMC

THE MAN AT LONE LAKE. London, Cassell, 1912. 309p [BVaU LC OTMC QMM

TREVELYAN'S LITTLE DAUGHTERS. Toronto, Briggs, 1898. 197p [BM BVa NBFU OKQ

**Shepherd, J.C.**

A FARMER'S THREE YEARS' EXPERIENCE IN MERCHANDISE. St. Thomas, Journal, 1891. 155p [OLU

**Sheppard, Edmund Ernest, 1855–1924**

A BAD MAN'S SWEETHEART. Toronto, Sheppard Pub. Co., 1889. 202p [OTU

DOLLY, THE YOUNG WIDDER UP TO FELDER'S. Toronto, Rose, 1886. 135p [BVaU OTU

WIDOWER JONES. A Faithful History of his "Loss" and Adventures in Search of a "Companion." A Realistic Story of Rural Life. Toronto, Sheppard Pub. Co., 1888. 197p [OTP

**Sherman, Ralph S.**
MOTHER NATURE STORIES. Toronto, Dent, 1924. 259p [BVaU NBFU OOP

**Sherwood, Roland Harold, 1902–**
STORY PARADE. Sackville, N.B., Tribune Press, 1948. 245p [NBFU OTU

**Shibley, Fred. Warner, 1864–**
A BUNDLE OF YARNS. Providence, R.I., Gregory, 1899. 249p [LC OTU

**Shinnick, J.**
THE BANKER'S DAUGHTER; or, Her First and Last Ball. A Novel. Montreal, Gazette Print., 1891. 74p [OTP

**Shipley, Nancy (Sommerville)**
THE SCARLET LILY. New York, Fell, 1959. 234p

**Shute, Evan Vere, 1905–**
SKY PAINTER. By Vere Jameson [pseud]. London, Ont., Hunter, 1950. 94p [OTU

**Silver, Barbara (pseud)**
OUR YOUNG BARBARIANS; or, Letters from Oxford. ... By Barbara Silver [pseud]. London, Macmillan, 1935. 305p [BM BVaU LC NBFU OTU QMM

**Sim, Mrs. R.S.**
UNDER THE MAPLES. Blandford Station, Ont., Author, n.d. 98p [AEU OTU

**Sime, Jessie Georgina, 1880–**
CANADA CHAPS. London, Lane, 1917. 271p [BM NBFU OTMC QMSS
INEZ AND HER ANGEL. By Georgina Sime & Frank Nicholson. London, Chapman & Hall, 1954. 141p
OUR LITTLE LIFE. A Novel of Today. New York, Stokes, 1921. 394p [BM LC NBFU OTMC QMM
SISTER WOMAN. London, Richards, 1919. 293p [BM NBFU OTMC QMM
A TALE OF TWO WORLDS. By Georgina Sime and Frank Nicholson. London, Chapman & Hall, 1953. 683p

**Simms, Florence Mary**
ETOFFE DU PAYS. Lower St. Lawrence Sketches. Toronto, Musson, [1913?]. 87p [BM BVaU NSHD OKQ

**Simon, Samuel William, 1893–**
THE FUR COAT. A Humorous True Story, Eye-witnessed by the Author. Montreal, Author, 1950. 96p [OONL

**Simonds, Peter, 1906–**
THE CASE OF CONSTABLE SHIELDS. By Richard Greaves [pseud]. Philadelphia, Dorrance, 1940. 341p [LC
RED SEPULCHRE. A Story of Adventure Behind the Iron Curtain. Montreal, Adanac Press, 1947. 391p [QMBM

**Simpson, Maria**

"BROTHER G.M. ROSE." A Temperance Story. Toronto, Hunter Rose, 1879. 236p [OTU

RONALD McFARLANE. A Temperance Story. Toronto, Hunter Rose, 1878. 74p [OTMC

ROSEVILLE SEMINARY. A Temperance Story. Toronto, Hunter Rose, 1878. 234p [AEU OLU OTMC

THE TORONTO RINE BOYS. A Temperance Story. Toronto, Author, 1878. 62p [OTP

**Sinclair, Bertrand William, 1878–**

BIG TIMBER. A Story of the Northwest. Boston, Little Brown, 1916. 321p [BM BVaU LC OTMC

BOTH SIDES OF THE LAW. London, Wright & Brown, 1955. 156p

BURNED BRIDGES. Toronto, Briggs, 1919. 308p [BM BVaU LC NBFU OTMC

DOWN THE DARK ALLEY. Boston, Little Brown, 1936. 291p [BM BVaU LC OTU

GUNPOWDER LIGHTNING. Boston, Little Brown, 1930. 298p [BM BVaU LC OTMC

THE HIDDEN PLACES. Toronto, Ryerson, 1922. 318p [BM BVaU LC NBFU OTMC

THE INVERTED PYRAMID. Boston, Little Brown, 1924. 339p [BM BVaU LC NBFU OTMC

THE LAND OF FROZEN SUNS. New York, Dillingham, 1910. 309p [BVaU LC OTMC

NORTH OF FIFTY-THREE. Boston, Little Brown, 1914. 345p [BM BVaU LC NBFU OTMC

PIRATES OF THE PLAINS. London, Hodder, 1928. 318p [BM BViPA

POOR MAN'S ROCK. Boston, Little Brown, 1920. 307p [BM BVaU LC NBFU OTMC

RAW GOLD. A Novel. New York, Dillingham, 1908. 311p [BVaU LC OTMC

ROOM FOR THE ROLLING M. London, Wright & Brown, 1954. 158p

WILD WEST. Toronto, Ryerson, 1926. 288p [BM BVaU LC OTMC

**Sinclair, Coll McLean**

THE DEAR OLD FARM. A Canadian Story. By Malcolm [pseud]. St. Thomas, The Journal, 1897. 198p [BM BVaU NSHPL OTP

**Sinclair, Mary R.**

CHILDREN OF THE PIONEERS. Toronto, Dent, 1931. 138p [OTMC

**Sirluck, Lesley (McNaught)**

GUP. Toronto, Ryerson, 1946. 48p [BVa OTMC

**Skelton, Mme. Henrietta**

THE CHRISTMAS TREE. A Story of German Domestic Life. Cincinnati, Walden & Stowe; New York, Phillips & Hunt, 1883. 279p [LC

GRACE MORTON. By Madame Skelton. Toronto, Irving, 1873. 212p [BVaU OTMC

A MAN TRAP, and THE FATAL INHERITANCE. Two Temperance Tales. By Mrs. H. Skelton. Toronto, Magurn, 1876. 152p [OTP

**Skelton, James, 1880–**

DOWN NORTH FOR ADVENTURE. Ilfracombe, Devon, Stockwell, 1958. 224p

HO! FOR THE LABRADOR. Ilfracombe, Devon, Stockwell, 1957. 159p

**Skinner, Constance Lindsay, 1879? –1939**

ANDY BREAKS TRAIL. New York, Macmillan, 1928. 199p [LC

BECKY LANDERS. Frontier Warrior. New York, Macmillan, 1928. 234p [LC

DEBBY BARNES, TRADER. New York, Macmillan, 1932. 244p [LC NBFU

"GOOD MORNING, ROSAMOND!" New York, Doubleday, 1917. 384p [BVaU LC NBFU OTMC

THE RANCH OF THE GOLDEN FLOWERS. New York, Macmillan, 1928. 182p [LC NBFU

RED MAN'S LUCK. New York, Coward-McCann, 1930. 251p [BVa LC NBFU

RED WILLOWS. Toronto, McClelland, 1929. 412p [BVaU LC MWU NBFU OTU

ROB ROY. The Frontier Twins. New York, Macmillan, 1934. 218p [LC

ROSELLE OF THE NORTH. New York, Macmillan, 1927. 256p [BVa LC NBFU QMM

SILENT SCOT, FRONTIER SCOUT. New York, Macmillan, 1925. 234p [BVa LC

THE SEARCH RELENTLESS. London, Methuen, 1925. 311p [BM BViPA LC NBFU OTMC

THE TIGER WHO WALKS ALONE. New York, Macmillan, 1927. 211p [LC NBFU OTMC

THE WHITE LEADER. New York, Macmillan, 1926. 219p [LC NBFU

**Sluman, Norma Pauline (Hardman), 1924–**

BLACKFOOT CROSSING. Toronto, Ryerson, 1959. 255p

**Smith, A. de Herries, 1881–**

DRUMS OF THE NORTH. New York, Macaulay, 1928. 312p [BVaU LC NBFU

**Smith, Donald Taylor, 1909–**

CHINA COASTER. A Novel of Suspense. New York, Holt, 1953. 211p

**Smith, Edgar Maurice, 1870–**

ANEROESTES THE GAUL. A Fragment of the Second Punic War. Montreal, Grafton, 1898. 242p [BM NSHD OTU

THE BARONESS OF DENONVILLE. Montreal, 1900. [BCF

A DAUGHTER OF HUMANITY. A Novel. Boston, Arena, 1895. 317p [BM LC

**Smith, Frank Clifford, 1865–1937**

A DAUGHTER OF PATRICIANS. Toronto, Publishers Synd., 1901. 327p [BVaU OTU

A LOVER IN HOMESPUN, AND OTHER STORIES. Toronto, Briggs, 1896. 201p [BVaU NSHD OTU QMBM

THE TRAITOR. Toronto, Briggs, 1912. 230p [OOP

**Smith, George, 1852–1930**

THE AMISHMAN. By Clyde Smith [pseud]. Toronto, Briggs, 1912. 132p [BM BVaU OTP

**Smith, George Washington, 1855–1945**

THE SMILEYS. A Tale of Hardwoodlands. Windsor, N.S., Anslow, 1901. 119p [BVaU NBFU QMM

**Smith, Jean Mitchell**

SUNSHINE-SHADDER. Sketches of Ontario Life. Toronto, Briggs, 1911. 80p [BM BVa OTMC

**Smith, Josephine**

PERTH-ON-THE-TAY. A Tale of the Transplanted Highlanders. Ottawa, Mortimer, 1901. 266p [BVaU NBFU OTP

**Smith, Minnie**

IS IT JUST? A Tale of British Columbia Life. Toronto, Briggs, 1911. 135p [BM BVaU NBFU OTU

**Smith, Rev. Oswald Jeffrey, 1889–**

THE ADVENTURES OF ANDY McGINNIS. Grand Rapids, Mich., Zondervan, 1945. 67p [BM LC

OSWALD SMITH'S SHORT STORIES. Grand Rapids, Mich., Zondervan, 1943. 163p [BM LC NBFU

**Smith, Thomas Barlow, 1839–1933**

ROSE CARNEY. A Story of Ever Shifting Scenes on Land and Sea. Windsor, N.S., Anslow, 1890. 204p [NSHD OOP

SERAPH ON THE SEA; or, The Career of a Highland Drummer Boy. ... Windsor, N.S., Anslow, 1891. 156p [NSHD

YOUNG LION OF THE WOODS; or, A Story of Early Colonial Days. Halifax, Nova Scotia Print., 1889. 147p [BVaU NSHD OTP

**Smythe, Albert Ernest Stafford, 1861–1947**

MRS. LOTHBURY'S GOSPEL. [A Story]. [Toronto], 1920. 36p [BM NSWA OTU

**Smythe, Carroll F.**

THE VAGABOND VENDER. Toronto, Dominion Bureau of Circulation, 1929. 65p [OTMC QSherU

**Sollows, Atlanta Sara, 1889–1954**

WHITHER THOU GOEST. Toronto, Allen, 1947. 211p [NBFU

**Somerville, Alexander, 1811–1885**

THE LIFE OF ROGER MOWBRAY. London, 1853. [BM

**Souster, Raymond, 1921–**

THE WINTER OF TIME. By Raymond Holmes [pseud]. New Toronto, Export Pub. Enterprises, 1949. 160p [Priv. info.

**Spang, Edward**

"COBALT," THE MASCOT OF COBALT SILVER CAMP, AND OTHER STORIES. Sudbury, Sudbury News, 1922. 134p [BM BVaU OTP

**Sparrow, Charles, 1877–**

A DOOMED MANSION. Toronto, Briggs, 1905. 139p [BVaU NSHD OTMC

THE HOUSE ON THE CLIFF. Toronto, Briggs, 1909. 122p [BVaU NSHD OTMC

THE ROMANCE OF THE HOUSE OF ARNOLD; or, Ravendale Manor. Toronto, Briggs, 1913. 168p [BM BVaU NSHD

SHADOWS OF THE DEEP. Toronto, Briggs, 1903. 176p [NSHD

THE TURNING POINT. Toronto, Briggs, 1911. 137p [BM BVaU NSHD OTMC

**Sparrow, Malcolm Weethie, 1862–1936**

THE LADY OF CHATEAU BLANC. An Historical Romance. By Max Moineau [pseud]. Toronto, Brough, 1896. 70p [BM

**Spedon, Andrew Learmont, 1831–1884**

CANADIAN SUMMER EVENING TALES. Montreal, Lovell, 1866. 208p [BVaU OTP

TALES FOR CANADIAN HOMES. [The Black-sealed Letter; The Poetic Wreath.] Montreal, Mitchell, 1872. 112p [BVaU OKQ

TALES OF THE CANADIAN FOREST. Montreal, Lovell, 1861. 221p [BVaU LC NBFU OTP QMM

**Sprague, Miss E.**

AN EARNEST TRIFLER. Toronto, Belfords, 1880. 254p [OKQ

**Sprigge, Elizabeth, 1900–**

CASTLE IN ANDALUSIA. London, Heinemann, 1935. 343p [BM BVaU LC NBFU OTMC

CHILDREN ALONE. London, Heinemann, 1935. 272p [BM

FAINT AMORIST. London, Knopf, 1927. 272p [BM LC NBFU

HOME IS THE HUNTER. By Henry Toke Munn and Elizabeth Sprigge. Toronto, Macmillan, 1930. 296p [BM OTMC

THE OLD MAN DIES. A Novel. London, Heinemann, 1933. 292p [BM BVaU LC NBFU OTMC

PONY TRACKS. New York, Scribner, 1936. 156p [BM LC NBFU OTU

THE RAVEN'S WING. London, Macmillan, 1940. 419p [BM LC NBFU OTMC

A SHADOWY THIRD. London, Knopf, 1927. 259p [BM

THE SON OF THE HOUSE. London, Collins, 1937. 315p [BM BVaU LC NBFU OTU

TWO LOST ON DARTMOOR. London, Eyre & Spottiswoode, 1940. 172p [BM OTU

**Starkey, Mrs. Allistene**

THE GRAFTED TWIG. New York, Arcadia House, 1940. 320p [LC NBFU

**Starr, J.R.L.**

MOST THOROUGH. A Father and Son Story. Toronto, Allen, 1927. 28p [OTMC

**Stavrakov, Marion**

CHESTER GNOMIE. And His Friends the Elves – and the Blueberries – and the Old Grey Goose. Montreal, Palm Pub., 1950. 24p [OONL

**Stead, Robert James Campbell, 1880–1959**

THE BAIL JUMPER. Toronto, Briggs, 1914. 335p [BM BVaU OTMC

THE COPPER DISC. New York, Doubleday, 1931. 321p [BM BVaU LC NBFU OTMC

THE COW PUNCHER. New York, Harper, 1918. 331p [BM BVaU LC NBFU OTMC

DENNISON GRANT. A Novel of Today. Toronto, Musson, 1920. 388p [BM BVaU NBFU OTMC

GRAIN. Toronto, McClelland, 1926. 281p [BM BVaU LC NBFU OTMC QMM

THE HOMESTEADERS. A Novel of the Canadian West. Toronto, Musson, 1916. 314p [BM BVaU NBFU OTMC

NEIGHBOURS. Toronto, Hodder, 1922. 315p [BVaU NBFU OTMC QMM

THE SMOKING FLAX. Toronto, McClelland, 1924. 301p [BM BVaU LC NBFU OTMC

ZEN OF THE Y.D. A Novel of the Foothills. [A revised ed. of DENNISON GRANT.] London, Hodder, 1925. 320p [BM

**Steele, Harwood Elmes Robert, 1897–**

GHOSTS RETURNING. Toronto, Ryerson, 1950. 272p [BVaU NBFU OTMC QMM

"I SHALL ARISE." London, Hodder, 1926. 320p [BM BVaU NBFU QMM

THE NINTH CIRCLE. New York, Doubleday, 1928. 312p [BM BVaU LC NBFU OORD QMM

SPIRIT-OF-IRON. An Authentic Novel of the North West Mounted Police. Toronto, McClelland, 1923. 358p [BM BVaU LC NBFU OTMC

TO EFFECT AN ARREST. Adventures of the Royal Canadian Mounted Police. Toronto, Ryerson, 1947. 311p [BM BVaU LC NBFU OTU QMBM

**Stefansson, Vilhjalmur, 1879–1962**

KAK, THE COPPER ESKIMO. By Vilhjalmur Stefansson and Violet Irwin. ... New York, Macmillan, 1924. 253p [BM BVaU LC NBFU OTP

THE MOUNTAIN OF JADE. By Violet Irwin and ——. London, Macmillan, 1926. 236p [BM LC OTMC

**Steinhouse, Herbert, 1922–**

TEN YEARS AFTER. London, Bodley Head, 1958. 371p

THE TIME OF THE JUGGERNAUT. New York, Morrow, 1958. 470p [Same as TEN YEARS AFTER.]

**Stephen, Alexander Maitland, 1882–1942**

THE GLEAMING ARCHWAY. London, Dent, 1929. 296p [BViPA NSHD OTMC QMM

THE KINGDOM OF THE SUN. A Romance of the Far West Coast. Toronto, Dent, 1927. 285p [BM BVaU NBFU OTMC QMM

**Stern, Karl, 1906–**

THROUGH DOOMS OF LOVE. A Novel. New York, Farrar Straus, 1960. 433p

**Stevens, Charles A.**

A SAILOR BOY'S EXPERIENCE. Napanee, Ont., 1892. 107p [OLU

**Stevens, George Roy, 1895–**

THE REMEMBRANCE OF SHERE JEHAN. By G.R.S. Montreal, Author, 1960. 16p

**Stevenson, Laura Agnes**

THE LADIES' BENEVOLENT AND INDUSTRIAL SALLYMAG SOCIETY. By L.S. Charlottetown, Bremner, 1868. 131p [LC NSHD OTP

**Stewart, Alexander Charles, 1867–1944**

THE DISCARD. Being the Historical Remnants of a Rough Neck. ... By Professor A.C.S. [pseud]. Toronto, Hunter Rose, 1919. 265p [BVaU NBFU OTMC

**Stewart, James Livingstone, 1872–1946**

THE GODDESS OF MERCY. A Tale of Love and Turmoil of Modern China. New York, Revell, 1927. 351p [BM LC NBFU OTMC

GODS OF WEALTH AND WAR. A Tale of Modern China. New York, Revell, 1931. 288p [BVaU LC OKQ

THE LAUGHING BUDDHA. A Tale of Love and Adventure in Western China. New York, Revell, 1925. 347p [BM LC NBFU OKQ

**Stilman, Abram, 1903–**

HEALER OF ALL FLESH. A Novel. New York, Whittier Books, 1959. 441p

**Stirling, Helen**

A SOLDIER OF THE KING. Toronto, Oxford U. Press, 1915. 55p [OTMC

**Stirling, Lilla May Elderkin, 1904–**

JOCKIE. A Story of Prince Edward Island. New York, Scribner, 1951. 202p

**Stobo, Rev. Edward John, 1838–1918**

THE O'ERTURN O' BOTANY BAY. By Aletheia [pseud]. Philadelphia, American Baptist Pub. Soc., 1901. 270p [LC

**Stockford, Lela E.**

MEDICO OF THE VALLEY. By Joan Hamilton-Stockford [pseud]. Philadelphia, Dorrance, 1939. 226p [LC

**Storey, Arthur George, 1915–**

PRAIRIE HARVEST. Toronto, Ryerson, 1959. 210p

**Stormont, Lan (pseud)**

TAN MING. A Fantasy. By Lan Stormont [pseud]. New York, Exposition Press, 1955. 471p

**Strange, William, 1902–**

SUNSET IN EBONY. Toronto, Macmillan, 1935. 305p [BM NBFU

**Stredder, Eleanor**

LOST IN THE WILDS. A Canadian Story. London, Nelson, 1896. 227p [BM NBFU OTU QMBM

**Stringer, Arthur John Arbuthnot, 1874–1950**

ARE ALL MEN ALIKE?–THE LOST TITIAN. [See TWIN TALES . ...]

THE CITY OF PERIL. New York, Knopf, 1923. 317p [BVaU LC NBFU OTU

CHRISTINA AND I. Indianapolis, Bobbs-Merrill, 1929. 301p [BM BVaU LC NBFU OTMC

THE DARK WING. New York, Bobbs-Merrill, 1939. 311p [BM LC NBFU OTU

THE DEVASTATOR. Toronto, McClelland, 1944. 198p [BM BVaU LC NBFU OTU

THE DIAMOND THIEVES. Indianapolis, Bobbs-Merrill, 1923. 416p [BM LC NBFU OTU

THE DOOR OF DREAD. A Secret Service Romance. Indianapolis, Bobbs-Merrill, 1916. 375p [BM LC NSWA OTMC

EMPTY HANDS. Indianapolis, Bobbs-Merrill, 1924. 360p [BM BVaU LC NBFU OTU

THE GHOST PLANE. Indianapolis, Bobbs-Merrill, 1940. 304p [BM BVaU LC NBFU OTU

THE GUN-RUNNER. A Novel. New York, Dodge, 1909. 370p [Also: Toronto, McClelland, 1923. 316p] [BM BVaU LC NBFU OTU QMM

THE HAND OF PERIL. New York, Macmillan, 1915. 331p [BVaU LC NBFU OTU

HEATHER OF THE HIGH HAND. A Novel of the North. New York, Bobbs-Merrill, 1937. 291p [BM BVaU LC NBFU OTU

THE HOUSE OF INTRIGUE. Indianapolis, Bobbs-Merrill, 1918. 363p [BM LC NBFU OTU

IN BAD WITH SINBAD. Indianapolis, Bobbs-Merrill, 1926. 185p [BM BVaU LC NBFU OTU

INTRUDERS IN EDEN. A Novel. Indianapolis, Bobbs-Merrill, 1942. 308p [BM BVaU LC OTMC

A LADY QUITE LOST. A Novel. Indianapolis, Bobbs-Merrill, 1931. 303p [Pub. in *Saturday Evening Post* under title: THE SQUAW WOMAN.] [BM BVaU LC NBFU OTMC

THE LAMP IN THE VALLEY. A Novel of Alaska. New York, Bobbs-Merrill, 1938. 314p [BM BVaU LC OTU

LONELY O'MALLEY. A Story of Boy Life. Boston, Houghton, 1905. 383p [Also: Toronto, McClelland, 1924. 383p] [BM BVaU LC OTU

THE LOOM OF DESTINY. Boston, Small Maynard, 1899. 208p [BM BVaU LC NBFU OTU

MAN LOST. Indianapolis, Bobbs-Merrill, 1934. 328p [BM BVaU LC OOP

THE MAN WHO COULDN'T SLEEP. Being a Relation of the Divers Strange Adventures which befell Witter Kerfoot ... along the Highways and Byways of Manhattan. Indianapolis, Bobbs-Merrill, 1919. 351p [BM BVaU LC NBFU OTU

MANHANDLED. By Arthur Stringer and Russell Holman. ... New York, Bobbs-Merrill, 1924. 312p [BM BVaU LC OTMC

MARRIAGE BY CAPTURE. Indianapolis, Bobbs-Merrill, 1933. 316p [BM LC NBFU OTU

THE MUD LARK. Indianapolis, Bobbs-Merrill, 1932. 331p [BM LC NBFU OTU QMM

NEVER-FAIL BLAKE. New York, Burt, 1924. 302p [Originally pub. under title: THE SHADOW.] [LC NBFU OTMC

NIGHT HAWK. A Novel. New York, Burt, 1926. 307p [LC

THE OCCASIONAL OFFENDER. [MOR'12

PHANTOM WIRES. Boston, Little Brown, 1907. 295p [Another ed., 1923.] [BM BVaU LC NBFU OTU

POWER. Indianapolis, Bobbs-Merrill, 1925. 308p [BM BVaU LC NSHD OTU

THE PRAIRIE CHILD. Indianapolis, Bobbs-Merrill, 1922. 382p [BM BVaU LC NBFU OTU QMM

THE PRAIRIE MOTHER. Toronto, McClelland, 1920. 359p [BM BVaU LC NBFU OTU

THE PRAIRIE OMNIBUS. Containing Two Complete Novels ... THE PRAIRIE WIFE, THE PRAIRIE MOTHER. New York, Grosset & Dunlap, n.d. 316 + 359p [OTMC QMG

PRAIRIE STORIES. Containing THE PRAIRIE WIFE, THE PRAIRIE MOTHER, THE PRAIRIE CHILD. New York, Burt, 1936. 1057p [OLU

THE PRAIRIE WIFE. A Novel. Indianapolis, Bobbs-Merrill, 1915. 316p [BM BVaU LC NBFU OTU

THE SHADOW. New York, Century, 1913. 302p [Later pub. under title: NEVER-FAIL BLAKE.] [BM BVaU LC OTMC

THE SILVER POPPY. A Novel. New York, Appleton, 1903. 291p [Another ed., 1924.] [BM BVaU LC NBFU OTMC

STAR IN A MIST. A Novel. Indianapolis, Bobbs-Merrill, 1943. 312p [BM LC NBFU OTMC

THE STORY WITHOUT A NAME. By Arthur Stringer and Russell Holman. New York, Grosset, 1924. 316p [BM BVaU LC NBFU OTMC

THE STRANGER. Toronto, Dominion Publicity Com. Victory Loan, 1919. 16p [NSHPL OTMC

TOOLOONA. A Novel of the North. London, Methuen, 1936. 248p [BM

TWIN TALES: ARE ALL MEN ALIKE? and THE LOST TITIAN. Indianapolis, Bobbs-Merrill, 1921. 288p [BVaU LC NBFU OTU QMM

THE UNDER GROOVE. A Novel. New York, McClure, 1908. 335p [BVaU LC NBFU OTMC

WHITE HANDS. Indianapolis, Bobbs-Merrill, 1927. 302p [BM BVaU LC OTU

THE WIFE TRADERS. A Tale of the North. Indianapolis, Bobbs-Merrill, 1936. 319p [BM BVaU LC NBFU OLU

THE WINE OF LIFE. New York, Knopf, 1921. 389p [BVaU LC NBFU OTU QMM

THE WIRE TAPPERS. Boston, Little Brown, 1906. 324p [Another ed., 1922.] [BM BVaU LC NBFU OTU

THE WOLF WOMAN. A Novel. Indianapolis, Bobbs-Merrill, 1928. 331p [BM BVaU LC NBFU OTMC

THE WOMAN WHO COULDN'T DIE. Indianapolis, Bobbs-Merrill, 1929. 314p [BVaU LC NBFU OTU

**Stroud, Amelia Panton**

DAISY DALTON'S DECISION. Toronto, Bain, 1894. 218p [OTMC

**Sullivan, Alan, 1868–1947**

"AND FROM THAT DAY." Toronto, Ryerson, 1944. 195p [BVaU LC NSHD OOP OTU QMM

ANTIDOTE. By Sinclair Murray [pseud]. London, J. Murray, 1932. 332p [BM LC

THE BIRTHMARK. London, Arnold, 1924. 319p [EngCat

BLANTYRE–ALIEN. London, Dent, 1914. 265p [BVaU NSHD OTMC

THE BROKEN MARRIAGE. By Sinclair Murray [pseud]. New York, Dutton, 1929. 319p [Also: London, Murray, 1928.] [BM LC

BROTHER BLACKFOOT. New York, Century, 1927. 300p [LC NBFU OOP

BROTHER ESKIMO. Toronto, McClelland, 1921. 249p [BVaU NBFU OTMC

THE CARIBOO ROAD. A Novel. Toronto, Nelson, 1946. 311p [BVaU NBFU OTMC QMM

COLONEL PLUCKETT. London, Ward Lock, 1932. 256p [LC NBFU

CORNISH INTERLUDE. By Sinclair Murray [pseud]. London, J. Murray, 1932. 303p [BM

THE CRUCIBLE. By Sinclair Murray [pseud]. London, Bles, 1925. 318p [BM LC NBFU

THE DAYS OF THEIR YOUTH. New York, Century, 1926. 332p [BVaU LC NBFU OTU

DOUBLE LIVES. By Sinclair Murray [pseud]. Toronto, Macmillan, 1929. 318p [Also: London, Murray, 1929. 318p] [BM NBFU

THE FUR MASTERS. London, Murray, 1938. 320p [BVaU LC NBFU OTU QMM

GOLDEN FOUNDLING. By Sinclair Murray [pseud]. Toronto, Macmillan, 1931. 338p [BM NBFU

THE GREAT DIVIDE. A Romance of the Canadian Pacific Railway. Toronto, Macmillan, 1935. 417p [BVaU LC NBFU OTU QMM

HUMAN CLAY. By Sinclair Murray [pseud] and B.V. Shann. London, J. Murray, 1926. 318p [BM OOP

IN THE BEGINNING. London, Hurst & Blackett, 1926. 280p [LC NBFU OTMC

THE INNER DOOR. New York, Century, 1917. 388p [LC NBFU OTMC

THE IRONMASTER. London, J. Murray, 1931. 345p [CBI

THE JADE GOD. London, Bles, 1924. 316p [Dramatized as 3-act play with same title by William Edwin Barry: New York, French, 1930. 77p –CBI] [BVaU LC NBFU OTMC

JOHN FRENSHAM, K.C. By Sinclair Murray [pseud]. New York, Dutton, 1928. 293p [Same title, but with B. V. Shann as jt. author: London, J. Murray, 1925. 320p –EngCat] [BM LC NBFU

A LITTLE WAY AHEAD. Toronto, Macmillan, 1930. 316p [LC NBFU OTU QMM

THE MAGIC MAKERS. London, J. Murray, 1930. 297p [NBS

MAN AT LONE TREE. London, Ward Lock, 1933. 256p [CBI

THE MONEY SPINNERS. By Sinclair Murray [pseud]. London, Low Marston, 1936. 378p [BM LC NBFU OTU

MR. ABSALOM. London, Murray, 1930. 316p [CBI

NO SECRETS ISLAND. London, Murray, 1931. 314p [CBI

THE OBSTINATE VIRGIN. London, Low Marston, 1934. 314p [BM

THE PASSING OF OUL-I-BUT AND OTHER TALES. Toronto, Dent, 1913. 302p [BVaU NSHD OTMC

QUEER PARTNERS. By Sinclair Murray [pseud]. Toronto, Macmillan, 1930. 313p [BM NBFU OOP

THE RAPIDS. Toronto, Copp Clark, 1922. 337p [BVaU LC NSHD OTU QMM

SANDS OF FORTUNE. By Sinclair Murray [pseud]. New York, Dutton, 1928. 300p [BM LC NBFU

THE SPLENDID SILENCE. New York, Dutton, 1929. 278p [LC NBFU OTMC

THE STORY OF ONE-EAR. London, Philip, 1929. 68p [CBI

THREE CAME TO VILLE MARIE. Toronto, Oxford U. Press, 1941. 391p [BVaU LC NSHD OTMC QMM

THE TRAINING OF THE SEA. London, Philip, 1929. 72p [CBI

UNDER THE NORTHERN LIGHTS. London, Dent, 1926. 218p [BVaU LC NSHD OTU QMM

THE VERDICT OF THE SEA. London, Hurst & Blackett, 1927. 288p [BVaU LC NBFU OTU

WHAT FOOLS MEN ARE! By Sinclair Murray [pseud]. London, Sampson Low, 1933. 316p [BM NBFU

WHISPERING LODGE. By Sinclair Murray [pseud]. Toronto, Ryerson, 1927. 336p [Also: London, Murray, 1927. 336p] [BM NBFU

WITH LOVE FROM RACHEL. By Sinclair Murray [pseud]. Toronto, Oxford U. Press, 1938. 312p [BM NBFU OTU

**Sullivan, Archibald Beresford Dennistown, 1886–1921**

THE LAUGHING BIRDS AND OTHER STORIES. Toronto, Macmillan, 1925. 283p [AEU BVaU NBFU OTMC

**Sullivan, Barry Seaghan**

FIBRE. London, Faber, 1945. 246p [BM LC

**Sutton, Mrs. Rose**

DRIFT. New York, Vantage Press, 1955. 157p

**Swabey, Maurice, 1832?–1902**

VOICES FROM ABEGWEET; or, The Home on the Wave. London, Nisbet, 1878. 71p [BM NSHD

**Swayze, James Frederick, 1907–1967**

RUN FOR YOUR LIFE! The Adventures of John Rutherfurd at Pontiac's Siege of Detroit, 1763. Toronto, Ryerson, 1960. 149p

**Sweatman, Mrs. Constance Travers**

HALF PRICE. Toronto, McClelland, 1927. 277p [BM BVaU LC NBFU OTMC

SINCE ADAM. A Novel. London, Hurst & Blackett, 1927. 287p [BM

TO LOVE AND TO CHERISH. Toronto, Macmillan, 1929. 342p [NBFU OTMC

YOUNG FOLK, OLD FOLK. A Novel of the Younger Set. Toronto, Allen, 1926. 304p [BM LC NBFU OTMC

**Sykes, Hon. Villum (pseud.)**

LETTERS TO HIS HEXCELLENT LORD CATHCART (GOV'NOR AS VOS) ... HEXPLAININ VOT IS VOT IN CANARDEY, AS VEL AS VOT HOUGHTN'T TO BE. By the Hon. Villum Sykes [pseud], late Hinspector hof Cabs and Lisenses. Montreal, Donoghue & Mantz, 1846. 38p [OTP

**Symons, Harry Lutz, 1893–**

THREE SHIPS WEST. ... Toronto, Ryerson, 1949. 315p [NBFU OTMC QMBM

**Taggart, William Stuart, 1859–1925**

"GUILTY." Forgiven—Reclaimed; "TRUTH IS STRANGER THAN FICTION." A Canadian Story from Real Life. By Lance Bilton [pseud]. Ottawa, Crain, 1906. 305p [BM BVaU OTMC

**Tait, George Edward, 1910–**

THE SADDLE OF CARLOS PEREZ. Toronto, Ryerson, 1949. 87p [OONL

THE SILENT GULLS. Toronto, Ryerson, 1950. 95p [OONL

**Tait, John, 1896? –1955**

GRANDMA TAKES A HAND. Toronto, Ryerson, 1956. 155p

**Talbot, Thomas, (fl. 1844–82)**

THE GRANVILLES. An Irish Tale. London, Sampson, 1882. 3v [BM

**Tapley, K.C.**

TAPPINGS. By Casey Tap [pseud]. Saint John, McMillan, 1884. 58p [NBS OONL

**Tate, Frank J., 1902–**

RED WILDERNESS. Toronto, Oxford U. Press, 1938. 461p [LC NBFU OTU QMBM

**Taylor, Archibald M'Alpine**

JEAN GRANT. A Novel. New York, Lovell, 1890. 242p [LC

**Taylor, Daphne**

POMPOUS PARROT, AND OTHER WEST INDIAN TALES. Toronto, Macmillan, 1947. 114p [CC

**Taylor, Miss E.A.**

BEATRICE OF OLD YORK. Toronto, Musson, 1929. 214p [BVaU NBFU OKQ

**Taylor, Gaie**

ANASTASIA'S DAUGHTER. Toronto, Ryerson, 1955. 256p

**Taylor, Gladys (Tall), 1917–**

THE KING TREE. Toronto, Ryerson, 1958. 335p

PINE ROOTS. Toronto, Ryerson, 1956. 238p

**Teetgen, Ada B.**

A WHITE PASSION. London, Gardner, 1913. 346p [BM BVaU OOP

**Tempest, Judith (pseud)**

MONKSWOLD. Saint John, Author, 1903. 156p [Earlier ed., 1895 –BCF] [BCF NBS

**Templeton-Armstrong, Mrs. I.**

THE OLD VICE AND THE NEW CHIVALRY. Toronto, Briggs, 1884. 178p [BVaU OTP

**Tennant, Margaret E.**

THE GOLDEN CHORD. A Story of Trial and Conquest. Almonte, Ont., McLeod & McEwen, 1899. 133p [BVaU

**Tennenhaus, Hanna (Faust), 1923–**
EVA. Bathurst, N.B., Aire Pub., 1959. 188p

**Teskey, Adeline Margaret, –1924**
ALEXANDER McBAIN, B.A. Prince in Penury. New York, Revell, 1906. 297p [LC OTU
CANDLELIGHT DAYS. London, Cassell, 1913. 344p [BM BVaU NSHD OTU
THE LITTLE CELESTIAL. Toronto, 1912. [DCB MOR'12
A LITTLE CHILD SHALL LEAD THEM. London, Hodder, 1911. 31p [AEU BM BVaS
THE VILLAGE ARTIST. New York, Revell, 1905. 216p [BM BVaU LC OTMC
WHERE THE SUGAR MAPLE GROWS. Idylls of a Canadian Village. New York, Fenno, 1901. 268p [BM BVaU LC NBFU OTU QMM
THE YELLOW PEARL. New York, Hodder, 1911. 208p [BM BVaU LC OTMC

**Thomas, Cyrus, 1836–1908**
THE FRONTIER SCHOOLMASTER. The Autobiography of a Teacher. ... Montreal, Lovell, 1880. 465p [BVaU OTMC QMM
THE REVEREND JOHN AND A FEW PHILANTHROPISTS. [A Novel.] Montreal, Lovell, 1903. 492p [BM BVaU NBFU OTMC QMM

**Thomas, Lillian (Beynon), 1874–1961**
NEW SECRET. Toronto, Allen, 1946. 214p [BVaU NBFU OTMC

**Thomas, Martha Banning**
STORMALONG GERT. New York, Green Circle Books, 1936. 318p [Pub. in England as: WOMAN OF THE SEA. London, Long, 1938. 254p] [LC OTU

**Thompson, Dora Olive, 1895? –1934**
ADELE IN SEARCH OF A HOME. London, Girl's Own Paper, 1926. 288p [BM
A DEALER IN SUNSHINE. London, Girl's Own Paper, 1926. 224p [BM
DIMPLES. London, Religious Tract Soc., 1929. 269p [BM
JOY MEREDITH. London, Religious Tract Soc., 1928. 255p [BM
KATHLEEN AND PETER. Toronto, Upper Canada Tract Soc., 1934. 271p [BM
LIZZIE ANNE. London, Girl's Own Paper, 1927. 288p [BM
NANCY-ROSE. London, Girl's Own Paper, n.d. 256p [NBS
THAT GIRL GINGER. London, Religious Tract Soc., 1931. 286p [BM

**Thompson, Mrs. James C.**
SKETCHES FROM LIFE. Being Tales on the Ten Commandments. Toronto, Hunter, 1876. 240p [OTMC

**Thompson, Sheila Sonia, 1917–**
LIKE A FLOWER. Toronto, Nelson, 1946. 208p [BM LC

**Thompson, Thomas Phillips, 1843–1933**
THE POLITICAL EXPERIENCES OF JIMUEL BRIGGS [pseud] ... AT TORONTO, OTTAWA AND ELSEWHERE. ... Toronto, Flint Morton, 1873. 126p [LC OTUV

**Thomson, Edward William, 1849–1924**

BETWEEN EARTH AND SKY, AND OTHER STRANGE STORIES OF DELIVERANCE. Toronto, Briggs, 1897. 297p [BM BVa OTUV

OLD MAN SAVARIN, AND OTHER STORIES. Toronto, Briggs, 1895. 289p [BM BVaU LC NBFU OTMC QMM

OLD MAN SAVARIN STORIES. Tales of Canada and Canadians. Toronto, Gundy, 1917. 344p [BM BVaU LC OTMC QMM

SMOKY DAYS. New York, Crowell, 1901. [AmCat

WALTER GIBBS, THE YOUNG BOSS; AND OTHER STORIES. A Book for Boys. Toronto, Briggs, 1896. 361p [BM BVa OOP QMM

**Thorold, William James, 1871–**

NEAR THE THRONE. New York, Meyer, 1899. 289p [LC

ZEROLA OF NAZARETH. By Louie Barron [pseud]. Toronto, Musson, 1895. 160p [BM OOP

**Tibbits, Ethel Caswell (Burnett), 1890–**

ON TO THE SUNSET. Toronto, Ryerson, 1953. 155p

**Tiller, Stanley C., 1902–**

STORMSWEPT. Toronto, Ryerson, 1950. 213p [BVaU NBFU OTMC

**Todd, Robert Henry, 1877–**

THE SOLVER OF MYSTERIES AND OTHER STORIES. Brampton, Charters, 1930. 292p [NBFU OTMC

**Tomkinson, Grace (Avard), 1890–**

THE CAPE AND THE RIVER. London, Johnson, 1947. 256p [Same as HER OWN PEOPLE, *q.v.*] [BM OWtU

HER OWN PEOPLE. A Novel. New York, Ives Washburn, 1945. 248p [Pub. in England as: THE CAPE AND THE RIVER, 1947.] [BVaU LC NBFU OTMC

WELCOME WILDERNESS. New York, Ives Washburn, 1946. 289p [BM BVaU NBFU OTU

**Toronto, Ont. Writers' Club**

... FICTION. Toronto, 1936. 48p [Selected from 300 mss submitted in a national competition.] [OTP

**Tovell, Ruth (Massey), 1889–**

THE CRIME IN THE BOULEVARD RASPAIL. By Ruth Massey. Edinburgh, Nelson, 1932. 318p [Also as: DEATH IN THE WIND. ... New York, Nelson, 1932.] [AEU BM CBI CC

**Townley, Alice Ashworth**

OPINIONS OF MARY. Toronto, Briggs, 1909. 229p [BM BVaU OTMC

**Traill, Catharine Parr (Strickland), 1802–1899**

ADVENTURES OF LITTLE DOWNY; THE FIELD MOUSE; and THE LITTLE PRINCESS, or Passion and Patience. By Miss Strickland. New ed. London, Dean, 1844.

78p [Attributed to Mrs. Traill by Agnes Fitzgibbon in sketch prefaced to Mrs. Traill's PEARLS AND PEBBLES.] [BM

AFAR IN THE FOREST; or, Pictures of Life and Scenery in the Wilds of Canada. London, Nelson, 1869. 207p [Various editions. Also pub. under titles: LADY MARY AND HER NURSE; LITTLE MARY AND HER NURSE; STORIES OF THE CANADIAN FOREST –OTP] [BM BVaU OKQ

THE CANADIAN CRUSOES. A Tale of the Rice Lake Plains. Ed. by Agnes Strickland. London, Hall, 1850. 368p [Also: Toronto, McClelland, 1923. 322p Other editions have title: LOST IN THE BACKWOODS. London, Nelson, 1882. Etc.] [BM BVaU NSHD OLU QMM

COT AND CRADLE STORIES. Ed. by Mary Agnes Fitzgibbon. ... Toronto, Briggs, 1895. 239p [BM BVaU LC MWU NBFU OKQ

IN THE FOREST; or, Pictures of Life and Scenery in the Woods of Canada. London, Nelson, 1886. 188p [See AFAR IN THE FOREST.] [BVaU NBFU QMBM

LADY MARY AND HER NURSE; or, A Peep into the Canadian Forest. London, Hall, 1856. 204p [See AFAR IN THE FOREST.] [BM OTU QMSS

LOST IN THE BACKWOODS. A Tale of the Canadian Forest. London, Nelson, 1882. 319p [See THE CANADIAN CRUSOES.] [BM BVaU NSHD QMM

PREJUDICE REPROVED; or, The History of the Negro Toy-Seller. By the Author of the "Tell-Tale" [i.e., Agnes Strickland], "Reformation" [i.e., Catharine P. Strickland], "Disobedience" [i.e., Elizabeth Strickland], "Early Lessons," etc. London, Harvey and Darton, 1826. 86p [BM

REFORMATION; or, The Cousin. London, 1819. [BM

STORIES OF THE CANADIAN FOREST; or, Little Mary and her Nurse. Boston, Crosby & Nichols, 1861. 240p [See also AFAR IN THE FOREST.] [BVaU NBFU OTP QMM

**Treleaven, Emma**

PEACE AT THE LAST. Ilfracombe, Devon, Stockwell, 1958. 287p

**Tremblay, Jean Jacques, 1926–**

TEN CANADIAN LEGENDS. Fredericton, Brunswick Press, 1955. 32p

**Trill, Matthew, 1887–**

GOOD KING WENCESLAS. A Tale of Old Gods and New Inspired by the Ancient Carol. By Hew Trill. Montreal, Ronalds, 1934. 21p [BVaU NBFU QMM

THE STRANGER WITHIN. New York, Stokes, 1935. 319p [BM LC NBFU OTMC

**Trueman, Stuart, 1911–**

COUSIN ELVA. Toronto, McClelland, 1955. 224p

**Tsyr, Paul**

G. DWYER, K.W. A Novel. Montreal, Lovell, 1895. 250p [NSHD OTP

**Tuck, Clyde Edwin**

THE BALD KNOBBERS. Indianapolis, Bowen, 1910. 325p [LC

FOR LOVE OF YOU. Indianapolis, Bowen, 1909. 87p [LC

**Tuckwell, Ronald Wesley, 1889–**

PHIL. ACTON'S PROMISE. London, Stockwell, 1932. 95p [BM

THE WINSTONE WAY ( AND OTHER STORIES OF WINSTONE SCHOOL). Ilfracombe, Devon, Stockwell, 1960. 128p

**Tupper, Kathryn (Munro)**

WHISKERS IN LILACTOWN. By Kathryn Munro. Kentville, N.S., Kentville Pub. Co., 1934. 61p [BVaU NBFU OTMC

**Tyrrell, Mary Edith (Carey), 1870? –1945**

FURRY AND FLUFFY. The Story My Children Loved Best. Toronto, Ryerson, 1946. 16p [OTU

**Uren, Alfred Ernest, 1881–**

BOB AND BILL GO FARMING. Toronto, Bob and Bill Pubs., 1935. 80p [CAR

**Urtica, R. (pseud)**

THE STORY OF JOHN AND JONATHAN. Ottawa, Bell, 1871. 28p [OKQ

**Vaczek, Louis Charles, 1913–**

THE FRIGHTENED DOVE. By Peter Hardin [pseud]. New York, Scribner, 1951. 192p

THE GOLDEN CALF. New York, Sloane, 1956. 317p

THE HIDDEN GRAVE. By Peter Hardin [pseud]. New York, Dell, 1955. 188p

RIVER AND EMPTY SEA. A Novel. Boston, Houghton, 1950. 372p [BM BVaU LC NBFU OTMC

**Van Der Mark, Christine, 1917–**

IN DUE SEASON. Toronto, Oxford U. Press, 1947. 363p [BVaU LC NBFU OTMC QMM

**Van Vogt, Alfred Elton, 1912–**

AWAY AND BEYOND. New York, Pellegrini, 1952. 300p

THE BOOK OF PTATH. ... Reading, Pa., Fantasy Press, 1947. 227p [LC

DESTINATION: UNIVERSE! New York, Pellegrini, 1952. 295p

THE HOUSE THAT STOOD STILL. New York, Greenberg, 1950. 210p [BM LC OONL

MASTERS OF TIME. Reading, Pa., Fantasy Press, 1950. 227p [LC NBFU OTMC

THE MIND CAGE. A Science-Fiction Novel. New York, Simon & Schuster, 1957. 190p

THE MIXED MEN. New York, Gnome Press, 1952. 223p

OUT OF THE UNKNOWN. Los Angeles, Fantasy Pub. Co., 1948. 141p [LC NBFU
SLAN. Sauk City, Wis., Arkham House, 1946. 216p [BM LC OONL
THE WEAPON MAKERS. Providence, R.I., Hadley, 1947. 224p [BM LC
THE WEAPON SHOPS OF ISHER. New York, Greenberg, 1952. 220p
THE VOYAGE OF THE SPACE BEAGLE. New York, Simon & Schuster, 1950. 240p [Reprinted as: MISSION: INTERPLANETARY. New York, New American Library (Signet Books), 1952. 174p] [BM LC OONL
THE WAR AGAINST THE RULL. New York, Simon & Schuster, 1959. 244p
THE WORLD OF Ā. New York, Simon & Schuster, 1948. 246p [LC NBFU OTMC

**Vaughan, Leslie**
CHARLIE OGILBIE. A Romance of Scotland and New Brunswick. Toronto, Bryce, 1889. 158p [NSHD OTU

**Verral, Charles Spain, 1904–**
CAPTAIN OF THE ICE. New York, Crowell, 1953. 151p
THE CASE OF THE MISSING MESSAGE. New York, Golden Press, 1959. 188p
CHAMPION OF THE COURT. New York, Crowell, 1954. 192p
HIGH DANGER. New York, Sterling Pub. Co., 1955. 192p
THE KING OF THE DIAMOND. New York, Crowell, 1955. 179p
RIN TIN TIN AND THE HIDDEN TREASURE. Authorized ed. New York, Simon & Schuster, 1958. 28p
THE WINNING QUARTERBACK. New York, Crowell, 1960. 248p

**Vial, Alexia Agnes**
GRIM TRUTH. A Short Story. Montreal, Lovell, 1890. 37p [NSHD OTP QMM

**Waagen, Mary Elizabeth (Hickson)**
THE CALL OF GOD. By Mary Elizabeth Hickson. Montreal, Author, 1911. [CAR
MADAME JANVIER'S CHURCH. By Mary Elizabeth Hickson. Toronto, Musson, [1911?]. 70p [BM BVaU NBFU OTMC QMBM
THE WAYSIDE CROSS. Toronto, Musson, 1924. 136p [BVaU NBFU OTP QMM

**Waitt, Georgina Seymour**
THREE GIRLS UNDER CANVAS. Victoria, "In Black and White," 1900. 154p [BVaU OTMC

**Wakeham, Pius Joseph, 1910–**
A BOOK OF NEWFOUNDLAND STORIES. St. John's, Long Bros., 1955. 258p
ISLAND ROMANCE. St. John's, Dicks & Co., 1959. 325p
MUTINY AT MIDNIGHT. A Thrilling Adventure Story. St. John's, Long Bros., 1951. 233p

THE ROYAL IMPOSTOR. St. John's, Dicks & Co., 1960. 398p
TWENTY NEWFOUNDLAND STORIES. St. John's, Long Bros., 1953. 322p

**Walford, Austin**
CONFESSION OF THE HILLS. Winnipeg, Middle West Pub. Co., 1915. 313p [BM LC OTMC

**Walker, Annie Louisa (Mrs. Henry Coghill), 1836–1907**
AGAINST HER WILL. A Novel. London, Tinsley, 1877. 3v [BM
A CANADIAN HEROINE. By the Author of LEAVES FROM THE BACKWOODS. London, Tinsley, 1873. 3v [OKQ
HOLLYWOOD. London, Tinsley, 1875. 3v [BM
LADY'S HOLM. A Novel. London, Tinsley, 1878. 3v [BM
TRIAL OF MARY BROOM. By Mrs. Coghill. London, Hutchinson, 1894. 149p [BM
TWO RIVAL LOVERS. A Novel. London, White, 1881. 3v [BM

**Walker, David Harry, 1911–**
DIGBY. A Novel. London, Collins, 1953. 254p
GEORDIE. Boston, Houghton, 1950. 209p [BM LC NBFU OTMC
HARRY BLACK. A Novel. London, Collins, 1956. 320p
THE PILLAR. Boston, Houghton, 1952. 313p [Also pub. as THE WIRE. Garden City, N.Y., Permabooks, 1953. 382p]
SANDY WAS A SOLDIER'S BOY. London, Collins, 1957. 159p
THE STORM AND THE SILENCE. Boston, Houghton, 1949. 248p [BM BVaU LC OTMC
WHERE THE HIGH WINDS BLOW. Boston, Houghton, 1960. 536p

**Walker, Ella May (Jacoby), 1892–1960**
FORTRESS NORTH. Toronto, Allen, 1947. 419p [2nd ed., rev.: Montreal, Renouf, 1956. xi + 423p] [BVaU NBFU OTMC QMBM

**Walker, Joan (Suter)**
REPENT AT LEISURE. Toronto, Ryerson, 1957. 284p

**Walker, Major Benson**
ON DOWN THE ROAD. Ottawa, Graphic, 1928. 253p [BVaU NBFU OTMC
SCOTTIE. The True Story of a Dog. Ottawa, Graphic, 1927. 176p [NBFU OTMC
"SKIPPER." The Story of a Dog. New York, Crowell, 1930. 238p [LC

**Walker, Rev. William Wesley, 1858–1945**
ALTER EGO. A Tale. Toronto, Briggs, 1907. 69p [BM BVaU NSHD OTMC QMBM
OCCIDENT AND ORIENT. A Tale. Toronto, Briggs, 1905. 113p [BM BVaU NSHD OTMC

**Wallace, Rev. Archer, 1884–1958**
ADVENTURES IN THE AIR. Toronto, Ryerson, 1932. 117p [BM QMSS

THE FIELD OF HONOR. Toronto, Ryerson, 1949. 157p [LC OTMC

ONE HUNDRED STORIES FOR BOYS. Nashville, Abingdon-Cokesbury, 1947. 171p [Also: Toronto, Ryerson, 1947. 264p] [BVaU LC OTMC

**Wallace, Frederick William, 1886–1958**

BLUE WATER. A Tale of the Deep Sea Fishermen. Toronto, Musson, 1907. 303p [Also: Toronto, Musson, 1935. 322p] [BM BVaU NBFU OTU

CAPTAIN SALVATION. Toronto, Musson, 1925. 397p [BM BVaU NSHD OTU QMM

SALT SEAS AND SAILORMEN. Toronto, Hodder, 1922. 288p [BM BVaU NBFU OKQ

THE SHACK-LOCKER. Yarns of the Deep Sea Fishing Fleets. Toronto, Hodder, 1916. 303p [BM BVaU NSHD OKQ QMM

TEA FROM CHINA, and Other Yarns of the Sea. Toronto, Musson, 1926. 326p [BM BVaU LC NSHD OTMC QMM

THE VIKING BLOOD. A Story of Seafaring. Toronto, Musson, 1920. 407p [BM BVaU NBFU OTU

**Wallace, Rev. Michael A., –1892**

WELL! WELL! A Tale Founded on Fact. New York, Sadlier, 1863. 312p [An earlier ed.: New York, Sadlier, 1856. —AmCat] [LC OOP

**Wallace, Paul Anthony Wilson, 1891–**

BAPTISTE LAROCQUE. Legends of French-Canada. Toronto, Musson, 1923. 129p [BM BVaU NSHD OTMC QMM

SELECTIONS FROM SAM SLICK (JUDGE HALIBURTON). Ed. by ——. Toronto, Ryerson, 1923. 150p [BM BVaU OTU QMM

THE TWIST AND OTHER STORIES. Toronto, Ryerson, 1923. 167p [BM BVaU NSHD OTP

THE WHITE ROOTS OF PEACE. [Indian Legends.] Philadelphia, U. of Penn. Press, 1946. 57p [BM BVa LC OTU QMM

**Wallis, Mrs. Ella Bell**

THE EXQUISITE GIFT. Ottawa, Ariston, 1930. 249p [BVaU NSHD OTP QMM

**Walsh, Henry Cecil**

BONHOMME. French-Canadian Stories and Sketches. Toronto, Briggs, 1899. 252p [BM BVaU NBFU OTP QMM

**Walsh, Leo P.**

THE SINFUL TOWN. A Novel. New York, Exposition Press, 1948. 208p [LC

**Walsh, William Emmett, 1868–**

THE DOOM OF CONAIRE-MOR (CONARY THE GREAT). New York, Carrier, 1929. 346p [LC NBFU OTMC

**Walshe, Elizabeth Hely, 1835? –1869**

CEDAR CREEK. From the Shanty to the Settlement. [Anon] London, Religious

Tract Soc., 1863. 269p [Later eds. under titles: CEDAR CREEK. A Tale of Canadian Life. London, R.T.S., 1902. 384p and KINGSTON'S REVENGE. ... London, R.T.S., 1917. 320p] [BM BVaU NBFU OTMC OTU

THE FOSTER BROTHERS OF DOON. A Tale of [the Irish Rebellion of] 1798. [Anon] London, Religious Tract Soc., 1866. [Later ed.: London, R.T.S., 1906. 382p] [BM OTMC

GOLDEN HILLS; A Tale of the Irish Famine. By the Author of "Cedar Creek." London, Religious Tract Soc., 1865. 272p [BM

KINGSTON'S REVENGE. ... See above under CEDAR CREEK.

THE MANUSCRIPT MAN; or, The Bible in Ireland. London, Religious Tract Soc., 1869. [BM

WITHIN SEA WALLS; or, How the Dutch Kept the Faith. By Elizabeth H. Walshe and George Etell Sargent. London, Religious Tract Soc., 1880. 378p [Also: Boston, Bradley, 1881. 378p] [BM BVaU LC

UNDER THE INQUISITION. Story of the Inquisition in Italy. London, Religious Tract Soc., 1904. 348p [BM

**Walters, Harry Macdonald**

WESBLOCK. The Autobiography of an Automaton. Toronto, Dent, 1914. 172p [BM BVaU OTMC

**Ward, James Edward, 1883–1958**

THE WAYFARER. Leaves from a Wanderer's Log. Toronto, Macmillan, 1922. 231p [BM BVaU LC NBFU OTMC QMM

**Warman, Cy, 1855–1914**

THE EXPRESS MESSENGER, and Other Tales of the Rail. New York, Scribner, 1897. 238p [BM BVa LC OTMC

FRONTIER STORIES. New York, Scribner, 1898. 246p [LC OTMC

THE LAST SPIKE, and Other Railroad Stories. New York, Scribner, 1906. 286p [BVaU LC NBFU OTMC

SHORT RAILS. New York, Scribner, 1900. 310p [BVaU LC

SNOW ON THE HEADLIGHT. A Story of the Great Burlington Strike. New York, Appleton, 1899. 248p [LC OTMC

TALES OF AN ENGINEER, with Rhymes of the Rail. New York, 1895. 242p [BVaU LC OLU

WEIGA OF TEMAGAMI, and Other Indian Tales. Toronto, McLeod & Allen, 1908. 206p [BM BVaU LC NSHD OTP QMM

THE WHITE MAIL. New York, Scribner, 1899. 197p [BVa LC QMM

**Warnock, Amelia Beers (Mrs. John Garvin), 1878–1956**

LEGENDS OF THE ST. LAWRENCE. Retold by Katherine Hale [pseud]. Montreal, Canadian Pacific Railway, 1926. 47p [BVaU NBFU OTMC

**Warren, Mrs. Sara Evangeline Matheson**

ANDY THE MILKMAN. Ilfracombe, Devon, Stockwell, 1957. 128p

**Warwick, Joseph, 1892–**

ANNA OF THE TROUBLED VALLEY. A Tale of Rural Life. Winnipeg, North Star Pub. Co., [1923]. 174p [ACG

**Watson, Muriel F.**

FIREWEED. Toronto, Hodder, 1924. 315p [BM BVaU NBFU OTMC

**Watson, Robert, 1882–1948**

A BOY OF THE GREAT NORTH-WEST. Ottawa, Graphic, 1930. 259p [BVaU LC NBFU OTMC QMSS

THE GIRL OF O.K. VALLEY. A Romance of the Okanagan. Toronto, McClelland, 1919. 297p [BVaU LC NBFU OTMC

GORDON OF THE LOST LAGOON. A Romance of the Pacific Coast. Toronto, Allen, 1924. 271p [BM BVaU LC NBFU OTP

HIGH HAZARD. A Romance of the Far Arctic. Montreal, Carrier, 1929. 346p [BM BVaU LC NBFU OTMC QMM

ME AND PETER. Toronto, Allen, 1926. 248p [BM NBFU OTMC

MY BRAVE AND GALLANT GENTLEMAN. A Romance of British Columbia. Toronto, McClelland, 1918. 339p [BM BVaU LC NBFU OTMC

THE SPOILERS OF THE VALLEY. New York, Doran, 1921. 395p [BM BVaU LC NBFU OTMC

STRONGER THAN HIS SEA. Toronto, McClelland, 1920. 307p [BM BVaU LC NBFU OTMC

WHEN CHRISTMAS CAME TO FORT GARRY. A Romance of the Early Red River Days. Toronto, Ryerson, 1935. 35p [BVaU NBFU OTMC

**Watson, Samuel James, 1837–1881**

THE PEACE KILLER; or, The Massacre of Lachine. Toronto, 1870. 30p [BCF NSWA QMSS

**Watson, Mrs. Sheila, 1919–**

THE DOUBLE HOOK. Toronto, McClelland, 1959. 127p

**Weatherby, Hugh Wallace, 1908–**

FIR FOREST FUN. Toronto, Ryerson, 1947. 132p [BVa OTMC

HOW THE FIR FOREST WAS SAVED. Victoria, British Columbia Forest Service, 1949. 54p [AEU OTMC

TALES THE TOTEMS TELL. Toronto, Macmillan, 1944, 96p [Also: Toronto, Macmillan, 1951. x + 96p] [BVaU LC OTP

TEDDY, DAPPY AND JOE. Toronto, Ryerson, 1948. 75p [OTMC

**Weaver, Emily Poynton, 1865–1943**

MY LADY NELL. An English Story of the Olden Time. London, Warne, 1890. 312p [Also: Boston, Congregational Church Pub. House, 1889. —AmCat] [BM

THE ONLY GIRL. A Tale of 1837. Toronto, Macmillan, 1925. 298p [OTP

PRINCE RUPERT'S NAME-SAKE; or, After the Restoration. Edinburgh, Oliphant,

1894. 394p [Also: Boston, Congregational Church Pub. House, 1893 —AmCat] [BM

THE RABBI'S SONS. A Story of the Days of St. Paul. London, Kelly, 1891. 270p [Also: Boston, Congregational Church Pub. House, 1891. —AmCat] [BM

THE RAINPROOF INVENTION. Boston, Congregational Sunday-School & Pub. Soc., 1897. 414p [LC

THE SEARCH FOR MOLLY MARLING. Toronto, Musson, [1903?]. 224p [BM NBFU

SOLDIERS OF LIBERTY. A Story of Wars in the Netherlands. Toronto, Briggs, 1892. 128p [BM OTU

THE TROUBLE MAN; or, The Wards of St. James. Toronto, Musson, [1911?]. 315p [BM BVaU NBFU OTMC

**Weaver, Robert Leigh, 1921–**

CANADIAN SHORT STORIES. Ed. by Robert Weaver and Helen James. Toronto, Oxford U. Press, 1952. 248p

CANADIAN SHORT STORIES. Selected and with an intro. by ——. London, Toronto, Oxford U. Press, 1960. xiii + 420p [Different selections from preceding title]

**Webber, Franklyn Millard, 1900–**

CODE OF THE RANGELAND. Edmonton, Author, 1959. 236p [mimeographed]

TWENTY PEBBLES AND OTHER STORIES. New York, Pageant Press, 1955. 89p

**Webber, William Lester, 1882–**

THE THUNDERBIRD "TOOTOOCH" LEGENDS. Folk Tales of the Indian Tribes of the Pacific Northwest. Seattle, Ace Print., 1936. xxi + 38p [Rev. ed., Vancouver, Author, 1952. 65p] [AEU LC OTMC

**Webling, Lucy**

ONE WAY STREET. A Novel. By Lucy Betty McRaye. London, Hutchinson, 1933. 286p [BM

CENTRE STAGE. By Lucy Betty McRaye. London, Hutchinson, 1938. 256p [BM

**Webling, Peggy**

THE AMBER MERCHANT. London, Hutchinson, 1925. 288p [BM

ANNA MARIA. London, Hutchinson, 1927. 284p [BM

ASPIDISTRA'S CAREER. London, Hutchinson, 1936. 320p [BM

BLUE JAY. New York, Reynolds, 1905. 378p [BM LC

BOUNDARY HOUSE. London, Hutchinson, 1916. 324p [BM LC OTMC

COMEDY CORNER. London, Hutchinson, 1920. 288p [BM

EDGAR CHIRRUP. New York, Putnam, 1915. 362p [BM LC OTMC

FELIX CHRISTIE. London, Methuen, 1912. 345p [BM

THE FRUITLESS ORCHARD. London, Hutchinson, 1922. 288p [BM

IN OUR STREET. London, Hutchinson, 1918. 256p [BM LC

THE LIFE OF ISOBEL ERNE. London, Hutchinson, 1922. 294p [BM OTMC

OPAL SCREENS. London, Hutchinson, 1937. 288p [BM

THE PEARL STRINGER. London, Methuen, 1913. 318p [BM
THE SCENT SHOP. London, Hutchinson, 1919. 288p [BM
A SPIRIT OF MIRTH. London, Methuen, 1910. 312p [BM LC
THE STORY OF VIRGINIA PERFECT. London, Methuen, 1909. 316p [BM
STRANGE ENCHANTMENT. London, Hutchinson, 1932. 288p [BM
VIRGINIA PERFECT. London, Methuen, 1911. 224p [*Cf.* THE STORY OF VIRGINIA PERFECT, 1909.] [EngCat
YOUNG LAETITIA. London, Hutchinson, 1939. 288p [BM

**Weekes, Mrs. Mary Loretto, 1885–**
ACADIAN BETRAYAL. Toronto, Burns & MacEachern, 1955. 301p
PAINTED ARROWS. New York, Nelson, 1941. 262p [Same title: Regina, School Aids & Text Book Pub. Co., 1949. 148p. — OOP] [BVa LC NBFU OTU
ROUND THE COUNCIL FIRES. Toronto, Ryerson, 1935. 113p [BVaU NBFU OTMC
THE SILVER PELT. London, Blackie, 1960. 174p

**Wees, Frances Shelley (Johnson), 1902–**
THE COUNTRY OF THE STRANGERS. Garden City, N.Y., Doubleday, 1960. 235p
DETECTIVES LTD. London, Eyre & Spottiswoode, 1933. 287p [First pub. as THE MAESTRO MURDERS, *q.v.*] [BM LC NBFU OOP
HONEYMOON MOUNTAIN. Philadelphia, Macrae Smith, 1934. 318p [LC OTMC
IT BEGAN IN EDEN. Philadelphia, Macrae Smith, 1936. 285p [BM LC NBFU OTU
THE KEYS OF MY PRISON. London, Jenkins, 1956. 190p
LOST HOUSE. Philadelphia, Macrae Smith, 1938. 285p [BM LC NBFU
THE MAESTRO MURDERS. New York, Mystery League, 1931. 286p [Pub. in England as DETECTIVES LTD., *q.v.*] [BM LC NBFU
MELODY UNHEARD. Philadelphia, Macrae Smith, 1950. 253p [BM LC NBFU OTMC
M'LORD, I AM NOT GUILTY. London, Jenkins, 1954. 192p
THE MYSTERY OF THE CREEPING MAN. Philadelphia, Macrae Smith, 1931. 330p [BM LC NBFU OTMC
ROMANCE ISLAND. Philadelphia, Macrae Smith, 1933. 296p [BM LC
SOMEONE CALLED MAGGIE LANE. Philadelphia, Macrae Smith, 1947. 244p [BM LC
A STAR FOR SUSAN. Philadelphia, Macrae Smith, 1940. 254p [BM LC OTMC
THIS NECESSARY MURDER. London, Jenkins, 1957. 190p
UNDER THE QUIET WATER. Philadelphia, Macrae Smith, 1949. 256p [BM LC NBFU OTMC
UNTRAVELLED WORLD. London, Eyre & Spottiswoode, 1936. 375p [BM OLU
WHERE IS JENNY NOW? London, Jenkins, 1958. 192p

**Weller, Mrs. Evelyn L.**
CARDINAL ROAD. Toronto, Burns & MacEachern, 1955. 254p

WINGS OF THE SPIRIT. Toronto, Musson, 1921. 244p [BM BVaU NBFU OTU QMSS

**Wemyss, Prof., F.R.S.A.**

THE HEATHER PRINCE; or, Scotland for Ever. Brockville, n.p., n.d. 50p [OOP

**Weston, Garnett James, 1890–**

CITIZENS—TO ARMS! London, Cassell, 1943. 287p [English title of THE MAN WITH THE MONOCLE.] [BM

DEAD MEN ARE DANGEROUS. New York, Stokes, 1937. 310p [BM LC NBFU OTMC

DEATH NEVER FORGETS. London, Hutchinson, 1935. 288p [BM

THE HIDDEN PORTAL. New York, Doubleday, 1946. 284p [LC NBFU OTMC

LEGACY OF FEAR. New York, Mill & Morrow, 1950. 245p [BM BViPA LC NBFU OONL

THE MAN WITH THE MONOCLE. New York, Doubleday, 1943. 245p [LC NBFU OTMC

MURDER IN HASTE. New York, Stokes, 1935. 310p [LC

MURDER ON SHADOW ISLAND. New York, Farrar & Rinehart, 1933. 309p [BM LC NBFU

POLDRATE STREET. New York, Messner, 1944. 256p [LC NBFU

THE UNDERTAKER DIES. London, Methuen, 1940. 288p [BM

**Wetherald, Agnes Ethelwyn, 1857 1940**

AN ALGONQUIN MAIDEN. A Romance of the Early Days of Upper Canada. By G. Mercer Adam and A. Ethelwyn Wetherald. Montreal, Lovell, 1887. 240p [BM BVaU LC NBFU OTU QMM

**Wherry, Edith Margaret**

JADE MOUNTAIN. London, Hutchinson, 1926. 268p [BM LC QMM

THE RED LANTERN. Being the Story of the Goddess of the Red Lantern Light. New York, Lane, 1911. 306p [BM LC OTMC QMM

THE WANDERER ON A THOUSAND HILLS. New York, Lane, 1917. 305p [BM LC QMM

**White, Samuel Alexander, 1885–1956**

AMBUSH. New York, Doubleday, 1920. 244p [BVa LC NBFU OTU

CALLED NORTHWEST. New York, Phoenix, 1943. 256p [LC OTU

THE CODE OF THE NORTHWEST. New York, Phoenix, 1940. 255p [BM BViPA LC NBFU OTU

EMPERY. A Story of Love and Battle in Rupert's Land. Toronto, Musson, 1913. 332p [Same as: LAW OF THE NORTH. A Story of Love and Battle in Rupert's Land. New York, Grosset, 1913. 332p] [BVaU LC NBFU OTU QMM

FLAMING FUR LANDS. Toronto, Ryerson, 1948. 153p [BVaU NBFU OTU QMBM

THE FOAMING FORE SHORE. New York, Doubleday, 1920. 248p [LC NBFU OTU

LAW OF THE NORTH. [See EMPERY, above.]
MAN SCENT. New York, Scribner, 1936. 286p [BM LC NBFU OTU
MORGAN OF THE MOUNTED. New York, Phoenix, 1939. 258p [BM LC NBFU OTU
NIGHTHAWK OF THE NORTHWEST. New York, Phoenix, 1938. 256p [BM LC OTU
NORTH OF THE BORDER. New York, Phoenix, 1940. 256p [BM LC NBFU OTU
NORTH OF THE LAW. New York, Doubleday, 1920. 250p [LC NBFU OTU
NORTH WEST CROSSING. New York, Phoenix, 1944. 256p [BM LC NBFU OTU
NORTHWEST LAW. New York, Phoenix, 1942. 256p [BViPA LC OTU
NORTHWEST PATROL. New York, Phoenix, 1943. 254p [BM LC OTU
NORTHWEST RAIDERS. New York, Phoenix, 1945. 256p [BM LC OTU
NORTHWEST WAGONS. New York, Phoenix, 1941. 254p [BM LC NBFU OTU
THE STAMPEDER. Toronto, Briggs, 1910. 275p [BM BVaU NBFU OTU
THE WILDCATTERS. A Tale of Cobalt. Toronto, Briggs, 1912. 219p [BM BVaU NBFU OTU
THE WONDERSTRANDS. Garden City, N.Y., Garden City Pub. Co., 1924. 120p [AEU BM OTU

**Whitehouse, Francis Cecil, 1879–**

PLAIN FOLKS. A Story of the Canadian Prairies. Ottawa, Graphic, 1926. 301p [BVaU NSHD OTP QMM

**Whitell, Evelyn**

THE BUILDER'S CROWN OF JEWELS. Los Angeles, Master Press, 1925. 142p [LC
A CALIFORNIA POPPY. The Story of a Child Healer. 4th ed. Los Angeles, Master Press, 1925. 33p [BViPA
CANADIAN TIM. Vancouver, Author, n.d. 101p [BViPA
EXTRAORDINARY MARY. Los Angeles, Master Mind Pub. Co., 1920. 72p [LC
THE GOLDEN AGE FAIRY TALES. Vancouver, Vancouver Bindery Ltd., 1942. 195p [BVaU
THE HEALING OF THE HAWAIIAN. A Story of the Hawaiian Islands. Los Angeles, Master Press, 1923. 155p [LC
THE LIGHT OF GAMBIER ISLAND. London, The Rally, n.d. 45p [BVaU
SHEKINAH. Los Angeles, De Vorss, 1937. 342p [LC NBSU
THE WOMAN HEALER. Los Angeles, Master Mind Pub. Co., 1920. 88p [BViPA LC

**Wild, Roland Gibson, 1903–**

NINE O'CLOCK GUN. London, Cassell, 1952. 223p

**Wilkinson, Anne Cochran (Boyd), 1910–1961**

SWANN & DAPHNE. Toronto, Oxford U. Press, 1960. 47p

**Williams, Charles R., –1859?**

THE RIVAL FAMILIES; or, Virtue and Vice, and THE STOLEN JEWELS; or, The Matchmaking Mamma. Cobourg, 1858. 147p [BibC

**Williams, Flos (Jewell), 1893–**

BROKEN GODS. Ottawa, Graphic, 1930. 304p [BVaU NBFU OTMC QMM

FOLD HOME. Toronto, Ryerson, 1950. 265p [NBFU OTMC

THE JUDGMENT OF SOLOMON. Toronto, Musson, 1925. 315p [BM BVaU LC NBFU OTMC

NEW FURROWS. A Story of the Alberta Foothills. Ottawa, Graphic, 1926. 303p [BVaU NBFU OTMC QMM

**Williams, Frances de Wolfe (Fenwick)**

THE ARCH-SATIRIST. Boston, Lothrop, 1910. 358p [LC NSHD OOP

A SOUL ON FIRE. New York, Lane, 1915. 316p [Pub. in England as THEODORA. A Soul on Fire. London, Lane, 1915.] [BM LC NSHD OOP QMM

VIKING'S REST. A Story of the Land of Evangeline. ... Toronto, Goodchild, 1924. 301p [BM BVaU LC NSHD OTMC QMSS

**Williams, Murray Edmund, 1877–1930**

GOLDEN DIVIDENDS. Toronto, McClelland, 1927. 411p [BVaU NBFU OTMC QMM

**Williamson, John, –1840**

THE NARRATIVE OF A COMMUTED PENSIONER. By J.W. Montreal, Starke, 1838. 320p [BVaU NSHD

**Williamson, Owen Templeton Garrett, 1883–**

MIKE MULLINS OF BOSTON CRICK. Toronto, Ryerson, 1953. xiv + 114p

**Willis, Arthur Robert**

NORTH OF THE YUKON. Toronto, Ryerson, 1956. 254p

**Willis, T.K.**

THE LETTERS OF A PRAIRIE DOG. Victoria, Colonist Print. & Pub. Co., 1945. 65p [BViPA

**Willison, Marjory (MacMurchy), –1938**

THE CHILD'S HOUSE. A Comedy of Vanessa from the Age of Eight. By Marjory MacMurchy. Toronto, Macmillan, 1923. 242p [BM BVaU LC NBFU OTU

THE LONGEST WAY ROUND. Toronto, Macmillan, 1937. 325p [BVaU NBFU OTU QMBM

**Willson, (Henry) Beckles, 1869–1942**

DRIFT. 1894. [MOR'98

HAROLD. A Race Experiment. 1891. [MOR'98

THE LOSING OF VIREL. 1892. [MOR'98

REDEMPTION. A Novel. By Beckles Willson. New York, Putnam, 1924. 399p [BM LC OKQ

**Wilson, Anna May**

THE DAYS OF MOHAMMED. Elgin, Cook, 1897. 95p [LC

A STAR IN PRISON. A Tale of Canada. Elgin, Cook, 1898. 96p [BVaU LC OTU

**Wilson, Clifford Parnell, 1902–**

ADVENTURERS ALL. Tales of Forgotten Heroes in New France. Toronto, Macmillan, 1933. 244p [BM BVaU OTMC NBFU QMBM

**Wilson, Cornelius, –1909**

RESCUED IN TIME. A Tale. Toronto, Briggs, 1894. 304p [OLU

**Wilson, Ethel Davis (Bryant), 1890–**

THE EQUATIONS OF LOVE: Tuesday and Wednesday; Lilly's story. Toronto, Macmillan, 1952. 280p

HETTY DORVAL. Toronto, Macmillan, 1947. 116p [BM BVaU NBFU OTU QMM

THE INNOCENT TRAVELLER. Toronto, Macmillan, 1949. 276p [BM BVaU LC NBFU OTP

LILLY'S STORY. New York, Harper, 1952. 208p [First pub. as part of THE EQUATIONS OF LOVE, *q.v.*]

LOVE AND SALT WATER. Toronto, Macmillan, 1956. ix + 202p

SWAMP ANGEL. Toronto, Macmillan, 1954. 215p

**Wilson, Herbert Emerson, 1881–**

GREED. Vancouver, Authors Agency Pub., n.d. 323p [BVaU OTU

**Wilson, Lawrence Maurice, 1896–**

THE CANADIAN MEMBER OF PARLIAMENT. A Satire. Montreal, Momus Press, 1958. 20p

**Wilson, May**

CARMICHAEL. By Anison North [pseud]. London, Ont., Weld, 1907. 338p [Also: New York, Doubleday, 1907. 338p] [BM LC NBFU OTMC

THE FORGING OF THE PIKES. A Romance of the Upper Canadian Rebellion of 1837. By Anison North [pseud]. New York, Doran, 1920. 319p [BM BVaU LC NBFU OTP

**Wilson, Rev. Robert, 1833–1912**

NEVER GIVE UP; or, Life in the Lower Provinces. ... Saint John, "Daily News," 1878. 287p [BVaU NSHD

TRIED BUT TRUE. A Tale. By Mark Mapleton [pseud]. Saint John, "Daily News," 1874. 293p [NSHD OOP

**Winlow, Alice Maud (Dudley), 1885–**

THE MORNIN'-GLORY GIRL. By Alice M. Winlow and Kathryn Pocklington. Toronto, McClelland, 1920. 224p [BVaU NBFU OTU

**Winslow, Elizabeth Bruce R.**

ROSAMONDE OF MONTERRE. A Canadian Pastoral. Boston, Four Seas Co., 1923. 102p [LC NBFU

**Wiseman, Adele, 1928–**

THE SACRIFICE. A Novel. Toronto, Macmillan, 1956. 346p

**Withrow, Rev. William Henry, 1839–1908**

BARBARA HECK. A Tale of Early Methodism in America. Toronto, Methodist Mission Rooms, 1895. 238p [BM BVaU LC NSHD OTP

THE KING'S MESSENGER; or, Lawrence Temple's Probation. A Story of Canadian Life. Toronto, Methodist Book, 1879. 232p [Several later editions.] [BM BVaU NBFU OTP

LIFE IN A PARSONAGE; or, Lights and Shadows of the Itinerancy. London, Woolmer, 1885. 160p [Also: Toronto, Briggs, 1886. 214p] [BM BVaU OTP

NEVILLE TRUEMAN, THE PIONEER PREACHER. A Tale of the War of 1812. Toronto, Briggs, 1880. 244p [Also as: A VICTORY AND ITS COST; or, Neville Trueman, the Pioneer Preacher. ... London, Wesleyan Methodist Sunday School Union, 1893. 224p] [BM BVaU LC NBFU OTU QMM

VALERIA. A Tale of Early Christian Life in Rome. Toronto, Briggs, 1882. 243p [BM BVaU NBFU OTU QMM

A VICTORY AND ITS COST. ... [See under NEVILLE TRUEMAN. ...]

**Wodson, Harry Milner, 1874–1952**

THE LAD FELIX. A Tragedy of *Ne Temere.* By Henry Milner [pseud]. Toronto, Briggs, 1912. 302p [BM OTP

**Wood, Edgar Allardyce, 1907–**

COWBOY YARNS FOR YOUNG FOLK. By Kerry Wood [pseud]. Toronto, Copp Clark, 1951. 137p

THREE MILE BEND. By Kerry Wood [pseud]. Toronto, Ryerson, 1945. 170p [BVa LC NBFU OTU

WILD WINTER. By Kerry Wood [pseud]. Boston, Houghton Mifflin, 1954. 175p

WILLOWDALE. By Kerry Wood [pseud]. Toronto, McClelland, 1956. 216p

**Wood, Esther, 1905–**

BELINDA BLUE. New York, Longmans, 1940. 31p [BM LC

GREAT SWEEPING DAY. New York, Longmans, 1936. 158p [BM LC

THE HOUSE IN THE HOO. New York, Longmans, 1941. 32p [LC

PEDRO'S COCONUT SKATES. New York, Longmans, 1938. 191p [BM LC

PEPPER MOON. New York, Longmans, 1940. 32p [BM LC

SILK AND SATIN LANE. New York, Longmans, 1939. 225p [BM LC

SILVER WIDGEON. New York, Longmans, 1942. 227p [BM LC OOP

**Wood, Ethel M.**

SALVAGE. Victoria, Victoria Pub. Co., 1945. 54p [BViPA OTMC

**Wood, Joanna E., –1919**

A DAUGHTER OF WITCHES. Toronto, Gage, 1900. 342p [BM OTUV

FARDEN HA'. London, Hurst & Blackett, 1901. 340p [BM

JUDITH MOORE; or, Fashioning a Pipe. Toronto, Ontario Pub. Co., 1898. 240p [BM BVaU NBFU OTP QMM

THE LYNCHPIN SENSATION. [MOR'12

A MARTYR TO LOVE. New York, Town Topics, 1903. [AmCat
THE UNTEMPERED WIND. New York, Tait, 1894. 314p [LC OTU
UNTO THE THIRD GENERATION. [MOR'12
WHERE WATERS BECKON. [MOR'12

**Woodley, Rev. Edward Carruthers, 1878–1955**
CANADIAN LEGENDS. Montreal, Northern Electric Co., 1950. 32p [OONL
LEGENDS OF FRENCH CANADA. Toronto, Nelson, 1931. 105p [BM BVaU LC NBFU OTP QMM
UNTOLD TALES OF OLD QUEBEC. Toronto, Dent, 1949. 216p [BVaU NBFU OTP QMM

**Woods, Alexandrina**
LITTLE GRAY DOORS. Springfield, Mass., Bradley, 1926. 120p [LC

**Wreford, Marjorie**
LITTLE WILDING. Toronto, Nelson, 1948. 156p [OTMC

**Wright, James Frederick Church, 1904–**
ALL CLEAR, CANADA! By Jim Wright. Toronto, Copp Clark, 1944. 160p [LC NBFU OTP

**Wrong, Edward Murray, 1889–1928**
CRIME AND DETECTION. Ed. by ——. New York, Oxford U. Press, 1926. 394p [An anthology of stories by famous authors.] [BM LC NBFU OTU QMM

**Yates, Abel**
TRUTH AND FICTION. [Canada?], 1898. 20p [BM
VIOLETS; or, Jasper Luckings. The Kanuck Landlord and California Gardiner. A Tragi-comedy in Four Acts. 1884. 47p [BCF OONL

**Yeigh, Kate (Westlake), 1856–1906**
A SPECIMEN SPINSTER. Toronto, Copp Clark, 1905. 314p [Also: Philadelphia, Griffith & Rowland, 1906.—OTUV] [BM OTU

**York, Eva Rose (Fitch), 1858–**
CHAON ORR. Portions of his Autobiography. Belleville, Sun Print., [1896]. 113p [OTP
THE WHITE LETTER. A Tale of Retribution and Reward. Toronto, Briggs, 1903. 107p [BM BVaU NSHD OTU

**Young, Rev. Egerton Ryerson, 1840–1909**
ALGONQUIN INDIAN TALES. Collected by ——. New York, Eaton & Mains, 1903. 258p [BM BVaU LC OTU
THE BATTLE OF THE BEARS. ... Reminiscences of Life in the Indian Country. London, R. Culley, [1907?]. 318p [ACG BViPA OTUV

CHILDREN OF THE FOREST. A Story of Indian Love. New York, Revell, 1904. 282p [BM LC NBFU OOP

DUCK LAKE. New York, Eaton & Mains, 1905. 191p [BM BVaU LC NBFU OTMC

HECTOR MY DOG. His Autobiography. Boston, Wilde, 1905. 332p [BM LC OTMC

OOWIKAPUN; or, How the Gospel Reached the Nelson River Indians. London, Kelly, 1895. 162p [BM BViPA LC NBFU OTP

STORIES FROM INDIAN WIGWAMS AND NORTHERN CAMP-FIRES. Toronto, Briggs, 1893. 293p [BM BVaU LC NSHD OTU QMM

THREE BOYS IN THE WILD NORTH LAND, SUMMER. New York, Eaton & Mains, 1896. 260p [BM LC OTMC

WINTER ADVENTURES OF THREE BOYS IN THE GREAT LONE LAND. New York, Eaton & Mains, 1899. 377p [BM BVa LC OTMC

**Young, Rev. Egerton Ryerson, 1869–**

THE CAMP DOCTOR, AND OTHER STORIES. London, Religious Tract Soc., n.d. 320p [BM OTUV

JUST DOGS. Philadelphia, Sunday School Times Co., 1926. 151p [LC

THREE ARROWS. New York, Friendship Press, 1932. 183p [BM LC OTMC

WHEN THE BLACKFEET WENT SOUTH AND OTHER STORIES. London, Boy's Own Paper, 1936. 128p [Also: London, Lutterworth Press, 1954. 95p [BM BVaU OTMC

**Young, Katherine A.**

STORIES OF THE MAPLE LAND. Tales of the Early Days of Canada for Children. Toronto, Copp Clark, 1898. 120p [BM BVaU NSHD OTU

**Young, Patricia Lucy, 1922–**

BLACK DAHLIA GIRL. London, Ward Lock, 1958. 191p

THE DEVIL AND HIS APPLE. London, Ward Lock, 1945. 188p [BM

DOCKSIDE SYMPHONY. London, Ward Lock, 1947. 192p [BM

EAST OF BOW BELLS. London, Ward Lock, 1950. 221p [BM NBFU OPAL

FAR FLUNG SEED. London, Ward Lock, 1943. 223p [BM

FOOLS' PENCE. London, Ward Lock, 1946. 192p [BM

THE GALLANT OPPORTUNIST. London, Ward Lock, 1949. 215p [BM

GIPSIES MARSH. London, Ward Lock, 1944. 220p [BM

HALF PAST YESTERDAY. London, Ward Lock, 1959. 187p

HUNGER FOR LOVE. London, Ward Lock, 1952. 191p

IF A MAN LOVE. London, Ward Lock, 1948. 190p [BM

LONDON'S CHILD. London, Ward Lock, 1954. 189p

A MAN AND HIS COUNTRY. London, Ward Lock, 1953. 187p

NARROW STREETS. London, Ward Lock, 1942. 192p [BM

PRIDE OF PRINCES. London, Ward Lock, 1950. 192p [BM

SILENCE IS THE SINNER. London, Ward Lock, 1956. 189p

SPECIAL SHOES. London, Ward Lock, 1948. 207p [BM
A STORY THEY TELL. London, Ward Lock, 1947. 191p [BM
TOMORROW'S DREAMS. London, Ward Lock, 1952. 188p

**Young, Phyllis (Brett)**
PSYCHE. A Novel. Toronto, Longmans, 1959. 319p
THE TORONTONIANS. Toronto, Longmans, 1960. 319p

**Young, Scott, 1918–**
BOY ON DEFENSE. Toronto, McClelland, 1953. 246p
THE FLOOD. Toronto, McClelland, 1956. 222p
SCRUBS ON SKATES. Toronto, McClelland, 1952. 218p

**Yule, Pamelia S. (Vining), 1825?–1897**
ADA EMORY; or, The Sister's Bible. By Mrs. J.C. Yule. Philadelphia, Am. Baptist Pub. Co., [1876?]. [AmCat
UP HILL; or, Paul Sutherland's Progress. By Mrs. J.C. Yule. Philadelphia, Am. Baptist Pub. Co., 1887. 416p [LC

**Zehnder, Meinrad, 1887–**
ANTHONY MARTIN'S FIRST LOVE. A First Love Story of Switzerland. Toronto, Author, 1929. 307p [OTMC QMM
ON BROKEN CRUTCHES. A Psychological Novel. Toronto, Author, 1932. 469p [NBFU OTMC

**Zero (pseud)**
ONE MISTAKE. A Manitoban Reminiscence. By Zero [pseud]. Montreal, Canada Bank Note Co., 1888. 120p [BVaU OLU

# DRAMA

## Stage and radio plays

**Aikins, Charles Carroll Colby, 1888–**

THE GOD OF GODS. A Play in Three Acts. British Columbia, priv. print., 1919. 51p [BM NBFU OTU

**Allan, Adam, 1757–1823**

THE NEW GENTLE SHEPHERD. A Pastoral Comedy Originally Written in the Scotch Dialect, by Allan Ramsay. Reduced to English by Lieutenant Adam Allan. To which is annexed a Description of the Great Falls of the River Saint John. ... London, Richardson, 1798. 75p [LC

**Allan, Marguerite Martha, 1895–1942**

ALL OF A SUMMER'S DAY. [DCB

SUMMER SOLSTICE. A Drama in One Act. By Martha Allan. Toronto, French, 1935. 36p [BM LC OTP

WHAT FOOLS WE MORTALS BE. [DCB

**Allen, Joseph Antisell, 1814–1900**

THE TRUE ROMANTIC LOVE-STORY OF COL. AND MRS. HUTCHINSON. A Drama in Verse. London, Elliot Stock, 1883. 88p [BM BVaU OTU

**Anderson, Clara (Rothwell), –1958**

... .AUNT SOPHIA SPEAKS. [Ottawa, Author, 19—?]. 24p [OH

A CHARACTER SKETCH ENTERTAINMENT, ENTITLED AFTERNOON TEA IN FRIENDLY VILLAGE, 1862. Ottawa, J. Hope, 1912. 40p [BM OONL

A CHARACTER SKETCH ENTERTAINMENT. ... ENTITLED THE YOUNG VILLAGE DOCTOR. Ottawa, J. Hope, 1915. 44p [BM OONL

THE JOGGSVILLE CONVENTION. A Play (for all women). Ottawa, Author, n.d. 36p [AEU

... "LET MARY LOU DO IT." [Ottawa, 19—?]. 40p [OH

... MARRYING ANNE? [Ottawa, 19—?]. 48p [OH

"MARTHA MADE OVER." Ottawa, Pattison, 1923. 48p [AEU

THE MINISTER'S BRIDE. A Character Entertainment for Young People's Societies, Bible Classes, and other Church Organizations. Ottawa, J. Hope, 1913. 38p [AEU BM OONL

AN OLD-TIME LADIES' AID BUSINESS MEETING AT MOHAWK CROSS-ROADS. [A Play]. Ottawa, J. Hope, 1912. 32p [AEU BM OONL

PLAY ENTITLED "THE YOUNG COUNTRY SCHOOLM'AM." Ottawa, J. Hope, 1920. 45p [AEU BM OTU

WANTED, A WIFE. [Ottawa, n.p., 19—?]. 41p [OH

**Anderson, William E.**

A ROMAN DRAMA IN FIVE ACTS ENTITLED LEO AND VENETIA. Pickering, Ont., Pickering Newsprint, 1895. [CAAE

**Anonymous**

DERMOT McMURROUGH. A Drama. [Anon] Toronto, Hunter Rose, 1882. [Bound with THE FIREWORSHIPPERS. A Drama.] [OTP

THE FIREWORSHIPPERS. A Drama. [Anon] Toronto, 1882. [Bound with DERMOT McMURROUGH. A Drama.] [OTP

THE LAND SWAP. A Satire. Montreal, 1875. 79p [OTP OTU

SIR JOHN AND SIR CHARLES; or, The Secrets of the Syndicate. Montreal, a Syndicate, 1881. 8p [BVaU OTP QQL

**Archibald, Edith Jessie (Mortimer), 1854–1938**

THE TOKEN. A Play in Three Acts of the Old Days in Cape Breton. ... Halifax, Royal Print., 1927. 56p [An earlier "suppressed edition" with title THE TOKEN. A Homespun Yarn of Old Cape Breton Days in Three Tangled Skeins. [Ottawa, Graphic], 1926. 66p is held by NSWA.] [BM NSHD OONL

**Armstrong, Louis Olivier, 1874–**

THE BOOK OF THE PLAY OF HIAWATHA, THE MOHAWK. ... [N.p.], 1909. 24p [?An earlier ed.: HIAWATHA; or, Manabozho, or, Ojibway Indian Play. Montreal, Author, 1901.] [BVaU LC

**Ascher, Isidore Gordon, 1835–1914**

CIRCUMSTANCES ALTER CASES. A Comedietta, in One Act. London, French, 1888. 20p [BM

LOVE, MARRIAGE AND HAPPINESS. By Isidore [pseud]. London, Digby & Long, 1894. 96p [BM

**Ascher, Mrs. Isidore Gordon**

PLAYS AND PROSE. London, Elliot Stock, 1929. 100p [BM

**Baker, Ida Emma (Fitch), 1858–1948**

DIALOGUES AND DRAMAS FOR SCHOOL AND HOME. Toronto, 1928. [Dora Hood cat. 84

THE STORY OF CANADA. Toronto, Musson, 1927. 27p [BVaU OONL QMM

**Baker, William King**

GEORGE AND MARGARET FOX. London, Routledge, 1926. 118p [BM NSHD OTU

**Baxter, Arthur Beverley, 1891–1964**

IT HAPPENED IN SEPTEMBER. A Play. London, Hutchinson, 1943. 120p [BM LC

**Bengough, John Wilson, 1851–1923**

THE BREACH OF PROMISE TRIAL BARDELL v PICKWICK. Adapted from *The Pickwick Papers* of Charles Dickens ... as presented by the Dickens Fellowship Company of Players at Toronto, May 9, 10, 15 and 28, 1907. Toronto, [Dickens Fellowship], 1907. 45p [AEU

BUNTHORNE ABROAD; or, the Lass that Loved a Pirate. Original Comic Opera in 2 Acts. Toronto, 1883. 28p [BVaU OONL

**Benson, Nathaniel Anketell Michael, 1903–1966**

THREE PLAYS FOR PATRIOTS. Ottawa, Graphic, 1930. 153p ["The Paths of Glory, 1812"; "The Patriot, 1837"; "The Leather Medal."] [BVaU NBFU OKQ QMM

**Bicknell, Minnie Evans**

RELIEF. A Play in One Act. Toronto, Macmillan, 1938. 28p [MW SRL

**Bidwell, Barnabas, 1763–1833**

THE MERCENARY MATCH. A Tragedy. By Barna [*sic*] Bidwell. New Haven, Meigs Bowen & Dana, [1784?] 57p [Reprinted: New York, McMurtrie, 1925. 57p] [BM LC NBFU

**Birney, Earle, 1904–**

TRIAL OF A CITY, and Other Verse. Toronto, Ryerson, 1952. 71p

**Braden, Bernard, 1916–**

THESE ENGLISH. Toronto, McClelland, 1948. 240p [OTP

**Brewer, George McKenzie, 1889–**

THE HOLY GRAIL. A Whitsuntide Mystery of the Quest of the Soul, Founded on Ancient Legends Derived from Various Sources. ... Montreal, Herald Press, 1933. 50p [BVaU LC OTP QMM

**Brickenden, Catharine (McCormick), 1896–**

A PIG IN A POKE. A Farce Comedy in Three Acts. Toronto, French, 1948. 72p [BVaU OTP

**Brooke, Frances (Moore), 1724–1789**

MARIAN. A Comic Opera in Two Acts. London, Longman, 1800. 31p [BM QMM

ROSINA. A Comic Opera in Two Acts. [Anon] London, Cadell, 1783. 46p [Many later editions.] [BM LC OTU QMM

THE SIEGE OF SINOPE. A Tragedy. London, Cadell, 1781. 71p [BM

VIRGINIA. A Tragedy. With Odes, Pastorals, and Translations. London, Author, 1756. 159p [BM

**Broughall, George, 1861–1927**

THE 90TH ON ACTIVE SERVICE; or, Campaigning in the North West. A Musical and Dramatic Burlesque in Two Acts, with an Introductory, Interlude and Final

Tableau. Written by Staff Sergeant Geo. Broughall. Songs by Major L. Buchan, Chaplain D.M. Gordon [and others]. Winnipeg, G. Bishop, 1885. 42p [Brown U NSWA

THE TEARFUL AND TRAGICAL TALE OF THE TRICKY TROUBADOUR; or, the Truant Tracked. A Topical and Tuneful Tradition Told in Travesty. A Four Act Burlesque. Winnipeg, Manitoba Free Press, 1886. 34p [BViPA

**Buckskin (pseud)**

THE PASSING OF THE BUFFALO. By Buckskin [pseud]. Vancouver, Selkirk, 1916. 47p [BM BVaU LC NSHD OTP SSU

**Bullock-Webster, Llewelyn, 1879–**

THE CURSE OF CHIRRA-POONJE. Victoria, B.C. Dramatic School, 1924. [T&C

HE PASSED THROUGH SAMARIA. A Religious Play in One Act. New York, Fitzgerald, 1932. 27p [BViP LC

REMORSE. A Play in One Act. Rock Island, Ill., Ingram, 1936. 24p [BVaU

THE SHADOW OF THE NILE. A Play in One Act. Toronto, French, 1935. 28p [BM BVaU LC OTP

**Burkholder, Mabel Grace (Clare), 1881–**

MR. SCROOGE ON MAIN STREET. A Pageant in 2 Scenes. Chicago, Hope Pub. Co., 1928. 16p [LC

A PAGEANT OF BETHLEHEM. In Four Scenes. Mount Hamilton, Author, 1922. 8p [BM

A PRINCE OF EGYPT. Mount Hamilton, Author, 1922. 16p [BM

THE TEN VIRGINS. In One Scene. Mount Hamilton, Author, 1922. 7p [BM

**Burnette, Norman L.**

ANGRY MEN. A Play in Four Episodes. By N.L. Burnette and Ella Monckton. Ottawa, Metropolitan Life Insurance Co., 1942. 42p [NSHPL

**Burton, Franklin Wicher**

ACHILLES. Toronto, U. of Toronto Press, 1928. 20p [The Jardine Prize for Poetry, 1927.] [BVaU NBFU OTU QMU

**Buschlen, John Preston, 1888–**

ASSEMBLY CALL. A Play by a Flyer's Dad. Hollywood, Murray & Gee, 1943. 102p [LC

THE PLEASURES OF THE WORLD. A Religious Comedy in Three Acts. By John Preston [pseud]. Lamoni, Ia., Herald, 1915. 64p [LC

TRUANTS. A Comedy in One Act. ... By John Preston [pseud]. Lamoni, Ia., Herald, 1915. 33p [LC

**Bush, Thomas**

SANTIAGO. A Drama in Five Acts. Toronto, Rollo & Adam, 1866. 55p [OTP

**Cadogan, Mrs. Elda Magill, 1916–**

THE INVISIBLE WORM. Durham, Ont., Durham House, 1953. 18p

THE OTHER HALF. Durham, Ont., Durham House, 1954. 23p

RISE AND SHINE. Durham, Ont., Durham Chronicle, 1952. 19p

**Caldwell, James Ernest, 1862–1954**

THE YELLOW BAG. A Drama [and Poems]. Ottawa, Thorburn, 1907. 74p [BM BVaU OTP

**Callan, J.B.**

A PAGEANT OF CANADIAN HISTORY. By J.B. Callan, T.C. Mulvihill, E.C. Scully. Toronto, French, 1938. 32p [Brown U OTP

**Cameron, George Frederick, 1854–1885**

LEO, THE ROYAL CADET. An entirely new and original Military Opera in Four Acts. Libretto by G.F. Cameron, music by Oscar F. Telgmann. Kingston, Henderson, [1889?]. 111p [OKQ

**Campbell, Wilfred, 1858–1918**

MORDRED AND HILDEBRAND. A Book of Tragedies. Ottawa, Durie, 1895. 168p [BVaU NBFU OTP

POETICAL TRAGEDIES. Toronto, Briggs, 1908. 316p [Contents: MORDRED; DAULAC; MORNING; HILDEBRAND.] [BM BVaU OTU NBFU QMM

**Canadian Authors' Association. Montreal Branch**

ONE-ACT PLAYS. By Canadian Authors. 19 Short Canadian Plays. Montreal, the Branch, 1926. 228p [BVaU NSHD OTP QMBM

**Candidus, Caroli (pseud)**

THE FEMALE CONSISTORY OF BROCKVILLE. A Melodrama in Three Acts. Brockville, Author, 1856. 60p [OTP

**Card, Patricia**

LIFE OF A TOY. Toronto, Author, 1940. 11p [CC

**Card, Raymond William George, 1893–**

GENERAL WOLFE. A One-Act Play. Toronto, Nelson, 1931. 28p [BVaU NBFU OTP

"ON GUARD FOR FREEDOM." An Empire Pageant. Toronto, Robinson Plays, 1940. 7p [CC

**Carleton, John Louis, 1861–1939**

HILDEBRAND. A Drama in Five Acts. Saint John, Author, 1903. 74p [OTP

A MEDIEVAL HUN. A Five Act Historical Drama. Boston, Cornhill, 1921. 165p [AEU LC NSHD OTP

MORE SINNED AGAINST THAN SINNING. New York, DeWitt, [1882].

**Carman, Bliss, 1861–1929**

DAUGHTERS OF DAWN. A Lyrical Pageant or Series of Historic Scenes for Presentation with Music and Dancing. By Bliss Carman and Mary Perry King. New York, Kennerley, 1913. 118p [BVaU LC NSHD OKQ

EARTH DEITIES, AND OTHER RHYTHMIC MASQUES. By Bliss Carman and Mary Perry King. New York, Kennerley, 1914. 85p [BVa LC NSHD OKQ

**Cecil-Smith, E.**

EIGHT MEN SPEAK. A Political Act in Six Acts. By E. Cecil-Smith, Oscar Ryan, H. Francis, and Mildred Goldberg. Toronto, Progressive Arts, 1934. 43p [BVaU OTU

**Chapman, Doris**

MIDNIGHT AND CHRISTMAS EVE. Toronto, Tower Print., [1932?]. 11p [OONL

**Chesnut, T. Herbert**

NINA, OR A CHRISTMAS IN THE MEDITERRANEAN. A Nautical Comic Operetta in Two Acts. Written for the Harmonic Club to whom it is Respectfully Dedicated. Hamilton, Author, n.d. 23p [NSWA

**Clarke, Wilfred John, 1896–1965**

TWO ONE-ACT PLAYS. Entitled "St. Paul's Defence" and "A Plea of Judas." [Fredericton, Usbell, 1950.] 19p [NBFU

**Coates, Carol**

THE JADE HEART. New York, Junior Leagues of America, Inc., 1946. [mimeographed] [CanLit No. 48, p56

**Cockings, George, –1802**

THE CONQUEST OF CANADA; or, The Siege of Quebec. An Historical Tragedy of Five Acts. London, Cooke Haysell, 1766. 76p [BM LC OTP

**Cohen, Maxwell Charles, 1926–**

THE MEMBER FROM TROIS-RIVIERES. A One Act Play based on the Life of Ezekiel Hart—the First Jew to be elected to Public Office in Canada. Montreal, Canadian Jewish Congress, 1959. 17p [mimeographed]

**Colquhoun, Kathryn E.**

HIS BLONDE DILEMMA. Toronto, Robinson, 1937. 50p [mimeographed] [CC

A RUN FOR HIS MONEY. A Comedy in One Act. Toronto, Robinson, 1937. 28p [Brown U

**Connor, Fredric Jarrett, 1920–**

THE STATES. [Poetic Drama.] By Fredric Jarrett [pseud]. Shawbridge, Que., Hart Severance, 1949. 104p [AEU BVaU NSHD OTP

**Conover, Dora Smith**

THE CAT AND THE MUSHROOMS. Toronto, Robinson, 1937. 24p [mimeographed] [CC

**Cooper, Douglas**

WIDOWS LEARN FAST. A Farcical Comedy in Three Acts. Toronto, Robinson, 1950. 76p [AEU OTP

**Corbett, Maurice William, 1900–**

WOMAN CALLED "X". Franklin, Ohio, Eldridge, 1951. 95p

**Cosentino, Nicholas**

BIGGEST HALL IN BROOKLYN. Chicago, Dramatic Pub. Co., 1937. [CAAE

MOON OVER MULBERRY STREET. Chicago, Dramatic Pub. Co., 1936. 109p [BVaU

**Coulter, John William, 1888–**

DEIRDRE OF THE SORROWS. An Ancient and Noble Tale Retold by John Coulter for Music by Healey Willan. Toronto, Macmillan, 1944. 72p [BVaU NBFU OTP

THE HOUSE IN THE QUIET GLEN, and THE FAMILY PORTRAIT. [Two Dramas.] Toronto, Macmillan, 1937. 124p [BVaU NBFU OTP

... TRANSIT THROUGH FIRE. Written by John Coulter for Music by Healey Willan. Toronto, Macmillan, 1942. 8p [OTP

**Cowan, John Bruce, 1882–**

CANUCK. A Play in Three Acts. Vancouver, Rose, Cowan & Latta, 1931. 149p [BVaU QMM

NUMBER FIVE CHEYNE ROW. A Play in Four Acts. Vancouver, Rose, Cowan & Latta, 1950. 128p [BVaU OTP

**Creighton, Anthony**

EPITAPH FOR GEORGE DILLON. A Play in Three Acts. By John Osborne and Anthony Creighton. New York, Criterion Books, 1958. 94p

**Crowell, Edwin, 1853–1926**

CHEVROSE, THE HERMIT OF CAPE SABLE. One Act Play. Yarmouth, N.S., Yarmouth Herald, 1925. 27p [NSHD QMBM

**Curzon, Mrs. Sarah Anne, 1833–1898**

LAURA SECORD, THE HEROINE OF 1812, A Drama; And Other Poems. Toronto, Robinson, 1887. 215p [BM BVaU LC MWU NSHD OTP QMM

**Cushing, Eliza Lanesford (Foster), 1794–**

ESTHER, A Sacred Drama; with JUDITH, A Poem. Boston, Dowe, 1840. 118p [BM LC OLU

**Dakin, Laurence B., 1904–**

IRENEO. A Tragedy in Three Acts. Portland, Me., Falmouth Book House, 1936. 54p [BM LC NSHD

MARCO POLO. A Drama in Four Acts. Portland, Me., Falmouth Book House, 1936. 53p [Another ed., 1946.] [BM BVaU LC NSHD

PROMETHEUS, THE FIRE GIVER. A Lyrical Drama in Three Acts. Paris, Obelisk Press, 1938. 84p [BM NSHD OTU

PYRAMUS AND THISBE. A Tragedy in Three Acts. Portland, Me., Falmouth Book House, 1939. 38p [BM LC NSHD OTU

TANCRED: PRINCE OF SALERNO. Toronto, Dent, 1948. 58p [BM BVaU NBFU OTU

**Davidson, Ida Marion**

THE ACADIAN TRAGEDY. Winnipeg, Manitoba Text Book Bureau, 1932. 28p (Canadian History Plays) [OORD PC

ALEXANDER MACKENZIE. Winnipeg, Manitoba Text Book Bureau, 1932. 28p (Canadian History Plays) [BViPA OORD

CANADIAN HISTORY PLAYS. Illus. by Evelyn Gowanlock. Winnipeg, Manitoba Text Book Bureau, 1929–1932. 6v [Contents: 1 "Alexander Mackenzie"; 2 "The Capture of Quebec" and "Madeline de Vercheres"; 3 "Gentlemen Adventurers"; 4 "Lord Selkirk"; 5 "Sir Isaac Brock" and "Laura Secord"; 6 "The Acadian Tragedy."] [OH

GENTLEMEN ADVENTURERS. Winnipeg, Manitoba Text Book Bureau, 1932. 36p [ACG OORD PC

LORD SELKIRK. Winnipeg, Manitoba Text Book Bureau, 1932. 48p [BVaU OTP PC

**Davidson, True, 1901–**

CANADA IN STORY AND SONG. A Pageant. Toronto, Dent, [1927]. 16p [BVaU NBS OLU

LA CLAIRE FONTAINE. Toronto, Author, n.d. 13p [mimeographed] [OTU

**Davies, Robertson, 1913–**

AT MY HEART'S CORE. Toronto, Clarke Irwin, 1950. 91p [BVaU NSHD OONL

EROS AT BREAKFAST, AND OTHER PLAYS. ... Toronto, Clarke Irwin, 1949. 129p [BVaU LC NSHD OKQ

FORTUNE MY FOE. Toronto, Clarke Irwin, 1949. 99p [BVaU NBFU OTU

A JIG FOR THE GYPSY. Toronto, Clarke Irwin, 1954. 98p

A MASQUE OF AESOP. Toronto, Clarke Irwin, 1952. 47p

OVERLAID. A Comedy. Toronto, French, 1948. 24p [BVaU OTU

SHAKESPEARE FOR YOUNG PLAYERS. A Junior Course. Toronto, Clarke Irwin, 1942. 255p [AEU NBSaM OONL

**Davin, Nicholas Flood, 1843–1901**

THE FAIR GRIT; or, The Advantages of Coalition. A Farce. Toronto, Belford, 1876. 35p [BM MWU NSHD OTU

**De La Roche, Mazo, 1879–1961**

COME TRUE. A Play. Toronto, Macmillan, 1927. 47p [BVaU NBFU OTU QMM

LOW LIFE. A Comedy in One Act. Toronto, Macmillan, 1925. 37p [BVaU NBFU OKQ

LOW LIFE AND OTHER PLAYS. Boston, Little Brown, 1929. 109p [BVaU LC NBFU OKQ

THE RETURN OF THE EMIGRANT. Boston, Little Brown, 1929. 34p [BM BVaU LC

WHITEOAKS. A Play. Boston, Little Brown, 1936. 124p [Also: London, Fox, n.d. 68p] [BM BVaU LC OTU

**Denison, Merrill, 1893–**

BROTHERS IN ARMS. A Play in One Act. New York, French, 1923. 27p [BM BVaU LC NBFU OTU

HAVEN OF THE SPIRIT. A Play in One Act. New York, Dramatists Play Service, 1939. 34p [BM BVaU LC

HENRY HUDSON AND OTHER PLAYS. Six Plays for the Microphone from the Romance of Canada Series. ... Toronto, Ryerson, 1931. 183p [BVaU LC NSHD OTU

ON CHRISTMAS NIGHT. A Play in One Act. London, French, 1934. 26p [BM LC

THE PRIZE WINNER. A Comedy in One Act. New York, Appleton, 1928. 35p [BM LC OLU

THE UNHEROIC NORTH. Four Canadian Plays. Toronto, McClelland, 1923. 183p [BM BVaU NSHD OKQ

THE U.S. VS. SUSAN B. ANTHONY. A Play in One Act. New York, Dramatists Play Service, 1941. 29p [LC

**Devlin, Edward Wade**

ROSE LATULIPPE. A Canadian Folk-Play in One Act. Toronto, French, 1935. 32p [BM BVaU OTP

**Dickie, Donalda James, 1883–**

CANADIAN SCHOOL PLAYS. By D.J. Dickie and Others. Toronto, Dent, 1931. 158p [BVaU OTU

**Dixon, Frederick Augustus, 1843–1919**

FIFINE, THE FISHER MAID; or, The Magic Shrimps. By F.A.D. Ottawa, Woodburn, 1877. 50p [NSHPL OLU

LITTLE NOBODY. A Fairy Play. By F.A.D. Toronto, Adam & Stevenson, 1875. 37p [AEU OTUV

MAIDEN MONA THE MERMAID. A Fairy Play for Fairy People. By F.A.D. Toronto, Belford, 1877. 42p [BVaU OTP QMSS

THE MAIRE OF ST. BRIEUX. An Operetta in One Act ... for H.E. the Countess of Dufferin's Private Theatricals ... Feb. 1875. Ottawa, [1875?]. 34p [Adelphi cat. 61

A MASQUE ENTITLED "CANADA'S WELCOME." Shown Before His Excellency the Marquis of Lorne and Her Royal Highness the Princess Louise, on Feb. 24th, 1879, at the Opera House. Written by Frederick A. Dixon; composed by Arthur A. Clappe. Ottawa, Maclean Roger, 1879. 19p [BVaU MWU NSHPL OTP

PIPANDOR. A Comic Opera. Ottawa, Citizen Print., 1884. 55p [AEU OOP

YE LAST SWEET THING IN CORNERS. Being ye Faithful Drama of ye Artists' Vendetta. By F.A.D. Philadelphia, Duncan & Hall, [1880]. 66p [OONL

**Doherty, Brian, 1906–**

FATHER MALACHY'S MIRACLE. A Play in Three Acts. New York, Random House, 1938. 201p [Dramatization of Bruce Marshall's novel of the same title.] [BM BVaU LC OLU

**Dollard, Rev. James Bernard, 1872–1946**

CLONTARF. An Irish National Drama in Four Acts. Dublin, Catholic Truth Soc., 1920. 48p [Also with imprint: Toronto, 1915. See T&C] [OH

**Doughty, Arthur George, 1860–1936**

BONNIE PRINCE CHARLIE. ... An Original Comic Opera in Two Acts. Montreal, Desbarats, 1892. 15p [BM

**Dowsett, Rev. Geoffrey Nevil**

THE BETRAYAL. A Passion Play in Three Acts. New York, French, 1942. 94p [BM LC OTP

**Duvar, John Hunter-, 1830–1899**

DE ROBERVAL, A Drama; also THE EMIGRATION OF THE FAIRIES, and THE TRIUMPH OF CONSTANCY, A Romaunt. Saint John, McMillan, 1888. 192p [BVaU LC MWU NSHD OKQ

THE ENAMORADO. A Drama. Summerside, Graves, 1879. 120p [BVaU NSHD OTP QMM

FIN DE SIECLE. A Comedy. [MOR'98

**Edgar, Mary Susanne, 1889–**

THE CHRISTMAS TREE BLUEBIRD. New York, Woman's Press, 1920. 19p [BVaU

THE WAYSIDE PIPER. New York, Nat'l Board Y.W.C.A., 1915. 27p [LC NSHD

**Edgerton, E. Maud**

RUBY OF MELCHIOR. Toronto, Robinson, 1937. 15p [UTQ'38

**Edmond, Reby**

GUEST HOUSE, VERY EXCLUSIVE. A Christmas Play in One Act. New York, French, 1937. 34p [BM LC

THE SPIRIT OF THE THING. A Comedy in One Act. New York, Fitzgerald, 1934. 34p [BVaU

**Fairbairn, Archibald Macdonald Duff**

PLAYS OF THE PACIFIC COAST. Toronto, French, 1935. 111p [Contains: EBB-TIDE, THE WAR DRUMS OF SKEDANS, THE TRAGEDY OF TANOO, and A PACIFIC COAST TRAGEDY.] [BVaU OTU QMM

**Fairbairn, Robert Edis, 1880–1951**

WHEN THE KING SMILED. A Drama of the Resurrection in Four Scenes. Toronto, French, 1935. 24p [BM BVaU OTP

**Farquharson, Mary Frederica (McLean)**

SURE OF A FOURTH. A Satirical Comedy in One Act. Toronto, French, 1935. 27p [BM BVaU LC OTP

THEY MEET AGAIN. A Comedy in One Act. Toronto, Macmillan, 1938. 26p [BVi QMM

**Ferguson, James P., 1900–**

COURAGE, MR. GREENE. A Comedy. Toronto, French, 1936. 20p [BM BVaU OTU

**Finch, Robert Duer Claydon, 1900–**

A CENTURY HAS ROOTS. A Masque performed at Hart House Theatre to commemorate the One Hundredth Anniversary of the Foundation of University College, Toronto, 1853. Toronto, U. of Toronto Press, 1953. 28p

**Fowke, Helen Shirley, 1914–**

A GIFT FOR BENJAMIN. A One-Act Christmas Play for Children. Fredericton, Brunswick Press, 1960. 16p

**Fraser, Donald Andrew, 1875–1948**

THE POTTER'S DREAM. A Playlet for Young Folks. Denver, Eldridge Entertainment House, 1928. 9p [LC

**Fraser, Hermia (Harris), 1902–**

HOB'S HEAVEN. Denver, Eldridge Entertainment House, 1937. 8p [LC

**Freund, Philip, 1909–**

MARIO'S WELL. A One Act Comedy. New York, French, 1937. 18p [BM LC

PRINCE HAMLET. A Play. New York, Bookman Associates, 1953. 70p [BVaU

**Fuller, William Henry**

H.M.S. "PARLIAMENT"; or, The Lady who Loved a Government Clerk. [Anon] Ottawa, Citizen Pub. Co., 1880. 37p [BVaU OTP

THE UNSPECIFIC SCANDAL. An Original, Political, Critical and Grittical Extravaganza, performed at the great Dominion Theatre, Ottawa, in the year of grace 1873. [Anon] Ottawa, Woodburn, 1874. 19p [BVaU OOA

**Gagnieur, Elizabeth**

CONFLICT AND TRIUMPH. A Drama in Three Acts. Montreal, Canadian Messenger Press, 1908. 339p [QMBM

**Garcia, A.E. de**

CANADA, FAIR CANADA. A Modern Romantic Tragedy. Montreal, Montreal Shorthand Institute & Business College, 1902. 100p [BM Brown U LC

**Garnier, John Hutchison, 1810? [1823?]–1898**

PRINCE PEDRO. A Tragedy. Toronto, Belford, 1877. 158p [BVaU OTU QMM

**Gibbon, John Murray, 1875–1952**

THE MAN COMES DOWN FROM THE MOON. Musical Playlet based on "Northland Songs." Toronto, Thompson, 1937. 15p [OTP

THE ORDER OF GOOD CHEER. From the French version of Louvigny de Montigny. Canadian-historical Ballad Opera of the First Settlers in Canada. Reconstructed by ——. Toronto, Dent, 1929. 30p [Brown U

**Goulding, Dorothy Jane, 1923–**

THE MASTER CAT AND OTHER PLAYS. Toronto, Dent, 1955. 138p

**Gowan, Elsie Park (Young), 1905–**

BREECHES FROM BOND STREET. A Comedy in One Act. New York, S. French, 1952. 24p

SHOP IN TOAD LANE. Edmonton, Alberta Co-operative Wholesale Assoc., 1940. 16p [UTQ'41

**Gray, James Orman**

ANTICHRIST. Vancouver, Thomson, 1912. 106p [At head of title: The Plays of James Orman Gray, L.L.B.] [BM BVaU

**Green, Harry A.V.**

THE DEATH OF PIERROT. A Trivial Tragedy in One Act. Winnipeg, Community Players, 1923. 25p [MWU OTU

**Greene, Barnet M.**

"WOMAN–THE MASTERPIECE," A Play in Four Episodes; and "THE GOD-INTOXICATED MAN," A Play in Three Acts. Toronto, Ryerson, 1923. 148p [BVaU NSHD OTU QMM

**Grey, Francis William, 1860–1939**

FOUR PLAYS. LOVE'S PILGRIMAGE, A Passiontide Mystery in a Prologue and Three Acts; BISHOP AND KING, Blessed Oliver Plunkett and Charles II; THE BRIDEGROOM COMETH, A Morality Play in One Act; THE VALIANT WOMAN, An Epiphany Masque. Ottawa, Miller, 1931. [Separate pagination.] [OOP

SIXTEEN-NINETY. A Series of Historical Tableaux. Ottawa, Mortimer, 1904. 42p [QMM

**Groves, Edith (Lelean), 1870–1931**

BRITANNIA. [A Play.] Toronto, McClelland, 1917. 18p [AEU OTU

CANADA CALLS. A Timely Patriotic Play, Dedicated to the Children of Canada. Toronto, McClelland, 1918. 22p [BM NSWA

A CANADIAN FAIRY TALE. A Patriotic Play. By Edith Lelean. Toronto, Briggs, 1916. 31p [BM Brown U BVaU

THE KEY OF JACK CANUCK'S TREAURE-HOUSE. Toronto, Briggs, 1916. 16p [BM BVaU

THE MAKING OF CANADA'S FLAG: A Patriotic Play. Toronto, Briggs, 1916. 20p [BM BVaU NSHPL OH

A PATRIOTIC AUCTION. Toronto, McClelland, 1918. 22p [OONL

THE WAR ON THE WESTERN FRONT. A Patriotic Play. Toronto, Briggs, 1916. 23p [BM Brown U BVaU

THE WOOING OF MISS CANADA. Toronto, McClelland, 1917. 32p [BM BVaU OTP

**Gustafson, Ralph Barker, 1909–**

ALFRED THE GREAT. London, Joseph, 1937. 119p [BM BVa NSHD OTU QMM

**Hailey, Arthur, 1920–**

CLOSE-UP ON WRITING FOR TELEVISION. [Six Plays.] Garden City, N.Y., Doubleday, 1960. 307p

**Hammond, George Arthur**

THE CROWNING TEST. A Drama. Kingsclear, N.B., Lahstok Rustic Press, 1901. 92p [NSWA

JASSOKET AND ANEMON. A Ramble. Kingsclear, N.B., Lahstok Pub., 156p [NBFU OTP

STARBORN THE CONJURER. A Dramatic Poem. Kingsclear, N.B., 1903. [Various pagings] [NSWA

A TRIAD. Lahstok, N.B., Rural Press, 1887. 3 parts in one. [Pt. 1: The Lake of Tears, an Allegory; Various Poems. Pt. 2: On the Strand, a Fable; Golden Circle Dirges. Pt. 3: Knud Iverson, a Dramatic Sketch; Twilight Cimmerian; Autumnal Musings; The Loiterer, a Fragment.] [OTP

THE TWO OFFERINGS. A Drama. [LAMECH. A Drama.] Kingsclear, N.B., Lahstok Rural Press, 1890. [Various pagings] [NSWA

**Hammond, Josephine, 1876–**

EVERYWOMAN'S ROAD. A Morality of Woman, Creator, Worker, Waster, Joy-Giver, and Keeper of the Flame. New York, Kennerley, 1911. 55p [BVaU LC

**Harper, John Murdoch, 1845–1919**

CHAMPLAIN. A Drama in Three Acts. With an Intro. entitled "Twenty Years and After," and a Chapter on "Champlain the Explorer." Toronto, Trade Pub. Co., 1908. 296p [BM BVaU LC NSHD OKQ

**Harris, Walter Eric, 1889–**

SUCH HARMONY. A Play in One Act. Toronto, French, 1936. 37p [OTP

TWENTY-FIVE CENTS. Toronto, French, 1936. 32p [NSHD OTP

**Harrison, Susie Frances (Riley), 1859–1935**

FOUR BALLADS AND A PLAY. By "Seranus" [pseud]. N.p., 1933. 18p [OTP

**Heavysege, Charles, 1816–1876**

COUNT FILIPPO; or, The Unequal Marriage. A Drama in Five Acts. By The Author of SAUL [pseud]. Montreal, Author, 1860. 153p [BM BVaU LC NBFU OKQ

SAUL. A Drama. In Three Parts. [Anon] Montreal, Rose, 1857. 315p [Second ed., rev.: Montreal, 1859. 328p] [Also pub. under title: SAUL: A Drama in Three Parts. By Charles Heavysege. A new and rev. ed. Boston, Fields Osgood, 1869. 436p] [BM BVaU LC MWU NSHD OTU QMM

**Henderson, J. Duff**

ALVIRA alias ORCA. The Nineteenth Century Story. [Also some Poems and some Dramas.] Toronto, Hunter Rose, 1899. 279p [BCF OTP

**Hensley, Sophia Margaret (Almon), 1866–**

PRINCESS MIGNON. A Musical Play in Three Acts. Founded on One of Andrew Lang's Fairy Tales. Written by Almon Hensley. New York, Kenworth, 1900. 30p [AEU LC

**Herman, Alan, 1916–**

DOUBLE IMAGE. A Play in three acts. By Roger MacDougall and Ted Allan [pseud]. Based on a story by Roy Vickers. London, French, 1957. 76p

THE MONEY MAKERS. By Ted Allan [pseud]. Trans. into Russian by V. Abramova. Moscow, Iskusstvo, 1958. 130p [Title and text in Russian. English title from t.p. verso. Translation of Russian Title: Mr. Finch Makes Money. First produced Toronto, 1953. Rewritten and produced, London, 1955, under title: "The Ghost Writers."]

**Hezzelwood, Oliver, 1861–1933**

POEMS. And a Play: "THE INVISIBLE URGE." Toronto, Ontario Press, 1926. 168p [BVaU OKQ QMM

**Hill, Thomas, –1860**

THE PROVINCIAL ASSOCIATION. A Tragi-Comedy in Verse. Fredericton, 1845. [NBB

**Hitchins, William English, 1910–**

"EVEN OUR FAITH." A Pageant depicting the Story of the Anglican Church in Canada from Pioneer Days. Toronto, General Board of Religious Education, [1952?]. xiii + 62p

**Hoare, John Edward, 1886–**

CASH AS CATCH CAN. A Comedy of Sicily in Two Scenes. London, French, 1937. 27p [BM LC

RED PLANET. By —— and John Lloyd Balderston. New York, French, 1931. 33p [PC

THE SHOEMAKERS OF SYRACUSE. A Play in One Act. London, French, 1948. 36p [BM LC

**Hooke, Hilda Mary, 1898–**

ONE ACT PLAYS FROM CANADIAN HISTORY. Toronto, Longmans, 1942. 157p [BVaU LC OTP

**Hooper, Dora M.**

WHERE THE BUFFALO ROAM. New York, French, 1940. [24p] [LC

**Ingraham, Mary (Kinley), 1874–1949**

ACADIA. A Play in Five Acts. Wolfville, Davidson, 1920. 19p [BVaU NBFU OTP

**Irvine, William, 1885–1962**

THE BRAINS WE TRUST. A Play in Three Acts. Toronto, Nelson, 1935. 48p [BVi OTP

YOU CAN'T DO THAT. A Play in Three Acts. Toronto, Nelson, 1936. 48p [OTP

**Jacob, Fred, 1882–1926**

ONE THIRD OF A BILL. Five Short Canadian Plays. Toronto, Macmillan, 1925. 140p [BVaU LC NSHD OTU

**Jacobson, Percy Nathanial, 1886–1952**

THE ACCIDENT. Rock Island, Ill., Ingram, 1937. 12p [CC

AND SENDETH RAIN. Rock Island, Ill., Ingram, 1934. [CC

NOT ONLY THE GUPPY. Rock Island, Ill., Ingram, 1934. [CC

RIDICULOUS AND SUBLIME. A Comedy in One Act. Boston, Baker, 1948. 38p [AEU

THE USUAL THREE. Comedy-Drama. Toronto, French, 1948. 20p [AEU OTP

**Jones, Emrys Maldwyn, 1905–**

CANADIAN SCHOOL PLAYS. Series One. Toronto, Ryerson, 1948. 201p [BVa LC OTU

**Jones, James Edmund, 1866–1939**

SCENES FROM DICKENS. Arranged by the Dickens Fellowship Players of Toronto. Ed. by ——. Toronto, McClelland, 1923. 335p [BVaU OTU

**Joudry, Patricia, 1921–**

TEACH ME HOW TO CRY. Drama in Three Acts. New York, Dramatists Play Service, 1955. 78p

**Keating, James W.**

THE SHRIEVALTY OF LYNDEN. A Tragedy in One Act. St. Catharines, Sherwood, 1889. 23p [AEU OTP

**Kerr, William Hastings, 1826–1888**

THE KIDNAPPERS. A Tragico-Comical Melodrama in Ten Acts. [Anon] Montreal, [1867?]. 8p [BVaU NSWA OTU QMSS

**Kirkconnell, Watson, 1895–**

THE MOD AT GRAND PRE. A Nova Scotian Light Opera in Two Acts. Wolfville, priv. print., 1955. 35p

**Knight, Mary A.**

PAGEANTS AND PLAYS. Four Plays which have been Awarded Prizes by the Imperial Order of the Daughters of the Empire. [Three plays by Mary A. Knight; one play by Marguerite Letson.] Toronto, Nelson, 1935. 57p [PC

**Knister, Raymond, 1900–1932**

YOUTH GOES WEST. A Play in One Act. [In *Poet Lore,* 39: 582–95. Boston, 1928.] [LC

**Knowles, A. Beatrice**

THE SAINT. A Play in One Act. New York, French, 1936. 32p [AEU OTP

**Knox, Alexander, 1907–**

OLD MASTER. A Comedy. London, Constable, 1940. 128p [BM Brown U OLU

**Lambie, Alexander, 1870–**

THE LADY OF LADORE. A Play-form Tale of Derwentdale. Vancouver, Author, 1928. 220p [BM BVaU NBFU

**Lane, Wilmot Burkmar, 1872–**

QUEBEC. Toronto, Macmillan, 1936. 40p [NSHD OTP

**Lanigan, John Alphonsus, 1854–1919**

EITHNE; or, The Siege of Armagh. A Drama in Four Acts. Buffalo, Express Steam Print., 1872. 49p [LC

**Leacock, Stephen Butler, 1869–1944**

"Q". A Farce in One Act. By Stephen Leacock and Basil Macdonald Hastings. New York, French, 1915. 23p [BM LC

**Lesperance, John Talon, 1838–1891**

ONE HUNDRED YEARS AGO. An Historical Drama of the War of Independence in 4 Acts and 20 Tableaux. [Anon] Montreal, "La Minerva" Steam Presses, 1876. 108p [LC

**Llwyd, Rev. John Plummer Derwent, 1861–1933**

THE VESTAL VIRGIN. A Dramatic Poem. Halifax, 1920. 58p [BM LC OOP

**Macbeth, Madge Hamilton (Lyons), 1878–1965**

CURIOSITY REWARDED. A Dialogue between Gilbert Knox and the Curious Public. Ottawa, Graphic, 1926. 12p [NBFU OTU

THE GOOSE'S SAUCE. A Comedy in One Act. Toronto, French, 1935. 20p [BM LC OTP

**McConkey, Hugh T., 1922–**

TRILOGY IN A GARDEN. A Play for Voices in Three Parts. New York, Exposition, [1955]. 58p

**MacDonald, Wilson**

IN SUNNY FRANCE. A Musical Comedy. Moose Jaw, 1924. 48p [OKQ

**Macdonell, Amice Anna Botham**

HISTORICAL PLAYS FOR CHILDREN. First Series. London, Allen, 1909. 249p [BM LC

HISTORICAL PLAYS FOR CHILDREN. Second Series. London, Allen, 1910. 272p [BM LC

THE NAME ON THE ROCK. A Play in Three Acts. London, Allen & Unwin, 1933. 61p [BM BViPA LC

THE SACRED FIRE. A Morality Play for the League of Nations. In One Act. Oxford, Blackwell, 1924. 24p [BM

THE STORY OF THE ARMADA. A Play for Children. In Three Acts. London, League of the Empire, 1908. 32p [BM

**McDonnell, William, 1814–1900**

MARINA, THE FISHERMAN'S DAUGHTER. An Operatic Romance in Three Acts. Toronto, Strange & Co., 1883. 48p [OTP

**MacDougall, James Brown, 1871–1950**

MISS CANADA'S RECEPTION. Toronto, McClelland, 1917. 12p [OTU

**McEvoy, Bernard, 1842–1932**

THE SPRATTS. A Comedy in Three Acts. Montreal, Southam, 1927. 28p [BVaU

**McGee, Thomas D'Arcy, 1825–1868**

SEBASTIAN; or, The Roman Martyr. A Drama. New York, 1861. 52p [OOP

**McIlwraith, Jean Newton, 1859–1938**

PTARMIGAN. ... [Comic Opera]. Hamilton, Spectator, 1895. 27p [OTU

**MacIntosh, Claire (Harris), 1882–**

TWO PLAYS FOR CHILD ACTORS. (FLOWERS, for six little girls; THE TEA PARTY AT THE SHOE.) 1934. 15p [NSHD

**MacKay, Isabel Ecclestone (Macpherson), 1875–1928**

GOBLIN GOLD. A Comedy Drama in Three Acts. New York, French, 1933. 89p [LC OTP

THE LAST CACHE. ... New York, French, 1927. 31p [BVaU

THE SECOND LIE. A Play in One Act. [In CANADIAN PLAYS FROM HART HOUSE THEATRE. Ed. by Vincent Massey. Toronto, Macmillan, 1926. V. 1, pp. 125–51.] [BVaU NBFU OTP QMM

TREASURE. A Play in One Act. New York, French, 1927. 25p [BM BVaU OTP QMM

TWO TOO MANY. A Comedy in Three Acts. Philadelphia, Penn. Pub. Co., 1927. 78p [A 3-act play which won third prize of $250 from the Penn. Pub. Co., of Philadelphia in 1927.] [BVaU OKQ

**MacKay, Louis Alexander, 1901–**

THE FREEDOM OF JEAN GUICHET. A Play in Three Acts. [In CANADIAN PLAYS FROM HART HOUSE THEATRE. Ed. by Vincent Massey. Toronto, Macmillan, 1927. V. 2, pp. 69–129.] [BVaU NBFU OTP QMM

**Mackenzie, James Bovell, 1851–1919**

THAYENDANEGEA. An Historico-Military Drama. Toronto, Briggs, 1898. 179p [Thayendanegea–Joseph Brant, Sachem of the Mohawks.] [BVaU NBFU OTP QMSS

**MacKenzie, Malcolm**

CANADA FOREVER; or, Home is the Roamer. Boston, Baker's Plays, 1950. 77p [BVaU

**Maclennan, J. Munro, 1900–**

SEVEN CAESARS' RANSOMS. A Dramatic Poem in 3 Acts. New York, Exposition Press, 1952. 149p

**Macphail, Andrew, 1864–1938**

THE LAND. A Play of Character. Montreal, University Magazine, 1914. 82p [BM QMM

**Mahon, James, 1910–**

THE IMAGINARY LINE. A Mystical Comedy. Toronto, Author, 1946. 56 leaves. [CC

**Mair, Charles, 1838–1927**

TECUMSEH. A Drama. Toronto, Hunter Rose, 1886. 205p [A second ed., with other poems: Toronto, Briggs, 1901.] [BM BVaU MWU NBFU OTP QMBM

**Mary Agnes, Sister [dramatist]**

THE ARCH OF SUCCESS. A Dialogue for Commencement Day. By S.M.A. Winnipeg, St. Mary's Academy, 1919. 11p [BM

THE BEST GIFT. (A May Festival. The Divine Guest. The Birthday of the Divine Child. Pearls for the Missions. Uncle Jerry's Silver Jubilee. Winnipeg, Sister Mary Agnes, 1924. 3pts. [BM

BETTER THAN GOLD. A Play for Girls. By S.M.A. Winnipeg, 1922. 27p [BM

THE EMPRESS HELENA; or, The Victory of the Cross. An Historical Drama for Girls. By S.M.A. Winnipeg, 1920. 27p [BM

AN IRISH PRINCESS. (Also: The Step Sisters. Old Friends and New.) By S.M.A. Winnipeg, St. Mary's Academy, 1917. 3pts. [BM

THE LAST OF THE VESTALS. (Also: At the Court of Isabella. Those Shamrocks from Ireland. A Patriot's Daughter. Choosing a Model.) By S.M.A. Winnipeg, 1914. 177p [BM

MARY MAGDALEN, AND OTHER PLAYS. By S.M.A. Winnipeg, St. Mary's Academy, 1918. 4pts. [BM

MOTHER'S BIRTHDAY. By S.M.A. St. Boniface, Le Manitoba, 1921. 19p [BM

THE QUEEN OF SHEBA. A Biblical Drama. (Also: Christmas Guests. That Millionaire's Daughter. A Shakespeare Pageant. Plans for The Holidays.) By S.M.A. Winnipeg, St. Mary's Academy, 1915. 5pts. [BM

SENSE AND SENTIMENT. A School Play for Girls. By S.M.A. Winnipeg, 1920. 23p [BM

ZUMA, THE PERUVIAN MAID; CROSS AND CHRYSANTHEMUM; SHORT PLAYS AND RECITATIONS. [Three Pamphlets in one volume.] Winnipeg, St. Mary's Academy, 1922. 37 + 48 + 45p [BM OOP

**Mason, Harold Campbell, 1895–**

SMITH BROADENS OUT. A Play in Two Acts. Toronto, 1923. 30p [BM

**Massey, Vincent, 1887–1967**

CANADIAN PLAYS FROM HART HOUSE THEATRE. Ed. by ——. Toronto, Macmillan, 1926–27. 2v [BM BVaU NBFU OTP QMM

**Maura, Sister (née Mary Power), 1881–1957**

VIA VITAE. By a Sister of Charity [pseud]. London, Milford, 1923. 24p [LC

**Merritt, Catharine Nina**

"WHEN GEORGE III WAS KING." An Historical Drama in Three Acts. Toronto, Rowsell & Hutchinson, 1897. 30p [BM BVaU

**Middleton, Jesse Edgar, 1872–1960**

PILGRIMS AND STRANGERS. A Picture in Two Lights. Toronto, Crocker, 1914. 39p [BM

**Miller, Hanson Orlo, 1911–**

"THIS WAS LONDON." [A Play in 3 Acts.] London, Ont., Author, 1955. 89p [mimeographed]

**Milligan, James Lewis, 1876–**

JUDAS ISCARIOT. A Poetical Play. Toronto, Ryerson, 1929. 31p [NBFU OKQ

**Milne, William Samuel, 1902–**

THE FAILURE. One-Act Comedy. Toronto, Robinson, 1937. 24p [OTU

THE LAMPSHADE. A Guignol Piece in One Scene. Toronto, French, 1936. 19p [BM LC OTP

**Mitchell, Ronald Elwy**

ANGELS AND SUCH. Comedy in One Act. New York, Dramatists Play Service, 1938. 29p [BM LC

BETTER DAYS. A Play in One Act. New York, French, 1934. 30p [BM LC

THE GOBLIN. A Welsh Comedy in One Act. New York, French, 1934. 23p [BM LC

A HANDFUL OF SHEEP. A Comedy of North Wales, in One Act. New York, French, 1935. 24p [BM LC

HE THAT HOPS. A Play for Young Children. New York, French, 1935. 20p [BM LC

THE HOLY DRAGON. A Play in One Act. New York, French, 1935. 22p [BM LC

A HUSBAND FOR BREAKFAST. Comedy in One Act. New York, Dramatists Play Service, 1937. 32p [Also pub. as: A HUSBAND FOR BREAKFAST. A Comedy in a Welsh Setting. London, French, 1937. 26p] [BM LC

THE MEDDLER IN MIRACLES. A One-Act Play. New York, French, 1936. 24p [BM LC

NO BOOTS IN BED. A Comedy in Three Acts. New York, French, 1942. 102p [LC

PANIC OVER PORTERHOUSE. A Comedy in One Act. London, French, 1937. 30p [BM LC

RESURRECTION EZRA. Comedy in One Act. New York, Dramatists Play Service, 1938. 35p [BM LC

A ROCKY WOOING. Comedy in One Act. New York, French, 1935. 28p [BM LC

A ROGUE IN BED. London, French, 1937. 25p [A version in Scots, by David Rorie, pub. as: A BEDFAST PROPHET. London, French, 1937. 25p] [BM LC

LA SANDRA. A Play in One Act. New York, French, 1936. 25p [BM LC

THE WAY TO LONDON. A Welsh Play in One Act. New York, French, 1935. 24p [BM LC

**Moray, Elspeth**

THE DREAM OF THE MONTHS. A New Year Pageant. Toronto, McClelland, 1918. 25p [BVaU NSWA

THE FESTIVAL OF THE WHEAT. A Play for the Little Folk. Toronto, McClelland, 1918. 11p [NSWA

**Morrison, Frank**

TZINQUAW. A Musical Dramatization of the Cowichan Indian Legend, the Thunderbird and the Killer-Whale. In Four Scenes. Vancouver, n.p., 1950. 16p [OONL

**Mountford, George Frederick, 1890–1950**

CROOKS FOR A MONTH. A Comedy in Three Acts. Chicago, Denison, 1926. 99p [LC

DO YOU TAKE THIS WOMAN? A One-Act Comedy. Chicago, Denison, 1929. 26p [LC

FRIDAY FOR LUCK. A Comedy in One Act. Chicago, Denison, 1924. 30p [LC

THE LOOSE BRICKS IN THE CHIMNEY. A One-Act Comedy. Chicago, Denison, 1935. 33p [LC

RATS! One-Act Farce. Chicago, Denison, 1924. 30p [LC

SAY IT WITH TAFFY. A One-Act Comedy. Chicago, Denison, 1927. 29p [LC

YOU CAN'T STOP CUPID. A One-Act Comedy. Chicago, Denison, 1930. 30p [LC

YOU'RE A CUCKOO. A One-Act Comedy. Chicago, Denison, 1925. 32p [LC

**Moyse, Charles Ebenezer, 1852–1924**

SHAKESPEARE'S SKULL AND FALSTAFF'S NOSE. A Fancy in Three Acts. By Belgrave Titmarsh [pseud]. London, Stock, 1889. 80p [BM OOU QMM

**Murray, David Graham, 1926–**

THE LINE. Durham, Ont., Durham House, 1954. 29p

**Norwood, Gilbert, 1880–1954**

THE ACHARNIANS. An Abridged Acting Edition. Arranged and trans. by Gilbert Norwood. Oxford, Blackwell, 1911. 67p [OTU

THE MOSTELLARIA OF PLAUTUS. Trans. into English verse, and ed. for Actors. Manchester, U. Press, 1908. 85p [OTU

**Norwood, Rev. Robert Winkworth, 1874–1932**

THE MAN OF KERIOTH. New York, Doran, 1919. 138p [BVaU LC NSHD OKQ

THE WITCH OF ENDOR. A Tragedy. New York, Doran, 1916. 121p [BVaU LC NBFU OKQ QMM

**O'Higgins, Harvey Jerrold, 1876–1929**

THE DUMMY. A Detective Comedy in Four Acts. By Harvey O'Higgins and Harriet Ford. New York, French, 1925. 113p [LC

MR. LAZARUS. A Comedy in Four Acts. By Harvey O'Higgins and Harriet Ford. New York, French, 1926. 134p [LC

OLD P.Q. A Play in Three Acts. By Harvey O'Higgins and Harriet Ford. New York, French, 1928. 81p [LC

ON THE HIRING LINE. A Comedy in Three Acts. By Harvey O'Higgins and Harriet Ford. New York, French, 1923. 116p [LC

ORPHAN AGGIE. A Romantic Comedy. By Harvey O'Higgins and Harriet Ford. New York, French, 1927. 96p [LC

"WHEN A FELLER NEEDS A FRIEND." A Play in Three Acts. By Harvey O'Higgins and Harriet Ford. [New York], 1920. 106p [LC

**O'Meara, Martin**

SITTING BILL. A Comedy in One Act. Toronto, French, 1949. 30p [OTU

**Osborne, Marian (Francis), 1871–1931**

SAPPHO AND PHAON. A Lyrical Drama. Toronto, Macmillan, 1926. 68p [BM BVaU NBFU OTU QMM

**Owens, Charles R.**

TATTERED ROSES. A Play in One Act. Mimico, Ont., Epworth Press, 1928. 38p [OKQ

**Pacaud, George Washington, 1879–**

SOCIAL IDOLATRY. New York, French, 1920. 93p [BM LC NSHD QMBM

**Palmer, George Alfred, 1869–**

MADAME VERITE AT BATH. A Comedy in One Act. Toronto, French, 1935. 24p [BM BVaU LC OTP

HAIL. An Original Domestic Drama in Two Acts. Regina, Author, 1933. 39p [Brown U

**Parker, Gilbert, 1862–1932**

ADAPTATION OF FAUST. 1888. [MOR'12

THE VENDETTA. 1889. [MOR'12

**Pearson, Harry Mitchell, 1891–1938**

THE LOVE GIFT. A Religious Mystery Play in Three Acts. Toronto, Ryerson, 1923. 31p [BM OTU

**Plunkett, M.W.**

CAPTAIN M.W. PLUNKETT, MANAGER AND OWNER, PRESENTS "THE DUMBELLS" IN BIFF-BING-BANG. N.p., 1921. 14p [BM

THE NEW DUMBELLS PLAY, "CARRY ON." N.p., 1923. 12p [BM

**Potter, Ida Elizabeth**

"ANNABEL'S M.I. CLUB." A Three-Act Play. [Portage la Prairie], Author, 1931. 20p [MBC

"AT HOPPER'S CORNERS." A Two-Act Play. N.p., Author, 1927. 32p [AEU

"FARMER MAXWELL'S CITY NIECE." A Three-Act Drama. N.p., Author, 1926. 39p [AEU

"MOTHER DUNN AND HER FAMILY." A Two-Act Comedy. Portage la Prairie, Author, 1924. [CC Rhod p824

WE ARE COMING. A Five-Act Modern Drama. Portage la Prairie, Author, 1923. [CC Rhod p824

**Price, Marjorie**

GOD CAESAR. A Comedy in One Act. Toronto, French, 1935. 24p [BM BVaU LC OTP

THE SIX QUEENS OF HENRY. An Historical Fantasy in One Act. Toronto, French, 1937. 39p [BM LC OTP

**Ramsay, Alexander**

COERCION. A One Act Play. Toronto, French, 1935. 28p [BM LC

**Reynolds, Lois**

NELLIE McNABB. A One-Act Farce Comedy. Toronto, French, 1937. 26p [BM BVaU LC OTP

SUMMER HOTEL. A Play in One Act. Chicago, Denison, 1936. 28p [BM

**Richards, Stanley, 1918–**

CANADA ON STAGE. A Collection of One-Act Plays. Ed. and intro. by ——. Toronto, Clarke Irwin, 1960. xvii + 324p

**Ringwood, Gwendolyn Margaret (Pharis), 1910–**

THE COURTING OF MARIE JENVRIN. A Comedy of the Far North. By Gwen Pharis. Toronto, French, 1951. 35p

DARK HARVEST. A Tragedy of the Canadian Prairies. By Gwen Pharis. With notes, acting suggestions, and questions by G.L. Broderson. Toronto, Nelson, 1945. 143p [BVaU NBFU OTUV

LAMENT FOR HARMONICA (MAYA). Ottawa, Little Theatre, [1960]. 20p

STILL STANDS THE HOUSE. A Drama in One Act. Toronto, French, 1939. 28p [OTU PC

**Roberts, Jessie (Alexander), –1907**

ENCORE! A New Book of Platform Sketches. By Jessie Alexander. Toronto, McClelland, 1922. 312p [BM BVaU OTP

JESSIE ALEXANDER'S PLATFORM SKETCHES. Original and adapted. Toronto, McClelland, 1916. 227p [BM BVaU OTP

SUCCESSFUL RECITATIONS. By Jessie Alexander. Toronto, McClelland, 1927. 240p [OTP

**Robinson, Hazel Alberta, 1913–1955**

POEMS AND A PLAY. Toronto, Ryerson, 1955. 39p [Radio play, "This Perilous Dream," presented on the CBC, Nov. 11, 1949.]

**Roddick, Amy (Redpath), –1954**

THE BIRTH OF MONTREAL (A Chronicle Play), and Other Poems. Montreal, Dougall, 1921. 174p [BM BVaU NSHD OTP QMM

IN A VENETIAN GARDEN; ST. URSULA. Two Plays. Montreal, Dougall, 1926. 119p [BVaU OTU QMM

THE SEEKERS. An Indian Mystery Play. Montreal, Dougall, 1920. 75p [BM BVaU LC NSHD OTP QMM

THARBIS. A Poetic Drama. Montreal, Dougall, 1937. 80p [BVaU LC OTP QMM

THE TOMAHAWK. A Playlet; And Other Poems. Montreal, Dougall, 1938. 76p [BVaU LC OTU QMM

**Rogers, Robert, 1731–1795**

PONTEACH; or, The Savages of America. A Tragedy. London, Author, 1766. 110p [New ed., with an intro. and biography of the author by Allan Nevins. Chicago, Caxton Club, 1914. 261p] [BM LC OTP QMM

**Roy, James Alexander, 1884–**

THE BREAKING OF THE BRIDGE. A Play in One Act. Kingston, Jackson, 1923. 19p [LC QMM

**Sadlier, Mary Anne (Madden), 1820–1903**

THE BABBLER. A Drama for Boys, in One Act. Adapted from the French. New York, Sadlier, 1863. 23p [AEU BM

ELDER BROTHER. New York, Sadlier, 187–? [AmCat 1876

INVISIBLE HAND. New York, Sadlier, 187–? [AmCat 1876

JULIA; or, The Gold Thimble. A Drama for Girls, In One Act. New York, Sadlier, 1861. [AmCat

THE SECRET. A Drama. London, Washbourne, 1880. 32p [An earlier ed.: New York, Sadlier, 1865. AmCat] [BM

THE TALISMAN. A Drama in Three Acts. New York, Sadlier, 1863. [AmCat BM

**Scott, Duncan Campbell, 1862–1947**

PIERRE. A Play in One Act. [CANADIAN PLAYS FROM HART HOUSE THEATRE. Ed. by Vincent Massey. Toronto, Macmillan, 1926. V.1, pp. 51–76.] [BM BVaU NBFU OTP QMM

**Scott, Elise Aylen, 1904–**

THE HOLY CROWN. By Elise Aylen. [In *The Best One-Act Plays of 1937.* Selected by J.W. Marriott. London, Harrap, 1938.] [BM

**Scott, Rev. Frederick George, 1861–1944**

THE KEY OF LIFE. A Mystery-Play. Quebec, Dussault, 1907. 42p [3rd ed., 1927.] [BM BVaU OTP QMM

**Scribble, Sam (pseud)**

DOLORSOLATIO. A Local Political Burlesque. Montreal, Lovell, 1865. 22p [OTP

NOT DEAD YET; or, The Skating Carnival. A Farce in One Act. Montreal, Lovell, 1865. 23p [OTUV

**Sellar, Robert, 1841–1919**

THE TRAGEDY OF WALLACE. Huntingdon, Que., Gleaner Book, 1919. 49p [BVaU OTP

**Seton, Ernest Thompson, 1860–1946**

THE WILD ANIMAL PLAY FOR CHILDREN. New York, Doubleday, 1900. 79p [BM LC NBFU OTP

**Sharman, Mrs. Lyon, 1872–**

A SOMERSAULT TO LOVE. A Comedy of Changing Manners in China. Toronto, Macmillan, 1926. 48p [BVaU OTU

**Sharpe, Lynch Lawdon**

THE VICEROY'S DREAM; or, The Canadian Government Not "Wide Awake." A Mono-Dramatico-Political Poem. London, Whittaker, 1838. 25p [BM LC OTP

**Ship, Reuben, 1915–**

THE INVESTIGATOR. A Narrative in Dialogue. London, Sidgwick and Jackson, 1956. 118p

**Sinclair, Lister Shedden, 1921–**

A PLAY ON WORDS AND OTHER RADIO PLAYS. Toronto, Dent, 1948. 298p [BVaU NBFU OTP QMM

SOCRATES. A Drama in Three Acts. Toronto, Book Society of Canada, 1957. 103p

WAYS OF MANKIND. Thirteen Dramas of Peoples of the World and How They Live. By Lister Sinclair [and others] . Ed. with commentary by Walter Goldschmidt. Boston, Beacon Press, 1954. 212p

**Skey, Francis W.**

RED RIDING-HOOD. An Operatic Interlude, in Two Acts. Quebec, 1854. 20p [NSWA

**Social Credit Board**

ALICE IN BLUNDERLAND. A Humorous Sketch in One Act. Edmonton, the Board, 1941. 12p [ACG

**Stephen, Alexander Maitland, 1882–1942**

CLASS-ROOM PLAYS FROM CANADIAN HISTORY. Toronto, Dent, 1929. 164p [AE BVa NSHPL OLU

**Stewart, Luke**

ANDREW McMURTY, IMMIGRANT. Toronto, French, 1938. 30p [BM BVaU LC QMBM

DAFT DANNY. A Comedy in One Act. Toronto, French, 1947. 26p [BVaU OTP

RELEASE. Toronto, French, 1937. 28p [BM BVaU LC QMBM

**Stratford, Phyllis (Coate), 1900–**

BRIGHT AND GLORIOUS. Toronto, French, 1938. 32p [BM BVaU OTP QMBM

**Stringer, Arthur John Arbuthnot, 1874–1950**

ALEXANDER WAS GREAT. Greek Burlesque in One Act. Toronto, French, 1937. 25p [Also included in THE CLEVEREST WOMAN IN THE WORLD. ...] [UTQ'38

THE BLOT. A Drama. [MOR'12

THE CLEVEREST WOMAN IN THE WORLD AND OTHER ONE-ACT PLAYS. New York, Bobbs-Merrill, 1939. 272p [BM LC OLU

**Telgmann, Heinrich Bertram**

AGAINST THE WORLD; or, Life in London. A Drama in Four Acts. Kingston, British Whig Office, 1889. 50p [BM LC

**Thomas, Lillian (Beynon), 1874–1961**

JIM BARBER'S SPITE FENCE. A Comedy in One Act. Toronto, French, 1935. 32p [BM BVaU NBFU

**Thompson, Elizabeth Jane (Sweetland), 1858–**

A DOUBLE LIFE. A Drama in 5 Acts. Toronto, Hill & Weir, 1884. 38p [OOP

**Thompson, John Sparrow**

CADETS OF TEMPERANCE. Entertainment for the Christmas Holidays. ... Halifax, Bowes, 1852. 25p [NSHD

**Thompson, Ruth C.**

BEYOND THE SKYLINE. A Play of Modern China (in Four Scenes). Toronto, Committee on Missionary Education, United Church of Canada, 1937. 14p [Brown U

**Thorlakson, E.J.**

PIONEER THEATRE SERIES. Bk. 1. MARIE HEBERT; THE KING'S GIRLS; FATHER LACOMBE; POET OF THE PLAINS. Edmonton, Institute of Applied Art, 1936. 36p [Brown U

**Tremayne, William Andrew, 1864–**

THE MAN WHO WENT. A Play in Four Acts. Boston, Baker, 1918. 96p [OTP

**Underhill, John**

DAMON AND PYTHIAS. A Drama of Quebec Liberalism. N.p., Author, 1891. 31p [MWU NSHD QMSS

**Voaden, Herman Arthur, 1903–**

A BOOK OF PLAYS FOR SCHOOLS AND COMMUNITY DRAMA GROUPS IN CANADA. Ed. by ——. Toronto, Macmillan, 1935. xviii + 316p [OTU

ON STAGE. Plays for School and Community. Ed. by ——. Toronto, Macmillan, 1945. 445p [BVaU OTP

SIX CANADIAN PLAYS. Ed. by ——. Toronto, Copp Clark, 1930. 136p [BVaU NSHD OTP QMM

**Waight, Quentin, 1894–**

PRELUDE TO GLORY. [Poems and a Play.] Seattle, Superior Pub. Co., 1951. xiv + 166p [Includes a one-act play.]

**Walker, Annie Louisa (Mrs. Harry Coghill), 1836–1907**

PLAYS FOR CHILDREN. London, Routledge, 1876. [BM

**Ward, James Edward, 1883–1958**

THE CRADLE IN THE HILLS. A Play of the Nativity. Toronto, Tyrrell, 1941. 30p [LC OTU

... GOD'S PLENTY. A Pastoral Idyll Founded on the Book of Ruth. With Incidental Lyrics. Toronto, Longmans, 1945. 66p [BVaU OTP

**Watson, Samuel James, 1837–1881**

THE LEGEND OF THE ROSES–A Poem; RAVLAN–A Drama. Toronto, Hunter Rose, 1876. 228p [BVaU NBFU OTU QMM

**Waygood, John**

LIKE AS TWO P'S. A Comedy in Four Acts. N.p., n.p., n.d. 24p [No title page. Bound with Alexander Begg's PRACTICAL HANDBOOK AND GUIDE TO MANITOBA. ...] [BViPA

**Williams, Minnie (Harvey)**

THE ROMANCE OF CANADA. An Historical Pageant. Toronto, Ryerson, 1923. 29p [BM OTP

**Williams, Norman, 1923–**

A BATTLE OF WITS. A Play in One Act. Toronto, French, 1956. 29p

WORLDS APART. Six Prize-Winning Plays. Toronto, Copp Clark, 1956. xii + 203p

**Winlow, Alice Maud (Dudley), 1885–**

THE BROKEN FLOWER. London, Fowler Wright, 1927. 16p [OKQ

THE MIRACLE OF ROSES. Vancouver, Chalmers, 1926. 94p [BVaU OTU QMM

**Wood, W.P.**

MINNIE TRAIL; or, The Woman of Wentworth. A Tragedy in Three Acts, &c. &c. Hamilton, Evening Times, 1871. 37p [OTUV

**Worth, Edward**

WORTH'S BURLESQUE RITUAL. Includes Initiation of a Candidate, Opening and Closing Ceremony, Minutes, Orders of Business, Etc., with General Instructions, Written for the Purpose of Creating Amusement at Anniversaries of Secret Societies and for Public Entertainments. ... Kent Bridge, Ont., Author, 1896. 19p [BM

**Wren, Frances**

THE EARLY HISTORY OF ST. ANDREWS AS SHOWN BY HISTORICAL TABLEAUS, AUGUST, 1942. [St. Andrews, N.B.? 1942?]. 12p [NBFU

**Young, David Leonard, 1886–**

THE LIGHT. A Play for Christmas or Easter. Boston, Baker, 1943. 29p [LC

# PART II

# BIOGRAPHY

## Including memoirs, memorial sermons, genealogy, autobiography, reminiscences, letters, diaries, etc.

**Abraham, Dorothy E., 1894–**
LONE CONE. A Journal of Life on the West Coast of Vancouver Island. 3rd ed. Victoria, Author, [1945]. 100p [Later eds., 1946, 1952, 1961.] [AEP BVi OTU

**Acadia University.**
THE ACADIA RECORD, 1838–1953. [4th ed., rev. and enl. by Watson Kirkconnell.] Wolfville, N.S., Acadia University, 1953. 565 p
RECORDS OF THE GRADUATES OF ACADIA UNIVERSITY, 1843–1926. Arranged by Classes. ... Wolfville, Associated Alumni, 1926. 296p [BVaU LC NSWA OTU

**Adam, Graeme Mercer, 1839–1912**
PROMINENT MEN OF CANADA. ... Ed. by ——. Toronto, Canadian Biographical Pub. Co., 1892. 476p [BM BVaU LC NSHD OTP

**Adams, Mrs. Mary, 1928–**
I MARRIED A MONK. Toronto, Evangelical Mission, [1951?]. 67p

**Adamson, Rev. William Agar, 1800–1868**
LETTERS AND ADDRESSES, presented to the Rev. W. Agar Adamson, D.C.L., Chaplain to the ... Legislative Council of Canada. Toronto, Lovell, 1856. 24p [OTP

**Aitken, Katherine (Scott), 1891–1971**
MAKING YOUR LIVING IS FUN. Toronto, Longmans, 1959. 213p
NEVER A DAY SO BRIGHT. Toronto, Longmans, 1956. 249p

**Albani, Emma, 1847–1930**
FORTY YEARS OF SONG. London, Mills & Boon, 1911. 285p [BM LC

**Alderton, Haddon,**
ONE MAN'S MEAT. London, Long, 1937. 288p [BM LC

**Alexander, James Edward, 1803–1885**
PASSAGES IN THE LIFE OF A SOLDIER. London, Hurst & Blackett, 1857. 300p [BM BVaU NSHD OTP

**Allan, Rev. David, 1860–1940**
"FROM THE LUMBER CAMP TO THE MINISTRY." The Autobiography of Rev. David Allan. Toronto, Evangelical Pubs., 1938. 230p [OTP

**Allan, Iris Constance (Sommerville), 1910–**

THE BOY IN BUCKSKINS (BOYHOOD OF JOHN McDOUGALL). Edmonton, Institute of Applied Art, 1959. 160p

**Allen, Grant, 1848–1899**

BIOGRAPHIES OF WORKING MEN. London, Soc. Pro. Christian Knowledge, 1885. 191p [NSHD OLU

... CHARLES DARWIN. New York, Appleton, 1885. 206p [BM LC OTU

IN MEMORIAM GEORGE PAUL MACDONELL. London, Lund, 1895. 64p [BM OTU

**Allen, Joseph Antisell, 1814–1900**

DR. RYERSON. A Review and a Study. Toronto, 1884. 10p [LC OTP

ORANGEISM, CATHOLICISM, AND SIR FRANCIS HINCKS. Toronto, 1877. [MWU

**Alline, Rev. Henry, 1748–1784**

LIFE AND JOURNALS OF THE REV. MR. HENRY ALLINE. Boston, Gilbert & Dean, 1806. 180p [NSWA OOP

**Allison, Leonard A., 1853–1903**

THE REV. OLIVER ARNOLD. Saint John, Sun Print., 1892. 30p [LC NSHD OONL

**Alward, Silas, 1842–1919**

AN ORATION ON PROF. C.F. HARTT, at Acadia College, N.S. Saint John, Knodell, 1884. 11p [NSWA QMBM

**Ambridge, Douglas White, 1898–**

FRANK HARRIS ANSON (1859–1923) PIONEER IN THE NORTH. New York, Montreal, Newcomen Society in North America, 1952. 24p

**Anahareo, 1907?– (Chippewa Woman)**

MY LIFE WITH GREY OWL. London, Davies, 1940. 230p [BM LC OTP

**Anderson, Rev. Duncan, 1828–1903**

SCOTTISH FOLK-LORE; or, Reminiscences of Aberdeenshire, from Pinafore to Gown. New York, Selwin Tait, 1895. 245p [BM OTP

**Anderson, Rev. John, 1823–1908**

REMINISCENCES AND INCIDENTS CONNECTED WITH THE LIFE ... OF THE REV. JOHN ANDERSON. Ed. by his son, the Rev. J.D. Anderson. Toronto, Briggs, 1910. 340p [BM BVaU OTU

**Anderson, Patrick, 1915–**

FIRST STEPS IN GREECE. London, Chatto, 1958. 211p

SEARCH ME. Autobiography–the Black Country, Canada and Spain. London, Chatto, 1957. 237p

SNAKE WINE. A Singapore Episode. London, Chatto, 1955. 288p

**Anderson, Pete, 1869–**

I, THAT'S ME. Escape from a German Prison and Other Adventures. Edmonton, Bradbury Print., [1920?]. 174p [AE

**Anderson, William James, 1813?–1873**

CANADIAN HISTORY AND BIOGRAPHY, AND PASSAGES IN THE LIVES OF A BRITISH PRINCE AND A CANADIAN SEIGNEUR, the Father of the Queen and the Hero of Chateauguay. A Paper read before the Literary and Historical Society of Quebec, December 19th, 1866. Quebec, Middleton & Dawson, 1867. 51p [BVaU LC QMSS

THE LIFE OF F.M., H.R.H. EDWARD, DUKE OF KENT. Illustrated by his Correspondence with the De Salaberry Family ... from 1791–1814. Toronto, Hunter Rose, 1870. 241p [BM BVaU LC NSWA OOU

**Andrew, Frederick William, 1879–**

KLINKER. A Country Doctor's Dog. Toronto, Author, 1948. 101p [BVaU OTP

**Angier, Mrs. Vena**

AT HOME IN THE WOODS. Living The Life of Thoreau Today. By Vena and Bradford Angier. New York, Sheridan House, 1951. 255p

**Annis, Levi Edward, 1858–1933**

ANNIS ANNALS, 1638–1931. Pickering, Printer's Guild, 1931. 56p [OTP

**Anonymous**

A BRIEF BIOGRAPHICAL SKETCH OF THE HON. ROBERT CHARLES WILKINS. Belleville, Chronicle Office, 1866. 8p [OTP

THE CANADIAN BIOGRAPHICAL DICTIONARY AND PORTRAIT GALLERY OF EMINENT AND SELF-MADE MEN. Quebec and Maritime Provinces Volume. Toronto, Am. Biographical Pub. Co., 1880. 778p [BVaU NBFU OLU

THE CANADIAN WHO'S WHO. Toronto, Musson, 1910. 243p [BVaU NSWA OTP

HEARTS OF GOLD. Being Chronicles of Heroism in Canadian History. [Toronto?], Ontario Women's Liberal Association, 1915. 30p [NSHD OLU QMU

JAMES STANLEY McLEAN. An Appreciation by a Group of his Friends. Toronto, R.C. Stone, 1957. 80p

LIFE OF RIGHT REVEREND PATRICK PHELAN, THIRD BISHOP OF KINGSTON. To Which is Added a Synopsis of the Lives of the Two First Bishops of Kingston. By the Clergyman who served Bishop Phelan's Last Mass. Kingston, Lightfoot, 1862. 46p [Haight Pt I

A MEMOIR OF THE LATE MR. WILLIAM RUTTAN. By a Friend. To Which is Prefixed a Sermon ... by the Rev. A.N. Bethune. Cobourg, Chatterton, 1837. 55p [OTP

NARRATIVE OF THE LIFE OF THE DARING MURDERER, HIGHWAYMAN AND BURGLAR, WILLIAM TOWNSEND, JUST TRIED AT THE HALDIMAND ASSIZES FOR THE MURDER OF MR. JOHN H. NELLES OF CAYUGA TOWNSHIP. ... Hamilton, Franklin Lightning Press, 1857. 14p [OTU

THE PEARL OF TROYES; or, Reminiscences of the Early Days of Ville-Marie. Revealed to us in the Heroic Life of Sister Marguerite Bourgeoys, Foundress and First Superior of the Congregation of Notre Dame. Montreal, Can. Print., 1878. 375p [NSWA OTU

PIONEER LIFE ON THE BAY OF QUINTE. Including Genealogies of old Families and Biographical Sketches of Representative Citizens. Toronto, Rolph, n.d. 1005p [BVa NSHD OTP

SKETCH OF THE LIFE OF CATHERINE BREITHAUPT, HER FAMILY AND TIMES. Berlin, Ont., 1911. [Hood cat. no. 87

**Anslow, Florence**

THE HALIBURTON MEMORIAL MUSEUM. Windsor, N.S., 1954. 21p

**Arcand, Mrs. Anne**

UNFORGETTABLE DAYS. [Quebec?], 1958. 15p

**Archer, William L.**

JOE ATKINSON'S TORONTO STAR. The Genius of Crooked Lane. Montreal, [194–?]. 20p [OTP

**Archibald, Edith Jessie (Mortimer), 1854–1938**

LIFE AND LETTERS OF SIR EDWARD MORTIMER ARCHIBALD. By his Daughter, ——. Toronto, Morang, 1924. 266p [BM BVaU LC NSHD OKQ

ONE OF THE WONDERS OF PERSONAL SUCCESS. By an Eyewitness [pseud]. N.p., n.d. 10p [OTU

**Archibald, Raymond Clare, 1875–1955**

CARLYLE'S FIRST LOVE, MARGARET GORDON, LADY BANNERMAN. London, Lane, 1910. 213p [BM BViP LC NSWA OLU

**Ardagh, Henry Hatton, 1853–1936**

LIFE OF HON. SIR JAMES ROBERT GOWAN, K.C.M.G., LL.D., SENATOR OF CANADA. By his Nephew, ——. Toronto, U. of Toronto Press, 1911. 328p [Rev. and enl. ed. of a memoir previously ed. by A.H.U. Colquhoun, *q.v.*] [BM OTP

**Armstrong, Rev. John**

THE LIFE AND LETTERS OF THE REV. GEORGE MORTIMER, RECTOR OF THORNHILL. London, Aylott & Jones, 1847. 308p [BM BVaU OTP

**Armstrong, Nevill Alexander Drummond, 1878?–**

YUKON YESTERDAYS. Thirty Years of Adventure in the Klondike. London, Long, 1936. 287p [BM BVaU LC OTU

**Arsenault, Aubin Edmond, 1870–**

MEMOIRS OF THE HON. A.E. ARSENAULT, Former Premier and Retired Justice, Supreme Court of Prince Edward Island. Charlottetown, Island Guardian Pub., 1951. 188p

**Ashbridge, Wellington Thomas, 1869–**
THE ASHBRIDGE BOOK. Relating to Past and Present Ashbridge Families in America. Toronto, Copp Clark, 1912. 182p [LC OOP

**Ashton, Harry, 1882–**
MADAME LAFAYETTE. Toronto, Macmillan, 1922. 292p [BM BVaU LC NSHD OTU

**Askin, John, 1739–1815**
THE JOHN ASKIN PAPERS. ... Ed. by Milo M. Quaife. [Detroit], Public Library Commission, 1928, 1931. 2v [BM BVaU LC NBFU OTU

**Asselstine, Kathryn Rachel**
A PIONEER FAMILY. [Genealogical history.] Windsor, Ont., priv. print., 1954. 75p

**Atherton, William Henry, 1867–1950**
A CANADIAN EDUCATIONIST OF THE 17TH CENTURY: THE VENERABLE MARGUERITE BOURGEOYS. Montreal, Gazette, 1920. 16p [OTL
THE SAINTLY LIFE OF JEANNE MANCE. First Lay Nurse in North America. St. Louis, Mo., Catholic Hospital Assoc., 1945. 95p [OTP

**Atlay, James Beresford, 1860–1912**
LORD HALIBURTON. A Memoir. ... Toronto, Briggs, 1909. 296p [BM BVaU NBFU OTU

**Ayscough, Florence (Wheelock), 1878–1942**
FLORENCE AYSCOUGH AND AMY LOWELL: CORRESPONDENCE OF A FRIENDSHIP. Ed. by Harley Farnsworth MacNair. Chicago, U. of Chicago Press, 1945. 288p [BM BVaU LC QMM

**Bagnall, F.W.**
NOT MENTIONED IN DESPATCHES. By Ex-Quaker [pseud]. North Vancouver, North Shore Press, 1933. 116p [BVaU NSWA

**Bailey, Jacob, 1731–1808**
THE FRONTIER MISSIONARY. A Memoir of the Life of the Rev. Jacob Bailey, Missionary at Pownalborough, Maine, Cornwallis and Annapolis, N.S. Ed. by Wm. S. Bartlet. Boston, Ide & Dutton, 1853. 365p [BM BVaU NBFU OTP

**Bailey, Joseph Whitman, 1865–1932**
THE CURIOUS STORY OF DR. MARSHALL WITH A FEW LIGHTS ON NAPOLEON AND OTHER PERSONS OF CONSEQUENCE. Cambridge, Mass., Murray, 1930. 113p [BM LC NBFU OTU
LORING WOART BAILEY. The Story of a Man of Science. Saint John, McMillan, 1925. 141p [BM BVaU NBFU OTU

**Bailey, Thomas Melville, 1912–**

TRACES, PLACES AND FACES. Links Between Canada and Scotland. Hamilton, Author, 1957. 67p

**Baines, Henry Edward, 1840–1866**

... THE CRUISE OF THE BREEZE. N.p., n.d. 40p [OTP

IN MEMORIAM, HENRY EDWARD BAINES. [Anon] London, Hunt, [1866?]. 30p [OTP

**Baird, Rev. Frank, 1870–1951**

ADDRESSES AT THE CELEBRATION OF THE ONE HUNDRED AND FIFTIETH ANNIVERSARY OF THE ARRIVAL IN NOVA SCOTIA OF REV. JAMES DRUMMOND MACGREGOR. ... Ed. by ——. Toronto, Presbyterian Pub., 1937. 310p [QMM

**Baird, William Thomas, 1819–1897**

SEVENTY YEARS OF NEW BRUNSWICK LIFE. Autobiographical Sketches. ... Saint John, Day, 1890. 358p [BVaU LC NSWA OTU QMM

**Baker, George Harold, 1877–1916**

A CANADIAN SOLDIER. [Letters ... and a Memoir by J.W. Cunliffe.] New York, priv. print., [1917?]. 83p [BVaU OOP

**Baker, William King**

JOHN T. DORLAND. ... Ed. and with a preface by Anne W. Richardson. London, Headley, 1898. 433p [BM BVaU OLU

A QUAKER WARRIOR. The Life of William Hobson. London, Headley, 1913. 178p [BM

**Baldwin, Harold, 1888–**

A FARM FOR TWO POUNDS. Being the Odyssey of an Emigrant. London, Murray, 1935. 300p [BM LC NSHD OTU QMM

"HOLDING THE LINE." Chicago, McClurg, 1918. 305p [BM LC NSHD OTU

**Balfour, Rev. Charles Wilfred, 1877–**

LIFE AND WORK AND MEMOIRS OF GEORGE THORNELOE, D.C.L., D.D., 1848–1935, BISHOP OF THE DIOCESE OF ALGOMA (1897–1927), METROPOLITAN OF ONTARIO AND ARCHBISHOP OF ONTARIO (1915–1926). By his son-in-law. Peterborough, Ont., Author, 1955. 112p

**Ball, Ernest A.**

JIMMY DAROU, THE KING OF COURAGE. Montreal, priv. print., 1938. 28p [QMBM

**Ball, Geraldine F.**

SOME EXTRACTS AND REMINISCENCES OF A LIFETIME. Regina, Leader, 1922. 165p [ACG SRL

**Ballantyne, Mabel (Erb), 1890–**

THE HISTORY OF THE BALLANTYNE FAMILY. Ed. by ——. N.p., Editor, 1952. 87p

**Banfill, Bessie Jane, 1899–**

LABRADOR NURSE. Toronto, Ryerson, 1952. 218p

**Banks, Margaret Amelia, 1928–**

EDWARD BLAKE, IRISH NATIONALIST. A Canadian Statesman in Irish Politics, 1892–1907. Toronto, U. of Toronto Press, 1957. xii + 370p

**Banwell, Selwyn, 1880–**

A FRONTIER JUDGE [Sir Matthew Begbie]. British Justice in the Earliest Days of Farthest West. Toronto, Rous & Mann, 1938. 30p [BVaU NSHPL OTP

**Baptist Union of Western Canada**

SOME BAPTIST PIONEERS. Edmonton, 1932. 64p [ACG

**Bapty, Walter, 1884–**

MEMOIRS. 1st print. N.p., W. Bapty, 1959. 1v (various pagings). [mimeographed]

**Barbeau, Charles Marius, 1883–1969**

CORNELIUS KRIEGHOFF. Pioneer Painter of North America. Toronto, Macmillan, 1934. 152p [BM BVaU LC NBFU OKQ QMM

COTE, THE WOOD CARVER. Toronto, Ryerson, 1943. 43p [BVaU NBFU OTU QMM

HENRI JULIEN. Toronto, Ryerson, 1941. 44p [BM BVaU LC NBFU OTU QMM

PAINTERS OF QUEBEC. Toronto, Ryerson, 1946. 48p [BVaU LC NSHD OTU QMM

**Barclay, Charles**

LETTERS FROM THE DORKING EMIGRANTS WHO WENT TO UPPER CANADA IN THE SPRING OF 1832. Edited by C. Barclay. London, J. & A. Arch, 1833. 44p [BM OTP

**Barclay, Rev. John, 1812–1887**

EXTRACT FROM A SERMON PREACHED IN ST. ANDREW'S CHURCH, TORONTO ... ON THE OCCASION OF THE SUDDEN DEATH OF COLONEL E.W. THOMSON, One of the Elders of the Congregation. Montreal, Lovell, 1865. 11p [OTP

A SERMON PREACHED ON THE OCCASION OF THE LAMENTED DEATH OF THE HON. ARCHIBALD McLEAN, President of Her Majesty's Court of Error and Appeal for Upper Canada. Toronto, Leader, 1865. 39p [OTP

**Bar-David, Molly (Lyons), 1910–**

MY PROMISED LAND. New York, Putnam, 1953. x + 307p

**Barnes, Rev. Joshua Ninyon, 1830–1915**

LIGHTS AND SHADOWS OF EIGHTY YEARS. An Autobiography. ... Rev. and ed. by his son, Edwin N.C. Barnes. Saint John, Barnes, 1911. 218p [NBFU OTP

**Barnes, William Morris, 1850–**

ROLLING HOME. When Ships were Ships and not Tin Pots. London, Cassell, 1931. 471p [BM LC NfSM

**Barrass, Rev. Edward, 1821–1898**

A GALLERY OF DISTINGUISHED MEN. Napanee, Author, 1870. 346p [BM BVaU OTP

SMILES AND TEARS; or, Sketches from Real Life. ... With intro. by Rev. W.H. Withrow. First Series. Toronto, Hunter Rose, 1879. 200p [BVaU OTP

**Bartlett, Rev. Leonard, 1872–1963**

"UNCLE JOE LITTLE." Life and Memoirs of Joseph Russell Little. Toronto, Briggs, 1903. 251p [BM BVaU OLU

**Bartlett, Robert Abram, 1875–1946**

THE LOG OF BOB BARTLETT. The True Story of Forty Years Seafaring and Exploration. New York, Putnam, 1928. 352p [Also: New York, Blue Ribbon Books, 1932.] [BM BVaU LC QMM

**Bateman, Reginald John Godfrey, 1884?–1918**

REGINALD BATEMAN, TEACHER AND SOLDIER. A Memorial Volume of Selections from his Lectures and other Writings. London, Sotheran, 1922. 147p [BVaU OOA

**Bates, Walter, 1760–1842**

COMPANION FOR CARABOO. A Narrative of the Conduct and Adventures of Henry Frederic Moon, Alias Henry Frederic More Smith ... his Unparalleled Artifices, Impostures, Mechanical Ingenuities. ... With an Introductory Description of New Brunswick; and a Postscript, containing Some Account of Caraboo, the late Female Impostor, at Bristol. ... 2nd ed. London, Allman, 1817. 84p [Various later editions, incorporating additional material under variant titles, such as: THE MYSTERIOUS STRANGER; or, THE ADVENTURES OF HENRY MORE SMITH. Charlottetown, Steam Press, 1855. 109p] [BM BVaU NSWA OTU

THE MYSTERIOUS STRANGER; or, The Adventures of Henry More Smith. [See note under preceding title.]

**Battell, Jud, 1867–1951**

JUD BATTELL'S STORY OF THE EARLY DAYS OF THE WEST. By [i.e., as told to] Evangeline Chapman. Moose Jaw, Bowes Publishers, 1953. 32p

**Baxter, Arthur Beverley, 1891–1964**

MEN, MARTYRS AND MOUNTEBANKS. Beverley Baxter's Inner Story of Personalities and Events Behind the War. London, Hutchinson, 1940. 286p [BM BVaU LC OTU QMM

STRANGE STREET. London, Hutchinson, 1935. 286p [BM BVaU LC NBFU OKQ QMM

WESTMINSTER WATCHTOWER. Toronto, Collins, 1938. 319p [BVaU NBFU OTU QMM

**Baxter, John Babington Maccaulay, 1868–**

SIMON BAXTER (The First United Empire Loyalist to Settle in New Brunswick),

His Ancestry and Descendants. Saint John, New Brunswick Museum, 1943. 46p [BVaU LC OOP

**Bayne, J.N.**

A BRIEF STORY OF JOHN WEIR [1840–1940] AND HIS WIFE. Regina, 1940. 42p [OOP

**Baynes, George Edgar**

EDGAR G. BAYNES, PIONEER OF THE WEST, 1870–1956. Vancouver, Author, 1957. 12p

**Beattie, Jessie Louise, 1896–**

ALONG THE ROAD. Toronto, Ryerson, 1954. 168p

BLACK MOSES, THE REAL UNCLE TOM. Toronto, Ryerson, 1957. xiii + 215p [Life of Josiah Henson]

JOHN CHRISTIE HOLLAND, MAN OF THE YEAR. Toronto, Ryerson, 1956. xiv + 169p

**Beattie, Kim, 1900–**

BROTHER, HERE'S A MAN! The Saga of Klondike Boyle. New York, Macmillan, 1940. 309p [BVa LC OTU

**Begg, Alexander, 1825–1905**

A SKETCH OF THE SUCCESSFUL MISSIONARY WORK OF WILLIAM DUNCAN, amongst the Indian Tribes in Northern British Columbia from 1858–1901. Victoria, 1901. 32p [BVa

**Begg, Alexander, 1839–1897**

SEVENTEEN YEARS IN THE CANADIAN NORTH-WEST. London, Spottiswoode, 1884. 35p [BM BVaU NSWA

**Beland, Henri Sévérin, 1869–1935**

MY THREE YEARS IN A GERMAN PRISON. Toronto, Briggs, 1919. 280p [BVaU LC OTU

**Belaney, George Stansfeld, 1888–1938**

A BIOGRAPHICAL NOTE, AND A DAY AT BEAVER LODGE. By Wa-Sha-Quon-Asin (Grey Owl) [pseud]. London, 1937. 13p [The material quoted in A DAY AT BEAVER LODGE is selected from Grey Owl's writings and published in this form as a souvenir of his visit to the United Kingdom in the autumn of 1937.] [UTQ'39

**Belcher, Edward, 1799–1877**

THE LAST OF THE ARCTIC VOYAGES. Being a Narrative of the Expedition ... in Search of Sir John Franklin, during the Years 1852–53–54. ... London, Reeve, 1855. 2v [BM BVaU LC NSWA OLU QMM

NARRATIVE OF A VOYAGE ROUND THE WORLD; Performed in Her Majesty's Ship Sulphur, during the Years 1836–1842. London, Colburn, 1843. 2v [BM BVaU LC NSHD

NARRATIVE OF THE VOYAGE OF H.M.S. SAMARANG, during the Years 1843–46; Employed Surveying the Islands of the Eastern Archipelago. Accompanied by a Brief Vocabulary of the Principal Languages. London, Reeve, 1848. 2v [BM BVaU LC NSHD

**Bell Telephone Company of Canada**

ALEXANDER GRAHAM BELL, SCIENTIST, TEACHER AND HUMANITARIAN WHOSE INVENTIVE GENIUS GAVE US THE TELEPHONE. Montreal, The Company, 1954. 31p [Rev. ed. First ed., 1947.]

**Bell, Andrew**

BRITISH-CANADIAN CENTENNIUM, 1759-1859. General James Wolfe, his Life and Death. A Lecture Delivered in ... Montreal. Montreal, Lovell, 1859. 48p [NSWA OTP

**Bell, Edwin Wallace, 1908–**

ISRAEL KENNY. His Children and Their Families. Ed. by Lilian M.B. Maxwell. [Vancouver], 1944. 111p [LC NBFU OTP

**Bell, Frederick McKelvey, 1878–1931**

THE FIRST CANADIANS IN FRANCE. The Chronicle of a Military Hospital in the War Zone. New York, Doran, 1917. 308p [LC NSWA OTU QMM

**Bell, Winthrop Pickard, 1884–**

BRIGADIER-GENERAL JEDIDIAH PREBLE (1707–1784) AND HIS PARTICIPATION IN NOVA SCOTIA HISTORY. Halifax, Halcraft Print., 1954. 39p

**Bellamy, Herbie**

A SKETCH OF THE LIFE OF HERBIE BELLAMY. Toronto, Women's Missionary Soc. of Methodist Church, 1902. 29p [Peel Supp

**Bender, Louis Prosper, 1844–1917**

OLD AND NEW CANADA, 1753–1844: Historic Scenes and Social Pictures; or, The Life of Joseph-François Perrault. Montreal, Dawson, 1882. 291p [BM BVaU LC MWU NSWA OTU QMM

**Benson, Nathaniel Anketell Michael, 1903–1966**

"IN MEMORIAM PRINCIPIS." A Memorial Tribute To My Honoured Friend The Right Honourable W.L. Mackenzie King, O.M., P.C. (1874–1950) on The First Anniversary of His Death, July 22nd, 1951. Toronto, 1951. 2 + vip

NONE OF IT CAME EASY. The Story of James Garfield Gardiner. Toronto, Burns & MacEachern, 1955. 272p

**Bergmann, Werner, 1915–**

DOCTORS ARE PEOPLE. By W. Berg Mann [pseud]. New York, Vantage Press 1954. 88p

**Bernier, Joseph Elzéar, 1852–1934**

MASTER MARINER AND ARCTIC EXPLORER. A Narrative of Sixty Years at Sea. ... Ottawa, Le Droit, 1939. 409p [BM BVaU LC OTU QMM

**Berton, Laura Beatrice (Thompson)**

I MARRIED THE KLONDIKE. Boston, Toronto, Little Brown, 1954. x + 269p

**Berton, Pierre Francis de Marigny, 1920–**

THE ROYAL FAMILY. The Story of the British Monarchy from Victoria to Elizabeth. Toronto, McClelland, 1954. 273p

**Bertrand, Elie-Oscar, 1894–**

NOTES, SOUVENIRS OF FORTY YEARS OF FAMILY LIFE, AND PUBLIC AND POLITICAL ACTIVITIES. ... Ottawa, Author, 1955. 88p

**Bethune, Rev. Alexander Neil, 1800–1879**

MEMOIR OF THE RIGHT REV. JOHN STRACHAN, FIRST BISHOP OF TORONTO. Toronto, Rowsell, 1870. 385p [BM BVaU LC NSWA OTU

A SERMON PREACHED ... ON OCCASION OF THE DEATH OF MRS. BOULTON, Wife of George Strange Boulton, Esquire, M.P.P. Cobourg, Chatterton, 1838. 21p [OTP

A SERMON PREACHED IN THE CHURCH OF ST. GEORGE THE MARTYR, TORONTO, ON SUNDAY, NOVEMBER 19, 1876, ON OCCASION OF THE DEATH OF THE HONORABLE JOHN HILLYARD CAMERON. Toronto, Rowsell & Hutchinson, 1876. 16p [NSWA OTP

SERMON. By ——. Prefixed to A MEMOIR OF THE LATE MR. WILLIAM RUTTAN. By a Friend. Cobourg, Chatterton, 1837. [OTP

**Bethune, Rev. John, 1791–1872**

A NARRATIVE OF THE CONNECTION OF THE REV. J. BETHUNE, D.D., WITH McGILL COLLEGE. ... Montreal, Lovell & Gibson, 1846. 56p [OTP

A SERMON ... ON THE OCCASION OF THE DEATH OF THE LATE HON. CHIEF JUSTICE REID. Montreal, Lovell & Gibson, 1848. 17p [BM NSHD QMM

**Beurling, George F.**

MALTA SPITFIRE. The Story of a Fighter Pilot. By Flying Officer F. Beurling and Leslie Roberts. Toronto, Oxford U. Press, 1943. 235p [BM BVaU OTU QMSS

**Bezanson, A. Maynard, 1878–1958**

SODBUSTERS INVADE THE PEACE. Toronto, Ryerson, 1954. 209p

**Bezanson, Rev. W.B.**

THE ROMANCE OF RELIGION. A Sketch of the Life of Henry Alline, in the Pioneer Days of the Maritime Provinces. Kentville, N.S., Kentville Pub. Co., 1927. 71p [NSWA OTP

**Biggar, Charles Robert Webster, 1847–1909**

SIR OLIVER MOWAT. A Biographical Sketch. Toronto, Warwick & Rutter, 1905. 2v [BM BVaU LC NSWA OTU QMM

**Biggar, Emerson Bristol, 1853–1921**

ANECDOTAL LIFE OF SIR JOHN MACDONALD. ... Montreal, Lovell, 1891. 332p [BM BVaU LC NSWA OKQ QMM

**Biggar, Henry Percival, 1872–1938**

A COLLECTION OF DOCUMENTS RELATING TO JACQUES CARTIER AND THE SIEUR DE ROBERVAL. Ottawa, Public Archives, 1930. 577p [BVaU NSHD OTU QMM

**Bilkey, Paul Ernest, 1878–**

PERSONS, PAPERS AND THINGS. Being the Casual Recollections of a Journalist, with some Flounderings in Philosophy. Toronto, Ryerson, 1940. 235p [BM BVaU NBFU OTU QMM

**Bingham, Helen E.**

AN IRISH SAINT. The Life Story of Ann Preston ("Holy Ann"). Toronto, Briggs, 1907. 155p [BM BVaU OTU

**Binnie-Clark, Georgina**

WHEAT AND WOMAN. Toronto, Bell & Cockburn, 1914. 413p [BM BVaU LC NSHD OTU

**Bird, William Richard, 1891–**

AND WE GO ON. Toronto, Hunter Rose, 1931. [OTU

THE TWO JACKS. The Amazing Adventures of Major Jack M. Veness and Major Jack L. Fairweather. Philadelphia, Smith, 1954. 209p

**Bishop, William Avery, 1894–1956**

THE FLYING SQUAD. By Colonel William A. Bishop and Major Rothesay Stuart-Wortley. New York, Doran, 1927. 260p [BM LC OTMC QMM

WINGED WARFARE. Hunting the Huns in the Air. London, Hodder, 1918. 301p [BM BVaU LC NSHD OTU QMM

**Black, Cyrus, 1811?–1900**

HISTORICAL RECORD OF THE POSTERITY OF WILLIAM BLACK WHO SETTLED IN THIS COUNTRY IN 1775. Brought up to the year 1885 by Cyrus Black of Amherst, N.S. The records from 1885 to 1959 were compiled by L.W. Black of Middle Sackville, N.B. Sackville, Tribune Press, 1959. 167p

**Black, Martha Louise (Munger), 1866–1957**

KLONDIKE DAYS. Whitehorse, priv. print., 1954. 38p

MY FIRST CHRISTMAS MEMORY DURING THE CHICAGO FIRE OF 1871. Whitehorse, priv. print., 1953. 11p

MY SEVENTY YEARS. By Mrs. George Black. ... As told to Elizabeth Bailey Price. ... London, Nelson, 1938. 317p [BM BVaU LC NSHD OTU QMM

TWO ROYAL ELIZABETHS. Whitehorse, priv. print., 1953. 16p

**Blakeny, Charles Hanford, 1888–1961**

THE STORY OF A BUSINESS AND ITS FOUNDERS. Moncton, N.B., priv. print., 1960. 160p [Record of the origin and development of Blakeny & Son Ltd., and Blakeny Concrete Products Ltd., 1900–60.]

**Blanchard, Henry Percy, 1862–**

THE ANCESTRAL McCURDYS. Their Origin and Remote History. London, Covenant, 1930. 42p [LC NSWA OOA

GENEALOGICAL RECORD & BIOGRAPHICAL SKETCHES OF THE McCURDYS OF NOVA SCOTIA. Comp. and ed. by ——. London, Covenant, 1930. xxi + 228p [BM LC NBFU

I REMEMBER. Sketches. N.p., Tribune Job Print., n.d. 58p [NSWA

**Bland, Salem Goldworth, 1859–1950**

JAMES HENDERSON, D.D. Toronto, McClelland, 1926. 360p [BM BVaU OTU QMM

**Blauveldt, Robert Brooks, 1894–**

THE BLAUVELDT FAMILY IN NOVA SCOTIA. Including all the Yarmouth County Lents and Many of the Van Nordens and Hatfields; with all these Lines Traced back to their Arrival in America in the Early 1600's. Comp. by ——. [Tusket? N.S., 1939.] 19p [BM LC NSHD

LEADERS OF NOVA SCOTIA, 1936. A "Who's Who" of the Political, Professional, Commercial and Moral Leaders of the Province. Ed. by ——. Yarmouth, Loyalist Press, 1936. 82p [BM LC OTP

**Blyth, Stephen Cleveland, 1771–**

THE CONVERSION OF STEPHEN CLEVELAND BLYTH, TO THE FAITH OF THE CATHOLIC, APOSTOLIC & ROMAN CHURCH. ... Montreal, Nahum Mower, 1822. 100p [OTP

**Bock, William George, 1884–**

THE BOOK OF SKELETONS. Saskatoon, Modern Press, 1960. 173p

**Boddy, Samuel Johnson, 1826–1905**

A BRIEF MEMOIR OF THE REV. SAMUEL B. ARDAGH. Toronto, Rowsell & Hutchinson, 1874. 174p [OTP

**Bogart, Marshall Campbell, 1847–**

SOME NOTES ON THE HISTORY OF THE BOGART FAMILY IN CANADA. With Genealogical Record of my Parents, Lewis Lazier Bogart and Elizabeth Cronk Bogart. Comp. by ——. Toronto, Briggs, 1918. 71p [LC OTP

**Boggs, William Edward, 1867–1935**

THE GENEALOGICAL RECORD OF THE BOGGS FAMILY, THE DESCENDANTS OF EZEKIEL BOGGS. Halifax, Royal Print., 1916. 105p [NSHD

**Bompas, Charlotte Selina (Cox), 1830–1917**

A HEROINE OF THE NORTH. Memoirs of Charlotte Selina Bompas (1830–1917), Wife of the First Bishop of Selkirk (Yukon). Comp. by S.A. Archer. Toronto, Macmillan, 1929. 187p [BM BVaU LC OTU QMM

**Bond, George John, 1850–**

SKIPPER GEORGE NETMAN. A Story of Outpost Methodism in Newfoundland. London, Woolmer, 1887. 126p [A later ed.: Toronto, 1911. 126p] [BM BVaU OTU

**Bone, Peter Turner, 1859–1945**

WHEN THE STEEL WENT THROUGH. Reminiscences of a Railroad Pioneer. Toronto, Macmillan, 1947. 180p [BVaU LC NSHD OTU QMM

**Boniface, Father, 1880–**

PIONEERING IN THE WEST. Memories of His Life and Experiences in the West with the Franciscans. Vancouver, Alverna Distributors, 1957. xiv + 277p

**Borden, Robert Laird, 1854–1937**

ROBERT LAIRD BORDEN: HIS MEMOIRS. Ed. and with a preface by Henry Borden, with an intro. by Arthur Meighen. Toronto, Macmillan, 1938. 2v [BM BVaU LC NSHD OTU QMM

**Borthwick, Rev. John Douglas, 1832–1912**

HISTORY AND BIOGRAPHICAL GAZETEER OF MONTREAL TO THE YEAR 1892. Montreal, Lovell, 1892. 531p [BVaU OTU QMM

MONTREAL, ITS HISTORY. To Which is Added Biographical Sketches. Montreal, Drysdale, 1875. 153p [BVaU LC NSWA QMM

**Bossin, Hye**

A SAINT IN STREET CLOTHES. Willie Frankel, His Life and Loyalties. Toronto, Newsboy's Benefit Fund, 1939. 33p [QMJ

**Boulton, Charles Arkoll, 1841–1899**

REMININSCENCES OF THE NORTH-WEST REBELLIONS ... and a Chapter on Canadian Social and Political Life. Toronto, Grip, 1886. 531p [BM BVaU NSWA OTP

**Bourinot, Arthur Stanley, 1893–1969**

EDWARD WILLIAM THOMSON (1849–1924). A Bibliography, with Notes and some Letters. Ottawa, Author, 1955. 28p

FIVE CANADIAN POETS: Duncan Campbell Scott, Archibald Lampman, William E. Marshall, Charles Sangster, George Frederick Cameron. Ottawa, Author, 1954. 26p [Rev. ed., 1956]

MORE LETTERS OF DUNCAN CAMPBELL SCOTT. ... (2nd series). Sel. and ed. by ——. (With some personal recollections by the editor.) Ottawa, Editor, 1960. 104p

SOME LETTERS OF DUNCAN CAMPBELL SCOTT, ARCHIBALD LAMPMAN & OTHERS. Ed. by ——. Ottawa, Editor, 1959. 63p

**Bourinot, John George, 1837–1902**

BUILDERS OF NOVA SCOTIA. Toronto, Copp Clark, 1900. 197p [BVaU LC NSWA OTU QMM

LORD ELGIN. Toronto, Morang, 1903. 276p [BM BVaU LC NSHD OTU QMM

**Boyd, John, 1864–1933**

SIR GEORGE ETIENNE CARTIER, BART. His Life and Times. A Political History of Canada from 1814 until 1873. Toronto, Macmillan, 1914. 439p [BM BVaU LC NSHD OKQ QMM

**Boyle, David, 1842–1911**

NOTES ON THE LIFE OF DR. JOSEPH WORKMAN. Toronto, 1894. [DCB

**Boyle, George, 1902–1956**

PIONEER IN PURPLE. The Life and Work of Archbishop Neil McNeil. Montreal, Palm Publishers, 1951. 290p

FATHER TOMPKINS OF NOVA SCOTIA. New York, Kenedy, 1953. 234p

THE POOR MAN'S PRAYER. The Story of Credit Union Beginnings. [Fictionized biography of Alphonse Desjardins.] New York, Harper, 1951. 207p

**Bradley, Mrs. Mary, 1771–**

A NARRATIVE OF THE LIFE AND CHRISTIAN EXPERIENCE OF MRS. MARY BRADLEY OF ST. JOHN, N.B. Written by herself. ... Boston, Strong & Brodhead, 1849. 374p [BVaU NBFU OOP

**Brady, Alexander, 1896–**

THOMAS D'ARCY McGEE. Toronto, Macmillan, 1925. 182p [BM BVaU LC NSHD OTU QMM

**Brandis, Maxine (van Vollenhoven), 1910–**

LAND FOR OUR SONS. London, Toronto, Hurst & Blackett, 1958. 195p

**Brasset, Edmund Alfred, 1907–**

A DOCTOR'S PILGRIMAGE. Philadelphia, Lippincott, 1951. 256p [Later ed. with title: BACKWOODS DOCTOR. London, Transworld Pubs., 1956. 253p]

**Bready, John Wesley, 1887–1953**

DOCTOR BARNARDO. Physician, Pioneer, Prophet. Child Life Yesterday and To-day. London, Allen & Unwin, 1931. 271p [BM BVaU LC NSHD OTU QMM

**Breckenridge, William, 1894–**

FROM VIMY TO MONS. A Historical Narrative. N.p., 1957. 251p [Autobiographical account of the author's experiences in World War 1.] [mimeographed]

**Bridgman, Rev. Wellington, 1853–1922**

BREAKING PRAIRIE SOD. The Story of a Pioneer Preacher in the Eighties. With a Discussion of the Burning Question of Today, "Shall the Alien Go?" Toronto, Musson, 1920. 265p [OTU

**Bridle, Augustus, 1869–1952**

SONS OF CANADA. Short Studies of Characteristic Canadians. Toronto, Dent, 1916. 279p [BM BVaU LC NSWA OTU QMM

**Brierley, James Samuel, 1858–1935**

1881 AND ONWARD. Reminiscences of St. Thomas and Elgin County Half a Century Ago. St. Thomas, Ont., Author, 1931. 47p [OLU

**Britnell, John**

BOOKS AND BOOKSELLERS IN ANCIENT AND MODERN TIMES. With Autobiographical Experiences of the Past Sixty Years. Toronto, priv. print., 1923. 32p [LC OTU

**Brock, Anna Maude (Cawthra)**

BROCK FAMILY RECORDS. Toronto, Stapleton, 1927. 153p [BM LC NSWA OTU

THE CAWTHRA FAMILY. Past and Present. Notes by Henry Cawthra and Others. Comp. by A. Maude (Cawthra) Brock, and ed. by A.H. Young. Toronto, 1924. 47p [BM OLU

THE MILLS, HOLTON, AND SMITH FAMILIES. Comp. by ——. Toronto, 1927. [BM OTU

**Brockington, Leonard Walter, 1888–**

MR. MACKENZIE KING'S PUBLIC BEQUESTS. A Commentary. C.B.C. National Network, Aug. 8, 1950. Ottawa, Estate of W.L.M. King, 1950. 7p [OONL

**Brodie, Neil**

TWELVE DAYS WITH THE INDIANS, MAY 14–MAY 26, 1885. ... Being his Experience in Poundmaker's Camp during the Rebellion of 1885. Battleford, Saskatchewan Herald, 1932. 8p [SSU

**Broley, Mrs. Myrtle Jeanne**

EAGLE MAN. Charles L. Broley's Field Adventures with American Eagles. New York, Pellegrini & Cudahy, 1952. xiv + 210p

**Brooks, Rev. Edward Arnold**

PADRE HOLMES. Portrait of a Ministry. Ed. by ——. Toronto, Editorial Department of the General Board of Religious Education for the Diocese of Niagara, 1958. 66p

**Brown, Audrey Alexândra, 1904–**

THE LOG OF A LAME DUCK. Toronto, Macmillan, 1938. 292p [BM BVaU LC NSHD OKQ

**Brown, Margaret Adeline (Porter), 1867–**

EXTRACTS FROM THE LIFE OF JOSEPH BRANT, and history of Six Nations Indians. Brantford, Moyer, 1941. 44p [Extracts from a book not then published.] [CC

LIFE OF JOSEPH BRANT. Comprising in Part the Origin and History of the Iroquois or Six Nations Indians. N.p., n.d. 166p [OTL OLU

**Brown, Rev. Robert Christopher Lundin, –1876**

KLATSASSAN, AND OTHER REMINISCENCES OF MISSIONARY LIFE IN BRITISH COLUMBIA. London, S.P.C.K., 1873. 199p [BM BVaU LC NBFU

**Brown, Thomas Storrow, 1803–1888**

1837: MY CONNECTION WITH IT. Quebec, Renault, 1898. 38p [BM BVaU NBFU OTU QMBM

**Brown, William Gordon, 1904–**

TO TESTIFY ... THE GRACE OF GOD. In Memoriam Pastor W.J.H. Brown. Toronto, Author, 1935. 60p [CC

**Bruce, Herbert Alexander, 1868–1963**

VARIED OPERATIONS. An Autobiography. Toronto, Longmans, 1958. xiv + 366p

**Bryce, Rev. George, 1844–1931**

JOHN BLACK, THE APOSTLE OF THE RED RIVER. Toronto, Briggs, 1898. 158p [BM BVaU NSWA OTP

THE LIFE OF LORD SELKIRK. Coloniser of Western Canada. Toronto, Musson, 1912. 95p [BVaU LC NSHD OKQ QMM

MACKENZIE, SELKIRK, SIMPSON. Toronto, Morang, 1905. 305p [BM BVaU LC NSHD OTU QMM

SKETCH OF THE LIFE AND DISCOVERIES OF ROBERT CAMPBELL. Winnipeg, Manitoba Free Press, 1898. 18p [LC OTP

**Bublitz, Mrs. Dorothea E. (Mackie), 1894–**

LIFE ON THE DOTTED LINE. New York, Vantage Press, 1960. 110p

**Buchanan, Arthur William Patrick, 1870–1939**

THE BENCH AND BAR OF LOWER CANADA DOWN TO 1850. Montreal, Burton's, 1925. 219p [BM BVaU LC NBFU OTU QMM

THE BUCHANAN BOOK. The Life of Alexander Buchanan, Q.C., of Montreal, Followed by an Account of the Family of Buchanan. Montreal, Author, 1911. 475p [BVaU LC OTU QMM

LATER LEAVES OF THE BUCHANAN BOOK. Montreal, Garand, 1929. 482p [QMM

**Buchanan, Donald William, 1908–1966**

JAMES WILSON MORRICE. Toronto, Ryerson, 1937. 187p [BM BVaU LC NSHD OTU QMM

**Buckingham, William, 1832–1915**

THE HON. ALEXANDER MACKENZIE. His Life and Times. By William Buckingham and Hon. Geo. W. Ross. Toronto, Rose, 1892. 678p [BM BVaU LC NSWA OTU QMM

**Buffalo Child Long Lance, Blood Indian Chief, –1932**

LONG LANCE. London, Transworld Publishers, 1956. 236p [First pub. New York, Cosmopolitan Book Corp., 1928.]

**Bull, William Perkins, 1870–1947**

FROM BROCK TO CURRIE. The Military Development and Exploits of Canadians in General and of the Men of Peel in Particular, 1791–1930. (Perkins Bull Hist. Ser.) Toronto, Perkins Bull Fdn., George J. McLeod, 1935. xxiv + 772p [BM BVaU NSHD OKQ OOA

**Bullock, Reginald Heber, 1828–**

A MEMOIR OF THE VERY REV. WILLIAM BULLOCK, DEAN OF NOVA SCOTIA. Halifax, Morton, 1899. 42p [NSWA OTU

**Bullock, Rev. William, 1797–1874**

THE RULER'S DAUGHTER RAISED. A Funeral Discourse on the Occasion of the Death of Miss Bliss. Halifax, 1851. 11p [BibC

**Bullock Family (Benjamin Bullock, 1792–1852). Canadian Branch.**

DESCENDANTS OF BENJAMIN BULLOCK III. Lethbridge, Paramount Print., 1956. 278p

**Burgess, Barry Hovey, 1888–**

BURGESS GENEALOGY, KING'S COUNTY, NOVA SCOTIA. New York, Fitchett, 1941. 93p [BVaU LC NSHD OTU QMM

**Burkholder, Mabel Grace (Clare), 1881–**

KIT. Comp. by ——. Niagara Falls, Evening Review, 1933. 16p [Life of Kathleen Blake Coleman.] [Brown U OTU

**Burnett, Rev. Andrew Ian, 1906–**

THE RIGHT HONOURABLE WILLIAM LYON MACKENZIE KING. P.C., O.M., December 17th, 1874–July 22nd, 1950. Memorial Addresses Delivered at St. Andrew's Church, Ottawa ... July 26th ... July 30th, 1950. Ottawa, Laurier House, 1950. 15p [OONL

**Burnham, John Hampden, 1860–1940**

CANADIANS IN THE IMPERIAL NAVAL AND MILITARY SERVICE ABROAD. Toronto, Williamson, 1891. 240p [BM BVaU NSHD OTU

**Burns, Rev. Robert Ferrier, 1826–1896**

THE LIFE AND TIMES OF THE REV. ROBERT BURNS. Including an Unfinished Autobiography. Ed. by his Son, ——. Toronto, Campbell, 1872. 462p [BVaU LC NSHD OOP QMM

**Burns, William C., 1857–1929?**

SEEING THE WORLD THROUGH THE EYES OF OTHERS. Edmonton, 1929. 16p [ACG

TWENTY YEARS OF THRILLING ADVENTURES IN THE SILENT PLACES OF THE NORTH. By W.C. Burns (blind), [with the assistance of Ruby Erwin. Edmonton, Douglas Print., 1929?]. 72p [AEU

**Burpee, Lawrence Johnstone, 1873–1946**

CHARLES HEAVYSEGE. A Monograph. Ottawa, Royal Society of Canada, 1901. 42p [NSHD OLU

PATHFINDERS OF THE GREAT PLAINS. A Chronicle of La Vérendrye and his Sons. Toronto, Glasgow Brook, 1914. 116p [BM BVaU LC NSWA OTU QMM

SANDFORD FLEMING, EMPIRE BUILDER. London, Oxford U. Press, 1915. 288p [BM BVaU LC NSHD OTU QMM

**Burris, Matthew George, 1887–1948**

MY PIONEER ANCESTORS. An Account of the Burris and Dean Families of Musquodoboit, Nova Scotia. ... [Truro, N.S.? 1950?]. 293p [OONL

**Burt, Silas Wright, 1830–1912**

AN ENGINEER ON THE GREAT WESTERN. A Selection from the Personal Reminiscences of Silas Wright Burt. Ed. by A.G. Bogue and Lilian R. Benson. London, Ont., Lawson Memorial Library, U. of Western Ontario, 1952. 35p

**Burton, Charles Luther, 1876–**

A SENSE OF URGENCY. Memoirs of a Canadian Merchant. Toronto, Clarke Irwin, 1952. 363p

**Burton, Jean, 1905–1952**

ELISABETH NEY. By Jan Fortune and Jean Burton. Toronto, Ryerson, 1943. 300p [BM BVaU LC QMM

GARIBALDI, KNIGHT OF LIBERTY. New York, Knopf, 1945. 225p [LC

HEYDAY OF A WIZARD: DANIEL HOME, THE MEDIUM. New York, Knopf, 1944. 275p [BM LC OTU QMM

KATHERINE FELTON AND HER SOCIAL WORK IN SAN FRANCISCO. Stanford U., Delkin, 1947. 274p [LC OTU

LYDIA PINKHAM IS HER NAME. New York, Farrar, 1949. 279p [LC OTU QMM

SIR RICHARD BURTON'S WIFE. New York, Knopf, 1941. 378p [BM BVaU LC OTU QMM

**Burwash, Rev. Nathanael, 1839–1918**

EGERTON RYERSON. Toronto, Morang, 1903. 303p [Pref.: "The little work is the product of joint labour with my ... colleague, Dr. A.H. Reynar."] [BM BVaU LC NSWA OTU QMM

MEMORIALS OF THE LIFE OF EDWARD & LYDIA ANN JACKSON. Toronto, Rose, 1876. 86p [BVaU LC OKQ

**Buschlen, John Preston, 1888–**

SENOR PLUMMER. The Life and Laughter of an Old Californian. By Don Juan [pseud]. Los Angeles, Times Mirror, 1942. 242p [BVaU LC

**Butler, William Francis, 1838–1910**

SIR WILLIAM BUTLER. An Autobiography. London, Constable, 1911. 476p [BM BVaU NSWA OTP QMM

**Byerly, Alpheus Edward, 1894–1960**

THE McCRAES OF GUELPH. Elora, Ont., Elora Express, 1932. 13p [BVaU OTP

**C., A.L.O. (pseud)**

THE STORY OF A DARK PLOT; or, Tyranny on the Frontier. By A.L.O.C. [pseud]. Montreal, Lovell, 1898. 197p [Also: Boston, Warren Press, 1903.] [On dismissal of Wm. W. Smith, temperance agitator, from the service of the C.P.R.] [BM BVaU OTU

**Calnek, William Arthur, 1822–1892**

A BRIEF MEMOIR OF THE LATE HON. JAMES WILLIAM JOHNSTON, FIRST JUDGE IN EQUITY OF NOVA SCOTIA. Saint John, Knodell, 1884. 49p [NSWA QMM

**Calvert, Reuben, 1865–1940**

THE STORY OF ABIGAIL BECKER, THE HEROINE OF LONG POINT. As Told by her Step-Daughter, Mrs. Henry Wheeler. Ed. by ——. Toronto, Briggs, 1899. 20p [OTP

**Cameron, James Malcolm, 1913–**

THE DESCENDANTS OF DONALD CAMERON, A HIGHLAND IMMIGRANT WHO SETTLED AT PITCHER'S FARM, COUNTY OF ANTIGONISH, NOVA SCOTIA, CANADA. New Glasgow, N.S., Hector Pub. Co., 1957. 73p

SHIPS AND SEAMEN OF NEW GLASGOW, NOVA SCOTIA. New Glasgow, Author, 1959. 45p

**Campbell, Mrs. Dorothy de Brissac**

DU BARRY. An Intimate Biography. New York, Covici Friede, 1931. 351p [BVaU LC QMM

THE INTRIGUING DUCHESS, MARIE DE ROHAN, DUCHESSE DE CHEVREUSE. New York, Covici Friede, 1930. 392p [BM LC NBFU OTP QMM

**Campbell, Gray, 1912–**

WE FOUND PEACE. Toronto, Ryerson, 1953. 244p

**Campbell, Jessie (Buchanan)**

THE PIONEER PASTOR. Some Reminiscences of the Life and Labours of the Rev. George Buchanan, M.D., First Presbyterian Minister of Beckwith, Lanark County, Upper Canada. Toronto, Author, 1900. 56p [Another ed., 1905.] [BVaU OLU

**Campbell, John Lorne, 1906–**
FR ALLAN McDONALD OF ERISKAY, 1859–1905, PRIEST, POET, AND FOLKLORIST. Based upon a Broadcast Talk Recorded at Antigonish, Nova Scotia, in May, 1953, and Printed to Mark the Fiftieth Anniversary of the Consecration of Eriskay Church, built by Fr. Allan. London, Oliver & Boyd, 1954. 31p

**Campbell, Marjorie Elliott (Wilkins), 1901–**
THE SOIL IS NOT ENOUGH. Toronto, Macmillan, 1938. 285p [Biography of her father, William Herbert Wilkins.] [BM BVaU LC OTU SSU

**Campbell, Marjorie (Freeman), 1896–**
HOLBROOK OF THE SAN. Toronto, Ryerson, 1953. xi + 212p

**Campbell, Milton Neil, 1881–**
REMINISCENCES OF PIONEER DAYS IN THE WEST. Hamilton, Author, [1960?]. 12p

**Campbell, Robert, 1808–1894**
TWO JOURNALS OF ROBERT CAMPBELL (CHIEF FACTOR, HUDSON'S BAY COMPANY) 1808 TO 1853. ... Seattle, 1958. 151p [Preface signed John W. Todd, Jr.] [mimeographed]

**Campbell, Robert Eldon, 1871–**
I WOULD DO IT AGAIN. Reminiscences of the Rockies. Toronto, Ryerson, 1959. ix + 204p

**Campbell, Robert McAlpine, 1907–**
WHEE! THE PEOPLE. A Collection of Election Yarns. Toronto, Nelson, 1957. 75p

**Camsell, Charles, 1876–1958**
SON OF THE NORTH. Toronto, Ryerson, 1954. xii + 244p

**Canadian Association of Children's Librarians.**
LILLIAN H. SMITH, A TRIBUTE FROM THE C.A.C.L. Ottawa, Canadian Library Association, 1952. 60p

**Canadian Daily Newspaper Publishers Association.**
RENOWNED EDITORS OF CANADIAN DAILY NEWSPAPERS. Toronto, Thomson Newspapers, 1957. 21p

**Canadian Music Library Association.**
A BIO-BIBLIOGRAPHICAL FINDING LIST OF CANADIAN MUSICIANS AND THOSE WHO HAVE CONTRIBUTED TO MUSIC IN CANADA, COMPILED BY A COMMITTEE OF THE CANADIAN MUSIC LIBRARY ASSOCIATION, 1960–61. Ottawa, Canadian Library Association, 1961. 53p [mimeographed]

**Canadian Newspaper Service**
REFERENCE BOOK, 1927+. Biographical Reference Data and Other General

Information for Library, Newspaper and Individual Use. Montreal, Can. Newspaper Service, 1928 +. [Title changed in 1936 to NATIONAL REFERENCE BOOK ON CANADIAN MEN AND WOMEN.] [BVaU LC NBFU OTU QMM

**Canadian Press Syndicate**

ENCYCLOPEDIA OF CANADIAN BIOGRAPHY. Containing Brief Sketches and Steel Engravings of Canada's Prominent Men. Montreal, Canadian Press Syndicate, 1904–7. 3v [OTU

**Canadian Publicity Co.**

PIONEERS AND PROMINENT PEOPLE OF MANITOBA. Winnipeg, Bulman, 1925. 367p [BVaU OTU

PIONEERS AND PROMINENT PEOPLE OF SASKATCHEWAN. Toronto, Ryerson, 1924. 343p [BVaU

PROMINENT PEOPLE OF THE MARITIME PROVINCES. Saint John, Canadian Pub. Co., 1922. 215p [OTU

PROMINENT PEOPLE OF THE PROVINCE OF ONTARIO. Ottawa, Can. Biographies, 1925. 274p [OTU

**Cannell, Kathleen Biggar (Eaton), 1891–**

JAM YESTERDAY. New York, Morrow, 1945. 239p [LC OTU QMM

**Careless, James Maurice Stockford, 1919–**

BROWN OF THE GLOBE. Toronto, Macmillan, 1959–63. 2v

**Carman, Bliss, 1861–1929**

BLISS CARMAN'S SCRAP BOOK. A Table of Contents. Ed. with a postscript by Lorne Pierce. Toronto, Ryerson, [1931]. 18p [An index of a scrap book kept by Carman of his fugitive writings, 1883–1919.] [BVaU LC NSHD QMM

**Carr, Emily, 1871–1945**

THE BOOK OF SMALL. Toronto, Oxford U. Press, 1942. 245p [BM BVaU LC NSHD OTU

EMILY CARR: HER PAINTINGS AND SKETCHES. Toronto, Oxford U. Press, 1945. 64p [BM BVaU LC NBFU OTU

GROWING PAINS. The Autobiography of Emily Carr. Toronto, Oxford U. Press, 1946. 381p [BM BVaU LC NSHD OTU QMM

THE HEART OF A PEACOCK. Ed. by Ira Dilworth. Toronto, Oxford U. Press, 1953. 234p

THE HOUSE OF ALL SORTS. Toronto, Oxford U. Press, 1944. 222p [BM BVaU LC NSHD OTU

KLEE WYCK. Toronto, Oxford U. Press, 1941. 155p [BM BVaU LC NBFU OKQ

**Carr, William James Guy, 1895–1959**

BRASS HATS AND BELL-BOTTOMED TROUSERS. Unforgettable and Splendid

Feats of the Harwich Patrol. Being volume two of BY GUESS AND BY GOD. London, Hutchinson, 1939. 272p [OTP

BY GUESS AND BY GOD. The Story of the British Submarines in the War. Garden City, Doubleday, 1930. 310p [BM BVaU LC OTU QMM

GOOD HUNTING. Being volume three of BY GUESS AND BY GOD. London, Hutchinson, 1940. 288p [BM OTP

HELL'S ANGELS OF THE DEEP. Toronto, Gundy, 1932. 288p [BM OTP

HIGH AND DRY. The Post-War Experiences of the Author of BY GUESS AND BY GOD. London, Hutchinson, 1938. 253p [BM LC NBFU OTU

**Carr-Harris, Bertha Hannah (Wright), 1863–1949**

LIGHTS AND SHADES OF MISSION WORK; or, Leaves from a Worker's Note Book. Being Reminiscences of Seven Years' Service at the Capital, 1885–1892. By B.H.W. [pseud]. Ottawa, Free Press, 1892. [Amtmann cat. 145

THE WHITE CHIEF OF THE OTTAWA. Toronto, Briggs, 1903. 252p [Biography of Philemon Wright.] [BM BVaU NBFU OTP QMM

**Carrel, Frank, 1870–1940**

IMPRESSIONS OF WAR. Quebec, Telegraph Print., 1919. 248p [BM OTP

**Carroll, Rev. John, 1809–1884**

CASE AND HIS CONTEMPORARIES; or, The Canadian Itinerants' Memorial. ... A Biographical History of Methodism in Canada. Toronto, Rose, 1867–77. 5v [BVaU LC NSWA OKQ

"FATHER CORSON"; or, The Old Style Canadian Itinerant. Embracing the Life and Gospel Labours of the Rev. Robert Corson. Toronto, Rose, 1879. 277p [BVaU OTP

MY BOY LIFE. Presented in a Succession of True Stories. Toronto, Briggs, 1882. 288p [BVaU LC NBFU OTP

THE STRIPLING PREACHER; or ... The Life ... of the Rev. Alexander S. Byrne. Toronto, Green, 1852. 255p [BVaU NSWA OTP

**Carroll, Peter Owen**

THE LIFE AND ADVENTURES OF DETECTIVE PETER OWEN CARROLL. N.p., n.pub., 1923. 80p [BVaU NSWA

**Carruthers, John, –1866**

RETROSPECT OF THIRTY-SIX YEARS' RESIDENCE IN CANADA WEST. Hamilton, M'Intosh, 1861. 253p [BVaU NSHD OTP QMM

**Carter, J. Smyth, 1877–**

DOCTOR M.W. LOCKE AND THE WILLIAMSBURG SCENE. Toronto, 1933. 138p [BVaU LC OTP

**Carter, S.M.**

WHO'S WHO IN BRITISH COLUMBIA, 1930+. An Illustrated Record. ... Ed. by ——. Victoria, Carter, 1930+. [A continuing serial.] [BVaU LC OOP

**Cartwright, Rev. Conway Edward, 1837–1920**

LIFE AND LETTERS OF THE LATE HON. RICHARD CARTWRIGHT. Ed. by ——. Toronto, Belford, 1876. 145p [BVaU LC NSWA OKQ

**Cartwright, George, 1739–1819**

CAPTAIN CARTWRIGHT AND HIS LABRADOR JOURNAL. Ed. by Charles Wendell Townsend. Boston, Estes, 1911. xxxiii + 385p [BM BVaU LC NSWA OTU

**Cartwright, Richard John, 1835–1912**

REMINISCENCES. Toronto, Briggs, 1912. 408p [BM BVaU LC NSWA OTP

**Case, Rev. William, 1780–1855**

A CIRCUIT RIDER ON THE RIVER THAMES. The Diary of William Case, 20 June–26 August 1809. Ed. by John S. Moir. London, Ont., Lawson Memorial Library, U. of Western Ontario, 1958. 22p

**Casey, Rev. David A., 1886–**

CAPT. THE REV. T.E. MOONEY. Kingston, Can. Register, n.d. 36p [OTU

**Cashman, Anthony Walcott, 1923–**

ERNEST C. MANNING. A Biographical Sketch. Edmonton, Alberta Social Credit League, 1958. 35p

THE VICE-REGAL COWBOY. Life and Times of Alberta's J.J. Bowlen. Edmonton, Institute of Applied Art, 1957. 200p

**Chadwick, Edward Marion, 1840–1921**

THE CHADWICKS OF GUELPH AND TORONTO AND THEIR COUSINS. Toronto, Davis & Henderson, 1914. 88p [Contains also genealogy of the Bell family.] [LC OTU

ONTARIAN FAMILIES. Genealogies of United-Empire-Loyalist and Other Pioneer Families of Upper Canada. Toronto, Rolph Smith, 1895–98. 2v [BM LC NSWA OTU QMM

**Chalmers, John West, 1910–**

FUR TRADE GOVERNOR, GEORGE SIMPSON, 1820–1860. Edmonton, Institute of Applied Art, 1960. 190p

**Charlesworth, Hector Willoughby, 1872–1945**

A CYCLOPAEDIA OF CANADIAN BIOGRAPHY. In the Twentieth Century. Ed. by ——. Toronto, Hunter Rose, 1919. 303p [BVaU LC OTU

GRENVILLE KLEISER, EXPONENT OF SELF-HELP. New York, Funk & Wagnalls, 1919. 19p [BM

**Chaureth, Sophie (Berthelette), 1799–**

SKETCHES OF THE LIFE, TROUBLES, AND GRIEVANCES OF A FRENCH CANADIAN LADY. Caused Especially by Civil and Religionist Political Persecution. Written by herself. Toronto, 1857. 32p [OTP

**Chester, Rev. Eldred Augustus, 1890–**

THIS I LEARNED. Toronto, Ryerson, 1957. 78p [Reminiscences of a Methodist minister.]

**Chiniquy, Rev. Charles Paschal Télesphore, 1809–1899**

FIFTY YEARS IN THE CHURCH OF ROME. Chicago, Craig & Barlow, 1885. 832p [Numerous later editions.] [BM BVaU LC NSWA OTU QMBM

FORTY YEARS IN THE CHURCH OF CHRIST. Chicago, Revell, 1900. 498p [BVaU BM LC NSWA QMSS

THE LIFE AND LABOURS OF THE REV. FATHER CHINIQUY. Glasgow, Religious Tract Soc., 1861. 33p [BM QMSS

THE TWO CHINIQUYS: FATHER CHINIQUY VERSUS MINISTER CHINIQUY. Montreal, True Witness, 1898. 24p [Earlier ed., 1893?] [BVaU QMSS

**Chisholm, Joseph Andrew, 1863–1950**

JOSEPH HOWE. A Sketch, with a Chronology. Halifax, Chronicle Print., 1909. 44p [BM NSWA QMM

**Chown, Alice Amelia, 1866–1949**

THE STAIRWAY. Boston, Cornhill, 1921. 340p [LC NBFU OTP

**Church, Herbert E., 1868–**

AN EMIGRANT IN THE CANADIAN NORTHWEST. London, Methuen, 1929. 134p [BM BVaU OTU SSU

MAKING A START IN CANADA. Letters from Two Young Emigrants, with an intro. by Alfred J. Church, M.A. By —— and Richard Church. London, Seeley, 1889. 224p [BM LC NSHD OOP SSU

**Chute, Rev. Arthur Crawley, 1853–1936**

BIOGRAPHY OF JOHN THOMAS. N.p., Baptist Book, 1893. 58p [NSWA

**Chute, Arthur Hunt, 1890–1929**

THE REAL FRONT. New York, Harper, 1918. 308p [BM BVaU LC NSWA QMM

**Clark, Jeremiah Simpson, 1872–1950**

RAND AND THE MICMACS. Charlottetown, Examiner, 1899. 81p [BM BVaU NSHD OTU QMM

**Clark, Mattie M.I.**

THE POSITIVE SIDE OF JOHN GRAVES SIMCOE. Toronto, Forward, 1943. 121p [OTU

**Clarke, Adele**

OLD MONTREAL. John Clarke—his Adventures, Friends and Family. By his daughter. Montreal, Herald, 1906. 47p [BVaU MWU OTU

**Clarke, Charles, 1826–1909**

SIXTY YEARS IN UPPER CANADA. With Autobiographical Recollections. Toronto, Briggs, 1908. 321p [BM BVaU NSHD OKQ

**Clarke, Henry J.**

A SHORT SKETCH OF THE LIFE OF THE HON. D'ARCY McGEE. Montreal, Lovell, 1868. 80p [BVaU OTU QMM

**Clarke, Peter Dooyentate**

ORIGIN AND TRADITIONAL HISTORY OF THE WYANDOTTS, AND SKETCHES OF OTHER INDIAN TRIBES OF NORTH AMERICA. True Traditional Stories of Tecumseh and his League in the Years 1811 and 1812. [Anon] Toronto, Hunter Rose, 1870. 158p [BVaU LC OTU

**Clarke, William Fletcher, 1824–1902**

"IN MEMORIAM": THE LATE REV. JOHN ROAF. Toronto, Chewett, [1863?]. 12p [OTP

**Clarke, William Henry, 1902–1955**

WILLIAM HENRY CLARKE, 1902–1955. A Memorial Volume, Containing Some Recent Speeches and Writing Chiefly Concerned with Publishing & Education in Canada over Thirty Years. Toronto, Clarke Irwin, 1956. xvii + 141p

**Clegg, Howard**

A CANUCK IN ENGLAND. Journal of a Canadian Soldier. London, Harrap, 1942. 160p [BVaU NBS OTP

**Clint, Mabel Brown, 1874–1939**

OUR BIT. Memories of War Service by a Nursing Sister. Montreal, Barwick, 1934. 177p [BVa NBSaM OTU QMSS

**Coates, M. Helen**

IN MYSTERIOUS WAYS. White Rock, B.C. [Printed by Bulman Bros., Winnipeg], 1952? 62p

**Coats, Robert Hamilton, 1874–1960**

SIR JAMES DOUGLAS. By Robert Hamilton Coats and R.E. Gosnell. De luxe ed. Toronto, Morang, 1908. 369p [Also: Toronto, Oxford U. Press, 1926. 386p] [BM BVaU LC NSHD OTU

**Coburn, Rev. John, 1874–1954**

I KEPT MY POWDER DRY. Toronto, Ryerson, 1950. 185p [BVaU NSHD OTU

GRACE, GRIT, AND GUMPTION. Toronto, Ryerson, 1952. 181p [Sequel to his I KEPT MY POWDER DRY.]

**Cochrane, Charles Norris, 1889–1945**
DAVID THOMPSON, THE EXPLORER. Toronto, Macmillan, 1924. 173p [BM BVaU LC NSHD OTU

**Cochrane, James Arthur, 1891–1947**
LAVOISIER. London, Constable, 1931. 264p [BM LC OTU QMM

**Cochrane, Rev. William, 1831–1898**
THE CANADIAN ALBUM. Men of Canada; or, Success by Example. ... Brantford, Bradley Garretson, 1891–96. 5v [BM BVaU NSWA OTP
MEMOIRS AND REMAINS OF THE REV. WALTER INGLIS, African Missionary and Canadian Pastor. Toronto, Robinson, 1887. 325p [BVaU OTP
A QUIET AND GENTLE LIFE. In Memoriam Mary Neilson Houstoun Cochrane [1834–1871]. Brantford, Hudson & Sutherland, 1871. 84p [OTP

**Cody, Hiram Alfred, 1872–1948**
AN APOSTLE OF THE NORTH. Memoirs of the Right Reverend William Carpenter Bompas, D.D., First Bishop of Athabaska, 1874–1884, First Bishop of Mackenzie River, 1884–1891, First Bishop of Selkirk (Yukon), 1891–1906. Toronto, Musson, 1908. 385p [BM BVaU LC NSWA OTU
ON TRAIL AND RAPID BY DOGSLED AND CANOE. The Story of Bishop Bompas's Life amongst the Red Indians and Eskimos. Told for Boys and Girls. Toronto, Musson, 1911. 203p [Also later editions.] [BM BVaU LC OTUV

**Colby, Charles Williams, 1867–1955**
THE FIGHTING GOVERNOR. A Chronicle of Frontenac. Toronto, Glasgow Brook, 1915. 167p [BM BVaU LC NSWA OTU
THE FOUNDER OF NEW FRANCE. A Chronicle of Champlain. Toronto, Glasgow Brook, 1915. 158p [BM BVaU LC NSWA OTU

**Colgate, William G., 1882–**
ARCHIBALD LAMPMAN, A DEDICATION AND A NOTE. Toronto, priv. print., 1957. 15p
ARTHUR HEMING. Recorder of the North. Toronto, Best, 1934. 13p [Another ed.: Toronto, Best, 1938. 16p] [OTP
C.W. JEFFERYS. Toronto, Ryerson, 1945. 42p [BVaU NBFU OTP
TWO LETTERS OF TOM THOMSON, 1915 AND 1916. Weston, Ont., Old Rectory Press, 1946. 15p (Printed as a Christmas message for Dr. and Mrs. A.D.A. Mason of Toronto.) [BVaU NBFU OTP

**Colley, B.W., 1852?–**
REMINISCENCES. Toronto, Author, 1944. 72p [OTP

**Collier, Eric, 1903–1966**
THREE AGAINST THE WILDERNESS. New York, Dutton, 1959. 349p

**Collins, Alice Helen (Roger), –1955**

A BIOGRAPHICAL SKETCH OF KATHERINE E. WALLIS, CANADIAN ARTIST. Fort Erie, Review Co., 1948. 52p [OTP

PEN PICTURES ... REAL PEOPLE, SKETCH NO. I: ABRAHAM GROVES. [Walkerton, Telescope, 1931.] 23p [OTP

PEN PICTURES ... REAL PEOPLE, SKETCH NO. II: MARION G. FERGUSON. Walkerton, Author, [1932?]. 18p [OTP

PEN PICTURES ... REAL PEOPLE, SKETCH NO. III: SIR CHARLES BRUCE ... AND LADY BRUCE AND THE ISLAND OF MAURITIUS. [Walkerton, Telescope, 1933.] 30p [OTP

PEN PICTURES ... REAL PEOPLE, SKETCH NO. IV: JULES TREMBLAY. [Walkerton, Telescope, 1934.] 34p [OTP

PEN PICTURES ... REAL PEOPLE, SKETCHES NO. V, VI, VII, VIII: ELIZABETH VEALS; PETER McARTHUR; ELLEN MARY KNOX; J.L. YULE. [Walkerton, Herald-Times, 1935.] 50p [OTP

PEN PICTURES ... REAL PEOPLE, SKETCHES NO. IX, X: HARRY M. FIELD; "THE GLIDDONS." London, Ont., Chapman, 1936. 77p [OTP

PEN PICTURES ... REAL PEOPLE, SKETCH NO. XI: IVY G. COVENTRY. Walkerton, Herald-Times, 1937. 19p [OTP

PEN PICTURES ... REAL PEOPLE, SKETCH NO. XII: MARGARET MACKELLER. Walkerton, Herald-Times, n.d. 36p [OTU

REAL PEOPLE, PEN PICTURES: AUGUSTUS STEPHEN VOGT. Sketch 12. Elora, Express Pr., n.d. 38p [UTQ'42

**Collins, Joseph Edmund, 1855–1892**

CANADA'S PATRIOTIC STATESMAN. The Life and Career of the Right Honorable Sir John A. Macdonald. Based on the work of Edmund Collins. Rev. by G. Mercer Adams. Toronto, Rose, 1891. 613p [First pub. under title: LIFE AND TIMES OF THE RIGHT HONORABLE SIR JOHN A. MACDONALD. Toronto, Rose, 1883. 642p] [BM BVaU LC NSHD OTP

**Collison, Rev. William Henry, 1847–1922**

IN THE WAKE OF THE WAR CANOE. A Stirring Record of Forty Years' Successful Labour, Peril & Adventure among the Savage Indian Tribes of the Pacific Coast, and the Piratical Head-hunting Haidas of the Queen Charlotte Islands, B.C. London, Seeley, 1915. 352p [BM BVaU LC NBFU OKQ

**Colquhoun, Arthur Hugh Urquhart, 1861–1936**

THE HON. JAMES R. GOWAN, MEMBER OF CANADIAN SENATE. A Memoir. Ed. by ——. Toronto, priv. print., 1894. 170p [BVaU NBFU OTU

PRESS, POLITICS AND PEOPLE. The Life and Letters of Sir John Willison, Journalist and Correspondent of *The Times.* Toronto, Macmillan, 1935. 306p [BM BVaU LC NSHD OTP

**Comfort, Charles Fraser, 1900–**
ARTIST AT WAR. Toronto, Ryerson, 1956. xvii + 187p

**Composers, Authors, and Publishers Association of Canada**
TRIBUTE TO A NATION BUILDER. An Appreciation of Dr. John Murray Gibbon. Toronto, The Association, 1946. 31p [NBFU OTP

**Connolly, Rev. Thomas Louis, 1815–1876**
FUNERAL ORATION ON THE LATE HON. THOMAS D'ARCY McGEE, Delivered in the Metropolitan Church of St. Mary's, Halifax, Nova Scotia. Halifax, Compton, 1868. 24p [NSWA

**Connon, John Robert, 1862–1931**
FLORENCE NIGHTINGALE'S LOVER ... The Life of the Rev. John Smithurst. [No title page.] 4p [OTU

**Constance, Arthur, 1891–**
THE GLAZIER. London, Laurie, 1956. 279p [Biography of H.J. Constance.]

**Cook, Frederick, 1858–1943**
THE CANADIAN WHO'S WHO. Ed. by ——. Toronto, 1910. [NBFU OOP

**Cook, Rev. John, 1805–1892**
A SERMON PREACHED ON THE OCCASION OF THE DEATH OF THE REV. ROBERT McGILL, Minister of St. Paul's Church, Montreal. Montreal, Ramsay, 1856. 27p [NSWA OTP

**Cooke, Martha Stoddard (Colby), 1865–1951**
ABOVE THE POST OFFICE. Memories, Sketches and Stories. Vancouver, priv. print., 1953. 38p

**Cooney, Rev. Robert, 1800–1870**
THE AUTOBIOGRAPHY OF A WESLEYAN METHODIST MISSIONARY (Formerly a Roman Catholic). ... Montreal, Pickup, 1856. 407p [NSWA OTP QMM

**Cooper, John Alexander, 1868–1956**
MEN OF CANADA. ... A Portrait Gallery. ... Ed. by ——. Montreal, Can. Historical Co., 1901–2. 296p [BVaU LC NSHD OTU QMM

**Cooper, William Barrett, 1857–**
LIFE AND WORK OF WILLIAM TINDALE. Toronto, Longmans, 1924. 54p [BM BVaU LC OTUV

**Copeland, Donalda Murray (McKillop), 1916–**
REMEMBER, NURSE. As Told to Eugenie Louise Myles. Toronto, Ryerson, 1960. 250p

**Copway, George, 1818–1863**
THE LIFE, HISTORY, AND TRAVELS OF KAH-GE-GA-GAH-BOWH (GEORGE COPWAY) ... Chief of the Ojebwa Nation ... and a Missionary to his People. ... Written by

himself. Philadelphia, Harmstead, 1847. 158p (2nd ed.) [BM LC NSWA OTP QMM

THE LIFE, LETTERS AND SPEECHES OF KAH-GE-GA-GAH-BOWH, or G. Copway. ... New York, Benedict, 1850. 224p [Includes THE LIFE, HISTORY, AND TRAVELS OF KAH-GE-GA-GAH-BOWH.] [BM LC OTP

RECOLLECTIONS OF A FOREST LIFE; or, The Life and Travels of Kah-ge-ga-gah-bowh, or George Copway, Chief of the Ojibway Nation. London, Gilpin, [Preface 1850]. 248p [BM BVaU OTP

RUNNING SKETCHES OF MEN AND PLACES, IN ENGLAND, FRANCE, GERMANY, BELGIUM, AND SCOTLAND. New York, Riker, 1851. 346p [BM LC OOU

**Corbett, Edward Annand, 1887–**

FATHER, GOD BLESS HIM. Toronto, Ryerson, 1953. 76p [Life of Thomas C. Corbett.]

HENRY MARSHALL TORY: BELOVED CANADIAN. Toronto, Ryerson, 1954. 242p

McQUEEN OF EDMONTON. Toronto, Ryerson, 1934. 125p [BVaU OTP SSU

WE HAVE WITH US TONIGHT. Toronto, Ryerson, 1957. xviii + 222p [Autobiographical account of the author's work in adult education, 1920–51.]

**Cormack, Barbara (Villy), 1903–**

THE RED CROSS LADY (MARY H. CONQUEST, M.B.E.) Edmonton, Institute of Applied Art, 1960. 92p

**Costain, Thomas Bertram, 1885–1965**

THE CHORD OF STEEL. The Story of the Invention of the Telephone. Garden City, N.Y., Doubleday, 1960. 238p

**Coventry, Ivy G.**

BIOGRAPHY OF JOHN COVENTRY, M.D., 1836–1902. Toronto, Author, n.d. 8p

**Cowan, Charles L.**

THE TRAIL OF THE SKY PILOT. Toronto, Westminster Press, 1929. 208p [BVaU NBFU OTMC

**Cowan, John Bruce, 1882–**

CANADA'S GOVERNORS-GENERAL, 1867–1952. Toronto, York Pub. Co., 1952. 210p

JOHN INNES, PAINTER OF THE CANADIAN WEST. Vancouver, Rose, Cowan & Latta, 1945. 33p [BVaU OTP SSU

**Cowans, David**

ANECDOTES OF A LIFE ON THE OCEAN. Being a Portion of the Experiences of Twenty-seven Years' Service in many Parts of the World. Montreal, Lovell, 1871. 198p [BVaU LC NSHD OKQ

**Cowie, Isaac, 1848–1917**

THE COMPANY OF ADVENTURERS. A Narrative of Seven Years in the Service of the Hudson's Bay Company during 1867–1874, on the Great Buffalo Plains, with Historical and Biographical Notes and Comments. Toronto, Briggs, 1913. 515p [BM BVaU LC NBFU SSU

**Cox, Corolyn**

CANADIAN STRENGTH. Biographical Sketches. Toronto, Ryerson, 1946. 192p [BM BVaU LC NSHD OTU

**Cox, Harold Robert Wakeford, 1907–**

GREENHORNS IN BLUE PASTURES. New York, Smith & Durrell, 1945. 162p [BVaU NSHPL OTP

**Cox, Ross, 1793–1853**

ADVENTURES ON THE COLUMBIA RIVER. Including the Narrative of a Residence of Six Years on the Western Side of the Rocky Mountains, among various Tribes of Indians hitherto unknown; Together with a Journey across the American Continent. London, Colburn & Bentley, 1831. 2v [Also pub. as: ADVENTURES ON THE COLUMBIA RIVER. ... New York, Harper, 1832. 335p; and London, Colburn & Bentley, 1832. 2v] [BM BVaU LC NSWA OTP SSU

**Coyne, James Henry, 1849–1942**

RICHARD MAURICE BUCKE. A Sketch. Toronto, Saunders, 1923. 77p [BM BVaU LC OTP

**Cragg, Kenneth C., 1904–1948**

FATHER ON THE FARM. Toronto, Longmans, 1947. 173p [BVaU LC NBFU OKQ QMM

**Craig, James Beverley, 1894–**

THE CRAIGS OF GOULBOURNE AND NORTH GOWER. Kingston, Hanson & Edgar, 1929. 220p [LC OLU

**Cramp, Rev. John Mockett, 1796–1881**

A MEMOIR OF MADAME FELLER. With an Account of the Origin and Progress of the Grande Ligne Mission. Comp. by ——. Montreal, Grafton & Drysdale, 1876. 254p [BVaU BM LC NSWA OTU QMM

A PORTRAITURE FROM LIFE. By a Bereaved Husband [pseud]. Halifax. Christian Messenger, 1862. 18p [Haight Pt I

**Cramp, Mary**

THE RADIANT LIFE. A Memoir of Ruth Marion Shatford-Holmes. By Mary Cramp and Maud C. Edgar. 55p [NSHD

**Cranston, James Herbert, 1880–1952**

ETIENNE BRULE: IMMORTAL SCOUNDREL. Toronto, Ryerson, 1949. 144p [BM BVaU LC NSHD OTU QMM

INK ON MY FINGERS. Toronto, Ryerson, 1953. 188p

**Crawley, Rev. Edmund Albern, 1799–1888**

FUNERAL DISCOURSE ... JANUARY 4, 1874, ON THE DEATH OF ... JAMES W. JOHNSTON, Judge in Equity for the Province of Nova Scotia. Halifax, Bowes, 1874. 20p [NSHP

A SERMON PREACHED IN ... HALIFAX, N.S., MARCH 12, 1837 ON THE OCCASION OF THE DECEASE OF ELIZA L. TREMAIN. Halifax, English & Blackadar, 1837. 17p [NSHD

**Creighton, Donald Grant, 1902–**

HAROLD ADAMS INNIS. Portrait of a Scholar. Toronto, U. of Toronto Press, 1957. 146p

JOHN A. MACDONALD. The Young Politician. Toronto, Macmillan, 1952. 524p

JOHN A. MACDONALD. The Old Chieftain. Toronto, Macmillan, 1955. 630p

**Creighton, William Black, 1864–1946**

ROUND 'BOUT SUN-UP. Some Memories that Live. Toronto, Ryerson, 1946. 55p [BVaU LC NBFU OTP QMM

**Crockett, Asa James, 1870–**

GEORGE MUNRO "THE PUBLISHER." Halifax, Dalhousie U. Press, 1957. 34p

**Crofton, Francis Blake, 1841–1912**

HALIBURTON, THE MAN AND THE WRITER. A Study. Winslow, N.S., Anslow, 1889. 73p [BM BVaU LC NBFU OTU QMM

**Crofton, Walter Cavendish, 1806?–1870**

A BRIEF SKETCH OF THE LIFE OF CHARLES, BARON METCALFE ... to the Period of his Resigning the Office of Governor General of the British North American Colonies, in 1845. Originally compiled for the "British Whig." By "Uncle Ben" [pseud]. Kingston, Atheneum, 1846, 37p [OTP

**Croil, James, 1821–1916**

LIFE OF JAMES CROIL, MONTREAL. An Autobiography, 1821–1916. Montreal, Mitchell & Wilson, 1918. 247p [BVaU OTUV

LIFE OF THE REV. ALEX. MATHIESON. [Anon] ... With a Funeral Sermon by the Rev. John Jenkins ... and three Discourses ... by Dr. Mathieson. Montreal, Dawson, 1870. 261p [The LIFE is often attributed to the Rev. John Jenkins.] [BM BVaU NSWA OTP QMSS

**Crompton, F.C.B.**

GLIMPSES OF EARLY CANADIANS: LAHONTAN. Toronto, Nelson, 1925. 101p [BM BVaU LC NBFU OTU

**Crosby, Rev. Thomas, 1840–1914**

DAVID SALIOSALTON. Toronto, Briggs, n.d. 62p [BViPA OTP

AMONG THE AN-KO-ME-NUMS OR FLATHEAD TRIBES OF INDIANS OF THE PACIFIC COAST. Toronto, Briggs, 1907. 243p [BM BVaU LC NSHD OTU

UP AND DOWN THE NORTH PACIFIC COAST BY CANOE AND MISSION SHIP. Toronto, The Missionary Soc., Methodist Church, 1914. 403p [BVaU LC NSHD OKQ

**Cross, Austin Fletcher, 1898–**

THE PEOPLE'S MOUTHS. Toronto, Macmillan, 1943. 171p [BVaU LC OTU QMM

**Crowe, John Congdon, 1888–**

IN THE DAYS OF THE WINDJAMMERS. Toronto, Ryerson, 1959. xi + 176p

**Crowell, William Arthur, 1879–**

THE ROAR OF THE SEA. Dartmouth, N.S., Author, 1955. 93p

**Crowfoot, Alfred Henchman, 1881–**

BENJAMIN CRONYN, FIRST BISHOP OF HURON. London, Ont., Incorporated Synod of the Diocese of Huron, 1957. 142p

**Cruikshank, Ernest Alexander, 1854–1939**

THE CORRESPONDENCE OF THE HONOURABLE PETER RUSSELL WITH ALLIED DOCUMENTS Relating to his Administration of the Government of Upper Canada. ... Coll. & ed. by E.A. Cruikshank and A.F. Hunter. Toronto, Ontario Hist. Soc., 1932–1936. 3v [BM NBFU OTU QMM

THE LIFE OF SIR HENRY MORGAN. With an Account of the English Settlement of the Island of Jamaica (1655–1688). Toronto, Macmillan, 1935. 448p [BM BVaU OTU

A MEMOIR OF COLONEL THE HONOURABLE JAMES KERBY. His Life in Letters. Welland, Hist. Soc., 1931. 349p [BM BVaU QMSS

THE POLITICAL ADVENTURES OF JOHN HENRY. The Record of an International Imbroglio. Toronto, Macmillan, 1936. 206p [BM BVaU OTU

**Cruikshank, Julia E. (Kennedy), –1921**

WHIRLPOOL HEIGHTS. The Dream-House on the Niagara River. London, Allen, 1915. 254p [BM OTL

**Currelly, Charles Trick, 1876–1957**

I BROUGHT THE AGES HOME. Toronto, Ryerson, 1956. xx + 312p

**Currie, Arthur William, 1875–1933**

SIX YEARS AT McGILL. A Review. [Montreal, McGill Univ., 1926.] 50p [BVaU NSHD OTU QMM

**Currie, Emma Augusta (Harvey), 1829–1913**

THE STORY OF LAURA SECORD AND CANADIAN REMINISCENCES. Toronto, Briggs, 1900. 195p [Same title: St. Catharines, Ont., 1913. 254p] [BM BVaU LC NSHD OKQ

**Currie, John Allister, 1868–1931**

"THE RED WATCH." With the First Canadian Division in Flanders. Toronto, McClelland, 1916. 308p [BM LC NSWA OTP

**Curtis, James Davis, 1868–**

ST. THOMAS AND ELGIN MEDICAL MEN OF THE PAST. St. Thomas, Ont., Elgin County Pioneer Museum, 1956. 122p

**Curwen, Samuel, 1715–1802**

JOURNAL AND LETTERS OF THE LATE SAMUEL CURWEN. ... To which are added, Biographical Notices of Many American Loyalists and Other Eminent Persons. By George Atkinson Ward. New York, Francis & Co., 1842. 578p [Several later editions.] [BM LC NSWA OTP QMSS

**Curzon, Mrs. Sarah Anne, 1833–1898**

THE STORY OF LAURA SECORD, 1813. Toronto, Williamson, 1891. 15p [Also: Welland, Ont., Telegraph, 1898. 16p] [BM BVaU LC NSWA OTU

**Cushing, Elmer**

AN APPEAL, ADDRESSED TO A CANDID PUBLIC ... WHEREIN IS DISPLAYED THE SINGULAR HISTORY OF THE AUTHOR TOGETHER WITH THAT OF OTHER AMERICANS SETTLED IN THE PROVINCE OF LOWER CANADA. Stanstead, Author, 1826. 88p [NSWA

**Cushing, James Stevenson, 1878–**

GENEALOGICAL RECORD OF THE DESCENDANTS OF JOHN WALTERS AND MARY DeVAISSAILLE. Montreal, 1944. [2nd ed. Montreal, 1952. 62p]

**Cushing, Lemuel**

THE GENEALOGY OF THE CUSHING FAMILY. Montreal, Lovell, 1877. 117p [NSWA OTP

**Cyr, Narcisse, 1823?–1894**

MEMOIR OF THE REV. C.H.O. COTE, M.D. ... With a Memoir of Mrs. M.Y. Cote, and a History of the Grande Ligne Mission, Canada East. Philadelphia, Am. Baptist Pub. Soc., 1852. 144p [BM LC NSWA OTU

**Dafoe, John Wesley, 1866–1944**

CLIFFORD SIFTON IN RELATION TO HIS TIMES. Toronto, Macmillan, 1931. 552p [BM BVaU LC MWU NSHD OTU

LAURIER. A Study in Canadian Politics. Toronto, Allen, 1922. 182p [BM BVaU LC NSWA OKQ

SIXTY YEARS IN JOURNALISM. Text of Address delivered ... Winnipeg Press Club. ... Winnipeg, Royal Alexandra Hotel, 1943. 13p [OTU

**Dale-Harris, Leslie Ruth (Howard), 1924–**
A QUITE REMARKABLE FATHER. By Leslie Ruth Howard. New York, Harcourt, 1959. 307p

**Daly, George Thomas, 1872–1956**
MY FATHER. The Life of an Exemplary Catholic Layman. Toronto, Catholic Truth Soc., 1945. 153p [OTU

**Darling, Rev. William Stewart, 1818–1886**
SKETCHES OF CANADIAN LIFE. Lay and Ecclesiastical. By a Presbyter of the Diocese of Toronto [pseud]. London, Bogue, 1849. 310p [BM BVaU LC NBFU OTU

**Darwin, Oliver, 1860–1961**
PIONEERING WITH PIONEERS. (An Autobiography). Toronto, United Church of Canada, 1949. 151p [BVaU

**Davidson, William Harold**
AN ACCOUNT OF THE LIFE OF WILLIAM DAVIDSON OTHERWISE JOHN GODSMAN. Saint John, New Brunswick Museum, 1947. 60p [BVaU NBFU

**Davidson, William McCartney, 1872–1942**
LOUIS RIEL, 1844–1885. A Biography. Calgary, Albertan Pub. Co., 1955. 214p [Complete ed.; to replace earlier THE LIFE AND TIMES OF LOUIS RIEL. Calgary, The Albertan, 1951. 114p]

**Davies, Blodwen, 1897–1966**
PADDLE AND PALETTE. The Story of Thom Thomson. ... Toronto, Ryerson, 1930. 35p [BVaU OTP
A STUDY OF TOM THOMSON. A Story of a Man who Looked for Beauty and for Truth in the Wilderness. Toronto, Discus Press, 1935. 133p [BVaU LC NBFU OTU

**Davies, Evan, 1881?–1959?**
BEYOND THE OLD BONE TRAIL. By Evan Davies and Aled Vaughan. London, Cassell, 1960. 172p

**Davies, William, 1831–1921**
LETTERS OF WILLIAM DAVIES, TORONTO, 1854–1861. Ed. by William Sherwood Fox. Toronto, U. of Toronto Press, 1945. 144p [BM BVaU LC NSHD OTU QMM

**Davin, Nicholas Flood, 1843–1901**
THE EARL OF BEACONSFIELD. With Disraeli anecdotes never before published. Regina, Leader Co., 1890. 12p [Earlier ed.: Toronto, Belford, 1876. 42p] [LC OTU
THE SECRETARY OF THE ROYAL SOCIETY OF CANADA (J.G. Bourinot). A Literary Fraud. Ottawa, 1882. 20p [BM LC NSHD OTU

**Davis, Bruce Pettit, and Davis, Carroll Langstaff**

THE DAVIS FAMILY & THE LEATHER INDUSTRY, 1834–1934. Toronto, Ryerson, 1934. 145p [BM BVaU LC OTU

**Davis, Herbert John, 1893–**

CHARLES DOUGHTY, 1843–1926. New York, Hammer, 1945. 31p [LC OTU

**Davis, Rev. John, 1803?–1875**

THE PATRIARCH OF WESTERN NOVA SCOTIA. Life and Times of the Late Rev. Harris Harding, Yarmouth, N.S. Comp. by ——. With an intro. by J.W. Nutting. Charlottetown, Bremner, 1866. xxii + 271p [BVaU NSWA OTP

**Dawson, Rev. Aeneas MacDonell, 1810–1894**

PIUS IX, AND HIS TIME. London, Coffey, 1880. 440p [BM OTU

SERMONS. D'Arcy McGee ... etc. Ottawa, 1868. [OTU

**Dawson, John William, 1820–1899**

BIOGRAPHICAL SKETCH OF JAMES McGILL. N.p., n. pub., 1859. 14p [NSWA

FIFTY YEARS OF WORK IN CANADA, SCIENTIFIC AND EDUCATIONAL. Being Autobiographical Notes by Sir William Dawson. ... Ed. by Rankine Dawson. London, Ballantyne, 1901. 308p [BM BVaU LC NSHD OTU QMM

IN MEMORIAM, PETER REDPATH. Governor and Benefactor of McGill University. ... Montreal, "Witness" Print., 1894. 39p [OLU QMM

**Dawson, Robert MacGregor, 1895–1958**

WILLIAM LYON MACKENZIE KING. A Political Biography. Toronto, U. of Toronto Press, 1958. V. 1: 1874–1923. 500p

**Day, Effie Jamieson**

ANNIE ELIZABETH BRADLEY. Toronto, Women's Missionary Society of the United Church of Canada, 1936. 31p [UTQ'37

**Day, Frank Parker, 1881–1950**

THE AUTOBIOGRAPHY OF A FISHERMAN. Garden City, Doubleday, 1927. 202p [Also: New York, Minton Balch, 1932.] [BM BVaU NBFU OKQ QMM

**Deacon, William Arthur, 1890–**

PETER McARTHUR. Toronto, Ryerson, 1923. 180p [BM BVaU NSHD OTU

**Deane, Richard Burton, 1848–1930**

MOUNTED POLICE LIFE IN CANADA. London, Cassell, 1916. 311p [BM BVaU NBFU OTU QMM

**Deans, Dorothea**

C.A. FLEMING. A Biography. Owen Sound, Ont., 1953. 162p

**De La Roche, Mazo, 1879–1961**

RINGING THE CHANGES. An Autobiography. Toronto, Macmillan, 1957. xvi + 304p

**De Mille, James, 1833–1880**

MANUSCRIPT COLLECTION. ... Letters ... Documents, Unpublished Manuscripts of James De Mille [and other members of the De Mille family], covering the years 1850–1881. [NSHD

**Denison, George Taylor, 1839–1925**

RECOLLECTIONS OF A POLICE MAGISTRATE. Toronto, Musson, 1920. 263p [BVaU LC NSHD OTU QMM

SOLDIERING IN CANADA. Recollections and Experiences. ... Toronto, Morang, 1901. 364p [BM BVaU LC NSWA OKQ

**Denison, Richard Lonton, 1910–**

THE CANADIAN PIONEER DENISON FAMILY OF COUNTY YORK, ENGLAND, AND COUNTY YORK, ONTARIO. A History, Genealogy and Biography. Toronto, Author, 1951–52. 3v.

**Denison, Septimus Julius Augustus, 1859–1937**

MEMOIRS. Toronto, Best, 1927. 174p [BM OTU QMM

**Dennis, William Alexander, 1903–1961**

THE DENNIS GENEALOGY. An Account of the Dennis Ancestry with Supplements on the Millers and Archibalds, Biographical and Genealogical with Portraits. Kentville, N.S., priv. print., 1959. 38 + 4p

**Denny, Cecil Edward, 1850–1928**

THE LAW MARCHES WEST. Toronto, Dent, 1939. 319p [BM BVaU OLU

THE RIDERS OF THE PLAINS. A Reminiscence. ... Calgary, Herald, 1905. 223p [BVaU OTUV QMM

**Dent, John Charles, 1841–1888**

THE CANADIAN PORTRAIT GALLERY. Toronto, Magurn, 1880–81. 4v [BVaU LC NSWA OKQ QMM

**Desaulniers, Abel, 1913–**

IN LOVE WITH WINGS. The Story of a Barnstorming Pilot. New York, Exposition Press, 1959. 78p

**Dewar, David G.**

QUEEN'S PROFILES. [Biographical Sketches of 14 Former Members of the Faculty at Queen's University.] Kingston, Queen's University, 1951. 124p

**DeWitt, Norman Wentworth, 1876–1958**

IN MEMORIAM ANDREW JAMES BELL, 1856–1932. ... Toronto, Clarke Irwin, 1934. 29p [OLU

**Dezell, Robert, 1866–**

FIRE AND FROST. The Meadow Lea Tragedy. Toronto, Briggs, 1907. 131p [Title changed same year to: A NIGHT ON THE PRAIRIE: The Meadow Lea Tragedy. Bound with THE LIFE STORY OF FINLAY BOOTH, by Hamilton Wigle.] [BM BVaU NSHD OTU

**Dick, Catharine (Bond), 1891–**

TRAILS I'VE RIDDEN. An Era in the Prairie-foothill Country of Alberta. Calgary, Dick, 1946. 63p [ACG LC

**Dickie, Charles Herbert, 1859–**

OUT OF THE PAST. By an M.P. [pseud]. N.p., [1934?]. 128p [OOP

**Dickson, Lovat, 1902–**

THE ANTE-ROOM. Toronto, Macmillan, 1959. 270p

THE GREEN LEAF. A Tribute to Grey Owl. Ed. by ——. London, Lovat Dickson, 1938. 109p [ACG BM LC NBFU OTU

HALF-BREED. The Story of Grey Owl (Wa-Sha-Quon-Asin). London, Davies, 1939. 345p [BM BVaU LC OKQ

RICHARD HILLARY. London, Macmillan, 1950. 201p [BM BVaU LC

**Diesel, Gladys Cynthia Rebecca (Shope), 1907–**

SALUTE TO THE PAST. Edmonton, Commercial Printers, 1957. 188p

**Dionne, Emil**

REMINISCING. Spokane, Wash., Evergreen Press, 1952. 64p

**Dixon, James Dunbar, 1819–**

HISTORY OF CHARLES DIXON. One of the Early Settlers of Sackville, N.B. Comp. by ——. Rockfort, Ill., Forest City Pub. Co., 1891. 200p [BVaU LC NSWA OTU

**Dodds, Edmund King, –1910**

CANADIAN TURF RECOLLECTIONS AND OTHER SKETCHES. Toronto, 1909. 304p [BM BVaU OTU

**Doherty, Rev. Patrick J., 1838–1872**

PRINCIPAL ENGLISH WRITINGS OF THE LATE REV. P.J. DOHERTY. With a Sketch of his Life. Quebec, Huot, 1873. 237p [BVaU OTP

**Dooner, Alfred James, 1865?–1949**

COLONEL JOHN MacDONELL. First Speaker of the House of Assembly of Upper Canada, 1750–1809. Toronto, Extension Print., n.d. 15p [OTU

HON. ALEXANDER McDONELL (COLLACHIE). Speaker of the Legislative Assembly of Upper Canada, 1762–1842. Toronto, Author, [194–?]. 24p [OTP

RIGHT REV. EDMUND BURKE., D.D. Apostle of Upper Canada ... Vicar Apostolic of Nova Scotia. Hull, Leclerc, 1941. 17p [CC

**Doran, George Henry, 1869–1956**

CHRONICLES OF BARABBAS, 1884–1934 and FURTHER CHRONICLES AND COMMENT, 1952. New York, Rinehart, 1952. xiii + 446p [First ed. of CHRONICLES OF BARABBAS: New York, Harcourt Brace, 1935.]

**Doughty, Arthur George, 1860–1936**

A DAUGHTER OF NEW FRANCE. Being a Story of the Life and Times of Magdelaine de Verchères, 1665–1692. Ottawa, Mortimer, 1916. 166p [BM BVaU LC NBFU OTU QMM

**Douglas, Alice Vibert, 1894–**

THE LIFE OF ARTHUR STANLEY EDDINGTON. London, Nelson, 1956. xi + 207p

**Douglas, James, 1800–1886**

JOURNALS AND REMINISCENCES OF JAMES DOUGLAS, M.D. Ed. by his son. New York, priv. print., 1910. 254p [BM BVaU LC OTU

**Douglas, James, 1837–1918**

A MEMOIR OF THOMAS STERRY HUNT. Philadelphia, MacCalla, 1898. 61p [LC OTU QMM

**Douglas, John Harvey, 1888–**

CAPTURED. Sixteen Months as a Prisoner of War. Toronto, McClelland, 1918. 195p [BVaU NSHD OTP QQL

**Doull, John, 1878–**

REVEREND ALEXANDER McGILLIVRAY, D.D. Halifax, Author, 1938. 24p [OTU

**Dow, Rev. John, 1885–**

ALFRED GANDIER. Man of Vision and Achievement. Toronto, United Church Pub. House, 1951. 138p

**Doyle, Sister St. Ignatius**

MARGUERITE BOURGEOYS AND HER CONGREGATION. Gardenvale, Que., Garden City Press, 1941. 325p [OTU

**Dressler, Marie, 1873–1934**

THE EMINENT AMERICAN COMEDIENNE MARIE DRESSLER. In the Life Story of an Ugly Duckling. An Autobiographical Fragment. ... New York, McBride, 1924. 234p [BM LC

MY OWN STORY AS TOLD TO MILDRED HARRINGTON. Boston, Little Brown, 1934. 289p [BM LC OTU QMM

**Drew, Andrew, 1792–1878**

THE BURNING OF THE CAROLINE, AND OTHER REMINISCENCES OF 1837–38. By Rear-Admiral Drew ... and Judge [Robert Stuart] Woods. Chatham, Ont., Banner, 1896. 20p [OTP

A NARRATIVE OF THE CAPTURE AND DESTRUCTION OF THE STEAMER 'CAROLINE,'

AND HER DESCENT OVER THE FALLS OF NIAGARA. ... London, Spottiswoode, 1864. 31p [BM OKQ

**Drummond, May Isobel (Harvey)**

THE GRAND OLD MAN OF DUDSWELL. Being the Memoirs of the Rev. Thos. Shaw Chapman, M.A., Rector of St. Paul's Church, Marbleton. Quebec, Telegraph, 1916. 182p [BVaU OTU

**Duff, Louis Blake, 1878–1959**

ADDRESS ... AT A DINNER ... ON THE OCCASION OF THE UNVEILING OF A BRONZE BUST OF STEPHEN LEACOCK BY ELIZABETH WYN WOOD, Orillia Public Library, Friday, 14th Sept., 1951. Fort Erie, Review Co., 1951. 16p

AMAZING STORY OF THE WINGHAMITE SECRETARY OF LOUIS RIEL. London, Ont., Lawson Memorial Library, U. of Western Ontario, 1955. 37p [Biography of William Henry Jackson.]

BURNABY. Welland, Tribune-Telegraph, 1926. 38p [BM BVaU OKQ QMM

JANE SUSAN DUFF ... HER BOOK. Welland, Baskerville Press, 1940. 44p [OTU

MUDDIMAN, THE FIRST EDITOR. Welland, Tribune-Telegraph, 1925. 9p [OTU

**Duncan, Dorothy, 1903–1957**

PARTNER IN THREE WORLDS. New York, Harper, 1944. 340p [Biography of Jan Rieger (pseud). Pub. in England under title: PORTRAIT OF JAN.] [BM BVaU LC NBFU OTU QMM

**Duncan, Eric, 1858–1944**

FIFTY SEVEN YEARS IN THE COMOX VALLEY. Courtenay, B.C., Comox Argus Co., 1934. 61p [BVaU OTP

FROM SHETLAND TO VANCOUVER ISLAND. Recollections of Seventy-five Years. Edinburgh, Oliver & Boyd, 1937. 277p [3rd ed., enl., 1939. 303p] [BM BVaU LC OTU

**Duncan, Norman, 1871–1916**

DR. GRENFELL'S PARISH: THE DEEP SEA FISHERMEN. Toronto, Revell, 1905. 155p [BM BVaU LC NSWA OTU

HIGGINS, A MAN'S CHRISTIAN. New York, Harper, 1909. 116p [Biography of Francis Edmund Higgins.] [BVaU LC OKQ

**Dunlop, William, 1792–1848**

RECOLLECTIONS OF THE AMERICAN WAR 1812–14. Ed. with a Biographical Sketch of the Author by A.H.U. Colquhoun. Toronto, Historical Pub. Co., 1905. 112p [BM BVaU LC NSHD OTP QMM

WILLIAM "TIGER" DUNLOP, "BLACKWOODIAN BACKWOODSMAN." Essays by and about Dunlop, sel. and ed. by Carl F. Klinck. Toronto, Ryerson, 1958. xii + 185p

**Durand, Charles, 1811–1905**

REMINISCENCES OF CHARLES DURAND OF TORONTO, BARRISTER. Toronto,

Hunter Rose, 1897, 1899. 663p [Pub. in two forms–one in 1897 with 536p and again with added material paged continuously, 537–663.] [BM BVaU LC MWU NBFU OLU

**Duval, Paul**

ALFRED JOSEPH CASSON, PRESIDENT, ROYAL CANADIAN ACADEMY. Toronto, Ryerson, 1952. 64p

**Earl, Lawrence, 1915–**

CROCODILE FEVER. A True Story of Adventure. New York, Knopf, 1954. x + 293p

**Eaton, Arthur Wentworth Hamilton, 1849–1937**

THE COCHRAN-INGLIS FAMILY OF HALIFAX. Halifax, Ruggles, 1899. 18p [BM BVaU LC NSWA

THE EATON FAMILY OF NOVA SCOTIA, 1760–1929. Cambridge, Mass., Murray, 1929. 247p [BM BVaU LC NSHD OTU

THE ELMWOOD EATONS. Kentville, N.S., Advertiser, 1895. 29p [BM LC NSWA OOA

FAMILIES OF EATON–SUTHERLAND, LAYTON-HILL. New York, priv. print., 1899. 20p [BM BVaU LC NSWA

THE FAMOUS MATHER BYLES, THE NOTED BOSTON TORY PREACHER, POET, AND WIT, 1707–1788. Boston, Butterfield, 1914. 258p [BM BVaU LC NSWA OTU

GENEALOGICAL SKETCH OF THE NOVA SCOTIA EATONS. Halifax, Morning Herald, 1885. 128p [BM BVaU LC NSWA OTU

LT. COL. OTHO HAMILTON OF OLIVESTOB ... MEMBER OF THE NOVA SCOTIA COUNCIL FROM 1731–1744; HIS SONS, CAPTAIN JOHN AND LIEUTENANT-COLONEL OTHO HAMILTON 2ND, AND HIS GRANDSON, SIR RALPH HAMILTON, KT. Halifax, Ruggles, 1899. 22p [BM BVaU NSWA OTP

MEMORIAL SKETCH OF WILLIAM EATON. New York, priv. print., 1893. 16p [BVaU NSWA OTP

THE OLIVESTOB HAMILTONS. New York, Author, 1893. 32p [BM BVaU LC NSWA

**Eaton, Evelyn Sybil Mary, 1902–**

EVERY MONTH WAS MAY. New York, Harper, 1947. 241p [BM BVi LC OOP QMM

THE NORTH STAR IS NEARER. New York, Farrar Straus, 1949. 232p [BM BVi LC OOP QMM

**Eaton, Flora McCrea, 1880–1970**

MEMORY'S WALL. The Autobiography of Flora McCrea Eaton. Toronto, Clarke Irwin, 1956. xii + 214p

**Eayrs, Hugh Smithurst, 1894–1940**

SIR ISAAC BROCK. An Historical Monograph. Toronto, Macmillan, 1918. 108p [Rev. ed., 1924.] [BM BVaU LC NSWA OKQ

**Eby, Ezra E., 1850–**

BIOGRAPHICAL HISTORY OF THE EBY FAMILY AND OF THEIR SETTLEMENT IN AMERICA. Berlin, Ont., Hett & Alby, 1889. 144p [LC OTU

**Eccles, William John, 1917–**

FRONTENAC, THE COURTIER GOVERNOR. Toronto, McClelland, 1959. ix + 406p

**Edgar, Helen Madeline (Boulton), –1933**

DAHABEAH DAYS. An Egyptian Winter Holiday. Toronto, Ryerson, 1923. 85p [BM BVaU OTU QMM

**Edgar, Matilda (Ridout), 1844–1910**

A COLONIAL GOVERNOR IN MARYLAND: HORATIO SHARPE AND HIS TIMES, 1753–1773. London, Longmans, 1912. 311p [BM BVaU NSHD OTU QMM

GENERAL BROCK. Toronto, Morang, 1904. 322p [Also: London, Oxford U. Press, 1926. 324p] [BM BVaU LC NSWA OTU

**Edwards, Charles Austin McNally, 1917–**

BROOK WATSON OF BEAUSEJOUR. Toronto, Ryerson, 1957. 183p

TAYLOR STATTEN. A Biography. With a foreword by J. Alex. Edmison. Toronto, Ryerson, 1960. xii + 161p

**Ellerby, John Williams, 1862–**

THE ELLERBY FAMILY TREE. Weston, Charters Pub. Co., 1935. 50p [CC

**Elliott, Sophy Louisa, 1880–**

OUR CANADIAN STATESMEN. Ed. by ——. Montreal, D'Arcy McGee Pub. Co., 1958. 36p

THE WOMEN PIONEERS OF NORTH AMERICA. Gardenvale, Que., Garden City Press, 1941. 299p [BVaU OTU

**Elliott, William Edmund, 1883–**

POLITICS IS FUNNY. Toronto, Britannia Printers, 1951. 128p [2nd ed., Toronto, Burns & MacEachern, 1952. 170p]

**Ellis, Jean MacLachlan**

FACE POWDER AND GUNPOWDER. By Jean M. Ellis with Isabel Dingman. Toronto, Saunders, 1947. 229p [BVaU OTU QMM

**Ermatinger, Edward, 1797–1876**

LIFE OF COLONEL TALBOT, AND THE TALBOT SETTLEMENT. Its Rise and Progress, with Sketches of ... Public Characters. ... St. Thomas, McLachlin, 1859. 230p [BVaU LC NSWA OTP QMM

**Estabrooks, Florence Cecilia, 1883–**

THE ESTABROOKS FAMILY IN CONCORD, MASSACHUSETTS AND ON THE SAINT JOHN RIVER, NEW BRUNSWICK, CANADA, ALSO IN HAVERHILL, MASSACHUSETTS. Saint John, Author, 1953–1956. 2v [mimeographed].

GENEALOGY OF THE ANGLO-DUTCH ESTABROOKS FAMILY OF THE SAINT JOHN RIVER, NEW BRUNSWICK. Rev. 1958. Saint John, Author, 1935 [i.e., 1959]. 210p

**Eustace, Cecil John, 1903–**

A CANADIAN FOUNDRESS. The Life of Aurelie Caouette, Foundress of the Institute of the Precious Blood. Toronto, Basilian Press, 1947. 31p [OTU

**Evans, Hubert Reginald, 1892–**

NORTH TO THE UNKNOWN. The Achievements and Adventures of David Thompson. New York, Dodd Mead, 1949. 224p [BVi LC OOP

**Evans, Rev. Richard C., 1861–**

AUTOBIOGRAPHY OF ELDER R.C. EVANS, One of the First Presidency of the Reorganized Church of Jesus Christ of Latter Day Saints. London, Ont., Advertiser, 1907. 358p [T&C

FORTY YEARS IN THE MORMON CHURCH: WHY I LEFT IT. Toronto, n.p. [pref. 1920]. [OTUV

**Factor, Alexander, 1896–**

OLD TIMES. Ilfracombe, Devon, Stockwell, 1956. 127p

**Fairbairn, Rev. Charles Victor, 1890–**

I CALL TO REMEMBRANCE. Winona Lake, Ind., Light and Life Press, 1960. 185p

**Fairley, Thomas Christopher, 1919–**

THE TRUE NORTH. The Story of Captain Joseph Bernier. By T.C. Fairley & Charles E. Israel. Toronto, Macmillan, 1957. 160p

**Falconer, Rev. James William, 1868–1956**

JOHN GEDDIE, HERO OF THE NEW HEBRIDES. Toronto, Presbyterian Church in Canada, 1915. 118p [NSHD OTUV QMM

**Fallis, Rev. George Oliver, 1885–1952**

A PADRE'S PILGRIMAGE. Toronto, Ryerson, 1953. xi + 166p

**Fanning, David, 1756?–1825**

THE NARRATIVE OF COL. DAVID FANNING. ... Giving an Account of his Adventures ... from 1775–1783. As Written by Himself. Ed. with intro. and notes. New York, J. Sabin's Reprints, 1865. xxvi + 86p [First printed in 1861 in Richmond, Va. Later re-edited by A.W. Savary and reprinted from *The Canadian Magazine* 1908.] [BVaU LC NSHPL OONL QMBM

**Farmer, Jones Hughes, 1858–1928**

E.W. DADSON: THE MAN AND HIS MESSAGE. Ed. by ——. Toronto, Briggs, 1902. 379p [NSWA OTU

**Farnalls, Paul L.**

MEMOIRS OF LIFE IN ALBERTA. N.p., [1960?] 46p

**Farquharson, Mrs. James**

RECOLLECTIONS OF A PIONEER MINISTER AND HIS WORK. By his Wife. N.p., 1927. 34p [MWUC

**Farthing, Rev. John Cragg, 1861–1947**

RECOLLECTIONS OF THE RIGHT REVEREND JOHN CRAGG FARTHING, BISHOP OF MONTREAL, 1909–1939. Toronto, Church House, 1945. 191p [BVaU OTP

**Fast, Gerhard Andrew, 1853–1924**

TO FIND THE DAILY BREAD. Pt. 1 written by Gerhard Andrew Fast. Pt. 2 by Jacob Fast. Saskatoon, Western Producer, 1954. 48p

**Faughnan, Thomas, fl. 1835–1883**

STIRRING INCIDENTS IN THE LIFE OF A BRITISH SOLDIER. An Autobiography. Toronto, Hunter Rose, 1879. 336p [Several later editions, same place and publisher, e.g., "3rd edition" in 1881, 360p, and one in 1885, "Twenty-second Thousand–Enlarged and Illustrated" 536p] [BVaU LC NSHD OTP QMBM

**Fawcett, Edgar, 1847–1923**

SOME REMINISCENCES OF OLD VICTORIA. Toronto, Briggs, 1912. 294p [BM BVaU NBFU OTU

**Fea, Rev. Samuel, 1872–1943**

IRISH NED, THE WINNIPEG NEWSY. Toronto, Briggs, 1910. 28p [BM BVaU OTU

**Fenety, George Edward, 1812–1899**

LIFE AND TIMES OF THE HON. JOSEPH HOWE. Saint John, Carter, 1896. 376p [BM BVaU NSWA OTP

**Ferguson, George Victor, 1897–**

JOHN W. DAFOE. Toronto, Ryerson, 1948. 127p [BM BVaU LC NSHD OTU QMM

**Fergusson, Charles Bruce, 1911–**

CHARLES FENERTY. The Life and Achievement of a Native of Sackville, Halifax County, N.S. Halifax, 1955. 15p

**Ferns, Henry Stanley, 1913–**

THE AGE OF MACKENZIE KING. By H.S. Ferns and B. Ostrey. V.1: The Rise of the Leader. London, Heinemann; Toronto, British Book Service, 1955. xii + 356p

**Ferrie, Adam, 1777–1863**

AUTOBIOGRAPHY, LATE HON. ADAM FERRIE. N.p., n.d. 36p [OTP

**Fetherstonhaugh, Robert Collier, 1892–1949**

CHARLES FLEETFORD SISE, 1834–1918. A Biography. Montreal, Gazette, 1944. 238p [BM BVaU OTU QMM

**Firbank, Thomas, 1910–**

I BOUGHT A STAR. London, Harrap, 1951. 240p [Author's military experiences.]

LOG HUT. London, Harrap, 1954. 200p

**Fisher, Claude Laing**

JAMES, CARDINAL McGUIGAN, ARCHBISHOP OF TORONTO. Toronto, McClelland, 1948. 133p [BVaU NBFU OTP

**Fitkin, Edward**

"COME ON, TEEDER!" The Story of Ted (Teeder) Kennedy, Captain of The Toronto Maple Leafs. Toronto, Baxter Pub. Co., 1950. 141p [OONL

FOOTLOOSE IN HOCKEY. Toronto, Baxter Pub. Co., 1951. 144p

THE GASHOUSE GANG OF HOCKEY. Toronto, Baxter Pub., 1951. 144p

MAURICE RICHARD, HOCKEY'S ROCKET. Toronto, Baxter Pub., 1951. 144p

MAX BENTLEY, HOCKEY'S DIPSY-DOODLE DANDY. Toronto, Baxter Pub., 1951. 144p

TURK BRODA OF THE LEAFS. The Story of One of Hockey's Greatest Goalkeepers. Toronto, Baxter Pub., 1950. 143p [OONL

**Fitzgibbon, Mary Agnes, 1851–1915**

A VETERAN OF 1812. The Life of James Fitzgibbon. Toronto, Briggs, 1894. 347p [BM BVaU LC NSHD OTP

**Fitzpatrick, Frank Joseph Emile, 1861–**

SERGEANT 331: Personal Recollections of a Member of the Canadian Northwest Mounted Police from 1879–1885. New York, Author, 1921. 126p [BVaU LC OTU

**Fleming, Rev. Archibald Lang, 1883–1953**

ARCHIBALD THE ARCTIC. New York, Appleton-Century-Crofts., 1956. 399p

THE HUNTER-HOME; or, Joseph Pudlo, a Life Obedient to a Commanding Purpose. Toronto, 1930. 43p [OLU

PERILS OF THE POLAR PACK; or, The Adventures of the Rev. E.W.T. Greenshield, of Blacklead Island, Baffin Land. Toronto, Missionary Society of Church of England in Canada, 1932. 175p [BM OTU

**Flenley, Ralph, 1886–1969**

SAMUEL DE CHAMPLAIN, FOUNDER OF NEW FRANCE. Toronto, Macmillan, 1924. 149p [BM BVaU LC NSHD OTU QMM

**Fontaine, Robert Louis, 1911–1965**
HELLO TO SPRINGTIME. New York, Crowell, 1955. 246p

**Footner, Hulbert, 1879–1944**
SAILOR OF FORTUNE. The Life and Adventures of Commodore Barney, U.S.N. New York, Harper, 1940. 323p [LC OONL

**Foran, Joseph Kearney, 1857–1931**
JEANNE MANCE; or, "The Angel of the Colony," Foundress of the Hotel-Dieu Hospital, Pioneer Nurse of North America, 1642–1673. Montreal, Herald, 1931. 192p [BVaU LC NBFU OTU QMM

**Ford, Arthur Rutherford, 1880–1968**
AS THE WORLD WAGS ON. The Autobiography of a Roving Editor. Toronto, Ryerson, 1950. 228p [BVaU NBFU OTUV

**Ford, Frederick Samuel Lampson, 1869–**
WILLIAM DUNLOP. Toronto, Britnell, 1934. 60p [BVaU OTP

**Fordyce, Alexander Dingwall, –1894**
EPITOME; or, Who? What? Where? When? respecting the Family of Dingwall Fordyce and Connexions, 1655–1884. Comp. by A.D.F. Fergus, Ont., 1884. 107p [OKQ
FAMILY RECORD OF THE NAME OF DINGWALL FORDYCE IN ABERDEENSHIRE. Showing Descent ... both Direct and Collateral. ... Comp. by ——. Fergus, Ont., n. pub., 1885–88. 2v [LC OLU
THE MONUMENTAL INSCRIPTIONS IN THE CEMETERY AT BELLESIDE, FERGUS. Fergus, Ont., Author, 1883. 80p [OTP

**Forster, John Wycliffe Lowes, 1850–1938**
UNDER THE STUDIO LIGHT. Leaves from a Portrait Painter's Sketch Book. Toronto, Macmillan, 1928. 244p [BVaU LC NBFU OTU QMM

**Foster, George Eulas, 1847–1931**
MEMOIRS. Ed. by W.S. Wallace. Toronto, Macmillan, 1933. 291p [BVaU NBFU OTUV

**Foster, William Alexander, 1840–1888**
CANADA FIRST. A Memorial of the Late William A. Foster, Q.C. With intro. by Goldwin Smith. Toronto, Hunter Rose, 1890. 221p [BVaU LC NSWA OKQ QMM

**Fox, William Sherwood, 1878–1967**
SILKEN LINES AND SILVER HOOKS. A Life-long Fisherman Recounts His Catch. Toronto, Copp Clark, 1954. xii + 152p

**Fraser, Alexander, 1860–1936**
BROCK CENTENARY, 1812–1912. Account of the Celebration at Queenston Heights,

Ontario on the 12th October 1912. Ed. by ——. Toronto, Briggs, 1913. 92p [BM BVaU LC NBFU OTU

**Fraser, Rev. Donald, 1826–1892**

AUTOBIOGRAPHY OF THE LATE D. FRASER. With a Selection from his Sermons. London, Nisbet, 1892. 243p [OTUV QMM

CANADA AS I REMEMBER IT, AND AS IT IS. [London, 1876.] 33p [BVaU NSWA

LEAVES FROM A MINISTER'S PORTFOLIO. London, Nisbet, 1858. 141p [NSWA LC OTU QMM

MARY JANE KINNAIRD. London, Nisbet, 1890. 160p [LC QMM

THOMAS CHALMERS, D.D., LL.D. New York, Armstrong, 1882. [LC OLU

**Fraser, Hermia (Harris), 1902–**

TALL BRIGADE. True Adventures of Tom McKay, Brigade Leader for the Early Hudson's Bay Company. Portland, Oregon, Binfords & Mort, 1956. 294p

**Fraser, Rev. Joshua, fl. 1858–1883**

SHANTY, FOREST AND RIVER LIFE IN THE BACKWOODS OF CANADA. By the author of THREE MONTHS AMONG THE MOOSE. Montreal, Lovell, 1883. 361p [BM BVaU LC MWU OTU QMM

THREE MONTHS AMONG THE MOOSE. "A Winter's Tale" of the Northern Wilds of Canada. By a Military Chaplain [pseud]. Montreal, Lovell, 1881. 168p [BVaU LC NSHD OTU QMM

**Fraser, Robert James, 1887–**

AS OTHERS SEE US. Scots of the Seaway Valley. Beamsville, Ont., Express, 1959. 328p

**Fraser, Roy, 1889–1957**

HAPPY JOURNEY. Toronto, Ryerson, 1958. xiv + 124p

**Fraser, Simon, 1776–1862**

LETTERS AND JOURNALS, 1806–1808. Ed. with an intro. by W. Kaye Lamb. Toronto, Macmillan, 1960. 292p

**Freed, Augustus Toplady, 1835–**

HANCOCK. The Life ... of Winfield Scott Hancock. Chicago, Summer, 1880. 74p [BM LC

**French, Maida (Parlow)**

APPLES DON'T JUST GROW. Toronto, McClelland, 1954. 226p

**Freshman, Rev. Charles, 1819–1875**

THE AUTOBIOGRAPHY OF THE REV. CHARLES FRESHMAN, late Rabbi of the Jewish Synagogue at Quebec ... at present German Wesleyan Minister at Preston, Ontario. ... Toronto, Rose, 1868. 316p [BVaU LC NSWA OTU QMM

**Fry, Henry**

A BIOGRAPHICAL SKETCH OF SIR N.F. BELLEAU. Quebec, Côté, 1894. 12p [QMSS

**Fudger, Harris Henry**

MEMOIR AND WRITINGS. Comp. by his Daughter. Toronto, priv. print., 1931. [BVaU OTUV

**Führer, Mrs. Charlotte H.**

THE MYSTERIES OF MONTREAL. Being Recollections of a Female Physician. Montreal, Lovell, 1881. 245p [BVaU LC NSWA OTU QMM

**Fulford, Rev. Francis, 1803–1868**

A SERMON ... AFTER THE DEATH OF H.R.H. THE PRINCE CONSORT. Montreal, Lovell, 1862. 15p [BM OTP

**Fuller, Peter, 1826–1890**

PETER FULLER, HIS STEPS AND HIS LIFE, PRINCIPALLY FROM HIS OWN DIARIES. On the Occasion of the Centennial of the Founding of Christ's Church, the Church of England, Meaford. Sel. by F. Stanley Knight. Meaford, Ont., 1959. 34p

**Fuller, Rev. Thomas Brock, 1810–1884**

MEMOIR OF MR. JOHN BEATTY, who died at Port Robinson, C.W., 15th February, 1861. Toronto, Rowsell, 1861. 24p [OTU

**Gaisford, John**

THEATRICAL THOUGHTS. By John Gaisford ... and Conundrums, Sent to John Gaisford. Montreal, Lovell, 1848. 75p [LC OTP

**Gallishaw, John, 1890–**

TRENCHING AT GALLIPOLI. Toronto, Gundy, 1916. 241p [NSHPL OTY

**Galloway, Margaret Agnes**

I LIVED IN PARADISE. Winnipeg, Bulman Bros., 1942. 257p [BViPA LC OLU

**Galt, Ont. Knox Church**

REV. DR. JOHN BAYNE, D.D., MINISTER OF KNOX CHURCH, GALT, 1835–1859. [Galt?], 1935. 16p [OTU

**Ganong, William Francis, 1864–1941**

A GENEALOGY OF THE NEW BRUNSWICK BRANCH OF THE DESCENDANTS OF THOMAS GANONG. ... Comp. by ——. Cambridge, Mass., Graves & Henry, 1893. 27p [BM LC OOP

**Garland, Bessie (Ford)**

THE OLD MAN'S DARLING. A Series of Character Sketches. Toronto, Author, 1881. 157p [BVaU OTP

**Garrioch, Rev. Alfred Campbell, 1848–1934**

A HATCHET MARK IN DUPLICATE. Toronto, Ryerson, 1929. 283p [BM BVaU OTU SSU

**Gates, William, 1815–**
RECOLLECTIONS OF LIFE IN VAN DIEMAN'S LAND. Lockport, N.Y., Crandall, 1850. 231p [NBFU OTP QMM

**Gaudin, Rev. Samuel D., 1861–1947?**
FORTY-FOUR YEARS WITH THE NORTHERN CREES. Toronto, Mundy-Goodfellow Print., 1942. 170p [AEU OTU

**Gemmill, John Alexander, 1847–1905**
THE OGILVIES OF MONTREAL WITH A GENEALOGICAL ACCOUNT OF THE DESCENDANTS OF THEIR GRANDFATHER, ARCHIBALD OGILVIE. [Ed. by J.A.G.] Montreal, Gazette, 1904. 98p [OTU

**Ghent, Percy Parker, 1888–1952**
JOHN READE AND HIS FRIENDS. Toronto, Belcher, 1925. 63p [BM BVaU NBFU OTP
LITERARY AND HISTORIC FRAGMENTS OF CANADIAN INTEREST. Adventures in Book and Autograph Collecting. Toronto, Belcher, 1927. 86p [BVaU NBFU OTP

**Gibbon, Mary Elizabeth, 1925–**
NORTHWARD MY CALLING. By Mary E. Hope [pseud]. Toronto, Ryerson, 1954. 170p

**Gibbons, Arthur**
A GUEST OF THE KAISER. The Plain Story of a Lucky Soldier. Toronto, Dent, 1919. xvi + 798p [LC NSHPL OTU

**Gibson, George Herbert Rae, 1881–1932**
MAPLE LEAVES IN FLANDER'S FIELDS. By Herbert Rae [pseud]. Toronto, Briggs, 1916. 268p [BM BVaU OTU QMM

**Gibson, Jesse**
THOMAS BONE, THE SAILOR'S FRIEND. The Story of his Work on the Welland Canal. Toronto, U.C. Tract Society, [1908?]. 158p [BVaU OTP

**Gifford, Rev. William Alva, 1877–1960**
JOHN WESLEY: PATRIOT AND STATESMAN. Toronto, Ryerson, 1922. 30p [BM OTUV

**Gilbert, Geoffrey, 1893–**
THE ANCESTORS OF MOSES HASKELL GILBERT OF VERMONT AND MONTREAL, 1790–1843. Pt. 1. The Ancestry of his Father, Solomon Gilbert. Pt. 2. The Ancestry of his Mother, Thankful Haskell. Gilbert Material comp. and ed. by Geoffrey Gilbert. Nineteen "stories" on Maternal Lines by Eva L. Moffatt. Victoria, Author, 1954. 144p [mimeographed]

GILBERTS OF NEW ENGLAND. Pt. 1. Descendants of John Gilbert of Dorchester. Comp. by George Gordon Gilbert and Geoffrey Gilbert. Pt. 2. Descendants of Matthew Gilbert of New Haven, Humphrey Gilbert of Ipswich, and William Gilbert of Boston. From the Gilbert Family Manuscript Genealogy by Homer W. Brainard and Clarence A. Torrey. ... Ed. by ——. Victoria, Author, 1959. xv + 484p

**Gillespie, Alexander, 1880–1948**

JOURNEY THROUGH LIFE. Biography of Alexander Gillespie, 1880–1948. Victoria, priv. print., 1954. 143p

**Gillespie, Gerald Joseph, 1911–**

BLUENOSE SKIPPER. Fredericton, Brunswick Press, 1955. 129p

**Gillis, Elsie (McCall)**

NORTH POLE BOARDING HOUSE. As Told by Elsie McCall Gillis to Eugenie Myles. Toronto, Ryerson, 1951. 206p

**Gillis, James Donald, 1870–**

THE CAPE BRETON GIANT. A Truthful Memoir. Montreal, Lovell, 1899. 102p [Also: Halifax, Allen, 1914 and 1919.] [BVaU NSWA OTU QMM

A LITTLE SKETCH OF MY LIFE. Halifax, Allen, n.d. 12p [NSHPL OTUV QMM

MY PALESTINE PILGRIMAGE. ... 1936 A.D. North Sydney, N.S., Herald Print., 1936. 72p [NSHD OTU QMBM

**Glass, Rev. Charles Gordon**

STRAY LEAVES FROM SCOTCH AND ENGLISH HISTORY. With the Life of Sir William Wallace. Montreal, Lovell, 1873. 400p [2nd ed.: Montreal, Stevenson, 1876. 399p] [BVaU NSHD OTU QMBM

**Glazebrook, George Parkin de Twenebrokes, 1900–**

SIR CHARLES BAGOT IN CANADA. A Study in British Colonial Government. London, Oxford U. Press, 1929. 160p [BM BVaU LC NSHD OTU

SIR EDMUND WALKER. London, Oxford U. Press, 1933. 160p [BM BVaU NBFU OTU

**Godfrey, Miss L.M.**

INDIRECT DOMESTIC INFLUENCE; or, Nova Scotia as it was, as it is, and as it may be. ... Combining Sketches of Provincial Character. ... By a Provincial [pseud]. Boston, Author, 1855. 64p [Enl. ed. under title: SECRET INQUISITIONS; or, Nova Scotia as it was, is, and may be. ... (Anon) Boston, French, 1856. 112p] [NSHD OTP

**Godsell, Jean Walker (Turner), 1896–**

I WAS NO LADY. I Followed the Call of the Wild. The Autobiography of a Fur Trader's Wife. ... Toronto, Ryerson, 1959. xiv + 212p

**Godsell, Philip Henry, 1889–1961**

PILOTS OF THE PURPLE TWILIGHT. The Story of Canada's Early Bush Flyers. Toronto, Ryerson, 1955. xii + 225p

**Goldbloom, Alton, 1890–**

SMALL PATIENTS. The Autobiography of a Children's Doctor. Toronto, Longmans, 1959. 316p

**Goldsmith, Oliver, 1794–1861**

THE AUTOBIOGRAPHY OF OLIVER GOLDSMITH. Published for the First Time from the Original Manuscript of the Author of "The Rising Village." With intro. and notes by Rev. Wilfrid E. Myatt. ... Toronto, Ryerson, 1943. 76p [BVaU NSHD OTP

**Good, William Charles, 1876–**

FARMER CITIZEN. My Fifty Years in the Canadian Farmers' Movement. Toronto, Ryerson, 1958. xiv + 294p

**Good Templar, A (pseud)**

RECOLLECTIONS OF A CHECKERED LIFE. By a Good Templar [pseud]. Napanee, Hamond, 1868. 116p [Reminiscences by member of a temperance organization.] [Haight Pt I OLU

**Goodfellow, Florence Askin (Agassiz)**

MEMORIES OF PIONEER LIFE IN BRITISH COLUMBIA. Wenatchee, Wash., Author, 1945. 43p [BVaU

**Goodhand, Henrietta McIntosh**

FOOT PRINTS. A Memoir. Minot, N.D., Author, 1948. 134p [Pioneer days in Ontario and Alberta.] [OTU

**Goodman, Alfred Edwin, 1860–**

GOODMAN, A FAMILY HISTORY. [Anon] Vancouver, Timms, 1916. 548p [BVaU

**Gordon, Rev. Charles William, 1860–1937**

THE LIFE OF JAMES ROBERTSON, Missionary Superintendent in the Northwest Territories. By Charles W. Gordon (Ralph Connor). Toronto, Westminster, 1908. 403p [BM BVaU LC NSWA OTU

POSTSCRIPT TO ADVENTURE. The Autobiography of Ralph Connor. New York, Farrar, 1938. 430p [BM BVaU LC NSHD OTU

**Gordon, Rev. James D., –1872**

THE LAST MARTYRS OF EROMANGA. Being a Memoir of the Rev. George N. Gordon, and Ellen Catherine Powell, His Wife. ... Halifax, McNab & Shaffer, 1863. 294p [BVaU NSHD

**Gordon, Robert Kay, 1887–**

JOHN GALT. Toronto, Oxford U. Press, 1920. 121p [BM LC OTU QMM

**Gordon, Wilhelmina, 1885–**

DANIEL M. GORDON, HIS LIFE. Toronto, Ryerson, 1941. 313p [BM BVaU NBFU OTU QMM

**Gosling, William Gilbert, 1863–1930**

THE LIFE OF SIR HUMPHREY GILBERT, England's First Empire Builder. London, Constable, 1911. 304p [BM BVaU LC NBFU OTU

**Gough, Thomas Bunbury**

BOYISH REMINISCENCES OF HIS MAJESTY THE KING'S VISIT TO CANADA IN 1860. London, Murray, 1910. 242p [BM BVaU LC NSWA OTU QMM

**Gourlay, Robert Fleming, 1778–1863**

THE BANISHED BRITON AND NEPTUNIAN. ... The Life ... of Robert Gourlay, Esq., now Robert Fleming Gourlay. Boston, Dickinson, 1843–46. [Issued in 38 parts proper, and an appendage. The Toronto Public Library's holdings are incomplete.] [BVaU OLU OTP

CHRONICLES OF CANADA. Being a Record of Robert Gourlay, Esq., now Robert Fleming Gourlay, "The Banished Briton." St. Catharines, "Journal," 1842. 40p [An abridged ed. with an additional section pub.: Ingersoll, C.W., "Chronicle," 1857. 40p] [LC OTP

MR. GOURLAY'S CASE BEFORE THE LEGISLATURE, WITH HIS SPEECH. Toronto, Globe, 1858. 29p [OTP

**Gouzenko, Svetlana (Gouseva)**

BEFORE IGOR. Memories of my Soviet Youth. New York, Norton, 1960. 252p

**Gowanlock, Mrs. Theresa, –1899**

TWO MONTHS IN THE CAMP OF BIG BEAR. The Life and Adventures of Theresa Gowanlock and Theresa Delaney. Parkdale, Times Office, 1885. 136p [BVaU NSWA OTUV SSU

**Gowland, John Stafford, 1898–**

SMOKE OVER SIKANASKA. London, Laurie, 1955. 224p

**Graham, Angus A., 1867–**

THE GOLDEN GRINDSTONE. The Adventures of George M. Mitchell. Recorded by Angus Graham. Toronto, Oxford U. Press, 1935. 304p [BM BVaU LC OTU

**Graham, Ellen Maud, 1876–**

A CANADIAN GIRL IN SOUTH AFRICA. Toronto, Briggs, 1905. 192p [NSHD OLU

**Graham, Percy Wentworth**

SIR ADAM BECK. London, Carl Smith, 1925. 64p [BVaU OTU

**Graham, William Creighton, 1887–1955**

JOHN WESLEY AS A LETTER WRITER. ... Toronto, Ryerson, 1923. 35p [OTUV

**Graham, William Roger, 1919–**

ARTHUR MEIGHEN. A Biography. Toronto, Clarke Irwin, 1960–65. 3v

**Grant, Douglas, 1921–1969**

THE FUEL OF THE FIRE. London, Cresset, 1950. 235p [BM BVaU NBFU OTU

**Grant, Rev. George Monro, 1835–1902**

JOSEPH HOWE. Halifax, MacKinlay, 1904. 83p [2nd ed., incl. Howe's essay on "The Organization of the Empire"· Halifax, MacKinlay, 1906. 110p] [BVaU NSWA OTP QMM

**Grant, Mrs. Hilda Kay, 1910–**

THE SALT-BOX. By Jan Hilliard [pseud]. New York, Norton, 1951. 212p [Reminiscences of author's girlhood in Nova Scotia.]

**Grant, Kenneth James, 1839–**

MY MISSIONARY MEMORIES. Halifax, Imperial, 1923. 203p [BVaU NSWA

**Grant, Rev. Robert, 1824?–1900**

EAST RIVER WORTHIES. ... New Glasgow, Scotia Printers, [1900?]. 66p [NSHL OTP

LIFE AND TIMES OF GEORGE R. YOUNG. ... New Glasgow, MacKenzie, 1886. 7p [NSHD

**Grant, Robert Neil, –1909**

LIFE OF REV. WILLIAM COCHRANE. Toronto, Briggs, 1899. 290p [BVaU OTU

**Grant, William Lawson, 1872–1935**

IN MEMORIAM, WILLIAM GEORGE McINTYRE. ... N.p., n.d. 38p [OTU

PRINCIPAL GRANT. By W.L. Grant and Frederick Hamilton. Toronto, Morang, 1904. 531p [Also as: GEORGE MONRO GRANT. Edinburgh, Jack, 1905. 531p] [BM BVaU LC NSWA OTU QMM

THE TRIBUNE OF NOVA SCOTIA. A Chronicle of Joseph Howe. Toronto, Glasgow Brook, 1915. 163p [BM BVaU LC NBFU OTU

**Gray, Edwin Roy**

IN ALL THY WAYS. Letters from a Canadian Flying Officer. ... Toronto, Oxford U. Press, 1944. 47p [OTUV

**Gray, John Morgan, 1907–**

A.W. MACKENZIE, M.A., D.D., THE GROVE, LAKEFIELD. A Memoir. Toronto, Grove Old Boys' Assoc., 1938. 25p [BVaU OTU

**Gray, Rev. John William Dering, 1797–1868**

A SERMON, UPON THE DEATH OF HIS LATE MAJESTY WILLIAM IV, and upon the Accession of our Present Sovereign, Queen Victoria. Saint John, Chubb, 1837. 16p [LC NSWA OTP

**Gray, William**

MORE LETTERS FROM BILLY. By the Author of A SUNNY SUBALTERN [pseud]. Toronto, McClelland, 1917. 121p [BVaU LC OLU

A SUNNY SUBALTERN. Billy's Letters from Flanders. [Anon] Toronto, McClelland, 1916. 175p [Also under title: A CANADIAN SUBALTERN. Billy's Letters to his Mother. London, Constable, 1917. 128p] [BM BVaU LC NSHD OLU

**Green, Rev. Anson, 1801–1879**

THE LIFE AND TIMES OF THE REV. ANSON GREEN, D.D. Written by himself. Toronto, Methodist Book Room, 1877. 448p [BVaU LC NBFU OTU QMM

**Green, Henry Gordon, 1912–**

THE SILVER DART. The Authentic Story of the Hon. J.A.D. McCurdy, Canada's First Pilot. Fredericton, Brunswick Press, 1959. xvi + 208p

**Greene, Barnet M.**

WHO'S WHO IN CANADA. ... Ed. by ——. Toronto, International Press, 1915/16. [A continuing series. Title varies, early vols. being entitled: WHO'S WHO AND WHY. ...] [BVaU LC MWU NSHD OTP QMM

**Greene, Rev. David Leslie, 1883–**

BY THE SWIFT WATERS. London, Colonial and Continental Church Society, [1943?]. 31p [OTU SSU

**Greene, Gordon Kay, 1927–**

DANIEL KENT GREENE, HIS LIFE & TIMES, 1851–1921, AND PART II, THE PROGENY OF EVAN MOLBOURNE GREENE, 1814–1960. Edmonton, Author, 1960. 151 + 157p

**Grenfell, Wilfred Thomason, 1865–1940**

FORTY YEARS FOR LABRADOR. Boston, Houghton, 1932. 372p [BM BVaU LC NSHD OTU QMM

A LABRADOR DOCTOR. The Autobiography of ——. Boston, Houghton, 1919. 441p [BM BVaU LC NSHD OTU QMM

A LABRADOR DOCTOR. ... London, Hodder, 1948. 349p [An " 'amalgam' of two previous autobiographies ... FORTY YEARS FOR LABRADOR and A LABRADOR DOCTOR."] [BM LC QMM

THE STORY OF A LABRADOR DOCTOR. London, Hodder, n.d. 300p [BM BVaU NSWA OTU

**Grierson, Frank, 1865–**

WILLIAM LYON MACKENZIE KING. A Memoir Presented for the Earnest Consideration of All Patriotic Canadians. Ottawa, priv. print., 1952. 110p

**Griesbach, William Antrobus, 1878–1945**

I REMEMBER. Toronto, Ryerson, 1946. 353p [BVaU LC OTU QMM

**Griffin, Frederick G., 1889–1946**

MAJOR-GENERAL SIR HENRY MILL PELLATT, C.VO., D.C.L., V.D. ... Toronto, Ontario Pub. Co., 1942. 30p [LC OTP

VARIETY SHOW. Twenty Years of Watching the News Parade. Toronto, Macmillan, 1936. 359p [LC OTU

**Griffin, Justin Alonzo, 1846?–**

ANCESTORS AND DESCENDANTS OF RICHARD GRIFFIN OF SMITHVILLE, ONTARIO. A Pioneer Family, with a Brief Account of Some Related Griffin Families in Canada. Hamilton, Griffin & Richmond, 1924. 168p [BM LC OTU

**Griffin, W.H.**

THE PRINTER OF GREEN GROVE FARM. Being a Biographical Sketch of the Late Adam L. Lewis. Montreal, Author, n.d. 30p [QMM

THREE SCORE YEARS. Toronto, Griffin Agency, 1948. 51p [UTQ'50

**Griffith, Margaret R.**

JEAN DOW, M.D. A Beloved Physician. Toronto, United Church, n.d. 63p [OTP

**Grigg, David Henry, 1883–**

FROM ONE TO SEVENTY. Vancouver, Mitchell, 1955. [c1953]. 199p

**Grove, Frederick Philip, 1879–1948**

IN SEARCH OF MYSELF. Toronto, Macmillan, 1946. 457p [BVaU LC NSHD OTU QMM

**Groves, Abraham, 1847–1935**

ALL IN THE DAY'S WORK. Leaves from a Doctor's Case-Book. Toronto, Macmillan, 1934. xv + 181p [AEU BVaU OLU QMM

**Gudlaugson, Magnus Gudmundur, 1880–**

THREE TIMES A PIONEER. Ed. by Holmfridur Danielson. Winnipeg, Author, 1958. 104p [mimeographed].

**Guernsey, Isabel Russell**

FREE TRIP TO BERLIN. Toronto, Macmillan, 1943. 230p [BVaU OTU QMM

**Guillet, Edwin Clarence, 1898–**

PATHFINDERS OF NORTH AMERICA. By E.C. and Mary Guillet. Toronto, Macmillan, 1939. 304p [BM BVaU OTU

THIS MAN HANGED HIMSELF! A Study of the Evidence in the King *versus* Newell. ... Toronto, Ontario Pub. Co., 1943. 210p [An account of the trial of Hugh William A. Newell for the murder of his wife Sept. 29, 1940.] [BVaU NBFU OTU QMM

**Gurd, Norman St. Clair, 1870–1943**

THE STORY OF TECUMSEH. Toronto, Briggs, 1912. 190p [BM BVaU LC NSHD OTP

**Hague, Rev. Dyson, 1857–1935**

BISHOP BALDWIN. A Brief Sketch of One of Canada's Greatest Preachers and Noblest Church Leaders. Toronto, Evangelical Pub., 1927. 63p [OTU QMM

THE LIFE AND WORK OF JOHN WYCLIFFE. 2nd ed., enl. London, Church Book Room, 1935. 200p [1st ed. pub. 1909.] [BM BVaU LC OTU

**Hahn, James Emanuel, 1892–**

FOR ACTION. The Autobiography of a Canadian Industrialist. Toronto, Clarke Irwin, 1954. xii + 305p

**Haig, Kennethe Macmahon**

BRAVE HARVEST. The Life Story of E. Cora Hind, LL.D. Toronto, Allen, 1945. 275p [BVaU NBFU OTP QMM

COLONEL J.B. MITCHELL, FOR WHOM A WINNIPEG SCHOOL IS NAMED. [Winnipeg, 1957?]. 32p

**Haig-Brown, Roderick Langmere, 1908–**

CAPTAIN OF THE DISCOVERY. The Story of Captain George Vancouver. Toronto, Macmillan, 1956. 181p

FISHERMAN'S WINTER. New York, Morrow, 1954. 288p

**Haight, Canniff, 1825–1901**

COUNTRY LIFE IN CANADA FIFTY YEARS AGO. Personal Recollections and Reminiscences of a Sexagenarian. Toronto, Hunter Rose, 1885. 303p [BM BVaU LC MWU NSWA OKQ

A GENEALOGICAL NARRATIVE OF THE DANIEL HAIGHT FAMILY. Toronto, Rowsell & Hutchison, 1899. 71p [LC OTP

**Haliburton, Robert Grant, 1831–1901**

MEN OF THE NORTH AND THEIR PLACE IN HISTORY. ... Montreal, Lovell, 1869. 12p [NSHD OTU

**Haliburton Club. King's College, Windsor, N.S.**

HALIBURTON. A Centenary Chaplet. With a bibliography by John Parker Anderson. Toronto, Briggs, 1897. 116p [BM BVaU LC OTU QMM

**Hallam, Lillian Gertrude (Best), –1939**

THE FIRST PROTESTANT MISSIONARY IN CANADA. By Mrs. W.T. Hallam. Toronto, Canadian Churchman, [19—?]. 14p [OTP

**Halliday, William May, 1866–**

POTLATCH AND TOTEM, AND THE RECOLLECTIONS OF AN INDIAN AGENT. Toronto, Dent, 1935. 240p [BM BVaU LC OTU

**Ham, George Henry, 1847–1926**

THE MIRACLE MAN OF MONTREAL. [Brother André]. Toronto, Musson, 1922. 68p [BM BVaU NSHD OTU QMM

REMINISCENCES OF A RACONTEUR, BETWEEN THE '40s AND THE '20s. Toronto, Musson, 1921. 330p [BM BVaU LC NSHD OTU

**Hamer-Jackson, Celesta (Grivot de Grandcourt)**

DISCOVERERS AND EXPLORERS OF NORTH AMERICA. Toronto, Nelson, 1931. 319p [BM BVaU OTP

**Hamil, Frederick Coyne, 1903–**

LAKE ERIE BARON. The Story of Colonel Thomas Talbot. Toronto, Macmillan, 1955. ix + 326p

**Hamilton, James Cleland, 1836–1907**

OSGOODE HALL. Reminiscences of the Bench and Bar. Toronto, Carswell, 1904. 196p [BM BVaU LC OTP

**Hamilton, Marie Albina (Bonneau), 1878–**

THESE ARE THE PRAIRIES. By Zachary MacCaulay Hamilton and Marie Albina Hamilton. Regina, School Aids & Text Book Pub. Co., 1954. [pref. 1948]. 277p

**Hamilton, Ross**

PROMINENT MEN OF CANADA, 1931–2. Ed. by ——. Montreal, National Pub. Co., 1932. 640p [BM BVaU LC OTU

**Hammond, Melvin Ormond, 1876–1934**

CANADIAN CONFEDERATION AND ITS LEADERS. New York, Doran, 1917. 333p [BM BVaU LC NSWA OTU

HORATIO WALKER: PAINTER OF THE HABITANT. N.p., n.pub., n.d. 36p [NSWA

A TRIBUTE TO SAMUEL T. WOOD. [Anon] Toronto, Author, 1917. 32p [NBFU

**Hanley, Annie Harvey (Ross) Foster, 1875–**

THE MOHAWK PRINCESS. Being some Account of the Life of Tekahion-wake (E. Pauline Johnson). By Mrs. W. Garland Foster. Vancouver, Lion's Gate Pub., 1931. 216p [BM BVaU LC NBFU OTP

**Hanna, David Blythe, 1858–1938**

TRAINS OF RECOLLECTION. Drawn from Fifty Years' Railway Service in Scotland and Canada. By D.B. Hanna, as told to Arthur Hawkes. Toronto, Macmillan, 1924. 340p [BM BVaU LC NSHD OTU

**Hannay, James, 1842–1910**

THE HEROINE OF ACADIA ... FRANCES MARIE JACQUELINE, WIFE OF SIEUR DE LATOUR. Saint John, Bowes, 1910. 24p [BVaU NSHD OTU

NINE YEARS A CAPTIVE; or, John Gyles' Experience among the Milicete Indians from 1689–1698. With an intro. and historical notes by ——. Saint John, "Daily Telegraph," 1875. 38p [NBB

SIR LEONARD TILLEY. [See under WILMOT & TILLEY.]

WILMOT & TILLEY. Toronto, Morang, 1907. 301p [Later pub. as: LEMUEL ALLAN WILMOT. Toronto, Oxford U. Press, 1926. 164p; and SIR LEONARD TILLEY. Toronto, Oxford U. Press, 1926. 156p [BM BVaU LC NSWA OTP QMM

**Hanning-Lee, Muriel, 1927?–1957**

HEAD IN THE CLOUDS. London, Hodder, 1958. 191p

**Hardy, Henry Reginald, 1903–**

MACKENZIE KING OF CANADA. A Biography. Toronto, Oxford U. Press, 1949. 390p [BVaU LC NBFU OLU

**Hargrave, Letitia (Mactavish), 1813–1854**

THE LETTERS OF LETITIA HARGRAVE. Ed. with intro. & notes by Mrs. Margaret Arnett MacLeod. Toronto, Champlain Soc., 1947. cliv + 310p [BM BVaU LC NBFU OLU

**Harrington, Bernard James, 1848–1907**

LIFE OF SIR WILLIAM E. LOGAN ... Chiefly Compiled from his Letters, Journals and Reports. Montreal, Dawson, 1883. 432p [BM BVaU LC NSHD OTU

**Harris, John Norman, 1915–1964**

KNIGHTS OF THE AIR. Canadian Aces of World War I. Toronto, Macmillan, 1958. 156p

**Harris, Rev. Joseph Hemington, 1800–1881**

A LETTER TO THE HON. & VEN. ARCHDEACON STRACHAN in Reply to ... his "Letter ... on the Life and Character of Bishop Hobart". ... York, [Correspondent Print.], 1833. 21p [OTP

**Harris, Reginald Vanderbilt, 1881–**

CATALOGUE OF PORTRAITS OF THE JUDGES OF THE SUPREME COURT OF NOVA SCOTIA. ... [Halifax? 1921?]. 111p [LC NSHD OOA

CHARLES INGLIS, Missionary, Loyalist, Bishop (1734–1816). Toronto, General Board of Religious Education, 1937. 186p [BVaU LC NBFU OTP

**Harrison, Charles Yale, 1898–1954**

CLARENCE DARROW. New York, Cape & Smith, 1931. 380p [BM LC OTU

**Harrold, Ernest William, 1889–1945**

THE DIARY OF OUR OWN PEPYS. E.W. Harrold's Record of Canadian Life. Ed. by I. Norman Smith. Toronto, Ryerson, 1947. 296p [BVaU LC NBFU OTP

**Hart, Margaret Janet (McPhee), 1867–1941**

OUR WEB OF LIFE. Some Account of Dougal McPhee, Pioneer to Eastern Nova Scotia, his Wife Mary McMillan, and their Family. Vancouver, 1959. 17 + 5p [mimeographed].

**Hart, Rev. William Edward, 1907–**
AN APPRECIATION OF JOHN HOWARD. Saint John, Author, 1959. 51p

**Hartley, Rev. H.A.S.**
TA TOU PRAGMA EMOU BIOU; or, Some Concerns of my Life. Amherst, 1890. 310p [NBFU

**Hartwell, George E.**
GRANARY OF HEAVEN. Toronto, United Church, 1939. 228p [BVaU OTUV

**Harvey, Athelstan George, 1884–1950**
DOUGLAS OF THE FIR. A Biography of David Douglas, Botanist. Cambridge, Mass., Harvard U. Press, 1947. 290p [BM BVaU LC OOA

**Harvey, Daniel Cobb, 1886–**
THE CENTENARY OF EDWARD WHELAN. Lecture delivered in Strand Theatre, Charlottetown, P.E.I., August 9, 1926. [Charlottetown?], Irwin, 1926. 21p [OTU
JOSEPH HOWE AND LOCAL PATRIOTISM. An Inaugural Lecture delivered on March 10th, 1921. Winnipeg, 1921. 28p [BVaU NSWA OKQ
LETTERS OF REV. NORMAN McLEOD, 1835–51. Ed. by ——. Halifax, Pub. Archives, 1939. 32p [UTQ'40
THOMAS D'ARCY McGEE. The Prophet of Canadian Nationality. A Popular Lecture. ... Winnipeg, U. of Manitoba, 1923. 30p [BM BVaU NSWA OKQ

**Harvey, Ruth (Walker), 1900–**
CURTAIN TIME. Toronto, Allen, 1949. 310p [BVaU NBFU OTU

**Hassard, Albert Richard, 1873–1940**
A NEW LIGHT ON LORD MACAULAY. Toronto, Rockingham Press, 1918. 76p [BM LC NSHD OTU QMM

**Hathaway, Ann, 1848–**
MUSKOKA MEMORIES. Sketches from Real Life. Toronto, Briggs, 1904. 127p [BM OTU

**Hathaway, Ernest Jackson, 1871–1930**
JESSE KETCHUM AND HIS TIMES. Being a Chronicle of the Social Life and Public Affairs of the Capital of the Province of Upper Canada during its First Half Century. Toronto, McClelland, 1929. 359p [BM BVaU LC NSHD OLU

**Hatzan, Alexander Leon, 1864–**
THE TRUE STORY OF HIAWATHA, AND HISTORY OF THE SIX NATION INDIANS. Toronto, McClelland, 1925. 298p [BM BVaU NSHD OTU QMSS

**Haultain, Theodore Arnold, 1857–1941**
GOLDWIN SMITH, HIS LIFE AND OPINIONS. London, Werner Laurie, 1913. 304p [BM BVaU LC NSWA OTU QMM

**Haw, Rev. William**

FIFTEEN YEARS IN CANADA. ... Edinburgh, Ziegler, 1850. 120p [BM LC OTP

**Hay, George Upham, 1843–1913**

MEMORIAL SKETCH OF PROF. C.F. HARTT. Saint John, 1881. [NBB

**Haydon, Andrew, 1867–1932**

MACKENZIE KING AND THE LIBERAL PARTY. Toronto, Allen, 1930. 54p [BVaU OTU

**Healy, William Joseph, 1867–1950**

WOMEN OF THE RED RIVER. Being a Book Written from the Recollections of Women Surviving from the Red River Era. ... Winnipeg, Russell Lang, 1923. 261p [BM BVaU NSHD OTU QMM

**Hearne, Samuel, 1745–1792**

COPPERMINE JOURNEY. An Account of a Great Adventure. Selected from the Journals of Samuel Hearne, by Farley Mowat. Toronto, McClelland, 1958. 144p

**Heeney, Rev. William Bertal, 1873–1955**

I WALK WITH A BISHOP [Charles James Stewart]. Toronto, Ontario Pub. Co., 1931. 113p [BVaU OKQ

JOHN WEST AND HIS RED RIVER MISSION. Toronto, Musson, 1920. 56p [AEU BVaU OTUV

**Helwig, Mrs. Solomon**

A HISTORY OF THE DIEBEL FAMILY. By Mrs. Solomon Helwig and Mrs. John A. Helwig. Hanover, Ont., Post Press, 1936. 93p [OTU

**Hemsley, Richard, 1846–1931**

LOOKING BACK. Montreal, Gazette, 1930. 175p [BM BVaU OTP QMM

**Henderson, Dorothy (McLaughlin), 1900–**

BIOGRAPHICAL SKETCHES OF SIX HUMANITARIANS WHOSE LIVES HAVE BEEN FOR THE GREATER GLORY. Toronto, Ryerson, 1958. 188p [Cover title: FOR THE GREATER GLORY.]

**Henderson, John**

GREAT MEN OF CANADA. Toronto, Southam, 1928. 239p [BVaU NBFU OTU

HOWARD FERGUSON. The Romance of a Personality. ... Toronto, Macmillan, 1930. 145p [BM BVaU NBFU OTP

**Henderson, Mary (Gillespie), 1840–1935**

MEMORIES OF MY EARLY YEARS. Montreal, Charters & Charters, 1937. 58p [BVaU LC OTU

**Henry, Lorne James, 1893–**

CANADIANS. A Book of Biographies. Toronto, Longmans, 1950. 153p [BVaU NBFU OONL

**Henry, Mrs. P.A.**

MEMOIR OF REV. THOMAS HENRY, Christian Minister, York Pioneer, and Soldier of 1812. Toronto, Hill, 1880. 192p [BVaU NSWA OTU

**Henry, Walter, 1791–1860**

TRIFLES FROM MY PORT-FOLIO; or, Recollections of ... France, the East Indies ... St. Helena during the Detention and until the Death of Napoleon, and Upper and Lower Canada. By a Staff Surgeon [pseud]. Quebec, Neilson, 1839. 2v [2nd ed. with alterations, under title: EVENTS OF A MILITARY LIFE. London, Pickering, 1843. 2v] [BM BVaU LC NSHD OTU QMM

**Henson, Josiah, 1789–1883**

AN AUTOBIOGRAPHY OF THE REV. JOSIAH HENSON ("Uncle Tom") from 1789 to 1881. With a Preface by Mrs. Harriet Beecher Stowe ... London, Ont., Schuyler Smith, 1881. 256p [OTP

"TRUTH IS STRANGER THAN FICTION." An Autobiography of the Rev. Josiah Henson (Mrs. Harriet Beecher Stowe's "Uncle Tom"), from 1789–1879. With a preface by Mrs. Harriet Beecher Stowe ... Wendell Phillips and John G. Whittier. ... Boston, Russell, 1879. 336p [LC

TRUTH STRANGER THAN FICTION. Father Henson's Story of his Own Life. With an intro. by Mrs. H.B. Stowe. Boston, Jewett, 1858. 212p [LC OTUV

THE LIFE OF JOSIAH HENSON, Formerly a Slave, Now an Inhabitant of Canada. As Narrated by himself. Boston, Phelps, 1849. 76p [Also: Dresden, Ont., 1965.] [BM BVaU LC

UNCLE TOM'S STORY OF HIMSELF. London, 1877. [BM

**Hereford, Sara Lillian (Jakes), 1887–**

OUR UNITED EMPIRE LOYALIST ANCESTRY. By Sally Hereford. Ottawa, Mutual Press, 1958. 27p [Descendants of John Chester, United Empire Loyalist.]

**Herklots, Rev. Hugh Gerard Gibson, 1903–**

THE FIRST WINTER. A Canadian Chronicle. Toronto, Dent, 1935. 176p [BM BVaU LC NBFU OTU

**Herman, Alan, 1916–**

THE SCALPEL, THE SWORD. The Story of Dr. Norman Bethune. By Ted Allan [pseud] and Sydney Gordon. Boston, Little Brown, [1952]. 336p

**Herrington, Walter Stevens, 1860–1947**

HEROINES OF CANADIAN HISTORY. Toronto, Briggs, 1909. 78p [BM BVaU NSHD OTP

THE MARTYRS OF NEW FRANCE. Toronto, Briggs, 1909. 159p [BM BVaU OKQ QMBM

**Hewitt, William Abraham, 1875–**

DOWN THE STRETCH. Recollections of a Pioneer Sportsman and Journalist. Toronto, Ryerson, 1958. xi + 239p

**Hickey, Rev. Raymond Myles, 1909–**

THE SCARLET DAWN. Campbellton, N.B., Tribune, 1949 [i.e. 1950]. 277p [BVaU OONL

**Hiemstra, Mary (Pinder), 1897–**

GULLY FARM. Toronto, McClelland, 1955. 311p

**Higgins, Rev. Thomas Alfred, 1823–1905**

THE LIFE OF JOHN MOCKETT CRAMP, D.D., 1796–1881, Late President of Acadia College. Montreal, Drysdale, 1887. 396p [BVaU NSHD OTP

**Higgins, W.H.**

THE LIFE AND TIMES OF JOSEPH GOULD. ... Struggles of the Early Canadian Settlers, Settlement of Uxbridge, Sketch of the History of the County of Ontario, the Rebellion of 1837, Parliamentary Career, etc. Reminiscences of Sixty Years of Active Political and Municipal Life. Toronto, Robinson, 1887. 304p [BM BVaU OTP

**Higginson, Thomas Boyd, 1912–**

DESCENDANTS OF THE REVEREND THOMAS HIGGINSON. London, Research Pub. Co., 1958. 64p

**Higginson, Thomas Tweed, 1828–1903**

DIARIES. Ed. by Thomas Boyd Higginson. London, Ont, Research Pub. Co., 1960. 91p

**Higinbotham, John David, 1864–1961**

WHEN THE WEST WAS YOUNG. Historical Reminiscences. ... Toronto, Ryerson, 1933. 328p [BM BVaU NBFU OTP

**Hill, Rev. Allan Massie, 1876–1943**

IT HAPPENED TO ME. Toronto, Thorn Press, 1942. 111p [LC OTP

**Hill, Rev. George William, 1824–1906**

IN MEMORY OF ROBERT FITZGERALD UNIACKE, Rector of St. George's Halifax. ... Halifax, Blackadar, 1870. 25p [BVaU NSHD

MEMOIR OF SIR BRENTON HALLIBURTON. Late Chief Justice of the Province of Nova Scotia. ... Halifax, Bowes, 1864. 207 + 47p [Appended is: JOHN BULL AND HIS CALVES; *see* **Halliburton, Brenton.**] [BM BVaU LC NSWA OTP

**Hill, Rev. James Edgar, 1842–1911**

MEMORIAL SERVICE, JANUARY 10TH, 1897, BEING THE SUNDAY AFTER THE FUNERAL OF SIR JOSEPH HICKSON. Montreal, Gazette, 1897. 16p [OTP

**Hilts, Rev. Joseph Henry, 1819–1903**

EXPERIENCES OF A BACKWOODS PREACHER; or, Facts & Incidents Culled from Thirty Years of Ministerial Life. Toronto, Briggs, 1887. 352p [BVaU OTP

**Hincks, Francis, 1807–1885**

REMINISCENCES OF HIS PUBLIC LIFE. Montreal, Drysdale, 1884. 450p [BM BVaU NSWA OTP

**Hines, Rev. John, 1850–1931**

THE RED INDIANS OF THE PLAINS. Thirty Years' Missionary Experience in Saskatchewan. London, S.P.C.K., 1915. 332p [BM BVaU NSHD OTP QMM

**Hobart, John Henry, 1902–**

QUAKER BY CONVINCEMENT. New York, McKay, 1951. 227p

**Hobson, Richmond Pearson, 1907–**

GRASS BEYOND THE MOUNTAINS. Discovering the Last Great Cattle Frontier on the North American Continent. Philadelphia, Lippincott, 1951. 256p

NOTHING TOO GOOD FOR A COWBOY. Philadelphia, Lippincott, 1955. 252p

**Hodgins, James Cobourg, 1866–1953**

THE REV. DR. HENDERSON & HIS CRITICS. Toronto, Hunter, 1916. 14p [OTU

**Hodgins, John George, 1821–1912**

THE REV. EGERTON RYERSON. ... Founder of the School System of Ontario. An Historical Retrospect. ... [Toronto? 1889.] 16p [LC OTU

RYERSON MEMORIAL VOLUME. ... Toronto, Warwick, 1889. 131p [BM BVaU NSHD OTU

SKETCH OF THE REVEREND DOCTOR RYERSON. [Toronto? 1894?] 15p [LC OTU

**Hoemberg, Elisabeth (Sims), 1909–**

THY PEOPLE, MY PEOPLE. London, Dent, 1950. 314p [OONL

**Holden, Mrs. John Rose**

A PRIMITIVE CIVILIZATION. THE BRANT FAMILY. N.p., Wentworth Historical Soc., [1904?]. 33p [OTU

**Holliday, Charles W., 1870–**

THE VALLEY OF YOUTH. Caldwell, Idaho, Caxton, 1948. 357p [BVaU LC OOA

**Holt, Miss C.E.**

AN AUTOBIOGRAPHICAL SKETCH OF A TEACHER'S LIFE, Including a Residence in the Northern and Southern States, California, Cuba and Peru. By Miss Holt. Quebec, Carrel, 1875. 117p [BVaU LC OTU QMSS

SUPPLEMENT TO MISS HOLT'S "AUTOBIOGRAPHICAL SKETCH." Quebec, 1875. 11p [QMSS

**Hood, Dora (Ridout), 1885–**

THE SIDE DOOR. Twenty-Six Years in my Book Room. Toronto, Ryerson, 1958. ix + 238p

**Hoover, Dorothy (Haines)**

J.W. BEATTY. Toronto, Ryerson, 1948. 37p [BVaU LC NBFU OTP

**Hopkins, Arthur George, 1869–**

GO WEST YOUNG MAN, I DID. Ilfracombe, Devon, Stockwell, 1956. 286p

**Hopkins, John Castell, 1864–1923**

LIFE AND WORK OF THE RT. HON. SIR JOHN THOMPSON ... Prime Minister of Canada. Toronto, United Pub., 1895. 479p [BVaU LC NSWA OTP

THE LIFE OF KING EDWARD VII. With a Sketch of the Career of George, Prince of Wales, and a History of the Royal Tour of the Empire in 1901. Toronto, Scull, 1910. 472p [BVaU NBFU OOU QMM

**Horan, John William, 1908–**

ON THE SIDE OF THE LAW. Biography of J.D. Nicholson, Formerly Assistant Superintendent, A.P.P. Edmonton, Institute of Applied Art, 1944. 275p [BVaU LC OTP

**Horner, Ralph Cecil, 1854–1921**

REMINISCENCES FROM HIS OWN PEN. Also Reports of Five Typical Sermons. Brockville, Mrs. A. Horner, n.d. 213p [OTU

**Horton, William**

MEMOIR OF THE LATE THOMAS SCRATCHERD. A Family Record. London, Ont., 1878. 262p [BVaU OTU

**Howard, John George, 1803–1890**

INCIDENTS IN THE LIFE OF JOHN G. HOWARD. ... Toronto, Copp, 1885. 36p [BVaU NSWA OTU

**Howard, Robert Palmer, 1823–1889**

A SKETCH OF THE LIFE OF THE LATE G.W. CAMPBELL ... Late Dean of the Medical Faculty, and a Summary of the History of the Faculty ... McGill University. Montreal, Gazette, 1882. 24p [BVaU NSWA OTP

**Howay, Frederic William, 1867–1943**

CAPTAIN GEORGE VANCOUVER. Toronto, Ryerson, 1932. 32p [BVaU

**Howe, Joseph, 1804–1873**

THE HEART OF HOWE. Selections from the Letters and Speeches. Ed. by D.C. Harvey. Toronto, Oxford U. Press, 1939. 197p [BVaU LC NSHD OTP

**Howell, Henry Spencer, 1857–1912**

AN ISLAND PARADISE AND REMINISCENCES OF TRAVEL. Toronto, Hart & Riddell, 1892. 296p [2nd ed.: Toronto, 1911.] [NBFU OKQ QMSS

**Howell, William Boyman, 1873–**

F.J. SHEPHERD–SURGEON. His Life and Times. Toronto, Dent, 1934. 251p [BVaU LC NBFU OTUV

**Howey, Mrs. Florence R., 1856?–1936**

PIONEERING ON THE C.P.R. Ed. by Mrs. George E. Mabee. Ottawa, Mutual Press, 1938. 141p [BM BViPA OLU

**Hubicz, Rev. Edward Michael, 1912–**

FATHER JOE–A MANITOBAN MISSIONARY. A Biographical Account of the Life of Father Ladislaus Joseph Kreciszewski. London, Veritas Foundation Pub. Centre, 1959. 95p

**Huestis, Rev. George Oxley, 1827–1905**

HISTORICAL ITEMS AND PERSONAL REMINISCENCES OF METHODISM IN CUMBERLAND COUNTY, NOVA SCOTIA. ... Windsor, N.S., Anslow, 1902. 20p [NSWA

MEMORIALS OF WESLEYAN MISSIONARIES AND MINISTERS, who have died within the Bounds of the Conference of Eastern British America, since the Introduction of Methodism into these Colonies. Halifax, Macnab, 1872. 147p [BVaU NSWA OTP

**Huey, John Alexander, 1882–1954**

THE WARDENS, COUNCILLORS, PARLIAMENTARY REPRESENTATIVES, JUDICIAL OFFICERS AND COUNTY OFFICIALS OF THE COUNTY OF LAMBTON FOR 100 YEARS FROM 1849 TO 1949. Comp. by ——. [Sarnia, Lambton] County Council, 1950. 111p [OONL

**Hughes, James Laughlin, 1846–1935**

THE REAL ROBERT BURNS. London, Chambers, 1922. 216p [BVa LC NSWA OKQ QMM

**Hughes, Katherine, –1925**

ARCHBISHOP O'BRIEN. Ottawa, Crain, 1906. 230p [BM BVaU NSWA OTP

FATHER LACOMBE, THE BLACK-ROBE VOYAGEUR. Toronto, Briggs, 1911. 467p [Several later editions.] [BM BVaU LC NSHD OTP QMM

**Hume, Blanche**

THE STRICKLAND SISTERS. Toronto, Ryerson, 1928. 32p [BVaU OTU

**Hunt, William Harold, 1884–**

BIRTHRIGHTS. A Genealogical Record of Canadian Branches of Hunt, Scott, Ives & Farwell Families, including the Lineage of John & Robert Hunt of Fitzroy Tps., Carleton Co., Ont., Daniel Scott of Dunham Tps., Mississquoi [*sic*] Co., Que., Joseph & Joel Hall Ives of Magog Tps., Stanstead Co., Que., Gladden Farwell of Compton Tps., Stanstead Co., Que., and Allied Families. Winnipeg, McCullough's Multigraphing, 1957. 1v. (various pagings). [Also: Supplement to Scott section. Winnipeg, 1961. 11 + 4p]

**Hunter, Edmund Robert, 1909–**

J.E.H. MACDONALD. A Biography and Catalogue of his Work. Toronto, Ryerson, 1940. 60p [BVa NBFU OTP QMM

THOREAU MACDONALD. Toronto, Ryerson, 1942. 43p [BVaU LC OTP

**Hutchinson, Rev. Gerald Middleton, 1914–**

MEMORIAL BOOKLET WRITTEN ON THE OCCASION OF THE 100TH ANNIVERSARY CELEBRATIONS HONORING THE ARRIVAL OF THE REVEREND THOMAS WOOLSEY AND THE REVEREND HENRY BIRD STEINHAUER IN SEPTEMBER, 1855. N.p., 1955. 23p [Cover title: "The roots of the province; Alberta's 50 years, and 100 years of Christian service."]

**Hutchison, Bruce, 1901–**

THE INCREDIBLE CANADIAN. A Candid Portrait of Mackenzie King: his Works, his Times, and his Nation. Toronto, Longmans, 1952. 454p [English title: MACKENZIE KING, THE INCREDIBLE CANADIAN. London, Longmans, 1953.]

**Hutton, Samuel King, 1877–**

BY ESKIMO DOG-SLED AND KYAK [*sic*]. A Description of a Missionary's Experiences and Adventures in Labrador. London, Seeley Service, 1919. 219p [BVaU LC NfSM OLU

A SHEPHERD IN THE SNOW. The Life Story of Walter Perret of Labrador. London, Hodder, 1936. 285p [LC NfSM OORD

**Ingraham, Mary (Kinley), 1874–1949**

ROBERT BRUCE KINLEY AND HIS FAMILY. Wolfville, Acadian, 1941. 4p [NSWA

**Innis, Harold Adams, 1894–1952**

PETER POND, FUR TRADER AND ADVENTURER. Toronto, Irwin & Gordon, 1930. 153p [BM BVaU LC NSHD OTP

**Jack, Isaac Allen, 1843–1903**

BIOGRAPHICAL REVIEW. This volume contains Biographical Sketches of Leading Citizens of the Province of New Brunswick. Editorial supervision of ——. Boston, Biographical Review Pub. Co., 1900. 508p [LC NSWA QMM

**Jackson, Alexander Young, 1882–**

BANTING AS AN ARTIST. With a memoir by F.W.W. Hipwell. Toronto, Ryerson, 1943. 37p [BVi LC OTU QMM

A PAINTER'S COUNTRY. The Autobiography of A.Y. Jackson. Toronto, Clarke Irwin, 1958. xv + 170p

**Jackson, Harold McGill, 1898–1961**

JUSTUS SHERWOOD, SOLDIER, LOYALIST AND NEGOTIATOR. [Aylmer East, Que.?], Author, 1958. 59p

**Jackson, William H.**

LIFE AND CONFESSIONS OF SOPHIA HAMILTON, who was Tried, Condemned, and Sentenced to be Hung, at Montreal, Jan. 22, 1845. Montreal, Jackson, 1845. 32p [NSWA

**James, Norman Bloomfield, 1872–1963**

THE AUTOBIOGRAPHY OF A NOBODY. Toronto, Dent, 1947. 239p [AEU BVaU OTP

**Jamieson, Mrs. Annie Straith**

WILLIAM KING, Friend and Champion of Slaves. Toronto, Missions of Evangelism, 1925. 209p [BVaU LC NSWA OTU QMM

**Jarvis, Julia, 1899–**

THREE CENTURIES OF ROBINSONS. The Story of a Family. Toronto, priv. print., 1953. 170p

**Jarvis, Peter Robinson, 1824–1906**

MEMOIRS OF P.R. JARVIS. N.p., n.d. 133p [OOP

**Jenkins, Rev. John, 1813–1898**

THE FAITHFUL MINISTER. A Memorial of the Late Rev. William Squire. ... Montreal, Wesleyan Book; London, Mason, 1853. 175p [NSWA OTP

**Jephson, Harriet Julia (Campbell), 1854–1930**

NOTES OF A NOMAD. London, Hutchinson, 1918. 368p [BM

**Job, Patrick Dalzel**

THE SETTLERS. By Peter Dalzel [pseud]. London, Constable, 1957. 209p

**Job, Robert Brown, 1873–**

JOHN JOB'S FAMILY. A Story of his Ancestors and Successors and their Business Connections with Newfoundland and Liverpool, 1730–1953. 2nd enl. ed. St. John's, Telegram Print. Co., 1954. 144p

**Johnson, Mrs. Amelia B., –1888**

FROM LIFE'S SCHOOL TO THE "FATHER'S HOUSE." A Brief Memoir of Amelia, Annie, & Thomas Johnson, with Letters. Comp. and ed. by M.R.J. Toronto, Hunter Rose, 1888. 204p [BVaU LC OTUV

**Johnson, Wellwood Robert, 1887–**

LEGEND OF LANGLEY. An Account of the Early History of Fort Langley and an Intimate Story of the Lives of some, but not all, of the early Pioneers of the District of Langley. Langley, B.C., the Centennial Committee, 1958. 183p

**Johnston, Blanche J. (Read), 1866–**

THE LADY WITH THE OTHER LAMP! The Story of Blanche Read Johnston. As told to Mary Morgan Dean. Toronto, McClelland, 1920. 282p [BM BVaU

THE LIFE OF JOHN READ. By Blanche J. Read. Toronto, Salvation Army Pub. House, [19—?]. 181p [OTP

**Johnston, Elizabeth (Lichtenstein), 1764–1848**

RECOLLECTIONS OF A GEORGIA LOYALIST. Written in 1836. Ed. by Arthur W. Eaton. New York, Mansfield, 1901. 224p [BM BVaU LC

**Johnston, Rev. Hugh, 1840–1922**

MEMORIAL OF THE LATE HON. SENATOR FERRIER, OF MONTREAL. A Sermon ... with an Account of the Funeral, and an Address by the Rev. John Potts. ... Toronto, Briggs, 1888. 42p [OTUV

MEMORIAL OF THE LATE ROBERT WALKER. Toronto, Briggs, 1885. 10p [OTUV

A MERCHANT PRINCE. Life of Hon. Senator John Macdonald. Toronto, Briggs, 1893. 321p [BVaU NSHD OKQ

A REVIEW OF REV. F.W. MACDONALD'S LIFE OF WILLIAM MORLEY PUNSHON. ... Toronto, Briggs, 1888. 182p [OKQ

TOWARDS THE SUNRISE. Being Sketches of Travel in Europe and the East, to which is added a Memorial Sketch of the Rev. William Morley Punshon. Toronto, Briggs, 1883. 459p [BVaU OTU

**Johnston, Mono (Troop)**

PROPHET, PRESBYTER, AND SERVANT OF MANKIND. A Memoir of Rev. Canon G. Osborne Troop, M.A. Comp. by Mono Troop Johnston, and ed. by Dyson Hague. Truro, News Pub. Co., 1935. 222p [UTQ

**Jones, Elizabeth, 1830–1837?**

MEMOIR OF ELIZABETH JONES, a Little Indian Girl, who lived at the River-Credit Mission, Upper Canada. [Anon] London, Mason, 1838. 34p [OTP

**Jones, James Edmund, 1866–1939**

DESCENDANTS OF PHILIP HENRY. New ed. Kingston, "British Whig," 1925. 32 + 68p [OTU

**Jones, Rev. John Gordon, 1901–**

THE FIVE LIVES OF WILLIAM CAREY. N.p., Baptist Federation of Canada, 1960. 23p

**Jones, Mrs. Nancy, 1890–1959**

FOR GOODNESS' SAKE. Toronto, Ryerson, 1949. 291p [BVaU LC NBFU OTP

**Jones, Rev. Peter (Chippewa Chief), 1802–1856**
LIFE AND JOURNALS OF KAH-KE-WA-QUON-A-BY (Rev. Peter Jones), Wesleyan Missionary. Toronto, Green, 1860. 424p [BM BVaU LC OTP QMM

**Jowett, Cecilia**
NO THOUGHT FOR TOMORROW. The Story of a Northern Nurse. Toronto, Ryerson, 1954. xii + 104p

**Joyal, Rev. Erwin Carlyle, 1875–**
A TERCENTENIAL [*sic*] HISTORY OF THE JOYAL FAMILY. By Rev. Erwin C. Joyal and Rev. Eleanor Ruth Joyal. Bath, N.B., the Authors, 1960. 3 pts in 2. [mimeographed]

**Kaiser, Thomas Erlin, 1863–1940**
THE KAISER FAMILIES OF THE COUNTY OF YORK, ONTARIO. Oshawa, Author, 1931. 22p [OTP

**Karr, Willliam John, –1938**
THE HISTORY OF CANADA THROUGH BIOGRAPHY. Explorers, Soldiers & Statesmen: Canadian Pacific History. Toronto, Dent, 1929. [Several volumes of different dates.] [BVaU LC NSHD OTU QMM

**Kay, Rev. John**
BIOGRAPHY OF THE REV. WILLIAM GUNDY. ... Twenty Years of Methodism in Canada. Toronto, Campbell, 1871. 176p [BVaU OTU

**Kean, Abram, 1855–1945**
OLD AND YOUNG AHEAD. A Millionaire in Seals. Being the Life History of Captain Abram Kean. ... London, Heath Cranton, 1935. 218p [BM BVaU LC OTU

**Kearley, Mark H.**
A FEW HINTS AND SUGGESTIONS ABOUT EMILY CARR AND HER WORK. An Informal Talk. ... [Victoria? Federation of Canadian Artists?], 1946. 14p [BVaU OKQ

**Kearney, Lawrence Cunningham**
THE LIFE OF COLONEL ... THOMAS TALBOT. ... Chatham, Rose, 1857. 51p [OTP

**Keefer, Rev. Robert, 1871–**
MEMOIRS OF THE KEEFER FAMILY. Norwood, Norwood, 1935. 30p [LC OTU

**Keene, Louis**
"CRUMPS." The Plain Story of a Canadian Who Went. With a prefatory note by General Leonard Wood. Boston, Houghton, 1917. 156p [LC NBFU OTU

**Kelley, Thomas Patrick, 1910–**

BAD MEN OF CANADA. A History of the Ten Most Desperate Men in Canadian Crime. N.p., Arrow Pub. Co., 1950. 158p [OONL

THE BLACK DONNELLYS. Toronto, Harlequin Books, 1954. 160p

**Kells, A. Edna, 1880–**

ELIZABETH McDOUGALL, PIONEER. Toronto, United Church Pub. House, 1933. 48p [AEU OTP

**Kelly, Fanny (Wiggins), 1845–**

NARRATIVE OF MY CAPTIVITY AMONG THE SIOUX INDIANS. With a Brief Account of General Sully's Indian Expedition of 1860, Bearing upon Events Occurring in my Captivity. Toronto, Maclear, 1872. 304p [1st ed.: Cincinnati, 1871.] [BVaU LC NBFU OTU

**Kemp, Harold Stuart Miller, 1892–**

NORTHERN TRADER. Toronto, Ryerson, 1956. 253p

**Kemp, Vernon Alfred Miller, 1895?–**

WITHOUT FEAR, FAVOUR OR AFFECTION. Thirty-five Years with the Royal Canadian Mounted Police. Toronto, Longmans, 1958. ix + 263p

**Kennedy, Howard Angus, 1861–1938**

FATHER LACOMBE.... Toronto, Ryerson, 1928. 32p [BVaU OTUV QMM

LORD STRATHCONA. Toronto, Ryerson, 1928. 32p [BViP NBS OLU QMSS

**Kennedy, Thomas Laird, 1878–1959**

TOM KENNEDY'S STORY. As told to Ralph Hyman. Toronto, the Globe, 1960. 62p

**Kennedy, William Paul McClure, 1879–1963**

ARCHBISHOP PARKER. London, Pitman, 1908. 306p [LC OTU

LORD ELGIN. London, Oxford U. Press, 1926. 272p [BM BVaU LC OTU QMM

**Kerby, Rev. George William, 1860–1944**

THE BROKEN TRAIL. Pages from a Pastor's Experience in Western Canada. Toronto, Briggs, 1909. 189p [BVaU NSHD OKQ SSU

**Kern, Hannah Aikman (Hammill), 1820–1885**

DIARY. Ed. by J.H. Holbrook and M.H. Farmer. London, Ont., Lawson Memorial Library, University of Western Ontario, 1958. 29p [mimeographed]

**Kerr, Donald Gordon Grady, 1913–**

SIR EDMUND HEAD, A SCHOLARLY GOVERNOR. By D.G.G. Kerr with the assistance of J.A. Gibson. Toronto, U. of Toronto Press in co-operation with Mount Allison University, 1954. xi + 259p

**Kerr, John Blaine**

BIOGRAPHICAL DICTIONARY OF WELL-KNOWN BRITISH COLUMBIANS. With a Historical Sketch. Vancouver, Kerr & Begg, 1890. 326p [BVi LC OOP

**Kerr, Wilfred Brenton, 1896–1950**

ARMS AND THE MAPLE LEAF. Memories of Canada's Corps, 1918. Seaforth, Ont., Huron Expositor, 1943. 90p [A continuation of "SHRIEKS AND CRASHES."] [BM LC OTP

FROM SCOTLAND TO HURON. A History of the Kerr Family. Seaforth, Ont., Huron Expositor, 1949. 48p [OTP

"SHRIEKS AND CRASHES." Being Memories of Canada's Corps, 1917. Toronto, Hunter Rose, 1929. 218p [BM BVaU LC OTP

**Ketcheson Family History Publication Committee**

A GENEALOGICAL HISTORY THROUGH EIGHT GENERATIONS IN CANADA OF THE KETCHESON FAMILY AND DESCENDANTS. N.p., 1958. 72p

**Ketchum, Creston Donald**

HIS PATH IS IN THE WATERS. New York, Prentice-Hall, 1955. 183p

**Ketchum, William, 1798–1876**

MEMOIR OF THE DISTINGUISHED MOHAWK INDIAN CHIEF, SACHEM, AND WARRIOR, CAPT. JOSEPH BRANT. [Anon] Brantford, Stewart, 1872. 89p [NSWA OTU

**Ketchum, Rev. William Quintard, 1818–1901**

THE LIFE AND WORK OF THE MOST REVEREND JOHN MEDLEY, D.D., First Bishop of Fredericton and Metropolitan of Canada. Saint John, McMillan, 1893. 335p [BM BVaU LC NSWA OTU

**Key, Sydney James, 1918–**

JOHN CONSTABLE. His Life and Work. Toronto, Dent, 1948. 128p [BM BVa LC OTU

**Kibbe, James Allen**

THE WOOD FAMILY, SACKVILLE, N.B. A Genealogy of the Line from Thomas Wood, of Rowley, Mass., born about 1634, to Josiah Wood, of Sackville, N.B., born in 1843. Gathered and arranged by ——. Sackville, Wood, 1904. 43p [BM BVaU LC NSHD OOP

**Kidd, Henry George, 1878–**

THE MEGANTIC OUTLAW. Toronto, 1948. 139p [NBFU OTP

**Kilbourn, William Morley, 1926–**

THE FIREBRAND. William Lyon Mackenzie and the Rebellion in Upper Canada. Toronto, Clarke Irwin, 1956. xv + 283p

**King, Rev. George Brockwell, –1956**

FOND MEMORY AND THE LIGHT OF OTHER DAYS. The Old Leslie Street School, and a Last Century Tragedy "over the Don." Toronto, priv. print. 195–. 10p

**King, Herbert Baxter, 1879–**

SOLOMON MUSSALLEM. A Biography. Haney, B.C., priv. print., 1955. ix + 143p

**King, John, 1843–1916**

McCAUL: CROFT: FORNERI. Personalities of Early University Days. Toronto, Macmillan, 1914. 256p [OTP

**King, Rev. John Mark, 1829–1899**

THE GOOD FIGHT. A Sermon Preached in the Presbyterian Church, Gould St., Toronto, on August 22nd, 1869, on Occasion of the Death of the Rev. Robert Burns. Toronto, Adam Stevenson, 1869. 23p [NSHD OTP

**King, William Cornwallis, 1845–1940**

TRADER KING. As Told to Mary Weekes. Regina, School Aids and Text Book Pub. Co., 1949. 184p [King was one of the last of the "Wintering Partners" of the Hudson's Bay Co., serving 40 years in the Northwest Territories.] [BVaU OTU

**King, William Lyon Mackenzie, 1874–1950**

ADDRESS ... ON ... YEARS OF LEADERSHIP–AND REASONS FOR RETIREMENT AS LEADER OF THE PARTY ... August 6, 1948. Ottawa, National Liberal Federation, 1948. 16p [OOL

THE MACKENZIE KING RECORD. Ed. by J.W. Pickersgill. Toronto, U. of Toronto Press, 1960. v. 1: 1939–1945.

THE SECRET OF HEROISM. A Memoir of Henry Albert Harper. Toronto, Revell, 1906. 161p [Also: Toronto, Musson, 1919.] [BM BVaU LC NBFU OTU

TRIBUTE TO LATE LORD TWEEDSMUIR, GOVERNOR GENERAL OF CANADA. ... Ottawa, King's Printer, 1940. 6p [UTQ'41

**Kingsford, Maurice Rooke, 1894–**

THE LIFE, WORK AND INFLUENCE OF WILLIAM HENRY GILES KINGSTON. Toronto, Ryerson, 1947. 220p [BVaU NSHD OTU

**Kingsford, William, 1819–1898**

SIR DANIEL WILSON. N.p., 1893. 10p [Reprinted from Trans. Roy. Soc. Can.] [NSWA

**Kingsmill, Col. William, 1794–1876**

THE GREENWOOD TRAGEDY. ... The Suicide of William Greenwood. Guelph, "Herald," 1864. 35p [BVaU OTP

**Kinton, Ada Florence, 1859–1905**

JUST ONE BLUE BONNET. The Life Story of Ada Florence Kinton, Artist and Salvationist. Told mostly by herself with pen and pencil. Ed. by her sister Sara A. Randleson. Toronto, Briggs, 1907. 192p [BM OOP

**Kirby, William, 1817–1906**

ALFRED, LORD TENNYSON AND WILLIAM KIRBY. Unpublished Correspondence, to which are added some Letters from Hallam, Lord Tennyson. Ed by Lorne Pierce. Toronto, Macmillan, 1929. 71p [BM BVaU OTU

REMINISCENCES OF A VISIT TO QUEBEC, JULY, 1839. Niagara, Author, 1903. 16p [BVaU OTP

THE SERVOS FAMILY. ... [Same as: THE UNITED EMPIRE LOYALISTS OF CANADA, *q.v.*] [NSWA

SIR JAMES LE MOINE. A Family Memoir. Together with "The Knight of Spencer Grange." Quebec, Author, 1898. 12p

THE UNITED EMPIRE LOYALISTS OF CANADA. Illustrated by Memorials of the Servos Family. Toronto, Briggs, 1884. 20p [LC OOP

**Kirkconnell, Watson, 1895–**

A CANADIAN HEADMASTER. A Brief Biography of Thomas Allison Kirkconnell, 1862–1934. Toronto, Clarke Irwin, 1935. 156p [BM BVaU LC NSHD OTU

**Kirkwood, Kenneth Porter, 1899–**

A GARDEN IN POLAND. Karachi, Process Pakistan, 1953. 34p [On Chopin.] [BM OTU

**Klengenberg, Capt. Christian, 1869–1931**

KLENGENBERG OF THE ARCTIC. An Autobiography. Ed. by Tom MacInnes. London, Cape, 1932. 360p [BM BVaU LC OTU QMM

**Klinck, Vernon Edward, 1904–**

THE KLINCK FAMILY. Leonard Klinck and Elizabeth Brown Grant, Their Parents and Descendants for Six Generations, Together with Notes concerning certain of the Early Members. Comp. and ed. by Vernon Edward Klinck, Harry Osborne Klinck, and Leonard Sylvanus Klinck. Stouffville, Ont., 1955. 72p [mimeographed]

**Knox, Ellen Mary, 1858–1924**

ELLEN MARY KNOX. A Memorial volume. [Anon] Toronto, Havergal College, [1925]. 107p [OLU

**Knox, Olive Elsie (Robinson)**

JOHN BLACK OF OLD KILDONAN. Toronto, Ryerson, 1958. 198p

LITTLE GIANT (MISS-TOP-ASHISH). The Story of Henry Kelsey. Toronto, Ryerson, 1951. 196p [Also: New York, Bouregy & Curl, 1954. 186p]

MRS. MINISTER. Philadelphia, Westminster Press, 1956. 190p

**Kristjanson, Wilhelm, 1896–**

GLIMPSES OF OXFORD. Winnipeg, Columbia Press, 1935. 68p [CC

**Lambert, Richard Stanton, 1894–**

ADVENTURE TO THE POLAR SEA. The Story of Sir John Franklin. ... Indianapolis, Bobbs-Merrill, 1950. 302p [LC OONL

FOR THE TIME IS AT HAND. An Account of the Prophecies of Henry Wentworth Monk of Ottawa, Friend of the Jews and Pioneer of World Peace. Toronto, Ryerson, 1947. 168p [BM BVaU OTU

FRANKLIN OF THE ARCTIC. A Life of Adventure. Toronto, McClelland, 1949. 354p [Also: London, Bodley Head, 1954. 354p] [BM BVaU NBFU OTU QMM

REDCOAT SAILOR. The Adventures of Sir Howard Douglas. Toronto, Macmillan, 1956. 160p

THEY WENT EXPLORING. Agincourt, Ont., Book Society of Canada, 1955. 168p

TRAILMAKER. The Story of Alexander Mackenzie. Toronto, McClelland, 1957. 160p

**Lambton County, Ont.**

COMMEMORATIVE BIOGRAPHICAL RECORD OF THE COUNTY OF LAMBTON. Toronto, Hill Bind. Co., 1906. 840p [OLU

**Lampman, Archibald, 1861–1899**

ARCHIBALD LAMPMAN'S LETTERS TO EDWARD WILLIAM THOMSON (1890-1898). Ed. with an intro., annotations, a bibliography with notes, and his "Essay on Happiness," by Arthur S. Bourinot. Ottawa, Editor, 1956. 74p

**Lamontagne, Père Onésime, 1913–**

ILLUSTRATED LIFE OF GOOD FATHER FREDERIC. Trois-Rivières, Editions Bon Père Frédéric, 1950. 77p [OONL

THIS IS GOOD FATHER FREDERIC. Trois-Rivières, Editions Bon Père Frédéric, 1950. 72p [OONL

**Land, Robert Ernest Augustus, 1847–1927**

FIFTY YEARS IN THE MALTA ORDER. Toronto, priv. print., 1928. 2v [BM LC OTU

**Lande, Lawrence Montague, 1906–**

CREDO and AN OPEN LETTER TO A SCIENTIST. Montreal, Author, 1950. 28p [OONL

THE 3rd DUKE OF RICHMOND. A Study in Early Canadian History. Montreal, Author, 1956. 138p

**Landon, Fred, 1880–1969**

AN EXILE FROM CANADA TO VAN DIEMEN'S LAND. Being the Story of Elijah Woodman transported overseas for Participation in the Upper Canada Troubles of 1837–38. Toronto, Longmans, 1960. 321p

**Langton, Anne, 1804?–1893**

A GENTLEWOMAN IN UPPER CANADA. The Journals of Anne Langton. Ed. by H.H. Langton. Toronto, Clarke Irwin, 1950. 249p [BVaU NBFU OTP

LANGTON RECORDS. Journals and Letters from Canada 1837–1846. [By Anne Langton and others.] Preface by Ellen Josephine Philips. Edinburgh, Clark, 1904. 369p (Printed for private circulation only.) [BM OTU

THE STORY OF OUR FAMILY. Manchester, Sowler, 1881. 204p [OTP

**Langton, Hugh Hornby, 1862–1953**

JAMES DOUGLAS. A Memoir. Toronto, U. of Toronto Press, 1940. 130p [BM BVaU LC OTU QMM

JAMES LOUDON AND THE UNIVERSITY OF TORONTO. Toronto, U. of Toronto Press, 1927. 32p [BVaU OTU QMM

SIR DANIEL WILSON. A Memoir. Toronto, Nelson, 1929. 250p [BM BVaU NSHD OTU

SIR JOHN CUNNINGHAM McLENNAN. A Memoir. Toronto, U. of Toronto Press, 1939. 123p [BM BVaU OTP

**Langton, John, 1808–1894**

EARLY DAYS IN UPPER CANADA. Letters of John Langton from the Backwoods of Upper Canada. ... Ed. by W.A. Langton. Toronto, Macmillan, 1926. 310p [BM BVaU LC NSHD OKQ QMM

**Laporte, Pierre, 1921–1970**

THE TRUE FACE OF DUPLESSIS. Montreal, Harvest House, 1960. 140p

**Lapp, Eula (Carscallen), 1905–**

A HISTORY OF ONE BRANCH OF THE CARSCALLEN FAMILY (THE DESCENDANTS OF EDWARD CARSCALLEN, U.E.L. ...) Meaford, Ont., 1956. vi + 68p [Cover title: "Seven generations of Carscallens."]

**Large, William Sydney, 1916–1943**

DIARY OF A CANADIAN FIGHTER PILOT. Toronto, Saunders, 1944. 64p [BVa OTU QMM

**Lathern, Rev. John, 1831–1905**

THE HON. JUDGE WILMOT. A Biographical Sketch. Halifax, Wesleyan Office, 1880. 133p [Rev. ed.: Toronto, Methodist Book House, 1881. 165p] [BM BVaU NSHD OKQ

**Laurie, Richard Carnie, 1858–1938**

REMINISCENCES OF EARLY DAYS IN BATTLEFORD AND WITH MIDDLETON'S COLUMN. ... Recollections of Incidents of Travel, Early Surveys, Poundmaker ... etc. Battleford, Saskatchewan Herald, 1935. 140p [SSU

**Laurier, Wilfrid, 1841–1919**

LETTERS TO MY FATHER AND MOTHER. Selected and ed. by Lucien Pacaud. Toronto, Ryerson, 1935. 148p [BM BVaU OLU

**Lauriston, Victor, 1881–**

POSTSCRIPT TO A POET. Off the Record Tales about Arthur Stringer. Chatham, Tiny Tree Club, 1941. 48p [BVaU OLU

**Laut, Agnes Christina, 1871–1936**

CADILLAC, KNIGHT ERRANT OF THE WILDERNESS, FOUNDER OF DETROIT. Indianapolis, Bobbs-Merrill, 1931. 298p [BM BVaU LC NSHD OKQ QMM

**Lawrence, Joseph Wilson, 1818–1892**

THE JUDGES OF NEW BRUNSWICK AND THEIR TIMES. From the Manuscript of the late Joseph Wilson Lawrence. Ed. and annotated by Alfred A. Stockton. ... Saint John, Jack, 1907. 532p [LC NSHD OOP OTU QMM

**Lawrence, Sheridan, 1870–1952**

SHERIDAN LAWRENCE, EMPEROR OF THE PEACE, 1870–1952. As told to his wife, Julia Lawrence. N.p., priv. print., n.d. 61p

**Laws, William Black, 1811–1875**

THE WRITING AND LIFE OF W.B. LAWS. Montreal, Lovell, 1895. 132p [BM LC OTUV

**Lawson, John Murray, 1848–1925**

YARMOUTH, PAST AND PRESENT. A Book of Reminiscences. Comp. by ——. Yarmouth, Herald, 1902. 647p [BM BVaU LC NSWA OKQ QMM

**Lawson, William, 1793–1875**

THE LIFE OF WILLIAM LAWSON, J.P., ONE OF THE BUILDERS OF CANADA. Written by Himself, with an intro. and notes by a grandson. Columbia, Mo., 1917. 38 + xp [OTP

**Leacock, Stephen Butler, 1869–1944**

BALDWIN, LAFONTAINE, HINCKS: Responsible Government. Toronto, Morang, 1907. 371p [BM BVaU LC NSWA OTP

THE BOY I LEFT BEHIND ME. Garden City, Doubleday, 1946. 184p [BM BVaU LC NSHD OKQ

MACKENZIE, BALDWIN, LAFONTAINE, HINCKS. Toronto, Oxford U. Press, 1926. 395p [An Expansion of BALDWIN, LAFONTAINE, HINCKS: Responsible Government. Toronto, Morang, 1907. 371p] [BM BVaU LC OTU QMM

MY MEMORIES AND MISERIES AS A SCHOOLMASTER. Toronto, Upper Canada College Endowment and Extension Fund, [19–?]. 15p [OTP

**Leatherbarrow, Mrs. Margaret F.**

GOLD IN THE GRASS. Toronto, Ryerson, 1954. 278p

**Lee, Norman, 1862–1939**

THE JOURNAL OF NORMAN LEE, 1898. ... The Account of a Cattle-drive from the Chilcotin Country to Teslin Lake by the Telegraph Trail. Prepared for pub. by Gordon R. Elliott. Vancouver, R. and F. Reid, 1959. x + 58p

KLONDIKE CATTLE DRIVE. The Journal of Norman Lee. Ed. by Gordon Elliott. Vancouver, Mitchell Press, 1960. xxii + 58p

**Lee, Thomas Roche, 1915–**

ALBERT H. ROBINSON, "THE PAINTER'S PAINTER." Montreal, priv. print., 1956. 45p

**Lees, John, fl. 1764–1775**

JOURNAL OF JOHN LEES, OF QUEBEC, Merchant. [Travel-diary, April–October,

1768 ... trip to New England, New York, and return.] Detroit, Speaker-Hines Press, 1911. 55p [BM BVaU LC OTU

**Leggo, William, 1822–1888**

THE HISTORY OF THE ADMINISTRATION OF THE RIGHT HONORABLE FREDERICK TEMPLE, Earl of Dufferin ... late Governor General of Canada. Montreal, Lovell, 1878. 901p [BM BVaU LC NSHD OTU QMM

**LeMoine, James MacPherson, 1825–1912**

THE HON. HENRY CALDWELL. 1904. [MOR'12

THE SWORD OF BRIGADIER-GENERAL RICHARD MONTGOMERY. ... A Memoir. Comp. by ——. Quebec, Middleton & Dawson, 1870. 36p [BVaU LC OKQ QMSS

**Leonard, Elijah, 1814–1891**

THE HONOURABLE ELIJAH LEONARD. A Memoir. [Anon] London, Ont., Advertiser, [1894?]. 51p [BVaU NSWA OTU

**Leslie, Percy Campbell, 1871–**

THE FAMILY OF LESLIE. Montreal, 1953. 14p

**Le Sueur, William Dawson, 1840–1917**

COUNT FRONTENAC. Toronto, Morang, 1906. 382p [BM BVaU LC NSWA OTU QMM

[LIFE OF WILLIAM LYON MACKENZIE.] N.p., n.d. 553p [No title page. "Author's proof Copy." Typewritten.] [OTU

**Levine, Albert Norman, 1923–**

CANADA MADE ME. London, Putnam, 1958. 277p

**Lewis, Ada Maria (Leigh), –1931**

THE LIFE OF JOHN TRAVERS LEWIS, D.D., First Archbishop of Ontario. By his Wife. ... Foreword by Sir Gilbert Parker. London, Skeffington, 1930. 160p [BM BVaU OTP

**Lewis, Charles Edward**

REVERIES OF AN OLD SMOKER. Interspersed with Reminiscences of Travel and Adventure. Toronto, Hunter Rose, 1881. 384p [BVaU OTP

**Lewis, John, 1858–1935**

GEORGE BROWN. Toronto, Morang, 1906. 281p [Also pub.: Toronto, Oxford U. Press, 1926.] [BM BVaU LC NSWA OTU QMM

MACKENZIE KING, THE MAN, HIS ACHIEVEMENTS. Toronto, Morang, 1925. 136p [Rev. and extended by Norman McLeod Rogers: Toronto, Nelson, 1935. 212p] [BM BVaU LC MWU NSWA OTP QMM

**Lewis, Thaddeus, 1793–**

AUTOBIOGRAPHY OF THADDEUS LEWIS, a Minister of the Methodist Episcopal

Church in Canada. Picton, "North American" Office, 1865. 205p [BVaU OTP

**Liedl, Charles**

HUNTING WITH RIFLE AND PENCIL. Fredericton, Brunswick Press, 1955. 186p

**Lighthall, William Douw, 1857–1954**

LA CORNE ST. LUC. The "General of the Indians." Montreal, n.p., 1908. 8p [NBFU OTU

THOMAS POWNALL: His Part in the Conquest of Canada. Ottawa, Hope, 1904. 5p [BVaU NBFU

**Lindsey, Charles, 1820–1908**

THE LIFE AND TIMES OF WM. LYON MACKENZIE. ... Toronto, Randall, 1862. 2v [Later ed. by G.G.S. Lindsey, with Additions, in "Makers of Canada" series: Toronto, Morang, 1908. 542p] [BM BVaU LC NSWA OTP QMM

**Linnell, J.B.**

THE STORY OF A PIONEER. As Told to his Daughter-in-law, Ruth Linnell at Summerberry, Sask., February, 1949. Grenfell, Sask., Grenfell Sun Print., 1949. 24p [BViPA SSU

**Little, George E., 1906–**

THE LITTLES OF GALLOWAY AND THE COUNTY OF KENT, N.B. Moncton, Author, 1956. 153p

**Little, Robert H., 1859?–**

REMINISCENCES OF MY PIONEERING EXPERIENCES IN TWP. 7, RANGE 12, CYPRESS RIVER LOCALITY, DURING THE WINTER OF 1879–1880. Treherne, Man., Times Print., 1931. 36p [MWP OTP

**Livesay, John Frederick Bligh, 1875–1944**

THE MAKING OF A CANADIAN. Ed. with a memoir by F.R. Livesay. Toronto, Ryerson, 1947. 181p [BM BVa LC NSHD OTP QMM

**Livingston, Helen Armina Mary, 1899–**

HER NAME WAS MINA HAGER. A Short Sketch. Hamilton, Ont., Livingston United Church, 1958. 12p [Biographical sketch of Mina Hager Livingston.]

**Lloyd-Owen, Frances**

GOLD NUGGET CHARLIE. A Narrative Compiled from the Notes of Charles E. Musson. London, Harrap, 1939. 260p [BM BVaU LC MWU

**Llwyd, Rev. John Plummer Derwent, 1861–1933**

SON OF THUNDER. A Study of the Life and Work of John of Bethsaida, Fisher of Men. New York, Long & Smith, 1932. 170p [BVa LC NSHD OTU

**Locke, George Herbert, 1870–1937**

THE QUEEN'S RANGERS. By G.H. Locke and Margaret Ray. Toronto, Public Library, 1923. 30p [BM NBFU OKQ

**Logan, Annie Robertson (Macfarlane), –1933**
AN ACCOUNT OF THE EXPLORATIONS AND DISCOVERIES OF SAMUEL DE CHAMPLAIN, AND OF THE FOUNDING OF QUEBEC. By Mrs. J.E. Logan. Montreal, Montreal News, 1908. 50p [OOP QMM

**Logan, John Daniel, 1869–1929**
LOVE'S PILGRIM ... [John Killick Bathurst]. Halifax, Allen, 1921. 22p [BM BVaU NBFU OOP
THOMAS CHANDLER HALIBURTON. Toronto, Ryerson, 1923. 176p [BM BVaU NSHD OTU

**Long, John, fl. 1768–1791**
JOHN LONG'S JOURNAL, 1768–1782. Cleveland, Clark, 1904. 329p [BVaU OTP

**Longley, James Wilberforce, 1849–1922**
JOSEPH HOWE. Toronto, Morang, 1904. 307p [BVaU LC NSWA OTP
SIR CHARLES TUPPER. Toronto, Morang, 1916. 304p [BVa LC NSWA OTU QMM

**Longley, Ronald Stewart, 1896–**
SIR FRANCIS HINCKS. Toronto, U. of Toronto Press, 1943. 480p [BM BVaU LC NBFU OTP

**Longstaffe Family**
THE HOUSE OF LONGSTAFFE, 70TH YEAR, 1888–1958. N.p., 1958. 12p [Genealogy of the descendants of Edwin and Lottie Longstaffe of Toronto.]

**Longworth, Israel**
THE LIFE OF S.G.W. ARCHIBALD. Halifax, Huestis, 1881. 179p [BM BVaU LC NSWA OKQ

**Lord, Rev. George A., 1820–**
A SHORT NARRATIVE OF THE LIFE AND CONVERSION OF REV. GEORGE A. LORD. ... Albany, N.Y., Author, 1847. 34p [Other eds.: N.p., 1854. 46p; Troy, N.Y., 1855. 36p] [BM OTP

**Loudon, William James, 1860–1951**
A CANADIAN GEOLOGIST. Toronto, Macmillan, 1930. 257p [Life of J.B. Tyrrell.] [BM BVaU NBFU OTP
SIR WILLIAM MULOCK. A Short Biography. Toronto, Macmillan, 1932. 384p [BM BVaU LC OTP QMBM

**Love, Christopher Charles**
FREDERICK CLARK STEPHENSON, 1864–1941. Toronto, Ryerson, 1957. 36p

**Lower, Arthur Reginald Marsden, 1889–**
UNCONVENTIONAL VOYAGES. Toronto, Ryerson, 1953. xii + 156p

**M., Mrs. E.M.**

RECOLLECTIONS OF A BELOVED PASTOR. By Mrs. E.M.M. Kingston, News, 1845. 37p [An appreciation of Rev. R.D. Cartwright.] [OTU

**McAleer, George, 1845–**

REMINISCENT AND OTHERWISE. Life in the Eastern Townships of the Province of Quebec, Canada, Fifty Years Ago. Worcester, Mass., Goddard, 1901. 20p [BM BVaU OTU QMSS

A STUDY IN THE ORIGIN AND SIGNIFICATION OF THE SURNAME McALEER, and a Contribution to the McAleer Genealogy. Comp. by ——. Worcester, Mass., McAleer, 1909. 103p [LC

**MacAlister, Alexander Wardrope Greenshields, 1876–**

THE BENCH AND BAR OF THE PROVINCES OF QUEBEC, NOVA SCOTIA, AND NEW BRUNSWICK. Ed. by ——. Montreal, Lovell, 1907. 371p [BM LC OLU

**McAlister, George Alexander**

HIGH-SKY! The Ups and Downs of a Pinfeather Pilot. Toronto, Ryerson, 1944. 124p [BVa LC OTP

**McAllister, George Clinton, 1804–1842**

THE JOURNAL OF CAPTAIN GEORGE C.McALLISTER, JANUARY 1, 1831 TO JULY 27, 1833. Copied from the original note books by Mary Hill, January, 1931. Intro. and notes by Evans Hill. St. Stephen, N.B., 1958. 121p

**McAllister, Ronald Nelson, 1917–**

FOOTBALL STARS TODAY AND YESTERDAY. From The Canadian Sports Album [Radio Programme]. Intro. by James Vipond. Toronto, McClelland, 1950. 120p [OONL

HOCKEY STARS TODAY AND YESTERDAY. From The Canadian Sports Album [Radio Programme]. Intro. by Elmer Ferguson. Toronto, McClelland, 1950. 126p [OONL

SWIM TO GLORY. The Story of Marilyn Bell and the Lakeshore Swimming Club. Toronto, McClelland, 1954. 128p

**McAra, Peter, 1862–1949**

SIXTY-TWO YEARS ON THE SASKATCHEWAN PRAIRIES. [Anon] Regina, 1945. 48p [SSU

**McAree, John Verner, 1876–1958**

CABBAGETOWN STORE. Toronto, Ryerson, 1953. 113p

**McArthur, Peter, 1866–1924**

SIR WILFRID LAURIER. Toronto, Dent, 1919. 183p [BM BVaU LC NSWA OKQ

**Macbeth, John Douglas**

SOMEWHERE IN ENGLAND. War Letters of a Canadian Officer on Overseas Service. Toronto, Macmillan, 1941. 32p [LC OTP

**Macbeth, Madge Hamilton (Lyons), 1878–1965**

BOULEVARD CAREER. Toronto, Kingswood House, 1957. x + 230p

OVER MY SHOULDER. Toronto, Ryerson, 1953. 170p

**MacBeth, Rev. Roderick George, 1858–1934**

THE MAKING OF THE CANADIAN WEST. Being the Reminiscences of an Eyewitness. Toronto, Briggs, 1898. 230p [2nd ed.: Toronto, Briggs, 1905. 280p] [BM BVaU LC NSWA OTP QMBM

PEACE RIVER LETTERS. Vancouver, White & Bindon, 1915. 31p [BVaU LC MWP OKQ

RECENT CANADIAN WEST LETTERS. Historical and Descriptive. Brantford, Hurley Print., 1912. 52p [OLU

SIR AUGUSTUS NANTON. A Biography. Toronto, Macmillan, 1931. 130p [BVaU LC NSHD OTU

**McCall, Delbert Thomas, 1871–**

GENEALOGY AND HISTORY OF THE NORFOLK McCALL FAMILY AND ASSOCIATED DESCENDANTS, 1796–1946. Comp. by ——. Simcoe, Norfolk McCall Soc., 1946. 215p [NBFU OTP

**McCarthy, Pearl, 1895–**

LEO SMITH. A Biographical Sketch. Toronto, U. of Toronto Press, 1956. ix + 53p

**McCaskill, Rev. John James, 1875–**

THE BUSINESS MAN AS HERO. Being a Memoir of Duncan Alexander McCaskill. ... 1908. [MOR'12

**McCharles, Aeneas, 1844–1906**

BEMOCKED OF DESTINY. The Actual Struggles and Experiences of a Canadian Pioneer, and the Recollections of a Lifetime. Toronto, Briggs, 1908. 244p [BM BVaU LC NSHD OTP

**McClung, Nellie Letitia (Mooney), 1873–1951**

CLEARING IN THE WEST. My Own Story. Toronto, Allen, 1935. 378p [BM BVaU LC NBFU OTU SSU

THE STREAM RUNS FAST. My Own Story. Toronto, Allen, 1945. 316p [BVaU NBFU OTP QMM SSU

**McCorkell, Edmund Joseph, 1891–**

CAPTAIN, THE REVEREND WILLIAM LEO MURRAY ... 1890–1937, First Pastor of St. John the Evangelist Church, Campbell's Bay, Quebec. ... A Memoir. Ed. by ——. Toronto, St. Michael's College, 1939. 48p [OTP

**McCourt, Edward Alexander, 1907–1972**

BUCKSKIN BRIGADIER. The Story of the Alberta Field Force. Toronto, Macmillan, 1955. 150p

**McCourt, Peter**

BIOGRAPHICAL SKETCH OF THE HONOURABLE EDWARD WHELAN. Together with a Compilation of his Principal Speeches. ... Charlottetown, Author, 1888. 301p [BVaU LC NSWA OLU

**McCulley, Joseph**

REFLECTIONS OF A HEADMASTER. Newmarket, Ont., Pickering College, 1938. 20p [OTU

**McCulloch, John Herries, 1892–**

NORTH RANGE. A Record of Hard Living and Adventure on the Colourful Northern Rim of the British Empire. London, Chambers, 1954. 191p

**McCulloch, Mercy Emma (Powell)**

THAT REMINDS ME OF N.A.P. ... By M.E.M. Toronto, Ryerson, 1942. 78p [Biography of Newton Albert Powell.] [BVaU LC OTP

**McCulloch, William, 1811–1895?**

LIFE OF THOMAS McCULLOCH D.D., PICTOU. ... Truro, priv. print., 1920. 218p [BVaU NSHD OTU

**McCully, Elizabeth A.**

A CORN OF WHEAT; or, The Life of Rev. W.J. McKenzie of Korea. Toronto, Westminster Co., 1903. 290p [BM BVaU NBFU

**McCurdy, Rev. James Frederick, 1847–1935**

LIFE AND WORK OF D.J. MACDONNELL, Minister of St. Andrew's Church, Toronto, with a Selection of Sermons and Prayers. Toronto, Briggs, 1897. 512p [BM BVaU NBFU OTP QMM

**MacDermot, Hugh Ernest, 1888–**

MAUD ABBOTT. A Memoir. Toronto, Macmillan, 1941. 264p [BVaU LC OTP QMBM

SIR THOMAS RODDICK. His Work in Medicine and Public Life. Toronto, Macmillan, 1938. 160p [BM BVaU OTU QMBM

**Macdonald, Adrian, 1889–**

CANADIAN PORTRAITS. Toronto, Ryerson, 1925. 230p [BM BVaU LC NSHD OTU

**MacDonald, Rev. Alexander, 1858–1941**

A BIT OF AUTOBIOGRAPHY. Victoria, Willows Press, 1920. 61p [BVaU NSHD

**Macdonald, Edward Mortimer, 1865–1940**

RECOLLECTIONS, POLITICAL AND PERSONAL. Toronto, Ryerson, 1938. 584p [BM BVaU LC NBFU OTP

**MacDonald, Eileen Harrison (Button)**

I MARRIED AN ARTIST. By Billy Button. Toronto, Ryerson, 1951. 238p

**MacDonald, Frank C.**

THE KAISER'S GUEST. Garden City, N.Y., Country Life Press, 1918. 250p [LC BViV

**Macdonald, Frederick Charles, –1936**

EDWARD ASHURST WELCH, M.A., D.C.L., LL.D., OF GATESHEAD, TORONTO, WAKEFIELD AND SOUTH CHURCH. A Memoir. Toronto, General Board of Religious Education, 1936. 93p [BM OTU

**MacDonald, Hugh N., 1856–**

MACDONALD AND MACKINNON FAMILIES. A Biographical Sketch. Whycomagh, N.S., Author, 1937. 32p [OTU

**Macdonald, James, 1878–**

DR. LOCKE, HEALER OF MEN. A Biography. Toronto, MacLean Pub., 1933. 83p [LC

**Macdonald, James Simon, 1837–1914**

BIOGRAPHICAL PAPERS READ BEFORE THE NOVA SCOTIA HISTORICAL SOCIETY, 1899–1904. Halifax, McAlpine, 1905. 100p [Re: Edward Cornwallis, 1713–1776; Charles Lawrence, 1709–1760; Richard Bulkeley, 1717–1800.] [LC OOP

MEMOIR OF GOVERNOR JOHN PARR. N.p., n.pub., n.d. 38p [NSWA

**Macdonald, John Alexander, 1815–1891**

CORRESPONDENCE OF SIR JOHN MACDONALD. Selections from the Correspondence of the Right Honourable Sir John Alexander Macdonald. ... Made by his Literary Executor, Sir Joseph Pope. Toronto, Oxford U. Press, 1921. 502p [BVaU LC NBFU OTP

**MacDonald, John Howard**

THE HONORABLE EDWARD CORNWALLIS. A Biographical Sketch. Kentville, N.S., D.A.R., 1930. 20p [NSWA

**Macdonald, R.C.**

SKETCHES OF HIGHLANDERS. With an Account of their Early Arrival in North America. ... Saint John, Chubb, 1843. 70p [BVaU NSWA OTU

**MacDonald, Ranald, 1824–1894**

RANALD MACDONALD. The Narrative of his Early Life under the Hudson's Bay Company's Regime; of his Experiences in the Pacific Whale Fishery; and of his Great Adventure to Japan; with a Sketch of his Later Life on the Western Frontier. Ed. and annotated ... by William S. Lewis and Naojiro Murakami. Spokane, Wash., Inland-American Print., 1923. 333p [BM BVaU NBFU OTU

**Macdonald, William John, 1832–1916**

A PIONEER, 1851. [Anon] N.p., n.pub., 1914. 30p [Macdonald lived on Vancouver Island, 1851–1916.] [BVaU OTU

**Macdonell, John Alexander, 1851–1930**

A SKETCH OF THE LIFE OF THE HONOURABLE AND RIGHT REVEREND ALEXANDER MACDONELL, Chaplain of the Glengarry Fencible. ... First Catholic Bishop of Upper Canada, and a Member of the Legislative Council. ... Alexandria, The Glengarrian, 1890. 86p [LC NSWA OTP QMM

**Macdonell, W.J.**

REMINISCENCES OF THE LATE HON. AND RIGHT REV. ALEX. MACDONELL, First Catholic Bishop of Upper Canada. ... [Anon] Toronto, Williamson, 1888. 55p [NSHD OTU

**Macdonnell, James Smellie, 1878?–**

STOPPING PLACES. A Biographic Journey. Pasadena, Calif., Star-News Press, 1946. 93p [BVaU OTU

**Macdougall, Rev. Archibald, 1849–1922**

THE LIFE AND LETTERS OF REV. DR. ARCHIBALD MACDOUGALL. Ed. by Helen J. McLean. Hyde Park, Mass., Editor, 1933. 116p [CC

**McDougall, Rev. John, 1842–1917**

GEORGE MILLWARD McDOUGALL, THE PIONEER, PATRIOT, AND MISSIONARY. Toronto, Briggs, 1888. 242p [BM BVaU NSWA OTP QMSS

**McDowall, Rev. James, 1826?–1864**

A BRIEF MEMOIR AND SOME REMAINS OF THE LATE REV. JAMES McDOWALL. Ed. by Rev. James Cameron. Toronto, 1866. 54p [BibC

**McDowell, Louise, 1872–**

PAST AND PRESENT. A Canadian Musician's Reminiscences. Kirkland Lake, Ont., priv. print., 1957. xvii + 211p

**McElheran, Irene Beatrice (Brock), 1879–1955**

THAT'S WHAT I'M HERE FOR. Robert B. McElheran, His Days and His Ways. Toronto, Ryerson, 1955. xvii + 122p

**MacEwan, Grant, 1902–**

EYE OPENER BOB. The Story of Bob Edwards. Edmonton, Institute of Applied Art, 1957. 227p

FIFTY MIGHTY MEN. Saskatoon, Modern Press, 1958. 342p

JOHN WARE'S COW COUNTRY. Edmonton, Institute of Applied Art, 1960. 261p

**McEwen, Thomas Alexander, 1891–**

HE WROTE FOR US. The Story of Bill Bennett, Pioneer Socialist Journalist. Vancouver, Tribune Pub. Co., 1951. 159p

**McGee, Thomas D'Arcy, 1825–1868**

HISTORICAL SKETCHES OF O'CONNELL AND HIS FRIENDS. ... With a Glance at the Future Destiny of Ireland. 3rd ed. Boston, Donahue & Rohan, 1845. 208p [BM BVaU LC NSWA OTP QMSS

A LIFE OF THE RT. REV. EDWARD MAGINN, Coadjutor Bishop of Derry. With Selections from his Correspondence. New York, O'Shea, 1857. 306p [BM LC OTP QMSS

A MEMOIR OF THE LIFE AND CONQUEST OF ART MACMURROGH, King of Leinster, from A.D. 1377 to A.D. 1417. Dublin, Duffy, 1886. 200p [An earlier edition in 1847.] [BM LC OLU

**McGibbon, Robert Davidson, 1857–1906**

THOMAS D'ARCY McGEE. An Address. ... Montreal, Dawson, 1884. 19p [BVaU LC NSHPL OKQ QMBM

**MacGill, Elizabeth Muriel Gregory, 1905–**

MY MOTHER, THE JUDGE. A Biography of Judge Helen Gregory MacGill. By Elsie Gregory MacGill. Toronto, Ryerson, 1955. xvi + 248p

**McGill University. Osler Society**

W.W. FRANCIS, TRIBUTES FROM HIS FRIENDS, ON THE OCCASION OF THE THIRTY-FIFTH ANNIVERSARY OF THE OSLER SOCIETY OF McGILL UNIVERSITY. Montreal, Society, 1956. xv + 123p

**McGillicuddy, Owen Ernest, 1887–1954**

THE MAKING OF A PREMIER–An Outline of the Life Story of the Right Hon. W.L. Mackenzie King. ... Toronto, Musson, 1922. 91p [BM BVaU NSHD OKQ QMM

**MacGillivray, C.J.**

TIMOTHY HIERLIHY AND HIS TIMES. The Story of the Founder of Antigonish, N.S. Antigonish, Casket Print, 1935. 173p [NSWA OTU

**M'Gillivray, Duncan, –1808**

THE JOURNAL OF DUNCAN M'GILLIVRAY OF THE NORTH-WEST COMPANY ... 1794–5. With intro., notes and appendix by A.S. Morton. Toronto, Macmillan, 1929. lxxviii + 79 + 24 + 6p [BM BVaU LC NBFU OTP QMSS

**McGoey, John Heck, 1915–**

NOR SCRIP NOR SHOES. Boston, Little Brown, 1958. 280p

**McGregor, Daniel Arthur**

MEMOIR OF D.A. McGREGOR, Late Principal of Toronto Baptist College. Toronto, The Alumni, 1891. [BVaU NSWA OTU

**MacGregor, James Grierson, 1905–**

BEHOLD THE SHINING MOUNTAINS. Being an Account of Anthony Henday, 1754–55, the First White Man to Enter Alberta. Edmonton, Applied Art Products, 1954. 276p

NORTH-WEST OF 16. Toronto, McClelland, 1958. 224p

**MacGregor, Mary Esther (Miller), 1876–1961**

THE BLACK BEARDED BARBARIAN. The Life of George Leslie Mackay of Formosa.

By Marian Keith [pseud]. New York, Missionary Education Movement, 1912. 307p [BVaU LC NBFU OTP

**Machar, Agnes Maule, 1837–1927**

FAITHFUL UNTO DEATH. A Memorial of John Anderson [1810–1859], Late Janitor of Queen's College, Kingston. ... [Anon] Kingston, Creighton, 1859. 66p [OKQ

HEROES OF CANADA. Based upon "Stories of New France." Toronto, Copp Clark, 1893. 96p [*See* STORIES OF NEW FRANCE, p. 885 below.] [OTU QMSS

**Machar, Rev. John, 1796–1863**

MEMORIALS OF THE LIFE AND MINISTRY OF THE REV. JOHN MACHAR, D.D., 1796–1863. Late Minister of St. Andrew's Church, Kingston. Ed. by Members of his Family. Toronto, Campbell, 1873. 301p [BVaU NSWA OTP

**Machum, George Cecil, 1896–1958**

CANADA'S V.C.'S, THE STORY OF CANADIANS WHO HAVE BEEN AWARDED THE VICTORIA CROSS. A Centenary Memorial, 1956. Comp. by ——. Toronto, McClelland, 1956. 208p

THE STORY OF THE "JEFF" RUSSEL MEMORIAL TROPHY. A Tribute to the Memory of a Great Athlete and Gentleman. Ed. by ——. Montreal, [Industrial Shops for the Deaf], 1958. 68p

**McIlwraith, Jean Newton, 1859–1938**

SIR FREDERICK HALDIMAND. Toronto, Morang, 1904. 356p [BM BVaU LC NSWA OTP

**MacInnis, Grace (Woodsworth), 1905–**

J.S. WOODSWORTH, A MAN TO REMEMBER. Toronto, Macmillan, 1953. xiv + 336p

**McIntosh (or Mackintosh), Hugh Fraser, 1862–**

FATHER LOUIS DELLA VAGNA, CAPUCHIN, Pastor of St. Mary's Church, Toronto, 1856–1857. Toronto, "Catholic Weekly Review," 1888. 22p [NSHD OTP

**McIntyre, Fred, 1877–**

THE TRUE LIFE STORY OF A PIONEER. Syracuse, Ind., Nonpareil Press, 1955. 240p

**Mack, Harry Wilson, 1892–**

THE MACK AND SINE FAMILIES. With Allied Families: Althouse, Sarles, Chard, Rosebush, Hills, Kromenaker, Grant and others. Detroit, Mich., E.P. Mack, 1955. 74p

**Mackay, Charles Angus, 1872–**

MEMOIRS OF THE LIFE OF CHARLES ANGUS MACKAY. By Himself. Victoria, Colonist, 1930. 50p [BVaU

**Mackay, Miss Janet**

CATHERINE OF BRAGANZA. London, Long, 1937. 315p [BM

LITTLE MADAM. A Biography of Henrietta Maria. London, Bell, 1939. 380p [BM NBS OWtU

**Mackay, Robert Walter Stuart, 1809?–1854**

THE CANADA DIRECTORY. Containing the Names of the Professional and Business Men of every description, in the Cities, Towns, and Principal Villages of Canada ... [etc.]. Montreal, Lovell, 1851. 692p [OTU QMBM

**MacKellar, Margaret, 1861–**

LIFE OF AMELIA J. HARRIS. Toronto, United Church of Canada, 1937. 16p [OTU

**Mackenzie, Alexander, 1822–1892**

THE LIFE AND SPEECHES OF HON. GEORGE BROWN. Toronto, Globe, 1882. 381p [BM BVaU LC NSWA OTP QMSS

**MacKenzie, Donald, 1908–**

FUGITIVES. An Autobiography. London, Elek Books, 1955. 206p [American title: OCCUPATION: THIEF. Indianapolis, Bobbs-Merrill, 1955. 260p]

GENTLEMEN AT CRIME. An Autobiography. London, Elek Books, 1956. 199p [Sequel to: FUGITIVES.]

**Mackenzie, John Joseph, 1865–1922**

NUMBER 4 CANADIAN HOSPITAL. The Letters of Professor J.J. Mackenzie from the Salonika Front. ... Toronto, Macmillan, 1933. 247p [BM LC OTU QMM

**Mackenzie, Kenneth Ferns, 1882–**

SABOTS AND SLIPPERS. Toronto, priv. print., 1954. 131p

**McKenzie, Nathaniel Murdoch William John, 1856–1943**

THE MEN OF THE HUDSON'S BAY COMPANY 1670 A.D.–1920 A.D. Fort William, Times-Journal, 1921. 214p [BM BVaU LC OTP

**McKenzie, Thomas, 1830–**

MY LIFE AS A SOLDIER. Saint John, McMillan, 1898. 202p [BVaU NSWA OTP QMSS

**Mackenzie, William Lyon, 1795–1861**

MACKENZIE'S OWN NARRATIVE OF THE LATE REBELLION. Toronto, Palladium Office, 1838. 23p [Same title: Toronto, Rous & Mann, 1937. 30p] [BVaU LC NSWA OTP QMSS

THE SONS OF THE EMERALD ISLE; or, Lives of One Thousand Remarkable Irishmen, including Memoirs of Noted Characters of Irish Parentage or Descent. New York, Burgess Stringer, 1845. 108p [LC, OTL and OTU copies have only 60 pages, rest missing; OTP copy has 108 pages, but is an incomplete copy with p. 109ff missing.] [LC OTL OTP OTU

**McKeown, Hugh Charles, 1841–1889**

THE LIFE AND LABORS OF MOST REV. JOHN JOSEPH LYNCH, D.D. Cong., Miss., First Archbishop of Toronto. Montreal & Toronto, Sadlier, 1886. 353p [BM BVaU LC OTP

**McKinley, Mabel (Burns)**

CANADIAN HEROES OF PIONEER DAYS. Toronto, Longmans, 1930. 119p [BM BViPA OLU

CANADIAN HEROINES OF PIONEER DAYS. New York, Longmans, 1929. 66p [LC QMSS

FAMOUS MEN AND WOMEN OF CANADA. Toronto, Longmans, 1938. 128p [BM BVa OOA

**Mackinnon, Rev. Clarence D., 1868–1937**

A BRIEF SKETCH OF THE LIFE OF THE REVEREND JOHN FRANKLIN FORBES. ... Saint John, Globe, 1905. 56p [NSWA OTU

THE LIFE OF PRINCIPAL OLIVER. ... Toronto, Ryerson, 1936. 162p [BM BViPA LC OKQ SSU

REMINISCENCES. Toronto, Ryerson, 1938. 236p [BM LC OTP

**McKinnon, John Angus, 1898–**

LACHLIN McKINNON, 1865-1948. Calgary, Author, 1956. 130p

**McKitrick, Thomas George, 1873–1952**

ANDREW STEWART OF THE PRAIRIE HOMESTEADS. Crystal City, Man., Author, 1950. 134p [BVaU OTU

**MacLane, Mary, 1881–1929**

I, MARY MacLANE. A Diary of Human Days. New York, Stokes, 1917. 317p [BM LC OH

MY FRIEND, ANNABEL LEE. Chicago, Stone, 1903. 262p [AEU LC OTU

THE STORY OF MARY MacLANE. By Herself. Chicago, Stone 1902. 322p [New ed., with added chapter, New York, Duffield, 1911. 354p] [BM LC NBFL OTMC

**McLaurin, Rev. Colin Campbell, 1854–1941**

SIXTY YEARS IN THE MINISTRY. Edmonton, Institute Press, 1937. 13p [OTU

**MacLean, Andrew Dyas, 1896–**

R.B. BENNETT, PRIME MINISTER OF CANADA. Toronto, Excelsior, 1934. 112p [BVaU LC NBFU OTP QMBM

**McLean, Charles Herbert, 1877–**

PROMINENT PEOPLE OF NEW BRUNSWICK IN THE RELIGIOUS, EDUCATIONAL, POLITICAL, PROFESSIONAL, COMMERCIAL, AND SOCIAL ACTIVITIES. ... Comp. by ——. With an introductory essay by A.G. Bailey. Saint John, Biographical Society of Canada, 1938. 261p [BM NBFU

**McLean, John, 1799–1890**

NOTES OF A TWENTY-FIVE YEARS' SERVICE IN THE HUDSON'S BAY TERRITORY. London, Bentley, 1849. 2v (Also: Ed. by W.S. Wallace. Toronto, Champlain Society, 1932. xxxvi + 402p) [BVaU LC NBFU OTP QMBM

**Maclean, Rev. John, 1851–1928**

HENRY B. STEINHAUER, His Work among the Cree Indians of the Western Plains of Canada. Toronto, Methodist Church Pub., n.d. 51p [BVaU OTUV

JAMES EVANS, Inventor of the Syllabic System of the Cree Language. Toronto, Briggs, 1890. 208p [BM BVaU LC OTU

McDOUGALL OF ALBERTA. A Life of Rev. John McDougall, D.D., Pathfinder of Empire and Prophet of the Plains. Toronto, Ryerson, 1927. 282p [BM BVaU NBFU OTP QMM

VANGUARDS OF CANADA. Toronto, Missionary Society of the Methodist Church, 1918. 262p [Biographies of missionaries across Canada.] [BM BViPA NSWA OTP SSU

THE WARDEN OF THE PLAINS, and Other Stories of Life in the Canadian North-west. Toronto, Briggs, 1896. 301p [BM BVaU LC MWP OKQ

WILLIAM BLACK, THE APOSTLE OF METHODISM IN THE MARITIME PROVINCES. ... Halifax, Methodist Book Room, 1907. 64p [BM BVaU NBFU OKQ

**McLeish, John Alexander Buchanan, 1913–**

SEPTEMBER GALE. A Study of Arthur Lismer of the Group of Seven. Toronto, Dent, 1955. xi + 212p

**McLennan, John Stewart, 1853–1939**

HUGH McLENNAN, 1825–1899. Montreal, Author, 1936. 100p [QMM

**McLeod, Donald [of Woodstock, Ont.]**

DONALD McLEOD'S GLOOMY MEMORIES IN THE HIGHLANDS OF SCOTLAND *versus* MRS. HARRIET BEECHER STOWE'S "SUNNY MEMORIES IN (ENGLAND) A FOREIGN LAND"; or, A Faithful Picture of the Extirpation of the Celtic Race from the Highlands of Scotland. Toronto, Thompson, 1857. 212p [NSHD OTU QMM

**McMahon, Hugh, 1836–1911**

REMINISCENCES. Toronto, 1908. 57p [OTU

**MacMechan, Archibald McKellar, 1862–1933**

WILLIAM GREENWOOD. N.p., n. pub., 1914. 12p [OTU

**MacMillan, Don A.**

ONLY THE STARS KNOW. Toronto, Dent, 1944. 138p [BVaU LC NBFU OTP QMSS

**McNab, Rev. John, 1887–**

FOUR CAMEOS, 1846–1946. ... Toronto, British & Foreign Bible Soc., 1946. 15p [OKQ

IN OTHER TONGUES. Tales of the Triumphs of Canadian Translators of Scripture. Toronto, Thorn Press, 1939. 141p [BVaU OTU

THEY WENT FORTH. Toronto, McClelland, 1933. 207p [Rev. ed., 1955. 240p] [Biogs. of missionaries.] [BVaU LC OTU

**McNabb, John H., 1880–1954**

THE HOMESTEAD DAYS OF JOHN H. AND ROBERT D. McNABB. Saskatoon, [1953?]. 24p

**McNaught, Kenneth William Kirkpatrick, 1918–**

A PROPHET IN POLITICS. A Biography of J.S. Woodsworth. Toronto, U. of Toronto Press, 1959. 339p

**Macnaughton, John, 1858–1943**

LORD STRATHCONA. London, Oxford U. Press, 1926. 391p [BM BVaU LC NSHD OTP QMM

**McNeill, William Everett, 1876–**

WALLACE OF QUEEN'S. [Kingston, Queen's University, 1951]. 12p

**MacNutt, William Stewart, 1908–**

DAYS OF LORNE. From the Private Papers of the Marquis of Lorne, 1878–1883, in the Possession of the Duke of Argyll at Inverary Castle, Scotland. Fredericton, Brunswick Press, 1955. x + 262p

**Macoun, John, 1831–1920**

AUTOBIOGRAPHY OF JOHN MACOUN, Canadian Explorer and Naturalist. A Memorial Volume. Ottawa, Field-Naturalists' Club, 1922. 305p [BM BVaU LC NBFU OTP

**McPhail, Alexander James, 1883–1931**

THE DIARY OF ALEXANDER JAMES McPHAIL. Ed. by Harold A. Innis. Toronto, U. of Toronto Press, 1940. 289p [BM BViPA LC NSHD OTP QMM

**Macphail, Andrew, 1864–1938**

THE MASTER'S WIFE. Montreal, Gnaedinger Print., 1939. 246p [BVaU NBFU OTP QMM

THREE PERSONS. 3rd ed. London, Murray, 1929. 346p [BM BVaU LC NSHD OTU QMM

**Macpherson, Charlotte Holt (Gethings), fl. 1828–1890**

OLD MEMORIES, AMUSING AND HISTORICAL. A sequel to REMINISCENCES OF OLD QUEBEC. By Mrs. Daniel Macpherson. ... Montreal, Author, 1890. 128p [BVaU LC NSWA OTP QMBM

REMINISCENCES OF OLD QUEBEC. By Mrs. Daniel Macpherson. Montreal, Lovell, 1890. 128p [BVaU LC NSWA OTP QMM

**Macpherson, James Pennington, 1839–1916**
LIFE OF THE RIGHT HON. SIR JOHN A. MACDONALD. ... By his Nephew. Saint John, Earle, 1891. 2v [BVaU LC NBFU OTP QMBM

**MacPherson, Stewart**
THE MIKE AND I. London, Home & Van Thal, 1948. 191p [BM OOP

**MacPhie, Rev. John Peter, 1854–1931**
PICTONIANS AT HOME AND ABROAD. Sketches of Professional Men and Women of Pictou County–Its History and Institutions. Boston, Pinkham, 1914. 232p [BVaU NBFU OTU

**McRae, James Archibald, 1889–**
CALL ME TOMORROW. Toronto, Ryerson, 1960. 240p

**McRaye, Walter Jackson, 1876–1946**
PAULINE JOHNSON AND HER FRIENDS. Toronto, Ryerson, 1947. 182p [NBFU OTP QMM
PIONEERS AND PROMINENT PEOPLE OF MANITOBA. Ed. by ——. Winnipeg, Can. Publicity Co., [1925?]. 353p [BViV SSU
TOWN HALL TONIGHT. Toronto, Ryerson, 1929. 256p [BVaU NBFU OTP

**McRobie, William Orme**
FIGHTING THE FLAMES; or, Twenty-Seven Years in the Montreal Fire Brigade. ... Montreal, "Witness" Print., 1881. 299p [BVaU NSWA OTP QMBM

**MacTavish, Newton McFaul, 1875–1941**
GEORGE HAM. Sketch of a Gentleman on Whom the Sun Never Sets. N.p., priv. print., n.d. 16p [NBFU

**McTavish, Rev. William Sharpe, 1858–1932**
MISSIONARY PATHFINDERS. Presbyterian Laborers at Home and Abroad. Ed. by ——. Toronto, Musson, 1907. 272p [BM BVaU OOP

**MacVicar, Rev. Donald Harvey, 1831–1902**
IN MEMORIAM: A SERMON PREACHED ON THE OCCASION OF THE DEATH OF JOHN REDPATH. Montreal, Lovell, 1869. 29p [NSWA

**Macvicar, Helena**
MARGARET SCOTT, A TRIBUTE: The Margaret Scott Nursing Mission. Winnipeg, Stovel, 1948. 28p [UTQ'50

**MacVicar, Rev. John Harvey, 1864–**
LIFE AND WORK OF DONALD HARVEY MacVICAR. Toronto, Westminster Co., 1904. 351p [BM BVaU OTP QMM

**Magrath, Charles Alexander, 1860–1949**
THE GALTS, FATHER AND SON, Pioneers in the Development of Southern Alberta. Lethbridge, Herald, 1936. 64p [BM BVaU LC NSHD OTP QMBM

**Malone, Richard Sankey, 1909–**

MISSING FROM THE RECORD. Toronto, Collins, 1946. 227p [BM BVaU LC NSHD OTU QMBM

**Manion, James Patrick, 1907–1959**

A CANADIAN ERRANT. Twenty-five Years in the Canadian Foreign Service. Ed. by Guy Sylvestre. Toronto, Ryerson, 1960. ix + 196p

**Manion, Robert James, 1881–1943**

LIFE IS AN ADVENTURE. Toronto, Ryerson, 1936. 360p [BVaU OTP QMM

A SURGEON IN ARMS. New York, Appleton, 1918. 310p [BM NSHD OTL

**Manly, Rev. John G., 1814–1908**

A PULPIT ESTIMATE OF WELLINGTON. ... London, 1852. [BM

**Marquis, Thomas Guthrie, 1864–1936**

BROCK, THE HERO OF UPPER CANADA. Toronto, Morang, 1912. 142p [BM BVaU OOP QMBM

BUILDERS OF CANADA FROM CARTIER TO LAURIER. ... Ed. by ——. Toronto, Winston, 1903. 570p [Also pub. as: GIANTS OF THE DOMINION FROM CARTIER TO LAURIER. Philadelphia, 1905.] [BVaU LC NSWA OTP QMSS

THE WAR CHIEF OF THE OTTAWAS. A Chronicle of the Pontiac War. Toronto, Glasgow Brook, 1915. 145p [BM BVaU LC NSWA OTU

**Mars, Alastair, 1915–**

COURT MARTIAL. London, Muller, 1954. 223p

**Marsden, Rev. Joshua, 1777–1837**

GRACE DISPLAYED. An Interesting Narrative of the Life, Conversion, Christian Experience, Ministry, and Missionary Labours of ——. New York, Paul & Thomas, 1813. 240p [LC OTUV

SKETCHES OF THE EARLY LIFE OF A SAILOR, NOW A PREACHER OF THE GOSPEL. Hull, Ross, 1820. N.p. [OTUV

**Marsh, D'Arcy Gilbert, 1906–**

THE TRAGEDY OF HENRY THORNTON. Toronto, Macmillan, 1935. 293p [BM BVaU LC NBFU OTP QMBM

**Marshall, James Stirrat, 1899–**

ADVENTURE IN TWO HEMISPHERES, INCLUDING CAPTAIN VANCOUVER'S VOYAGE. By James Stirrat Marshall and Carrie Marshall. Vancouver, Talex Print., 1955. xii + 208p

**Marshall, John George, 1786–1880**

PERSONAL NARRATIVES. With Reflections and Remarks. ... Halifax, Chamberlain, 1866. 154p [NSHD OOP

**Marsters, Joseph Dimock**

GENEALOGY OF THE DIMOCK FAMILY FROM THE YEAR 1637. Windsor, N.S., Anslow, 1899. 44p [NSWA

**Martin, Alfred Tobias John**

THE REMAINS OF THE LATE T. [i.e., Tobias] MARTIN. ... With a memoir of the author. Helston, 1831. [BM

**Martin, Chester Bailey, 1882–1958**

LORD SELKIRK'S WORK IN CANADA. Oxford, Clarendon, 1916. 240p [BM BVaU LC NSHD OTP

**Marty, Aletta Elise, 1866–1929**

MY EDUCATIONAL CREED. Toronto, Ryerson, 1924. 52p [BM BVaU NSHD OKQ

**Marwick, Alice (Stinson), 1892–1956**

THE HONOURABLE FRANK COCHRANE. A Tribute. Cochrane, Ont., Author, 1950. 22p [OONL

**Mason, Rev. George**

IN MEMORY OF SIR JAS. DOUGLAS. N.p., n.d. 3p [BViPA

**Massey, Hart Almerrin, 1823–1896**

HART ALMERRIN MASSEY. Pioneer Farmer, Farm Implement Manufacturer, Public-Spirited Citizen, Philanthropist. ... [Anon] Toronto, priv. print., [1896]. 35p [OOP

**Matheson, Charles Winfield, 1878–**

THE THREE RICHARDS OF THE DALHOUSIE LAW SCHOOL WHO BECAME KNIGHTS [Richard McBride, Richard Bennett, and Richard Squires]. Calgary, priv. print., 1954. 4p

**Mathieson, Rev. Alexander, 1795–1890**

SERMON ON THE DEATH OF MR. ROBERT WATSON. Montreal, 1827. [BibC

A TRIBUTE OF RESPECT TO THE MEMORY OF A GOOD MAN. A Sermon on the Death of Hugh Brodie, Esq. Montreal, 1852. 44p [BibC

**Matthews, Richard F., 1832–**

DIARY [January 28th, 1863 to March 17, 1899]. London, Ont., 1947. 3v [LC

**Matthews, Matthew George**

MATTHEWS' FAMOUS STORIES AND WORK. Windsor, Ont., Jaques & Sons, 1915. 234p [OTP

**Mavor, James, 1854–1925**

MY WINDOWS ON THE STREET OF THE WORLD. New York, Dutton, 1923. 2v [BM BVaU LC NSHD OTP QMBM

**Mayerhoffer, Rev. Vincent Philip, 1784–1859**

TWELVE YEARS A ROMAN CATHOLIC PRIEST; or, The Autobiography of ——. Toronto, Rowsell & Ellis, 1861. 340p [BVaU LC NSWA OTP QMM

**Meilicke, Emil Julius, 1852–1934**

LEAVES FROM THE LIFE OF A PIONEER. Being the Autobiography of Sometime Senator Emil Julius Meilicke (with Editorial Notes). Vancouver, Wrigley, 1948. 163p [BVaU OTP SSU

**Mellick, Henry George, 1857–1937**

TIMOTHY'S BOYHOOD; or, Pioneer Country Life on Prince Edward Island. By Timothy, a Country Boy [pseud]. Kentville, N.S., Kentville Pub. Co., 1933. [Rhod p683

**Mellor, T.C.**

SKETCH OF THE LIFE OF HIS HONOUR JUDGE SAVARY DELIVERED BEFORE THE HISTORICAL ASSOCIATION OF ANNAPOLIS ROYAL. ... Annapolis Royal, Spectator, 1922. 41p [NSWA

**Merkel, Andrew Doane, 1884–1954**

LETTERS FROM THE FRONT. ... Halifax, Ross Print., [Preface 1914]. 128p [NSHD

**Merkley, E. May**

OUR DOCTOR. Morrisburg, Ont., Leader Pub., 1933. 61p [On Dr. Mahlon W. Locke.] [LC OTU

**Merrick, Rev. Earl Chauncey, 1905–**

JOHN BATES McLAURIN ... A Biography. Toronto, priv. print. by Mrs. J.B. McLaurin, 1955. x + 134p

**Merritt, Jedediah Prendergast, 1820–1901**

BIOGRAPHY OF THE HON. W.H. MERRITT, M.P., of Lincoln, District of Niagara. St. Catharines, Leavenworth, 1875. 429p [BM BVaU LC NSHD OTU QMSS

**Methodius, Brother**

REVEREND BROTHER STANISLAUS JOSEPH. Yorkton, Sask., St. Joseph's College, 1953. 30p

**Middleton, Jesse Edgar, 1872–1960**

NATIONAL ENCYCLOPEDIA OF CANADIAN BIOGRAPHY. Ed. by Jesse Edgar Middleton and W. Scott Downs. Toronto, Dominion Pub., 1935. 383p [Also in 1937. 336p] [BVaU NSHD OTU

**Middleton, Samuel H., 1884–**

KOOTENAI BROWN, ADVENTURER, PIONEER, PLAINSMAN, PARK WARDEN. ... Lethbridge, Herald, 1954. 64p

**Mikel, William Charles, 1867–1950**

GODLOVE MIKEL (UNITED EMPIRE LOYALIST). Historical Notes Concerning

One of the Old Log Cabin Family. Trenton, Quinte Sun, 1939. 63p [BVaU OTP

**Miller, John Ormsby, 1861–1936**

BRIEF BIOGRAPHIES SUPPLEMENTING CANADIAN HISTORY (Heroes of the Northland). Toronto, Copp Clark, 1902. 152p [BM BVaU NSWA OTU

**Miller, Linus Wilson, 1818?–1880**

NOTES OF AN EXILE TO VAN DIEMEN'S LAND. Fredonia, N.Y., McKinstry, 1846. 378p [Reprinted New York, Johnson Reprint, 1968.] [BVaU LC OTP QQL

**Miller, William**

INCIDENTS IN THE POLITICAL CAREER OF THE LATE SIR JOHN THOMPSON NOT CONTAINED IN MR. J. CASTELL HOPKINS' BOOK. ... N.p., [1895?]. 21p [NSWA OTU

**Millman, Rev. Thomas Reagh, 1905–**

LIFE OF ... CHARLES JAMES STEWART, D.D., SECOND LORD BISHOP OF QUEBEC. Edinburgh, Stewart, [1948]. 12p [BM OTU

LIFE OF THE RT. REV. THE HON. CHARLES JAMES STEWART. London, Ont., Huron College, 1953. 237p

JACOB MOUNTAIN. First Lord Bishop of Quebec. Toronto, U. of Toronto Press, 1947. 310p [BM BVaU LC NBFU OTP QMM

A SKETCH OF THE LIFE AND WORK OF THE RIGHT REVEREND JACOB MOUNTAIN, D.D., FIRST LORD BISHOP OF QUEBEC. A Sermon preached on Sunday, October 31, 1943 ... on the Occasion of the 150th Anniversary of the Arrival of the Bishop. Durham, P.Q., Author, 1943. 10p [BM OTP

**Mills, Stanley, 1863–**

GENEALOGICAL AND HISTORICAL RECORDS OF THE MILLS AND GAGE FAMILIES, 1776–1926. ... Comp. by ——. Hamilton, Reid Press, 1926. 101p [BM BVaU LC OKQ

**Milner, William Cochrane, 1846–1939**

OUR LIEUTENANT GOVERNORS. Saint John, Busy East Press, 1928. 60p [BVaU NSWA OOA

**Miner, Jack (John Thomas Miner), 1865–1944**

JACK MINER AND THE BIRDS; and Some Things I Know about Nature. Toronto, Ryerson, 1923. 178p [BM BVaU LC NBFU OTU QMM

**Moberly, Henry John, 1835–1931**

WHEN FUR WAS KING. By ——. In collaboration with William Bleasdell Cameron. ... Toronto, Dent, 1929. 237p [BM BVaU LC NSHD OLU QMM

**Mockridge, Rev. Charles Henry, 1844–1913**

THE BISHOPS OF THE CHURCH OF ENGLAND IN CANADA AND NEWFOUNDLAND. Toronto, Brown, 1896. 380p [BM BVaU LC NBFU OLU QMM

**Moffat, Eva L., –1947**

THE ANCESTORS OF DANIEL FREEMAN BRITTON OF WESTMORELAND, N.H., AND GANANOQUE, ONT., 1808–1887. Pt. 1. The Ancestry of his Father, Daniel Britton. Pt. 2. The Ancestry of his Mother, Sally Wood. Comp. by ——. Ed. and correlated by Geoffrey Gilbert. Victoria, Editor, 1953. 135 + 81p [mimeographed]

THE ANCESTORS OF NANCY MARIA MOFFATT, WIFE OF DANIEL FREEMAN BRITTON. Pt. 1. The Ancestry of her Mother, Nancy Treadway. Pt. 2. The Ancestry of her Father, Melvin Moffatt. Comp. by ——. Ed. and correlated by Geoffrey Gilbert. Victoria, Editor, 1952. 159 + 69p

THE ANCESTRY OF EZRA HOLTON OF NORTHFIELD, MASS., AND SOPERTON, ONT., 1785–1824. Twenty-eight "Stories." Comp. by ——. Ed. and correlated by Geoffrey Gilbert. Victoria, Editor, 1953. 158p

THE ANCESTRY OF WILLIAM FORBES OF BARRE, MASS., AND MONTREAL, QUE., 1778–1833. Thirteen "Stories." Ed. and correlated by Geoffrey Gilbert. Victoria, Editor, 1953. 103p

**Montgomery, Lucy Maud, 1874–1942**

THE GREEN GABLES LETTERS, FROM L.M. MONTGOMERY TO EPHRAIM WEBER, 1905–1909. Ed. by Wilfrid Eggleston. Toronto, Ryerson, 1960. 102p

**Montreal, Que. Jewish Public Library**

TRIBUTE TO ISRAEL RABINOVITCH ON HIS SIXTIETH BIRTHDAY. Observed Sunday Evening in The Library Auditorium, December 26, 1954. Montreal, 1954. 24p

**Montreal, Que. Zion Church**

JUBILEE SERVICES ... TO CELEBRATE THE 50TH ANNIVERSARY OF THE MINISTERIAL WORK OF REV. HENRY WILKES. Montreal, The Church, 1878. 39p [NSWA

**Montreuil, Mrs. Anna B., 1886–**

THREE CAME WITH GIFTS. The Story of the First Hospital, the First School, and the First Cloister in Canada and their Heroic Founders [the Duchesse d'Aiguillon, Madame de la Peltrie, and Mère Marie de l'Incarnation]. Toronto, Ryerson, 1955. 60p

**Monture, Mrs. Ethel Brant, 1894–**

FAMOUS INDIANS: Brant, Crowfoot, Oronhyatekha. Toronto, Clarke Irwin, 1960. 160p

**Moodie, John Wedderburn Dunbar, 1797–1869**

SCENES AND ADVENTURES AS A SOLDIER AND SETTLER DURING HALF A CENTURY. Montreal, Lovell, 1866. 299p [BVaU LC NSWA OTP QMM

**Moodie, Susanna (Strickland), 1803–1885**

THE HISTORY OF MARY PRINCE, A WEST INDIAN SLAVE. [Anon] London, Maunder, 1831. [Authorship identified by C. Ballstadt in *Can. Notes & Queries*, Nov. 1971] [BM

LIFE IN THE BACKWOODS. A Sequel to ROUGHING IT IN THE BUSH. New York, Lovell, 1887. 224p [LC OTUV QMM

LIFE IN THE CLEARING VERSUS THE BUSH. London, Bentley, 1853. 384p [Also: ed. with an intro. by Robert L. McDougall. Toronto, Macmillan, 1959. xxxiii + 298p] [BM BVaU NSHD OTP QMM

NEGRO SLAVERY DESCRIBED BY A NEGRO. Being the Narrative of Ashton Warner, a Native of St. Vincents. ... [Anon] London, Maunder, 1831. [Authorship identified by C. Ballstadt in *Can. Notes & Queries*, Nov. 1971] [National Library, Scotland

ROUGHING IT IN THE BUSH; or, Life in Canada. London, Bentley, 1852. 2v [Many later editions.] [BM BVaU LC NSHD OTP QMM

**Moody, James, 1744?–1809**

NARRATIVE OF HIS EXERTIONS AND SUFFERINGS IN THE CAUSE OF GOVERNMENT SINCE THE YEAR 1776. London, Richardson & Urquhart, 1783. 64p [First pub. in 1782] [NSHP OHM

**Moody, Joseph Palmer, 1919–**

ARCTIC DOCTOR. An Account of Strange Adventures among the Eskimos. By Joseph P. Moody with W. de Groot van Embden. London, Odhams Press, 1955. 256p

**Mooney, Daniel, 1860?–**

THE TRAVELS AND PHILOSOPHY AND LIFE AND TIMES OF DANIEL MOONEY, Born in the Year 1860 on the Dublin Road between Banbridge and Drommore, County Down, Ireland. An Irish Exile. Winnipeg, Author, 1930. 442p [OTP

**Moore, Rev. Arthur Henry, 1869–1938**

A MINISTRY OF LOVE. A Sermon preached in All Saints Cathedral, Halifax ... at a Memorial Service to the Rev. Dr. Robert Norwood ..., Oct. 23, 1932. N.p., 1932. 13p [NSHD

**Moore, Cay**

SHE SKATED INTO OUR HEARTS. [Story of Barbara Ann Scott, figure skater.] Toronto, McClelland, 1948. 117p [QMBM

**Moore, Irene, 1876–1947**

VALIANT LA VERANRYE [*sic*! VERANDRYE]. Quebec, Proulx, 1927. 382p [BM BVaU LC NSHD OKQ

**Moreton, Rev. Julian, 1825–1900**

LIFE AND WORK IN NEWFOUNDLAND. Reminiscences of Thirteen Years Spent There. London, Rivingtons, 1863. 106p [BM BVaU LC NSHD OTP

**Morgan, Henry James, 1842–1913**

AD MULTOS ANNOS. A Tribute to Sir Charles Tupper on his Political Birthday, 1900. Toronto, Briggs, 1900. 16p [BM LC NSHD OTP QMBM

THE CANADIAN MEN AND WOMEN OF THE TIME. A Handbook of Canadian Biography. Ed. by ——. Toronto, Briggs, 1898. 1118p [2nd ed., much enl.:

Toronto, Briggs, 1912. 1218p] [BM BVaU LC NBFU OTU QMM

IN MEMORIAM: RECOLLECTIONS OF FATHER DAWSON. ... To which are added a Portion of a Sermon preached by the Rev. W.T. Herridge referring to Dr. Dawson's Example and Career, and Other Tributes to his Memory. Ottawa, Paynter & Abbott, 1895. 16p [NSHD OTP QMSS

SKETCHES OF CELEBRATED CANADIANS AND PERSONS CONNECTED WITH CANADA. Quebec, Hunter Rose, 1862. 779p [BM BVaU LC NBFU OTP

TYPES OF CANADIAN WOMEN, and of Women who are or have been Connected with Canada. Toronto, Briggs, 1903. v. 1. 382p [No more published.] [BM BVaU LC NBFU OTU QMM

**Morice, Rev. Adrian Gabriel, 1859–1938**

FIFTY YEARS IN WESTERN CANADA. Being the Abridged Memoirs of ——. Toronto, Ryerson, 1930. 267p [BM BVaU LC OTU

**Morphy, Edward M., 1820–1905**

LIFE PICTURES. A York Pioneer's Recollections of Youthful Days in the Emerald Isle ... his Emigration and first Impressions of Canada, especially Toronto (late York), and its Inhabitants when the City was only one Year old. Toronto, Author, 1893. 35p [OTU QMBM

SAINTY SMITH AND "THE SCHOOL UPON THE HILL." A Reminiscence .... Toronto, Author, [1890?]. 16p [OTP

A YORK PIONEER LOOKING BACK, 1834–1884. ... With Amusing Incidents and Anecdotes. ... Toronto, Press of the Budget, 1890. 32p [OLU

**Morphy, J.**

RECOLLECTIONS OF A VISIT TO GREAT BRITAIN AND IRELAND IN THE SUMMER OF 1862. Quebec, Palmer, 1863. 95p [BVaU LC OTP QMM

**Morris, John M., 1856–1936**

A KERFOOT HISTORY, CANADIAN BRANCH. London, Ont., Watt Letter Service, 1953. 187p [mimeographed]

**Morrison, Edith (Lennox)**

WILLIAM TYRRELL OF WESTON. By Edith Lennox Morrison and J.E. Middleton. Toronto, Macmillan, 1937. 152p [BVaU OTP

**Morrissey, Sister Helen**

ETHAN ALLEN'S DAUGHTER. Gardenvale, Que., Garden City Press, 1940. 134p [LC OTU

**Morse, William Inglis, 1874–1952**

AUTOBIOGRAPHICAL RECORDS OF WILLIAM INGLIS MORSE 1874–1905. ... Boston, McIver-Johnson, 1943. 56p [BM LC

THE DIARY OF A MUSKETEER. Boston, Sawyer, 1926. 71p [LC NSWA

EWART GLADSTONE MORSE, 1892–1935. A Memoir. Boston, Sawyer, 1940. 23p [NSHD

GENEALOGIAE; or, Data Concerning the Families of Morse, Chipman, Phinney, Ensign and Whiting. Ed. by ——. Boston, Sawyer, 1925. 189p [BM LC NSHD OTP
PIERRE DU GUA, SIEUR DE MONTS. Records, Colonial and "Saintongeois." Collected and ed. by ——. London, Quaritch, 1939. 67p [BM LC OTP
RICORDATI, 1874–1924. By W.I.M. Boston, Sawyer, 1925. 56p [LC NSWA

**Morton, Arthur Silver, 1870–1945**
SIR GEORGE SIMPSON, Overseas Governor of the Hudson's Bay Company. ... Toronto, Dent, 1944. 310p [BVaU LC NBFU OTP QMM

**Morton, James [of Victoria, B.C.], 1870?–1967**
HONEST JOHN OLIVER. The Life Story of the Honourable John Oliver, Premier of British Columbia, 1918–1927. Toronto, Dent, 1933. 272p [BM BVaU OTP

**Morton, Sarah Etter (Silver)**
JOHN MORTON OF TRINIDAD. ... Journals, Letters and Papers. ... Ed. by Sarah E. Morton and Arthur S. Morton. Toronto, Westminister, 1916. 491p [NSHD OLU
THE STORY OF JOSEPH ANNAJEE. ... Halifax, Nova Scotia Print. Co., 1879. 27p [NSHD

**Moser, Rev. Charles**
REMINISCENCES OF THE WEST COAST OF VANCOUVER ISLAND. Comp. by ——. Victoria, Acme Press, 1926. 192p [BM BVa LC OTP

**Moss, Thomas Patteson, 1915–1936**
PAT MOSS: CANADIAN AND ENGLISH LETTERS, 1924–36. Toronto, U. of Toronto Press, 1940. 425p [BM BVaU LC OTP

**Mountain, Armine Wale, 1823–1885**
A MEMOIR OF GEORGE JEHOSHAPHAT MOUNTAIN, D.D., D.C.L., Late Bishop of Quebec. ... By his son, Armine W. Mountain. ... London, Low & Marston; Montreal, Lovell, 1866. 477p [BM BVaU LC NSHD OTP QMM

**Mountain, Mrs. Armine Simcoe Henry**
MEMOIRS AND LETTERS OF THE LATE COLONEL ARMINE S.H. MOUNTAIN. ... Ed. by ——. London, Longman, 1857. 319p [BM NSWA
SOME ACCOUNT OF A SOWING TIME ON THE RUGGED SHORES OF NEWFOUNDLAND. With a Memoir of the Author. London, Society for the Propagation of the Gospel, 1857. 38p [NSWA

**Mountain, Rev. George Jehoshaphat, 1789–1863**
A SERMON PREACHED ... 1819, AFTER ... THE DEATH OF ... THE DUKE OF RICHMOND. ... Quebec, Neilson, 1819. 17p [OTP

**Mowat, Farley McGill, 1921–**
THE DOG WHO WOULDN'T BE. Boston, Little Brown, 1957. 238p

**Mullally, Emmet J.**
A SKETCH OF THE LIFE AND TIMES OF THE RIGHT REVEREND ANGUS BERNARD

MACEACHREN, THE FIRST BISHOP OF THE DIOCESE OF CHARLOTTETOWN. ... Montreal, [Can. Catholic Hist. Assoc.], 1947. 38p [OLU PCL QMM

**Munday, Mrs. Luta**

A MOUNTY'S WIFE. Being the Life Story of One Attached to the Force, but not of it. London, Sheldon Press, 1930. 217p [BM BVaU LC NBFU OTP

**Munroe, Jack**

MOPPING UP! Through the Eyes of Bobbie Burns, Regimental Mascot [dog]. New York, H.K. Fly, 1918. 319p [BViP OTU

**Murdoch, Rev. Benedict Joseph, 1886–**

FAR AWAY PLACE. Francestown, N.H., M. Jones Co., 1952. 185p

THE RED VINEYARD. Cedar Rapids, Iowa, Torch Press, 1923. 313p [BVaU LC NBFU OTP

**Murphy, Belva Gene (Atkinson)**

AT HOME WITH THE MURPHYS. Chicago, Moody Press, 1959. 127p

MOMMIE OF THE MIXING BOWL. Biography of Doris Coffin Aldrich. Chicago, Moody Press, 1959. 192p

**Murphy, George Henry, 1875–1958**

WOOD, HAY AND STUBBLE. Antigonish, N.S., Casket Print., 1956. 143p

**Murray, Frances Elizabeth**

IN MEMORIAM: FREDERICK HERVEY JOHN BRIGSTOCKE, Archdeacon of St. John. [Anon] Saint John, McMillan, 1899. 159p [BVaU NBFU OLU

MEMOIR OF LeBARON BOTSFORD, M.D. By his Niece. ... Saint John, McMillan, 1892. 285p [NBFU OLU

**Murray, John Wilson, 1840–1906**

MEMOIRS OF A GREAT DETECTIVE. Incidents in the Life of John Wilson Murray. Ed. by Victor Speer. ... New York, Baker & Taylor, 1905. 484p [Earlier ed.: London, Heinemann, 1904. 455p] [BM BVaU LC OTU

**Nannary, Miss M.A.**

MEMOIRS OF THE LIFE OF REV. E.J. DUNPHY. Saint John, Weekly Herald, 1877. 128p [OTP

**Narraway, Rev. J.R.**

SERMON ON THE OCCASION OF THE DEATH OF CHARLES F. ALLISON, Founder of Mount Allison Academy. Halifax, Wesleyan Conference Steam Press, 1859. 19p [NSHD

**Nasmith, George Gallie, 1877–1965**

ON THE FRINGE OF THE GREAT FIGHT. Toronto, McClelland, 1917. 263p [BM LC NBFU OTP QMM

TIMOTHY EATON. Toronto, McClelland, 1923. 312p [BM BVaU OTU

**Need, Thomas, 1808–**

SIX YEARS IN THE BUSH; or, Extracts from the Journal of a Settler in Upper Canada, 1832–1838. [Anon] London, Simpkin Marshall, 1838. 126p [Sometimes attributed to Susanna Moodie.] [BM BVaU LC NSWA OTP

**Needler, George Henry, 1866–1962**

COLONEL ANTHONY VAN EGMOND. From Napoleon and Waterloo to Mackenzie and Rebellion. Toronto, Burns & MacEachern, 1956. 63p

LETTERS OF ANNA JAMESON TO OTTILIE von GOETHE. Ed. by ——. London, Oxford U. Press, 1939. 247p [BM BVaU OTU

LOUIS RIEL. The Rebellion of 1885. Toronto, Burns & MacEachern, 1957. 81p

OTANABEE PIONEERS. The Story of the Stewarts, the Stricklands, the Traills, and the Moodies. Toronto, Burns & MacEachern, 1953. 172p

**Neilson, Joseph, 1813–1888**

MEMORIES OF RUFUS CHOATE.... Boston, Houghton, 1884. 460p [BM LC QMM

**Nelson, George, 1785?–**

A WINTER IN THE ST. CROIX VALLEY. George Nelson's Reminiscences, 1802–03. Ed. with an intro. and notes by Richard Bardon and Grace Lee Nute. St. Paul, Minnesota Hist. Soc., 1948. 46p [OTP

**Nelson, Hugh Spence, 1865–1946**

FOUR MONTHS UNDER ARMS. A Reminiscence of Events prior to and during the Second Riel Rebellion. Nelson, B.C., Daily News, n.d. 20p [BVaU OOA

**Nesbitt, James Knight, 1908–**

ALBUM OF VICTORIA OLD HOMES AND FAMILIES. Victoria, Hebden Print., 1956. 63p

**New, Chester William, 1882–1960**

LORD DURHAM. A Biography. Oxford, Clarendon, 1929. 612p [BM BVaU LC NBFU OTP QMM

**Newman, Peter Charles, 1929–**

FLAME OF POWER. Intimate Profiles of Canada's Greatest Businessmen. Toronto, Longmans, 1959. 263p

**Newton, Rev. William, 1828–1910**

TWENTY YEARS ON THE SASKATCHEWAN. London, Stock, 1897. 184p [BM BVaU LC OTP QMBM

**Nicolson, Alexander Wylie, –1903**

MEMORIES OF JAMES BAIN MORROW. Toronto, Methodist Book & Pub. House. 1881. 179p [BVaU NSWA OTP

**Niven, Frederick John, 1878–1944**

COLOURED SPECTACLES. London, Collins, 1938. 352p [BM BVaU LC NBFU OTU

THE STORY OF ALEXANDER SELKIRK. London, Wells Gardner, 1929. 119p [BM

**Norris, Armine Frank, –1918**
"MAINLY FOR MOTHER." Toronto, Ryerson, 1919. 219p [OTU

**Nourse, Hugh Campbell Boyd, 1892–**
RECORDS OF NOURSE AND BOYD DESCENDANTS BASED ON THE FAMILY AND CONNECTIONS OF ALFRED T. NOURSE. Comp. by ——. Montreal, Compiler, 1954. 43p

**Nursey, Walter R., 1847–1927**
THE STORY OF ISAAC BROCK, HERO, DEFENDER AND SAVIOUR OF UPPER CANADA, 1812. Toronto, Briggs, 1908. 181p [Also: Toronto, McClelland, 1923. 238p] [BM BVaU LC NBFU OTU QMM

**Obodiac, Stanlee, 1922–**
MY EXPERIENCES AT A CANADIAN AUTHORS' CONVENTION. Saskatoon, Modern Press, 1958. 133p

**O'Brien, Arthur Henry, 1865–**
HALIBURTON ("SAM SLICK"). A Sketch and Bibliography. 2nd ed. Montreal, Gazette, 1909. 26p [BM BVaU NBFU OTU QMSS

**O'Brien, Rev. Cornelius, 1843–1906**
FUNERAL SERMON ON SIR JOHN THOMPSON. Halifax, Meagher, 1906. 23p [BVaU NSWA OTU QMSS
MEMOIRS OF RT. REV. EDMUND BURKE, First Vicar Apostolic of Nova Scotia. Ottawa, Thorburn, 1894. 154p [BM LC NBFU OTP

**O'Connor, Daniel, 1796–1858**
DIARY AND OTHER MEMOIRS OF DANIEL O'CONNOR ... One of the Pioneers of By-Town ... 1827. Ottawa, priv. print., 1901. 45p [OOP

**O'Connor, John, 1824–1887**
WANDERINGS OF A VAGABOND. An Autobiography. Ed. by John Morris [pseud]. New York, Author, 1873. 492p [LC

**Odle, E.V.**
GREAT STORIES OF HUMAN COURAGE. Selected and edited by ——. London, Lane, 1933. 645p [BM MWU OHM
QUEST AND CONQUEST. An Anthology of Personal Adventures. Comp. by ——. Toronto, Macmillan, 1938. 231p [BM OONL QMSS

**O'Donnell, John Harrison, 1844–1912**
MANITOBA AS I SAW IT. From 1869 to Date. ... Toronto, Musson, 1909. 158p [BVaU LC NSHD OTP

**O'Hagan, Howard, 1902–**
WILDERNESS MEN. Garden City, N.Y., Doubleday, 1958. 263p

**O'Hagan, Thomas, 1855–1939**
FATHER MORICE. (On the Missionary Work of Adrian Gabriel Morice in North-West Canada.) Toronto, Ryerson, 1928. 31p [BM BViP NBSaM OTU QMSS

**Oldfield, Mabel (Dimock), 1878–**
WITH YOU ALWAY. The Life of a South China Missionary. Halifax, Author, 1958. 252p

**Oliver, William Sandford, 1751?–1813**
A COLLECTION OF PAPERS AND FACTS RELATIVE TO THE DISMISSION OF WILLIAM SANDFORD OLIVER, ESQ., FROM THE OFFICE OF SHERIFF OF THE CITY AND COUNTY OF ST. JOHN ... N.B. [Saint John?], 1791. 24p [OTP

**Olson, Oscar, 1908–**
I JOINED THE MOUNTIES. New York, Pageant Press, 1956. 183p

**O'Malley, James**
LIFE OF JAMES O'MALLEY. Montreal, Desaulniers, 1893. 192p [BVaU NBFU OTP QMM

**One of Them (pseud)**
UNKNOWN SOLDIERS. By One of Them. New York, Vantage Press, 1959. 170p [Veteran's account of service with the Canadian Expeditionary Force during World War I.]

**Orillia, Ont. Historical Society**
A MEDONTE PIONEER AND HIS FAMOUS SON [Sir Samuel B. Steele]. Orillia, Ont., the Society, 1954. 15p

**Osler, Featherstone Lake, 1805–1895**
RECORDS OF THE LIVES OF ELLEN FREE PICKTON AND FEATHERSTONE LAKE OSLER. London, priv. print., 1915. 257p [OTP

**Osler, William, 1849–1919**
MICHAEL SERVETUS. London, Frowde, 1909. 35p [BM LC OTP
THOMAS LINACRE. Cambridge, The University Press, 1908. 64p [BM BVaU LC OTU

**Ossinger, Mrs. June Eileen**
LAMP IN THE WILDERNESS. By June Lydiard Spencer [pseud]. New York, Vantage Press, 1955. 135p

**Ostenso, Martha, 1900–1963**
AND THEY SHALL WALK. The Life Story of Sister Elizabeth Kenny. Written in Collaboration with Martha Ostenso. New York, Dodd Mead, 1943. 282p [BM BVaU OTU

**Ostrander, Manly, 1874–**
THE HOUSE OF OSTRANDER. ... Deseronto, Ont., 1942. 32p [LC OTP

MEMORIAL TO CAPTAIN BRADSHAW. Comp. by —— and Charles G. Crouse. Oshawa, C.G. Crouse, 1942. 31p [LC OTP

**Otheman, Edward**

MEMOIR AND WRITINGS OF MRS. HANNAH MAYNARD PICKARD. Late Wife of Rev. Humphrey Pickard, A.M., Principal of the Wesleyan Academy at Sackville, N.B. Boston, Ela, 1845. 311p [NSWA OTP

**Ottawa, Ont. National Gallery of Canada**

EMILY CARR, HER PAINTINGS AND SKETCHES. Toronto, Oxford U. Press, 1945. 64p [BM NSHD

**Owen, William, 1738?–1778**

THE JOURNAL OF CAPTAIN WILLIAM OWEN ... DURING HIS RESIDENCE ON CAMPOBELLO IN 1770–1771. Ed. by W.F. Ganong, Saint John, Sun Print., 1899. 27p [BVaU LC NSWA QMBM

**Owen Sound, Ont. Junior Chamber of Commerce**

TOM THOMSON, 1877–1917. A Tribute. Owen Sound, 1956. 12p

**Page, Frank E.**

HOMER WATSON, ARTIST AND MAN. Kitchener, Commercial Print., 1939. 182p [BM OTP

**Paget, Rev. Edward Clarence, 1851–1927**

MEMOIR OF THE HON. SIR CHARLES PAGET, G.C.H., 1778–1839. With a Short History of the Paget Family. London, Longmans, 1913. 131p [First printed: Toronto, Briggs, 1911. 100p] [BM OTP QMM

A YEAR UNDER THE SHADOW OF ST. PAUL'S. Early Undergraduate Days in Keble College, Oxford, and Other Papers. Calgary, Author, 1908. 213p [ACG BVaU

**Panabaker, Frank Shirley, 1904–**

REFLECTED LIGHTS. Toronto, Ryerson, 1957. xvi + 159p

**Parent, Rev. Amand, 1818–1907**

THE LIFE OF REV. AMAND PARENT, THE FIRST FRENCH-CANADIAN ORDAINED BY THE METHODIST CHURCH. Forty-Seven Years' Experience in the Evangelical Work in Canada. Toronto, Briggs, 1887. 235p [BM BVaU NSWA OTP QMBM

**Parham, Henry James, 1870–**

A NATURE LOVER IN BRITISH COLUMBIA. London, Witherby, 1938. 202p [ACG BVaU OKQ

**Parker, William Frederick, 1860–1918**

DANIEL McNEILL PARKER, M.D. His Ancestry and a Memoir of his Life. Toronto, Briggs, 1910. 604p [BM BVaU NSWA OOP

**Parkin, George Robert, 1846–1922**

EDWARD THRING, HEADMASTER OF UPPINGHAM SCHOOL. Life, Diary and Letters. London, Macmillan, 1898. 2v [BM BVaU LC NSHD OTP QMM

SIR JOHN A. MACDONALD. Toronto, Morang, 1908. 372p [BM BVaU LC NSWA OTP QMM

**Patrick, Mary Niven (Cattanach), 1884–1954**

GROWING OLD IN VICTORIA. Victoria, priv. print., 1954. 6p

**Patterson, Andrew Dickson, 1854–1930**

WILLIAM RICE, POET AND BOOKMAN. Biographical Sketch and Portraits. Toronto, Author, 1904. 11p [OOP

**Patterson, Frank Harris, 1891–**

JOHN PATTERSON, THE FOUNDER OF PICTOU TOWN. By his Great-Grandson. Truro, N.S., Truro Print., 1955. 110p

MARY DICKSON. By Her Great-Grandson. Truro, N.S., Truro Print., 1952. 60p

STEWART KISSLEPAUGH. Truro, N.S., Truro Print., 1953. 28p

**Patterson, Rev. George, 1824–1897**

A BRIEF SKETCH OF THE LIFE AND LABOURS OF THE LATE REV. JOHN KEIR, D.D., S.T.P. Pictou, 1859. 43p [BibC

MEMOIR OF THE REV. JAMES MACGREGOR, D.D., Missionary ... to Pictou, Nova Scotia, 1786–1830. By his Grandson, ——. Philadelphia [etc.], Wilson [etc.], 1859. 533p [BM BVaU NBFU OTP QMM

MEMOIRS OF THE REV. S.F. JOHNSTON, THE REV. J.W. MATHESON, AND MRS. MARY JOHNSTON MATHESON, MISSIONARIES ON TANNA. With Selections from their Diaries and Correspondence. Philadelphia, Martien, [1864]. 504p [NSWA OTU

MISSIONARY LIFE AMONG THE CANNIBALS. Being the Life of the Rev. John Geddie, First Missionary to the New Hebrides. Toronto, Campbell, 1882. 512p [NSHD OTU

SKETCH OF THE LIFE AND LABORS OF THE REV. JOHN CAMPBELL, OF ST. MARY'S, N.S. New Glasgow, MacKenzie, 1889. 37p [NSWA

**Patterson, Raymond Murray, 1898–**

DANGEROUS RIVER. New York, Sloane, 1954. 314p

**Pattillo, Thomas Richard, 1833–1910**

MOOSE-HUNTING, SALMON-FISHING, AND OTHER SKETCHES OF SPORT. Being the Record of Personal Experiences ... in Canada. Toronto, Briggs, 1902. 299p [BVaU LC NSWA OTP QMSS

**Pearce, Bruce M., 1900–**

FIRST GRAND MASTER. A Biography of William Mercer Wilson, First Grand Master of the Grand Lodge of Canada, A.F. & A.M. Simcoe, Pearce Pub. Co., 1932. 189p [BM OTP

**Pearce, Richard**

MAROONED IN THE ARCTIC. Diary of the Dominion Explorers' Expedition to the Arctic, August to December, 1929. Toronto, 1931. 71p [BVaU OTP

**Pearson, Carol (Williams), 1910–**

EMILY CARR AS I KNEW HER. Toronto, Clarke Irwin, 1954. x + 162p

**Pearson, James Johnston, 1884–**

LAY ON, MACDUFF! Dublin, priv. print., 1960. xi + 107p

**Peat, Harold Reginald, 1893–1960**

PRIVATE PEAT. His Own Story. Toronto, McLeod, 1917. 235p [BM BVaU LC NSHD OTU QMM

**Peat, Louisa (Watson)**

MRS. PRIVATE PEAT. By Herself. Indianapolis, Bobbs-Merrill, 1918. 236p [BM LC

**Pedley, James Henry, 1892–1945**

ONLY THIS– A War Retrospect. Ottawa, Graphic, 1927. 371p [BVaU OTU

**Pedley, James William, 1856–1933**

BIOGRAPHY OF LORD STRATHCONA AND MOUNT ROYAL. Toronto, Nichols, 1915. 187p [BM BVaU LC OTP QMBM

**Pelley, Richard**

TALES OF THE SEA. Hamilton, Time Job Print., 1926. 204p [OKQ

**Pennefather, John Pyne, 1833–1913**

THIRTEEN YEARS ON THE PRAIRIES. From Winnipeg to Cold Lake, Fifteen Hundred Miles. London, Kegan Paul, 1892. 127p [BVaU OTP QMSS

**Pennington, Myles, 1814–1898**

RAILWAYS AND OTHER WAYS. Being Reminiscences of Canal and Railway Life during a Period of Sixty-seven Years. Toronto, Williamson, 1894. 407p [BM BVaU LC NSWA OTP QMM

**Penny, Arthur Guy, 1886–1963**

THE SHIRT-SLEEVED GENERATION. An Account of the Life and Times of a Canadian Newspaper Man. ... Quebec, Chronicle-Telegraph, 1953. 335p

**Perkins, Simeon, 1735–1812**

DIARY. 1780–1789. Ed. with an intro. by D.C. Harvey, with notes by C. Bruce Fergusson. Toronto, Champlain Society, 1958. lviii + 531 + xvip

THE DIARY OF SIMEON PERKINS, 1766–1780. Ed. with intro. and notes by Harold A. Innis. Toronto, Champlain Society, 1948. 298p [BM BVaU LC NBFU OTP QMM

**Perry, Rev. Charles Ebenezer, 1835–1917**

THE HON. N. CLARKE WALLACE, GRAND MASTER, LOYAL ORANGE ASSOCIATION

OF BRITISH AMERICA. His Action on the "Remedial Bill" and what led up to it. With an appendix by W.W. Colpitts. N.p., 1897. 138p [BVaU NfSM OOP QMBM

**Perry, James Black, 1845–1936**

HAPPENINGS IN A HAPPY LIFE. An Autobiography. Kingston, Jackson Press, 1925. 125p [OKQ

**Phelan, Josephine, 1905–**

THE ARDENT EXILE. The Life and Times of Thos. D'Arcy McGee. Toronto, Macmillan, 1951. 317p

THE BOLD HEART. The Story of Father Lacombe. Toronto, Macmillan, 1956. 182p

**Phillips, Mrs. Bluebell Stewart, 1904–**

SOMETHING ALWAYS TURNED UP. Toronto, Ryerson, 1958 [i.e. 1959]. 134p

**Phillipps-Wolley, Clive Oldnall, 1854–1918**

SPORT IN THE CRIMEA AND CAUCASUS. London, Bentley, 1881. 370p [BVaU OTP

**Pichette, J.A. Robert**

A BOOK OF MOTTOES. [Gives Mottoes of Leading English-speaking New Brunswick Families.] Edmundston, N.B., "Le Madawaska," n.d. 12p

**Pickering, Joseph**

EMIGRATION, OR NO EMIGRATION. Being the Narrative of the Author (an English Farmer) from the Year 1824 to 1830. London, Longman Rees, 1830. 132p [3rd ed. pub. under title: INQUIRIES OF AN EMIGRANT. London, Wilson, 1832. 207p] [BM BVaU LC OOP

**Pickersgill, Frank H.D., 1915–1944**

THE PICKERSGILL LETTERS. Written during the Period 1934–1943. Ed. with a memoir by George H. Ford. Toronto, Ryerson, 1948. 229p [BVa LC NSHD OTU QMM

**Pickford, Mary, 1893–**

THE FILM LIFE OF MARY PICKFORD. London, Page & Thomas, 1914. [BM

MY STRANGE LIFE. The Intimate Life Story of a Moving Picture Actress. New York, Grosset & Dunlap, 1915. 280p [OONL

SUNSHINE AND SHADOW. Garden City, N.Y., Doubleday, 1955. 382p

**Pidhainy, Semen Aleksandrovich, 1907–**

ISLANDS OF DEATH. Toronto, Burns & MacEachern, 1953. 240p [Experiences in Russian prison camps.]

**Pierce, Lorne Albert, 1890–1961**

ALBERT DURRANT WATSON. An Appraisal. Toronto, Ryerson, 1923. 10p [BM BVaU LC NBFU OTP QMM

E. GRACE COOMBS (MRS. JAMES SHARP LAWSON), A.O.C.A., O.S.A. Toronto, Ryerson, 1949. 32p [BM BVaU LC NSHD OTP

FIFTY YEARS OF PUBLIC SERVICE: A LIFE OF JAMES L. HUGHES. Toronto, Oxford U. Press, 1924. 256p [BM BVaU LC NBFU OTP

IN MEMORIAM: CHARLES W. JEFFERYS, 1869–1951. N.p., 1951. 4p

MARJORIE PICKTHALL. A Book of Remembrance. Toronto, Ryerson, [1925]. 217p [BM BVaU NBFU OTP QMM

MARJORIE PICKTHALL. A Memorial Address. Toronto, Ryerson, 1943. 20p [BM BVaU LC NBFU OTP QMM

A POSTSCRIPT OF J.E.H. MACDONALD, 1873–1932. Toronto, Ryerson, 1940. 12p [BM BVaU LC NBFU OTP QMM

THOREAU MACDONALD. Toronto, Ryerson, 1942. 8p [BM BVaU LC NBFU OTP QMM

THREE FREDERICTON POETS: WRITERS OF THE UNIVERSITY OF NEW BRUNSWICK AND THE NEW DOMINION. Toronto, Ryerson, 1933. 30p [BM BVaU NBFU OTP QMM

WILLIAM KIRBY. The Portrait of a Tory Loyalist. Toronto, Macmillan, 1929. 477p [BM BVaU LC NBFU OTP QMM

**Pierce, Rev. William Henry, 1856–1948**

FROM POTLATCH TO PULPIT. Being the Autobiography of the Rev. William Henry Pierce. Ed. by Rev. J.P. Hicks. Vancouver, Vancouver Bindery, 1933. 176p [BM BVaU LC NBFU OTP

**Piers, Harry, 1870–1940**

BIOGRAPHICAL REVIEW. Biographical Sketches of Leading Citizens of the Province of Nova Scotia. Ed. by ——. Boston, Biographical Review Pub. Co., 1900. 487p [NSWA

ROBERT FIELD. Portrait Painter in Oils, Miniature, Water-Colours, and Engraver. New York, Sherman, 1927. 202p [NSHD OTU

**Piersol, Mary Cameron (Blackadar)**

THE RECORDS OF THE VAN EVERY FAMILY, UNITED EMPIRE LOYALISTS, New York State, 1653–1784, Canada, 1784–1947. Toronto, Best, 1947. 131p [OTP

**Pinkerton, Kathrene Sutherland (Gedney), 1887–**

BRIGHT WITH SILVER. New York, Sloane, 1947. 347p [Story of Fromm Bros., Inc.] [BVa LC OOP

TWO ENDS TO OUR SHOESTRING. New York, Harcourt, 1941. 362p [BM BVaU LC OTU QMM

**Pitblado, Rev. Charles Bruce, 1836–1913**

ROBERT BURNS, HIS LIFE AND POETRY. An Address Delivered in Selkirk Hall, Winnipeg, Manitoba, February 25th, 1884. Winnipeg, Isaac Pitblado, 1955. 43p

**Plewman, William Rothwell, 1880–**

ADAM BECK AND THE ONTARIO HYDRO. Toronto, Ryerson, 1947. 494p [BVaU LC NSHD OTP QMM

MY DIARY OF THE GREAT WAR. Being a Current History of the World's Greatest Struggle. Toronto, Ontario Press, 1918. 203p [OTP

**Plummer, John Orme, 1894–**

CANADIAN PIONEERS. History of the Plummer Family. Toronto, priv. print., 1958. 35p

**Plunkett, Albert William, 1899?–1957**

AL PLUNKETT, THE FAMOUS DUMBELL. By Patrise Earle, as told by Al Plunkett. New York, Pageant Press, 1956. 107p

**Pocock, Roger, 1865–1941**

CAPTAINS OF ADVENTURE. Indianapolis, Bobbs-Merrill, 1913. 376p [BViPA LC NBSaM

CHORUS TO ADVENTURERS. Being the Later Life of Roger Pocock, ("A Frontiersman"). London, Lane, 1931. 304p [BM LC OTU QMM

A FRONTIERSMAN. London, Methuen, 1903. 307p [Pub. also under title: FOLLOWING THE FRONTIER. New York, McClure, 1903. 338p] [BM BVaU LC OLU QMM

**Pollard, William Correll, 1878–**

LIFE ON THE FRONTIER. A Sketch of the Parry Sound Colonists. London, Stockwell, n.d. 112p [Also pub. under title: PIONEERING IN THE PRAIRIE WEST. 2nd ed. Uxbridge, Ont., Cave, 1925; London, Stockwell, 1933. 110p] [BM BVaU OTP QMSS

**Pollett, Ronald, 1900–**

PETER THE GRATE. St. John's, Guardian Associates, 1952. 64p ["An outport character study."]

**Pomeroy, Elsie May, 1886–**

SIR CHARLES G.D. ROBERTS. A Biography. Toronto, Ryerson, 1943. 371p [BM BVaU LC NBFU OTP QMM

TRIBUTES THROUGH THE YEARS. The Centenary of the Birth of Sir Charles G.D. Roberts, January 10, 1960. Ed. by ——. Toronto, priv. print., 1959. 19p

WILLIAM SAUNDERS AND HIS FIVE SONS. The Story of The Marquis Wheat Family. Toronto, Ryerson, 1956. xiii + 192p

**Poole, Evelyn Lavina, 1907–**

THE HISTORY OF THE MACFARLANES, 1831–1931. London, Ont., Middlesex, 1931. 80p [OTU

**Poole, Rev. William Henry, 1820–1896**

A SERMON, OCCASIONED BY THE DEATH OF EDWARD JACKSON, ESQ. Toronto, Wesleyan, 1872. 32p [OTUV

**Pope, Joseph, 1854–1926**

THE DAY OF SIR JOHN MACDONALD. Toronto, Brook, 1915. 195p [BM BVaU LC NBFU OTP QMM

JACQUES CARTIER. His Life and Voyages. Ottawa, Woodburn, 1890. 168p [BM BVaU LC NBFU OTU QMM

MEMOIRS OF THE RIGHT HONOURABLE SIR JOHN ALEXANDER MACDONALD. London, Arnold, 1894. 2v [Also: Toronto, Oxford U. Press, 1930. 816p] [BM BVaU LC NBFU OTP QMM

PUBLIC SERVANT. The Memoirs of Sir Joseph Pope. Ed. and completed by Maurice Pope. Toronto, Oxford U. Press, 1960. 312p

SIR JOHN A. MACDONALD VINDICATED. A Review of the Right Hon. Sir Richard Cartwright's Reminiscences. Toronto, Publishers' Association, 1912. 24p [BM BVaU NBFU OTU QMSS

**Portlock, Rosa (Elliott), 1839–1928**

TWENTY-FIVE YEARS OF CANADIAN LIFE. With a Study on Bible Prophecy. Toronto, Briggs, 1901. 195p [BVaU OTP

**Powell, Oscar Reginald, 1884–**

SO SOON FORGOTTEN. By Dick Fairfax [pseud]. Saskatoon, Modern Press, 1955. 132p [Life on the Canadian Prairies, 1904–20.]

**Pratt, Viola Leone (Whitney), 1892–**

FAMOUS DOCTORS: Osler, Banting, Penfield. Toronto, Clarke Irwin, 1956. xi + 160p

**Preston, Richard Arthur, 1910–**

GORGES OF PLYMOUTH FORT. A Life of Sir Ferdinando Gorges, Captain of Plymouth Fort, Governor of New England, and Lord of the Province of Maine. Toronto, U. of Toronto Press in cooperation with the Royal Military College of Canada, 1953. 495p

**Preston, William Thomas Rochester, 1851–1942**

THE LIFE AND TIMES OF LORD STRATHCONA. Toronto, McClelland, 1914. 324p [BM BVaU NSWA OTP QMM

MY GENERATION OF POLITICS AND POLITICIANS. Toronto, Rose, 1927. 462p [BVaU LC NSHD OTP QMSS

**Pringle, Rev. George Charles Fraser, 1873–1949**

ADVENTURES IN SERVICE. Toronto, McClelland, 1929. 282p [BVaU OOP

**Pringle, Jacob Farrand, 1816–1901**

THE GENEALOGY OF JACOB FARRAND PRINGLE AND ... ISABELLA FRASER PRINGLE. Cornwall, 1892. 35p [OTU

**Provencher, Paul, 1902–**

I LIVE IN THE WOODS. A Book of Personal Recollections and Woodland Lore. Fredericton, Brunswick Press, 1953. 188p

**Prychodko, Nicholas, 1904–**
ONE OF THE FIFTEEN MILLION. Toronto, Dent, 1952. 169p [Account of prison experiences in USSR, and escape into western Europe.]

**Pugsley, William Howard, 1912–**
SAILOR REMEMBER. Toronto, Collins, 1948. 185p [BVa OTU QMBM
SAINTS, DEVILS, AND ORDINARY SEAMEN. Life on the Royal Canadian Navy's Lower Deck. Toronto, Collins, 1945. 241p [BM BVaU LC NBFU OLU QMM

**Purkis, Leslie S.**
THE FIRE KINDLERS. The Story of the Purkis Family. Hamilton, Davis-Lisson, 1939. 55p [BM OOA QMBM

**Putman, John Harold, 1866–1940**
EGERTON RYERSON AND EDUCATION IN UPPER CANADA. Toronto, Briggs, 1912. 270p [BM BVaU NSWA OTU QMM
FIFTY YEARS AT SCHOOL. An Educationist Looks at Life. Toronto, Clarke Irwin, 1938. 253p [BM OTU
SCHOOLMASTERS ABROAD. A 1937 Diary. Toronto, Clarke Irwin, 1937. 98p [BVaU OTU

**Putnam, Ben**
FIFTY YEARS OF PROGRESS. Chiefly the Story of the Pioneers of the Watson District from 1900–1910. Ed. by Ben Putnam and Others. Muenster, Sask., St. Peter's Press, 1951. 111p

**Raber, Jessie (Browne), 1885?–**
PIONEERING IN ALBERTA. New York, Exposition Press, 1951. 171p

**Randell, Jack, 1879–**
I'M ALONE. Indianapolis, Bobbs-Merrill, 1930. 317p [AEU LC NSHPL OKQ

**Ransford, Henry, 1804–**
DATES AND EVENTS CONNECTED WITH MY FAMILY (1667–1881). London, Ont., Library, U. of Western Ontario, 1959. 81p [mimeographed].

**Rasky, Frank, 1923–**
GAY CANADIAN ROGUES. Swindlers, Gold-Diggers and Spies. Toronto, Nelson, 1958. 190p

**Ravenhill, Alice, 1859–1954**
ALICE RAVENHILL, THE MEMOIRS OF AN EDUCATIONAL PIONEER. With a foreword by Norman MacKenzie. Toronto, Dent, 1951. 241p

**Rawlinson, James H.**
THROUGH ST. DUNSTAN'S TO LIGHT. Toronto, Allen, 1919. 90p [BM BVaU OTP

**Raymond, Ethel T.**

TECUMSEH. A Chronicle of the Last Great Leader of his People. Toronto, Glasgow Brook, 1915. 159p [BM BVaU NSWA OTU

**Read, David Breakenridge, 1823–1904**

THE LIEUTENANT-GOVERNORS OF UPPER CANADA AND ONTARIO, 1792–1899. Toronto, Briggs, 1900. 253p [BM BVaU LC NBFU OTP QMM

THE LIFE AND TIMES OF GEN. JOHN GRAVES SIMCOE, First Governor of Upper Canada. Toronto, Virtue, 1890. 305p [BM BVaU LC NBFU OTP QMM

THE LIFE AND TIMES OF MAJOR-GENERAL SIR ISAAC BROCK. Toronto, Briggs, 1894. 266p [BM BVaU LC NSHD OTP QMM

THE LIVES OF THE JUDGES OF UPPER CANADA AND ONTARIO FROM 1791 TO THE PRESENT TIME. Toronto, Rowsell & Hutchinson, 1888. 486p [BM BVaU LC NBFU OTP QMM

**Reesor, A.D. (presumed author)**

THE REESOR FAMILY IN CANADA. Genealogical and Historical Records, 1804–1950. Markham, Ont., A.D. Reesor, 1950. 160p [OONL

**Remits, Ernest Lorand, 1901–**

JOTTINGS FROM THE NEW AND OLD COUNTRIES. Ottawa, Progressive, 1935. 116p [OOU

**Renison, Rev. Robert John, 1875–1957**

ONE DAY AT A TIME. The Autobiography of Robert John Renison. Ed. by Margaret Blackstock. Toronto, Kingswood House, 1957. x + 322p

**Reynolds, William Kilby, 1848–1902**

THE REV. WILLIAM DONALD, D.D., OF ST. ANDREW'S CHURCH, ST. JOHN, N.B. A Sketch of his Life and Character. Mobile, Ala., Mobile Stationery Co., 1898. 84p [NSWA QMM

**Richan, Sarah (Hopkins), 1871–**

THE BOOK OF RICHAN ... A.D. 938 to ... 1936. Comp. and ed. by ——. Barrington & Yarmouth, N.S., Author, 1936. 39p [BM OOA

**Richardson, Evelyn May (Fox), 1902–**

MY OTHER ISLANDS. Toronto, Ryerson, 1960. 213p

WE KEEP A LIGHT. Toronto, Ryerson, 1945. 260p [Also, with added chapter, Toronto, Ryerson, 1961. 271p Pub. in the U.S. as: WE BOUGHT AN ISLAND. Philadelphia, Macrae Smith, 1954. 281p] [BM BVa LC NBFU OTP QMM

**Richardson, John, 1796–1852**

CORRESPONDENCE, Submitted to Parliament, between Major Richardson, Late Superintendent of Police on the Welland Canal, and the Hon. Dominick Daly, Provincial Secretary. Montreal, Donoghue, 1846. 62p [NSWA OTP

EIGHT YEARS IN CANADA. Embracing a Review of the Administrations of Lords

Durham and Sydenham, Sir Chas. Bagot, and Lord Metcalfe; and Including Numerous Interesting Letters from Lord Durham, Mr. Chas. Buller, and other well-known Public Characters. Montreal, Cunningham, 1847. 232p [BM BVaU LC NSWA OTU QMM

THE GUARDS IN CANADA; or, The Point of Honor. Being a Sequel to Major Richardson's EIGHT YEARS IN CANADA. Montreal, Cunningham, 1848. 54p [BM BVaU NSWA OTP QMM

JOURNAL OF THE MOVEMENTS OF THE BRITISH LEGION. By an Officer [J. Richardson]. London, Effingham Wilson, 1836. 262p [BM OTP

MOVEMENTS OF THE BRITISH LEGION, with Strictures on the Course of Conduct Pursued by Lieutenant-General Evans. 2nd ed. To which is added ... a Continuation of the Operations from the 5th of May, 1836, to the close of March, 1837. London, Simpkin Marshall, 1837. 330p [1st ed.: London, 1836.] [BM BVaU LC NSHD OTU QMBM

PERSONAL MEMOIRS OF MAJOR RICHARDSON ... as Connected with the Singular Oppression of that Officer while in Spain. Montreal, Armour & Ramsay, 1838. 145p [BM BVaU LC NSWA OTU QMSS

SKETCH OF THE LATE BATTLE OF THE WIND MILL, NEAR PRESCOTT, IN NOVEMBER, 1838. Prescott, 1839. 12p [In *Papers of the Bibliog. Soc. of Canada,* v.4, Morley says of this title: "almost certainly not" by Richardson.] [QMM

TECUMSEH AND RICHARDSON. The Story of a Trip to Walpole Island and Port Sarnia. With an Intro. and Biographical Sketch by A.H.U. Colquhoun. Toronto, Ontario Book Co., [1924]. 124p [The "Trip ..." was originally pub. anonymously in the *Literary Garland,* Jan., 1849.] [BM BVaU LC NSHD OLU QMM

WAR OF 1812. First Series. [Brockville, Author], 1842. 182p [Reprinted from Richardson's *The New Era or Canadian Chronicle,* v. 2, no. 1–15, Mar. 2–July 22, 1842.] (Ed. with extended biography and a full bibliography of Richardson's work by Alexander Clark Casselman. Toronto, Historical Pub. Co., and Musson, 1902. lviii + 320p) [BM BVaU LC NSWA OTP QMM

**Richey, Rev. Matthew, 1803–1883**

A MEMOIR OF THE LATE REV. WILLIAM BLACK, Wesleyan Minister, Halifax, N.S. Including an Account of the Rise and Progress of Methodism in Nova Scotia. Halifax, Cunnabell, 1839. 370p [NBFU OTP

SERMON ON OCCASION OF THE DEATH OF THE REV. WILLIAM BENNETT, Preached ... Dec. 27, 1857. Halifax, Wesleyan, 1858. 19p [NSHD

A SERMON OCCASIONED BY THE DEATH OF THE REV. WILLIAM CROSCOMBE. Halifax, Wesleyan, 1859. 27p [NSWA

SERMON ON THE DEATH OF THE REV. WILLIAM McDONALD, Late Wesleyan Missionary. Halifax, 1834. 32p [NSWA

**Rickard, Thomas Arthur, 1864–1953**

RETROSPECT. An Autobiography. Toronto, McLeod, 1937. [BVaU OTU

**Riddell, Robert Gerald, 1908–1951**

CANADIAN PORTRAITS. C.B.C. Broadcasts. Ed. by ——. Toronto, Oxford U. Press, 1940. 154p [BVaU LC NSHD OTP QMM

**Riddell, William Renwick, 1852–1945**

JOHN RICHARDSON. Toronto, Ryerson, [1923]. 226p [BM BVaU LC NBFU OTU

THE LIFE OF JOHN GRAVES SIMCOE. Toronto, McClelland, [1926]. 492p [BM BVaU LC NSHD OTP QMM

THE LIFE OF WILLIAM DUMMER POWELL, First Judge at Detroit and Fifth Chief Justice of Upper Canada. Lansing, Michigan Historical Commission, 1924. 305p [BM BVaU LC NSHD OTP QMM

WILLIAM KIRBY. Toronto, Ryerson, 1923. 176p [BM BVaU NSWA OTU

**Ridley, Hilda M., –1960**

THE STORY OF L.M. MONTGOMERY. Toronto, Ryerson, 1956. xiii + 137p

**Riley, Robert Thomas, 1851–1944**

MEMOIRS. Winnipeg, C.S. Riley, 1947. 119p [BViPA MWU SSU

**Rintoul, Rev. David**

MEMOIR OF ROBERT POLLOK, A.M. Toronto, Cleland, 1845. 61p [NSWA OTU

**Ritchie, Mary Christine**

MAJOR-GENERAL SIR GEOFFREY TWINING. A Biographical Sketch and the Story of his East African Diaries. Montreal, Chapman, 1922. 102p [NSWA OTP QMSS

**Rivard, Edmond Samuel, 1861–**

NOTES ON THE LIFE OF REV. LAURENT E. RIVARD. By his son, ——. Montreal, Janes-Rondeau, 1944. 80p [OTP

**Roberton, Thomas Beattie, 1879–1936**

THE FIGHTING BISHOP, JOHN STRACHAN ... AND OTHER ESSAYS IN HIS TIMES. Ottawa, Graphic, 1926. 179p [BM BVaU NBFU OTU QMM

**Roberts, Charles George Douglas, 1860–1943**

THE CANADIAN WHO'S WHO. Ed. by Charles G.D. Roberts and Arthur L. Tunnell. Toronto, Trans-Canada Press, 1938–. [A continuing serial of irregular issue.] [BVaU NSHD OTP QMM

A STANDARD DICTIONARY OF CANADIAN BIOGRAPHY. The Canadian Who Was Who. Ed. by Charles G.D. Roberts and Arthur L. Tunnell. Toronto, Trans-Canada press, 1934–1938. 2v [No more pub.] [BM BVaU NBFU OTP QMM

**Roberts, Leslie, 1896–**

C.D. The Life and Times of Clarence Decatur Howe. Toronto, Clarke Irwin, 1957. 246p

MALTA SPITFIRE. The Story of a Fighter Pilot. By Flying Officer F. Beurling and Leslie Roberts. Toronto, Oxford U. Press, 1943. 235p [BM BVaU OTU QMSS

THESE BE YOUR GODS. Toronto, Musson, 1929. 319p [BVaU OTU QMM

**Roberts, Lloyd, 1884–1966**

THE BOOK OF ROBERTS. Toronto, Ryerson, 1923. 147p [BM BVaU NBFU OTP

**Roberts, Theodore Goodridge, 1877–1953**

LOYALISTS. A Compilation of Histories, Biographies, and Genealogies of United Empire Loyalists and their Descendants. Pt. 1. Toronto, Roberts, 1937–. [LC NBFU OTU

THIRTY CANADIAN V.C.'S. London, Skeffington, 1918. 96p [BM BVaU OLU

**Robertson, Jessie Ewart, 1859–1888**

A TEACHER'S LIFE: JESSIE E. ROBERTSON. With Extracts from her Diaries, Essays, and Letters. By her Sisters and Friends. Ed. by Robert McQueen. Hamilton, Griffin & Kidner, 1890. [OTUV

**Robertson, John Kellock, 1885–1958**

TAYVILLE. Toronto, Ryerson, 1932. 136p [BVaU NSHD OKQ

**Robertson, John Ross, 1841–1918**

THE DIARY OF MRS. JOHN GRAVES SIMCOE, Wife of the First Lieutenant-Governor of Upper Canada, 1792–6. Ed. by ——. Toronto, Briggs, 1911. 440p [BM BVaU LC NSHD OTU QMM

**Robertson, William Norrie, 1855–**

YUKON MEMORIES. Sourdough Tells of Chaos and Changes in the Klondike Vale. Toronto, Hunter Rose, 1930. 359p [BM BVaU NBFU OTP

**Robinson, Charles Walker, 1836–1924**

LIFE OF SIR JOHN BEVERLY ROBINSON, Chief Justice of Upper Canada. Toronto, Morang, 1904. 490p [BM BVaU LC NBFU OTP QMM

**Robinson, Judith**

TOM CULLEN OF BALTIMORE. Toronto, Oxford U. Press, 1949. 435p [BM BVaU LC NBFU OTP QMM

**Robinson, Noel, 1880–**

BLAZING THE TRAIL THROUGH THE ROCKIES. The Story of Walter Moberley and his Share in the Making of Vancouver. Vancouver, News-Advertiser, 1913. 118p [BVaU LC NSHD OTP QMM

**Robson, Elizabeth**

EARLY DAYS IN CANADA. London, Stockwell, 1939. 108p [BM OTU

**Roe, Rev. Henry, 1829–1909**

MEMOIR OF THE REV. ARCHIBALD CAMPBELL SCARTH. Sherbrooke, Stevens & Price, 1904. 46p [OTU

**Rogers, Robert, 1731–1795**

JOURNALS OF MAJOR ROBERT ROGERS ... during the Late War. London, Author, 1765. 236p [New ed. by Franklin B. Hough. Albany, Munsell, 1883. 297p] [BM LC NSHD OLU

REMINISCENCES OF THE FRENCH WAR. Containing Rogers' Expeditions with the New-England Rangers ... as published in London in 1765. To which is added an Account of the Life ... of Maj. Gen. John Stark. Concord, N.H., Luther Roby, 1831. 275p [BM BVaU LC NBFU OTP QMM

**Roher, Martin, 1924–1954**

DAYS OF LIVING. The Journal of Martin Roher. Ed. by Joseph Pollick. Toronto, Ryerson, 1959. xii + 145p

**Rokeby-Thomas, Rev. Howard Rokeby, 1907–**

CHRONICLES OF THE ROOKS AND RAVENS. [Port Stanley, Ont.?], Author, 1951. 1v. (unpaged) [Genealogy of Thomas, Rokeby, and related families.]

**Rolph, William Kirby, 1917–1953**

HENRY WISE WOOD OF ALBERTA. Toronto, U. of Toronto Press, 1950. 235p [BM BVaU NSHD OTU

**Romaniuk, Gus, 1902–**

TAKING ROOT IN CANADA. An Autobiography. Winnipeg, Columbia Press, 1954. 283p

**Rose, George MacLean, 1829-1898**

A CYCLOPAEDIA OF CANADIAN BIOGRAPHY. Being Chiefly Men of the Time. Ed. by ——. Toronto, Rose, 1886–1919. 3v [Cover title: REPRESENTATIVE CANADIANS.] [BM BVaU LC NBFU OTP QMM

IN MEMORY OF THE LATE HON. WILLIAM COSTELLO KENNEDY, P.C., M.P. Toronto, Hunter Rose, 1923. [OLU

**Rosewarne, Winnifred Marguerite (Grindell), 1892–**

THE FAMILY HISTORY OF HENRY GRINDELL AND HIS DESCENDANTS, 1832–1956. By Winnifred & Robert Rosewarne. Ottawa, Authors, 1957. viii + 65 + 13p [mimeographed]

**Ross, Alexander, 1783–1856**

LETTERS OF A PIONEER, ALEXANDER ROSS. Ed. by George Bryce. Winnipeg, Manitoba Free Press, 1903. 15p [BViPA LC OTP

**Ross, Alexander Milton, 1832–1897**

MEMOIRS OF A REFORMER (1832–1892). Toronto, Hunter Rose, 1893. 271p [BVaU NBFU OTP

RECOLLECTIONS AND EXPERIENCES OF AN ABOLITIONIST, FROM 1855–1865. Toronto, Rowsell & Hutchinson, 1875. 224p [BM NSWA OTP

**Ross, Mrs. Anna**
THE MAN WITH THE BOOK; or, Memoirs of "John Ross of Brucefield." Toronto, McLean, 1897. 264p [BVaU OTP

**Ross, George William, 1841–1914**
GETTING INTO PARLIAMENT AND AFTER. Toronto, Briggs, 1913. 342p [BM BVaU NSWA OTU

**Ross, Hugh Robert, 1870–1937**
THIRTY-FIVE YEARS IN THE LIMELIGHT. Sir Rodmond P. Roblin and his Times. ... Winnipeg, Farmer's Advocate, 1936. 205p [BM BViPA OTP

**Ross, J.L.W.**
MEDICAL STUDENT'S LETTERS TO HIS PARENTS. By "Scugog" [pseud]. Toronto, Murray Print., 1909. 139p [OTP SSU

**Ross, James K.M.**
BOOTS AND SADDLES. The Story of the Fabulous Ross Stable in the Golden Days of Racing. New York, Dutton, 1956. 272p

**Ross, Margaret, 1846?–1935**
SIR GEORGE W. ROSS. A Biographical Sketch. Toronto, Ryerson, 1923. 195p [BM BVaU OTP

**Ross, Philip Dansken, 1858–1949**
RETROSPECTS OF A NEWSPAPER PERSON. Toronto, Oxford U. Press, 1931. 327p [BVaU LC NSHD OTP QMM

**Ross, Victoria (Burrill), 1877–**
MOMENTS MAKE A YEAR. Sackville, Tribune, [1958]. 216p [Log of Mount Allison Ladies College]

**Rouse, Rev. John James, 1869–**
PIONEER WORK IN CANADA, PRACTICALLY PRESENTED. Kilmarnock, Scotland, Ritchie, 1935. 181p [Autobiography.] [AEP BVaU OTU

**Rowley, Owsley Robert, 1868–1949**
THE HOUSE OF BISHOPS. Portraits of the Living Archbishops and Bishops of the Church of England in Canada. Comp. by ——. Montreal, Morton Phillips, 1907. 55p [BM BVaU NSWA OLU

**Roy, James Alexander, 1884–**
THE HEART IS HIGHLAND. Toronto, McClelland, 1947. 262p [BVaU NBFU OTP QMBM
JOSEPH HOWE. A Study in Achievement and Frustration. Toronto, Macmillan, 1935. 347p [BM BVaU LC NSHD OTP QMBM

**Rundle, Edwin George, 1838–**
A SOLDIER'S LIFE. Being ... Personal Reminiscences. Toronto, Briggs, 1909. 127p [BVaU BViPA LC OTU

**Russell, Benjamin, 1849–1935**

AUTOBIOGRAPHY OF BENJAMIN RUSSELL. Halifax, Royal, 1932. 307p [BM BVaU LC NSWA OTP QMM

NOVA SCOTIA BLUE BOOK AND ENCYCLOPAEDIA. Toronto, Historical Pub. Assoc., 1932. 127p [LC NSWA OTU

**Russell, Rev. George Stanley, 1883–1957**

THE ROAD BEHIND ME. Toronto, Macmillan, 1936. 287p [BM BVaU LC OTP

**Rutledge, Stanley**

PEN PICTURES FROM THE TRENCHES. Toronto, Briggs, 1918. 125p [BM BVaU OKQ

**Ryder, Mrs. Huia Gwendoline, 1904–**

EDWARD JOHN RUSSELL, MARINE ARTIST. With a Catalogue of the Artist's Marine Paintings compiled by George MacBeath. Saint John, New Brunswick Museum, 1953. 27p

**Ryerson, Rev. Adolphus Egerton, 1803–1882**

CHRISTIANS ON EARTH AND IN HEAVEN ... Discourse delivered in ... Toronto ... October 29th, 1848, on the Occasion of the death of Mrs. Sanderson, late wife of the Rev. Geo. Sanderson, Ed. of the "Christian Guardian." Toronto, 1848. 34p [OTU

MY DEAREST SOPHIE. Letters from Egerton Ryerson to his Daughter. Ed. by C.B. Sissons. Toronto, Ryerson, 1955. xxxvi + 350p

"THE STORY OF MY LIFE." ... Being Reminiscences of Sixty Years' Public Service in Canada. Prepared under the Supervision of his Literary Trustees. ... Ed. by J. George Hodgins. Toronto, Briggs, 1883. 612p [BM BVaU LC NBFU OTP QMM

**Ryerson, Geoffrey Parker**

MEMOIRS OF A CANADIAN SECRETARY. Toronto, Greenleaf & Kirkland, 1928. 42p [NBSM QMBM

**Ryerson, George Ansel Sterling, 1854–1925**

LOOKING BACKWARD. Toronto, Ryerson, 1924. 264p [BM BVaU NSHD OKQ

**Sage, Walter Noble, 1888–1963**

THE CHRONICLES OF THOMAS SPROTT. Kingston, 1916. 12p [BVaU NBFU OLU QMM

SIR ALEXANDER MACKENZIE AND HIS INFLUENCE ON THE HISTORY OF THE NORTHWEST. Kingston, Jackson, 1922. 18p [BVaU LC NBFU OLU QMM

SIR GEORGE ARTHUR AND HIS ADMINISTRATION OF UPPER CANADA. Kingston, Jackson, 1918. 32p [BM BVaU LC NBFU OTP QMM

SIR JAMES DOUGLAS AND BRITISH COLUMBIA. Toronto, U. of Toronto Press, 1930. 398p [BM BVaU LC OTP QMM

**Sanders, Byrne Hope, 1902–**

EMILY MURPHY, CRUSADER ("JANEY CANUCK"). With intro. by Nellie L. McClung. Toronto, Macmillan, 1945. 355p [BM BVaU LC NBFU OKQ QMM

FAMOUS WOMEN. Carr, Hind, Gullen, Murphy. Toronto, Clarke Irwin, 1958. ix + 145p

**Sanderson, Camilla**

JOHN SANDERSON THE FIRST; or, A Pioneer Preacher at Home. ... With intro. by F.W. Wallace. Toronto, Briggs, 1910. 237p [BM BVaU OTP

**Sanderson, Rev. Joseph Edward, 1830–1913**

MESSENGERS OF THE CHURCH. ... Pioneer Missionaries. Toronto, Briggs, 1900–01. 2v [BVaU OTP

**Sandwell, Bernard Keble, 1876–1954**

THE MOLSON FAMILY. With a foreword by Herbert Molson. Montreal, priv. print., 1933. 256p [BM OTU QMM

**Sandys, Edwyn William, 1860–1909**

SPORTING SKETCHES. New York, Macmillan, 1905. 389p [BM BVaU LC

**Saskatchewan, University of**

ARTHUR SILVER MORTON. Professor of History and Librarian, 1914–40. Saskatoon, the University, 1943. 23p [BM BVaU NSHD OTU

**Saunders, Rev. Edward Manning, 1829–1916**

THE LIFE AND LETTERS OF THE RT. HON. SIR CHARLES TUPPER. Ed. by ——. London, Cassell, 1916. 2v [BM BVaU LC NBFU OTP QMM

THE LIFE AND TIMES OF REV. JOHN WISWALL, M.A., AN EPISCOPAL UNITED EMPIRE LOYALIST. Halifax, Nova Scotia Hist. Soc., 1908. 73p [NSWA

THREE PREMIERS OF NOVA SCOTIA: THE HON. J.W. JOHNSTONE, THE HON. JOSEPH HOWE, THE HON. CHARLES TUPPER. Toronto, Briggs, 1909. 628p [BM BVaU LC NBFU OTP QMM

**Savary, Alfred William, 1831–1920**

ANCESTRY OF GENERAL SIR WILLIAM FENWICK WILLIAMS OF KARS. Exeter, Pollard, 1911. 15p [NSWA OTU

A GENEALOGICAL AND BIOGRAPHICAL RECORD OF THE SAVARY FAMILIES ... AND OF THE SEVERY FAMILY. ... By A.W. Savary and L.A. Savary. Boston, Collins, 1893. 266p [Supplement pub.: Boston, 1905.] [BM NSWA OTP

**Scadding, Rev. Henry, 1813–1901**

EXTRACTS FROM THE DIARY OF THE REV. HENRY SCADDING, 1837–1838. Toronto, 1906. 32p [LC

THE FIRST BISHOP OF TORONTO. A Review and a Study. Toronto, Chewett, 1868. 85p [Life of John Strachan, D.D.] [BVaU OTU QMM

A MEMORIAL OF THE REV. WILLIAM HONEYWOOD RIPLEY, Classical Master in Upper Canada College. Toronto, 1849. [BibC

**Schofield, Mrs. Emily M.**

CHARLES DEBEVER SCHOFIELD, Late Bishop of British Columbia. Victoria, Author, 1941. 69p [BVaU OTU

**Schull, Joseph, 1910–**

BATTLE FOR THE ROCK. The Story of Wolfe and Montcalm. Toronto, Macmillan, 1960. 158p

THE SALT–WATER MEN. Canada's Deep-Sea Sailors. Toronto, Macmillan, 1957. 144p

**Schuster, Rev. Anselm, 1834?–1885**

THE LIFE AND LABOURS OF REV. ANSELM SCHUSTER. Ed. by David Mitchell. Belleville, Daily Intelligencer Steam Print., 1886. 167p [OOP

**Scott, Rev. Alexander Hugh, 1853–1931**

TEN YEARS IN MY FIRST CHARGE. Toronto, Hart, 1891. 357p [BVaU NBFU OTP

**Scott, Barbara Ann, 1928–**

SKATE WITH ME. Garden City, N.Y., Doubleday, 1950. 159p [OONL

**Scott, Duncan Campbell, 1862–1947**

JOHN GRAVES SIMCOE. Toronto, Morang, 1905. 241p [BM BVaU LC NSHD OTP QMM

WALTER J. PHILLIPS, R.C.A. Toronto, Ryerson, 1947. 59p [BVaU LC NBFU OTP QMM

**Scott, Rev. Frederick George, 1861–1944**

THE GREAT WAR AS I SAW IT. Toronto, Goodchild, 1922. 328p [BM BVaU NSWA OTP QMM

**Scott, Jonathan, 1744–1819**

A BRIEF VIEW OF THE RELIGIOUS TENETS AND SENTIMENTS, LATELY PUBLISHED AND SPREAD IN ... "TWO MITES" ... PUBLICATIONS OF MR. HENRY ALLINE. Halifax, Howe, 1784. 334p [NSHP QMBM

**Scott, Robert C.**

MY CAPTAIN OLIVER. A Story of Two Missionaries on the B.C. Coast. Toronto, United Church, 1947. 200p [BVaU OTU

**Scott, William Louis, 1862–1947**

THE MACDONNELLS OF LEEK, COLLACHIE, AND ABERCHALDER. Ottawa, Author, 1935. 12p [OTP

**Segall, Jean (Brown)**

WINGS OF THE MORNING. Toronto, Macmillan, 1945. 152p [Biography of Canadian pilot, Mark Henry Brown.] [BVa LC MWP

**Sellar, Robert, 1841–1919**

GEORGE BROWN AND CONFEDERATION. Huntingdon, Que., 1917. 32p [Same as following title?] [BVaU

GEORGE BROWN, THE GLOBE, CONFEDERATION. Toronto, Britnell, 1917. 32p [BVa OTP SSU

**Service, Robert William, 1874–1958**

HARPER OF HEAVEN. New York, Dodd Mead, 1948. 452p [V. 2 of Service's autobiography. See also: PLOUGHMAN OF THE MOON.] [BM BVaU LC OTU QMM

PLOUGHMAN OF THE MOON. An Adventure into Memory. New York, Dodd Mead, 1945. 472p [V. 1 of Service's autobiography. See also: HARPER OF HEAVEN.] [BM BVaU LC NSHD OKQ QMM

**Seton, Ernest Thompson, 1860–1946**

TRAIL OF AN ARTIST-NATURALIST. The Autobiography of ——. New York, Scribner, 1940. 412p [BM BVaU LC NBFU OTU QMM

**Shand, Margaret (Clark), 1851–1943**

THE SUMMIT AND BEYOND. By Margaret Clark Shand and Ora M. Shand. Caldwell, Idaho, Caxton Printers, 1959. xix + 326p

**Shanly, Walter, 1819–1899**

DAYLIGHT THROUGH THE MOUNTAIN. Letters and Labours of Civil Engineers, Walter and Francis Shanly. Ed. by Frank Norman Walker. Research by Gladys Chantler Walker. Montreal, Engineering Institute of Canada, 1957. xiii + 442p

**Shapiro, Lionel Sebastian Berk, 1908–1958**

THEY LEFT THE BACK DOOR OPEN. A Chronicle of the Allied Campaign in Sicily and Italy. Toronto, Ryerson, 1944. 191p [BM BVaU LC OTP QMM

**Sharcott, Margaret (Brampton), 1928–**

A PLACE OF MANY WINDS. London, Davies, 1960. 236p

**Sharman, Mrs. Lyon, 1872–**

SUN YAT-SEN, HIS LIFE AND ITS MEANING. A Critical Biography. New York, Day, 1934. 418p [BM BVaU LC OTU

**Shatford, Rev. Allan Pearson, 1873–1935**

HE ... YET SPEAKETH. Glimpses of the Life Work of Canon Allan P. Shatford. ... With an intro. by Dr. Arthur H. Moore. Toronto, Musson, 1938. 250p [BVaU OTU QMBM

**Shaw, Bertha Mary Constance, 1880–**

BORN TO GROW OLD. Timmins, Northern Stationery & Print., 1960. 163p

BROKEN THREADS. Memories of a Northern Ontario Schoolteacher. New York, Exposition Press, 1955. 153p

LAUGHTER AND TEARS. Memoirs from between the Limestone Hills and the Blue Georgian Bay, Ontario. New York, Exposition Press, 1957. 183p [Reminiscences of an Ontario schoolteacher.]

**Shaw, Lloyd Ethelbert, 1878–1960**

MY LIFE IN THE BRICK INDUSTRY. [Halifax?], Author, 1955. 92p

**Shaw, Margaret Mason, 1904–**

GEOLOGISTS AND PROSPECTORS. Toronto, Clarke Irwin, 1958. xi + 190p

HE CONQUERED DEATH. The Story of Frederick Grant Banting. Toronto, Macmillan, 1946. 111p [BVaU LC OTP QMM

**Shearwood, Mary Howard (Henderson), 1869–1962**

BY WATER AND THE WORD. A Transcription of the Diary of the Right Reverend J.A. Newnham ... while Plying the Waters and Ice Fields of Northern Canada in the Diocese of Moosonee. By Mrs. F.P. Shearwood. Toronto, Macmillan, 1943. 216p [BVaU LC MWP NSHPL OTP QMBM

**Shenton, Mrs. M.J. (Lodge)**

A BIOGRAPHICAL SKETCH OF THE LATE REV. JOB SHENTON. With Some of his Sermons and Lectures. Saint John, McMillan, 1902. 160p [NSWA

**Shepherd, Francis John, 1851–1929**

SIR WILLIAM OSLER, BART. Montreal, 1921. 105p [LC

REMINISCENCES OF STUDENT DAYS AND DISSECTING ROOM. Montreal, priv. print., 1919. 28p [QMM

**Shepherd, Peter**

WITH GLOWING HEARTS. True Stories of Canadians in the Making. Toronto, United Church of Canada, 1946. 138p [OTU

**Shier, Morley, 1888?–**

FIRESIDE MINING. A Compendium of Mining Stories. Vancouver, Author, 1958. 78p

**Shipley, Nancy (Sommerville)**

ANNA AND THE INDIANS. Toronto, Ryerson, 1955. 237p [Life of Anna, wife of Rev. Samuel Gaudin, missionary in northern Manitoba.]

FRANCES AND THE CREES. Toronto, Ryerson, 1957. ix + 181p [Life of Frances (Pickell) Stevens, wife of Dr. Fred Stevens, missionary in the Fisher River area, Manitoba. Covers the years 1897–1946.]

**Shortt, Adam, 1859–1931**

LORD SYDENHAM. Toronto, Morang, 1908. 367p [BM BVaU LC NSWA OTP QMM

**Shulman, Milton, 1913–**

HOW TO BE A CELEBRITY. [With] Caricatures by Vicky of the [London] *News Chronicle.* London, Reinhardt & Evans, 1950. 215p [OONL

**Sibbald, Susan (Mein), 1783–1866**

THE MEMOIRS OF SUSAN SIBBALD (1783–1812). Ed. by ... Francis Paget Hett. London, Lane, 1926. 339p [BM BVaU LC NSHD OTP QMM

**Sibbald, Thomas, 1810–1890**

REMINISCENCES OF A BRITISH NAVAL OFFICER. By an Old Salt [pseud]. Toronto, Bain, 1885. 124p [BM

**Sifton, Clifford, 1893–**

THE SIFTON FAMILY RECORD. Information that has been Collected from Miscellaneous Sources, pertaining to the Family of Charles and Rebecca Sifton, who came from County Tipperary, Ireland, to London Township, Middlesex County, in Upper Canada in 1819, and their Descendants and Espouses. Toronto, Author, 1956. 136p

**Sillitoe, Violet E. (Pelly)**

PIONEER DAYS IN BRITISH COLUMBIA. Reminiscences. Vancouver, Evans & Hastings, [1922?]. 32p [BVaU LC OTU QMM

**Simcoe, Elizabeth Posthuma (Gwillim), 1766–1850**

THE DIARY OF MRS. JOHN GRAVES SIMCOE, Wife of the First Lieutenant-Governor of ... Upper Canada, 1792–6. With Notes and a Biography by J. Ross Robertson. Toronto, Briggs, 1911. xxix + 440p [BM BVaU LC NSHD OTP QMM

A SIMCOE RELIC AMONG THE THOUSAND ISLES IN 1796. Fragment of a MS. Journal of Mrs. Simcoe. Ed. by Rev. H. Scadding. Toronto, 1896. 7p [OTP QMM

**Simcoe, John Graves, 1752–1806**

THE CORRESPONDENCE, WITH ALLIED DOCUMENTS RELATING TO HIS ADMINISTRATION OF UPPER CANADA. Coll. and ed. by E.A. Cruickshank. Toronto, Ontario Hist. Soc., 1923–1936. 5v [BM BVaU NSHD OTU QMM

**Sime, Jessie Georgina, 1880–**

BRAVE SPIRITS. By Georgina Sime and Frank Nicholson. London, priv. print., 1952. 165p

**Simmons, Mervin C.**

THREE TIMES AND OUT. Told by Private [Mervin C.] Simmons. Written by Nellie McClung. Toronto, Allen, 1918. 247p [BVaU LC OTU

**Simms, Lewis Wesley, 1885–**

A TRIBUTE TO THE MEMORY OF T.S. SIMMS, on the Occasion of the Centennial of his Birth. Saint John, Author, 1945. 49p [OTP

**Sinclair, Alexander, 1818–1897**

PIONEER REMINISCENCES. Toronto, Warwick & Rutter, 1898. 22p [OTP

**Sinclair, Rev. Alexander Maclean, 1840–1924**

CLAN GILLEAN. ... Charlottetown, Haszard & Moore, 1899. 529p [BM NSHD

THE MACKENZIES OF APPLECROSS. Charlottetown, Mackenzie, 1901. 11p [NSWA

THE SINCLAIRS OF ROSLIN, CAITHNESS, AND GOSHEN. Charlottetown, Examiner, 1901. 44p [NSWA

**Sinclair, John H., 1848–**

CAPTAIN GEORGE McKENZIE. An Appreciation. Ottawa, Hope, [1920?]. 24p [BVaU NSWA OOP

THE LIFE OF JAMES WILLIAM CARMICHAEL, AND SOME TALES OF THE SEA. Halifax, Allen, [1911]. 180p [BM NSHD OTU

**Sinton, Robert, 1854–1952**

LOOKING BACKWARD FROM THE EIGHTIETH MILESTONE, 1935–1854. Memories Recalled. Regina, Paragon Business College, 1935. 102p [mimeographed] [SSU

**Sissons, Charles Bruce, 1879–1965**

EGERTON RYERSON. His Life and Letters. ... Toronto, Clarke Irwin, 1937–47. 2v [BM BVaU LC NBFU OTP QMM

LETTERS OF MARY LEWIS RYERSON FROM 1832–1942. Ed. by ——. Toronto, Victoria U. Library, 1948. 18p [BM NBFU OTUV

**Sissons, Constance (Kerr), 1875–**

JOHN KERR. Toronto, Oxford U. Press, 1946. 282p [BM BVaU LC NSHD OTP

**Sisterhood of St. John The Divine, Toronto**

A MEMOIR OF THE LIFE AND WORK OF HANNAH GRIER COOME, Mother-Foundress of the Sisterhood of St. John the Divine, Toronto, Canada. London, Oxford U. Press, 1933. 294p [OTP

**Skelton, Isabel (Murphy)**

ISAAC JOGUES. Toronto, Ryerson, 1928. 32p [BVa OTU

THE LIFE OF THOMAS D'ARCY McGEE. Gardenvale, Que., Garden City Press, 1925. 554p [BM BVaU NSHD OTP QMM

A MAN AUSTERE. William Bell, Parson and Pioneer. Toronto, Ryerson, 1947. 337p [BVaU LC NBFU OTP QMM

**Skelton, Oscar Douglas, 1878–1941**

THE DAY OF SIR WILFRID LAURIER. A Chronicle of our own Times. Toronto, Glasgow Brook, 1916. 340p [BM BVaU MWU NSWA OLU QMM

LIFE AND LETTERS OF SIR WILFRID LAURIER. Toronto, Gundy, 1921. 2v [BM BVaU LC MWU NBFU OTP QMM

THE LIFE AND TIMES OF SIR ALEXANDER TILLOCH GALT. Toronto, Oxford U. Press, 1920. 586p [BM BVaU NSWA OTP QMM

**Smallwood, Joseph Roberts, 1900–**
COAKER OF NEWFOUNDLAND. The Man who led the Deep-sea Fishermen to Political Power. London, Labour Pub. Co., 1927. 96p [BM OTU

**Smellie, George, 1811–1896**
MEMOIR OF THE REV. JOHN BAYNE, D.D., OF GALT. ... With Dr. Bayne's Essay on Man's Responsibility for his Belief. Toronto, Campbell, 1871. 139p [BVaU NSWA OTP

**Smith, Rev. Albert Edward, 1871–1947**
ALL MY LIFE. An Autobiography. Toronto, Progress Books, 1949. 224p [BVaU NfSM OTP QMBM

**Smith, George Havens, 1884–**
LOUIS BLAKE DUFF, THE COMPOSITE MAN. Port Colborne, Ont., priv. print., 1959. 23p

**Smith, Goldwin, 1823–1910**
THE MORAL CRUSADER, WILLIAM LLOYD GARRISON. Toronto, Williamson, 1892. 190p [BM BVaU LC NSWA OTU QMM
MY MEMORY OF GLADSTONE. Toronto, Tyrrell, 1904. 87p [BM BVaU NSHD OTU QMM
REMINISCENCES. Ed. by Arnold Haultain. New York, Macmillan, 1910. 477p [BM BVaU LC NSHD OTU QMM

**Smith, Henry Robert**
A GLIMPSE OF THE PAST. Ottawa, 1912. [Matthews

**Smith, Irving Norman, 1909–**
J.F.B. LIVESAY. A Memory. Ottawa, Mortimer, 1944. 53p [OTP QMM

**Smith, Rev. James Frazer, 1858–1948**
LIFE'S WAKING PART. Toronto, Nelson, 1937. 345p [LC OTP

**Smith, Nicholas**
FIFTY-TWO YEARS AT THE LABRADOR FISHERY. London, Stockwell, 1936. 199p [BVaU OTU

**Smith, Rev. Oswald Jeffrey, 1889–**
THE STORY OF MY LIFE. Toronto, Peoples Press, 1950. 104p [Title varies with later eds.] [LC SRL OLH

**Smith, Waldo Edward Lovel, 1901–**
WHAT TIME THE TEMPEST. An Army Chaplain's Story. Toronto, Ryerson, 1953. 305p

**Smith, William, 1728–1793**
HISTORICAL MEMOIRS OF WILLIAM SMITH, HISTORIAN OF THE PROVINCE OF NEW YORK, MEMBER OF THE GOVERNOR'S COUNCIL AND LAST CHIEF JUSTICE OF

THAT PROVINCE UNDER THE CROWN, CHIEF JUSTICE OF QUEBEC. Ed. with an intro., biography and notes by William H.W. Sabine. From the previously unpublished manuscript in the New York Public Library. New York, Colburn & Tegg, 1956–58. 2v

**Smith, William, 1859–1932**

POLITICAL LEADERS OF UPPER CANADA. Toronto, Nelson, 1931. 292p [BM BVaU NSHD OTU QMM

ROBERT GOURLAY. Kingston, Jackson, 1926. 20p [BM BVaU NBFU OLU QMM

**Smith, William Edward, 1864–1944**

A CANADIAN DOCTOR IN WEST CHINA. Forty Years under Three Flags. Toronto, Ryerson, 1939. 278p [BM OTU

**Smyth, Eleanor Caroline (Hill), 1831–1926**

AN OCTOGENARIAN'S REMINISCENCES. ... [Anon] N.p., Author, [1916]. 131p [BViPA

**Snider, David William, 1859–1924**

THE LIFE AND WORK OF W.K. SNIDER, GTR CONDUCTOR. Also Sermons and Lectures. Toronto, Briggs, 1898. 116p [BM OTP

**Snodgrass, Rev. William, 1827–1906**

THE NIGHT OF DEATH. A Sermon preached ... after the Funeral of the Hon. Peter M'Gill. Montreal, Owler, 1860. 37p [NSWA

SERMON ON THE DEATH OF HEW RAMSAY, ESQ. Montreal, Lovell, 1857. 27p [NSWA

**Snow, Samuel**

THE EXILE'S RETURN. Cleveland, Smead & Cowles, 1846. 32p [Autobiography of an 1837 rebel.] [QMBM

**Somers, Hugh Joseph, 1902–**

THE LIFE AND TIMES OF THE HON. AND RT. REV. ALEXANDER MACDONELL, First Bishop of Upper Canada, 1762–1840. Washington, Catholic Univ. of America, 1931. 232p [BVaU LC NSHD OLU

**Somerville, Alexander, 1811–1885**

THE AUTOBIOGRAPHY OF A WORKING MAN. By "One who has Whistled at a Plough." London, Gilpin, 1848. 511p [Later ed.: with an intro. by John Carswell. London, Turnstile Press, 1951. xxxiv + 283p] [BM BVaU LC OTU

CONSERVATIVE SCIENCE OF NATIONS. Being the First Complete Narrative of Somerville's Diligent Life in the Service of Public Safety in Britain. Montreal, Lovell, 1860. 320p [Extracted from his AUTOBIOGRAPHY.] [BM BVaU LC NSHD OTP QMM

NARRATIVE OF AN EVENTFUL LIFE. A Contribution to the Conservative Science of Nations. Hamilton, 1863. 320p [OTP

**Soward, Frederic Hubert, 1899–**

MOULDERS OF NATIONAL DESTINIES. London, Oxford U. Press, 1938. 203p [Rev. ed.: London, Oxford U. Press, 1939. 248p] [BM BVaU OTU QMM

**Spaight, George**

TRIAL OF PATRICK J. WHELAN FOR THE MURDER OF THE HON. D'ARCY McGEE. ... Ottawa, Desbarats, 1868. 88p [NSWA

**Spark, Rev. Alexander, 1762–1819**

A SERMON. ... By the Late Rev. Alex. Spark, D.D. on the ... Day of his Death. Also a Funeral Sermon. [With intro. signed Daniel Wilkie.] Quebec, Neilson, 1819. 26p [Contains a biographical and bibliographical note.] [LC OTP

**Springett, Evelyn Cartier (Galt)**

FOR MY CHILDREN'S CHILDREN. Montreal, Unity, 1937. 204p [BM BViPA LC OTU QMM

**Sprott, Rev. John, 1790–1869**

MEMORIALS OF THE REV. JOHN SPROTT. Ed. by his son, George W. Sprott. Edinburgh, Morton, 1906. 232p [NSWA OOP

**Squair, John, 1850–1928**

THE AUTOBIOGRAPHY OF A TEACHER OF FRENCH. Toronto, U. of Toronto Press, 1928. 292p [BVaU OTP

**Stackhouse, Cyril, 1886–**

THE CHURCHES OF ST. JOHN THE DIVINE, DERBY (1859) – YALE (1860) IN THE CROWN COLONY OF BRITISH COLUMBIA, AND THEIR FIRST RECTOR, THE REVEREND WILLIAM BURTON CRICKMER, M.A. (Oxon.). Vancouver, Archives Society of Vancouver, 1960. 32p

**Stairs, William James, 1819–1906**

FAMILY HISTORY: STAIRS, MORROW, including Letters, Diaries, Essays, Poems, etc. Comp. by W.J. Stairs and Mrs. S.M. Stairs. Halifax, McAlpine, 1906. 264p [BVaU LC NSHD

**Stansford, Joshua**

FIFTY YEARS OF MY LIFE. Ilfracombe, Devon, Stockwell, 1952. 216p [Journal of a Newfoundland Fisherman between the Years 1904 and 1950.]

**Steele, Harwood Elmes Robert, 1897–**

THE MARCHING CALL. Toronto, Nelson, 1955. x + 249p

**Steele, Samuel Benfield, 1849–1919**

FORTY YEARS IN CANADA. Reminiscences of the Great North-West. London, Jenkins, 1915. 428p [BM BVaU LC NSHD OTP QMM

**Steeves, Dorothy Gretchen (Biersteker), 1895–**

THE COMPASSIONATE REBEL. Ernest E. Winch and his Times. Vancouver, Evergreen Press, 1960. xi + 227p

**Stephens, Hiram B.**

JACQUES CARTIER AND HIS FOUR VOYAGES TO CANADA. An Essay. Toronto, Musson, 1890. 163p [BM BVaU NBFU OTP QMM

**Stern, Karl, 1906–**

THE PILLAR OF FIRE. [An Autobiography.] New York, Harcourt, 1951. 310p

**Stevens, Gerald Francis, 1909–**

FREDERICK SIMPSON COBURN, R.C.A. Toronto, Ryerson, 1958. xi + 72p

THE OLD STONE HOUSE. Toronto, Ryerson, 1954. 119p

**Stevens, Muriel G.**

MRS. AGNES DENNIS, C.B.E. Her Life. [Halifax, 1938.] 13p [NSWA

**Stevenson, Lionel, 1902–**

THE WILD IRISH GIRL. The Life of Sydney Owenson, Lady Morgan, 1766–1859. London, Chapman & Hall, 1936. 330p [BM BVaU LC OKQ QMM

**Stevenson, Lloyd Grenfell, 1918–**

NOBEL PRIZE WINNERS IN MEDICINE AND PHYSIOLOGY, 1901–1950. New York, Schuman, 1953. xi + 291p

SIR FREDERICK BANTING. Toronto, Ryerson, 1946. 446p [BM BVaU LC NBFU OTP QMM

**Stevenson, Orlando John, 1869–1950**

REMINISCENCES. N.p., n.d. 32p [OTU

THE TALKING WIRE. New York, Messner, 1947. 207p [The story of Alexander Graham Bell.] [BM BVaU LC OTU

**Steward, Austin, 1794–**

TWENTY-TWO YEARS A SLAVE, and Forty Years a Freeman. Rochester, N.Y., Alling, 1857. 360p [Includes a Life of the Author while in Canada, 1831–1857.] [BM LC OTP

**Stewart, Frances (Browne), 1794–1872**

OUR FOREST HOME. Being Extracts from the Correspondence of the Late Frances Stewart. Ed. by her daughter, E.S. Dunlop. Toronto, Presbyterian Printing, 1889. 210p [Also: Montreal, Gazette, 1902. 300 + xcip] [BVa BVaU MWU OTP QMM

**Stewart, Margaret Dorothy (McCall), 1904–**

ASK NO QUARTER. A Biography of Agnes Macphail. By Margaret Stewart and Doris French. Toronto, Longmans, 1959. 311p

**Stokes, William Edward Herbert, 1869–1948**
THE RED MAN'S RELIGION, AND FIVE TRUE TALES OF MY HAPPY CAREER. Regina, Caxton Press, 1910. 78p [BVaU MWP QMBM

**Stong, Daniel Alexander, 1883–**
THE STONG GENEALOGY OF CANADA AND UNITED STATES. Weston, Ont., Author, 1958. 79p

**Story, Duncan Albert, 1853–**
THE DeLANCEYS. A Romance of a Great Family. With Notes on those Allied Families who Remained Loyal to the British Crown during the Revolutionary War. N.p., Author, 1931. 180p [NSHD OTP

**Stothers, Robert**
A BIOGRAPHICAL MEMORIAL TO ROBERT HENRY COWLEY, 1859–1927. Toronto, Nelson, 1935. xix + 151p [LC OTP
A TRIBUTE OF APPRECIATION TO THE MEMORY OF THE LATE LIEUT. ROBERT ERIC GREENE, of the 38th Ottawa Battalion, C.E.F. Ottawa, 1916. 11p [OTU

**Stovel, Joseph Hodder, 1880–**
A MINING TRAIL, 1902–1945. N.p., [1956?]. 68p

**Strachan, Rev. John, 1778–1867**
A SERMON ON THE DEATH OF THE HONORABLE RICHARD CARTWRIGHT. With a short Account of his Life. Preached at Kingston on the 3rd of September, 1815. Montreal, Gray, 1816. 56p [NSWA OTP
A SERMON PREACHED AT YORK ... THIRD OF JULY, ON THE DEATH OF THE LATE LORD BISHOP OF QUEBEC [Rev. Jacob Mountain, 1749–1825]. Kingston, Macfarlane, 1826. 34p [OTP

**Strang, Rev. Peter, 1856–1934**
AUTOBIOGRAPHY. Regina, Author, 1933. 53p [mimeographed] [MWP SSU

**Strange, Kathleen (Redman), 1896–1968**
NEVER A DULL MOMENT. By Harry and Kathleen Strange. Toronto, Macmillan, 1941. 373p [BVaU OTP QMM
WITH THE WEST IN HER EYES. The Story of a Modern Pioneer. Toronto, McLeod, 1937. 292p [Later ed., 1945, with added foreword and an epilogue.] [BM BVaU LC NBFU OTP QMM

**Strange, Thomas Bland, 1831–1925**
GUNNER JINGO'S JUBILEE. An Autobiography. 3rd ed. London, Macqueen, 1896. 346p [BM BVaU LC NSHD OTU

**Strange, William, 1902–**
INTO THE BLITZ. A British Journey. Toronto, Macmillan, 1941. 266p [BVaU OTP

**Strickland, Samuel, 1804–1867**

TWENTY-SEVEN YEARS IN CANADA WEST; or, The Experience of an Early Settler. By Major Strickland. Ed. by Agnes Strickland. London, Bentley, 1853. 2v [BM BVaU LC NSWA OTP QMM

**Strickland, William Thomas**

ADRIFT ... ON THE BANKS IN A DORY! St. John's, Author, 1953. 15p

**Stuart, Arabella Mary (pseud)**

ARABELLA'S LETTERS, TOGETHER WITH THE CONTENTS OF HER SMALL DIARY, 1823–1828. Ed. by Mrs. Percy Domville. Toronto, Musson, 1927. 300p [BM LC OTP QMBM

**Stuart, Campbell, 1885–**

OPPORTUNITY KNOCKS ONCE. London, Collins, 1952. 248p

**Stubbs, Roy St. George, 1907–**

LAWYERS AND LAYMEN OF WESTERN CANADA. Toronto, Ryerson, 1939. 197p [BVaU LC NSHD OTP

PRAIRIE PORTRAITS. Toronto, McClelland, 1954. ix + 176p

**Student Christian Movement of Canada**

THIS ONE THING. A Tribute to Henry Burton Sharman, ... 1865–1953. Prepared by a group of friends. Toronto, Student Christian Movement of Canada, 1959. 96p

**Swayze, James Frederick, 1907–1967**

THE FIGHTING LE MOYNES. Toronto, Ryerson, 1958. 201p

FRONTENAC AND THE IROQUOIS. The Fighting Governor of New France. Toronto, Macmillan, 1959. 158p

TONTY OF THE IRON HAND. Toronto, Ryerson, 1957. 194p [Story of Henri de Tonty]

**Swayze, Nansi, 1936–**

THE MAN HUNTERS: JENNESS, BARBEAU, WINTEMBERG. Toronto, Clarke Irwin, 1960. xi + 180p

**Symonds, Rev. Herbert, 1860–1921**

HERBERT SYMONDS. A Memoir. Comp. by Friends. Montreal, Renouf, 1921. 319p [BM OTU QMSS

**Symons, John, 1808–1902**

THE BATTLE OF QUEENSTON HEIGHTS. Being a Narrative of the Opening of the War of 1812, with Notices of the Life of Major-General Sir Isaac Brock. ... Toronto, Thompson, 1859. 39p [OTP QMM

**Tait, George, 1828–**

AUTOBIOGRAPHY OF G. TAIT, a Deaf Mute who first gave Instructions to the Deaf and Dumb in the City of Halifax. Halifax, Bowes, 1892. 32p [NSHD

**Tait, Rev. Robert Cowie, 1884–**

A LITTLE KNOWN CHAPTER IN CANADIAN HISTORY. Sherbrooke, Que., 1958. 12p [Story of the watchmaking industry, carried on in Lennoxville, Que., in the 19th century, by Charles and George Henry.]

**Taylor, Fennings, 1817–1882**

THE HON. THOS. D'ARCY McGEE. A Sketch of his Life and Death. Montreal, Lovell, 1864. 40p [New ed., rev. & enl., Montreal, Lovell, 1868. 60p] [BVaU MWU NBFU OTU

THE LAST THREE BISHOPS APPOINTED BY THE CROWN FOR THE ANGLICAN CHURCH OF CANADA. Montreal, Lovell, 1869. 281p [Also: Montreal, Dawson, 1870. 281p] [BM BVaU LC NSWA OLU QMM

PORTRAITS OF BRITISH AMERICANS. By W. Notman. ... With Biographical Sketches by Fennings Taylor. Montreal, Notman, 1865–68. 3v [BM BVaU NSWA OTP QMM

**Taylor, James P., fl. 1851–1899**

HOW A SCHOOLMASTER BECAME A CATHOLIC. Renfrew, Gravelle, 1889. 140p [Rev. ed.: Lindsay, Canada Post Book Dept., 1890. 214p] [OTP OTU

**Taylor, Thomas Griffith, 1880–**

JOURNEYMAN TAYLOR. The Education of a Scientist. Abridged and ed. by Alasdair Alpin MacGregor. London, Hale, 1958. 352p

WITH SCOTT. The Silver Lining. New York, Dodd Mead, 1916. 464p [BM LC OTU QMM

**Taylor, Rev. William, 1803–1876**

IN MEMORIAM. REV. WILLIAM TAYLOR. Montreal, Erskine Church, 1876. 51p [NSWA

**Thompson, George S., 1848–**

UP TO DATE; or, The Life of a Lumberman. Peterboro, Times Print., 1895. 126p [BVaU MWU OTUV

**Thompson, John Henry, 1853–**

GENEALOGY: THOMPSON-SPAFFORD, 1630–1830; CHASE-GORDON, 1788–1930; OSBORN-GADSBY, GADSBY-WOODCOCK. ... Comp. by ——. Thorold, Ont., Author, [1930?]. 120p [LC

**Thompson, Samuel, 1810–1886**

REMINISCENCES OF A CANADIAN PIONEER FOR THE LAST FIFTY YEARS. An Autobiography. Toronto, Hunter Rose, 1884. 392p [BM BVaU NSWA OTU QMM

**Thompson, Thomas, 1832–1909**

THE TWO YORKS; or, Sitting at the "King's Table." Written ... for his Golden Wedding. ... N.p., [1905?]. 36p [Deals with the Thompson family of Toronto.] [OTP

**Thomson, Dale C., 1923–**
ALEXANDER MACKENZIE, CLEAR GRIT. Toronto, Macmillan, 1960. 436p

**Thomson, Edward William, 1849–1924**
THE LETTERS OF EDWARD WILLIAM THOMSON TO ARCHIBALD LAMPMAN (1891–1897). Ed. with notes, a bibliography and other material on Thomson and Lampman by Arthur S. Bourinot. Ottawa, Editor, 1957. 49p

**Thomson, Watson, –1969**
PIONEER IN COMMUNITY. Henri Lasserre's contribution to the Fully Cooperative Society. Toronto, Ryerson, 1949. 123p [BVa OTP QMM

**Thornhill, Mary Elizabeth, 1865–**
BETWEEN FRIENDS. Toronto, Saunders, 1935. 252p [BVaU OTU QMM

**Throop, Herbert David, 1899–**
THROOP GENEALOGY. With Special Reference to the Throops of Grenville County, Ontario. ... Ottawa, Author, 1931. 33p [BM LC OTP

**Tolboom, Wanda (Neill)**
ARCTIC BRIDE. Toronto, Ryerson, 1956. x + 256p

**Tollemache, Stratford Haliday Robert Louis, 1864–1937**
REMINISCENCES OF THE YUKON. Toronto, Briggs, 1912. 316p [BM BVaU LC OTU

**Tomkinson, Constance, 1915–**
LES GIRLS. Boston, Little Brown, 1956. 274p

**Toronto, Ont. Baptist College. Alumni**
MEMOIR OF DANIEL ARTHUR McGREGOR, Late Principal of Toronto Baptist College. Pub. by the Alumni Association of Toronto Baptist College. Toronto, Dudley & Burns, 1891. 248p [BVaU NSWA OTP

**Toronto, Ont. Ryerson School. Old Boys' Association**
MEMORIAL OF SAMUEL McALLISTER, Principal of Ryerson School. ... 1877–1906. Toronto, The Association, 1907. 45p [NBFU

**Toronto, University of**
THE INSTALLATION OF CLAUDE THOMAS BISSELL, EIGHTH PRESIDENT, UNIVERSITY OF TORONTO, OCTOBER 1958. Toronto, U. of Toronto Press, 1958. 55p

**Toronto, University of. Victoria College**
IN MEMORIAM, MARGARET ADDISON, 1868–1940. Toronto, Clarke Irwin, 1941. 26p [UTQ'42

**Toronto Scottish Officers' Association**
COLONEL COLIN CLARKE HARBOTTLE, C.M.G., D.S.O., V.D. Ed. by H.M. Jackson. Toronto, the Association, 1958. 20p

**Townsend, Rev. Arthur Herbert, 1912–**

SOD-BUSTERS. New York, Vantage Press, 1957. 180p

**Townshend, Charles James, 1844–1924**

LIFE OF HONOURABLE ALEXANDER STEWART. N.p., n.d. 114p [NSWA

**Trotter, Beecham, –1933?**

A HORSEMAN AND THE WEST. Reminiscences as told to Arthur Hawkes. Toronto, Macmillan, 1925. 304p [BM BVaU OTU

**Tuck, Clyde Edwin**

BIOGRAPHICAL SKETCHES OF REPRESENTATIVE CITIZENS [OF NOVA SCOTIA] AND GENEALOGICAL RECORDS OF OLD FAMILIES. [V. 3 of David Allison's HISTORY OF NOVA SCOTIA. Halifax, Bowen, 1916. 3v] [BVaU LC NSWA OTP

**Tunnell, Arthur L.**

THE CANADIAN WHO'S WHO. Ed. by Charles G.D. Roberts and Arthur L. Tunnel. Toronto, Trans-Canada Press, 1938–. [A continuing serial of irregular issue.] [BVaU NSHD OTP QMM

A STANDARD DICTIONARY OF CANADIAN BIOGRAPHY. ... Ed. by Charles G.D. Roberts and Arthur L. Tunnell. Toronto, Trans-Canada Press, 1934–1938. 2v [No more pub.] [BM BVaU NBFU OTP QMM

**Tupper, Charles, 1821–1915**

A LETTER TO THE RIGHT HONOURABLE THE EARL OF CARNARVAN. ... London, Westerton, 1866. 78p [BVaU NSHD OTU

POLITICAL REMINISCENCES OF THE RIGHT HONOURABLE SIR CHARLES TUPPER. Transcribed and ed. by the late W.A. Harkin. With a Biographical Sketch. London, Constable, 1914. 303p [BM BVaU LC NSHD OTP

RECOLLECTIONS OF SIXTY YEARS. London, Cassell, 1914. 414p [BM BVaU LC NSWA OTU QMM

**Tupper, Charles Hibbert, 1855–1927**

SUPPLEMENT TO THE LIFE AND LETTERS OF THE RT. HON. SIR CHARLES TUPPER, BART. Toronto, Ryerson, 1926. 199p [BM BVaU NSHD OTU QMM

**Tupper, Ferdinand Brock**

FAMILY RECORDS. Containing Memoirs of Major-General Sir Isaac Brock, Lieut. E.W. Tupper, and Col. William de Vic Tupper. ... Guernsey, Barbet, 1835. 218p [BVaU NSHD OTU

THE LIFE AND CORRESPONDENCE OF MAJOR-GENERAL SIR ISAAC BROCK, K.B. Interspersed with Notices of ... Tecumseh; and Comprising Brief Memoirs of D. DeLisle Brock, Lieut. E.W. Tupper, R.N., and Colonel W. DeVic Tupper. Ed. by ——. London, Simpkin Marshall, 1845. 468p [2nd ed., "considerably enlarged," 492p] [BM BVaU NSHD OLU

**Tupper, Reginald H.**

VICTOR GORDON TUPPER. A Brother's Tribute. ... London, Oxford U. Press, 1921. 66p [BM BVaU NSHD

**Turnbull, John Fulton, 1894–**

HISTORY OF THE TURNBULL FAMILY OF DIGBY, NOVA SCOTIA. Agincourt, Book Society of Canada, 1960. 18 + 29p

**Turney, Stephen, 1811–1847**

THE REMARKABLE LIFE AND CONFESSIONS OF STEPHEN TURNEY, who was Executed at Toronto ... 1847, for ... Murder..... Reduced to Writing by J.B. Townsend, Police Constable. Also: The Confession of James Hamilton, who was Executed ... for ... Murder. Toronto, Townsend, 1847. 16p [OTP

**Tyre, Robert, 1908–**

SADDLEBAG SURGEON. The Story of Murrough O'Brien, M.D. Toronto, Dent, 1954. 261p

**Tyrrell, Mary Edith (Carey), 1870?–1945**

I WAS THERE. A Book of Reminiscences. Toronto, Ryerson, 1938. 131p [BVaU LC NSHD OTP

**Underhill, Frank Hawkins, 1889–1971**

JAMES SHAVER WOODSWORTH. Untypical Canadian. An Address. ... [Toronto], Ontario Woodsworth Memorial Foundation, 1944. 34p [NBFU OTP

**Unwin, Charles, 1829–1918**

AUTOBIOGRAPHICAL SKETCH. Toronto, 1910. [Matthews

**Urquhart, Hugh MacIntyre, 1880–1950**

ARTHUR CURRIE. The Biography of a Great Canadian. Toronto, Dent, 1950. xix + 363p [BVaU NSHD OONL

**VanDusen, Rev. Conrad, 1801?–1878**

THE INDIAN CHIEF. ... The Labours, Losses, Sufferings, and Oppression of Ke-zig-ko-e-ne-ne (David Sawyer), a Chief of the Ojibbeway Indians in Canada West. By Enemikeese [pseud]. London, Nichols, 1867. 204p [BVaU LC NSWA OTP QMM

THE PRODIGY. A Brief Account of the Bright Career of ... Dr. G.E.A. Winans. ... Toronto, Dredge, 1870. 171p [BVaU NSWA MWU OTP

THE SUCCESSFUL YOUNG EVANGELIST. An Account of the Brief but Brilliant Career of Wm. Henry Winans, Wesleyan Preacher. ... Toronto, Dredge, 1870. 168p [OTP

**Vaudry, Mary Olive**

A SKETCH OF THE LIFE OF CAPTAIN JOHN SAVAGE, J.P., First Settler in Shefford County, 1792. Also the Early History of St. John's Church, West Shefford, Que., 1821–1921. [Toronto, 1921?] 20p [OTU QMM

**Vaughan, Harold Withrow**

THE LIVING CHURCH. A Book in Memory of the Life and Work of Rev. Richard Davidson, Principal of Emmanuel College, Toronto. Ed. by ——. Toronto, United Church Pub. House, 1949. 193p [OTU

**Vaughan, Walter, 1865–1922**

THE LIFE AND WORK OF SIR W. VAN HORNE. New York, Century, 1920. 388p [Also in "Makers of Canada" series: Toronto, 1926. vol. 10.] [BM BVaU LC NSWA OTU QMM

**Verral, Charles Spain, 1904–**

MIGHTY MEN OF BASEBALL. New York, Aladdin Books, 1955. 140p

**Vieth, Frederick Harris Dawes, –1910**

RECOLLECTIONS OF THE CRIMEAN CAMPAIGN AND THE EXPEDITION TO KINBURN IN 1855. Including also Sporting and Dramatic Incidents in Connection with Garrison Life in the Canadian Lower Provinces. Montreal, Lovell, 1907. 308p [BM BVaU LC NSHD OOP

**Vining, Charles Arthur McLaren, 1897–**

BIGWIGS. Canadians Wise and Otherwise. By R.T.L. (Charles Vining). Toronto, Macmillan, 1935. 149p [BM BVaU LC OTP QMM

**Vonlandsburg, John G.**

"THE NOBLEMAN'S SON." THE LIFE AND ADVENTURES OF DR. JOHN G. VONLANDSBURG, BARON OF WORMSTALL, HANOVER AND HESSON CASTELL. Halifax, 1845. 108p [BibC

**Wade, G.V.**

A WHO'S WHO IN SASKATCHEWAN. A Biographical Directory. Ed. by ——. 1st. ed. Saskatoon, Western Canada Directories, 1958 [c1956]. 275p

**Wade, Mark Sweeten, 1858–1929**

MACKENZIE OF CANADA. The Life and Adventures of Alexander Mackenzie. London, Blackwood, 1927. 332p [BM BVaU LC NSHD OTU QMM

**Wakeham, Pius Joseph, 1910–**

SISTER THACKERY. St. John's, Dicks & Co., 1956. 349p

**Waldron, Malcolm Thomas, 1903–1931**

SNOW MAN. John Hornby in the Barren Lands. Boston, Houghton, 1931. 292p [BM BVaU LC OTU QMM

**Waldron, Samuel J.**

REMINISCENCES OF MY LIFE. Ed. by Frances Ebbs-Canavan. Victoria, Author, 1938. 29p [BVa OTU

**Walker, (Sergeant) Alexander, fl. 1848–1867**

HOURS OFF AND ON SENTRY; or, Personal Recollections of Military Adventure in Great Britain, Portugal and Canada. Montreal, Lovell, 1859. 248p [BVaU OTP

**Walker, Rev. William Wesley, 1858–1945**

BY NORTHERN LAKES. Reminiscences of Life in Ontario Mission Fields. Toronto, Briggs, 1896. 168p [BM BVaU LC NSWA OTU

**Wallace, Rev. Archer, 1884–1958**

CANADIAN HEROES OF MISSION FIELDS OVERSEAS. Toronto, Can. Council of Missionary Educ., 1920. 88p [BM NSWA OOP

DEEDS OF DARING. New York, Harper, 1934. 97p [LC OKQ QMSS

HANDS AROUND THE WORLD. New York, Smith, 1930. 134p [LC OKQ

HEROES OF PEACE. Toronto, Musson, 1929. 133p [BM LC OTP

I BELIEVE IN PEOPLE. New York, Round Table, 1936. 210p [BM LC OKQ

IN SPITE OF ALL. Toronto, Ryerson, 1944. 137p [BVa LC OTP QMM

MEN WHO PLAYED THE GAME. New York, Smith, 1931. 127p [BM LC OKQ

MORE STORIES OF GRIT. New York, Smith, 1930. 140p [Also: Toronto, Musson, 1930.] [BM BVaU LC NSHD OKQ

MOTHERS OF FAMOUS MEN. Toronto, Musson, 1931. 112p [BM LC OKQ

OVERCOMING HANDICAPS. New York, Doran, 1927. 140p [BM LC

POOR MEN WHO MADE US RICH. Toronto, Ryerson, 1933. 130p [BM LC OKQ

THE RELIGIOUS FAITH OF GREAT MEN. New York, Round Table, 1934. 217p [LC OKQ

STORIES OF GRIT. Toronto, Musson, 1925. 133p [BM LC OKQ

**Wallace, Elisabeth, 1910–**

GOLDWIN SMITH, Victorian Liberal. Toronto, U. of Toronto Press, 1957. x + 297p

**Wallace, Elizabeth, 1906–**

THE SINGING HEART. [A Biography of Mother Mary Ward, Foundress of the Institute of the Blessed Virgin Mary.] Toronto, Dent, 1954. 96p

**Wallace, Frederick William, 1886–1958**

ROVING FISHERMAN. An Autobiography, Recounting Personal Experiences in the Commercial Fishing Fleets and Fish Industry of Canada and the United States, 1911-1924. Gardenvale, Que., *Canadian Fisherman,* 1955. xxi + 512p

**Wallace, Rev. Isaiah, 1826–1907**

AUTO-BIOGRAPHICAL SKETCH. With Reminiscences of Revival Work. Halifax, Burgoyne, [1903]. 181p [NSHD

**Wallace, Paul Anthony Wilson, 1891–**

CONRAD WEISER, 1696–1760. Friend of Colonist and Mohawk. Philadelphia, U. of Penn. Press, 1945. 648p [BM LC OTU QMM

**Wallace, Robert Charles, 1881–1955**

SOME GREAT MEN OF QUEEN'S: GRANT, WATSON, DUPUIS, CAPPON, JORDAN, SHORTT. Ed. by ——. Toronto, Ryerson, 1941. 133p [BVaU NSHD OTU

**Wallace, William Stewart, 1884–1970**

THE DICTIONARY OF CANADIAN BIOGRAPHY. Comp. by ——. Toronto, Macmillan, 1926. 433p [2nd ed.: Toronto, Macmillan, 1945. 2v] [BM BVaU LC NSHD OTU QMM

A DICTIONARY OF NORTH AMERICAN AUTHORS DECEASED BEFORE 1950. Comp. by ——. Toronto, Ryerson, 1951. 525p

THE KNIGHT OF DUNDURN. Toronto, Rous & Mann, 1960. 22p [About Sir Allan MacNab, 1798–1862.]

THE MASERES LETTERS, 1766, 1768. Ed. by ——. Toronto, University Library, 1919. 131p [BM BVaU NSWA OTP

THE MEMOIRS OF THE RIGHT HON. SIR GEORGE FOSTER. Toronto, Macmillan, 1933. 291p [BM BVaU LC NSHD OTU QMM

SIR JOHN MACDONALD. Toronto, Macmillan, 1924. 132p [BM BVaU LC NSHD OTU QMM

THE STORY OF LAURA SECORD. A Study in Historical Evidence. Toronto, Macmillan, 1932. 26p [BVaU LC OLU

**Walsh, Leo J.**

DROSS REFINED. A Biography on the Life of "Fighting" Billy Matheson, Ex-pugilist and Ex-bartender. London, Ont., Hayden Press, 1932. 212p [OLU

**Walton, Jesse M.**

FROM THE AUCTION BLOCK ... TO THE ROSTRUM. The Life of William Allan. Aurora, Walton, 1938. 8p [OTU

**Warder, Richard C., 1901–**

NORTHERN EXPOSURE. Tales of the North Country. New York, Pageant Press, 1957. 179p

**Warnica, George and Phoebe**

MEMOIRS OF GEORGE AND PHOEBE WARNICA, PIONEERS OF INNISFIL. Ed. by A.F. Hunter. Barrie, Examiner, 1891. 28p [OTL

**Warren, Ernest Herbert Falkland, 1888?–**

SEVENTY SOUTH ALBERTA YEARS. ... Autobiography of ——, ... as written by S. Evangeline Warren. Ilfracombe, Devon, Stockwell, 1960. 255p

**Waterston, Margaret Elizabeth (Hillman), 1922–**

PIONEERS IN AGRICULTURE: Massey, McIntosh, Saunders. Toronto, Clarke Irwin, 1957. 136p

**Waterton, William Arthur, 1916–**

THE QUICK AND THE DEAD. London, F. Muller, 1956. 237p

**Watetch, Abel, 1883–**

PAYEPOT AND HIS PEOPLE. As told to Blodwen Davies. Regina, Saskatchewan History and Folklore Soc., 1959. 66p

**Watkin, Edward William, 1819–1901**

ALDERMAN COBDEN OF MANCHESTER. Letters and Reminiscences of Richard Cobden. New York, Ward Lock, 1891. 218p [BM LC

CANADA AND THE STATES. Recollections, 1851 to 1886. New York, Ward Lock, 1887. 524p [BM BVaU LC NSWA OTU QMM

**Watson, Albert Durrant, 1859–1926**

ROBERT NORWOOD. Toronto, Ryerson, 1923. 124p [BM BVaU LC NSHD OTU

**Watson, William Ritchie, 1904–**

I GIVE YOU YESTERDAY. Toronto, Macmillan, 1938. 238p [BVaU OTU

MY DESIRE. Edmonton, U. of Alberta Press, 1932. 84p [AEU OTU

**Watson, William Robinson, 1887–**

MAURICE CULLEN, R.C.A. A Record of Struggle and Achievement. Toronto, Ryerson, 1931. 45p [QMM

**Waugh, William Templeton, 1884–1932**

JAMES WOLFE, MAN AND SOLDIER. Montreal, Carrier, 1928. 333p [BM BVaU LC NSWA OTU QMM

**Weaver, Emily Poynton, 1865–1943**

BUILDERS OF THE DOMINION. Men of the East. Toronto, Copp Clark, 1904. 116p [BM NBFU

**Webling, Peggy**

PEGGY. The Story of One Score Years and Ten. London, Hutchinson, 1924. 303p [BM OTL

**Webster, John Clarence, 1863–1950**

THE CAREER OF THE ABBE LE LOUTRE IN NOVA SCOTIA. With a Translation of his Autobiography. Shediac, priv. print., 1933. 50p [BM BVaU NBFU OTU QMM

CHARLES DES CHAMPS DE BOISHEBERT. A Canadian Soldier in Acadia. Priv. print., 1931. 38p [BM BVaU NSWA OTU QMM

CORNELIS STEENWYCK, DUTCH GOVERNOR OF ACADIE. ... Shediac, priv. print., 1929. 12p [BVaU NSWA OLU QMM

EDINBURGH MEMORIES AND ROBERT LOUIS STEVENSON. Sackville, Tribune Press, 1943. 19p [BVaU NBFU OTP QMM

THE JOURNAL OF JOSHUA WINSLOW ... 1760. Ed. by ——. Saint John, New Brunswick Museum, 1936. 40p [NBFU OTU QMBM

JOURNALS OF BEAUSEJOUR: DIARY OF JOHN THOMAS: JOURNAL OF LOUIS DE COURVILLE. Ed. by ——. Sackville, Tribune, 1937. 54p [BVaU LC NSWA OLU QMM

LIFE OF JOHN MONTRESOR. Ottawa, Royal Soc. of Canada, 1928. 31p [BVaU NBSM OKQ

THE LIFE OF JOSEPH FREDERICK WALLET DES BARRES. Shediac, priv. print., 1933. 70p [BM BVaU LC NSWA OTU QMM

SAMUEL VETCH. [First British Governor of Nova Scotia after the Conquest of 1710]. An Address. Shediac, priv. print., 1929. 23p [BM BVaU NSWA OTP

SIR BROOK WATSON. Friend of the Loyalists, first Agent of New Brunswick in London. Sackville, Mount Allison University, 1924. 25p [BM BVaU NSWA OTP QMM

THOMAS PICHON. "The Spy of Beausejour." Sackville, Tribune, 1937. 161p [BM BVaU LC NSWA OTP QMM

THOSE CROWDED YEARS, 1863–1944. Shediac, priv. print., 1944. 51p [Reminiscences.] [BVaU LC NBFU OTP

WILLIAM FRANCIS GANONG MEMORIAL. Ed. by ——. Saint John, New Brunswick Museum, 1942. 31p [BVaU LC NBFU OTU QMM

WOLFE AND THE ARTISTS. A Study of his Portraiture. Toronto, Ryerson, 1930. 74p [BM BVaU LC NSHD OTU

WOLFIANA. A Potpourri of Facts and Fantasies. Arranged by ——. Shediac, priv. print., 1927. 47p [BM BVaU LC NSWA OTU QMM

**Webster, Rev. Thomas, 1809–1901**

LIFE OF REV. JAMES RICHARDSON. Bishop of the Methodist Episcopal Church in Canada. Toronto, Magurn, 1876. 240p [BVaU LC OTP

**Weekes, Mrs. Mary Loretto, 1885–**

THE LAST BUFFALO HUNTER. As Told to her by Norbert Welsh. Toronto, Nelson, 1939. 304p [BViPA OTU QMSS

**Weir, John, 1906–**

BARD OF UKRAINE. An Introduction to the Life and Works of Taras Shevchenko. Toronto, National Jubilee Committee of the Association of United Ukrainian Canadians, 1951. 64p

**Weir, William, 1823–1905**

SIXTY YEARS IN CANADA. Montreal, Lovell, 1903. 268p [BM BVaU NSWA OTU QMM

**Weldon, William S., 1883–**

THE FAMILY OF WELDON IN CANADA, 1732–1952. Including their Lineage to the First Progenitor in England, in 1066 A.D. Altona, Man., D.W. Friesen, 1953. x + 125p

**Wells, Clifford Almon, 1892–1917**

FROM MONTREAL TO VIMY RIDGE AND BEYOND. The Correspondence of Lieut. Clifford Almon Wells B.A. of the 8th Battalion, Canadian B.E.F. Ed. by O.C.S. Wallace. Toronto, McClelland, 1917. 321p [BVaU LC NSHD OTU

**Wells, Daniel**

CAMP FIRES GLEAMING. New York, Outing Pub. Co., 1911. 142p [OONL

**Wells, James Edward, 1836–1898**

LIFE AND LABORS OF ROBERT ALEX. FYFE, D.D. Founder and ... Principal of the Canadian Literary Institute, now Woodstock College. ... Toronto, Gage, [189–?]. 466p [BVaU NSWA OTP

**Welton, Rev. Daniel Morse, 1831–1904**

JOHN LIGHTFOOT, THE ENGLISH HEBRAIST. An Historical Essay Presented to Obtain the Doctorate of Philosophy. Leipzig, Ackermann, 1878. 47p [BM NSWA

**Weston, Thomas Chesmer, 1832–1911**

REMINISCENCES AMONG THE ROCKS. In Connection with the Geological Survey of Canada. Toronto, Warwick, 1899. 328p [BM BVaU LC OTU QMM

**Wheeler, Frances Ellen, 1895–**

THE AWAKENING OF THE LAURENTIANS. A Fabulous Woman, Lucile Wheeler, and her Family who made the Laurentians Famous. New York, Vantage Press, 1958. 93p

**Whidden, David Graham, 1857–1941**

GENEALOGICAL RECORD OF THE ANTIGONISH WHIDDENS. Wolfville, n.p., 1930. 24p [NSWA OTU

**Whillans, Rev. James William, 1880–1954?**

FIRST IN THE WEST. The Story of Henry Kelsey, Discoverer of Canadian Prairies. Edmonton, Applied Art Products, 1955. 175p

**Whitaker, Rev. George, 1810?–1882**

A SERMON ... ON OCCASION OF THE DEATH OF THE REV. THOMAS SMITH KENNEDY. ... Toronto, Rowsell & Ellis, 1863. 12p [OTP

**White, James Edward, 1822–**

A GENEALOGICAL HISTORY OF THE DESCENDANTS OF PETER WHITE OF NEW JERSEY, FROM 1670, AND OF WILLIAM WHITE AND DEBORAH TILTON, HIS WIFE, LOYALISTS. Saint John, Barnes, 1906. 89p [BVaU LC NSHD OTU

**White, Rev. William Charles, 1873–1960**

CANON CODY OF ST. PAUL'S CHURCH. Toronto, Ryerson, 1953. 220p

**Whiteside, William Carleton, 1900–**

THE NOMADIC LIFE OF A SURGEON. Edmonton, Douglas Print., 1950. 89p [OONL

**Whittaker, Rev. Charles Edward, 1864–1947**

ARCTIC ESKIMO. A Record of Fifty Years' Experience & Observation among the Eskimo. ... London, Seeley Service, 1937. 259p [BM BVaU OTP

**Wicksteed, Gustavus William, 1799–1898**

IN MEMORIAM. GEORGE ETIENNE CARTIER. Ottawa, 1885. 19p [BM OOP QMBM

**Wigle, Rev. Hamilton A., 1858–1934**

HISTORY OF THE WIGLE FAMILY AND THEIR DESCENDANTS. ... Ed. by ——. N.p., 1931. 248p [OTP

THE LIFE STORY OF FINLAY BOOTH. Toronto, Briggs, 1900. 123p [Another ed., bound with A NIGHT ON THE PRAIRIE. By R. Dezell. Toronto, Briggs, 1907. 55p] [BM BVaU NSHD OTU

**Wild, Roland Gibson, 1903–**

AMOR DE COSMOS. Toronto, Ryerson, 1958. xi + 146p

ARCTIC COMMAND. The Story of Smellie of the *Nascopie*. Toronto, Ryerson, 1955. xxii + 194p

**Wilkes, Rev. Henry, 1805–1886**

DEATH IN THE CITY. Address at the Funeral of the late John Easton Mills, Mayor of the City of Montreal. ... Montreal, Becket, 1848. 19p [BM QMM

**Wilkinson, Anne Cochran (Boyd), 1910–1961**

LIONS IN THE WAY. A Discursive History of the Oslers. Toronto, Macmillan, 1956. 274p

**Willinsky, Abraham Isaac, 1885–**

A DOCTOR'S MEMOIRS. Toronto, Macmillan, 1960. x + 183p

**Willis-O'Connor, Henry, 1886–**

INSIDE GOVERNMENT HOUSE. As Told by Colonel H. Willis-O'Connor to Madge Macbeth. Toronto, Ryerson, 1954. xi + 163p

**Willison, John Stephen, 1856–1927**

REMINISCENCES, POLITICAL AND PERSONAL. Toronto, McClelland, 1919. 351p [BM BVaU LC NSHD OTU QMM

SIR GEORGE PARKIN. A Biography. London, Macmillan, 1929. 278p [BM BVaU NSHD OTP QMM

SIR WILFRID LAURIER. Toronto, Oxford U. Press, 1926. 472 + 526p [First 27 chapters "were ... published in ... 1903."] [BM BVaU LC OTU

SIR WILFRID LAURIER AND THE LIBERAL PARTY. A Political History. Toronto, Morang, 1903. 2v [BM BVaU NSHD OTP QMM

**Willson, David, 1778?–1866**

A COLLECTION OF ITEMS OF THE LIFE OF DAVID WILLSON. From the Year 1801 to 1852. ... Newmarket, Porter, 1852. 10p [OTP

THE PRACTICAL LIFE OF THE AUTHOR, FROM THE YEAR 1801 TO 1860. Newmarket, Jackson, 1860. 80p [OTP

**Willson, (Henry) Beckles, 1869–1942**

FROM QUEBEC TO PICCADILLY. ... Some Anglo-Canadian Memories. ... London, Cape, 1929. 366p [BM BVaU NSHD OTP

THE LIFE AND LETTERS OF JAMES WOLFE. London, Heinemann, 1909. 522p [BM BVaU LC NSWA OTP QMM

THE LIFE OF LORD STRATHCONA & MOUNT ROYAL. ... London, Cassell, 1915. 631p [BM BVaU LC NBFU OTU QMM

LORD STRATHCONA, THE STORY OF HIS LIFE. ... London, Methuen, 1902. 288p [BM BVaU LC NSHD OTU

**Wilson, Daniel, 1816–1892**

THE LIFE OF JANE McCREA. With an Account of Burgoyne's Expedition in 1777. New York, Baker, 1853. 155p [OTL

REMINISCENCES OF OLD EDINBURGH. Edinburgh, Hamilton, 1878. 2v [BM BVaU LC OTU

WILLIAM NELSON. A Memoir. Edinburgh, Nelson, 1889. 254p [BM OTP

**Wilson, George Earl, 1891–**

THE LIFE OF ROBERT BALDWIN. A Study in the Struggle for Responsible Government. Toronto, Ryerson, 1933. 312p [BM BVaU LC NSHD OTP QMM

**Wilson, Herbert Emerson, 1881–**

I STOLE $16,000,000. New York, New American Library, 1956. 141p

**Wilson, Rev. Robert, 1833–1912**

PIETY PORTRAYED IN THE LIVES AND DEATHS OF MR. AND MRS. ISAAC BURPEE OF SHEFFIELD, N.B. Saint John, Chubb, 1870. 14p [NBB

**Winnipeg Free Press**

JOHN WESLEY DAFOE. Editor-in-Chief, Winnipeg Free Press, 1901–1944. Winnipeg, Free Press, 1944. 42p [OTP

**Winslow, Edward, 1746–1815**

WINSLOW PAPERS, A.D. 1778–1826. Ed. by Rev. W.O. Raymond. Saint John, Sun Print., 1901. 732p [BM BVaU NSWA OTP QMM

**Winslow, Joshua, 1727–1801**

THE JOURNAL OF JOSHUA WINSLOW. Recording his Participation in the Events of the Year 1750. Ed. with Intro. and Notes by Dr. J.C. Webster. ... Saint John, New Brunswick Museum, 1936. 40p [BM BVaU LC NSHD OTU QMM

**Winter, Charles Francis, 1863–1946**

LIEUTENANT-GENERAL SIR SAM HUGHES. ... Canada's War Minister, 1911–1916. Toronto, Macmillan, 1931. 182p [BM BVaU LC NBFU OTUV

**Withrow, Rev. William Henry, 1839–1908**

BEACON LIGHTS OF THE REFORMATION. Toronto, Briggs, 1899. 304p [BM NSHD OTP QMM

WORTHIES OF EARLY METHODISM. Toronto, Rose, 1878. 165p [OTP

**Wood, Edgar Allardyce, 1907–**

THE GREAT CHIEF. Maskepetoon, Warrior of the Crees. By Kerry Wood [pseud]. Toronto, Macmillan, 1957. 160p

THE MAP-MAKER. The Story of David Thompson. By Kerry Wood [pseud]. Toronto, Macmillan, 1955. 185p

THE QUEEN'S COWBOY. Colonel Macleod of the Mounties. By Kerry Wood [pseud]. Toronto, Macmillan, 1960. 157p

THE SANCTUARY. By Kerry Wood [pseud]. Red Deer, Alta., Author, 1952. 105p

**Wood, Rev. John**

MEMOIR OF HENRY WILKES. His Life and Times. Montreal, Grafton, 1887. 280p [BM BVaU NSWA OTU QMSS

**Wood, Louis Aubrey Lorne, 1883–1955**

THE WAR CHIEF OF THE SIX NATIONS. A Chronicle of Joseph Brant. ... Toronto, Glasgow Brook, 1914. 147p [BM BVaU LC NSWA OTU QMM

**Wood, William Charles Henry, 1864–1947**

THE FATHER OF BRITISH CANADA. A Chronicle of Carleton. Toronto, Glasgow Brook, 1916. 239p [BM BVaU LC NSWA OTU QMM

MONTCALM. The Hero of a Lost Cause. Toronto, Morang, 1912. 154p [BM

THE PASSING OF NEW FRANCE. A Chronicle of Montcalm. ... Toronto, Glasgow Brook, 1914. 149p [BM BVaU LC NSWA OOA QMM

THE WINNING OF CANADA. A Chronicle of Wolfe. Toronto, Glasgow Brook, 1914. 152p [BM BVaU LC NSWA OOA QMM

WOLFE. The Hero of Quebec. Toronto, Robert Glasgow, 1912. 156p [BM OOP

**Woodruff, Norris Counsell, 1901–**

TWELVE GENERATIONS FROM THE COLONY OF CONNECTICUT IN NEW ENGLAND AND THE PROVINCE OF UPPER CANADA, 1636–1959. A Woodruff Genealogy. Hamilton, Author, 1959. 101p

**Woods, Robert Stuart, 1819–1906**

THE CUTTING OUT OF THE CAROLINE AND OTHER REMINISCENCES OF 1837–38. N.p., [1885?]. 8p [OTP

**Woods, Walter Sainsbury, 1884–**

THE MEN WHO CAME BACK. A Book of Memories. Toronto, Ryerson, 1956. 175p

**Woodsworth, Rev. James, 1843–1917**

THIRTY YEARS IN THE CANADIAN NORTH-WEST. Toronto, McClelland, 1917. 259p [BM BVaU LC NSHD OTU QMM

**Woollacott, Arthur Philip, 1875–1958**

MACKENZIE AND HIS VOYAGEURS. By Canoe to the Arctic and the Pacific, 1789–93. Toronto, Dent, 1927. 237p [BVaU NBFU OTU QMM

**Worthington, Edward Dagge, 1820–1895**

REMINISCENCES OF STUDENT LIFE AND PRACTICE. Sherbrooke, Walton, 1897. 119p [OTU QMSS

**Wotherspoon, Mildred Faith (Cumberland)**

THE STORY OF A HOME, "DUNAIN," 1857–1957. [Port Hope, Ont.?], Author, 1958. 18p

**Wright, Esther Isabell (Clark), 1895–**

ALEXANDER CLARK, LOYALIST. A Contribution to the History of New Brunswick. Kentville, Kentville Pub. Co., 1940. 81p [BVaU NBFU OTU

GRANDMOTHER'S CHILD. The Life of Harriet H.R. Clark. Ottawa, Author, 1959. 110p

THE LOYALISTS OF NEW BRUNSWICK. Fredericton, Author, 1955. 365p

**Wright, Frederick Keays, 1865–**

GENEALOGY OF THE WRIGHT FAMILY, 1631–1950. Calgary, Albertan Printers, 1950. 28p [Revision to 1950 of his GENEALOGY OF THE WRIGHT FAMILY 1631–1930.] [OONL

**Wrong, Edward Murray, 1889–1928**

CHARLES BULLER AND RESPONSIBLE GOVERNMENT. Oxford, Clarendon Press, 1926. 352p [BM BVaU NSHD OLU

**Wrong, George McKinnon, 1860–1948**

THE EARL OF ELGIN. London, Methuen, 1905. 300p [BVaU LC NSHD OTU QMM

**Wrong, Humphrey Hume, 1894–1954**

SIR ALEXANDER MACKENZIE. Explorer and Fur-Trader. By Hume Wrong. Toronto, Macmillan, 1927. 171p [BM BVaU LC NBFU OTU QMM

**York, Eva Rose (Fitch), 1858–**

WHEN MY DREAM CAME TRUE. A Brief Autobiography in which the Author is Seen Seeking and Finding Abiding Joy. Toronto, Evangelical Pub., 1935. 62p [OTU

**York County, Ont.**

COMMEMORATIVE BIOGRAPHICAL RECORD OF THE COUNTY OF YORK. Toronto, Beers, 1907. 673p [BVaU

**Youmans, Letitia (Creighton), 1827–1896**

CAMPAIGN ECHOES. The Autobiography of Mrs. Letitia Youmans, the Pioneer of the White Ribbon Movement in Canada. Toronto, Briggs, 1893. 311p [BM BVaU LC OTP QMM

**Young, Anna Grace Peterson, 1898–**

OFF WATCH. Today and Yesterday on the Great Lakes. Toronto, Ryerson, 1957. xviii + 156p

**Young, Archibald Hope, 1863–1935**

THE REVD. JOHN STUART, D.D., U.E.L., of Kingston, U.C., and his Family. A Genealogical Study. Kingston, Whig Press, 1920. 64p [BVaU LC NSHD OLU QMM

**Young, Rev. Arminius**

A METHODIST MISSIONARY IN LABRADOR. [Toronto], S. and A. Young, 1916. 180p [BM NSHD OTU

**Young, Rev. Egerton Ryerson, 1840–1909**

THE APOSTLE OF THE NORTH, REV. JAMES EVANS. New York, Revell, 1899. 262p [BM BVaU LC MWU NSWA OTP

THE BATTLE OF THE BEARS, AND REMINISCENCES OF LIFE IN THE INDIAN COUNTRY. London, Culley, 1907. 318p [BM LC OTU

**Young, Rev. George, 1821–1910**

MANITOBA MEMORIES ... 1868–1884. Toronto, Briggs, 1897. 364p [BM BVaU LC NSWA OKQ

**Young, James, 1835–1913**

PUBLIC MEN AND PUBLIC LIFE IN CANADA. The Story of the Canadian Confederacy. Being Recollections of Parliament and the Press. Toronto, Briggs, 1912. 2v [Earlier ed., in one vol., in 1902.] [BM BVaU NSWA OTU QMBM

**Yule, Pamelia S. (Vining), 1825?–1897**

SOWING AND REAPING; or, Records of the Ellisson Family. Toronto, Briggs, 1899. 404p [Ryerson Impt

**Ziegler, Olive Irene**

WOODSWORTH: SOCIAL PIONEER. Toronto, Ontario Pub. Co., 1934. 202p [BVaU OTP

# ESSAYS AND SPEECHES

Addresses, personal and general essays, nature writings, monographs, sketches, lectures, etc.

**Adamson, Rev. William Agar, 1800–1868**

SALMON-FISHING IN CANADA. By a Resident [pseud]. Ed. by Sir James Edward Alexander. London, Longman, 1860. 350p [BVaU NSWA OKQ QMM

**Alexander, William Hardy, 1878–1962**

THESE TWENTY-FIVE YEARS. A Symposium by W.H. Alexander, E.K. Broadus, F.J. Lewis, and J.M. MacEachran of the University of Alberta. Toronto, Macmillan, 1933. 113p [BVaU NBFU OTP QMM

**Alexander, William John, 1855–1944**

THE STUDY OF LITERATURE. Inaugural Address Delivered at the Convocation of Dalhousie University ... Oct. 28, 1884. Halifax, Nova Scotia Print., [1884]. 22p [OTU

**Allen, Egbert Chesley, 1882–1947**

THE OUT-OF-DOORS. Toronto, Ryerson, 1932. 141p [AEU NSHP OTP QMM

**Allen, Grant, 1848–1899**

COLIN CLOUT'S CALENDAR. The Record of a Summer, April to October. London, Chatto, 1882. 237p [BM OTU

COUNTY AND TOWN IN ENGLAND. Together with Some Annals of Churnside. With an intro. by Frederick York Powell. London, Grant Richards, 1901. 274p [BVaU SSU

FALLING IN LOVE, WITH OTHER ESSAYS. London, Smith Elder, 1889. 356p [BM LC OTU

FLASHLIGHTS ON NATURE. London, Newnes, 1899. 312p [BM BVaU OTU

THE HAND OF GOD, AND OTHER POSTHUMOUS ESSAYS. London, Watts, 1909. 114p [BM OTU

IN NATURE'S WORKSHOP. London, Newnes, 1901. 240p [BM OLU

NATURAL INEQUALITY. London, Clarion Office, [189–?]. 20p [Reprinted from *Forecasts of the Coming Century.*] [LC

POST-PRANDIAL PHILOSOPHY. London, Chatto, 1894. 214p [BM OTU

SCIENCE IN ARCADY. London, Lawrence & Bullen, 1892. 304p [BM LC OTU

VIGNETTES FROM NATURE. London, Chatto, 1881. 229p [BM OTU

**Allen, Robert Thomas, 1911–**

THE GRASS IS NEVER GREENER. The Hilarious Adventures of a Family in Search of the Perfect Place to Live. Toronto, McClelland, 1956. 204p

TIME FOR EVERYTHING. New York, Crowell, 1955. 218p

**Allison, Gerald Carlyle, 1907–1972**

THE CORNER CUPBOARD. Winnipeg, Harlequin Books, 1958. 192p

**Allison, William Talbot, 1874–1941**

THE HISTORY OF JOURNALISM. A Lecture Delivered Aug. 9, 1921 to the Conference of Western Journalists ... Winnipeg. Winnipeg, Manitoba Dept. of Agriculture, [1921?]. 24p [OTU MWP

THIS FOR REMEMBRANCE. Comp. by Carlyle Allison. Toronto, Ryerson, 1949. 50p [BVaU LC NBFU OTP

**Alward, Silas, 1842–1919**

"OUR WESTERN HERITAGE." "THEN AND NOW"; or, "Thirty Years After." Lectures delivered by ——. Saint John, Globe, 1910. 58p [BViPA NBFU

**Anderson, Margaret Pauline, 1870–**

SICK ROOM THOUGHTS AND GLEANINGS. 3rd ed. Saint John, "Progress" Book and Job, 1895. 142p [1st ed., 1893.] [BVaU LC NBFU OLU QMM

**Angus, Marion Isabel (Hand), 1902–1951**

WOMAN UNVEILED. Vancouver, Vancouver Bindery, 1932. 95p [BVaU

**Anonymous**

ESSAY ON MARRIAGE. Quebec, Ruthven, 1829. 113 + 64p [NBFU OTP

EURIDICE AHOY! A Yacht Cruise on Lake Champlain in 1880. By the Author of "One More Unfortunate." Montreal, Lovell, 1881. 66p [OTP QMSS

THE NEW PARTI NATIONAL. ... A Satire. Tracts for the Times in Canada, No. 1. N.p., n.d. 16p [OTP QMBM

**Ayscough, Florence (Wheelock), 1878–1942**

A CHINESE MIRROR. Being Reflections of the Reality behind Appearance. Boston, Houghton, 1925. 464p [BM LC OTP

**Barber, Frank Louis, 1877–1945**

IN MEMORIAM FRANK LOUIS BARBER, 1877–1945. [Contains two essays by Dr. Barber, and a Memorial Address by W.T. Brown.] Toronto, Victoria Univ., 1948. 19p [OTUV

**Barber, Mrs. Mary Josephine Axford, 1913–**

CHRISTMAS IN CANADA. The Early Days. From Sea to Sea. Spirit of Christmas Past. Spirit of Christmas Present. Ed. by Mary Barber & Flora McPherson. Toronto, Dent, 1959. 134p

**Barr, Alfred Tennyson, 1890–**

WHY NOT THINK IT OVER? Essays on Popular Fallacies. New York, Exposition Press, 1954. 163p

**Barrass, Rev. Edward, 1821–1898**
CLASS MEETINGS. Their Origin, and Advantages. Sherbrooke, Walton, 1865. 21p [NSWA OTUV QMSS

**Baxter, Arthur Beverley, 1891–1964**
FIRST NIGHTS AND FOOTLIGHTS. London, Hutchinson, 1955. 256p
FIRST NIGHTS AND NOISES OFF. London, Hutchinson, 1949. 239p [LC NBFU OTP

**Baylis, Samuel Mathewson, 1854–1941**
ENCHANTING METIS. [Montreal], 1928. 18p [OTU QMM

**Beers, William George, 1843–1900**
PATRIOTIC SPEECH ... YOUNG CANADA'S REPLY TO "ANNEXATION". ... Montreal, n.p., 1888. 7p [BVaU OTP QMM

**Belaney, George Stansfeld, 1888–1938**
A BOOK OF GREY OWL. Pages from the Writing of Wa-Sha-Quon-Asin. Ed. by E.E. Reynolds. ... London, Davies, 1938. 324p [Same title, but with an intro. by Hugh Eayrs: Toronto, Macmillan, 1938. xxi+324p] [BM LC NBFU OTMC
FAREWELL TO THE CHILDREN OF THE BRITISH ISLES. By Wa-Sha-Quon-Asin (Grey Owl) [pseud]. London, Dickson, 1938. 12p [BM OTU
PILGRIMS OF THE WILD. By Wa-Sha-Quon-Asin (Grey Owl) [pseud]. London, Dickson, 1934. 282p [BM BVaU LC NBFU OTMC
TALES OF AN EMPTY CABIN. By Wa-Sha-Quon-Asin (Grey Owl) [pseud]. Toronto, Macmillan, 1936. 335p [BM BVaU LC NBFU OKQ

**Belcher, Alexander Emerson, 1844–1926**
WHAT I KNOW ABOUT COMMERCIAL TRAVELLING. Who We Are, What We Do, and How We Do It. Toronto, Hunter Rose, 1883. 149p [BVaU LC OTU

**Bell, Charles William, 1876–1938**
WHO SAID MURDER? Toronto, Macmillan, 1935. 403p [Essays on famous Canadian murders.] [BM BVaU OKQ QMM

**Bell, Rev. Clifford Ritchie, 1905–**
PURPLE VAPOURS. Sherbrooke, Page, 1927. [Also a 2nd series in 1931.]

**Bender, Louis Prosper, 1844–1917**
VISIONS OF OLD QUEBEC. Quebec, 1911. 23p [OTL

**Bengough, John Wilson, 1851–1923**
BENGOUGH'S CHALK-TALKS. A Series of Platform Addresses on Various Topics. Toronto, Musson, 1922. 162p [BM BVaU NSHD OKQ
THE DECLINE AND FALL OF KEEWATIN; or, The Free-trade Redskins. A Satire Illus. by J.W. Bengough. Toronto, "Grip" Office, 1876. 28p [BVaU NSHD OTP
THE GIN MILL PRIMER. A Book of Easy Reading Lessons for Children of All Ages, Especially for Boys who have Votes. Toronto, Briggs, 1898. 78p [BM BVaU OOP

THE PROHIBITION AESOP. A Book of Fables. Hamilton, Royal Templar Pub., n.d. 39p [BVaU OTU

THE UP-TO-DATE PRIMER. A First Book of Lessons for Little Political Economists, in Words of One Syllable with Pictures. New York, Funk & Wagnalls, 1896. 75p [BM BVaU LC NSWA OLU

THE WHOLE HOG BOOK. Being George's Thoro' Going Work "Protection or Free-Trade?" Rendered into Words of One Syllable, and Illustrated with Pictures; or, A Dry Subject Made Juicy. Boston, American Free-Trade League, 1908. 99p [LC

THE GRIP-SACK. A Receptacle of Light Literature, Fun and Fancy. Toronto, Grip, 1882. 2v [NSHD OTU

**Berton, Pierre Francis de Marigny, 1920–**

ADVENTURES OF A COLUMNIST. Toronto, McClelland, 1960. 211p

JUST ADD WATER AND STIR. Being a Random Collection of Satirical Essays, Rude Remarks, Used Anecdotes, Thumbnail Sketches, Ancient Wheezes, Old Nostalgias, Wry Comments, Limp Doggerel, Intemperate Recipes, Vagrant Opinions and Crude Drawings. Toronto, McClelland, 1959. 222p

**Bethune, Rev. John, 1791–1872**

ADDRESS. Delivered by the Principal of McGill College. Montreal, Lovell & Gibson, 1843. 14p [OTP

**Bezanson, Rev. W.B.**

STORIES OF ACADIA. Halifax, Nova Print., 1941. 57p (Birch Bark Series No. 4) [Series apparently began in 1924 with a Dartmouth imprint. 44p] [BVaU OKQ OTP

**Bidwell, Barnabas, 1763–1833**

THE PROMPTER. A Series of Essays on Civil and Social Duties. [Anon]. Kingston, Thomson, 1821. 56p [OTP

**Biggar, Emerson Bristol, 1853–1921**

CANADA: A MEMORIAL VOLUME. General Reference Book of Canada. Ed. by ——. Montreal, Biggar, 1889. 953p [BM BVaU OTU

**Binmore, Charles J.**

THE CANADIAN NATIONALITY. Montreal, Drysdale, 1888. 16p [BM OTU QMBM

**Bird, William Richard, 1891–**

THE COMMUNICATION TRENCH. Amherst, N.S., Author, 1933. 336p [BVaU NSWA OTP

THE STORY OF VIMY-RIDGE. [Arras (France), I.N.S.A.P.], 1932. 24p [LC

THIRTEEN YEARS AFTER. Toronto, MacLean, 1932. 180p [BVaU NBFU

**Bishop, Leslie Gurney, 1908–**

BEES FROM THE UNDERGRADUATE BONNET. Oxford, Blackwell, 1929. 103p [BM

**Blake, Edward, 1833–1912**

"A NATIONAL SENTIMENT!" Speech of Hon. Edward Blake at Aurora. Ottawa, Perry, 1874. 107p [BVaU OTU

... SPEECHES BY HON. EDWARD BLAKE ON THE POLITICAL QUESTIONS OF THE DAY, DELIVERED IN THE PROVINCE OF ONTARIO. ... Toronto, Hunter Rose, 1887. 424p [OLU QMU

**Blake, William Hume, 1861–1924**

BROWN WATERS, AND OTHER SKETCHES. Toronto, Macmillan, 1915. 264p [Many later editions.] [BM BVaU LC NSHD OKQ

A FISHERMAN'S CREED. Toronto, Macmillan, 1923. 40p [BM BVaU NSHD OKQ QMM

IN A FISHING COUNTRY. Toronto, Macmillan, 1922. 263p [BM BVaU LC NSHD OKQ QMM

**Bock, William George, 1884–**

THE BOOK OF HUMBUG. Saskatoon, Modern Press, 1958. 132p

**Bourinot, Arthur Stanley, 1893–1969**

THE QUICK AND THE DEAD. Views and Reviews On Poetry. Ottawa, Author, 1955. 21p

**Bourque, Romuald, 1889–**

OUR CENTURY. Montreal, Editorial Associates, 1950. 157p [OONL

**Bracken, John, 1883–**

JOHN BRACKEN SAYS. Toronto, Oxford U. Press, 1944. 134p [BM BVaU OTU

**Bready, John Wesley, 1887–1953**

FAITH AND FREEDOM, THE ROOTS OF DEMOCRACY. Winona Lake, Ind., Light and Life Press, 1952. 151p

**Bridle, Augustus, 1869–1952**

THE MASQUES OF OTTAWA. By "Domino" [pseūd]. Toronto, Macmillan, 1921. 283p [BM BVaU LC NSHD OTU QMM

THE OLD 24TH OF MAY. Toronto, McLean, [19–?]. 8p [OTP

**Broadus, Edmund Kemper, 1876–1936**

SATURDAY AND SUNDAY. Toronto, Macmillan, 1935. 260p [BVaU LC NBFU OTP

**Brockington, Leonard Walter, 1888–**

ADDRESS ... [at the] Opening of Mackenzie House, 82 Bond Street, Toronto, Tuesday, May 9th, 1950. Toronto, W.L. Mackenzie Homestead Foundation, 1950. 10p [OONL

**Brooke, Frances (Moore), 1724–1789**

THE OLD MAID. By Mary Singleton, Spinster [pseud]. London, Millar, 1764. 304p [A bound periodical.] [BM OTU

**Brooks, Anne (Sutherland)**

THE ODD LITTLE SOUL. By Anne Sutherland. Guelph, Author, 1933. 62p [CC

**Brown, Audrey Alexandra, 1904–**

POETRY AND LIFE. An Address. Toronto, Macmillan, 1941. 10p [BVaU OTU QMM

**Bruce, Herbert Alexander, 1868–1963**

FRIENDSHIP: THE KEY TO PEACE, AND OTHER ADDRESSES. Toronto, Macmillan, 1937. 364p [BM BVaU LC NBFU OTU QMM

OUR HERITAGE, AND OTHER ADDRESSES. Toronto, Macmillan, 1934. 392p [BM BVaU LC OTU QMM

**Brundle, John, 1882–**

BROMESWELL DICK'S AND JOHNNY PIPER'S RAPHSODY [*sic*]. From the Pen of John, a Suffolk Herd Boy. Roche's Point, Ont., Author, 1953. 30p

**Bryce, Rev. George, 1844–1931**

CANADIAN LOYALTY. Winnipeg, Manitoba Free Press, 1902. 20p [LC QMBM

**Bryce, Peter Henderson, 1853–**

THE ILLUMINATION OF JOSEPH KEELER, ESQ.; or, On to the Land. Boston, American Journal of Public Health, 1915. 97p [BVaU NSHD OTU

**Bucke, Richard Maurice, 1837–1902**

COSMIC CONSCIOUSNESS. A Paper read before the American Medico-Psychological Association ... 18 May 1894. Philadephia, The Conservator, 1894. 18p [OLU

**Burgess, Rev. Edwin Harcus, 1858–**

FOR CANADA AND THE OLD FLAG. Halifax, Knight, 1893. 46p [NSHD QMM

**Burke, Luke**

PHRENOLOGICAL ENQUIRIES. Pts. I and II. Quebec, Cowan, 1840. 40p [QMSS

**Burn, William Scott, –1851**

THE CONNECTION BETWEEN LITERATURE AND COMMERCE. In Two Essays read before the Literary and Historical Society of Toronto. Toronto, Rowsell, 1845. 16p [OTP

**Burpee, Lawrence Johnstone, 1873–1946**

BY CANADIAN STREAMS. Toronto, Musson, 1909. 87p [BVaU OTU QMM

CANADIAN ELOQUENCE. Ed. and arranged by ——. Toronto, Musson, 1910. 112p [BVaU OTU QMM

GOOD NEIGHBOURS. Toronto, Ryerson, 1940. 30p [OTU

**Buschlen, John Preston, 1888–**

THE DESERT BATTALION. By Jack Preston [pseud] and Mrs. Edward G. Robinson. Hollywood, Murray & Gee, 1944. 97p [LC

THE DONKEY, THE ELEPHANT AND THE GOAT. [Great Falls, Mont., Montana Print., 1920.] 16p [LC

ROMANCE AND THE WEST. Falling Petals. By John Preston [pseud]. Boston, Cornhill, 1918. 49p [LC

**Calamo, C.**

A GRAB BAG; or, Junk from an Attic Storage. Winnipeg, Winnipeg Print., n.d. 32p [BVaS

PUG-NOSE; or, From the Ridiculous to the Sublime. [Winnipeg], Winnipeg Print., n.d. 190p [AEU MWU

**Campbell, Rollo, 1803–1871**

TWO LECTURES ON CANADA. Greenock, Mackenzie, 1857. 45p [Also: Toronto, 1857. 47p] [BM LC NSWA OTP QMM

**Canadian Authors' Association. Western Ontario Branch**

ADDRESSES ... AT ... ARCHIBALD LAMPMAN MEMORIAL CAIRN. ... London, Ont., The Branch, 1930. 16p [OTU

**Canniff, William, 1830–1910**

CANADIAN NATIONALITY. Its Growth and Development. Toronto, Hart & Rawlinson, 1875. 20p [BM OTP

**Carman, Bliss, 1861–1929**

ADDRESS TO THE GRADUATING CLASS 1911 OF THE UNITRINIAN SCHOOL OF PERSONAL HARMONIZING. ... New York, Tabord Press, 1911. 27p [BVaU LC NBFU OKQ

THE FRIENDSHIP OF ART. Boston, Page, 1904. 303p [BM BVaU LC NSHD OKQ

THE KINSHIP OF NATURE. Boston, Page, 1904. [Pub. 1903.] 298p [BM BVaU LC NSHD OTU QMM

THE MAKING OF PERSONALITY. By Bliss Carman [with Mary Perry King]. Boston, Page, 1908. 375p [BM BVaU LC NSHD OTU QMM

TALKS ON POETRY AND LIFE. Five Lectures Delivered before the Univeristy of Toronto, December 1925. [Transcribed and ed. by Blanche Hume.] Toronto, Ryerson, 1926. 58p [BVaU LC NBFU OTU QMM

THE POETRY OF LIFE. Boston, Page, 1905. 258p [BM BVaU LC NSHD OTUV QMM

**Carr, Emily, 1871–1945**

AN ADDRESS BY EMILY CARR. With an intro. by Ira Dilworth. Toronto, Oxford U. Press, 1955. ix + 13p

PAUSE, A SKETCH BOOK. Toronto, Clarke Irwin, 1953. 148p

**Cash, Gwen (Goldsmid), 1891–**
A MILLION MILES FROM OTTAWA. Toronto, Macmillan, 1942. 152p [BVaU LC OTU QMM

**Charlesworth, Hector Willoughby, 1872–1945**
THE CANADIAN SCENE. Sketches: Political and Historical. Toronto, Macmillan, 1927. 235p [BM BVaU LC NSHD OKQ
CANDID CHRONICLES. Leaves from the Note Book of a Canadian Journalist. Toronto, Macmillan 1925. 404p [BM BVaU LC NBFU OTU
I'M TELLING YOU. Being ... Further Candid Chronicles. Toronto, Macmillan, 1937. 344p [BVaU LC NBFU OTU
MORE CANDID CHRONICLES. Further Leaves from the Note Book of a Canadian Journalist. Toronto, Macmillan, 1928. 429p [BM BVaU LC OKQ

**Charlton, John, 1829–1910**
SPEECHES AND ADDRESSES, POLITICAL, LITERARY, AND RELIGIOUS. Toronto, Morang, 1905. 499p [BM BVaU NBFU OTU

**Chisholme, David, 1796?–1842**
THE LOWER-CANADA WATCHMAN. [Anon] Kingston, Macfarlane, 1829. 491p [BVaU LC NSWA OTU

**Clark, Gregory, 1892–**
THE BEST OF GREGORY CLARK. Foreword by Craig Ballantyne. Toronto, Ryerson, 1959. 174p
SO WHAT? Toronto, Saunders, 1937. 252p [BVaU OTU
WHICH WE DID. Toronto, Saunders, 1936. 221p [BVaU NBFU OTU

**Clarke, Andrew David, 1882–1948**
ANDY CLARKE AND HIS NEIGHBOURLY NEWS. With an intro. by Greg. Clark. Toronto, Ryerson, 1949. 158p [OTP

**Coffin, William Foster, 1808–1878**
QUIRKS OF DIPLOMACY. Read before the Literary & Scientific Society of Ottawa, Jan. 22, 1874. Montreal, Lovell, 1874. 31p [BVaU LC OTU

**Collier, Della**
ECHOES FROM AN OLD GARDEN. New Westminster, Jackson, 1944. 104p [BVaU

**Cook, Marjorie Grant**
VERDUN DAYS IN PARIS. By Marjorie Grant. London, Collins, 1918. 239p [BM QMM

**Cooke, Ronald John Victor, 1913–**
WRITING FOR THE TRADE JOURNALS. Windsor, Non-Fiction Press, [1949?]. 48p [CC

**Copleston, Mrs. Edward**
CANADA: Why We Live in It, and Why We Like It. London, Parker & Bourn, 1861. 121p [BM BVaU LC OTP

**Cordner, Rev. John, 1816–1894**

THE FOUNDATIONS OF NATIONALITY. Montreal, Rose, 1856. 28p (Discourse preached in the Unitarian Church, Montreal, on the Sunday after the great railway celebration, Nov. 1856.) [BM BVaU NSWA OTU QMM

**Corry, James Alexander, 1899–**

CIVIL LIBERTIES IN TRYING TIMES. Fredericton, U. of New Brunswick, 1953. 16p

**Coulon, Emile**

POETICAL LEISURE HOURS AND TORONTONIAN DESCRIPTIONS. In French Verse and English Essays. ... Toronto, Rowsell, 1897. 39p [BM Brown U OTU

**Cowan, Mary Edith**

RAINBOW OF LIFE. Ottawa, Canadian Research and Editorial Institute, 1945. 52p [BVaU OKQ

**Craik, Robert Henry, 1829–1906**

PAPERS AND ADDRESSES. Montreal, Gazette, 1907. 222p [BVaU OTU QMM

**Cramp, Rev. John Mockett, 1796–1881**

LECTURES FOR THESE TIMES. London, Houlston & Stoneman, 1844. 308p [BM NSWA OTUV

**Cramp, Mary**

ETERNAL YOUTH: Addresses to Girls, 1913–1930. By Mary Cramp and Maud C. Edgar. Toronto, Macmillan, 1931. 262p [BM BVaU NBFU OTU

**Creighton, Donald Grant, 1902–**

FOUNDERS' DAY ADDRESS, UNIVERSITY OF NEW BRUNSWICK ... WRITING OF HISTORY IN CANADA. Fredericton, The University, 1945. 18p [BM NBFU OTU

**Crofton, Francis Blake, 1841–1912**

FOR CLOSER UNION. ... Halifax, Mackinlay, 1897. 57p [BM NSHD OTU

IS IT TOO LATE? London, Author, n.d. 20p [NSHD

**Crombie, Keith**

SACKCLOTH AND SPLASHES—Fragments from "The Goblin." By Keith Crombie and J.E. MacDougall. Toronto, McClelland, 1923. 256p [BM BVaU OTU

**Crone, Kennedy, 1883–**

THE SPIRIT OF MONTREAL (NON-ALCOHOLIC). An Analysis for Americans. Montreal, Woodward Press, 1929. 39p [QMBM

**Crooks, Adam, 1827–1885**

SPEECHES. Toronto, Robinson, 1879. 48p [NSWA OTU

**Crowley, Cornelius Patrick Joseph, 1914–**

THE HUMAN IMAGE. Twenty-six Scripts of Radio Talks as Given on CBC. Windsor, Ont., Assumption U. of Windsor Press, 1960. 88p

**Cumming, Robert Dalziel, 1871–**

SKOOKUM CHUCK FABLES. Bits of History through the Microscope (Some of which Appeared in the Ashcroft Joùrnal). By Skookum Chuck [pseud]. N.p., 1915. 167p [BVaU

**Currie, Arthur William, 1875–1933**

THE NEW CANADIANISM. An Address delivered before the 8th Annual Conference of Heads of Canadian Universities held at Winnipeg, June 16th, 1922. [Montreal], 1922. 10p [NSWA OLU QMM

**Currie, Margaret (Gill), 1843–**

MARGARET CURRIE: HER BOOK. Toronto, Hunter Rose, 1924. 352p [NBFU OTP QMSS

**Dafoe, John Wesley, 1866–1944**

CANADA, AN AMERICAN NATION. New York, Columbia U. Press, 1935. 134p [BM BVaU NSHD OKQ QMM

**Daor, Francis**

SKETCHES [Reprinted from the Montreal *Herald*]. N.p., n.p., n.d. 69p [BVaU

**Davidson, S.**

STRAY SHOTS FROM SOLOMON. By James Acton [pseud]. Toronto, Acton Pub. Co., 1907. 160p [Same title: Toronto, Acton Pub. Co., 1929. 28p] [BM BVaU OTU

**Davies, Blodwen, 1897–1966**

YOUTH SPEAKS ITS MIND. Toronto, Ryerson, 1948. 232p [Survey of Canadian Youth Commission.] [BVaU LC OTU

**Davies, Robertson, 1913–**

THE DIARY OF SAMUEL MARCHBANKS. Toronto, Clarke Irwin, 1947. 204p [BVaU LC NBFU OTU

RENOWN AT STRATFORD. A Record of the Shakespeare Festival in Canada 1953. By Tyrone Guthrie, Robertson Davies, and Grant Macdonald. Toronto, Clarke Irwin, 1953. 127p

THE TABLE TALK OF SAMUEL MARCHBANKS. ... Toronto, Clarke Irwin, 1949. 248p [BM BVaU LC NSHD OKQ

THRICE THE BRINDED CAT HATH MEW'D. A Record of the Stratford Shakespearean Festival in Canada, 1955. By Robertson Davies, Tyrone Guthrie, Boyd Neel, and Tanya Moiseiwitsch. Toronto, Clarke Irwin, 1955. xii + 178p

TWICE HAVE THE TRUMPETS SOUNDED. A Record of the Stratford Shakespearean Festival in Canada, 1954. By Tyrone Guthrie, Robertson Davies, and Grant Macdonald. Toronto, Clarke Irwin, 1954. 192p

A VOICE FROM THE ATTIC. Toronto, McClelland, 1960. ix + 360 + xp [Pub. in England as THE PERSONAL ART, Reading to Good Purpose. London, Secker, 1961. 268p]

**Davin, Nicholas Flood, 1843–1901**

BRITISH VERSUS AMERICAN CIVILIZATION. A Lecture. ... Toronto, Adam Stevenson, 1873. 45p [LC NSHD OTU

CULTURE AND PRACTICAL POWER. An Address delivered at the Opening of Lansdowne College, Portage la Prairie. ... Regina, Leader Co., 1889. 16p [BM LC NSWA OOA

IRELAND AND THE EMPIRE. A Speech ... delivered before the St. Patrick's Society ... Montreal, on St. Patrick's Day 1885. Ottawa, Citizen Print., 1885. 18p [BM NSHD

STRATHCONA HORSE. Speech at Lansdowne Park, March 7th, A.D. 1900. ... Ottawa, Hope, 1900. 20p [BM NSWA OTU

**Davis, Herbert John, 1893–**

CHALLENGE TO THE INTELLECT. Three Addresses. Northampton, Mass., Hampshire Bookshop, 1941. 44p [LC

**Dawson, John William, 1820–1899**

THE CANADIAN STUDENT. N.p., n. pub., 1891. 8p [NSWA OTU

CREATIVE DEVELOPMENT AND EVOLUTION. Frome, Butler & Tanner, n.d. 36p [QMM

DUTIES OF EDUCATED YOUNG MEN IN BRITISH AMERICA. Montreal, Lovell, 1863. 24p [LC NSHD OTP

EDUCATED WOMEN. An Address. ... [N.p., priv. circ., 1889.] 14p [NSWA

**Dawson, Samuel Edward, 1833–1916**

THE NORTHERN KINGDOM. By a Colonist [pseud]. Montreal, Dawson, [1866?]. 18p [BM NSWA OTU QMM

A PLEA FOR LITERATURE. Presidential Address before the Royal Society. ... Montreal, Renouf, 1908. 26p [LC OTU QMM

**Day, Frank Parker, 1881–1950**

A GOOD CITIZEN. Sackville, Mt. Allison Univ., 1947. 134p [NSHD OLU

**Deacon, William Arthur, 1890–**

MY VISION OF CANADA. Toronto, Ontario Pub. Co., 1933. 309p [BM BVaU LC NSHD OTU QMM

OPEN HOUSE. Ed. by W.A. Deacon and Wilfred Reeves. Ottawa, Graphic, 1931. 319p [BM BVaU NSHD OKQ

PENS AND PIRATES. Toronto, Ryerson, 1923. 325p [BM BVaU NSHD OTP

POTEEN. A Pot-Pourri of Canadian Essays. Ottawa, Graphic, 1926. 241p [BM BVaU NSHD OKQ

SH-H-H ... HERE COMES THE CENSOR! An Address to the Ontario Library Association, March 28, 1940. Toronto, Macmillan, 1940. 16p [OTU

**Dean, J.K.**

THE SAYINGS AND DOINGS OF THE SELF-STYLED ROYAL FAMILY, THE MAGRATHS, OF MACKENZIE'S CASTLE, SPRINGFIELD. Toronto, 1844. 47p [OTP

**Dehan, Aiken A.**

WASHING THE HANDS. Toronto, McClelland, 1936. 37p [OTU

**De La Roche, Mazo, 1879–1961**

PORTRAIT OF A DOG. Boston, Little Brown, 1930. 199p [BM BVaU LC NBFU OTU QMM

**Dewart, Rev. Edward Hartley, 1828–1903**

ESSAYS FOR THE TIMES. Studies of Eminent Men and Important Living Questions. Toronto, Briggs, 1898. 198p [BM BVaU OTUV

**Dezell, Robert, 1866–**

"I SEZ, SEZ I." A Series of Talks to Talkers on what to say and how to say it. Allenford, Ont., Author, 1911. 199p [LC

MOIKE SPAKES HIS MOIND. Toronto, Allen, 1937. 62p [LC

**Dixon, Frederick John, 1881–1931**

DIXON'S ADDRESS TO THE JURY IN DEFENCE OF FREEDOM OF SPEECH ... And Judge Galt's Charge to the Jury in Rex v. Dixon. Winnipeg, Defence Committee, [1920]. 126p [Peel

**Dolman, Claude Ernest, 1906–**

A LAYMAN VIEWS THE ARTIST. Vancouver, Art Gallery, 1946. 9p [BVaU

SCIENCE AND THE HUMANITIES. An Address. ... Vancouver, U. of British Columbia, 1950. 19p [BVaU OTU

**Donovan, Rev. P.J.**

DAD'S MUSINGS. A Household Philosopher's Kindly and Practical Reflections on the Affairs of Average Citizens. ... Chicago, Meier, 1926. 123p [LC

**Donovan, Peter, 1884–**

IMPERFECTLY PROPER. By P. O'D. [pseud]. Toronto, McClelland, 1920. 379p [BM BVaU NBFU OTU QMM

OVER 'ERE AND BACK HOME. Random Impressions of an Earnest Soul. By P. O'D. [pseud]. Toronto, McClelland, 1922. 355p [Earlier ed. in paper covers: Toronto, McClelland, 1918.] [BM BVaU NBFU OTP QMM

**Douglas, Frances Mary**

BRITANNIA WAIVES THE RULES. A Confidential Guide to the Customs, Manners and Habits of the "Nation of Shopkeepers." By Frances Douglas (Who has never been there) and Thelma Lecocq (Who has). Toronto, Dent, 1934. 112p [BM NBFU OTU QMM

**Douglas, Robert W., –1931**

HOW BOOKS MAY HELP YOU. Vancouver, Burrard Pub. Co., 1914. 22p [BVaU

**Duff, Louis Blake, 1878–1959**

IMMORTAL MEMORY. An Address before the Burns Literary Society. Fort Erie, Ont., Review Co., 1945. 16p [OTU

A STUDY OF VANITY. ... Welland, Ont., Author, 1952. 14p

**Duggan, Joseph Jenkins, 1874–**

THE UNFORGOTTEN VALLEY. Studies of Life and Character on the Welsh Border. Toronto, Ryerson, 1926. 177p [OTP QMM

**Duncan, Sara Jeannette (Mrs. Everard Cotes), 1861–1922**

THE CROW'S NEST. New York, Dodd Mead, 1901. 248p [Pub. in Eng. as: ON THE OTHER SIDE OF THE LATCH. London, Methuen, 1901. 266p] [BM BVaU LC OTP

ON THE OTHER SIDE OF THE LATCH. [See under THE CROW'S NEST.]

**Dunlop, William, 1792–1848**

AN ADDRESS DELIVERED TO THE YORK MECHANICS' INSTITUTION, March, 1832. York, Coates, 1832. 16p [OTU

**Dunton, (Arnold) Davidson, 1912–**

FREEDOM FOR MINDS, 1957. Fredericton, U. of New Brunswick, 1957. 12p

**Eayrs, Hugh Smithurst, 1894–1940**

THE BAROMETER POINTS TO CHANGE. An Address delivered to the Toronto Branch of the Canadian Authors' Association ... 1938. Toronto, Macmillan, 1938. 27p [OKQ

IT ISN'T GOOD ENOUGH. An Address delivered to the Annual Meeting of the Canadian Authors' Association ... 1939. Toronto, Macmillan, 1939. 16p [BViP OKQ

**Edmonds, Walter Everard, 1875–**

BROAD HORIZONS. Maple Leaf Sketches from a Prairie Studio. ... Toronto, Musson, 1919. 224p [BVa LC OTP

THE CANADIAN FLAG DAY BOOK. Toronto, Longmans, 1927. 154p [BVa OKQ

IN A COLLEGE LIBRARY. Edmonton, Esdale Press, 1920. 91p [ACG BM

**Eisendrath, Maurice Nathan, 1902–**

THE NEVER FAILING STREAM. Toronto, Macmillan, 1939. 398p [BM BVaU LC OTP

READING IN WAR-TIME. Toronto, Macmillan, 1941. 31p [BVaU LC OTP

**Emberson, Frederick C., –1913**

HOW TO BE HAPPY. Introduction to Secrets of Joy. ... Montreal, Foster Brown, [18–?]. 64p [OTP QMSS

**Empire Club of Canada, Toronto.**

ADDRESSES. Toronto, T.H. Best, 1903–. xiii + 361p [A continuing annual publication since 1903. Publisher and pagination vary.] [AEU BVaU NBFU OTP

**Ewart, John Skirving, 1849–1933**

THE KINGDOM OF CANADA ... and Other Essays. Toronto, Morang, 1908. 370p [BM BVaU LC NSWA OKQ

**Ewing, John Morton, 1889–**

REFLECTIONS OF A DOMINIE. Toronto, Nelson, 1932. 96p [BVaU OTU QMM

**Fairchild, George Moore, 1854–1912**

CANADIAN LEAVES. History, Art, Science, Literature, Commerce. A Series of New Papers read before the Canadian Club of New York. Ed. by ——. New York, Thompson, 1887. 289p [BM BVaU LC NBFU OTU

**Fairchild, Queenie, –1950**

MY FRENCH CANADIAN NEIGHBOURS, AND OTHER SKETCHES. Quebec, Telegraph Print., 1916. 121p [BVaU NBFU OTU

**Falconer, Robert Alexander, 1867–1943**

CITIZENSHIP IN AN ENLARGING WORLD. Sackville, Mount Allison U., 1928. 85p [BM BVaU NBFU OKQ

IDEALISM IN NATIONAL CHARACTER. London, Hodder, 1920. 216p [BM BVaU NSHD OTP

**Ferguson, George Victor, 1897–**

THE NEWSPAPER IN A FREE SOCIETY. [Sesquicentennial lectures, 1950.] Fredericton, U. of New Brunswick, [1950]. 11p [OONL

**Fewster, Ernest Philip, 1868–1947**

MY GARDEN DREAMS. Ottawa, Graphic, 1926. 175p [BVaU NSHD OTU QMM

**Fisher, John Wiggins, 1913–**

JOHN FISHER REPORTS. An Anthology of Radio Scripts. Hamilton, Niagara Editorial Bureau, 1949. 185p [BVa OLU

**Fisher, Raymond Anderson, 1900–**

THE PSYCHOLOGY OF DESIRE; or, A Measure for Men. Saskatoon, Elliott Print., 1930. 158p [BVa OTP

**Fitch, Adelaide P.**

EAST AND WEST. Essays and Sketches. Toronto, Briggs, 1911. 198p [BM BVaU NBFU

**Flenley, Ralph, 1886–1969**

ESSAYS IN CANADIAN HISTORY. Presented to George McKinnon Wrong for his Eightieth Birthday. Ed. by ——. Toronto, Macmillan, 1939. 372p [BM BVaU LC NSHD OTU QMM

**Fontaine, Robert Louis, 1911–1965**

THAT'S A GOOD QUESTION. Boston, Author, 1960. x + 139p

**Ford, Paul**

OUR NATIONAL PIE AND WHAT IT CONTAINED. Being a Report of the Proceedings of the Anglo-Franco-Hibernian-Scottish-Canadian-National Society ... 1876. Montreal, Drysdale, 1877. 19p [BVaU NSWA OTU QMSS

**Forster, John Wycliffe Lowes, 1850–1938**

SIGHT AND INSIGHT. Foreword by Sir Robert Falconer. Toronto, Oxford U. Press, 1941. 176p [BVi OTP

**Foster, George Eulas, 1847–1931**

CANADIAN ADDRESSES. Ed. by Arnold Winterbotham. Toronto, Bell & Cockburn, 1914. 324p [BM BVaU LC NSHD OTU QMM

CITIZENSHIP. ... Sackville, Mount Allison Univ., 1926. 85p [BVaU NBFU OTU

**Foster, William Alexander, 1840–1888**

CANADA FIRST; or, Our New Nationality. An Address. Toronto, Adam-Stevenson, 1871. 36p [BVaU OTP QMBM

**Fox, Marion Wathen, 1871–1956**

CANADA'S NEW FLAG. Toronto, Hunter-Rose, 1917. 15p [NBFL OKQ

**Fraser, John, 1820–1899**

CANADIAN PEN AND INK SKETCHES. Montreal, Gazette, 1890. 391p [BM BVaU LC NSHD OTU QMM

**Fraser, William Alexander, 1859–1933**

SORROW AND OLD FRIENDS. Philadelphia, Altemus, [1901]. 41p [LC

**French, Sarah**

A BOOK FOR THE YOUNG. Dedicated by Permission to the Hon. Mrs. Manners Sutton. By a Lady [pseud]. Saint John, McMillan, 1856. 175p [NBFU OTU

LETTERS TO A YOUNG LADY ON LEAVING SCHOOL AND ENTERING THE WORLD. Dedicated by Permission to Lady Head. By a Lady [pseud]. Boston, 1855. 158p [NBB

**Frost, Rex Hanby, 1896–**

THE PASSING SHOW. [Selections from his Radio Talks on Canada.] Toronto, Ryerson, 1946. 121p [BVaU LC OTU

**Frye, Northrop, 1912–**

ADDRESS BY H. NORTHROP FRYE ON THE OCCASION OF HIS INSTALLATION AS PRINCIPAL OF VICTORIA COLLEGE, OCTOBER 21, 1959. Toronto, Clarke Irwin, 1959. 23p

**Fulford, Rev. Francis, 1803–1868**

FIVE OCCASIONAL LECTURES, DELIVERED IN MONTREAL. Montreal, Lovell, 1859. 118p [BM BVaU NSHD OTP

**Fuller, William Henry**

A DREAM OF PURE POLITICIANS. [MOR '98

FLAPDOODLE. A Political Encyclopedia and Manual for Public Men. Ed. by an ex-Minister [pseud]. Toronto, 1881. 28p [Attributed to John Wilson Bengough in NSHD.] [NSHD OTU QMSS

**Gale, Samuel, 1783–1865**

NERVA; or, A Collection of Papers Published in the Montreal Herald. [Anon] Montreal, Gray, 1814. 45p [LC OTP QMM

**Galloway, Thomas**

LECTURES. Uxbridge, 1896. [Earlier ed. in 1882?] [OLU OOP OTU

**Garison, Isabel**

LOOKING FORWARD. Montreal, Robinson, 1890. 227p [OOP QMSS

**Garvie, William**

BARNEY ROONEY'S LETTERS ON CONFEDERATION, BOTHERATION, AND POLITICAL TRANSMOGRIFICATION. Halifax, 1865. 56p [BibC

THE LIGHT AND THE SHADOWS; or, Christianity the Ideal of Our Race. A Lecture. Halifax, 1860. 38p [NSWA

**Gates, Hartley Baxter**

THE DOMINION OF CANADA. Its Interests, Prospects, and Policy. An Address. ... Montreal, Lovell, 1872. 34p [OTU QMM

**George, Rev. James, 1801?–1870**

THE RELATION BETWEEN PIETY AND INTELLECTUAL LABOR. An Address. ... Kingston, Daily News, 1855. 24p [OTP

THE VALUE OF EARNESTNESS. An Address. Kingston, Daily News, [1854?]. 16p [OTP

**Gillis, James Donald, 1870–**

MODERN ENGLISH. A Canadian Grammar. "Leave the Old to the Old." Halifax, Allen, 1913. 65p [NSHD OTU QMBM

**Gould, Benjamin Apthorp, 1870–1937**

THE GREATER TRAGEDY, AND OTHER THINGS. Toronto, Dent, 1916. 189p [BM LC NSHD OLU

WAR THOUGHTS OF AN OPTIMIST. Toronto, Dent, 1915. 200p [BM LC OLU

**Graham, Emma (Jeffers), –1922**

ETCHINGS FROM A PARSONAGE VERANDA. ... Toronto, Briggs, 1895. 187p [BVaU NSHD OTU

**Graham, James E., 1904–**

THE TIME OF YOUR LIFE. Toronto, George Weston Ltd., 1951. 47p

**Graham, William Creighton, 1887–1955**

EDUCATION AND THE NEW AGE. A Series of Addresses Delivered at United College, Winnipeg. ... Toronto, Ryerson, 1947. 81p [BVaU LC NBFU OTU

**Grenfell, Wilfred Thomason, 1865–1940**

THE ATTRACTIVE WAY. Boston, Pilgrim, 1913. 59p [LC

YOURSELF AND YOUR BODY. New York, Scribner, 1924. 324p [BM LC NBFU

**Grove, Frederick Philip, 1879–1948**

IT NEEDS TO BE SAID. Toronto, Macmillan, 1929. 163p [BVaU NSHD OKQ

OVER PRAIRIE TRAILS. Toronto, McClelland, 1922. 231p [Also, with intro. by Malcolm Ross. Toronto, McClelland, 1957. xiv + 146p] [BM BVaU LC NSHD OKQ

THE TURN OF THE YEAR. Toronto, McClelland, 1923. 237p [BM BVaU LC NSHD OTU

**Hague, John, 1829–1906**

CANADA FOR CANADIANS. A Royalist "Roland" for the Annexationist "Oliver." ... A Paper read before the Toronto Branch of the Imperial Federation League ... 23rd January, 1889. Toronto, Hart, 1889. 40p [NSWA OTP

**Haig-Brown, Roderick Langmere, 1908–**

FISHERMAN'S SPRING. Toronto, Collins, 1951. 222p

FISHERMAN'S SUMMER. Toronto, Collins, 1959. 253p

MEASURE OF THE YEAR. Toronto, Collins, 1950. 279p [Also: New York, Morrow, 1950. 260p] [BVaU LC NBFU OTMC QMM

POOL AND RAPID. The Story of a River. Toronto, McClelland, 1932. 239p [Also: London, Cape, 1936.] [BM BVaU LC NBFU OTU

RETURN TO THE RIVER. A Story of the Chinook Run. New York, Morrow, 1941. 259p [BM BVaU LC NBFU OTU QMM

A RIVER NEVER SLEEPS. New York, Morrow, 1946. 352p [BM BVaU LC NBFU OTUV QMM

SILVER. The Life of an Atlantic Salmon. London, Black, 1931. 96p [BM BVaU LC OTUV

SPRING CONGREGATION ADDRESS 1952: Power and People. Vancouver, U. of British Columbia, 1952. 5p

THE WESTERN ANGLER. An Account of Pacific Salmon and Western Trout in British Columbia. 2nd ed. New York, Morrow, 1947. 356p [First pub. in limited ed.: New York, Derrydale Press, 1939. 2v] [BVaU LC NBFU OTP

**Haliburton, Thomas Chandler, 1796–1865**

AN ADDRESS ON THE PRESENT CONDITION, RESOURCES AND PROSPECTS OF BRITISH NORTH AMERICA. ... London, Hurst & Blackett, 1857. 44p [Also: Montreal, Lovell, 1857. 17p] [BM LC NSWA OKQ

THE ENGLISH IN AMERICA. By the Author of "Sam Slick, the Clockmaker". ... London, Colburn, 1851. 2v [Subsequently re-titled RULE AND MISRULE OF THE ENGLISH IN AMERICA: The English in America. London, Colburn, 1851. 2v] [BM BVaU LC NSWA OKQ

A REPLY TO THE REPORT OF THE EARL OF DURHAM. By a Colonist [pseud]. London, Bentley, 1839. 91p [BM OTP

RULE AND MISRULE OF THE ENGLISH IN AMERICA. ... [See under THE ENGLISH IN AMERICA.]

**Halliburton, Brenton, 1775–1860**

OBSERVATIONS ON THE IMPORTANCE OF THE NORTH AMERICAN COLONIES TO GREAT BRITAIN. By an Old Inhabitant of British America [pseud]. Halifax, Royal Gazette, 1825. 34p [Also: London, Murray, 1831. 49p] [BM BVaU LC NSWA OTU

**Hambleton, John O. ("Jack"), 1901–1961**

FISHERMAN'S PARADISE. Toronto, Longmans, 1946. 172p [BVa OTP

**Hamilton, James H.**

LOVE OF LEARNING. The Annual Lecture of the Mutual Improvement Union, delivered at Hantsport, N.S., Sept. 27, 1866. ... Wolfville, Theakston, 1866. 32p [NSHD

**Hansson, Gertrude Edith, 1917–**

WE ARE BLIND. Winnipeg, Columbia Press, 1953. 63p

**Harper, John Murdoch, 1845–1919**

DOMINUS DOMI; or, The Chateau St. Louis. Quebec, Chien d'Or, 1898. 23p [OTP

**Harris, Lawren Stewart, 1885–1970**

ABSTRACT PAINTING, A DISQUISITION. Toronto, Rous & Mann, 1954. 16p

**Harris, Walter Eric, 1889–**

ACHATES; or, The Future of Canada. Toronto, Musson, 1929. 93p [BVaU OTU

STAND TO YOUR WORK. Toronto, Musson, 1927. 269p [BVaU NSWA OTP

**Harvey, Rev. Moses, 1820?–1901**

WHERE ARE WE AND WHITHER TENDING? Three Lectures on the Reality and Worth of Human Progress. Boston, Doyle & Whittle, 1886. 134p [BM LC NSWA QMM

**Harvey, William Earl, 1898–**

THE PSYCHOLOGY OF COMPOSITION. St. Paul, Minn., Review Pub., 1927. 78p [LC

**Hatheway, Warren Franklin, 1850–1923**

CANADIAN NATIONALITY. The Cry of Labor, and Other Essays. Toronto, Briggs, 1906. 230p [BM BVaU LC NBFU OTP

**Haultain, Theodore Arnold, 1857–1941**

A CHRISTMAS CHAT. A Fragmentary Dialogue on Love and Religion. Toronto, Ellis, Moore & Bangs, 1887. 23p [OTP

HINTS FOR LOVERS. Boston, Houghton, 1909. 308p [BM LC NBFU OTU

THE MYSTERY OF GOLF. A Brief Account of Games in General, their Origine, Antiquity, and Rampancie, and of the Game ycleped Golfe in Particular &c &c. Boston, Houghton, 1908. 152p [BM NBFU OTU

OF WALKS AND WALKING TOURS. An Attempt to Find a Philosophy and a Creed. London, Werner Laurie, 1914. 230p [BM NSHD OTU QMM

TWO COUNTRY WALKS IN CANADA. Toronto, Morang, 1903. 93p [BM BVaU LC NSHD OTP

**Hawkes, Arthur, 1871–1933**

THE BIRTHRIGHT. A Search for the Canadian Canadian and the Larger Loyalty. Toronto, Dent, 1919. 380p [BM BVaU LC NSHD OLU

**Hayes, E.H.**

CANADIANS AS WE SEE 'EM. Cartoons, Penportraits, Caricatures. [Montreal? 1900?] [unpaged] [BVaU OKQ

**Henderson, Dorothy (McLaughlin), 1900–**

I LIVE AND MOVE. A Series of Sketches with Related Readings. New York, Philosophical Library, 1953. 104p

**Hensley, Sophia Margaret (Almon), 1866–**

LOVE AND THE WOMAN OF TOMORROW. By Almon Hensley [pseud]. London, Drane's, 1913. 216p [BM

WOMAN AND THE RACE. By Gordon Hart [pseud]. New York, Ariel, 1908. 280p [AmCat MOR'12

**Herridge, Rev. William Thomas, 1857–1929**

THE CALL OF THE WAR. Ottawa, Author, 1915. 12p [BM OTU

**Heywood, Edward Percival, 1885–**

WONDERS OF THE WORLD. Ilfracombe, Devon, Stockwell, 1959. 186p

**Hill, Rev. Allan Massie, 1876–1943**

SWEEPINGS FRAE THE CURLING RINK. Yarmouth, N.S., 1910. 162p [T&C

**Hill, Philip Carteret, 1821–1894**

UNITED STATES AND BRITISH PROVINCES. Contrasted from Personal Observation. ... Halifax, Barnes, 1859. 30p [NSHD

**Hill, Mrs. Vivian Wood, 1900–**

CROSS ROADS PANORAMA. Toledo, Ont., Author, 1940. 55p [OTU

HOMEWARD JOURNEY. N.p., Author, [1945?]. 50p [OTU

**Hill-Tout, Charles, 1858–1944**

MAN AND HIS ANCESTORS, IN THE LIGHT OF ORGANIC EVOLUTION. Vancouver, Cowan Brookhouse, 1925. 157p [BVaU OOA

**Hodgins, John George, 1821–1912**

AN HOSPITAL SUNDAY FOR TORONTO. A Paper. ... Toronto, Mail, 1887. 15p [NSWA

**Hodgins, Samuel Raymond Norris, 1895–**

SOME CANADIAN ESSAYS. Ed. by ——. Toronto, Nelson, 1932. 239p [BM BVaU NSHD OTU QMM

**Holmes, Francis Joseph Sloan, 1908–**

DUCKS ARE DIFFERENT. Caricatures and Candid Stories of your Favorite Waterfowl. Winnipeg, Author, 1949. 38p [MWP

**Hossack, Donald Calvin, 1862–1937**

ILLUSTRIOUS MEN. Addresses. Toronto, Rose, 1903. 110p [BM OTP

**Howe, Joseph, 1804–1873**

ADDRESS DELIVERED ... at the Howe Festival, Framingham, Massachusetts, August 31, 1871. Boston, Rockwell & Churchill, 1871. 21p [NSHD QMSS

ADDRESS DELIVERED BEFORE THE HALIFAX MECHANICS' INSTITUTE, ON THE 5th OF NOV., 1834. Halifax, 1834. 23p [NSHD

ADDRESS DELIVERED ... before the Young Men's Christian Assoc., Ottawa, Feb. 27, 1872. Ottawa, Taylor, 1872. [NSHD

CONFEDERATION CONSIDERED IN RELATION TO THE INTERESTS OF THE EMPIRE. London, Stanford, 1866. 37p [BM BVaU NSWA OTP

SHAKESPEARE. Oration Delivered at the Request of the St. George's Society, Halifax, Nova Scotia, 23rd April, 1864. Halifax, "Citizen," 1864. 25p [BM NSHD OLU QMM

THE SPEECHES AND PUBLIC LETTERS OF THE HON. JOSEPH HOWE. Ed. by William Annand. Boston, Jewett; Halifax, Mackinlay; Montreal, Dawson; London, Sampson Low, 1858. 2v [Revised and augmented edition ed. by Joseph Andrew Chisholm: Halifax, Chronicle Pub. Co., 1909. 2v] [BM BVaU LC NSHD OKQ QMM

TRIAL FOR LIBEL, ON THE MAGISTRATES OF HALIFAX ... before the Chief Justice and a Special Jury. ... Halifax, 1835. 102p [NSHP

**Howes, Ernest Albert, 1872–1940**

WITH A GLANCE BACKWARD. Toronto, Oxford U. Press, 1939. 196p [BVaU NSHD OTP

**Howley, Rev. Michael Francis, 1843–1914**

CABOT'S VOYAGES. A Lecture. ... St. John's, Devine & O'Mara, 1897. 39p [BM LC NSHD QMSS

**Hunt, Rev. John**

REVERIES, REVIEWS, RECOLLECTIONS. Toronto, Briggs, 1887. 155p [BVaU NSWA OTP

**Huntington, Lucius Seth, 1827–1886**

INDEPENDENCE OF CANADA. ... Montreal, Herald Steam Press, 1869. 14p [NSHD

**Hutton, Maurice, 1856–1940**

ALL THE RIVERS RUN INTO THE SEA. Toronto, Musson, 1928. 288p [BM BVaU LC NSHD OTU QMM

MANY MINDS. London, Hodder, 1927. 300p [BM LC NSHD OKQ QMM

THE SISTERS, JEST AND EARNEST. London, Hodder, 1930. 288p [Earlier ed.: Toronto, Musson, 192–?] [BM BVaU OLU QMM

**Iles, George, 1852–1942**

THE APPRAISAL OF LITERATURE. Speech at International Library Conference, London, July 13–16, 1897. New York, 1897. 16p [NSHPL OTU

BOOKS IN THE BALANCE. [Lecture delivered June 21st, 1922 to McGill Summer Library School.] Montreal, 1922. 10p [OTU QMM

**Imrie, John, 1846–1902**

THE SCOT AT HOME AND ABROAD. Toronto, Imrie & Graham, 1898. 29p [BM QMSS

**Innis, Harold Adams, 1894–1952**

A PLEA FOR TIME. Fredericton, U. of New Brunswick, 1950. 21p [OONL

**Jack, Annie L. (Hayr), 1839–1912**

THE CANADIAN GARDEN. A Pocket Help for the Amateur. Toronto, Musson, 1910. 120p [BM NSHD OTU QMG

**Jephson, Harriet Julia (Campbell), 1854–1930**

A CANADIAN SCRAP-BOOK. A Volume of Essays and Stories. London, Marshall Russell, 1897. 183p [BM OTP

**Johnson, Charles Nelson, 1860–**
THE HAND CLASP. Chicago, 1919. 76p [LC

**Johnson, Rev. John H., 1826–**
INAUGURAL ADDRESS AS PRINCIPAL OF THE BELLEVILLE SEMINARY. Hamilton, 1857. [BibC
MAN, THE ARCHITECT OF HIS OWN FORTUNE. A Lecture. Montreal, Wilson, 1862. 24p [QMSS

**Johnson, Walter Seely, 1880–**
ESSAYS OF NOON AND SHADOW. Montreal, Burton's Ltd., 1934. 158p [BVaU OTU QMM

**Johnston, Blanche J. (Read), 1866–**
... OUR NEW CITIZENSHIP. 2nd ed. Toronto, McClelland, 1919. 64p [First ed., 1917.] [BM OKQ

**Johnston, John George, 1895–**
OF THIS AND THAT. By J.G. Johnston, J.L. Charlesworth, and R.G. Everson. Toronto, Authors, 1940. 64p [CC

**Jones, Rev. Peter, Chippewa Chief (Kah-Ke-Wa-Quon-A-By), 1802–1856**
THE SERMON AND SPEECHES OF THE REV. PETER JONES ... 1831. Leeds, Spink, n.d. 24p [OTP

**Jordan, Rev. William George, 1852–1939**
ENGLAND REVISITED. ... Toronto, Ryerson, 1926. 71p [OTUV

**Keate, Stuart, 1913–**
PRESS AND PUBLIC. The Annual Canadian Club Lecture Delivered at the University of British Columbia, December 10, 1955. Vancouver, U. of British Columbia, 1956. 18p

**Keefer, Thomas Coltrin, 1821–1915**
THE CANALS OF CANADA. Their Prospects and Influence. [A Prize Essay.] Toronto, Armour, 1850. 111p [BM BVaU LC NSWA OTU QMM
"MONTREAL" AND "THE OTTAWA": Two Lectures. ... Montreal, Lovell, 1854. 73p [BM BVaU NSHP OLU QMM

**Kennedy, Howard Angus, 1861–1938**
ROBERT BURNS IN THE TWENTIETH CENTURY. New York, Caledonian Pub., 1923. 23p [OTU

**Kennedy, Roderick Stuart, 1889–1953**
LAUGHTONES. Being a Series of Humorous and Inaccurate Biographical Sketches of certain leading Canadian Advertising Managers as they appeared to an Observer

with insufficient Opportunity to become acquainted with his Subjects and of too mean an Intellect to do them Justice, the whole embellished with twenty-six portraits. ... [Anon] Montreal, Family Herald, 1937. 63p [OTP

**Kerr, Estelle Muriel, 1879–1971**

THE TOWN CRIER OF GEVREY. New York, Macmillan, 1930. 129p [LC OTU

**King, Amabel (Reeves), 1899–**

RELICS OF A V.A.D. Toronto, Leslie Press, 1935. 21p [OTU

**King, Reginald Harold**

CLASSICAL MYTHOLOGY IN SONG AND STORY. Pts. I and II by Reginald Harold King and Neil Kenneth McKecknie. Toronto, Copp Clark, 1937, 1939. 2v [CC

**King, William Lyon Mackenzie, 1874–1950**

THE MESSAGE OF THE CARILLON, AND OTHER ADDRESSES. Toronto, Macmillan, 1927. 274p [BM BVaU LC NSHD OTP

THE STRUGGLE FOR ENDURING PEACE. An Address Given at the Canadian Corps Reunion, Toronto, July 30th, 1938. Ottawa, King's Printer, 1938. [OTU

**Kiriline, Louise (Flach) de, 1894–**

THE LOGHOUSE NEST. Toronto, Saunders, 1945. 173p [BVaU OKQ

**Kirkconnell, Watson, 1895–**

TWILIGHT OF LIBERTY. London, Oxford U. Press, 1941. 193p [BM BVaU NSHD OTU

**Kirkwood, Kenneth Porter, 1899–**

EXCURSIONS AMONG BOOKS. Buenos Aires, Mitchell's Bookstore, 1945. 431p [BM LC OKQ

**Kirkwood, Mossie May (Waddington), 1890–**

FOR COLLEGE WOMEN ... AND MEN. Toronto, Oxford U. Press, 1938. 81p [BVaU OLU QMM

**Knight, John Thomas Philip, 1851–1914**

INCIDENTALLY. Being Some Account of Incidents in the Life of a Mere Man. J.K. Montreal, Westmount News, 1913. 152p [BVaU NSHD OKQ

**Knox, Ellen Mary, 1858–1924**

THE GIRL OF THE NEW DAY. Toronto, McClelland, 1919. 241p [BM BVaU NSHD OTU

**Kristjansson, Adalsteinn**

IN THE STARLIGHT. ... Winnipeg, Columbia Press, 1931. 255p [BM BVaU OTP

SUPERSTITION IN THE TWILIGHT. Winnipeg, Columbia Press, 1929. 47p [LC

**Lamb, William Kaye, 1904–**

A PLEA FOR QUALITY AND INEQUALITY. Vancouver, U. of British Columbia, 1957. 16p

**Lambert, Richard Stanton, 1894–**

HOME FRONT. Intimate Letters, both Grave and Gay, Telling how Great Britain Faces the War. ... Collected and ed. by ——. Toronto, Ryerson, 1940. 123p [LC OTU

**Lanceley, Rev. John Ellis, 1848–1900**

THE DEVIL OF NAMES, AND OTHER LECTURES AND SERMONS. Ed. by his Brother, with Intro. by the Rev. Joseph Parker ... and a Biographical Sketch by the Rev. N. Burwash. Toronto, Briggs, 1900. 284p [BM BVaU LC OKQ

**Lande, Lawrence Montague, 1906–**

THE LADDER. A Discourse before the St. James Literary Society. Montreal, Author, 1958. 29p

**Langton, John, 1808–1894**

THE CENSUS OF 1861. A Paper Read before the Literary and Historical Society of Quebec. Quebec, Hunter Rose, 1864. 22p [OTP

**Laurier, Wilfrid, 1841–1919**

LECTURE ON POLITICAL LIBERALISM. ... Quebec, Budget Steam Print., 1877. 44p [BVaU NSHD OTU

WILFRID LAURIER ON THE PLATFORM. Collection of the Principal Speeches made in Parliament or before the People. Comp. by Ulric Barthe. ... Quebec, Turcotte & Menard, 1890. 624p [BVaU LC NBFU OKQ

**Lawson, Jessie (Kerr), 1838–1917**

THE EPISTLES O' HUGH AIRLIE [pseud]. (Formerly o'Scotland, Presently Conneckit wi' Tam Tamson's Warehoose in Toronto). Illus. by J.W. Bengough. Toronto, Grip Print., 1888. 103p [BM NSHD OTP

**Leacock, Stephen Butler, 1869–1944**

ALL RIGHT, MR. ROOSEVELT (Canada and the United States). Toronto, Oxford U. Press, 1939. 40p [BM OTU QMM

ESSAYS AND LITERARY STUDIES. London, Lane, 1916. 310p [BM BVaU LC NSHD OKQ

GREATER CANADA. An Appeal. Let Us No Longer Be a Colony. Montreal, Montreal News, 1907. 10p [BM NSWA OTU QMM

HOW TO WRITE. New York, Dodd Mead, 1943. 261p [BM BVaU NSHD OTU QMM

LINCOLN FREES THE SLAVES. New York, Putnam, 1934. 178p [BM BVaU LC NBFU OTU QMM

MY DISCOVERY OF ENGLAND. London, Lane, 1922. 219p [BM BVaU NSHD OKQ QMM

MY DISCOVERY OF THE WEST. A Discussion of East and West in Canada. Toronto, Allen, 1937. 272p [BM BVaU LC NBFU OTU QMM

"MY OLD COLLEGE" 1843–1943. [Montreal], Author, 1943. 16p [QMM

OUR HERITAGE OF LIBERTY. Its Origin, Its Achievement, Its Crisis. A Book for War Time. New York, Dodd Mead, 1942. 86p [BM BVaU OTU QMM

THE PROPER LIMITATIONS OF STATE INTERFERENCE. Toronto, 1924. 14p [QMM

THE PURSUIT OF KNOWLEDGE. A Discussion of Freedom and Compulsion in Education. New York, Liveright, 1934. 48p [BVaU LC NBFU OTU

STEPHEN LEACOCK'S PLAN TO RELIEVE THE DEPRESSION IN 6 DAYS, TO REMOVE IT IN 6 MONTHS, TO ERADICATE IT IN 6 YEARS. Toronto, Macmillan, 1933. 18p [BVaU NBFU OTU QMM

TOO MUCH COLLEGE; or, Education Eating Up Life. With Kindred Essays in Education and Humour. New York, Dodd Mead, 1939. 255p [BM BVaU LC NSHD OKQ QMM

**LeClaire, Gordon, 1905–**

MORE LIFE IN LIVING. Through the Seven Miracles of Mind. N.p., Author, [1947]. 61p [BVaU

**LeMoine, James MacPherson, 1825–1912**

THE EXPLORATION OF JONATHAN OLDBUCK, F.R.S.Q., IN EASTERN LATITUDES. Canadian History–Legends. ... Quebec, Demers, 1889. 265p [BM BVaU LC NSHD OTU

MAPLE LEAVES. A Budget of Legendary, Historical, Critical and Sporting Intelligence. Seven Series. Quebec, Hunter Rose, 1863–1906. 7v [BM BVaU NSHD OTU QMM

THE SCOT IN NEW FRANCE. An Ethnological Study. Inaugural Address ... Literary Society of Quebec, 29th November, 1880. Montreal, Dawson Bros., 1881. 83p [BVaU NSWA OTP

**Lett, William Pittman, 1819–1892**

THE ANTLERED KINGS. A Lecture. Ottawa, 1884. [OOP

**Lighthall, William Douw, 1857–1954**

AN ACCOUNT OF THE BATTLE OF CHATEAUGUAY. Being a Lecture. Montreal, Drysdale, 1889. 32p [BM BVaU LC NSWA OTU

GOVERNANCE OF EMPIRE. ... Montreal, Author, 1910. 15p [BM NSHD OTU

**Lloyd, Cecil Richard Francis, 1884–1938**

MALVERN ESSAYS. Toronto, Ryerson, 1930. 51p [BVaU NBFU OTP

SUNLIGHT AND SHADOW. Toronto, Hunter Rose, 1928. 83p [BM OTP QMM

**Llwyd, Rev. John Plummer Derwent, 1861–1933**

THE MESSAGE OF AN INDIAN RELIC. Seattle, Lowman & Hanford, 1909. 21p [BViPA

MYSTICISM AND OTHER ESSAYS. Toronto, Macmillan, 1926. 108p [BVa NSHD OTP

**Locke, Clark, 1890–**

COUNTRY HOURS. Toronto, Ryerson, 1959. 105p

**Locke, George Herbert, 1870–1937**

BUILDERS OF THE CANADIAN COMMONWEALTH. Toronto, Ryerson, 1923. 317p [A selection of speeches by Canadian statesmen.] [BM BVaU LC NBFU OTP QMM

**Lodge, Rupert Clendon, 1886–**

MANITOBA ESSAYS. Ed. by ——. Toronto, Macmillan, 1937. 432p [BM BVaU NBFU OTU

**Logan, John Daniel, 1869–1929**

THE INN AT THE END OF THE WORLD. ... Halifax, Allen, 1923. 27p [BVaU OOP

**Long, John Henry**

SLIPS OF TONGUE AND PEN. Toronto, Copp Clark, 1886. 101p [OTU QMM

**Loudon, William James, 1860–1951**

STUDIES OF STUDENT LIFE. Toronto, Macmillan, 1923–37. 8v [BM BVaU NBFU OTU QMM

**Lovegrove, F. Francis**

RUMINATIONS. Toronto, Ryerson, 1923. 63p [BM BVaU LC OKQ

**Low, Rev. George Jacobs, 1836–1906**

A PARSON'S PONDERINGS. Toronto, Briggs, 1906. 184p [BM NSHD OTP

**McAleer, George, 1845–**

GATHERED WAIFLETS. Worcester, Mass., Author, 1913. 505p [LC

**McAree, John Verner, 1876–1958**

THE FOURTH COLUMN. Toronto, Macmillan, 1934. 332p [BVaU NBFU OTP

**McArthur, Peter, 1866–1924**

THE AFFABLE STRANGER. Toronto, Allen, 1920. 216p [BVaU LC NBFU OKQ

AROUND HOME. ... Toronto, Musson, 1925. 250p [BVaU LC NSHD OKQ QMSS

A CHANT OF MAMMONISM. Waterloo, Ont., Ont. Equitable Life, [1922]. 6p [NBFU OTU

FAMILIAR FIELDS. London, Dent, [1925?]. 157p [BM BVaU NSHD OTP

FRIENDLY ACRES. Toronto, Musson, 1927. 239p [BVaU NSHD OTP QMM

IN PASTURES GREEN. Toronto, Dent, 1915. 363p [Also: Toronto, Dent, 1948. 298p] [BM BVaU LC NSHD OTP

THE LAST LAW-BROTHERHOOD. Toronto, Allen, 1921. 57p [BM BVaU NSHD OKQ

THE RED COW AND HER FRIENDS. Toronto, Dent, 1919. 287p [BVaU LC NSHD OTU

TO BE TAKEN WITH SALT. Being an Essay in Teaching one's Grandmother to Suck Eggs. London, Limpus Baker, 1903. 196p [BM BVaU OTP

**MacCallum, Duncan Campbell**

ADDRESSES. Montreal, Desbarats, 1901. 168p [BVaU OOP QMSS

**McCarroll, James, 1815–1896**

LETTERS OF TERRY FINNEGAN [pseud], to the Hon. Thomas d'Arcy McGee. Volume 1. Complete in Itself. Toronto, 1863. 104p [OTP

**McCarthy, Eugene**

A TALE OF LAKE ST. JOHN. Comprising a Bit of History, a Quantity of Facts, and a Plentitude of Fish Stories. Montreal, Desbarats, [1903?]. 65p [BVaU OOP QMBM

**McCawley, Stuart**

STANDING THE GAFF. The Cape Breton Mines and Miners. N.p., n.d. 30p [NSHP

**McClung, Nellie Letitia (Mooney), 1873–1951**

IN TIMES LIKE THESE. Addresses. New York, Appleton, 1915. 217p [BM BVaU LC NBFU OTU

THE NEXT OF KIN. Stories of Those Who Wait and Wonder. Boston, Houghton, 1917. 256p [BVaU LC NBFU OTU

**McCord, Frederick Augustus, 1856–1908**

ERRORS IN CANADIAN HISTORY CULLED FROM "PRIZE ANSWERS." Montreal, Dawson, 1880. 45p [BVaU NSWA OTP QMM

**McCowan, Daniel, 1882–1956**

ANIMALS OF THE CANADIAN ROCKIES. Toronto, Macmillan, 1936. 302p [BM BVaU LC OTP QMM

A NATURALIST IN CANADA. Toronto, Macmillan, 1941. 284p [BM BVaU LC NBFU OTP QMSS

OUTDOORS WITH A CAMERA IN CANADA. Toronto, Macmillan, 1945. 102p [BM BVaU LC OTP QMBM

TIDEWATER TO TIMBERLINE. Toronto, Macmillan, 1951. x + 205p

**McCulloch, Rev. Thomas, 1776–1843**

THE NATURE AND USES OF A LIBERAL EDUCATION ILLUSTRATED. Being a Lecture Delivered at the Opening of the Pictou Academical Institution. Halifax, Holland, 1819. 24p [NSWA

**McCurdy, John Alexander Douglas, 1886–**

"NOVA SCOTIA" AND THE MEN WHO LIVED ON HER SOIL. New York, Montreal, Newcomen Society in North America, 1953. 28p

**Macdonald, Angus Lewis, 1890–1954**

SPEECHES. With a Biographical Note by A.T. Crerar. Toronto, Longmans, 1960. xxvii + 227p

**Macdonald, Rev. James Alexander, 1862–1923**

MEMORIES OF HALLOWE'EN. At the Annual Banquet of the Caledonian Society of Toronto on Hallowe'en, 1906. Toronto, 1906. 15p [OTP

THE NORTH AMERICAN IDEA. New York, Revell, 1917. 240p [BVaU LC NSWA OTP

**Macdonald, John Alexander, 1815–1891**

ADDRESS TO THE ELECTORS OF THE CITY OF KINGSTON. N.p., 1861. 153p [NSHD OTU

**McDonnell, William, 1814–1900**

OUR STRANGE GUEST. Lindsay, Wilson & Wilson, [1876?]. 14p [OTP

**MacDougall, James Brown, 1871–1950**

THE REAL MOTHER GOOSE. The Reality Behind the Rhyme. Toronto, Ryerson, 1940. 57p [BVaU LC OTU QMM

**McDougall, Robert Lorne, 1918–**

OUR LIVING TRADITION. Second and third series. Ed. by ——. Toronto, pub. in association with Carleton University by U. of Toronto Press, 1959. xvi + 288p

**McEvoy, Bernard, 1842–1932**

WHICH WAY, CANADA? By Diogenes, B.A. [pseud]. N.p., n.d. 15p [QMSS

**McGee, Thomas D'Arcy, 1825–1868**

1825–D'ARCY McGEE–1925. A Collection of Speeches and Addresses. Selected ... by the Hon. Charles Murphy. Toronto, Macmillan, 1937. 366p [BM BVaU LC NBFU OTP QMM

THE POLITICAL CAUSES AND CONSEQUENCES OF THE PROTESTANT "REFORMATION." A Lecture. New York, Sadlier & Co., 1853. 27p [BM LC NSWA OTU

**McGillen, Pete**

OUTDOORS WITH PETE McGILLEN. Toronto, Ryerson, 1955. xii + 177p

**McGillicuddy, Paul Clark, 1918–1942**

BETWEEN LECTURES. Some Tips to Canadian Undergraduates–and their Enemies–and Friends. Toronto, Age Publications, 1939. 63p [NBFU OTP QMM

**MacGregor, Rev. James, 1759–1830**

A FEW REMAINS OF THE REV. JAMES MacGREGOR. Ed. by his grandson, the Rev. George Patterson. Philadelphia, Wilson, 1859. 274p [BM BVaU NSWA OTP

**McGuire, James Leonard**

OAT-CAKES AND SULPHUR. Brockville, Recorder Print., 1927. 81p [BVaU OTP QMSS

**Machar, Agnes Maule, 1837–1927**

YOUNG SOLDIER HEARTS OF FRANCE. Toronto, Musson, 1919. 300p [OTU

**MacInnes, Thomas Robert Edward, 1867–1951**

THE TEACHING OF THE OLD BOY. London, Dent, 1927. 227p [BM BVaU NBFU OLU

**MacKay, Isabel Ecclestone (Macpherson), 1875–1928**

THE TIMELESS TRAVELLERS. Toronto, Best, n.d. 16p [BVaU

**Mackenzie, Alexander, 1822–1892**

POLITICAL POINTS AND PENCILLINGS. Being Selections from Various Addresses Delivered by the Hon. Alex. Mackenzie. Toronto, "Grip" Office, 1878. 36p [NSHD OTP

SPEECHES DURING HIS RECENT VISIT TO SCOTLAND. With his Principal Speeches in Canada since the Session of 1875. With Sketch of his Life. Toronto, Campbell, 1876. 219p [BM BVaU NBFU OTP QMM

**MacKenzie, Norman Archibald MacRae, 1894–**

ADDRESS AT SPECIAL CONVOCATION OF MOUNT ALLISON UNIVERSITY, JAN. 31, 1941. Sackville, Mount Allison U., 1941. [OTU

**Mackenzie, William Lyon, 1795–1861**

SELECTED WRITINGS, 1824–1837. Ed. by Margaret Fairley. Toronto, Oxford U. Press, 1960. 383p

**MacKinnon, John [of P.E.I.]**

A SKETCH BOOK COMPRISING HISTORICAL INCIDENTS, TRADITIONAL TALES AND TRANSLATIONS. Saint John, Barnes, 1915. 213p [BM OTU

**McLaren, John W.**

LET'S ALL HATE TORONTO. Narration, Illustration & Exhortation. By Jack McLaren. Toronto, Kingswood House, 1956. xi + 66p

**Maclean, Rev. John, 1851–1928**

LONE LAND LIGHTS. First series. Toronto, Briggs, 1882. 75p [BVaU LC OTP SSU

**MacLennan, Hugh, 1907–**

CANADIAN UNITY AND QUEBEC. By Emile Vaillancourt, J.P. Humphrey, and Hugh MacLennan. Montreal, 1942. 16p [OTU QMM

CROSS COUNTRY. Toronto, Collins, 1949. 172p [BVaU NBFU OLU QMBM

THE FUTURE OF THE NOVEL AS AN ART FORM. Toronto, U. of Toronto Press, [1959?]. 11p

THE PRESENT WORLD AS SEEN IN ITS LITERATURE. Fredericton, U. of New Brunswick, 1952. 12p

SCOTCHMAN'S RETURN AND OTHER ESSAYS. Toronto, Macmillan, 1960. 279p

THIRTY & THREE. Ed. by Dorothy Duncan. Toronto, Macmillan, 1954. xi + 261p

**McLennan, William, 1856–1904**

LITERARY PAMPHLETS, CANADA. [No title page.] 19v in 1. [QMM

**MacLeod, Margaret Marie (Furness)**

"FOUR SCRIPTS." Trans-Canada-Matinée. Inspired by Childhood Memories in Prince Edward Island. Montreal, Author, 1956. 19p [mimeographed]

**McLeod, Robert Randall, 1839–1909**

FURTHER STUDIES IN NATURE. Halifax, Commercial Print., 1910. 120p [NSHD

IN THE ACADIAN LAND. Nature Studies. Boston, Whidden, 1899. 166p [BM BVaU LC OKQ NSHD

**McLuhan, Herbert Marshall, 1911–**

COUNTERBLAST 1954. Toronto, priv. print., [1954?]. 17p

**MacMechan, Archibald McKellar, 1862–1933**

THE BOOK OF ULTIMA THULE. Toronto, McClelland, 1927. 368p [BM BVaU NSHD OKQ

THE LIFE OF A LITTLE COLLEGE, AND OTHER PAPERS. Boston, Houghton, 1914. 308p [BVaU LC NSHD OTU

THE LOG OF A HALIFAX PRIVATEER. Nova Scotia Chapbook No. 6. Halifax, Marshall, 1921. [BVaU NBFU OTU

THE MEMORIAL TOWER. Nova Scotia Chapbook. Halifax, Marshall, 1922. 12p [BVaU OTP

NOVA SCOTIA CHAP-BOOKS. Halifax, Marshall, 1919–192–?. 16v: 1, Three Sea Songs. 2, The Nova Scotia-ness of Nova Scotia. 3, Storied Halifax. 4, The Memorial Tower. 5, The Orchards of Ultima Thule. 6, The Log of a Halifax Privateer. 7, Glamming; the Neredi's Embrace; the Two Games. 8, The Loss of the Atalante. 9, "Nova Scarcity"; The Literature of Nova Scotia. 10, The Pleasance; From Minas to the Wotan Line. 11, The Sky-Line; Old King's. 12, Spring in Ultima Thule; The Potato Patch. 13, The Luck of the Grilse. 14, Twelve Profitable Sonnets. 15, Twelve Unprofitable Sonnets. 16, Afoot in Ultima Thule. [Files at the libraries are incomplete.] [BVaU NBFU NSHD OTP

THE NOVA SCOTIA-NESS OF NOVA SCOTIA. Nova Scotia Chap-Book No. 2. Halifax, Allen, 1924. 12p [The numbering is irrelevant to order of publication, since "four other" chapbooks have preceded this one.] [BVaU OTU

THE ORCHARDS OF ULTIMA THULE. Nova Scotia Chapbook. Halifax, Marshall, 1919. 13p [BVaU NBFU OKQ

THE PORTER OF BAGDAD, and other Fantasies. Toronto, Morang, 1901. 150p [BM NBFU NSHD OTU

**MacMillan, Ernest Campbell, 1893–**

SOME PROBLEMS OF THE CANADIAN COMPOSER. Charlottetown, Prince of Wales College, 1956. 14p

**Macnaughton, John, 1858–1943**

ESSAYS AND ADDRESSES. Selected by D.D. Calvin. Kingston, Queen's U., 1946. 319p [BVaU LC NSHD OTP QMM

**Macphail, Andrew, 1864–1938**

ESSAYS IN FALLACY. New York, Longmans, 1910. 359p [BM BVaU LC NSHD OTU QMM

ESSAYS IN POLITICS. London, Longmans, 1909. 301p [BM BVaU LC NBFU OLU QMM

ESSAYS IN PURITANISM. Boston, Houghton, 1905. 339p [BM BVaU LC NBFU OTU QMBM

**MacRae, Archibald Oswald, 1869–**

WHAT IS THE MATTER WITH CANADA? Addresses. ... By "Politicus" [pseud]. London, Stockwell, 1928. 96p [BM BVaU NSHD OTP

**MacTavish, Newton McFaul, 1875–1941**

THROWN IN. Toronto, Macmillan, 1923. 196p [BM BVaU NBFU OTP

**Madison, Grant**

RIVER FOR MY SIDEWALK. Toronto, Dent, 1953. 135p

**Malone, Richard Sankey, 1909–**

BOOKSHELF FREE PRESS. A Selection from the Winnipeg *Free Press.* V. 1, 1955–56. Ed. by ——. Winnipeg, Winnipeg *Free Press*, 1956. 256p [No more published.]

**Marsh, Edith Louise, –1960**

BIRDS OF PEASEMARSH. Toronto, Musson, 1919. 233p [BM LC OTP

WITH THE BIRDS. Toronto, Dent, 1935. 86p [CC

**Marshall, Mortimer Villiers, 1898–**

AN APPLE FOR TEACHER. Wolfville, N.S., Bookstore, Acadia U., 1954. 40p

**Mason, Louise, –1946**

AFTER THE HONEYMOON. Toronto, McClelland, [1913]. 58p [Another ed.: Toronto, McClelland, 1922.] [BM CC T&C

**Massey, Denton, 1900–**

THE STUFF MEN ARE MADE OF. With an intro. by Rev. G. Stanley Russell. Toronto, Saunders, 1935. 254p [LC

**Massey, Rev. Samuel, 1817–**

"HOME SWEET HOME" – A Lecture ... on "Our City Homes, and How to make them Healthy and Sweet." Delivered in St. John's Church, Montreal. Montreal, [18—?]. 8p [OTP

**Massey, Vincent, 1887–1967**

AN ADDRESS AT HART HOUSE IN THE UNIVERSITY OF TORONTO BEFORE THE ASSOCIATION OF AMERICAN UNIVERSITY PRESSES. ... Toronto, U. of Toronto Press, 1951. 15p

GOOD NEIGHBOURHOOD, AND OTHER ADDRESSES IN THE UNITED STATES. Toronto, Macmillan, 1930. 362p [BM BVaU LC NSHD OTP QMM

THE MAKING OF A NATION. Boston, Houghton, 1928. 44p [BVaU LC NSHD OTP

ON BEING CANADIAN. Toronto, Dent, 1948. 198p [BM BVaU NBFU OTP QMM

ON BOOKS AND READING. The Address ... at the 125th Anniversary Dinner of the United Church Publishing House and the Ryerson Press ... October 19th, 1954. Toronto, Ryerson, 1954. 12p

SPEAKING OF CANADA. Addresses. Toronto, Macmillan, 1959. x + 244p

THE SWORD OF LIONHEART AND OTHER WARTIME SPEECHES. Toronto, Ryerson, 1942. 117p [BM BVaU LC NSHD OTP

UNCERTAIN SOUNDS. Sackville, N.B., Mount Allison University, 1957. 32p [On language.]

**Matthews, James Skitt, 1878–**

THE DEDICATION OF STANLEY PARK, 1889. [An Address. ...] Vancouver, City Archives, 1952. 16p

**Matthews, Robertson, 1879–**

HIS LOST CHORD. Glimpses of Man's Deepest Emotion in Restraint. Bolton, Ont., Bolton Enterprise, 1959. 48p

**May, Rev. John, 1834–**

ESSAYS ON EDUCATIONAL SUBJECTS. Ottawa, Woodburn, 1880. 52p [OTP

**Medley, Rev. John, 1804–1892**

ELEMENTARY REMARKS ON CHURCH ARCHITECTURE. Exeter, Hannaford, 1841. 40p [OTP

**Meighen, Arthur, 1874–1960**

"THE GREATEST ENGLISHMAN OF HISTORY" [Shakespeare]. An Address. Toronto, Gundy, 1936. 39p [Also: Fort Erie, Review Co., 1954. 43p] [BVaU NSHD OTU

OVERSEA ADDRESSES, JUNE–JULY, 1921. Toronto, Musson, 1921. 82p [BVaU NBFU OTP QMBM

UNREVISED AND UNREPENTED. Debating Speeches and Others. With a foreword by M. Grattan O'Leary. Toronto, Clarke Irwin, 1949. 470p [BVaU NBFU OTP QMBM

**Millard, Frederick Payne, 1878–**

THE HARP OF LIFE. Toronto, McClelland, 1928. 287p [BVaU NBFU

NO OLDER AT NIGHT. Boston, Christopher Pub. House, 1926. 178p [LC QMM

THROUGH THE FOG. Kirksville, Mo., Journal Print., 1927. 262p [LC QMM

**Miller, John Ormsby, 1861–1936**

THE NEW ERA IN CANADA. Essays Dealing with the Upbuilding of the Canadian Commonwealth. Ed. by ——. Toronto, Dent, 1917. 421p [BVaU LC NBFU OLU QMM

**Miller, Robert**

THE LAW AND THE LOVE OF UNITY EXHIBITED IN THE CREATION. A Lecture. Halifax, Barnes, 1858. 40p [NSHD

TRUE GREATNESS. A Lecture. ... Halifax, Barnes, 1859. 29p [NSHD QMM

**Milliken, Lorene Frances (Ritz)**

INTERLUDES. Prose Pieces. Winnipeg, Author, 1957. 62p

**Miner, Jack (John Thomas Miner), 1865–1944**

JACK MINER ON CURRENT TOPICS. Toronto, Ryerson, 1929. 111p [BVaU OTP

**Mines, Robert Frederick, 1925–**

MY MIND WENT ALL TO PIECES. The Funniest Things that Patients have said to their Psychiatrists. New York, Dial Press, 1958. 93p

**Mitchell, John, 1880–**

THE KINGDOM OF AMERICA. The Canadian Creed. Brampton, Banner & Times, 1930. 90p [BVaU LC NBFU OTUV

**Mitchell, Roy, 1884–1944**

THEOSOPHIC STUDY and A WHITE LOTUS DAY ADDRESS. Toronto, Blavatsky Institute, 1953. 83p

**Montgomery, Lucy Maud, 1874–1942**

COURAGEOUS WOMEN. By L.M. Montgomery, Marian Keith [pseud], and Mabel Burns McKinley. Toronto, McClelland, 1934. 203p [BVa LC NBFU OTU

**Montreal, Que. Literary Society**

ESSAYS READ IN MONTREAL DURING THE WINTER OF 1880–81. Montreal, 1881. 54p [QMM

**Moore, William Henry, 1872–1960**

BY THEIR FRUITS. Pickering, Printers' Guild, 1949. 136p [BVaU OTP QMM

THE COMMANDMENTS OF MEN. Toronto, Printers' Guild, 1925. 197p [BM BVaU LC OTP QMSS

GREY DAYS. Pickering, Printers' Guild, 1946. 145p [BVaU OTP

PUBLIC LIFE. Pickering, priv. print., 1936. 64p [OTP QMSS

UNDERNEATH IT ALL. Pickering, Printers' Guild, 1942. 143p [BVa LC OTP QMM

WHEN THE IRON IS HOT. Pickering, Printers' Guild, 1943. 124p [BVaU LC NSHD OTP

**Morgan, Henry James, 1842–1913**

THE PLACE BRITISH AMERICANS HAVE WON IN HISTORY. Ottawa, Hunter Rose, 1866. 22p [BM LC NSWA OKQ

**Morgan, Lorne Thompson, 1897–**

THE PERMANENT WAR; or, Homo the Sap. Toronto, Workers' Educational Assoc., 1943. 64p [BVaU OTU

**Morgan-Powell, Samuel, 1898–**

MEMORIES THAT LIVE. Toronto, Macmillan, 1929. 282p [BM BVaU NBFU OTP QMBM

THIS CANADIAN LITERATURE. Being an Address. ... Toronto, Macmillan, 1940. 14p [LC OTP

**Morse, William Inglis, 1874–1952**

ECCENTRICS IN PARADISE, AND OTHER ESSAYS. Boston, Sawyer, 1926. 94p [LC

INTERLUDES FOR DUST EATERS (ANCIENT AND MODERN). With a Monologue. By W.I.M. Boston, Sawyer, 1923. 27p [LC

**Muir, James, 1892?–1960**

THE LAND WE LEFT. An Address to the Illinois Saint Andrew Society ... in ... Chicago ... December 3rd, 1949. Montreal, Royal Bank of Canada, n.d. 52p

SCOTLAND AND SAINT ANDREW. An Address to the North British Society ... in ... Halifax, ... November 30th, 1953. Montreal, Royal Bank of Canada, n.d. 45p

**Muldrew, William Hawthorne, 1867–1904**

SYLVAN ONTARIO. A Guide to our Native Trees and Shrubs. Toronto, Briggs, 1901. 67p [BM LC NBFU OTP

**Murray, E.G.D.**

STUDIA VARIA. Royal Society of Canada Literary and Scientific Papers. Ed. by ——. Toronto, Published for the Society by U. of Toronto Press, 1957. 127p

**Murray, Mrs. Margaret L.**

LITTLE TRAVELS TO WINDY RIDGE AND OTHER PLACES. ... Vancouver, Lillooet Pubs., 1944. 150p [BViPA OTU

**Neatby, Hilda Marion Ada, 1904–**

THE DEBT OF OUR REASON. Toronto, Clarke Irwin, 1954. 23p

A TEMPERATE DISPUTE. Toronto, Clarke Irwin, 1954. 97p

**Newton, Frances (pseud)**

LIGHT LIKE THE SUN. By Frances Newton [pseud]. New York, Dodd Mead, 1937. 25p [On cremation.] [OTU

**Nicholson, Byron, 1857–1916**

IN OLD QUEBEC, AND OTHER SKETCHES. Quebec, Commercial Print., 1908. 162p [BVaU LC NSHD OLU QMM

**Nicol, Eric Patrick, 1919–**

GIRDLE ME A GLOBE. Toronto, Ryerson, 1957. xii + 134p

A HISTORY OF CANADA. [Cover title: An Uninhibited History of Canada.] Montreal, D. Hackett, 1959. 1v. [unpaged]

IN DARKEST DOMESTICA. Toronto, Ryerson, 1959. xi + 113p

THE ROVING I. Toronto, Ryerson, 1950. 134p [BVaU NBFU OTP

SENSE AND NONSENSE. Toronto, Ryerson, 1947. 148p [BVaU NBFU OTU QMBM

SHALL WE JOIN THE LADIES? Toronto, Ryerson, 1955. xi + 156p

TWICE OVER LIGHTLY. Toronto, Ryerson, 1953. 137p [BVaU NBFU OTUV

**Nobile, Achilles Alexander, 1833–**

HERE AND THERE THROUGH THE HISTORY OF ITALY. A Lecture. ... Followed by MANZONI AND RATTAZZI, An Address. ... Toronto, Williams, 1884. 37p [Bound with his MISCELLANEOUS POEMS, Translated. ...] [BVaU LC OTU QMBM

**Norwood, Gilbert, 1880–1954**

SPOKEN IN JEST. Toronto, Macmillan, 1938. 209p [BM BVaU LC NBFU OTU QMM

THE WOODEN MAN AND OTHER STORIES AND ESSAYS. New York, Macmillan, 1926. 240p [BM LC OTU

**Odlum, Edward, 1850–1935**

WHO ARE THE JAPANESE? London, Covenant, [1932?]. 31p [LC

**O'Hagan, Thomas, 1855–1939**

CANADIAN ESSAYS, CRITICAL AND HISTORICAL. Toronto, Briggs, 1901. 222p [BM BVaU LC NBFU OTP

CHATS BY THE FIRESIDE. A Study in Life, Art and Literature. Somerset, Ohio, Rosary Press, [Pref. 1911]. 150p [LC OTP

ESSAYS, LITERARY, CRITICAL, AND HISTORICAL. Toronto, Briggs, 1909. 112p [BM BVaU LC NSHD OTP

ESSAYS ON CATHOLIC LIFE. Baltimore, Murphy, 1916. 166p [LC OKQ

INTIMACIES IN CANADIAN LIFE AND LETTERS. Ottawa, Graphic, 1927. 94p [BVaU LC NBFU OTP

SPAIN AND HER DAUGHTERS. Toronto, Hunter Rose, 1931. 123p [BVaU LC NSHD OTP

WITH STAFF AND SCRIP. Toronto, Ryerson, 1924. 156p [BVaU NBFU OTP

**O'Higgins, Harvey Jerrold, 1876–1929**

THE AMERICAN MIND IN ACTION. By Harvey O'Higgins and Edward H. Reede. New York, Harper, 1924. 336p [LC

**O'Loughlin, A.J., –1884?**

MAN, A MATERIAL, MENTAL AND SPIRITUAL BEING. A Lecture Delivered in ... Kingston, C.W., Jan. 6th, 1860. Kingston, Creighton, 1860. 66p [OTP

**O'Malley, Rev. Andrew, 1863–1921**

ESSAYS AND LECTURES. Barrie, Gazette, [1916?]. 189p [BVaU LC OLU

**O'Neill, Rev. Arthur Barry, 1858–**

CLERICAL COLLOQUIES. Essays. Notre Dame, Ind., University Press, 1916. 270p [LC OOSU

PRIESTLY PRACTICE. Familiar Essays on Clerical Topics. 2nd ed. Notre Dame, Ind., University Press, 1914. 249p [LC OOU

**Osler, William, 1849–1919**

AEQUANIMITAS. OTHER ESSAYS TO MEDICAL STUDENTS. ... London, Lewis, 1904. 398p [Various later editions.] [BM BVaU LC NBFU OTU

AN ALABAMA STUDENT, AND OTHER BIOGRAPHICAL ESSAYS. New York, Oxford U. Press, 1908. 334p [BM BVaU LC NBFU OTU QMM

COUNSELS AND IDEALS. Selections. ... Oxford, Clarendon Press, 1905. 292p [Various other eds.] [BM BVaU LC OTU

THE OLD HUMANITIES AND THE NEW SCIENCE. London, Murray, 1919. 32p [Also: Boston, Houghton, 1920.] [BM BVaU LC OTU QMM

SCIENCE AND WAR. An Address. Oxford, Clarendon Press, 1915. 39p [BM OTU

SELECTED WRITINGS. 12 July 1849 to 20 December 1919. ... London, Oxford U. Press, 1951. 278p [Editor's note, by A.W. Franklin.]

SIR WILLIAM OSLER. Aphorisms from his Bedside Teachings and Writings. ... Collected by R.B. Bean; ed. by W.B. Bean. New York, Schuman, 1950. 159p [LC OTU QMM

THE STUDENT LIFE. The Philosophy of Sir William Osler. Ed. by Richard E. Verney. Toronto, Macmillan, 1957. xiii + 214p

THE STUDENT LIFE AND OTHER ESSAYS. With an Intro. by H.H. Bashford. London, Constable, 1928. 36 + 145p [BM BVa LC OTU QMM

A WAY OF LIFE. An Address Delivered to Yale Students Sunday Evening, April 20, 1913. London, Constable, 1913. 62p [Also: New York, Hoeber, 1937.] [BM BVaU NBFU OTU QMM

**Parker, Gilbert, 1862–1932**

THE UNITED STATES AND THIS WAR. A Word in Season. Speech delivered ... to the Pilgrim's Society ... London, on the 15th April, 1915, on the Occasion of the Fiftieth Anniversary of the Death of Abraham Lincoln. London, Darling & Son, 1915. 10p [BM LC OTP

**Penfield, Wilder Graves, 1891–**

THE LIBERAL ARTS IN CANADA. Charlottetown, Prince of Wales College, 1958. 11p

**Peterson, William, 1856–1921**

CANADIAN ESSAYS AND ADDRESSES. London, Longmans, 1915. 373p [BM BVaU LC NSHD OTP QMM

**Phelps, Arthur Leonard, 1887–1970**

CANADIAN WRITERS. Toronto, McClelland, 1951. 119p

COMMUNITY AND CULTURE. The Founders' Day Address at the University of New Brunswick. Fredericton, U. of New Brunswick, 1947. 17p [BVaU NBFU OTP

THIS CANADA. Toronto, CBC Pub. Branch, 1940. 63p [LC NBFU OOA

THESE UNITED STATES. Toronto, CBC Pub. Branch, 1941. 60p [LC OTU

**Pierce, Lorne Albert, 1890–1961**

THE ARMOURY IN OUR HALLS. Toronto, Ryerson, 1941. 19p [BM BVaU LC NBFU OTP QMM

THE BELOVED COMMUNITY. Toronto, Ryerson, 1924. 72p [Ryerson Impt.

A CANADIAN NATION. Toronto, Ryerson, 1960. 42p

A CANADIAN PEOPLE. Toronto, Ryerson, 1945. 84p [BVaU LC NBFU OTP QMM

THE CANADA BOOK OF PROSE AND VERSE. Ed. by Lorne Pierce and Dora Whitefield (Mrs. Hugh S. Eayrs). Toronto, Ryerson, 1932. 3v [BVaU NBFU OLU

CHRISTIANITY AND CULTURE IN OUR TIME. Toronto, Ryerson, 1947. 12p [BVaU LC NBFU OTP

AN EDITOR'S CREED. Toronto, Ryerson, 1960. 14p

NEW HISTORY FOR OLD. Discussions on Aims and Methods in Writing and Teaching History. Toronto, Ryerson, 1931. 72p [BVaU NBFU OKQ

ON PUBLISHERS AND PUBLISHING. Toronto, Ryerson, 1951. 19p

"PRIME MINISTERS TO THE BOOK." Toronto, Ryerson, 1944. 11p [BM BVaU LC NBFU OTP QMM

**Poole, Rev. William Henry, 1820–1896**

THE ODD MAN AND HIS ODDITIES. Detroit, Detroit Pub. Co., 1891. 143p [LC OLU

**Pyper, Charles B.**

ONE THING AFTER ANOTHER. Toronto, Dent, 1948. 262p [BVaU OTP

**Pyramus (pseud)**
GEIKIE VERSUS ELIOTT; or, The King's Canvas Bag. Halifax, 1852. 8p [NSHP

**Quebec Literary and Historical Society**
TRANSACTIONS. ... 1829–. [A continuing serial.] [NSHP OTU

**Queen's Quarterly, Editors of**
HOW CAN UNIVERSITIES BEST BENEFIT THE PROFESSION OF JOURNALISM AS A MEANS OF MOULDING AND ELEVATING PUBLIC OPINION? A Collection of Essays. Ed. by the editors of Queen's Quarterly. Kingston, Queen's University, 1903. 300p [BVaU NSHD OKQ

**Reid, D. Clifford**
HORIZONS OF THOUGHT. Seattle, Lowman & Hanford, 1935. 249p [BVaU LC

**Richey, Rev. Matthew, 1803–1883**
AN ADDRESS AT THE INAUGURATION OF THE YOUNG MEN'S CHRISTIAN ASSOCIATION. Halifax, Bowes, 1854. 26p [NSHD

**Ridley, Hilda M., –1960**
THE POST-WAR WOMAN. Intro. by W.D. Calvert. Toronto, Ryerson, 1941. 39p [OTP QMM

**Rintoul, Rev. David**
TWO LECTURES ON RHETORIC. Toronto, Scobie, 1844. 48p [OLU

**Robb, Wallace Havelock, 1888–**
INDIAN LORE OF THE BAY OF QUINTE. Kingston, Author, 1952. 12p

**Robbins, John Everett, 1903–**
CANADA BETWEEN COVERS. An Address to the Rotary Club of Ottawa, January 7, and to the Rotary Club of Ottawa West, February 12th, 1957. Ottawa, Author, 1957. 10p
THE IDEA OF AN ENCYCLOPEDIA DEFINED AND ILLUSTRATED. An Address to the Newman Club of Ottawa ... March 24, 1957. Ottawa, Author, 1957. 9p

**Robbins, William, 1909–**
HUMANISTIC VALUES IN ENGLISH LITERATURE. Five Radio Talks as heard on CBC University of the Air. Toronto, Canadian Broadcasting Corporation, 1960. 56p

**Roberton, Thomas Beattie, 1879–1936**
A SECOND HELPING OF NEWSPAPER PIECES. By "T.B.R." Toronto, Macmillan, 1937. 157p [BVaU NBFU OTP
T.B.R. Newspaper Pieces. Toronto, Macmillan, 1936. 142p [BM BVaU LC NSHD OTU

**Roberts, Leslie, 1896–**

WE MUST BE FREE. Reflections of a Democrat. Toronto, Macmillan, 1939. 248p [BM BVaU OTP QMM

**Robertson, John Charles, 1864–1956**

MIXED COMPANY. Toronto, Dent, 1939. 200p [BM BVa LC NSHD OTP

**Robertson, John Ross, 1841–1918**

TALKS WITH CRAFTSMEN, AND PENCILLINGS BY THE WAYSIDE. Toronto, Hunter Rose, 1890. 191p [BM NSHD OTU

**Robins, John Daniel, 1884–1952**

COTTAGE CHEESE. Toronto, Collins, 1951. 232p

THE INCOMPLETE ANGLERS. Toronto, Collins, 1943. 229p [BVaU LC NBFU OTP QMM

**Roe, Rev. Henry, 1829–1909**

ADVANTAGES AND MEANS OF KEEPING UP HABITS OF READING AMONG THE CLERGY. A Paper read before the Clergy assembled in Lennoxville ... 6th July, 1864. Montreal, Lovell, 1864. 23p [NSWA OTP

**Ross, Alexander Milton, 1832–1897**

LETTERS ON CANADIAN INDEPENDENCE. Toronto, 1865. 11p [OTP

**Ross, Rev. Ebenezer E.**

THE MANLINESS OF PIETY. A Lecture. ... Halifax, Wesleyan, 1860. 24p [NSHD

**Ross, Malcolm Mackenzie, 1911–**

OUR SENSE OF IDENTITY. A Book of Canadian Essays. Ed. by ——. Toronto, Ryerson, 1954. xvi + 348p

**Ruark, Fletcher, 1880–1952**

SKETCHES FROM LIFE. Windsor, Ont., Curtis, 1942. 94p [BVaU OTP QMM

**Ryder, Kenneth Walter, 1904–**

DEAR PATRICIA. Letters written to Patricia Ryder by her Father when she was in Ottawa. N.p., priv. print., 1957. 18p

**Ryerson, Rev. Adolphus Egerton, 1803–1882**

CIVIL GOVERNMENT, THE LATE CONSPIRACY. A Discourse delivered in Kingston, U.C., December 31, 1837. Toronto, Conference Office, 1838. 20p [BVaU OTP

LETTERS ... TO THE HON. AND REVEREND DOCTOR STRACHAN. ... Kingston, Herald Office, 1828. 42p [OTP

**Salter, Frederick Millet, 1895–1962**

"THIS BANK AND SHOAL OF TIME." An Address to the Annual Assembly of Victoria College, Victoria, B.C., October 18, 1957. Victoria, Daily Colonist, 1957. 8p

**Sandwell, Bernard Keble, 1876–1954**

THE DIVERSIONS OF DUCHESSTOWN AND OTHER ESSAYS. With an intro. by Robertson Davies. Toronto, Dent, 1955. xii + 84p

THE GODS IN TWILIGHT. Vancouver, U. of British Columbia, 1948. 18p [BVaU LC OTP QMM

THE PRIVACITY AGENT AND OTHER MODEST PROPOSALS. Toronto, Dent, 1928. 223p [BM BVaU LC NBFU OTU QMM

WESTING. Montreal, priv. print., 1918. 31p [BVa OKQ

**Saunders, Margaret Marshall, 1861–1947**

MY PETS. Real Happenings in my Aviary. Philadelphia, Griffith & Rowland, 1908. 283p [Also: Toronto, Ryerson, 1935. 256p] [BM LC NBFU OLU

**Saxe, Mary Sollace, 1868–1942**

OUR LITTLE QUEBEC COUSIN. Boston, Page, 1919. 122p [BVaU LC QMSS

**Scadding, Rev. Henry, 1813–1901**

THE EASTERN ORIEL OPENED. An Address on the Laying of the Foundation Stone of the University of Toronto. Toronto, 1842. 11p [BibC

THE MAPLE LEAF AS AN EMBLEM OF CANADA. Toronto, Boyle, 1891. 6p [NSWA OTU

THE PRESIDENT'S VALEDICTORY ADDRESS, DELIVERED BEFORE THE ATHENAEUM OF TORONTO. Toronto, 1846. 12p [BibC

**Schrag, Alexander Andrew, 1907–**

MORTGAGE MANOR. By Lex Schrag. Aided and abetted by Jim Reidford. Toronto, Ryerson, 1955. xix + 156p

**Scott, Duncan Campbell, 1862–1947**

THE ADMINISTRATION OF INDIAN AFFAIRS IN CANADA. ... Prepared for the Fourth Bi-Annual Conference of the Institute of Pacific Relations ... October 18 – November 3, 1931. Toronto, Canadian Institute of International Affairs, 1931. 27p [BM BVaU NBFU OKQ

**Scott, Jack**

FROM OUR TOWN. Toronto, McClelland, 1959. 224p

**Sedgewick, Rev. Robert**

AMUSEMENTS FOR YOUTH. A Lecture. Halifax, Barnes, 1858. 29p [NSHD

THE PROPER SPHERE AND INFLUENCE OF WOMAN IN CHRISTIAN SOCIETY. A Lecture. Halifax, Barnes, 1856. 47p [BM NSWA

**Service, Robert William, 1874–1958**

WHY NOT GROW YOUNG? or, Living for Longevity. New York, Barse, 1928. 266p [BM BVaU LC OLU

**Seton, Ernest Thompson, 1860–1946**

ANIMAL TRACKS AND HUNTER SIGNS. Garden City, N.Y., Doubleday, 1958. 160p

... ANIMALS, Selected from "LIFE-HISTORIES OF NORTHERN ANIMALS." New York, Doubleday, 1926. 299p [BVa LC OTU

ANIMALS WORTH KNOWING. Selected from "LIFE-HISTORIES OF NORTHERN ANIMALS." New York, Doubleday, 1934. 299p [LC

THE GOSPEL OF THE REDMAN. An Indian Bible. Comp. by Ernest Thompson Seton and Julia M. Seton. Garden City, Doubleday, 1936. 121p [BM BVa LC NBFU OTP

LIFE-HISTORIES OF NORTHERN ANIMALS. An Account of the Mammals of Manitoba. New York, Scribner, 1909. 2v [BM BVaU LC OTP QMM

LIVES OF GAME ANIMALS. New York, Doubleday, 1925–28. 4v [BM BVaU NBFU OTP QMM

MAINLY ABOUT WOLVES. London, Methuen, 1937. 319p [ACG BM OWtU

THE WAR DANCE AND THE FIRE-FLY DANCE. New York, Doubleday, 1910. 10p [LC

**Shatford, Rev. Allan Pearson, 1873–1935**

THE INNOCENTS. A Christmas Study. Montreal, Lovell, 1912. 58p [QMSS

**Sigbjornsson, Mrs. Rannveig Kristin G., 1880–**

PEBBLES ON THE BEACH. Treherne, Man., Treherne Times, 1936. 17p [OTU

**Simcoe, John Graves, 1752–1806**

LETTER TO SIR JOSEPH BANKS ... 1792. ... To which is Added Five Official Speeches, delivered ... in [Upper Canada]. With a prefatory notice by Rev. Dr. Scadding. Toronto, Copp Clark, 1892. 18p [OLU

**Sime, Jessie Georgina, 1880–**

THE LAND OF DREAMS. Toronto, Macmillan, 1940. 273p [BM OOU QMM

ORPHEUS IN QUEBEC. London, Allen & Unwin, 1942. 47p [BM BVaU NBFU OTU QMM

**Smith, Arthur James Marshall, 1902–**

UNIVERSITY OF NEW BRUNSWICK, FOUNDERS' DAY ADDRESS. With Opening Remarks by D.L. MacLaren ... 1946. Fredericton, University, 1946. 19p [OKQ QMM

**Smith, Goldwin, 1823–1910**

DOES THE BIBLE SANCTION AMERICAN SLAVERY? Cambridge, Sever & Francis, 1863. 107p [BM BVaU LC NBFU OTU QMM

THE EARLY DAYS OF CORNELL. Ithaca, priv. print., 1904. 25p [OTU

THE EMPIRE. A Series of Letters Published in "The Daily News," 1862, 1863. Oxford, 1863. 306p [BM BVaU NBFU OTU QMM

ESSAYS ON QUESTIONS OF THE DAY, POLITICAL AND SOCIAL. New York, Macmillan, 1893. 360p [BM BVaU LC NSHD OTU QMM

FALSE HOPES; or, Fallacies, Socialistic and Semi-Socialistic, Briefly Answered. ... New York, Lovell, 1883. 69p [BM NBFU

THE FOUNDATION OF THE AMERICAN COLONIES. ... Oxford, 1861. [BM NBFU

KEEPING CHRISTMAS. Toronto, Robinson, 1888. 12p [BVaU LC NBFU OTU

LECTURES AND ESSAYS. Toronto, Hunter Rose, 1881. 336p [BM BVaU LC NSHD OKQ QMM

LECTURES ON MODERN HISTORY. Delivered in Oxford, 1859–61. Oxford, Parker, 1861. [2nd ed.: 1865. 190p] [BM NSWA OTU QMM

LOYALTY. An Address ... before the Young Men's Liberal Club, Toronto, on Feb. 2, 1891. Toronto, Hunter Rose, 1891. 20p [OTU

LOYALTY, ARISTOCRACY AND JINGOISM. Three Lectures. ... Toronto, Hunter Rose, 1891. 96p [BM BVaU LC NBFU OTU

ON SOME SUPPOSED CONSEQUENCES OF THE DOCTRINE OF HISTORICAL PROGRESS. ... Oxford, Parker, 1861. 47p [BM NBFU

OXFORD AND HER COLLEGES. London, Macmillan, 1894. 99p [Also: New York, 1895. 170p] [BM BVaU NBFU OTU QMM

THE POLITICAL DESTINY OF CANADA. With a Reply by Sir Francis Hincks. ... Toronto, Willing & Williamson, 1878. 197p [NSHD has: Toronto, Belford, 1877. 32p Without Hincks' REPLY?] [BM BVaU NSWA OTU QMM

PROGRESS OR REVOLUTION? A Letter to a Labour Friend. Toronto, Tyrrell, 1906. 30p [NBFU OTU

A SELECTION FROM GOLDWIN SMITH'S CORRESPONDENCE ... BETWEEN THE YEARS 1846 AND 1910. Ed. by Arnold Haultain. ... London, Laurie, [1913?]. 540p [BM BVaU LC NSHD OTU QMM

THE STUDY OF HISTORY. Two Lectures. London, Oxford U. Press, 1859. 35p [BM BVaU NBFU

**Smith, Irving Norman, 1909–**

A REPORTER REPORTS. Toronto, Ryerson, 1954. x + 145p

**Smith, Sidney Earle, 1897–1959**

UNITY OF KNOWLEDGE: THE SCIENCES AND THE HUMANITIES. An Address before the Royal Canadian Institute, February 23, 1952. Toronto, U. of Toronto Press, 1952. 12p

**Smith, Thomas Barlow, 1839–1933**

BACKWARD GLANCES. Halifax, Bowes, 1898. 254p [BM BVaU NSWA OTP QMM

NOVA SCOTIA. Trial and Relief. Windsor, "Hants," 1929. 42p [BM QMBM

**Smith, Rev. William Wye, 1827–1917**

VETULIA; or, Going to the Bottom of Things. Toronto, Dudley & Burns, 1891. 78p [OTP

**Smythe, Carroll F.**

SMILE, STRIVE, STICK. Success Boiled Down to Three Words. Toronto, L.R. Steel Service Corp., [1921]. 32p [OTP

**Sommerville, Rev. William, 1800–1878**

SOUTHERN SLAVERY NOT FOUNDED ON SCRIPTURE WARRANT. A Lecture. Saint John, Barnes, 1864. 27p [NSWA

**Spark, Rev. Alexander, 1762–1819**

AN ORATION AT THE DEDICATION OF FREE-MASON'S HALL, QUEBEC, CANADA. Quebec, Brown, 1790. 16p [BM QMSS

**Sproat, Gilbert Malcolm, 1832–1913**

CANADA AND THE EMPIRE.... London, n.p., 1873. 35p [BM NSWA OTU

**Stead, Robert James Campbell, 1880–1959**

THE MAPLE'S PRAISE OF FRANKLIN DELANO ROOSEVELT, 1882–1945. Canadian Tributes. By Robert J.C. Stead, Dorothy Dumbrille, Nathaniel A. Benson. Ottawa, Tower Books, 1945. 18p [OTU

WORDS. Winnipeg, Public Press, 1945. 21p [UTQ

**Stefansson, Vilhjalmur, 1879–1962**

ADVENTURES IN ERROR. Toronto, McLeod, 1936. 299p [BVaU OTP

**Stevenson, Orlando John, 1869–1950**

THE STUDY OF LITERATURE. Toronto, Morang, 1904. 31p [BM OTU

THROUGH THE YEARS. Toronto, Ryerson, 1952. 45p

**Stewart, Herbert Leslie, 1882–1953**

FROM A LIBRARY WINDOW. Reflections of a Radio Commentator. Toronto, Macmillan, 1940. 323p [BM BVaU LC NSHD OTP

OBITER SCRIPTA. Halifax, 1914–1936. 3v [Essays on many different subjects collected by their author, from the various magazines in which they were published, and bound together.] [NSHD

**Stirling, John Bertram, 1888–**

THE FIRST HUNDRED YEARS. Fredericton, U. of New Brunswick, 1954. 13p

**Strachan, Rev. John, 1778–1867**

THE JOHN STRACHAN LETTER BOOK: 1812–1834. Ed. by George W. Spragge. Toronto, Ontario Hist. Soc., 1946. 279p [BM BVaU LC NBFU OTP QMM

A LETTER FROM THE HON. AND VENERABLE DR. STRACHAN, U.C., TO DR. LEE, D.D. Kingston, Herald, 1829. 19p [OTU

**Sullivan, Alan, 1868–1947**

I BELIEVE THAT ——. Toronto, Tyrrell, 1912. 59p [BM BVaU OTP

**Sykes, Frederick Henry, 1863–1918**

MEMORIALS. Address at the Celebration of the Twenty-fifth Anniversary of the Bill Memorial Library, Groton, Conn., October 15th, 1913. Groton, Bill Mem. Lib. Assoc., 1913. 20p [BM OTU

**Symons, Harry Lutz, 1893–**

THE BORED MEETING. Toronto, Ryerson, 1951. 121p

FRIENDSHIP. Toronto, Macmillan, 1943. 265p [BVaU OTU QMM
OJIBWAY MELODY. Stories of Georgian Bay. Toronto, Best, 1946. 294p [BVaU NBFU OTP QMBM
THE ORANGE BELT SPECIAL. Toronto, Nelson, 1956. xii + 210p

**Thomas, Robert Brockholes**
SHORT SPECULATIVE ESSAYS. Charlottetown, 1882. 91p [BM OLU

**Thompson, Drew [Andrew Ruthven], 1894–**
HYSTERIC HISTORIES. Ottawa, le Droit, 1941. 64p [OOP

**Thompson, John Sparrow David, 1844–1894**
THE EXECUTION OF LOUIS RIEL. Speech ... Delivered March 22, 1886. N.p., n.p., [1886?]. 31p [BViPA NSWA OTP

**Thomson, Watson, –1969**
"I ACCUSE." Winnipeg, Contemporary Pub., 1943. 32p [OTU

**Tocque, Rev. Philip, 1814–1899**
KALEIDOSCOPE ECHOES. Being Historical, Philosophical, Scientific, and Theological Sketches from the Miscellaneous Writings. ... Ed. by his daughter, Annie S.W. Tocque. Toronto, Hunter, 1895. 300p [BVaU OTP

**Todd, Henry Cook, –1862**
ITEMS (IN LIFE OF AN USHER) ON TRAVEL, ANECDOTE, AND POPULAR ERRORS. By One in Retirement [pseud]. Montreal, 1850. 266p [Also: Quebec, 1855. 306p] [LC OLU OTP

**Toronto, Ont. National Club**
MAPLE LEAVES. Being the Papers read before the National Club ... during the Winter 1890–1891. Toronto, the Club, [1891?]. 136p [NSHD OTU

**Toronto Arts & Letters Club**
YEAR BOOK OF CANADIAN ART. Literature, Architecture, Music, Painting, Sculpture. Toronto, Dent, [1913]. V. 1. [No more pub.] [BM NBS OTU QMG

**Tory, James Cranswick, 1862–**
ADDRESSES. ... Ottawa, Mortimer, 1932. 291p [NSHD

**Traill, Catharine Parr (Strickland), 1802–1899**
CANADIAN WILD FLOWERS. Painted and Lithographed by Agnes Fitz Gibbon, with Botanical Descriptions by C.P. Traill. ... Montreal, Lovell, 1868. 86p [Several later editions.] [BM BVaU LC OLU
PEARLS AND PEBBLES; or, Notes of an Old Naturalist. With Biographical Sketch by Mary Agnes Fitz Gibbon. Toronto, Briggs, 1894. 241p [BM BVaU MWU NSHD OTP QMM

STUDIES OF PLANT LIFE IN CANADA; or, Gleanings from Forest, Lake and Plain. By Mrs. C.P. Trail. ... Illus. ... by Mrs. Chamblin. Ottawa, Woodburn, 1885. 288p [New and rev. ed., 1906.] [BM BVaU LC NSHD OTU

**Twain, Mathew (pseud)**

THE CRAZY QUILT SERIES. V. 1, No. 1. A Compendium of Wit, Humor and Pathos. By Mathew Twain [pseud]. Toronto, 1888. [BVaU

**Voorhis, Ernest, 1859–1933**

WINTER IN CANADA. [Ottawa, 1926?]. 14p [NBFU OKQ

**Wallace, Rev. Archer, 1884–1958**

THE FAITH OF MORN. New York, Round Table, 1940. 150p [LC OTU

THE SILVER LINING. New York, Round Table, 1937. 94p [BVaU LC

**Wallace, Robert Charles, 1881–1955**

THEN AND NOW. Founder's Day Address, University of New Brunswick. Fredericton, the University, 1950. 15p [BM BVaU OKQ

**Ward, Norman, 1918–**

MICE IN THE BEER. Toronto, Longmans, 1960. xii + 206p

**Warman, Cy, 1855–1914**

THE WHITE ELEPHANT. Montreal, Canada Pub., 1905. 33p [QMBM

**Watson, Albert Durrant, 1859–1926**

THE SOVEREIGNTY OF IDEALS. ... Westwood, Mass., Ariel Press, 1903. 38p [LC OKQ

THREE COMRADES OF JESUS. Toronto, Ryerson, 1919. 73p [BM BVaU NSWA OKQ

**Watson, John, 1847–1939**

EDUCATION AND LIFE. An Address delivered at the Opening of the 32nd Session of Queen's University. Kingston, Alma Mater Society, n.d. 20p [Amtmann cat. 145

**Watson, Robert, 1882–1948**

HOW TO WRITE, BY THOSE WHO CAN. ... Comp. by ——. Ottawa, Graphic, [1928?]. 16p [OTP

**Watson, William Ritchie, 1904–**

... AND ALL YOUR BEAUTY. Toronto, Macmillan, 1948. 385p [BVaU NBFU OTP

**Webber, Rev. George, 1838–1907**

LECTURES AND SERMONS. London, Ont., Advertiser Print., 1883. 219p [OTU

**Webber, William Lester, 1882–**
THE ORIGINAL THUNDER BIRD STICK GAME. Vancouver, Author, 1939. 14p [BViPA

**Webling, Peggy**
GUESTS OF THE HEART. London, Baines & Scarsbrook, 1917. 65p [BM BVaU

**Webster, John Clarence, 1863–1950**
THE CLASSICS OF ACADIA. Ottawa, "Progressive," 1933. 8p [QMBM
PRESENT DAY ASPECTS OF CANADIAN NATIONALISM. [An Address delivered at Mt. Allison University ... November 15, 1922.] N.p., 1922. 19p [OTP

**Weekes, Mrs. Mary Loretto, 1885–**
THE WHEATLAND. Regina, Western Printers, 1937. 29p [BVaU LC NBFU OTU

**Wells, Kenneth McNeill, 1905–**
BY JUMPING CAT BRIDGE. London, Heinemann; Toronto, British Book Service, 1956. 268p
BY MOONSTONE CREEK. Toronto, Dent, 1949. 280p [BVaU NBFU OTP
THE OWL PEN. Toronto, Dent, 1947. 289p [BVaU NBFU OTP QMM
UP MEDONTE WAY. Toronto, Dent, 1951. 247p

**Welton, Rev. Daniel Morse, 1831–1904**
THE IMITATIVE FACULTY, ITS USE AND ABUSE. A Lecture. Halifax, Christian Messenger, 1858. 27p [NSHP

**West, Bruce, 1912–**
A CHANGE OF PACE. Toronto, U. of Toronto Press, 1956. x + 158p

**West, Paul Noden, 1930–**
THE GROWTH OF THE NOVEL. Eight Radio Talks as heard on CBC University of the Air. Toronto, Canadian Broadcasting Corporation, 1959. 84p

**Whelan, Edward, 1824–1867**
BIOGRAPHICAL SKETCH OF THE HONOURABLE EDWARD WHELAN TOGETHER WITH A COMPILATION OF HIS PRINCIPAL SPEECHES. By Peter McCourt. Charlottetown, Author, 1888. 301p [BVaU LC NSWA OLU

**White, Thomas, 1830–1888**
OUR GREAT WEST. A Lecture. ... Montreal, Dawson, 1873. 32p [BM LC OTP

**Whitton, Charlotte Elizabeth, 1896–**
THE DECAY OF DEMOCRACY. Charlottetown, Prince of Wales College, 1955. 19p

**Wilkes, Rev. Henry, 1805–1886**
LECTURE ON FREEDOM OF MIND ... And Speech of His Excellency the Right Hon. the Earl of Elgin & Kincardine delivered before the Mercantile Library Association of Montreal. ... Montreal, Potts, 1848. 27p [OTP

**Williams, Mrs. Mary Elizabeth, 1877–**
IT SEEMS TO ME. New York, Vantage Press, 1960. 195p

**Williamson, Owen Templeton Garrett, 1883–**
CIVVY STREET. Red Light or Green? Toronto Ryerson, 1945. 28p [OTP

**Willison, John Stephen, 1856–1927**
PARTNERS IN PEACE. The Dominion, The Empire, and The Republic. Addresses. ... Toronto, Warwick & Rutter, 1923. 94p [BM BVaU NSHD OTU

**Willison, Marjory (MacMurchy), –1938**
THE KING'S CROWNING. Toronto, Briggs, 1911. 12p [OTU

**Wills, Harold Arthur, 1907–**
FIRST PERSON PLURAL. Being Editorials for these Troubled Times; a Golden Jubilee Collection of Editorials. Cochrane, Northland Post, 1960. xii + 276p

**Wilson, Clifford Parnell, 1902–**
NORTHERN TREASURY. Selections from the *Beaver.* Ed. by ——. Edinburgh, Toronto, Nelson, 1955. 238p

**Wilson, Daniel, 1816–1892**
PIPES AND TOBACCO. An Ethnographic Sketch. Toronto, Lovell & Gibson, 1857. 52p [BM LC QMM

**Wilson, Rev. Robert, 1833–1912**
THE TOBACCO NUISANCE. Saint John, McMillan, 1890. 18p [NSWA

**Winson, J.W.**
OPEN AIR JOTTINGS. Being Notes on Nature ... in British Columbia. By Wildwood [pseud]. Vancouver, Murphy & Chapman, 1937. 23p [BVaU
WEATHER AND WINGS. Nature Essays. Toronto, Nelson, 1932. 172p [BVaU
WILDWOOD TRAILS. Vancouver, Chapman & Warich, 1946. 203p [BVaU OTU

**Wodson, Harry Milner, 1874–1952**
THE JUSTICE SHOP. Toronto, Sovereign Press, 1931. 119p [BVaU OKQ
PRIVATE WARWICK. Musings of a Canuck in Khaki. Toronto, Sovereign Press, 1915. 96p [BM OTU
THE WHIRLPOOL. Scenes from Toronto Police Court. Toronto, priv. print., 1917. 208p [BM BVaU OTP

**Wood, Edgar Allardyce, 1907–**
ROBBING THE ROOST. The Marquis of Roostburg Rules governing the Ancient and Dishonorable Sport. Red Deer, priv. print., n.d. 8p [ACG

**Wood, Samuel Thomas, 1860–1917**
RAMBLES OF A CANADIAN NATURALIST. Toronto, Dent, 1916. 247p [BVaU LC NSHD OTU QMM

**Woodcock, George, 1912–**

ANARCHY OR CHAOS. London, Freedom Press, 1944. 124p [BM LC

RAILWAYS AND SOCIETY. London, Freedom Press, 1943. 31p [BM LC

THE WRITER AND POLITICS. London, Porcupine, 1948. 248p [BM BVaU LC

**Woodsworth, Rev. James Shaver, 1874–1942**

HOURS THAT STAND APART. Ottawa, Mutual Press, 1927. 40p [OTU

LABOR'S CASE IN PARLIAMENT. A Summary and Compilation of the Speeches of J.S. Woodsworth, M.P. in the Canadian House of Commons, 1921–1928. Ottawa, Canadian Brotherhood of Railroad Employees, 1929. 92p [OTP

TOWARDS SOCIALISM. Selections from the Writings of J.S. Woodsworth. Ed. by Edith Fowke. Toronto, Ontario Woodsworth Memorial Foundation, 1948. 48p [NBFU OTP

**Young, Archibald Hope, 1863–1935**

TRINITY COLLEGE. A Causerie, delivered ... March 14th, 1925. [Toronto, 1925.] 19p [BM OTP

UPPER CANADA COLLEGE, TORONTO, 1829–1929. Toronto, [1929?]. 12p [BM NBFU OTP QMM

**Young, George Paxton, 1819–1889**

FREEDOM AND NECESSITY. A Lecture delivered in Knox College ... 1870. Toronto, Adam & Stevenson, 1870. 19p [OTP

**Yule, James Colton, 1839–1876**

RECORDS OF A VANISHED LIFE. Lectures, Addresses, etc., of James Colton Yule ... late professor of New Testament Interpretation. ... in the Canadian Literary Institute. A Memoir by his Wife. Toronto, Baptist Pub. Co., 1876. 174p [NBFU OKQ

# LOCAL HISTORY AND DESCRIPTION

## Historical studies and recent descriptions of communities, provinces, regions

**Abraham, Dorothy E., 1894–**

ROMANTIC VANCOUVER ISLAND. Victoria, Yesterday and Today. Victoria, Acme, 1947. 118p [2nd ed., 1949; 3rd ed., 1956.] [BVaU OOA

**Acton, Ont. Free Press**

ACTON'S EARLY DAYS. Recollections of "the Old Man" as Published in the Acton Free Press. Acton, Free Press, 1939. 285p [BVaU OTU

**Adam, Graeme Mercer, 1839–1912**

THE CANADIAN NORTH-WEST ... from the Early Days of the Fur-Trade to the Era of the Railway and the Settler. Toronto, etc., Rose, etc., 1885. 408p [BM BVaU LC NBFU OTP QMBM

ILLUSTRATED QUEBEC ... Under French and English Occupancy. Ed. by ——. Montreal, McConniff, 1891. 90p [BVaU LC NSWA OTP

MUSKOKA ILLUSTRATED. With Descriptive Narrative of the Picturesque Region. Toronto, Bryce, 1888. 20p [OLU

TORONTO, OLD AND NEW: ... Historical, Descriptive and Pictorial ... to mark the Hundredth Anniversary of the Passing of the Constitutional Act of 1791 ... with Some Sketches of the Men who have made or are making the Provincial Capital. By G. Mercer Adam and the Rev. Henry Scadding. Toronto, Mail, 1891. 212p [BVaU LC NSWA OTP

**Adanac, Sask., Jubilee Association**

THE STORY OF ADANAC. Adanac, Sask., 1955. 48p

**Affleck, Edward Lloyd, 1924–**

STERNWHEELERS, SANDBARS, AND SWITCHBACKS. A Chronicle of Steam Transportation in Southeastern British Columbia. Vancouver, 1958. 65p [mimeographed]

**Aitken, Martha Alice (Duff), 1882–**

THE BOOK OF TURNBERRY, 1857–1957. N.p., 1957. 59p

**Akins, Thomas Beamish, 1809–1891**

HISTORY OF HALIFAX CITY. Halifax, Nova Scotia Hist. Soc., 1895. 272p [BM NSWA OTP QMM

PRIZE ESSAY ON THE HISTORY OF THE SETTLEMENT OF HALIFAX. Halifax, English & Blackadar, 1847. 62p [NSHD

SELECTIONS FROM THE PUBLIC DOCUMENTS OF ... NOVA SCOTIA. Ed. by ——. Halifax, Annand, 1869. 755p [Papers relating to Acadian and English settlement, 1714–61.] [BM BVaU NSWA OTP

**Alexander, James Edward, 1803–1885**

THE BURNING OF THE ST. LOUIS THEATRE, QUEBEC. Quebec, 1846. 8p [LC OTP

**Alexander, Mary H.T. (Strachan)**

OLD FORT PRINCE OF WALES. Toronto, Ryerson, 1930. 30p [BVaU OTU

**Allison, David, 1836–1924**

HISTORY OF NOVA SCOTIA. By David Allison [and Clyde Edwin Tuck]. Halifax, Bowen, 1916. 3v [V. 3, by C.E. Tuck, is subtitled: BIOGRAPHICAL SKETCHES OF REPRESENTATIVE CITIZENS AND GENEALOGICAL RECORDS OF THE OLD FAMILIES.] [BVaU LC NSWA OTP

**Alloway, Mary H. (Wilson), 1848–1919**

FAMOUS FIRESIDES OF FRENCH CANADA. Montreal, Lovell, 1899. 217p [BM BVaU LC NSWA OTU QMM

**Almon, Albert, 1873–**

LOUISBOURG. The Dream City of America. Truro, News Pub. Co., 1934. 85p [NSHD OTP QMBM

ROCHEFORT POINT. A Silent City in Louisbourg. Glace Bay, Macdonald, 1940. 44p [LC NSHP QMM

**Ames, Herbert Brown, 1863–1954**

"THE CITY BELOW THE HILL." A Sociological Study of a Portion of the City of Montreal. Montreal, Bishop, 1897. 72p [BVaU OTP

**Anderson, Mrs. Aili Sophia, 1906–**

HISTORY OF SOINTULA. Sointula, B.C., Sointula Centennial Committee, 1958. 16p

**Anderson, Carr**

KEMPTVILLE, PAST AND PRESENT. Kemptville, 1903. [OOP

**Anderson, Rev. David, 1814–1885**

NOTES OF THE FLOOD AT THE RED RIVER, 1852. By the Bishop of Rupert's Land. London, Hatchard, 1852. 124p [BM BVaU LC NSWA OTP

**Anderson, William James, 1813?–1873**

THE LOWER ST. LAWRENCE. Its Scenery, Navigation, and Commerce, forming a Complete Tourist's Guide. Quebec, "Morning Chronicle," 1872. 49p [NSHPL OLU QMBM

**Andrew, Frederick William, 1879–**

THE STORY OF SUMMERLAND. Penticton, Herald, 1945. 55p [BVaU

**Aneroid, Sask. High School**

HISTORY OF ANEROID. Aneroid, Sask., 1955. 13 + 3p

**Angus, Alexander David, 1911–1941**

OLD QUEBEC IN THE DAYS BEFORE OUR DAY. Montreal, Carrier, 1949. 232p [BVaU NBFU OTP

**Annapolis Royal, N.S. 350th Anniversary Celebration Committee**

WELCOME TO ANNAPOLIS ROYAL'S 350TH ANNIVERSARY. Annapolis Royal, 1955. 88p

**Anonymous**

A DESCRIPTION OF PRINCE EDWARD ISLAND ... AND A FEW CURSORY OBSERVATIONS RESPECTING THE CLIMATE, NATURAL PRODUCTIONS, AND ADVANTAGES OF ITS SITUATION IN REGARD TO AGRICULTURE AND COMMERCE. By a Person Many Years Resident There. London, Ashey, n.d. 22p [Describes P.E.I. in 1795.] [OTU QMU

GLIMPSES IN AND ABOUT HALIFAX ... ITS PICTURESQUE BEAUTIES AND ATTRACTIVE SURROUNDINGS ILLUSTRATED AND DESCRIBED. [Halifax], Howard, n.d. [c1900?]. 79p [NSHPL OTU

AN INTERESTING ACCOUNT ... OF THE CELEBRATED HORDE OF ROBBERS KNOWN AS THE MARKHAM GANG. Toronto, 1846. 24p [OTP

THE PONOKA BOOK. Published as a Tribute to the Pioneers who Opened up the District and to Commemorate the Town's Fiftieth Anniversary, 1904–1954. Ponoka, Alta., 1954. 93p

**Anspach, Rev. Lewis Amadeus**

A HISTORY OF THE ISLAND OF NEWFOUNDLAND. London, Author, 1819. xxviii + 512p [BM BVaU LC NSWA OLU

**Archer, John Hall, 1914–**

HISTORIC SASKATOON [1882–1947]. A Concise Illustrated History of Saskatoon. Comp. by John H. Archer and Joseph C. Bates. Saskatoon, Junior Chamber of Commerce, 1948. 63p [BVaU NSHD OTU

**Armstrong, Edith Vernette (Akeley), 1905–**

A WHEATLAND HERITAGE. Eston, Sask., Board of Trade, 1956. 275p [History of the Rural Municipality of Snipe Lake No. 259, Saskatchewan, 1906–1916.]

**Arrell, Alex H.**

A SHORT HISTORY OF CALEDONIA. Ed. by ——. Caledonia, Ont., Sachem Print., 1950. 131p [OONL

**Assiniboia, Sask. Golden Jubilee Committee**

GOLDEN MEMORIES. Assiniboia, Sask., 1955. 88p [A history of the Assiniboia district.]

**Atherton, William Henry, 1867–1950**
MONTREAL, 1535–1914. Montreal, Clarke, 1914. 3v [BM LC NSHD OTP

**Babbitt, George W.**
FREDERICTON IN THE EIGHTIES, WITH GLIMPSES OF SAINT JOHN, MONCTON, AND ST. ANDREWS. N.p., [1954?]. 20p

**Bagg, Stanley Clark, 1820–**
ANTIQUITIES AND LEGENDS OF DURHAM. A Lecture. Montreal, Rose, 1866. 21p [BM BVaU LC NSWA QMM

**Baird, Rev. Frank, 1870–1951**
HISTORY OF THE PARISH OF STANLEY AND ITS FAMOUS FAIR. Fredericton, McMurray Book, 1950. 159p [OONL

**Baker, Edna**
PRAIRIE PLACE NAMES. Toronto, Ryerson, 1928. 28p [NBFU OTU SSU

**Baldwin, Mrs. Alice Murray Sharples, 1906–**
METIS, WEE SCOTLAND OF THE GASPE. N.p., 1960. 64p [History of Métis Beach, Que.]

**Barbeau, Charles Marius, 1883–1969**
THE KINGDOM OF SAGUENAY. Toronto, Macmillan, 1936. 167p [BM BVaU LC NBFU OTU QMM
QUEBEC, WHERE ANCIENT FRANCE LINGERS. Toronto, Macmillan, 1936. 173p [BM BVaU NSHD OTU QMBM

**Barnes, Clarence James, 1884–**
SEVENTY YEARS IN SOUTHWESTERN MANITOBA. Medora, Man., 1954. 48p

**Barnwell, Alta. Church Of Jesus Christ Of Latter Day Saints**
BARNWELL HISTORY. Comp. by Barnwell Relief Society. Ann Arbor, Mich., Edwards Bros., 1952. 10 + 401 + 28p [History of the Relief Society founded in 1842 and of the village of Barnwell.]

**Barschel, J.F. Paul, 1875–**
A HISTORY OF CANORA AND DISTRICT. Canora, Sask., Canora Golden Jubilee Committee, 1960. 189p

**Bates, Jane Eliza (Woolf), 1873–1951**
FOUNDING OF CARDSTON AND VICINITY. Pioneer Problems. By Jane E. Woolf Bates. Comp. by Zina Woolf Hickman. Salt Lake City, Utah, W.L. Woolf, 1960. 214p [On Mormon settlement in Alberta.]

**Bates, Walter, 1760–1842**
KINGSTON AND THE LOYALISTS OF THE "SPRING FLEET" OF A.D. 1783. ... To

which is Appended a Diary written by Sarah Frost on her Voyage to St. John, N.B., with the Loyalists of 1783. Ed. with notes by W.O. Raymond. Saint John, Barnes, 1889. 30p [LC NSWA OTP QMM

**Beavan, Mrs. F.**

SKETCHES AND TALES ILLUSTRATIVE OF LIFE IN THE BACKWOODS OF NEW BRUNSWICK. ... London, Routledge, 1845. 142p [Photostat copy /negative/; bound as PIONEER LIFE IN NEW BRUNSWICK.] [NBFU

**Bédard, Rev. Roméo**

HISTORY, MONTMARTRE, SASK., 1893–1953. [Trans. by Sister Marie Helena]. Montmartre, Sask., 1953. 97p [mimeographed]

**Bedore, Bernard Vance, 1923–**

THE BROAD VALLEY OF THE OTTAWA. Comp. by ——. Arnprior, Ont., Ottawa Valley Pub., 1957. 70p

**Begg, Alexander, 1825–1905**

HISTORY OF BRITISH COLUMBIA. ... Toronto, Briggs, 1894. 568p [BM BVaU LC MWU NSWA OTU QMM

**Begg, Alexander, 1839–1897**

THE CREATION OF MANITOBA; or, A History of the Red River Troubles. Toronto, Hovey, 1871. 408p [BM BVaU LC NSHD OKQ

THE GREAT CANADIAN NORTH WEST. Its Past History, Present Condition, and Glorious Prospects. Montreal, Lovell, 1881. 135p [BM BVaU LC NSWA OTU QMM

HISTORY OF THE NORTH-WEST. Toronto, Hunter Rose, 1894–95. 3v [BM BVaU LC NBFU OKQ QMM

RED RIVER JOURNAL AND OTHER PAPERS RELATIVE TO THE RED RIVER RESISTANCE OF 1869–1870. Ed. with an intro. by W.L. Morton. Toronto, Champlain Society, 1956. xxiii + 636 + xvip

TEN YEARS IN WINNIPEG. A Narration of the Principal Events in the History of the City of Winnipeg from ... 1870 to ... 1879. By Alexander Begg and Walter R. Nursey. Winnipeg, Times, 1879. 226p [BM BVaU LC NSWA OTU QMM

**Bell, Charles Napier, 1854–1936**

... OLD FORTS OF WINNIPEG (1738–1927). Winnipeg, Dawson Richardson, 1927. 39p [BVaU NSHD

THE SELKIRK SETTLEMENT AND THE SETTLERS. A Concise History of the Red River Country from its Discovery, Including Information Extracted from Original Documents lately discovered, and Notes Obtained from Selkirk Settlement Colonists. Winnipeg, "Commercial," 1887. 44p [BVaU OTU QMM

SOME HISTORICAL NAMES AND PLACES OF THE CANADIAN NORTH-WEST. Winnipeg, Manitoba Free Press, 1885. 8p [LC OTP

... SOME RED RIVER SETTLEMENT HISTORY. ... Winnipeg, Call, 1887. 8p [LC OTP

**Bell, Fannie Chandler**

A HISTORY OF OLD SHEDIAC, NEW BRUNSWICK. Moncton, National Print., 1937. 63p [NBFU OTP

**Belsham, Alice Ada (Carroll), 1922–**

HISTORY OF FORT FRASER. Comp. by Alice Belsham and J. Philip Myers. Fort Fraser, B.C., Author, 1958. 11p

**Belyea, Myrtle**

HISTORY OF NEREPIS, N.B. N.p., 1924. 10p [NBFU

**Berry, Gerald Lloyd, 1915–**

THE WHOOP-UP TRAIL (ALBERTA-MONTANA RELATIONSHIPS). Edmonton, Applied Art Products, 1953. 143p

**Berry, James P., 1867–1953**

CLOVER BAR IN THE MAKING, 1881–1931. [Edmonton?], 1931. 32p [ACG

**Berton, Pierre Francis de Marigny, 1920–**

THE GOLDEN TRAIL. The Story of the Klondike Rush. Toronto, Macmillan, 1954. 147p

KLONDIKE. The Life and Death of the Last Great Gold Rush. Toronto, McClelland, 1958. viii + 457 + xixp [American ed. (New York, Knopf, 1958) has title: KLONDIKE FEVER. The Life and Death of the Last Great Gold Rush.]

**Bertrand, Joseph Placide, 1881–**

HIGHWAY OF DESTINY. An Epic Story of Canadian Development. New York, Vantage Press, 1959. 301p [History of northwestern Ontario.]

PORT ARTHUR CENTENNIAL, 1857–1957, JULY 27 TO AUGUST 3. Official Programme. Ed. by J.P. Bertrand and A. Phillips. Port Arthur, Ont., City Clerk's Office, 1957. 84p

**Bezanson, A. Maynard, 1878–1958**

THE PEACE RIVER TRAIL. [Anon] Edmonton, Journal Co., 1907. 73p [AEP BM

**Bible, George Potter, 1858–**

AN HISTORICAL SKETCH OF THE ACADIANS, Their Deportation and Wanderings, together with an Historical Basis for Longfellow's poem Evangeline; with Extracts from the Original Documents Bearing upon the Subject, and Illustrations of Scenes in and around Grand Pré and Annapolis, Nova Scotia, "the Land of Evangeline." Philadelphia, Ferris & Leach, 1906. 205p [BM BVaU LC OTU

**Bienfait, Sask. High School. Student Council**

HISTORY OF BIENFAIT. Bienfait, Sask., 1955. 34p [mimeographed]

**Biggar, Charles L.**

A TALE OF EARLY DAYS ON LUNDY'S LANE. Niagara Falls, Niagara Pub., 1947. 10p [OOA

**Bill, Fred Alexander**

LIFE ON THE RED RIVER OF THE NORTH, 1857 TO 1887. Being the History of Navigation on the Red River. ... Life on the River Town of Fargo and Moorhead, by J.W. Riggs. Baltimore, Wirth, 1947. 122p [BVaU MWP

**Bird, William Richard, 1891–**

A CENTURY AT CHIGNECTO, THE KEY TO OLD ACADIA. Toronto, Ryerson, 1928. 245p [BVaU LC NSWA OKQ

DONE AT GRAND PRE. Toronto, Ryerson, 1955. xii + 179p

HISTORIC NOVA SCOTIA. Prepared by ——. Halifax, Govt. of N.S., [194–?]. 114p [BVaU LC NBFU OTP

**Black, Norman Fergus, 1876–1964**

HISTORY OF SASKATCHEWAN AND THE OLD NORTH WEST. Regina, North West Historical Co., 1913. 605p [BVaU NBFU OTU QMM

**Blaine Lake, Sask. School**

OUR HISTORICAL BLAINE LAKE. Blaine Lake, Sask., 1957. 27 + 6p [mimeographed]

**Blakeley, Phyllis Ruth, 1922–**

GLIMPSES OF HALIFAX, 1867–1900. Halifax, Public Archives of N.S., 1949. 216p [BM NSHD OLU

**Blanchard, Kathleen Helen (Barrett), 1872–**

THE GOSSAMER THREAD. A True Story of Bishop Grisdale, and the Legend of Qu'Appelle. N.p., n.d. 13p [OTU

**Blue, John, 1875–1945**

ALBERTA, PAST AND PRESENT. Chicago, Pioneer Hist. Pub. Co., 1924. 3v [BVaU

**Bohrson, S.D. No. 1644, Sask. School**

50TH ANNIVERSARY OF BOHRSON SCHOOL DISTRICT NO. 1644, 1906–1956. Hanley, Sask., 1956. 31p

**Boissevan, Man. Jubilee Book Committee**

BECKONING HILLS. Boissevan, 1956. 260p

**Bompas, Charlotte Selina (Cox), 1830–1917**

OWINDIA. A True Tale of the Mackenzie River Indians, North-west America. [signed C.S.B.] London, Wells Gardner, 1886. 60p [BM OTP

**Borthwick, Rev. John Douglas, 1832–1912**

FROM DARKNESS TO LIGHT. History of the Eight Prisons which have been, or are now, in Montreal, 1760–1907. Montreal, Gazette, 1907. 142p [BVaU LC OTU QMM

HISTORY AND BIOGRAPHICAL GAZETEER OF MONTREAL TO THE YEAR 1892. Montreal, Lovell, 1892. 531p [BVaU OOP QMM

HISTORY OF MONTREAL, INCLUDING THE STREETS OF MONTREAL. Their Origin and History. Montreal, Gallagher, 1897. 288p [BM BVaU LC NSWA OTU QMM

HISTORY OF THE MONTREAL PRISON, FROM A.D. 1784 TO A.D. 1886. ... Montreal, Periard, 1886. 270p [BM BVaU LC NSWA OTU QMM

MONTREAL, ITS HISTORY. To Which is added Biographical Sketches. Montreal, Drysdale, 1875. 153p [BVaU LC NSWA OTU QMM

**Bosworth, Newton, 1776?–1848**

HOCHELAGA DEPICTA. The Early History and Present State of ... Montreal. Ed. by ——. Montreal, Greig, 1839. 284p [Also: Toronto, Congdon & Britnell, 1901]. [BM BVaU LC NSWA OKQ QMM

HOCHELAGA DEPICTA; or, A New Picture of Montreal. ... Ed. by ——. Montreal, Mackay, 1846. 27 + 284p [New ed.] [BVaU LC NBFU OTP QMM

**Bothwell, Jessie (Robson), 1884–**

A HEALTH TO REGINA. N.p., 1927. 20p [ACG OTU

"PIONEERS! O PIONEERS!" Regina, 1955. 92p

**Botsford, David Patterson, 1898–**

AMHERSTBURG'S PLACE IN AMERICAN HISTORY. ... Amherstburg, Amherstburg Echo, 1959. 16p

**Bourinot, John George, 1837–1902**

HISTORICAL AND DESCRIPTIVE ACCOUNT OF THE ISLAND OF CAPE BRETON, and of its Memorials of the French Régime. ... Montreal, Brown, 1892. 183p [BM BVaU LC NSWA OTU QMM

MEMORIES OF DUNDURN AND BURLINGTON HEIGHTS. An Address delivered at Hamilton, Ontario. ... With Historical Notes. Toronto, Copp Clark, 1900. 32p [OTP

**Bowen, Noel Hill, –1872**

AN HISTORICAL SKETCH OF THE ISLE OF ORLEANS. Quebec, "Mercury," 1860. 40p [BVaU LC OTP QMM

**Boyle, David, 1842–1911**

THE TOWNSHIP OF SCARBORO 1796–1896. Ed. by ——. Toronto, Briggs, 1896. 302p [BM BVaU LC OTU

**Boylen, John Chancellor**

YORK TOWNSHIP, AN HISTORICAL SUMMARY [1850–1954]. Toronto, Municipal Corporation of the Township of York and Board of Education of the Township of York, 1954. 131p

**Bramley-Moore, Alwyn, 1877–1916**

CANADA AND HER COLONIES; or, Home Rule for Alberta. London, Stewart, 1911. 185p [BVaU NBFU OTU SSU

**Brebner, John Bartlet, 1895–1957**

THE NEUTRAL YANKEES OF NOVA SCOTIA. ... New York, Columbia U. Press, 1937. 388p [BM BVaU LC NSHD OTU QMM

NEW ENGLAND'S OUTPOST. Acadia before the Conquest of Canada. New York, Columbia U. Press, 1927. 293p [BM BVaU LC NSWA OTU QMM

**Bredenbury, Sask. High School**

HISTORY OF BREDENBURY, 1883–1955. Bredenbury, Sask., 1955. 26p [mimeographed]

**Bremner, Archibald, 1849–1901**

CITY OF LONDON, ONTARIO, CANADA. The Pioneer Period and the London of To-day. [Anon] London, London Print. & Lith., 1897. 136p [BM BVaU OTP

**Bremner, Benjamin, 1851–1938**

AN ISLAND SCRAP BOOK ... Sequel to MEMORIES OF LONG AGO. ... Charlottetown, Irwin, 1932. 161p [BM BVaU OTU QMM

MEMORIES OF LONG AGO ... Charlottetown in the Past. Charlottetown, Irwin, 1930. 96p [BVaU OTP

TALES OF ABEGWEIT [Prince Edward Island]. Containing Historical, Biographical and Humorous Sketches. ... With an Appendix of Place-names in Prince Edward Island, with their Origins or Meanings. Charlottetown, Irwin, 1936. 132p [BM LC NBSaM OTU

**Brewster, Winfield, 1879–**

THE FLOODGATE. Random Writings of Our Ain Folk. Hespeler, Ont., priv. print., 1952. 44p

HESPELER YARNS. Odds and Ends about the Textile Trade at Hespeler, and Some of the People who were Concerned therewith. Hespeler, Ont., Author, 1953. 46p

J. HESPELER, NEW HOPE, C.W. Hespeler, Ont., T. & T. Press, 1951. 34p

**Brighton, Ont. Centennial Book Committee**

CENTENNIAL OF THE INCORPORATION OF THE VILLAGE OF BRIGHTON, 1859–1959. Brighton, 1959. 90p

**Britton, Freeman**

SOUVENIR OF GANANOQUE AND THOUSAND ISLANDS. With short Sketch of First Owners, Early Settlement and Other Historical Notes of the Town. Gananoque, Ont., 1901. 80p [OOA

**Broadview, Sask. School**

THE GOOD OLD DAYS OF BROADVIEW. Ed. by Mavis Anderson, Assistant ed., Orville Fitzgerald. Broadview, Sask., 1955. 46p

**Brome County, Que. Historical Society**

INDEX OF BOOKS AND PAMPHLETS ... CONCERNING THE EARLY HISTORY AND SETTLERS IN THE EASTERN TOWNSHIPS. Knowlton, Que., the Society, 1949. 83p [BVaU OLU

**Brown, George Stayley**

YARMOUTH, NOVA SCOTIA. A Sequel to Campbell's HISTORY. Boston, Rand Avery, 1888. 524p [BVaU LC NSWA OTU QMSS

**Brown, Harrison, 1893–**

ADMIRALS, ADVENTURERS AND ABLE SEAMEN. Forgotten Stories about Places on our British Columbia Coast and how they got their Names. Vancouver, Keystone Press, 1954. 30p

**Brown, Lewis, 1858–1930**

A HISTORY OF SIMCOE, 1829–1929. ... Simcoe, Pearce, 1929. 108p [LC OTP

**Brown, Mrs. O.E.A.**

SETTLERS OF THE PLAINS. By O.E.A. Brown, assisted by C. Finnen. [Gilbert Plains, Man.?], 1953. 15 + 188p

**Brown, Richard**

A HISTORY OF THE ISLAND OF CAPE BRETON. With some Account of the Discovery and Settlement of Canada, Nova Scotia, and Newfoundland. London, Sampson Low, 1869. 464p [BM BVaU LC NSWA OTU

**Brown, Rev. Robert Christopher Lundin, –1876**

BRITISH COLUMBIA. An Essay. New Westminster, Royal Engineer Press, 1863. 64 + xxxiiip [BVaU LC OTP

**Brown, Thomas J.**

PLACE NAMES OF THE PROVINCE OF NOVA SCOTIA. Halifax, Royal Print., 1922. 158p [BVaU LC NSWA OTU

**Brown, Thomas Storrow, 1803–1888**

MONTREAL FIFTY YEARS AGO. [Montreal, 1868.] 11p [QMM

**Brown, Wallace William, 1923–**

HISTORY OF PORT MELLON, 1908–1958. By W.W. Brown and J.B. Stewart. Port Mellon, B.C., Port Mellon Community Association, 1959. 36p

**Browne, Rev. Patrick William, 1864–1937**

WHERE THE FISHERS GO. The Story of Labrador. Toronto, Musson, 1909. 370p [BM BVaU LC NSHD OTU

**Brownlee, Sask. Jubilee Committee**

BROWNLEE DISTRICT, 1905–1955. Comp. and printed by the Citizens of the Community of Brownlee, Saskatchewan, on the Occasion of the Celebration of Saskatchewan's Jubilee Year – 1955. Brownlee, Sask., 1955. 84p [mimeographed]

**Bryce, Rev. George, 1844–1931**

CANADIAN PAMPHLETS. (37 items in 1.) Winnipeg, Manitoba Free Press, 1875–1909. [Contains many essays separately published.] [OTP

A HISTORY OF MANITOBA. Toronto, Canadian History Co., 1906. 693p [BVaU OTUV

MANITOBA: ITS INFANCY, GROWTH, AND PRESENT CONDITION. London, Low Marston, 1882. 367p [BM BVaU LC NSWA OTU QMM

THE ROMANTIC SETTLEMENT OF LORD SELKIRK'S COLONISTS. (The Pioneers of Manitoba). Toronto, Musson, 1909. 328p [BM BVaU LC MWU NSHD OKQ QMM

... "SEVEN OAKS." An Account of the Affair of Seven Oaks. ... Winnipeg, Manitoba Free Press, [1891?]. 38p [OTP

WILLIAM SILVERING'S SURRENDER. A Story of Western Experiences. ... [Anon] Winnipeg, Winnipeg Forestry Assoc., 1901. 96p [NBFU OKQ QMSS

**Bryce, Marion (Samuel), 1839–1920**

EARLY RED RIVER CULTURE. By Mrs. George Bryce. Winnipeg, Manitoba Free Press, 1901. 16p [OTP QMM SSU

**Buckaway, Mrs. Catherine Margaret, 1919–**

THE PRAIRIE ROSE STORY. 50th Anniversary. Jansen, Sask., 1960. 43p

**Bugeia, Julia H.S.**

IN OLD MISSISQUOI. With History and Reminiscences of Stanbridge Academy. By Julia H.S. Bugeia and Theodora Cornell Moore. Montreal, Lovell, 1910. 211p [BVaU OTU

**Bull, William Perkins, 1870–1947**

FROM THE BOYNE TO BRAMPTON; or, John the Orangeman at Home and Abroad. Toronto, Perkins Bull Foundation, 1936. 326p [BM BVaU LC OTP

FROM OXFORD TO ONTARIO. A History of the Downsview Community. Toronto, Perkins Bull Foundation, 1941. 310p [BM OKQ

THE PERKINS BULL COLLECTIONS. Historical Paintings by Canadian Artists illustrating Pioneers and Pioneering in the County of Peel. Brampton, Author, 1934. 144p [BM BVaU NSHD OKQ QMM

**Bullock, Mrs. Ellen Guthrie**

PIONEERS OF THE PIPESTONE. Brandon, Sun. Pub. Co., 1929. 63p [MWP

**Burge, Thomas Ashlee, 1922–**

"THIS IS SALTSPRING." 2nd ed. Ganges, B.C., The Spotlight, 1953. 32p

**Burkholder, Mabel Grace (Clare), 1881–**

BARTON ON THE MOUNTAIN. A Short History of that Part of Barton Township which is Situated on the Mountain above the City of Hamilton, from Days of Early Settlement to the Openings [*sic*] Years of the Twentieth Century. [Hamilton?], Author, 1956. 48p

THE STORY OF HAMILTON. Hamilton, Davis-Lisson, 1938. 183p [LC OTU QMM

**Burns, Rev. Robert Ferrier, 1826–1896**

OUR MODERN BABYLON. A Discourse Delivered in Fort Massey Church, Halifax, N.S. on ... the Sabbath succeeding the "Chiniquy Riot." ... With an appendix. Halifax, Nova Scotia Print., 1876. 22p [NSHD

**Burns, William M., 1863–1943**

A HISTORY AND STORY OF BOTSFORD [N.B.]. Sackville, Tribune Print., 1933. 106p [Reprinted 1962.] [NBSaM

**Burrows, Charles Acton, 1853–1948**

THE ANNALS OF THE TOWN OF GUELPH, 1827–1877. Comp. under the direction of ——. Guelph, Herald, 1877. 170p [BVaU LC NSWA OTU QMM

**Burt, Alfred LeRoy, 1888–**

THE OLD PROVINCE OF QUEBEC. Toronto, Ryerson, 1933. 551p [BM BVaU LC NBFU OTU QMM

THE ROMANCE OF THE PRAIRIE PROVINCES. Toronto, Gage, 1931. 262p [BM BVaU LC OTU

**Byerly, Alpheus Edward, 1894–1960**

THE BEGINNING OF THINGS IN WELLINGTON AND WATERLOO COUNTIES, WITH PARTICULAR REFERENCE TO GUELPH, GALT AND KITCHENER. Guelph, Guelph Pub. Co., 1935. 106p [BM OTU

FERGUS, OR THE FERGUSSON-WEBSTER SETTLEMENT. ... Elora, Ont., Elora Express, 1932–34. 372p [BM BVaU OTP

THE HISTORY OF LOWER NICHOL. Fergus, News, 1930. 16p [OTU

**Byrnes, Harold**

PIONEER DAYS AT CECIL LAKE [B.C.]. By Slim Byrnes. N.p., 1959. 64p

**Byrnes, John Maclay**

THE PATHS TO YESTERDAY. Memories of Old St. John's, Newfoundland, including a number of typical Newfoundland poems, each from the gifted pen of a Terra Novian. Boston, Meador, 1931. 235p [BVaU LC OTU

**Calgary, Alta.**

CALGARY, ALBERTA, "THE CITY WITH EVERYTHING UNDER THE SUN." Calgary, 1951. 100p

**Calkin, John Burgess, 1829–1918**

THE GEOGRAPHY AND HISTORY OF NOVA SCOTIA. Halifax, MacKinlay, 1859. 102p [Several later editions.] [BVaU NSWA OTP QMM

**Calnek, William Arthur, 1822–1892**

HISTORY OF THE COUNTY OF ANNAPOLIS. ... With Memoirs of its Representatives in the Provincial Parliament, and Biographical and Genealogical Sketches of its Early English Settlers and their Families. ... Ed. and completed by A.W. Savary. Toronto, Briggs, 1897. 660p [BM BVaU LC NSWA OTU QMM

**Calverley, Eva**

AND SO ... NINETTE, 1879–1919. Comp. by ——. Ninette, Man., [1958?]. 113p

**Calvin, Delano Dexter, 1881–1948**

A SAGA OF THE ST. LAWRENCE. Timber and Shipping through Three Generations. Toronto, Ryerson, 1945. 176p [BVaU LC NSHD OTU QMM

**Cameron, William Bleasdell, 1862–1951**

THE WAR TRAIL OF BIG BEAR. Being the Story of the Connection of Big Bear and other Cree Indian Chiefs and their Followers with the Canadian North-west Rebellion of 1885. ... Toronto, Ryerson, 1926. 256p [4th ed., rev., pub. under title: BLOOD RED THE SUN. ... Calgary, Kenway, 1950. 225p] [BM BVaU LC NBFU OTU QMM

**Campbell, Alice A. (Hallonquist), 1892–**

MILK RIVER COUNTRY. Lethbridge, Alta., Herald, 1959. 439p

**Campbell, Clarence Thomas, 1843–1922**

PIONEER DAYS IN LONDON. Some Account of Men and Things in London before it became a City. London, Ont., Advertiser Print., 1921. 128p [BVaU LC NSHD OTP

THE SETTLEMENT OF LONDON, ONT. N.p., [1911?]. 51p [OLU

**Campbell, Duncan, 1819?–1886**

HISTORY OF PRINCE EDWARD ISLAND. Charlottetown, Bremner, 1875. 224p [BM BVaU LC NSWA OTU QMM

NOVA SCOTIA. Its Historical, Mercantile and Industrial Relations. Montreal, Lovell, 1873. 548p [BM BVaU LC NSWA OTU QMM

**Campbell, George Graham, 1904–**

THE HISTORY OF NOVA SCOTIA. Toronto, Ryerson, 1948. 288p [BVaU LC NSHD OTU QMM

**Campbell, Isabelle, 1896–**

A HIBBERT REVIEW, COUNTY OF PERTH. Seaforth, Ont., Huron Expositor, 1953. 109p

A HIBBERT REVIEW (Part Two). Including the Lots Contained in Concessions I to VII, inclusive. Seaforth, Ont., Huron Expositor, 1959. 1v [unpaged]

THE STORY OF HIBBERT TOWNSHIP, COUNTY OF PERTH. Seaforth, Ont., Huron Expositor, 1952. 66p

**Campbell, Rev. John Roy, 1841–1926**

AN ANSWER TO SOME STRICTURES IN BROWN'S SEQUEL TO CAMPBELL'S "HISTORY OF YARMOUTH. ..." Halifax, McMillan, 1889. 18p [NSWA

A HISTORY OF THE COUNTY OF YARMOUTH, N.S. Saint John, McMillan 1876. 200p [See also: YARMOUTH, NOVA SCOTIA. A Sequel to Campbell's HISTORY. By George S. Brown. ... Boston, Rand Avery, 1888.] [BViP LC NSWA OTP QMSS

**Campbell, Marjorie Elliott (Wilkins), 1901–**

THE SASKATCHEWAN. ... New York, Rinehart, 1950. 400p [BVaU LC NSHD OKQ QMM

**Campbell, Marjorie (Freeman), 1896–**

NIAGARA, HINGE OF THE GOLDEN ARC. Toronto, Ryerson, 1958. xviii + 356p

**Campbell, Mrs. Sara L.**

BROOKE TOWNSHIP HISTORY, 1833–1933. Alvinston, Ont., Brooke Women's Institute, 1936. 171p [LC OTP

**Camrose Canadian, The**

THE GOLDEN TRAIL. Ed. by the staff of the Camrose *Canadian.* Camrose, Alta., Lions Club, 1955. 136p [A history of Camrose and area.]

**Camrose Historical Society**

EARLY HISTORY OF CAMROSE, ALBERTA, AND DISTRICT. [Camrose?], the Society, 1947. 36p [ACG SSU

**Cando, Sask. School**

THE STORY OF CANDO AND COMMUNITY. Cando, Sask., Cando School Students Council, 1955. 2v [mimeographed]

**Canniff, William, 1830–1910**

HISTORY OF THE PROVINCE OF ONTARIO. ... Toronto, Hovey, 1872. xxxi + 670p [BVaU LC NSWA OTU

HISTORY OF THE SETTLEMENT OF UPPER CANADA. With Special Reference to the Bay of Quinte. Toronto, Dudley & Burns, 1869. xxxi + 671p [BM BVaU LC NSWA OTU QMM

**Canso, N.S.**

HISTORIC CANSO. N.p., n.p., 1928. 63p [NSWA

**Cantelon, Robert Alvin**

EDMONTON, CROSSROADS OF THE WORLD. A Brief View of the City's Development, and its Place in the Post-war World. Edmonton, Civic Enterprises, 1944. 80p [BVa OTP

**Capp, Edward Henry, 1871–**

THE STORY OF BAW-A-TING. Being the Annals of Sault Sainte Marie. Sault Sainte Marie, 1907. 261p [An earlier ed., 1904.] [BVaU LC OTP

**Carberry Agricultural Society. Carberry Plains Anniversary Book Committee**

THE CARBERRY PLAINS. 75 Years of Progress. Carberry, Man., the Committee, 1959. 160p

**Card, Brigham Young, 1914–**

THE CANADIAN PRAIRIE PROVINCES FROM 1870 to 1950. A Sociological Introduction. Toronto, Dent, 1960. xi + 46p

**Carlson, William E.**

HISTORY OF EMERSON, FEATURING HISTORICAL SKETCHES OF SURROUNDING DISTRICTS. Emerson, Man., Journal, 1950. 80p [OTP

**Carlyle, Sask. School**

CARLYLE. Carlyle, Sask., 1955. 38p [mimeographed]

**Carnochan, Janet, 1839–1926**

HISTORY OF NIAGARA (in part). Toronto, Briggs, 1914. 333p [BM BVaU LC OTU QMM

INSCRIPTIONS AND GRAVES IN THE NIAGARA PENINSULA. Niagara, Ont., The Times, [1902?]. 72p [2nd ed.: with Additions and Corrections. Welland, The Tribune, 1910. 126p] [See also Niagara Hist. Soc. reprint with additions and corrections: Niagara-on-the-Lake, The Society, 1931. 147p] [BM LC OTP

NIAGARA ONE HUNDRED YEARS AGO. The Ancient Capital and its Vicinity. Welland, Ont., Tribune, 1892. 35p [BVaU LC NSWA OTU QMM

**Carrel, Frank, 1870–1940**

GUIDE TO THE CITY OF QUEBEC. ... Quebec, Carrel, 1899. 154p [Earlier ed., 1896. Many later editions, gradually lengthening; 45th ed. entitled: CARREL'S ILLUSTRATED GUIDE & MAP OF QUEBEC. ... Quebec, Chronicle-Telegraph, 1937. 213p] [BVaU LC OTP

THE QUEBEC TERCENTENARY COMMEMORATIVE HISTORY. Comp. and ed. by Frank Carrel and Louis Feiczewicz. ... Quebec, Daily Telegraph, 1908. 178p [BM LC NBFU OTP

**Carter, Dyson, 1910–**

SEA OF DESTINY. The Story of Hudson Bay – our Undefended Back Door. New York, Greenberg, 1940. 236p [ACU BM LC NfSG OONL

**Carter, J. Smyth, 1877–**

THE STORY OF DUNDAS ... from 1784 to 1904. Iroquois, Ont., St. Lawrence News, 1905. 463p [BVaU LC NSHD OTU QMM

**Cartwright, George, 1739–1819**

A JOURNAL OF TRANSACTIONS AND EVENTS, DURING A RESIDENCE OF NEARLY SIXTEEN YEARS ON THE COAST OF LABRADOR. Containing many interesting Particulars, both of the Country and its Inhabitants, not hitherto Known. ... Newark, Allin & Ridge, 1792. 3v [A later ed., Saint John, 1882.] [ACG NBFU OTP QMBM

**Cartwright, Man. Citizens**

MEMORIES ALONG THE BADGER. Seventy Five Years of our History, 1885–1960. A Story of the Village of Cartwright, Manitoba. Steinbach, Man., Derksen Printers, 1960. 147p [Prepared by P.A. Watts and others.]

**Cashman, Anthony Walcott, 1923–**

THE EDMONTON STORY. The Life and Times of Edmonton, Alberta. Edmonton, Institute of Applied Art, 1956. 279p

MORE EDMONTON STORIES. The Life and Times of Edmonton, Alberta. Edmonton, Institute of Applied Art, 1958. 261p

**Cebryk, M. Alex**

THE PROGRESS OF FISKE. Fiske, Sask., 1955. 28p [mimeographed]

**Chalmers, John West, 1910–**

RED RIVER ADVENTURE. The Story of the Selkirk Settlers. Toronto, Macmillan, 1956. 158p

**Channell, Leonard Stewart, 1868–**

HISTORY OF COMPTON COUNTY AND SKETCHES OF THE EASTERN TOWNSHIPS, DISTRICT OF ST. FRANCIS, AND SHERBROOKE COUNTY. Comp. by ——. Including Biography of the Late Hon. John Henry Pope, by Hon. C.H. Mackintosh. Cookshire, Que., L.S. Channell, 1896. 289p [BM BVaU LC OTP

**Charles, Evelyn**

THE HISTORY OF MULDREW LAKE [MUSKOKA]. A Record of By-gone Days in and around the Lake, from the Archives of the Muldrew Lake Cottagers' Club. Ed. by ——. Toronto, the Club, 1953. 15p [mimeographed]

**Charlottetown, P.E.I. Centennial Committee**

THE CHARLOTTETOWN CENTENNIAL, 1855–1955. Official Souvenir Booklet. Charlottetown, [1955?]. 101p

**Chase, Reta, 1940–**

A HISTORY OF BURFORD. Burford, Ont., Advance, 1960. 39p

**Chiel, Rabbi Arthur Abraham, 1920–**

JEWISH EXPERIENCES IN EARLY MANITOBA. Winnipeg, Manitoba Jewish Publications, 1955. xiii + 125p

**Chisholm, Joseph Andrew, 1863–1950**

THE HALIFAX MEMORIAL TOWER. Halifax, Canadian Club, 1913. 76p [BM LC NSWA OTU QMM SSU

**Chittick, Hattie**

HANTSPORT, THE SMALLEST TOWN. Hantsport, N.S., Women's Institute, 1940. 46p [Rev. ed., 1954, with title: HANTSPORT ON AVON.] [NSWA

**Christie, James R., 1877–**

THE STORY OF OKANAGAN FALLS. By Jas. R. Christie and Isabel Christie MacNaughton. Okanagan Falls, B.C., Centennial Committee, 1958. 44p

**Christie, Robert, 1788–1856**

A HISTORY OF THE LATE PROVINCE OF LOWER CANADA, Parliamentary and Political, from the Commencement to the Close of its Existence as a Separate Province ... 1791 ... 1841. ... Quebec, Cary, 1848–55. 6v [BM BVaU LC NSWA OTP QMM

**Clark, Andrew Hill, 1911–**

THREE CENTURIES AND THE ISLAND. A Historical Geography of Settlement and Agriculture in Prince Edward Island, Canada. Toronto, U. of Toronto Press, 1959. xiii + 287p

**Clarke, George Frederick, 1883–**

EXPULSION OF THE ACADIANS. The True Story (Documented). Fredericton, Brunswick Press, 1955. 31p

TOO SMALL A WORLD. The Story of Acadia. Fredericton, Brunswick Press, 1958. 423p

**Clarke, Gwendoline Pattie (Fitz-Gordon), 1893–**

HALTON'S PAGES OF THE PAST. Acton, Ont., Dills Print., 1955. 191p [History of Halton County, Ont.]

**Clarke, W.W.**

CLARKE'S HISTORY OF THE EARLIEST RAILWAYS IN NOVA SCOTIA. Windsor, N.S., Hants Journal Press, [1925?]. 63p [Cover title.] [BVaU NBFU OTU

**Clay, Charles, 1906–**

THE LEASIDE STORY. Leaside, Ont., the Council, 1958. 64p

**Cleasby, Henry Standley, 1868–**

THE NICOLA VALLEY IN REVIEW. Merritt, B.C., Herald, 1958. V. 1.

**Cleveland, Rev. Edward, 1804–1886**

A SKETCH OF THE EARLY SETTLEMENT AND HISTORY OF SHIPTON, CANADA EAST. Canada East, "Richmond County Advocate," 1858. 78p [BM LC NSWA OTP QMM

**Clingan, Ruth Mary Ida (Thompson), 1874–**

THE VIRDEN STORY. Virden, Man., 1957. 13 + 264p

**Cochrane, James Arthur, 1891–1947**
THE STORY OF NEWFOUNDLAND. Boston, Ginn, 1938. 256p [Rev. ed.: Toronto, Ginn, 1949. 288p] [BVaU LC NSWA OTU QMM

**Cohoon, William Albert, 1886–**
JUBILEE REMINISCENCES AND HISTORY OF THE MACRORIE AND BRATTON DISTRICT, WITH BIOGRAPHIES OF THE PEOPLE. London, Ont., Middlesex Print., 1956. 103p [2nd ed., 1957. 120p]

**Colborne, Ont. Centennial Committee**
COLBORNE CENTENNIAL, JUNE 27 – JULY 1ST, 1959. Colborne, Ont., 1959. 93p [Editor: D. Peebles.]

**Colborne Township, Ont. Centenary Celebration Committee**
ONE HUNDRED YEARS OF MUNICIPAL GOVERNMENT IN THE TOWNSHIP OF COLBORNE, 1850–1950. With Contributed Articles on the Evolution of Educational, Agricultural, Industrial and other Activities in the Township Centennial Celebration and Reunion, June 30, 1950, at Benmiller. Goderich, Ont., 1950. 26p [OONL

**Coleman, John T.**
HISTORY OF THE EARLY SETTLEMENT OF BOWMANVILLE AND VICINITY. Bowmanville, West Durham Print., 1875. 43p [BVaU OTP

**Coleman, MacDonald, 1919–**
THE FACE OF YESTERDAY. The Story of Brandon, Manitoba. Brandon, Junior Chamber of Commerce, 1957. 106p

**Coleman, Alta. Board of Trade**
COLEMAN'S 50TH ANNIVERSARY BOOKLET. Coleman, Alta., [1953?]. 70p

**Collier, Herbert B.**
REMEMBER WHEN? History of the Viking District. Edmonton, Commercial Print., [1937?]. 72p [AEU

**Collins, Rev. Donald St. Clair, 1922–**
"THIS WAY, HOMESTEADER." By Rev. Don Collins and Margaret Dunham. Carnduff, Sask., Carnduff Jubilee Committee, 1955. 25p [History of Carnduff, 1905–55.]

**Colonsay, Sask. High School**
COLONSAY MEMOIRS, 1905–1955. Colonsay, 1955. 56p [mimeographed]

**Community Clubs of Alexis Creek, B.C., and Other Districts**
HISTORY AND LEGENDS OF THE CHILCOTIN. Williams Lake, B.C., Cariboo Press, 1958. 48p

**Complin, Margaret (Robertson) –1951**
WINGED MOCCASINS TO WINGED WORDS. Regina, Western Print., 1937. 23p [On Northwest Territories.] [OTP SSU

**Connon, John Robert, 1862–1931**
"ELORA." Elora, Ont., Elora Express & Fergus News-Record, 1930. 207p [BVaU OTP

**Conquest, Sask. Homemakers' Club. Pioneer History Committee**
THIS CONQUEST OF OURS, 1905–1948. Conquest, the Club, [1949]. 51p [UTQ'51

**Consolidated Mining and Smelting Company of Canada Limited**
TRAIL'S GOLDEN JUBILEE OLD TIMERS, 1901–1951. Trail, B.C., 1952. 38p

**Cook, John Thomas**
NIPAWIN. Moose Jaw, Quality Press, 1946. 51p [SSU

**Coombs, Albert Ernest, 1871–1957**
CITY OF ST. CATHARINES. Historical Facts. St. Catharines, The Standard, 1947. 52p [OTU
HISTORY OF THE NIAGARA PENINSULA AND THE NEW WELLAND CANAL. Toronto, Historical Publishers, 1930. 428p [BM OTU

**Coombs, William Gordon, 1884–**
FROM OX TEAM TO COMBINE. Local History of Buckland District from 1907 to 1955. Buckland, Sask., Homemakers' Club, 1955. 34p [mimeographed]

**Cooney, Rev. Robert, 1800–1870**
A COMPENDIOUS HISTORY OF THE NORTHERN PART OF ... NEW BRUNSWICK, AND OF THE DISTRICT OF GASPE, IN LOWER CANADA. Halifax, Howe, 1832. 288p [BM BVaU LC MWU NSHD OTP

**Cooper, Charles William, 1819?–1893**
FRONTENAC, LENNOX & ADDINGTON. Prize Essay. Kingston, Creighton, 1856. 105p [LC NSWA OTP

**Cooper, John Irwin, 1905–**
THE HISTORY OF THE MONTREAL HUNT 1826–1953. Montreal, Montreal Hunt, 1953. 18 + 131 + 43p
MONTREAL. THE STORY OF THREE HUNDRED YEARS. Montreal, Lamirande, 1942. 133p [BM BVaU LC OTU QMM

**Cope, Leila M. (Sutton)**
A HISTORY OF THE VILLAGE OF PORT CARLING. Bracebridge, Ont., Herald-Gazette Press, 1956. 87p

**Corbitt, Harry Wellington, 1889–**
THE HISTORY OF KALEDEN. Kaleden, B.C., Centenial Committee, 1958. 61p

**Corey, Rowland H., 1864?–**
HISTORICAL SKETCH OF THE FIRST SETTLERS OF NEW CANAAN. [Sussex, N.B.?], priv. print., 1946. 30p [NBFU

**Cornell, John A., 1841–**

THE PIONEERS OF BEVERLEY. A Series of Sketches. ... With Supplementary Articles on the Municipal History ... Educational Matters ... Agricultural Society [by other hands]. Dundas, Somerville, 1889. 186p [BVaU OTU

**Corner, Raymond Westley, 1894–**

GLENMORE, THE APPLE VALLEY. Kelowna, B.C., Glenmore Centennial Committee, 1958. 57p

**Cornwall, Ont. Old Boys' Reunion**

CORNWALL AND THE UNITED COUNTIES OF STORMONT, DUNDAS AND GLENGARRY. Souvenir of the Old Boys' Reunion ... [1906]. Cornwall, The Freeholder, 1906. 171p [OTP

**Cotton, William Lawson, 1848–1928**

CHAPTERS IN OUR ISLAND STORY. Rev. and repub. by request. Charlottetown, Irwin Print., 1927. 162p [BVaU NBFU OTP

**Coutts, Mrs. Marjorie Ellen, 1914–**

DAWSON CREEK, PAST AND PRESENT. An Historical Sketch. Ed. by ——. Dawson Creek, B.C., Dawson Creek Historical Society, 1958. 115p

**Cowan, Hugh, 1870–1943**

THE DETROIT RIVER DISTRICT. Toronto, Algonquin Hist. Soc., 1929. 319p [BVaU OTP

GOLD AND SILVER JUBILEE, Sault Ste. Marie, Ont. N.p., 1938. 32p [Anon] [OTP

**Coward, Mrs. Elizabeth Ruggles, 1887–1959**

BRIDGETOWN, NOVA SCOTIA. Its History to 1900. Bridgetown, N.S., Author, 1955. 253p

**Cowie, Isaac, 1848–1917**

THE WESTERN PLAINS OF CANADA REDISCOVERED. [Winnipeg], 1903. 40p [ACG

**Coyne, James Henry, 1849–1942**

THE COUNTRY OF THE NEUTRALS (as far as comprised in the County of Elgin) from Champlain to Talbot. St. Thomas, Times Print., 1895. 44p [LC OTU

**Craick, William Arnot, 1880–1969**

PORT HOPE. Historical Sketches. Port Hope, Williamson Press, 1901. 138p [BM BVaU OTU

**Craig, John Roderick, 1837–**

RANCHING WITH LORDS AND COMMONS; or, Twenty Years on the Range. Being a Record of Actual Facts and Conditions Relating to the Cattle Industry of the North-west Territories of Canada. Toronto, Briggs, 1903. 293p [BM BVaU LC OTU SSU

**Craig, Martha**

THE GARDEN OF CANADA. Burlington, Oakville ana District. Toronto, Briggs, 1902. 96p [Ryerson Impt

**Cranston, James Herbert, 1880–1952**

HURONIA. The Cradle of Ontario's History. 3rd ed. Midland, Huronia Historic Sites, 1951. 80p [First ed., 1949. 24p] [OLU OTP

**Crerar, Thomas Alexander, 1876–**

SILVER CREEK DISTRICT IN THE EARLY DAYS. Winnipeg, priv. print., 1955. 15p

**Croil, James, 1821–1916**

DUNDAS; or, A Sketch of Canadian History, and More Particularly of the County of Dundas. ... Montreal, Dawson, 1861. 352p [BM BVaU LC NSWA OTU QMM

**Crosskill, William Hay, 1861–**

PRINCE EDWARD ISLAND, GARDEN PROVINCE OF CANADA. Its History, Interests, and Resources. ... Charlottetown, Murley & Garnhum, 1899. 79p [Later rev. and enl. eds. in 1904 and 1906.] [BVaU LC NSWA OTP QQL

**Crowell, Edwin, 1853–1926**

A HISTORY OF BARRINGTON TOWNSHIP AND VICINITY, SHELBURNE COUNTY, NOVA SCOTIA, 1604–1870. With a Biographical and Genealogical Appendix. Yarmouth, Author, 1923. 603p [BM BVaU LC NSWA OTU QMM

**Crown Zellerbach Canada Limited. Richmond Division**

A HISTORY OF THE MUNICIPALITY OF RICHMOND. Richmond, B.C., 1958. 28p

**Cruickshank, Frederick David**

HISTORY OF WESTON. By F.D. Cruickshank and J. Nason. Weston, Ont., Times & Guide, 1937. 162p [BVaU OTP

**Cruikshank, Ernest Alexander, 1854–1939**

A CENTURY OF MUNICIPAL HISTORY, 1792–1892. Comp. from the Municipal Records of the County of Welland. Welland, Tribune Print., 1892–93. 2v in 1. [OTP

COLLECTION OF CONTEMPORARY LETTERS AND DOCUMENTS, JANUARY TO JULY, 1813. Ed. by ——. Niagara-on-the-Lake, Niagara Hist. Soc., 1939. 87p [UTQ'41

THE FIGHT IN THE BEECHWOODS. A Study in Canadian History. Welland, Sawle, 1895. 32p [BM BVaU NSHD OTU

HISTORICAL AND DESCRIPTIVE SKETCH OF THE COUNTY OF WELLAND, 1792–1841. Welland, County Council, 1886. [OTU

THE SETTLEMENT OF THE UNITED EMPIRE LOYALISTS ON THE UPPER ST.

LAWRENCE AND BAY OF QUINTE IN 1784. A Documentary Record, Transcribed and ed. by ——. Toronto, Ontario Hist. Soc., 1934. 188p [BM LC NBFU OTU QMM

THE STORY OF BUTLER'S RANGERS AND THE SETTLEMENT OF NIAGARA. Welland, Tribune Print., 1893. 114p [BM BVaU NSWA OTU

TEN YEARS OF THE COLONY OF NIAGARA, 1780–1790. Welland, Tribune Print., 1908. 50p [BVaU

**Cumberland, Frederic Barlow, 1846–1913**

A CENTURY OF SAIL AND STEAM ON THE NIAGARA. Toronto, Musson, 1913. 198p [BM BVaU LC OTU QMM

THE NORTHERN LAKES OF CANADA. ... A Guide. ... Toronto, Hunter Rose, 1886. 198p [BVaU OTP

**Cumberland, Robert William, 1895–**

THE UNITED EMPIRE LOYALIST SETTLEMENTS BETWEEN KINGSTON AND ADOLPHUSTOWN. Kingston, Jackson Press, 1923. 24p [BVaU NBFU OKQ

**Cumberland, W.G.E.**

A BRIEF HISTORY OF ALLISTON, FROM THE FOUNDING OF THE FIRST SETTLEMENT BY WILLIAM FLETCHER UNTIL YEAR OF CENTENNIAL, 1947. ... Comp. by ——. Alliston, Ont., City Clerk, 1947. 128p [BViP OLU

**Currie, Mary Olive, 1909–**

SO MUCH TO REMEMBER AND TO LOOK FORWARD TO ... STRASBOURG, SASKATCHEWAN, 1905–1955. Strasbourg, Sask., Strasbourg and Community Booster Club, 1955. 20p

**Dahlman, Laura Rose (Thorn), 1895–**

TWELVE MILE LAKE HISTORY. By Mrs. Laura Dahlman and Mrs. George Cristo. Twelve Mile Lake, Sask., Authors, 1955. 10p [mimeographed]

**Dartmouth, N.S. Bicentennial Committee**

OFFICIAL BICENTENNIAL PROGRAM AND GUIDE BOOK OF DARTMOUTH, N.S. Halifax, Scott Publications, 1950. 95p [OONL

**Davies, Blodwen, 1897–1966**

OTTAWA. Portrait of a Capital. Toronto, McGraw-Hill, 1954. 185p

QUEBEC, PORTRAIT OF A PROVINCE. New York, Greenberg, 1951. xiii + 258p

THE STORIED STREETS OF QUEBEC. Montreal, Carrier, 1929. 94p [BVaU LC NBFU OTU QMM

STORIED YORK. Toronto Old and New. Toronto, Ryerson, 1931. 127p [NBFU OTU

**Dawson, Carl Addington, 1887–**

PIONEERING IN THE PRAIRIE PROVINCES: THE SOCIAL SIDE OF THE SETTLEMENT

PROCESS. By C.A. Dawson and Eva R. Younge. Toronto, Macmillan, 1940. 338p [BM BVaU LC NSHD OTU QMM SSU

THE SETTLEMENT OF THE PEACE RIVER COUNTRY. A Study of a Pioneer Area. Toronto, Macmillan, 1934. 284p [BM BVaU LC NSHD OTU QMM SSU

**Dawson, Samuel Edward, 1833–1916**

HANDBOOK TO THE CITY OF MONTREAL. With Carnival Supplement. [Anon] [Montreal, Dawson Bros., 1884.] 23 + 143p [NSHPL OLU QMBM

THE SAINT LAWRENCE BASIN. London, Lawrence & Bullen, 1905. 451p [BM BVaU LC NSWA OTU

**Day, Catherine Matilda (Townsend), 1815–1899**

HISTORY OF THE EASTERN TOWNSHIPS, PROVINCE OF QUEBEC. ... Montreal, Lovell, 1869. 475p [BM BVaU NSWA OTU QMM

PIONEERS OF THE EASTERN TOWNSHIPS. ... Montreal, Lovell, 1863. 171p [BM BVaU LC NSWA OTU QMM

**Day, Frank, 1887?–**

HERE AND THERE IN ERAMOSA. An Historical Sketch of the Early Years and of the People and Events Contributing to the Growth and Development of the Township. Rockwood, Ont., 1953. 199p

**DeGarthe, William Edward, 1907–**

THIS IS PEGGY'S COVE, NOVA SCOTIA, CANADA. Halifax, Author, 1956. 35p

**Deloraine, Man. Deloraine and District Chamber of Commerce**

DELORAINE, MANITOBA, 1880–1955. [A History.] 75th Anniversary Celebration, Sunday, June 19th to Thursday, June 23rd. Deloraine, Man., 1955. 74p

**Denison, George Taylor, 1839–1925**

THE FENIAN RAID ON FORT ERIE. Toronto, Rollo & Adam, 1866. 92p [BVaU OTU

**Denton, Vernon Llewellyn, 1881–1944**

THE FAR WEST COAST. Toronto, Dent, 1924. 297p [BM BVaU NSHD OTU

**DesBarres, Joseph Frederic Wallet, 1722–1824**

LETTERS TO LORD —— on A Caveat against Emigration to America, with the state of the Island of Cape Breton ... 1784 to the present. ... London, Bensley, 1804. 228p [A CAVEAT AGAINST EMIGRATION TO AMERICA, by William Smith, Chief Justice of Cape Breton, was pub. in London in 1803.] [LC

**Des Brisay, Mather Byles, 1828–1896**

HISTORY OF THE COUNTY OF LUNENBURG. Halifax, Bowes, 1870. 264p [2nd ed.: Toronto, Briggs, 1895. 585p] [BM BVaU LC NSHD OTU

**Devine, Rev. Edward James, 1860–1927**

HISTORIC CAUGHNAWAGA. Montreal, Messenger Press, 1922. 443p [BVaU OTU QMM

OLD FORT STE. MARIE: HOME OF THE CANADIAN MARTYRS 1639–1649. Toronto, Canadian Messenger, 1925. 52p [Earlier ed., Toronto, 1915. 58p] [NBFU OLU QMM

**Devine, Patrick Kevin, 1859–1950**

YE OLDE ST. JOHN'S, 1750–1939. St. John's, Robinson, 1939. 175p [LC NSHD OTU

**Devore, Roy William, 1891–**

THE HISTORY OF WALTERDALE. Edmonton, Author, 1956. 17p

**Dimock, Celia C. (Gillis), –1959**

CHILDREN OF THE SHEILING. Sydney, N.S., Lynk Print., n.d. 98p [NSHP

ISLE ROYALE: "THE FRONT DOOR OF CANADA." Halifax, Allen, 1929. 81p [2nd ed., 1946.] [AEU NSHL OKQ

**Doane, Frank Augustus, 1862–1950**

OLD TIMES IN BARRINGTON. Truro, Truro Pub. Co., 1948. 95p [NSHD QMM

**Dobbin, Francis Hincks, 1850–1923**

OUR OLD HOME TOWN. Toronto, Dent, 1943. 246p [About Peterborough, Ont.] [BM BVaU LC OTU

**Doe, Ernest**

HISTORY OF SALMON ARM, 1885–1912. Comp. by ——. Salmon Arm, B.C., Salmon Arm Observer, 1947. 83p [BVaU OTP

SALMON ARM. A Basic History ... to 1912. Comp. by ——. Salmon Arm, B.C., 1939. 64p [BVaU

**Donohoe, E.F.**

KITCHENER CENTENNIAL, 1854–1954. Ed. by ——. Kitchener, Ont., Kitchener-Waterloo Record, 1954. 108p

**Dooner, Alfred James, 1865?–1949**

CATHOLIC PIONEERS IN UPPER CANADA. Toronto, Macmillan, 1947. 251p [BVaU LC OTP

**Dorian, Charles Edward, 1881–**

THE FIRST 75 YEARS. A Headline History of Sudbury, Canada. Ilfracombe, Devon, Stockwell, 1959. xi + 300p

**Doughty, Arthur George, 1860–1936**

THE ACADIAN EXILES. A Chronicle of the Land of Evangeline. Toronto, Glasgow Brook, 1916. 178p [BM BVaU LC NSHD OTU QMM

THE CRADLE OF NEW FRANCE. A Story of the City Founded by Champlain. Montreal, Cambridge Corp., 1908. 314p [BM BVaU LC NSWA OTU QMM

THE FORTRESS OF QUEBEC, 1608–1903. Quebec, Dussault & Proulx, 1904. 126p [BM LC NSWA

THE KING'S BOOK OF QUEBEC. Comp. by A.G. Doughty and W.C.H. Wood. Ottawa, Mortimer, 1911. 2v [Memorial of tercentenary celebrations of 1908.] [BM NBFU OTU

QUEBEC OF YESTER-YEAR. Toronto, Nelson, 1932. 198p [BM BVaU LC NSHD OTU QMM

QUEBEC UNDER TWO FLAGS. A Brief History of the City. ... By A.G. Doughty and N.E. Dionne. Quebec, Quebec News, 1903. 424p [BM BVaU NSWA OTU QMM

THE SIEGE OF QUEBEC AND THE BATTLE OF THE PLAINS OF ABRAHAM. [In collab. with G.W. Parmelee.] Quebec, Dussault & Proulx, 1901–2. 6v [BM BVaU NBFU OTU

**Douglas, Mrs. Helen Frances, 1898–**

GOLDEN KERNELS OF GRANUM. The Story of the Early Settlers of Granum. Granum, Alta., Author, n.d. 79p

**Douglas, James, 1837–1918**

OLD FRANCE IN THE NEW WORLD. Quebec in the Seventeenth Century. Cleveland, Burrows, 1905. 597p [BM BVaU NSHD OTU

**Douglas, Robert, 1881–1930**

PLACE-NAMES OF PRINCE EDWARD ISLAND, WITH MEANINGS. Comp. by ——. Ottawa, King's Printer, 1925. 55p [BM BVaU OLU OONL

**Downs, Arthur George, 1924–**

QUESNEL, BRITISH COLUMBIA. Quesnel, B.C., Cariboo Digest, 1954. 30p

WAGON ROAD NORTH. The Story of the Cariboo Gold Rush in Historical Photos. Quesnel, B.C., Northwest Digest, 1960. 76p

**Drake, Earl Gordon, 1928–**

REGINA, THE QUEEN CITY. Toronto, McClelland, 1955. ix + 260p

**Draper, William George, –1868**

HISTORY OF THE CITY OF KINGSTON. Kingston, Creighton, 1862. 28p [OTP

**Driver, Sask. School**

HISTORY OF DRIVER S.D. NO. 811 AND VICINITY. Driver, Sask., 1955. 1v (unpaged) [mimeographed]

**Drouin, Lucien Henri, 1919–**

HISTORY OF ST. PAUL. Histoire de Saint-Paul. 1909–1959. By L.H. Drouin and others. St. Paul, Alta., St. Paul Journal, 1960. 232p [Text partly in English, partly in French.]

**Drury, Ernest Charles, 1878–**

ALL FOR A BEAVER HAT. A History of Early Simcoe County. Toronto, Ryerson, 1959. xvi + 160p

THE STORY OF SIMCOE COUNTY, LAND OF HOLIDAY AND HISTORY. Barrie, Ont., County Council of Simcoe, 1955. 28p

**Duff, Louis Blake, 1878–1959**

CROWLAND. Welland, Baskerville, 1928. 60p [BM BVaU NBFU OTU QMM

**Dumbrille, Dorothy, 1898–**

BRAGGART IN MY STEP. More Stories of Glengarry. Toronto, Ryerson, 1956. ix + 173p

UP AND DOWN THE GLENS. The Story of Glengarry. Toronto, Ryerson, 1954. 139p

**Duncan, Mrs. Frances Imogene, 1926–**

THE SAYWARD-KELSEY BAY SAGA. Courtenay, B.C., Argus Pub. Co., 1958. 51p

**Dundas County, Ont.**

HISTORY OF THE COUNTY OF DUNDAS FROM 1784 TO 1904. Iroquois, 1905. [BVaU NBFU OOP

**Dundurn, Sask. School**

DUNDURN. The Village and District of Dundurn Throughout the Years. Dundurn, Sask., 1955. 89p [mimeographed]

**Dunham, Bertha Mabel, 1881–1957**

GRAND RIVER. Toronto, McClelland, 1945. 299p [BVaU NBFU OKQ QMM

**Dunn, Charles William, 1915–**

HIGHLAND SETTLER. A Portrait of the Scottish Gael in Nova Scotia. Toronto, U. of Toronto Press, 1953. 179p

**Duquette, Rev. Carson W., 1913–**

GENTLE PEOPLE. Gatineau Story. Ottawa, 1955. 72 + 78p [History of the town of Gatineau, Que. Text in English and French.]

**Earle, Emily Mae (Waite), 1882–**

FOOTPRINTS IN NEW BRUNSWICK. An Historical Account of Victoria County, New Brunswick. Perth, N.B., 1959. 175p

**Earle, Evelyn Purvis**

LEEDS THE LOVELY. Toronto, Ryerson, 1951. 174p

**Eastern Irrigation District, Brooks, Alta.**

THE HISTORY OF THE EASTERN IRRIGATION DISTRICT. 25th Anniversary, May 1st, 1960. Brooks, Alta., the District, 1960. 64p

**Eaton, Arthur Wentworth Hamilton, 1849–1937**

THE HISTORY OF KING'S COUNTY, NOVA SCOTIA. Giving a Sketch of the French and their Expulsion and a History of the New England Planters ... 1604–1910. Salem, Mass., Salem Press, 1910. 898p [BM BVaU LC NSWA OTU QMSS

**Eaton, Mrs. Grace Elvira, 1905–**

GREEN HILL. The Story of a Prairie Community and its Pioneers. By Grace E. Eaton and Lloyd L. Vallée. Carlyle, Sask., Authors, 1955. [unpaged]

**Eatonia, Sask. School**

AS FAR AS I REMEMBER. Comp. and pub. by Eatonia School staff and pupils. Eatonia, Sask., The Enterprise, 1955. 8p

**Eby, Ezra E., 1850–**

A BIOGRAPHICAL HISTORY OF WATERLOO TOWNSHIP AND OTHER TOWNSHIPS OF THE COUNTY. Being a History of the Early Settlers and their Descendants &c. Berlin, Ont., n.p., 1895–96. 2v [OTU

**Edgar, Matilda (Ridout), 1844–1910**

TEN YEARS OF UPPER CANADA IN PEACE AND WAR, 1805–1815. Being the Ridout Letters. With annotations by ——. (Appendix: THE NARRATIVE OF THE CAPTIVITY AMONG THE SHAWANESE INDIANS, IN 1788, OF THOS. RIDOUT.) Toronto, Briggs, 1890. 389p [BM BVaU LC NSHD OTP

**Edmonds, Walter Everard, 1875–**

EDMONTON, PAST AND PRESENT. Edmonton, Douglas, 1943. 32p [BVaU OTP SSU

**Edstrom, Mrs. Sylvia, 1914–**

MEMOIRS OF THE EDBERG PIONEERS. Comp. by Sylvia Edstrom and Florence Lundstrom. Edberg, Alta., 1956. 121p

**Edwards, Joseph Plimsoll, 1857–1930**

LOUISBOURG. An Historical Sketch. ... Halifax, Nova Scotia Print., 1895. 62p [BM NSWA OTU QMM

**Elder, Annie Edna (Vallis), 1882–**

HISTORY OF NEW JERUSALEM [in Queen's County, N.B.]. Fredericton, priv. print., 1953. 97p

**Elliott, George B.**

WINNIPEG AS IT IS IN 1874; and as it was in 1860. ... Ottawa, Free Press Office, 1875. 36p [ACG NSHPL OTP QMSS

**Elliott, Gordon Raymond, 1920–**

QUESNEL. Commercial Centre of the Cariboo Gold Rush. Quesnel, B.C., Cariboo Historical Society, 1958. 190p

**Elstow, Sask. High School**

SOD SHACK TO ATOMIC AGE. Elstow-Clavet. Elstow, Sask., 1955. 36p [mimeographed]

**Emigrant Lady (pseud)**

LETTERS FROM MUSKOKA. By an Emigrant Lady [pseud]. London, Bentley, 1878. xii + 289p [BM LC OTU

**England, Robert, 1894–**

THE COLONIZATION OF WESTERN CANADA. A Study of Contemporary Land Settlement (1896–1934). London, King, 1936. 341p [BM BVaU LC OTU QMM

**English, Leo Edward Francis, 1887–**

OUTLINE OF NEWFOUNDLAND HISTORY. London, Toronto, Nelson, [1929]. 109p [2nd ed., rev., with title: NEWFOUNDLAND PAST AND PRESENT. Toronto, Nelson, 1949. 128p] [BM NfSM OTP

**Entremont, H. Leander d', 1862–**

THE BARONNIE DE POMBCOUP AND THE ACADIANS. Yarmouth, Herald-Telegram, 1931. 192p [BM BVaU NSWA OTU

THE FORTS OF CAPE SABLE OF THE SEVENTEENTH CENTURY. Centre East Pubnico, N.S., Davis, 1938. 106p [LC NBFU OTU

**Ermatinger, Charles Oakes Zaccheus, 1851–1921**

RECORD OF THE CELEBRATION OF THE CENTENARY OF THE TALBOT SETTLEMENT ... 1903. St. Thomas, Elgin Historical and Scientific Institute, 1910. 72p [OLU OTU

THE TALBOT REGIME; or, The First Half Century of the Talbot Settlement. St. Thomas, Municipal World, 1904. 393p [BM BVaU LC NBFU OTU QMM

**Essex County, Ont.**

COMMEMORATIVE BIOGRAPHICAL RECORD OF THE COUNTY OF ESSEX. ... Toronto, Beers, 1905. 676p [OLU

**Essex County, Ont. Tourist Association**

ESSEX COUNTY SKETCHES. Windsor, Ont., Herald Press, 1947. 50p [OTU

**Evans, Len**

THE COPELAND STORY, 1905–1955. By Len Evans and others. Wynyard, Sask., Wynyard Advance, 1955. 15p

**Ewart, John Skirving, 1849–1933**

THE MANITOBA SCHOOL QUESTION. An Historical Account of the Red River Outbreak in 1869 and 1870. ... Toronto, Copp Clark, 1894. 401p [BM BVaU LC NSHD OTU

**Fahrni, Margaret (Morton)**

THIRD CROSSING. A History of the First Quarter Century of the Town and District of Gladstone in the Province of Manitoba. By Margaret Morton Fahrni and William Lewis Morton. Winnipeg, Advocate Press, 1946. 118p [BVaU LC QMM SSU

**Fairchild, George Moore, 1854–1912**

FROM MY QUEBEC SCRAP BOOK. Quebec, Carrel, 1907. 316p [BM BVaU OTU QMM

GLEANINGS FROM QUEBEC. Quebec, Carrel, 1908. 216p [BM BVaU LC OTU

A HISTORY OF THE QUEBEC WINTER CARNIVAL. Quebec, Carrel, 1894. 140p [BM BVa OTU

JOURNAL OF AN AMERICAN PRISONER AT FORT MALDEN AND QUEBEC IN THE WAR OF 1812. Ed. by ——. Quebec, Carrel, 1909. 32p [BVaU OTU

A SHORT ACCOUNT OF YE QUEBEC WINTER CARNIVAL HOLDEN IN 1894. Quebec, Daily Telegraph, 1894. [BVaU

**Farewell, John Edwin Chandler, 1840–1923**

COUNTY OF ONTARIO. Short Notes as to the Early Settlement and Progress of the County, and Brief References to the Pioneers and some Ontario County Men who have taken a Prominent Part in Provincial and Dominion Affairs. Whitby, Gazette-Chronicle, 1907. 318p [BVaU OTU

**Farm Women's Union of Alberta. Beddington Local**

THE NOSE CREEK STORY FROM 1792. Prepared and Written by Members of the Community. Calgary, 1960. 156p [History of the district between Calgary and Airdrie, Alta.]

**Farmer, Samuel, 1871–1948**

ON THE SHORES OF THE SCUGOG. Rev. and enl. ed. Port Perry, Ont., Port Perry Star, 1934. 256p [First pub. in 1913.] [OTP

**Farquharson, Donald Robert**

TALES AND MEMOIRS OF CROMAR AND CANADA. Chatham, Planet, [1930?]. 215p [BVaU NBFU OLU

**Ferrier, Alexander David, 1813–1890**

REMINISCENCES OF CANADA AND THE EARLY DAYS OF FERGUS. Being Three Lectures delivered ... in 1864 and 1865. Fergus, Ont., News-Record, 1923. 47p [First pub. in 1866.] [BVaU OTP

**Fife Lake, Sask. School**

FIFE LAKE, A LOCAL HISTORY. Saskatchewan Jubilee, 1955. Fife Lake, 1956. 10p [mimeographed]

**Finch Township, Ont. Teachers**

PIONEER HISTORY OF FINCH TOWNSHIP. Comp. by the teachers of Finch Township. Finch, Ont., 1957. 47p [mimeographed]

**Findlay, J.W.M.**

THE PEMBROKE CENTENNIAL SOUVENIR BOOK. ... Commemorating the Centennial of Pembroke's Incorporation as a Village in 1858. ... Ed. by ——. Pembroke, Ont., Pembroke Observer, 1958. 156p

**Finn, T.D.**

CENTENARY OF OTTAWA, 1854–1954. "The Capital Chosen by a Queen." Ed. by ——. Ottawa, 1954. 76p

**Fisher, Peter, 1782–1848**

HISTORY OF NEW BRUNSWICK ... As Originally Published in 1825. Saint John, New Brunswick Historical Soc., 1921. 133p [1st ed. under title: SKETCHES OF NEW BRUNSWICK. Containing an Account of the First Settlement of the Province. By an Inhabitant of the Province [pseud]. Saint John, Chubb & Sears, 1825. 108p] [BM BVaU NSWA OLU

NOTITIA OF NEW-BRUNSWICK, FOR 1836, AND EXTENDING INTO 1837. ... By an Inhabitant. Saint John, Chubb, 1838. 134p [NSWA OTP

SKETCHES OF NEW BRUNSWICK. ... [See under HISTORY OF NEW BRUNSWICK].

**Fitzgerald, James Edward, 1818–1896**

AN EXAMINATION OF THE CHARTER AND PROCEEDINGS OF THE HUDSON'S BAY COMPANY, WITH REFERENCE TO ... VANCOUVER'S ISLAND. London, Saunders, 1849. 293p [BM BVaU OTU

**Fleming, John, 1786?–1832**

POLITICAL ANNALS OF LOWER CANADA. Being a Review of the Political and Legislative History ... under the Act of the Imperial Parliament ... Which Established a House of Assembly and Legislative Council. Showing the Defects. ... By a British Settler [pseud]. Montreal, Herald & Gazette, 1828. lxxviii + 180p [Covers period 1759–1811, and ends with the words: "End of the first part." No more published.] [BM BVaU LC NSWA OTP QMM

**Fleming, Sandford, 1827–1915**

MEMORIAL OF THE PEOPLE OF RED RIVER ... ON THE COLONIZATION ... AND THE ESTABLISHMENT OF A GREAT TERRITORIAL ROAD ... TO BRITISH COLUMBIA. Quebec, Hunter Rose, 1863. 57p [BViPA

**Fonthill, Ont. Women's Institute**

HISTORY OF THE VILLAGE OF FONTHILL. Welland, the Institute, 1944. 51p [OTU

**Forest, Ont. Centennial Committee**

FOREST AND DISTRICT CENTENNIAL 1859–1959. Forest, 1959. 195p

**Fort Erie, Ont. Times-Review**

FORT ERIE CENTENNIAL, 1857–1957. Fort Erie, Review Co., 1957. 56p

GOLDEN JUBILEE SUPPLEMENT, July 18, 1945. Fort Erie, Times Review, 1945. 48p [OTU

**Fox, William Sherwood, 1878–1967**

THE BRUCE BECKONS. The Story of Lake Huron's Great Peninsula. Toronto, U. of Toronto Press, 1952. xviii + 235p

'T AIN'T RUNNIN' NO MORE. The Story of Grand Bend, the Pinery and the Old

River Bed. ... London, Ont., Holmes, 1946. 55p [BVaU LC NBFU OKQ

'T AIN'T RUNNIN' NO MORE–TWENTY YEARS AFTER. The Story of Grand Bend, the Pinery and the Watershed of the Aux Sables River. London, Ont., Oxford Book Shop, 1958. xii + 89p

**Frame, Archibald**

SELMAH IN 1853. A Paper read before the Presbyterian Social in Selmah, N.S. Halifax, Herald Print., 1894. 18p [NSHP OKQ

**Frame, Elizabeth, 1820–1913**

A LIST OF MICMAC NAMES OF PLACES, RIVERS, ETC., IN NOVA SCOTIA. Comp. by ——. Cambridge, Wilson, 1892. 12p [BM LC NSWA OTU

**Fraser, Alexander, 1860–1936**

A HISTORY OF ONTARIO. Toronto, Canada Hist. Co., 1907. 2v [BVaU LC OTU QMM

THE LAST LAIRD OF MACNAB. An Episode in the Settlement of MacNab Township, Upper Canada. Toronto, Imrie Graham, 1899. 218p [BVaU LC OTP

TORONTO, HISTORICAL, DESCRIPTIVE AND PICTORIAL. Toronto, Waverley Press, 1901. 46p [BM BVaU OTU

**Fraser, George B.**

MORRIS, MANITOBA, GROWTH AND PROGRESS. With Personal Sketches. Morris, Herald Print., 1882. 31p [Peel

**Fraser, George Johnston, 1872–**

THE STORY OF OSOYOOS, SEPTEMBER 1811 TO DECEMBER 1952. Penticton, B.C., Penticton Herald, 1952. 212p

**Fraser, John, 1820–1899**

HISTORIC CANADIAN GROUND. The LaSalle Homestead of 1666 and Other Old Landmarks of French Canada. ... Montreal, Witness, 1892. 30p [BM BVaU LC NSHD OTU QMM

**Fraser, L.R., 1873?–**

HISTORY OF MUSKOKA. Bracebridge, Ont., Thomas, 1946. 152p [BVaU OTP

**Fredericton, N.B. City Council**

FREDERICTON'S 100 YEARS: Then and Now. Fredericton, the Council, 1948. 267p [NBFU OTU

**Frith, B.M.**

A SHORT HISTORY OF THE WAKOW DISTRICT. Wakow, Recorder, 1932. 60p [SSU

**Fryer, Charles Edmund, 1876–**

A HISTORY OF QUEBEC, ITS RESOURCES AND ITS PEOPLE. By Benjamin Sulte ... C.E. Fryer ... L.O. David. Montreal & Toronto, Canada History Co., 1908. 2v [BM LC OLU

**Gabriel, Theresa**

VERNON, BRITISH COLUMBIA. A Brief History. Vernon, Centennial Committee, 1958. 63p

**Gaetz, Annie Louise (Siddall), 1881–**

THE PARK COUNTRY. A History of Red Deer and District. Red Deer, Alta., Author, 1948. 173p [Rev. ed., 1960.] [AEU BVaU OTU

TRAILS OF YESTERDAY. Folk Lore of the Red Deer District. Red Deer, Alta., Author, 1952. 99p

**Gaetz, Rev. Leonard, 1841–1907**

REPORT OF SIX YEARS' EXPERIENCE OF A FARMER IN THE RED DEER DISTRICT. Ottawa, Dawson, 1892. 31p [OTU SSU

**Gale, George Gordon, 1857–1940**

HISTORIC TALES OF OLD QUEBEC. Quebec, Telegraph, 1920. 245p [Rev. and enl.: 1923. 344p] [BM BVaU LC NSHD OTU QMM

QUEBEC 'TWIXT OLD AND NEW. Quebec, Telegraph, 1915. 296p [BM BVaU LC NBFU OTU

**Gallagher, Edward L.**

HISTORY OF OLD KINGSTON AND REXTON. Sussex, N.B., Maritime, 1948. 51p [NBFU OTU QMM

**Galloway, Hazel Frances (Dempsey), 1921–**

A HISTORY OF THE CEDAR, BRIGHT, CRANBERRY AND OYSTER DISTRICTS ON VANCOUVER ISLAND, B.C. Comp. by Mrs. Allan Galloway and Robert Strachan. Ladysmith, B.C., Cedar Centennial Committee, 1958. 26p [mimeographed]

**Ganong, William Francis, 1864–1941**

THE HISTORY OF CARAQUET & POKEMOUCHE. Rev. and Enl. from the Author's MS. Notes. Ed. by Susan Brittain Ganong. Saint John, New Brunswick Museum, 1948. 62p [OTU

THE HISTORY OF MISCOU AND SHIPPEGAN. Rev. and Enl. from the Author's MS. Notes. Ed. by Susan Brittain Ganong. Saint John, New Brunswick Museum, 1946. 92p [BVaU NSWA OTU

A MONOGRAPH OF HISTORIC SITES IN THE PROVINCE OF NEW BRUNSWICK. Ottawa, Hope, 1899. 357p [BVaU OLU

STE. CROIX (DOUCHET) ISLAND. Ed. by Susan Brittain Ganong. Saint John, 1945. 125p [LC NSWA OKQ

**Gardiner, Herbert Fairbairn, 1849–1924**

NOTHING BUT NAMES.... Toronto, Morang, 1899. 561p [BVaU NSHD OTP

**Garratt, Alfred Webster, 1871–**

HISTORY OF MILESTONE, 1893–1910. Milestone, Sask., Author, 1948. 129p [BVaU OOA SSU

**Garrett, Anne (Evans)**

THE BOWEN ISLAND STORY. Bowen Island, B.C., 1957. 16p

**Garrett, Rev. John C.**

... HISTORIC BUILDINGS; THE CENTENNIAL – AN OLD CANADIAN FORT. Welland, Tribune, 1911. 57p [LC OLU

**Garrioch, Rev. Alfred Campbell, 1848–1934**

THE CORRECTION LINE. Winnipeg, Stovel, 1933. 414p [BM BVaU OTU

FIRST FURROWS. A History of the Early Settlement of the Red River Country, including that of Portage la Prairie. Winnipeg, Stovel, 1923. 336p [BM BVaU LC OTU SSU

**Gayton, Albert, 1840–1923**

KEMPTVILLE, YARMOUTH COUNTY, NOVA SCOTIA. An Historical Sketch. Yarmouth, Vickery, 1911. 19p [NSWA OOA

**Gellatly, Dorothy (Hewlett)**

A BIT OF OKANAGAN HISTORY. Kelowna, Kelowna Print., 1932. 80p [Rev. Centennial ed., Kelowna, Orchard City Press, 1958. 133p] [BVaU OTU

**Gerein, Rev. Frank**

HISTORY OF ODESSA. To Commemorate the 50th Anniversary of the Advent of Odessa's First Settlers and the 40th Anniversary of the Founding of Holy Family Parish, Odessa, Saskatchewan. ... Regina, Western Printers, 1954. 68p

**Gershaw, Frederick William, 1883–**

MEDICINE HAT. Sidelights on Early Days in Medicine Hat and Vicinity. N.p., [1950?]. 66p [OOP

"MEDICINE HAT." Early Days in Southern Alberta. N.p., [1954?]. 70p [Same as preceding title?]

RANCHING IN SOUTHERN ALBERTA. [Medicine Hat, Modern Press], n.d. 24p [OTU

"THE SHORT GRASS AREA." A Brief History of Southern Alberta. N.p., [1956?]. 123p

**Ghent, Percy Parker, 1888–1952**

YULETIDE IN LITTLE YORK. Sleigh Ride through the Quaint Town that Became the City of Toronto. Toronto, Bond, 1937. 11p [OTU

**Ghost Pine Community Group**

MEMOIRS OF THE GHOST PINE HOMESTEADERS. Three Hills, Alta., Capital Printers, 1954. 196p

**Gibbon, John Murray, 1875–1952**

TIME AND TIDE IN THE ATLANTIC PROVINCES. By John Murray Gibbon and Leo Cox. Sackville, N.B., Enamel and Heating Products Ltd., 1952, 46p

OUR OLD MONTREAL. Toronto, McClelland, 1947. 266p [BVaU LC QMM

**Gilbert, George, 1867?–1957**
BATHURST, 1891–1951. Bathurst, N.B., n.d. 18p

**Gilpin, John Bernard, 1810–1892**
SABLE ISLAND. Its Past History, Present Appearance, Natural History, Etc. Halifax, Wesleyan Conference, 1858. 34p [Bound with a lecture by Joseph Darby and a poem by Joseph Howe.] [LC NSWA OTP QMM

**Gilroy, Marion**
LOYALISTS AND LAND SETTLEMENT IN NOVA SCOTIA. Comp. by ——. Halifax, Nova Scotia Archives, 1937. 154p [BM BVaU NSHD OLU QMBM

**Given, Robert A.**
THE STORY OF ETOBICOKE. Etobicoke, Ont., 1950. 76p [OONL

**Glover, Terrot Reaveley, 1869–1943**
A CORNER OF EMPIRE, THE OLD ONTARIO STRAND. By T.R. Glover and D.D. Calvin. Toronto, Macmillan, 1937. 178p [BVaU NBFU OKQ QMM

**Gogo, Jean Louise, 1901–**
LIGHTS ON THE ST. LAWRENCE. An Anthology. Ed. by ——. Toronto, Ryerson, 1958. 303p

**Golden, B.C. Centennial Committee. Historical Branch**
GOLDEN MEMORIES OF THE TOWN WHERE THE TURBULENT KICKING HORSE MEETS THE MIGHTY COLUMBIA. Golden, B.C., the Committee, 1958. 91p [mimeographed]

**Goodchild, Frederick Henry, 1892–1955**
BRITISH COLUMBIA. Its History, People and Industry. London, Allen & Unwin, 1951. 219p

**Goodfellow, John Christie, 1890–**
THE STORY OF SIMILKAMEEN. Princeton, B.C., Similkameen Spotlight, 1958. V. 1.
TOTEM POLES IN STANLEY PARK. Vancouver, Art Historical and Scientific Assn., 1924. 44p [BM BVaU LC OTU

**Goodyear, Hedley John, 1886–1918**
NEWFOUNDLAND AND ITS POLITICAL AND COMMERCIAL RELATION TO CANADA. Toronto, U. of Toronto Press, [1913]. 48p [NfSM OTUV

**Gordon, George Lawson, 1853–1919**
RIVER JOHN, ITS PASTORS AND PEOPLE. New Glasgow, N.S., Author, 1911. 152p [BVaU NSWA OTP

**Gordon, William Austin, 1885–**
LAKE ERIE'S ISLE OF ROMANCE. Port Dover, Ont., Author, 1934. 56p [OTU

**Gosling, William Gilbert, 1863–1930**

LABRADOR. Its Discovery, Exploration and Development. London, Rivers, 1910. 574p [BM BVaU LC NSWA OKQ QMU

**Gosnell, R. Edward, 1860–1931**

A HISTORY: BRITISH COLUMBIA. [Victoria?], Hill Binding Co., 1906. 783p [BVaU OOP

LAND OF THE OKANAGAN, BRITISH COLUMBIA. Vancouver, Daily Telegram, [1891?]. 48p [OOA

**Gourlay, John Lowry, 1821–1904**

HISTORY OF THE OTTAWA VALLEY. A Collection of Facts, Events and Reminiscences for over half a Century. Ottawa, 1896. 288p [BM BVaU LC MWU NSWA OTU QMM

**Gow, John Milne, 1844–1898**

CAPE BRETON ILLUSTRATED. Historic, Picturesque and Descriptive. ... Toronto, Briggs, 1893. 423p [BM BVaU LC NSWA OTU QMM

**Graham, Audrey, 1912–**

HISTORIC ST. JOHN'S AT YORK MILLS, 1816–43. Comp. by ——. Toronto, Hendrick-Jewell, 1935. 61p [BVaU OTP

**Graham, Clara**

FUR AND GOLD IN THE KOOTENAYS. Vancouver, Wrigley, 1945. 206p [BVaU NBFU OTP

**Graham, Janet (Pollock), 1880–**

THE WATER HIGHWAY OF ARGENTEUIL AND ITS CENTENNIAL ANNIVERSARY. Lachute, Que., Watchman, 1933. 16p [OTP

**Graham, Myrtle E., 1892–**

DALRYMPLE ON THE LAKE, 1855–1955. By Myrtle Graham, Grace Deverell, and Margaret Stewart. Sebright, Ont., 1956. 47p

**Grant, Rev. George Monro, 1835–1902**

THE EASTERNMOST RIDGE OF THE CONTINENT. Historical and Descriptive Sketch of the Scenery and Life in New Brunswick, Nova Scotia, and Prince Edward Island. Ed. by ——. Chicago, Belford, 1899. 216p [BVaU LC NBFU OLU QMBM

FRENCH CANADIAN LIFE AND CHARACTER. With Historical and Descriptive Sketches of the Scenery and Life in Quebec, Montreal, Ottawa, and Surrounding Country. Ed. by ——. Chicago, Belford, 1899. 249p [BVaU LC OTP

**Grant, Rev. Robert, 1824?–1900**

EAST RIVER SKETCHES: HISTORICAL AND BIOGRAPHICAL. New Glasgow, MacKenzie, 1895. 92p [NSWA OTU

**Grant, Robert W.**

THE HUMBOLDT STORY, 1903–1953. A Brief History of the Town of Humboldt, its Pioneers and Development. Humboldt, Sask., Board of Trade, 1954. 65p

**Gray, Clayton, 1918–**

THE MONTREAL STORY. Montreal, Whitcombe & Gilmour, 1949. 84p [OONL

**Greeley, Hugh Payne, 1884–**

WORK AND PLAY IN THE GRENFELL MISSION. ... By Hugh Payne Greeley and Floretta Elmore Greeley. With an intro. by Dr. Wilfred T. Grenfell. Toronto, Revell, 1920. 192p [BVaU LC OTU

**Green, Ernest, 1882–1947**

LINCOLN AT BAY. A Sketch of 1814. Welland, Tribune-Telegraph, 1923. 78p [BVaU LC NSHD OTU QMM

SOME GRAVES IN LUNDY'S LANE. Niagara, Historical Soc., 1912. 82p [LC OTP

**Green, George, –1955**

HISTORY OF BURNABY AND VICINITY. ... North Vancouver, Author, 1947. 233p [BVaU LC OTU

**Greening, Roy M., 1925–**

THE KNOTTY SERPENT. A Tale of Ogopogo. Kelowna, B.C., Author, 1957. 17p

**Greenwood, Rev. Walter R.**

HISTORY OF FREEPORT, N.S., 1784–1934. Freeport, Davis, 1934. 46p [LC NSWA OOA

**Greig, Emma (Danard), 1889–**

THE SWAN RIVER VALLEY, 1898–1958. Comp. by ——. N.p., 1958. 80p

**Griffin, Harold John Michael, 1912–**

BRITISH COLUMBIA. The People's Early Story. Vancouver, Tribune Pub., 1958. 95p

**Guardian Associates Ltd.**

GRAND FALLS, BOTWOOD, BISHOP'S FALLS, BADGER, MILLERTOWN, TERRA NOVA, NEWFOUNDLAND. Paper and Pulpwood Towns of the Interior. Montreal, 1951. 48p [Story by Ewart Young.]

ST. JOHN'S NEWFOUNDLAND. The Oldest City in North America, Capital of Canada's Newest Province. Montreal, St. John's Publicity Committee of the Newfoundland Board of Trade, 1950. 64p [OONL

**Guillet, Edwin Clarence, 1898–**

COBOURG, 1798–1948. ... Oshawa, Goodfellow, 1948. 259p [BVaU OTP

THE COBOURG CONSPIRACY. An Account of a Little-Known Episode in the disturbed Times which followed the Rebellion of 1837. ... Toronto, 1949. 27p [OTP

EARLY LIFE IN UPPER CANADA. Toronto, Ontario Pub. Co., 1933. 782p [BM BVaU LC NBFU OTP QMM

THE LIVES AND TIMES OF THE PATRIOTS. An Account of the Rebellion in Upper Canada, 1837–1838, and the Patriot Agitation in the United States, 1837–1842. Toronto, Nelson, 1938. 304p [BM BVaU LC NBFU OTU QMM

PIONEER LIFE IN THE COUNTY OF YORK. Toronto, Hess-Trade Typesetting Co., 1946. 166p [OTU

TORONTO FROM TRADING POST TO GREAT CITY. Toronto, Ontario Pub. Co., 1934. 495p [BM BVaU LC NSHD OKQ

THE VALLEY OF THE TRENT. Ed. by ——. Toronto, Champlain Society for the Government of Ontario, 1957. lviii + 474p

**Gunn, Donald, 1797–1878**

HISTORY OF MANITOBA. From the Earliest Settlement till 1835. Ottawa, Maclean, 1880. 482p [BM BVaU LC NSWA OTU QMM

**Gunn, John J., 1861–1907**

ECHOES OF THE RED. A Reprint of Some of the Early Writings of the Author depicting Pioneer Days in the Red River Settlements. ... Toronto, Macmillan, 1930. 246p [BM BVaU LC OTU

**Hafford, Sask. District History Committee**

SKETCHES OF HAFFORD AND DISTRICT. Hafford, Sask., 1955. 9p

**Hahn, Josephine Elizabeth**

HOME OF MY YOUTH, HANOVER. Hanover, Ont., Author, 1947. 298p [OTP

**Haig-Brown, Roderick Langmere, 1908–**

THE FARTHEST SHORES. Toronto, Longmans Green, 1960. ix + 127p [Radio dramatizations of the exploration of British Columbia, produced over the CBC national network during 1958.]

**Haliburton, Robert Grant, 1831–1901**

THE PAST AND FUTURE OF NOVA SCOTIA. An Address on the 113th Anniversary of the Settlement of that Province. Halifax, 1862. 27p [BM NSWA

**Haliburton, Thomas Chandler, 1796–1865**

AN HISTORICAL AND STATISTICAL ACCOUNT OF NOVA SCOTIA. ... Halifax, Howe, 1829. 2v [BM BVaU LC NSWA OTU QMM

**Hall, Mrs. Mary Georgina Caroline**

A LADY'S LIFE ON A FARM IN MANITOBA. By Mrs. Cecil Hall. London, Allen, 1884. 171p [BVaU OTP

**Hallam, Lillian Gertrude (Best), –1939**

WHEN YOU ARE IN HALIFAX. Sketches of Life in the First English Settlement in Canada. By Mrs. W.T. Hallam. Toronto, Church Book Room, 1937. 83p [BVaU LC NSHD OTP

**Halliwell, Mrs. Gladys M., 1892–**

THREE SCORE AND TEN, 1886–1956. A Story of the Swedish settlement of Stockholm and District. By Gladys M. Halliwell and M. Zetta D. Persson. Yorkton, Sask., Redeemer's Voice Press, 1959. 192p

**Hambley, Rev. George Henry, 1896–**

HISTORICAL RECORDS AND ACCOUNTS OF THE EARLY PIONEERS OF THE DISTRICT OF SWAN LAKE, MANITOBA, FROM ITS EARLY SETTLEMENT, 1873–1950. N.p., 1952. 280p [Jacket title: PIONEERS, OH! PIONEERS.]

TRAILS OF THE PIONEERS. Records, Accounts, Historical Studies, Data, Reports, Letters of the Section of Manitoba, Canada, Lying Southwest of Winnipeg in the Red River Valley and Centered on the Town of Roland, Manitoba. Altona, Man., D.W. Friesen, 1956. xiii + 295p

**Hamil, Frederick Coyne, 1903–**

THE VALLEY OF THE LOWER THAMES, 1640 TO 1850. Toronto, U. of Toronto Press, 1951. xi + 390p

**Hamilton, Basil G.**

THE LEGEND OF WINDERMERE. 2nd ed. Invermere, B.C., Author, 1921. 12p [BViPA OONM

NAMING OF COLUMBIA RIVER AND THE PROVINCE OF BRITISH COLUMBIA. [Cranbrook, B.C.], Cranbrook Courier, [1921]. 16p [BVaU OORD

**Hamilton, James Herbert, 1879–**

WESTERN SHORES. Narratives of the Pacific Coast. By Captain Kettle [pseud]. Vancouver, Progress, 1932. 218p [BM BVaU NBFU OTU

**Hamilton, Reuben, 1888–**

MOUNT PLEASANT EARLY DAYS. Memories of Reuben Hamilton, Pioneer, 1890. Vancouver, City Archives, 1957. 64p

**Hamilton, Ont. Spectator**

HAMILTON SPECTATOR, 100th ANNIVERSARY, 1846–1946. Reflections of a Hundred Years. Hamilton, Spectator, 1946. 84p [OTU

WENTWORTH LANDMARKS. [Collected from the Columns of the Hamilton Spectator.] Hamilton, Spectator, n.d. 147p [OOP

**Hamlyn, Rupert Gladstone, 1887–**

BOWMANVILLE. A Retrospect by Rupert G. Hamlyn, Elsie Carruthers Lunney, and David R. Morrison. Bowmanville, Ont., Centennial Committee, 1958. 10 + 80p

**Hannay, James, 1842–1910**

THE HISTORY OF ACADIA. From its First Discovery to its Surrender to England, by the Treaty of Paris. Saint John, McMillan, 1879. 440p [BM BVaU LC NBFU OKQ QMU

HISTORY OF NEW BRUNSWICK. Saint John, Bowes, 1909. 2v [BM BVaU LC NSWA OTU

LIFE AND TIMES OF SIR LEONARD TILLEY. Being a Political History of New Brunswick, for the past Seventy Years. Saint John, 1897. 400p [BM BVaU NSHD OTU

THE STORY OF ACADIA. Kentville, Dominion Atlantic Railway, [19—?]. 128p [An abridgement of THE HISTORY OF ACADIA.] [BVaU NSHD OLU

**Hanley, Sask. High School**

HANLEY. The Story of the Town and District. Prepared by the pupils of Hanley High School, Saskatchewan, 1954–1955, Jubilee year. Hanley, Sask., 1955. 134p [mimeographed]

**Hanson, Mrs. Sarah Foss**

HOMESTEADING AT CLAVET, SASKATCHEWAN. Clavet, Sask., Homemakers' Club, 1956. 24p

**Hargrave, Joseph James, 1841–1894**

RED RIVER. Montreal, Lovell, 1871. 506p [BM BVaU LC NSWA OTP SSU

**Harker, Douglas Edward, 1911–**

THE CITY AND THE STORE. Vancouver, Woodward Stores, 1958. 29p

**Harkness, John Graham, 1865–1948**

STORMONT, DUNDAS, AND GLENGARRY. A History, 1784–1945. Morrisburg, Author, 1946. 601p [BVaU NSWA OTU

**Harnett, Legh**

TWO LECTURES ON BRITISH COLUMBIA. Victoria, Higgins & Long, 1868. 50p [BVaU NSHP

**Harper, J. Russell**

THE EARLY HISTORY OF HALDIMAND COUNTY. Caledonia, Ont., Grand River Sachem, 1950. 78p [OKQ

PORTLAND POINT, CROSSROADS OF NEW BRUNSWICK HISTORY. Preliminary Report of the 1955 Excavation. Saint John, New Brunswick Museum, 1956. 51p

**Harper, John Murdoch, 1845–1919**

THE HISTORY OF NEW BRUNSWICK AND THE OTHER MARITIME PROVINCES. Saint John, McMillan, 1876. 158p [BVaU NSWA OOA

THE MONTGOMERY SIEGE. Quebec, Michaels, [1908?]. 102p [Quebec City siege, 1775–76.] [BVaU LC NBFU OOP

... THEN AND NOW: THE EARLIEST BEGINNINGS OF CANADA: THE SILLERY MISSION. Toronto, Trade Pub. Co., [1908?]. 26 + 104 + 27p [BVaU OTP

**Harris, Edward William, 1832–1925**

RECOLLECTIONS OF LONG POINT. Toronto, Warwick, 1918. 48p [OTU

**Harris, Reginald Vanderbilt, 1881–**

THE OAK ISLAND MYSTERY. Toronto, Ryerson, 1958. xii + 211p [Refers to buried treasure on Oak Island, N.S.]

**Harris, Rev. William Richard, 1847–1923**

TADOUSSAC AND ITS INDIAN CHAPEL, 1617–1920. N.p., n.d. 66p [OTU

**Hart, George Edward**

THE STORY OF OLD ABEGWEIT. A Sketch of Prince Edward Island History. ... [Charlottetown, 1936?]. 79p [NBFU OKQ PCPW

**Hart, Gerald Ephraim, 1849–1936**

THE FALL OF NEW FRANCE, 1755–1760. Montreal, Drysdale, 1888. 175p [BM BVaU LC NSWA OTP

**Harvey, Arthur, 1834–1905**

A STATISTICAL ACCOUNT OF BRITISH COLUMBIA. Ottawa, Desbarats, 1867. 41p [BVaU LC NSHP OTU

**Harvey, Daniel Cobb, 1886–**

THE FRENCH REGIME IN PRINCE EDWARD ISLAND. New Haven, Yale U. Press, 1926. 265p [BM BVaU LC NSHD OTU QMBM

HOLLAND'S DESCRIPTION OF CAPE BRETON ISLAND AND OTHER DOCUMENTS. Comp. by ——. Halifax, Pub. Archives, 1935. 168p [BVaU NSHD OLU

LOYALISTS AND LAND SETTLEMENT IN NOVA SCOTIA. A list comp. under the direction of ——. Halifax, Pub. Archives, 1937. 154p [BVa

**Harvey, Rev. Moses, 1820–1901**

NEWFOUNDLAND. Its History, its Present Condition and its Prospects. By Joseph Hatton and M. Harvey. Boston, Doyle & Whittle, 1883. 431p [BM BVaU LC NBFU OTU

NEWFOUNDLAND AT THE BEGINNING OF THE TWENTIETH CENTURY. A Treatise of History and Development. ... New York, South, 1902. 118p [BVaU NSHD OTP

NEWFOUNDLAND IN 1897. Being Queen Victoria's Diamond Jubilee. London, Low Marston, 1897. 203p [BM BVaU NSWA OTU

NEWFOUNDLAND IN 1900. St. John's, Garland, 1900. 196p [BVaU LC NSHD OLU

A SHORT HISTORY OF NEWFOUNDLAND. England's Oldest Colony. London, Chapman Hall, 1883. 489p [BM BVaU LC NSHD OLU

**Harvie, Fred W.**

TOWN OF THOROLD CENTENNIAL, 1850–1950. Ed. by ——. Thorold, Ont., the Town, 1950. 128p [OONL

**Hathaway, Ernest Jackson, 1871–1930**

THE STORY OF THE OLD FORT AT TORONTO. Toronto, Macmillan, 1934. 35p [BVaU NBFU OTP

**Hatheway, Calvin L., 1796–1866**

THE HISTORY OF NEW BRUNSWICK, FROM ITS FIRST SETTLEMENT. Fredericton, Phillips, 1846. 81p [BM BVaU LC NSHD OTP QMM

**Haultain, Theodore Arnold, 1857–1941**

A HISTORY OF RIEL'S SECOND REBELLION AND HOW IT WAS QUELLED. Toronto, Grip, 1885. 44p [BVaU LC NSWA OLU

**Hawarden, Sask. Bethlehem Scandinavian Lutheran Church. Ladies' Aid**

A SHORT HISTORY OF BETHLEHEM COMMUNITY, HAWARDEN, SASK., 1902–1955. Comp. by Marion Pederson. Hawarden, Sask., Mrs. O.N. Pederson, 1955. 16p

**Hawarden, Sask. Homemakers' Club**

THE HISTORY OF HAWARDEN AND COMMUNITY. Saskatoon, Midwest Litho Ltd., 1950. 32p [SSU

**Hawkes, John, 1851–1931**

THE STORY OF SASKATCHEWAN AND ITS PEOPLE. Chicago, Clarke, 1924. 3v [BVaU OTP SSU

**Hawkins, Alfred, 1802?–1854**

HAWKINS'S PICTURE OF QUEBEC. With Historical Recollections. Quebec, Neilson & Cowan, 1834. 477p [BM BVaU LC NSWA OTU QMM

**Hawthorn, Harry Bertram, 1910–**

THE INDIANS OF BRITISH COLUMBIA. A Study of Contemporary Social Adjustment. By H.B. Hawthorn, C.S. Belshaw and S.M. Jamieson. Toronto, U. of Toronto Press and U. of British Columbia, 1958. ix + 499p

**Haydon, Andrew, 1867–1932**

PIONEER SKETCHES IN THE DISTRICT OF BATHURST. V. 1. Toronto, Ryerson, 1925. 291p [BM BVaU LC NSHD OTU QMM

**Hayes, Catherine E. (Simpson), 1852–1943**

THE LEGEND OF THE WEST. Victoria, Author, 1908. [Unpaged.] [BViPA OOP

**Healey, Elizabeth, 1912–**

HISTORY OF ALERT BAY AND DISTRICT. Comp. by ——. Alert Bay, B.C., Centennial Committee, 1958. 101p

**Healy, William Joseph, 1867–1950**

WINNIPEG'S EARLY DAYS. A Short Historical Sketch. ... Winnipeg, Stovel, 1927. 59p [BVaU OTP QMM

**Heartwell, Joseph Woolsey, 1882–**

PIONEER DAYS – SASKATCHEWAN, IN TOWNSHIP 30, RANGE 15, WEST OF THE 3RD MER. A Comedy of Errors, 1905–1909. Meadow Lake, Sask., 1955. (Unpaged.) [Early history of the Rosetown District, Saskatchewan.] [mimeographed]

**Heeney, Rev. William Bertal, 1873–1955**

THE FOUNDING OF RUPERT'S LAND AND ITS FIRST BISHOP. Winnipeg, McIntyre Print., 1929. 33p [Peel

**Hendrie, Lilian Margaret, 1870–1952**

EARLY DAYS IN MONTREAL, AND RAMBLES IN THE NEIGHBOURHOOD. Montreal, Mercury, 1932. 70p [BVaU LC OTU QMM

**Henry, Lorne James, 1893–**

PIONEER DAYS IN ONTARIO. By Lorne J. Henry and Gilbert Paterson. Toronto, Ryerson, 1938. 234p [BM OTU QMM

**Hepburn, Agnes Marion, 1881–**

HISTORICAL SKETCH OF THE VILLAGE OF PORT STANLEY. Comp. by ——. Port Stanley, Ont., Women's Institute, 1952. 54p

**Herbert, Sask. School**

THESE GOLDEN YEARS. Herbert, Sask., 1955. 50p

**Herbin, John Frederic, 1860–1923**

GRAND-PRE. A Sketch of the Acadian Occupation. ... A Guide to Tourists. Toronto, Briggs, 1898. 127p [Other editions under title: THE HISTORY OF GRAND-PRE. ... E.g., 3rd ed.: Toronto, Briggs, 1907. 171p] [BM BVaU LC NSWA OLU QMM

THE HISTORY OF GRAND-PRE. [See under GRAND-PRE.]

THE LAND OF EVANGELINE. The Authentic Story of her Country and her People. Toronto, Musson, 1921. 84p [BVaU NSHD OTU QMBM

**Herrington, Walter Stevens, 1860–1947**

THE EVOLUTION OF THE PRAIRIE PROVINCES. Toronto, Briggs, 1911. 144p [BM BVaU OTP SSU

HISTORY OF THE COUNTY OF LENNOX AND ADDINGTON. Toronto, Macmillan, 1913. 427p [BM BVaU LC NSHD OLU

**Hett, Francis Paget, 1878–**

GEORGINA. A Type Study of Early Settlement and Church Buildings in Upper Canada. Toronto, Macmillan, 1939. 128p [BM LC OLU

**Hewitt, Grace Henderson**

EARLY DAYS IN SIMCOE COUNTY. Orillia, Women's Canadian Club, [1927?]. 20p [BVa OTP QMM

**High River Pioneers' And Old Timers' Association**

LEAVES FROM THE MEDICINE TREE. A History of the Area influenced by the Tree, and Biographies of Pioneers and Old Timers who came under its Spell prior to 1900. Lethbridge, Alta., Herald, 1960. 529p

**Hill, Rev. Allan Massie, 1876–1943**

SOME CHAPTERS IN THE HISTORY OF DIGBY COUNTY. Halifax, McAlpine, 1901. 115p [NSWA

**Hill, Rev. George William, 1824–1906**

NOVA-SCOTIA AND NOVA-SCOTIANS. ... Halifax, Bowes, 1858. 49p [BVaU LC NSHD OTP

**Hill, Hamnett Pinhey, 1876–1942**

ROBERT RANDALL AND THE LE BRETON FLATS. An Account of the Early Legal and Political Controversies respecting the Ownership of a large Portion of the Present City of Ottawa. Ottawa, Hope, 1919. 62p [BM BVaU LC NSHD OTP

**Hill, Hazel A.E.**

TALES OF THE ALBERNI VALLEY. Edmonton, Hamly Press, 1952. 48p

**Hill, Robert Brown, 1843–1900**

MANITOBA: HISTORY OF ITS EARLY SETTLEMENT, DEVELOPMENT, AND RESOURCES. Toronto, Briggs, 1890. 764p [BM BVaU NSWA OTP SSU

**Hind, Henry Youle, 1823–1908**

HISTORICAL GLEANINGS. No. 1–11. [Windsor, N.S.? 189–?] 48p [BM LC NSWA OTU

MANITOBA AND THE NORTH-WEST FRAUDS. ... Windsor, Ont., Knowles, 1883. 40p [BM NSWA

SKETCH OF THE OLD PARISH BURYING GROUND OF WINDSOR, NOVA SCOTIA. With an Appeal for its Protection. ... Windsor, N.S., Anslow, 1889. 99p [BM LC NSWA OTP QMM

**Hiscock, Eric Dixon Cave, 1911–**

NEWFOUNDLAND'S FIRST FIFTY YEARS. Ilfracombe, Devon, Stockwell, 1957. 46p

**Hislop, Mary**

THE STREETS OF WINNIPEG. Winnipeg, Taylor, 1912. 46p [BM SSU

**Historical Society of Alberta**

THE EARLY WEST. Ed. by H.A. Dempsey. Edmonton, the Society, 1957. 36p

**Historical Society of the City and County of Peterborough**

PETERBOROUGH, A TENTATIVE GUIDE. Peterborough, Ont., [1955?]. 12p

**Hodgins, John George, 1821–1912**

THE CITY OF TORONTO. [Anon] Toronto, Campbell, 1860. 63p [NSWA QMM

**Hoffer, Clara (Schwartz)**

LAND OF HOPE. By Clara Hoffer and F.H. Kahan. Saskatoon, Modern Press, 1960. 157p [On life of Jewish pioneers in southeastern Saskatchewan.]

**Hoig, David Scott**

REMINISCENCES AND RECOLLECTIONS. An Interesting Pen Picture of Early Days, Characters, and Events in Oshawa. Oshawa, Mundy-Goodfellow Print., 1933. 227p [BVaU OTP

**Holley, George Washington, 1810–1897**

NIAGARA. Its History and Geology, Incidents and Poetry. ... Toronto, Hunter Rose, 1872. 165p [Later ed.: THE FALLS OF NIAGARA AND OTHER FAMOUS CATARACTS. London, Hodder & Stoughton, 1882. xv + 185p] [BVaU OHM OLU

**Holman, Carrie Ellen, 1877–**

OUR ISLAND STORY. Broadcasts given over CFCY Charlottetown. ... Sackville, N.B., Tribune Press, 1949. 119p [5th ed., 1963.] [NBFU OTP

**Hope, Ethel Penman, –1958**

EARLY SETTLEMENT OF MEECH LAKE. [Ottawa, Author, 1957?] 10p [mimeographed]

**Hope, William**

SCRAPS FROM CANADA TO OLD COUNTRY FRIENDS. By a Hamiltonian [pseud]. Hamilton, Times, 1877. 62p [OTL

**Hopkins, John Castell, 1864–1923**

FRENCH CANADA AND THE ST. LAWRENCE. Historic, Picturesque and Descriptive. Toronto, Bell, 1913. 431p [BM BVaU LC NSHD OOA

**Horan, John William, 1908–**

"WEST, NOR'WEST." A History of Alberta. Edmonton, Northgate Books, 1945. 184p [BM BVaU LC OOA SSU

**Horsey, Edwin Ernest, 1870–**

KINGSTON, A CENTURY AGO. Kingston, Kingston Historical Society, 1938. 37p [BVaU NBFU OTP

**Hotson, Zella May, 1893–**

THE EARLY DAYS OF INNERKIP DISTRICT. Innerkip, Ont., Author, 1952. 176p

**Howay, Frederic William, 1867–1943**

BRITISH COLUMBIA AND THE UNITED STATES. The North Pacific Slope from Fur Trade to Aviation. By F.W. Howay, W.N. Sage, and H.F. Angus. Ed. by H.F. Angus. Toronto, Ryerson, 1942. 408p [BM BVaU NSHD OTP QMSS

BRITISH COLUMBIA, THE MAKING OF A PROVINCE. Toronto, Ryerson, 1928. 289p [BM BVaU LC NSHD OTU QMM

BUILDERS OF THE WEST. A Book of Heroes. Ed. by ——. Toronto, Ryerson, 1929. 251p [BM BVaU LC NSHD OTP

THE DIXON-MEARES CONTROVERSY. Containing Remarks on the Voyages of John Meares, by George Dixon; An Answer to Mr. George Dixon, by John Meares, and further remarks. ... Ed. by ——. Toronto, Ryerson, 1929. 156p [BVaU LC NBFU OKQ QMBM

... THE EARLY HISTORY OF THE FRASER RIVER MINES. Victoria, Banfield, 1926. 126p [BM BVaU LC OKQ

THE OVERLAND JOURNEY OF THE ARGONAUTS OF 1862. Ottawa, Royal Society, 1920. 55p [BVaU OTP

THE WORK OF THE ROYAL ENGINEERS IN BRITISH COLUMBIA, 1858–1863. Victoria, Wolfenden, 1910. 17p [BVaU LC OKQ

**Hubbard, Benjamin F., 1798–**

FORESTS AND CLEARINGS. The History of Stanstead County, Province of Quebec, with Sketches of more than Five Hundred Families. The whole revised, abridged and pub. with additions and illus. by John Lawrence. Montreal, Lovell Print. and Pub. Co., 1874. [Reprinted by Page-Sangster Print. Co., 1963, viii + 367p]

**Hudson Bay, Sask. High School**

THE HUDSON BAY STORY. Hudson Bay, Sask., 1955. 62p [mimeographed]

**Hultgren, Peter, 1885–**

A BRIEF HISTORY OF MIDALE AND DISTRICT, 1903–1953. Midale, Sask., Board of Trade, 1953. 31p

**Hunter, Andrew Frederick, 1863–1940**

A HISTORY OF SIMCOE COUNTY. Barrie, County Council, 1909. 2v [BM BVaU LC NSHD OTU QMM

LAKE SIMCOE AND ITS ENVIRONS. Barrie, Examiner, 1893. 44p [BVaU OTP

**Hutchison, Bruce, 1901–**

THE FRASER. New York, Rinehart, 1950. 368p [BVaU NSHD OTU QMM

**Hutton, Samuel King, 1877–**

AMONG THE ESKIMOS OF LABRADOR. A Record of Five Years Close Intercourse with the Eskimo Tribes of Labrador. Toronto, Musson, 1912. 343p [BVaU LC NSHPL OTUV QMBM

AN ESKIMO VILLAGE. London, S.P.C.K., 1929. 156p [An abridgement of AMONG THE ESKIMOS.] [ACG LC NSHPL OTP

**Huxtable, Thompson Russell, 1875–1959**

DOWN MEMORIES LANE. Shelburne, Ont., Free Press, 1959. 80p [Stories of early days in Ontario, especially around Horning's Mills.]

**Imrie, John Mills, 1883–1942**

PEACE RIVER. An Empire in the Making. Edmonton, Journal, 1930. 32p [BVa

**Innes, John, 1864–1941**

... THE EPIC OF WESTERN CANADA. ... Vancouver, Gehrke's, 1928. 15p [BViPA

**Innisfil, Ont. Book Committee**

HISTORICAL REVIEW. A Record of 100 Years of Progress ... 1850–1950. Innisfil, Township Council, 1951. 184p [Same as following title?]

**Innisfil Township, Ont.**

INNISFIL TOWNSHIP CENTENNIAL, 1850–1950. N.p., 1950. 185p [BVaU OTU

**Instow, Sask. School**

PIONEER DAYS IN THE INSTOW COMMUNITY. Instow, Sask., 1955. 35p [mimeographed]

**Inwood, Ont. Women's Institute**

INWOOD VILLAGE HISTORY, 1873–1947. Inwood, Women's Institute, 1947. 69p [Also, 1948. 80p] [OLU OTU

**Jack, David Russell, 1864–1913**

CENTENNIAL PRIZE ESSAY ON THE HISTORY OF THE CITY AND COUNTY OF ST. JOHN. Saint John, McMillan, 1883. 178p [BVaU LC NSHD OTU QMM

**Jackes, Lyman Bruce, 1889–1958**

TALES OF NORTH TORONTO. Toronto, North Toronto Business Men's Assoc., 1948. 28p [BVaU OTU

TALES OF NORTH TORONTO. V. 2. Toronto, Canadian Historical Press, 1952. 64p

**Jackson, Mary (Percy), 1904–**

ON THE LAST FRONTIER. Pioneering in the Peace River Block. Letters. ... London, Sheldon Press, 1933. 118p [BM BVaU OTU SSU

**James, Charles Canniff, 1863–1916**

EARLY HISTORY OF THE TOWN OF AMHERSTBURG. Amherstburg, Ont., Echo Print. Co., 1902. 23p [BVaU LC NSWA OTU QMM

**James, Rev. Thomas Henry, 1871–1931**

NEWFOUNDLAND: Its Resources and Discovery, and Settlements of John Guy at Cuper's Cove, Conception Bay. St. John's, Evening Telegram, 1910. 20p [NBSaM

**James, William T., 1861–**

TORONTO, AS IT WAS AND IS. A Graphic Historical Sketch. Toronto, James, 1903. 32p [BVaU OTU

**Jamieson, Heber Carss, 1879–1962**

EARLY MEDICINE IN ALBERTA. The First 75 Years. Edmonton, C.M.A. (Alta. Div.), 1947. 214p [AEU BViPA QMM

**Jefferson, Robert, 1856–**

FIFTY YEARS ON THE SASKATCHEWAN. Being a History of the Cree Indian Domestic Life and the Difficulties which led to ... Conflict of 1885 in the Battleford Locality. ... Battleford, N.W. Hist. Soc., 1929. 160p [BM BViPA OTU SSU

**Jeffery, Ranald Angus, 1880–**

MACNAB. Foleyet, Ont., Macnab Hist. Assoc., 1946. 27p [OOA

**Jelly, William, 1865–**

PROCEEDINGS OF THE JOHNSTOWN DISTRICT COUNCIL, 1842–1849. Comp. by ——. Brockville, Farrow, 1929. 100p [OTU

**Johnson, Henry Smith**

NORFOLK COUNTY. An Illustrated Review. ... Simcoe, Ont., Norfolk Chamber of Commerce, Norfolk County Council and Simcoe Town Council, 1939. 40p [OTU

**Johnson, Kate (Bailey), 1885–**

PIONEER DAYS OF NAKUSP AND THE ARROW LAKES. Comp. by ——. "1892, Nakusp Diamond Jubilee, 1952." Nakusp, B.C., Author, 1951. 146p [Rev. ed., 1964. 240p]

**Johnson, Patricia Mary, 1913–**

A SHORT HISTORY OF NANAIMO. Nanaimo, B.C., Centennial Committee, 1958. 55p

**Johnston, Charles Murray, 1926–**

THE HEAD OF THE LAKE. A History of Wentworth County. Hamilton, Wentworth County Council, 1958. 345p

**Johnston, John George, 1895–**

FROM A HUNDREDWEIGHT OF PI. ... Fort Erie, Review Co., 1933. 28p [History of newspaper.] [OKQ

**Johnston, William, 1840–1917**

HISTORY OF THE COUNTY OF PERTH FROM 1825 TO 1902. Stratford, Ont., O'Beirne, 1903. 565p [BVaU LC NSHD OTU

THE PIONEERS OF BLANSHARD, with a Historical Sketch of the Township. Toronto, Briggs, 1899. 278p [BVaU LC NSHD OTU

**Jones, George Poole**

WINDSOR [N.S.]. Its History, Points of Interest, and Representative Business Men. Windsor, N.S., Anslow, 1893. 52p [NSWA OOA

**Jones, Harold Saunders, 1880–**

HISTORY AND REMINISCENCES OF EASTEND AND DISTRICT. By H.S. Jones and others. Eastend, Sask., Author, 1955. 35p

**Jones, James Edmund, 1866–1939**

PIONEER CRIMES AND PUNISHMENTS IN TORONTO AND THE HOME DISTRICT. ... Toronto, Morang, 1924. 195p [BM BVaU LC NSWA OLU QMM

**Jones, Reg.**

THE SASKATCHEWAN STORY. Powell River, Powell River News, 1949. 30p [OKQ

**Jordon, John A., 1843–1917**

THE GROSSE-ISLE TRAGEDY AND THE MONUMENT TO THE IRISH FEVER VICTIMS, 1847. Quebec, Telegraph Print., 1909. 136p [OOP

**Jost, Arthur Cranswick, 1875–1958**

GUYSBOROUGH SKETCHES AND ESSAYS. Guysborough, N.S., Jost, 1950. 414p [LC NSHL OTU QMM

**Jury, William Wilfrid, 1898–**

CLEARVILLE PREHISTORIC VILLAGE SITE IN ORFORD TOWNSHIP, KENT COUNTY, ONTARIO. London, Ont., 1941. [Unpaged.] [LC

CRAWFORD PREHISTORIC VILLAGE SITE. ... London, Ont., U. of Western Ontario, 1948. 18p [LC OTP

FAIRFIELD ON THE THAMES. Report of Excavations made on the Site of the Early Mission Village. London, Ont., 1945. 35p [LC OTP

SAINTE-MARIE AMONG THE HURONS. ... Toronto, Oxford U. Press, 1954. xiii + 128p

**Kaiser, Thomas Erlin, 1863–1940**

HISTORIC SKETCHES OF OSHAWA. Oshawa, Reformer Print., 1921. 216p [BVaU OTU

**Kalamalka Women's Institute**

TWEEDSMUIR HISTORY OF OYAMA, BRITISH COLUMBIA. Oyama, B.C., 1951. 38p [mimeographed]

**Kamloops, B.C. Centenary Celebration, 1912**

THE DAYS OF OLD AND DAYS OF GOLD. Victoria, King's Printer, 1912. 15p [BVaU OTU

**Kamloops, B.C. High School. Junior Historical Club**

KAMLOOPS, 1812–1937. A History. Kamloops, the Club, 1937. 107p [BVaU OTU

**Kaslo, B.C. Historical Committee**

HISTORY OF KASLO. Kaslo Diamond Jubilee, 1893–1953. Kaslo, 1953. 64p

**Kelly, Leroy Victor, 1880–1956**

THE RANGE MEN. The Story of the Ranchers and Indians of Alberta. Toronto, Briggs, 1913. 468p [AEU BM BVaU NBFU OKQ

**Kelly, Orval Edgar, 1903–**

IN THE BEGINNING. The Story from the Early Days in and around Presqu'Ile Point and Brighton, Ontario. Brighton, Ensign Print., 1942. 28p [LC OTP

**Kelsey, Vera, 1891?–1961**

RED RIVER RUNS NORTH. Toronto, Musson, 1951. xviii + 297p

**Kemptville, Ont. Centennial Committee**

HISTORICAL REVIEW OF KEMPTVILLE AND DISTRICT ON THE OCCASION OF THE 100TH ANNIVERSARY OF THE INCORPORATION OF THE VILLAGE OF KEMPTVILLE, JUNE 30TH TO JULY 6TH, INCLUSIVE, 1857–1957. Kemptville, Ont., 1957. 158p

**Kendrick, Mary Fletcher**

DOWN THE ROAD TO YESTERDAY. A History of Springfield, Annapolis County, Nova Scotia. Bridgewater, Macpherson, 1941. 141p [NSWA OOP

**Kennedy, Charles E., 1888–**

CRAIK'S GOLDEN JUBILEE STORY. Craik, Sask., Craik Agricultural Society, 1955. 58 + 28 + 28p

**Kennedy, David, 1828–1903**

INCIDENTS OF PIONEER DAYS AT GUELPH, AND THE COUNTY OF BRUCE. Toronto, Author, 1903. 135p [BM OTU

**Kennedy, Fred**

THE CALGARY STAMPEDE STORY. Calgary, T.E. Thonger, 1952. 236p

**Kennedy, Howard Angus, 1861–1938**

THE BOOK OF THE WEST. The Story of Western Canada, its Birth and Early Adventures, and its Present Ways. Toronto, Ryerson, 1925. 205p [BM BVaU LC NSHD OTU QMM SSU

**Kenney, James Francis, 1884–1946**

THE FOUNDING OF CHURCHILL. Being the Journal of Captain James Knight, Governor-in-chief in Hudson Bay from the 14th of July to the 13th of September, 1717. Ed. with an historical intro. and notes by ——. Toronto, Dent, 1932. 213p [BM BVaU OTU SSU

**Kent County, Ont.**

COMMEMORATIVE BIOGRAPHICAL RECORD OF THE COUNTY OF KENT. Toronto, Beers, 1904. 874p [OLU

**Kent Historical Society (Chatham, Ont.)**

KENTIANA. The Story of the Settlement and Development of the County of Kent. Summarized from the Published Records of the Society. [Chatham, Ont.], the Society, 1939. 105p [OTU QMM

PAPERS AND ADDRESSES. Chatham, Ont., the Society, 1914–. [A continuing serial.] [BVaU LC OTP

**Kenton, Man. History Committee**
FROM CRADLE TO COMBINE. Kenton, 1881–1956. Elkhorn, Man., Woodworth Times, 1956. 91p

**Kernighan, Thomas**
DUFFERIN AND CARMAN, MANITOBA. Being Recollections of an Eyewitness. Vancouver, Author, 1923. 74p [MWP

**Kerr, Wilfred Brenton, 1896–1950**
THE MARITIME PROVINCES OF BRITISH NORTH AMERICA AND THE AMERICAN REVOLUTION. Sackville, N.B., Busy East Press, 1941. 172p [BVaU LC NBFU OTU QMM

**Kerrisdale Courier**
THE KERRISDALE STORY. Vancouver, 1955. 85p

**Kerrobert, Sask. High School**
HISTORY OF KERROBERT. Kerrobert, Sask., 1955. 64p [mimeographed]

**Ketchum, Thomas Carleton Lee, 1862?–1927**
A SHORT HISTORY OF CARLETON COUNTY, NEW BRUNSWICK. Woodstock, N.B., Sentinel Pub., 1922. 86p [BM BVaU LC NBFU OTP

**Keys, David Reid, 1856–1939**
TORONTO, AN HISTORICAL AND DESCRIPTIVE SKETCH. Toronto, 1913. 33p [OTP

**Kidd, Mrs. Margaret Isabel, 1891–1951**
THIS WAS THEIR LIFE. A Story of the Pioneers of Fairmede and Adjacent Districts. Kindersley, Sask., 1955. 84p

**Killaly, Sask. High School**
50 YEARS OF PROGRESS OF THE COMMUNITY OF KILLALY. Prepared by the Principal, Jack H. Hanowski, and students of the Killaly High School. Killaly, Sask., 1955. 12p

**Killarney, Man. Women's Institute**
STORIES OF PIONEER DAYS AT KILLARNEY. Killarney, Man., Women's Institute, 1930. 47p [BVaU MWP OTU

**Kindersley, Sask.**
THE TOWN OF KINDERSLEY. 50 Years of Progress, 1910–1960. Kindersley, Sask., M. Arikado, 1960. 100p

**King, John, 1843–1916**
THE OTHER SIDE OF THE "STORY": BEING SOME REVIEWS OF MR. J.C. DENT'S FIRST VOLUME OF "THE STORY OF THE UPPER CANADIAN REBELLION," and the Letters in the Mackenzie-Rolph Controversy; Also a Critique, hitherto unpublished, on "The New Story." [Anon] Toronto, Murray, 1886. 150p [BVaU NSWA OTP

**Kingston, Ont. Kingston Historical Society**

HISTORIC KINGSTON. Being the Transactions of the Kingston Historical Society. No. 1, 1951/52. Kingston, Ont., the Society, 1952. [A continuing serial.]

**Kingsville, Ont. Centennial Committee, Historical Section**

KINGSVILLE THROUGH THE YEARS 1783–1952. Kingsville, Lakeshore Publishers, 1952. 105p

**Kinney, J.E.**

THE PORT OF YARMOUTH AND ITS DEVELOPMENT. Yarmouth, Herald, 1931. 14p [NSWA

**Kirby, William, 1817–1906**

ANNALS OF NIAGARA. Welland, Tribune, 1896. 269p [Also: Toronto, Macmillan, 1927. 329p] [BVaU LC NSHD OKQ

**Kirkconnell, Watson, 1895–**

KAPUSKASING. An Historical Sketch. Kingston, Jackson Press, 1921. 15p [BM BVaU LC NSWA OTUV QMM

VICTORIA COUNTY CENTENNIAL HISTORY. Lindsay, Ont., Watchman-Warder Press, 1921. 261p [BM BVa NSHD OTP

**Kitchener-Waterloo Record**

KITCHENER'S FIRST 100 YEARS, 1854–1954. Kitchener, Ont., 1954. 40p

**Kittson, Arthur**

THE SAGA OF SHERBROOKE STREET YESTERDAY AND TO-DAY. A Pictorial Record of Montreal's Most Colourful Thoroughfare from 1853 to 1949. Montmagny, Que., Marquis, 1949. 47p [BVaU OTU

**Kitwanga, B.C. Superior School**

GITWANGAG 1858 TO KITWANGA 1958. Kitwanga, B.C., the School, 1958. 33p [mimeographed]

**Knight, Fulton Stanley, 1883–**

THIS IS MEAFORD, 1875–1956. A Little Sketch of the Origin of our Names, Saint Vincent – Meaford, the Background of these Names, and a Short History of John Jervis, Admiral of the Fleet. ... Meaford, Ont., Author, 1956. 35p

**Lacadena, Sask. Women's Association**

HISTORY OF THE LACADENA COMMUNITY. Comp. by Mrs. Jean Minogue. Lacadena, Sask., 1955. 15p [mimeographed]

**Lagace, Anita**

HOW GRAND FALLS GREW. Grand Falls, N.B., Author, 1945. 77p [NBFU OTU QMBM

**Landon, Fred, 1880–1969**

UP THE PROOF LINE. The Story of a Rural Community. By Fred Landon and Orlo Miller. London, Ont., D.B. Weldon, 1955. 85p [History of the Proof Line Road and London Township.]

TRIAL AND PUNISHMENT OF THE PATRIOTS, captured at Windsor in December, 1838. London, Ont., Author, 1934. 8p [NSHD OTU

WESTERN ONTARIO AND THE AMERICAN FRONTIER. Toronto, Ryerson, 1941. 305p [BM BVaU LC NSHD OTU QMM

**Landstrom, Oscar, 1871–**

PIONEER HOMESTEAD STORIES, FROM 1868 TO PRESENT TIME. Govan, Sask., Western Printers, 1942. 32p [SSU

**Lane, Myrtle Eliza (Mack)**

LAND OF SHINING MOUNTAINS. British Columbia in Legend and Story. By Myrtle E. Lane, Margaret G. Steer and Mary Carr Wright. Toronto, Dent, 1957. 354p

**Langrish, William**

PIONEER DAYS IN THE OXBOW AND GLEN EWEN DISTRICTS. Containing Histories written by William Langrish, Ambrose Dowkes and Edith Campbell. Oxbow, Sask., Herald, 1955. 38p

**Lanigan, Sask. Jubilee Committee**

LANIGAN, 1905–1955. A Brief History of the Town and District, Written in Conjunction with Saskatchewan's Golden Jubilee. Lanigan, Sask., 1955. 68p

**Large, Richard Geddes, 1901–**

THE SKEENA, RIVER OF DESTINY. Vancouver, Mitchell Press, 1957. ix + 180p

**Laurie, William, 1856–1927**

THE BATTLE RIVER VALLEY. ... The Advantages of the country drained by the Battle and Saskatchewan Rivers as a Field for Settlement. Battleford, P.G. Laurie, 1883. 104p [SSU

**Lauriston, Victor, 1881–**

LAMBTON'S HUNDRED YEARS, 1849–1949. Sarnia, Haines Frontier Print., 1949. 335p [OLU

ROMANTIC KENT. More than Three Centuries of History, 1626–1952. Chatham, Ont., Shepherd Print., 1952. 784p [Cover title: THE STORY OF A COUNTY.]

**Laut, Agnes Christina, 1871–1936**

THE CARIBOO TRAIL. A Chronicle of the Gold-fields of British Columbia. Toronto, Glasgow Brook, 1916. 116p [BM BVaU LC NSHD OTU QMM

PIONEERS OF THE PACIFIC COAST. A Chronicle of Sea Rovers and Fur Hunters. Toronto, Glasgow Brook, 1915. 139p [BM BVaU LC NSWA OTU

**Lawrence, Joseph Collins, 1918–**

THE SOUTH-WEST COAST OF VANCOUVER ISLAND. From Metchosin to Bamfield, including Sooke, Otter, River Jordan and Port Renfrew. Sooke, B.C., Women's Institute, 1959. 73p [Cover title: A BRIEF HISTORY OF SOOKE DISTRICT.]

**Lawrence, Joseph Wilson, 1818–1892**

1783–1883. FOOT-PRINTS; or, Incidents in Early History of New Brunswick. Saint John, McMillan, 1883. 108p [BVaU LC NSWA OKQ QMM

**Lawson, John Murray, 1848–1925**

RECORD OF THE SHIPPING OF YARMOUTH, N.S. Containing a List of Vessels owned in the County of Yarmouth since its Settlement in 1761 ... ; also List of Vessels Lost ... and other Information in Reference to the Mercantile Marine. ... Comp. by ——. Yarmouth, 1876. 258p [LC NSHD OOP

**Lawson, Mary Jane (Katzmann), 1828–1890**

HISTORY OF THE TOWNSHIPS OF DARTMOUTH, PRESTON, AND LAWRENCETOWN, HALIFAX COUNTY, N.S. (Akins Historical Prize Essay.) By Mrs. William Lawson (Mary Jane Katzmann). Ed. by Harry Piers. Halifax, Morton, 1893. 260p [BVaU LC NSWA OTU

**Lawton, John Thomas, 1860–1961**

OLD KING'S COVE. [By J.T. Lawton and P.K. Devine.] [St. John's?], 1944. 106p [NfSM

**Lay, Gregory S., 1865?–**

MEMORIES OF EARLY DAYS ON ST. JOSEPH'S ISLAND. The Garden of Algoma and Tourists' Paradise. Kirkland Lake, Ont., Sutherland Print., 1951. 20p

**Leavitt, Thaddeus W.H., 1844?–1909**

HISTORY OF LEEDS AND GRENVILLE, ONTARIO, FROM 1749 TO 1879. With ... Biographical Sketches of some of its Prominent Men and Pioneers. Brockville, Recorder Press, 1879. 200p [BVaU LC NSWA OTU

**Legget, Robert Ferguson, 1904–**

RIDEAU WATERWAY. Toronto, U. of Toronto Press, 1955. xiv + 249p

**LeMessurier, Henry William, 1848–1931**

LECTURE: "ANCIENT ST. JOHN'S." [St. John's], Herald Print., [1915?]. 20p [NfSM

A LECTURE ON PLACENTIA. ... [St. John's, Total Abstinence Society, 1910.] 34p [NBSM

**LeMoine, James MacPherson, 1825–1912**

CHATEAU-BIGOT: HISTORY AND ROMANCE. Historical Sketch of the Ruins of the French Chateau ... with all the Romantic Memories which Attach to it. By the Author of MAPLE LEAVES [pseud]. Quebec, 1874. 21p [BVaU OKQ QMM

THE CHRONICLES OF THE ST. LAWRENCE. Montreal, Dawson, 1878. 380p [BM BVaU LC NSWA OTU

GLIMPSES OF QUEBEC DURING THE LAST TEN YEARS OF FRENCH DOMINATION IN CANADA, 1749–1759. With Observations on the Past and on the Present. Quebec, Morning Chronicle, 1879. 42p [NSWA OTU QMSS

HISTORICAL NOTES ON QUEBEC AND ITS ENVIRONS. ... Drive to Indian Lorette. Indian Lorette. Tahourenche, the Huron Chief. The St. Louis and the Ste. Foy roads. Château Bigot. Laval University, Picture Gallery. ... 2nd ed. Quebec, Darveau, 1887. 59p [LC OTU

HISTORICAL NOTES ON QUEBEC AND ITS ENVIRONS. Montreal to Quebec by Steamer–Round Town–Quebec to Jacques Cartier Monument–Quebec to Montmorency Falls–Drive to Indian Lorette–Indian Lorette. ... 5th ed. Quebec, Darveau, 1890. 152p [BM LC OLU QMSS

ORIGIN OF THE FESTIVAL OF SAINT-JEAN-BAPTISTE. QUEBEC, ITS GATES AND ENVIRONS. ... Quebec, Morning Chronicle, 1880. 94p [BM NSWA

THE PORT OF QUEBEC, ITS ANNALS, 1535–1900. Quebec, Chronicle Print., 1901. 95p [BM BVaU OKQ QMM

QUEBEC PAST AND PRESENT ... 1608–1876. Quebec, Coté, 1876. 466p [BM BVaU NSWA OTU

QUEEN'S BIRTHDAY, 1880. QUEBEC, ITS GATES AND ENVIRONS: Something about the Streets, Lanes and Early History of the Ancient Capital. Quebec, Morning Chronicle, 1880. 94p [*Cf. above:* ORIGIN OF THE FESTIVAL. ... ] [BM BVaU OTU QMM

ST LOUIS STREET AND ITS STORIED PAST. A Christmas Sketch Specially Printed. Quebec, Morning Chronicle, 1891. 19p [BVaU LC OOP

**Lethbridge, Alta. Booklet Committee**

LETHBRIDGE. Alberta's Golden Jubilee. Lethbridge, 1955. 68p

**Lett, William Pittman, 1819–1892**

THE CITY OF OTTAWA AND ITS SURROUNDINGS. Ottawa, Woodburn, 1884. 22p [BM NSWA

RECOLLECTIONS OF BYTOWN AND ITS OLD INHABITANTS. Ottawa, "Citizen" Print., 1874. 95p [BVaU OTU QMM

**Levy, Herman David**

A HISTORY OF SHERWOOD IN THE COUNTY OF LUNENBURG. Truro, N.S., Truro Print., 1953. 98p

**Lewis, Ella N.**

EARLY MEDICAL MEN OF ELGIN COUNTY. St. Thomas, Sutherland, 1931. 60p [OLU QMM

EAST ELGIN PLACE NAMES. St. Thomas, Elgin Hist. Soc., 1935. 25p [LC OTP

SIDELIGHTS ON THE TALBOT SETTLEMENT. St. Thomas, Elgin Hist. Soc., 1938. 28p [CC

**Lewis, Jennie (Raycraft), 1899–**

BIRR AND BEYOND. Comp. by —— *et al.* [London, Ont.?], Birr Women's Institute, 1958. 176p [History of North London Township, Ont., and district.]

**Liberty, Sask. Book Committee (Jubilee)**

FIFTY YEARS OF LIBERTY, 1904–1955. Liberty, Sask., 1955. 112p

**Lincoln County, Ont. Council**

LINCOLN COUNTY, 1856–1956. St. Catharines, Ont., the Council, 1956. 152p

**Lindsay, Frederick William, 1903–**

THE CARIBOO STORY, PUBLISHED IN B.C.'S CENTENNIAL YEAR. Quesnel, B.C., Quesnel Advertiser, 1958. 52p

**Lizars, Kathleen Macfarlane, –1931**

THE VALLEY OF THE HUMBER, 1615–1913. Toronto, Briggs, 1913. 170p [BM BVaU LC NBFU OTP

**Long, Harold Gordon, 1888–**

FORT MACLEOD. The Story of the North West Mounted Police, 1874–1904, Royal North West Mounted Police, 1904–1920, Royal Canadian Mounted Police, 1920 to Present Time. Ed. by ——. Fort Macleod, Alta., Fort Macleod Historical Association, 1958. 96p

**Longstaff, Frederick Victor, 1879–1961**

ESQUIMALT NAVAL BASE. A History of its Work and its Defences. Victoria, Victoria Book & Stationery, 1941. 189p [BM BVaU OTU

**Loreburn, Sask. School**

HISTORY OF LOREBURN, 1905–1955. Loreburn, Sask., 1955. 21p [mimeographed]

**Lorimer, John G., 1807–1897**

HISTORY OF ISLANDS AND ISLETS IN THE BAY OF FUNDY, CHARLOTTE COUNTY, NEW BRUNSWICK. ... St. Stephens, N.B., Saint Croix Courier, 1876. 132p [LC NBSM OTP QMBM

**Low, David, 1913–**

KINGSTON, ONTARIO, CANADA. Kingston, Whig-Standard, 1960. 60p [Calendar, with sketches and historical outline.]

ST. THOMAS, ONTARIO, CANADA, A CENTRE OF INFLUENCE IN ELGIN COUNTY. St. Thomas, Times-Journal, 1960. 71p

**Lucas, Frederick C.**

AN HISTORICAL SOUVENIR DIARY OF THE CITY OF WINNIPEG. ... Comp. and ed. by ——. Winnipeg, Cartwright & Lucas, 1923. 240p [BM BVaU LC SSU

**Ludditt, Alfred William, 1907–**

GOLD IN THE CARIBOO. Vancouver, Evergreen Press, 1958. 40p

**Lugrin, Charles Henry, 1846–1917**

VANCOUVER ISLAND AND RAILWAY DEVELOPMENT. Victoria, Colonist, 1909. 37p [BViPA LC OTU

**Lugrin, Nellie de Bertrand, 1874–**
THE PIONEER WOMEN OF VANCOUVER ISLAND, 1843–1866. Written by N. de Bertrand Lugrin [Mrs. Charles Henry Shaw]. Ed. by John Hosie. Victoria, Women's Can. Club of Victoria, 1928. 312p [BM BVaU NBFU OKQ

**Lundar, Man.**
LUNDAR DIAMOND JUBILEE, 1887–1947. Winnipeg, Viking, 1948. 175p [BVa OTP

**Lynch-Staunton, Mrs. Emma, 1885–1949**
A HISTORY OF THE EARLY DAYS OF PINCHER CREEK, OF THE DISTRICT AND OF THE SOUTHERN MOUNTAINS.... Lethbridge, Herald Print., 1926. 56p [SSU

**Lyons, Chester Peter, 1915–**
MILESTONES ON VANCOUVER ISLAND. The Story of this "Island to the West," its Past, and its Present. Vancouver, priv. print., 1958. 314p

**MacBeath, George Boyd, 1924–**
CHAMPLAIN AND THE ST. JOHN, 1604–1954. Ed. by —— *et al.* Saint John, New Brunswick Historical Society, 1954. 80p
THE STORY OF THE RESTIGOUCHE. Covering the Indian, French, and English Periods of the Restigouche Area. Saint John, New Brunswick Museum, 1954. 25p

**MacBeth, Malcolm, 1868–**
MORNINGTON AND ITS PIONEERS. Milverton, Ont., Milverton "Sun," 1933. 96p [OTU

**MacBeth, Rev. Roderick George, 1858–1934**
THE ROMANCE OF WESTERN CANADA. Toronto, Briggs, 1918. 309p [BM BVaU LC NSHD OTP QMSS
THE SELKIRK SETTLERS IN REAL LIFE. Toronto, Briggs, 1897. 119p [BM BVaU LC NSHD OTP QMSS

**McCague, John Joseph E., 1899–**
A CENTURY OF PROGRESS. The Centennial Review of the Township of Essa, 1850–1950. Ed. by ——. Thornton, Ont., the Township, 1950. [unpaged] [OTU

**McCall, Ralph Lewis, 1925–**
THE ACME STORY, 1910–1960. Acme, Alta., 1960. 5 + 43p

**McColl, Hugh**
SOME SKETCHES OF THE EARLY HIGHLAND PIONEERS OF THE COUNTY OF MIDDLESEX. Strathroy, Ont., Gaelic Society of Toronto, 1904. 58p [OTP

**McCowan, Daniel, 1882–1956**

UPLAND TRAILS. Toronto, Macmillan, 1955. xiv + 158p

**MacDermot, Hugh Ernest, 1888–**

A HISTORY OF THE MONTREAL GENERAL HOSPITAL. Montreal, the Hospital, 1950. 135p [BVaU NBFU

HISTORY OF SCHOOL OF NURSING OF MONTREAL GENERAL HOSPITAL. Montreal, Alumnae Assoc., the Hospital, 1940. 125p [BVaU

**MacDonald, Rev. Alexander, 1858–1941**

THE BRITISH COLUMBIA ORPHANS' FRIEND HISTORICAL NUMBER. ... Victoria, Press Pub. Co., 1913. 208p [BVaU

**McDonald, Archibald, 1790–1853**

NARRATIVE RESPECTING THE DESTRUCTION OF THE EARL OF SELKIRK'S SETTLEMENT UPON RED RIVER, IN THE YEAR 1815. London, Brettell, 1816. 14p [BViPA OTP

REPLY TO THE LETTER ADDRESSED TO THE EARL OF SELKIRK BY JOHN STRACHAN ... concerning the Settlement on Red River. Montreal, Gray, 1816. 50p [Reprinted from Montreal "Herald." Bound with two others.] [QMM

**Macdonald, Charles Ochiltree, 1870–**

THE LAST SIEGE OF LOUISBURG. London, Cassell, [1907?]. 176p [BVaU LC NSWA OTP QMM

**MacDonald, D., 1855–**

CAPE NORTH AND VICINITY. Pioneer Families, History and Chronicles. ... [Port Hastings, N.S.], Author, 1933. 160 + xivp [NBFU

**MacDonald, George Heath**

EDMONTON. Fort, House, Factory. Edmonton, Douglas Print., 1959. 236p

FORT AUGUSTUS–EDMONTON. Northwest Trails and Traffic. Edmonton, Douglas Print., 1954. 255p

**Macdonell, Alexander Greenfield, –1835**

A NARRATIVE OF TRANSACTIONS IN THE RED RIVER COUNTRY. From the Commencement of the Operations of the Earl of Selkirk till the Summer of the Year 1816. London, Macmillan, 1819. 85p [BM BVaU LC OTU

**Macdonell, John Alexander, 1851–1930**

SKETCHES ILLUSTRATING THE EARLY SETTLEMENT AND HISTORY OF GLENGARRY IN CANADA. ... Montreal, Foster Brown, 1893. 337p [BM BVaU LC NSWA OTP QMSS

**Macdougall, A.W.**

BLACK RIVER AND ITS FIRST SETTLERS. Comp. by Louise Manny. [Chatham, N.B.?], 1935. 56p [NBFU

**McDougall, Rev. John, 1842–1917**

FOREST, LAKE, AND PRAIRIE. Twenty Years of Frontier Life in Western Canada–1842–1862. Toronto, Briggs, 1895. 267p [BM BVaU LC NBFU OTU QMSS

IN THE DAYS OF THE RED RIVER REBELLION. Life and Adventure in the Far West of Canada (1868–1872). Toronto, Briggs, 1903. 303p [BM BVaU OTP

ON WESTERN TRAILS IN THE EARLY SEVENTIES. Frontier Life in the Canadian Northwest. Toronto, Briggs, 1911. 279p [BM BVaU LC OKQ

PATHFINDING ON PLAIN AND PRAIRIE. Stirring Scenes of Life in the Canadian North-west. Toronto, Briggs, 1898. 277p [BM BVaU LC OKQ

SADDLE, SLED AND SNOWSHOE. Pioneering on the Saskatchewan in the Sixties. Toronto, Briggs, 1896. 282p [BM BVaU LC OTP

**MacDougall, John L.**

HISTORY OF INVERNESS COUNTY, NOVA SCOTIA. Truro, News Pub. Co., 1922. 690p [LC NBFU OTP

**McEvoy, John Millar, 1864–1935**

THE ONTARIO TOWNSHIP.... Toronto, Warwick, 1889. 42p [BM NSHP OTP

**MacEwan, Grant, 1902–**

CALGARY CAVALCADE FROM FORT TO FORTUNE. Edmonton, Institute of Applied Art, 1958. x + 246p

**Macfie, Charles Maitland, 1872–**

APPIN, ONTARIO, 1847–1947. A Century's Story of the Growth of a Village and Community from the Primeval Forest to the Privileged Condition of Today. Appin, Ont., Women's Institute, 1947. 35p [OOA

EKFRID TOWNSHIP, 1821–1949. Appin, Ont., Author, 1949. 48p [OOA

**Macfie, Matthew**

VANCOUVER ISLAND AND BRITISH COLUMBIA, THEIR HISTORY, RESOURCES, AND PROSPECTS. London, Longmans, 1865. xxi + 574p [BVa NBSM OONL QMSS

**MacGregor, James Grierson, 1905–**

BLANKETS AND BEADS. A History of the Saskatchewan River. Edmonton, Institute of Applied Art, 1949. 278p [BVaU OTP

THE LAND OF TWELVE-FOOT DAVIS. A History of the Peace River Country. Edmonton, Applied Arts Products, 1952. 395p

**MacGregor, John, 1797–1857**

HISTORICAL AND DESCRIPTIVE SKETCHES OF THE MARITIME COLONIES OF BRITISH AMERICA. London, Longman etc., 1828. 266p [LC NSWA OTP

**Machar, Agnes Maule, 1837–1927**

THE STORY OF OLD KINGSTON. Toronto, Musson, 1908. 291p [BM BVaU LC NSWA OTU

**MacInnes, Alexander P., 1868–**

CHRONICLES OF THE CARIBOO. Dunlevy's Discovery of Gold on the Horsefly. Lillooet, B.C., Lillooet Pub., 1938. 27p [BVaU

**MacInnes, Charles Malcolm, 1891–**

IN THE SHADOW OF THE ROCKIES. London, Rivingtons, 1930. 347p [A history of the development of ranching in southern Alberta.] [BM BVaU LC NBFU OTU SSU

**McIntosh, Donald J.**

FORT ST. JAMES, PAST AND PRESENT. Vancouver, 1933. 22p [BVaU

**Mack, Hazel L. (Spencer), 1903–**

HISTORICAL HIGHLIGHTS OF WELLINGTON COUNTY. [Rockwood, Ont.?], Author, 1955. 44p

HISTORY OF EDEN MILLS AND VICINITY. Rockwood, Ont., Eden Crest and Eden Mills Women's Institutes, 1954. 56p

**Mackay, Corday**

HELMCKEN HOUSE, HISTORIC MUSEUM, VICTORIA, BRITISH COLUMBIA. Victoria, n.p., n.d. 20p

**MacKay, Elsie Annie Myrtle, 1905–**

SELKIRK'S 75th ANNIVERSARY. Ed. by ——. Selkirk, Man., 75th Anniversary Committee, 1957. 80p

THE STONE FORT, LOWER FORT GARRY. Selkirk, Man., the Author, 1960. 28p

**McKay, Kenneth W.**

THE COURT HOUSES OF A CENTURY. A Brief Historical Sketch of the Court Houses of the London District, the County of Middlesex and County of Elgin. Comp. by ——. St. Thomas, Ont., Times Print., 1901. 26p [LC OOP

**MacKay, Rev. William Alexander, 1842–1905**

PIONEER LIFE IN ZORRA. Toronto, Briggs, 1899. 400p [BM BVaU LC OTP QMBM

ZORRA BOYS AT HOME AND ABROAD; or, How to Succeed. Toronto, Briggs, 1900. 228p [2nd ed. under title: SUCCESS ILLUSTRATED BY EXAMPLE, 1901.] [BM BVaU NSHD OTP QMBM

**McKelvie, Bruce Alistair, 1889–1960**

EARLY HISTORY OF THE PROVINCE OF BRITISH COLUMBIA. London, Dent, 1926. 118p [BVaU OOA

FORT LANGLEY, OUTPOST OF EMPIRE. Vancouver, "Daily Province," 1947. 98p [BM BVaU LC NBFU OTP

HBC IN B.C. Winnipeg, Hudson's Bay Company, 1958. 26p

MAQUINNA THE MAGNIFICENT. Vancouver, "Daily Province," 1946. 65p [BVaU OTP QMBM

PAGEANT OF B.C. Glimpses into the Romantic Development of Canada's Far Western Province. Toronto, Nelson, 1955. 263p
TALES OF CONFLICT. Vancouver, "Daily Province," 1949. 99p [BVaU OTP

**McKenzie, Ina Campbell, 1897–**

BRADFORD, 1857–1957. One Hundred Years in Picture and Story. Comp. and arr. by Ina and Stewart McKenzie. Bradford, Ont., 1957. 128p

**MacKinnon, Donald Alexander, 1863–**

PAST AND PRESENT OF PRINCE EDWARD ISLAND. ... A Concise Review of its Early Settlement, Development and Present Condition. By the ... Authors of the Province. ... Ed. by D.A. MacKinnon ... and A.B. Warburton ... [with] Life Sketches of Representative Men and Families. ... Charlottetown, Bowen, 1906. 731p [NSHD

**Mackinnon, Frank, 1919–**

THE GOVERNMENT OF PRINCE EDWARD ISLAND. Toronto, U. of Toronto Press, 1951. 385p

**MacKinnon, Ian F., 1898–**

SETTLEMENTS AND CHURCHES IN NOVA SCOTIA, 1749–1776. Montreal, Walker, 1930. 111p [BM BVaU NBFU OTP

**MacKinnon, J.G.**

OLD SYDNEY. Sketches of the Town and its People in Days Gone By. Sydney, N.S., Don MacKinnon, 1918. 143p [BVaU NSWA OOP

**MacKinnon, James N., 1871–1946**

MOOSOMIN AND ITS PIONEERS. Including Humorous Incidents and Up-to-date Sketches. Moosomin, World-Spectator, 1937. 67p [SSU
A SHORT HISTORY OF THE PIONEER SCOTCH SETTLERS OF ST. ANDREWS, SASK. Regina, Courier, 1921. 30p [SRL

**McKitrick, Thomas George, 1873–1952**

CORNER STONES OF EMPIRE. The Settlement of Crystal City and District in the Rock Lake Country. Crystal City, Man., Courier Pub. Co., [194–?]. 201p [BVa MWP

**Macklin, Sask. Home and School Association**

A SHORT HISTORY OF MACKLIN AND COMMUNITY, ON THE OCCASION OF SASKATCHEWAN'S GOLDEN JUBILEE YEAR. Macklin, Sask., 1955. 32p [mimeographed]

**MacLaren, George**

THE PICTOU BOOK. Stories of Our Past. New Glasgow, Hector Pub., 1955. 267p

**McLaren, J.L.**

STORIES OF THE DANFORTH. A Collection of Familiar Stories of the Danforth

District. Comp. by ——, from many reliable sources. Toronto, n.p., 1921. 21p [BM OTP

**McLennan, John Stewart, 1853–1939**

LOUISBOURG, FROM ITS FOUNDATIONS TO ITS FALL, 1713–1758. Toronto, Macmillan, 1918. 454p [2nd ed.: Sydney, N.S., Fortress Press, 1957. 330p] [BVaU LC NBFU OTU QMSS

**McLennan, Mary Louise, 1879–1938**

A HISTORY OF THE NORTH EASTHOPE PIONEERS, COUNTY OF PERTH, CANADA, FROM PERTHSHIRE, SCOTLAND. With an Intro. by Donald Scott. [Stratford, Ont.?], Author, 1937. 185p [BM OOA

**McLeod, Donald, 1779–1879**

A BRIEF REVIEW OF THE SETTLEMENT OF UPPER CANADA BY THE U.E. LOYALISTS AND SCOTCH HIGHLANDERS IN 1783, AND OF THE GRIEVANCES WHICH COMPELLED THE CANADAS TO HAVE RECOURSE TO ARMS IN DEFENCE OF THEIR RIGHTS AND LIBERTIES IN ... 1837 AND 1838. ... Cleveland, Penniman, 1841. 292p [BVaU LC NSWA OTP QMBM

**McLeod, Margaret (Arnett), 1877–1966**

BELLS OF RED RIVER. Winnipeg, Stovel, 1938. 41p [BVaU NSWA OTP QMBM

LOWER FORT GARRY. Winnipeg, priv. print., 1957. 12p

**MacLeod, N.W.**

PICTURESQUE CARDSTON AND ENVIRONMENTS. A Story of Colonization and Progress in Southern Alberta. Cardston, Author, 1900. 116p [Reprinted as souvenir for Cardston Golden Jubilee, June 28–July 3, 1937.] [AEP

**McLeod, Robert Randall, 1839–1909**

MARKLAND OR NOVA SCOTIA. Its History, Natural Resources, etc. [Berwick, N.S.], Markland Pub. Co., 1903. 603p [BM BVaU LC NBFU OTP QMM

**MacMartin, Belle D.**

VERNON YESTERDAY AND TO-DAY. By Belle D. MacMartin and Beatrice R. Porteous. Vernon, Ont., Women's Institute, 1950. 24p [OONL

**MacMechan, Archibald McKellar, 1862–1933**

OLD PROVINCE TALES. ... Toronto, McClelland, 1924. 345p [BM BVaU LC NSHD OKQ

ORIGINAL MINUTES OF HIS MAJESTY'S COUNCIL AT ANNAPOLIS ROYAL, 1720–1739. Ed. by ——. Halifax, McAlpine Pub. Co., 1908. 408p [BM NSHD OTP QMSS

PROVINCE HOUSE. Halifax, Author, 1927. 8p [BVaU OKQ

RED SNOW ON GRAND PRE. Toronto, McClelland, 1931. 224p [BM BVaU LC NBFU OTU

SAGAS OF THE SEA. Toronto, Dent, 1924. 156p [BM BVaU LC NSHD OKQ

STORIED HALIFAX. (Nova Scotia Chapbook). Halifax, Allen, 1922. 17p [BVaU OTP

TALES OF THE SEA. Foreword by T.H. Raddall. Toronto, McClelland, 1947. 230p [NBFU OTP QMBM

THERE GO THE SHIPS. Toronto, McClelland, 1928. 293p [BM BVaU NBFU OTP

**McMeekan, John Murray**

A SHORT HISTORY OF YELLOWKNIFE. Toronto, Cooper, 1944. 4p [CC

**McMorran, Gordon Alexander, 1885–**

THE SOURIS PLAINS. From Pemmican to Wheat, 1881–1956. Commemorating the 75th Anniversary of Souris and District, July 1956. Ed. by ——. Souris, Man., Souris Plaindealer, 1956. 68p

**McMurray, Thomas, 1831–**

THE FREE GRANT LANDS OF CANADA, from Practical Experience of Bush Farming in the Free Grant Lands of Muskoka and Parry Sound. Bracebridge, Northern Advocate, 1871. 146p [OTUV

**MacNeil, Neil, 1891–**

THE HIGHLAND HEART IN NOVA SCOTIA. New York, Scribner, 1948. 199p [Also: Toronto, Saunders, 1958.] [BVaU LC NBFU OTP QMM

**McNeill, Leishman, 1896–**

TALES OF THE OLD TOWN. Calgary, 1875–1950. Calgary, Herald, 1951. 92p [Reprint of articles published in *The Herald* during Calgary's 75th anniversary celebrations, 1950.]

**MacNutt, William Stewart, 1908–**

NEW BRUNSWICK AND ITS PEOPLE. The Biography of a Canadian Province. Ed. by A.W. Trueman. Fredericton, New Brunswick Travel Bureau, 1952. 46p

**MacQueen, Malcolm Alexander, 1878–1960**

HEBRIDEAN PIONEERS. Winnipeg, Henderson Directories, 1957. 104p [An account of emigrants to Belfast, P.E.I.]

SKYE PIONEERS AND "THE ISLAND." Winnipeg, Stovel, 1929. 162p [BM BVaU LC NSHD OLU QMBM

**MacRae, Archibald Oswald, 1869–**

HISTORY OF THE PROVINCE OF ALBERTA. Calgary, Western Canada History Co., 1912. 2v [BVaU LC NSHD OTP QMSS

**MacVicar, William Mortimer, 1851–1928**

A SHORT HISTORY OF ANNAPOLIS ROYAL ... 1604 to 1854. Toronto, Copp Clark, 1897. 127p [BM BVaU LC NSWA OTP QMM

**Macwatt, Daniel Fraser, 1853–1920**

SHORT SKETCHES, WITH PHOTOGRAPHS, OF WARDENS, PARLIAMENTARY REPRESENTATIVES, JUDICIAL OFFICERS AND COUNTY OFFICIALS OF THE COUNTY OF LAMBTON FROM 1852–1917. Sarnia, County Council, 1917. 55p [OTU

**McWilliams, Margaret (Stovel), 1875–1952**

MANITOBA MILESTONES. Toronto, Dent, 1928. 249p [BM BVaU LC NSHD OTP QMBM

**Maidstone, Sask. Jubilee Committee**

BETWEEN THE RIVERS ... MAIDSTONE, SASKATCHEWAN, 1905–1955. Maidstone, Sask., 1955. 88p

**Main Centre, Sask. School**

GREEN GRASS TO GOLDEN GRAIN, MAIN CENTRE. Main Centre, Sask., 1955. 18p [mimeographed]

**Major, Frederick William, 1874–**

MANITOULIN, THE ISLE OF THE OTTAWAS. Being a Handbook of Historical and other Information on the Grand Manitoulin Island. Gore Bay, Ont., Recorder Press, 1934. 84p [OTP

**Manning, Mrs. Mary Ethel, 1919–**

A VILLAGE LIBRARY. The Story of the Streetsville Library, 1854–1959. Comp. by Mrs. Mary Manning and Rev. T.D. Jones. Streetsville, Ont., W.G. Tolton, 1959. 24p

**Manny, Louise, 1890–1971**

SHIPS OF MIRAMICHI. A History of Shipbuilding on the Miramichi River, N.B., 1773–1919. Saint John, New Brunswick Museum, 1960. 84p

**Manotick, Ont. Centennial Committee**

MANOTICK'S CENTENNIAL YEAR SOUVENIR BOOK, 1859–1959. Containing the Manotick Story ... also Historical Reports of each of Manotick's Churches and of the various Social and Fraternal Orders and Associations. ... Manotick, the Committee, 1959. 75p

**Mantario, Sask. Homemakers' Club**

FROM OXEN TO AIRPLANE: MANTARIO, 1908–1950. Comp. by C. Evans Sargent. [Saskatoon, Midwest Litho Co., 1950.] 91p [Cf. title listed under Shipley, Mrs. R.L., below.] [SRL SSU

**Markham Township, Ont. Historical Committee**

HISTORICAL SKETCH OF MARKHAM TOWNSHIP, 1793–1950. Centennial Celebration of Municipal Government, 1850–1950. Unionville, Ont., the Township, 1950. 106p [OTU

**Marsh, Edith Louise, –1960**

A HISTORY OF THE COUNTY OF GREY. ... Owen Sound, Fleming, 1931. 487p [BVaU OTP

WHERE THE BUFFALO ROAMED. The Story of Western Canada Told for the Young. ... Toronto, Briggs, 1908. 242p [Also: Toronto, Macmillan, 1923. 257p] [BM BVaU LC NSHD OLU

**Marshall, John George, 1786–1880**

BRIEF HISTORY OF PUBLIC PROCEEDINGS & EVENTS ... during the Earliest Years of the Present Century. ... Halifax, "Wesleyan," [1878?]. 69p [NSWA OTL

**Martin, Chester Bailey, 1882–1958**

RED RIVER SETTLEMENT. Papers in the Canadian Archives Relating to the Pioneers. Sel. and ed. by ——. Ottawa, the Archives, 1910. 27p [BM BVaU NSHD OOC QMSS

**Martin, John Patrick, 1886–**

THE STORY OF DARTMOUTH. Dartmouth, N.S., priv. print., 1957. 550p

**Marwick, Alice (Stinson), 1892–1956**

NORTHLAND POST. The Story of the Town of Cochrane. Cochrane, Author, 1950. 342p [BM BVaU OTU

**Mary Theodore, Sister, 1856–1951**

PIONEER NUNS OF BRITISH COLUMBIA. Sisters of St. Ann. Victoria, Colonist, 1931. 146p [BVaU

**Mason, Douglas H.C.**

MUSKOKA. The First Islanders. Bracebridge, Ont., Herald-Gazette, 1957. 30p

**Masters, Donald Campbell Charles, 1908–**

THE RISE OF TORONTO, 1850–1890. Toronto, U. of Toronto Press, 1947. 239p [BVaU LC OTP QMM

THE WINNIPEG GENERAL STRIKE. Toronto, U. of Toronto Press, 1950. 159p [BM BVaU NBFU OTP

**Masterton, Mrs. I.V.**

HISTORY OF EMERSON, FEATURING HISTORICAL SKETCHES OF SURROUNDING DISTRICTS. Ed. by —— and W.E. Carlson. Emerson, Man., W.E. Carlson, 1953. 80p

**Mather, Barry, 1909–**

NEW WESTMINSTER, THE ROYAL CITY. By Barry Mather and Margaret McDonald. Vancouver, Dent and the Corporation of the City of New Westminster, 1958. xxvii + 192p

**Mathews, Hazel (Chisholm)**

OAKVILLE AND THE SIXTEEN. The History of an Ontario Port. Toronto, U. of Toronto Press, 1953. xxv + 521p

**Maurice, Varney, 1879–**

FIFTY YEARS IN THE PEACE RIVER COUNTRY, and the Story of the Alaska Highway. High Prairie, Alta., 1947. 143p [AEU

**Maxwell, Lilian Mary (Beckwith), 1877–1956**

HOW NEW BRUNSWICK GREW. Sackville, Tribune Press, 1943. 95p [LC NBFU OTP

THE OLD GRAVE-YARD, FREDERICTON, NEW BRUNSWICK, EPITAPHS. ... Ed. by ——. Sackville, Busy East Press, [1938?]. 139p [BVaU OTP

AN OUTLINE OF THE HISTORY OF CENTRAL NEW BRUNSWICK TO THE TIME OF CONFEDERATION. Sackville, Tribune Press, 1937. 183p [BM BVaU LC NBFU OTP QMM

**Maymont, Sask. Golden Jubilee Committee**

THE STORY OF MAYMONT. Maymont, Sask., 1955. 50p

**Meldrum, Frances Muriel (Tanner), 1909–**

KITIMAT: THE FIRST FIVE YEARS. Kitimat, B.C., Corporation of the District of Kitimat, 1959. 40p

**Melfort, Sask. Board of Trade**

MELFORT, SASKATCHEWAN, CANADA, THE HEART OF THE CARROT RIVER VALLEY. Melfort, Sask., 1952. 20p

**Melville, Sask. Board of Trade**

MELVILLE, THE WEST'S WONDER TOWN. Melville, Canadian Office, 1910. 44p [SSU

**Melville, Sask. High School**

THE MELVILLE STORY. [Freda Lawrence, history editor.] Melville, Sask., 1955. 57p [mimeographed]

**Mendham, Sask. School**

MENDHAM AFTER FIFTY YEARS. Mendham, Sask., 1955. 16p

**Meredith, Mrs. Alden G.**

MARY'S ROSEDALE AND GOSSIP OF "LITTLE YORK." Ottawa, Graphic, 1928. 280p [BVaU NBFU OTP QMSS

**Merkel, Andrew Doane, 1884–1954**

SCHOONER BLUENOSE. Toronto, Ryerson, 1948. 70p [BVaU LC NSHD OTP QMM

**Merritt, Jedediah Prendergast, 1820–1901**

CANADA SEVENTY YEARS AGO; or, Prince Edward's Visit to Niagara. ... 3rd ed. St. Catharines, 1860. 13p [OTP

**Metcalfe, Joseph Henry, 1870–1938**

THE TREAD OF THE PIONEERS. Under the Distinguished Patronage of the Government of the Province of Manitoba, the Corporation of the City of Portage la Prairie, the Council of the Rural Municipality of Portage la Prairie. Ed. by ——. Toronto, Portage la Prairie & District Old Timers' Association, 1932. 305p [BVaU OTP

**Metzler, Norbert**

ILLUSTRATED HALIFAX, ITS CIVIL, MILITARY, AND NAVAL HISTORY. With a Brief Sketch of Acadian Annals. Montreal, McConniff, 1891. 80p [NSWA OTP QMM

**Middleton, Jesse Edgar, 1872–1960**

THE MUNICIPALITY OF TORONTO. A History. Toronto, Dominion Pub., 1923. 3v [BM BVaU LC OTP

THE PROVINCE OF ONTARIO–A History–1615-1927. By Jesse Edgar Middleton ... and Fred Landon. ... Toronto, Dominion Pub., 1927–28. 5v [BVaU LC NBFU OLU QMM

TORONTO'S 100 YEARS. Toronto, Centennial Committee, 1934. 228p [BM BVaU LC OTP QMM

**Mikel, William Charles, 1867–1950**

CITY OF BELLEVILLE HISTORY. Comp. by ——. Picton, Ont., Gazette Pub., 1943. 322p [BVaU LC OTP QMM

SOME BAY OF QUINTE REMINISCENCES. An Address before the U.E.L. Association at Toronto ... April 27th, 1922. Belleville, Cherry Press, [193–?]. 24p [OTP

**Milestone, Sask. School**

MILESTONE HISTORY. Saskatchewan Golden Jubilee. Milestone, Sask., 1955. 37p

**Miller, Hanson Orlo, 1911–**

A CENTURY OF WESTERN ONTARIO. The Story of London, "The Free Press," and Western Ontario, 1849–1949. Toronto, Ryerson, 1949. 289p [OLU QMM

**Miller, Maud (Henderson), 1866–**

HISTORY OF UPPER WOODSTOCK. Saint John, Globe Print., 1940. 165p [BViP LC NBFU OTP

**Miller, Thomas, 1803–**

HISTORICAL AND GENEALOGICAL RECORD OF THE FIRST SETTLERS OF COLCHESTER COUNTY, DOWN TO THE PRESENT TIME. ... Halifax, MacKinlay, 1873. 400p [BVaU LC NSHD OTU

**Mills, Edward Robert Rufus, 1886–**

THE STORY OF STONY MOUNTAIN AND DISTRICT. Winnipeg, De Montfort Press, 1960. 140p

**Mills, Stanley, 1863–**

LAKE MEDAD AND WATERDOWN. Hamilton, Author, 1937. 114p [OKQ

**Milner, William Cochrane, 1846–1939**

THE BASIN OF MINAS AND ITS EARLY SETTLERS. N.p., [193–?]. 132p [BVaU NSWA OTP QMM

EARLY HISTORY OF DORCHESTER AND OTHER PARTS OF NEW BRUNSWICK. N.p., 1932. 32p [Earlier ed., 1915.] [BVaU NSWA OLU

HISTORY OF SACKVILLE, NEW BRUNSWICK. Sackville, Tribune, 1934. 185p [BVaU LC NBFU OTP QMM

RECORDS OF CHIGNECTO. N.p., Nova Scotia Hist. Soc., 1916. 86p [BVaU NSWA OONL

SAINT JOHN IN THE FORTIES. N.p., Daily Telegraph, 1923. 23p [NSWA OONL

**Minden, Ont. Centennial Planning Board**

MINDEN CENTENNIAL, 1859–1959. Minden, Ont., 1959. 100p

**Minnedosa, Man. 75th Anniversary History Section**

A HISTORY OF MINNEDOSA AND SURROUNDING DISTRICTS. Minnedosa, Man., 1958. 1v [unpaged]

**Minter, Roy Seymour, 1916–**

A YUKON POT POURRI. Vancouver, priv. print., 1958. 24p

**Mitchell, John, 1882–1951**

THE SETTLEMENT OF YORK COUNTY. Toronto, Municipal Corporation of the County of York, 1952. 114p

**Moffatt, Charles W.**

INTRODUCING SACKVILLE, N.B. ... Comp. by ——. Sackville, Tribune, 1946. 89p [BVaU LC NBSM OTP

**Moir, George Thomson, 1871–**

SINNERS AND SAINTS. A True Story of Early [Railroad] Days in the Farthest West. By an Old Timer, Written and Told by Himself. Victoria, Wooding, 1948. 165p [mimeographed] [BVaU OTU

**Monk, Harry Albert Jervis, 1913–**

A HISTORY OF COQUITLAM AND FRASER MILLS, 1858–1958. By H.A.J. Monk and John Stewart. New Westminster, B.C., District of Coquitlam–Fraser Mills Centennial Commission, 1958. 76p

**Monro, Alexander, 1813–1896**

NEW BRUNSWICK. With a Brief Outline of Nova Scotia, and Prince Edward Island. ... Halifax, Nugent, 1855. 384p [BM BVaU LC NBFU OTP QMM

**Montreal, Que. Tercentenary Commission**

MONTREAL–SOREL, 1642–1942. Montreal's Pageant of Progress and its Nation Builders. ... Montreal, Bull Dog, 1942. 44p [OTU QMM

**Moore, Rev. Arthur Henry, 1869–1938**

THE VALLEY OF THE RICHELIEU. An Historical Study. St. John, Que., Smith, 1929. 46p [NSHD OTU QMM

**Moose Jaw, Sask. Golden Jubilee Committee**

GOLDEN JUBILEE, 1903–1953. Moose Jaw, the Committee, 1953. 50p

**More, James F.**

THE HISTORY OF QUEENS COUNTY, N.S. ... Halifax, Nova Scotia Print., 1873. 250p [BM BVaU LC NSWA OTU QMU

**Morgan, Joan Elson, 1917–**

CASTLE OF QUEBEC. Toronto, Dent, 1949. 186p [BVa NBFU OTU

**Morice, Rev. Adrian Gabriel, 1859–1938**

A CRITICAL HISTORY OF THE RED RIVER INSURRECTION, after Official Documents and Non-Catholic Sources. Winnipeg, Canadian Publishers, 1935. 375p [BM BVaU LC NBFU OTP QMBM

THE HISTORY OF THE NORTHERN INTERIOR OF BRITISH COLUMBIA, FORMERLY NEW CALEDONIA [1660–1880]. Toronto, Briggs, 1904. 349p [BM BVaU LC NSWA OTP QMSS

**Mornington Township, Ont. Centennial Committee**

MORNINGTON CENTENNIAL AND MILVERTON OLD BOYS & GIRLS REUNION, AUGUST 2 TO AUGUST 5. Souvenir Booklet and Programme. Milverton, Ont., 1957. 108p

**Morris, Rev. M.**

THE PROPOSED RAILWAY ACROSS NEWFOUNDLAND. A Lecture. ... St. John's, Nfld., "Public Ledger" Office, 1875. 46p [LC

**Morrison, Clifford Jennings, 1906–**

DO YOU REMEMBER? The First Fifty Years in the Spalding District. Prepared by C.J. Morrison from information secured by Mrs. Matt. Dircks. Spalding, Sask., Jubilee Committee, 1955. 19p

**Morrison, Mrs. Elsie C.**

CALGARY, 1875–1950. A Souvenir of Calgary's Seventy-Fifth Anniversary. Ed. by Elsie C. Morrison and P.N.R. Morrison. Calgary, Calgary Pub. Co., 1950. 247p [OONL

**Morrison, Neil Farquharson, 1896–**

GARDEN GATEWAY TO CANADA. One Hundred Years of Windsor and Essex County, 1854–1954. Toronto, Ryerson, 1954. ix + 344p

**Morrow, James William, 1869–1932**

EARLY HISTORY OF THE MEDICINE HAT COUNTRY. Medicine Hat, News, 1923. 65p [OTU SSU

**Morrow, Robert A.H.**

STORY OF THE SPRINGHILL DISASTER. Comprising a Full and Authentic Account of the Great Coal Mining Explosion at Springhill Mines, Nova Scotia, February 21st, 1891, including a History of Springhill and its Collieries. ... 2nd ed. Saint John, Morrow, 1891. 311p [BVaU LC NSWA OTU

**Morse, John Jesse, 1906–**

KAMLOOPS, THE INLAND CAPITAL. A Condensed History. Kamloops, B.C., Kamloops Museum Association for the Kamloops Centennial Committee, 1957. 40p

**Morse, William Inglis, 1874–1952**

ACADIENSIA NOVA (1598–1779). ... New and Unpublished Documents and Other Data Relating to Acadia. Collected and ed. by ——. London, Quaritch, 1935. 2v [BM BVaU LC NSWA OTP

GRAVESTONES OF ACADIE, AND OTHER ESSAYS ON LOCAL HISTORY. London, Smith, 1929. 110p [BM BVaU LC NBFU OTP QMM

THE LAND OF THE NEW ADVENTURE (THE GEORGIAN ERA IN NOVA SCOTIA). London, Quaritch, 1932. 158p [BM BVaU LC NSWA OLU QMBM

LOCAL HISTORY OF PARADISE, ANNAPOLIS COUNTY, NOVA SCOTIA (1684–1936). Boston, Sawyer, 1937. 65p [Supplement–to 1938: Boston, Sawyer, 1938. 79p] [BM LC NSHD OTP QMM

**Morton, Arthur Silver, 1870–1945**

HISTORY OF PRAIRIE SETTLEMENT. Toronto, Macmillan, 1938. 571p [BM BVaU LC NBFU OTP QMM

A HISTORY OF THE CANADIAN WEST TO 1870–71. Being a History of Rupert's Land (the Hudson's Bay Company's Territory) and of the North-west Territory (including the Pacific Slope). Toronto, Nelson, 1939. 987p [BM BVaU LC NBFU OTP QMM

**Morton, William Lewis, 1908–**

MANITOBA. A History. Toronto, U. of Toronto Press, 1957. xii + 519p

**Mowat, Grace Helen, 1875–1964**

THE DIVERTING HISTORY OF A LOYALIST TOWN. St. Andrew's, N.B., Charlotte County Cottage Craft, 1932. 140p [2nd ed., Fredericton, Brunswick Press, 1953. 152p] [BVaU LC NBFU OTP

THE HOUSE THAT HURRICANE JACK BUILT. Fredericton, Brunswick Press, 1954. 14p [History of the Bayside area of New Brunswick and of the house built there by John Mowat.]

**Muir, Robert Cuthbertson, 1856–1935**

THE EARLY POLITICAL AND MILITARY HISTORY OF BURFORD, ONT. Quebec, Imprimerie Commerciale, 1913. 371p [OTP QMSS

**Mulholland, A.H.R.**

NEARLY HALF A CENTURY. London, Ont., Lawson Memorial Library, U. of Western Ontario, 1945. 7 leaves [OTU

**Mullane, George, 1850–1938**

FOOTPRINTS AROUND AND ABOUT BEDFORD BASIN, a District Brimful of Romantic Associations. Some Interesting Facts about its Early History. Halifax, [19—?]. 46p [BVaU OTP

MONOGRAPH OF ST. PAUL'S CEMETERY. ... Halifax, Burgoyne, 1902. 24p [NSHD

**Mullins, Janet Elizabeth**

LIVERPOOL PRIVATEERING, 1756–1815. Comp. by ——. Liverpool, N.S., Queen's County Hist. Soc., 1936. 68p [NBSaM QMG

SOME LIVERPOOL CHRONICLES. ... Liverpool, N.S., Advance, 1941. 297p [NSHPL

**Mullock, Rev. John Thomas, 1807–1869**

TWO LECTURES ON NEWFOUNDLAND DELIVERED AT ST. BONAVENTURE'S COLLEGE. ... New York, Mullaly, 1860. 60p [BM OONL QMSS

**Mulvany, Charles Pelham, 1835–1885**

THE HISTORY OF THE COUNTY OF BRANT. ... By C. Pelham Mulvany and others. Toronto, Warner Beers, 1883. 689p [OLU

HISTORY OF THE COUNTY OF PETERBOROUGH, ONTARIO. [By C. Pelham Mulvany and others.] Toronto, Robinson, 1884. 783p [OTU

THE HISTORY OF THE NORTH-WEST REBELLION OF 1885. Toronto, Hovey, 1885. 424p [BM BVaU LC NSHD OTP QMM

HISTORY OF TORONTO AND COUNTY OF YORK, ONTARIO. By C. Pelham Mulvany, G.M. Adam, and others. Toronto, Robinson, 1885. 2v [BM NSWA OTU

TORONTO, PAST AND PRESENT. Toronto, Caiger, 1884. 320p [BM BVaU LC NSWA OTP QMSS

**Munday, Walter Alfred Don, 1890–1950**

THE UNKNOWN MOUNTAIN. By Don Munday. London, Hodder, 1948. 268p [Mount Waddington, B.C.] [BM BVaU OTP

**Murdoch, Beamish, 1800–1876**

A HISTORY OF NOVA SCOTIA, OR ACADIE. Halifax, Barnes, 1865–67. 3v [BM BVaU LC NBFU OTP QMM

**Murphy, James, 1867–1931**

A CENTURY OF EVENTS IN NEWFOUNDLAND. St. John's, Author, 1924. 28p [NfSG

ENGLAND'S OLDEST POSSESSION, THE COLONY OF NEWFOUNDLAND. A useful Compilation of Events in her History. ... St. John's, Author, 1924. 42p [NfSM

MURPHY'S OLD SEALING DAYS. St. John's, Murphy, 1916. 46p [NfSM

THE MUSTY PAST. Incidents of Newfoundland History for 73 Years. St. John's, Barnes, 1906. 28p [NfSG

**Murphy, John Michael, 1915–**

THE LONDONDERRY HEIRS. A Story of the Settlement of the Townships of Truro, Onslow, and Londonderry. Truro, N.S., Author, 1960. 133p ["Pub. on the Occasion of Truro's Bicentenary Celebrations, 1960."]

**Namao, Alta. United Farm Women of Alberta, Local No. 61**

A CAMEO OF THE WEST. Story of the Pioneers of the Sturgeon River District, 1879–1900. Edmonton, Commercial Print., 1936. 54p [AEP

**Naramata, B.C. Centennial Committee**

NARAMATA IN RETROSPECT. Namarata, B.C., the Committee, 1958. 15p [mimeographed]

**Nase, Edith Rowena**

WESTFIELD [N.B.]. An Historical Sketch. N.p., Author, [1925?]. 88p [NBSM OTP

**Neal, Frederick**

THE TOWNSHIP OF SANDWICH, PAST AND PRESENT. An Interesting History of the Canadian Frontier along the Detroit River. Ed. by ——. Windsor, Ont., Record Print., 1909. 232p [BM BVaU LC NBFU OTU

**Neal, May**

A SOUVENIR OF REGINA, "QUEEN CITY OF THE PLAINS." Ed. by ——. Regina, Western Printers, 1954. 132p

**Neatby, Leslie Hamilton, 1902–**

IN QUEST OF THE NORTH WEST PASSAGE. Toronto, Longmans, 1958. 194p

THE LINK BETWEEN THE OCEANS. Toronto, Longmans, 1960. 139p [On the search for Sir John Franklin's Expedition.]

**Neilburg, Sask. Jubilee Committee**

A GLANCE BACK, 1955 TO 1905. By Mrs. Jennie Johnson and others. Neilburg, Sask., 1955. 119p [History of Neilburg.]

**Nelson, Denys, 1876–1929**

FORT LANGLEY, 1827–1927. A Century of Settlement in the Valley of the Lower Fraser River. Vancouver, Evans & Hastings, 1927. 31p [BM BVaU LC OTP

**New Brunswick Historical Society**

COLLECTIONS. Saint John, Daily Telegraph, Barnes, 1894–. [A continuing serial.] [BM BVaU NSHD OTP QMSS

LOYALIST SOUVENIR. One Hundred and Fiftieth Anniversary of the Landing of the Loyalists in the Province of New Brunswick, 1783–1933. Saint John, the Society, 1933. 31p [BVaU LC NSHD OLU

LOYALIST'S CENTENNIAL SOUVENIR. ... Saint John, McMillan, 1887. 183p [BVaU NBFU OOA

**New Liskeard, Ont. St. Paul's United Church**

NEW LISKEARD THEN AND NOW. New Liskeard, Ont., [1950?]. 128p [Editor: D.K. Kitchen.] [OONL

**Newmarket, Ont.**

PINE ORCHARD HISTORY, 1800–1936. [Newmarket], Newmarket Era, 1936. 22p [OTU

**Niagara Historical Society**
PUBLICATIONS. ... Niagara, the Society, 1896–. [A continuing serial.] [BVaU LC OTP

**Nicholls, Mrs. Margaret Alexandria, 1915–**
A HISTORY OF NANOOSE BAY. Nanoose Bay, B.C., Nanoose Centennial Committee, 1958. 54p [mimeographed]

**Nickle, Carl Olof, 1914–**
THE VALLEY OF WONDERS. The Story of Turner Valley. Calgary, Oil Bulletin, 1942. 40p [CC

**Nicolls, John Pethybridge, 1870–**
REAL ESTATE VALUES IN VANCOUVER. A Reminiscence. Vancouver, City Archives, 1954. 39p

**Norcross, Elizabeth Blanche, 1920–**
THE WARM LAND. Duncan, B.C., Author, 1959. xi + 112p [History of the Cowichan Valley, B.C.]

**Nordra S.D. No. 1947, Sask. School**
A BRIEF HISTORY OF THE NORDRA DISTRICT. Wynyard, Sask., 1954. 16p

**Norris, Frederick Corbett, 1880–**
THEN AND NOW. A Condensed History of Turtle Mountain Municipality and the Town of Killarney, marking their 75th and 50th Anniversaries, July 11th to 14th, 1957. Comp. and ed. by —— *et al.* Killarney, Man., Killarney Guide, 1957. 125p

**Norrish, Joshua**
THE EARLY HISTORY OF NASAGIWEYA. Guelph, Hough, 1889. 99p [Reprinted in: NASSAGAWEYA CENTENNIAL, 1850–1950; an Historical Volume of Nassagaweya Township in Halton County ... including the Early History of Nassagaweya as Written by the Late Joshua Norrish, an Early Settler. Acton, Ont., Free Press, [1950?]. 90p] [OOA

**North Battleford, Sask. Golden Jubilee Committee**
SKYLINE ... THE PANORAMIC PATTERN OF A CITY. North Battleford's Golden Jubilee Story. Editor and Historic Committee Chairman: C. Irwin McIntosh. North Battleford, McIntosh Pub. Co., 1955. 84p

**Nottawasaga, Ont. Centennial Celebration**
NOTTAWASAGA. The Outburst of the Iroquois. Nottawasaga, Historical Committee, 1934. 122p [OTP

**Nova Scotia Historical Society**
COLLECTIONS. Halifax, Morning Herald, 1879–. [A continuing serial.] [BM BVaU NSHD OTP

**Noyes, John Powell, 1842–1923**

THE CANADIAN LOYALISTS AND EARLY SETTLERS IN THE DISTRICT OF BEDFORD. St. John, Que., the News, 1900. 20p [BVaU LC NSWA OTP QMM

SKETCHES OF SOME EARLY SHEFFORD PIONEERS. [Anon] Montreal, Gazette, 1905. 126p [BVaU OLU

**Oak Bay, B.C. Municipal Council. Anniversary Committee**

THE CORPORATION OF THE DISTRICT OF OAK BAY. Golden Jubilee, 1906–1956: Fifty Years of Growth. Oak Bay, the Council, 1956. 28p

**Oblates of Mary Immaculate. St. Joseph's Colony, Sask.**

RIPENING HARVEST. The Story of St. Joseph's Colony, 1905–1955. Denzil, Sask., 1955. 44p

**Ogema, Sask. School**

OGEMA'S HISTORY. Ogema, Sask., 1955. 23p [mimeographed]

**Ogilvie, William, 1846–1912**

EARLY DAYS ON THE YUKON. The Story of its Gold Finds. Ottawa, Thorburn Abbott, 1913. 306p [BM BVaU LC NSWA OTU QMM

**Okanagan Historical Society. Penticton Branch**

HISTORICAL SOUVENIR OF PENTICTION, B.C., 1908–1958. ... Penticton, City of Penticton, 1958. 164p

**O'Leary, A.E.**

RAMBLES THRO' MEMORY LANE WITH CHARACTERS I KNEW. [Richibucto, N.B.], Author, 1937. 109p [AEU NBSM OTP

**Oliver, Edmund Henry, 1882–1935**

THE CANADIAN NORTHWEST. Its Early Development and Legislative Records, Minutes of the Councils of the Red River Colony. Ed. by ——. Ottawa, Government Print. Bureau, 1914–15. 2v [BM BVaU NSHD OTP

**O'Neill, William John, 1882–**

STEAMBOAT DAYS ON THE SKEENA RIVER, BRITISH COLUMBIA. Ed. by Stan Rough. Kitimat, B.C., Northern Sentinel, 1960. 35p

TIME AND PLACE: STORIES OF NORTHERN BRITISH COLUMBIA. Stories of the West Coast, Skeena River, Bulkley Valley, Douglas Channel, and the old and new Kitimat. By Wiggs O'Neill [and others]. Prince Rupert, priv. print., 1958. 53p

WHITEWATER MEN OF THE SKEENA. Ed. by Stan Rough. Kitimat, B.C., 1960. 28p

**Ontario Centennial Committee, 1892**

CENTENNIAL OF THE PROVINCE OF UPPER CANADA, 1792–1892. ... [Toronto?], Arbuthnot & Adamson, 1893. 33p [NSHD OLU

**Ontario Historical Society**
PAPERS AND RECORDS. ... Toronto, Briggs, 1899–. [A continuing serial.] [BM BVaU NSHD OTU

**Ormsby, Margaret Anchoretta, 1909–**
BRITISH COLUMBIA. A History. Toronto, Macmillan, 1958. x + 558p

**Owen, Egbert Americus, –1908**
PIONEER SKETCHES OF LONG POINT SETTLEMENT; or, Norfolk's Foundation Builders and their Family Genealogies. Toronto, Briggs, 1898. 578p [BVaU LC NBFU OTP

**Owen, William, 1738?–1778**
NARRATIVE OF AMERICAN VOYAGES AND TRAVELS, AND SETTLEMENT OF THE ISLAND OF CAMPOBELLO ... 1766–71. Ed. by V.H. Paltsits. New York, Public Library, 1942. 169p [BM NBFU OTP

**Oxner, Mrs. Effie G., 1874–**
HISTORY OF CHESTER BASIN, 1760–1951. Comp. by Effie Oxner, Olive Turner and Jean Countway. Chester Basin, N.S., 1952. 12p

**Page, Frank E.**
THE STORY OF SMITHVILLE. Welland, Tribune-Telegraph, 1923. 90p [BM BVaU LC OTP

**Pain, Sidney Albert, 1896–**
THREE MILES OF GOLD. The Story of Kirkland Lake. Toronto, Ryerson, 1960. 109p

**Pambrun, Sask. Intermediate School**
THE HISTORY OF PAMBRUN AND ITS COMMUNITY. Comp. by Mrs. E. Mumby and her pupils of Pambrun Intermediate School. Pambrun, Sask., 1957. 31p

**Parker, Gilbert, 1862–1932**
OLD QUEBEC, THE FORTRESS OF NEW FRANCE. By Gilbert Parker and Claude G. Bryan. New York, Macmillan, 1903. 486p [BM BVaU LC NBFU OTP QMM

**Parkinson, Hazel (McDonald), 1898–**
THE MERE LIVING. A Biography of the Hartney District. Altona, Man., D.W. Friesen, 1957. 301p

**Paterson, Gilbert Clarence, 1887–**
LAND SETTLEMENT IN UPPER CANADA 1783–1840. Toronto, James, 1921. 278p [BVaU OLU QMM

**Patterson, Frank Harris, 1891–**
ACADIAN TATAMAGOUCHE AND FORT FRANKLIN. Truro, N.S., Truro Print., 1947. 84p [NSWA OTP

A HISTORY OF TATAMAGOUCHE, NOVA SCOTIA. Halifax, Royal Print., 1917. 143p [BVaU NSWA OTP QMM

**Patterson, Rev. George, 1824–1897**

A HISTORY OF THE COUNTY OF PICTOU. Montreal, Dawson, 1877. 471p [Reprinted: Pictou, "Advocate," 1916. 296p] [BVaU NSWA OTP QMM

SABLE ISLAND. Its History and Phenomena. Montreal, Drysdale; Halifax, Knight, 1894. 49p [BM BVaU LC NSWA OTU

**Patterson, George Geddie, 1864–1951**

MORE STUDIES IN NOVA SCOTIAN HISTORY. Halifax, Imperial, 1941. 180p [BVaU NSWA OTP QMBM

STUDIES IN NOVA SCOTIAN HISTORY. Halifax, Imperial, 1940. 125p [BVaU NSWA OTP

**Payzant, Harry Young, 1881–1953**

"PEOPLE." A Story of the People of Nova Scotia. Truro, N.S., News Pub. Co., 1935. 369p [BM BVaU LC NBFU OTU

**Pearce, F.M.**

EARLY DAYS IN WATERFORD. Waterford, Ont., Author, 1941. 20p [OTP

**Pearson, John, 1900–**

LAND OF THE PEACE ARCH. Cloverdale, B.C., Surrey Centennial Committee, 1958. xii + 159p [History of the Municipal District of Surrey, B.C.]

**Pearson, William Henry, 1831–1920**

RECOLLECTIONS AND RECORDS OF TORONTO OF OLD. With References to Brantford, Kingston and Other ... Towns. Toronto, Briggs, 1914. 372p [BVaU LC OTP

**Pedley, Rev. Charles, 1821–1872**

THE HISTORY OF NEWFOUNDLAND, FROM THE EARLIEST TIMES TO THE YEAR 1860. London, Longmans, 1863. 531p [BM BVaU LC NSWA OTP QMM

**Peel, Bruce Braden, 1916–**

THE SASKATOON STORY, 1882–1952. By Bruce Peel and Eric Knowles. Saskatoon, M.A. East, 1952. 86p

**Pellerin, Mrs. Maude Gage, 1884–**

THE STORY OF HATLEY. Hatley, Que., Author, 1951. 84p

**Perkins, Charlotte Isabella**

THE OLDEST HOUSES ALONG ST. GEORGE STREET, ANNAPOLIS ROYAL, N.S. Saint John, Barnes, 1925. 41p [BM NSWA

THE ROMANCE OF OLD ANNAPOLIS ROYAL, N.S. Annapolis Royal, Author, 1935. 101p [Rev. ed., 1954. 121p] [BVaU NBFU OTP

**Perlin, Albert B., 1901–**

THE STORY OF NEWFOUNDLAND. Comprising a new Outline of the Island's History from 1497 to 1958. ... St. John's, Dicks & Co., 1959. 248p

**Petty, Thomas, 1890–**

ECHOES OF THE QU'APPELLE LAKES DISTRICT. A Guide to Some Historic Sites, Trails and Scenes of the Qu'Appelle Lakes District. Indian Head, Sask., Author, 1955. 55p

**Pick, Harry, 1881–**

NEXT YEAR. A Semi-Historical Account of the Exploitations of the Far-Famed Barr Colonists ... led by an Unscrupulous Church of England Parson ... in the Early Years of the Twentieth Century. Toronto, Ryerson, 1928. 254p [BM BVaU OTU

**Piers, Harry, 1870–1940**

A CHRONOLOGICAL TABLE OF DARTMOUTH, PRESTON, AND LAWRENCETOWN, COUNTY OF HALIFAX, N.S. Halifax, n.p., 1894. 12p [NSWA

THE EVOLUTION OF THE HALIFAX FORTRESS, 1749–1928. ... Ed. by ——. Halifax, Public Archives of Nova Scotia, 1947. 155p [BM BVaU LC NSHD OTP

MASTER GOLDSMITHS AND SILVERSMITHS OF NOVA SCOTIA. Halifax, Antiquarian Club, 1948. 161p [BVaU NSHD OTU

**Pilot Mound, Man. Reunion Committee**

REUNION, PILOT MOUND 50, DISTRICT 75, JULY 1954. Pilot Mound, Man., 1954. 64p [50th Anniversary of the ... Village and 75th of the ... district.]

**Pincher Creek, Alta. Old Timers Association**

PINCHER CREEK OLD TIMERS SOUVENIR ALBUM, 1878–1958. Pincher Creek, Alta., the Association, 1958. 69p

**Piper, William Samuel, 1863–**

THE EAGLE OF THUNDER CAPE. Toronto, Warwick & Rutter, 1926. 301p [BVaU OONL QMBM

**Pirie, Alexander Fraser, 1849–1903**

PICTURESQUE DUNDAS. Dundas, Ont., A.F. Pirie, 1896. 192p [DCB attributes this title to A.F. Pirie, but OLU attributes it to "Charles N. Pirie and W.A. Davidson" as co-compilers.] [DCB OLU

**Plato, Sask. Golden Jubilee Committee**

PLATO, SASKATCHEWAN, 1905–1955. Plato, Sask., 1955. 16p

**Pollard, James B.**

HISTORICAL SKETCH OF THE EASTERN REGIONS OF NEW FRANCE ... ALSO PRINCE EDWARD ISLAND: Military and Civil. ... Charlottetown, Coombs, 1898. 235p [BVaU LC NSWA OTU QMSS

**Ponteix S.D. 2369, Sask. School**

PONTEIX, 1955. Ponteix, Sask., 1955. 24p [mimeographed]

**Poole, Edmund Duval**

ANNALS OF YARMOUTH AND BARRINGTON (NOVA SCOTIA) IN THE REVOLUTIONARY WAR. Comp. by ——, from Original Manuscripts, etc., contained in the Office of the Secretary of the Commonwealth, State House, Boston, Mass. Yarmouth, Lawson, 1899. 133p [LC NSWA OTU

**Poole, Thomas Wesley, 1831?–1905**

A SKETCH OF THE EARLY SETTLEMENT AND SUBSEQUENT PROGRESS OF THE TOWN OF PETERBOROUGH, AND OF EACH TOWNSHIP IN THE COUNTY OF PETERBOROUGH. Peterborough, Review Office, 1867. 220p [A reprint of this work, with additional material bringing the history down to 1941, was published by the Centennial Committee of the Peterborough County Council: Peterborough, Peterborough Print., 1941. 220 + 44 + 72p] [BVaU LC NSWA OTP QMM

**Porcupine, Ont. Golden Anniversary Committee**

SOUVENIR BOOKLET CELEBRATING THE GOLDEN ANNIVERSARY OF THE PORCUPINE GOLD RUSH, JULY 1–5, 1959. [Porcupine, Committee, 1959.] 100p

**Porter, Lancelot, 1882–**

BURTON, BRITISH COLUMBIA: "Our Days Before Yesterday," as told by Bob Hewatson [pseud] to Mrs. H.D. McCormack. Burton, B.C., Burton Centennial Committee, 1958. 31p

**Powell River News**

BRITISH COLUMBIA CENTENNIAL, 1858–1958. Westview, B.C., 1958. 56p

**Powers, John Weston, 1852–1905**

THE HISTORY OF REGINA. Its Foundation and Growth. ... Regina, Leader Co., 1887. 93p [OOA SSU

**Powley, Mrs. Ellen Frances Gladys, 1884–**

EARLY DAYS OF WINFIELD, B.C. Comp. by ——. Winfield, B.C., Women's Institute, 1957. 30p

**Prentice, Wilbur Miller, 1908–**

RANDOM STORIES FROM GEORGIAN BAY. Toronto, Author, 1958. 16p [mimeographed]

**Preston, Richard Arthur, 1910–**

KINGSTON BEFORE THE WAR OF 1812. A Collection of Documents. Ed. by ——. Toronto, Champlain Society for the Government of Ontario, U. of Toronto Press, 1959. cxvi + 428p

ROYAL FORT FRONTENAC. Texts selected and translated from the French by

Richard A. Preston. Ed. with intro. and notes by Leopold Lamontagne. Toronto, Champlain Society for the Government of Ontario, U. of Toronto Press, 1958. xxx + 503p

**Price, Bertha Maud (Weston), 1872–1955**

GLIMPSES INTO THE PAST. Sherbrooke, Que., Daily Record, 1955. 152p [Refers to the Eastern Townships of Quebec.]

**Prince Albert, Sask. Schools**

SASKATCHEWAN GOLDEN JUBILEE PROGRAM, PRINCE ALBERT SCHOOLS, MAY 25, 1955. Prince Albert, 1955. 16p [mimeographed. Chiefly a history of Prince Albert.]

**Prince Edward Island Historical Society**

HISTORIC HIGHLIGHTS OF PRINCE EDWARD ISLAND. Charlottetown, the Society, 1955. 127p [Also: 1956. 98p]

**Pringle, Jacob Farrand, 1816–1901**

LUNENBURGH; or, THE OLD EASTERN DISTRICT. Its Settlement and Early Progress, with Personal Recollections of the Town of Cornwall, from 1824. ... Cornwall, Standard, 1890. 424p [BVaU LC NSHD OTP QMM

**Pritchard, John, 1777–1856**

GLIMPSES OF THE PAST IN THE RED RIVER SETTLEMENT. From Letters ... 1805–1836. Notes by Rev. Dr. Bryce. Middlechurch, Man., Rupert's Land Indian Industrial School Press, 1892. 23p [BViPA OTP

NARRATIVES OF JOHN PRITCHARD, PIERRE CHRYSOLOGUE PAMBRUN, AND FREDERICK DAMIEN HEURTER, Respecting the Aggressions of the North-west Company, against the Earl of Selkirk's Settlement upon Red River. London, Murray, 1819. 91p [BM BViPA LC OTP QMM

**Prowse, Daniel Woodley, 1834–1914**

EPISODES IN OUR EARLY HISTORY. ... St. John's, Nfld., "Morning Chronicle," 1878. 29p [NSHD QMBM

A HISTORY OF NEWFOUNDLAND. ... With a prefatory note by Edmund Gosse. London, Macmillan, 1895. 742p [2nd ed., rev. and corrected: London, Eyre, 1896. 634p] [BM BVaU NSWA OTP QMM

**Prowse, George Robert Farrar, 1860–**

EXPLORATION OF THE GULF OF ST. LAWRENCE, 1499–1525. Winnipeg, Author, 1933. 32p [BM BVaU NSWA OTU

**Pubnico, N.S. Tricentennial Committee**

TRICENTENAIRE DE PUBNICO – PUBNICO'S TERCENTENARY, 1651–1951. Album-Souvenir, Souvenir Booklet, August 21–25, 1951. Pubnico, N.S., 1951. 64p

**Pumphrey, Ronald**

STRANGE FACTS ABOUT NEWFOUNDLAND. By Ron Pumphrey and L.E.F. English. St. John's, Guardian Associates, 1952. 44p

**Puslinch, Ont. Historical Committee**

ANNALS OF PUSLINCH, 1850–1950. Acton, Ont., Free Press, 1950. 120p [OONL

**Quebec, Que.**

REPORT OF THE COMMISSIONERS APPOINTED TO INQUIRE INTO THE CONDUCT OF THE POLICE AUTHORITIES ON THE OCCASION OF THE RIOT AT CHALMERS' CHURCH ON THE 6th OF JUNE, 1853. ... Quebec, Campbell, 1854. 127p [QMM

REPORT OF THE STATE TRIALS before a General Court Martial held in Montreal in 1838–9. Exhibiting a Complete History of the late Rebellion in Lower Canada. Montreal, Armour & Ramsay, 1839. 2v [OTU QMM

**Quene Yip**

VANCOUVER CHINATOWN. Specially Prepared for the Vancouver Golden Jubilee 1886–1936. ... Vancouver, Pacific Printers, 1936. 48p [BViPA

**Quill Lake, Sask. School**

QUILL LAKE HISTORY. A Tribute to the Community and its Builders. Editors, Mrs. B. McBeath and V. Gabriel. Quill Lake, 1955. 47p [mimeographed]

**Raddall, Thomas Head, 1903–**

HALIFAX, WARDEN OF THE NORTH. ... Toronto, McClelland, 1948. 348p [BM BVaU LC NBFU OTP QMM

**Rand, Rev. Silas Tertius, 1810–1889**

A SHORT STATEMENT OF FACTS RELATING TO THE HISTORY, MANNERS, CUSTOMS, LANGUAGE, AND LITERATURE OF THE MICMAC TRIBE OF INDIANS IN NOVA SCOTIA AND P.E. ISLAND. Halifax, Bowes, 1850. 40p [BM NSWA OTP QMM

**Randall, Mrs. Evelina Belle, 1889–**

HEALING WATERS. History of Harrison Hot Springs and Port Douglas Area. Harrison Hot Springs, B.C., Author, 1958. 34p

**Rankin, Rev. Duncan Joseph, 1874–1954**

A HISTORY OF THE COUNTY OF ANTIGONISH, NOVA SCOTIA. Toronto, Macmillan, 1929. 390p [BVaU LC NBFU OKQ QMM

**Rannie, William Fraser, 1915–**

CAVE SPRINGS FARM. Fact and Fancy about one of the Historic Places of the Niagara Peninsula. 2nd ed. Beamsville, Ont., Beamsville Express, 1960. 35p [1st ed., 1952]

**Ravenhill, Alice, 1859–1954**

A CORNER STONE OF CANADIAN CULTURE. An Outline of the Arts and Crafts of the Indian Tribes of British Columbia. Victoria, Banfield, 1944. 103p [BVaU OTP QMM

FOLKLORE OF THE FAR WEST. With Some Clues to Characteristics and Customs. Victoria, n.p., 1953. 87p

THE NATIVE TRIBES OF BRITISH COLUMBIA. Victoria, Banfield, 1938. 142p [BM BVaU LC OTP QMBM

**Raymond, Rev. William Odber, 1853–1923**

GLIMPSES OF THE PAST. History of the River St. John, 1604–1784. Saint John, 1905. 375p [Later pub. under title: THE RIVER ST. JOHN. Its Physical Features, Legends and History from 1604 to 1784. Saint John, Bowes, 1910. 552p Cf. also same title: Sackville, N.B., Tribune Press, 1943. 280p] [BM BVaU LC NBFU OTP QMM

**Ream, Rev. Peter Tennant, 1925–**

THE FORT ON THE SASKATCHEWAN. A History of Fort Saskatchewan. ... Edmonton, Douglas Print. Co., 1957. 155p [With APPENDIX, 1962. 18p]

**Reeves, Helena K.**

IN THE SHADOW OF THE SLEEPING GIANT. An Historical Sketch of Port Arthur, Ontario. Port Arthur, Chamber of Commerce, 1947. 24p [OOA

**Regan, John William, 1873–1945**

DARTMOUTH, NOVA SCOTIA: "The Great Harbour." ... By John Quinpool [pseud]. Halifax, 1942. 24p [LC NSHP OTP

FIRST THINGS IN ACADIA, "THE BIRTHPLACE OF A CONTINENT." ... By John Quinpool [pseud]. Halifax, First Things Pub., 1936. 304p [BM BVaU LC NSWA OTP QMM

HALIFAX, NOVA SCOTIA: "The Great Harbour." ... By John Quinpool [pseud]. Halifax, 1941. 24p [LC NSHP OTP

SKETCHES AND TRADITIONS OF THE NORTHWEST ARM. Halifax, McAlpine, 1908. 191p [BM BVaU LC NSWA OTP QMM

**Reid, William, 1880–**

MEMORIES OF PIONEER DAYS AT PILOT MOUND. [Anon] Pilot Mound, "Sentinel" Print., 1930. 54p [MWP OTP

**Renown, Sask. High School**

RENOWN, OUR STORY. By Students of Grades XI and XII and Teachers of Renown High School. Renown, Sask., 1955. 84 + 12p [mimeographed]

**Revenue, Sask. High School**

REVENUE REMEMBERS, 1905–1955. Revenue, Sask., 1955. 47p [mimeographed]

**Reville, Frederick Douglas, 1866–1944**

HISTORY OF THE COUNTY OF BRANT. Brantford, Hurley, 1920. 2v [BM BVaU OTP QMM

**Reynolds, William Kilby, 1848–1902**

... OLD TIME TRAGEDIES. Celebrated Cases before the Courts in St. John, N.B. ... Saint John, "Progress" Electric Print., 1895. 104p [BVaU NSHD

**Rich, E.E.**

MOOSE FORT JOURNALS 1783–85. Ed. by ——, assisted by A.M. Johnson. London, Hudson's Bay Record Society, 1954. xxx + 392p

**Richardson, Burton Taylor, 1906–**

TORONTO '59. One Hundred and Twenty Fifth Anniversary. Ed. by ——. Toronto, City Council, 1959. 168p

**Rickard, Thomas Arthur, 1864–1953**

HISTORIC BACKGROUNDS OF BRITISH COLUMBIA. Vancouver, Wrigley, 1948. 358p [BVaU NBFU OTP QMM

**Ricker, Jackson**

HISTORICAL SKETCHES OF GLENWOOD AND THE ARGYLES, YARMOUTH COUNTY, NOVA SCOTIA. ... Truro, Truro Print., 1941. 134p [NSHD

**Riddell, Walter, 1814–1904**

HISTORICAL SKETCH OF THE TOWNSHIP OF HAMILTON. Cobourg, 1897. [OOP

**Riddell, William Renwick, 1852–1945**

OLD PROVINCE TALES. Upper Canada. Toronto, Brook, 1920. 280p [LC NSHD OTP QMM

UPPER CANADA SKETCHES. Incidents in the Early Times of the Province. Toronto, Carswell, 1922. 156p [BVaU LC OTP

**Rimbey, Alta. History Committee**

HISTORY OF RIMBEY, ALBERTA. 50 Years of Progress. Rimbey, Alta., 1952. 60p

**Ritchie, Mrs. Mary Houston, –1961**

A TOWNSHIP ON THE LAKE: BEAVERTON AND THORAH, 1820–1952. Beaverton, Ont., [1952?]. 78p

**Roberts, Leslie, 1896–**

THE MACKENZIE. New York, Rinehart, 1949. 276p [BVaU LC NBFU OTP QMM

NORANDA. Toronto, Clarke Irwin, 1956. xiii + 223p

**Robertson, John Ross, 1841–1918**

LANDMARKS OF TORONTO. A Collection of Historical Sketches of the Old Town of York from 1792 until 1833, and of Toronto from 1834 to 1908. Toronto, Author, 1894–1914. 6v [BM BVaU LC NSWA OTU QMM

OLD TORONTO. A Selection of Excerpts from LANDMARKS OF TORONTO. Ed. by E.C. Kyte. Toronto, Macmillan, 1954. xi + 346p

**Robertson, Norman, 1845–1936**

THE HISTORY OF THE COUNTY OF BRUCE. Toronto, Briggs, 1906. 560p [BM BVaU LC NSHD OTU QMSS

**Robinson, Leigh Burpee**

ESQUIMALT. "Place of Shoaling Waters." Victoria, Quality Press, 1947. 126p [BVaU NSHD OTP QMBM

**Robinson, Noel, 1880–**

HISTORY OF THE ART, HISTORICAL AND SCIENTIFIC ASSOCIATION. Vancouver's First Cultural Association. Vancouver, the Association, 1944. 20p [BM BVaU OTP

**Robinson, Percy James, 1873–1953**

TORONTO DURING THE FRENCH REGIME ... 1615–1793. Toronto, Ryerson, 1933. 254p [BM BVaU LC NBFU OTP QMM

**Robinson, Ross, 1904–**

DELISLE AND DISTRICT IN REVIEW. Delisle, Sask., 1955. 32p

**Robsart, Sask. Jubilee Committee**

ROBSART PIONEERS REVIEW THE YEARS. Robsart, Sask., 1956. 115p

**Roche Percée, Sask. School**

HISTORY OF ROCHE PERCEE, SASKATCHEWAN. Roche Percée, Sask., 1955. 14p

**Rockwood-Woodlands Historical Society**

ROCKWOOD ECHOES: 90 YEARS OF PROGRESS, 1870–1960. A History of the Men and Women who Pioneered the Rockwood Municipality. Stonewall, Man., the Society, 1960. 375p

**Roger, Charles, 1819–1878**

OTTAWA PAST AND PRESENT. ... Ottawa, Times Pub. Co., 1871. 124p [BM BVaU OOP

QUEBEC: AS IT WAS, AND AS IT IS. ... 5th ed. Quebec, Author, 1867. 138p [Earlier editions (1857, 1860, etc.) appeared under the name of Willis Russell, but were probably written by Roger.] [BVaU NSWA OTP QMBM

STADACONA DEPICTA; or, Quebec and its Environs. ... Ed. by ——. Quebec, Carey, 1857. 198p [BM OTP QMBM

**Rogers, Grace Dean (McLeod), 1865–1958**

LOUISBURG. Toronto, Ryerson, 1928. 32p [BViP NSWA OTU QMSS

PIONEER MISSIONARIES IN THE ATLANTIC PROVINCES. 1930. Toronto, Ryerson, 1930. 64p [NSWA OTU

**Rogers, Mrs. Mary A.**

THE STORY OF SCOTSGUARD AND VICINITY. By Mrs. Rogers and Mrs. J. Fortney. Scotsguard, Sask., Jubilee Committee, 1955. 20p

**Rome, David**

THE FIRST TWO YEARS. A Record of the Jewish Pioneers on Canada's Pacific Coast, 1858–1860. Montreal, Caiserman, 1942. 120p [BVaU OTP QMM

**Ross, Alan Henderson, 1874–**

REMINISCENCES OF NORTH SYDENHAM. A Retrospective Sketch of the Villages of Leith and Annan, Grey County, Ontario. By A.H.R. Owen Sound, Richardson, Bond & Wright, 1924. 256p [BVaU LC OTP

**Ross, Alexander, 1783–1856**

THE RED RIVER SETTLEMENT. ... London, Smith Elder, 1856. 416p [BM BVaU LC NSWA OTP QMM

**Ross, Alexander Herbert Douglas, –1950**

OTTAWA, PAST AND PRESENT. Toronto, Musson, 1927. 224p [BM BVaU LC NSHD OTP QMM

**Ross, Daniel Keith, 1874–**

THE PIONEERS AND CHURCHES. The Pioneers and Families of Big Brook and West Branch E.R. and Surrounding Sections, including Lorne, Glengarry, Elgin, Centerdale, Hopewell, Marshdale, Foxbrook. New Glasgow, N.S., Hector Pub. Co., 1957. 239p

**Rossland, B.C. Centennial Committee**

THE GOLDEN CITY CENTENNIAL AND FALL FAIR PROGRAMME. ... Rossland, B.C., the Committee, 1958. 27p

**Round Hill, Alta.**

GOLDEN JUBILEE, ROUND HILL, ALBERTA, 1905–1955. N.p., 1955. 16p

**Roy, James Alexander, 1884–**

KINGSTON, THE KING'S TOWN. Toronto, McClelland, 1952. 364p

**Runnalls, Rev. Frank E.**

A HISTORY OF PRINCE GEORGE. Prince George, B.C., Author, 1946. 197p [BVaU LC NBFU OTP QMBM

**Russell, Ralph Clifford**

THE CARLTON TRAIL. The Broad Highway into the Saskatchewan Country from the Red River Settlement, 1840–1880. Saskatoon, Saskatchewan Golden Jubilee Committee, 1955. 102p

**Russell, Willis, 1814–1887**

QUEBEC: AS IT WAS, AND AS IT IS. ... [See under **Roger, Charles.**]

**Rutland, B.C. Centennial Committee**

HISTORY OF THE DISTRICT OF RUTLAND, BRITISH COLUMBIA, 1858–1958. Kelowna, B.C., Orchard City Press, 1958. 127p

**Ryan, Timothy Joseph, 1918–**

VOICES OF THE PAST. A History of Melfort and District. Melfort, Sask., Melfort and District Golden Jubilee Committee, 1955. 138p

**St. Andrews, N.B.**

ST. ANDREWS, NEW BRUNSWICK, ON PASSAMAQUODY BAY. N.p., n.p., n.d. 45p [NSWA

**St. Barbe, Charles, –1929**

FIRST HISTORY OF NELSON, B.C. With Sketches of Some of its Prominent Citizens. ... N.p., Rohrabacher, n.d. 24p [BViPA

**St. Basile, N.B. Madawaska Centennial Exhibition**

MADAWASKA 1859–1959, ST. BASILE, N.B., 4–7 SEPT. [St. Basile, Centennial Exhibition, 1959.] 80p

**St. John, William Charles**

CATECHISM OF THE HISTORY OF NEWFOUNDLAND. ... Rev. ed. Boston, Rand, 1855. 72p [First ed., 1835.] [LC NfSG OTP

**Saint John, N.B.**

OLD TIME TRAGEDIES [in Saint John]. Saint John, 1895. [OOP

ST. JOHN, N.B., CITY OF THE LOYALISTS. N.p., n.p., n.d. 40p [NSWA

**Sandham, Alfred, 1838–1910**

VILLE-MARIE; or, Sketches of Montreal, Past and Present. Montreal, Bishop, 1870. 393p [BM BVaU LC NSWA OTU QMSS

**Santha, Rev. Paul, 1890–**

THREE GENERATIONS, 1901–1957. The Hungarian Colony at Stockholm, Saskatchewan, Canada. Stockholm, Sask., Author, 1959. 94p [Includes the history of St. Elizabeth's Parish.]

**Saskatoon, Sask. Historical Association**

NARRATIVES OF SASKATOON, 1882–1912. By Men of the City. Saskatoon, University Book-store, 1927. [BVaU OTU

**Savary, Alfred William, 1831–1920**

SUPPLEMENT TO THE HISTORY OF THE COUNTY OF ANNAPOLIS [by W.A. Calnek]. ... Toronto, Briggs, 1913. 142p [BVaU LC NSWA OTU

**Sawden, Stephen, 1867–**

HISTORY OF DUFFERIN COUNTY. Orangeville, Ont., Orangeville Banner, 1952. 182p

**Sawdon, Herbert H.**

THE WOODBRIDGE [ONT.] STORY. N.p., [1960?]. 177p

**Sawle, George Robert Tregerthen, 1877–**

HOMETOWN. Historical Sketches of Persons & Spicy Incidents from the late Years of the Nineteenth Century and the early Decades of the Twentieth. Welland, Author, 1959. 92p

**Scadding, Rev. Henry, 1813–1901**

EARLY NOTICES OF TORONTO. Toronto, Chewett, 1865. 26p [BM LC OTP

HISTORY OF THE OLD FRENCH FORT AT TORONTO. Toronto, Copp Clark, 1887. 48p [BVaU LC NSWA OTP QMM

TORONTO OF OLD. Collections and Recollections Illustrative of the Early Settlement and Social Life of the Capital of Ontario. Toronto, Adam & Stevenson, 1873. 594p [BM BVaU LC NBFU OKQ QMM

TORONTO, PAST AND PRESENT. Historical and Descriptive. A Memorial Volume for the Semi-Centennial of 1884. By the Rev. Henry Scadding and John Charles Dent. Toronto, Hunter Rose, 1884. 330p [BM BVaU LC NSWA OTP

TORONTO'S FIRST GERM (FORT TORONTO). ... Toronto, "Guardian" Office, 1878. 12p [BM OTP

**Schofield, Frank Howard, 1859–1929**

THE STORY OF MANITOBA. Winnipeg, Clarke, 1913. 3v [BVaU LC OTP

**Scholefield, Ethelbert Olaf Stuart, 1875–1919**

BRITISH COLUMBIA. From the Earliest Times to the Present. By E.O.S. Scholefield and F.W. Howay. Vancouver, Clarke, 1913. 39p [A prospectus of their proposed four-volume history.] [BVaU QMM

BRITISH COLUMBIA FROM THE EARLIEST TIMES TO THE PRESENT. By E.O.S. Scholefield and F.W. Howay. Vancouver, Clarke, 1914. 4v [BM BVaU LC NBFU OTP QMM

A HISTORY OF BRITISH COLUMBIA. Part One, being a Survey of Events from the Earliest Times down to the Union of the Crown Colony of British Columbia with the Dominion of Canada. By E.O.S. Scholefield. Part Two, being a History ... since Confederation. ... By R.E. Gosnell. Vancouver, B.C. Hist. Assoc., 1913. 436p [BVaU OTP QMM

**Scott, Bertha Isabel, 1881–1946**

SPRINGHILL. A Hilltop in Cumberland. Springhill, N.S., n.p., 1926. 119p [BViP NSHD

**Scott, Duncan Campbell, 1862–1947**

NOTES ON THE MEETING PLACE OF THE FIRST PARLIAMENT OF UPPER CANADA AND THE EARLY BUILDINGS AT NIAGARA. Ottawa, Royal Society, 1913. 15p [NSWA

**Scott, H. Percy, 1856–1937**

HISTORIC DATA OF FORT EDWARD. ... Windsor, N.S., Tribune Pub., [1926]. 16p [Caption title: HISTORIC WINDSOR.] [NSHL

**Scott, James, 1916–**

HURON COUNTY IN PIONEER TIMES. Seaforth, Ont., Huron County Historical Committee, 1954. 87p

**Scott, Richard William, 1825–1913**

THE CHOICE OF THE CAPITAL. Ottawa, Mortimer, 1907. 44p [LC OOA

RECOLLECTIONS OF BYTOWN. Some Incidents in the History of Ottawa. Ottawa, Mortimer Press, [1911]. 31p [BVaU NSWA OTP QMM

**Seaman, Holly Skiff, 1884?–1952**

MANITOBA LANDMARKS AND RED LETTER DAYS, 1610 TO 1920. Winnipeg, n.p., 1920. 92p [BM BVaU NSHD OTP QMBM

**Seary, Edgar Ronald, 1908–**

TOPONYMY OF THE ISLAND OF NEWFOUNDLAND. St. John's, Memorial University, 1959. [mimeographed]

**Seary, Victor Perrin, 1903–**

THE ROMANCE OF THE MARITIME PROVINCES. Toronto, Gage, 1931. 243p [BVaU LC NSHD OLU QMBM

**Sederberg, Mrs. Lilian Margaret, 1926–**

THE SERPENT'S TAIL. Malakwa, B.C., Centennial Committee, 1958. 15p [History of Eagle Valley, B.C.]

**Sellar, Robert, 1841–1919**

THE HISTORY OF THE COUNTY OF HUNTINGDON [Quebec] AND OF THE SEIGNORIES OF CHATEAUGAY AND BEAUHARNOIS. From their First Settlement to the Year 1838. Huntingdon, Que., Canadian Gleaner, 1888. 584p [BVaU LC NSWA OTP QMM

LETTERS RELATIVE TO THE RIGHTS AND PRESENT POSITION OF THE QUEBEC MINORITY. [Huntingdon, Que.], "Gleaner," 1890. 145p [BVaU OTP

THE TRAGEDY OF QUEBEC: THE EXPULSION OF ITS PROTESTANT FARMERS. Huntingdon, Que., "Gleaner," 1907. 120p [Several later editions.] [BM BVaU LC NBFU OTP QMM

THE U.S. CAMPAIGN OF 1813 TO CAPTURE MONTREAL. ... Huntingdon, Que., "Gleaner," 1913. 33p [BM OTU

**Semmens, Rev. John, 1850–1921**

THE FIELD AND THE WORK. Sketches of Missionary Life in the Far North. Toronto, Methodist Book Room, 1884. 199p [BVaU OTP

**Shaunavon, Sask. Public School**

SHAUNAVON, TOWN AND COMMUNITY. Comp. by the pupils of the Shaunavon Public and High Schools. Shaunavon, Sask., 1955. 32p

**Shenston, Thomas Strahan, 1822–1895**

THE OXFORD GAZETTEER. ... History of the County of Oxford. Hamilton, Chatterton & Helliwell, 1852. 216p [BVaU LC NSWA OTP

TELANGOO MISSION SCRAP BOOK. Brantford, Expositor Book & Job Print., 1888. 251p [OLU

**Shepherd, Francis John, 1851–1929**

ORIGIN AND HISTORY OF THE MONTREAL GENERAL HOSPITAL. Montreal, Gazette Print., n.d. 47p [OTU

**Sherk, Michael Gonder, 1862?–1927**

PEN PICTURES OF EARLY PIONEER LIFE IN UPPER CANADA. By a "Canuck" (of the Fifth Generation). Toronto, Briggs, 1905. 280p [BVaU NSWA OTP

**Sherwood, Roland Harold, 1902–**

OUT OF THE PAST. Vignettes of Historical Significance in Pictou County. Pictou, N.S., Coastal Publishers, 1954. 120p

PICTOU PARADE. Sackville, N.B., Tribune Press, 1945. 114p [NBFU OTU

**Shibley, Fred. Warner, 1864–**

ASPINWALL ISLAND. New York, Author, 1916. 167p [OTL

**Shipley, Mrs. R.L.**

FROM OXEN TO AIRPLANE. Mantario, 1908–1950. Ed. by ——. Mantario, Sask., Homemakers' Club, 1950. 104p [Cf. title listed under Mantario, Sask., above.] [OONL

**Shoal Lake, Man. Anniversary Committee**

BRIDGING THE YEARS ... SHOAL LAKE AND DISTRICT. Municipality, 1884–1959, Village, 1904–1959. Brandon, 1959. 31p

**Shufelt, Harry Ball, 1896–**

ALONG THE OLD ROADS. Reflections, Recollections, Romance of Eastern Townships History. Knowlton, Que., 1956. 48p

**Simpson, Jenny Russell**

GUIDE TO THE BYTOWN AND OTTAWA HISTORICAL MUSEUM. Comp. and ed. by the Curator, ——. Ottawa, the Museum, 1929. 31p [LC

**Simpson, John Garbutt, 1889–**

THE STORY OF DUMMER THROUGH THE YEARS. Dummer, Sask., Dummer Ladies' Community Club, 1955. 20p

**Sioux Lookout, Ont. Junior Chamber of Commerce**

SIOUX LOOKOUT, A PROGRESSIVE NORTHWESTERN ONTARIO COMMUNITY. Sioux Lookout, 1953. 19p

**Smallfield, W.E.**

THE STORY OF RENFREW. From the Coming of the First Settlers about 1820. ... By W.E. Smallfield and Rev. Robert Campbell. V.1. Renfrew, Smallfield, 1919. [BM NSHD OTU

**Smith, Alexander William, 1911–**

IN THOSE DAYS. A History of North Hastings and of South Nipissing, by the People Who Live it. Ed. by ——. Bancroft, Ont., the Editor, 1956. 56p [mimeographed]

**Smith, Donald Alexander, 1905–**
AT THE FORKS OF THE GRAND. 20 Historical Essays on Paris, Ontario. By Donald A. Smith, with one essay by John P. Pickell. Paris, Ont., Centennial Committee, 1956. 302p

**Smith, Joseph Henry, 1839–1917**
HISTORICAL SKETCH OF THE COUNTY OF WENTWORTH. Hamilton, County Council, 1897. 140p [OTU

**Smith, Stanley K.**
THE DRAMA OF A CITY. The Story of Stricken Halifax. New York, Weir, 1918. 178p [OTP
HEART THROBS OF THE HALIFAX HORROR. Halifax, Weir, 1918. 120p [On the Halifax explosion] [OTU

**Smith, William Loe, 1855–1945**
THE PIONEERS OF OLD ONTARIO. Toronto, Morang, 1923. 343p [BM BVaU NSHD OTP QMM

**Smith, Rev. William Wye, 1827–1917**
GAZETTEER OF THE COUNTY OF GREY FOR 1865–6. Owen Sound, 1865. 332p [OTU

**Smitheram, Henry Arthur, 1918–**
KNOW THY NEIGHBOUR. Merritt, B.C., Author, 1953. 11p [On Indians of The Nicola Valley, B.C.]

**Smiths Falls, Ont.**
75 YEARS OF PROGRESS, 1882–1957, TOWN OF SMITHS FALLS, INCORPORATED APRIL 25TH, 1882, 75TH BIRTHDAY CELEBRATION, THURSDAY, APRIL 25TH, 1957. Comp. by Mrs. W.A. Graham. Smiths Falls, Record-News Press, 1957. 4p

**Smyth, Fred J.**
TALES OF THE KOOTENAYS. Cranbrook, B.C., Courier, 1938. 200p [2nd ed., 1942] [BM BVaU LC OTP

**Somerville, Alexander, 1811–1885**
NARRATIVE OF THE FENIAN INVASION. Hamilton, Author, 1866. 128p [BM LC OTP

**Sonningdale, Sask. Spartan High School**
THE SONNINGDALE STORY. Sonningdale, Sask., 1955. 22p [mimeographed]

**Southampton, Ont. Centennial Committee**
SOUTHAMPTON CENTENNIAL. Stories of the Past, 1858–1958. Southampton, Ont., 1958. 28p [Prepared by J.F. Morton.]

**South Dumfries, Ont. Centennial Committee**
THE TOWNSHIP OF SOUTH DUMFRIES CENTENNIAL, 1852–1952. South Dumfries, Ont., 1952. 43 + 4p

**Sparling, Mrs. Reita Bambridge**

REMINISCENCES OF THE ROSSBURN PIONEERS. Rossburn, Man., Women's Institute, 1951. 131p

**Spinks, William Ward, 1851–1937**

TALES OF THE BRITISH COLUMBIA FRONTIER. Toronto, Ryerson, 1933. 134p [BM BVaU LC NSHD OTU QMM

**Springfield, P.E.I. Women's Institute**

SPRINGFIELD, 1828–1953. Springfield, P.E.I., 1954. 122p [mimeographed]

**Squair, John, 1850–1928**

THE TOWNSHIPS OF DARLINGTON AND CLARKE ... ONTARIO. ... Toronto, U. of Toronto Press, 1927. 609p [BVaU LC NSHD OTP QMM

**Squamish, B.C. Centennial Committee**

A CENTENNIAL COMMENTARY UPON THE EARLY DAYS OF SQUAMISH, BRITISH COLUMBIA. Squamish, B.C., the Committee, 1958. 32p

**Stanley, George Francis Gilman, 1907–**

THE BIRTH OF WESTERN CANADA. A History of the Riel Rebellion. London, Longmans, 1936. xiv + 475p [Reprinted: Toronto, U. of Toronto Press, 1960.] [BViP NSHPL OTP QMSS

A SHORT HISTORY OF KINGSTON AS A MILITARY AND NAVAL CENTRE. Kingston, Royal Military College, 1950. 37p [Rev. ed., with Richard A. Preston, 1951. 39p] [OONL

**Star City, Sask. Jubilee Editorial Committee**

STAR CITY ... PIONEER DAYS TO JUBILEE YEAR. Star City, Sask., Star City and District Board of Trade, 1955. 201p

**Starratt, Mrs. David, 1842?–**

HISTORY OF FALKLAND RIDGE, ANNAPOLIS COUNTY, NOVA SCOTIA. Ed. by Mary F. Kendrick. N.p. n.p., 1923. 12p [NSWA

**Steen, Ragna, –1962**

PIONEER DAYS IN BARDO, ALBERTA. Including Sketches of Early Surrounding Settlements. By Ragna Steen and Magda Hendrickson. Winnipeg, Dahl, 1944. 228p [SSU

**Steeves, Helen Isabelle (Harper), 1873–**

THE STORY OF MONCTON'S FIRST STORE AND STORE-KEEPER. Life around "the Bend" a Century Ago. Saint John, McMillan, 1924. 178p [BM BVaU LC NBFU OTP QMM

**Stephen, Irene Simmons (Phelan), 1902–**

WINGED CANOES AT NOOTKA AND OTHER STORIES OF THE EVERGREEN COAST. Toronto, Dent, 1955. x + 227p

**Stevens, Arthur Herbert, 1880–**
CLIMAX BEFORE AND AFTER. Comp. by ——. Climax, Sask., Board of Trade, 1955. 12p

**Stevenson, Douglas Andrew, 1888–**
A HISTORY OF THE FONTHILL PUBLIC LIBRARY. Prepared in Celebration of the One Hundredth Anniversary of its Opening—on Feb. 2, 1853. Fonthill, Ont., Library Board, 1953. 25p

**Stewart, David Alexander, 1874–1937**
GLIMPSES AT MANITOBA HISTORY. An Address. Winnipeg, n.p., 1932. 15p [BViPA NSWA OTU

**Stewart, George, 1848–1906**
THE STORY OF THE GREAT FIRE IN ST. JOHN, N.B. JUNE 20, 1877. Toronto, Belford, 1877. 272p [BVaU LC NBFU OTP

**Stewart, Herbert Leslie, 1882–1953**
THE IRISH IN NOVA SCOTIA. Annals of the Charitable Irish Society of Halifax (1786–1836). Kentville, N.S., Kentville Pub. Co., 1949. 199p [NSHD OTP QMM

**Stewart, McLeod, 1847–1926**
THE FIRST HALF CENTURY OF OTTAWA. Ottawa, Esdale, 1910. 84p [BM BVaU LC OTU QMM

**Stewart, William James, 1889–**
FROM WIGWAM TO SKYSCRAPER. Toronto, Centennial Office, 1934. [CC

**Stewart Valley, Sask. School**
CLIMBING THE STAIRS AT STEWART VALLEY. Stewart Valley, 1955. 28p [mimeographed. A history of Stewart Valley.]

**Stewiacke, N.S.**
CELEBRATION OF THE 100TH ANNIVERSARY ... Held on October 6, 1880. Truro, Guardian, 1880. 64p [Also accounts of later celebrations pub. in subsequent years.] [BVaU NSHP

**Stone, Harry A.**
A SHORT HISTORY OF CAULFEILD VILLAGE. Vancouver, Wrigley, [1940?]. 25p [BVaU OOA

**Stone, Sask. Jubilee Committee**
THE STORY OF THE STONE COMMUNITY. Stone, 1956. 12p

**Stout, Clarence H., 1887–**
FROM FRONTIER DAYS IN LEDUC AND DISTRICT. Ed. by ——. Leduc, Alta., 1957. 184p

**Strachan, Rev. John, 1778–1867**

A LETTER to the ... Earl of Selkirk, on his Settlement at the Red River. ... London, Longman, Hurst, Rees, Orme & Brown, 1816. 76p [LC NSWA OTP

**Stratford Police Association**

STRATFORD TOURIST GUIDE. Old Boys Reunion and Centennial Celebration, 1853–1953. [Stratford, Ont., 1953?] 72p

**Stretton, R.W.**

DUNNVILLE, ONTARIO, CENTENNIAL YEAR 1950. 100 Years of Progress. Ed. by ——. Dunnville, Centennial Book Committee, 1950. 112p [OONL

**Summerland, B.C. Board of Trade**

SUMMERLAND GOLDEN JUBILEE, 1906–1956. Summerland, 1956. 28p

**Sussex Emigrants**

EMIGRATION: Letters from Sussex Emigrants ... 1832 ... for Upper Canada. Petworth, Phillips; London, Longman, 1833. 103 + 16p (Intro. signed: T. Sockett, Petworth.) [BM OTP

LETTERS FROM SUSSEX EMIGRANTS... to Upper Canada. Chichester, Mason, 1837. 10p [OTP

**Sutherland, George, 1830–1893**

A MANUAL OF THE GEOGRAPHY AND NATURAL AND CIVIL HISTORY OF PRINCE EDWARD ISLAND. Charlottetown, Ross, 1861. 164p [BM BVaU NSWA OTP

**Sutherland, James**

SUTHERLAND'S CITY OF HAMILTON AND COUNTY OF WENTWORTH DIRECTORY, for 1867–8. Published Annually. Comp. by ——. Ottawa, Hunter Rose; Hamilton, Eastwood, [Preface 1867]. xxxii + 454p [OTP

**Sutton Township, Que.**

SESQUICENTENNIAL OF SUTTON, 1802–1952. Sutton, Que., n.p., 1952. 69p

**Swainson, J.L.**

OUR ANCESTORS ARRIVE IN MANITOBA. Early Settlers of Fort Ellice, Birtle, Russell, Seeburn, Rossburn and Surrounding Districts; also Winnipeg as it was at the Turn of the Century. Winnipeg, De Montfort Press, [1958?]. 70p

**Swallow, Harry Sparling, 1884–**

FROM OX-TRAILS TO HIGHWAYS IN 60 YEARS. Yorkton District. Yorkton, Sask., Author, 1955. 111p

**Swarthmore, Sask. Jubilee Association**

GOLDEN THREADS. The Tapestry of Swarthmore. Swarthmore, 1955. 48p

**Swift Current, Sask. Collegiate Institute**

EVER ONWARD. The Story of the Frontier City. Pub. by the Grade XI and XII students. Swift Current, 1955. 20p [mimeographed]

GOLDEN WAVES. Comp. by the grade ten students. Ed. by Colleen Dand and others. Swift Current, 1955. 46p [mimeographed]

**Swift Current, Sask. Local Council of Women**

GOLDEN FURROWS. [An Historical Chronicle of Swift Current.] Swift Current, 1954. 55p

**Sydney, N.S. Junior Chamber of Commerce**

CAPE BRETON TOURIST GUIDE. 1957. Sydney, 1957. 80p

**Sylvester, Alfred**

SKETCHES OF TORONTO.... Toronto, Holiwell, 1858. 120p [OTP

**Taber, Alta. Booklet Committee**

GOLDEN JUBILEE, COMMEMORATING FIFTY YEARS OF PICTURE HISTORY OF TABER, ALBERTA, 1905–1955. Taber, 1955. 204p

**Tait, Robert Holland**

NEWFOUNDLAND. A Summary of the History and Development of Britain's oldest Colony from 1497 to 1939. [Harrington Park, N.J., Harrington Press, 1939.] 260p [BM LC NfSG OKQ

**Taylor, Andrew Winton, 1907–**

OUR YESTERDAYS. A History of the Township of North Dumfries, Ontario, Canada. 1816–1952. Galt, Ont., Author, 1952. 128p

**Taylor, Conyngham Crawford, 1823–1898**

... TORONTO "CALLED BACK," FROM 1897 TO 1847. Toronto, Briggs, 1887. 398p [Several other editions, with various dates.] [BM BVaU LC NBFU OKQ

**Taylor, Rev. Ernest Manly, 1848–1941**

HISTORY OF BROME COUNTY, QUEBEC, FROM THE DATE OF GRANTS OF LAND THEREIN TO THE PRESENT TIME. With Records of Some Early Families. Montreal, Lovell, 1908–1937. 2v [BM BVaU LC OLU QMM

**Taylor, Gordon de Rupe, 1923–**

DELTA'S CENTURY OF PROGRESS. Cloverdale, B.C., Kerfoot-Holmes Print., 1958. 96p

**Taylor, Henry Edwin, 1889–**

POWELL RIVER'S FIRST 50 YEARS. Comp. by ——. Westview, B.C., Powell River News, 1960. 1v [unpaged]

**Templin, Hugh Charles, 1896–**

A BRIEF HISTORY OF WELLINGTON COUNTY. Fergus, Ont., News-Record, 1946. 28p [OTU

FERGUS, AND THE REBELLION OF 1837. N.p., 1937. 14p [OTU

FERGUS, THE STORY OF A LITTLE TOWN. Fergus, Ont., News-Record, 1933. 311p [BVaU OTU

**Tennant, Joseph Francis, 1848–**

ROUGH TIMES, 1870–1920. ... A Souvenir of the 50th Anniversary of the Red River Expedition and the Formation of the Province of Manitoba. [Winnipeg?], 1920. 271p [AE BViPA OTP SSU

**Texada Island, B.C. Centennial Committee**

TEXADA. Vananda, B.C., the Committee, 1960. xii + 51p

**Thomas, Cyrus, 1836–1908**

CONTRIBUTIONS TO THE HISTORY OF THE EASTERN TOWNSHIPS. Montreal, Lovell, 1866. 376p [BVaU LC MWU NSWA OTP QMM

HISTORY OF THE COUNTIES OF ARGENTEUIL, QUE. AND PRESCOTT, ONT., FROM THE EARLIEST SETTLEMENT TO THE PRESENT. Montreal, Lovell, 1896. 665p [OTP QMM

THE HISTORY OF SHEFFORD. Civil, Ecclesiastical, Biographical and Statistical. Montreal, Lovell, 1877. 143p [NSWA OTP QMM

**Thomas, Lewis Gwynne, 1914–**

THE LIBERAL PARTY IN ALBERTA. A History of Politics in the Province of Alberta, 1905–1921. Toronto, U. of Toronto Press, 1959. xii + 230p

**Thompson, John Henry, 1853–**

JUBILEE HISTORY OF THOROLD TOWNSHIP AND TOWN FROM THE TIME OF THE REDMAN TO THE PRESENT. Thorold, Ont., Thorold Post, 1897–98. 212 + 77p [BM OTU

THIRTY-FIVE YEARS LATER. Supplement to the Jubilee History of Thorold, 1897 to 1932. [Anon] Thorold, Ont., Thorold Post, 1932. 80p [OTU

**Thompson, Muriel Lillian, 1898–**

NEW HOPE ON THE PRAIRIES. A History of Stoughton, Heward, Forget, Handsworth Districts. Weyburn, Sask., Weyburn Review, 1956. 99p

**Thompson, Robert, 1816–**

A BRIEF SKETCH OF THE EARLY HISTORY OF GUELPH. Guelph, Mercury Steam Print., 1877. [Reprinted as AN EARLY VIEW OF GUELPH. Ed. by Hugh Douglass. London, Ont., U. of Western Ontario Library, 1958. 19p] [OTP

**Thomson, Thomas Muir, 1894–**

HAMILTON CITY SKETCHES. Ed. by ——. Hamilton, Board of Education, 1954. 62p

**Tisdale, Sask. Composite School**

FIFTY YEARS ALONG THE DOGHIDE. A History of the Development of Tisdale and District. Tisdale, 1955. 51p

**Tombs, Guy, 1877–**

THE HARBOUR OF MONTREAL. An Address given ... before the St. James Literary Society of Montreal. Montreal, 1932. 56p [OTP QMM

**Toronto, Ont. United Empire Loyalist Centennial Committee**

THE CENTENNIAL OF THE SETTLEMENT OF UPPER CANADA BY UNITED EMPIRE LOYALISTS, 1784–1884. The Celebration at Adolphustown, Toronto and Niagara. With an Appendix containing a Copy of the U.E. List Preserved in the Crown Lands Department at Toronto. ... Toronto, Rose Pub. Co., 1885. 334p [BVaU Brown U OTU

**Townshend, Charles James, 1844–1924**

HISTORY OF THE COURT OF CHANCERY IN NOVA SCOTIA. Toronto, Carswell, 1900. 98p [BVaU LC NSWA

**Toye, William, 1926–**

THE ST. LAWRENCE. Toronto, Oxford U. Press, 1959. 296p

**Trail, B.C. Board of Trade**

TRAIL, B.C. A Brief Story of the History and Development of the Most Important Industrial Center in Interior of British Columbia. Trail, Board of Trade, 1931. 52p [OTP

**Trail, B.C. Golden Jubilee Society**

TRAIL, B.C. A Half Century, 1901–1951. Trail, the Society, [1951?]. 48p

**Tramping Lake, Sask. School**

50 GOLDEN YEARS. Tramping Lake, 1905–1955. Tramping Lake, 1955. 41p [mimeographed]

**Traquair, Ramsay, 1874–**

THE OLD ARCHITECTURE OF QUEBEC. A Study of the Buildings Erected in New France from the Earliest Explorers to the Middle of the Nineteenth century. Toronto, Macmillan, 1947. 324p [BVaU NSHD OLU QMM

THE OLD SILVER OF QUEBEC. ... Toronto, Macmillan, 1940. 169p [BM BVaU NSHD OTU QMM

**Trueman, Howard Thompson, 1837–1908**

THE CHIGNECTO ISTHMUS AND ITS FIRST SETTLERS. Toronto, Briggs, 1902. 268p [BVaU LC NSWA OTU

EARLY AGRICULTURE IN THE ATLANTIC PROVINCES. ... Moncton, "Times" Print., 1907. 131p [NSHD OTU

**Tuck, Clyde Edwin**

HISTORY OF NOVA SCOTIA. V.3 Biographical Sketches. ... [For full entry, see under **Allison, David**, in Local History.]

**Tuck, Esme (Gardner), 1887–**

A BRIEF HISTORY OF POUCE COUPE VILLAGE AND DISTRICT, BRITISH COLUMBIA, CANADA. Pouce Coupé, B.C., Women's Institute, 1954. 28p

**Tucker, Rev. William Bowman, 1859–1934**

THE CAMDEN COLONY; or, The Seed of the Righteous. A Story of the United Empire Loyalists. ... Montreal, Lovell, 1908. 216p [2nd ed. under title: THE ROMANCE OF THE PALATINE MILLERS. ...] [BM BVaU NSHD OTU QMM

THE ROMANCE OF THE PALATINE MILLERS. A Tale of Palatine Irish-Americans and United Empire Loyalists. Montreal, Southam Press, 1929. 369p [2nd ed., rev. and enl., of THE CAMDEN COLONY. ...] [BM BVaU OTUV

**Turner, Adam, 1852–1944**

SOME RAMBLING HISTORICAL NOTES AND REMINISCENCES OF THE EARLY DAYS IN SASKATOON. ... Saskatoon, Modern Press, 1932. 27p [BVaU

**Tutt, Nellie (Hereron), 1895–**

THE HISTORY OF ELLISON DISTRICT, 1858–1958. Comp. by Mrs. D. Tutt. Kelowna, B.C., Ellison Centennial Committee, 1959. 116p

**Tyrrell, Joseph Burr, 1858–1957**

DOCUMENTS RELATING TO THE EARLY HISTORY OF HUDSON BAY. Ed. by ——. Toronto, Champlain Society, 1931. 419p [BM BVaU NSHD OTP

**Upton, Primrose (Walker), 1915–**

THE HISTORY OF OKANAGAN MISSION. A Centennial Retrospect. Okanagan Mission, B.C., Centennial Committee, 1958. 81p

**Ure, George P., –1860**

THE HAND-BOOK OF TORONTO. By a Member of the Press [pseud]. Toronto, Lovell & Gibson, 1858. 272p [OTP QMM

**Uttley, William Velores, 1865–1944**

A HISTORY OF KITCHENER, ONTARIO. Kitchener, Chronicle, 1937. 433p [BVaU LC OKQ

**Val Marie, Sask. High School**

VAL-ECHO. A History of Val Marie. By the Teachers and Pupils of Val Marie High School. Val Marie, "Val-Echo," 1955. 61p [mimeographed]

**Vallance, James Dunlop, 1903–**

UNTRODDEN WAYS. Victoria, Hebden Print., 1958. 150p [History of British Columbia.]

**Van Cortlandt, Gertrude**
RECORDS OF THE RISE AND PROGRESS OF THE CITY OF OTTAWA. Ottawa, Citizen. 1858. 23p [LC OTP QMM

**Vancouver Exhibition Association**
VANCOUVER EXHIBITION ASSOCIATION 1886–1936. Fifty Years of Progress. Vancouver, The Assoc., 1936. 47p [OTP

**Vernon, Rev. Charles William, 1871–1934**
CAPE BRETON, CANADA, AT THE BEGINNING OF THE TWENTIETH CENTURY. Toronto, Nation Pub. Co., 1903. 337p [BVaU LC NSWA OTU QMM

**Vibank, Sask. Elsas High School**
VIBANK. Vibank, 1955. 52p [mimeographed]

**Virgin, Victor Ernest, 1892–**
HISTORY OF NORTH AND SOUTH SAANICH PIONEERS AND DISTRICT. Victoria, Saanich Pioneer Soc., 1959. 79p

**Viscount, Sask. Golden Jubilee Committee**
THE VISCOUNT STORY. Viscount, 1955. 64p

**Waddington, Alfred Penderill, 1801–1872**
THE FRASER MINES VINDICATED; or, The History of Four Months. Victoria, P. De Garro, 1858. 49p [Reprinted: Vancouver, Private Press of Robert R. Reid, 1949. With an intro. by W.K. Lamb. xv + 95p] [BVaU OTP QMM
THE NECESSITY OF REFORM. A Tract for the Times. Addressed to the Colonists of Vancouver Island. By One of the People [pseud]. Victoria, British Colonist Office, 1859. 15p [BVaU NSWA OOA

**Wade, Lennie D.**
HISTORIC GLIMPSES OF PICTURESQUE BEAR RIVER, NOVA SCOTIA. [Digby, Courier Press, 1907?]. 34p [NSHL

**Wade, Mark Sweeten, 1858–1929**
THE FOUNDING OF KAMLOOPS. A Story of 100 Years Ago. Kamloops, Inland Sentinel, [1912]. 15p [BVaU LC OTU
THE THOMPSON COUNTRY. Being Notes on the History of Southern British Columbia, and particularly the City of Kamloops. Kamloops, Inland Sentinel, 1907. 136p [BVaU LC NSHD OTU

**Wade, Robert William Gorman, 1884–**
EARLY HISTORY OF HOWICK TOWNSHIP IN HURON COUNTY. Gorrie, Ont., priv. print., 1952. 64p

**Walbran, John Thomas, 1848–1913**

BRITISH COLUMBIA COAST NAMES, 1592–1906. Ottawa, Govt. Print. Bureau, 1909. 546p [BVaU LC NBFU OTU QMM

**Waldie, Jean Hall, 1916–**

THE COUNTY OF BRANT. Centennial Sketches. Brantford, Brant County Council, 1952. 51p

**Wales, Benjamin Nathaniel, 1851–**

MEMORIES OF OLD ST. ANDREWS AND HISTORICAL SKETCHES OF THE SEIGNIORY OF ARGENTEUIL. Lachute, Watchman Press, 1934. 135p [BVaU OTU QMM

**Walkem, William Wymond, 1850–1919**

STORIES OF EARLY BRITISH COLUMBIA. Vancouver, News-Advertiser, 1914. 287p [BVaU LC NBFU

**Walker, Harry James William, 1892–**

THE OTTAWA STORY THROUGH 150 YEARS. Ottawa, Ottawa Journal, 1953. 94p

RENFREW AND ITS FAIR THROUGH 100 YEARS. Renfrew, Ont., South Renfrew Agricultural Society, [1953]. 104p

**Wallace, Frederick William, 1886–1958**

THE ROMANCE OF A GREAT PORT. The Story of St. John, N.B. Saint John, Barnes, 1935. 64p [BViP LC NSWA OTU QMSS

**Wallace, James Nevin, 1871–1941**

THE WINTERING PARTNERS ON PEACE RIVER. From the Earliest Records to the Union in 1821. With a Summary of the Dunvegan Journal, 1806. ... Ottawa, Thorburn & Abbott, 1929. 139p [BM BViPA LC NBFU OTP

**Walter, Margaret (Shaw)**

EARLY DAYS AMONG THE GULF ISLANDS OF B.C. Victoria, Diggon-Hibben, 1946. 68p [2nd ed., Victoria, Hebden Print. Co., [1959?]. 67p] [BVaU LC OTP

**Walton, Avis Carroll, 1911–**

ABOUT VICTORIA AND VANCOUVER ISLAND. Ed. by ——. [2nd ed.] Victoria, New Neighbour Services, 1958. 212p

**Walton, Jesse M.**

THE STORY OF KETTLEBY. Aurora, Ont., Banner Press, [1939?]. 28p [NBFU OTP

**Warburton, Alexander Bannerman, 1852–1929**

A HISTORY OF PRINCE EDWARD ISLAND FROM ITS DISCOVERY IN 1534 UNTIL THE DEPARTURE OF LIEUTENANT-GOVERNOR READY IN A.D. 1831. Saint John, Barnes, 1923. 494p [BM BVaU LC NSWA OTU QMM

PRINCE EDWARD ISLAND. A Historical Sketch. Charlottetown, 1906. 59p [NSHD

**Ward, Edmund, 1787–1853**
AN ACCOUNT OF THE RIVER ST. JOHN, WITH ITS TRIBUTARY RIVERS AND LAKES. Fredericton, Sentinel, 1841. 96p [LC NSHD OTU

**Warman, Sask. School**
WARMAN'S 50 YEARS OF PROGRESS. From Ox-cart to Airplane. Warman, 1955. 20p [mimeographed]

**Warnock, Amelia Beers, 1878–1956**
TORONTO. Romance of a Great City. By Katherine Hale [pseud]. Toronto, Cassell, 1956. 262p

**Warnock, Robert**
A SKETCH OF THE COUNTY OF HALTON, CANADA WEST. Toronto, Leader Steam-Press, 1862. 56p [OTP

**Waterford and Townsend, Ont. Old Timers**
OLD TIMERS' REUNION, WATERFORD AND TOWNSEND [1878–1960]. Waterford, Ont., 1960. 92p

**Waterloo, Ont. Centennial Advertising Committee**
WATERLOO 1857–1957. Centennial Band and Folk Festival ... Souvenir Programme. Waterloo, the Committee, 1957. 98p

**Waterloo, Ont. Trust and Savings Company**
A GUIDE TO PLEASANT PLACES AND JOURNEYS OF HISTORIC INTEREST WITHIN THE COUNTY OF WATERLOO. Waterloo, Ont., the Company, 1956. 46p

**Watson, Omar Kern, 1869–**
MEMORIES OF THE OLD HOME TOWN–RIDGETOWN, 1930. Comp. by ——. Ridgetown, Dominion, 1930. 71p [OTP

**Watson, Robert, 1882–1948**
FAMOUS FORTS OF MANITOBA. Winnipeg, Dept. of Education, 1929. 29p [BVa
LOWER FORT GARRY. A History of the Stone Fort. Winnipeg, Hudson's Bay Co., 1928. 69p [BVaU LC NSHD OTU

**Weaver, Emily Poynton, 1865–1943**
OLD QUEBEC, THE CITY OF CHAMPLAIN. Illus. by Annie E. Weaver. Toronto, Briggs, 1907. 60p [BVaU OTP QMM
THE STORY OF THE COUNTIES OF ONTARIO. Toronto, Bell & Cockburn, 1913. 318p [BVaU OTU QMM

**Weber, Manasseh, 1872–1957**
SUCH WAS LIFE. Calgary, 1956. 72p [Rhymed history of Didsbury, Alta.]

**Webster, Mrs. Deborah**
THE THOMSON HOUSE, CHARLOTTE LANE, SHELBURNE, NOVA SCOTIA. ... Rev. ed. Shelburne, Historical Society, 1955. 11p [First ed. 1949.]

**Webster, John Clarence, 1863–1950**

ACADIA AT THE END OF THE SEVENTEENTH CENTURY. Letters, Journals and Memoirs of Joseph Robineau de Villebon, Commandant in Acadia, 1690–1700. Saint John, New Brunswick Museum, 1934. 232p [BVaU LC NSWA OLU QMM

THE BUILDING OF FORT LAWRENCE IN CHIGNECTO. ... Ed. by ——. Saint John, New Brunswick Museum, 1941. 23p [BVaU LC NSWA OTP QMBM

THE FORTS OF CHIGNECTO. A Study of the Eighteenth Century Conflict between France and Great Britain in Acadia. ... Shediac, N.B., Author, 1930. 142p [BM BVaU NBFU OTU QMM

AN HISTORICAL GUIDE TO NEW BRUNSWICK. Fredericton, New Brunswick Tourist Assoc., 1928. 106p [Rev. eds. 1930, 1936, 1938, 1942, 1944.] [BM BVaU LC NSWA OTU QMM

HISTORY IN A GOVERNMENT HOUSE. [Halifax?], 1926. 16p [NSWA OTU

A HISTORY OF SHEDIAC, NEW BRUNSWICK. Shediac, N.B., priv. print., 1928. 22p [Reprinted by the New Brunswick Museum, 1953.] [BM BVaU LC NSWA OLU QMM

THE RECAPTURE OF ST. JOHN'S, NEWFOUNDLAND, IN 1762, AS DESCRIBED IN THE JOURNAL OF LT.-COL. WILLIAM AMHERST. Ed. by ——. Shediac, N.B., Author, 1928. [BM NBFU OLU

SOME EPISODES IN THE RELATION BETWEEN THE MARITIME PROVINCES AND THE AMERICAN ATLANTIC STATES. N.p., [1927?]. 20p [BM NSHD OTP QMM

**Weir, Rev. F.G.**

SCUGOG AND ITS ENVIRONS. Port Perry, Ont., Star Print., 1927. 143p [BVaU OTU

**Welland, Ont. Centennial Committee**

SOUVENIR BOOKLET. Welland, Ont., 1958. 83p [Cover title: "Welland Centennial, 1858–1958."]

**Wellington County, Ont. Centennial Committee**

CENTENNIAL, 1854–1954, THE COUNTY OF WELLINGTON. Fergus, Ont., 1954. 28p

**Wells, Catherine Boott (Gannett), 1838–1911**

CAMPOBELLO. An Historical Sketch. By Kate Gannett Wells. [Boston, 1893]. 47p [LC NSWA OTU QMM

**Wells, William Benjamin, 1809–1881**

CANADIANA. Containing Sketches of Upper Canada, and the Crisis in its Political Affairs. ... London, Reynell, 1837. 2 Parts: 84p and 85–202p [BVaU LC OTP

**Wessel, Mrs. H.**

SAGA OF WESTWOLD. By Mrs. H. Wessel, Mrs. L. Jones and Mrs. L. Ness. Westwold, B.C., Women's Institute, 1954. 12p

**Wetherell, Margaret Hubner (Smith), –1933**

JUBILEE HISTORY OF THOROLD TOWNSHIP. ... Thorold, Ont., Post Print., 1897. 212p [Another ed., 1933.] [OTU

**Wetmore, Ralph W.**

HISTORICAL MEMOIRS OF CLIFTON, N.B. Saint John, Day, 1912. 32p [NBSM OTU

**Wetton, Cecilia (Chidlow), 1893–**

HISTORIC BATTLEFORD. Through the Years, 1875–1955. Battleford, Sask., Board of Trade Jubilee Committee, 1955. 72p

THE PROMISED LAND. The Story of the Barr Colonists. Lloydminster, Sask., Times, 1953. 73p

**Weyburn, Sask. Golden Jubilee Committee**

PIONEER DAYS OF WEYBURN. Weyburn, 1955. 40p

**Whidden, David Graham, 1857–1941**

THE HISTORY OF THE TOWN OF ANTIGONISH. Wolfville, 1934. 209p [BVaU LC NSWA OTU QMM

**Whitby, Ont. Centennial Committee**

WHITBY, ONTARIO, CANADA, THE TOWN OF OPPORTUNITY, RESIDENTIAL, INDUSTRIAL. Ed. by Charles H. Chaytor. Whitby, 1955. 68p

**White, G.A.**

HALIFAX AND ITS BUSINESS. An Historical Sketch and Description of the City. Halifax, Nova Scotia Print., 1876. 173p [NSHD OLU

**White, James, 1863–1928**

PLACE-NAMES IN GEORGIAN BAY. Toronto, Ontario Hist. Soc., 1913. 81p [BVaU LC

PLACE NAMES [IN] QUEBEC, THE THOUSAND ISLANDS, AND NORTHERN CANADA. Ottawa, [Govt. Print. Bureau?], 1910. 302p [BVa NBFU OTU QMM

PLACE-NAMES IN THE THOUSAND ISLANDS, ST. LAWRENCE RIVER. Ottawa, Govt. Print. Bureau, 1910. 7p [BM BVaU LC OOA QMM

**White, Walter Sydney, 1909–**

PAGES FROM THE HISTORY OF SOREL, 1642–1958. Sorel, Que., Author, n.d. 175p

**Whittaker, Lance H.**

ROSSLAND, THE GOLDEN CITY. Ed. by ——. Rossland, Rossland Miner, 1949. [BVaU OTP

**Whitton, Charlotte Elizabeth, 1896–**

A HUNDRED YEARS A-FELLIN'. Some Passages from the Timber Saga of the Ottawa in the Century ... 1842–1942. Comp. by ——. Ottawa, Runge Press, 1943. 172p [BVaU OKQ

"I BELONG ON THE OTTAWA." A Few Odd Jottings for the Casual Visitor taken from the Notebooks of Her Worship, the Mayor of Ottawa, and reproduced herewith from Articles appearing in the Ottawa Citizen in 1950–51. Ottawa, 1952. 12p

**Wilkes, Rev. Frederick Alfred, 1919–**

THEY ROSE FROM THE DUST. Saskatoon, Modern Press, 1958. 249p [An account of pioneer days in south central Saskatchewan.]

**Wilkie, Sask. Jubilee Committee**

DISTRICT OF WILKIE, SASKATCHEWAN. Ed. and comp. by W.A. Hook and others. Wilkie, Historical Section of the Jubilee Committee, 1955. 45p

**Wilkinson, Douglas, 1919–**

LAND OF THE LONG DAY. Toronto, Clarke Irwin, 1955. 261p [Account of a year spent on Baffin Island.]

**Williamson, Owen Templeton Garrett, 1883–**

THE NORTHLAND. The Romance of Northern Ontario. Toronto, Ryerson, 1946. 110p [BVaU LC OTP QMM

**Willoughby, J.**

THE LAND OF THE MAYFLOWER; or, The Past and Present of Nova Scotia. Halifax, Barnes, 1860. 64p [NSWA OTP

**Willson, (Henry) Beckles, 1869–1942**

NOVA SCOTIA. The Province That has been Passed By. London, Constable, 1911. 256p [BM BVaU LC NSWA OTU QMM

QUEBEC. The Laurentian Province. Toronto, Bell & Cockburn, 1912. 271p [BM BVaU LC NSHD OLU QMM

THE TENTH ISLAND. Being some Account of Newfoundland, its People, its Politics, its Problems, and its Peculiarities. London, Richards, 1897. 208p [Rev. ed.: THE TRUTH ABOUT NEWFOUNDLAND. ... London, Richards, 1901. 228p] [BM BVaU LC NSWA OLU QMM

**Wilson, Andrew**

A HISTORY OF OLD BYTOWN AND VICINITY, NOW THE CITY OF OTTAWA. ... Ottawa, "News," 1876. 89p [NSWA OTU

**Wilson, Ann MacLean**

HISTORY OF "BLANSHARD IN REVIEW," 1951. Comp. by ——. Blanshard Township, Ont., Historical Committee, 1951. 111p

**Wilson, Isaiah Woodworth, 1848–1928**

A GEOGRAPHY AND HISTORY OF THE COUNTY OF DIGBY, NOVA SCOTIA. Halifax, Holloway, 1900. 471p [BVaU LC NSWA OTU

**Wilson, Lawrence Maurice, 1896–**

THIS WAS MONTREAL IN 1814, 1815, 1816 AND 1817. (Life in Canada's Metropolis as culled Verbatim from the Editorial, News and Advertising Columns of *The Montreal Herald*.) Comp. by ——. Montreal, priv. print., 1960. 205p

**Wilton Rural Municipality No. 472, Sask.**
RURAL MUNICIPALITY OF WILTON, NO. 472, MARSHALL, SASKATCHEWAN, 1905–1955. ... Marshall, 1955. 36p

**Wingfield, Alexander Hamilton, 1898–**
THE HAMILTON CENTENNIAL, 1846–1946. Ed. by ——. [Hamilton], Hamilton Centennial Committee, 1946. 122p [LC OOA

**Winkler, Man. Burwalde School District**
DIAMOND JUBILEE YEAR BOOK OF THE BURWALDE SCHOOL AT WINKLER, MANITOBA, 1888–1948. [Winkler?], 1948. 48p [SSU

**Winnipeg Daily Tribune**
CITY OF WINNIPEG. ... A General Historical, Statistical, and Descriptive Review. Winnipeg, Daily Tribune, 1891. 26p [NSWA OLU

**Wintemberg, William John, 1876–1941**
FOLK-LORE OF WATERLOO COUNTY, ONTARIO. Ottawa, King's Printer, 1950. 68p [BM BVaU OLU

**Winter, James Spearman, 1845–1911**
FRENCH TREATY RIGHTS IN NEWFOUNDLAND. The Case for the Colony stated by the People's Delegates, Sir J.S. Winter ... P.J. Scott ... and A.B. Morine. London, King, 1890. 130p [BM BVaU OTP

**Women's Institute. Canada. Arundel Women's Institute, Que.**
ARUNDEL, QUEBEC, CANADA, 1856–1954. Arundel, Que., the Institute, 1954. 35p

**Women's Institute. Canada. Bancroft Women's Institute, Alta.**
THE HERITAGE OF BANCROFT. Calgary, the Institute, [1961?]. 276p

**Women's Institute. Canada. Bessborough Women's Institute, B.C.**
THE BESSBOROUGH DISTRICT. Comp. June 1958, in Recognition of the British Columbia Centennial. Bessborough, the Institute, 1958. 19p [mimeographed]

**Women's Institute. Canada. Bounty Homemakers' Club, Sask.**
BOUNTY. Bounty, Sask., the Club, 1956. 331p [History of the Bounty District, Sask.]

**Women's Institute. Canada. Burnham Homemakers' Club, Sask.**
50 YEARS ALONG THE CUTBANK. Comp. by Mrs. Edna B. Linklater. Burnham, Sask., the Club, 1955. 16p

**Women's Institute. Canada. Crapaud Women's Institute, P.E.I.**
HISTORY OF CRAPAUD, PRINCE EDWARD ISLAND. Crapaud, the Institute, 1958. 129p

**Women's Institute. Canada. Fruitvale Women's Institute, B.C.**
HISTORY OF BEAVER VALLEY & PEND d'OREILLE DISTRICTS. Fruitvale, B.C., the Institute, 1958. 16p

**Women's Institute. Canada. Great Village Women's Institute, N.S.**
GREAT VILLAGE HISTORY. Commemorating the 40th Anniversary of Great Village Women's Institute, 1920–1960. ... Great Village, N.S., the Institute, 1960. 155p

**Women's Institute. Canada. Hamiota Women's Institute, Man.**
A HISTORY OF HAMIOTA VILLAGE AND MUNICIPALITY, 1879–1956. Hamiota, Man., the Institute, [1956?]. 1v [unpaged].

**Women's Institute. Canada. Jonesville Homemakers' Club, Sask.**
A HISTORY OF BEECHY, SASK. AND DISTRICT. Beechy, the Club, 1955. 66p

**Women's Institute. Canada. Louisbourg Women's Institute, N.S.**
LOUISBOURG, 1758–1958. Louisbourg, the Institute, 1958. 89p

**Women's Institute. Canada. Port Clyde Women's Institute, N.S.**
HISTORY OF PORT CLYDE. Shelburne, N.S., 1954. 82p

**Women's Institute. Canada. Tregarva Homemakers' Club, Sask.**
THIS IS TREGARVA. Tregarva, the Club, 1956. 39p

**Wood, Louis Aubrey Lorne, 1883–1955**
THE RED RIVER COLONY. A Chronicle of the Beginnings of Manitoba. Toronto, Glasgow Brook, 1915. 152p [BM BVaU LC NSWA OTU QMM

**Wood, William Charles Henry, 1864–1947**
THE GREAT FORTRESS. A Chronicle of Louisbourg 1720–1760. ... Toronto, Glasgow Brook, 1915. 144p [BM BVaU LC NSWA OTU QMSS
IN THE HEART OF OLD CANADA. Toronto, Briggs, 1913. 310p [BVaU LC NSHD OTP
THE STORIED PROVINCE OF QUEBEC, PAST AND PRESENT. Ed. by ——. Toronto, Dominion, 1931–32. 5v [BM BVaU LC NBFU OOA QMM
UNIQUE QUEBEC. A Vade-Mecum. Quebec, Lit. & Hist. Society of Quebec, 1924. 109p [BM BVaU LC NSWA OTP QMM

**Wood, William Robertson, 1874–1947**
PAST YEARS IN PICKERING. Sketches of the History of the Community. Toronto, Briggs, 1911. 316p [BVaU LC NSHD OTU

**Wood River, Sask. Old Timers' Association. Historical Committee**
PIONEER DAYS IN WOOD RIVER DISTRICT. Comp. by Historical Committee, Wood River Old Timers' Association, and George Douglas. Ed. by Allan R. Turner. Saskatoon, the Association, 1960. 116p

**Woodley, Rev. Edward Carruthers, 1878–1955**

CANADA'S ROMANTIC HERITAGE. The Story of New France. Toronto, Dent, 1940. 288p [BM BVaU OTP

OLD QUEBEC. Trails and Homes. Toronto, Ryerson, 1946. 137p [BVaU LC OTP QMM

THE PROVINCE OF QUEBEC THROUGH FOUR CENTURIES. ... Toronto, Gage, 1944. 230p [LC OTP

**Woodrow, James**

SAINT JOHN: PAST AND FUTURE. Readings in Congregational Church. ... Saint John, "Globe" Press, 1882. 24p [NBSaM

**Woods, John Jex, 1895–**

THE AGASSIZ-HARRISON VALLEY. History and Development. 2nd ed. Sidney, B.C., pub. for the Kent Centennial Committee by the Peninsula Print. Co., 1958. 113p

HISTORY AND DEVELOPMENT OF AGASSIZ-HARRISON VALLEY. Agassiz, Agassiz-Harrison Advance, 1941. 68p [BVaU OTU

**Woods, Robert Stuart, 1819–1906**

HARRISON HALL AND ITS ASSOCIATIONS; or, A History of the Municipal, Judicial, and Educational Interests of the Western Peninsula. ... Chatham, Ont., Planet, 1896. 150p [Early history of Kent County, etc.] [BVaU NSHD OLU QMM

**Woods, William Carson, 1860–1902**

THE ISLE OF THE MASSACRE. [Adapted from the French of the late J.C. Taché.] Toronto, Publishers Synd., 1901. 98p [BVaU NBFU OTU

**Worden, Marquis Dufferin**

THE STORY OF VANSCOY COMMUNITY. Vanscoy, Sask., Ladies Service Club, 1955. 23p

**Wright, Arthur Walker, 1855–1944**

MEMORIES OF MOUNT FOREST AND SURROUNDING TOWNSHIPS, Minto, Arthur, West Luther, Normanby, Egremont, Proton. ... Ed. by ——. Mount Forest, Ont., the Confederate, [1928?]. 202p [OTP

NOW AND THEN: PIONEER JOURNALISM IN THE COUNTY OF WELLINGTON. Prepared for the Ontario Historical Society. N.p., n.d. 25p [OTU

PIONEER DAYS IN NICHOL ... FERGUS, ELORA AND SALEM TOWNSHIPS. Ed. by ——. Mount Forest, Ont., Editor, 1924. 132p [2nd ed., enl.: 1933. 313p] [BM BVaU LC OKQ

SKETCHES OF THE EARLY DAYS OF FERGUS AND VICINITY. Comp. by ——. Mount Forest, Ont., n.d. 128p [OOA

**Wright, Esther Isabell (Clark), 1895–**

BLOMIDON ROSE. Toronto, Ryerson, 1957. 206p [Account of Cape Blomidon and the Annapolis Valley, Nova Scotia.]

THE MIRAMICHI. A Study of the New Brunswick River and of the People who Settled along it. Sackville, Tribune Press, 1944. 79p [LC NSWA OLU QMM

THE PETITCODIAC. A Study of the New Brunswick River and the People who Settled along it. Sackville, Tribune Press, 1945. 72p [BVaU NSWA OTP QMM

THE SAINT JOHN RIVER. Toronto, McClelland, 1949. 254p [NSWA OTP QMM

**Wright, James Frederick Church, 1904–**

SASKATCHEWAN, THE HISTORY OF A PROVINCE. Toronto, McClelland, 1955. xi + 292p

**Wright, Norman Ernest**

IN VIEW OF THE TURTLE HILL. A Survey of the History of Southwestern Manitoba to 1900. Deloraine, Man., Times Pub. Co., 1951. 146p

**Yarmouth, N.S. Town Council**

YARMOUTH'S 175TH ANNIVERSARY, 1936. ... [Kentville, Kentville Pub., 1936]. 94p [BViP NSHL OTP

**Youmans, Harriet Phelps**

GRIMSBY PARK, HISTORICAL AND DESCRIPTIVE. Toronto, Briggs, 1900. 75p [BM OTU

**Young, Archibald Hope, 1863–1935**

THE PARISH REGISTER OF KINGSTON, UPPER CANADA, 1785–1811. Ed. with Notes and intro. by ——. Kingston, "British Whig," 1921. 207p [BM BVaU NSHD OTU QMSS

**Young, Cecil J.**

OAKVILLE'S 100 YEARS, 1857–1957. [N.p., Author, 1957?] 48p

**Young, Ewart, 1913–**

CORNER BROOK, NEWFOUNDLAND, 1923–1948. 25 Years of Progress. [Corner Brook, Western Pub., 1948?]. 64p [NfSG OOA

ST. JOHN'S, NEWFOUNDLAND, CAPITAL OF CANADA'S NEWEST PROVINCE. [Montreal, Guardian Associates, 1949.] 64p ["3rd printing": St. John's, Guardian Ltd., 1955.] [NfSM OOA

THIS IS NEWFOUNDLAND. Ed. by ——. With a Prologue by E.J. Pratt. ... Toronto, Ryerson, 1949. 104p [BVaU LC NSHD OLU QMM

**Young, George Renny, 1802–1853**

... THE "ESCHEAT QUESTION" IN THE ISLAND OF PRINCE EDWARD ISLAND. Together with the Causes of the Late Agitation. ... London, Swale, 1838. 72p [BM OTP

**Young, James, 1835–1913**

REMINISCENCES OF THE EARLY HISTORY OF GALT AND THE SETTLEMENT OF DUMFRIES. Toronto, Hunter Rose, 1880. 272p [BM BVaU LC NSWA OTU

**Young, William Frederick Hackett, 1898–**
HISTORICAL DIRECTORY, CHIPPAWA CENTENNIAL–ANNIVERSARY, 1850–1950. "The Romance of a Village." Comp. by ——. Chippawa, Ont., F.H. Young, Associates, 1950. 32p [OONL

**Zelma, Sask. Homemakers' Club**
THE COMMUNITY OF ZELMA, 1904–1949. Saskatoon, Saskatoon Printers, 1949. 26p [ACG BVa OOP SRL

**Zurich, Ont. Historical Committee**
A CENTURY OF PROGRESS, ZURICH 1856–1956. Zurich, 1956. 64p

# RELIGION AND MORALITY

## Sermons, denominational history, histories of local churches, doctrine, controversy, homiletics, etc.

**Adams, Frank Dawson, 1859–1942**

A HISTORY OF CHRIST CHURCH CATHEDRAL, MONTREAL. Montreal, Burton's Ltd., 1941. 226p [BVaU LC OTP

**Adams, Robert Chamblet, 1839–**

EVOLUTION: A SUMMARY OF EVIDENCE. A Lecture. ... New York, Putnam, 1883. 44p [BM LC

GOOD WITHOUT GOD. New York, Eckler, 1902. 113p [LC

PIONEER PITH. The Gist of Lectures on Rationalism. New York, Truth Seeker Co., [1889]. 99p [OLU QMSS

TRAVELS IN FAITH FROM TRADITION TO REASON. New York, Putnam, 1884. 238p [BM LC

**Adamson, Rev. William Agar, 1800–1868**

THINGS TO BE REMEMBERED. A Sermon. Montreal, Armour & Ramsay, 1846. 29p [NSWA QMSS

**Aitken, Everett Melville, 1899–**

A WORLD IN WAITING. Toronto, Ryerson, 1952. 87p

**Aiton, Grace**

HISTORY OF ST. PAUL'S UNITED CHURCH, SUSSEX, N.B. Sussex, The Church, 1949. 51p [OTU

**Akins, Thomas Beamish, 1809–1891**

A SKETCH OF THE RISE AND PROGRESS OF THE CHURCH OF ENGLAND IN THE BRITISH NORTH AMERICAN PROVINCES. Halifax, Cunnabell, 1849. 151p [NSWA OTP QMM

**Alexander, William Hardy, 1878–1962**

COLLEGE AND RELIGION. Talks to College Students. Boston, Badger, 1920. 107p [LC OOCC

**Allan, William, 1885–1939**

CROWDED WAYS. A Second Series of Meditations Broadcast from ... CFRB, Toronto. Toronto, Nelson, 1935. 147p [BM BViP OTU

MEMORIES OF BLINKBONNIE. A Second Book of Musings. Toronto, Nelson, 1939. 117p [BVaU NBFU OTU

MUSINGS. Toronto, Nelson, 1937. 125p [OTU

THE QUIET PLACE. Toronto, Nelson, 1933. 127p [NBFU OTU

**Allen, Grant, 1848–1899**

THE EVOLUTION OF THE IDEA OF GOD. New York, Holt, 1897. 447p [Rev. and abridged by Franklin P. Richards. London, Watts, 1903.] [BM BVaU LC NSHD OTU

THE EVOLUTIONIST AT LARGE. New York, Fitzgerald, 1881. 50p [Same title: London, Chatto, 1881. 215p] [BM LC OTU

THE NEW HEDONISM. New York, Tucker, 1900. 30p [LC

**Alley, Herbert Ruttan, 1892–**

THINKING OF ROME? Think Twice! Toronto, United Church Pub. House, 1958. 68p

**Alline, Rev. Henry, 1748–1784**

THE ANTI-TRADITIONALIST. [Halifax, Anthony Henry, 1783.] 70p [Tremaine

A GOSPEL CALL TO SINNERS. A Sermon. Newburyport, Blunt & March, 1795. 35p [NSWA

A SERMON ON A DAY OF THANKSGIVING PREACHED AT LIVERPOOL. Halifax, Henry, 1782. 40p [LC

A SERMON PREACHED ON THE 19TH OF FEB. 1783, AT FORT MIDWAY. Halifax, Henry, 1783. 44p [NSHP

A SERMON PREACHED TO, AND AT THE REQUEST OF, A RELIGIOUS SOCIETY OF YOUNG MEN ... IN LIVERPOOL. Halifax, Henry, 1782. 36p [NSWA

TWO MITES ON SOME OF THE MOST IMPORTANT AND MUCH DISPUTED POINTS OF DIVINITY. Halifax, Henry, 1781. 342p [Reprinted as TWO MITES CAST INTO THE OFFERING. ... By Henry Alline. ... With some amendments by Benjamin Randle. Dover, N.H., 1804. 250p] [NSHD

**Anderson, Rev. Arthur Edward Oswald**

SAINT PETER'S, CARLINGTON, OTTAWA, 1921–1951. Ottawa, Author, 1951. 12p

**Anderson, Rev. David, 1814–1885**

BRITAIN'S ANSWER TO THE NATIONS. A Missionary Sermon. London, Hatchard, 1857. 36p [BM BViPA OTP

CHILDREN INSTEAD OF FATHERS. ... London, Hatchard, 1854. 32p [BM BViPA OTP

CHRISTIAN PRIVILEGE AND DUTY. A Sermon preached in St. John's Cathedral, Red River Settlement ... May 10th, 1868. ... Winnipeg, Nor'Western Office, 1868. 11p [OOA

THE CIRCLE OF LIGHT; or, The Conjuror's Confession. London, Hatchard, 1857. 16p [BM

FAITHFUL AND FRUITFUL. Two Sermons. ... Bristol, Chillcott, 1872. 38p [BM

THE GOSPEL IN THE REGIONS BEYOND. ... London, Hatchard, 1874. 16p [BM OTP

THE HEART GIVEN TO GOD AND THE WORK. ... London, Hatchard, 1857. 24p [BM BViPA OTP

PAPAMAS; or, The Chief's Address. London, Hatchard, 1857. 16p [BM

THE SEAL OF APOSTLESHIP. London, Hatchard, 1851. 31p [BM MWP OTP

THE TRUTH AND THE CONSCIENCE. ... London, Hatchard, 1861. 35p [BM OTP

TWO SERMONS PREACHED IN ST. JAMES' MEMORIAL CHURCH, CLIFTON. ... London, Hamilton Adams, 1876. 31p [BM

THE WINNER OF SOULS. ... London, Hatchard, 1856. 32p [BM OTP

THE WORDS OF THE WISE. ... London, R.T.S., 1857. 30p [BM

**Anglican Church of Canada. Dioceses. Nova Scotia**

TWO HUNDRED AND FIFTY YEARS YOUNG. Our Diocesan Story, 1710–1960. Halifax, 1960. 168p

**Angwin, J.G.**

METHODISM IN CAPE BRETON, 1789–1914. A Retrospect. ... Sydney Mines, 1914. 65p [BVaU NSHD OLU

**Anonymous**

THE EPISCOPAL CONTROVERSY. Being a Series of Letters written by the Respective Friends of the Ven. Archdeacon Bethune and Dr. Cronyn, the two Candidates for the Bishopric of the Western Diocese. London, Ont., Free Press, 1857. 79p [OTU

EPISCOPAL TESTIMONIES AGAINST DOCTRINES ADVOCATED IN THE "TRACTS FOR THE TIMES" PUBLISHED AT OXFORD. Kingston, The Times, 1844. 32p [OTU

THE JUDGMENTS OF THE CANADIAN BISHOPS, on ... Trinity College in Relation to the Theological Teaching of the College. Toronto, Rowsell & Ellis, 1863. 24p [OTU

REMARKS ON A PAMPHLET ENTITLED "POPERY CONDEMNED BY SCRIPTURE AND THE FATHERS." Halifax, Howe, 1809. 403p [NSWA

A VOICE FROM THE WILDERNESS OF CANADA. Addressed to All in General, and Presbyterians in Particular. Toronto, Globe Print., 1870. 234p [BVaU OTP

**Armitage, Rev. William James, 1860–1929**

THE CHURCH YEAR STUDIES FOR THE SUNDAYS, SACRED SEASONS AND SAINTS' DAYS OF THE CHRISTIAN YEAR. Oxford, Frowde, 1908. 229p [BM NSWA

THE CITIES OF REFUGE. Pictures of Gospel Principles, Gospel Promises, and Gospel Privileges. London, Marshall, 1908., 88p [BM NSWA OLU

THE FRUIT OF THE SPIRIT. London, Marshall, 1909. 104p [First pub. 1907.] [BM LC NSWA

THE SOLDIERS OF THE KING. ... London, Marshall, n.d. 135p [BM NSWA

THE STORY OF THE CANADIAN REVISION OF THE PRAYER BOOK. Cambridge, Eng., Cambridge U. Press, 1922. 442p [BM BVaU LC NSWA OTU QMM

**Armstrong, Mrs. Allan**

WAWEIG UNITED CHURCH THROUGH THE YEARS, 1848–1948. Waweig, N.B., The Church, 1949. 36p [OTU

**Armstrong, Rev. Maurice Whitman, 1905–1968**

THE GREAT AWAKENING IN NOVA SCOTIA, 1776–1809. Hartford, Conn., Am. Soc. of Church History, 1947. 141p [AEU LC NBSM OTU

THE PRESBYTERIAN ENTERPRISE. Sources of American Presbyterian History. Ed. by Maurice W. Armstrong, Lefferts A. Loetscher and Charles A. Anderson. Philadelphia, Westminster Press, 1956. 336p

**Atkinson, Rev. Abraham Fuller, 1803?–1866**

THE LEADING DOCTRINES OF THE GOSPEL. Montreal, Armour & Ramsay, 1836. 24p [NSWA OTP

**Austin, Rev. Benjamin Fish, 1850–1932**

GLIMPSES OF THE UNSEEN. Toronto, Bradley-Garretson, 1898. 504p [BM

THE GOSPEL TO THE POOR VERSUS PEW RENTS. Toronto, Briggs, 1884. 110p [OTP

THE JESUITS. Their Origin, History, Aims, Principles, Immoral Teaching. London, Ont., Advertiser, 1889. 40p [BVaU NSWA OTU QMSS

THE METHODIST EPISCOPAL PULPIT. A Volume of Sermons by the Members of the Niagara and Bay of Quinte Conferences. ... V. 1. Toronto, Hunter, 1879. 315p [OTU

POPULAR SINS. A Series of Sermons against the Sins of the Times. Toronto, Hunter Rose, 1880. 115p [OTUV

WHAT CONVERTED ME TO SPIRITUALISM. Toronto, Austin, 1901. 205p [BM

**Aylmer, Que. United Church**

LIVING STONES IN A SPIRITUAL HOME. The History of Aylmer United Church, 1828–1956. Aylmer, 1956. 16p

**Bagnall, Lucy A. (Lowe)**

AT THE SIXTIETH MILESTONE. The Story of the First Baptist Church, Calgary, Alberta, 1888–1948. Calgary, First Baptist Church, 1948. 81p [AC

**Bagnall, Rev. Walter E.**

ST. JOHN'S CHURCH, PRESTON, ONTARIO. Forty Five Years. Toronto, Livingstone, 1935. 30p [OTU

**Baker, Ida Emma (Fitch), 1858–1948**

HOW THEY FOUND JESUS. Toronto, Mundy, n.d. 121p [OTU

**Baldwin, Rev. Maurice Scollard, 1836–1904**

A BREAK IN THE OCEAN CABLE. 3rd ed., rev. Montreal, 1880. [BM OOP

A LIFE IN A LOOK. Montreal, Dawson, 1879. 113p [Also: Toronto, Briggs, n.d. 104p] [BM BVaU NSWA OLU

**Ballantyne, Murray, 1909–**

ALL OR NOTHING. New York, Sheed & Ward, 1956. 216p

**Banner, Ont. United Church**

CENTENNIAL, 1857–1957, BANNER UNITED CHURCH. Banner, [1957?]. 34p

**Bannister, J.A.**

A CENTENNIAL HISTORY OF GRACE UNITED CHURCH, PORT DOVER, ONTARIO, 1847–1947. Port Dover, Author, 1947. 24p [OTP

**Barber, Frank Louis, 1877–1945**

THE PHILOSOPHY OF JOHN WESLEY. Toronto, Ryerson, 1923. 19p [BM OTUV

**Barclay, Rev. John, 1812–1887**

THRONE ESTABLISHED BY RIGHTEOUSNESS. ... A Discourse preached ... on ... the Anniversary of the Birthday of ... Queen Victoria. Toronto, Lovell & Gibson, 1863. 24p [NSHD OTU

THE TIMES OF OLD AND THEIR HAPPY MEMORIES. A Discourse ... preached on the Occasion of the ... Tricentenary of the Scottish Reformation. Toronto, Leader, 1861. 46p [NSWA QMSS

**Barnhill, William Perley, 1897–**

THE FIRST UNITED BAPTIST CHURCH, LANCASTER, NEW BRUNSWICK. Historical Record [1881–1956]. Comp. by ——. Ed. by W. Gordon Ross and Stanley C. Ross. Lancaster, N.B., the Church, 1956. 18 + 22 + 9p [mimeographed]

**Barrett, F.**

A BRIEF HISTORY OF METHODISM IN WINDSOR, NOVA SCOTIA ... 1782–1925. Windsor, N.S., Hants Journal Press, 1925. 62p [NSWA

**Barrowclough, Edna I. (Hill), 1902–**

THE STORY OF WESLEYVILLE UNITED CHURCH AND ITS PEOPLE. Port Hope, Ont., the Author, 1960. 45p

**Bates, Walter, 1760–1842**

A SERIOUS CONFERENCE ... ON THE SUBJECT OF RELIGIOUS WORSHIP. Saint John, Durant, 1826. 80p [OTU

**Bayer, Charles Walter, 1893–**

CHRIST CHURCH, DARTMOUTH, NOVA SCOTIA, 1817 TO 1959. Dartmouth, the Church, 1960. 165p

**Bayne, Rev. John, 1806–1859**

IS MAN RESPONSIBLE FOR HIS BELIEF? Galt, Ainslie, 1851. 32p [Also included in George Smellie's MEMOIR OF ... JOHN BAYNE, *q.v.*] [BVaU NSWA OTP

WAS THE RECENT DISRUPTION OF THE SYNOD IN CANADA, IN CONNECTION WITH THE CHURCH OF SCOTLAND, CALLED FOR? An Address to the Presbyterians of Canada. ... [Anon] Galt, Ainslie, 1846. 83p [OTU

**Beadle, The Venerable (pseud)**

A SEASONABLE SHOVE TO THE MEMBERS OF THE ANGLICAN CHURCH IN THE DIOCESE OF QUEBEC. Quebec, Middleton, 1858. 30p [NSWA

**Beattie, Rev. Francis Robert, 1848–1906**

APOLOGETICS; or, THE RATIONAL VINDICATION OF CHRISTIANITY. Richmond, Va., Presbyterian Committee of Publications, 1903. 605p [LC OTU

EXAMINATION OF THE UTILITARIAN THEORY OF MORALS. Brantford, Sutherland, 1885. 222p [OTU QMM

THE HIGHER CRITICISM. Modern Critical Theories as to the Origin and Contents of the Literature and Religion found in the Holy Scriptures. Toronto, Briggs, 1888. 56p [OLU

THE PRESBYTERIAN STANDARDS. An Exposition of the Westminster Confession of Faith and Catechisms. Richmond, Va., Presbyterian Committee of Publications, 1896. [OTUV

**Beaubien, Père Irénée, 1916–**

TOWARDS CHRISTIAN UNITY IN CANADA. A Catholic Approach. Montreal, Palm Publisher [*sic*], 1956. 184p

**Beaven, Rev. James, 1801–1875**

"ASK FOR THE OLD PATHS." Cobourg, Diocesan Press, 1844. 19p [NSWA OTP

ELEMENTS OF NATURAL THEOLOGY. London, Rivington, 1850. 240p [OTP

S. IRENAEUS, BISHOP OF LYONS. The Doctrine, Discipline, Practices, and History of the Church, and the Tenets and Practices of the Gnostic Heretics, During the Second Century. London, Rivington, 1841. xxviii + 334p [LC

"THAT THEY ALL MAY BE ONE." Toronto, Rowsell & Ellis, 1859. 16p [NSWA OTP

**Beck, Lily Adams (Moresby), –1931**

THE LIFE OF THE BUDDHA. London, Collins, 1939. 287p [BM LC QMSS

THE SPLENDOUR OF ASIA. The Story and Teaching of the Buddha. New York, Dodd Mead, 1926. 269p [Repub. as THE LIFE OF THE BUDDHA. With an intro. by George F. Maine. London, Collins, 1959. xxxix + 256p] [BM BVaU LC NSHD OONL QMM

THE STORY OF ORIENTAL PHILOSOPHY. New York, Cosmopolitan Book, 1928. 429p [BM BVaU LC NBFU OTU QMM

THE WAY OF POWER. Studies in the Occult. New York, Cosmopolitan Book, 1928. 285p [BM LC QMM

**Bellamy, Lora (Davis), 1855–1937**

PIONEER DAYS OF THE FIRST BAPTIST CHURCH IN NORTHERN ALBERTA. Edmonton, 1925. 15p [History of First Baptist Church in Edmonton.] [AE

**Bennett, Rev. James, 1817–1901**

THE WISDOM OF THE KING; or, Studies in Ecclesiastes. Edinburgh, Oliphant, 1870. 426p [EngCat NBB

**Bentley, Mrs. Verna Bessie, 1904–**

ST. BARNABAS' CHURCH, Fiftieth Anniversary, 1885–1935. By Mrs. O.C. Bentley. Toronto, The Church, 1935. 15p [OTP

**Bentom, Rev. Clark**

A STATEMENT OF FACTS AND LAW. Relative to the Prosecution of the Rev. Clark Bentom, Protestant Missionary from the London Missionary Society, for the Assumption of the Office of a Dissenting Minister of the Gospel in Quebec, by the King's Attorney General of Lower Canada. Troy, N.Y., Penniman, 1804. 32p [BM LC OTP

TALEBEARING A GREAT SIN. A Sermon preached Lord's Day, February 22, 1801. ... Quebec, Neilson, 1801. 31p [OTP

**Berry, Rev. William George, 1903–**

THIS INCREDIBLE THING–EVANGELISM. Toronto, Ryerson, 1959. ix + 32p

**Bethune, Rev. Alexander Neil, 1800–1879**

THE CHURCH OF THE LIVING GOD. A Sermon preached ... in St. Peter's Church, Cobourg. Toronto, Rowsell, 1864. 12p [NSWA OTP

THE CLERGY RESERVE QUESTION IN CANADA. London, Clay, 1853. 24p [BM BVaU OTU QMM

FOUR SERMONS ON THE HOLY SACRAMENT OF THE LORD'S SUPPER. Toronto, Plees, 1852. 52p [OTUV

LECTURES, EXPOSITORY AND PRACTICAL, ON THE LITURGY OF THE CHURCH OF ENGLAND. Toronto, Rowsell, 1862. 170p [BM BVaU NSWA OLU QMBM

LECTURES UPON HISTORICAL PORTIONS OF THE OLD TESTAMENT. New York, Stanford, 1857. 213p [OLU

NATIONAL JUDGMENTS PROVOKED BY NATIONAL SINS. Cobourg, Chatterton, 1838. 24p [BM

A SERMON PREACHED IN ST. PETER'S CHURCH, COBOURG, U.C., on ... the day appointed for a general thanksgiving to Almighty God for having removed the heavy judgments with which these provinces have recently been afflicted. Cobourg, Chatterton, 1833. 22p [OTP

SERMONS ON THE LITURGY OF THE CHURCH OF ENGLAND. York, Stanton, 1829. 76p [OTP

THOUGHTS UPON THE LAWFULNESS AND EXPEDIENCY OF CHURCH ESTABLISHMENTS ... in a Letter to C.A. Hagerman. Cobourg, Chatterton, 1836. 32p [OTP

**Bethune, Rev. John, 1791–1872**

BAPTIST MISREPRESENTATION ON BAPTISM, WITH AN EXPOSURE OF THE SYSTEMATIC POLICY OF BAPTIST CHURCH PUBLICATIONS OF MISQUOTATIONS &C. Toronto, Presbyterian Print. House, 1876. 176p [BVaU OTU

A SERMON PREACHED AT BROCKVILLE, U.C., on the 18th of June, 1816, being a Day of General Thanksgiving. Montreal, Gray, 1816. 25p [OKQ

A SERMON PREACHED IN CHRIST'S CHURCH, MONTREAL, on Friday, the 4th May, 1832. Being the Day Appointed for a Public Fast, Occasioned by the Apprehension of being Visited by the Pestilence which is Scourging the Nations of Europe. Montreal, Bull, 1832. 19p [QMM

A SERMON PREACHED ON WEDNESDAY, FEBRUARY 6, 1833. Being the Day appointed ... for a General Thanksgiving to Almighty God for having Removed the Heavy Judgment of the Pestilence. Montreal, Armour, 1833. 16p [QMM

**Bettridge, Rev. William Craddock, 1791–1879**

A BRIEF HISTORY OF THE CHURCH IN UPPER CANADA. ... London, Painter, 1838. 143p [BM BVaU LC NSWA OOP QMM

**Bezanson, Rev. W.B.**

FUEL FOR MISSIONS. Kentville, Kentville Pub. Co., 1934. 60p [OTP

**Bill, Rev. Ingraham E., 1805–1891**

FIFTY YEARS WITH THE BAPTIST MINISTERS AND CHURCHES OF THE MARITIME PROVINCES OF CANADA. Saint John, Barnes, 1880. 778p [BM BVaU NSHD OTU

**Black, William G.**

THE CHURCH AND SOCIAL PROBLEMS. Brantford, Ont., Baptist Federation of Canada, 1959. 48p

**Bland, Salem Goldworth, 1859–1950**

THE NEW CHRISTIANITY; or, The Religion of the New Age. Toronto, McClelland, 1920. 168p [BM BVaU OTUV

**Blewett, George John, 1873–1912**

THE CHRISTIAN VIEW OF THE WORLD. Nathaniel William Taylor Lectures for 1910–1911, Delivered before the Divinity School of Yale University. New Haven, Yale U. Press, 1912. 344p [BM BVaU LC OTU

THE STUDY OF NATURE AND THE VISION OF GOD. With Other Essays in Philosophy. Toronto, Briggs, 1907. 358p [BM BVaU LC OTU QMM

**Bompas, Rev. William Carpenter, 1834–1906**

DIOCESE OF MACKENZIE RIVER. London, S.P.C.K., 1888. 108p [BM BVaU NSWA OLU

NORTHERN LIGHTS ON THE BIBLE. Drawn from a Bishop's Experience during Twenty-Five Years in the Great Northwest. London, Nisbet, 1893. 211p [BM BVaU OKQ

**Boniface, Father, 1880–**

THE HISTORY OF SAINT FRANCIS PARISH, VANCOUVER. Vancouver, 1959. xii + 174p

**Bonis, Rev. Robert Raynes, 1906–**

THE STORY OF ST. MARGARET'S CHURCH, WEST HILL, AND THE PARISH OF SCARBOROUGH, 1833–1953. West Hill, St. Margaret's Church, 1953. 19p

**Borland, Rev. John, 1809–1888**

AN APPEAL TO THE MONTREAL CONFERENCE AND METHODIST CHURCH

GENERALLY FROM A CHARGE BY REV. WILLIAM SCOTT. Montreal, "Witness," 1883. 40p [NSWA OTP

DIALOGUES BETWEEN TWO METHODISTS. ... Toronto, Author, 1856. 46p [OTP

LETTERS TO A MEMBER OF THE WESLYAN METHODIST CHURCH. Montreal, "Witness," 1873. 43p [NSWA

OBSERVATIONS ON THE MORAL AGENCY OF MAN ... in which the Obliquity of Universalism is Exhibited. ... Sherbrooke, Walton, 1848. 161p [NSWA OTP

**Borthwick, Rev. John Douglas, 1832–1912**

HISTORY OF THE DIOCESE OF MONTREAL, 1850–1910. Montreal, Lovell, 1910. 230p [BVaU LC OTU

**Bovell, James, 1817–1880**

DEFENCE OF DOCTRINAL STATEMENTS. Addressed to the Right Rev. the Lord Bishop of Toronto, the Right Rev. the Lord Bishop of Huron, and the Corporation of Trinity College. ... Toronto, Rowsell & Ellis, 1860. 60p [OTP

LETTERS, Addressed to the Rev. Mr. Fletcher and Others, Framers of a Series of Resolutions on "Ritual." Toronto, Hill, 1867. 64p [OTP

OUTLINES OF NATURAL THEOLOGY FOR THE USE OF THE CANADIAN STUDENT. ... Toronto, Rowsell & Ellis, 1859. 649p [NSHD OTP

PASSING THOUGHTS ON MAN'S RELATION TO GOD AND ON GOD'S RELATION TO MAN. Toronto, Rowsell & Ellis, 1862. 427p [OTP

PREPARATION FOR THE CHRISTIAN SACRIFICE; OR, HOLY COMMUNION. Toronto, Rowsell, 1859. 294p [OTTC

THE WORLD AT THE ADVENT OF THE LORD JESUS. Toronto, Chewett, 1868. 412p [OTU QMM

**Brady, Buckskin**

STORIES AND SERMONS BY BUCKSKIN BRADY, THE COWBOY EVANGELIST. Toronto, Briggs, 1905. 135p [BM LC

**Braeside, Ont. Braeside United Church**

HISTORY OF THE BRAESIDE UNITED CHURCH, FORMERLY THE BRAESIDE PRESBYTERIAN CHURCH, 1885–1952. Braeside, the Church, 1952. 23p

**Brandon, Horace G.**

THE THREE LAST BATTLES. A Prophetic Preview of the Last Three Struggles of a Dying World Order, Covered up in Symbolic Terms as "Wind," "Earthquake" and "Fire." Comp. from the Scriptures and arranged by ——. Vancouver, Ireland & Allan Ltd., n.d. xiii + 209p

**Bready, John Wesley, 1887–1953**

THIS FREEDOM–WHENCE? With an intro. by Rutherford L. Decker. 12th print., rev. Winona Lake, Indiana, Light and Life Press, 1950. xviii + 365p [Abridgment and revision of his ENGLAND: BEFORE AND AFTER WESLEY. London, Hodder, 1938.] [OONL

**Breckenridge, Rev. James, –1879**
PREDESTINATION. A Sermon. Toronto, Presbyterian Print., 1876. 50p [BVaU

**Brewing, Rev. Willard, 1881–**
FAITH FOR THESE TIMES. London, Collins, 1945. 159p [BVaU OTP

**Brice, Edward, 1879–**
THE HISTORY OF THE WORLD A.D. 1960 TO A.D. 2000. Edmonton, Author, 1960. 249p [On history and Biblical prophecy.]

**Brigstocke, Rev. Frederick Hervey John, 1841–1899**
HISTORY OF TRINITY CHURCH, SAINT JOHN, NEW BRUNSWICK, 1791–1891. Comp. and ed. by ——. Saint John, McMillan, 1892. 202p [BVaU NSHD OOA

**Broadus, Eleanor (Hammond)**
A BOOK OF THE CHRIST CHILD. New York, Appleton, 1910. 158p [BM LC

**Brooker, Bertram, 1888–1955**
ELIJAH. With illustrated drawings. New York, Rudge, 1930. 26p [LC OTUV

**Brosnan, Rev. Michael, 1894?–1943**
PIONEER HISTORY OF ST. GEORGE'S DIOCESE, NEWFOUNDLAND. [Toronto, Western Pub. Co., 1948.] 172p [NBFL OOA

**Broughall, James Samuel, 1866–**
OUTLINE OF THE HISTORY OF GRACE CHURCH-ON-THE-HILL, TORONTO 1911–1932. Toronto, Author, 1932. 19p [OTU

**Brown, Rev. Andrew, –1834**
THE PERILS OF THE TIME, AND THE PURPOSES FOR WHICH THEY ARE APPOINTED. A Sermon. ... Halifax, Howe & M'Kinstry, 1795. 40p [NSHD

**Brown, Arnold, 1913–**
WHAT HATH GOD WROUGHT? The History of the Salvation Army in Canada. Toronto, Salvation Army Print. and Pub. House, 1952. 130p [2nd ed., 1957]

**Brown, Rev. John Willoughby, 1857–1940**
AN HISTORICAL SKETCH OF THE EARLY SETTLEMENT OF NEW CANAAN [N.B.] AND THE HISTORIES OF THE NEW CANAAN, HAVELOCK, AND ALBERT BAPTIST CHURCHES. N.p., [1905?]. 39p [NSWA

**Brown, Rev. Robert Christopher Lundin, –1876**
THE LIFE OF PEACE. London, Masters, 1876. 160p [BM

**Bryce, Rev. George, 1844–1931**
THE PRESBYTERIAN CHURCH IN CANADA, AND THE CANADIAN NORTH-WEST. Toronto, British American Presbyterian Office, 1875. 21p [LC NSWA OTUV

**Bryden, Rev. Walter Williamson, 1883–1952**
SEPARATED UNTO THE GOSPEL. Toronto, Burns & MacEachern, 1956. xiv + 218p

**Brymner, Douglas, 1823–1902**

ENDOWMENTS OF THE CHURCH OF SCOTLAND IN CANADA. Toronto, Hunter, 1883. 42p [OTU QMBM

FAULTS AND FAILURES OF THE LATE PRESBYTERIAN UNION IN CANADA. London, Ont., Free Press, 1879. 43p [OTU

**Bucke, Richard Maurice, 1837–1902**

MAN'S MORAL NATURE. An Essay. New York, Putnam, 1879. 200p [BM BVaU LC OTU QMM

THE MORAL NATURE AND THE GREAT SYMPATHETIC. Utica, Roberts, 1878. 27p [OTP

**Buffett, Rev. Frederick M.**

THE STORY OF THE CHURCH [OF ENGLAND] IN NEWFOUNDLAND. Toronto, General Board of Religious Education, [1939]. 96p [NfSM OLU

**Bull, William Perkins, 1870–1947**

FROM MACDONELL TO McGUIGAN. The History of the Growth of the Roman Catholic Church in Upper Canada. Toronto, Perkins Bull Fdn, 1939. 501p [BM LC OKQ

FROM STRACHAN TO OWEN. How the Church of England was Planted and Tended in British North America. Toronto, Perkins Bull Fdn, 1938. 495p [BVaU LC NBFU OKQ

SPADUNK; or, From Paganism to Davenport United. Toronto, Perkins Bull Fdn, 1935. 467p [BM BVaU LC OLU

**Bullock, Rev. William, 1797–1874**

THE BAPTISTS ANSWERED. The Doctrine of Infant Baptism as Taught in the Scripture, and Practiced in the Church. Boston, Clapp, 1843. 18p [NSHP

A WARNING TO ICE-HUNTERS. A Sermon on the Profanation of the Sabbath, Preached ... previous to the Departure of the Vessels Engaged in the Seal Fishery, 1832. [Anon] St. John's, Ryan & Withers, [1832]. 15p [OTP

**Burgess, Rev. Edwin Harcus, 1858–**

AT THE PLACE WHICH IS CALLED CALVARY. New York, Randolph, 1890. [NSWA

LOYALTY. New York, Randolph, [1892]. 54p [LC

**Burke, Rev. Edmund, 1753–1820**

CONTINUATION OF THE FIRST PRINCIPLES OF CHRISTIANITY. Halifax, Howe, 1810. 451p [NSWA QMSS

LETTER OF INSTRUCTION TO THE CATHOLIC MISSIONARIES OF NOVA-SCOTIA. Halifax, Gay, 1804. 58p [NSWA OTP

REMARKS ON A PAMPHLET ENTITLED POPERY CONDEMNED BY SCRIPTURE AND THE FATHERS. [*See* **McCulloch, Thomas.**] Halifax, Howe, 1809. 403p [BM NSWA OTP

REMARKS ON THE REV. MR. STANSER'S EXAMINATION OF THE REV. MR. BURKE'S LETTER OF INSTRUCTION TO THE C.M. OF NOVA-SCOTIA, Together with a Reply to the Rev. Mr. Cochran's Fifth and Last Letter to Mr. B. ... also a Short Review of his Former Letters and the Replies which were made. Halifax, Gay, 1805. 2v [BM NSHD OTP

A TREATISE ON THE FIRST PRINCIPLES OF CHRISTIANITY. Halifax, Howe, 1808–10. 2v [BM BVaU NSWA OTP

**Burkholder, Lewis J., 1875–**

A BRIEF HISTORY OF THE MENNONITES IN ONTARIO. [Toronto, Livingstone], 1935. 358p [BM BVaU LC OLU

**Burnett, Rev. Andrew Ian, 1906–**

LORD OF ALL LIFE. Toronto, Clarke Irwin, 1952. xi + 205p

**Burnfield, Rev. George**

VOICES FROM THE ORIENT; or, The Testimony of the Monuments ... and of the Customs and Traditions of the People in the Orient to the Veracity of the Sacred Record. 2nd ed. Toronto, Robinson, 1884. 491p [LC OTU

**Burns, Rev. George, 1790–1876**

LECTURES AND SERMONS. Saint John, Reynolds, 1820. 400p [NSWA OTP

A VIEW OF THE PRINCIPLES AND FORMS OF THE CHURCH OF SCOTLAND AS BY LAW ESTABLISHED. Saint John, 1817. 32p [NBB

**Burns, Rev. Robert Ferrier, 1826–1896**

THE PRESBYTERIAN CHURCH IN CANADA. Her Principles, Position and Prospects. A Lecture. Halifax, Nova Scotia Print., 1876. 29p [NSHD

**Burwash, Rev. Nathanael, 1839–1918**

INDUCTIVE STUDIES IN THEOLOGY. Including the Doctrines of Sin and the Atonement. Toronto, Briggs, 1896. 87p [OTU

MANUAL OF CHRISTIAN THEOLOGY ON THE INDUCTIVE METHOD. London, Marshall, 1900. 2v [BM BVaU OTU

THE RELATION OF CHILDREN TO THE FALL, THE ATONEMENT, AND THE CHURCH. Toronto, Briggs, 1882. 31p [OTU

WESLEY'S DOCTRINAL STANDARDS. Pt. I. The Sermons. With introduction, analysis, and notes. Toronto, Briggs, 1881. xxvii + 523p [Several later editions.] [OTU Ryerson Impt

**Burwell, Rev. Adam Hood, 1790–1849**

DOCTRINE OF THE HOLY SPIRIT. ... Toronto, Coates, 1835. 124p [BM OTP

ON THE PHILOSOPHY OF HUMAN PERFECTION AND HAPPINESS. Montreal, Lovell & Gibson, 1849. 29p [BM

A VOICE OF WARNING AND INSTRUCTION CONCERNING THE SIGNS OF THE TIMES. Kingston, Herald, 1835. 225p [OLU

**Butchart, Reuben, 1863–1963**

THE DISCIPLES OF CHRIST IN CANADA SINCE 1830. Toronto, Churches of Christ, Canada Pub., 1949. 674p [NBFU OTU QMM

OLD EVERTON AND THE PIONEER MOVEMENT AMONGST THE DISCIPLES OF CHRIST IN ERAMOSA TOWNSHIP, UPPER CANADA, FROM 1830. Everton, Ont., Church of Christ (Disciples), 1941. 58p [OTP

A PRIMER OF DISCIPLE HISTORY IN CANADA. Toronto, College of the Churches of Christ in Canada, 1942. 17p [OTP

**Byerly, Alpheus Edward, 1894–1960**

ONE HUNDRED YEARS AT KNOX PRESBYTERIAN CHURCH, GUELPH, ONTARIO, 1844–1944. Guelph, Author, 1944. 56p [OTP

ONE HUNDRED YEARS OF NASSAGAWEYA PRESBYTERIAN CHURCH, 1836–1936, Guelph, Author, 1936. 24p [OTU

**Cahill, Rev. Joseph Allison, 1847–1914**

SANCTIFICATION INSTANTANEOUS AND COMPLETE IN THIS LIFE IS UNSCRIPTURAL. Saint John, Barnes, 1885. 58p [NBB

**Caird, George Bradford, 1917–**

PRINCIPALITIES AND POWERS. A Study in Pauline Theology. Oxford, Clarendon, 1956. xi + 106p

**Caldwell, William, 1863–1942**

THE IDEA OF CREATION. Its Origin and its Value. Fort Worth, Keystone, 1909. 48p [LC QMM

**Cameron, Agnes Deans, 1863–1912**

A BRIEF HISTORY OF GROVE PRESBYTERIAN CHURCH, FROM ITS INCEPTION TO THE PRESENT DATE. Comp. by ——. Halifax, 1892. 14p [NSWA

**Cameron, Frank**

BOTANY CHURCH. Record and Memories of Botany Presbyterian Church and its Successor, St. John's United Church, 1858–1941. Howard, Ont., Author, 1941. 37p [OTU

**Cameron, Viola Mary**

GOD'S PLAN AND MAN'S DESTINY. With a pref. by Cornelius Van Til. Truro, N.S., Author, 1952. 164p

**Cameron, Rev. William A., 1882–1956**

THE CLINIC OF A CLERIC. Toronto, McClelland, 1931. 249p [OTU

THE GIFT OF GOD, AND OTHER SERMONS. Toronto, McClelland, [1925]. 230p [BM BVaU OTU QMM

JESUS AND THE RISING GENERATION. Toronto, McClelland, 1932. 228p [OTP

NO ROOM IN THE INN. A Christmas Sermon and Prayer. Toronto, McClelland, 1926. 43p [BVaU OTP

NOT BY EASTERN WINDOWS ONLY. Messages from Modern Prophets. Toronto, McClelland, 1929. 244p [BM BVaU NSHD OLU

THE POTTER'S WHEEL. Toronto, McClelland, 1927. 255p [BVaU NSWA OTUV QMM

RAINBOWS THROUGH THE RAIN. Yorkminster Sermons. Toronto, McClelland, 1938. 239p [LC OTP

SONGS OF THE AGES. Toronto, McClelland, 1934. 201p [LC OTP

**Campbell, Rev. John, 1840–1904**

A CONCISE HISTORY OF FRENCH-CANADIAN PROTESTANTISM. Montreal, Board of French Evangelization of the Presbyterian Church in Canada, 1896. 32p [OTP

THE GREAT ELECTION. Montreal, Lovell, 1894. 30p [QMSS

NEW LIGHT ON THE OLD PRAYER. Toronto, Briggs, 1895. 28p [OTP

PROTEST AGAINST THE DECISION OF THE PRESBYTERY OF MONTREAL AND APPEAL TO THE SYNOD OF MONTREAL AND OTTAWA. N.p., 1894. 25p [OTU

**Campbell, Norman**

HISTORY OF WESLEY UNITED CHURCH, PEMBROKE, ONTARIO, 1835–1935. Comp. by ——. Pembroke, Standard-Observer Print. Co., 1935. 66p [OTU QMM

**Campbell, Rev. Robert, 1835–1921**

HISTORY OF THE SCOTCH PRESBYTERIAN CHURCH, ST. GABRIEL STREET, MONTREAL. Montreal, Drysdale, 1887. 807p [BVaU NSWA OTU QMM

THE PRETENSIONS EXPOSED OF MESSRS. BURNET & CO., TO BE "THE PRESBYTERIAN CHURCH OF CANADA IN CONNEXION WITH THE CHURCH OF SCOTLAND." Montreal, Drysdale, 1878. 34p [NSWA QMM

THE RELATIONS OF THE CHRISTIAN CHURCHES TO ONE ANOTHER; and Problems Growing out of them, Especially in Canada. Toronto, Briggs, 1913. 337p [BM BVaU OTU

ON THE UNION OF PRESBYTERIANS IN CANADA. Prize Essay. Montreal, Grafton, 1871. 55p [NSWA

**Canadian Layman, A (pseud)**

"ESSAYS AND REVIEWS" CONSIDERED. Toronto, Chewett, 1862. 50p [NSWA OTP

**Carman, Albert, 1833–1917**

THE GUIDING EYE; or, The Holy Spirit's Guidance of the Believer. Toronto, Briggs, 1889. 221p [OTP

THE SUPERNATURAL. Toronto, Haynes Press, n.d. 20p [OONL

**Carman, Albert Richardson, 1865–1939**

THE ETHICS OF IMPERIALISM. An Enquiry whether Christian Ethics and Imperialism are Antagonistic. Boston, Turner, 1905. 177p [BM BVaU OTU

**Carmichael, Rev. James, 1835–1908**

CHURCH YEAR. A Series of Sermons for the Sacred Seasons. Montreal, 1893. 353p [BVaU QMM

DESIGN AND DARWINISM. Toronto, Hunter, 1880. 50p [NSWA

THE ERRORS OF THE PLYMOUTH BRETHREN. Montreal, Montreal Press & Pub. Co., 1869. 43p [Also: Montreal, Drysdale, 1888. 23p] [NSWA QMSS

HOW TWO DOCUMENTS MAY BE FOUND IN ONE. A Monograph in Connection with the Higher Criticism. Montreal, Gazette Print., 1895. 22p [BM NSWA QMSS

IS THERE A GOD FOR MAN TO KNOW? Toronto, Church of England, 1900. 113p [BM LC OTU

ORGANIC UNION OF CANADIAN CHURCHES. Montreal, Dawson, 1887. 88p [LC NSWA OTU QMM

WHY SOME FAIRLY INTELLIGENT PERSONS DO NOT ENDORSE THE HYPOTHESIS OF EVOLUTION. A Plea for Divine Intention in Creation. Montreal, Gazette Print., 1898. 48p [NSWA OTP

**Carnochan, Janet, 1839–1926**

ANNIVERSARY OF ST. ANDREW'S CHURCH, NIAGARA. Welland, Tribune, 1911. 13p [OTU

CENTENNIAL ST. ANDREW'S, NIAGARA, 1794–1894. Toronto, Briggs, 1895. 70p [BVaU LC OTP QMBM

CENTENNIAL, ST. MARK'S [EPISCOPAL] CHURCH, NIAGARA, 1792–1892. Toronto, Bain, 1892. 56p [LC OTP

ST. ANDREW'S, NIAGARA, 1794–1894. Toronto, Briggs, 1895. 31p [OTU

TWO FRONTIER CHURCHES. Niagara, 1890. 20p [OTU

**Carr-Harris, Bertha Hannah (Wright), 1863–1949**

THE HIEROGLYPHICS OF THE HEAVENS; or, The Enigma of the Ages. Toronto, Armac Press, 1933. 3v in 1. [OTP

**Carrington, Rev. Philip, 1892–**

ACCORDING TO MARK. A Running Commentary on the Oldest Gospel. Cambridge, Eng., U. Press, 1960. xi + 384p

THE EARLY CHRISTIAN CHURCH. Cambridge, Eng., U. Press, 1957. 2v

OUR LORD AND SAVIOUR. His Life and Teachings. Greenwich, Conn., Seabury Press, 1959. 138p

THE PRIMITIVE CHRISTIAN CALENDAR. A Study in The Making of the Marcan Gospel. Cambridge, Eng., U. Press, 1952. V. 1

THE STORY OF THE CHRIST. Toronto, General Board of Religious Education of the Anglican Church of Canada, 1956. 157p

**Carroll, Rev. John, 1809–1884**

THE BESIEGERS' PRAYER; or, A Christian Nation's Appeal to the God of Battles, for Success in the Righteous War. Toronto, Guardian, 1855. 25p [OTP

THE "EXPOSITION" EXPOUNDED, DEFENDED, AND SUPPLEMENTED. Toronto, Methodist Book, 1881. 159p [LC OTU

PAST AND PRESENT; or, A Description of ... Canadian Methodism for the Last Forty Years. By a Spectator of the Scenes [pseud]. Toronto, Dredge, 1860. 331p [NSWA OTP QMM

**Carry, Rev. John, 1824–1891**

SERMONS, DOCTRINAL, DEVOTIONAL AND PRACTICAL. Quebec, Lovell, 1860. 202p [NSWA OTU QMM

**Carter, Rev. Alexander, 1909–**

ANSWERS FROM FATHER CARTER'S QUESTION BOX. Montreal, Palm Publishers, 1953. xv + 227p

**Carter, Rev. Gerald Emmett, 1912–**

PSYCHOLOGY AND THE CROSS. Milwaukee, Bruce Pub., 1959. xvi + 135p

**Cartwright, Robert David, 1804–1843**

THE FIRST AND LAST WORDS OF A PASTOR TO HIS PEOPLE. [Anon] Kingston, Watson, 1843. 23p [OTP

**Case, Rev. William, 1780–1855**

JUBILEE SERMON. Toronto, Sanderson, 1855. 64p [OTU

**Casey, Maurice**

THE PARISH OF ST. PATRICK OF OTTAWA AND WHAT LED TO IT. An Historical Sketch. [Anon] Ottawa, Mortimer, 1900. 103p [OOU

**Caven, Rev. William, 1830–1904**

CHRIST'S TEACHING CONCERNING THE LAST THINGS, AND OTHER PAPERS. [With a biog. sketch of the Author, by James A. Macdonald.] London, Hodder, 1908. xxxii + 328p [BM BVaU OTU

THE TESTIMONY OF CHRIST TO THE OLD TESTAMENT. Toronto, Haynes, n.d. 35p [OTU

**Celebrated Astronomer, A (pseud)**

PORTRAIT OF A PUSEYITE. Taken in the Moon by a Celebrated Astronomer [pseud]. Halifax, Kirk, 1846. 24p [NSWA

**Central Canada Baptist Conference**

GOLDEN JUBILEE OF THE CENTRAL CANADA BAPTIST CONFERENCE. A Commemoration of Fifty Years, 1907–1957. Saskatoon, Gospel Press, [1957?]. 57p

**Chalmers, Rev. Randolph Carleton, 1908–**

CHALLENGE AND RESPONSE. Modern Ideas and Religion. Ed. by R.C. Chalmers and John A. Irving. Toronto, Ryerson, 1959. 130p

A GOSPEL TO PROCLAIM. Toronto, Ryerson, 1960. x + 118p

THE LIGHT AND THE FLAME. Modern Knowledge and Religion. Ed. by R.C. Chalmers and John A. Irving. Toronto, Ryerson, 1956. xii + 143p

THE PROTESTANT SPIRIT. Toronto, Ryerson, 1955. 90p

**Champion, Thomas Edward, 1842–1910**

THE ANGLICAN CHURCH IN CANADA. Toronto, Hunter Rose, 1898. 19p [OTP

THE METHODIST CHURCHES OF TORONTO. With Biographical Sketches of many of the Clergy and Laity. Toronto, Rose, 1899. 388p [BM OTP

**Cheetham, William**

CHRISTIANITY REVIEWED. Brockville, Recorder Print., 1896. 296p [BM OTP

**Chiniquy, Rev. Charles Paschal Télesphore, 1809–1899**

THE CHURCH OF ROME IS THE ENEMY OF THE HOLY VIRGIN AND OF JESUS CHRIST. Trans. by Fannie Macpherson. Stratford, Maddocks, 1866. 59p [NSHD OTP

PAPAL IDOLATRY. An Exposure of the Dogma of Transubstantiation and Mariolatry. Chicago, Craig Press, 1889. 58p [BM NSWA QMSS

THE PERVERSION OF DR. NEWMAN TO THE CHURCH OF ROME. In the Light of His Own Explanations, Common Sense, and the Word of God. 3rd ed. Montreal, Witness Print., 1896. 40p [BM

PRESIDENT LINCOLN'S ASSASSINATION. Traced Directly to the Doors of Rome. Cincinnati, Mercer, [1894?]. 46p [LC

THE PRIEST, THE WOMAN, AND THE CONFESSIONAL. London, Gibson, 1874. 192p [Also: Montreal, Grafton, 1875. 184p. Several other later eds.] [BM BVaU NSWA OLU QMSS

**Chown, Rev. Samuel Dwight, 1853–1933**

SOME CAUSES OF THE DECLINE OF THE EARLIER TYPICAL EVANGELISM. Toronto, Ryerson, 1930. 50p [OTUV

THE STORY OF CHURCH UNION IN CANADA. Toronto, Ryerson, 1930. 156p [BM BVaU LC OTP

**Church of England in Canada. Huron Diocese**

HURON DIOCESE. A Jubilee Memorial. The Story of the Church [of England] and First Fifty Years of the Diocese of Huron, 1857–1907. London, Ont., London Print., [1907]. 122p [OLU

**Church of England in Canada. Niagara Diocese**

THE HISTORY OF THE DIOCESE OF NIAGARA TO 1950. Hamilton, Synod of Niagara, 1950. 98p [OONL

**Churchill, Rev. Charles, fl. 1837–1879**

MEMORIALS OF MISSIONARY LIFE, IN NOVA SCOTIA. London, Mason; Hamilton, Adams; Nottingham, Dearden, 1845. 206p [BM LC NSWA OTP

**Chute, Rev. Arthur Crawley, 1853–1936**

THE RELIGIOUS LIFE OF ACADIA. With Chapters on its Earlier History by W.B. Boggs. Wolfville, [Acadia U.], 1933. 249p [BVaU NBFU QMM

**Clark, Rev. Howard Hewlett, 1903–**

THE CHRISTIAN LIFE ACCORDING TO THE PRAYER BOOK. Toronto, Anglican Church of Canada, 1956. 165p

**Clark, John Artemas, 1878–**

THE HISTORY OF FIRST BAPTIST CHURCH, CHARLOTTETOWN. Written on the Occasion of the Opening of the new Church Edifice, Sunday, May 17, 1959. Charlottetown, the Church, 1959. 24p

**Clark, Samuel Delbert, 1910–**

CHURCH AND SECT IN CANADA. Toronto, U. of Toronto Press, 1948. 458p [BM BVaU LC NSHD OTU QMM

**Clark, Rev. William Robinson, 1829–1912**

THE ANGLICAN REFORMATION. New York, Christian Literature Co., 1897. 482p [BM LC OTP

THE PARACLETE. A Series of Discourses on the Person and Work of the Holy Spirit. Toronto, Morang, 1900. 236p [BM LC OTP

PASCAL AND THE PORT ROYALISTS. Edinburgh, Clark, 1902. 235p [BM LC OTP

THE SUFFERINGS OF CHRIST, THEIR ORIGIN, NATURE AND RESULTS. Mission Sermons. Detroit, Young Men's Assoc. of Grace Church, 1889. 32p [LC

WITNESSES TO CHRIST. A Contribution to Christian Apologetics. Chicago, McClurg, 1888. 300p [BM OTU

**Clarke, Kathleen Margaret (Cunningham), 1905–**

LETTERS TO MY HEAVENLY FATHER. Grand Rapids, Mich., Zondervan Pub. House, 1960. 115p

**Clarke, William Fletcher, 1824–1902**

CANADIAN BICENTENARY PAPERS. No. I. The History of Nonconformity in England in 1662. By W.F. Clarke. No. II. The Reasons for Nonconformity in Canada in 1862. By Rev. F.H. Marling. Toronto, Chewett, 1862. 69p [OTP

**Clayton, Hazel Maud (Snow), 1900–**

HISTORY OF THE SMITHS COVE UNITED BAPTIST CHURCH. Smiths Cove, N.S., Author, 1957. 17p [mimeographed]

**Cleaver, Solomon, 1855–1939**

THE AGES ASK. ... Toronto, Mundy-Goodfellow, [1934]. 36p [BVaU OTU

AND CHRISTMAS CAME TO THE DESERT. Toronto, Mundy-Goodfellow, [1936]. 29p [NBFU OTU

THE HOUSE THAT LOVE BUILT. Toronto, Mundy-Goodfellow, 1937. 32p [OTU

LIFE'S GREAT ADVENTURE, PRAYER. Toronto, Ryerson, 1931. 163p [LC OTUV

AND WE ARE THE SHEEP. Toronto, Mundy-Goodfellow, 1933. 29p [OTU

**Cliffe, Albert Edward, 1892–**

LESSONS IN LIVING. Practical Faith in Practice. Montreal, Author, 1949. [2nd ed., rev. and enl., London, Hodder, 1952. 152p]

**Clifford, Rev. Paul Rowntree, 1913–**

THE PASTORAL CALLING. London, Carey Kingsgate Press, 1959. xiii + 162p

**Cochrane, Rev. William, 1831–1898**

THE CHURCH AND THE COMMONWEALTH. Discussions and Orations on Questions of the Day, Practical, Biographical, Educational and Doctrinal, Written during a Twenty Years' Ministry. Brantford, Bradley Garretson, 1887. 560p [NSWA OTP

FUTURE PUNISHMENT; or, Does Death End Probation?—with Illustrative Notes from the Writings of Eminent British & American Theologians—Illus. by the celebrated French artist, Gustav Doré. Brantford, Bradley, 1886. 528p [BVaU NSWA OTU

THE HEAVENLY VISION; AND OTHER SERMONS (1863–73). ... Toronto, Adam, 1874. 367p [NSWA OTU

**Coffey, John F.**

THE CITY AND DIOCESE OF LONDON, ONTARIO. An Historical Sketch. ... London, Catholic Register, 1885. 78p [OLU QMBM

**Cogswell, Rev. William, 1810–1847**

FOUR SERMONS PREACHED ... DURING THE SEASON OF ADVENT, A.D. 1840. Halifax, Gossip & Coade, 1841. 75p [NSHD

SERMONS, CHIEFLY UPON CHAP. XVII OF ST. JOHN'S GOSPEL. ... London, Hatchard, 1839. 497p [BM NSHD

SERMONS, PREACHED IN THE PARISH CHURCH OF ST. PAUL, HALIFAX, N.S., chiefly during the year 1845. London, Nisbet, 1847. 505p [BM NSHD

SEVEN LECTURES OF THE ACTS OF THE APOSTLES, delivered in the Parish Church of St. Paul, Halifax, N.S. during the Season of Lent, A.D. 1837. Halifax, Ward, 1837. 174p [BM NSHD

**Coleman, Rev. Michael Edward, 1902–**

THE CROSS, THE EUCHARIST AND YOU. Toronto, Anglican Church of Canada, [1959?]. 166p

**Collingwood, Ont. All Saints' Church**

ONE HUNDRED YEARS OF HISTORY OF ALL SAINTS' CHURCH IN THE TOWN OF COLLINGWOOD, 1855–1955. N.p., 1955. 32p

**Colquette, Richard Daniel, 1881–**

ONE HUNDRED YEARS AT ST. MARK'S, UNITED CHURCH OF CANADA (FORMERLY FAIRVILLE METHODIST CHURCH) 1859–1959. Comp. by ——. Lancaster, N.B. the Church, 1959. 80p

**Cook, Rev. John, 1805–1892**

SERMONS PREACHED IN ST. ANDREW'S CHURCH, QUEBEC. Montreal, Dawson, 1888. 354p [NSHD OTUV QMM

**Cookstown, Ont. Methodist Church**

ONE HUNDRED YEARS OF METHODISM IN COOKSTOWN, 1825–1925. Cookstown, Methodist Church, 1925. [OTU

**Cooney, Rev. Robert, 1800–1870**

THE GLORY OF THE GOD OF ISRAEL. Halifax, Novascotian, 1836. 34p [OTP

THE JUDGMENT SEAT OF CHRIST. A Sermon. Halifax, Cunnabell, 1838. 23p [NSHD OTP

THE LORD IS ON OUR SIDE. ... First Anniversary of the Battle [at Odelltown]. Montreal, Campbell & Becket, 1840. 40p [NSWA OTP

**Cooper, John Irwin, 1905–**

THE BLESSED COMMUNION. The Origins and History of the Diocese of Montreal, 1760–1960. Montreal, the Diocese, 1960. 266p

**Cordner, Rev. John, 1816–1894**

A BRIEF STATEMENT OF REASONS FOR DECLINING TO RECEIVE THE DOCTRINE OF THE TRINITY. Boston, Crosby & Nichols, 1846. 35p [BM

CHRIST, THE SON OF GOD. A Discourse in Review of the Rev. Dr. Wilkes' Sermon entitled "Who is Christ?" ... Montreal, Potts, 1851. 28p [OTP QMSS

THE CHRISTIAN IDEA OF SACRIFICE. Montreal, Rose, 1858. 29p [BM OTU

IS PROTESTANTISM A FAILURE? The Question Considered in Five Lectures. Also a Discourse on Christian Monotheism. Montreal, Lovell, 1869. 96p [OTP QMU

A PASTORAL LETTER TO THE CHRISTIAN CONGREGATION ASSEMBLING FOR WORSHIP AND EDIFICATION IN THE UNITARIAN CHURCH, MONTREAL. Montreal, Rose, 1853. 15p [OTL

THE PHILOSOPHIC ORIGIN AND HISTORIC PROGRESS OF THE DOCTRINE OF THE TRINITY. A Lecture delivered in the Unitarian Church, Montreal ... 1851. Montreal, Becket, 1851. 22p [Same title: Boston, Crosby & Nichols, [1849?]. 34p] [BM OTP

RIGHTEOUSNESS EXALTETH A NATION. A Discourse Concerning the Relation of Morality to National Well-being. ... Montreal, Rose, 1860. 19p [NSWA OTUV

TWENTY-FIVE SERMONS. A Memorial of 25 Years' Ministry. Montreal, Lovell, 1868. 395p [NSWA OTP

**Cormican, Leo Alphonsus, 1902–**

INVITATION TO LOVE. Ottawa, Association of Mary Immaculate, 1954. 170p

**Cornell, John A., 1841–**

THE FIRST CHURCH OF BEVERLEY. A History and a Memorial. Toronto, McClelland, 1921. 124p [BVaU OTU

**Cornish, George Henry, 1834–1912**

CYCLOPAEDIA OF METHODISM IN CANADA. Toronto, Methodist Pub. House, 1881–1903. 2v [BM BVaU NSWA MWU OTU

HAND-BOOK OF CANADIAN METHODISM. Being [a List] of all the Ministers and Preachers ... [of] Canadian Methodism. Toronto, Wesleyan Print., 1867. 238p [Later expanded as CYCLOPAEDIA OF METHODISM IN CANADA, *q.v.*] [BVaU LC NSWA OTP

**Cornwall, Ont. St. Columban's Church**

AN HISTORICAL SKETCH OF ST. COLUMBAN'S PARISH ... Commemorative of the Opening of the New Church, June, 1896. Cornwall, Standard Print., 1896. 36p [OTP

**Cornwallis, N.S. St. John's Church**

HISTORICAL SKETCH ... 1760–1910. Halifax, Macnab, [1910?]. 16p [NSWA

**Coster, Rev. Frederick**

THE "COMPANION TO THE PRAYER BOOK" DEFENDED AGAINST UNFOUNDED OBJECTIONS OF THE REV. J.W.D. GRAY. Saint John, 1851. [NBB

**Coster, Rev. George, 1794–1859**

A SERMON PREACHED IN CHRIST CHURCH, FREDERICTON. Saint John, Avery, 1842. 16p [OTU

**Cowan, Hugh, 1870–1943**

THE GREAT DRAMA OF HUMAN LIFE. ... Toronto, Religious Progress Assoc., 1937. 128p [NBFU OTU

**Cragg, Edward, 1904–**

PROTESTANT FAITH AND LIFE. Toronto, Ryerson, 1958. 58p

**Craig, H.A.**

ST. STEPHEN'S CHURCH, WESTMOUNT, ONE-HUNDRETH ANNIVERSARY, 1848–1948. [Anon] Westmount, The Church, 1948. 36p [OTP

**Cramp, Rev. John Mockett, 1796–1881**

BAPTIST HISTORY ... TO THE CLOSE OF THE 18TH CENTURY. London, Stock, 1868. 559p [BM LC NSHD OTU

CASE OF THE BAPTISTS, STATED AND EXPLAINED. ... Halifax, "Christian Messenger," 1873. 16p [NSHD

CATECHISM OF CHRISTIAN BAPTISM. ... Halifax, "Christian Messenger," 1866. 90p [NSHD

THE CENTENARY OF THE BAPTISTS IN NOVA SCOTIA. Halifax, "Christian Messenger," 1860. 30p [NSHD OTP

"FUTURE" OF THE BAPTISTS AND THEIR DUTY TO PREPARE FOR IT. A Lecture delivered at Wolfville, N.S. Halifax, Naylor, 1852. 28p [NSHD

THE GREAT EJECTMENT OF 1662. A Lecture. ... Halifax, "Christian Messenger," 1862. 40p [NSHD

LETTERS ON CHURCH RATES. Addressed to the Rev. J.E.N. Molesworth, M.A. of Canterbury. London, Wightman, 1837. 36p [BM NSHD

THE LAMB OF GOD. London, Yates, 1871. 201p [BM NSWA

PAUL AND CHRIST. A Portraiture and an Argument. London, Yates & Alexander, 1873. 198p [BM NSHD QMM

SCRIPTURE AND TRADITION. A Reply to Mr. Maturin's Letter on "The Claims of the Catholic Church." Halifax, "Christian Messenger," 1859. 64p [NSHD

THE SECOND COMING OF OUR LORD. An Essay. Halifax, "Christian Messenger," 1879. 19p [NSHD

SUCCESSION OF MARTYRS. A Sermon. ... Halifax, "Christian Messenger," 1859. 15p [NSHD

A TEXTBOOK OF POPERY. Comprising a Brief History of the Council of Trent. ... London, Holdsworth & Ball, 1831. 439p [Two later editions.] [BM NSHD OTU QMM

WHAT WILL BECOME OF THE WICKED? An Address. Halifax, "Christian Messenger." 1860. 24p [NSHP

**Crawford, Alexander Wellington, 1866–1933**

GERMANY'S MORAL DOWNFALL. The Tragedy of Academic Materialism. New York, Abingdon, 1919. 217p [LC OTUV QMM

**Crawford, John**

DEBATE ON THE POINTS OF DIFFERENCE IN FAITH AND PRACTICE BETWEEN THE TWO RELIGIOUS BODIES KNOWN AS THE DISCIPLES OF CHRIST AND THE REGULAR BAPTISTS. Held in Springfield, Elgin County, Ont. ... (Debaters: John Crawford and J.S. Sweeny). Toronto, Sheppard, 1875. 295p [OTU

**Crawford, John White, 1883–**

A HISTORICAL SKETCH OF GRACE PRESBYTERIAN CHURCH, CALGARY, ALBERTA. Calgary, David Print., 1935. 28p [OTU

**Crawley, Rev. Edmund Albern, 1799–1888**

TREATISE ON BAPTISM. ... Containing a Reply to Mr. Elder's Letters on Infant Baptism, and a solemn Appeal in Favor of a Spiritual Church. Halifax, Spike, 1835. 199p [NSHD OTUV

**Creedy, Frederick, 1883–**

THE NEXT STEP IN CIVILIZATION, A STAR TO STEER BY. Toronto, Ryerson, 1955. 217p

**Creighton, William Black, 1864–1946**

ALL IN THE DAY'S WORK. Brief Essays for Busy People. Toronto, Ryerson, 1923. 409p [BM NSHD OTP

LIFE IS LIKE THAT. Toronto, Ryerson, 1945. 254p [LC OTP

**Creswicke, May (Spry), 1870–**

THE HISTORY OF TRINITY CHURCH, BARRIE, ONTARIO, CANADA, 1835–1935. Comp. by Mrs. A.E.H. Creswicke. Barrie, 1935. 60p [OTP

**Cridge, Edward, 1817–1913**

SKETCH OF THE RISE AND PROGRESS OF METLAHKATLAH, IN THE DIOCESE OF BRITISH COLUMBIA. London, Church Missionary Soc., 1868. 16p [OTUV

**Croil, James, 1821–1916**

THE GENESIS OF CHURCHES IN THE UNITED STATES OF AMERICA, IN NEWFOUNDLAND AND THE DOMINION OF CANADA. Montreal, Foster Brown, 1907. 307p [BM BVaU LC NSWA OTU QMM

A HISTORICAL AND STATISTICAL REPORT OF THE PRESBYTERIAN CHURCH OF CANADA, in Connection with the Church of Scotland, for the year 1866. Montreal, Lovell, 1867. 172p [OTP

THE MISSIONARY PROBLEM. Containing a History of Protestant Missions. ... Toronto, Briggs, 1883. 224p [NSHD OTP

**Cronin, Kay**

CROSS IN THE WILDERNESS. Vancouver, Mitchell Press, 1960. xxiii + 255p [History of the pioneer Oblate Fathers of British Columbia.]

**Cronyn, Rev. Benjamin, 1802–1871**

THE BISHOP OF HURON'S OBJECTIONS TO THE THEOLOGICAL TEACHING OF TRINITY COLLEGE, WITH THE PROVOST'S REPLY. Toronto, Rowsell & Ellis, 1862. 84p [BM NSHP OTP

THE GOSPEL IN CANADA: AND ITS RELATION TO HURON COLLEGE. In Addresses by the Lord Bishop of Huron; ... Bishop of Ohio; ... Assistant Bishop of Ohio. ... With an intro. by the Rev. T.R. Birks. London, Hunt, [1865?]. 112p [OTP

**Dalby, George E.**

HISTORICAL MEMORANDUM, COLLEGE STREET PRESBYTERIAN CHURCH, TORONTO ... 1872–1917. Comp. by ——. Toronto, College Press, 1918. 34p †OTP

**Daly, George Thomas, 1872–1956**

CATHOLIC PROBLEMS IN WESTERN CANADA. Toronto, Macmillan, 1921. 352p [BM BVaU NBS OONL QMSS

**Dartmouth, N.S. Christ Church**

THE STORY OF CHRIST CHURCH ... SPECIALLY WRITTEN FOR THE CENTENNIAL CELEBRATION. ... Halifax, Weekes, 1917. 219p [BVaU NSWA

**Dartmouth, N.S. Grace United Church**

THE ONE HUNDREDTH ANNIVERSARY, GRACE UNITED CHURCH, 1853–1953. Dartmouth, the Church, 1953. 25p [mimeographed]

**Davenport, Rev. John M.**

MESSIAH (GOD INCARNATE), NOT MESSIAH'S MOTHER, THE "BRUISER OF THE SERPENT'S HEAD." Saint John, McMillan, 1891. 168p [NBB

PAPAL INFALLIBILITY. "Catholic's" Replies to "Cleophas." Saint John, McMillan, 1885. 106p [NBB

**Davies, Trevor Hughes, 1871–**

THE INNER CIRCLE. Studies in the Associates of Jesus. New York, Doran, 1924. 315p [BM LC OKQ

**Davis, Rev. E.A.**

COMMEMORATIVE REVIEW OF THE METHODIST, PRESBYTERIAN, AND CONGREGATIONAL CHURCHES IN BRITISH COLUMBIA. ... Comp. and pub. by Joseph Lee. Ed. by ——. Vancouver, Lee, 1925. xxxii + 380p [BVaU OTU

**Davis, Rev. John, 1803?–1875**

CIRCUMCISION AND BAPTISM. ... Charlottetown, Author, 1867. 24p [NSWA

**Davison, Rev. William Holmes, 1884–**

HE SHALL SPEAK PEACE. A Good Friday Devotion for the Three Hours Watch by the Cross. Toronto, Church of England in Canada, 1952. 54p

**Dawson, Rev. Aeneas MacDonell, 1810–1894**

SKETCH OF THE PARISH OF ST. MARY, ALMONTE, ONT. Almonte, 1885. [OOP

**Dawson, John William, 1820–1899**

ARCHAIA; or, Studies of the Cosmogony and Natural History of the Hebrew Scriptures. ... Montreal, Dawson, 1860. 406p [BM BVaU NSHD OTU

EDEN LOST AND WON. Studies of the early History and final Destiny of Man as taught in Nature and Revelation. London, Hodder, 1895. 226p [BM BVaU LC OTUV

EPISCOPAL ELECTIONS ANCIENT AND MODERN. A Study in Ecclesiastical Polity. ... Montreal, Dawson, 1877. 53p [NSHD

HISTORICAL DELUGE, IN ITS RELATION TO SCIENTIFIC DISCOVERY AND TO PRESENT QUESTIONS. New York, Revell, 1895. 56p [BM LC OTU QMBM

THE MEETING-PLACE OF GEOLOGY AND HISTORY. London, Religious Tract Soc., 1895. 223p [Also: New York, Revell, [1894].] [BM LC NSHD OTU

MODERN IDEAS OF EVOLUTION AS RELATED TO REVELATION AND SCIENCE. London, Religious Tract Soc., 1890. 240p [BM NSWA OTP QMM

MODERN SCIENCE IN BIBLE LANDS. Montreal, Dawson, 1888. 606p [BM LC NSWA OTU QMM

NATURE AND THE BIBLE. A Course of Lectures delivered in New York ... on the Morse Foundation of the Union Theological Seminary. New York, Carter, 1875. 257p [BM LC NSWA OTUV QMM

THE ORIGIN OF THE WORLD, ACCORDING TO REVELATION AND SCIENCE. Montreal, Dawson, 1877. 438p [BM BVaU NSWA OTU

POINTS OF CONTACT BETWEEN REVELATION AND NATURAL SCIENCE. London, Religious Tract Soc., [1885]. 64p [BM NSWA

THE TESTIMONY OF THE HOLY SCRIPTURES RESPECTING WINE AND STRONG DRINK. Pictou, Macdonald, 1858. 46p [3rd ed., rev.: Montreal, Grafton, 1898. 52p] [LC NSHD OTP QMM

**Dawson, William Bell, 1854–**

THE BIBLE CONFIRMED BY SCIENCE. London, Marshall, 1936. 159p [BM OTU

EVOLUTION CONTRASTED WITH SCRIPTURE'S TRUTH. Chicago, Bible Institute, 1926. 63p [LC

**De Blois, Stephen William, 1827–1884**

HISTORICAL SKETCH OF THE FIRST HORTON BAPTIST CHURCH, WOLFVILLE, for the period of one hundred years, from A.D. 1778 to A.D. 1878. Halifax, Messenger, 1879. 29p [NSHD

**Delafosse, Frederick Montague, 1860–1950**

CENTENARY HISTORY, ST. JOHN'S CHURCH, PETERBOROUGH, [1827–1927]. ... Peterborough, Review Press, 1927. 97p [OTP

**Devine, Rev. Edward James, 1860–1927**

THE CANADIAN MARTYRS. The Story of the ... Death of Eight Missionaries at the Hands of the Iroquois, 1642–1649. 2nd ed. Montreal, Canadian Messenger, 1923. 168p [3rd ed. under title: THE JESUIT MARTYRS. ...] [BVaU OOA QMBM

**Dewart, Rev. Edward Hartley, 1828–1903**

THE BIBLE UNDER HIGH CRITICISM. A Review of Current Evolutionary Theories about the Old Testament. Toronto, Briggs, 1900. 214p [BM NSWA OTUV

BRIEF OUTLINE OF CHRISTIAN DOCTRINE: Designed for Senior Epworth Leagues and all Bible Students. Toronto, Briggs, 1898. 67p [BM NBSaM OTUV

BROKEN REEDS; or, The Heresies of the Plymouth Brethren, shown to be Contrary to Reason and Scripture. Toronto, Wesleyan, 1869. 34p [OTP

HIGH CHURCH PRETENSIONS DISPROVED; or, Methodism and the Church of England. Toronto, Methodist Book Room, 1877. 59p [NSWA OTUV

JESUS THE MESSIAH IN PROPHECY AND FULFILMENT. A Review and Refutation of the Negative Theory of Messianic Prophecy. Toronto, Briggs, 1890. 256p [BVaU LC NSWA OTP

LIVING EPISTLES; or, Christ's Witnesses in the World, &c. &c. Toronto, Christian Guardian, 1878. 288p [OTUV

MODERN CRITICISM AND THE TEACHING OF THE OLD TESTAMENT. A brief Review of the Theories Advocated in Professor George Adam Smith's Yale Lectures. Toronto, Briggs, 1902. 32p [BM

**Dezell, Robert, 1866–**

LOST TRACK OF A DAY. A Stricture on Seventh Day Teaching and Sabbath Desecration. ... Owen Sound, Rutherford, 1899. 108p [BM OTUV

**Dickinson, Rev. Clarence Heber, 1899–**

SEVEN DAYS & THE SEVEN WORDS. Toronto, Ryerson, 1952. 54p

**Dickson, James A.R., 1839–1915**

"EBENEZER": A HISTORY OF THE CENTRAL PRESBYTERIAN CHURCH, GALT, ONTARIO. With Brief Sketches of Some of its Members. ... Toronto, Briggs, 1904. 394p [BM OTUV

**Dorland, Arthur Garratt, 1887–**

A HISTORY OF THE SOCIETY OF FRIENDS (QUAKERS) IN CANADA. Toronto, Macmillan, 1927. 343p [BM BVaU LC NSHD OTU QMM

**Dougall, Lily, 1858–1923**

ABSENTE REO. By the Author of "Pro Christo et Ecclesia" [pseud]. London, Macmillan, 1910. 357p [LC OTU QMM

THE CHRISTIAN DOCTRINE OF HEALTH. A Handbook on the Relation of Bodily to Spiritual and Moral Health. London, Macmillan, 1916. 197p [Also: New York, Macmillan, 1923. 181p] [BM LC OTU

CHRISTUS FUTURUS. By the Author of "Pro Christo et Ecclesia" [pseud]. London, Macmillan, 1907. 404p [Pub. in the U.S. under title: THE CHRIST THAT IS TO BE.] [BVaU LC OTU QMM

GOD'S WAY WITH MAN. ... With intro. and biog. note by Canon B.H. Streeter. London, Student Christian Movement, 1924. 123p [BM BVaU LC OTU

THE LORD OF THOUGHT. A Study of the Problems which Confronted Jesus. ... By Lily Dougall and Cyril W. Emmet. London, Student Christian Movement, 1922. 324p [BM BVaU LC OTUV

THE PRACTICE OF CHRISTIANITY. By the Author of "Pro Christo et Ecclesia" [pseud]. London, Macmillan, 1913. 291p [BM LC OTU QMM

PRO CHRISTO ET ECCLESIA. ... [Anon] London, Macmillan, 1900. 191p [Rev. ed.: 1910.] [BM BVaU LC QMM

VOLUNTAS DEI. By the Author of "Pro Christo et Ecclesia" [pseud]. London, Macmillan, 1912. 276p [QMM

**Dowe, Marjorie Jean (Pierce), 1922–**

144TH ANNIVERSARY, 1810–1954, THE CLEMENTSVALE UNITED BAPTIST CHURCH, CLEMENTSVALE, N.S. Clementsvale, the Church, 1954. 10p

**Downer, Alfred Wallace**

NOTTAWASAGA ANGLICAN CHURCHES, ONTARIO, HISTORICAL SKETCHES. Christ Church, Batteau, 1865–1935; Church of the Redeemer, Duntroon, 1875–1935; St. Paul's Church, Singhampton, 1875–1935. Comp. by ——. N.p., 1935. 58p [OTP

**Driscoll, Frederick, 1834–1907**

SKETCH OF THE CANADIAN MINISTRY. Montreal, 1866. 130p [NSWA OTP QMM

**Duckworth, Rev. Henry Thomas Forbes, 1868–1927**

THE CHURCH OF THE HOLY SEPULCHRE. Toronto, Hodder, 1922. 299p [BM BVaU OTU QMM

**Duff, Louis Blake, 1878–1959**

HUNDREDTH ANNIVERSARY OF TRINITY CHURCH, CHIPPEWA. The Story of the Centennial Ceremonies and the History of the Church the Past Century, 1820–1920. Welland, Tribune, [1920?]. 20p [OTU

**Du Moulin, John Philip, 1836–1911**

THE ETERNAL LAW. Toronto, Musson, 1903. 191p [The Slocum Lectures, 1901.] [BM LC OLU

**Duncan, Jessie**

MANNA FROM HEAVEN. N.p., n.d. 102p [BVaU OH

WINDOWS TOWARDS HEAVEN. N.p., n.d. 95p [OH OTUV

**Duncan, B.C. St. John's Church**

ANNALS OF AN UNIMPORTANT PARISH. Notes on the History of St. John's Church, Duncan, British Columbia, 1905–1956. Duncan, B.C., 1956. 17p [mimeographed]

**Dunham, Bertha Mabel, 1881–1957**

SO GREAT A HERITAGE. Historical Narrative of Trinity United Church [Kitchener, Ont.], 1841–1941. Ed. by ——. Kitchener, Cober Print., 1941. 70p [OTU

**Eaton, Arthur Wentworth Hamilton, 1849–1937**

THE CHURCH OF ENGLAND IN NOVA SCOTIA AND THE TORY CLERGY OF THE REVOLUTION. New York, Whittaker, 1891. 320p [BM BVaU LC NSHD OTU

THE HEART OF THE CREEDS: HISTORICAL RELIGION IN THE LIGHT OF MODERN THOUGHT. New York, Putnam, 1888. 200p [LC NSHD

**Eaton, Rev. Charles Aubrey, 1868–1953**

FOR TROUBLED HEARTS. Toronto, Poole, 1899. 130p [BM NSWA OTU

THE OLD EVANGEL AND THE NEW EVANGELISM. Chicago, Revell, 1901. 162p [BVaU LC NSWA OTU

**Eby, Charles Samuel, 1845–1925**

CHRISTIANITY AND HUMANITY. A Course of Lectures. ... Yokohama, Meiklejohn, 1883. 296p [BVaU LC OTP

METHODISM AND THE MISSIONARY PROBLEM. Toronto, Briggs, 1886. 66p [OTUV

**Edmonton, Alta. McDougall United Church**

DIAMOND JUBILEE, 1871–1931. Edmonton, 1931. 24p [AE

**Elder, William, 1784–1848**

INFANT SPRINKLING, Weighed in the Balance of the Sanctuary, and found wanting. In Five Letters addressed to the Rev. George Jackson. ... Halifax, Author, 1823. 56p [NSHD

**Emberson, Frederick C., –1913**

ARE WE IMMORTAL? Montreal, n.d. 108p [NSWA QMM

**Embury, Jean Thompson (MacMillan)**

HISTORY OF THE DIOCESE OF QU'APPELLE. Regina, the Diocese, 1959. 72p

**Esquesing, Ont. Churchill United Church**

CHURCHILL UNITED CHURCH 1838–1938. Acton, Free Press, 1938. 22p [OTU

**Estabrooks, Robert Ernest, 1873–**

THE HISTORY OF THE UNITED BAPTIST CHURCH AT MIDDLE SACKVILLE, 1763–1953. N.p., 1953. 15p

**Eustace, Cecil John, 1903–**

HOUSE OF BREAD. A Catholic Journey. Toronto, Longmans, 1943. 159p [BM BVaU LC OTP

AN INFINITY OF QUESTIONS. A Study of the Religion of Art, and of the Art of Religion in the Lives of Five Women. ... London, Dobson, 1946. 170p [BM LC OTU

MIND AND MYSTERY. A Catholic Explanation. Toronto, Longmans, 1937. 314p [BM OTU QMSS

ROMEWARDS. London, Washbourne & Bogan, 1933. 329p [BM LC OWA

**Evans, Rev. Richard C., 1861–**

SERMONS. London, Ont., Advertiser, 1912. 420p [BVaU OTU

**Eylands, Valdimar Jonsson, 1901–**

LUTHERANS IN CANADA. Winnipeg, Icelandic Evangelical Lutheran Synod, 1945. 326p [BVaU OTP

**Fackenheim, Rabbi Emil Ludwig, 1916–**

PATHS TO JEWISH BELIEF. A Systematic Introduction. New York, Behrman House, 1960. 157p

**Fairbairn, Robert Edis, 1880–1951**

APOSTATE CHRISTENDOM. London, Ken-Pax Pub. Co., n.d. 92p [BVi OTUV

AN APPEAL TO REALITY. New York, Abingdon Press, 1927. 192p [LC OTUV

**Fairweather, Rev. Eugene Rathbone, 1920–**

EPISCOPACY AND REUNION. By E.R. Fairweather and R.F. Hettlinger. Toronto, General Board of Religious Education of the Church of England in Canada, 1952. ix + 118p

**Falconer, Rev. James William, 1868–1956**

FROM APOSTLE TO PRIEST. A Study of Early Church Organization. ... Edinburgh, Clark, 1900. 292p [NSHD OTUV

THE PASSION ACCORDING TO ST. JOHN. Toronto, United Church Pub. House, 1944. 43p [LC OTU

THE THREE CROSSES. London, Hodder, 1907. 101p [NSHD OTUV

**Falconer, Robert Alexander, 1867–1943**

THE HEART OF THE NEW TESTAMENT. Toronto, United Church Pub. House, 1943. 46p [LC OTP

THE IDEA OF IMMORTALITY AND WESTERN CIVILIZATION. Cambridge, Mass., Harvard U. Press, 1930. 61p [BM LC OTU

THE PASTORAL EPISTLES. Introduction, Translation and Notes. Oxford, Clarendon, 1937. 164p [BVaU LC OTP

THE TRUTH OF THE APOSTOLIC GOSPEL. New York, Int'l Committee of Y.M.C.A., 1904. 148p [LC NSWA OTP

**Farmer, Mary Harrington, 1905–**

THE CHURCH OF THE ASCENSION, HAMILTON. A Short History, 1850–1950. Hamilton, Kinder Print. Co., 1950. 83p [OTU

**Farmer, Thomas Devey Jermyn**

A HISTORY OF THE PARISH OF ST. JOHN'S CHURCH, ANCASTER. With many Biographical Sketches. Guelph, Gummer Press, 1924. 304p [BVaU OTU

**Farncomb, Dora, 1863–1938**

THE VISION OF HIS FACE. London, Ont., Weld Co., 1909. 224p [BM LC OTUV

**Fee, Norman, 1889–**

KNOX PRESBYTERIAN CHURCH CENTENARY. A History of the Congregation. Ottawa, Mortimer, 1944. 78p [OTP

**Ferguson, James**

THE HISTORY OF ST. ANDREW'S CHURCH, BARRIE, ONTARIO, 1849–1949. Barrie, Presb. Church in Canada, 1949. 44p [UTQ'51

**Ferres, James, 1905–**

THE FIRST FIFTY YEARS, 1907–1957. Toronto, Anglican Church of St. Michael and All Angels, 1957. 65p

**Ferrier, Rev. Andrew, –1861**

CHRIST WOUNDED IN THE HOUSE OF HIS FRIENDS. A Brief Review of Proceedings in Different Courts of the Presbyterian Church of Canada. 2nd ed. Brantford, Herald, 1851. 52p [NSHD OTP

THE TOWER OF BABEL; or, Confusion in Language on Points Connected with the Question of Civil Establishments of Religion. Hamilton, Gazette, 1849. 93p [BVaU

**Fischer, William Joseph, 1879–1921**

THE YEARS BETWEEN. Techny, Ill., Soc. of the Divine Word, 1912. 242p [CBI MOR'12

**Fitch, Ernest Robert, 1878–1935**

THE BAPTISTS OF CANADA. A History of their Progress and Achievement. Ed. by E.R.F. Toronto, Standard, 1911. 304p [NSWA OTUV

**Fitzgerald, Doris Marion (Chapman), 1898–**

A CHRONICLE OF THE PARISH OF TRINITY CHURCH, THORNHILL, 1830–1955. Ed. by S.A.R. Wood. [Thornhill, Ont.?], 1955. 32p

**Fitzroy Harbour, Ont. St. Andrew's Church**

ST. ANDREW'S KIRK, 1858–1958. Fitzroy Harbour, Ont., the Church, 1958. 8p [mimeographed]

**Fitzwilliam, William**

THE QUODDY HERMIT; or, Conversations at Fairfield on Religion and Superstition. Boston, Dickinson, 1841. 194p [NSHD

**Fleming, Rev. Archibald Lang, 1883–1953**

ALL SAINTS CATHEDRAL, AKLAVIK. N.p., [1939?] 20p [OTU

A BOOK OF REMEMBRANCE; or, The History of St. John's Church. Saint John, Barnes, 1925. 416p [BM BVaU NSWA OTP

DWELLERS IN ARCTIC NIGHT. Toronto, Missionary Soc. of Church of England in Canada, 1928. 176p [BM BVaU NSWA OTU

FOR US: MEDITATIONS ON THE SEVEN WORDS FROM THE CROSS. London, Marshall, [1924]. 80p [BM NSWA

**Folyard, Rev. W.**

A THEOLOGICAL AND UNIVERSAL HISTORY. Describing Heaven, Earth and Hell in Panoramic Order. Saint John, Barnes, 1867. 64p [NBB

**Foran, Joseph Kearney, 1857–1931**

BLOSSOMS OF THE PAST, 1857–1931. Montreal, Gazette, 1935. 205p [BVaU LC NSHD OTU QMM

THE SPIRIT OF THE AGE; or, Faith and Infidelity. An Essay. Montreal, Sadlier, 1885. 184p [OTP

**Forbes, Elmer Vincent, 1890–**

THE STORY OF ONE HUNDRED AND FIFTY YEARS IN ST. JAMES UNITED CHURCH, ANTIGONISH, NOVA SCOTIA, 1804–1954. Antigonish, N.S., 1954. 13p [mimeographed]

**Forbes, George**

THE HISTORY OF ST. PETER'S PARISH (OBLATE FATHERS), NEW WESTMINSTER, B.C., 1860–1960. New Westminster, Author, 1960. 48p

**Forbes, Jean (Gordon), 1880–**

WIDE WINDOWS. The Story of the Woman's Missionary Society of the United Church of Canada. Toronto, United Church, 1951. 208p

**Ford, Rev. John Alexander**

HISTORICAL SKETCH OF THE EAST POINT BAPTIST CHURCH, P.E.I. Centennial 1833–1933. With Biographical Sketches and Account of Early Settlement. By —— and Rev. Henry George Mellick. [Kentville, N.S., Kentville Pub., 1933.] 83p [NSWA

**Ford, Thomas G.**

SHORT HISTORY OF ST. PAUL'S, HARBOR GRACE, PARISH (1764–1935) AND CHURCH (1835–1935). [Harbour Grace, Nfld.], Standard Print., 1935. 88p [NfSM

**Forsyth, Alexander E.**

REMINISCENCES OF ... THE EARLY FORMATION OF THE METHODIST CHURCH IN EASTERN ONTARIO. Cornwall, Standard, 1907. 56p [OKQ

**Fortin, Rev. Octave, 1842–1927**

SIXTY YEARS AND AFTER. An Historical Sketch of Holy Trinity Parish, Winnipeg. Written for the most part by the late Venerable Archdeacon Fortin. Also an Outline of Present Day Activities and Possible Future Developments, by Rev. C. Carruthers. Winnipeg, Dawson Richardson, 1928. 138p [MWP OTUV

**Foulds, Elsie G.**

FARRINGDON CHURCH. Its History and Background from 1833 to 1951 and the Church today. Comp. by Elsie G. Foulds and Helen M. Kippax. [Brantford, the Church], 1951. 36p

**Fox, Charles James**

AN HISTORICAL SKETCH OF THE PARISH OF WILMOT, 1828–1913, Diocese of Huron, Ontario. [Anon] New Hamburg, n.p., [1913]. 71p [OTU

**Fox, William Sherwood, 1878–1967**

A CENTURY OF SERVICE. A History of the Talbot Street Baptist Church, 1845–1945. London, Ont., Talbot Street Baptist Church, 1945. 103p [OTP

SAINT IGNACE, CANADIAN ALTAR OF MARTYRDOM. By William Sherwood Fox, with the collaboration of Wilfrid Jury. Toronto, McClelland, 1949. 175p [BVaU NBFU OTP

**Franchetti, Rev. Nicolo, 1879–**

A CHURCHMAN'S POCKET DICTIONARY. Toronto, General Board of Religious Education. 1959. 114p

**Frankel, Rabbi Israel, 1909–**

PESHAT (PLAIN EXEGESIS) IN TALMUDIC AND MIDRASHIC LITERATURE. Toronto, La Salle Press, 1956. 211p

**Fraser, James MacDonell, 1882–**

ST. MUNGO'S CENTENNIAL, 1836–1936. The Story of One Hundred Years at Cushing–within the Church of Scotland, the Presbyterian Church in Canada and the United Church of Canada. Cushing, Que., St. Mungo's Church, 1937. 72p [OTP

**Fraser, Lennox**

THE PRODIGAL FATHER. [A Sermon] Montreal, Author, 1929. [OTP QMM

**Fraser, Rev. Thomas**

SERMONS. Montreal, Lovell, 1867. 229p [NSHPL OTP

**Fredericton, N.B. Christ Church Cathedral**

CHRIST CHURCH CATHEDRAL, FREDERICTON, N.B. Fredericton, the Cathedral, 1955. 26p

**Fredericton, N.B. Methodist Church**

FIFTY YEARS IN THE FREDERICTON METHODIST CHURCH, and an Account in Detail of Semi-Centennial Jubilee Exercises in December, 1902. Fredericton, Herald, 1902. 74p [NSWA

**Fredericton, N.B. St. Paul's Church**

A CENTURY OF SERVICE. The History of St. Paul's Church, Fredericton, 1832–1932. Fredericton, [1932?]. 99p [NBFU

**Freeman, John Dolliver, 1864–1943**

CONCERNING THE CHRIST. New York, Armstrong, 1908. 241p [BM LC NSWA OTUV

THE EDGE OF THE AGE. London, Hodder, 1917. 288p [BM OTU NSWA

LIFE ON THE UPLANDS. An Interpretation of the Twenty-Third Psalm. Toronto, Briggs, 1906. 127p [Also: New York, Armstrong, 1907. 139p] [BM BVaU LC NSWA OTU QMM

**Frerichs, Natalie H.M., 1887–**

HISTORY OF TRINITY CHURCH, OTTAWA, 1876–1956. Ottawa, Trinity Church, 1956. 20p [mimeographed]

**Freshman, Rev. Charles, 1819–1875**

THE PENTATEUCH. Its Genuineness and Authenticity Proved and Defended against ... Bishop Colenso. Toronto, Green, 1864. 140p [OTP

**Frith, Rowley Campbell, 1897–**

FIRST BAPTIST CHURCH, OTTAWA, 1857–1957. By Rowley Frith and others. Ottawa, the Church, 1957. 47p

**Fulford, Rev. Francis, 1803–1868**

THE CONTROVERSY BETWEEN THE LORD BISHOP OF MONTREAL AND THE VEN. ARCHDEACON HELLMUTH. London, Taylor, 1863. 16 + 26 + 75p [Mostly replies to Fulford.] [BM OTP

SERMONS, ADDRESSES AND STATISTICS OF THE DIOCESE OF MONTREAL. Montreal, Dawson, 1865. 308p [BM NSWA OTU QMM

**Fyfe, Rev. Robert Alexander, 1816–1878**

BAPTIST SENTIMENTS CONFIRMED BY THE AUTHORITY OF THE MOST LEARNED PEDOBAPTISTS. Toronto, Globe, 1856. 28p [NSWA OTU

SUGGESTIONS TO CANADIAN BAPTIST CHURCHES, PASTORS, AND DEACONS. Toronto, Canadian Baptist, 1866. 43p [OLU

**Galbraith, J.F.**

THE MENNONITES IN MANITOBA, 1875–1900. A Review of their Coming, their Progress and their Present Prosperity. Morden, Man., Chronicle, 1900. 48p [LC OTP

**Gandier, Alfred, 1861–1932**

THE DOCTRINAL BASIS OF UNION AND ITS RELATION TO THE HISTORIC CREEDS. Toronto, Ryerson, 1926. 50p [OTUV

THE SON OF MAN COMING IN HIS KINGDOM. A Study of the Apocalyptic Element in the Teaching of Jesus. New York, Doran, 1922. 154p [BVaU LC OTUV

**Ganges, Salt Spring Island, B.C. St. Mark's Church**

ST. MARK'S CHURCH, PARISH OF SALT SPRING ISLAND. Ganges, B.C., 1952. 12p

**Gant, Mrs. Sophia, 1891–**

BLESSINGS GALORE. Proven Treasures of Wisdom. New York, Pageant Press, 1959. 84p

**Garland, Rev. Peter Bernard, 1923–**

THE DEFINITION OF SACRAMENT ACCORDING TO SAINT THOMAS. Ottawa, U. of Ottawa Press, 1959. x + 115p

**Garstin, Lawrence Hamilton, 1918–**

EACH AGE IS A DREAM. A Study in Ideologies. Toronto, Ryerson, 1953. xi + 143p

**Gaynor, Rev. William Cleophas, 1855–**

PAPAL INFALLIBILITY. Letters of "Cleophas." Saint John, McMillan, 1885. 104p [NSHD

**Geddes, Rev. John Gamble, 1811–1891**

THE MINISTERIAL CHARACTER. A Sermon. Toronto, Rowsell, 1857. 18p [NSWA OTP

**Gedye, Frank William, 1881–**

AN HISTORICAL SKETCH OF THE PARISH OF BROME. Granby, Que., Simms Print., 1952. 48p

**Geikie, John Cunningham, 1824–1906**

THE ENGLISH REFORMATION. How It Came About, and Why We Should Uphold It. New York, Appleton, 1879. 512p [BM LC OTUV QMM

HOURS WITH THE BIBLE; or, The Scriptures in the Light of Modern Knowledge. An entirely new ed., rev. throughout and largely rewritten. ... New York, Pott, 1893. 6v [Earlier ed.: London, Partridge, 1881.] [BM BVaU LC OTUV

THE LIFE AND WORDS OF CHRIST. New York, Appleton, 1879. 2v [BM BVaU LC OTU

OLD TESTAMENT CHARACTERS. New York, Pott, 1888. 484p [BM LC

**George, Rev. James, 1801?–1870**

CHRIST CRUCIFIED. A Sermon. ... Toronto, Coates, 1837. 27p [OTP

THE DUTIES OF SUBJECTS TO THEIR RULERS. With a Special View to the Present Times. A Sermon. Toronto, Coates, 1838. 32p [NSWA OTP

THOUGHTS ON HIGH THEMES. Being a Collection of Sermons. Toronto, Campbell, 1874. 262p [OTU

**Gifford, Rev. William Alva, 1877–1960**

THE SEEKERS. A Mirror for Orthodoxy. London, Skeffington, 1955. 256p [First pub. Boston, Beacon Press, 1954, under title: *The Seekers:* Why Christian Orthodoxy is Obsolete.]

THE STORY OF THE FAITH. A Survey of Christian History for the Undogmatic. New York, Macmillan, 1946. 622p [BM BVaU LC NBFU OTP

**Gillies, Rev. Archibald C., 1834–1887**

POPERY DISSECTED. Its Absurd, Inhuman, Unscriptural, Idolatrous and Anti-christian Assumptions, Principles and Practices Exposed from its own Standard Works. ... Pictou, Harris, 1874. 83p [NSHD OTP

**Gilmour, Rev. George Peel, 1900–**

THE MEMOIRS CALLED GOSPELS. Toronto, Clarke Irwin, 1959. x + 299p

**Glanford, Ont. St. Paul's Church**

ST. PAUL'S CHURCH, (ANGLICAN), GLANFORD, ONTARIO. 100th Anniversary, July 1st, 1951. Glanford, Ont., 1951. 11p

**Glover, George Henry Wilson, 1881–**

HISTORY OF THE UNITED CHURCH OF CANADA, NORTH AND SOUTH SAANICH AREAS. Saanichton, B.C., Author, 1956. 35p

**Glover, Terrot Reaveley, 1869–1943**

DEMOCRACY AND RELIGION. Sackville, Mount Allison Univ., 1932. 108p [BVaU NSHD OTU

**Goodspeed, Rev. Calvin, 1842–1912**

BAPTISM VERSUS RANTISM. ... A Reply to the Misstatements and Fallacies of Rev. W.A. McKay. Woodstock, "Times" Office, 1880. 46p [NSHD OTU

THE MESSIAH'S SECOND ADVENT. A Study in Eschatology. Toronto, Briggs, 1900. 288p [BM OTUV

PECULIAR PRINCIPLES OF THE BAPTISTS. ... Toronto, Dudley & Burns, 1876. 43p [NSHD OTU

**Gordon, Rev. Charles William, 1860–1937**

THE ANGEL AND THE STAR. By Ralph Connor [pseud]. Toronto, Westminster, 1908. 24p [BM BVaU LC OTU

CHRISTIAN HOPE. By Ralph Connor [pseud]. London, Hodder, 1912. 31p [BM SSU

THE DAWN BY GALILEE. A Story of the Christ. By Ralph Connor [pseud]. London, Hodder, 1909. 30p [BM BVaU LC NBFU OTU

A FIGHT FOR FREEDOM. By Ralph Connor [pseud]. Toronto, McClelland, 1917. 13p [BM

THE RECALL OF LOVE. A Message of Hope. By Ralph Connor [pseud]. London, Hodder, 1910. 23p [BM BVaU LC OTU

**Graham, Rev. Hugh, 1758–1829**

THE RELATION AND RELATIVE DUTIES OF PASTOR AND PEOPLE, ILLUSTRATED IN TWO SERMONS. Halifax, 1799. [BibC

SERMONS AND ADDRESSES. Halifax, 1799. [DCB

**Graham, William Creighton, 1887–1955**

THE MEANING OF THE CROSS. Toronto, Ryerson, 1923. 100p [BVaU OKQ

**Grant, Rev. George Monro, 1835–1902**

REFORMERS OF THE NINETEENTH CENTURY. Halifax, Bowes, 1867. 32p [NSWA

THE RELIGIONS OF THE WORLD. New York, Revell, [1894?]. 137p [Also: London, Black, 1911. 137p] [BM BVaU OTP QMM

**Grant, Rev. John Webster, 1919–**

THE SHIP UNDER THE CROSS. Toronto, Ryerson, 1960. 106p

WORLD CHURCH. Achievement or Hope? Toronto, United Church Pub. House, 1956. 51p

**Gray, Rev. Archibald**

SERMON, PREACHED ON 10TH AUGUST 1804: The Day Appointed, by Government, for a General Fast. ... Halifax, Howe, 1804. 38p [NSHD

**Gray, Rev. John William Dering, 1797–1868**

A BRIEF VIEW OF THE SCRIPTURAL AUTHORITY AND HISTORICAL EVIDENCE OF INFANT BAPTISM. Halifax, Cunnabell, 1837. 308p [NSWA OTUV

A LETTER TO MEMBERS OF THE CHURCH OF ENGLAND IN REPLY TO A LETTER FROM EDWARD MATURIN.... Saint John, McMillan, 1859. 124p [NSHP OTUV

A REPLY TO THE REV. F. COSTER'S DEFENCE OF THE "COMPANION TO THE PRAYER BOOK." ... Saint John, McMillan, 1849. 48p [NSHP

A REPLY TO THE STATEMENT OF THE REV. MR. WIGGINS. Saint John, McMillan, 1851. 48p [NSHP OTP

A SERMON PREACHED AT TRINITY CHURCH IN THE PARISH OF SAINT JOHN, N.B., AND DESIGNED TO RECOMMEND THE PRINCIPLES OF THE LOYALISTS OF 1783. Saint John, Macmillan, 1857. 15p [OTU

**Greene, Rev. David Leslie, 1883–**

AN HISTORICAL SKETCH, CHRIST CHURCH, THE PAS, MANITOBA. N.p., 1931. 24p [OORD SSU

**Gregg, William, 1817–1909**

HISTORY OF THE PRESBYTERIAN CHURCH IN THE DOMINION OF CANADA. From the Earliest Times to 1834. Toronto, Presbyterian Print., 1885. 646p [BVaU LC NSWA OTU QMM

SHORT HISTORY OF THE PRESBYTERIAN CHURCH IN THE DOMINION OF CANADA FROM THE EARLIEST TO THE PRESENT TIME. Toronto, Robinson, 1892. 248p [BVaU LC NBFU OTP

**Grenfell, Wilfred Thomason, 1865–1940**

THE ADVENTURE OF LIFE. Being the William Belden Noble Lectures for 1911. Boston, Houghton, 1912. 157p [BM BVaU LC OLU QMM

THE FISHERMEN'S SAINT. New York, Scribner, 1930. 56p [BM LC OTUV

A LABRADOR LOGBOOK. Boston, Little Brown, 1938. 372p [Another ed., London, Hodder, 1939.] [BM BVaU LC OTUV

A MAN'S FAITH. Boston, Pilgrim, 1908. 48p [New ed., 1926. 87p] [BM LC OTU QMM

A MAN'S HELPERS. Boston, Pilgrim, 1910. 76p [LC

ON IMMORTALITY. Boston, Pilgrim, 1912. 35p [BM LC

THE PRIZE OF LIFE. Boston, Pilgrim, 1914. 32p [LC

RELIGION IN EVERYDAY LIFE. Chicago, American Library Assoc., 1926. 30p [BVa LC

WHAT CAN JESUS CHRIST DO WITH ME. Boston, Pilgrim, 1912. 26p [LC

WHAT CHRIST MEANS TO ME. Boston, Houghton, 1927. 81p [Another ed., London, Hodder, 1926.] [BM BVaU LC OTU QMM

WHAT LIFE MEANS TO ME. Boston, Pilgrim, 1910. 32p [BM LC OLU

WHAT THE CHURCH MEANS TO ME. A Frank Confession and a Friendly Estimate by an Insider. Boston, Pilgrim, 1911. 36p [BVa LC

WHAT WILL YOU DO WITH JESUS CHRIST. Boston, Pilgrim, 1910. 30p [LC

**Griffith, Rev. Arthur Leonard, 1920–**

THE ROMAN LETTER TODAY. Toronto, Ryerson, 1959. 77p

**Guelph, Ont. St. George's Church**

HISTORY OF ST. GEORGE'S PARISH, GUELPH, ONT., 1832–1932. Guelph, Gummer, 1932. 91p [OTU

**Gunn, Rev. William Thomas, 1867–1930**

HIS DOMINION. ... Toronto, Canadian Council of the Missionary Education Movement, 1917. 269p [BM BVaU NSHD OTP

HOMELY HOMILIES. New York, Smith, 1930. 147p [LC OTUV

**Hague, Rev. Dyson, 1857–1935**

THE CHURCH OF ENGLAND BEFORE THE REFORMATION. With an Introductory Note by H.C. Moule. London, Thynne, 1897. 399p [BM OTU

THE CHURCH OF ENGLAND, THE CENTRE OF UNITY. ... Halifax, Morton, 1892. 86p [NSHD

THE HIGHER CRITICISM. Toronto, Evangelical Pub., 1923. 36p [OTP

THE PROTESTANTISM OF THE PRAYER BOOK. ... Toronto, Bryant, 1890. 171p [BM NSHD OTUV

THROUGH THE PRAYER BOOK. An Exposition of its Teaching and Language, the Origins and Contents of its Services; with Special Reference to the more Recent Features of the Canadian Prayer Book. London, Longmans, 1932. 399p [BM BVaU LC OTU

ST. ANDREW'S WORK. ... Halifax, Halloway, n.d. 86p [NSWA

THE STORY OF THE ENGLISH PRAYER BOOK, its Origin and Developments. With Special Chapters on the Scottish, Irish, American, and Canadian Prayer Books. London, Longmans, 1926. 279p [BM BVa LC OTU QMM

WHO ARE THE HIGHER CRITICS? Priv. pub., 1910. 36p [OTU

**Haig, Kennethe Macmahon**

WHAT MEAN THESE STONES. Story of Old Kildonan Church. Winnipeg, the Church, 1951. 33p

**Hall, Samuel**

SCIENCE AND THEOLOGY. ... The Creator and the Created. ... Hamilton, Author, 1875. 60p [Haight Pt I

**Hall, Rev. William Lashley, –1947**

THE CONTINUITY OF REVELATION. Toronto, Briggs, 1908. 197p [BM BVaU OTUV

**Hallam, William Thomas Thompson, 1878–1956**

THE VICTORY OF FAITH. A Study in Christian Missions. Toronto, Church of England in Canada, 1952. 94p

**Hamilton, Kenneth Morrison, 1917–**

THE PROTESTANT WAY. London, Epworth Press, 1956. 264p

**Hamilton, Margaret Lillian, 1909–**
IS SURVIVAL A FACT? Winnipeg, Free Press, 1957. 35p

**Hamilton, Ont. Westdale United Church**
ANNIVERSARY SERVICES, 25 YEARS, 1930–1955. Hamilton, the Church, 1955. 18p

**Harding, J.A.**
DEBATE ON BAPTISM, EMBRACING MODE AND SUBJECTS. Between Elder J.A. Harding, and Rev. T.L. Wilkinson. Held in Meaford, Ont., Commencing December 15th, 1884 ... stenographically reported. Toronto, Briggs, 1886. 406p [OKQ

**Harman, H.M.**
THE STORY OF THE CHURCH OF ST. GEORGE THE MARTYR [ANGLICAN] OF TORONTO [1845–1945]. Comp. by H.M. Harman and W.G. Upshall. Toronto, Rous & Mann, 1945. 52p [OOA

**Harris, John**
THE BIBLE READ BY THE LIGHT OF IDEAL SCIENCE. By Kuklos (J.H.) [pseud]. Montreal, 1874. 26p [BM QMM
THE LIFE OF THE REV. FRANCIS METHERALL AND THE HISTORY OF THE BIBLE CHRISTIAN CHURCH IN PRINCE EDWARD ISLAND. London, Bible Christian Book, 1883. n.p. [NSWA OTUV

**Harris, Rev. Joseph Hemington, 1800–1881**
A SERMON ... IN AID OF THE SUNDAY SCHOOL SOCIETY. ... York, Stanton, [1833?]. 23p [OTP

**Harris, Reginald Vanderbilt, 1881–**
THE CHURCH OF SAINT PAUL IN HALIFAX, NOVA SCOTIA, 1749–1949. Toronto, Ryerson, 1949. 310p [BVaU NSHD OTP QMM

**Harris, Rev. William Richard, 1847–1923**
THE CATHOLIC CHURCH IN THE NIAGARA PENINSULA, 1626–1895. Toronto, Briggs, 1895. 352p [BM BVaU LC NSHD OTU
THE CROSS-BEARERS OF THE SAGUENAY. Toronto, Dent, 1920. 202p [BVaU LC NBFU OOA
ESSAYS IN OCCULTISM, SPIRITISM, AND DEMONOLOGY. Toronto, McClelland, 1919. 181p [BM LC NSHD OOU
HISTORY OF THE EARLY MISSIONS IN WESTERN CANADA. Toronto, Hunter Rose, 1893. 339p [BVaU LC NBFU OTP
PIONEERS OF THE CROSS IN CANADA. Toronto, McClelland, 1912. 240p [A 3rd ed.: Toronto, 1930.] [BVaU LC NSWA OLU

**Hart, Lewis Alexander, 1847–**
A JEWISH REPLY TO CHRISTIAN EVANGELISTS. New York, Bloch, 1906. 239p [BM LC QMM

**Hart, Walter T., 1868–1948**

SIXTY-THREE YEARS OF UNINTERRUPTED SERVICE: FORT ROUGE METHODIST CHURCH, 1883–1925; ... CRESCENT-FORT ROUGE UNITED CHURCH, 1935–1945: Historical Sketch. Winnipeg, Bishop Print., 1947. 91p [OTU

**Hartley, Rev. G.A.**

IMMORTALITY VERSUS ANNIHILATION. Saint John, Barnes, 1867. 53p [NBB

**Harvey, Rev. Moses, 1820–1901**

LECTURES ON EGYPT AND ITS MONUMENTS, AS ILLUSTRATIVE OF SCRIPTURE. ... St. John's, McConnan, 1857. 95p [NSHD

LECTURES ON THE HARMONY OF SCIENCE AND REVELATION. ... Halifax, Barnes, 1856. 104p [NSHD

**Hawkins, Ernest, 1802–1868**

ANNALS OF THE DIOCESE OF FREDERICTON. London, S.P.C.K., 1847. 74p [BM BVaU NSWA OTU QMM

ANNALS OF THE DIOCESE OF QUEBEC. London, S.P.C.K., 1848–1849. 2v [BM BVaU NSWA OTU QMM

ANNALS OF THE DIOCESE OF TORONTO. London, S.P.C.K., 1848. 246p [BVaU NSWA OTP

DOCUMENTS RELATIVE TO THE ERECTION AND ENDOWMENT OF ADDITIONAL BISHOPRICS IN THE COLONIES. ... Ed. by ——. London, Rivington, etc., 1844. xxxi + 62p [BM OTP

HISTORICAL NOTICES OF THE MISSIONS OF THE CHURCH OF ENGLAND IN THE NORTH AMERICAN COLONIES. ... London, Fellowes, 1845. 447p [BM NSWA OTU QMM

**Heeney, Rev. William Bertal, 1873–1955**

CENTENARY ADDRESSES & SERMONS. Collected & Arranged. ... The Rupert's Land Celebration Held in Winnipeg, October 10th to 17th, 1920. N.p., n.pub., n.d. 127p [BViPA SSU

EVOLUTION AND RELIGION. Winnipeg, Laymen of St. Luke's, [1927?]. 76p [OKQ

LEADERS OF THE CANADIAN CHURCH. Ed. by ——. Toronto, Musson, 1918. 319p [2nd series, 1920; 3rd series, 1943.] [BM BVaU LC NSWA OKQ QMM

SECRET OF POWER. Addresses on the Holy Spirit. Toronto, Ryerson, 1944. 38p [BVi OTP

WHAT OUR CHURCH STANDS FOR. The Anglican Church in Canadian Life. By William Bertal Heeney [and others]. Toronto, McClelland, 1932. 292p [BVa OTP

**Hendel, Charles William, 1890–**

CIVILIZATION AND RELIGION. An Argument about Values in Human Life. The Rockwell Lectures on Religion at the Rice Institute. ... New Haven, Yale U. Press, 1948. 78p [BM BVi LC NBFU QMM

**Henderson, George A.**

EARLY SAINT JOHN METHODISM AND HISTORY OF CENTENARY METHODIST CHURCH, SAINT JOHN, N.B. A Jubilee Souvenir. Ed. by ——. Saint John, Day, 1890. 176p [NBFU

**Hendy, Rev. Albert Edward, 1905–**

ST. PAUL'S CHURCH, NANAIMO, B.C. A Brief History since its Foundation, 1859–1952. Nanaimo, St. Paul's Church, 1953. 36p

**Herklots, Rev. Hugh Gerard Gibson, 1903–**

AMSTERDAM 1948. An Account of the First Assembly of the World Council of Churches. London, S.C.M. Press, 1948. 88p [BM LC NSHD

THESE DENOMINATIONS. An Informal Introduction. ... London, S.C.M. Press, 1946. 143p [BM NSHD OTUV

THE EPISTLE OF ST. PAUL TO THE PHILIPPIANS. A Devotional Commentary. London, Lutterworth, 1946. n.p. [BM OTUV

A FRESH APPROACH TO THE NEW TESTAMENT. London, S.C.M. Press, 1950. n.p. [BM BVaU OTUV

HOW THE CHURCHES ARE UNITING. London, S.P.C.K., 1943. 29p [BM LC

PILGRIMAGE TO AMSTERDAM. By H.G.G. Herklots and Henry Smith Leiper. New York, Morehouse-Gorham, 1947. 90p [BM LC

PIONEER DAYS IN THE WESTERN CHURCH. N.p., 1933. 24p [NSWA OKQ

**Herridge, Rev. William Thomas, 1857–1929**

THE COIGN OF VANTAGE. New York, Revell, 1908. 160p [BM QMM

THE ORBIT OF LIFE. Studies in Human Experience. New York, Revell, 1906. 147p [BM NSHD OKQ

**Herzer, John E.**

HOMESTEADING FOR GOD. The Story of the Lutheran Church (Missouri Synod) in Alberta and British Columbia. Edmonton, Commercial Print., [1946?]. 70p [ACG

**Hezzelwood, Oliver, 1861–1933**

TRINITY WAR BOOK. ... A Partial Description of Various War Efforts Participated in by the People of the Trinity Methodist Church, Toronto, Containing One Hundred New Stories from the War Front. ... Toronto, Trinity Methodist Church, 1921. 368p [BM BVa OTU

**Hill, Rev. George William, 1824–1906**

LETTER TO THE PARISHIONERS OF ST. PAUL'S, HALIFAX. Halifax, Macnab & Shaffer, 1866. 48p [BM NSHD

RECORDS OF THE CHURCH OF ENGLAND IN RAWDON FROM ITS ORIGIN UNTIL THE PRESENT DATE. Halifax, Bowes, 1858. 28p [NSHP

RECORDS OF THE CHURCH OF ENGLAND IN NEWPORT, FROM ITS ORIGIN UNTIL THE PRESENT DATE. Halifax, Bowes, 1858. 22p [NSHP

REVIEW OF THE RISE AND PROGRESS OF THE CHURCH OF ENGLAND IN NOVA SCOTIA. Halifax, King's College Alumni, 1858. 33p [NSWA

**Hill, Hamnett Pinhey, 1876–1942**

HISTORY OF CHRIST CHURCH CATHEDRAL, OTTAWA, 1832–1932. Ottawa, Runge Press, 1932. 122p [OTP

**Hill, Rev. James Edgar, 1842–1911**

QUEEN CHARITY, AND OTHER SERMONS. Montreal, 1890. 415p [BVaU OTUV QMM

**Hill, Philip Carteret, 1821–1894**

DRIFTING AWAY. London, Bemrose, 1885. 46p [BM NSHD

**Hirschfelder, Jacob Maier, 1819–1902**

BIBLICAL EXPOSITOR AND PEOPLE'S COMMENTARY. 2v Vol 1, Introduction. History of Hebrew Literature. Vol 2, Commentary on Genesis. Toronto, Rowsell, 1882–5. [OTU

THE CREATION. Being Two Lectures on the Mosaic Account. ... Toronto, Rowsell, 1874. 75p [NSHP

THE SCRIPTURES DEFENDED. Being a Reply to Bishop Colenso's Book on the Pentateuch and the Book of Joshua. Toronto, Rowsell, 1863. 215p [OTP

**Hodgins, John George, 1821–1912**

HISTORICAL SKETCH OF THE DIOCESE OF TORONTO, 1839–1889. By J.G. Hodgins and Henry Scadding. N.p., n.d. 28p [OTU

**Hofer, Peter, 1885–**

THE HUTTERIAN BRETHREN AND THEIR BELIEFS. Starbuck, Man., Hutterian Brethren of Manitoba, 1955. 48p

**Hominuke, J.**

A CENTENARY OF UKRAINIAN BAPTISTS. A Century of Struggle and Martyrdom for the "Faith once delivered to the Saints." Winnipeg, Ukrainian Evangelical-Baptist Alliance, 1952. 32p

**Hopewell, N.S. Union (Presbyterian) Church**

HISTORY OF HOPEWELL UNION (PRESBYTERIAN) CHURCH [Pictou, N.S.] N.p., n.p., 1921. 23p [NSWA

**Hopper, Jane (Agar), –1922**

OLD-TIME PRIMITIVE METHODISM IN CANADA (1829–1884). By Mrs. R.P. Hopper. Toronto, Briggs, 1904. 336p [BM BVaU LC NBFU OKQ

**Hopper, John Elisha Peck, 1841–1895**

ECCE AGNUS DEI. A Reply to ECCE HOMO. Saint John, "Christian Visitor," 1879. [NBB

1492–1892; or, Four Hundred Years of Progress. Halifax, "Herald," 1894. [NBB
RECOGNITION OF FRIENDS IN HEAVEN. Saint John, "Progress," 1894. 100p [NBB

**Hordern, Rev. William Edward, 1920–**

THE CASE FOR A NEW REFORMATION THEOLOGY. Philadelphia, Westminster Press, 1959. 176p
CHRISTIANITY, COMMUNISM, AND HISTORY. Nashville, Tenn., Abingdon Press, 1954. 174p

**Horner, Ralph Cecil, 1854–1921**

ORIGINAL AND INBRED SIN. Ottawa, Crain, 1896. 148p [BM OLU
PENTECOST. Toronto, Briggs, 1891. 143p [Ryerson Impt

**Hoskin, Mary**

HISTORY OF ST. BASIL'S PARISH, ST. JOSEPH ST., TORONTO. Toronto, Catholic Register, 1912. 172p [OTU

**Hotson, Zella May, 1893–**

PIONEER BAPTIST WORK IN OXFORD COUNTY. Woodstock, Commercial, 1939. 52p [OTP

**Howley, Rev. Michael Francis, 1843–1914**

ECCLESIASTICAL HISTORY OF NEWFOUNDLAND. Boston, Doyle & Whittle, 1888. 426p [BM BVaU LC NSWA OOA

**Howse, Rev. Ernest Marshall, 1902–**

THE LAW AND THE PROPHETS. A Series of Sermons on the Making of the Old Testament. Toronto, Ryerson, 1947. 69p [LC OTU
THE LIVELY ORACLES. London, Allen & Unwin; Toronto, Nelson, 1956. 224p
OUR PROPHETIC HERITAGE. Toronto, Ryerson, 1945. 66p [LC NSHD OTP

**Hubicz, Rev. Edward Michael, 1912–**

THE HISTORY OF OUR LADY OF THE LAKE CHURCH, WINNIPEG BEACH, MANITOBA, 1911 TO 1956. An Historical Study of the Founding of a Church and of its Development over a Period of Forty-Five Years. Winnipeg, 1956. 49p

**Huestis, Rev. Charles Herbert, 1863–1951**

SUNDAY IN THE MAKING. A Historical & Critical Study of the Sabbath Principle in Inheritance and Development. New York, Abingdon Press, 1929. 256p [LC OTUV

**Hughes, James Laughlin, 1846–1935**

SKETCHES OF THE SHARON TEMPLE AND OF ITS FOUNDER, DAVID WILLSON. Toronto, Federal Print., [1918?]. 16p [OTU

**Humbert, Stephen, 1768?–1849**

THE RISE AND PROGRESS OF METHODISM, IN THE PROVINCE OF NEW BRUNSWICK ... UNTIL ... 1805. Saint John, Durant, 1836. 43p [NBB

**Humphrey, W.H.**

THE SABBATH. A Moral and Positive Institution. Being Two Sermons. ... Halifax, "Christian Messenger," 1860. 32p [NSHD

**Hunter, Alexander Jardine, 1868–1940**

A FRIENDLY ADVENTURE. The Story of the United Church Mission among New Canadians at Teulon, Manitoba. Toronto, United Church, 1929. 145p [BViPA MWP OTUV

**Hunter, James Hogg, 1890–**

THE BOW IN THE CLOUD. Toronto, Evangelical Pub., 1948. 154p [CC

THE GREAT DECEPTION. Toronto, Evangelical Pub., 1945. 126p [CC

THINE IS THE KINGDOM. Toronto, Evangelical Pub., 1951. 288p

**Hunter, Rev. William John, 1835–1911**

THE PLEASURE DANCE IN ITS RELATION TO RELIGION AND MORALITY. A Sermon Preached in the Bloor Street Methodist Church. ... Toronto, Methodist Book, 1881. 26p [OTUV

**Huntsman, Archibald Gowanlock, 1883–**

LIFE AND THE UNIVERSE. Toronto, Distributed by U. of Toronto Press Book Dept., [c1959]. x + 112p

**Hutchinson, Rev. Daniel Falloon**

AN ASTRONOMICAL PHILOSOPHY; or, The Study of the Heavens Made Easy. Kingston, Author, 1855. 146p [OTUV

THE GOOD OLD WAY. A Discourse on the Nature, Importance and Subjects of Christian Baptism. ... Halifax, Macnab & Shaffer, 1864. 40p [NSHD OTP

**Hutchison, Rev. Harry, 1923–**

THE CHURCH AND SPIRITUAL HEALING. Foreword by the Very Rev. Geo. Johnstone Jeffrey. London, Rider, 1955. 164p

A FAITH TO LIVE BY. Natick, Mass., Wilde Co., 1959. 92p

**Hutton, Samuel King, 1877–**

BY PATIENCE AND THE WORD. The Story of the Moravian Missions. London, Hodder, 1935. 252p [LC OTUV NSHPL

**Inglis, Rev. Charles, 1734–1816**

A VINDICATION OF THE BISHOP OF LANDAFF'S SERMON FROM THE GROSS MISREPRESENTATIONS, AND ABUSIVE REFLECTIONS CONTAINED IN MR. WILLIAM LIVINGSTON'S LETTER TO HIS LORDSHIP. ... By a Lover of Truth and Decency [pseud]. New York, Holt, 1768. 82p [LC

**Inglis, Rev. David, 1825–1877**

RIGHTEOUSNESS EXALTETH A NATION. ... Hamilton, "Spectator," 1866. 14p [NSWA OTP

SYSTEMATIC THEOLOGY IN ITS RELATION TO MODERN THOUGHT. A Lecture delivered at Knox College. Toronto, Adam, 1870. 23p [NSWA

**Inglis, Rev. John, 1777–1850**

THE JUDGEMENT SEAT OF CHRIST. A Sermon. ... Halifax, Royal Gazette, [1835?]. 20p [BM LC

**Ingraham, Mary (Kinley), 1874–1949**

SEVENTY-FIVE YEARS. Historical Sketch of the United Baptist Women's Missionary Union. Kentville, N.S. [1947?]. 68p [NBFL

**Innes, Rev. Thomas Christie, 1909–**

BATTLE-TESTED RELIGION. New York, American Tract Soc., 1944. 191p [LC

CHRISTIAN AND SOLDIER. Toronto, Nelson, 1939. 12p [OTU

LOVE'S BLEEDING HEART. Radio and Other Messages. Toronto, Thorn Press, 1942. 142p [LC

**Irving, Rev. George Clerk, –1866**

PARISH, SCHOOL, AND COLLEGE SERMONS. [With a memoir of the author's life by the Rev. George Whitaker.] Montreal, Lovell, 1867. 236p [BVaU NSWA OLU QMSS

**Irwin, William Andrew, 1884–**

THE OLD TESTAMENT. Keystone of Human Culture. New York, Schuman, 1952. 293p

**Ivison, Ernest Hauber Stuart, 1906–**

THE BAPTISTS IN UPPER AND LOWER CANADA BEFORE 1820. By Stuart Ivison and Fred Rosser. Toronto, U. of Toronto Press, 1956. 193p

**Jack, David Russell, 1864–1913**

HISTORY OF SAINT ANDREW'S CHURCH, SAINT JOHN, N.B. Saint John, Barnes, 1913. 407p [BVaU NBFU OTP QMM

**Jackson, Alan Bart, 1894–**

FOR CHRISTIANS ONLY. Simcoe, Ont., 1959. ix + 107p

**Jackson, Rev. William**

THE PORTRAIT OF THE REV. THOMAS TAYLOR; or, The Hypocrite Unmasked. Halifax, Blackadar, 1835. 27p [NSWA

MAN OF SORROWS; or, The Providence of God Displayed. ... Balt, Wooddy, 1834. 339p [NSHD

**Jackson, William, 1840–1915**

IMMORTALITY VERSUS ANNIHILATION. An Inquiry Concerning the Nature and Destiny of the Human Soul. Montreal, Grafton, 1872. 252p [OTP

**Jacob, Rev. Edwin, 1795?–1868**

SERMONS. Intended for the Propagation of the Gospel. Fredericton, Simpson, 1835. 164p [BM NSWA

**James, Percy**

A HISTORY OF ST. MARY'S CHURCH, OAK BAY, VICTORIA, B.C. Victoria, Parker Buckle, n.d. 28p [BViPA

**Jameson, John**

FROM WENTWORTH MISSION TO ST. ANDREWS CHURCH, 1856–1935. Hamilton, Modern Printery, 1935. 68p [OTU

**Jamieson, Mrs. R.E. and Smith, W.H.**

THE FIRST TEN YEARS. A Brief History of Shaughnessy Heights United Church up to November 30, 1937. [Anon] Vancouver, The Church, 1938. 15p [BViPA OTU

**Janzen, Jacob H.**

TALES FROM MENNONITE HISTORY. Waterloo, Ont., Author, 1945. 96p [OTP

**Jaques, G.E.**

CHRONICLES OF THE ST. JAMES ST. METHODIST CHURCH, MONTREAL. Toronto, Briggs, 1888. 116p [BVaU OTU

**Jarvis, Thomas Stinson, 1854–1926**

THE ASCENT OF LIFE; or, The Psychic Laws and Forces in Nature. Boston, Arena, 1894. 120p [LC

THE PRICE OF PEACE. Los Angeles, Rowny Press, 1921. 126p [LC

**Jefferson, Rev. Robert, 1881–**

FAITH OF OUR FATHERS. The Story of the Diocese of Ottawa. About the Building of the Diocese by the Right Reverend Robert Jefferson and about the People and their Churches by Leonard L. Johnson. Ottawa, Anglican Book Society, 1957. 230p

**Jelfs, George Frederick**

COMMENTARIES ON SIN. Boston, Sherman French, 1910. 105p [LC

MAN'S NATURAL, MORAL AND SOCIAL DUTIES. Words of Wisdom and Good Counsel, Selected ... from the Writings and Sayings of Eminent Authors, Ancient and Modern. Ed. by ——. Hamilton, Cloke's Bookstore, 1925. 227p [OTU

THE TRUE OBJECT OF LIFE. Hamilton, Spectator, 1906. 215p [BM OTU

**Jenkins, Rev. John, 1813–1898**

A PROTESTANT'S APPEAL TO THE DOUAY BIBLE, and Other Roman Catholic Standards, in Support of the Doctrines of the Reformation. Montreal, Wesleyan Book, 1853. 424p [LC OTP QMM

**Jennings, Rev. John, 1814–1876**

REASON OR REVELATION; or, The Religion, Philosophy of the Ancient Heathen,

Contrasted with Christianity and its Legitimate Consequences. ... Toronto, Cleland, 1852. 48p [NSHD OTUV

SAY NO. Toronto, 1865. 59p [BibC

**Johnston, Rev. Angus Anthony, 1897–**

A HISTORY OF THE CATHOLIC CHURCH IN EASTERN NOVA SCOTIA. V. 1: 1611–1827. Antigonish, St. Francis Xavier U. Press, 1960. 555p

**Johnston, Rev. Hugh, 1840–1922**

BEYOND DEATH. New York, Eaton & Mains, 1903. 330p [LC

**Johnston, Robert, 1862–**

PRESBYTERIAN WORSHIP. Its Spirit, Method and History. Toronto, Publishers' Syndicate, 1901. 163p [OTP

**Johnstone, Rev. Robert Cuthbert, 1857–1934**

THE STORY OF THE CHURCH OF ENGLAND IN RUPERTSLAND. Winnipeg, Bulman, 1920. 46p [OTUV SSU

**Jordan, Alfred McKay**

THE BOOK OF THE ONE LAW. Vancouver, Sun Job Presses, 1918. 171p [BM BVaU OOP

**Jordan, Rev. Louis Henry, 1855–1923**

COMPARATIVE RELIGION. Its Adjuncts and Allies. London, Milford, 1915. xxxii + 574p [BM BVaU LC NSHD OTP

COMPARATIVE RELIGION. Its Genesis and Growth. Edinburgh, Clark, 1905. 668p [BM LC NSHD OTU

COMPARATIVE RELIGION. Its Method and Scope. A Paper read in part at the Third International Congress of the History of Religions, Oxford, Sept. 17, 1908. Oxford, Frowde, 1908. 20p [BM NSHD OKQ

COMPARATIVE RELIGION. Its Origin and Outlook. A Lecture. London, Milford, 1913. 16p [BM NSHD OLU

COMPARATIVE RELIGION. Its Range and Limitations. A Lecture. Oxford, Milford, 1916. 15p [BM NSHD OKQ

COMPARATIVE RELIGION. A Survey of Its Recent Literature. ... Reprinted from the *Review of Theology and Religion.* 2 pts. Edinburgh, Schulze, 1906. [2nd ed., 1910. 72p Another edition, "revised and augmented": London, Milford, 1920. 160p] [BM BVaU LC NSHD OTP

**Jordan, Mabel Ellen (Tremlett), 1908–**

THE McDOUGALL MEMORIAL UNITED CHURCH, MORLEY, ALBERTA, THE CHURCH OF THE MOUNTAIN STONEYS. A Souvenir Booklet. Calgary, the Church, 1957. 8p

**Jordan, Rev. William George, 1852–1939**

ANCIENT HEBREW STORIES AND THEIR MODERN INTERPRETATION. London, Hodder, 1922. 344p [BM LC OKQ QMM

BIBLICAL CRITICISM AND MODERN THOUGHT; or, The Place of the Old Testament Documents in the Life of To-day. Edinburgh, Clark, 1909. 322p [BM BVaU OKQ

THE BOOK OF JOB. Its Substance and Spirit. New York, Macmillan, 1929. 193p [BVa LC OOSU

THE CHALLENGE OF THE BOOK; or, The Modern Interpretation of the Old Testament. Kingston, Jackson Press, 1921. [BVaU OTL

COMMENTARY ON THE BOOK OF DEUTERONOMY. New York, Macmillan, 1911. 263p [BVaU OKQ

HISTORY AND REVELATION. The Individuality of Israel. London, Clarke, 1926. 287p [BM BVaU OKQ

PROPHETIC IDEAS AND IDEALS. A Series of Short Studies in the Prophetic Literature of the Hebrew People. Chicago, Revell, 1902. 363p [BM BVaU OKQ QMM

RELIGION IN SONG; or, Studies in the Psalter. London, Clarke, 1918. 275p [BM BVaU OTU

THE RELIGION OF ISRAEL. Kingston, n.p., 1919. 54p [OTU

THE SONG AND THE SOIL; or, The Missionary Idea in the Old Testament. New York, Scribner, 1913. 141p [Another ed., Edinburgh, Clark, 1912.] [BM BVaU OKQ

SONGS OF SERVICE AND SACRIFICE. A Study of *Isaiah* xl–lv. London, Clarke, 1924. 188p [BM BVaU OKQ

**Jose, Rev. Murray Burkholder, 1913–**

MEDITATIONS AT THE LORD'S TABLE. Toronto, Ryerson, 1959. 66p

**K., J. (Cobourg author)**

THE CHURCH AND THE WESLEYANS. By J.K. Cobourg, Chatterton, 1838. 16p [OTP

**Kaufman, Carolyn Reesor, 1883–**

HISTORIC CHURCHES OF ALBERTA AND THE CANADIAN NORTH WEST. Edmonton, Author, 1958. 80p

**Kaulbach, J.A.**

THE HISTORY OF THE PARISH OF ST. JOHN'S, TRURO, COLCHESTER, NOVA SCOTIA. ... Ed. by W.P. Robertson. [Truro?,1913]. 117p [BVaU NSWA

**Kelly, Rev. Edward, 1875–1937**

THE STORY OF ST. PAUL'S PARISH, TORONTO. ... Commemorating the Centenary of the First Parish Church in the Archdiocese of Toronto. Comp. and Ed. by ——. Toronto, priv. print., 1922. 329p [BVaU OTP

**Kelwood, Man. Knox United Church**

A SHORT HISTORICAL SKETCH OF CHURCH WORK IN THE KELWOOD FIELD, UP TO AND AFTER UNION, COMPILED AND PRINTED TO MARK THE OCCASION OF THE 50TH ANNIVERSARY OF THE BUILDING OF KNOX CHURCH, KELWOOD. Gladstone, Man., 1955. 12p

**Kennedy, Henry Dawson, 1869–1925**

MISUNDERSTOOD. Toronto, Briggs, 1903. 105p [BM OTU

**Kenner, Henry, 1832–1916**

POPULAR AMUSEMENTS. The Duty of the Officers and Members of the Methodist Church in Relation Thereto. An Essay. ... Toronto, Briggs, 1882. 15p [OTAr

**Kent, Herbert Harold**

AN ARCHITECT PREACHES. London, Independent Press, 1957. 205p [Sermons.]

**Ker, Rev. Robert, 1843–**

ST. GEORGE'S PARISH CHURCH, ST. CATHARINES. Jubilee Celebration and Historic and Centenary Review. Ed. by ——. St. Catharines, Star Print., [1892?]. 186p [BVaU LC NSWA OTU QMM

**Kerr, Rev. Alexander Enoch, 1898–**

IN THE LAST ANALYSIS. Toronto, Ryerson, 1958. 98p [Sermons and addresses.]

PREFACE TO CHRISTMAS. Toronto, Ryerson, 1951. 104p

**Kerr, Hugh Thomson, 1909–**

MYSTERY AND MEANING IN THE CHRISTIAN FAITH. Toronto, Ryerson, 1958. 51p

**Kilpatrick, Thomas Buchanan, 1858–1930**

NEW TESTAMENT EVANGELISM. ... London, Hodder, 1911. 313p [LC OTUV

OUR COMMON FAITH. With a Brief History of the Church Union Movement in Canada, by K.H. Cousland. Toronto, Ryerson, 1928. 216p [BVaU LC OTUV QMM

**King, Basil, 1859–1928**

THE ABOLISHING OF DEATH. New York, Cosmopolitan, 1919. 197p [LC OTUV

ABRAHAM'S BOSOM. London, Harper, 1918. 53p [BVaU LC OTMC

ADVENTURES IN RELIGION. Garden City, Doubleday, 1929. 252p [BM LC

THE BIBLE AND COMMON SENSE. London, Harper, 1924. 168p [LC NSHD

THE CONQUEST OF FEAR. Garden City, Doubleday, 1921. 270p [BM BVaU LC NSWA OTU QMM

THE DISCOVERY OF GOD. Toronto, Copp Clark, 1923. 265p [BM BVaU NSWA OTP

FAITH AND SUCCESS. Garden City, Doubleday, 1925. 266p [BM LC NSHD OTU

THE SEVEN TORCHES OF CHARACTER. Garden City, Doubleday, 1929. 260p [BM LC

**Kingsbridge, Ont. St. Joseph's Parish**

HISTORY OF ST. JOSEPH'S PARISH, KINGSBRIDGE, ONTARIO. Kingsbridge, the Church, 1938. 40p [OTU

**Kingston, Rev. George Frederick, 1889–1950**

THE FOUNDATIONS OF FAITH. Toronto, Ryerson, 1928. 75p [NSWA OTU

**Kirkwall, Ont. Kirkwall Church**

KIRKWALL CHURCH AND COMMUNITY, 1833–1933. Kirkwall, The Church, 1933. 120p [OTU

**Kirkwood, Mossie May (Waddington), 1890–**

DUTY AND HAPPINESS IN A CHANGED WORLD. Toronto, Macmillan, 1933. 207p [BM BVaU LC OTU QMM

**Kittson, Rev. Henry, 1848–1925**

CHURCH HISTORY FROM THE ARCHIVES. A Study. Kingston, Jackson, [1912?]. 39p [BM NSWA OTP QMSS

**Kromminga, Rev. John H., 1918–**

IN THE MIRROR. An Appraisal of the Christian Reformed Church. Hamilton, Guardian Pub. Co., 1957. 178p

**Krumpelmann, Rev. Cosmas W.**

IN THIS SIGN THEY CONQUERED. Being the Centenary of the Grey Nuns of St. Boniface, 1844–1944. Muenster, Sask., St. Peter's Press, 1944. 33p [MWP

**Kulbeck, Gloria Grace**

WHAT GOD HATH WROUGHT. A History of the Pentecostal Assemblies of Canada. Ed. by Walter E. McAlister and George R. Upton. Toronto, Pentecostal Assemblies of Canada, 1958. 364p

**Lahey, Mrs. Vivian Gwendolyn Davis, 1893–**

THE WOMAN'S ASSOCIATION OF LUNDY'S LANE UNITED CHURCH, 1858–1958. Niagara Falls, Ont., the Church, 1958. 6p

**Lanceley, Rev. John Ellis, 1848–1900**

THE DOMESTIC SANCTUARY; or, The Importance of Family Religion. Hamilton, Spectator Print., 1878. 132p [LC OLU

THE VIRGIN MARY AND OTHER SERMONS, Preached in the New Richmond Methodist Church, McCaul Street, Toronto. ... Toronto, Briggs, 1891. 301p [OTP

**Lande, Lawrence Montague, 1906–**

TOWARD THE QUIET MIND. A Guide to Self-Discovery through the Study of the *Book of Job.* Toronto, McClelland, 1954. 101p

**Landon, Fred, 1880–1969**

A HISTORY OF THE FIRST HUNDRED YEARS OF THE FIRST UNITED CHURCH, LONDON, ONTARIO ... 1832–1932. London, Ont., 1932. 59p [LC OTP

**Langford, Rev. Norman Frederick, 1914–**

BARRIERS TO BELIEF. Philadelphia, Westminster Press, 1958. 96p

THE TWO-EDGED SWORD: SERMONS. Philadelphia, Westminster Press, 1945. 194p [BVaU

**Langtry, Rev. John, 1834–1906**

CATHOLIC VERSUS ROMAN; or, Some of the Fundamental Points of Difference between the Catholic Church and the Roman Church. In Ten Lectures, delivered in St. Luke's Church, Toronto, in 1885. Toronto, Hunter Rose, 1886. 225p [BVaU NSWA OTP

COME HOME. An Appeal on Behalf of Reunion. Toronto, Church of England Pub. Co., 1900. 399p [BM BVaU OOU

HISTORY OF THE CHURCH IN EASTERN CANADA AND NEWFOUNDLAND. London, S.P.C.K., 1892. 256p [BM BVaU NBFU OTP

A STRUGGLE FOR LIFE. Higher Criticism Criticized. Toronto, Briggs, 1905. 328p [BM OTP

**Lanton, Rev. Henry, 1809?–1888**

LECTURES ON THE SECOND ADVENT OF CHRIST. Montreal, Wilson, 1855. 452p [BVaU NSWA OTU

**Lappin, Rev. Maitland M.**

BAPTISTS IN THE PROTESTANT TRADITION. Toronto, Ryerson, 1947. 112p [BVaU OTU

**Lathern, Rev. John, 1831–1905**

BAPTISMA. A Three-fold Testimony. Water-baptism, Spirit-baptism, and the Baptism of Fire. ... Charlottetown, Haszard, 1877. 72p [NSHD

BAPTISMA. The Mode and Subjects of Christian Baptism. Halifax, Pickard, 1879. 265p [NSHD OTU

**Law, Rev. Robert, 1860–1919**

THE EMOTIONS OF JESUS. Edinburgh, Clark, 1915. 155p [BM OTU

THE GRAND ADVENTURE, AND OTHER SERMONS. New York, Hodder, 1916. 219p [LC NBFU OLU

THE HOPE OF OUR CALLING. Toronto, McClelland, 1918. 185p [T&C

OPTIMISM AND OTHER SERMONS. Toronto, McClelland, 1919. 203p [BM OTU

THE TESTS OF LIFE. A Study of the First Epistle of St. John. 2nd ed. Edinburgh, Clark, 1909. 422p [BM BVaU LC OTU QMM

**Lawson, James Reid, 1820–1891**

THE MILLENIUM. A Discourse. Saint John, Barnes, 1864. 24p [NSHD

**Laycock, Samuel Ralph, 1891–1971**

PASTORAL COUNSELLING FOR MENTAL HEALTH. Toronto, Ryerson, 1958 x + 94p

**Leach, Rev. William Turnbull, 1805–1886**

AN ADDRESS ON RECHABITISM, Delivered [to] ... the Independent Order of Rechabites ... 18th July, 1845. Montreal, Brother J.C. Becket, 1845. 12p [Sermon to a secret society which promoted temperance.] [OTP

A DISCOURSE DELIVERED IN ST. ANDREW'S CHURCH, TORONTO, ON THE FOURTEENTH DAY OF DECEMBER, 1838. Being a Day of Public Fasting and Humiliation. ... Toronto, "British Colonist," 1839. 16p [OTP

DISCOURSE ON THE NATURE AND DUTIES OF THE MILITARY PROFESSION. ... Toronto, Scobie, 1840. 19p [OTU

**Leard, George Artemas, 1908–**

HISTORIC BEDEQUE, THE LOYALISTS AT WORK AND WORSHIP IN PRINCE EDWARD ISLAND. A History of Bedeque United Church. Bedeque, P.E.I., Bedeque United Church, 1948. 172p [NBFU OTP

SUMMERSIDE SAINTS AND SINNERS. A History of Trinity United Church, Summerside, P.E.I. Summerside, the Church, 1958. 62p

**Lee, George Herbert, 1854–1905**

AN HISTORICAL SKETCH OF THE FIRST FIFTY YEARS OF THE CHURCH OF ENGLAND IN THE PROVINCE OF NEW BRUNSWICK, 1783–1833. Saint John, Sun Pub. Co., 1880. 141p [BVaU NSWA OTU

**Legal, Emile Joseph, 1849–1920**

SHORT SKETCHES OF THE HISTORY OF THE CATHOLIC CHURCHES AND MISSIONS IN CENTRAL ALBERTA. Comp. by ——. Winnipeg, West Canada Pub. Co., 1914. 174p [AEU BVaU OTP QMBM

**Legge, Rev. Arthur Ernest Edgar, 1889–**

THE ANGLICAN CHURCH IN THREE RIVERS, QUEBEC, 1768–1956. Russell, Ont., Author, 1956. xv + 191p

**Leith, Ont. United Church**

THE EARLY HISTORY OF LEITH UNITED CHURCH. Leith, The Church, 1942. 17p [OTP

**Lench, Rev. Charles, 1860–1931**

AN ACCOUNT OF THE RISE AND PROGRESS OF METHODISM ON THE GRAND BANK AND FORTUNE CIRCUITS FROM 1816 TO 1916. ... [St. John's, Barnes], 1916. 80p [NfSM

THE STORY OF METHODISM IN BONAVISTA, AND THE SETTLEMENTS VISITED BY THE EARLY PREACHERS. ... [Bonavista, Nfld.], Author, 1919. 206p [NfSM OTU

**LeSage, Rev. J.L.**

ST. PATRICK'S CHURCH CENTENNIAL, 1855–1955. Comp. by ——. Ottawa, the Church, 1955. 44p

**Leslie, Rev. Charles Whitney, 1905–**

NO GRAVEN IMAGES. The Contemporary Relevance of the Ten Commandments. Toronto, Ryerson, 1954. xx + 88p

**Le Sueur, William Dawson, 1840–1917**

A DEFENCE OF MODERN THOUGHT. In Reply to a Recent Pamphlet, by the Bishop of Ontario on "Agnosticism." Toronto, Hunter Rose, 1884. 40p [NSWA OTP

EVOLUTION AND THE POSITIVE ASPECTS OF MODERN THOUGHT. In Reply to the Bishop of Ontario's Second Lecture on Agnosticism. Ottawa, Woodburn, 1884. 43p [BM QMSS

**Levy, George Edward, 1902–**

THE BAPTISTS OF THE MARITIME PROVINCES, 1753–1946. Saint John, Barnes-Hopkins, 1946. 336p [LC NBFU OTP

**Levy, Herman David**

A HISTORY OF FIRST BAPTIST CHURCH, TRURO, N.S. Truro, the Church, 1958. 51p [A centennial history.]

**Lewis, Fred**

LO, THE LIGHT SHINETH, AND MAKETH CLEAR THE DARKNESS. Winnipeg, Author, 1943. 94p [OTP

**Lewis, Rev. John Travers, 1825–1901**

AGNOSTICISM. ... Kingston, Author, 1883. 32p [NSHD OTU

**Lightbourn, Alexander Harvey, 1890–**

SAINT JUDE'S CHURCH, OAKVILLE, 1842–1957. An Historical Sketch. Rev. ed. Oakville, Ont., St. Jude's Church, 1957. 31p [First pub. in 1953.]

**Lindeman, Harold Roy, 1931–**

A HISTORY OF ZION EVANGELICAL LUTHERAN CHURCH, SHERWOOD, ONTARIO, 1806–1956. ... Comp. by ——. Sherwood, Ont., Author, 1956. [mimeographed]

**Lindsey, Charles, 1820–1908**

THE CLERGY RESERVES. ... By Charles Lindsay [*sic*]. Toronto, North American Press, 1851. 59p [NSWA OTP

**Line, Rev. John, 1885–**

THE DOCTRINE OF THE CHRISTIAN MINISTRY. London, Lutterworth Press, 1959. 190p

**Linscott, Rev. Thomas S., 1846–1919**

THE HEART OF CHRISTIANITY. Philadelphia, Bradley-Garretson, 1906–7. 2v [BM LC

**Lockhart, Rev. Wilfred Cornett, 1906–**

BETHLEHEM. The Meaning and Significance of Christmas for our Day. Toronto, United Church Pub. House, 1955. 53p

IN SUCH AN AGE. Younger Voices in the Canadian Church. Ed. by ——. Toronto, McClelland, 1951. xxiii + 215p

**Lodge, Rupert Clendon, 1886–**

APPLIED PHILOSOPHY. London, Routledge and Paul, 1951. xi + 243p [American ed. (Boston, Beacon Press) has title: APPLYING PHILOSOPHY.]

**London, Ont. First United Church**

A HISTORY OF THE FIRST HUNDRED YEARS OF THE FIRST UNITED CHURCH, LONDON, ONTARIO (Formerly the First Presbyterian Church), 1832–1932. London, the Church, 1932. 59p [OLU

**Longley, James Wilberforce, 1849–1922**

LOVE. Toronto, Copp Clark, 1898. 158p [BM BVaU NSWA OLU QMBM

**Longley, Ronald Stewart, 1896–**

THE WOLFVILLE UNITED BAPTIST CHURCH. Wolfville, N.S., the Church, 1953. 87p

**Longstaff, Frederick Victor, 1879–1961**

CHRIST CHURCH CATHEDRAL, VICTORIA, B.C. A Short History. Victoria, Author, 1951. 23p

**Low, Rev. George Jacobs, 1836–1906**

THE FIRST MIRACLE OF CHRIST AND PROHIBITION. A Sermon preached in St. Peter's Church, Brockville ... 1886. Toronto, Robinson, 1886. 14p [NSWA OTP QMBM

THE OLD FAITH AND THE NEW PHILOSOPHY. ... With an intro. by Principal Grant. Toronto, Briggs, 1900. 160p [BM NSWA OTU

**Lowe, John, 1899–1960**

SAINT PETER. New York, Oxford U. Press, 1956. 65p

**Lumsden, James**

THE SKIPPER PARSON ON THE BAYS AND BARRENS OF NEWFOUNDLAND. ... Toronto, Briggs, 1906. 212p [Earlier eds., London, Kelly, 1905; New York, Eaton, 1905.] [BM BVaU NSWA OTU

**Lunenburg, N.S. Methodist Church**

HISTORY OF A CENTURY. ... Lunenburg, The Church, 1914. 28p [NSWA

**Luxton, Rev. George Nasmith, 1901–**

THE OLD PARISH CHURCH OF ST. CATHARINES. Historical Sermons. ... With the Book of Remembrance of St. George's Church. St. Catharines, The Church, 1935. 34p [OTU

THE BUILDING OF OLD ST. GEORGE'S, 1835–1840. St. Catharines, The Church, [1937?]. 16p [OTP

**Lyall, Rev. William, 1811–1890**

INTELLECT, THE EMOTIONS AND THE MORAL NATURE. Edinburgh, Constable, 1855. 627p [BM BVaU NSHD OTU QMM

THE PHILOSOPHY OF THOUGHT. A Lecture delivered at the Opening of the Free Church College, Halifax, N.S., Session 1852–3. Halifax, Barnes, 1853. 15p [NSWA OTU

STRICTURES ON THE IDEA OF POWER. Edinburgh, Johnstone, 1842. 52p [OTU

**Lynch-Staunton, Betty (Frankish), 1895–**

A SHORT HISTORY OF THE CHURCH OF ST. JOHN THE EVANGELIST, PINCHER CREEK, ALBERTA. Pincher Creek, the Church, 1954. 12p

**M., H.R.**

ST. PETER'S SANCTUARY GUILD. A Brief History of the Parish of St. Peter's Church, Brockville, Ontario. By H.R.M. Brockville, The Guild, 1927. [OTU

**M., W.**

THE RELATIVE THEORY. Is or Is Not the Bible Infallible? and THE CRITIC CRITICISED COMBINED; or, Truth Vindicated & Error Confounded. Toronto, 1859. 56p [Preface signed: W.M.] [OTP

**McBeth, Margaret Elliot**

THE STORY OF KILDONAN PRESBYTERIAN CHURCH, 1851–1951. Commemorating the Coming of Dr. John Black and the Organization of the Congregation. Winnipeg, Kildonan Presbyterian Church, 1951. 16p

**MacBeth, Rev. Roderick George, 1858–1934**

THE BURNING BUSH AND CANADA. Toronto, Upper Canada Tract Soc., 1925. 160p [Also: Vancouver, Cowan Brookhouse, 1925.] [BVaU OKQ

OUR TASK IN CANADA. [Home Missions, Presbyterian Church.] Toronto, Westminster, 1912. 146p [BVaU LC OTU

**McCall, Oswald Walter Samuel, 1885–**

THE HAND OF GOD. 4th ed. New York, Harper, 1939. 158p [BM BVa

THE USES OF LITERATURE IN THE PULPIT. London, Harper, 1932. 127p [BM BVa LC OTUV

**McCann, Rev. Leonard Albert, 1908–**

THE DOCTRINE OF THE VOID. The Doctrine of the Void as Propounded by St. John of the Cross in his Major Prose Works and as Viewed in the Light of Thomistic Principles. Toronto, Basilian Press, 1955. 146p

**McCaskill, Kenneth**

THE CENTENARY: KNOX PRESBYTERIAN CHURCH, McDONALD'S CORNERS, ONTARIO ... 1845–1945. Lanark, Ont., Era Press, 1945. 62p [OKQ

**McCaul, Rev. John, 1807–1887**

EMIGRATION TO A BETTER COUNTRY. A Sermon preached ... Toronto ... 1842. Toronto, Rowsell, 1842. 15p [OTP

"LOVE OF GOD AND OUR NEIGHBOUR." A Sermon preached ... March 17, 1840. Toronto, Rowsell, 1840. 18p [NSWA OTP

**McCausland, Rev. John George Alban Patrick**

THE CHURCH OF YOUR CHOICE. The Faith, Position and Practice of the Religious Bodies in Canada. Bracebridge, Ont., Society of St. John the Evangelist, 1954. 73p

THE CHURCH'S ANSWERS. Bracebridge, Ont., Society of Saint John the Evangelist, 1950. 107p [Reprinted, 1951, 1952, 1954.] [OONL

A PRIMER OF CHRISTIAN TRUTH. Bracebridge, Ont., Society of St. John the Evangelist, 1955. 114p

**MacClung, Burt Ward**

HISTORY OF THE DEVIL. Regina, 1913. 188p [BM

**McCreary, Man. Knox United Church**

FIFTY YEARS IN OUR CHURCH, 1905–1955. Gladstone, Man., 1955. 9p

**McCulloch, Rev. Thomas, 1776–1843**

CALVINISM, THE DOCTRINE OF THE SCRIPTURES. Glasgow, Collins, [1849]. 270p [NSHD OTU

MEMORIAL FROM THE COMMITTEE OF MISSIONS OF THE PRESBYTERIAN CHURCH OF NOVA SCOTIA TO THE GLASGOW SOCIETY FOR PROMOTING THE RELIGIOUS INTERESTS OF THE SCOTTISH SETTLERS IN BRITISH NORTH AMERICA. With Observations on the Constitution of that Society. ... Edinburgh, Oliver & Boyd, 1826. 75p [NSHD

POPERY CONDEMNED BY SCRIPTURE AND THE FATHERS. Being a Refutation of the Principal Popish Doctrines and Assertions maintained in the Remarks on the Rev. Mr. Stanser's Examination of the Rev. Mr. Burke's Letter of Instruction to the Catholic Missionaries of Nova Scoita. ... Edinburgh, Pillans, 1808. 385p [Also as: POPERY AGAIN CONDEMNED. ... Edinburgh, Neill, 1810. 429p [NSHD OTP

THE PROSPERITY OF THE CHURCH IN TROUBLOUS TIMES. A Sermon preached ... Feb. 25, 1814. New Glasgow, Mackenzie, 1882. 18p [NSHP

A REVIEW OF THE SUPPLEMENT TO THE FIRST ANNUAL REPORT OF THE SOCIETY FOR PROMOTING THE RELIGIOUS INTERESTS OF SCOTTISH SETTLERS IN BRITISH NORTH AMERICA. In a Series of Letters to the Rev. Robert Burns. ... Glasgow, Young, 1828. 50p [OTP

WORDS OF PEACE. Being an Address delivered to the Congregation of Halifax ... in Consequence of some Congregational Disputes. ... Halifax, Ward, 1817. 16p [NSHD

**McCulloch, William, 1811–1895?**

EXISTING CHURCH THOUGHT AND ACTIVITY IN RELATION TO REVEALED CHARACTER AND OBJECTS. A Sermon preached before the Synod of the Presbyterian Church of the Lower Provinces of British North America, June 24th, 1868. ... Halifax, Barnes, 1869. 18p [NSHD OTUV

**McCurdy, Rev. James Frederick, 1847–1935**

HISTORY, PROPHECY AND THE MONUMENTS; or, Israel and the Nations. London, Macmillan, 1897–1901. 3v [BM BVaU LC NBFU OTU QMM

**MacDermot, Hugh Ernest, 1888–**

CHRIST CHURCH CATHEDRAL. A Century in Retrospect. Montreal, Christ Church Cathedral, 1959. 63p

**MacDonald, Rev. Alexander, 1858–1941**

THE MERCIES OF THE SACRED HEART. Twelve Sermons for the First Fridays. New York, Wagner, 1904. 56p [LC

THE SACRAMENTS. A Course of Seven Sermons. New York, Wagner, 1906. 82p [LC

THE SYMBOL IN SERMONS. A Series of Twenty-five Short Sermons on the Articles of the Creed. New York, Christian Press Assoc., 1903. 214p [OOU

THE SYMBOL OF THE APOSTLES. A Vindication of the Apostolic Authorship of the Creed on the Lines of Catholic Tradition. New York, Christian Press Assoc., 1903. 377p [NSHD OOU

**Macdonald, Donald Bruce, 1872–**

SUNDAY EVENINGS AT ST. ANDREW'S COLLEGE. Sermons in the College Chapel. Toronto, McClelland, 1946. 256p [CC

**McDonald, Donald Gordon, 1843–1931**

BIBLE BAPTISMA AND ITS QUALIFICATIONS – VERSUS REV. J. LATHERN'S "BAPTISMA." ... Charlottetown, Coombe, 1878. 200p [NSHD

**McDonald, Rev. Donald, 1783–1867**

THE PLAN OF SALVATION. Charlottetown, Bremner, 1874. 211p [NSWA

THE SUBJECTS OF THE MILLENIUM. Traced in their Downward Progress from their Ancestry through the Pre-Millennial Dispensations. Charlottetown, Haszard, 1849. 417p [NSWA

TREATISE ON THE HOLY ORDINANCE OF BAPTISM. Containing Scriptural Views of the Baptism of John: A Defence of the Doctrine of Infant Baptism. ... Charlottetown, Haszard & Moore, 1898. 264p [First pub. in 1845?] [NSHD

**Macdonald, Malcolm Campbell, 1898–**

FROM LAKES TO NORTHERN LIGHTS. [Toronto], United Church Committee on Missionary Education, [1951]. xii + 202p

**Macdonnell, Rev. George, 1812?–1871**

AID TO SACRAMENTAL COMMUNION. Montreal, Lovell, 1864. 211p [OKQ OLU

BOOK OF DEVOTIONS AND SERMONS. Montreal, Armour, 1851. 362p [NSWA

**McDowall, Rev. Robert, 1769?–1841**

DISCOURSES. Albany, Webster & Skinner, 1806. 123p [OTU

A SERMON ON THE NATURE OF JUSTIFICATION. ... York, U.C., 1805. [DCB

**MacFarlane, Rev. Duncan Herbert, 1898–**

PASSPORT TO PARADISE. [Sermons.] New York, Vantage Press, 1959. 106p

**MacGeorge, Rev. Robert Jackson, 1811?–1884**

THE PERFECT LAW OF LIBERTY. ... Toronto, The Church Office, 1846. 12p [S&T

**McGill, Rev. Robert, 1798–1856**

DISCOURSES PREACHED ON VARIOUS OCCASIONS IN THE COURSE OF MINISTERIAL DUTY. Montreal, Ramsay, 1853. 338p [BVaU LC NSWA OTP QMM

**Macgillivray, Rev. John M., 1883–1966**

ST. ANDREW'S PRESBYTERIAN CHURCH, SARNIA, ONTARIO ... 1841–1941. Sarnia, the Church, 1941. 63p [OLU

**MacGregor, Mary Esther (Miller), 1876–1961**

GLAD DAYS IN GALILEE. A Story of the Boyhood of Jesus. By Marian Keith [pseud]. Toronto, McClelland, 1935. 141p [OTMC

**McGregor, Rev. P.G.**

GALILEO AND THE COPERNICAN SYSTEM. How Treated by Rome. A Lecture, delivered February 7, 1867, in St. Andrew's Hall, Antigonish. ... Halifax, Compton, 1867. 34p [NSHD

PROVIDENCE IN REFERENCE TO NATIONS. A Lecture delivered before the Halifax YMCA, April 6, 1858. ... Halifax, Barnes, 1858. 31p [NSHD

**Machar, Rev. John, 1796–1863**

A PASTOR'S LAST WORDS TO HIS PEOPLE. Kingston, Creighton, 1863. 12p [OTUV

**McIntosh, William Donald, 1881–**

ONE HUNDRED YEARS IN THE ZORRA CHURCH [Knox United, Embro]. Toronto, Ryerson, 1930. 192p [BVaU OTP

**Mackay, Rev. Alexander Bisset, 1842–1901**

GOSPEL OF THE REV. B. FAY MILLS TESTED BY SCRIPTURE. ... Montreal, Morton Phillips, 1894. 23p [NSHD

THE TRUE GNOSTICS. A Sermon preached in Crescent Street Presbyterian Church, Montreal. Montreal, Drysdale, 1880. 13p [OTP

**Mackay, Rev. W.P.**

ABUNDANT GRACE. Selected Addresses. Toronto, Briggs, 1885. 232p [OKQ

GRACE AND TRUTH UNDER TWELVE DIFFERENT ASPECTS. Saint John, Barnes, 1881. 235p [NSWA

THE SEEKING SAVIOUR AND OTHER BIBLE THEMES. Toronto, Briggs, n.d., 247p [NSWA

**MacKay, Rev. William Alexander, 1842–1905**

IMMERSION PROVED TO BE NOT A SCRIPTURAL MODE OF BAPTISM BUT A ROMISH INVENTION; and Immersionists shewn to be disregarding Divine Authority in refusing Baptism to the Infant Children of Believers. Toronto, Briggs, n.d. 130p [3rd ed., 1881.] [NSHD OTU QMSS

**McKellar, Rev. Hugh, 1841–1934?**

PRESBYTERIAN PIONEER MINISTERS. Presbyterian Pioneer Missionaries in Manitoba, Saskatchewan, Alberta and British Columbia. Toronto, Murray Print., 1924. 249p [BM BVaU OTP SSU

**MacKenzie, Archibald J.**

HISTORY OF CHRISTMAS ISLAND PARISH. ... [Christmas Island, N.S.?], 1926. 167p [NSHP OTU

**McKenzie, Rev. Donald**

AN EXPOSITION OF OLD TESTAMENT SACRIFICES. Toronto, Briggs, 1900. 368p [NSWA

**McKenzie, Rev. William Patrick, 1861–1942**

CHRISTIAN SCIENCE. God's Lovingkindness Proved to Men. A Lecture. Boston, Christian Science Pub., 1914. 32p [LC

**MacKinnon, John Y., 1886–1951**

THE PROTESTANT DOCTRINE OF REVELATION. ... Toronto, Ryerson, 1946. 117p [BVaU LC OTP

WHAT PROTESTANTS BELIEVE AND WHY. Toronto, United Church Pub. House, 1944. 41p [LC OTP

**MacKinnon, Murdoch Archibald, 1871–1954**

THE CHORUS OF LIFE. Toronto, Ryerson, 1930. 267p [BVa LC OTU

THE IMPRISONED SPLENDOUR. London, Allenson, 1922. 159p [BM

**McKinnon, Rev. William Charles, –1862**

DIVINE SOVEREIGNTY. A Sermon ... preached at Elmsdale, April 14th, 1861. ... Halifax, Conference Job Print., 1861. 19p [NSHD

PAPACY: THE SACRIFICE OF THE MASS – Third Lecture delivered before the Protestant Alliance of Nova Scotia ... Jan. 11th, 1859. ... Halifax, Wesleyan Conference Steam Press, 1859. 28p [NSHD

**Maclaren, William**

LITERATURE AND DOGMA. An Inaugural Lecture ... on the Occasion of his Induction as Professor of Systematic Theology in Knox College. Toronto, Willing & Williamson, 1873. 24p [OTUV

THE ROMISH DOCTRINE OF THE RULE OF FAITH EXAMINED. A Lecture. With an appendix in which certain statements of Rev. Father Damen and Rev. Dr. O'Connor are considered. Ottawa, Henderson, [1872?]. 40p [OTUV

**McLaurin, Rev. Colin Campbell, 1854–1941**

MY OLD HOME CHURCH IN RURAL ONTARIO. Edmonton, Institute Press, 1937. 134p [OTP

PIONEERING IN WESTERN CANADA. A Story of the Baptists. Calgary, Author, 1939. 401p [BVaU LC OTP QMM SSU

**Maclean, Alexander, 1822–1916**

THE STORY OF THE KIRK IN NOVA SCOTIA. Pictou, Pictou Advocate, 1911. 102p [BVaU NSWA OTP

**McLean, Alexander, 1827–1864**

THE MORE PRIESTS THE MORE CRIME; or, The Challengers Defeated. Being a Series of Letters ... in Reply to the Challenge of the Catholic Citizen and Montreal True Witness. By a Protestant [pseud]. [OTP QMBM

**MacLean, Rev. Donald Alexander, 1886–**

CATHOLIC SCHOOLS IN WESTERN CANADA. Their Legal Status. ... Toronto, Extension Print., 1923. 162p [BM LC OTUV

**Maclean, Rev. John Brown**

THE SECRET OF THE STREAM. London, Allenson, 1907. 187p [BM NSHD OTU

**McLelland, Rev. Joseph Cumming, 1925–**

THE OTHER SIX DAYS. The Christian Meaning of Work and Property. Toronto, Burns & MacEachern, 1959. x + 121p

**MacLennan, Rev. David Alexander, 1903–**

JOYOUS ADVENTURE. Sermons for the Christian Year. Toronto, Clarke Irwin, 1952. 192p

A PREACHER'S PRIMER. Toronto, Clarke Irwin, 1950. 113p [OONL

RESOURCES FOR SERMON PREPARATION. Philadelphia, Westminster Press, 1957. 239p

THE STORY OF OUR CHURCH. A Little Guide for Visitors to Timothy Eaton Memorial Church. Toronto, United Church Pub., 1947. 31p [Ryerson Impt

**McLeod, Rev. Alexander W.**

THE METHODIST MINISTRY DEFENDED. ... Halifax, Cunnabell, 1839. 107p [NSHP

METHODIST MINISTRY FURTHER DEFENDED ... in ... Letters ... to the Rev. Charles J. Shreve. ... Pictou, Stiles, 1840. 228p [NSHD

UNIVERSALISM IN ITS MODERN AND ANCIENT FORM BROUGHT TO THE TEST AND SHOWN TO BE UNSCRIPTURAL. Halifax, Cunnabell, 1837. 163p [NSWA OTUV

**MacLeod, Rev. John M., 1825–**

HISTORY OF PRESBYTERIANISM ON PRINCE EDWARD ISLAND. Chicago, Winona Pub. Co., 1904. 279p [BVaU LC NSWA OTP QMBM

**McMillan, Donald**

HISTORY OF PRESBYTERIANISM IN CAPE BRETON. With brief Memorial Sketches of the Lives of Rev. Hugh McLeod, D.D., Rev. Matthew Wilson, Rev. Alexander Farquharson, and Other Pioneer Ministers. ... 3rd ed. Inverness, Inverness News, 1905. 73p [NSWA

**Macmillan, Rev. John C., 1862–1926**

THE EARLY HISTORY OF THE CATHOLIC CHURCH IN PRINCE EDWARD ISLAND. Quebec, Evénement Print., 1905. 304p [OTP QMBM

THE HISTORY OF THE CATHOLIC CHURCH IN PRINCE EDWARD ISLAND, from 1835 to 1891. Quebec, Evénement Print., 1913. 486p [BVaU LC OTU

**Macmillan, John Walker, 1868–1932**

HAPPINESS AND GOODWILL, and Other Essays on Christian Living. Toronto, McClelland, 1922. 154p [BVaU LC NSWA

**McMullen, John Mercier, 1820–1907**

THE SUPREMACY OF THE BIBLE, and its Relations to Speculative Science, Remote Ancient History, and the Higher Criticism. Toronto, Briggs, 1905. 479p [LC OTU QMM

**McNab, Rev. John, 1887–**

OUR HERITAGE AND OUR FAITH: "Our Priceless Heritage," by John McNab, and "The Essence of Our Faith," by F. Scott Mackenzie. Toronto, 75th Anniversary Committee, Presbyterian Church in Canada, 1950. 127p [OTP

**McNaughton, Rev. Duncan**

LAURA CLARENCE. A Treatise on Baptism. Toronto, Robinson, 1882. 148p [AEU OTUV

**MacNeill, Rev. John James, 1874–1937**

MANY MANSIONS. Sermons on the Future Life. Toronto, McClelland, 1926. 224p [BVaU OTP QMM

WORLD POWER: THE EMPIRE OF CHRIST. Toronto, McClelland, 1914. 203p [BVaU NSWA OTU

**McNeill, Rev. John Thomas, 1885–**

BOOKS OF FAITH AND POWER. New York, Harper, 1947. 183p [BM BVaU LC OTP

THE HISTORY AND CHARACTER OF CALVINISM. New York, Oxford U. Press, 1954. x + 466p

A HISTORY OF THE CURE OF SOULS. New York, Harper, 1951. xii + 371p

MODERN CHRISTIAN MOVEMENTS. Philadelphia, Westminster Press, 1954. 197p

THE PRESBYTERIAN CHURCH IN CANADA, 1875–1925. Toronto, General Board, Presbyterian Church in Canada, 1925. 276p [BM BVaU LC NBFU OTP QMM

**Macphail, Andrew, 1864–1938**

THE BIBLE IN SCOTLAND. London, Murray, 1931. 130p [BM OTU QMM

**Macphail, John Goodwill, 1877–**

ST. ANDREW'S CHURCH, OTTAWA. The First Hundred Years, 1828–1928. Ottawa, Dadson-Merrill Press, 1931. 169p [BVaU OTP

**McTavish, Rev. William Sharpe, 1858–1932**

REAPERS IN MANY FIELDS. A Survey of Canadian Presbyterian Missions. Toronto, 1904. 285p [BM BVaU OTU QMM

**Maddox, David Crisp**

FOR GOD AND PEACE. Ottawa, Author, 1937. 62p [OTU

**Maine, Star Floyd, 1893–**

EARLY METHODISM IN UPPER CANADA. Chicago, U. of Chicago, 1934. 120p [Earlier ed., 1932.] [LC OLU QMM

**Maloney, John James**

ROME IN CANADA. Vancouver, Columbia Protestant, 1935. 167p [OTP

**Manly, Rev. John G., 1814–1908**

ECCLESIOGRAPHY; or, The Biblical Church Analytically Delineated. London, Partridge & Oakey, 1852. 389p [BM LC OLU

THE NATURE, ORIGIN, PROGRESS, PRESENT STATE AND CHARACTER OF WESLEYAN METHODISM. A Sermon preached at Picton ... 25th October, 1839. ... Kingston, Author, 1840. 76p [NSHD OTP

THE RELIGION OF LIFE; or, Christ and Nicodemus. Toronto, Christian Guardian Office, 1875. 155p [OTP

**Mann, James**

THE VICTORIOUS KING. An Allegory. ... Richmond Hill, James Mann, Printer, 1878. [Amtmann cat. 145

**Mann, Rev. William Edward, 1918–**

SECT, CULT, AND CHURCH IN ALBERTA. Toronto, U. of Toronto Press, 1955. xiii + 166p

**Marling, Rev. Francis Henry, 1825–**

QUARTER-CENTURY MEMORIAL, 1849–1874: Bond Street Congregational Church, Toronto. Comp. by ——. Toronto, Dudley & Burns, 1874. 56p [OTP

**Marquis, Thomas Guthrie, 1864–1936**

THE JESUIT MISSIONS. A Chronicle of the Cross in the Wilderness. Toronto, Glasgow Brook, 1916. 152p [BM BVaU LC NSHD OTU

**Marshall, John**

HISTORY OF EBENEZER CHURCH, NASSAGAWEGA, COMPILED FOR THE OCCASION OF CENTENNIAL CELEBRATION OF THE FIRST CHURCH BUILDING, 1832. [Acton, Ont., Free Press, 1932.] 22p [OTU OH

**Marshall, John George, 1786–1880**

ANSWER TO DOCTRINAL AND HISTORICAL ERRORS IN ARCHBISHOP CONNOLLY'S RECENT LECTURES. Halifax, MacNab, 1872. 38p [NSHD

ANSWERS TO "ESSAYS AND REVIEWS." Halifax, n.p., 1862. 224p [BM BVaU NSWA

BIBLE TRUTH VERSUS "OPPOSITIONS OF SCIENCE, FALSELY SO CALLED." Being an Answer to ... Professor Alexr. McKnight ... on Creation. Halifax, MacNab, 1876. 24p [NSHP

DOCTRINAL ERRORS in a Pamphlet by G.W. Olver ... Tested and Condemned by Scripture and Wesleyan Methodism. ... [Halifax?], n.d. 30p [NSHD

ERRORS AND FALLACIES in a Pamphlet Entitled "Catholicity and Methodism," Exposed and Refuted. ... Halifax, Nova Scotia Print., 1877. 56p [NSHD

ERRORS REVIEWED AND FALLACIES EXPOSED. Being a Protestant Answer to E. Maturin's Catholic Claims. Halifax, Wesleyan Conference Steam Press, 1859. 71p [NSWA QMSS

EXPOSURE AND REFUTATION of Unscriptural Opinions on the Lord's Second Coming. ... Halifax, "Wesleyan," n.d. 31p [NSHD

FICTIONS AND ERRORS, in a Book on "The Origin of the World According to Revelation and Science" by J.W. Dawson, Exposed and Condemned on the Authority of Divine Revelation. Halifax, Methodist Book Room, 1877. 82p [NSWA

FULL REVIEW AND EXPOSURE OF BISHOP COLENSO'S ERRORS ... in his ... "The Pentateuch and Book of Joshua Critically Examined". ... London, Freeman, 1863–64. 2pts. [NSHD

FULL REVIEW OF THE LATE LECTURE BY REV. G.M. GRANT ON THE REFORMERS OF THE NINETEENTH CENTURY, SHOWING ITS UNSCRIPTURAL AND ERRONEOUS CHARACTER. Halifax, Chamberlain, 1867. 32p [NSHD

ON SCRIPTURAL CONVERSION. The Modern Style of Preaching and the State of the Churches. Halifax, MacNab, 1871. 32p [NSWA QMSS

A PROTESTANT'S ANSWER TO PART I OF MR. EDMUND MATURIN'S "DEFENCE OF THE CLAIMS OF THE CATHOLIC CHURCH." Halifax, Bowes, 1859. 72p [NSHD QMSS

REVIEW AND REFUTATION OF LECTURES BY PROFESSOR J.M. HIRSCHFELDER ON CREATION. Halifax, MacNab, 1874. 34p [NSHP

SCRIPTURAL ANSWER TO A PAMPHLET BY A. SUTHERLAND ON THE MORAL STATUS

OF CHILDREN AND THEIR RELATION TO CHRIST AND HIS CHURCH. Halifax, Nova Scotia Print., 1877. 23p [NSHD OTUV

SCRIPTURE TESTIMONIES TO DOCTRINES AND DUTIES OF CHRISTIANITY. ... Carefully compiled. ... Halifax, MacNab, 1873. 216p [NSHP

SERMONS ON SOME OF THE PRINCIPAL DOCTRINES AND DUTIES OF CHRISTIANITY. ... Halifax, Cunnabell, 1862. 296p [NSHD

TESTIMONY OF THE BIBLE CONCERNING EVERLASTING PUNISHMENT. Halifax, Wesleyan Book, 1878. 35p [QMSS

TESTIMONY OF THE SCRIPTURES TO THEIR DIVINE INSPIRATION. London, Burns, 1865. 48p [NSHP

A TREATISE ON THE DIVINE GOODNESS AND JUSTICE, AS REVEALED IN THE HOLY SCRIPTURES. Halifax, MacNab, 1875. 36p [NSWA QMSS

**Mary Agnes, Sister, (historian) 1875–**

THE CONGREGATION OF THE SISTERS OF ST. JOSEPH: LE PUY, LYONS, ST. LOUIS, TORONTO. Toronto, St. Joseph's Convent, 1951. xvii + 225p

**Mary Murphy, Sister**

ST. BONIFACE HEROINES OF MERCY. Commemorating the Centenary of the Grey Nuns of St. Boniface, 1844–1944. Muenster, Sask., St. Peter's Press, 1944. 20p [MWP

**Mason, Gershom William, 1878–**

THE LEGISLATIVE STRUGGLE FOR CHURCH UNION. Toronto, Ryerson, 1956. 162p

**Massey, Rev. Samuel, 1817–**

HISTORICAL SKETCHES OF THE PROTESTANT CHURCHES AND MINISTERS OF MONTREAL. Montreal, Witness Print., 1885. 8p [QMBM

**Mathieson, Rev. Alexander, 1795–1870**

THE MORAL AND RELIGIOUS INFLUENCES OF AUTUMN. A Sermon in Three Parts. Montreal, Starke, 1849. 72p [NSHD OTUV

**Matthews, Rev. Walter McNeill, 1885–**

TWO CENTURIES OF CHRISTIAN WITNESS IN TRURO, N.S. First United Church, 1760–1960. Truro, the Church, 1960. 85p

**Maura, Sister, 1881–1957**

THE SISTERS OF CHARITY, HALIFAX. Toronto, Ryerson, 1956. xxvi + 269p

**Maxwell, Leslie Earl, 1895–**

CROWDED TO CHRIST. Grand Rapids, Mich., Eerdmans Pub. Co., 1950. 354p [OONL

**May, Rev. Edward Geoffrey, 1869–1953**

A HUNDRED YEARS OF CHRIST CHURCH, ST. ANDREW, P.Q. An Historical Sketch of the Pioneer Church of the Ottawa Valley. ... St. John, Que., Smith, 1919. 71p [BVaU OLU

**Mayes, Rev. Percival**

THE STORY OF THE HISTORIC CHURCH OF ALL SAINTS, NIAGARA FALLS, ONTARIO. Niagara Falls, the Church, 1951. 16p

**Meacham, Albert Gallatin**

A COMPENDIOUS HISTORY OF THE RISE AND PROGRESS OF THE METHODIST CHURCH, BOTH IN EUROPE AND AMERICA. ... Hallowell, Ont., Wilson, 1832. 503p [BVaU NBFU OTP

**Meagher, Nicholas Hogan, 1842–1932**

THE RELIGIOUS WARFARE IN NOVA SCOTIA, 1855–1860. ... Joseph Howe's Part in it and the Attitude of Catholics. ... Halifax, [1927?]. 193p [BVaU NSWA OTP QMM

**Medicine Hat, Alta. Westminster Presbyterian Church**

AN HISTORICAL SKETCH OF WESTMINSTER PRESBYTERIAN CHURCH, MEDICINE HAT, ALBERTA, 1914–1921. Medicine Hat, 1921. 19p [MWUC

**Medley, Rev. John, 1804–1892**

THE EPISCOPAL FORM OF CHURCH GOVERNMENT. ... Saint John, Avery, 1845. 46p [BM NSHD

FOUR CHARGES TO THE CLERGY OF THE DIOCESE. By John, Lord Bishop of Fredericton, at his Triennial Visitations, holden in Christ Church Cathedral, Fredericton, 1853, 1856, 1859, 1862. With Notes upon New Brunswick. Oxford, Hammans, 1863. [BM NBFU

SERMONS. Published at the Request of Many of his late Parishioners. Exeter, Hannaford, 1845. 467p [BM NBFU OTP

**Mellish, Rev. Henry Frederick, 1828–1899**

NO POPERY; or, a Defence of the Book of Common Prayer. The False Charges of the so-called Reformed Episcopal Church Examined and fully Refuted. Caledonia, Sawle, 1878. 215p [OTP

**Melville, Sask. All Saints' Anglican Church**

ALL SAINTS' ANGLICAN CHURCH, MELVILLE, SASKATCHEWAN, GOLDEN JUBILEE, 1909–1959. Melville, the Church, 1959. 24p

**Mercer, William Henry Edgar, 1883–**

CENTENNIAL SOUVENIR, THE UNITED CHURCH OF CANADA, TWILLINGATE, NEWFOUNDLAND. A Century of Methodism in Twillingate and Notre Dame Bay ... 1831–1931. Twillingate, Sun Office, [1933]. 163p [NfSM OONL

**Methodist Church of Canada**

CENTENARY OF METHODISM IN EASTERN BRITISH AMERICA, 1782–1882. ... Halifax, Huestis, [1882]. 123p [NSHD

CENTENNIAL OF CANADIAN METHODISM. ... Published by the Direction of the General Conference. Toronto, Briggs, 1891. 339p [BVaU OTU

**Mildmay, Rev. Aubrey Neville St. John, 1865–**

LAUREATES OF THE CROSS. Six Sermons. With an Intro. by W.J. Knox-Little. London, Elliot Stock, 1896. 91p [BM

**Miller, Rev. Harry Baxter**

ST. PATRICK'S CHURCH, ANGLICAN, HUDSON BAY, SASKATCHEWAN, CANADA. Golden Jubilee, 1903–1953. Hudson Bay, Sask., [1953?]. 49p

**Millman, Rev. Thomas Reagh, 1905–**

A HISTORY OF THE PARISH OF NEW LONDON, PRINCE EDWARD ISLAND. With Notes on the Larger Life of the Parish and Community during the First Three Quarters of the Nineteenth Century. Toronto, 1959. 71p

A SHORT HISTORY OF THE PARISH OF DUNHAM, QUEBEC. Granby, Que., Granby Print., 1946. 66p [BM OTP QMBM

THE STORY OF ST. GEORGE'S CHURCH, GRAFTON. Cobourg, Cobourg World, 1935. 30p [OTU

**Milton, Ont. St. Paul's United Church**

ST. PAUL'S UNITED CHURCH, MILTON, ONTARIO, 1852–1952. Comp. by Mima Alma Hume *et al.* Milton, Historical Committee, 1952. 34p

**Mitchell, Roy, 1884–1944**

THEOSOPHY IN ACTION. Toronto, Blavatsky Institute, 1951. 86p

THROUGH TEMPLE DOORS. Studies in Occult Masonry. Toronto, Blavatsky Institute, 1950. 157p [OONL

**Moir, John Sargent, 1926–**

CHURCH AND STATE IN CANADA WEST. Three Studies in the Relation of Denominationalism and Nationalism, 1841–1867. Toronto, U. of Toronto Press, 1959. xv + 223p

**Mollison, John**

"WHAT IS MAN?–(THAT THOU ART MINDFUL OF HIM)." Summerside, P.E.I., Journal Pub., 1932. 251p [BM NSWA

**Moncton, N.B. First United Baptist Church**

FIRST MONCTON UNITED BAPTIST CHURCH, 1828–1928. Centennial Services and Church History. Moncton, the Church, 1928. 20p [NSWA

**Montreal, Que. Calvary Church**

MANUAL OF CALVARY CHURCH AND REPORTS FOR THE YEAR 1884. Montreal, "Witness," 1885. 72p [QMBM

**Montreal, Que. Erskine Church**

SERMONS AND ADDRESSES DELIVERED AT JUBILEE. Montreal, Bentley, 1883. 65p [NSWA

**Moore, Rev. Arthur Henry, 1869–1938**

HISTORY OF THE GOLDEN RULE LODGE (1803–1903), STANSTEAD, QUE. Toronto, Briggs, 1905. 219p [BM

**Moore, Rev. William, 1838–1915**

HISTORY OF BANK STREET PRESBYTERIAN CHURCH, OTTAWA, 1865–1911. [Ottawa, 1911.] 90p [OLU

A LECTURE DELIVERED ... IN THE BANK STREET PRESBYTERIAN CHURCH, Sunday, 31st December. Subject: "Is the Church of Rome Infallible?" Ottawa, Taylor [1871?]. 15p [OTP QMSS

REPORT ON THE CONDITION AND WORKING OF THE PRINCE ALBERT PRESBYTERIAN MISSION TO THE INDIANS ON THE SASKATCHEWAN. ... Ottawa, Woodburn, 1873. 52p [NSWA OKQ

**Moreton, Rev. Julian, 1825–1900**

A LETTER TO THE REV. H. BAILEY, IN REPLY TO RECENT STRICTURES UPON MISSIONARY SOCIETIES AND MISSIONARIES. London, Oxford U. Press, 1864. [BM

**Morice, Rev. Adrian Gabriel, 1859–1938**

THE CATHOLIC CHURCH IN THE CANADIAN NORTHWEST. Winnipeg, Author, 1936. 86p [BVaU OTU

HISTORY OF THE CATHOLIC CHURCH IN WESTERN CANADA, FROM LAKE SUPERIOR TO THE PACIFIC (1659–1895). Toronto, Musson, 1910. 2v [BVaU LC NSHD OTU

**Morley, Rev. Frank Selkirk, 1904–**

PERSONAL PEACE AND POWER. Calgary, Albertan Pub. Co., 1956. 109p

A WAY OF LIFE. Calgary, Author, 1958. 36p

WHY A PRESBYTERIAN CHURCH. Calgary, Author, 1955. 40p

**Morrison, Rev. George W., 1909?–1950**

COUNTRY PARSON. Ed. by William H. Cranston. Toronto, Ryerson, 1953. xi + 140p

**Morrison, Rev. John, 1857–1924**

THE CENTRAL METHODIST CHURCH, 1832–1919. Sarnia, the Church, 1919. 60p [OLU

**Morrow, Ernest Lloyd, 1884–1951**

CHURCH UNION IN CANADA. Its History, Motives, Doctrines and Government. Toronto, Allen, 1923. 450p [BVaU NBFU OTP QMM

**Morton, Arthur Silver, 1870–1945**

THE WAY TO UNION. Being a Study of the Principles of the Foundation and of the Historic Development of the Christian Church as bearing on the Proposed

Union of the Presbyterian, Methodist and Congregational Churches in Canada. ... Toronto, Briggs, 1912. 284p [BM BVaU NSHD OLU

**Mott, Henry**

JUBILEE HISTORY OF TRINITY CHURCH, MONTREAL 1840–1890. Comp. by ——. Montreal, Lovell, 1890. 64p [NSWA OOP

**Mountain, Rev. George Jehoshaphat, 1789–1863**

CANADIAN CHURCH DESTITUTION. Reprint of the Report made by the Right Rev. the Lord Bishop of Montreal, to the Right Hon. the Earl of Durham ... 1838. Hexham, Hatchard, n.d. 12p [OTP

A CIRCULAR LETTER FROM THE BISHOP OF MONTREAL, to the Clergy of his Diocese, on Church Vestments. London, Rivington, 1845. 39p [BM OTP

CIRCUMSTANCES PREVENTING COALITION WITH THE COLONIAL CHURCH & SCHOOL SOCIETY. Quebec, Mercury Office, 1859. 16p [OTP

THE DUTY OF THE CHRISTIAN MINISTER IN FOLLOWING CHRIST. New York, Church Depository, 1854. 32p [OTP

A FAST-DAY SERMON. Quebec, Mercury Office, 1857. 20p [OTP

THE FOUNDATION AND CONSTITUTION OF THE CHRISTIAN MINISTRY. Quebec, Neilson & Cowan, 1826. 39p [NSWA OTP QMSS

THE HOUSE OF THE LORD GOD. Two Sermons. Fredericton, Simpson, 1853. 24p [NSHD OTP

A LETTER TO MR. S.C. BLYTH, Occasioned by the Recent Publication of the Narrative of his Conversion to the Romish Faith. In 4 parts. By a Catholic Christian [pseud]. Montreal, Mower, 1822. 288p [BM OTP QMSS

A LETTER TO THE PRESIDENT OF THE ST. GEORGE'S SOCIETY OF QUEBEC, in Relation to the Choral Service of the Church of England. Quebec, Mercury Office, 1857. 8p [OTP

THE LOVE OF COUNTRY, Considered upon Christian Principles, with a Special Application to the Case of Englishmen. ... Quebec, Kemble, 1844. 17p [OTP QMSS

A PASTORAL LETTER ... UPON THE QUESTION OF AFFORDING THE USE OF CHURCHES AND CHAPELS OF THE CHURCH OF ENGLAND, FOR THE PURPOSES OF DISSENTING WORSHIP. Quebec, Cary, 1845. 18p [BM NSWA QMBM

A SERMON ON THE EDUCATION OF THE POOR ... Diffusing the Gospel, and ... Family Religion. ... Quebec, Neilson, 1822. 28p [OTP

SERMONS. London, Bell & Daldy; Cambridge, Deighton Bell, 1865. 262p [BM BVaU NSWA OTP QMBM

THE SOLDIER'S THANKSGIVING. A Sermon. Quebec, Cary, 1843. 16p [OTP

THE SPIRITUAL IMPROVEMENT of the Annual Observances of the Church. ... Quebec, Lovell & Lamoureux, 1855. 24p [OTP

THOUGHTS ON "ANNEXATION," in Connection with the Duty and the Interest of Members of the Church of England. Quebec, Cary, 1849. 28p [BVaU OTP QMM

A VALEDICTORY SERMON, Preached ... Fredericton ... 1817. Fredericton, Lugrin, 1817. 15p [OTP

**Mowat, Oliver, 1820–1903**

CHRISTIANITY AND ITS INFLUENCE. An Address. ... Toronto, Hunter Rose, 1898. 26p [OTU

CHRISTIANITY AND SOME OF ITS EVIDENCES POPULARLY STATED. Toronto, Williamson, 1890. 90p [2nd ed. rev. and enl.: Toronto, Briggs, 1901. 121p] [BVaU NSHD OTP

**Mowatt, Rev. Andrew Joseph, 1838–1911**

WORDS OF LIFE. ... Fredericton, Reporter Office, 1890. 352p [NSHD

**Muckleston, William Jeffryes, 1849–**

ROMAN METHODS OF CONTROVERSY, as Exemplified by the "Catholic Truth Society." A Lecture. ... Ottawa, Paynter & Abbott, 1893. 36p [NSHD OTU

**Mulock, John A., –1897**

METHODISM UNMASKED. In a Review of "A Vindication of the Methodist Church" (so called) "in a Pastoral Address" by Benjamin Nankevill, Wesleyan Minister. Carleton Place, Ont., Smith & Oswell, 1850. 54p [OTP

**Murdoch, Rev. Benedict Joseph, 1886–**

ALONE WITH THEE. Readings for the Holy Hour. Milwaukee, Bruce, 1934. 173p [LC NBFU OOSU

**Murphy, Rev. James J.**

FATHER MURPHY'S REPLY TO THE "WITNESS" CORRESPONDENCE EVOKED BY HIS DEFENCE OF PAPAL INFALLIBILITY. A Lecture delivered October 18th, 1875. Montreal, Sadlier, 1875. 30p [QMSS

**Murphy, Rev. William Leo, 1899–**

THE COBBLE STONES OF GALILEE. St. Nazianz, Wis., Society of the Divine Savior, 1946. 136p [LC

**Murray, Rev. John, 1843–1935**

THE HISTORY OF THE PRESBYTERIAN CHURCH IN CAPE BRETON. Truro, N.S., News Pub. Co., 1921. 282p [BVaU NBFU OTP

SCOTSBURN CONGREGATION, PICTOU COUNTY, NOVA SCOTIA. Its History, Professional Men. ... Truro, News Pub. Co., 1925. 161p [ACU NSHD OTP

**Murray, Mrs. Margaret L.**

ST. MARY'S OF LILLOOET. [Lillooet, B.C., 1935.] 8p [BViPA

**Mussen, Joseph M.**

THE CHURCH OF ST. MARK, A.D. 1792, NIAGARA-ON-THE-LAKE, ONTARIO, CANADA. Niagara-on-the-Lake, Author, 1934. 40p [OTU

**Nankevill, Benjamin, 1799–1856**

LETTERS TO THE REV. J.A. MULOCK. ... A Reply to Certain Charges against the Methodists. ... Carleton Place, Poole, 1850. 142p [NBFU OTP

**Neal, Lucille Alethea (Schoonover), 1916–**

LIKE A TREE PLANTED. New York, Pageant Press, 1955. 133p

**New, Chester William, 1882–1960**

CENTENARY HISTORY OF JAMES STREET BAPTIST CHURCH. By —— and George P. Gilmour. Hamilton, the Church, 1944. 78p [OLU

**Newnham, Miss Sophie**

THE BABES IN THE WOOD. Montreal, Lovell, 1895. 24p [NSWA OOA SSU

**Nichols, John W.**

A CENTURY OF METHODISM IN ST. JOHN'S NEWFOUNDLAND, 1815–1915. Ed. by ——. [St. John's], Dicks & Co., [1915]. 36p [NfSM

**Nichols, Thomas E.**

THE HISTORY OF THE DIOCESE OF NIAGARA TO 1950 A.D. Ed. by ——. Hamilton, Niagara Synod, 1950. 98p [NSHD OTU

**Nicol, John Lennox**

THROUGH THE YEARS WITH KNOX. Celebrating Sixty-five Years of Service as a Pastoral Charge, 1885–1950, and the Fiftieth Anniversary of the Opening of the First Knox Church, 1900–1950. Comp. by ——. Saskatoon, the Church, 1950. 60p [OONL SSU

**Noel, Beatrice Maxine (Thistle)**

THE STORY OF ONE HUNDRED YEARS AND A CHURCH, 1859–1959. ... Southampton, Ont., St. Paul's Anglican Church, 1959. 31p

**Norman, Rev. Richard Whitmore, 1829–1906**

CONSIDERATIONS ON THE REVISED EDITION OF THE NEW TESTAMENT. ... Montreal, Gazette, 1881. 55p [NSHD

THE IMPORTANCE OF RELIGIOUS RESERVE AND THE TEACHING OF THE CHURCH OF ENGLAND UPON CONFESSION AND ABSOLUTION. Three Sermons. Montreal, Lovell, 1873. 38p [NSWA QMSS

**Norwood, Rev. Robert Winkworth, 1874–1932**

HIS GLORIOUS BODY. New York, Scribner, 1930. 229p [BM LC NSHD

INCREASING CHRISTHOOD. New York, Scribner, 1932. 332p [BM LC

THE MAN WHO DARED TO BE GOD. A Story of Jesus. New York, Scribner, 1929. 324p [BM LC NSHD

PAUL TO TIMOTHY. An Epistle. N.p., [1914?]. 8p [NSHD

THE STEEP ASCENT. Noontide Meditations. ... New York, Scribner, 1928. 197p [BM NSHD

**Nunn, Norman Alfred, 1900–**
THE GREAT CHURCH OF ST. PAUL'S, TORONTO, CANADA. Toronto, the Church, 1954. x + 42p

**O'Brien, Rev. Cornelius, 1843–1906**
PHILOSOPHY OF THE BIBLE VINDICATED. Charlottetown, Bremner, 1876. 291p [BM NSHD OTP

**O'Byrne, Michael Cyprian**
UPON THIS ROCK. A Life-Chronicle of the Last Century of Christian Civilization. Toronto, Ellis, 1889. 434p [OONL

**Odlum, Edward, 1850–1935**
GOD'S COVENANT-MAN: BRITISH ISRAEL. Toronto, Briggs, 1916. 296p [BM BVaU

**O'Donnell, A.M.**
A BRIEF HISTORY AND SOUVENIR BOOKLET OF KNOX PRESBYTERIAN CHURCH, TRAIL, B.C., 1896–1921. Trail, Trail News, 1921. 19p [BViPA

**O'Hara, Margaret, 1855–**
LEAF OF THE LOTUS. Toronto, Poole, 1931. 188p [BVaU OTP

**O'Higgins, Harvey Jerrold, 1876–1929**
THE BEAST. A Story of Denver. By Judge Ben B. Lindsey and Harvey J. O'Higgins. Boston, Doubleday, 1910. 340p [LC OTU

**O'Leary, James M.**
HISTORY OF THE IRISH CATHOLICS OF QUEBEC. Saint Patrick's Church to the Death of Rev. P. McMahon. Quebec, Daily Telegraph, 1895. 48p [QMSS

**Oliver, Mrs. Althea Pearleen, 1917–**
A BRIEF HISTORY OF THE COLORED BAPTISTS OF NOVA SCOTIA, 1782–1953. In Commemoration of Centennial Celebrations of the African United Baptist Association of Nova Scotia. Halifax, African United Baptist Assoc. of N.S., 1953. 84p

**Oliver, Edmund Henry, 1882–1935**
HIS DOMINION OF CANADA. A Study in the Background, Development and Challenge of the Missions of the United Church of Canada. Toronto, Ryerson, 1932. 304p [BVaU OTU
THE SOCIAL ACHIEVEMENTS OF THE CHRISTIAN CHURCH. Toronto, Board of Evangelism and Social Service of the United Church of Canada, 1930. 192p [BVaU LC
TRACTS FOR DIFFICULT TIMES. By Edmund S. [!] Oliver. New York, Round Table Press, 1933. 212p [LC OLU

THE WINNING OF THE FRONTIER. Toronto, United Church Pub. House, 1930. 271p ["A study in the religious history of Canada."] [BM BVaU LC NSWA OTU

**O'Neill, Rev. Arthur Barry, 1858–**

SACERDOTAL SAFEGUARDS. Notre Dame, Ind., U. Press, 1918. 304p [LC NBFU

**Orillia, Ont. St. James's Parish**

FIRST HUNDRED YEARS. Story of St. James's Parish, Orillia. Orillia, Packet-Times Press, 1941. [UTQ'42

**Osborne, William Frederick, 1873–1950**

THE FAITH OF A LAYMAN. Toronto, Cassell, 1910. 238p [BM BVaU LC NSWA

**Osler, William, 1849–1919**

MAN'S REDEMPTION OF MAN. A Lay Sermon. London, Constable, 1910. 60p [Also: New York, Hoebner, 1913. 63p] [BM BVaU OTP QMM

SCIENCE AND IMMORTALITY. Boston, Houghton, 1904. 54p [BVaU LC NBFU QMM

**O'Sullivan, Dennis Ambrose, 1848–1892**

ESSAYS ON THE CHURCH IN CANADA. With an intro. by His Grace, the Archbishop of Toronto. Toronto, Catholic Truth Soc., 1890. 134p [BVaU NSWA OTP

**Ottawa, Ont. Congregation Adath Jeshurun**

CONGREGATION ADATH JESHURUN COMMEMORATES ... THE SIXTIETH ANNIVERSARY OF THE FOUNDING OF OUR SYNAGOGUE. Ed. by Herman S. Roodman. Ottawa, 1952. 24p

**Ottawa, Ont. Congregation Beth Shalom**

DEDICATION BETH SHALOM SYNAGOGUE, 1957. ... Ed. by Herman S. Roodman. Ottawa, the Synagogue, 1957. 32p

**Ottawa, Ont. St. Andrew's Church**

ST. ANDREW'S CHURCH, OTTAWA. The First Hundred Years, 1828–1928. Ottawa, Dadson-Merrill, 1931. 169p [BVaU

**Owen, Rev. Derwyn Randulph Grier, 1914–**

BODY AND SOUL. A Study on the Christian View of Man. Philadelphia, Westminster Press, 1956. 239p

SCIENTISM, MAN, AND RELIGION. Philadelphia, Westminster Press, 1952. 208p

**Owen, Epenetus, 1815–**

STRUCK BY LIGHTNING. ... With Incidents, Experiences, and Anecdotes for Old and Young. New ed. Otterville, Ont., A. Sims, [1891]. 190p [OONL

**Page, Mrs. Elizabeth Merwin, 1889–**
IN CAMP AND TEPEE. An Indian Mission Story. New York, Revell, 1915. 245p [LC

**Park, Mary Olga (Bracewell), 1891–**
BETWEEN TIME AND ETERNITY. New York, Vantage Press, 1960. 105p

**Parker, Rev. Stuart Crawford, 1888–1950**
THE BOOK OF ST. ANDREW'S. A Short History of St. Andrew's Presbyterian Church, Toronto. Toronto, St. Andrew's Church, 1930. 142p [BVaU OTP
THE CHURCH AND RECONSTRUCTION. (An Address). London, Scott, 1919. 56p [BM
THE GUEST CHAMBER. Toronto, Thorn Press, 1938. 125p [OTU
JESUS ASKS A QUESTION. Toronto, Thorn Press, 1937. 126p [OTU
LITTLE TALES OF JESUS. Toronto, Presbyterian Pub., 1935. 133p [OTU
YET NOT CONSUMED. A Short Account of the History and Antecedents of the Presbyterian Church in Canada. Toronto, Thorn Press, 1947. 204p [OTP

**Parsons, Henry M.**
BIOGRAPHICAL SKETCHES AND REVIEW. First Presbyterian Church in Toronto and Knox Church, 1820–1890. [Anon] Toronto, Timms, 1890. 46p [Haight Pt I

**Paterson, Rev. James J., 1870–1928**
ST. ANDREW'S CHURCH, SARNIA, 1843–1918. Sarnia, the Church, 1918. 69p [OLU

**Patrick, Rev. William, 1852–1911**
JAMES, THE LORD'S BROTHER. Edinburgh, Clark, 1906. 369p [BM BVaU LC OTU

**Patstone, Arthur Job, 1881–**
A SHORT HISTORY OF ST. PAUL'S CHURCH, NEWMARKET, ONTARIO. Toronto, Church of England, 1934. 16p [OTP

**Patterson, Rev. George, 1824–1897**
DOCTRINE OF THE TRINITY UNDERLYING THE REVELATION OF REDEMPTION. Edinburgh, Oliphant, 1870. 244p [BM BVaU NSHD OLU
HEATHEN WORLD. Its Need of the Gospel. Toronto, Briggs, 1884. 293p [NSHD OTU
"IT IS WELL." Two Sermons preached in Salem Church, Green Hill, on Sabbath, 6th August, 1854 ... on the Occasion of the Death of his Only Child. ... Halifax, Bowes, 1854. 27p [NSHD
PRESENT TRUTH. A Sermon. Halifax, Barnes, 1858. 22p [NSHD

**Peake, Frank Alexander, 1913–**
HEROES OF THE CHURCH IN BRITISH COLUMBIA. Special Missionary Lessons,

Epiphany, 1958. Vancouver, Diocese of New Westminister, Board of Religious Education, 1957. 67p

**Pearson, Rev. Leslie Trayer Holt, 1906–**

THE MEMOIRS OF A CATHEDRAL. A Century of Christian Activity, 1859–1959. New Westminster, Holy Trinity Cathedral, 1959. 71p

**Pelton, Sandford H.**

HISTORICAL SKETCH OF SAINT JOHN'S PRESBYTERIAN CHURCH, YARMOUTH, NOVA SCOTIA, 1840–1915. Yarmouth, Herald, 1915. 43p [Amtmann

**Penner, Rev. Archie, 1917–**

THE CHRISTIAN, THE STATE, AND THE NEW TESTAMENT. Altona, Man., D.W. Friesen, 1959. 128p

**Petrolia, Ont. Christ Church Booklet Committee**

CHRIST CHURCH, PETROLIA, ONT., 1866–1959. [Petrolia, Ont., 1959?]. 70p

**Phelps, Edward**

A HISTORY OF BLACKWELL UNITED CHURCH AND BLACKWELL COMMUNITY. Blackwell, Ont., the Church, 1958. 54p

**Pickel, Weldon U.**

1891–1951 DIAMOND JUBILEE. History of the First Baptist Church, Regina, Sask. Comp. by ——. Regina, the Church, 1951. 16p [mimeographed]

**Pickford, Mary, 1893–**

MY RENDEZVOUS WITH LIFE. New York, Kinsey, 1935. 37p [LC

WHY NOT LOOK BEYOND? London, Methuen, 1936. 39p [BM

WHY NOT TRY GOD? New York, Kinsey, 1934. 35p [BM LC NSHPL

**Pidgeon, Rev. George Campbell, 1872–1971**

THE COMMUNION OF SAINTS. Toronto, Ryerson, 1935. 63p [OTUV

THE INDWELLING CHRIST. New York, Oxford U. Press, 1948. 208p [BVaU LC OTP QMM

THE UNITED CHURCH OF CANADA. The Story of the Union. Toronto, Ryerson, 1950. 107p [BVaU LC NBFU OTP

THE VICARIOUS LIFE. Toronto, Oxford U. Press, 1945. 187p [BM BVaU LC OTP

THE WAY OF SALVATION. Toronto, Clarke Irwin, 1954. 98p

**Pierce, Lorne Albert, 1890–1961**

THE CHRONICLE OF A CENTURY, 1829–1929. The Record of One Hundred Years of Progress in the Publishing Concerns of the Methodist, Presbyterian, and Congregational Churches in Canada. Ed. by ——. Toronto, United Church Pub. House, 1929. 271p [BVaU OTP

IN CONFERENCE WITH THE BEST MINDS. Toronto, Ryerson, 1927. 272p [LC NSWA OTP QMM

METHODISM AND THE NEW CATHOLICISM. Toronto, Ryerson, 1923. 70p [Probably same as following title.] [Ryerson Impt

PRIMITIVE METHODISM AND THE NEW CATHOLICISM. Toronto, Methodist Book, 1923. 70p [BVaU NBFU OKQ

**Pilot Mound, Man. United Church**

70TH ANNIVERSARY, PILOT MOUND UNITED CHURCH, 1888–1958. Pilot Mound, Man., the Church, 1958. 46p [mimeographed]

**Platt, Mrs. Harriet Louise**

THE STORY OF THE YEARS. A History of the Women's Missionary Society of the Methodist Church, Canada, from 1881 to 1906. V. 1: Canada. V. 2: Beyond Seas. V. 3: Canada, 1906–1916. By Elizabeth S. Strachan. Toronto, Briggs, 1908, 1909, 1917. 155p, 148p, 338p [BM BVaU OTP

**Playter, Rev. George Frederick, 1811–1866**

THE HISTORY OF METHODISM IN CANADA. With an Account of the Rise and Progress of the Work of God among the Canadian Indian Tribes, and Occasional Notices of the Civil Affairs of the Province. Toronto, Green, 1862. 414p [BVaU NBFU OTP QMM

**Plewman, Harold Ernest, 1879–**

THE STORY OF RYERSON UNITED CHURCH ... 50TH ANNIVERSARY. Hamilton, the Church, 1958. 28p

**Pond, Douglas Daaman, 1915–**

ONE HUNDREDTH ANNIVERSARY, 1857–1957, UNITED BAPTIST CHURCH, MARYSVILLE, NEW BRUNSWICK. By D.D. Pond and G.W. Crandlemire. Marysville, the Church, 1957. 32p

**Poole, Rev. Aquila James, 1908–**

CENTENARY FESTIVAL, 1860–1960 ... A BRIEF HISTORY OF THE PARISH. Comp. by ——. Ottawa, 1960. 26p [On St. John's Anglican Church, Richmond, Ont.]

**Poole, Rev. William Henry, 1820–1896**

ANGLO-ISRAEL; or, The Saxon Race Proved to be the Lost Tribes of Israel. In nine lectures. Intro. by the Rev. W.H. Withrow. Toronto, Briggs, 1889. 686p [BM BVaU LC NBFU OTP QMM

**Pope, Joseph, 1854–1926**

TRADITIONS. Ottawa, Durie, 1891. 20p [NSHD

**Pope, Rev. William Robert, 1923–**

TRIUMPH OF THE SPIRIT. Toronto, Ryerson, 1960. 62p

**Port Dalhousie, Ont. St. Andrew's United Church**

CENTENNIAL, 1852–1952. Port Dalhousie, Ont., the Church, 1952. 24p

**Port Hope, Ont. Methodist Church**

HISTORICAL SKETCH OF METHODISM IN CANADA AND PORT HOPE. Port Hope, Commercial Press, 1925. 39p [OTP

**Porter, Jane**

THE CHRISTIAN'S WEDDING RING. Containing Five Letters written by a Lady [pseud]. With the Sincere Desire of Sowing the Seeds of Union in the Christian Church. [Anon] Montreal, Lovell, 1874. 287p [9 pts in one, paginated separately.] [OTP QMSS

**Porter, Rev. William Henry, 1840–1928**

SERMON ON BAPTISM AND THE LORD'S SUPPER. With Things that Baptists DO NOT Believe, and Things that they DO Believe. Brantford, Daily Expositor, 1876. 32p [NSHD

SMOOTH STONES FROM RUNNING BROOKS. A Sermon on Baptism and the Lord's Supper. Brantford, Daily Expositor, 1876. 32p [OTUV

**Pounder, Roy Mason, 1883–**

ARTIST, THINKER, AND SAINT. Toronto, Ryerson, 1936. 225p [BVaU OTU

**Powell, Mrs. R. Janet (Pettit), 1886–**

THE HISTORY OF ST. ANDREW'S CHURCH, GRIMSBY, ONTARIO, 1794–1944. By Mrs. R.J. Powell and Harriet Walsh. Grimsby, the Church, 1944. 36p [OTU

**Pratt, Edwin John, 1883–1964**

STUDIES IN PAULINE ESCHATOLOGY, AND ITS BACKGROUND. Toronto, Briggs, 1917. 203p [BVaU MWU OTUV

**Pratt, Viola Leone (Whitney), 1892–**

ONE FAMILY. Toronto, United Church, 1937. 96p [CC

**Presbyterian Church in Canada**

HISTORIC SKETCHES OF THE PIONEER WORK AND THE MISSIONARY, EDUCATIONAL, AND BENEVOLENT AGENCIES OF THE PRESBYTERIAN CHURCH IN CANADA. Ed. by a Committee. Toronto, Murray Print., 1903. 128p [BVaU LC MWU OTU

**Presbyterian Church in Canada. Hymn Book Committee**

OUR HYMN WRITERS. ... Biographical Notices. ... Toronto, Campbell, 1880. 40p [NSHD OTU

**Prince, Rev. Samuel Henry, 1883–1960**

THE DYKES OF CIVILIZATION. Toronto, Anglican Church of Canada, 1958. 144p

**Pringle, Rev. George Charles Fraser, 1873–1949**

ABOARD "THE SKY PILOT" ON THE PACIFIC. N.p., Board of Home Missions, Presbyterian Church in Canada, 1923. 16p [BViPA

IN GREAT WATERS. The Story of the United Church Marine Missions. Toronto, Ryerson, 1928. 178p [BVaU OTP QMM

**Proudfoot, Rev. John James Aitchison, 1821–1903**

SYSTEMATIC HOMILETICS. Ed. by Rev. J.A. Turnbull and Rev. A.J. MacGillivray. Chicago, Revell, 1903. 320p [LC

**Prower, Nelson, 1856–**

THEOLOGY AND MORALITY. Montreal, Gazette Print., n.d. 60p [QMBM

**Prowse, Daniel Woodley, 1834–1914**

HISTORY OF THE CHURCHES IN NEWFOUNDLAND. London, 1895. 56p [A supp. to his HISTORY OF NEWFOUNDLAND.] [NBFU OTU QMM

**Putnam, Ada MacLeod**

THE SELKIRK SETTLERS AND THE CHURCH THEY BUILT AT BELFAST [P.E.I.]. Toronto, Presbyterian Pubs., 1939. 57p [NBFU OTP QMM

**Pyper, James**

ANIMADVERSIONS UPON THE REV. JOHN ROAF'S TWO SERMONS ON BAPTISM. Toronto, Carter & Thomas, 1851. 37p [NSWA

**Quigley, Richard Francis, –1918**

IPSE, IPSA; IPSE, IPSA, IPSUM; WHICH? (Latin Various Readings, Genesis iii.15). Controversial Letters ... in Vindication of the Position Assigned by the Catholic Church to the Ever-Blessed Mother of the World's Redeemer. ... In Reply to the Right Reverend Dr. Kingdon and John M. Davenport. New York, Pustet, 1890. 471p [BM BVaU NBFU OTP QMSS

**Radford, Ruth, 1898–**

MAYBE. An Allegory. Bowen Island, B.C., priv. print., 1954. 16p

**Rae, James Penman, 1924–**

THOUGHTS [Book 1]. Embodying a Doctrine of Influences. Perth, Ont., Author, 1955. 15p

THOUGHTS. Book 2. Perth, Ont., Author, 1956. 65p

**Rand, Jennie Elizabeth (Magee), 1912–**

HISTORICAL SKETCH OF CHURCH OF ST. JOHN, 1810–1960, AND THE PARISH OF CORNWALLIS, NOVA SCOTIA, 1760–1960. N.p., 1960. 22p

**Rand, Rev. Silas Tertius, 1810–1889**

A HISTORICAL SKETCH OF THE NOVA SCOTIA BAPTIST ASSOCIATION. Charlottetown, Haszard, 1849. 31p [NSHD

**Rankin, A.**

JESUITS' ESTATES IN CANADA. Montreal, Becket, 1850. 134p [BM OTU

**Reid, William Stanford, 1913–**

THE CHURCH OF SCOTLAND IN LOWER CANADA. Toronto, Presbyterian Pub., 1936. 190p [BM BVaU LC OTU QMM

**Renison, Rev. Robert John, 1875–1957**

FOR SUCH A TIME AS THIS. Toronto, McClelland, 1947. 368p [BVaU LC OTP

WEDNESDAY MORNING. Toronto, McClelland, 1944. 275p [BVaU LC OTP

**Reynar, Rev. Alfred Henry, 1840–1921**

EBENEZER. Address on Methodism. Toronto, Briggs, 1900. 16p [OTU

**Reynolds, Rev. Arthur Guy, 1909–**

THE EARLY HISTORY OF LEITH UNITED CHURCH. Owen Sound, 1942. 20p [OTU

THE MEANS OF GRACE. Toronto, United Church Pub. House, 1952. 56p

WHAT'S THE DIFFERENCE? Protestant and Roman Catholic Beliefs Compared. Toronto, United Church Pub. House, 1954. 64p

**Reynolds, Henry Dunbar, 1820–1864**

THE NIAGARA CHURCH CASE. ... Toronto, Maclear, 1857. 113p [OTP

**Richey, Rev. Matthew, 1803–1883**

A PLAIN STATEMENT of Facts, Connected with the Union and Separation of the British Canadian Conferences. By J. Stinson and M. Richey. Toronto, Stanton, 1840. 56p [OTU QMSS

SERMONS DELIVERED ON VARIOUS OCCASIONS. Toronto, Ryerson, 1840. 280p [NSWA OTP

TWO LETTERS Addressed to the Editor of the "Church," Exposing the Intolerant Bigotry of that Journal. ... Toronto, Rogers Thompson, 1843. 18p [OTP

**Riddell, John Henry, 1863–1952**

METHODISM IN THE MIDDLE WEST. Toronto, Ryerson, 1946. 371p [BVaU LC OTP

**Riddell, Walter, 1814–1904**

DIARY OF VOYAGE FROM SCOTLAND TO CANADA IN 1833, and Story of St. Andrew's Presbyterian Church, Cobourg, Ontario. With Occasional Notes by the Honourable William Renwick Riddell. Toronto, Associated Printers, 1932. 32p [NSHD OTP QMM

**Riddell, Walter Alexander, 1881–**

THE RISE OF ECCLESIASTICAL CONTROL IN QUEBEC. New York, Columbia U. Press, 1916. 195p [LC NBFU

**Ritchie, David Lakie, 1864–1951**

THE GENIUS OF CONGREGATIONALISM. ... Toronto, Ryerson, 1926. 36p [OTUV

THE GOSPEL AS THE POWER OF GOD. Montreal, 1927. 10p [OKQ

**Ritchie, Eliza, 1850–1933**

THE PROBLEM OF PERSONALITY. ... Ithaca, Andrus & Church, 1889. 42p [LC NSHD

**Roaf, Rev. John, 1801–1862**

LECTURES ON THE MILLENIUM. Toronto, 1844. 173p [BVaU NSWA OTP

RELIGIOUS LIBERTY. Being a Letter to the Editor of the "Palladium," upon the Thanksgiving Proclamation of ... Sir F.B. Head, and a Second to the Editors of the "Patriot," "Christian Guardian," & "Commercial Herald". ... Toronto, Palladium Office, 1838. 8p [BM OTP

TWO SERMONS ON BAPTISM. ... Toronto, Carter & Thomas, 1850. 31p [BM NSWA OTP

**Roberts, Rev. Richard, 1874–1945**

THE CHRISTIAN GOD. New York, Macmillan, 1929. 154p [BM BVaU OTP

THE CONTEMPORARY CHRIST. New York, Macmillan, 1938. 148p [BM OTU

FOR GOD AND FREEDOM. Sackville, Mount Allison U., 1945. 45p [BVaU LC NBFU OTU QMM

THE GOSPEL AT CORINTH. New York, Macmillan, 1924. 173p [BM QMM

THE RED CAP ON THE CROSS. London, Hedley Bros., 1918. 127p [BM OTP

THE RENASCENCE OF FAITH. New York, Cassell, 1912. 308p [BM LC

THE SPIRIT OF GOD AND THE FAITH OF TODAY. New York, Willett Clark Colby, 1930. 185p [BVaU LC

THAT STRANGE MAN UPON HIS CROSS. New York, Abingdon, 1934. 139p [BVaU LC QMM

THE UNTRIED DOOR. An Attempt to Discover the Mind of Jesus for Today. New York, Women's Press, 1921. 174p [LC

WHAT'S BEST WORTH SAYING. New York, Doran, 1922. 131p [LC

**Robertson, Rev. Hugh John, 1868–1952**

THE STORY OF KNOX CHURCH, WINNIPEG. Seventy-five Years, 1872–1947. Winnipeg, the Church, [1947?]. 48p [MWP

**Robertson, Rev. James, 1801?–1878**

HISTORY OF THE MISSION OF THE SECESSION CHURCH TO NOVA SCOTIA AND PRINCE EDWARD ISLAND, FROM ITS COMMENCEMENT IN 1765. Edinburgh, Johnstone, 1847. 292p [NSWA OTP QMSS

A TREATISE ON INFANT BAPTISM. Shewing the Scriptural Grounds and Historical Evidence. ... Halifax, "The Novascotian" Office, 1836. xxiv + 291p [NBFU OTP

**Robinson, Frank Alfred, 1874–**

RELIGIOUS REVIVAL AND SOCIAL BETTERMENT. Boston, Gorham, 1918. 54p [LC

**Robson, Alexander Ritchie**

WEST OF THE WEST. A Sketch of Early Mission Days in North-Western Canada. Toronto, Musson, n.d. 136p [AEU OTU

**Robson, Rev. Ebenezer, 1835–1915**

HOW METHODISM CAME TO BRITISH COLUMBIA. Toronto, Methodist, 1905. 31p [BViPA OKQ

**Roddan, Rev. Andrew, –1948**

THE CHRIST OF THE WIRELESS WAY. Vancouver, Clarke & Stuart, 1932. 216p [BVaU NSWA

THE CHURCH IN THE MODERN CITY. The Story of Three Score Years of Practical Christian Service, 1885–1945, First United Church, Vancouver, B.C. Vancouver, Dunsmuir Print., n.d. 61p [BVaU

**Roe, Rev. Henry, 1829–1909**

BICENTENARY SERMONS. Two Sermons on the History and Scriptural Authority of the Book of Common Prayer. Montreal, Lovell, 1862. [NSWA

THE CONTINUITY OF THE CHURCH OF ENGLAND AND THE PAPAL ENCYCLICAL APOSTOLIC CURAE. Quebec, n.pub., 1897. 87p [NSWA

FAREWELL SERMON PREACHED IN ST. STEPHEN'S, OR 2ND INVERNESS CHURCH, MEGANTIC, ON THE 22ND OCTOBER, 1854. Montreal, Lovell, 1854. 40p [OTP

PURGATORY, TRANSUBSTANTIATION, AND THE MASS. Three Sermons. ... 2nd ed. Montreal, Lovell, 1863. 111p [NSWA OLU

STORY OF THE FIRST HUNDRED YEARS OF THE DIOCESE OF QUEBEC. Quebec, "Morning Chronicle," 1893. 63p [BVaU NSWA OTP

**Rokeby-Thomas, Rev. Howard Rokeby, 1907–**

CHURCH IN THE VALLEY. Port Stanley, Ont., Christ Church, 1949. 96p [OLU

**Roman Collar (pseud)**

THE PARSON HITS BACK. Toronto, Thorn Press, 1937. 126p [CC

**Rose, Albert, 1917–**

A PEOPLE AND ITS FAITH. Essays on Jews and Reform Judaism in a Changing Canada. Ed. by ——. Toronto, U. of Toronto Press, 1959. xiv + 204p

**Rosenberg, Rabbi Stuart E., 1922–**

MAN IS FREE. Sermons and Addresses. New York, Bloch Pub. Co., 1957. xii + 155p

THE ROAD TO CONFIDENCE. Toronto, Copp Clark, 1959. ix + 166p

A TIME TO SPEAK, OF MAN, FAITH AND SOCIETY. New York, Bloch Pub. Co., 1960. 181p

**Ross, Mrs. Anna**

THE NEW COVENANT. A Lost Secret. ... Toronto, Briggs, 1901. 193p [BM NSWA OTU

**Ross, Rev. Duncan, 1770?–1834**

BAPTISM CONSIDERED IN ITS SUBJECTS AND MODE. In Three Letters to the Rev. William Elder. Pictou, Weir Durham, 1825. 78p [NSHD

STRICTURES ON A PUBLICATION ENTITLED "BELIEVER IMMERSION." Pictou, Weir Durham, 1828. 38p [NSHD OTP

**Ross, Rev. John Jacob, 1871–**

BREAKING THE SEALS. A Spiritual and Devotional Study of All the Symbols in the Central Chapters of the Book of Revelation. New York, Revell, 1924. 221p [LC

DANIEL'S HALF-WEEK NOW CLOSING. New York, 1922. 115p [LC

THE KINGDOM IN MYSTERY. New York, 1920. 379p [LC

OUR GLORIOUS HOPE. New York, Revell, 1922. 160p [LC

PEARLS FROM PATMOS. New York, Revell, 1923. 231p [LC

THINKING THROUGH THE NEW TESTAMENT. New York, Revell, 1921. 254p [LC

**Roth, Rev. D. Luther**

ACADIE AND THE ACADIANS. Philadelphia, Lutheran Pub. Soc., 1890. 427p [Concerns the Lutheran Church in Nova Scotia] [BVaU LC NBFU OTP QMBM

OUR SCHOOLMASTER. A Series of Lectures on the Commandments. Halifax, Nova Scotia Print., 1880. xv + 136p [NSHPL

**Rowley, Owsley Robert, 1868–1949**

THE ANGLICAN EPISCOPATE OF CANADA AND NEWFOUNDLAND. Milwaukee, Morehouse, 1928. 280p [BM BVaU NSWA OTP QMM

**Roy, Rev. James, 1834–1922**

BAPTISM AND SALVATION. Montreal, Rivard, 1882. 46p [OTP

CATHOLICITY AND METHODISM; or, The Relation of John Wesley to Modern Thought. Montreal, Burland-Desbarats, 1877. 109p [BM NSWA OTP QMSS

HOW TO INTERPRET OUR BIBLE. New York, Broadway, 1911. 119p [LC NSHD QMM

**Royal Oak, Vancouver Island, B.C. St. Michael and All Angels' Church**

ST. MICHAEL AND ALL ANGELS' CHURCH, WEST SAANICH ROAD, ROYAL OAK, VANCOUVER ISLAND, BRITISH COLUMBIA, 1883 TO 1953. Victoria, n.p., 1953. 20p

**Royle, Rev. Edward Cecil, 1912–**

AN HISTORICAL STUDY OF THE ANGLICAN PARISH OF VAUDREUIL. Hudson Heights, Que., Author, 1952. 76p [mimeographed]

THE HISTORY OF THE ANGLICAN PARISH OF VAUDREUIL. [2nd ed. rev. and enl.] Hudson Heights, Que., Author, 1955. 221p

**Russell, Francis W.**

HISTORY OF ST. MARY'S CATHEDRAL PARISH, WINNIPEG, MANITOBA. Diamond Jubilee Edition. Winnipeg, 1936. 95p [MWP

**Russell, Rev. George Stanley, 1883–1957**

THE CHURCH IN THE MODERN WORLD. Toronto, Allen, 1931. 179p [BVaU LC NSHD OTP

THE FACE OF GOD. New York, Harper, 1935. 114p [BM

**Ryerson, Rev. Adolphus Egerton, 1803–1882**

CANADIAN METHODISM, ITS EPOCHS AND CHARACTERISTICS. ... Toronto, Briggs, 1882. 440p [BVaU NBFU OTP

CLAIMS OF THE CHURCHMEN AND DISSENTERS OF UPPER CANADA. Brought to the Test in a Controversy between Several Members of the Church of England and a Methodist Preacher. [Anon] Kingston, Herald Office, 1828. 232p [OTP QMSS

THE CLERGY RESERVE QUESTION AS A MATTER OF HISTORY, A QUESTION OF LAW AND A SUBJECT OF LEGISLATION. In a Series of Letters to the Hon. W.H. Draper. Toronto, Lawrence, 1839. 156p [BM BVaU OTP QMSS

SCRIPTURAL RIGHTS OF THE MEMBERS OF CHRIST'S VISIBLE CHURCH; or, Correspondence Containing the Reasons of Dr. Ryerson's Resignation of Office in the Wesleyan Methodist Church. Toronto, Brewer McPhail, 1854. [BM NSWA OTP

WESLEYAN METHODISM IN UPPER CANADA. A Sermon. ... Toronto, Conference Office, 1837. 27p [BVaU NSWA OTP

**Sackville, N.B. St. Paul's Church**

100TH ANNIVERSARY, ST. PAUL'S CHURCH, SACKVILLE, N.B. Sackville, the Church, 1958. 24p

**Sadlier, Mary Anne (Madden), 1820–1903**

PURGATORY: DOCTRINAL, HISTORICAL AND POETICAL. New York, Sadlier, 1886. 500p [LC OWA QQL

**Saint John, N.B. Exmouth Street United Church. Historical Committee**

ONE HUNDREDTH ANNIVERSARY, EXMOUTH STREET UNITED CHURCH, 1857–1957. Saint John, the Church, 1957. 36p

**Saint John, N.B. St. Andrew's Kirk. Historical Committee**

ST. ANDREW'S KIRK, SAINT JOHN, N.B., THE UNITED CHURCH OF CANADA. One Hundred and Seventy-fifth Anniversary, May 18th, 1784–May 18th, 1959. Saint John, the Church, 1959. 113p

**Saint John, N.B. St. Paul's Church**

ST. PAUL'S CHURCH, SAINT JOHN, NEW BRUNSWICK, ESTABLISHED MAY 1ST, 1856. Saint John, N.B., the Church, 1958. 8p

**Saint John, N.B. West Side Kirk of the United Church of Canada**

THE WEST SIDE KIRK OF THE UNITED CHURCH OF CANADA. A Century of Service, 1857–1957. Ed. by Gerald Keith. Saint John, the Church, 1957. 101p

**St. Laurent, Charles F. (pseud)**

LANGUAGE AND NATIONALITY IN THE LIGHT OF REVELATION AND HISTORY. Montreal, Author, 1896. 104p [OTP

**St. Mary's, Ont. Knox Presbyterian Church**

AN HISTORICAL SKETCH OF KNOX PRESBYTERIAN CHURCH, ST. MARY'S, ONTARIO, MAY 6TH, 1956. A Souvenir of the Golden Jubilee, 1906–1956. St. Mary's, the Church, 1956. 8p

**St. Paul, Mother M.**

FROM DESENZANO TO "THE PINES." A Sketch of the History of the Ursulines of Ontario. ... Toronto, Macmillan, 1941. 387p [OLU QMBM

**Salter, Walter Frederick, 1884–**

TRUTH AS I SEE IT. Haliburton, Ont., Author, [1959?]. 14 + 129p

**Sanderson, Rev. Joseph Edward, 1830–1913**

THE FIRST CENTURY OF METHODISM IN CANADA. Toronto, Briggs, 1908–1910. 2v [BVaU NSWA OTP

**Sangster, James Lewis, 1891–**

75 YEARS OF SERVICE. A History of Olivet Baptist Church, 1878–1953. New Westminster, Olivet Board of Management, 1953. 77p

**Saskatoon, Sask. Grace United Church**

GRACE UNITED CHURCH, SASKATOON, 1886–1951. Saskatoon, the Church, 1951. 32p

**Saskatoon, Sask. Third Avenue United Church**

GOLDEN JUBILEE OF THIRD AVENUE UNITED CHURCH, SASKATOON, SASKATCHEWAN, 50TH ANNIVERSARY. A Record of Service and Achievement down through the years, 1901–1951. Saskatoon, the Church, 1951. 32p

**Saunders, Rev. Edward Manning, 1829–1916**

HISTORY OF THE BAPTISTS OF THE MARITIME PROVINCES. Halifax, Burgoyne, 1902. 520p [BVaU NBFU OTP

A SKETCH OF THE ORIGIN AND HISTORY OF THE GRANVILLE STREET BAPTIST CHURCH. Halifax, Christian Messenger, 1877. 78p [NSHD

**Saunders, Henry Scholey, 1864–1951**

THE HIGHER CONSCIOUSNESS. A Little Introduction to Dr. Richard Maurice Bucke's "Cosmic Consciousness." Toronto, Author, 1924. 47p [OTP

**Savary, Alfred William, 1831–1920**

FRENCH AND ANGLICAN CHURCHES AT ANNAPOLIS ROYAL. ... Annapolis Royal, Spectator, 1910. 15p [NSWA

**Scadding, Rev. Henry, 1813–1901**

CHRISTIAN PANTHEISM. An Address. ... Toronto, Rollo, 1865. 11p [NSWA OTU

JUBILEE OF THE DIOCESE OF TORONTO. 1839 to 1889. ... By Henry Scadding and J.G. Hodgins. Toronto, Rowsell & Hutchinson, 1890. 235p [BVaU NSWA OTU

**Schrepfer, Luke**

PIONEER MONKS IN NOVA SCOTIA. Tracadie, N.S., St. Augustine's Monastery, 1947. 228p [BVaU

**Scollard, Robert Joseph L., 1908–**

BASILIAN FATHERS. A Short Account of History, Life and Works of Congregation of Priests of St. Basil. Toronto, Basilian Press, 1940. 32p [OTU

**Scott, Charles Sumner, 1858–**

CHRIST CHURCH CATHEDRAL, HAMILTON, 1835–1935. Hamilton, Davis-Lisson, 1935. 88p [OTP

**Scott, Rev. Frederick George, 1861–1944**

THE EMPIRE AND THE COLOURS OF THE FLAG; A Sermon Addressed to the Canadian Volunteers for the War. London, Christian Knowledge Society, 1900. 8p [BM

**Scott, Mary Jane, 1894–**

MY ADVENTURES WITH GOD. Toronto, Nelson, 1956. 139p

**Scott, Rev. Robert Balgarnie Young, 1899–**

THE ORIGINAL LANGUAGE OF THE APOCALYPSE. Toronto, U. of Toronto Press, 1928. 25p [BM LC OTU

THE RELEVANCE OF THE PROPHETS. New York, Macmillan, 1944. 237p [BVaU LC OTP

TOWARDS THE CHRISTIAN REVOLUTION. Ed. by R.B.Y. Scott and Gregory Vlastos. Chicago, Willett Clark, 1936. 254p [BM BVaU LC OTP QMM

**Scott, William Louis, 1862–1947**

EASTERN CATHOLICS. With Special Reference to the Ruthenians in Canada. Toronto, Catholic Truth Soc., 1923. 47p [OTP

**Scrimger, Rev. John, 1849–**

JESUIT MORALS. On the Errors in the Moral Teaching of the Jesuits. Montreal, Drysdale, 1890. 89p [OTP QMM

**Sedgewick, Rev. Robert**

HOLY AND HAPPY CHURCH THE ABODE OF THE GOD OF LOVE. A Sermon. Aberdeen, Smith, 1849. 36p [NSHD

THE PAPACY: THE IDOLATRY OF ROME. A Lecture. Halifax, Wesleyan, 1859. 59p [NSHP

WINE OF THE KINGDOM; or, Fellowship with Christ. Dundee, Middleton, 1846. 155p [BM NSHD

**Seely, Rev. Ralph Arthur, 1930–**

APPALLING APOSTASY. Central Bedeque, P.E.I., Author, 1955. 39p

**Sellar, Robert, 1841–1919**

THE PAPAL MENACE. Canada is Threatened with Papal rather than French Domination. Toronto, Sentinel Pub. Co., [1912?]. 46p [BVaU OTP

**Semmens, Rev. John, 1850–1921**

THE HANDBOOK TO SCRIPTURE TRUTHS. Toronto, Methodist Mission Rooms, 1893. 46p [LC

**Seymour, Rev. James Cooke, 1839–1902**

CHRIST THE APOCALYPSE. New York, Eaton & Mains, 1902. 350p [LC

THE RIVER OF LIFE. An Exposition of Ezekiel's Vision. Toronto, Wesleyan, 1869. 169p [Ryerson Impt

VOICES FROM THE THRONE; or, God's Call to Faith and Obedience. Toronto, Methodist Book, 1881. 153p [OTP

**Shatford, Rev. Allan Pearson, 1873–1935**

SIX MARKS OF A CHRISTIAN. Philadelphia, Winston, 1925. 122p [LC

SIX ROLES OF A CHRISTIAN. Toronto, McClelland, 1928. [CC

THE YEAR OF JUBILEE. A Brief Sketch of Fifty Years' Work in the Church of St. James the Apostle, Montreal, 1864–1914. Montreal, Lovell, 1914. 68p [BVaU NSWA OLU QMSS

**Shaw, Gordon, 1893–**

THE ROAD TO REALITY. New York, Pageant Press, 1952. xiii + 121p

**Shaw, John Arthur, 1862–**

SOME FEATURES OF THE FAITH. A Popular Discussion of Certain Cardinal Points of Christian Doctrine. Milwaukee, Young Churchman, 1902. 306p [LC OTU

**Shaw, Rev. John Mackintosh, 1879–**

THE BELIEF IN THE HOLY SPIRIT. Stirling, Drummond Tract Depot, n.d. 16p [OTU

CHRISTIAN DOCTRINE. A One-Volume Outline of Christian Belief. London, Lutterworth Press, 1953. 378p

THE CHRISTIAN GOSPEL OF THE FATHERHOOD OF GOD. London, Hodder, 1925. 191p [BM BVaU LC NSHD

LIFE AFTER DEATH. The Christian View of the Future Life. Toronto, Ryerson, 1945. 110p [BVa LC OTP

THE RESURRECTION OF CHRIST. Edinburgh, Clark, 1920. 215p [BM BVaU LC NSWA QMM

THE WONDER OF THE CHRISTIAN GOSPEL. Toronto, Ryerson, 1959. 143p

**Shaw, Robert**

EXISTENCE AND DEITY. Illustrated and Explained. In Two Parts. Montreal, Author, 1872. 900p [OONL QMBM

**Shaw, Rev. Robert Elwell, 1910–**

HISTORICAL SKETCH, 1831–1956, DISCIPLES OF CHRIST, NORTH STREET CHRISTIAN CHURCH, HALIFAX, N.S. Halifax, the Church, [1956?]. 22p

**Shaw, Rev. William Isaac, 1841–1911**

DIGEST OF THE DOCTRINAL STANDARDS OF THE METHODIST CHURCH. Toronto, Briggs, 1895. 141p [BM OTU

**Shaw, William John, 1886–**

ST. ANDREW'S–ST. PAUL'S, 1857–1957. Hamilton, St. Paul's Church, 1957. 57p

ST. PAUL'S CHURCH (PRESBYTERIAN), HAMILTON. A Century of Service. Hamilton, Author, 1933. 93p [OTP

**Shenston, Thomas Strahan, 1822–1895**

GLEANINGS. By T.S.S. Guelph, Hough, 1893. 176p [OTP

A JUBILEE REVIEW OF THE FIRST BAPTIST CHURCH, BRANTFORD, 1833 TO 1884. ... Toronto, Bingham & Webber, 1890. 203p [OTP

**Sheppard, Edmund Ernest, 1855–1924**

THE THINKING UNIVERSE. Reason as Applied to the Manifestations of the Infinite. Los Angeles, Author's Co., 1915. 347p [BM LC OTU

**Sheraton, Rev. James Peterson, 1841–1906**

CHRISTIAN SCIENCE. N.p., 1891. 44p [NSWA OTU

THE HIGHER CRITICISM. Toronto, 1904. 69p [OTP QMM

THE INSPIRATION AND AUTHORITY OF THE HOLY SCRIPTURES. Toronto, Bryant, 1893. 58p [OTU

OUR LORD'S TEACHING CONCERNING HIMSELF. N.p., 1904. 55p [OTU

**Sherbrooke, Que. Plymouth United Church**

PLYMOUTH CHURCH, PAST AND PRESENT. A Brief History of Plymouth United Church. ... [1835–1955]. Sherbrooke, the Church, 1956. ix + 65p

**Shields, Thomas Todhunter, 1873–1955**

"OTHER LITTLE SHIPS" FREIGHTED WITH COMFORT. Toronto, Hunter Rose, 1935. 261p [BM

**Sidey, John James**

THE CENTENNIAL OF THE BEDEQUE BAPTIST CHURCH, P.E.I. "Overcoming"; or,

"The Victory of the Gospel". ... A Scenic Pageant, showing the early History of the Bedeques and the Founding of the Baptist Church. [Bedeque?], 1926. [59]p [NSWA

**Sigsworth, John Wilkins, 1915–**

THE BATTLE WAS THE LORD'S. A History of the Free Methodist Church in Canada. Oshawa, Sage Publishers, 1960. 301p

**Silcox, Rev. Claris Edwin, 1888–1961**

CATHOLICS, JEWS AND PROTESTANTS. A Study in Relationships in the United States and Canada. By Claris Edwin Silcox and Galen M. Fisher. New York, Harper, 1934. 369p [BM BVaU LC OTP QMM

CHURCH UNION IN CANADA. New York, Inst. of Social and Religious Research, 1933. 493p [BM BVaU LC NSHD OTP

THE CONSECRATION OF POWER AND INTELLIGENCE. Toronto, Ryerson, 1945. 22p [BVaU OTU

AN EPISTLE TO THE HEBREWS. By John Cournos and C.E. Silcox. Toronto, Ryerson, 1938. 32p [OTU QMM

"FROM WAR TO PEACE." Sermons Preached in Newport, R.I., during the Great War. Newport, Milne Print., 1919. n.p. [OTU

PHYSICIANS, HUMAN AND DIVINE. A Sermon. Fairfield, Conn., 1922. 17p [OTU

PROTESTANT-CATHOLIC RELATIONS IN CANADA. Toronto, United Church Pub., 1938. 32p [BVaU OTU

THE RELATION OF CHURCH AND STATE. A Sermon. N.p., 1921. 18p [OTU

THE WAR AND RELIGION. Toronto, Macmillan, 1941. 30p [BVaU OTU

**Sims, Rev. Albert**

REMARKABLE NARRATIVES; or, Records of Powerful Revivals, Striking Providences, Wonderful Religious Experiences, Tragic Death-bed Scenes and Other Authentic Incidents. ... Kingston, Author, 1896. 352p [Another ed.: Pittsburgh, Hague, 1902. 352p] [BM BVaU LC

**Sinclair, Rev. Alexander Maclean, 1840–1924**

LETTERS ON THE ANGLO-ISRAEL FOLLY. Truro, McConnell, 1880. 41p [NSWA

**Sinclair, John D., 1874–1947**

WESTMINSTER CHURCH, THE UNITED CHURCH OF CANADA, WINNIPEG, FORTY-FIFTH YEAR. Souvenir of the Silver Jubilee of the present Church Building. Winnipeg, 1937. 101p [MWP

**Sisters of St. Ann. St. Ann's Academy**

THE SISTERS OF ST. ANN IN BRITISH COLUMBIA, YUKON, AND ALASKA, 1858–1958. Victoria, St. Ann's Academy, 1958. 100p

**Sisters of St. Ann. Saint Joseph Province**

CENTENNIAL ANNIVERSARY OF THE ARRIVAL OF THE PIONEER NUNS IN VICTORIA, B.C., JUNE 5, 1858–JUNE 5, 1958. Victoria, 1958. 63p

**Sleigh, William Willcocks, 1796–**

THE CHRISTIAN'S DEFENSIVE DICTIONARY. Philadelphia, Biddle, 1837. 437p [BM LC

AN EXPOSURE OF MARIA MONK'S PRETENDED ABDUCTION. Philadelphia, Collins, 1837. 36p [OTP

**Slight, Rev. Benjamin, 1798?–1858**

THE APOCALYPSE EXPLAINED. In Two Series of Discourses on the Entire Book of the Revelation of St. John. Montreal, Miller, 1855. 516p [BM LC OTP

**Smart, Rev. James Dick, 1906–**

THE RECOVERY OF HUMANITY. Philadelphia, Westminster Press, 1953. 157p

**Smith, Goldwin, 1823–1910**

DOES THE BIBLE SANCTION AMERICAN SLAVERY? Oxford & London, Henry & Parker, 1863. 107p [AEU NBFU OKQ

THE FOUNDER OF CHRISTENDOM. Boston, American Unitarian Assoc., 1903. 44p [BM BVaU LC NBFU OTP QMM

GUESSES AT THE RIDDLE OF EXISTENCE, AND OTHER ESSAYS ON KINDRED SUBJECTS. New York, Macmillan, 1897. 244p [BM BVaU LC NBFU OTU QMM

IN QUEST OF LIGHT. New York, Macmillan, 1906. 177p [BVaU LC NSHD OLU QMM

KEEPING CHRISTMAS. Toronto, Robinson, 1888. 12p [MWU NBFU OKQ

LINES OF RELIGIOUS ENQUIRY. Toronto, Copp Clark, 1897. 21p [AEU BM NBFU OTU

NO REFUGE BUT IN TRUTH. Toronto, Tyrrell, 1909. 93p [BM BVaU NBFU OKQ QMM

RATIONAL RELIGION, AND THE RATIONALISTIC OBJECTIONS OF THE BAMPTON LECTURES FOR 1858. Oxford, Wheeler, 1861. 146p [BM BVaU LC NBFU OTU QMM

**Smith, Rev. Oswald Jeffrey, 1889–**

BACK TO PENTECOST. New York, Christian Alliance, 1926. 124p [LC

THE BAPTISM WITH THE HOLY SPIRIT. New York, Christian Alliance, 1925. 54p [LC

CAN ORGANIZED RELIGION SURVIVE? Toronto, Tabernacle Pub., 1932. 299p [OWtL

THE CLOUDS ARE LIFTING. London, Marshall, Morgan & Scott, 1939. 96p [BM BVaU

THE DAWN IS BREAKING. London, Marshall, Morgan & Scott, [19—]. 96p [BM BVaU

THE DAY OF SALVATION. London, Marshall, Morgan & Scott, 1955. 127p

THE ENDUEMENT OF POWER. London, Marshall, Morgan & Scott, [19—]. 119p [BM BVaU OLU

FROM DEATH TO LIFE. New York, Christian Alliance, 1925. 128p [LC

THE GREAT PHYSICIAN. New York, Christian Alliance, 1927. 128p [LC
IS THE ANTICHRIST AT HAND?–WHAT OF MUSSOLINI. New York, Christian Alliance, 1927. 128p [LC
THE LORD IS CALLING. London, Marshall, Morgan & Scott, [19—]. 95p [BM BVaU
THE MAN GOD USES. New York, Christian Alliance, 1925. 133p [BM BVaU LC
THE MAN IN THE WELL. Chicago, Bible Inst., 1934. 31p [LC
THE PASSION FOR SOULS. London, Marshall, Morgan & Scott, 1950. 128p [BM
PROPHECY–WHAT LIES AHEAD? London, Marshall, Morgan & Scott, 1943. 190p [BM LC
THE REVIVAL WE NEED. New York, Christian Alliance, 1925. 125p [BM LC
THE SALVATION OF GOD. 2nd ed. London, Marshall, Morgan & Scott, 1937. 128p [BM BVaU
THE SPIRIT IS WORKING. London, Marshall, Morgan & Scott, [19—]. 120p [BM BVaU
THE SPIRIT-FILLED LIFE. New York, Christian Alliance, 1926. 126p [LC
WHEN ANTICHRIST REIGNS. New York, Christian Alliance, 1927. 148p [LC
THE WORK GOD BLESSES. London, Marshall, Morgan & Scott, [19—]. 128p [BM BVaU

**Smith, Thomas Watson, 1836–1902**

HISTORY OF THE METHODIST CHURCH WITHIN THE TERRITORIES EMBRACED IN THE LATE CONFERENCE OF EASTERN BRITISH AMERICA. Including Nova Scotia, New Brunswick, Prince Edward Island, and Bermuda. Halifax, Methodist Book Room, 1877–1890. 2v [BVaU LC NBFU OTP

**Smith, Rev. William Wye, 1827–1917**

THE PRINT OF HIS SHOE; or, Following Christ. Boston, Congregational Sunday-school, 1887. 160p [OTP

**Smyth, Rev. John Paterson, 1852–1932**

THE BIBLE IN THE MAKING, IN THE LIGHT OF MODERN RESEARCH. Toronto, 1914. 219p [BVaU QMM
GOD AND THE WAR. New York, Hodder, 1915. 190p [BM LC NSHD QMM
GOD, CONSCIENCE AND THE BIBLE. New York, Pott, 1924. 164p [BM LC
THE GOSPEL OF THE HEREAFTER. New York, Revell, 1910. 224p [BM BVaU LC NSHD OTU QMM
HOW GOD INSPIRED THE BIBLE. Dublin, Eason, 1892. 222p [Also: New York, Pott, 1918.] [BM LC
HOW WE GOT OUR BIBLE. An Answer to Questions Suggested by the New Revision. London, Bagster, 1885. 127p [Several later editions.] [BM BVaU LC OLU QMM
MARRIAGE AND ROMANCE, WITH OTHER STUDIES. New York, Revell, 1930. 160p [BM LC

MYSELF, AND OTHER PROBLEMS. New York, Revell, 1927. 194p [BM LC

THE OLD DOCUMENTS AND THE NEW BIBLE. London, Bagster, 1890. 216p [BM BVaU QMM

ON THE RIM OF THE WORLD. New York, Revell, 1922. 83p [BM LC NSHD OTU

A PEOPLE'S LIFE OF CHRIST. Toronto, Musson, 1920. 505p [BM BVaU LC QMM

THE PREACHER AND HIS SERMON. London, Nisbet, 1907. 124p [Also: New York, Doran, 1922. 143p] [BM BVaU LC QMM

SOCIAL SERVICE IDEALS. London, Sands, 1900. 152p [BM LC

THE STORY OF ST. PAUL'S LIFE AND LETTERS. New York, Pott, 1917. 223p [New ed.: Toronto, Musson, 1924.] [BM BVaU LC OTU QMM

**Smythe, Albert Ernest Stafford, 1861–1947**

AFTER FORTY-EIGHT YEARS. Some Reflections on Theosophy in Canada, 1922–1923. Toronto, Author, 1923. 29p [NSWA OKQ

**Snodgrass, Rev. William, 1827–1906**

THE TWO BUILDERS; or, The Conclusion of the Matter. Montreal, Lovell, 1863. 23p [NSWA

**Sommerville, Rev. William, 1800–1878**

ANTIPEDOBAPTISM. A Letter to the Rev. John Pryor, A.M. Halifax, Cunnabell, 1838. 53p [NSWA

BAPTISMAL IMMERSION NOT OF GOD. Arguments Pro and Con. Saint John, McKillop, 1876. 77p [NSWA

A DISSERTATION ON THE NATURE AND ADMINISTRATION OF THE ORDINANCE OF BAPTISM. Part 1. Halifax, Nova Scotian Office, 1845. 57p [Also: Paisley, Gardner, 1866. 319p] [NSHD NSWA

THE EXCLUSIVE CLAIMS OF DAVID'S PSALMS. Saint John, Barnes, 1855. 189p [NSHD NSWA

THE SOCIAL POSITION OF REFORMED PRESBYTERIANS OR CAMERONIANS. Londonderry, MacPherson, 1869. 38p [NSWA

**Sovereign, Rev. Arthur Henry, 1881–**

A TREE GROWS IN VERNON. The History of All Saints' Parish, Vernon, B.C. The Diamond Jubilee, 1893–1953. Vernon, B.C., Author, 1955. 36p

**Spark, Rev. Alexander, 1762–1819**

THE CONNEXION BETWEEN THE CIVIL AND RELIGIOUS STATE OF SOCIETY. Quebec, Neilson, 1811. 28p [BVaU OTP

**Speight-Humberstone, Clara E., 1862–**

SPIRITISM: THE HIDDEN SECRET IN EINSTEIN'S THEORY OF RELATIVITY. Kitchener, Ont., Commercial, 1922. 232p [BM LC

**Spencer, Rev. James, 1812–1863**

SERMONS. Toronto, Green, 1864. 391p [LC OTP

**Spetz, Rev. Theobald, 1850–1921**

THE CATHOLIC CHURCH IN WATERLOO COUNTY. [Toronto], Catholic Register & Extension, 1916. 262p [OTU QMSS

**Spiritus (pseud)**

BRIGHTER SPHERES. By Spiritus [pseud]. Dictated through the Mediumship of Annie F.S. With an intro. by E.J.C. Montreal, Lovell, 1890. 221p [BVaU LC OLU

**Squires, Susan Katherine (Dayton), 1869–1951**

ONE HUNDRED YEARS IN LEMUEL ALLAN WILMOT'S CHURCH, WITH A BRIEF SKETCH OF THE EARLIER DAYS OF METHODISM IN CENTRAL NEW BRUNSWICK. Fredericton, Wilmot United Church, 1952. 44p

**Stafford, Rev. Ezra Adams, 1839–1891**

THE GUIDING HAND; or, Some Phases of the Religious Life of the Day. Toronto, Briggs, 1887. 189p [OTP

THE NEED OF MINSTRELSY, AND OTHER SERMONS. Memorial Volume of the late Rev. E.A. Stafford. ... Toronto, Briggs, 1892. 317p [OTP

**Starr, Rev. George Lothrop, 1872–1925**

OLD ST. GEORGE'S. Being the Story of a Church and its Ministers in an Historic Centre of Upper Canada. Kingston, Uglow, 1913. 86p [BM BVaU OTU

**Stauffer, Rev. Byron H., 1870–1922**

THE BATTLE NOBODY SAW AND OTHER SERMONS. Toronto, Ryerson, 1919. 200p [OTUV

YOUR MOTHER'S APRON STRINGS, AND OTHER TALKS TO YOUNG MEN. Toronto, Briggs, 1910. 224p [BM BVaU OTUV

**Steele, Rev. David Allan, 1838–1931**

A HISTORY OF THE AMHERST BAPTIST CHURCH. To which is appended Historical Notes of the Town of Amherst. Amherst, N.S., Black, 1895. 44p [NSHD

**Steiner, Florence B., 1877–1946**

ONE HUNDRED YEARS OF SERVICE. 1845–1945, FIRST UNITARIAN CHURCH, TORONTO. Toronto, the Church, 1945. 32p [OTP

**Stephens, William A., 1809–1891**

PAPAL INFALLIBILITY. As seen in the Light of Catholicism, stated and defended by the Rev. M.J. Ferguson ... and as seen in the Light of Revelation, examined and exhibited by William A. Stephens. Owen Sound, 1871. 69p [BM

**Stephenson, Annie Devina (Swinton)**

ONE HUNDRED YEARS OF CANADIAN METHODIST MISSIONS, 1824–1924. By Mrs. Frederick G. Stephenson. Toronto, Missionary Society of the Methodist Church, 1925. 265p [BVaU OKQ

THAT THEY MAY BE ONE. An Introduction to the Study of the Work of the Board of Home Missions of the United Church of Canada. ... By Mrs. Frederick G. Stephenson and Sara Vance. Toronto, Board of Home Missions, 1929. 222p [BVaU NBSaM OTUV

**Stern, Rabbi Harry Joshua, 1897–**

MARTYRDOM AND MIRACLE. A Collection of Addresses. New York, Bloch Pub. Co., 1950. 246p [OONL

**Stevens, Rev. Lorenzo Graham**

A REVIEW OF THE FIRST HALF CENTURY'S HISTORY OF ST. LUKE'S CHURCH, PORTLAND, ST. JOHN, N.B. Ed. by ——. Saint John, McMillan, 1889. 198p [BVaU NSWA OLU

**Stewart, Alexander, –1840**

TWO ESSAYS. The First, on the Gospel; the Second, on the Kingdom of Christ: and a Sermon on Baptism, with an Appendix Containing Remarks on Late Publications. York, U.C., W.L. Mackenzie, [1827?]. 96p [NSWA OTP

**Stewart, Rev. Charles James, 1775–1837**

TWO SERMONS ON FAMILY PRAYER. Montreal, Mower, 1814. 394p [LC NSWA OTP QMM

**Stewart, Herbert Leslie, 1882–1953**

A CENTURY OF ANGLO-CATHOLICISM. Toronto, Dent, 1929. 404p [BM BVaU LC NSHD

MODERNISM, PAST AND PRESENT. London, Murray, 1932. 369p [BM LC NSHD OTU

**Stewart, James Livingstone, 1872–1946**

CHINESE CULTURE AND CHRISTIANITY. New York, Revell, 1926. 316p [BM LC OTP QMM

**Stewart, Robert, 1853–**

ST. ANDREW'S CHURCH (PRESBYTERIAN), QUEBEC. Quebec, Chronicle-Telegraph, 1928. 91p [OTP QMM

**Stewart, Rev. Thomas Millon, 1855–1923**

TOWARD THE SUNRISING AND OTHER SERMONS. With a Biographical Sketch by George S. Carson. Toronto, McClelland, 1923. 219p [BVaU NSHD OTP

**Stimson, Rev. Elam Rush, 1825?–1888**

HISTORY OF THE SEPARATION OF CHURCH AND STATE IN CANADA. Ed. by ——. Toronto, 1887. 201p [BM BVaU LC NBFU OTP QMM

**Stobo, Rev. Edward John, 1867–1922**

THE GLORY OF HIS ROBE. Meditations for the Quiet Hour. New York, Doran, 1922. 269p [LC NSWA

**Storrs, Monica**

THE NORTH PEACE RIVER PARISH, DIOCESE OF CALEDONIA. A Brief History. By Monica Storrs *et al.* Fort St. John, B.C., Alaska Highway News, 1954. 22p

**Stothers, Isaac Flexman, 1891–**

INVASION BY SADDLEBAG AND BUCKBOARD. Tisdale, Sask., [1959?]. 58p [History of the Methodist and Presbyterian Church in the Carrot River Valley, Sask., now St. Paul's United Church, Tisdale.] [mimeographed]

**Stott, William**

THE STORY OF ST. ANDREW'S UNITED CHURCH, NORTH VANCOUVER, 1865–1937. Vancouver, North Shore Press, 1937. 34p [BVaU OTU

**Strachan, Rev. John, 1778–1867**

THE CHRISTIAN RELIGION, RECOMMENDED IN A LETTER TO HIS PUPILS. Montreal, Mower, 1807. 32p [NSWA OTP QMM

THE CLERGY RESERVES. A Letter from the Bishop of Toronto to the Hon. A. N. Morin. Toronto, Thompson, 1854. 27p [BVaU OTP

THE CLERGY RESERVES. A Letter from the Lord Bishop of Toronto to the Duke of Newcastle, Her Majesty's Secretary for the Colonies. Toronto, "Churchman" Office, 1853. 27p [OTP

A LETTER TO THE CONGREGATION OF ST. JAMES' CHURCH, YORK, U. CANADA, OCCASIONED BY THE HON. JOHN ELMSLEY'S PUBLICATION OF THE BP. OF STRASBOURG'S OBSERVATIONS ON THE 6TH CHAPTER OF ST. JOHN'S GOSPEL. York, Stanton, 1834. 96p [BVaU NSWA OTU

A LETTER TO THE RIGHT HONORABLE THOMAS FRANKLAND LEWIS, M.P. [on Clergy Reserves]. York, Stanton, 1830. 112p [OTP

LETTERS TO THE HONORABLE WILLIAM MORRIS. Being Strictures on the Correspondence of that Gentleman with the Colonial Office, as a Delegate from the Presbyterian Body in Canada. Cobourg, Chatterton, 1838. 57p [OTP

OBSERVATIONS on the Provision made for the Maintenance of a Protestant Clergy, in the Provinces of Upper and Lower Canada. ... London, Gilbert, 1827. 44p [BVaU OTP

THE POOR MAN'S PRESERVATIVE AGAINST POPERY. ... Toronto, Bull, 1834. 54p [BM BVaU NSWA OTU

THE REPORT OF THE BISHOP OF TORONTO TO THE MOST HON. THE DUKE OF NEWCASTLE ON THE SUBJECT OF THE COLONIAL CHURCH. Toronto, Plees, 1853. 26p [QMM

SECULAR STATE OF THE CHURCH, IN THE DIOCESE OF TORONTO. Toronto, Diocesan Press, [1849?]. 40 + xixp [OTP QMM

A SPEECH, OF THE VENERABLE JOHN STRACHAN ... IN THE LEGISLATIVE COUNCIL ... SIXTH MARCH, 1828, ON THE SUBJECT OF THE CLERGY RESERVES. York, Stanton, [1828?]. 43p [OTP

**Straith, Rev. John, 1826–1885**

THE FIDELITY OF THE BIBLE. Being a Review of Colenso's Writings against the Pentateuch and Book of Joshua. Ingersoll, Ont., 1864. 64p [BibC

**Strang, Rev. Peter, 1856–1934**

HISTORY OF MISSIONS IN SOUTHERN SASKATCHEWAN. Regina, Author, 1929. 277p [BVaU OTU SRL

**Stratford, Ont. Avonton Presbyterian Church. Historical Committee**

CENTENNIAL, AVONTON PRESBYTERIAN CHURCH, 1857–1957. Stratford, Ont., the Committee, 1957. 28p

**Stratford, Ont. Central United Church**

CENTENNIAL HISTORY 1845–1945. Stratford, the Church, 1945. 96p [OOA

**Stuart, Rev. Henry Coleridge, 1844–1909**

THE CHURCH OF ENGLAND IN CANADA, 1759–1793. ... Montreal, Lovell, 1893. 117p [BVaU LC MWU NBFU OTP QMM

**Sutherland, Rev. Alexander, 1833–1910**

THE KINGDOM OF GOD, AND PROBLEMS OF TO-DAY. Toronto, Briggs, 1898. 240p [OTU

METHODISM IN CANADA. Its Work and its Story. London, Kelly, 1903. 350p [BM BVaU LC NBFU OTP

THE METHODIST CHURCH AND MISSIONS IN CANADA AND NEWFOUNDLAND. A Brief Account of the Methodist Church in Canada. What it is and what it has done. Toronto, Methodist Church Pub., 1906. 316p [BVaU OTU

**Sutherland, Donald**

THE CREATION; with its Glorious Prospect. Halifax, McAlpine, 1901. 32p [BM

**Symonds, Rev. Herbert, 1860–1921**

THE ANGLICAN CHURCH AND THE DOCTRINE OF APOSTOLIC SUCCESSION. Montreal, Renouf, 1907. 53p [QMM

THE BROAD CHURCH. A Sermon. ... Montreal, Witness Press, 1907. 14p [BVaU OTUV QMSS

LECTURES ON CHRISTIAN UNITY. Toronto, Briggs, 1899. 174p [OKQ

A SPIRITUAL FORWARD MOVEMENT. An Open Letter to Rev. Dr. Fraser. Montreal, Crites, n.d. 25p [BM OTU

**Tait, James, 1829–1899**

MIND IN MATTER. A Short Argument on Theism. London, Griffin, [1884]. 219p [BM

**Talling, Rev. Marshall P., 1857–1921**

COMMUNION WITH GOD. Extempore Prayer, its Principles, Preparation and Practice. New York, Revell, 1902. 302p [Pub. in England as: EXTEMPORE PRAYER. ...] [BM LC OTU

INTER-COMMUNION WITH GOD. New York, Revell, 1905. 206p [BM LC OTU

THE SCIENCE OF SPIRITUAL LIFE. New York, Revell, 1912. 320p [BM BVaU LC

**Tara, Ont. Knox Presbyterian Church**

HISTORICAL SKETCH ... READ AT THE TIME OF THE 75th ANNIVERSARY IN JUNE 1933. Tara, Leader Print., 1935. 20p [OTU

**Taylor, Andrew Winton, 1907–**

BANNERS UNFURLED. The History of First United Church, Galt, Canada, 1824–1949. Galt, Author, 1949. 60p [BVaU

**Taylor, Rev. Thomas**

THE BAPTIST COMMENTATOR REVIEWED. Two Letters to the Rev. William Jackson on Christian Baptism. ... Halifax, Cunnabell, 1835. 137p [NSWA

**Taylor, Rev. William, 1803–1876**

A DISCOURSE DELIVERED BEFORE THE LOYAL MONTREAL LODGE ... OF THE I.O.O.F., at their First Anniversary, Nov. 7, 1843. Montreal, Becket, 1843. 32p [QMSS

HINTS ON THE PROPER EMPLOYMENT OF HUMAN LIFE. Montreal, Campbell & Becket, 1838. 131p [BM BVaU NSWA OTP QMM

**Templeton, Charles Bradley, 1915–**

EVANGELISM FOR TOMORROW. New York, Harper, 1957. ix + 175p

LIFE LOOKS UP. [Sermons.] New York, Harper, 1955. 192p

**Templin, Hugh Charles, 1896–**

MELVILLE CHURCH, FERGUS. A History of the Congregation from 1845 to 1945. Written by Hugh Templin, John M. Imlah. ... Fergus, Ont., News-Record, 1945. 52p [OTP

**Ten Broeke, Rev. James, 1859–1937**

A CONSTRUCTIVE BASIS FOR THEOLOGY. London, Macmillan, 1914. 400p [BM BVaU OTU

THE MORAL LIFE AND RELIGION. A Study of Moral and Religious Personality. New York, Macmillan, 1922. 244p [BM OTP

**Therrien, Eugene Alphonse, 1895–1941**

BAPTIST WORK IN FRENCH CANADA. Toronto, Grande Ligne Mission, n.d. 126p [Same title: Toronto, Grande Ligne Mission, [1954]. 67p] [NSWA OTU

**Thirkell, Rev. Frederick William, 1930–**

THE FIRST TWO HUNDRED YEARS. The Story of the Parish of Newport and Walton. Newport, N.S., 1959. xviii + 107p

**Thomas, Rev. Benjamin Daniel, 1843–1917**

THE SECRET OF THE DIVINE SILENCE AND OTHER SERMONS. Toronto, Briggs, 1903. 241p [BVaU NSWA OTP

**Thompson, Rev. John, 1834–1903**

JESUS MY SAVIOUR. Being Brought Nigh by his Blood. New York, Revell, 1895. 121p [LC

THE LAMBS IN THE FOLD. New York, 1893. [DCB

**Thompson, John S.T.**

SCRIPTURE SKETCHES. Halifax, 1829. 280p [BibC

**Thomson, Donald Walter, 1906–**

THESE SIXTY YEARS, 1892–1952: THE STORY OF PARKDALE UNITED CHURCH, OTTAWA, AND ITS FOUNDING CONGREGATIONS. A Diamond Jubilee Record of Christian Service and Achievement in Canada's Capital. Ed. by ——. Ottawa, The Church, 1952. 31p

**Thomson, Rev. James Sutherland, 1892–**

THE HOPE OF THE GOSPEL. ... Toronto, Ryerson, 1955. 187p

**Tobin, Patrick Gerald**

OUR PARISH, PASTORS, PRIESTS. Diamond Jubilee of Our Lady of Mercy Church, Sarnia, Ontario. Petrolia, Advertiser-Topic, 1938. 82p [OLU

**Tombs, Guy, 1877–**

ONE HUNDRED YEARS OF ERSKINE CHURCH, MONTREAL, 1833–1933. United Church of Canada. Montreal, the Church, 1934. 122p [OOA

**Toombs, Rev. Herbert Wesley, 1870–1934**

MORMONISM. [Toronto?], Board of Home Missions, Presbyterian Church in Canada, [1916?]. 50p [OTP SSU

**Toronto, Ont. Church of the Epiphany**

GOLDEN JUBILEE, 1887–1937. Historical Review. Toronto, U. of Toronto Press, 1937. 32p [OTU

**Toronto, Ont. Church of St. John The Baptist, Norway**

THE STORY OF 100 YEARS OF THE CHURCH OF ST. JOHN THE BAPTIST, NORWAY. Toronto, the Church, 1950. 53p [OONL

**Toronto, Ont. Kew Beach United Church**

75TH ANNIVERSARY, 1882–1957. Toronto, the Church, 1957. 32p

**Toronto, Ont. Rhodes Avenue United Church. 50th Anniversary Year Committee**
RHODES AVENUE UNITED CHURCH. 50 Years of Blessing and Christian Witness, 1906–1956. Toronto, the Church, 1956. 8p

**Toronto, Ont. St. Clement's Church**
ST. CLEMENT'S CHURCH [Anglican]. A History of the Church, 1891–1941. Toronto, the Church, 1941. 16p [OTP

**Toronto, University of. Trinity College**
THE BISHOP OF HURON'S OBJECTIONS TO THE THEOLOGICAL TEACHING OF TRINITY COLLEGE. With the Provost's Reply. Toronto, Rowsell & Ellis, 1862. 84p [BM OTP
STRICTURES ON THE TWO LETTERS OF PROVOST WHITAKER. In Answer to Charges Brought by the Lord Bishop of Huron against the Teaching of Trinity College. By a Presbyter [pseud]. London, Ont., Evans, 1861. 96p [OTP

**Toronto Theosophical Society**
THEOSOPHY, AN ATTITUDE TOWARD LIFE; and Other Essays. Toronto, Toronto Theosophical Soc., 1944. 110p [OTP

**Townley, Rev. Adam, 1808–1887**
TEN LETTERS ON THE CHURCH AND CHURCH ESTABLISHMENTS. By an Anglo-Canadian [pseud]. Toronto, Commercial Herald Office, 1839. 79p [LC NSWA OTP

**Tracy, G. Frederick, 1862–1951**
BROKEN LIGHTS. Toronto, U. of Toronto Press, 1935. 140p [BVaU LC OTP

**Trewhella, Ethel Willson**
THE YONGE STREET QUAKERS. The Story of "The Friends" in the Early Days of York County, Ontario. Aurora, Walton, 1937. 15p [OTP

**Trinier, Rev. Harold Urban, 1912–**
A CENTURY OF SERVICE. Story of *The Canadian Baptist,* 1854–1954. Toronto, Board of Publication of the Baptist Convention of Ontario & Quebec, 1958. x + 149p

**Trotter, Thomas, 1781?–1855**
LETTERS ON THE MEANING OF BAPTIZED IN THE NEW TESTAMENT. In Reply to the Views of the Rev. Chas. Tupper. ... Pictou, "Eastern Chronicle," 1848. 76p [NSHD

**Tucker, Rev. Lewis Norman, 1852–**
FROM SEA TO SEA. The Dominion. 2nd ed. Toronto, Prayer and Study Union of the M.S.C.C., [1911?]. 181p [BVaU NSWA OTP
WESTERN CANADA. Toronto, Musson, [1907]. 164p (Handbooks of English Church Expansion.) [BM BVaU LC NSWA OTU QMSS

**Tucker, Sarah, –1859?**

THE BRIER AND MYRTLE;or, Heathenism and Christianity Illustrated in the History of Mary. London, 1851. [BM

THE RAINBOW IN THE NORTH. A Short Account of the First Establishment of Christianity in Rupert's Land. London, Nisbet, 1851. 222p [Several later editions.] [BM BVaU LC NSWA OLU QMM

**Tupper, Rev. Charles, 1794–1881**

BAPTIST PRINCIPLES VINDICATED. In Reply to the Rev. J.W.D. Gray's Work on Baptism. Halifax, Christian Messenger, 1844. 190p [NSHP

**Turney, William Charles, 1885–**

CHURCH OR SECT. Some Answers to Current Errors. Winnipeg, Author, [1956?]. 16p

**Turnley, Francis Ronald, 1895?–1948**

THE ALPHABET OF WISDOM. Introducing Planetarianism. Vancouver, Author, 1928. 175p [mimeographed] [BVaU BViPA

**United Church of Canada. Woman's Missionary Society**

THE HISTORY OF THE WOMAN'S MISSIONARY SOCIETY IN ALBERTA, THE UNITED CHURCH OF CANADA. ... Calgary, the Society, 1951. 86p

**Upton, Primrose (Walker), 1915–**

A HISTORY OF ST. ANDREW'S CHURCH, FEBRUARY 19TH, 1911 TO FEBRUARY 19TH, 1961. ... Okanagan Mission, B.C., the Church, 1961. 17p

**Ursuline Community**

GLIMPSES OF THE MONASTERY. A Brief Sketch of the History of the Ursulines during 200 years, 1639–1759. By a Member of the Community. Quebec, Darveau, 1875. 2v [2nd ed.: Brought up to 1839. Quebec, 1897.] [OTU OOP

**Vancouver, B.C. Chinese United Church**

A HUNDRED YEARS OF CHRISTIAN CHINESE WORK IN BRITISH COLUMBIA, 1859–1959. Vancouver, the Church, 1959. 12p

**Vancouver, B.C. Schara Tzedeck Synagogue**

50TH ANNIVERSARY YEAR BOOK, SCHARA TZEDECK SYNAGOGUE. ... Vancouver, the Synagogue, [1957?]. 72p

**Vanderburgh, Marjorie Kathleen (Hillman), 1899–**

THE HISTORY OF SUMMERLAND BAPTIST CHURCH, 1905–1955. West Summerland, B.C., the Church, 1955. 31p

**Vernon, Rev. Charles William, 1871–1934**

BICENTENARY SKETCHES AND EARLY DAYS OF THE CHURCH IN NOVA SCOTIA. With ... a Chapter on King's College, by Rev. Canon Vroom. Halifax, Chronicle Print., 1910. 259p [BM BVaU NSWA OTP

THE OLD CHURCH IN THE NEW DOMINION. The Story of the Anglican Church in Canada. London, S.P.C.K., 1929. 214p [BM BVaU NSWA OLU

THE STORY OF CHRIST CHURCH, DARTMOUTH. A Hundred Years and More in the Life of a Nova Scotian Parish. Halifax, Weeks Pub. Co., 1917. 219p [BVaU NSHD

**Vial, Frank Gifford, 1872–**

THREE MEASURES OF MEAL. A Study in Religion. London, Oxford U. Press, 1923. 342p [BM LC NSHD OTU QMM

**Viets, Rev. Roger, 1738–1811**

ON CENSORIOUSNESS AND EVIL SPEAKING. Oct. 26, 1788. A Sermon. Digby, N.S. [NSHP

A SERMON, ON THE DUTY OF ATTENDING THE PUBLIC WORSHIP OF GOD. Preached at Digby in Nova-Scotia, April 19th, 1789. Hartford, Conn., Hudson & Goodwin, 1789. 43p [Book includes two other sermons.] [LC NSHP

A SERMON, PREACHED AT SISSABOO, NOW CALLED WEYMOUTH, IN NOVA-SCOTIA, ON THE 15TH OCTOBER, 1797. Saint John, Author, 1799. 15p [Tremaine

**Voaden, Thomas**

CHRISTIANITY AND SOCIALISM. A Lecture. ... Toronto, Briggs, 1913. 75p [NBFU OTUV

CHRIST'S COMING AGAIN. An Exposition of His Teachings on that Subject and a Refutation of Pre-Millenial Views. Toronto, McClelland, 1918. xxiv + 279p [OHM

**Vokey, Rev. Edward Philip, 1933–**

THE 175TH ANNIVERSARY HISTORY OF THE PARISH OF CHRIST CHURCH, SOREL, QUE. Sorel, the Church, 1959. 70p

**Vroom, Rev. Fenwick Williams, 1856–1944**

AN INTRODUCTION TO THE PRAYER BOOK. New York, Macmillan, 1930. 230p [Also: London, S.P.C.K., 1953.] [BM BVaU LC

**Waddilove, Rev. William James Darley, 1785?–1859**

CANADIAN CHURCH ROBBERY. Newcastle-upon-Tyne, Hernaman, 1840. 38p [Re: Clergy reserves.] [BM OTP

THE STEWART MISSIONS. ... The Spiritual Destitution of the Emigrants Settled in the Remote Parts of Upper Canada. To which is Prefixed a Brief Memoir of the Late Hon. & Rt. Rev. Chas. James Stewart, Lord Bishop of Quebec. Ed. by ——. London, Hatchard, 1838. 252p [BM BVaU NSWA OTP QMM

**Walker, Rev. Algernon Stanley, 1890–1953**

THOUGHTS FOR THE TIMES. Toronto, Dent, 1955. ix + 118p

**Walker, Millidge**

AN HISTORICAL ADDRESS ... ON THE ONE HUNDREDTH ANNIVERSARY OF ST. PAUL'S PARISH, HAMPTON, N.B. Saint John, Barnes, 1910. 18p [NBSM

**Walker, Rev. William Wesley, 1858–1945**

SABRE THRUSTS AT FREE-THOUGHT; or, A Defence of Divine Inspiration. Toronto, Briggs, 1898. 136p [BM NSWA OTUV

**Wallace, Rev. Archer, 1884–1958**

THE AUTOGRAPH OF GOD. Toronto, Ryerson, 1952. 150p

BLAZING NEW TRAILS. Toronto, Musson, 1928. 149p [BM BVaU LC OTP

IN GRATEFUL REMEMBRANCE. Toronto, Ryerson, 1955. 128p

LEAVES OF HEALING. London, Harper, 1942. 168p [BVa LC OTP

STARS IN THE SKY. Toronto, Ryerson, 1938. 147p [LC OTU

**Wallace, Francis Huston, 1851–1930**

THE INTERPRETATION OF THE APOCALYPSE. Toronto, Briggs, 1903. 39p [OTU

WITNESSES FOR CHRIST; or, A Sketch of the History of Preaching. Lectures delivered under the Auspices of the Theological Union of Victoria University. Cobourg, Briggs, 1885. 155p [OOP

**Wallace, Robert Charles, 1881–1955**

RELIGION, SCIENCE AND THE MODERN WORLD. Toronto, Ryerson, 1952. 66p

**Wallace, Rev. William George, 1858–1949**

A HALF CENTURY OF SERVICE ... 1882–1932. Toronto, Halliday, 1932. 64p [History of Deer Park United Church, Toronto.] [OTU

THESE FORTY YEARS–AND AFTER. Toronto, Rous, 1927. 101p [History of Bloor Street United Church, Toronto.] [OTU

**Walsh, Henry Horace, 1899–**

THE CHRISTIAN CHURCH IN CANADA. Toronto, Ryerson, 1956. ix + 355p

**Walton, Jesse M.**

LOYALIST QUAKER SETTLEMENT, PENNFIELD, N.B., 1783. Aurora, Ont., Author, 1941. [UTQ'42

**Ward, James Edward, 1883–1958**

THE MASTER ON THE MOUNT. Toronto, Longmans, 1943. 137p [BVaU LC OTP

THE WINDOW OF LIFE. Toronto, Macmillan, 1925. [CC

**Ward, John William George, 1879–**

CAMEOS FROM CALVARY. New York, Doran, 1924. 263p [LC NSWA OTW

THE MASTER AND THE TWELVE. New York, Doran, 1924. 255p [BViPA NSHPL OTU QMBM

**Ware, Francis B.**

HISTORY OF CRONYN MEMORIAL CHURCH, LONDON, ONT., 1873–1949. London, the Church, 1949. 329p [OTU

**Warner, Rev. David Victor, 1879–**

THE CHURCH AND MODERN SOCIALISM. An Essay. Truro, News, 1909. 47p [BM NSWA

**Warner, Howard Willard, 1908–**

AND JACOB CALLED THE NAME OF THAT PLACE BETHEL. The History of Bethel United Church, South Augusta, Ontario, 1878–1948. Ottawa, Author, 1948. 171p [OTU

**Waters, Frederick William, 1889–**

PROTESTANTISM–A BAPTIST INTERPRETATION. A Treatise from the Pens and Discussion of a Number of Ministers of the Baptist Convention of Ontario and Quebec, re-cast and re-written. Toronto, Baptist Convention of Ontario and Quebec, 1958. 67p

**Watson, Albert Durrant, 1859–1926**

BIRTH THROUGH DEATH. The Ethics of the Twentieth Plane. A Revelation received through the Psychic Consciousness of Louis Benjamin. Toronto, McClelland, 1920. 374p [NSWA QMM

MEDIUMS AND MYSTICS. A Study in Spiritual Laws and Psychic Forces. By A.D. Watson and Margaret Lawrence. Toronto, Ryerson Press, 1923. 62p [BM NSWA OTUV

THE SOVEREIGNTY OF CHARACTER. Lessons from the Life of Jesus. ... Toronto, Briggs, 1903. 301p [BM OTU

THE TWENTIETH PLANE. A Psychic Revelation. Toronto, McClelland, 1918. 241p [BM BVaU LC NSHD OKQ

**Watt, John Robert, 1919–**

LET NOT YOUR HEART BE TROUBLED. Comfort for the Bereaved. New York, Nashville, Abingdon Press, 1957. 125p

**Weaver, Emily Poynton, 1865–1943**

SISTERS OF ST. BONIFACE. Toronto, Ryerson, [1930]. 32p [ACG OTUV

**Webber, Rev. George, 1838–1907**

THE PULPIT THE AGE NEEDS. Toronto, Briggs, 1886. 198p [OTUV

**Webling, Peggy**

SAINTS AND THEIR STORIES. London, Nisbet, 1919. 311p [BM BVaU LC

**Webster, Rev. Thomas, 1809–1901**

HISTORY OF THE METHODIST EPISCOPAL CHURCH IN CANADA. Hamilton, Christian Advocate, 1870. 424p [BVaU LC OTP QMM

THE UNION CONSIDERED, AND THE METHODIST EPISCOPAL CHURCH IN CANADA DEFENDED. Belleville, Victoria Chronicle Office, 1842. 100p [OTP

**Welton, Rev. Daniel Morse, 1831–1904**

CHRISTIAN BAPTISM. A Sermon in Reply to Rev. Dr. Richey's two Sermons on the same Subject. Also Strictures on Rev. Mr. Annand's Lectures on the Mode of Baptism. ... Halifax, Christian Messenger, 1870. 77p [NSHD

**Wentworth, Ont. Baptist Church**

BRIEF SKETCH FOR THE HISTORY OF THE WENTWORTH BAPTIST CHURCH OF HAMILTON. N.p., n.p., 1924. 43p [NSWA

**Westgate, Rev. Harrison Palmer, 1878–**

ST. JOHN'S CHURCH, SANDWICH, WINDSOR, ONTARIO, 1802–1952. The Beginnings of the Anglican Church in the Western District. Windsor, Author, 1952. 85p

**Weyburn, Sask. Calvary Baptist Church**

CALVARY BAPTIST CHURCH OF WEYBURN, SASKATCHEWAN, JUBILEE, 1905–1956. Weyburn, the Church, 1956. 40p [mimeographed]

**Whitaker, Rev. George, 1810?–1882**

SERMONS PREACHED IN TORONTO, FOR THE MOST PART IN THE CHAPEL OF TRINITY COLLEGE. London, Rivingtons, 1882. 323p [BM OTP

TWO LETTERS TO THE LORD BISHOP OF TORONTO. In Reply to Charges Brought by the Lord Bishop of Huron against the Theological Teaching of Trinity College. ... Toronto, Rowsell & Ellis, 1860. 96p [BM OTP

**White, Rev. George Robert, 1854–1910**

SPARKS FOR YOUR TINDER. Montreal, Drysdale, 1893. 200p [NSWA QMSS

**Whitell, Evelyn**

LOVINGLY IN THE HANDS OF THE FATHER. Kansas City, Unity School of Christianity, 1931. 125p [LC

THE MOTHERHOOD OF MAN. Vancouver, Author, n.d. 242p [BViPA

THE TWENTY-THIRD PSALM IN SILENCE. Los Angeles, Master Press, 1926. 61p [LC

**Wiggins, Ezekiel Stone, 1839–1910**

THE ARCHITECTURE OF THE HEAVENS. ... In Opposition to the Views of Dr. Colenso. Montreal, Lovell, 1864. 304p [BVaU LC NSWA OLU

UNIVERSALISM UNFOUNDED. Being a Complete Analysis and Refutation of the System. Napanee, Henry, 1867. 331p [NSWA OTP

**Wild, Rev. Joseph, 1834–1908**

CANADA AND THE JESUITS. Being a Series of Six Sermons. Toronto, "Canadian Advance," [1889?]. 79p [BVaU NBFU OTP

TALKS FOR THE TIMES. Toronto, Selby, 1886. 345p [OTP

**Wilkes, Rev. Henry, 1805–1886**
THE BRIGHT AND MORNING STAR AND OTHER SERMONS. London, 1889. 336p [BVaU QMM

**Wilkie, Rev. Duncan, 1906–**
THIS SUNDAY EVENING. [Collection of Brief Sermons for Broadcast.] Saskatoon, priv. print., 1951. 68p

**Wilkinson, Grace Marjorie (Floyd), 1908–**
THE LIVING BRANCH. Meditations on Spiritual Growth. Toronto, Ryerson, 1960. 88p

**Williams, Helen Ernestine**
THREE CHURCHES. St. Paul's, 1843–1892–1941. Knowlton, Que., St. Paul's Church, 1941. 50p [QMM

**Williamstown, Ont. St. Andrew's Presbyterian Church**
REPORT OF THE CENTENARY CELEBRATIONS OF ST. ANDREW'S PRESBYTERIAN CHURCH, WILLIAMSTOWN ... 1912. Cornwall, Standard, 1916. 100p [OTU

**Willis, Rev. Michael, 1799–1879**
DEATH MADE TRIBUTARY TO THE GLORY OF GOD. A Sermon preached in Gould Street Presbyterian Church, Toronto ... on Occasion of the Death of Rev. Dr. Burns. Toronto, Adam & Stevenson, 1869. 36p [NSWA OTP
WALKING WITH GOD, AND ITS HAPPY ISSUE. A Sermon on the Death of his Father, with Extracts from his Diary. Glasgow, 1827. [BibC

**Willson, David, 1778?–1866**
THE CHILDREN OF PEACE. Newmarket, Jackson, 1866. 80p [OTU
THE IMPRESSIONS OF THE MIND. To Which are added some Remarks on Church and State Discipline, and The Acting Principles of Life. Toronto, Lawrence, 1835. 358p [BM LC OTP QMM
LETTERS TO THE JEWS. Toronto, Coates, 1835. 71p [BM LC OTP
MYSTERIES OF THE MIND; or, Operations of Grace. By David Wilson [*sic*]. Toronto, Leader & Patriot, 1858. 85p [OTP
THE RIGHTS OF CHRIST, ACCORDING TO THE PRINCIPLES AND DOCTRINES OF THE CHILDREN OF PEACE. Philadelphia, Author, 1815. 59p [OTP
SELECTIONS FROM THE WRITINGS AND SERMONS OF DAVID WILLSON. Ed. by J.L. Hughes. Toronto, Federal Print., n.d. 16p [BVaU OTU

**Willson, (Henry) Beckles, 1869–1942**
OCCULTISM AND COMMON-SENSE. London, Laurie, [1908]. 290p [BM LC OTL

**Wilson, Rev. Alexander James, 1884–**
THE CHRISTIAN AND PEACE. Toronto, United Church Pub. House, 1953. 68p

**Wilson, Rev. Robert, 1833–1912**
JUDEA AND THE JEWS. ... Saint John, Day, 1861. 48p [NBB

THE PAPAL SUPREMACY EXAMINED. ... Halifax, Wesleyan Conference Steam Press, 1859. 37p [NSWA QMSS

**Wilson, Rev. William, 1800?–1870**

NEWFOUNDLAND AND ITS MISSIONARIES. Cambridge, Mass., Dakin & Metcalf, 1866. 448p [BVaU LC NSWA OTU QMM

**Windschiegl, Rev. Peter, 1879–**

FIFTY GOLDEN YEARS, 1903–1953. A Brief History of the Order of St. Benedict in the Abbacy Nullius of St. Peter, Muenster, Saskatchewan. Muenster, Sask., St. Peter's Abbey, 1954. 223p

**Winnipeg (Archdiocese). Immaculate Conception Parish**

SOUVENIR PROGRAMME. 70th Anniversary, 1883–1953, Immaculate Conception Parish, Winnipeg, Manitoba. Winnipeg, the Church, 1953. 16p

**Winnipeg, Man. St. John's Cathedral**

OUR HERITAGE, COMMEMORATING THE 25TH ANNIVERSARY OF THE PRESENT (THE THIRD) ST. JOHN'S CATHEDRAL, 1926–1951, AND THE 131ST ANNIVERSARY OF THE FOUNDING AND THE BIRTH-PLACE OF ST. JOHN'S MISSION CHURCH, THE MOTHER CHURCH OF THE CHURCH OF ENGLAND IN WESTERN CANADA, 1820–1951. Winnipeg, the Cathedral, 1951. 104p

**Wishart, Rev. William Thomas, –1853**

THE DECALOGUE. The Best System of Ethics. Halifax, Bowes, 1842. 100p [NSWA

A SERIES OF OUTLINES; or, Theological Essays on Various Subjects connected with Christian Doctrine and Practice. ... Saint John, Nelson, 1846. 447p [BVaU NBFU OLU

SIX DISQUISITIONS ON DOCTRINAL AND PRACTICAL THEOLOGY. Saint John, McMillan, 1853. 246p [BVaU NSWA OTP

A SYSTEM OF TEMPORAL RETRIBUTION. Vindicated by Various Considerations, Drawn from Scripture and Observation. Halifax, MacKinlay, 1841. 70p [NSWA

**Withrow, Rev. William Henry, 1839–1908**

THE CATACOMBS OF ROME, AND THEIR TESTIMONY RELATIVE TO PRIMITIVE CHRISTIANITY. New York, Nelson & Phillips, 1874. 560p [Other eds. in 1888 and 1901.] [BM BVaU LC NSHD OTU

MAKERS OF METHODISM. New York, Eaton & Mains, 1898. 310p [BM BVaU LC OTU

RELIGIOUS PROGRESS IN THE CENTURY. London, Linscott, 1900. xxii + 468p [BM BVaU LC NSWA OTP

THE ROMANCE OF MISSIONS. Toronto, Rose, 1879. 152p [OTU

**Wix, Rev. Edward, 1802–1866**

A RETROSPECT OF THE OPERATIONS OF THE SOCIETY FOR THE PROPAGATION

OF THE GOSPEL IN NORTH AMERICA. A Sermon preached ... at St. John's Church, Newfoundland. St. John's, M'Coubrey, 1833. 22p [BM OTP

**Wolsey, William Franklin, 1903–**
THE MORE ABUNDANT LIFE. Vancouver, B.C., Canadian Temple of the More Abundant Life, 1952. 103p

**Wood, William Charles Henry, 1864–1947**
AN URSULINE EPIC. Ottawa, 1908. 59p [OTU

**Woodley, Rev. Edward Carruthers, 1878–1955**
THE BIBLE IN CANADA. The Story of the British and Foreign Bible Society of Canada. Toronto, Dent, 1953. 320p

**Woodley, Elsie Caroline, 1909–**
WITH ONE VOICE. Messages from the Bible and Literature. Toronto, 1947. [QMM

**Woodworth, Hugh MacCallum, 1906–**
SANITY, UNHEARD OF. Victoria, Sumas Pub. Co., 1958. 109p

**Working Man, A (pseud)**
A REPLY TO THE REV. FATHER GRAHAM'S LECTURE ON MODERN INFIDELITY. By a Working Man [pseud]. Montreal, Cosmopolitan, 1881. 38p [NSWA

**Workman, Rev. George Coulson, 1848–1936**
ARMAGEDDON; or, The World Movement. Toronto, Briggs, 1917. 68p [BM OTU
ATONEMENT. New York, Revell, 1911. 237p [BM LC
DIVINE HEALING; or, True Science vs. Christian Science and Faith-Cure. Toronto, Ryerson, 1923. 63p [BM BVaU NSWA
IS JESUS COMING AGAIN? Toronto, Ryerson, 1922. 37p [OTUV
JESUS THE MAN, AND CHRIST THE SPIRIT. New York, Macmillan, 1928. 343p [BM BVa LC OTP
MESSIANIC PROPHECY VINDICATED; or, An Explanation and Defence of the Ethical Theory. Toronto, Briggs, 1899. 83p [NSWA OKQ
THE OLD TESTAMENT VINDICATED AS CHRISTIANITY'S FOUNDATION-STONE. With an intro. by Nathanael Burwash. Toronto, Briggs, 1897. 153p [BM NSWA OTU
THE SERVANT OF JEHOVAH. New York, Longmans, 1907. 250p [BM BVaU LC OKQ

**Wright, Henry Wilkes, 1878–**
FAITH JUSTIFIED BY PROGRESS. New York, Scribner, 1916. 287p [LC
THE MORAL STANDARDS OF DEMOCRACY. New York, Appleton, 1925. 309p [LC QMM
THE RELIGIOUS RESPONSE. New York, Harper, 1929. 256p [LC OTU
SELF-REALISATION. An Outline of Ethics. New York, Holt, 1913. 429p [LC OTU

**Young, Rev. Arminius**

ONE HUNDRED YEARS OF MISSION WORK IN THE WILDS OF LABRADOR. London, Stockwell, [1931]. 98p [BM LC NfSM OLU QMBM

**Young, George Paxton, 1819–1889**

THE ETHICS OF FREEDOM. Notes selected, trans. and arranged by his pupil, J.G. Hume. Toronto, U. of Toronto Press, 1911. 76p [BVaU OTU

MISCELLANEOUS DISCOURSES AND EXPOSITIONS OF SCRIPTURE. Edinburgh, Johnstone, 1854. 348p [BM NSHD OTU

**Young, Mildred J.**

THE ANGLICAN CHURCH OF CANADA, SAINT JAMES' CHURCH, SUTTON WEST, ONTARIO ... CENTENNIAL, 1857–1957. N.p., [1957?]. 16p

**Young, Rev. William Harold, 1892–**

GREAT CANADIAN PREACHING. Ed. by ——. New York, Doran, 1925. 297p [BVa LC NSHD

WHY ARE WE PROTESTANTS? Toronto, United Church Pub. House, [19—?]. 16p [LC

**Zavitz, Charles Ambrose, 1863–1942**

SPIRITUAL LIFE. Personal Thoughts. London, Ont., Talbot, 1932. 30p [NBFU OTU QMM

**Zehnder, Meinrad, 1887–**

UNIVERSE AND REALITY; or, Proportion of Spirit and Letter. Toronto, Author, 1929. xxxii + 736p [BVaU NSHD OTP QMM

# SOCIAL HISTORY

## Customs, social movements, racial groups, communications, organizations, professions, etc.

**Abbott, Maude Elizabeth Seymour, 1869–1940**

HISTORY OF MEDICINE IN THE PROVINCE OF QUEBEC. Montreal, McGill U., 1931. 97p [Pub. also with imprint date 1932, as No. 63 of McGill University Publications Series viii (Medicine).] [BM BVaU LC OTP

**Allen, Joseph Antisell, 1814–1900**

A REPLY TO THE SPEECH OF THE HON. EDWARD BLAKE AGAINST THE ORANGE INCORPORATION BILL. Kingston, 1884. 52p [OTP

**Angus, Henry Forbes, 1891–**

CANADA AND HER GREAT NEIGHBOUR. Sociological Surveys of Opinions and Attitudes concerning the United States. ... Ed. by ——. Toronto, Ryerson, 1938. 451p [BM BVaU LC NSHD OTP

**Anonymous**

ORONHYATEKHA. History of the Independent Order of Foresters. Toronto, Hunter Rose, 1894. 862p [BVa OTP QMU

**Armstrong, Charles Harold Algeo, 1888–**

THE HONOURABLE SOCIETY OF OSGOODE HALL. With an Appendix on the History and Architecture of the Fabric by E.R. Arthur. Toronto, Clarke Irwin, 1952. 60p

**Armstrong, George Henry, 1858–1938**

THE ORIGIN AND MEANING OF PLACE NAMES IN CANADA. Toronto, Macmillan, 1930. 312p [BM BVaU LC NSHD OKQ

**Armstrong, Rinaldo William**

THE SALT OF THE EARTH. A Study in Rural Life and Social Progress. Ottawa, Graphic, 1930. 233p [BM BVaU NBFU OTU

**Baby, William Lewis, 1812–1897**

SOUVENIRS OF THE PAST. The Customs and Habits of the Pioneers of Canada. Windsor, Ont., 1896. 266p [BVaU LC NSWA OKQ

**Bailey, Alfred Goldsworthy, 1905–**

THE CONFLICT OF EUROPEAN AND EASTERN ALGONKIAN CULTURES, 1504–1700. A Study in Canadian Civilization. Sackville, Tribune, 1937. 206p [BVaU NSHD OTP

**Barbeau, Charles Marius, 1883–1969**

INDIAN DAYS IN THE CANADIAN ROCKIES. ... Toronto, Macmillan, 1923. 208p [BM BVaU LC NSHD OKQ QMM

TOTEM POLES. Ottawa, King's Printer, 1950. 2v [BVaU NSHD OTU QMM

TOTEM POLES OF THE GITKSAN, UPPER SKEENA RIVER, BRITISH COLUMBIA. ... Ottawa, King's Printer, 1929. 275p [BM BVaU NBFU OTUV

**The Barrie Examiner**

SPECIAL CENTENNIAL SOUVENIR ED. FOR OLD HOME WEEK, AUG. 1–9, 1953. Barrie, Ont., 1953. 100p

**Bass, Charles, 1803–1863**

LECTURES ON CANADA. Its Present Position ... Its Onward Progress ... Its Future Destiny. Hamilton, Spectator, 1863. 45p [OTP QMM

**Bayard, William**

HISTORY OF THE GENERAL PUBLIC HOSPITAL IN THE CITY OF ST. JOHN, N.B. ... Saint John, 1896. 47p [NSWA

**Beaton, Allan**

LAUGH WITH AL BEATON. Cartoons from *The Province.* The Best of Beaton for 1956. Vancouver, Vancouver Province, [1957?]. 62p

**Bellasis, Margaret**

"RISE, CANADIANS!" [Story of the Rebellion of 1837 in Upper Canada.] Montreal, Palm Publishers, 1955. xv + 271p

**Belliveau, John Edward, 1913–**

THE COFFIN MURDER CASE. Toronto, Kingswood House, 1956. 154p

**Bengough, John Wilson, 1851–1923**

A CARICATURE HISTORY OF CANADIAN POLITICS. Events from the Union of 1841, as Illustrated by Cartoons from "Grip," and Various Other Sources. Toronto, Grip, 1886. 2v [BM BVaU LC NSWA OKQ QMM

CARTOONS OF THE CAMPAIGN. Dominion of Canada General Election, 1900. Toronto, Poole, [1900?]. 22 plates [BVaU NBFU OTP

THE GRIP CARTOONS: Vols. I and II, May 1873 to May 1874. ... Toronto, Rogers & Larminie, 1875. 110p [BVaU NSHD OTP

**Benson, George Frederick, 1864–1953**

HISTORICAL RECORD OF THE EDWARDSBURG & CANADA STARCH COMPANIES. Montreal, Canada Starch Co., 1950. 233p [OONL

**Biggar, Henry Percival, 1872–1938**

THE EARLY TRADING COMPANIES OF NEW FRANCE. ... Toronto, U. of Toronto Library, 1901. 308p [BVaU NSHD OTU

**Blake, Edward, 1833–1912**

THE ORANGE ASSOCIATION UNMASKED. ... Speech in the House of Commons, March 17, 1884. ... Montreal, Post Print., 1884. 24p [OTP

**Blue, John, 1875–1945**

THE JUBILEE OF CONFEDERATION, 1867–1917. Manitoba, Government, 1917. 34p [OTL

**Book Publishers' Association, Toronto**

SUBMISSION TO THE ROYAL COMMISSION ON PATENTS, COPYRIGHTS, TRADE MARKS AND INDUSTRIAL DESIGNS FROM THE BOOK PUBLISHERS' ASSOCIATION. Toronto, 1955. 32p [mimeographed]

**Borden, Robert Laird, 1854–1937**

CANADA IN THE COMMONWEALTH. From Conflict to Co-operation. ... Oxford, Clarendon Press, 1929. 144p [BM BVaU NSWA OTU

THE WAR AND THE FUTURE. Being a Narrative Compiled from Speeches Delivered at Various Periods of the War in Canada, the United States, and Great Britain. ... London, Hodder, 1917. 164p [BM BVaU LC NSWA OTU QMM

**Brady, Alexander, 1896–**

DEMOCRACY IN THE DOMINIONS. A Comparative Study in Institutions. Toronto, U. of Toronto Press, 1947. 475p [2nd ed., 1952. 604p] [BM BVaU NSHD OTP

**Brebner, John Bartlet, 1895–1957**

THE MINGLING OF THE CANADIAN AND AMERICAN PEOPLES. V. I: Historical. By Marcus Lee Hansen [1892–1938]. Completed and Prepared for Publication by John Bartlet Brebner. Toronto, Ryerson, 1940. 274p [BVaU LC NBFU OTU

NORTH ATLANTIC TRIANGLE. The Interplay of Canada, the United States and Great Britain. New Haven, Yale U. Press; Toronto, Ryerson, 1945. 385p [BVaU LC NSHD OTU QMM

PAUL MASCARENE OF ANNAPOLIS ROYAL. N.p., n.d. 16p [OTU

**Brennan, Joseph Fletcher**

A GENERAL HISTORY OF FREEMASONRY, BASED UPON ANCIENT DOCUMENTS. Trans. and Comp. from the Masonic Histories of Emmanuel Rebold. And, Added thereto, a History of Freemasonry in the Maritime Provinces and British North America ... 1737 to ... 1841, by J. Fletcher Brennan. Cincinnati, American Masonic Pub. Co., 1875. 442p [LC NBFU OLU

**Brown, Evelyn Marjorie, 1911–**

EDUCATING EVE. Montreal, Palm Publishers, 1957. xvi + 186p [Account of the Quebec Family Institutes.]

**Brown, George, 1818–1880**

THE AMERICAN WAR AND SLAVERY. Speech ... at ... the Anti-Slavery Society. [N.p., 1863?] 11p [BM OTP

**Brown, George Williams, 1894–1963**

CANADIAN DEMOCRACY IN ACTION. Toronto, Dent, 1945. [Rev. ed., 1951; new ed., 1952. 136p] [BVaU NBFU OONL QMBM

**Brown, Paola**

ADDRESS ... ON SLAVERY. Hamilton, Author, 1851. 64p [OTP

**Brown, Peter, 1784–1863**

THE FAME AND GLORY OF ENGLAND VINDICATED. Being an Answer to THE GLORY AND SHAME OF ENGLAND [By C. Edwards Lester]. ... By Libertas [pseud]. New York, Wiley & Putnam, 1842. 306p [BM LC OTU QMM

**Brown, Thomas Storrow, 1803–1888**

A HISTORY OF THE GRAND TRUNK RAILWAY OF CANADA. ... Quebec, Author, 1864. 54p [OTP QMM

**Bryce, Rev. George, 1844–1931**

REMARKABLE HISTORY OF HUDSON'S BAY COMPANY. Toronto, Briggs, 1900. 501p [BM BVaU LC NSWA OTU QMM

A SHORT HISTORY OF THE CANADIAN PEOPLE. London, Low Marston, 1887. 528p [Rev. ed.: Toronto, Briggs, 1914. 621p] [BM BVaU NSHD OTU

**Buck, Timothy, 1892?–**

1917–1957, FORTY YEARS OF GREAT CHANGE. Canada and the Great Russian Revolution. Toronto, Progress Books, 1957. 44p

OUR FIGHT FOR CANADA. Selected Writings (1923–1959). Toronto, Progress Books, 1959. 407p

THIRTY YEARS, 1922–1952. The Story of the Communist Movement in Canada. Toronto, Progress Books, 1952. 224p

**Bull, William Perkins, 1870–1947**

FROM MEDICINE MAN TO MEDICAL MAN. A Record of a Century and a Half of Progress in Health and Sanitation as Exemplified by Developments in Peel. Toronto, Perkins Bull Foundation, 1934. 457p [BM OTU

FROM RATTLESNAKE HUNT TO HOCKEY. The History of Sports in Canada and of the Sportsmen of Peel, 1798–1934. Toronto, Perkins Bull Foundation, 1934. 564p [BM BVaU OKQ

**Burnet, Jean Robertson, 1920–**

NEXT-YEAR COUNTRY. A Study of Rural Social Organization in Alberta. Toronto, U. of Toronto Press, 1951. xv + 188p

**Burpee, Lawrence Johnstone, 1873–1946**

CANADIAN LIFE IN TOWN AND COUNTRY. By Henry J. Morgan and Lawrence J. Burpee. London, Newnes, 1905. 267p [BM OTU QMSS

THE DISCOVERY OF CANADA. Sackville, 1927. 68p [Same title: Ottawa, Graphic, 1930. 96p Also: Toronto, Macmillan, 1944. 280p] [BM BVaU LC NSWA OTU QMM

**Calkin, John Burgess, 1829–1918**

OLD TIME CUSTOMS, MEMORIES AND TRADITIONS AND OTHER ESSAYS. Halifax, Mackinlay, 1918. 188p [BVaU LC NSHD OKQ

**Cameron, Stewart,**

NO MATTER HOW THIN YOU SLICE IT. 63 Cartoons. Calgary, Herald, [1938?]. 64p [BVaU OOA

**Campbell, Marjorie Elliott (Wilkins), 1901–**

THE NORTH WEST COMPANY. Toronto, Macmillan, 1957. xiv + 295p

THE NOR'WESTERS. The Fight for the Fur Trade. Toronto Macmillan, 1954. 176p

**Campbell, Wilfred, 1858–1918**

REPORT ON MANUSCRIPT LISTS IN THE ARCHIVES RELATING TO THE UNITED EMPIRE LOYALISTS, WITH REFERENCE TO OTHER SOURCES. [Ottawa], Archives Branch, 1909. 30p [NSWA OTP

THE SCOTSMAN IN CANADA. By Wilfred Campbell and George Bryce. London, Sampson Low, [1911]. 2v [Campbell wrote V. 1 on eastern Canada; Bryce wrote V. 2 on western Canada.] [BM BVaU MWU NSHD OTP QMM

**Canadian Association of University Teachers**

THE UNIVERSITY TEACHER AND THE CRISIS OF HIGHER EDUCATION IN CANADA. A Brief Presented to the Royal Commission on Canada's Economic Prospects, at Ottawa, Ontario, on March 9, 1956. Saskatoon, the Association, 1956. 41p

**Canadian Broadcasting Corporation**

FIVE YEARS OF ACHIEVEMENT, 1936–1941. NO. 7: MUSIC. Toronto, The Corporation, 1941. 13p [BM OLU

FIVE YEARS OF ACHIEVEMENT, 1936–1941. NO. 8: DRAMA AND FEATURES. Toronto, The Corporation, 1941. 13p [BM OLU

**Canniff, William, 1830–1910**

THE MEDICAL PROFESSION IN UPPER CANADA 1783–1850. ... Toronto, Briggs, 1894. 688p [BM BVaU LC NSWA OTP QMM

**Card, Raymond**

THE ONTARIO ASSOCIATION OF ARCHITECTS, 1890–1950. [Toronto], U. of Toronto Press, 1960. 45p

**Carry, Rev. John, 1824–1891**

AN EXPOSURE OF THE MISCHIEVOUS PERVERSIONS OF HOLY SCRIPTURE IN THE NATIONAL TEMPERANCE SOCIETY'S PUBLICATIONS. Addressed to Men of Sense and Candour. Toronto, Rowsell & Hutchison, 1885. 81p [LC NSWA OTP

**Case, George, 1821–**

OUR CONSTITUTIONAL RIGHTS VINDICATED; or, An Argument for the Legal Prescription of the Traffic in Alcoholic Beverages. In Six Letters to the Hon. Francis Hincks. Toronto, Bentley, 1854. 22p [OTP

**Chadwick, Edward Marion, 1840–1921**

THE PEOPLE OF THE LONGHOUSE [i.e. the Iroquois Indians]. Toronto, Church of England Publishing House, 1897. 166p [BM BVaU NBFU OTP

**Chafe, James Warren, 1900–**

EARLY LIFE IN CANADA. Toronto, Ryerson, 1943. 135p (Guidebook Series in Social Studies.) [BM LC

**Chambers, Ernest John, 1862–1925**

THE ROYAL NORTH-WEST MOUNTED POLICE. A Corps History. Montreal, Mortimer, 1906. 160p [BM BVaU LC OTU

**Chevrier, Lionel, 1903–**

THE ST. LAWRENCE SEAWAY. Toronto, Macmillan, 1959. x + 174p

**Christie, Robert, 1788–1856**

THE MILITARY AND NAVAL OPERATIONS IN THE CANADAS DURING THE LATE WAR WITH THE UNITED STATES. Including also the Political History of Lower-Canada during the Administrations of Sir James Henry Craig and Sir George Prevost. ... Quebec, 1818. 235p New York, Oran & Mott, 1818. 235p [BM LC NSWA QMM

**Clark, C.S.**

OF TORONTO THE GOOD. A Social Study. The Queen City of Canada as It Is. Montreal, Toronto Pub. Co., 1898. 210p [BVaU

**Clark, Samuel Delbert, 1910–**

MOVEMENTS OF POLITICAL PROTEST IN CANADA, 1640–1840. Toronto, U. of Toronto Press, 1959. 518p

THE SOCIAL DEVELOPMENT OF CANADA. An Introductory Study with Select Documents. Toronto, U. of Toronto Press, 1942. 484p [BM BVaU NSHD OTU QMSS

**Cleverdon, Catherine Lyle**

THE WOMAN SUFFRAGE MOVEMENT IN CANADA. Toronto, U. of Toronto Press, 1950. 324p [OONL

**Clint, Mabel Brown, 1874–1939**

IMPERIAL ANNIVERSARY BOOK. Comp. by Harold Saxon [pseud]. Toronto, Briggs, 1909. 306p [BM OTP

**Coffin, William Foster, 1808–1878**

1812: THE WAR AND ITS MORAL. A Canadian Chronicle. Montreal, Lovell, 1864. 296p [BM BVaU LC NSWA OTU

**Colby, Charles William, 1867–1955**

CANADIAN TYPES OF THE OLD REGIME, 1608–1698. New York, Holt, 1908. 366p [BM BVaU LC NSHD OTU QMM

**Collard, Edgar Andrew, 1911–**

CANADIAN YESTERDAYS. Toronto, Longmans, 1955. 327p

A TRADITION LIVES. The Story of *The Gazette,* Montreal, Founded June 3, 1778. Ed. by ——. Montreal Gazette Print., 1953. 56p

**Collins, John Alton, 1917–**

CARTOONS, 1955–1959. With an intro. by Edgar Andrew Collard. Montreal, Montreal Gazette, 1960. 1v [unpaged]

**Conant, Thomas, 1842–1905**

LIFE IN CANADA. Toronto, Briggs, 1903. 290p [BM BVaU LC NBFU OTU

UPPER CANADA SKETCHES. Toronto, Briggs, 1898. 243p [BVaU BM LC NBFU OTP

**Cooper, Francis Collier**

IN THE CANADIAN BUSH. London, Heath Cranton, 1914. 90p [BM LC OOP

**Copeland, John Morison, 1878–**

THE TRAIL OF THE SWINGING LANTERNS. A Racy, Railroading Review of Transportation Matters, Methods and Men. Comp. by ——. Toronto, Addison & Mainprice, 1918. 149p [BVaU LC OTP

**Copway, George, 1818–1863**

THE TRADITIONAL HISTORY AND CHARACTERISTIC SKETCHES OF THE OJIBWAY NATION. London, Black, 1850. 298p [BM LC OTP QMSS

**Corbett, Edward Annand, 1887–**

BLACKFOOT TRAILS. Toronto, Macmillan, 1934. 139p [On history and legends of Blackfoot Indians.] [BM BVaU OTP SSU

**Costain, Thomas Bertram, 1885–1965**

THE WHITE AND THE GOLD. The French Regime in Canada. Toronto, Doubleday, 1954. xii + 482p

**Coughlin, William Garnet, 1912–**

HERBIE [War cartoons]. By Bing Coughlin. Text by J.D.M. [J. Douglas MacFarlane]. Toronto, Nelson, [1946]. 192p [3rd ed., 1959.] [BVa NSHPL OTMC QQL

THIS ARMY. A Portfolio of Cartoons Drawn on the Italian Battle Front. Especially for *The Maple Leaf,* Canadian Army Newspaper. By Bing Coughlin. Rome, Italy, No. 2 Canadian Public Relations Group, 1945. 63p [OKR SRL

**Cowan, Helen I.**

BRITISH EMIGRATION TO BRITISH NORTH AMERICA. Rev. and enl. ed. Toronto, U. of Toronto Press, 1961. xi + 321p [First ed.: Toronto, U. of Toronto Library, 1928.]

**Cragg, Robert Cecil, 1905–**

CANADIAN DEMOCRACY AND THE ECONOMIC SETTLEMENT. Toronto, Ryerson, [1947]. 262p [BVaU LC NBFU OTU QMM

**Craick, William Arnot, 1880–1969**

HALLOWE'EN PRANKS IN CANADA. 1911. 11p [BM

**Cramp, Mary**

RETROSPECTS. A History of the Formation and Progress of the Women's Aid Societies of the Maritime Provinces. ... Halifax, Holloway Bros., 1892. 49p [NSHD

**Creighton, Donald Grant, 1902–**

THE COMMERCIAL EMPIRE OF THE ST. LAWRENCE (1760–1850). Toronto, Ryerson, 1937. 441p [Reprinted as: THE EMPIRE OF THE ST. LAWRENCE. Toronto, Macmillan, 1956. 441p] [BM BVaU NSHD OTU

**Creighton, Helen, 1899–**

BLUENOSE GHOSTS. Toronto, Ryerson, 1957. xiii + 280p

**Cross, Harold Clark, 1889–**

ONE HUNDRED YEARS OF SERVICE WITH YOUTH. The Story of the Montreal YMCA. Montreal, Metropolitan YMCA Montreal, 1951. 367 + xiiip

**Croteau, John Tougas, 1910–**

CRADLED IN THE WAVES. The Story of a People's Co-Operative Achievement in Economic Betterment on Prince Edward Island, Canada. Toronto, Ryerson, 1951. 149p

**Cumberland, Frederic Barlow, 1846–1913**

THE STORY OF THE UNION JACK. How it grew and what it is, particularly in its Connection with the History of Canada. Toronto, Briggs, 1897. 231p [Several later editions under title: THE HISTORY OF THE UNION JACK. ...] [BM BVaU LC OTU QMBM

**Cumberland, Robert William, 1895–**

PIONEER PROBLEMS IN UPPER CANADA. Kingston, Jackson, 1923. 19p [BVaU NSWA OTUV

**Dafoe, John Wesley, 1866–1944**

THE VOICE OF DAFOE. A Selection of Editorials on Collective Security, 1931–1944. ... Ed. by W.L. Morton. Toronto, Macmillan, 1945. 293p [BVaU NSHD OLU

**D'Albertanson, Leonard**

THE STORY OF ALBERTA DIVISION, CANADIAN WEEKLY NEWSPAPERS ASSOCIATION. Comp. by —— *et al.* Wainwright, Alta., the Association, [1955?]. 110p

**Dale, Archibald, 1882–1962**

THE DOO DADS IN THE WONDERLAND OF DOO. Winnipeg, 1919. 96p [BM

FIVE YEARS OF R.B. BENNETT. ... [Cartoons]. Winnipeg, Free Press, 1935. 84p [MWU OTP

THE LEFT AND THE RIGHT. ... [Cartoons]. Winnipeg, Free Press, 1945. 63p [ACG SRL

$25.00 A MONTH. Adventures in Aberhartia with Arch Dale and the Winnipeg Free Press. Winnipeg, Free Press, 1938. 60p [Cartoons about Social Credit.] [BViPA OTU

**Davidson, Gordon A.**

THE UKRAINIANS IN CANADA. A Study in Canadian Immigration. [Montreal, 1947.] 23p [BVaU NBSaM OTU QMU

**Davidson, Gordon Charles, 1884–1922**

THE NORTH WEST COMPANY. Berkeley, U. of California Press, 1918. 349p [BVaU NBFU OTU QMM

**Davin, Nicholas Flood, 1843–1901**

THE IRISHMAN IN CANADA. Toronto, Maclear, 1877. 692p [BM BVaU LC NSWA OKQ

**Davis, Robert, 1798?–1838**

THE CANADIAN FARMER'S TRAVELS IN THE UNITED STATES OF AMERICA. ... Remarks ... on the Arbitrary Colonial Policy Practiced in Canada. Buffalo, Steele's Press, 1837. 107p [OTP

**Dawson, Carl Addington, 1887–**

GROUP SETTLEMENT: ETHNIC COMMUNITIES IN WESTERN CANADA. Toronto, Macmillan, 1936. xx + 395p [BM BVaU LC NSHD OTP QMU

**Dawson, Samuel Edward, 1833–1916**

COPYRIGHT IN BOOKS. An Inquiry into its Origin, and an Account of its Present State in Canada. ... Montreal, Dawson, 1882. 40p [BM LC NSWA OTU QMM

**Denison, Merrill, 1893–**

ADVANCING AMERICA. The Drama of Transportation and Communication. New York, Dodd Mead, 1936. 303p [BM BVaU OTY QMSS

THE BARLEY AND THE STREAM. The Molson Story, A Footnote to Canadian History. Toronto, McClelland, 1955. xiv + 398p

HARVEST TRIUMPHANT. The Story of Massey-Harris. Toronto, McClelland, 1948. 351p [BM BVaU NBFU OTU

THIS IS SIMPSON'S. A Story of Canadian Achievement told in Celebration of the 75th Anniversary of One of her Great Institutions. Toronto, Simpson's, 1947. 18p [OTU

**Dent, John Charles, 1841–1888**

THE LAST FORTY YEARS: CANADA SINCE THE UNION OF 1841. Toronto, Virtue, 1881. 2v [BM BVaU NSWA OKQ

THE STORY OF THE UPPER CANADIAN REBELLION. Toronto, Robinson, 1885. 2v [BM BVaU NSWA OTU

**Douglas, William**

FREEMASONRY IN MANITOBA, 1884–1925. Winnipeg, Grand Lodge of Manitoba, A.F. & A.M., 1925. 6p [OTU SSU

THE HOUSE OF SHEA. The Story of a Pioneer Industry. Winnipeg, Bulman Bros., 1947. 109p [History of a Winnipeg brewery.] [OTU SSU

**Duff, Louis Blake, 1878–1959**

THE COUNTY KERCHIEF. Toronto, Ryerson, 1949. 224p [Accounts of death by hanging.] [OTP

**Eastman, Samuel Mack, 1882–**

CHURCH AND STATE IN EARLY CANADA. Edinburgh, Constable, 1915. 301p [BVaU LC NSHD OTP

**Edgar, James David, 1841–1899**

CANADA AND ITS CAPITAL. With Sketches of Political and Social Life at Ottawa. Toronto, Morang, 1898. 217p [BM BVaU MWU NSWA OTU

**Edwards, Nina Lorraine, 1914–**

THE STORY OF THE FIRST CANADIAN CLUB. Told on the Occasion of its Diamond Jubilee, 1893–1953. Hamilton, Canadian Club of Hamilton, 1953. 32p

**Eggleston, Wilfrid, 1901–**

SCIENTISTS AT WAR. Toronto, Oxford U. Press, 1950. x + 291p [OONL

**Ellis, Frank Henry**

CANADA'S FLYING HERITAGE. Toronto, U. of Toronto Press, 1954. xiv + 388p

**England, Robert, 1894–**

THE CENTRAL EUROPEAN IMMIGRANT IN CANADA. Toronto, Macmillan, 1929. 238p [BM BVaU LC NBFU OTU QMM

TWENTY MILLION WORLD WAR VETERANS. Toronto, Oxford U. Press, 1950. 227p [BM BVaU LC NBFU OTU

**Ermatinger, Edward, 1797–1876**

THE HUDSON'S BAY TERRITORIES. A Series of Letters on this Important Question. Toronto, Maclear, 1858. 32p [LC OTP QMM SSU

**Estimauville, Robert Anne d', Chevalier de Beaumouchel, 1754–1831**

CURSORY VIEW OF THE LOCAL, SOCIAL, MORAL, AND POLITICAL STATE OF THE COLONY OF LOWER CANADA. Quebec, Cary, 1829. 57p [BM QMBM

**Falconer, Robert Alexander, 1867–1943**

THE GERMAN TRAGEDY AND ITS MEANING FOR CANADA. Toronto, U. of Toronto Press, 1915. 90p [BM BVaU LC NSHD OTU

THE UNITED STATES AS A NEIGHBOUR. From a Canadian Point of View. Cambridge, Mass., U. Press, 1925. 259p [BM BVaU LC NSWA OTU

**Farmer, Thomas William Devey, 1910–**

HISTORY OF THE ROYAL CANADIAN HUMANE ASSOCIATION. Hamilton, Royal Canadian Humane Association, 1952. 11p

**Farrar, Frederick Sleigh, –1955**

ARCTIC ASSIGNMENT. The Story of the St. Roch. Ed. by Barrett Bonnezen. Toronto, Macmillan, 1955. 180p

**Fergusson, Charles Bruce, 1911–**

A CENTURY OF SERVICE TO THE PUBLIC, 1850–1950. Halifax, Nova Scotia Savings, Loan and Building Society, 1950. 40p [NSHP

**Ferrie, Adam, 1777–1863**

LETTER TO THE RIGHT HON. EARL GREY ... IN RELATION TO EMIGRATION TO CANADA DURING ... 1847. Montreal, "Pilot," 1847. 16p [BM NSWA OTP QMM

**Fidler, Rev. Isaac, 1795–1864**

OBSERVATIONS ON PROFESSIONS, LITERATURE, MANNERS, AND EMIGRATION, IN THE UNITED STATES AND CANADA ... IN 1832. London, Whittaker, 1833. 434p [BM BVaU LC NSWA OTP QMM

**Fitzgerald, James**

A PLAN OF SETTLEMENT & COLONIZATION. Adapted to all the British North American Provinces. Contained in a Series of Letters ... to a Friend in Ireland. Toronto, Judd, 1850. 63p [OOA

**Fitzgibbon, Mary Agnès (Bernard), 1862–1933**

THE CANADIAN DOUKHOBOR SETTLEMENTS. A Series of Letters ... Reprinted by Permission from "The Globe," Toronto. By Lally Bernard [pseud]. Toronto, Briggs, 1899. 68p [BM BVaU OTU QMSS

**Fitzpatrick, Alfred, 1862–1936**

HANDBOOK FOR NEW CANADIANS. Toronto, Ryerson, 1910. 327p [BM NSWA OTU QMM

**Flatt, W.D.**

THE TRAIL OF LOVE. An Appreciation of Canadian Pioneers and Pioneer Life. Toronto, Briggs, 1916. 263p [BM BVaU OTP

**Fleming, John, 1786?–1832**

SOME CONSIDERATIONS ON THIS QUESTION: WHETHER THE BRITISH GOVERNMENT

ACTED WISELY IN GRANTING TO CANADA HER PRESENT CONSTITUTION? ... By a British Settler [pseud]. Montreal, Brown, 1810. 26p [NSWA OTP QMM

**Fleming, Sandford, 1827–1915**

THE INTERCOLONIAL. A Historical Sketch of the Inception, Location, Construction and Completion of the Line of Railway Uniting the Inland and Atlantic Provinces of the Dominions. Montreal, Dawson, 1876. 268p [BM BVaU NSWA OTU

**Fortier, Loftus Morton**

THE BOOK OF REMEMBRANCE OF THE HISTORICAL ASSOCIATION OF ANNAPOLIS ROYAL, A.D. 1921. Ed. by ——. Toronto, U. of Toronto Press, 1921. 96p [OORD QMSS

CHAMPLAIN'S ORDER OF GOOD CHEER AND SOME BRIEF NOTES RELATING TO ITS FOUNDER. Toronto, Nelson, 1928. 28p [BVaU NSHPL OTP QMBM

**Fosdick, Lucian John, 1849–**

THE FRENCH BLOOD IN AMERICA. New York, Revell, 1906. 448p [BM LC OTU

**Foster, George Eulas, 1847–1931**

CANADIAN PROHIBITIONISTS' HAND BOOK. Montreal, "Witness," 1884. 116p [NSWA

**Foster, Mrs. Margaret Helen, 1896–**

THE FIRST FIFTY YEARS. A History of the University Women's Club of Toronto, 1903–1953. Toronto, the Club, 1953. 50p

**Fraser, Alexander, 1860–1936**

THE CLAN FRASER IN CANADA. Souvenir of the First Annual Gathering. Toronto, Mail Print., 1895. 112p [BM OTP

RECORDS OF THE EARLY COURTS OF JUSTICE OF UPPER CANADA. Toronto, Wilgress, 1918. 478p [LC OLU

**French, Donald Graham, 1873–1945**

FAMOUS CANADIAN STORIES. Re-told for Boys and Girls. ... Ed. by ——. New and enl. ed. Toronto, McClelland, 1931. 470p [First pub., 1923.] [BM BVaU LC QMM

MORE FAMOUS CANADIAN STORIES. Retold for Boys and Girls. Toronto, McClelland, 1926. 363p [BVa OTUV QMM

**Friedmann, Wolfgang Gaston, 1907–**

GERMAN IMMIGRATION INTO CANADA. Toronto, Ryerson, 1952. 63p

**Galt, Alexander Tilloch, 1817–1893**

CHURCH AND STATE. Montreal, Dawson, 1876. 41p [BM BVaU NSWA OTU QMM

**Geikie, John Cunningham, 1824–1906**

GEORGE STANLEY; or, LIFE IN THE WOODS. A Boy's Narrative of the Adventures of a Settler's Family in Canada. Ed. by ——. London, Routledge, 1864. 408p [Also pub. under titles: LIFE IN THE WOODS. A true story of the Canadian bush. London, Strahan, 1873. 405p; and ADVENTURES IN CANADA; or, Life in the Woods. Philadelphia, Porter, [1882?]. 408p]. [BM BVaU LC OTP QMM

**Gibbon, John Murray, 1875–1952**

CANADIAN MOSAIC. The Making of a Northern Nation. Toronto, McClelland, 1938. 455p [BM BVaU NBFU OKQ QMM

THE NEW CANADIAN LOYALISTS. Toronto, Macmillan, 1941. 39p [BVaU LC OKQ

NEW COLOUR FOR THE CANADIAN MOSAIC. The Displaced Person. Toronto, McClelland, 1951. 30p

THE ROMANCE OF THE CANADIAN CANOE. Toronto, Ryerson, 1951. 145p

SCOTS IN CANADA. A History of the Settlement of the Dominion from the Earliest Days to the Present Time. London, Kegan Paul, 1911. 162p [BM BVaU NSHD OTU QMM

STEEL OF EMPIRE. The Romantic History of the Canadian Pacific Railway, the Northwest Passage of Today. Toronto, McClelland, 1935. 423p [BM BVaU NSHD OTU QMM

THREE CENTURIES OF CANADIAN NURSING. By J. Murray Gibbon and Mary S. Mathewson. Toronto, Macmillan, 1947. 505p [BVaU LC NBFU OTU

THE VICTORIAN ORDER OF NURSES FOR CANADA. Fiftieth Anniversary, 1897–1947. Montreal, Southam, 1947. 124p [BVaU OTU

**Gillis, Duncan Hugh, 1918–**

DEMOCRACY IN THE CANADAS, 1759–1867. Toronto, Oxford U. Press, 1951. x + 217p

**Glazebrook, George Parkin de Twenebrokes, 1900–**

A HISTORY OF TRANSPORTATION IN CANADA. Toronto, Ryerson, 1938. 475p [BM BVaU LC NSHD OTU

**Godsell, Philip Henry, 1889–1961**

THEY GOT THEIR MAN. On Patrol with the North West Mounted. London, Hale, 1941. 287p [Earlier ed.: Toronto, Ryerson, 1939.] [BM BVa LC OLU

THE VANISHING FRONTIER. A Saga of Traders, Mounties and Men of the last North West. London, Hale, 1939. 285p [BM BVaU LC OTU QMM

**Gordon, Rev. James D., –1872**

HALIFAX. Its Sins and Sorrows. Halifax, 1862. 41p [BibC

**Gosnell, R. Edward, 1860–1931**

THE STORY OF CONFEDERATION. With a Postscript on the Quebec Situation. Victoria, Colonist, 1918. 156p [BM BVaU LC NSHD OTU

**Gourlay, Robert Fleming, 1778–1863**

ADDRESS TO THE JURY, AT KINGSTON ASSIZES, IN THE CASE OF THE KING V. ROBERT GOURLAY, FOR LIBEL. Kingston, Gazette, 1818. 24p [OTP

AN APPEAL TO ... THE BRITISH NATION. By Robert Gourlay. ... Now, and for the last Two Years, Imprisoned without fair Examination or Trial. London, Sherwood etc., 1826. xc + 196p [BM LC OTP

CANADA, AND CORN-LAWS; or, NO CORN-LAWS, NO CANADA. By Robert Gourlay, Esq., now Robert Fleming Gourlay. Edinburgh, Wood, 1852. 12p [OTP

EMIGRATION AND SETTLEMENT ON WILD LAND. By Rob. Gourlay, Esq., now Robert Fleming Gourlay. Cupar-Fife, Fife Herald, 1849. 20p [OTP

**Gowans, Alan Wilbert, 1923–**

LOOKING AT ARCHITECTURE IN CANADA. Toronto, Oxford U. Press, 1958. 232p

**Graham, John Hamilton, 1826–1900?**

OUTLINES OF THE HISTORY OF FREEMASONRY IN THE PROVINCE OF QUEBEC. Montreal, Lovell, 1892. 645p [BM BVaU LC NSHD OTU QMM

**Gray, Elma Edith (Lawson)**

WILDERNESS CHRISTIANS. The Moravian Mission to the Delaware Indians. By ——, in collaboration with Leslie Robb Gray. Toronto, Macmillan, 1956. xi + 354p

**Green, Gavin Hamilton, 1862–**

THE OLD LOG HOUSE AND BYGONE DAYS IN OUR VILLAGES. Goderich, Signal-Star, 1948. 203p [BVaU OLU

THE OLD LOG SCHOOL AND HURON OLD BOYS IN PIONEER DAYS. Goderich, Signal-Star, 1939. 217p [BM BVaU LC OLU

**Greenough, William Parker**

CANADIAN FOLK-LIFE AND FOLK-LORE. New York, Richmond, 1897. 199p [BVaU LC NSWA OTUV

**Griffin, Selwyn Powell**

OPEN SECRETS. Off the Beaten Track in Canada's Story. With Illustrations by T.G. Greene. Toronto, Macmillan, 1929. 328p [BM BVaU LC NBFU OTU

**Griffin, Watson, 1860–1952**

PROVINCES AND THE STATES: WHY CANADA DOES NOT WANT ANNEXATION. ... Toronto, Moore, 1884. 85p [BVaU NSHD OTU

**Guillet, Edwin Clarence, 1898–**

THE GREAT MIGRATION. The Atlantic Crossing by Sailing Ship since 1770. Toronto, Nelson, 1937. 284p [Reissued, with a supplement, 1962.] [BM BVaU LC NBFU OTU QMM

PIONEER ARTS AND CRAFTS. Toronto, Ontario Pub. Co., 1940. 102p [New ed. of sec. 5 of EARLY LIFE IN UPPER CANADA.] [BVaU LC OTP

PIONEER INNS AND TAVERNS. Toronto, the Author, 1954–62. 5v [Vols. 2-4 have imprint: Toronto, Ontario Pub. Co.]

PIONEER TRAVEL. Toronto, Ontario Pub. Co., 1939. 176p [New ed. of sec. 4 of EARLY LIFE IN UPPER CANADA.] [OTU

**Haight, Canniff, 1825–1901**

BEFORE THE COMING OF THE LOYALISTS. Toronto, Haight & Co., 1897. 23p [BVaU LC NSWA OTP

COMING OF THE LOYALISTS. Toronto, Haight and Co., 1899. 20p [BVaU LC NSWA OTP

**Hallam, Lillian Gertrude (Best), –1939**

SLAVE DAYS IN CANADA. By Mrs. W.T. Hallam. Toronto, Canadian Churchman, 1919. 15p [OTUV QMBM

**Hamil, Frederick Coyne, 1903–**

WHEN BEAVER WAS KING. Ed. by Joe L. Norris. Detroit, Wayne U. Press, 1951. 20p

**Hamilton, James Cleland, 1836–1907**

JOHN BROWN IN CANADA. A Monograph. [Toronto? 1894?] 21p [BM LC OTP

THE PANIS. An Historical Outline of Canadian Indian Slavery in the Eighteenth Century. Toronto, Arbuthnot, 1897. 27p [LC OTP

**Hamilton, Pierce Stevens, 1826–1893**

BRITISH AMERICAN UNION. A Review of Hon. Joseph Howe's Essay, Entitled CONFEDERATION CONSIDERED IN RELATION TO THE INTERESTS OF THE EMPIRE. Halifax, Grant, 1866. 25p [NSHD OTP

UNION OF THE COLONIES OF BRITISH NORTH AMERICA. Being Three Papers upon this Subject, Originally Published between the Years 1854 and 1861. ... Montreal, Lovell, 1864. 103p [NSHD OTU

**Hamilton Association for the Advancement of Literature, Science, and Art**

100TH ANNIVERSARY, 1857–1957. Hamilton, the Association, 1958. 78p

**Hannay, James, 1842–1910**

HISTORY OF THE WAR OF 1812. Saint John, Bowes, 1901. 410p [Also: Toronto, Morang, 1905. 372p; Pub. in England as: HOW CANADA WAS HELD FOR THE EMPIRE. ... London, Jack, 1905. 372p] [BM BVaU LC NSWA OTP QMBM

HOW CANADA WAS HELD FOR THE EMPIRE. [See preceding title.]

**Hardy, William George, 1896–**

FROM SEA UNTO SEA. Canada – 1850–1910: the Road to Nationhood. Garden City, N.Y., Doubleday, 1960. 528p

**Harper, John Murdock, 1845–1919**

THE GREATEST EVENT IN CANADIAN HISTORY: THE BATTLE OF THE PLAINS. Toronto, Musson, 1909. 269p [BM BVaU NSHD OTU QMBM

**Harris, Edward William, 1832–1925**

... HISTORY AND HISTORIETTES: The United Empire Loyalists. Toronto, Briggs, 1897. 18p [BVaU NSWA OTP

**Harris, Martha Douglas, 1854–1933**

HISTORY AND FOLKLORE OF THE COWICHAN INDIANS. By M.D.H. Victoria, Colonist Print., 1901. 89p [BVaU LC OKQ

**Hart, Arthur Daniel**

THE JEW IN CANADA. A Complete Record of Canadian Jewry from the Days of the French Regime to the Present Time. Comp. and ed. by ——. Toronto, Canadian Jewish Pub., 1926. 575p [BM BVaU LC OTU

**Harvey, Daniel Cobb, 1886–**

THE COLONIZATION OF CANADA. Toronto, Clarke Irwin, 1936. 154p [BM BVaU NSHD OTU

**Hassard, Albert Richard, 1873–1940**

FAMOUS CANADIAN TRIALS. Toronto, Carswell, 1924. 246p [BM BVaU OTU

NOT GUILTY AND OTHER TRIALS. Toronto, Lee-Collins, 1926. 352p [BM BVaU LC OTU

**Hathaway, Ernest Jackson, 1871–1930**

THE STORY OF THE HURONS. Toronto, Ontario Hist. Soc., 1915. 27p [BVaU LC OTU QMM

**Heagerty, John Joseph, 1879–1946**

FOUR CENTURIES OF MEDICAL HISTORY IN CANADA. ... Toronto, Macmillan, 1928. 2v [BM BVaU LC NBFU OTU

THE ROMANCE OF MEDICINE IN CANADA. Toronto, Ryerson, 1940. 113p [BVaU LC NSHD OTU

**Heriot, George, 1766–1844**

THE HISTORY OF CANADA FROM ITS FIRST DISCOVERY. Comprehending an Account of the Original Settlement of the Colony of Louisiana. London, Longman & Rees, 1804. 616p [BVaU LC QMM

**Herridge, Rev. William Thomas, 1857–1929**

FRENCH AND ENGLISH IN CANADA AND ACROSS THE SEA. A Sermon. Ottawa, Canadian Print., 1917. 11p [OTU

**Herrington, Walter Stevens, 1860–1947**

THE HISTORY OF THE GRAND LODGE OF CANADA IN ... ONTARIO, 1855–1930. Hamilton, Duncan, 1930. 354p [BVaU OTU

PIONEER LIFE AMONG THE LOYALISTS IN UPPER CANADA. Toronto, Macmillan, 1915. 107p [BM BVaU LC NSHD OLU

THE WAR WORK OF THE COUNTY OF LENNOX AND ADDINGTON. ... Napanee, Beaver Press, 1922. 278p [BVa MW NBFU OTU QMBM

**Hewitt, Foster William, 1902–**

"HE SHOOTS, HE SCORES!" Toronto, Allen, 1949. 145p [OTU

HELLO CANADA, AND HOCKEY FANS IN THE UNITED STATES. Toronto, Allen, 1950. 143p [BVaU OONL

**Hill-Tout, Charles, 1858–1944**

BRITISH NORTH AMERICA: 1. The Far West, the Home of the Salish and Déné. London, Constable, 1907. 263p [BVaU LC OLU

... NOTES ON THE COSMOGONY AND HISTORY OF THE SQUAMISH INDIANS OF BRITISH COLUMBIA. Ottawa, Durie, 1897. 90p [BVaU LC

**Hincks, Francis, 1807–1885**

REPLY TO THE SPEECH OF THE HON. JOSEPH HOWE ... ON THE UNION OF THE NORTH AMERICAN PROVINCES. ... London, Ridgway, 1855. 43p [BM OTP

**Hodgins, J. Herbert**

WOMEN AT WAR. Comp. by —— *et al.* Montreal, Maclean, 1943. 190p [AEU MWP OTU SSU

**Hodgins, John George, 1821–1912**

THE GEOGRAPHY AND HISTORY OF BRITISH AMERICA, AND OF THE OTHER COLONIES. ... To which is added a Sketch of the various Indian Tribes of Canada, with Brief Biographical Notices of Eminent Persons connected with the History of Canada. Toronto, Maclear, 1857. 128p [BM BViPA LC NSHD OTP QMM

IRISHMEN IN CANADA. Their Union not Inconsistent with the Development of Canadian National Feeling. Toronto, Lovell, 1875. 24p [BM OTP

**Hopkins, John Castell, 1864–1923**

CANADA: AN ENCYCLOPEDIA OF THE COUNTRY. By a Corps of Eminent Writers and Specialists. Ed. by ——. Toronto, Linscott, 1898–1900. 6v [BM BVaU LC NSWA OLU

HISTORICAL SKETCH OF A GREAT NEWSPAPER. Montreal, Star Pub. Co., 1910. 16p [OTU

PROGRESS OF CANADA IN THE NINETEENTH CENTURY. Toronto, Progress of Canada Pub. Co., 1900. 538p [BM BVi NSWA OTP

**Horetsky, Charles G., 1840–1900**

SOME STARTLING FACTS RELATING TO THE CANADIAN PACIFIC RAILWAY AND THE NORTH-WEST LANDS, ALSO A BRIEF DISCUSSION REGARDING THE ROUTE, THE WESTERN TERMINUS, AND THE LANDS AVAILABLE FOR SETTLEMENT. Ottawa, "Free Press," 1880. 76p [BVaU LC NSWA OTP

**Howard, Rev. Allen Leslie, 1875?–**

7000 FACTS ABOUT TEMPERANCE. ... Toronto, Briggs, 1908. 120p [BM OTP

**Howard, Clifford S.**

CANADIAN BANKS AND BANK-NOTES. A Record. Toronto, Author, 1951. 48p

**Hughes, James Laughlin, 1846–1935**

EQUAL SUFFRAGE. Toronto, Briggs, 1895. 53p [NSHD OTP

**Hunter, Arthur Thomas, 1872–1949**

CHRONICLE OF ALCOHOLIC BEVERAGES IN THE NORTHWEST TERRITORIES AND SASKATCHEWAN. Regina, Commercial Print., [1946?]. 32p [SRL

**Hunter, Rev. William John, 1835–1911**

MANHOOD WRECKED AND RESCUED. ... Toronto, Briggs, 1894. 241p [BVaU OTU

**Hutchison, Bruce, 1901–**

CANADA, TOMORROW'S GIANT. Toronto, Longmans, 1957. 325p

THE STRUGGLE FOR THE BORDER. Toronto, Longmans, 1955. x + 500p

WINDS OF CHANCE. Montreal, Northern Electric Co., 1951. 31p

**Inglis, Rev. Charles, 1734–1816**

THE LETTERS OF PAPINIAN: In Which the Conduct, Present State and Prospects of the American Congress are Examined. ... New York, Gaine, 1779. 130p [LC

PLAIN TRUTH ... Containing Remarks on a Late Pamphlet, entitled "Common Sense. ..." By Candidus [pseud]. London, Almon, 1776. 47p (2nd ed.) [Long attributed to Charles Inglis; also to Wm. Smith and others. See S&T.] [BM LC OTP

THE TRUE INTEREST OF AMERICA IMPARTIALLY STATED. In certain Strictures on a Pamphlet intitled "Common Sense." By an American [pseud]. Philadelphia, Humphreys, 1776. 71p [BM LC

**Innes, John, 1864–1941**

FROM TRAIL TO RAIL. The Epic of Transportation ... told in Twenty-One Oil Paintings. [Vancouver, Gehrke's, 1930.] 19p [BViPA

**Innis, Harold Adams, 1894–1952**

BIAS OF COMMUNICATION. Toronto, U. of Toronto Press, 1951. 226p

CHANGING CONCEPTS OF TIME. Toronto, U. of Toronto Press, 1952. 142p [Includes THE STRATEGY OF CULTURE, *q.v.*]

THE COD FISHERIES. The History of an International Economy. New Haven, Yale U. Press, 1940. 520p [Rev. ed., 1954.] [BM BVaU LC NBFU OTU

EMPIRE AND COMMUNICATIONS. ... Oxford, Clarendon, 1950. 230p [BM BVaU NSHD OTU

THE FUR TRADE IN CANADA. An Introduction to Canadian Economic History. Rev. ed. Toronto, U. of Toronto Press, 1956. xi + 463p [First pub.: New Haven, Conn., Yale U. Press, 1930.]

A HISTORY OF THE CANADIAN PACIFIC RAILWAY. Toronto, McClelland, 1923. 365p [BM BVaU NSHD OLU

THE PRESS: A NEGLECTED FACTOR IN THE HISTORY OF THE TWENTIETH CENTURY. London, Oxford U. Press, 1949. 48p [BM LC NBFU OTU

THE STRATEGY OF CULTURE. Toronto, U. of Toronto Press, 1952. 45p

**Innis, Mary E. (Quayle), 1899–**

UNFOLD THE YEARS. A History of the Young Women's Christian Association in Canada. Toronto, McClelland, 1949. 243p [BVaU OTP QMM

**Irving, John Allan, 1903–**

THE SOCIAL CREDIT MOVEMENT IN ALBERTA. Toronto, U. of Toronto Press, 1959. xi + 369p

**Jack, Isaac Allen, 1843–1903**

HISTORY OF ST. ANDREW'S SOCIETY OF ST. JOHN, N.B., CANADA, 1798–1903. Saint John, McMillan, 1903. 260p [BVaU NSWA OTP

**Jackes, Lyman Bruce, 1889–1958**

HOW CANADA GOT ITS FIRST POSTAGE STAMPS. Toronto, Author, 1948. 16p [CC

**Jackson, Louis**

OUR CAUGHNAWAGAS IN EGYPT. A Narrative of what was seen and accomplished by the Contingent of North American Indian Voyageurs who led the British Boat Expedition for the Relief of Khartoum. Montreal, Drysdale, 1885. 35p [BM OTU

**Jamieson, Rev. William Henry, 1849–**

THE NATION AND THE SABBATH. Toronto, Briggs, 1901. 148p [OTUV

**Jefferys, Charles William, 1869–1951**

CANADA'S PAST IN PICTURES. Written and illus. by ——. Toronto, Ryerson, 1934. 131p [BVaU OKQ

DRAMATIC EPISODES IN CANADA'S STORY. Written and illus. by ——. Toronto, Hunter Rose, 1930. 74p [BVaU NSHD OKQ

PICTURE GALLERY OF CANADIAN HISTORY. Illustrations drawn and collected by C.W. Jeffreys, assisted by T.W. McLean. Toronto, Ryerson, 1942–50. 3v [BM BVaU NSHD OTU

**Johns, Ethel, 1881–**

THE WINNIPEG GENERAL HOSPITAL SCHOOL OF NURSING, 1887–1953. [Winnipeg?], 1957. 85p

**Jones, Charles Hugh LePailleur, 1876–**

THE MARKLAND SAGAS. With a Discussion of their Relation to Nova Scotia. By C.H.L. Jones and T.H. Raddall. Montreal, Gazette, 1934. 118p [BVa NSHD OOA QMM

THE SAGA OF THE ROVER. By C.H.L. Jones, Thomas H. Raddall, Thomas W. Hayhurst. Halifax, Royal Print. & Litho. Ltd., [1932?]. 92p [OTU

**Jones, Cyril Meredith, 1904–**

INDIAN, PSEUDO-INDIAN PLACE NAMES IN THE CANADIAN WEST. Winnipeg, Ukrainian Free Academy of Sciences, 1956. 19p

**Jones, James Edmund, 1866–1939**

CAMPING AND CANOEING. What to Take, How to Travel, How to Cook, Where to Go. Toronto, Briggs, 1903. 154p [BM OTU

**Jones, Rev. Peter, Chippewa Chief (Kah-Ke-Wa-Quon-A-By), 1802–1856**

HISTORY OF THE OJEBWAY INDIANS. With Especial Reference to their Conversion to Christianity. [Includes a brief memoir of the writer.] London, Bennett, [1861?]. 278p [BM BVaU LC NSWA OTP QMM

**Kaiser, Thomas Erlin, 1863–1940**

A HISTORY OF THE MEDICAL PROFESSION OF THE COUNTY OF ONTARIO. Ed. by ——. Oshawa, County Medical Assoc., 1934. 126p [OTP

**Kallmann, Helmut, 1922–**

A HISTORY OF MUSIC IN CANADA, 1534–1914. Toronto, U. of Toronto Press, 1960. xiv + 311p

**Kaye, Vladimir Julian, 1896–**

PARTICIPATION OF UKRAINIANS IN THE POLITICAL LIFE OF CANADA. Ottawa, Author, 1957. 24p

**Keenleyside, Hugh Llewellyn, 1898–**

CANADA AND THE UNITED STATES. Some Aspects of their Historical Relations. Rev. and enl. ed. By H. Ll. Keenleyside and G.S. Brown. Intro. by W.P.M. Kennedy. New York, Knopf, 1952. 406p [1st ed., 1929.] [BM BVaU NSHD OTU QMM

**Keen, George, 1869?–1953**

THE BIRTH OF A MOVEMENT. Reminiscences of a Co-Operator. [Toronto, Co-Operative Union of Ontario, 1950.] 62p [OONL

**Keil, Doris Amelia Parkin, 1900–**

CHATHAM'S THIRTEEN PUBLIC LIBRARIES FROM 1839–1903. ... Chatham, Ont., Public Library, 1953. 16p

**Kelly, John Hall, 1879–1941**

THE POSITION OF THE SETTLER IN THE PROVINCE OF QUEBEC. N.p., [1906]. 59p [QMSS

**Kennedy, Cecil Howard, 1910–**

THE KINGSTON GENERAL HOSPITAL. A Summary of its Growth, 1835–1954. Kingston, Ont., the Hospital, 1955. 35p [mimeographed]

**Kennedy, Howard Angus, 1861–1938**

NEW CANADA AND THE NEW CANADIANS. Toronto, Musson, 1907. 264p [BM BVaU LC NSHD OKQ QMM

**Kenney, James Francis, 1884–1946**

A BRITISH REPORT ON CANADA, 1711. Toronto, U. of Toronto Press, 1920. 54p [BM OTU

**Kerr, Donald Gordon Grady, 1913–**

A HISTORICAL ATLAS OF CANADA. Ed. by ——. Toronto, Nelson, 1960. ix + 120p

**Ketchum, Thomas Carleton Lee, 1862?–1927**

HIGH SPOTS IN CANADIAN HISTORY. Saint John, Globe, 1926. 123p [LC NBFU OTP

**King, John, 1843–1916**

A DECADE IN THE HISTORY OF NEWSPAPER LIBEL. A Paper read at the Annual Meeting of the Canadian Press Association ... Ottawa, March 6-7, 1892. Woodstock, Sentinel-Review, 1892. 50p [OKQ OTU

**King, William Lyon Mackenzie, 1874–1950**

THE BRIDGE-BUILDERS. Address at Dedication of Thousand Islands International Bridge at Ivy Lea, Ont., Aug. 18th, 1938. Ottawa, King's Printer, 1938. 9p [OTU

CANADA AND THE FIGHT FOR FREEDOM. Toronto, Macmillan, 1944. 326p [BM BVaU NBFU OTU QMM

CANADA AND THE WAR. Victory: Reconstruction and Peace. A Series of Addresses. ... Ottawa, 1945. 142p [BVaU NSHD OTU

CANADA AT BRITAIN'S SIDE. Toronto, Macmillan, 1941. 332p [BM BVaU NBFU OTU QMSS

**Kingsford, William, 1819–1898**

THE CANADIAN CANALS. Their History and Cost, with an Inquiry into the Policy to Advance the Well-Being of the Province. Toronto, Rollo & Adam, 1865. 191p [BM BVaU LC NSHD OTU QMM

A CANADIAN POLITICAL COIN. A Monograph. ... Ottawa, Perry, 1874. 24p [BM BVaU NSHD OTU

**Kirby, William, 1817–1906**

COUNTER MANIFESTO TO THE ANNEXATIONISTS OF MONTREAL. By Britannicus [pseud]. Niagara, Davidson, 1849. 16p [OTP

**Kirkconnell, Watson, 1895–**

CANADIANS ALL. A Primer of Canadian National Unity. Ottawa, Director Public Information, 1941. 42p [LC OLU

**Lancefield, Richard Thomas, 1854–1911**

NOTES ON COPYRIGHT ... Domestic and International. Hamilton, Canadian Literary Bureau, 1896. 92p [2nd ed., 1897. 108p] [BM LC OTP QMM

**Large, Richard Geddes, 1901–**

SOOGWILIS. A Collection of Kwakiutl Indian Designs and Legends. Toronto, Ryerson, 1951. 77 + 10p

**Larmour, Robert, 1841–**

CANADA'S OPPORTUNITY. A Review of Butler's GREAT LONE LAND in its Relation to Present Day Conditions and Future Prospects. Toronto, Briggs, 1907. 32p [BVaU LC OTU

**Laut, Agnes Christina, 1871–1936**

THE 'ADVENTURERS OF ENGLAND' ON HUDSON BAY. A Chronicle of the Fur Trade in the North. Toronto, Glasgow Brook, 1914. 133p [BVaU LC NSWA OTU QMM

CANADA AT THE CROSS ROADS. Toronto, Macmillan, 1921. 279p [BVaU NSHD OKQ

THE CONQUEST OF THE GREAT NORTHWEST. Being the Story of the Adventurers of England known as the Hudson's Bay Company. New York, Outing Pub., 1908. 2v [BVaU LC NSWA OTU

THE FUR TRADE OF AMERICA. New York, Macmillan, 1921. 341p [BVaU NBFU

THE STORY OF THE TRAPPER. Toronto, Briggs, 1902. 284p [BVaU NSWA OTU

**Leacock, Stephen Butler, 1869–1944**

BACK TO PROSPERITY. The Great Opportunity of the Empire Conference. ... New York, Macmillan, 1932. 108p [BM BVaU LC NSHD OTU

CANADA: THE FOUNDATIONS OF ITS FUTURE. Montreal, Distillers Corp. Ltd., 1941. 257p [BM BVaU NSHD OKQ

CANADA AND THE SEA. Montreal, Beatty, 1944. 63p [OTU QMSS

ECONOMIC PROSPERITY IN THE BRITISH EMPIRE. ... Toronto, Macmillan, 1930. 245p [BM BVaU NSHD OTU

THE UNSOLVED RIDDLE OF SOCIAL JUSTICE. New York, Lane, 1920. 152p [BM BVaU LC NSHD OKQ

WHILE THERE IS TIME. The Case against Social Catastrophe. Toronto, McClelland, 1945. 136p [BVaU OTU QMM

**Lebourdais, Donat Marc, 1887–**

CANADA'S CENTURY. ... Toronto, Methuen, 1951. 214p

SUDBURY BASIN. The Story of Nickel. Toronto, Ryerson, 1953. xiv + 210p

**Lewis, Ada Maria (Leigh), –1931**

HOMELESS IN PARIS. The Founding of the "Ada Leigh" Homes. London, S.P.C.K., 1920. 147p [BM QMM

**Lighthall, William Douw, 1857–1954**

CANADA, A MODERN NATION. Montreal, Witness, 1904. 78p [LC NSHD OTU QMSS

**Lillie, Rev. Adam, 1803–1869**

CANADA, ITS GROWTH AND PROSPECTS. ... Brockville, Wylie, 1852. 60p [Also: Toronto, Bentley, 1852. 47p] [BM BVaU LC NSWA OTP

**Lindal, Walter Jacobson, 1887–**

THE SASKATCHEWAN ICELANDERS, A STRAND OF THE CANADIAN FABRIC. Winnipeg, Columbia Press, 1955. 363p

**Lindsey, Charles, 1820–1908**

ROME IN CANADA. The Ultramontane Struggle for Supremacy over the Civil Authority. Toronto, Lovell, 1877. 398p [BM BVaU NBFU OKQ QMM

**Linton, John James Edmonstoune, 1804–1869**

THE LIFE OF A BACKWOODSMAN; or, Particulars of the Emigrant's Situation in ... Canada. By a Settler, at Stratford [pseud]. London, Marchant Singer and Smith, 1843. 31p [OTP

[STATEMENTS FROM SETTLERS ON THE CANADA COMPANY LAND IN THE HURON DISTRICT.] London, Marchant Singer and Smith, [1842?]. 30p [No title page; information from colophon.] [OTP

**Livesay, John Frederick Bligh, 1875–1944**

THE CANADIAN PRESS, ITS BIRTH AND DEVELOPMENT. Quebec, Chronicle-Telegraph, 1939. 19p [OTU

**Lizars, Robina, –1918**

HUMOURS OF '37. Grave, Gay and Grim. Rebellion Times in the Canadas. By Robina and Kathleen M. Lizars. Toronto, Briggs, 1897. 370p [BM BVaU NBFU OTP

IN THE DAYS OF THE CANADA COMPANY. The Story of the Settlement of the Huron Tract and a View of the Social Life of the Period. 1825–1850. By Robina and Kathleen M. Lizars. Toronto, Briggs, 1896. 494p [BM BVaU LC NSWA OTP QMM

**Locke, George Herbert, 1870–1937**

WHEN CANADA WAS NEW FRANCE. Toronto, Dent, 1919. 154p [BM BVaU LC NBFU OTP

**Logan, John Daniel, 1869–1929**

DEMOCRACY, EDUCATION AND THE NEW DISPENSATION. A Constructive Essay on Social Theory. ... Toronto, Briggs, 1908. 20p [NSWA OKQ

**Long, John Robert, 1874–1937**

CANADIAN POLITICS. With Speeches by the Leaders of Reform and Progress in Canadian Politics and Government. St. Catharines, "Journal," 1903. 260p [BVaU LC OTP QMSS

**Longstreth, Thomas Morris, 1900–**

THE FORCE CARRIES ON. The Sequel to THE SCARLET FORCE. Toronto, Macmillan, 1954. ix + 182p

THE SCARLET FORCE. The Making of the Mounted Police. Toronto, Macmillan, 1953. ix + 182p

**Low, Rev. George Jacobs, 1836–1906**

PAPERS ON PROHIBITION. New York, United States Brewers' Assoc., 1887. 79p [LC QMBM

**Lower, Arthur Reginald Marsden, 1889–**

CANADA, NATION AND NEIGHBOUR. ... Toronto, Ryerson, 1952. 202p

CANADIANS IN THE MAKING. A Social History of Canada. Toronto, Longmans, 1958. xxiv + 475p

COLONY TO NATION. A History of Canada. Toronto, Longmans, 1946. 600p [BM BVaU NSHD OTU

SETTLEMENT AND THE FOREST FRONTIER IN EASTERN CANADA. ... With SETTLEMENT AND THE MINING FRONTIER. By H.A. Innis. Toronto, Macmillan, 1936. 424p [BM BVaU NBFU OTU QMM

THIS MOST FAMOUS STREAM. The Liberal Democratic Way of Life. Toronto, Ryerson, 1954. xii + 193p

**Loyal Orange Association of British America. Committee on Orange History**

HISTORY OF THE ORANGE ASSOCIATION IN THE DOMINION OF CANADA. No. 1. One Man's Loyalty. By Rev. Walter McCleary. Toronto, the Committee, 1953. 95p

**Lucas, Rev. Daniel Vannorman, 1834–1911**

TWINS. A Reply to the Anti-Scott Act Address of Mrs. Goldwin Smith at St. Catharines, Ont. ... Montreal, Witness, 1885. 28p [NSHD

**Lumsden, James**

THROUGH CANADA IN HARVEST TIME. A Study of Life and Labour in the Golden West. London, Unwin, 1903. 363p [BM BVaU NSHD OTU

**Lyle-Smythe, Alan, 1914–**

THE SHAKESPEARE FESTIVAL, A SHORT HISTORY OF THE INITIAL FIVE YEARS OF CANADA'S FIRST SHAKESPEARE FESTIVAL, 1949–1954. By Alan Caillou [pseud], Arnold M. Walter, and Frank Chappell. Toronto, Ryerson, 1954. 48p

**Lysenko, Vera**

MEN IN SHEEPSKIN COATS. A Study in Assimilation. Toronto, Ryerson, 1947. 312p [BVaU LC NBFU OTU QMM

**Macauley, John**

LETTERS TO MY HOMELESS ORPHANS AND TO THE PEOPLE OF CANADA. ["Revealing bigotry, perfidy, perjury, prosecution & plunder of orphans !! and judicial jugglery and ministerial delinquency in the County of Ottawa, P.Q." —— from cover.] Ottawa, n.p., 1879. 66p [BVaU OTP

**Macbeth, Madge Hamilton (Lyons), 1878–1965**

THE LADY STANLEY INSTITUTE FOR TRAINED NURSES. [A History.] Ottawa, Lady Stanley Institute Alumnae Association, 1959. 101p

**MacBeth, Rev. Roderick George, 1858–1934**

POLICING THE PLAINS. Being the Real-Life Record of the famous North-West

Mounted Police. New York, Hodder, 1921. 320p [Rev. and enl. ed.: Toronto, Musson, 1931. 352p] [BM BVaU LC NSWA OTP QMBM

ROMANCE OF THE CANADIAN PACIFIC RAILWAY. ... Toronto, Ryerson, 1924. 263p [BM BVaU NSHD OTU

**McConnell, Newton, 1877?–1940**

VANITY FAIR. A Portfolio of Caricatures. Preface by J.E. Middleton. Toronto, Johnston, 1912. 334p [BM BVaU OTU

**McCord, Frederick Augustus, 1856–1908**

HAND-BOOK OF CANADIAN DATES. Ed. by ——. Montreal, Dawson, 1888. 102p [BM BVaU LC NBFU OTP QMM

**MacCormack, John Patrick, 1895–1958**

CANADA: AMERICA'S PROBLEM. New York, Viking, 1940. 287p [BVaU OLU

**McCrea, Frances (Morden), 1880–**

HISTORY IN WOOD. The McCrea Models. Toronto, Royal Ontario Museum, 1957. 63p

**McCrimmon, Abraham Lincoln, 1865–1935**

THE WOMAN MOVEMENT. Philadelphia, Griffith, 1915. 254p [LC NSWA

**McCully, Jonathan, 1809–1877**

BRITISH AMERICA. Arguments against a Union of the Provinces Reviewed, with Further Reasons for Confederation. London, Algar, 1867. 32p [BM NSWA OTP QMSS

**MacDermot, Hugh Ernest, 1888–**

HISTORY OF THE CANADIAN MEDICAL ASSOCIATION, 1867–1921. Toronto, Murray, 1935. 209p [V.2, covering 1920–1956. Toronto, Murray, 1958. 153p] [BM BVaU OTP QMBM

A HISTORY OF THE MONTREAL GENERAL HOSPITAL. Montreal, the Hospital, 1950. 135p [OONL

**Macdonald, Helen Grace, 1888–**

CANADIAN PUBLIC OPINION ON THE AMERICAN CIVIL WAR. New York, Columbia U., 1926. 237p [BM BVaU LC NSWA OTP QMSS

**Macdonald, Rev. James Alexander, 1862–1923**

DEMOCRACY AND THE NATIONS. A Canadian View. ... New York, Doran, 1915. 244p [BM BVaU NSHD OLU

**Macdonald, James Simon, 1837–1914**

ANNALS OF THE NORTH BRITISH SOCIETY OF HALIFAX ... FROM ITS FOUNDATION, IN 1768 TO ... 1868. Comp. by ——. Halifax, "Citizen" Steam Print., 1868. 288p [AEU NSHP OKQ

**MacDonald, John Alexander, 1846–1922**

TROUBLOUS TIMES IN CANADA. A History of the Fenian Raids of 1866 and 1870. Toronto, Johnston, 1910. 255p [BVaU LC NSWA OTP QMSS

**Macdonald, Thoreau, 1901–**

A FEW OF THE OLD GATES AT THORNHILL AND SOME NEARBY FARMS. Toronto, Woodchuck Press, 1933. [OTU

SOME TOOLS OF THE PIONEERS. Drawn by Thoreau Macdonald. Thornhill, Woodchuck Press, 1936. 14p [OTP

A SPECIMEN BOOK OF CUTS USED BY THE WOODCHUCK PRESS. Drawn by Thoreau Macdonald. Toronto, Ryerson, 1946. 21p [LC NBFU OTP

**McDougall, Rev. John, 1842–1917**

RURAL LIFE IN CANADA. Its Trends and Tasks. By John MacDougall [*sic*]. ... Toronto, Westminster, 1913. 248p [BM BVaU LC NSHD OTP QMM

**MacEwan, Grant, 1902–**

AGRICULTURE ON PARADE. The Story of the Fairs and Exhibitions of Western Canada. Toronto, Nelson, 1950. 200p [BVaU OTP SSU

THE SODBUSTERS. Toronto, Nelson, 1948. 240p [BVaU OTP SSU

**McGee, Thomas D'Arcy, 1825–1868**

THE CROWN AND THE CONFEDERATION. Three Letters to the Hon. John Alexander McDonald. ... By a Backwoodsman [pseud]. Montreal, Lovell, 1864. 36p [NSWA OTP QMBM

EMIGRATION AND COLONIZATION IN CANADA. A Speech Delivered in the House of Assembly, Quebec, 25th April, 1862. Quebec, Hunter, 1862. 25p [NSWA

A HISTORY OF THE IRISH SETTLERS IN NORTH AMERICA. From the Earliest Period to the Census of 1850. Boston, "American Celt," 1851. 180p [5th ed.: Boston, Donahoe, 1852. 240p] [BM BVaU LC NSWA OTP QMBM

THE IRISH POSITION IN BRITISH AND IN REPUBLICAN NORTH AMERICA. A Letter to the Editors of the Irish Press. ... Montreal, Longmoore, 1866. 45p [BVaU LC MWU NSHD OTP QMM

SPEECHES AND ADDRESSES CHIEFLY ON THE SUBJECT OF BRITISH AMERICAN UNION. London, Chapman & Hall, 1865. 308p [BM BVaU LC NSWA OTP QMSS

TWO SPEECHES ON THE UNION OF THE PROVINCES. Quebec, Hunter Rose, 1865. 34p [BVaU NSWA OTP QMM

**McGill, Rev. Robert, 1798–1856**

THE LOVE OF COUNTRY. A Discourse preached at St. Andrew's Church, Niagara, on Tuesday, the 6th February, 1838. (A Day appointed for Public Thanksgiving, on Account of our Deliverance from the Miseries of the Late Insurrection.) Niagara, Sewell, 1838. 22p [BVaU NSWA OTP QMBM

**Machar, Agnes Maule, 1837–1927**

STORIES OF THE BRITISH EMPIRE FOR YOUNG FOLKS AND BUSY FOLKS. ... Series

I and II. London, Elliot Stock; Toronto, Briggs, 1913. 2v in 1 [OTUM

STORIES OF NEW FRANCE. Being Tales of Adventure and Heroism from the early History of Canada. In two series. First series by Agnes Maule Machar; Second Series by Thomas G. Marquis. Boston, Lothrop, 1890. 313p [BM BVaU LC NSHD OTU QMM

**McInnes, Graham Campbell, 1912–**

A SHORT HISTORY OF CANADIAN ART. Toronto, Macmillan, 1939. 125p [Rev. and enl. ed. pub. under title: CANADIAN ART. Toronto, Macmillan, 1950. 140p] [BM BVaU LC NSHD OTP QMM

**MacInnes, Thomas Robert Edward, 1867–1951**

ORIENTAL OCCUPATION OF BRITISH COLUMBIA. Vancouver, Sun. Pub. Co., 1927. 170p [BVaU LC NBFU OTP

**MacKay, Douglas, 1900–1938**

THE HONOURABLE COMPANY. A History of the Hudson's Bay Company. ... Indianapolis, Bobbs-Merrill, 1936. 396p [Rev. ed.: Toronto, McClelland, 1949. 397p] [BM BVaU LC NBFU OTP QMM

**Mackenzie, Alexander, 1822–1892**

ADDRESS ... TO THE TORONTO WORKINGMEN ON THE "NATIONAL POLICY." ... Toronto, Globe, 1878. 32p [NSHD OTU

**Mackenzie, James Bovell, 1851–1919**

TREATISE ON THE SIX-NATION INDIANS. ... Toronto, Guardian, 1882. 63p [Also as: THE SIX-NATION INDIANS IN CANADA [1896].] [BVaU NSHD OLU

**Mackenzie, William Lyon, 1795–1861**

AN ALMANAC OF INDEPENDENCE & FREEDOM FOR THE YEAR 1860. Containing a Plea for the Relief of the Inhabitants of Canada from a State of Colonial Vassalage or Irresponsible Rule. ... Toronto, Author, 1860. 62p [OTP

THE LEGISLATIVE BLACK LIST OF UPPER CANADA; or, Official Corruption and Hypocrisy Unmasked. York, Colonial Advocate, 1828. 39p [BVaU OTP

A NEW ALMANAC FOR THE CANADIAN TRUE BLUES. With which is Incorporated the Constitutional Reformer's Text Book, for the Millenial and Prophetical Year of the Grand General Election for Upper Canada and Total and Everlasting Downfall of Toryism in the British Empire. By Patrick Swift [pseud]. 2nd ed. York, Baxter, [1833?]. 23p [OTP

"POOR RICHARD"; or, The Yorkshire Almanac. ... By Patrick Swift [pseud]. York, Mackenzie, [1931?]. 16p (Continued annually.) [OTP

THE SEVENTH REPORT FROM THE SELECT COMMITTEE OF THE HOUSE OF ASSEMBLY OF UPPER CANADA ON GRIEVANCES ... W.L. Mackenzie, esq., chairman. Toronto, Reynolds, 1835. 470p [NSWA OOA

SKETCHES OF CANADA AND THE UNITED STATES. London, Effingham Wilson, 1833. 504p [BM BVaU LC OTP QMSS

**Maclean, Rev. John, 1851–1928**

CANADIAN SAVAGE FOLK. The Native Tribes of Canada. Toronto, Briggs, 1896. 641p [BM BVaU LC NSHD OTU

THE INDIANS, THEIR MANNERS AND CUSTOMS. London, Kelly, 1889. 351p [BVa LC OKQ

**McLoughlin, John, 1784–1857**

LETTERS OF DR. JOHN McLOUGHLIN, written at Fort Vancouver 1829–1832. Ed. by B.B. Barker. Portland, Ore., Binfords & Mort, 1948. 376p [BVaU LC NBFU OTP QMM

THE LETTERS OF JOHN McLOUGHLIN ... FROM FORT VANCOUVER TO THE GOVERNOR AND COMMITTEE. ... Ed. by E.E. Rich. With intro. by W. Kaye Lamb. Toronto, Champlain Society, 1941–44. 3v [BM BVaU LC NBFU OTP

**Macmillan Company of Canada**

A CANADIAN PUBLISHING HOUSE. Toronto, Macmillan, 1923. [BVaU OTU

**McPhedran, Marie (Green), 1904–**

CARGOES ON THE GREAT LAKES. Toronto, Macmillan, 1952. 226p

**Macpherson, Crawford Brough**

DEMOCRACY IN ALBERTA. The Theory and Practice of a Quasi-Party System. Toronto, U. of Toronto Press, 1953 [i.e., 1954]. xii + 258p

**Macpherson, Duncan Ian, 1924–**

TORONTO DAILY STAR CARTOONS. Toronto, Toronto Star, 1959. 1v [unpaged]

**MacPherson, Mrs. Lydia Eliza, 1883–**

HISTORICAL SKETCH OF THE WOMAN'S CHRISTIAN TEMPERANCE UNION OF BRITISH COLUMBIA, COMMEMORATING SEVENTY YEARS OF SERVICE, 1883–1953. Vancouver, n.p., 1953. 11p

**McWilliams, Margaret (Stovel), 1875–1952**

THIS NEW CANADA. London, Dent, 1948. 328p [BM BVa LC NBFU OTP QMM

**Mair, John, 1798–1877**

NEPHALEIA; or, Total Abstinence from Intoxicating Liquors in Man's Normal State of Health. The Doctrine of the Bible in a Series of Letters with Addenda, to Edward C. Delavan. New York, Sheldon, 1861. 302p [LC OTP

**Marquis, Thomas Guthrie, 1864–1936**

STORIES FROM CANADIAN HISTORY. Toronto, Copp Clark, 1936. 157p [Earlier ed.: Toronto, Copp Clark, 1893.] [BVaU LC OTU

**Marshall, John George, 1786–1880**

THE CANADIAN DOMINION TESTED BY THE EVIDENCE OF SCRIPTURE AND HISTORY. ... Halifax, Strong, 1868. 39p [NSHD QMSS

THE JUSTICE OF THE PEACE, AND COUNTY AND TOWNSHIP OFFICERS FOR NOVA SCOTIA. Halifax, Gossip & Coade, 1837–45. 646p [BVaU NSHPL OTP QMML

**Martin, Chester Bailey, 1882–1958**

FOUNDATIONS OF CANADIAN NATIONHOOD. Toronto, U. of Toronto Press, 1955. xx + 554p

**Martin, Horace Tassie, 1859–1905?**

CASTOROLOGIA; or, the History and Traditions of the Canadian Beaver. Montreal, Drysdale, 1892. 238p [BM BVaU LC OTU

**Mavor, James, 1854–1925**

NOTES ON APPRECIATION OF ART AND ON ART IN ONTARIO. With Remarks on the Exhibition of the Ontario Society of Artists, 1898. Toronto, Morang, 1898. 28p [OTP

**Merriken, Ellenor Ranghild (Olsen), 1899–**

THE NOSE HILLS COUNTRY. Federalsburg, Md., 1960. 133p [Autobiography of pioneer life in Alberta.]

**Mewburn, John, 1788–1864**

A LETTER TO MR. STICKNEY, OF HOLDERNESS, ON EMIGRATION TO CANADA. Darlington, Coates & Farmer, 1833. 12p [BM NSWA OTP

**Meyers, Leonard William, 1917–**

TWENTY-THREE SKIDOO. Toronto, Kingswood House, 1958. x + 227p

**Miller, Hanson Orlo, 1911–**

RAIDERS OF THE MOHAWK. The Story of Butler's Rangers. Toronto, Macmillan, 1954. ix + 182p

**Miller, John James, 1860–1950**

EARLY HISTORY OF THE VANCOUVER EXHIBITION ASSOCIATION. ... Vancouver, City Archives, 1953. 46p

**Mitchell, Rosslyn Brough, 1880–**

MEDICINE IN MANITOBA. The Story of its Beginnings. Winnipeg, 1955. 141p

**Moberly, Walter, 1832–1915**

THE EARLY HISTORY OF THE CANADIAN PACIFIC ROAD. Vancouver, 1909. 15p [BM BVaU LC NSWA OTU

**Monro, Alexander, 1813–1896**

ANNEXATION; or, Union with the United States is the Manifest Destiny of British North America. Saint John, Barnes, 1868. 52p [LC

THE UNITED STATES AND THE DOMINION OF CANADA. Their Future. Saint John, Barnes, 1879. 192p [BVaU LC NBFU OTU

**Montague, Sydney Robert**

RIDERS IN SCARLET. The Way of Life of the Mounties. Evanston, Ill., Row Peterson, 1941. 64p [BVa LC OOA

**Montgomery, George Hugh Alexander, 1874–1951**

MISSISSQUOI BAY. (Philipsburg, Que.) Granby, Que., Granby Pub., 1950. 132p [OTU

**Montreal, Que. Pen and Pencil Club**

THE PEN AND PENCIL CLUB, 1890–1959. Montreal, the Club, 1959. 15p

**Montreal, Que. Shakespeare Dramatic and Literary Club**

ANNUAL REPORT, for the year 1844. Montreal, 1845. 11p [QMM

**Moore, Gordon, 1922–**

AROUND OUR TOWN. Montreal, Whitcombe & Gilmour, 1948. 131p [OTP

**Moore, William Henry, 1872–1960**

THE CLASH. A Study in Nationalities. Toronto, Dent, 1918. 356p [BM BVaU LC NBFU OTP QMM

THE IRRESPONSIBLE FIVE. A New Family Compact. Toronto, McClelland, 1917. 67p [BM BVaU OTP QMSS

**Moorhouse, Arthur Herbert Joseph, 1882–**

DEEP FURROWS. Which Tells of Pioneer Trails along which the Farmers of Western Canada fought their way to Great Achievements in Co-operation. By Hopkins Moorhouse [pseud]. Toronto, McLeod, 1918. 229p [BM BVaU LC NSWA OOA QMM

**Morgan, Henry James, 1842–1913**

CANADIAN LIFE IN TOWN & COUNTRY. By Henry J. Morgan and Lawrence J. Burpee. ... London, Newnes, 1905. 266p [BM BVaU LC OTP

DOMINION ANNUAL REGISTER AND REVIEW, 1878–1886. Ed. by ——. Montreal, Dawson, 1879–1887. 7v [BM BVaU NBFU OTU

**Morris, Alexander, 1826–1889**

CANADA AND HER RESOURCES. [A Prize Essay.] Montreal, Lovell, 1855. 156p [2nd ed.: Montreal, Dawson, 1855. 119p] [BM BVaU LC NSWA OTP

NOVA BRITANNIA; or, British North America, its Extent and Future. A Lecture. Montreal, Lovell, 1858. 67p [BM BVaU LC NSWA OTP QMM

NOVA BRITANNIA; or, Our New Canadian Dominion Foreshadowed. Being a Series of Lectures. Toronto, Hunter Rose, 1884. 187p [BM BVaU LC NBFU OTP QMM

**Morton, William Lewis, 1908–**

THE PROGRESSIVE PARTY IN CANADA. Toronto, U. of Toronto Press, 1950. 331p [OONL

**Mountain, Rev. George Jehoshaphat, 1789–1863**

A RETROSPECT OF THE SUMMER AND AUTUMN OF 1832. ... Quebec, Cary, 1833. 33p [Appendix, on facts of a recent plague.] [BM OTP QMSS

**Munro, Robert Ross, 1913–**

GAUNTLET TO OVERLORD. The Story of the Canadian Army. Toronto, Macmillan, 1945. 477p [BM BVaU LC OTP QMM

**Munro, William F.**

THE BACKWOODS' LIFE. Toronto, Hunter Rose, 1869. 79p [Republished as: THE BACKWOODS' LIFE. An Interesting Story of Pioneer Days in Melancthon Township. Shelburne, Free Press Office, 1910. 59p] [BVaU LC NSHD OTP QMSS

**Murphy, Emily Gowan (Ferguson), 1868–1933**

THE BLACK CANDLE. Toronto, Allen, 1922. 405p [Re: Drug traffic.] [BM BVaU LC NSWA OTP QMM

**Murphy, Herbert H., 1881–**

ROYAL JUBILEE HOSPITAL, VICTORIA, B.C., 1858–1958. ... Victoria, Hebden Print., 1958. 160p

**Murray, N.**

THE EXPERIENCE OF AN OLD COUNTRY PEDLER AMONG THE MONTREAL SERVANT GIRLS AND THEIR MISTRESSES. Ottawa, Gov't., 1891. 16p [NSWA

**Murray, Norman, 1853–**

THE CELTIC TRAGEDY. British Races, Languages and Religions—the Anglo-Saxon Myth and Orange Fanaticism. Montreal, Murray, 1919–21. [OTU

**Nasmith, George Gallie, 1877–1965**

CANADA'S SONS AND GREAT BRITAIN IN THE WORLD WAR. Toronto, Winston, 1919. 607p [BM BVaU NSHD OTP

**National Council of Women of Canada**

WOMEN OF CANADA, THEIR LIFE AND WORK. Comp. by ——. N.p., the Council, 1900. 422p [BVaU NSWA OTP QMM

**Newman, Fred C.**

THE FIRST FIFTY YEARS. A Brief History of the St. James Literary Society. ... Montreal, the Society, 1948. 22p [OTP

**Newspaper Cartoonists' Association of Manitoba**

MANITOBANS AS WE SEE 'EM, 1908 and 1909. Winnipeg, the Association, 1909. 227 plates. [Cartoons of prominent Manitobans.] [BVaU SSU

**Nichols, Thomas E.**

THESE WERE THE THIRTIES. By T.E. Nichols. With Cartoons by the Late Ivan Glassco. Hamilton, Spectator, 1949. 102p [BViV OH

**Nicholson, Anna Mary**

100 YEARS OF MEDICINE, 1849–1949. Ed. by ——. Saskatoon, Modern Press, 1949. 44p [About women pioneers in medicine.] [SSU

**Nicholson, Byron, 1857–1916**

THE FRENCH-CANADIAN. A Sketch of his More Prominent Characteristics. Toronto, Bryant Press, 1902. 132p [BM BVaU OKQ QMM

**Norris, Leonard Matheson, 1913–**

THE BEST OF NORRIS, AS SELECTED BY HIMSELF. Toronto, McClelland, 1955. 123p

NORRIS CARTOONS IN THE VANCOUVER SUN. His World and You're in it. Vancouver, Sun. Pub. Co., 1952. 100p [An annual publication. Title varies.]

**North Renfrew, Ont. Agricultural Society. Centennial Committee**

CENTENNIAL, NORTH RENFREW AGRICULTURAL SOCIETY, 1857–1957. Pembroke, Ont., the Society, 1957. 134p [Comp. by Mrs. Carl Price.]

**O'Connor, John, 1824–1887**

LETTERS OF JOHN O'CONNOR, ESQ., M.P., ON FENIANISM. Toronto, Rose, 1870. 17p [QMBM

**Ord, Lewis Redman, 1856–1942**

REMINISCENCES OF A BUNGLE. By One of the Bunglers [pseud]. Toronto, Grip Print., 1887. 66p [On Riel Rebellion.] [OOA

**Ottawa, Ont. National Gallery of Canada**

THE MASSEY COLLECTION OF ENGLISH PAINTING. Ottawa, 1946. 30p [BM BVaU LC

CATALOGUE OF PAINTINGS, DRAWINGS, ETCHINGS AND SCULPTURE. Ottawa, Government Print. Bureau, 1912. 152p [LC

**Paget, Amelia Anne (McLean), 1867–1922**

THE PEOPLE OF THE PLAINS. Ed. with intro. by D.C. Scott. Toronto, Briggs, 1909. 199p [On North American Indians.] [BVaU LC NBFU OTP

**Paluk, William, 1914–**

CANADIAN COSSACKS. Essays, Articles, and Stories on Ukrainian-Canadian Life. Winnipeg, Canadian Ukrainian Rev., 1943. 129p [MWP OTP

**Parker, Gilbert, 1862–1932**

THE WORLD IN THE CRUCIBLE. An Account of the Origin and Conduct of the Great War. London, Murray, 1915. 432p [BM BVaU LC OTU

**Parkin, George Robert, 1846–1922**

IMPERIAL FEDERATION. The Problem of Imperial Unity. London, Macmillan, 1892. 314p [BM BVaU LC NBFU OONL QMSS

**Paterson, Isabel M. (Bowler)**

THE GOD OF THE MACHINE. New York, Putnam, 1943. 292p [BVaU OTU QMSS

**Peat, Louisa (Watson)**

GRANDMA DID IT THIS WAY. New York, Holt, 1950. 247p [BVa LC

**Phillips, Alan, 1916–**

THE LIVING LEGEND. The Story of the Royal Canadian Mounted Police. Winnipeg, Harlequin Books, 1960. 192p [Earlier eds.: Boston, Little Brown; London, Cassell, 1957.]

**Pierce, Lorne Albert, 1890–1961**

THE HOUSE OF RYERSON, 1829–1954. Toronto, Ryerson, 1954. ix + 52p

MASTER BUILDERS. Toronto, Ryerson, 1937. 45p [On Masonic order.] [BVaU OKQ

TOWARD THE BONNE ENTENTE. Toronto, Ryerson, 1929. 43p [BVaU NBFU OTU QMM

**Poole, Rev. William Henry, 1820–1896**

TOBACCO, SMOKING, CHEWING, SNUFFING. A Lecture. Brockville, Wylie, 1866. 30p [OTP

**Powell, Robert Wynyard, 1856–1935**

THE DOCTOR IN CANADA. His Whereabouts and the Laws which Govern him. A Ready Book of Reference. Montreal, Gazette, 1890. 342p [BVaU NSWA OTP QMSS

**Quebec Literary and Historical Society**

THE CENTENARY VOLUME, 1824–1924. Quebec, Evénement, 1924. 196p [BVaU QMM

**Racey, Arthur George, 1870–1942**

CANADIAN MEN OF AFFAIRS IN CARTOON. Illus. by A.G. Racey. Montreal, Southam Press, 1922. 129p [OTU

THE ENGLISHMAN IN CANADA. [Cartoons.] Montreal, Montreal News Co., 1902. 22p [BM OLU

**Raddall, Thomas Head, 1903–**

THE PATH OF DESTINY. Canada from the British Conquest to Home Rule: 1763–1850. Toronto, Doubleday, 1957. x + 468p

**Ramsey, Bruce, 1924–**

A HISTORY OF THE GERMAN-CANADIANS IN BRITISH COLUMBIA. Winnipeg, National Publishers, 1958. 69p

**Rattray, William Jordan, 1835–1883**

THE SCOT IN BRITISH NORTH AMERICA. Toronto, Maclear, 1880–84. 4v [BM BVaU LC NBFU OTP QMM

**Raymond, Rev. William Odber, 1853–1923**

THE UNITED EMPIRE LOYALISTS. Saint Stephen, N.B., St. Croix Pub. Co., 1893. 46p [NSHD OTP QMM

**Read, David Breakenridge, 1823–1904**

THE CANADIAN REBELLION OF 1837. Toronto, Robinson, 1896. 372p [BM BVaU NBFU OTP QMM

**Reaman, George Elmore, 1889–**

THE TRAIL OF THE BLACK WALNUT. Toronto, McClelland, 1957. xx + 256p [A study of the Pennsylvania Germans and related ethnic groups who migrated to Ontario during the American Revolution.]

**Rhinewine, Abraham, 1887–1932**

LOOKING BACK A CENTURY ON THE CENTENNIAL OF JEWISH POLITICAL EQUALITY IN CANADA. Rev. and enl. by Isidore Goldstick. Toronto, Kraft, 1932. 148p [BM BVaU LC NSHD OTP QMM

**Richardson, Evelyn May (Fox), 1902–**

THE WRECKWOOD CHAIR. Sagas of the Sea told in Wood. Comp. for the Shelburne Historical Society. Shelburne, N.S., the Society, 1957. 51p

**Rickard, Thomas Arthur, 1864–1953**

THE ROMANCE OF MINING. Toronto, Macmillan, 1944. 450p [BVaU LC NBFU OTP QMM

**Riddell, William Renwick, 1852–1945**

THE BAR AND THE COURTS OF THE PROVINCE OF UPPER CANADA OR ONTARIO. Toronto, Macmillan, 1928. 251p [LC OTU

THE LEGAL PROFESSION IN UPPER CANADA IN ITS EARLY PERIODS. Toronto, Law Society, 1916. 194p [BVaU NSWA OTU

SOME EARLY LEGISLATION AND LEGISLATORS IN UPPER CANADA. Toronto, Carswell, 1913. 39p [OTU QMM

**Roberts, Charles George Douglas, 1860–1943**

CANADA IN FLANDERS. With a Preface by Lord Beaverbrook. V. 3. London, Hodder, 1918. 144p [BM BVaU NBFU OTU QMSS

THE CANADIANS OF OLD. By Philippe Aubert de Gaspé. Trans. by Charles G.D. Roberts. New York, Appleton, 1890. 287p [New ed. under title: CAMERON OF LOCHIEL. Boston, Page, 1905. 287p] [BVaU LC OTU

A HISTORY OF CANADA, for High Schools and Academies. Boston, Lamson Wolffe, 1897. 493p [BM BVaU LC NSWA OTU

**Roberts, Leslie, 1896–**

CANADA: THE GOLDEN HINGE. Toronto, Clarke Irwin, 1952. 288p

**Robertson, John Ross, 1841–1918**

THE HISTORY OF FREEMASONRY IN CANADA, FROM ITS INTRODUCTION IN 1749. ... Toronto, Hunter Rose, 1899. 2v [BM BVaU NSWA OTU

HISTORY OF THE KNIGHTS TEMPLARS OF CANADA, FROM THE FOUNDATION ... IN A.D. 1800 TO THE PRESENT TIME. ... Toronto, Hunter Rose, 1890. 401p [BM BViP OLU

LANDMARKS OF CANADA. What Art has done for Canadian History. A Guide to the J. Ross Robertson Collection in the Public Reference Library, Toronto. Toronto, Author, 1917. 566p [BVaU NSHD OOP QMSS

**Robinson, William Gordon, 1918–**

TALES OF KITAMAAT. A Selection of Legends, Folk Stories and Customs of the Haisla People, a Branch of the Kwakiutl Indian Language-Group who live on the West Coast of British Columbia. Kitimat, B.C., 1956. 46p

**Roddan, Rev. Andrew, –1948**

CANADA'S UNTOUCHABLES. The Story of the Man without a Home. Vancouver, Clarke & Stewart, 1932. 111p [BVaU

GOD IN THE JUNGLES. The Story of the Man without a Home. Vancouver, 1931. 64p [BVaU OKQ

**Roger, Charles, 1819–1878**

THE RISE OF CANADA FROM BARBARISM TO WEALTH AND CIVILIZATION. Quebec, Sinclair, 1856. V. 1 [History to 1824.] 412p [No more published.] [BM BVaU NSWA OLU QMM

**Rohold, Rev. Sabetti B.**

THE JEWS IN CANADA. 2nd ed. N.p., Home Missions, 1913. 24p [NSWA

**Rome, David**

CANADIAN JEWS IN WORLD WAR II. Pt. 1, Decorations; Pt. 2, Casualties. Ed. by ——. Montreal, Canadian Jewish Congress, 1947–8. 2v in 1. [BM NBFU OLU QMM

**Rosenberg, Louis, 1893–**

CANADA'S JEWS. A Social and Economic Study. ... Montreal, Canadian Jewish Congress, 1939. 418p [BM BVaU LC NSHD OTU

CHRONOLOGY OF CANADIAN JEWISH HISTORY. Montreal, National Bicentenary Committee, Canadian Jewish Congress, 1959. 24p

A STUDY OF THE GROWTH AND CHANGES IN THE DISTRIBUTION OF THE JEWISH POPULATION OF MONTREAL 1851–1951. Montreal, Bureau of Social and Economic Research, Canadian Jewish Congress, 1955. 51p

**Ross, Murray George, 1911–**

THE Y.M.C.A. IN CANADA. The Chronicle of a Century. Toronto, Ryerson, 1951. xvii + 517p

**Ross, William**

EARLY HISTORY OF FREEMASONRY IN NOVA SCOTIA. Halifax, Chronicle, 1910. 32p [NSWA

**Rosser, Frederick Thomas**

THE WELSH SETTLEMENT IN UPPER CANADA. London, Ont., Lawson Memorial Library, U. of Western Ontario, 1954. 150p

**Roy, James Alexander, 1884–**

THE SCOT AND CANADA. Toronto, McClelland, 1947. 117p [BVaU NSHD OTP QMM

**Roy, Mgr. Maurice, 1905–**

THE PARISH AND DEMOCRACY IN FRENCH CANADA. Toronto, U. of Toronto Press, 1950. 37p [OONL

**Ryan, Alonzo**

CARICATURE POLITIQUE AU CANADA. Free Lance Political Caricature in Canada. Introductions by Lucien Lasalle and H.M. Williams. Montreal, Chapman, 1904. 112p [NSWA OTP QMSS

**Ryerson, Rev. Adolphus Egerton, 1803–1882**

DR. RYERSON'S LETTERS IN REPLY TO THE ATTACKS OF THE HON. GEORGE BROWN. Toronto, Lovell & Gibson; and Caverhill, 1859. 110p [BM BVaU LC NSWA OTP

THE HON. R.B. SULLIVAN'S ATTACKS UPON SIR CHARLES METCALFE, REFUTED BY EGERTON RYERSON. ... Being a Reply to the Letters of "Legion" [pseud]. Toronto, British Colonist, 1844. 63p [LC OTP

THE LOYALISTS OF AMERICA AND THEIR TIMES. From 1620 to 1816. Toronto, Briggs, 1880. 2v [BM BVaU NBFU OTP QMM

SIR CHARLES METCALFE DEFENDED AGAINST THE ATTACKS OF HIS LATE COUNSELLORS. Toronto, British Colonist, 1844. [Probably same as THE HON. R.B. SULLIVAN'S ATTACKS. ..., above.] [BVaU

**Ryerson, George Ansel Sterling, 1854–1925**

THE AFTERMATH OF A REVOLUTION. Being the Inaugural Address as President of the United Empire Loyalist Association ... Nov. 12, 1896. Toronto, Briggs, 1896. 16p [OTU

**Sack, Benjamin Gutelius, 1889–1967**

HISTORY OF THE JEWS IN CANADA, FROM THE EARLIEST BEGINNINGS TO THE

PRESENT DAY. Montreal, Canadian Jewish Congress, 1945–. [V. 1: FROM THE FRENCH REGIME TO THE END OF THE NINETEENTH CENTURY. 273p] [BM BVaU LC NSHD OTU

**Safarian, Albert Edward, 1924–**

THE CANADIAN ECONOMY IN THE GREAT DEPRESSION. Toronto, U. of Toronto Press, 1959. xii + 185p

**Sandham, Alfred, 1838–1910**

COINS, TOKENS AND MEDALS OF THE DOMINION OF CANADA. Montreal, Rose, 1869. 72p [BM BVaU LC NSWA OTU

HISTORY OF THE MONTREAL YOUNG MEN'S CHRISTIAN ASSOCIATION. ... Montreal, 1873. 120p [QMM

**Sandwell, Bernard Keble, 1876–1954**

THE CANADIAN PEOPLES. London, Oxford U. Press, 1941. 128p [BVaU LC MWU NSHD OTP QMM

**Saskatoon Star-Phoenix**

50TH ANNIVERSARY OF THE SASKATOON STAR-PHOENIX, 1902–1952. 70th Anniversary of the City of Saskatoon, 1882–1952. Saskatoon, 1952. 104p

**Scadding, Rev. Henry, 1813–1901**

CANADA IN SCULPTURE. A Paper Read before the Canadian Institute. ... Toronto, Copp, 1887. 12p [BVaU NSWA OTU

**Schull, Joseph, 1910–**

THE FAR DISTANT SHIPS. An Official Account of Canadian Naval Operations in the Second World War. Ottawa, King's Printer, 1950. 515p [BVaU NSHD OTP QMM

**Sclater, William, 1906–**

HAIDA. With an intro. by Rt. Hon. A.V. Alexander. Toronto, Oxford U. Press, 1946. 221p [An account of the destroyer "Haida."] [BM BVaU LC NSHD OTP QMM

**Scott, Francis Reginald, 1899–**

CANADA AND THE UNITED STATES. Boston, World Peace Foundation, 1941. 80p [BVaU NBFU OTU

CANADA TO-DAY. A Study of her National Interests and National Policy. London, Oxford U. Press, 1938. 184p [BM BVaU LC NBFU OTU

MAKE THIS *your* CANADA. A Review of C.C.F. History and Policy. By D. Lewis and F. Scott. With a foreword by M.J. Coldwell. Toronto, Central Canada Pub. Co., 1943. 223p [BVaU NBFU OLU QMM

**Scott, H. Percy, 1856–1937**

THE NEW SLAVERY. Toronto, Briggs, 1914. 190p [BM NSWA OTU QMM

**Scott, Rev. William, 1812?–1891**

THE TEETOTALER'S HAND-BOOK. In Four Parts. Being a Compilation of Valuable Information for the Use of all Classes. Toronto, Dredge, 1860. 408p [OKQ

**Seaborn, Edwin, 1872–1951**

THE MARCH OF MEDICINE IN WESTERN ONTARIO. Toronto, Ryerson, 1944. 386p [BVaU LC OTP QMM

**Secretan, James Henry Edward, 1852–1926**

CANADA'S GREAT HIGHWAY. From the First Stake to the Last Spike. London, Lane, 1924. 252p [BM BVaU NBFU OTU QMM

**Shannon, James A.**

HARD TIMES IN ONTARIO. A Pretty Story Certainly. ... Kingston, Daily News, 1872. 36p [NSHD

**Shortt, Adam, 1859–1931**

CANADA AND ITS PROVINCES. A History of the Canadian People and their Institutions. Ed. by Adam Shortt and Arthur G. Doughty. Toronto, Constable, 1913–17. 23v [BM BVaU LC NSWA OTU QMM

LIFE OF THE SETTLER IN WESTERN CANADA BEFORE THE WAR OF 1812. Kingston, Jackson, 1914. 18p [BM BVaU LC NSWA OTP QMM

**Simonds, Peter, 1906–**

MAPLE LEAF UP–MAPLE LEAF DOWN. The Story of Canadians in the Second World War. Toronto, Saunders, [1947]. 356p [BM BVaU OTP QMM

**Simpkins, James Nathaniel, 1910–**

JASPER. New York, Rinehart; Toronto, Burns & MacEachern, 1960. 1v [unpaged] [Cartoons, mainly previously published in *Maclean's* magazine.]

**Simpson, John, 1788–1873**

ESSAY ON MODERN REFORMERS. ... Kingston, Miles, 1818. 19p [Attack on the Reform Party, with a letter to Robert Gourlay.] [OTP

**Simpson, Maria**

SAYINGS AND DOINGS OF NOTED TEMPERANCE ADVOCATES. Toronto, Hunter Rose, 1879. 170p [OTP

**Skelton, Isabel (Murphy)**

THE BACKWOODSWOMAN. A Chronicle of Pioneer Home Life in Upper and Lower Canada. Toronto, Ryerson, 1924. 261p [BM BVaU LC NSHD OKQ QMM

**Skelton, Oscar Douglas, 1878–1941**

THE RAILWAY BUILDERS. Toronto, Glasgow Brook, 1916. 254p [BM BVaU NSWA OTU

**Skinner, Constance Lindsay, 1879?–1939**

ADVENTURERS OF OREGON. A Chronicle of the Fur Trade. New Haven, Yale U. Press, 1920. 290p [BM BVaU LC NSHD OTU

BEAVER KINGS AND CABINS. New York, Macmillan, 1933. 272p [BM BVaU LC NBFU OTU QMM

**Slight, Rev. Benjamin, 1798?–1858**

INDIAN RESEARCHES; or, Facts concerning the North American Indians. Montreal, Miller, 1844. 179p [BM LC NSWA OTP QMM

**Smith, Goldwin, 1823–1910**

CANADA AND THE CANADIAN QUESTION. Toronto, Hunter Rose, 1891. 325p [Also: 1892. 346p] [BM BVaU NSHD OKQ QMM

**Smith, William, 1769–1847**

HISTORY OF CANADA, FROM ITS FIRST DISCOVERY, TO THE YEAR 1791. Quebec, Neilson, 1815. 2v [BM BVaU LC NBFU OTP QMM

**Smith, William, 1859–1932**

THE EVOLUTION OF GOVERNMENT IN CANADA. Montreal, Gazette, 1928. 273p [BM BVaU NSHD OTU QMM

FIRST DAYS OF BRITISH RULE IN CANADA. Kingston, Jackson, 1922. 18p [BM BVaU NBFU OKQ

THE HISTORY OF THE POST OFFICE IN BRITISH NORTH AMERICA, 1639–1870. Cambridge, U. Press, 1920. 356p [BM BVaU LC NSHD OTU QMM

**Smith, William George, 1872–1943**

BUILDING THE NATION. A Study of some Problems Concerning the Churches' Relation to the Immigrants. Toronto, Canadian Council of the Missionary Education Movement, 1922. 202p [BM BVaU NSWA OKQ

A STUDY IN CANADIAN IMMIGRATION. Toronto, Ryerson, 1920. 406p [BM BVaU LC NSWA OKQ

**Smith, William Peter (pseud?)**

THE VICTORIA DIAMOND JUBILEE HISTORY OF CANADA. By William Peter Smith, Esq., M.A., F.R.C.S. [and others]. ... Toronto, Rose, 1897. 174p [NSHPL OTP

**Snider, Charles Henry Jeremiah, 1879–1971**

THE GLORIOUS "SHANNON'S" OLD BLUE DUSTER, AND OTHER FADED FLAGS OF FADELESS FAME. Toronto, McClelland, 1923. 430p [BM BVaU LC NBFU OTU

THE GRIFFON. Toronto, Rous & Mann Press, 1956. 23p [About La Salle's *Griffon*, first ship on the Great Lakes.]

IN THE WAKE OF THE EIGHTEENTWELVERS. Toronto, Bell & Cockburn, 1913. 291p [Later eds. under title: STORY OF THE "NANCY" AND OTHER EIGHTEEN-TWELVERS.] [BM BVaU LC NSHD OTU

LEAVES FROM THE WAR LOG OF THE "NANCY," EIGHTEEN HUNDRED AND THIRTEEN. Ed. by ——. Toronto, Rous & Mann, 1936. [LC

STORY OF THE "NANCY" AND OTHER EIGHTEENTWELVERS. Toronto, McClelland, 1926. 334p [BM BVaU LC NSHD OTU

TARRY BREEKS AND VELVET GARTERS. Sail on the Great Lakes of America, in War, Discovery, and the Fur Trade, under the Fleur-de-lys. Toronto, Ryerson, 1958. xvii + 148p

UNDER THE RED JACK. Privateers of the Maritime Provinces of Canada in the War of 1812. ... London, Hopkinson, 1928. 268p [BM BVaU LC NSHD NBFU

**Spence, Ruth Elizabeth, 1890–**

PROHIBITION IN CANADA. A Memorial to Francis Stephens Spence. Toronto, Dominion Alliance, 1919. 624p [BM BVaU NSWA OTP

**Spendlove, Francis St. George, 1897–1962**

THE FACE OF EARLY CANADA. Pictures of Canada which have Helped to Make History. Toronto, Ryerson, 1958. xxi + 162p

**Stacey, Charles Perry, 1906–**

CANADA AND THE BRITISH ARMY, 1846–1871. ... New York, Longmans, 1936. 287p [BM BVaU LC NSHD OTU

THE CANADIAN ARMY, 1939–1945. An Official Historical Summary. Ottawa, King's Printer, 1948. 354p [BM BVaU LC NSHD OTU

**Stanley, George Francis Gilman, 1907–**

CANADA'S SOLDIERS, 1604–1954. The Military History of an Unmilitary People. Toronto, Macmillan, 1954. 401p [BVaU NBFU OTP QMBM

**Stearns, Anna (Seidner), 1904–**

NEW CANADIANS OF SLAVIC ORIGIN. A Problem in Creative Reorientation. Winnipeg, Montreal, Ukrainian Free Academy of Sciences, 1960. 144p

**Steele, Harwood Elmes Robert, 1897–**

THE CANADIANS IN FRANCE, 1915–1918. Toronto, Copp Clark, 1920. 364p [BM NSHD OTU QMM

**Stephenson, Harry Edward, 1874–1940**

THE STORY OF ADVERTISING IN CANADA. A Chronicle of Fifty Years. By H.E. Stephenson and Carlton McNaught. Toronto, Ryerson, 1940. 364p [BVaU LC NBFU OTU

**Stevens, Gerald Francis, 1909–**

THE CANADIAN COLLECTOR. Glass, Pottery, Furniture, Firearms, of the Nineteenth Century. Toronto, Ryerson, 1957. xvii + 100p

**Stewart, George, 1848–1906**

CANADA UNDER THE ADMINISTRATION OF THE EARL OF DUFFERIN. Toronto, Rose-Belford, 1878. 696p [BM BVaU NSWA OKQ QMM

**Strachan, Rev. John, 1778–1867**

OBSERVATIONS ON THE HISTORY AND RECENT PROCEEDINGS OF THE CANADA COMPANY. Addresses in Four Letters to Frederick Widder. ... N.p., 1845. 54p [OLU

PASTORAL LETTER ... on the Subject of the Cholera. Toronto, Diocesan Press, 1848. 14p [OTP

**Sullivan, Robert Baldwin, 1802–1853**

ADDRESS ON EMIGRATION AND COLONIZATION. ... Toronto, Brown's Print., 1847. 41p [OTP

LETTERS ON RESPONSIBLE GOVERNMENT. By Legion [pseud]. Toronto, Examiner, 1844. 216p [OTP QMM

**Sutherland, Rev. Alexander, 1833–1910**

ERRING THROUGH WINE. A Discourse delivered in the Richmond Street Church, Toronto ... December 18, 1870. Toronto, Burnett, 1871. 16p [OTP

**Symons, Harry Lutz, 1893–**

FENCES. Toronto, Ryerson, 1958. x + 155p

**Talbot, Mrs. Marjorie, 1882–**

OLD LEGENDS AND CUSTOMS OF THE BRITISH COLUMBIA COAST INDIANS. New Westminster, Author, 1952. 8p

**Talman, James John, 1904–**

LOYALIST NARRATIVES FROM UPPER CANADA. Ed. by ——. Toronto, Champlain Society, 1946. 411p [BM BVaU LC NSHD OTU QMM

**Taylor, Henry, fl. 1819–1860**

ON THE PRESENT CONDITION OF UNITED CANADA. ... Montreal, Author, [1843?]. 104p [Same title: London, Ont., Sutherland, 1849. 168p — OOP] [BVaU NBFU OTP

**Taylor, Thomas Griffith, 1880–**

CANADA. A Study of Cool Continental Environments and their Effect on British and French Settlement. Toronto, Saunders, 1947. 542p [Rev. ed., 1950.] [BVaU LC NSHD OTU QMM

ENVIRONMENT, RACE, AND MIGRATION. ... Toronto, U. of Toronto Press, 1937. 483p [Special reference to Canada and Australia.] [BVaU LC NSHD OTU QMM

**Taylor, Rev. William, 1803–1876**

A TESTIMONY AGAINST DUELLING. A Sermon. ... Montreal, Campbell & Becket, 1838. 32p [QMM

**Textor, Lucy Elizabeth**

A COLONY OF EMIGRES IN CANADA, 1798–1816. Toronto, U. of Toronto Library, 1905. 86p [BM BVaU LC NSWA OTU

**Thomson, Donald Walter, 1906–**

THE FOUNDATION AND THE MAN. By Walter Dawson [pseud]. Toronto, priv. print., 1959. 23p [History of the Canadian Writers' Foundation founded by Dr. Pelham Edgar.]

**Timar, Leslie Joseph, 1899–**

A SHORT HISTORY OF THE HUNGARIAN PEOPLE IN CANADA. Toronto, Across Canada Press, 1957. 19p

**Toronto, Ont. Public Library**

RECORDING TORONTO. A Catalogue of Selected Pictures of early Buildings and Street Scenes in the Town of York and the City of Toronto from the John Ross Robertson Historical Collection and other Picture Collections of the Toronto Public Libraries. Comp. by Elspeth Smith. Toronto, the Library, 1960. 36p

**Toronto Arts & Letters Club**

FIFTY YEARS, 1908–1958. Toronto, the Club, 1958. 8p

**Toronto Literary Association**

TORONTO LITERARY ASSOCIATION. Laws of the Toronto Literary Association, Instituted 7th July, 1853. Toronto, Leader Office, 1856. 16p [OTP

**Toronto Transportation Commission**

PICTURE STORY. Public Transportation in Toronto. Toronto, the Commission, 1950. 30p [OONL

**Tory, Henry Marshall, 1864–1947**

A HISTORY OF SCIENCE IN CANADA. By Frank Dawson Adams *et al.* Ed. by ——. Toronto, Ryerson, 1939. 152p [BM BVaU NBFU OTU QMSS

**Townsley, Benjamin Franklin, 1890–1939**

MINE-FINDERS. The History and Romance of Canadian Mineral Discoveries. Toronto, Sat. Night Press, 1935. 246p [BM BVaU LC OTU QMM

**Tremaine, Marie**

CANADIAN BOOK OF PRINTING. How Printing Came to Canada and the Story of the Graphic Arts. Told Mainly in Pictures. Ed. by ——. Toronto, Public Libraries, 1940. 130p [BVaU LC NSHD OLU

EARLY PRINTING IN CANADA. Toronto, Golden Dog Press, 1934. 13p [BVaU NSWA OTP QMM

**Trotter, Rev. Thomas, 1853–1918**

LIFE PICTURES FROM RUM'S GALLERY; or, Sketches written from Personal

Knowledge of Persons who have been ruined through Liquor. Toronto, Briggs, 1886. 364p [BVaU OTP

**Tucker, Gilbert Norman, 1898–1955**
THE NAVAL SERVICE OF CANADA. Its Official History. Ottawa, King's Printer, 1952. 2v

**Tupper, Rev. Charles, 1794–1881**
PROHIBITION AND ANTI-PROHIBITION. Being a Series of Letters ... in Favor of Prohibition, and Replies to the Same, by John Bent. ... Saint John, Barnes, 1856. 40p [NSHP QMSS

**Turek, Victor, 1910–**
THE POLISH PAST IN CANADA. Contributions to the History of the Poles in Canada and of the Polish Canadian Relations. Ed. by ——. Toronto, Polish Alliance Press, 1960. 138p

**Turner, John Peter, 1879–1948**
THE NORTH-WEST MOUNTED POLICE, 1873–1893. ... Ottawa, King's Printer, 1950. 2v [BM BVaU LC NSHD OTU

**U.E.L. Centennial Committee**
THE CENTENNIAL OF THE SETTLEMENT OF UPPER CANADA BY THE UNITED EMPIRE LOYALISTS, 1784–1884. The Celebrations at Adolphustown, Toronto, and Niagara, with an Appendix containing a Copy of the U.E.L. List, Preserved in the Crown Lands Department at Toronto. Toronto, Rose, 1885. 334p [BVaU LC OTU

**Ure, George P., –1860**
THE MAINE LAW ILLUSTRATED. Being the Result of an Investigation made in the Maine Law States. By A. Farewell and G.P. Ure. Toronto, Can. Prohibitory Liquor Law League, 1855. 94p [OTU QMM

**Vancouver, B.C. Community Arts Survey Committee**
"THE ARTS AND OUR TOWN." Vancouver, Keystone Press, 1946. 201p [BVaU

**Vlassis, George Demetrios, 1897–**
THE GREEKS IN CANADA. 2nd ed. Ottawa, LeClerc Printers, 1953. 364p [1st ed., 1942.]

**Voorhis, Ernest, 1859–1933**
HISTORIC FORTS AND TRADING POSTS OF THE FRENCH REGIME AND OF THE ENGLISH FUR TRADING COMPANIES. Ottawa, Dept. of the Interior, 1930. 188p [BM BVaU NSHD OTP

**Walker, Annie**

FIFTY YEARS OF ACHIEVEMENT: ... 50th Anniversary of the Founding of the Women's Institute of Ontario. Toronto, Federated Women's Insts. of Ont., 1948. 163p [OTU

**Walker, Frank Norman, 1892–**

FOUR WHISTLES TO WOOD-UP! Stories of the Northern Railway of Canada. Toronto, Upper Canada Railway Society, 1953. 64p

**Wallace, Frederick William, 1886–1958**

IN THE WAKE OF THE WIND SHIPS. Notes, Records, and Biographies. Toronto, Musson, 1927. 282p [BM BVaU NSWA OTU

WOODEN SHIPS AND IRON MEN. The Story of the Square-rigged Merchant Marine of British North America. ... Toronto, Hodder, 1923. 337p [BM BVaU NSHD OTU QMM

**Wallace, William Stewart, 1884–1970**

THE FAMILY COMPACT. A Chronicle of the Rebellion in Upper Canada. Toronto, Glasgow Brook, 1915. 172p [BVaU LC NSWA OTU QMM

THE GROWTH OF CANADIAN NATIONAL FEELING. Toronto, Macmillan, 1927. 85p [BVaU LC NSHD OTU QMBM

MURDERS AND MYSTERIES. A Canadian Series. Toronto, Macmillan, 1931. 333p [BVaU LC NBFU OTU QMM

THE PEDLARS FROM QUEBEC AND OTHER PAPERS ON THE NOR'WESTERS. Toronto, Ryerson, 1954. xii + 101p

THE ROYAL CANADIAN INSTITUTE CENTENNIAL VOLUME, 1849–1949. Toronto, The Institute, 1949. 232p [BVaU OTU

A SKETCH OF THE HISTORY OF THE CHAMPLAIN SOCIETY. Toronto, The Society, 1937. 8p [Rev. ed., 1957. 15p] [BVaU LC NBFU OTU

THE UNITED EMPIRE LOYALISTS. A Chronicle of the Great Migration. ... Toronto, Glasgow Brook, 1914. 148p [BVaU LC NSWA OOU QMM

**Warnock, Amelia Beers (Mrs. John Garvin), 1878–1956**

CANADA'S PEACE TOWER AND MEMORIAL CHAMBER. ... Toronto, Mundy-Goodfellow, 1935. 29p [BVaU OKQ

**Warwick Bros. and Rutter, Ltd.**

THE STORY OF THE BUSINESS, 1848–1923. As Told, Printed, and Published on its 75th Anniversary. Toronto, Warwick & Rutter, 1923. 97p [OTU

**Watson, Samuel James, 1837–1881**

THE POWERS OF CANADIAN PARLIAMENTS. ... Toronto, Robinson, 1880. 160p [BVaU NSHD OTU

**Weaver, Emily Poynton, 1865–1943**

CANADA AND THE BRITISH IMMIGRANT. London, Religious Tract Soc., 1914. 312p [BM BVaU LC OTP

**Webster, John Clarence, 1863–1950**

THE DISTRESSED MARITIMES. A Study of Educational and Cultural Conditions in Canada. Toronto, Ryerson, 1926. 46p [BM BVaU NSWA OTP QMM

**Wetherell, James Elgin, 1851–1940**

THREE CENTURIES OF CANADIAN STORIES FROM JOHN CABOT TO JOHN FRANKLIN. Toronto, Musson, 1928. [BM OTU

**Whelan, Edward, 1824–1867**

THE UNION OF THE BRITISH PROVINCES. A Brief Account of the Several Conferences held in the Maritime Provinces and in Canada, in September and October, 1864. Together with a Report of the Speeches delivered by the Delegates. ... Charlottetown, Haszard, 1865. 231p [BM BVaU NSWA OTU QMSS

**White, Thomas, 1830–1888**

NEWSPAPERS, THEIR DEVELOPMENT IN THE PROVINCE OF QUEBEC. A Lecture. ... Montreal, 1883. 15p [OTP QMM

**White, William, 1830–1912**

THE ANNALS OF CANADA. [Pt. 1, 1492–1760; pt. 2, 1763–1814.] Comp. by —— Toronto, Adam & Stevenson, 1875–8. 138p [Issued as supplement to *Canadian Monthly & National Revue.*] [BVaU LC OOA

**Whitton, Charlotte Elizabeth, 1896–**

THE DAWN OF AMPLER LIFE. ... Contains Summaries of Marsh, Heagerty and Beveridge Reports. Toronto, Macmillan, 1943. 154p [BVaU NSHD OTU

GOD'S GOOD TIDE. Toronto, Ryerson, 1941. 20p [BVaU OTU

**Wightman, Rev. Frederick Arnold, 1860–1939**

OUR CANADIAN HERITAGE. Its Resources and Possibilities. Toronto, Briggs, 1905. 287p [BM BVaU NBFU OKQ

**Wilder, H.E.**

THE 100TH ANNIVERSARY OF JEWISH EMANCIPATION IN CANADA (1832–1932) AND THE 50TH ANNIVERSARY OF THE JEW IN THE WEST. Winnipeg, Israelite Daily Press, 1932. 60 + 60p [Text in English and Hebrew] [OTU

**Williams, Helen Ernestine**

SPINNING WHEELS AND HOMESPUN. Toronto, McClelland, 1923. 314p [BM BVaU LC NSHD OTU QMM

**Willison, John Stephen, 1856–1927**

THE NEW CANADA. A Survey of the Conditions and Problems of the Dominion. By the Canadian Correspondent of "The Times." London, The Times, 1912. 118p [NBFU OTP

**Willison, Marjory (MacMurchy), –1938**

THE WOMAN–BLESS HER. Not as Amiable a Book as it Sounds. ... Toronto, Gundy, 1916. 155p [BVaU LC NSHD OTU

WOMEN OF TODAY AND TOMORROW. Toronto, Reconstruction Assoc., 1919 [CAR

**Willson, (Henry) Beckles, 1869–1942**

THE GREAT COMPANY. A History of the Honourable Company of Merchants-Adventurers trading into Hudson's Bay. With an intro. by Lord Strathcona. Toronto, Copp Clark, 1899. 541p [BM BVaU LC NSWA OTU QMM

IN THE YPRES SALIENT. ... London, Simpkin Marshall, 1916. 80p [BM BVaU NSHD OTU

YOUTH BE DAMNED! Being a Protest and an Exhortation. London, Laurie, 1938. 214p [OTU

**Withrow, Oswald Charles Joseph, 1878–1946**

THE ROMANCE OF THE CANADIAN NATIONAL EXHIBITION. Toronto, Saunders, 1936. 157p [OTU

SHACKLING THE TRANSGRESSOR. An Indictment of the Canadian Penal System. ... Toronto, Nelson, 1933. 229p [BVaU LC NSHD OTP

**Withrow, Rev. William Henry, 1839–1908**

THE BIBLE AND THE TEMPERANCE QUESTION. Toronto, Rose, 1876. 29p [OTUV

INTEMPERANCE. Its Evils and their Remedies. Napanee, Can. Temperance Union, 1869. 58p [OTP

**Wood, A.C.**

OLD DAYS ON THE FARM. Toronto, McClelland, 1918. 255p [BVaU OKQ

**Wood, Louis Aubrey Lorne, 1883–1955**

A HISTORY OF FARMERS' MOVEMENTS IN CANADA. Toronto, Ryerson, 1924. 372p [BM BVaU LC NSHD OTU QMM

**Wood, William Charles Henry, 1864–1947**

ALL AFLOAT. A Chronicle of Craft and Waterways. Toronto, Glasgow Brook, 1914. 199p [BM BVaU LC NSWA OTP

**Woodsworth, Rev. James Shaver, 1874–1942**

ON THE WATERFRONT. With the Workers on the Docks at Vancouver. Some Observations and Experiences. Ottawa, Montreal Print., [1918?]. 31p [BVaU OTU

STRANGERS WITHIN OUR GATES; or, Coming Canadians. Toronto, Missionary Society of the Methodist Church, 1909. 356p [BM BVaU LC NSWA OTP QMM

**Wright, James Frederick Church, 1904–**

SLAVA BOHU. The Story of the Doukhobors. New York, Farrar & Rinehart, 1940. 438p [BM BVaU LC NBFU OLU QMM

**Wrong, Dennis Hume, 1923–**

AMERICAN AND CANADIAN VIEWPOINTS. Prepared for the Canada–United States Committee on Education. Washington, D.C., American Council on Education, 1955. 62p [A comparison of national values.]

**Wrong, George McKinnon, 1860–1948**

CANADA AND THE AMERICAN REVOLUTION. The Disruption of the First British Empire. Toronto, Macmillan, 1935. 497p [BM BVaU NSHD OTU QMM

A CANADIAN MANOR AND ITS SEIGNEURS, 1761–1860. Toronto, Macmillan, 1908. 295p [An account of Murray Bay, Quebec, and the Nairne Family. ...] [BM BVaU LC NSHD OTU QMM

CHRONICLES OF CANADA. Ed. by G.M. Wrong and H.H. Langton. Toronto, Glasgow Brook, 1914–16. 32v [BM BVaU LC NBFU OTU QMM

THE CONQUEST OF NEW FRANCE. A Chronicle of the Colonial Wars. New Haven, Yale U. Press, 1918. 246p [BM BVaU LC NSHD OTU

THE UNITED STATES AND CANADA. A Political Study. New York, Abingdon Press, 1921. 191p [BM BVaU LC NBFU OTU

**York, Eva Rose (Fitch), 1858–**

FEATHERS WITH YELLOW GOLD. Ed. by Ray Palmer Baker and Eva Rose York. Toronto, Evangelical Pub., 1920. 235p [OTU

**Young, James, 1835–1913**

OUR NATIONAL FUTURE. Being Four Letters ... in Opposition to Commercial Union ... and Imperial Federation. ... Galt, Collie & McGiverin, 1887. 19p [OTP

**Young, Katherine A.**

EARLY DAYS IN THE MAPLE LAND. Stories for Children of Stirring Deeds under Three Flags. New York, Pott & Co., 1901. 120p [OONL

**Yuzyk, Paul, 1913–**

THE UKRAINIANS IN MANITOBA. A Social History. Toronto, U. of Toronto Press, 1953. xv + 232p

# SCHOLARSHIP

## Studies and criticism in literature and the other humanities

**Abell, Walter Halsey, 1897–1956**

REPRESENTATION AND FORM. A Study of Aesthetic Values in Representational Art. New York, Scribner, 1936. 172p [BM BVaU NBFU OTU

**Adair, Mary**

SHORT STORY STUDIES, IN SHORT STORY CLASSICS. ... Boston, Badger, 1930. 344p [LC OTP

**Adams, Sinclair MacLardy, 1891–**

SOPHOCLES THE PLAYWRIGHT. Toronto, U. of Toronto Press, 1957. 182p

**Alexander, Henry, 1893–**

THE STORY OF OUR LANGUAGE. Toronto, Nelson, 1940. 242p [Earlier ed.: Garden City, N.Y., Doubleday, 1926.] [BVaU LC NSHD OTU

**Alexander, William Hardy, 1878–1962**

THE AMIABLE TYRANNY OF PEISISTRATUS; or, The Future of Classical Studies. Edmonton, U. of Alberta Press, 1931. 20p [OTU

AUREA MEDIOCRITAS. An Address ... on the ... Two Thousandth Anniversary of the Birth of Horace. Edmonton, U. of Alberta Press, 1935. 17p [BM BVaU OTP

NOTES AND EMENDATIONS TO THE XII DIALOGES OF L. ANNAEUS SENECA. Edmonton, U. of Alberta Press, 1934. 33p [BM NSHD OLU QMM

NOTES AND EMENDATIONS TO THE EPISTULAE MORALES OF L. ANNAEUS SENECA. Edmonton, U. of Alberta Press, 1932. 15p [BM LC OTP

PENTASYLLABIC ENDINGS IN THE LATIN HEXAMETER WITH PARTICULAR REFERENCE TO THE VERSE OF LUCRETIUS. N.p., 1900. 32p [OTU

PUBLIUS VERGILIUS MARO, THE POET OF A LAND AND OF A RACE. Bimillenary Celebration Lecture given at the University of Alberta. N.p., 1930. 21p [OTU

SENECA'S DIALOGI. Los Angeles, U. of California Press, 1943–45. 3v [BM BVaU LC

SENECA'S EPISTULAE MORALES. The Text Emended and Explained. Berkeley, U. of California Press, 1940. [BM BVaU LC NSHD OTU

SENECA'S NATURALES QUAESTIONES. Berkeley, U. of California Press, 1948. 332p [BM BVaU LC OLU

SOME TEXTUAL CRITICISMS ON THE EIGHTH BOOK OF THE DE VITA CAESARUM OF SUETONIUS. Berkeley, U. of California Press, 1908. 33p [BM BVaU LC OLU

**Alexander, William John, 1855–1944**

AN INTRODUCTION TO THE POETRY OF ROBERT BROWNING. Boston, Ginn, 1899. 212p [BM BVaU LC NSHD OTU

THE STUDY OF LITERATURE. Inaugural Lecture Delivered in the Convocation Hall, October 12th, 1889. Toronto, Rowsell & Hutchinson, 1889. 34p [OTP

**Allen, Grant, 1848–1899**

THE COLOUR SENSE: ITS ORIGIN AND DEVELOPMENT. An Essay in Comparative Psychology. London, Trubner, 1879. 282p [BM OTU

EVOLUTION IN ITALIAN ART. London, Richards, 1908. 368p [BM OTU

FORCE AND ENERGY. A Theory of Dynamics. London, Longmans, 1888. 161p [BM OTU

THE MISCELLANEOUS AND POSTHUMOUS WORKS OF H.T. BUCKLE. Abridged ed. Ed. by ——. London, Longmans, 1885. 2v [BM OTU

THE NATURAL HISTORY OF SELBORNE. By Gilbert White. Ed. with notes by ——. London, Lane, 1899. 568p [BM BVaU

PHYSIOLOGICAL AESTHETICS. London, King, 1877. 283p [BM OTU

**Allison, William Talbot, 1874–1941**

BLAZING A NEW TRAIL. [Anon] Toronto, Musson, 1920. [On Canadian authors.]

BOLSHEVISM IN ENGLISH LITERATURE. An Inaugural Lecture. Winnipeg, U. of Manitoba, 1921. 21p [OTUV

**Anderson, Fulton Henry, 1895–1968**

THE ARGUMENT OF PLATO. Toronto, Dent, 1934. 216p [BM BVaU LC NSHD OTP

THE INFLUENCE OF CONTEMPORARY SCIENCE ON LOCKE'S METHOD AND RESULTS. Toronto, University Library, 1923. 31p [BVaU LC NSWA OTU

THE PHILOSOPHY OF FRANCIS BACON. Chicago, U. of Chicago Press, 1948. 312p [BM BVaU LC NSHD OTP

**Anstensen, Ansten, 1899–**

THE PROVERB IN IBSEN. Proverbial Sayings and Citations as Elements in His Style. New York, Columbia U. Press, 1936. 255p [BM LC OTU QMM

**Ashton, Harry, 1882–**

THE FRENCH NOVEL. London, Benn, 1928. 80p [BM BVaU OTU

MOLIERE. London, Routledge, 1930. 263p [BM BVaU LC NSHD OTU

A PREFACE TO MOLIERE. Toronto, Longmans, 1927. 177p [BM BVaU LC OTU

**Ayscough, Florence (Wheelock), 1878–1942**

TU FU. The Autobiography of a Chinese Poet, A.D. 712–770. Arranged from his Poems. Boston, Houghton, 1928. 450p [BM BVaU NSHD OTU

**Bagnani, Gilbert**

ARBITER OF ELEGANCE. A Study of the Life and Works of C. Petronius. Toronto, U. of Toronto Press, 1954. xi + 91p

**Baker, Ray Palmer, 1883–**

A HISTORY OF ENGLISH-CANADIAN LITERATURE TO THE CONFEDERATION. Cambridge, Harvard U. Press, 1920. 200p [BM BVaU LC NSHD OTU

**Barker, Arthur Edward, 1911–**

MILTON AND THE PURITAN DILEMMA, 1641–1660. Toronto, U. of Toronto Press, 1942. xxiv + 440p [Reprinted, 1955.] [BM BVaU NSHD OTP

**Barnes, Duane Clayton, 1905–**

WORDLORE. New York, Dutton, 1948. 135p [BViP LC

**Baylis, Samuel Mathewson, 1854–1941**

"SHAKE-SPEARE." An Enquiry. Paper read before the St. James Literary Society, Montreal. Toronto, Briggs, 1910. 32p [BM OTP

**Beaugrand, Honoré, 1849–1906**

NEW STUDIES OF CANADIAN FOLK LORE. Montreal, Renouf, 1904. 130p [BVaU LC NBFU OTUV

**Beck, Lily Adams (Moresby), –1931**

THE GHOST PLAYS OF JAPAN. New York, Japan Society, 1933. 35p [BVaU LC OTU

**Bedford-Jones, Henry James O'Brien, 1887–1949**

THE GRADUATE FICTIONEER. Denver, Col., Author & Journalist Pub. Co., 1932. 126p [LC

THIS FICTION BUSINESS. New York, Covici Friede, 1929. 178p [First pub. as: THE FICTION BUSINESS. Evansville, Ind., 1922. 72p] [BVaU LC

**Bell, Andrew James, 1856–1932**

THE LATIN DUAL AND POETIC DICTION. London, Oxford U. Press, 1923. 468p [BM LC NBFU OTU

**Bell, Inglis Freeman, 1917–**

THE ENGLISH NOVEL, 1578–1956. A Checklist of Twentieth-Century Criticisms. By Inglis F. Bell and Donald Baird. Denver, A. Swallow, 1959 [c1958]. xii + 169p

**Bender, Louis Prosper, 1844–1917**

LITERARY SHEAVES; or, La Littérature au Canada Français. The Drama, History, Romance, Poetry, Lectures, Sketches, &c. Montreal, Dawson, 1881. 215p [BM BVaU LC NBFU OTU QMM

**Berlis, Rudolph John**

CITY UNDER SIEGE. Montreal, Author, 1940. 8p [CC

**Birch, Thomas Albany, 1897–**

THE ENGLISH MIND AS REFLECTED IN LITERATURE. Montreal, Renouf Pub. Co., 1956. xi + 332p

**Bissell, Claude Thomas, 1916–**

OUR LIVING TRADITION. Seven Canadians. Ed. by ——. Toronto, Published in association with Carleton University by U. of Toronto Press, 1957. x + 149p [Public lectures given at Carleton University, Ottawa, 1957.]

**Black, Norman Fergus, 1876–1964**

ENGLISH FOR THE NON ENGLISH. Regina, Regina Book Shop, 1913. 211p [BM OTU

**Blanchard, Kathleen Helen (Barrett), 1872–**

STORIES OF BEAUTIFUL HYMNS. Grand Rapids, Mich., Zondervan, 1942. 117p [BVa LC

STORIES OF FAVORITE HYMNS. Grand Rapids, Mich., Zondervan, 1941. 118p [BVa LC

STORIES OF POPULAR HYMNS. Grand Rapids, Mich., Zondervan, 1939. 142p [BVa LC OTUV

STORIES OF WONDERFUL HYMNS. Grand Rapids, Mich., Zondervan, 1947. 109p [BVa

**Borneman, Ernst Wilhelm Julius, 1915–**

A CRITIC LOOKS AT JAZZ. London, Jazz Music Books, 1946. 53p [LC

**Bossin, Hye**

STARS OF DAVID. Toronto, Jewish Standard, 1956. 39p [Account of the Jewish contribution to the theatre in Toronto.]

**Bourinot, Arthur Stanley, 1893–1969**

AT THE MERMAID INN. By A. Lampman, W.W. Campbell, Duncan C. Scott. Being Selections from Essays on Life and Literature which appeared in the Toronto Globe, 1892–1893. Ed., annotated, and selected by ——. Ottawa, Bourinot, 1958. 96p

**Bourinot, John George, 1837–1902**

THE INTELLECTUAL DEVELOPMENT OF THE CANADIAN PEOPLE. An Historical Review. Toronto, Hunter Rose, 1881. 128p [BM BVaU LC MWU NSHD OTU QMM

OUR INTELLECTUAL STRENGTH AND WEAKNESS. A Short Historical and Critical Review of Literature, Art and Education in Canada. Montreal, Brown, 1893. 99p [BM BVaU LC NSHD OTU QMM

**Brebner, John Bartlet, 1895–1957**

SCHOLARSHIP FOR CANADA. The Function of Graduate Studies. Ottawa, Social Science Research Council, 1945. 90p [BVaU LC NSHD OTU QMM

**Brennan, Joseph Fletcher**

A POPULAR ILLUSTRATED HISTORY OF THE FINE ARTS OF PAINTING AND SCULPTURE FROM THE EARLIEST AGES TO THE PRESENT. Cincinnati, Franklin Type, 1884. 320p [LC

**Brett, George Sidney, 1879–1944**

THE GOVERNMENT OF MAN. An Introduction to Ethics and Politics. London, Bell, 1920. 318p [BM BVaU LC OLU

THE HISTORY OF PSYCHOLOGY, ANCIENT AND PATRISTIC. London, Allen, 1912–21. 3v [Abridged ed. in one vol., 1953.] [BM BVaU LC NBFU OTU

THE PHILOSOPHY OF GASSENDI. London, Macmillan, 1908. 310p [BM BVaU LC OTU

PSYCHOLOGY, ANCIENT AND MODERN. New York, Longmans, 1928. 164p [BM BVaU LC NSHD OTU QMM

**Bridle, Augustus, 1869–1952**

THE STORY OF THE CLUB. Toronto, Arts and Letters Club, 1945. 83p [NBFU OTP

**Broadus, Edmund Kemper, 1876–1936**

BOOKS AND IDEALS. An Anthology Selected and Arranged by ——. London, Oxford U. Press, 1921. 212p [BM LC QMM

THE LAUREATESHIP. A Study of the Office of Poet Laureate in England with Some Account of the Poets. Oxford, Clarendon Press, 1921. 239p [BM LC NSHD OTU QMM

THE STORY OF ENGLISH LITERATURE. New York, Macmillan, 1931. 624p [Rev. ed.: Toronto, Macmillan, 1936. 818p] [BM BVaU LC OTU QMM

**Brown, Edward Killoran, 1905–1951**

EDITH WHARTON. Paris, Didier, 1938. 11p [OTU

EDITH WHARTON, ETUDE CRITIQUE. Paris, Droz, 1935. 348p [BM OTU

MATTHEW ARNOLD. A Study in Conflict. Toronto, Ryerson, 1948. 223p [BM BVaU NSHD OTU QMM

ON CANADIAN POETRY. Toronto, Ryerson, 1943. 157p [Rev. and enl. ed.: Toronto, Ryerson, 1944. 172p] [BM BVaU LC NSHD OTU QMM

REPRESENTATIVE ESSAYS OF MATTHEW ARNOLD. Ed. by ——. Toronto, Macmillan, 1936. 240p [BVaU OTU

RHYTHM IN THE NOVEL. Toronto, U. of Toronto Press, 1950. 118p [BM BVaU NSHD OTU QMM

STUDIES IN THE TEXT OF MATTHEW ARNOLD'S PROSE WORKS. Paris, André, 1935. 139p [BM LC OTU

WILLA CATHER. A Critical Biography. ... Completed by Leon Edel. New York, Knopf, 1953. 351p

VICTORIAN POETRY. Ed. by ——. New York, Ronald, 1942. 912p [BVaU LC NBFU OTU

**Bryce, Rev. George, 1844–1931**

A POET'S MESSAGE. [Winnipeg? 1909?] 15p [On David, the Psalmist] [LC OTU

**Buchanan, Donald William, 1908–1966**

CANADIAN PAINTERS. From Paul Kane to the Group of Seven. Ed. by ——. Oxford, Phaidon, 1945. 25p (87 plates.) [BM BVaU LC NSHD OTU QMM

EDUCATIONAL AND CULTURAL FILMS IN CANADA. A Survey of the Situation, together with Recommendations, &c. Ottawa, n.p., 1936. 23p [BVaU OTU

THE GROWTH OF CANADIAN PAINTING. Toronto, Collins, 1950. 112p [BM BVaU NSHD OTU

**Buchanan, Milton Alexander, 1878–1952**

THE CHRONOLOGY OF LOPE DE VEGA'S PLAYS. Toronto, University Library, 1922. 25p [BM BVaU LC OTU QMM

SPANISH POETRY OF THE GOLDEN AGE. Ed. by ——. Toronto, U. of Toronto Press, 1942. 149p [2nd ed. 1947.] [BVaU LC NSHD OTU QMM

**Bucke, Richard Maurice, 1837–1902**

COSMIC CONSCIOUSNESS. A Study in the Evolution of the Human Mind. Philadelphia, Innes, 1901. 318p [Many later editions.] [BM BVaU LC OTU QMM

IN RE WALT WHITMAN. Edited by his Literary Executors, H.L. Traubel, R.M. Bucke, T.B. Larned. Philadelphia, McKay, 1893. 452p [LC OLU QMM

WALT WHITMAN. Philadelphia, McKay, 1883. 236p [BM BVaU LC OTU QMM

THE WOUND DRESSER. Letters written to his [Walt Whitman's] Mother from the Hospitals in Washington during the Civil War. Ed. by ——. With an intro. by Oscar Cargill. New York, Bodley Press, 1949. 200p [Earlier ed.: Boston, Small Maynard, 1897.] [BM BVaU LC

**Buckley, Jerome Hamilton, 1917–**

THE VICTORIAN TEMPER. A Study in Literary Culture. Cambridge, Mass., Harvard U. Press, 1951. viii + 282p

**Buckley, Joan**

THE TECHNIQUE OF POETRY. Hints on Verse-Writing. Vancouver, Clarke & Stuart, 1944. 63p [BVaU OKQ

**Burpee, Lawrence Johnstone, 1873–1946**

CANADIAN NOVELS AND NOVELISTS. N.p., [1901]. 28p [BVaU OTP

A LITTLE BOOK OF CANADIAN ESSAYS. Toronto, Musson, 1909. 87p [BVaU LC NBFU OKQ QMM

**Burrell, Martin, 1858–1938**

BETWIXT HEAVEN AND CHARING CROSS. Toronto, Macmillan, 1928. 328p [BM BVaU LC NSHD OTU QMM

CRUMBS ARE ALSO BREAD. Toronto, Macmillan, 1934. 340p [BM BVaU LC NSHD OTU QMM

**Burton, Alice Elizabeth, 1908–**

THE ELIZABETHANS AT HOME. London, Secker & Warburg, 1958. 276p

**Caldwell, William, 1863–1942**

PRAGMATISM AND IDEALISM. London, Black, 1913. 268p [BM BVaU LC NBFU OTU QMM

SCHOPENHAUER'S SYSTEM IN ITS PHILOSOPHICAL SIGNIFICANCE. Edinburgh, Blackwood, 1896. 538p [BM BVaU OTU QMM

**Campbell, Colin D.**

THE NATURE OF LITERATURE. (1) The Definition. Regina, Leader Pub. Co., 1926. 19p [OKQ

WHAT IS ART? Regina, Commercial Printers, 1934. 15p [OKQ

**Campbell, Rev. John, 1840–1904**

THE HITTITES. Their Inscriptions and History. Toronto, Williamson, 1890. 2v [BM BVaU OTU

**Campbell-McInnes, James, 1874–**

THE MUSIC OF LANGUAGE. London, Harris, 1939. 92p [BVaU LC OTU

**Canada. Royal Commission on National Development in the Arts, Letters and Sciences, 1949–1951**

REPORT. Ottawa, King's Printer, 1951. xxi + 517p [Vincent Massey, Chairman.]

ROYAL COMMISSION STUDIES. A Selection of Essays. Ottawa, King's Printer, 1951. 430p

**Canadian Broadcasting Corporation**

CANADIAN LITERATURE TO-DAY. Series of broadcasts sponsored by CBC. Toronto, U. of Toronto Press, 1938. 70p [Contributors: E.K. Brown, P. Child, W.E. Collin, F.P. Grove, W. Kirkconnell, J.F. Macdonald, E. McInnis, A.L. Phelps, W. Tyrrell.] [BM BVaU LC OTU

**Canadian Press Association**

A HISTORY OF CANADIAN JOURNALISM IN THE SEVERAL PORTIONS OF THE DOMINION. With a Sketch of the Canadian Press Association 1859–1908. Ed. by a Committee of the Association. Toronto, Murray Print., 1908. 242p [The sequel, V. 2, was authored by William Arnot Craick, *q.v.*] [BVaU LC NBFU OTU

**Cappon, James, 1854–1939**

BLISS CARMAN AND THE LITERARY CURRENTS AND INFLUENCES OF HIS TIME. Toronto, Ryerson, 1930. 340p [BM BVaU LC NSHD OTU QMM

CHARLES G.D. ROBERTS. Toronto, Ryerson, [1925]. 148p [BM BVaU NSHD OTU

ROBERTS AND THE INFLUENCES OF HIS TIME. Toronto, Briggs, 1905. 88p [Studies in Canadian Poetry, No. 1.] [NSHD OTP QMM

VICTOR HUGO. Edinburgh, Blackwood, 1885. 394p [BM LC OLU

WHAT CLASSICAL EDUCATION MEANS. Kingston, Jackson, n.d. 13p [OTU

**Carman, Bliss, 1861–1929**

JAMES WHITCOMB RILEY. An Essay by Bliss Carman, and Some Letters to him from James Whitcomb Riley [August 30, 1898–October 12, 1915]. ... New York, priv. print. for George D. Smith, [1917]. [Reprinted: Metuchen, N.J., Heartman, 1925–1926. 86p] [BM BVaU LC NSHD OKQ

**Carter, Alfred Edward, 1914–**

THE IDEA OF DECADENCE IN FRENCH LITERATURE, 1830–1900. Toronto, U. of Toronto Press, 1958. ix + 154p

**Chittick, Victor Lovitt Oakes, 1882–**

THOMAS CHANDLER HALIBURTON ("Sam Slick"). A Study in Provincial Toryism. New York, Columbia U. Press, 1924. 695p [BM BVaU LC NSHD OTU

**Clark, Alexander Frederick Bruce, 1884–**

BOILEAU AND THE FRENCH CLASSICAL CRITICS IN ENGLAND (1660–1830). Paris, Champion, 1925. 534p [BM BVaU LC NSHD OTU

JEAN RACINE. Cambridge, Harvard U. Press, 1939. 354p [BM BVaU LC NSHD OTU

**Clarke, George Herbert, 1873–1953**

THE ESSAYS OR COUNSELS CIVIL AND MORAL OF FRANCIS BACON. Ed. with intro. and notes by ——. New York, Macmillan, 1905. 318p [BM LC

SELECTED POEMS OF PERCY BYSSHE SHELLEY. Ed. with intro. and notes by ——. Boston, Houghton, 1907. 266p [BM LC OTU

SOME REMINISCENCES AND EARLY LETTERS OF SIDNEY LANIER. Macon, Ga., Burke, 1907. 27p [BM LC NSWA

**Coburn, Kathleen Hazel, 1905–**

INQUIRING SPIRIT. A New Presentation of Coleridge from His Published and Unpublished Prose Writings. Ed. by ——. London, Routledge, 1951. 454p

NOTEBOOKS OF SAMUEL TAYLOR COLERIDGE. New York, Pantheon Books; London, Routledge–Paul, 1957–. Ed. by ——. [V. 1 in two parts, text and notes, 1794–1804, pub. in 1957; other volumes to follow.]

THE PHILOSOPHICAL LECTURES OF SAMUEL TAYLOR COLERIDGE, HITHERTO UNPUBLISHED. Ed. by ——. London, Pilot Press, 1949. 480p [BM BVaU LC NBFU OTU

**Cochrane, Charles Norris, 1889–1945**

CHRISTIANITY AND CLASSICAL CULTURE. A Study of Thought and Action from Augustus to Augustine. Oxford, Clarendon Press, 1940. 523p [BM BVaU LC NSHD OTU

THUCYDIDES AND THE SCIENCE OF HISTORY. London, Oxford U. Press, 1929. 180p [BM BVaU LC NSHD OTU

**Colgate, William G., 1882–**

CANADIAN ART. Its Origin and Development. Toronto, Ryerson, 1943. 278p [BM BVaU NSHD OTU QMM

**Collin, William Edwin, 1893–**

CLOCKMAKER OF SOULS. A Study of Paul-Jean Toulet. New York, Kendall, 1933. 203p [BM LC OLU QMSS

THE WHITE SAVANNAHS. Toronto, Macmillan, 1936. 288p [On Canadian poets.] [BM BVaU LC NSHD OKQ

**Connor, Carl Yoder, 1890–**

ARCHIBALD LAMPMAN, CANADIAN POET OF NATURE. New York & Montreal, Carrier, 1929. 210p [BM BVaU LC NSWA OTU QMM

**Corrigan, Beatrice Marion, 1903–**

CURIOUS ANNALS. New Documents Relating to Browning's Roman Murder Story. Translated, edited, and with an intro. by ——. Toronto, U. of Toronto Press, 1956. 142p

**Coulter, John William, 1888–**

RADIO DRAMA IS NOT THEATRE. By John Coulter and Ivor Lewis. Toronto, Macmillan, 1937. 10p [OTP

**Coventry, George, 1793–1870**

A CRITICAL ENQUIRY REGARDING THE REAL AUTHOR OF THE LETTERS OF JUNIUS. Proving them to have been Written by Lord Viscount Sackville. London, Phillips, 1825. 382p [BM BVaU LC OTU QMM

**Cragg, Rev. Gerald Robertson, 1908–**

FROM PURITANISM TO THE AGE OF REASON. A Study of Changes in Religious Thought within the Church of England. 1660 to 1700. Cambridge, Eng., U. Press, 1950. 247p [OONL

PURITANISM IN THE PERIOD OF THE GREAT PERSECUTION, 1660–1688. Cambridge, Eng., University Press, 1957. ix + 325p

**Craick, William Arnot, 1880–1969**

A HISTORY OF CANADIAN JOURNALISM. V. 2: Last Years of the Canadian Press Association, with a Continuing Record of the Canadian Daily Newspaper Publishers Association, 1919–1959. Toronto, Ont. Pub. Co., [1959]. 311p [Sequel to A HISTORY OF CANADIAN JOURNALISM IN THE SEVERAL PORTIONS OF THE DOMINION, WITH A SKETCH OF THE CANADIAN PRESS ASSOCIATION, 1859–1908. By the Canadian Press Association. Toronto, Murray Print., 1908. 242p]

**Crawford, Alexander Wellington, 1866–1933**

THE GENIUS OF KEATS. An Interpretation. London, Stockwell, 1932. 202p [BM LC OTU

HAMLET, AN IDEAL PRINCE, AND OTHER ESSAYS IN SHAKESPEARIAN INTERPRETATION.... Boston, Badger, 1916. 317p [BM BVaU LC OTU

THE PHILOSOPHY OF F.H. JACOBI.... New York, Macmillan, 1905. 90p [BM LC OTU

**Creighton, Helen, 1899–**

FOLKLORE OF LUNENBURG COUNTY, NOVA SCOTIA. Ottawa, King's Printer, 1950. 163p [BM BVaU LC NSHD OTP

**Cridge, Edward, 1817–1913**

AS IT WAS IN THE BEGINNING; or, The Historic Principle Applied to the Mosaic Scriptures. Chicago, Revell, 1900. 121p [BVaU LC

**Dalton, Annie Charlotte (Armitage), 1865–1938**

THE FUTURE OF OUR POETRY. Vancouver, priv. print., 1931. 16p [BVaU

**Daniells, Roy, 1902–**

THOMAS TRAHERNE, A SERIOUS AND PATHETIC CONTEMPLATION OF MERCIES OF GOD, IN SEVERAL MOST DEVOUT AND SUBLIME THANKSGIVINGS FOR THE SAME. Ed. by ——. Toronto, U. of Toronto Press, 1941. 127p [BM BVaU OTU

**Davies, Blodwen, 1897–1966**

PLANETARY DEMOCRACY. An Introduction to Scientific Humanism and Applied Semantics. By Oliver L. Reiser and Blodwen Davies. New York, Creative Age, 1944. 242p [OTU QMM

**Davies, Robertson, 1913–**

SHAKESPEARE'S BOY ACTORS. London, Dent, 1939. 208p [Also: New York, Russell, 1964.] [BM BVaU OTU

**Davies, Trevor Hughes, 1871–**

SPIRITUAL VOICES IN MODERN LITERATURE. Toronto, Ryerson, 1919. 312p [BM BVaU LC OTU QMM

TO LIVE IN CHRIST. London, Oxford U. Press, 1938. 250p [Lectures on Augustine, Dante, Kingsley, Osler, etc.] [LC OTU

**Davis, Herbert John, 1893–**

NINETEENTH CENTURY STUDIES. Collected and ed. by ——. Ithaca, Cornell U. Press, 1940. 303p [BM BVaU LC OTU

THE PROSE WORKS OF JONATHAN SWIFT. Ed. by ——. Oxford, Shakespeare Head Press, 1939–62. 14v [BM BVaU LC OTU

THE SATIRE OF JONATHAN SWIFT. New York, Macmillan, 1947. 109p [BM BVaU LC NSHD OTU QMM

STELLA. A Gentlewoman of the Eighteenth Century. New York, Macmillan, 1942. 103p [BM BVaU LC NSHD OTU QMM

**Dawson, Robert MacGregor, 1927–**

PLACE NAMES IN NOVA SCOTIA. A Paper Read before the Linguistic Circle of Manitoba and North Dakota on May 16th, 1959. Winnipeg, Ukrainian Free Academy of Science, 1960. 16p

**Dawson, Samuel Edward, 1833–1916**

THE PROSE WRITERS OF CANADA. An Address Delivered before the Teachers of the City and District of Montreal, Renouf, 1901. 39p [BVaU LC NSHD OTU QMM

A STUDY WITH CRITICAL AND EXPLANATORY NOTES OF ALFRED TENNYSON'S POEM "THE PRINCESS." Montreal, Dawson, 1882. 120p [BM BVaU LC NSHD OTU

**Deacon, William Arthur, 1890–**

THE FOUR JAMESES. Ottawa, Graphic, 1927. 224p [Rev. ed., Toronto, Ryerson, 1953. 210p] [BVaU NSHD OTU QMM

**De Mille, Alban Bertram, 1873–**

AMERICAN POETRY. Edited with Intro., Notes, Questions, and Biographical Sketches. Boston, Allyn & Bacon, 1923. 339p [BVa

LITERATURE IN THE CENTURY. (The Nineteenth Century Series. V. 2.) Philadelphia, Bradley Garretson, 1903. 548p [Earlier ed.: London, Linscott, 1900.] [BM BVaU LC NSHD OTP

**De Mille, James, 1833–1880**

THE ELEMENTS OF RHETORIC. New York, Harper, 1878. 564p [BVaU LC NSHD OTU QMM

**de Pauley, Rev. William Cecil, 1893–**

THE CANDLE OF THE LORD. Studies in the Cambridge Platonists. New York, Macmillan, 1937. 248p [BM BVaU LC OTU

**Devine, Patrick Kevin, 1859–1950**

DEVINE'S FOLK LORE OF NEWFOUNDLAND IN OLD WORDS, PHRASES AND EXPRESSIONS, THEIR ORIGIN AND MEANING. St. John's, Robinson, 1937. 80p [NSHD OTU

**DeWitt, Norman Wentworth, 1876–1958**

THE DIDO EPISODE IN THE AENEID OF VIRGIL. ... Toronto, Briggs, 1907. 78p [LC OTU QMM

EPICURUS AND HIS PHILOSOPHY. Minneapolis, U. of Minnesota Press, 1954. 388p

ST. PAUL AND EPICURUS. Toronto, Ryerson, 1954. 201p

VIRGIL'S BIOGRAPHIA LITTERARIA. Toronto, Victoria College Press, 1923. 192p [BM BVaU LC NSHD OTU

**Doughty, Arthur George, 1860–1936**

THE CANADIAN ARCHIVES AND ITS ACTIVITIES. Ottawa, Acland, 1924. 88p [BM BVaU LC NSWA OTU QMM

**Dray, William Herbert, 1921–**

LAWS AND EXPLANATION IN HISTORY. London, Oxford U. Press, 1957. 174p

**Dudek, Louis, 1918–**

LITERATURE AND THE PRESS. A History of Printing, Printed Media, and their Relation to Literature. Toronto, Ryerson, 1960. 238p

**Duncan, Alastair Robert Campbell, 1915–**

PRACTICAL REASON AND MORALITY. A Study of Immanuel Kant's Foundations for the Metaphysics of Morals. London, Nelson, 1957. xviii + 182p

**Duvar, John Hunter–, 1830–1899**

THE STONE, BRONZE AND IRON AGES. A Popular Treatise on Early Archaeology. London, Swan Sonnenschein, 1892. 285p [BM LC

**Edgar, Oscar Pelham, 1871–1948**

ACROSS MY PATH. Ed. by Northrop Frye. Toronto, Ryerson, 1952. 167p

THE ART OF THE NOVEL FROM 1700 TO THE PRESENT TIME. New York, Macmillan, 1933. 493p [BM BVaU LC NSHD OTU

COLERIDGE AND WORDSWORTH. Select Poems. With intro. and notes. Ed. by ——. Toronto, Morang, 1902. 244p [BM OTUV

HENRY JAMES, MAN AND AUTHOR. Boston, Houghton, 1927. 351p [Earlier ed.: London, Richards, 1925.] [BM BVaU LC NSHD OTU

A STUDY OF SHELLEY, WITH SPECIAL REFERENCE TO HIS NATURE POETRY. Toronto, Briggs, 1899. 155p [BM LC NBFU

**Eggleston, Wilfrid, 1901–**

THE FRONTIER & CANADIAN LETTERS. Toronto, Ryerson, 1957. ix + 164p

**Engel, Srul Morris von, 1931–**

THE PROBLEM OF TRAGEDY. Fredericton, Brunswick Press, 1960. 81p

**Fairley, Barker, 1887–**

CHARLES M. DOUGHTY. A Critical Study. London. Cape, 1927. 256p [BM BVaU LC NSHD OTU QMM

GOETHE AS REVEALED IN HIS POETRY. London, Dent, 1932. 210p [BM BVaU LC NSHD OTU QMM

GOETHE'S "FAUST." Six Essays. Oxford, Clarendon, 1953. 132p

HEINRICH HEINE, AN INTERPRETATION. Oxford, Clarendon, 1954. 176p

SELECTED POEMS OF JOHANN WOLFGANG VON GOETHE. Ed. by ——. New York, Rinehart, 1955. xxvii + 221p [First pub. London, Heinemann, 1954.]

A STUDY OF GOETHE. Oxford, Clarendon, 1947. 280p [BM BVaU LC NSHD OTU QMM

**Fairweather, Rev. Eugene Rathbone, 1920–**

A SCHOLASTIC MISCELLANY. Anselm to Ockham. Ed. by ——. London, SCM Press, 1956. 457p

**Ferguson, Rev. George Dalrymple, 1829–1926**

LECTURES ON THE HISTORY OF THE MIDDLE AGES. Kingston, Uglow, 1904. 634p [BM LC OTU QMM

**Fitzgerald, Rev. D.**

A LECTURE ON THE REFORMATION. Charlottetown, Haszard, 1859. 94p [NSHP

**Flenley, Ralph, 1886–1969**

A HISTORY OF MONTREAL, 1640–1672. From the French of François Dollier de Casson. Trans. and ed. with a life of the author. London, Dent, 1928. 384p [BM BVaU OTU

**Ford, George Harry, 1914–**

KEATS AND THE VICTORIANS. A Study of his Influence and Rise to Fame, 1821–1895. New Haven, Yale U. Press, 1944. 200p [BM BVaU LC NBFU OTU QMM

**Fox, William Sherwood, 1878–1967**

GREEK AND ROMAN MYTHOLOGY. Boston, Marshall Jones, 1916. lxii + 354p [Later ed., 1928. 402p] [BM BVa LC NSHD OLU QMM

GREEK INSCRIPTIONS IN THE ROYAL ONTARIO MUSEUM. London, Ont., 1917. 14p [OTU

**French, Donald Graham, 1873–1945**

THE APPEAL OF POETRY. Toronto, McClelland, 1923. 137p [BM BVaU NSHD OKQ

THE CANADIAN WRITERS' NOTE BOOK. Toronto, Writers' Studio, 1932. 73p [OTU

POINTS ABOUT POETRY. Ridgewood, N.J., Editor Co., 1910. 85p [BVaU LC OTP

**Freshman, Rev. Charles, 1819–1875**

THE JEWS AND THE ISRAELITES. Their Religion, Philosophy, Traditions and Literature. Toronto, Dredge, 1870. 456p [NSHD OTU QMM

**Freund, Philip, 1909–**

HOW TO BECOME A LITERARY CRITIC. New York, Beechhurst, 1947. 200p [BVaU LC QMM

**Frye, Northrop, 1912–**

ANATOMY OF CRITICISM. Four Essays. Princeton, N.J., Princeton U. Press, 1957. x + 383p

FEARFUL SYMMETRY. A Study of William Blake. Princeton, N.J., Princeton U. Press, 1947. 462p [BM BVaU LC NSHD OTU QMM

SOUND AND POETRY. Ed. with an intro. by ——. New York, Columbia U. Press, 1957. xxvii + 156p

**Geikie, John Cunningham, 1824–1906**

RALPH WALDO EMERSON: HIS WRITINGS AND OPINIONS. A Lecture. Toronto, Geikie, 1859. 28p [NSWA OTP

**George, Rev. James, 1801?–1870**

A BRIEF INQUIRY INTO THE CAUSES OF THE POETIC ELEMENT IN THE SCOTTISH MIND. A Lecture. ... Kingston, Creighton, 1857. 60p [NSWA OLU

**Gibbon, John Murray, 1875–1952**

THE MAGIC OF MELODY. London, Dent, [1933]. 128p [BVaU OKQ QMM

MELODY AND THE LYRIC, FROM CHAUCER TO THE CAVALIERS. London, Dent, [1930]. 204p [BVaU NBFU OTU QMM

**Glazebrook, George Parkin de Twenebrokes, 1900–**

THE HARGRAVE CORRESPONDENCE, 1821–1843. Ed. by ——. Toronto, Champlain Society, 1938. 472p [BM BVaU LC NSHD OTU

**Gordon, Robert Kay, 1887–**

ANGLO-SAXON POETRY. Selected and trans. by ——. London, Dent, 1927. 367p [BM BVaU LC NBFU OTU

THE STORY OF TROILUS. As Told by Benoit de Saint-Maure, Giovanni Boccaccio (translated into English prose), Geoffrey Chaucer, and Robert Henryson. Trans. and intro. by ——. London, Dent, 1934. 388p [BM BVaU LC NBFU OTU QMM

**Goudge, Thomas Anderson, 1910–**

THE THOUGHTS OF C.S. PEIRCE. Toronto, U. of Toronto Press, 1950. 360p [BM BVaU LC NBFU OTU

**Graff, Willem Laurens, 1890–**

LANGUAGE AND LANGUAGES. An Introduction to Linguistics. New York, Appleton, 1932. 487p [BM BVaU OTU

RAINER MARIA RILKE. Creative Anguish of a Modern Poet. Princeton, N.J., Princeton U. Press, 1956. x + 353p

**Grafstein, Melech W.**

ISAAC LEIBUSH PERETZ. Published in Commemoration of his 100th Birthday. Ed. by ——. London, Ont., Jewish Observer, [1951?] 55 + 57p

**Graham, Franklin Thomas, 1869–**

HISTRIONIC MONTREAL. Annals of the Montreal Stage, with Biographical and Critical Notices of the Plays and Players of a Century. 2nd ed. Montreal, Lovell, 1902. 303p [BVaU OTU

**Graham, William Creighton, 1887–1955**

THE PROPHETS AND ISRAEL'S CULTURE. Chicago, U. of Chicago Press, 1934. 117p [BM BVaU LC NBFU OTU

**Grant, Douglas, 1921–1969**

JAMES THOMSON, POET OF "THE SEASONS." London, Cresset, 1951. 308p

**Grant, George Parkin, 1918–**

PHILOSOPHY IN THE MASS AGE. Toronto, Copp Clark, 1959. ix + 117p

**Grant, Rev. Robert, 1824?–1900**

ROBERT BURNS: VINDICATED. Halifax, Nova Scotia Print., 1883. 15p [NSWA

**Grant, William Lawson, 1872–1935**

A PURITAN AT THE COURT OF LOUIS XIV. Kingston, Jackson, 1913. 17p [BVaU LC NBFU OTUV QMM

**Greene, Donald Johnson, 1916–**

THE POLITICS OF SAMUEL JOHNSON. New Haven, Yale U. Press, 1960. xix + 354p

**Greenshields, Edward Black, 1850–**

LANDSCAPE PAINTING AND MODERN DUTCH ARTISTS. Toronto, Copp Clark, 1906. 229p [BVaU LC NSHD OTU QMM

SUBJECTIVE VIEW OF LANDSCAPE PAINTING. With Special Reference to J.H. Weissenbruch and Illustrations from Works of His in Canada. Montreal, Desbarats, 1904. 58p [QMM

**Griffin, Arthur Kent, 1893–**

ARISTOTLE'S PSYCHOLOGY OF CONDUCT. London, Williams & Norgate, 1932. 186p [Ph.D. Thesis, U. of Toronto.] [BVaU LC NSHD OTU

**Griffin, Frederick, 1798–1879**

JUNIUS DISCOVERED. Boston, Little Brown, 1854. 310p [An attempt to identify Junius with Thomas Pownall, 1722–1805.] [BM LC NSHD OLU QMM

**Groom, Bernard, 1892–**

THE DICTION OF POETRY FROM SPENSER TO BRIDGES. Toronto, U. of Toronto Press, in association with McMaster University, 1955. 284p

**Grube, Georges Maximilien Antoine, 1899–**

THE DRAMA OF EURIPIDES. London, Methuen, [1941]. 456p [BM BVaU LC NSHD OTU QMM

PLATO'S THOUGHT. London, Methuen, 1935. 320p [Reprinted, 1958.] [BM BVaU LC NSHD OTU QMM

**Guillet, Edwin Clarence, 1898–**

EARLY CANADIAN LITERATURE. Literary Pioneers of the Old Newcastle District. Toronto, 1942. 2v [Letters re Stricklands, Traills, Moodies, etc.] [OTP

**Guthrie, Norman Gregor, 1877–1929**

THE POETRY OF ARCHIBALD LAMPMAN. Toronto, Musson, 1927. 58p [BVaU MWU NBFU OTP

**Hall, Fernau**

AN ANATOMY OF BALLET. London, Melrose, 1953. 470p

**Hamilton, Robert Morris, 1912–**

CANADIAN QUOTATIONS AND PHRASES, LITERARY AND HISTORICAL. Comp. by ——. Toronto, McClelland, 1952. 272p

**Hammond, Melvin Ormond, 1876–1934**

PAINTING AND SCULPTURE IN CANADA. Toronto, Ryerson, 1930. 72p [BVaU LC NSHD OTU QMM

**Harper, John Murdoch, 1845–1919**

THE ORIGIN AND DEVELOPMENT OF THE GREEK DRAMA. Quebec, "Morning Chronicle," 1883. 35p [OTU

**Harris, John**

A REVIEW OF MACAULAY'S TEACHING ON THE RELATIONSHIP OF THEOLOGY TO THE SCIENCE OF GOVERNMENT. ... By Kuklos (J.H.) [pseud]. Montreal, 1874. 2v [BM OLU QMM

**Harris, Rev. William Richard, 1847–1923**

THE CATHOLIC ATMOSPHERE OF SHAKESPEARE'S DRAMAS. Toronto, "The Rainbow" (Loretto Abbey), [1917?]. 13p [OTU

**Hartley, Rev. H.A.S.**

CLASSICAL TRANSLATIONS. ... Saint John, McMillan, 1889. 134p [NSHD

**Harvey, Rev. Moses, 1820–1901**

LECTURES, LITERARY AND BIOGRAPHICAL. Edinburgh, Elliot, 1864. 512p [LC NSHD

THOUGHTS ON THE POETRY AND LITERATURE OF THE BIBLE. St. John's, McConnan, 1853. 28p [NSWA

**Hemlow, Joyce, 1906–**

THE HISTORY OF FANNY BURNEY. Oxford, Clarendon, 1958. xvi + 528p

**Hendel, Charles William, 1890–**

JEAN-JACQUES ROUSSEAU, MORALIST. London, Oxford U. Press, 1934. 2v [BM BVaU LC NSHD OTU QMM

STUDIES IN THE PHILOSOPHY OF DAVID HUME. Princeton, Princeton U. Press, 1925. 420p [BM BVaU LC NBFU OTU QMM

**Heuser, Alan, 1926–**

THE SHAPING VISION OF GERARD MANLEY HOPKINS. London, Toronto, Oxford U. Press, 1958. 128p

**Hines, Rev. Bede, 1918–**

THE SOCIAL WORLD OF ALDOUS HUXLEY. Montreal, Author, 1954. 104p

**Hirschfelder, Jacob Maier, 1819–1902**

AN ESSAY ON THE SPIRIT AND CHARACTERISTICS OF HEBREW POETRY. [Toronto? 1855?] 37p [OTP

**Hoare, John Edward, 1886–**

THE PSYCHOLOGY OF PLAYWRITING. New York, Dramatists Play Service, 1949. 211p [BM BVaU

**Hopkins, John Castell, 1864–1923**

LIFE AND WORK OF MR. GLADSTONE. Toronto, Bradley-Garretson, 1895. 498p [BVaU NBFU OTP QMU

**Housser, Frederick Broughton, 1889–1936**

A CANADIAN ART MOVEMENT. The Story of the Group of Seven. Toronto, Macmillan, 1926. 221p [BM BVaU NSHD OTU QMM

**Howay, Frederick William, 1867–1943**

PRESIDENTIAL ADDRESS: THE EARLY LITERATURE OF THE NORTHWEST COAST. Ottawa, Royal Society, 1924. 31p [BVaU OTP

**Howse, Rev. Ernest Marshall, 1902–**

SPIRITUAL VALUES IN SHAKESPEARE. New York, Abingdon Press, 1955. 158p

**Hubbard, Robert Hamilton, 1916–**

AN ANTHOLOGY OF CANADIAN ART. Ed. by ——. Toronto, Oxford U. Press, 1960. 187p

EUROPEAN PAINTINGS IN CANADIAN COLLECTIONS. Earlier Schools, edited with an Essay on Picture Collecting in Canada. Toronto, Oxford U. Press, 1956. xxv + 154p

**Hughes, James Laughlin, 1846–1935**

DICKENS AS AN EDUCATOR. New York, Appleton, 1901. 319p [BM BVaU LC NBFU OTP QMM

**Hurst, George Leopold, 1868–**

THE LITERARY BACKGROUND OF THE NEW TESTAMENT. New York, Macmillan, 1928. 163p [BM BVa OTU

AN OUTLINE OF THE HISTORY OF CHRISTIAN LITERATURE. New York, Macmillan, 1926. 547p [BM OTP QMM

SACRED LITERATURE. London, Dent, 1905. 152p [BM NSHD

**Hutchinson, Rev. Daniel Falloon**

A CLASS BOOK ON RHETORIC, WHEREIN ARE EXHIBITED THE GRACES AND STYLE OF ENGLISH COMPOSITION AND PUBLIC ORATORY. Belleville, Bowell & Moore, 1850. 103p [BM LC NSHD OTP

**Hutton, Maurice, 1856–1940**

THE GREEK POINT OF VIEW. London, Hodder, 1925. 207p [BM BVaU LC NSHD OKQ QMM

**Irving, John Allan, 1903–**

PHILOSOPHY IN CANADA. A Symposium. Ed. by ——. Toronto, U. of Toronto Press, 1952. 48p

SCIENCE AND VALUES. Explorations in Philosophy and the Social Sciences. Toronto, Ryerson, 1952. xi + 148p

**Irving, William Henry, 1891–**

THE PROVIDENCE OF WIT IN THE ENGLISH LETTER WRITERS. Durham, N.C., Duke U. Press, 1955. 382p

**James, Charles Canniff, 1863–1916**

A TENNYSON PILGRIMAGE, and TENNYSON THE IMPERIALIST. Toronto, 1910. 22p [LC OTP

**Jefferys, Charles William, 1869–1951**

SAM SLICK IN PICTURES. The Best of the Humour of Thomas Chandler Haliburton. Ed. by Lorne Pierce. Toronto, Ryerson, 1956. xx + 204p

**Jetter, Marianne Rose (Weiss), 1911–**

THE "ISLAND MOTIF" IN PROSE WORKS OF ERNST WIECHERT. Vancouver, Continental Book Centre, 1957. 96p

**Johnson, Allison Heartz, 1910–**

WHITEHEAD'S PHILOSOPHY OF CIVILIZATION. Boston, Beacon Press, 1958. xi + 211p

WHITEHEAD'S THEORY OF REALITY. Boston, Beacon Press, 1952. xiii + 262p

THE WIT AND WISDOM OF ALBERT WHITEHEAD. Ed. by ——. Boston, Beacon Press, 1947. 102p [LC NBFU

THE WIT AND WISDOM OF JOHN DEWEY. Ed. by ——. Boston, Beacon Press, 1949. 111p [LC OTU

**Johnstone, John Keith, 1923–**

THE BLOOMSBURY GROUP. A Study of E.M. Forster, Lytton Strachey, Virginia Woolf, and their Circle. London, Secker & Warburg, 1954. x + 383p

**Jordan, Rev. William George, 1852–1939**

VOLTAIRE, THE CRUSADER. Toronto, Ryerson, 1930. 64p [OTU

**Kennedy, Roderick Stuart, 1889–1953**

BIBLIOGRAPHY OF G.A. HENTY & HENTYANA. By R.S. Kennedy & B.J. Farmer. London, B.J. Farmer, 1956. 93p [mimeographed]

**Kenner, William Hugh, 1923–**

DUBLIN'S JOYCE. London, Chatto & Windus, 1955. xi + 372p

GNOMON. Essays on Contemporary Literature. New York, McDowell Obolensky, 1958. 300p

WYNDHAM LEWIS. London, Methuen, 1954. xv + 169p

**King, Rev. John Mark, 1829–1899**

A CRITICAL STUDY OF "IN MEMORIAM." Toronto, Morang, 1898. 253p [BVaU OTP

**King, Thomas Davies, 1819–1884**

BACON VERSUS SHAKESPEARE. A Plea for the Defendant. Montreal, Lovell, 1875. 187p [BVaU OTP

LECTURE OF "SHAKESPEARE AND HIS MORAL INFLUENCES." Montreal, Salter, 1859. [OOC

SHALL WE OPEN SHAKESPEARE'S GRAVE? NO. A Reply ... to ... J. Parker Norris. ... Montreal, Robinson, 1884. 30p [BM BVaU OTP

**King, William Lyon Mackenzie, 1874–1950**

INDUSTRY AND HUMANITY. A Study in the Principles underlying Industrial Reconstruction. Toronto, Allen, 1918. 567p [BM BVaU NSHD OTP QMBM

**Kirkconnell, Watson, 1895–**

THE CELESTIAL CYCLE. The Theme of Paradise Lost in World Literature, with Translations of the Major Analogues. Toronto, U. of Toronto Press, 1952. 701p

THE EUROPEAN HERITAGE. A Synopsis of European Cultural Achievement. Toronto, Dent, 1930. 184p [BM BVaU LC NSHD OTP

THE HUMANITIES IN CANADA. By Watson Kirkconnell and A.S.P. Woodhouse. Ottawa, Humanities Research Council, 1947. 287p [BM BVaU LC NSHD OKQ QMM

**Kirkwood, Kenneth Porter, 1899–**

ARNOLD J. TOYNBEE, PHILOSOPHER OF HISTORY. An Address Given at the British Council, Karachi, March 29, 1953. Karachi, priv. print., 1953. 30p

DID SHAKESPEARE VISIT DENMARK? Karachi, Process Pakistan, 1953. 74p

A GARDEN IN POLAND. [On Chopin] Karachi, priv. print., 1953. 34p

THE IMMORTAL MEMORY OF ROBERT BURNS. Ottawa, priv. print., 1958. 7 + 68p

MAUD. An Essay on Tennyson's Poem. Ottawa, Le Droit, 1951. 216p

OPHELIA OF ELSINORE. Ottawa, priv. print., 1958. 162p

RENAISSANCE IN JAPAN. A Cultural Survey of the Seventeenth Century. Tokyo, Meiji Press, 1938. 414p [BM BVaU OTU QMM

UNFAMILIAR LAFCADIO HEARN. Tokyo, Hokuseido Press, 1936, 97p [LC QMM

**Kirkwood, Mossie May (Waddington), 1890–**

THE DEVELOPMENT OF BRITISH THOUGHT FROM 1820 TO 1890. With Special Reference to German Influences. By Mossie May Waddington. Toronto, Dent, 1919. 194p [BM BVaU LC OTP

**Klinck, Carl Frederick, 1908–**

EDWIN J. PRATT, THE MAN AND HIS POETRY. By Henry W. Wells and Carl F. Klinck. Toronto, Ryerson, 1947. 197p [BVaU LC NBFU OTU QMM

WILFRED CAMPBELL. A Study in Late Provincial Victorianism. Toronto, Ryerson, 1942. 289p [BM BVaU LC MWU NSHD OTU QMM

**Lacey, Alexander, 1887–**

PIXERECOURT AND THE FRENCH ROMANTIC DRAMA. Toronto, U. of Toronto Press, 1928. 88p [BM BVaU LC OTP

**Lambert, Richard Stanton, 1894–**

THE ADVENTURE OF CANADIAN PAINTING. Toronto, McClelland, 1947. 226p [BVaU NBFU OTU QMM

THE FORTUNATE TRAVELLER. A Short History of Touring and Travel for Pleasure. London, Melrose, 1950. 242p [OONL

PICTURES FOR LASTING PLEASURE, BY SIX CANADIAN ARTISTS. Toronto, Laing Galleries, 1943. 23p [BVa

**Lande, Lawrence Montague, 1906–**

OLD LAMPS AGLOW. An Appreciation of Early Canadian Poetry. Montreal, Author, 1957. xiv + 329p

**Lapp, John Clarke, 1917–**

ASPECTS OF RACINIAN TRAGEDY. Toronto, U. of Toronto Press, 1955. x + 195p

**Lathern, Rev. John, 1831–1905**

INSTITUTE LECTURES: Cromwell, Cobden, Havelock and the English Reformers. Saint John, McMillan, 1871. 106p [NBFU OOP

**Lauriston, Victor, 1881–**

ARTHUR STRINGER, SON OF THE NORTH. Biography and Anthology. Toronto, Ryerson, 1941. 178p [BM BVaU LC NSHD OTU QMM

**Lavell, Cecil Fairfield, 1872–1948**

A BIOGRAPHY OF THE GREEK PEOPLE. Boston, Houghton, 1934. 297p [BM BVa LC NSHD OTU QMM

THE EVOLUTION OF GREEK MORAL EDUCATION. ... Kingston, Jackson Press, 1911. 97p [LC

**Lawrence, Margaret Isabel**

THE SCHOOL OF FEMININITY. A Book for and about Women as they are Interpreted through Feminine Writers of Yesterday and Today. Toronto, Nelson, 1936. 382p [Pub. in England as: WE WRITE AS WOMEN. London, Joseph, 1937. 314p] [BM BVa OLU QMM

**Leacock, Stephen Butler, 1869–1944**

CHARLES DICKENS, HIS LIFE AND WORK. London, Davies, 1933. 275p [BM BVaU LC NSHD OTU

ELEMENTS OF POLITICAL SCIENCE. ... Boston, Houghton, 1906. 417p [Several later eds.] [BM BVaU NSHD OTU

THE GREATEST PAGES OF AMERICAN HUMOR. Selected and discussed by ——. Garden City, Doubleday, 1916. 293p [BM BVaU LC OTU QMM

THE GREATEST PAGES OF CHARLES DICKENS. A Biographical Reader and a Chronological Selection from the Works of Dickens. With a Commentary on his Life and Art. Garden City, Doubleday, 1934. 233p [QMM

HUMOUR AND HUMANITY. An Introduction to the Study of Humour. London, Butterworth, 1937. 254p [BM BVaU LC NBFU OTU QMM

HUMOR, ITS THEORY AND TECHNIQUE. With Examples and Samples: A Book of Discovery. Toronto, Dodd Mead, 1935. 268p [BM BVaU OTU QMM

LAHONTAN'S VOYAGES. Ed. with intro. and notes by ——. Ottawa, Graphic, 1932. 348p [BM BVaU NBFU QMM

MARK TWAIN. London, Davies, 1932. 167p [BM BVaU LC OTU QMM

**LeRossignol, James Edward, 1866–**

THE ETHICAL PHILOSOPHY OF SAMUEL CLARKE. Leipzig, 1892. 98p [Dissertation for Ph.D. degree at Leipzig.] [OLU QMM

**Leroy, Albert**

THE FORMS OF VALUE. The Extension of Hedonistic Axiology. Toronto, Oxford U. Press, 1950. 352p

**Lewis, Jay, 1881–1947**

OTHER MEN'S MINDS. The Critical Writings of Jay Lewis. New York, Putnam, 1948. 172p [LC

**Lighthall, William Douw, 1857–1954**

THE COSMIC ASPECT OF THE OUTER CONSCIOUSNESS. Montreal, Author, 1924. 16p [BVaU OKQ QMM

THE PERSON OF EVOLUTION; THE OUTER CONSCIOUSNESS; THE OUTER KNOWLEDGE; THE DIRECTIVE POWER. Studies of Instinct as Contributions to a Philosophy of Evolution. Montreal, Kennedy, 1930. 216p [Enlarged ed.: Toronto, Macmillan, 1933. 246p] [BM BVaU NSWA OTP QMM

A PHILOSOPHY OF PURPOSE. Montreal, Author, 1920. 15p [OTU

SKETCH OF NEW UTILITARIANISM, INCLUDING A CRITICISM OF THE ORDINARY ARGUMENT FROM DESIGN AND OTHER MATTER. Montreal, Witness, 1887. 40p [BM QMM

SPIRITUALIZED HAPPINESS-THEORY; OR, NEW UTILITARIANISM. A Lecture before the Farmington School of Philosophy. Montreal, Witness, 1890. 22p [BM NSWA OTU

SUPERPERSONALISM. The Outer Consciousness, a Biological Entity. ... Montreal, Witness, 1926. 115p [BM BVaU NSHD OKQ QMM

THE TELEOLOGY OF THE OUTER CONSCIOUSNESS. Montreal, Author, 1924. 13p [BVaU OTU

**Lodge, Rupert Clendon, 1886–**

THE GREAT THINKERS. London, Routledge, 1949. 310p [BM LC NSHD OTU QMM

AN INTRODUCTION TO MODERN LOGIC. Minneapolis, Perine Book Co., 1920. 361p [BM BVaU LC QMM

THE MEANING AND FUNCTION OF SIMPLE MODES IN THE PHILOSOPHY OF JOHN LOCKE. Minneapolis, U. of Minnesota, 1918. 86p [BM BVaU LC NSHD OTU QMM

PHILOSOPHY OF EDUCATION. London, Harper, 1937. 328p [BM BVaU LC NBFU OOSU QMM

THE PHILOSOPHY OF PLATO. London, Routledge-Paul, 1956. ix + 347p

PLATO'S THEORY OF ART. London, Routledge-Paul, 1953. 316p

PLATO'S THEORY OF EDUCATION. ... London, Kegan Paul, 1947. 322p [BM BVaU LC NSHD OTP QMM

PLATO'S THEORY OF ETHICS. The Moral Criterion, and the Highest Good. London, Kegan Paul, 1928. 558p [BM BVaU LC NBFU OLU QMM

THE QUESTIONING MIND. A Survey of Philosophical Tendencies. London, Dent, 1937. 311p [BM LC OTP

**Logan, John Daniel, 1869–1929**

AESTHETIC CRITICISM IN CANADA. Its Aims, Methods and Status. ... Toronto, McClelland, 1917. 29p [BM NBFU OTP

DALHOUSIE UNIVERSITY AND CANADIAN LITERATURE. Being the History of an Attempt to have Canadian Literature included in the Curriculum of Dalhousie University. With a Criticism and a Justification. Halifax, Author, 1922. 24p [BVaU NBFU OTP

HIGHWAYS OF CANADIAN LITERATURE. A Synoptic Introduction to the Literary History of Canada (English) from 1760 to 1924. By J.D. Logan and Donald G. French. Toronto, McClelland, 1924. 418p [BM BVaU LC NBFU OTP

A LITERARY CHAMELEON. A New Estimate of Mr. H.L. Mencken. Milwaukee, Author, 1926. 26p [LC NBFU OTP

MARJORIE PICKTHALL. Her Poetic Genius and Art. Halifax, Allen, 1922. 44p [BM BVaU NSHD OTP

THE RELIGIOUS FUNCTIONS OF COMEDY. 1907. [NBFU

SCOTT AND HALIBURTON. An Essay in the Psychology of Creative Satiric Humor. Halifax, Allen, 1921. 22p [BM BVaU NBFU OTP

**Lomer, Gerhard Richard, 1882–1970**

STEPHEN LEACOCK. A Check-List and Index of his Writings. Ottawa, National Library, 1954. 153p

**Long, Marcus, –1968**

THE SPIRIT OF PHILOSOPHY. Toronto, U. of Toronto Press, 1953. 306p

**Luckyj, George Stephen Nestor, 1919–**

LITERARY POLITICS IN THE SOVIET UKRAINE, 1917–1934. New York, Columbia U. Press, 1956. x + 323p

**McAleer, George, 1845–**

A STUDY IN THE ETYMOLOGY OF THE INDIAN PLACE NAME MISSISQUOI. Worcester, Blanchard Press, 1906. 104p [BM BVaU OLU

**McArthur, Peter, 1866–1924**

STEPHEN LEACOCK. Toronto, Ryerson, 1923. 176p [BM LC NSHD OTU

**MacCallum, Reid, 1897–1949**

IMITATION & DESIGN AND OTHER ESSAYS. Ed. by William Blissett. Toronto, U. of Toronto Press, 1953. xvii + 209p

TIME LOST AND REGAINED. The Theme of Eliot's Four Quartets. Toronto, priv. print., [1949?]. 26p [BVaU OTP

**McCaul, Rev. John, 1807–1887**

BRITANNO-ROMAN INSCRIPTIONS, WITH CRITICAL NOTES. Toronto, Rowsell, 1863. 290p [OTU

CHRISTIAN EPITAPHS OF THE FIRST SIX CENTURIES. Toronto, Chewett, 1869. 72p [OTP

THE METERS OF THE GREEK TRAGEDIES EXPLAINED AND ILLUSTRATED. Dublin, Milliken, 1828. 115p [OTP

**McCourt, Edward Alexander, 1907–1972**

THE CANADIAN WEST IN FICTION. Toronto, Ryerson, 1949. 131p [BVaU NBFU OTU QMBM

**Macdonald, Daniel Joseph, 1881–**

THE RADICALISM OF SHELLEY AND ITS SOURCES. Washington, Catholic Education Press, 1912. 143p [BM BVaU LC NSHD OTU

**Macdonald, John Ford, 1878–**

WILLIAM HENRY DRUMMOND. Toronto, Ryerson, [1923?]. 132p [BM BVaU LC NSHD OTU QMBM

**MacDonald, John Harry**

MARJORIE PICKTHALL. Sunny Brae, N.S., 1927. 109p [An M.A. thesis.] [NSHD

**Macdonald, Thoreau, 1901–**

THE GROUP OF SEVEN. Toronto, Ryerson, 1944. 34p [3rd ed., 1952.] [BVaU LC NSHD OTP QMM

**MacDonald, Wilbert Lorne, 1879–**

BEGINNINGS OF THE ENGLISH ESSAY. Toronto, U. of Toronto Library, 1914. 122p [BM BVaU LC OTP QMM

POPE AND HIS CRITICS. A Study in Eighteenth Century Personalities. London, Dent, 1951. 340p

**McGee, Thomas D'Arcy, 1825–1868**

GALLERY OF IRISH WRITERS. The Irish Writers of the Seventeenth Century. Dublin, 1846. [BM OLU

**MacGillivray, James Robertson**

KEATS. A Bibliography and Reference Guide, with an Essay on Keats' Reputation. Toronto, U. of Toronto Press, 1949. 210p [BM BVaU LC NBFU OTP QMM

**McGregor, Patrick, 1816–1882**

A SYSTEM OF LOGIC, COMPRISING A DISCUSSION OF THE VARIOUS MEANS OF ACQUIRING AND RETAINING KNOWLEDGE AND AVOIDING ERROR. New York, 1862. 469p [NBFU

**McIlwraith, Jean Newton, 1859–1938**

A BOOK ABOUT LONGFELLOW. London, Nelson, 1900. 165p [BM OTP

A BOOK ABOUT SHAKESPEARE. London, Nelson, 1898. 222p [BM OLU

**MacKay, Louis Alexander, 1901–**

THE WRATH OF HOMER. Toronto, U. of Toronto Press, 1948. 131p [BVaU LC NSHD OTP QMM

**Macklem, Michael**

THE ANATOMY OF THE WORLD. Relations between Natural and Moral Law from Donne to Pope. Minneapolis, U. of Minnesota Press, 1958. 189p

**MacLean, Kenneth**

AGRARIAN AGE. A Background for Wordsworth. New Haven, Yale U. Press, 1950. 103p [BM BVaU LC NSHD OTUV

JOHN LOCKE AND ENGLISH LITERATURE OF THE EIGHTEENTH CENTURY. New Haven, Yale U. Press, 1936. 176p [BM BVaU OTU QMM

**McLelland, Rev. Joseph Cumming, 1925–**

THE VISIBLE WORDS OF GOD. An Exposition of the Sacramental Theology of Peter Martyr Vermigli, A.D. 1500–1562. Edinburgh, Oliver & Boyd, 1957. ix + 291p

**MacLennan, Hugh, 1907–**

OXYRHYNCHUS. An Economic and Social Study. Princeton, Princeton U., 1935. 93p [LC OTU

**McLuhan, (Herbert) Marshall, 1911–**

THE MECHANICAL BRIDE. Folklore of Industrial Man. New York, Vanguard Press, 1951. 157p

**MacLure, Millar, 1917–**

THE PAUL'S CROSS SERMONS, 1534–1642. Toronto, U. of Toronto Press, 1958. 261p

**MacMechan, Archibald McKellar, 1862–1933**

HEAD-WATERS OF CANADIAN LITERATURE. Toronto, McClelland, 1924. 247p [BM BVaU LC NSHD OTP

THE CENTENARY OF HALIBURTON'S "NOVA-SCOTIA." Halifax, Author, 1930. 15p [BVaU NSHD OTP QMM

CONCERNING THE OLDEST ENGLISH LITERATURE. Halifax, Bowes, 1889. 22p [OTU

THE RELATION OF HANS SACHS TO THE DECAMERON, AS SHOWN IN AN EXAMINATION OF THE THIRTEEN SHROVETIDE PLAYS DRAWN FROM THAT SOURCE. Halifax, Nova Scotia Print., 1889. 81p [BM NSHD OTU

VERGIL. [An Appreciation.] N.p., 1897. 25p [OTU

**MacMurchy, Archibald, 1832–1912**

HANDBOOK OF CANADIAN LITERATURE (ENGLISH). Toronto, Briggs, 1906. 236p [BM BVaU LC NBFU OTP QMBM

**McRae, Douglas George Wallis, 1908–**

THE ARTS AND CRAFTS OF CANADA. Toronto, Macmillan, 1944. 80p [BM BVaU LC OTP QMM

**MacTavish, Newton McFaul, 1875–1941**

ARS LONGA. Toronto, Ontario Pub. Co., 1938. 236p [BVaU LC OTP

THE FINE ARTS IN CANADA. Toronto, Macmillan, 1925. 181p [BM BVaU LC NSHD OTP QMM

**Mahon, Rev. Alexander Wylie, 1853–1930**

CANADIAN HYMNS AND HYMN WRITERS. Saint John, Globe, 1908. 56p [BVaU LC NBFU OTP QMBM

**Marquis, Thomas Guthrie, 1864–1936**

ENGLISH-CANADIAN LITERATURE. Toronto, Glasgow Brook, 1913. 103p [BM BVaU NBFU OTP QMM

**Martin, Burns, 1895–**

ALLAN RAMSAY. A Study of his Life and Works. Cambridge, Mass., Harvard U. Press, 1931. 203p [BVaU NBFU OTY

**Masta, Henry Lorne, 1853–**

ABENAKI INDIAN LEGENDS, GRAMMAR, AND PLACE NAMES. Victoriaville, Que., La Voix des Bois-Francs, 1932. 110p [BViV NBSM OTP QMBM

**Maura, Sister (née Mary Power), 1881–1957**

SHAKESPEARE'S CATHOLICISM. Cambridge, Riverside Press, 1924. 171p [BVaU LC NBFU QMM

**Medley, Rev. John, 1804–1892**

THE BOOK OF JOB. Trans. from the Hebrew Text, with an Intro., a Summary of each Chapter, and Brief Notes in Explanation of Obscure Passages. ... Saint John, McMillan, 1879. 149p [NBFU OLU

**Meek, Theophile James, 1881–**

HEBREW ORIGINS. The Haskell Lectures for 1933–34, the Graduate School of Theology, Oberlin College. New York, Harper, 1936. 220p [Rev. ed., Toronto, U. of Toronto Press, 1951. 246p] [BM BVaU LC NSHD OTP

**Meikle, W.**

THE CANADIAN NEWSPAPER DIRECTORY. Containing a Complete List of all the Newspapers in Canada, the Circulation of each, and all Information in Reference thereto. Toronto, Blackburn's City Steam Press, 1858. 60p [OTU

**Michener, Norah Eveline (Willis), 1902–**

MARITAIN ON THE NATURE OF MAN IN A CHRISTIAN DEMOCRACY. Hull, Editions "L'Eclair," 1955. xiii + 149p

**Middleton, Jesse Edgar, 1872–1960**

THE FIRST CANADIAN CHRISTMAS CAROL. Toronto, Rous, 1927. 15p [OTU

**Miller, Muriel, 1908–**

BLISS CARMAN. A Portrait. Toronto, Ryerson, 1935. 136p [BVaU LC NBFU OTP QMM

G.A. REID, CANADIAN ARTIST. Toronto, Ryerson, 1946. 230p [BM LC NBFU OTP QMBM

HOMER WATSON, THE MAN OF DOON. Toronto, Ryerson, 1938. 164p [LC OTP QMM

**Mitchell, Roy, 1884–1944**

CREATIVE THEATRE. New York, Day, 1929. 256p [BM BVaU LC OTP QMM

THE SCHOOL-THEATRE. A Handbook of Theory and Practice. Toronto, Nat. Council of Education, 1925. 104p [BM BVaU LC OTP QMM

SHAKESPEARE FOR COMMUNITY PLAYERS. Toronto, Dent, 1919. 142p [BM BVa LC OTP QMM

**Mitchell, Thomas H., 1865–1945**

THE DRAMA OF LIFE. A Series of Reflections on Shakespeare's "Seven Ages." Toronto, Allen, 1922. 183p [BM BVaU LC OTU

**Moore, William Francis, 1851–1935**

INDIAN PLACE NAMES IN ONTARIO. Toronto, Macmillan, 1930. 48p [BVaU OLU QMM

**Morgan, Henry James, 1842–1913**

BIBLIOTHECA CANADENSIS; or, A Manual of Canadian Literature. Ottawa, Desbarats, 1867. 411p [BM BVaU LC NBFU OTP

**Morris, Edmund Montague, 1871–1913**

ART IN CANADA: The Early Painters. [Toronto, 1911?] 40p [BM LC OTP QMBM

**Morrison, A.H.**

THE ART GALLERY OF THE ENGLISH LANGUAGE. Toronto, Williamson, 1886. 282p [BM NSWA OKQ

**Morse, William Inglis, 1874–1952**

BLISS CARMAN. Bibliography, Letters, Fugitive Verses, and Other Data. Windham, Conn., Hawthorne House, 1941. 86p [BM BVaU LC NSHD OKQ

**Moyse, Charles Ebenezer, 1852–1924**

DRAMATIC ART OF SHAKESPEARE. With Special Reference to "A Midsummer Night's Dream." Montreal, 1879. 34p [NSHPL QMM

POETRY AS A FINE ART. A University Lecture delivered in McGill College, Montreal. Montreal, "Witness," 1882. 30p [Also: London, 1883. 79p] [BM BVaU OTP QMM

**Muddiman, Bernard**

THE MEN OF THE NINETIES. London, Danielson, 1920. 145p [BM BVaU LC OTU

**Munn, Allan Macgregor, 1920–**

FREE-WILL AND DETERMINISM. Toronto,, U. of Toronto Press, 1960. 218p

**Murphy, George Henry, 1875–1958**

SHAKESPEARE AND THE ORDINARY MAN. Toronto, Ryerson, 1939. 41p [BM LC NBFU OTU

**Murray, Rev. John Clark, 1836–1917**

THE BALLADS AND SONGS OF SCOTLAND. In View of their Influence on the Character of the People. London, Macmillan, 1874. 205p [BM LC NSHD OTP QMM

A HANDBOOK OF PSYCHOLOGY. London, Gardner, 1885. 422p [Also: Boston, DeWolfe Fiske, 1897.] [BVaU NSHD QMM

A HANDBOOK OF CHRISTIAN ETHICS. Edinburgh, Clark, 1908. 328p [BM LC OLU QMM

AN INTRODUCTION TO ETHICS. Boston, De Wolfe Fiske, 1891. 407p [BM LC NSHD QMM

OUTLINE OF SIR WILLIAM HAMILTON'S PHILOSOPHY. ... Boston, Gould & Lincoln, 1870. 257p [BM BVaU LC NBFU

**Murray, John Tucker**

ENGLISH DRAMATIC COMPANIES, 1558–1642. London, Constable, 1910. 2v [BM BVaU LC NSHD OTP QMM

**Mustard, Wilfred Pirt, 1864–1932**

CLASSICAL ECHOES IN TENNYSON. New York, Macmillan, 1904. 164p [BM LC NSHD OTU QMM

TENNYSON AND VIRGIL. Baltimore, Author, 1899. 11p [OTU

**Needler, George Henry, 1866–1962**

GOETHE AND SCOTT. Toronto, Oxford U. Press, 1950. 140p [BM BVaU NBFU OTP

JOHN GALT'S DRAMAS. A Brief Review. Toronto, U. of Toronto Press, 1945. 39p [BM LC OTP

THE LONE SHIELING. Origin and Authorship of the Blackwood "Canadian Boat-Song." Toronto, U. of Toronto Press, 1941. 109p [BM BVaU LC NBFU OTP QMM

MOORE AND HIS CANADIAN BOAT SONG. Toronto, Ryerson, 1950. 14p [NSHD OTP

RICHARD COEUR DE LION IN LITERATURE. Leipzig, Fock, 1890. 75p [BM BVaU OTU

**Neville, Kenneth Percival Rutherford, 1876–**

THE CASE CONSTRUCTION AFTER THE COMPARATIVE IN LATIN. Ithaca, N.Y., Cornell U., 1901. 86p [Also in Cornell Studies in Classical Philology, XV.] [BM LC NSHD OTU

**Nichols, Mark Edgar, 1873–1961**

(CP) THE STORY OF THE CANADIAN PRESS. Toronto, Ryerson, 1948. 327p [BM BVaU LC OTU QMM

**Norwood, Gilbert, 1880–1954**

THE ART OF TERENCE. Oxford, Blackwell, 1923. 156p [BM BVaU LC NSHD OTU QMM

ESSAYS ON EURIPIDEAN DRAMA. Berkeley, U. of California Press; London, Cambridge U. Press; Toronto, U. of Toronto Press, 1954. 197p

EURIPIDES AND SHAW WITH OTHER ESSAYS. Boston, Luce, 1921. 226p [BM BVaU LC NBFU OTU QMM

GREEK COMEDY. London, Methuen, 1931. 413p [BM BVaU LC NBFU OTP QMM

GREEK TRAGEDY. London, Methuen, 1920. 394p [4th ed., 1948] [BM BVaU LC NSHD OOU QMM

PINDAR. Berkeley, U. of California Press, 1945. 302p [BM BVaU LC NBFU OTU QMM

PLAUTUS AND TERENCE. New York, Longmans, 1932. 212p [BM BVaU LC NBFU OTU QMM

THE RIDDLE OF "THE BACCHAE." The Last Stage of Euripides' Religious Views. Manchester, U. Press, 1908. 188p [BM LC NSHD OTU

THE WRITERS OF GREECE. London, Oxford U. Press, 1925. 142p [BM BVa LC NSHD OTU QMM

**O'Donnell, J. Reginald, 1907–**

NINE MEDIAEVAL THINKERS. A Collection of Hitherto Unedited Texts. Ed. by ——. Toronto, Pontifical Institute of Mediaeval Studies, 1955. xi + 382p

**O'Hagan, Thomas, 1855–1939**

THE GENESIS OF CHRISTIAN ART. New York, Macmillan, 1926. 170p [BM LC OTP

STUDIES IN POETRY: CRITICAL. Boston, Marlier & Callanan, 1900. 114p [BM LC

WHAT SHAKESPEARE IS NOT. Toronto, Hunter Rose, 1936. 115p [LC OTU QMM

**O'Higgins, Harvey Jerrold, 1876–1929**

ALIAS WALT WHITMAN. Newark, N.J., Carteret, 1930. 49p [LC

**Osborne, William Frederick, 1873–1950**

THE GENIUS OF SHAKESPEARE, AND OTHER ESSAYS. Toronto, Briggs, 1908. 149p [BM BVaU NSHD OKQ

**Osler, William, 1849–1919**

JOHN KEATS, THE APOTHECARY POET. Baltimore, Friedenwald, 1896. 18p [LC

**Owen, Eric Trevor, 1882–1948**

THE HARMONY OF AESCHYLUS. Toronto, Clarke Irwin, 1952. 130p

THE STORY OF THE ILIAD. As Told in the Iliad. Toronto, Clarke Irwin, 1946. 248p [BM BVaU LC MWU NBFU OTU

**Pacey, Desmond, 1917–**

CREATIVE WRITING IN CANADA. A Short History of English-Canadian Literature. Toronto, Ryerson, 1952. 220p [2nd ed., rev. & enl., 1961. 314p]

FREDERICK PHILIP GROVE. Toronto, Ryerson, 1945. 150p [BVaU LC NBFU OTP

TEN CANADIAN POETS. A Group of Biographical and Critical Essays. Toronto, Ryerson, 1958. ix + 350p

**Patterson, Rev. George, 1824–1897**

NOTES ON THE DIALECT OF THE PEOPLE OF NEWFOUNDLAND. [Montreal? 1894.] 19p [NSWA QMM

NOTES ON THE FOLK-LORE OF NEWFOUNDLAND. [No title page.] 6p [NSWA QMM

NEWFOUNDLAND FOLK-LORE AND DIALECT. Boston, American Folk-Lore Society, 1895. 40p [OTP

**Peardon, Thomas Preston, 1899–**

THE TRANSITION IN ENGLISH HISTORICAL WRITING 1760–1830. New York, Columbia U. Press, 1933. 341p [BM BVaU LC NBFU QMM

**Percival, Walter Pilling, 1885–1966**

LEADING CANADIAN POETS. Ed. by ——. Toronto, Ryerson, 1948. 271p [BVaU LC NBFU OTP QMM

**Peter, John Desmond, 1921–**

COMPLAINT AND SATIRE IN EARLY ENGLISH LITERATURE. Oxford, Clarendon, 1956. 323p

A CRITIQUE OF PARADISE LOST. New York, Columbia U. Press, 1960. ix + 172p

**Peterson, William, 1856–1921**

COLLATIONS FROM THE CODEX CLUNIACENSIS S. HOLKHAMICUS. A Ninth Century Manuscript of Cicero. With Hitherto Unpublished Scholia, and a History of the Codex. Oxford, Clarendon, 1901. 62 + 14p [BM LC QMM

**Pierce, Lorne Albert, 1890–1961**

ALFRED, LORD TENNYSON AND WILLIAM KIRBY. Unpublished Correspondence, to which are added Some Letters from Hallam, Lord Tennyson. Toronto, Macmillan, 1929. 71p [BM BVaU OTP QMSS

BLISS CARMAN'S SCRAP-BOOK. A Table of Contents. Ed. with a postscript by ——. Toronto, Ryerson, 1931. 19p [An index to Carman's scrapbook of his fugitive verse, 1883–1921.] [BM BVaU LC NBFU OTP QMM

ENGLISH CANADIAN LITERATURE, 1882–1932. Ottawa, 1932. 8p [BVaU NBFU OTP QMM

THE HOUSE OF RYERSON. Toronto, Ryerson, 1954. 52p

AN OUTLINE OF CANADIAN LITERATURE (French and English). Toronto, Ryerson, 1927. 251p [BM BVaU LC NSHD OTU QMM

UNEXPLORED FIELDS OF CANADIAN LITERATURE. Toronto, Ryerson, 1932. 32p [BVaU NBFU OTP QMM

**Pomeroy, Elsie May, 1886–**

G.B. LANCASTER: 1873–1945. A Canadian Tribune. Toronto, priv. print., 1948. 16p [NBFU OTP

**Porter, Harry Culverwell**

REFORMATION AND REACTION IN TUDOR CAMBRIDGE. Cambridge, Eng., University Press, 1958. x + 461p

**Priestley, Francis Ethelbert Louis, 1905–**

WILLIAM GODWIN'S ENQUIRY CONCERNING POLITICAL JUSTICE AND ITS INFLUENCE ON MORALS AND HAPPINESS. Photographic facsimile of the 3rd ed., corrected and ed. with variant readings, and with a critical intro. and notes by ——. Toronto, U. of Toronto Press, 1946. 3v [BM BVaU LC OTU

**Raftis, James Ambrose, 1922–**

THE ESTATES OF RAMSEY ABBEY. A Study in Economic Growth and Organization. Toronto, Pontifical Institute of Mediaeval Studies, 1957. xvii + 341p

**Rand, Rev. Silas Tertius, 1810–1889**

DICTIONARY OF THE LANGUAGE OF THE MICMAC INDIANS, who Reside in N.S.,

N.B., P.E.I., Cape Breton and Newfoundland. Halifax, Nova Scotia Print., 1888. 286p [BM BVaU LC NBFU OTU QMM

A FIRST READING BOOK IN THE MICMAC LANGUAGE. Halifax, Nova Scotia Print., 1875. 108p [BM NSHD OTU

MICMAC PLACE NAMES IN THE MARITIME PROVINCES AND GASPE PENINSULA ... 1852 ... 1890. Ottawa, Surveyor's Office, 1919. 116p [BVaU LC OTU

**Rashley, Richard Ernest, 1909–**

POETRY IN CANADA, THE FIRST THREE STEPS. Toronto, Ryerson, 1958. xvii + 166p

**Raymond, Rev. William Odber, 1853–1923**

SELECTIONS FROM SWINBURNE. Ed. by William Odber Raymond. New York, Harcourt, 1925. 392p [OTU

**Raymond, William Odber, 1880–**

THE INFINITE MOMENT AND OTHER ESSAYS IN ROBERT BROWNING. Toronto, U. of Toronto Press, 1950. 249p [BM BVa NBFU OTP QMM

**Rhodenizer, Vernon Blair, 1886–1968**

AT THE SIGN OF THE HAND AND PEN. Nova-Scotian Authors. N.p., Canadian Authors' Association., Nova Scotia Branch, 1948. 43p [BVaU NSWA OTP

A HANDBOOK OF CANADIAN LITERATURE. Ottawa, Graphic, 1930. 295p [Also: Toronto, Nelson, 1932. 295p] [BM BVaU LC NBFU OTP QMM

**Ridington, John, 1868–1945**

LIBRARIES IN CANADA. A Study of Library Conditions and Needs. By the Commission of Enquiry, John Ridington, Chairman, Mary J.L. Black, George H. Locke. Toronto, Ryerson, 1933. 153p [BVaU LC NBFU OTU

THE POETRY OF THE WAR. An Address delivered before the Pacific Northwest Library Association ... Portland, Oregon. ... Vancouver, priv. print., 1917. 40p [BVaU LC

**Robbins, William, 1909–**

THE ETHICAL IDEALISM OF MATTHEW ARNOLD. A Study of the Nature and Sources of his Moral and Religious Ideas. Toronto, U. of Toronto Press, 1959. xi + 259p

**Roberts, Charles George Douglas, 1860–1943**

ALASTOR AND ADONAIS. By Percy Bysshe Shelley. Ed. with an Essay on "The Pastoral Elegy" by ——. Boston, Silver Burdett, 1902. 108p [LC

**Roberts, Rev. Richard, 1874–1945**

THE PREACHER AS MAN OF LETTERS. London, Dent, 1931. 216p [BM BVaU OTP

THAT ONE FACE. Studies of the Place of Jesus in the Minds of Poets and Prophets. New York, Association Press, 1919. 199p [BVaU LC OLU

**Robertson, John Charles, 1864–1956**

THE GORGIANIC FIGURES IN EARLY GREEK PROSE. Baltimore, Friedenwald, 1893. 41p [BM OTU

THE STORY OF GREECE AND ROME, THEIR GROWTH AND THEIR LEGACY TO OUR WESTERN WORLD. By J.C. Robertson and H.G. Robertson. London, Dent, 1928. 352p [BM BVaU OTU QMM

**Robertson, Percy, 1874–**

CONTEMPORARY AUTHORS OF FORMER TIMES. A Chart and an Index. Comp. by ——. Toronto, [1944?]. [BM OTP QMM

**Robins, John Daniel, 1884–1952**

A BOOK OF CANADIAN HUMOUR. Ed. by J.D. Robins and Margaret V. Ray. Toronto, Ryerson, 1951. 308p

**Robson, Albert Henry, 1882–1939**

A.Y. JACKSON. Toronto, Ryerson, 1938. 32p [BVaU LC NBFU OTP QMBM

CANADIAN LANDSCAPE PAINTERS. Toronto, Ryerson, 1932. 227p [BM BVaU LC NBFU OTP, QMM

CLARENCE A. GAGNON, R.C.A., LL.D. Toronto, Ryerson, 1938. 32p [BVaU LC NBFU OTP QMBM

CORNELIUS KRIEGHOFF. Toronto, Ryerson, 1937. 32p [BVaU NBFU OTP QMM

J.E.H. MACDONALD. Toronto, Ryerson, 1937. 32p [BVaU LC NBFU OTP QMM

PAUL KANE. Toronto, Ryerson, 1938. 32p [BVaU LC NBFU OTP QMBM

TOM THOMSON. Toronto, Ryerson, 1937. 32p [BVaU LC OTP QMM

**Ross, Malcolm Mackenzie, 1911–**

THE ARTS IN CANADA. Stock-taking at Mid-Century. ... Ed. by ——. Toronto, Macmillan, 1958. 176p

MILTON'S ROYALISM. A Study of the Conflict of Symbol and Idea in the Poems. Ithaca, Cornell U. Press, 1943. 152p [BM BVaU NSHD OTU

POETRY & DOGMA. The Transfiguration of Eucharistic Symbols in Seventeenth Century English Poetry. New Brunswick, N.J., Rutgers U. Press, 1954. xii + 256p

**Ross, Philip Dansken, 1858–1949**

CANADIAN POETS AND THE SHORT WORD. Ottawa, Author, 1938. 23p [OTU

SHORT WORD IN ENGLISH POETRY. Ottawa, Author, 1937. [UTQ

**Rothstein, Samuel, 1921–**

THE DEVELOPMENT OF REFERENCE SERVICES THROUGH ACADEMIC TRADITIONS, PUBLIC LIBRARY PRACTICE, AND SPECIAL LIBRARIANSHIP. Chicago, Association of College and Reference Libraries, 1955. ix + 124p

**Roy, Rev. James, 1834–1922**

LAW IN LANGUAGE. A Thesis. Montreal, Witness, 1883. 23p [NSWA

**Roy, James Alexander, 1884–**

COWPER AND HIS POETRY. London, Harrap, 1914. 181p [BM LC OTU

IS THERE A SCOTTISH LITERATURE? Kingston, Queen's University, 1945. 16p [LC OTP

JAMES MATTHEW BARRIE. An Appreciation. London, Jarrolds, 1937. 255p [BM BVa LC NSHD OTP QMM

**Salmon, Edward Togo, 1905–**

A HISTORY OF THE ROMAN WORLD FROM 30 B.C. TO A.D. 138. 3rd ed. London, Methuen, 1957. xiii + 365p [First pub. 1944. 2nd ed. rev. 1950.]

**Salter, Frederick Millet, 1895–1962**

MEDIAEVAL DRAMA IN CHESTER. Toronto, U. of Toronto press, 1955. xi + 138p

**Sandilands, John**

WESTERN CANADIAN DICTIONARY AND PHRASE BOOKS. Explaining in Plain English ... the Meaning of the Most Popular Canadianisms, Colloquialisms, and Slang. ... 2nd ed. Winnipeg, Telegram, 1912. 30p [BM BVaU LC OTU

**Sandwell, Bernard Keble, 1876–1954**

THE MUSICAL RED BOOK OF MONTREAL. A Record of Music in Montreal from 1895 to 1907. Ed. by ——. Montreal, 1907. 229p [QMM

**Saunders, Henry Scholey, 1864–1951**

ILLUSTRATIONS TO WALT WHITMAN'S LEAVES OF GRASS. Toronto, Author, n.d. 122p [Edition limited to 10 copies.] [LC

AN INTRODUCTION TO WALT WHITMAN. Toronto, Author, 1934. 25p [LC OTP QMM

PARODIES ON WALT WHITMAN. Comp. by ——. New York, American Library Service, 1923. 171p [LC OTU

PORTRAIT GALLERY OF WHITMAN WRITERS. With Quotations. Comp. by ——. Toronto, Author, 1927. 122p [Ten copies made.] [LC

WHITMAN MUSIC. Comp. by ——. Toronto, Saunders, 1940. 16p [Typewritten.] [LC

WHITMAN PORTRAITS. With Notes. Comp. by ——. Toronto, Author, 1922. 73p [Nine copies made.] [LC

WHITMAN PORTRAITS. With Notes. Comp. by ——. Toronto, Author, 1923. 114p [Contains over 500 mounted photographs with typewritten descriptions. Four copies made.] [LC

**Scadding, Rev. Henry, 1813–1901**

FIRST GAZETTEER OF UPPER CANADA. Toronto, Copp, 1876. 23p [OTU

SHAKESPEARE, THE SEER, THE INTERPRETER. Address delivered before the St. George's Society ... April 23, 1864. Toronto, Copp Clark, 1864. 88p [OTP

SOME CANADIAN NOMS-DE-PLUME IDENTIFIED. Toronto, Copp Clark, 1877. 57p [LC NSWA OTP

SOME LAPSED NAMES IN CANADIAN LOCAL NOMENCLATURE. 1897. [OTU

**Sedgewick, Garnett Gladwin, 1882–1949**

OF IRONY, ESPECIALLY IN DRAMA. Toronto, U. of Toronto Press, 1935. 100p [Also: Toronto, U. of Toronto Press, 1948. 127p [BM BVaU LC NSHD OTP QMM

**Shaw, James Eustace, 1876–1962**

ESSAYS ON THE VITA NUOVA. Princeton, U. Press, 1929. 236p [BM BVaU LC OTU

GUIDO CAVALCANTI'S THEORY OF LOVE. ... Toronto, U. of Toronto Press, 1949. 228p [BM LC OTP

THE LADY "PHILOSOPHY" IN THE CONVIVIO. Cambridge, Mass., Dante Society, 1938. 29p [BM LC OTU

**Shea, Albert A.**

CULTURE IN CANADA. A Study of the Findings of the Royal Commission on National Development in the Arts, Letters and Sciences, (1949-1951). Ed. by —— Toronto, CORE Pub., 1952. 65p

**Shoolman, Regina Lenore, 1909–**

THE ENJOYMENT OF ART IN AMERICA. A Survey of the Permanent Collections of Painting, Sculpture, Ceramics & Decorative Arts in American and Canadian Museums. By Regina Shoolman and Charles E. Slatkin. Philadelphia, Lippincott, 1942. 792p [LC OTP QMM

SIX CENTURIES OF FRENCH MASTER DRAWINGS IN AMERICA. By Regina Shoolman and Charles E. Slatkin. New York, Oxford U. Press, 1950. 256p [LC OTP

THE STORY OF ART. The Lives and Times of the Great Masters. By Regina Shoolman and Charles Slatkin. New York, Halcyon, 1940. 332p [LC QMM

**Sime, Jessie Georgina, 1880–**

THOMAS HARDY OF THE WESSEX NOVELS. An Essay and Biographical Note. Montreal, Carrier, 1928. 58p [BVaU NBFU OTU QMSS

**Sinden, Margaret Jane, 1915–**

GERHART HAUPTMANN. The Prose Plays. Toronto, U. of Toronto Press, 1957. 238p

**Slater, Rev. Robert Henry Lawson, 1896–**

PARADOX AND NIRVANA. A Study of Religious Ultimates, with Special Reference to Burmese Buddhism. Chicago, U. of Chicago Press, 1951. 145p

**Smith, Arthur James Marshall, 1902–**

THE POETRY OF ROBERT BRIDGES. Montreal, Burton's, n.d. 15p [QMM

**Smith, Goldwin, 1823–1910**

THE ALLUSIONS IN "LOTHAIR." N.p., n.d. 4p [OTU

COWPER. New York, Harper, 1880. 128p [Same title: New York, Acme Library, 1880. Series 2. 363p] [BM BVaU LC NBFU OTU QMM

THE FEDERALIST. Collection of Essays by Alexander Hamilton, John Jay, and James Madison. With a special intro. by ——. New York, Colonial Press, 1901. 488p [OTU

LIFE OF COWPER. New York, Lovell, 1884. 82p [Same title: Toronto, Copp Clark, 1894. 166p] [LC NSWA OTU

LIFE OF JANE AUSTEN. London, Scott, 1890. 195p [BM BVaU LC NBFU OKQ QMM

QUAENAM FUERIT MULIERUM APUD VETERES GRAECOS CONDITIO? [Inquiry into the Status of Woman in Ancient Greece.] Oxford, Macpherson, 1846. 32p [OTU

SHAKESPEARE, THE MAN. An Attempt to find Traces of the Dramatist's Character in his Drama. Toronto, Morang, 1899. 60p [BM BVaU LC MWU NBFU OTP QMM

SPECIMENS OF GREEK TRAGEDY. Trans. by ——. New York, Macmillan, 1893. 2v [BM NBFU

**Smith, Grant F.O., 1877–1949**

THE MAN ROBERT BURNS. Toronto, Ryerson, 1940. 396p [BM BVaU LC NBFU OTU

ROBERT BURNS, 1759–1796. Comp. by ——. Toronto, 1936. 47p [MWP OTU

**Smith, Marion (Bodwell), 1912–**

MARLOWE'S IMAGERY AND THE MARLOWE CANON. Philadelphia, 1940. 213p [BVaU LC QMM

**Smith, Wilfred Cantwell, 1916–**

ISLAM IN MODERN HISTORY. Princeton, N.J., Princeton U. Press, 1957. ix + 317p

**Sprigge, Elizabeth, 1900–**

THE STRANGE LIFE OF AUGUST STRINDBERG. London, Hamilton, 1949. 246p [BM BVaU NBFU OTP

**Sproat, Gilbert Malcolm, 1832–1913**

SIR WALTER SCOTT AS A POET. Edinburgh, Montreal, 1871. [BM

**Sprott, Samuel Ernest**

MILTON'S ART OF PROSODY. Oxford, Blackwell, 1953. xi + 147p

**Stanley, Carleton Wellesley, 1886–1971**

MATTHEW ARNOLD. Toronto, U. of Toronto Press, 1938. 163p [BM BVaU LC NSHD OTP QMM

ROOTS OF THE TREE. Toronto, Oxford U. Press, 1936. 107p [BM LC NBFU OTP QMM

**Stern, Karl, 1906–**

THE THIRD REVOLUTION. A Study of Psychiatry and Religion. New York, Harcourt, 1954. xii + 306p

**Stevenson, Lionel, 1902–**

APPRAISALS OF CANADIAN LITERATURE. Toronto, Macmillan, 1926. 272p [BM BVaU LC NBFU OTP QMM

DARWIN AMONG THE POETS. Chicago, U. Press, 1932. 357p [BM BVaU LC NBFU OTU

DR. QUICKSILVER. The Life of Charles Lever. London, Chapman & Hall, 1939. 308p [BM BVaU LC OTP QMM

THE ENGLISH NOVEL. A Panorama. Boston, Houghton, 1960. 539p

THE ORDEAL OF GEORGE MEREDITH. New York, Scribner, 1953. 368p

THE SHOWMAN OF VANITY FAIR. The Life of William Makepeace Thackeray. New York, Scribner, 1947. 405p [BM BVaU LC NBFU OTP QMM

**Stevenson, Orlando John, 1869–1950**

A PEOPLE'S BEST. Toronto, Musson, 1927. 266p [BVaU NBFU OTU QMBM

**Stewart, Alexander Charles, 1867–1944**

THE POETICAL REVIEW. A Brief Notice of Canadian Poets and Poetry. Toronto, Anderson, 1896. 24p [OTP

**Stewart, George, 1848–1906**

ESSAYS FROM REVIEWS. First series: Quebec, Dawson, 1892. 171p [Second series: Quebec, Dawson, 1893. 159p] [BM BVaU NSHD OTP QMM

EVENINGS IN THE LIBRARY. Bits of Gossip about Books and those who Write them. Saint John, Morrow, 1878. 254p [BVaU LC NBFU OTP QMM

THE GENIUS AND LIFE-WORK OF LONGFELLOW. A Paper read before the Literary and Historical Society of Quebec. Quebec, Chronicle, 1883. 26p [NSWA

LECTURE ON ALCOTT. Delivered before the Literary and Historical Society of Quebec. Quebec, Chronicle, 1880. 27p [NSWA

THOREAU. The Hermit of Walden. Quebec, Morning Chronicle, 1882. 30p [NSHD OTP

**Stewart, Herbert Leslie, 1882–1953**

ANATOLE FRANCE, THE PARISIAN. Toronto, Dodd Mead, 1927. 394p [BVaU LC NSHD OTP QMM

NIETZSCHE AND THE IDEALS OF MODERN GERMANY. London, Arnold, 1915. 235p [BVaU LC NSHD OTU QMM

QUESTIONS OF THE DAY IN PHILOSOPHY AND PSYCHOLOGY. London, Arnold, 1912. 284p [BVaU LC NSHD OTU QMM

WINGED WORDS. Sir Winston Churchill as Writer and Speaker. Toronto, Ryerson, 1953. 114p

**Stewart, James McGregor, 1889–1955**

RUDYARD KIPLING. A Bibliographical Catalogue. Ed. by A.W. Yeats. Toronto, Dalhousie U. Press and U. of Toronto Press, 1959. xv + 673p

**Stockelbach, Mrs. Lavonia Ruth**

THE BIRDS OF SHAKESPEARE. London, Batsford, 1954. xiv + 94p

**Stone, Rev. James Samuel, 1852–**

RICHARD HOOKER. A Sketch of his Life, Writings, and Times. Toronto, Hunter, 1882. 48p [NSWA OTU

THOMAS CRANMER, ARCHBISHOP AND MARTYR. An Essay. Toronto, Hunter, 1882. 83p [NSWA OTP

**Story, George Morley, 1927–**

A NEWFOUNDLAND DIALECT DICTIONARY. A Survey of the Problems. St. John's, Memorial University, 1956. 14p

**Stratton, Thomas, 1816–1886**

THE AFFINITY BETWEEN THE HEBREW LANGUAGE AND THE CELTIC. 2nd ed., 1870. [3rd ed., Edinburgh, 1872.] [BM OLU

ILLUSTRATIONS OF THE AFFINITY OF THE LATIN LANGUAGE TO THE GAELIC OR CELTIC OF SCOTLAND. Toronto, Scobie, 1840. 26p [BM OTP

ILLUSTRATIONS OF THE AFFINITY OF THE LATIN LANGUAGE TO THE GAELIC OR CELTIC OF SCOTLAND AND TO THE LANGUAGE SPOKEN IN THE COUNTRY OF GLENGARRY, UPPER CANADA. Kingston, 1839. 91p [Manuscript.] [BM QMM

PROOFS OF THE CELTIC ORIGIN OF A GREAT PART OF THE GREEK LANGUAGE. Kingston, Chronicle & Gazette Office, 1840. 8p [BM OTP

**Stringer, Arthur John Arbuthnot, 1874–1950**

RED WINE OF YOUTH. A Life of Rupert Brooke. Indianapolis, Bobbs-Merrill, 1948. 287p [BVa LC NBFU OTU QMM

A STUDY IN KING LEAR. [MOR'12

**Sutherland, John, 1919–1956**

THE POETRY OF E.J. PRATT. A New Interpretation. Toronto, Ryerson, 1956. 109p

**Sykes, Frederick Henry, 1863–1918**

FRENCH ELEMENTS IN MIDDLE ENGLISH. Oxford, Hart, 1899. 64p [BM LC OTP QMM

POEMS OF ALFRED TENNYSON AND ROBERT BROWNING. With intro. and notes by ——. Toronto, Gage, 1907. 224p [BM OTU

SYLLABUS OF A COURSE OF SIX LECTURES ON ENGLISH WRITERS OF THE PRESENT ERA: Carlyle, Newman, Kingsley, Ruskin, Matthew Arnold, Kipling. Philadelphia, American Soc. for Extension of University Teaching, 1899. 35p [OTU

SYLLABUS OF A COLLEGIATE COURSE OF THIRTY LECTURES ON SHAKESPEARE. New York, Teachers' College, Columbia U., 1903. 31p [LC

**Talbot, Thomas, fl. 1844–1882**

GREECE AND THE GREEKS; or, A Historic Sketch of Attic Life and Manners. London, Sampson Low, etc., 1881. 334p [BM OTP

THE HEBREWS AT HOME; or, An Historical Sketch ... of the Ancient Hebrews. Montreat, Lovell, 1874. 270p [BM

**Tardivel, Jules Paul, 1857–1905**

BORROWED AND STOLEN FEATHERS; or, A Glance through Mr. J.M. Lemoine's latest work, THE CHRONICLES OF THE ST. LAWRENCE. Quebec, "Le Canadien," 1878. 33p [BVaU LC NSWA OTP QMM

**Taylor, Henry, fl. 1819–1860**

AN ATTEMPT TO FORM A SYSTEM OF THE CREATION OF OUR GLOBE, OF THE PLANETS, AND THE SUN OF OUR SYSTEM. ... Toronto, Coates, 1836. 119p [2nd ed. rev. and enl.: Quebec, Cowan, 1840. 136p] [3rd ed. rev. and enl.: Montreal, Becket, 1842. 156p] [9th ed. rev. and enl.: Quebec, Bureau & Marcotte, 1854. 213p] [Haight quotes from preface: "The original manuscript of this work was composed between the years 1819 and 1825."] [BM NSWA OOA QMM

CLASSIC ART. An Exponent of Religious Sentiment. A Lecture delivered ... Belleville, Ont., June 21st, 1875. New York, Great American Print., 1875. 28p [NSWA

**Taylor, Rev. William Edington, 1877–**

THE ETHICAL AND RELIGIOUS THEORIES OF BISHOP BUTLER. Toronto, Bryant, 1903. 79p [BM BVaU OTU

**Thomas, Clara Eileen (McCandless), 1919–**

CANADIAN NOVELISTS, 1920–1945. Toronto, Longmans, 1946. 141p [BM BVaU LC NBFU OTU QMM

**Thompson, Claude Willett**

HUMANISM IN ACTION. Toronto, Pitman, 1950. 275p [BVaU OTU

WILLIAM WOOD, CANADIAN HISTORIAN AND AUTHOR: BIBLIOGRAPHY. Forty Years of Study and Writing, 1896–1936. Montreal, n.p., 1939. 12p [OTU

**Todd, Henry Cook, –1862**

A MANUAL OF ORTHOEPY. With Numerous Notes upon the Origin and Abuse of

Words. 4th ed. with large additions and corrections. [Anon] York, Office of the Guardian, 1833. 104p [First pub. in London, 1832.] [BM OTP QMM

**Toronto, Ont. Public Libraries**

CANADIAN PERIODICAL INDEX, 1931–. Toronto, Public Libraries, 1931–. [A continuing serial, which suspended publication 1933–37.] [BM BVaU LC NSHD OTP QMM

**Toronto, University of. University College**

STUDIES IN ENGLISH. By Members of University College. Collected by ... Malcolm W. Wallace. Toronto, U. of Toronto Press, 1931. 254p [BVaU NBFU OTU

**Tovell, Ruth (Massey), 1889–**

FLEMISH ARTISTS OF THE VALOIS COURTS. ... Toronto, U. of Toronto Press, 1950. 157p [BM BVaU LC OTP

**Tracy, Clarence, 1908–**

THE ARTIFICIAL BASTARD. A Biography of Richard Savage. Toronto, pub. in co-operation with the U. of Saskatchewan by U. of Toronto Press, 1953. xvii + 164p

**Turnbull, Jane Mason, 1896–**

ESSENTIAL TRAITS OF FRENCH-CANADIAN POETRY. Toronto, Macmillan, 1938. 225p [An abstract was pub. at the U. of Chicago, 1937. 27p] [BM BVaU LC NSHD OTU

**Ullman, Solomon Baruch, 1908–**

CULTURE AND JUDAISM. Selected Essays. Toronto, Lieberman's Jewish Book Centre, 1956. 184p

**Vickery, Mrs. Olga Westland, 1925–**

THE NOVELS OF WILLIAM FAULKNER. A Critical Interpretation. Baton Rouge, Louisiana State U. Press, 1959. x + 269p

WILLIAM FAULKNER. Three Decades of Criticism. Ed. with an intro. and bibliography by Frederick J. Hoffman and Olga W. Vickery. New ed. East Lansing, Michigan State U. Press, 1960. xi + 428p [First ed. 1951.]

**Wallace, Malcolm William, 1873–1960**

ENGLISH CHARACTER AND THE ENGLISH LITERARY TRADITION. Toronto, U. of Toronto Press, 1952. viii + 78p

THE LIFE OF SIR PHILIP SIDNEY. Cambridge, U. Press, 1915. 428p [BM BVaU LC NBFU OTP QMM

**Walter, Hermann, 1863–1952**

HEINRICH HEINE. A Critical Examination of the Poet and his Works. London, Dent, 1930. 322p [MWU NSHPL OTY

MOSES MENDELSSOHN, CRITIC AND PHILOSOPHER. New York, Bloch, 1930. 220p [MWU OLU NSHPL

**Warnock, Amelia Beers (Mrs. John Garvin), 1878–1956**

ISABELLA VALANCY CRAWFORD. By Katherine Hale [pseud]. Toronto, Ryerson, 1923. 125p [BM BVaU NSHD OTU

**Watson, John, 1847–1939**

CHRISTIANITY AND IDEALISM. New York, Macmillan, 1897. xxxvii + 292p [BM BVaU LC NSHD OTU QMM

COMTE, MILL, AND SPENCER. New York, Macmillan, 1895. 302p [BM BVaU NSHD OTU QMM

HEDONISTIC THEORIES FROM ARISTIPPUS TO SPENCER. New York, Macmillan, 1895. 248p [BM BVaU LC NSHD OTP QMM

THE INTERPRETATION OF RELIGIOUS EXPERIENCE. Glasgow, Maclehose, 1912. 2v [BM BVaU LC OTP

KANT AND HIS ENGLISH CRITICS. A Comparison of Critical and Empirical Philosophy. Glasgow, Maclehose, 1881. 402p [BM BVaU LC NSHD OTP QMM

AN OUTLINE OF PHILOSOPHY. With Notes Historical and Critical. ... New York, Macmillan, 1898. 489p [2nd ed. of COMTE, MILL, AND SPENCER.] [BM BVaU LC NSHD OTP QMM

THE PHILOSOPHICAL BASIS OF RELIGION. A Series of Lectures. Glasgow, Maclehose, 1907. 485p [BM BVaU LC NSHD OTP QMM

THE PHILOSOPHY OF KANT EXPLAINED. Glasgow, Maclehose, 1908. 515p [BM BVaU LC NBFU OTP

THE RELATION OF PHILOSOPHY TO SCIENCE. An Inaugural Lecture ... Queen's University, Kingston ... October 16th, 1872. Kingston, Bailie, 1872. 37p [OTP

SCHELLING'S TRANSCENDENTAL IDEALISM. Chicago, Griggs, 1882. 251p [BM LC NSHD OTU QMM

THE STATE IN PEACE AND WAR. Toronto, Macmillan, 1919. 296p [BM NBFU OLU QMM

**Webling, Peggy**

A SKETCH OF JOHN RUSKIN. London, Baines & Scarsbrook, 1916. 29p [BM BVaU

**West, Paul Noden, 1930–**

BYRON AND THE SPOILER'S ART. London, Chatto & Windus, 1960. 155p

THE FOSSILS OF PIETY. Literary Humanism in Decline. ... New York, Vantage Press, 1959. 85p

**Wetmore, Jessie Helen Louise**

SENECA'S CONCEPTION OF THE STOIC SAGE AS SHOWN IN HIS PROSE WORKS. Edmonton, U. of Alberta Press, 1936. 66p [BM BVaU OTU

**Whalley, George, 1915–**

COLERIDGE AND SARA HUTCHINSON AND THE ASRA POEMS. Toronto, U. of Toronto Press, 1955. xxi + 188p

THE POETIC PROCESS. An Essay in Poetics. London, Routledge, 1953. 256p

**Wharton, Lewis, 1885–**

FRANCOIS VILLON. Blackguard and Immortal. Vancouver, Seymour Press, 1931. 29p [BM BVaU LC OOP QMSS

**White, Mary E., 1908–**

STUDIES IN HONOUR OF GILBERT NORWOOD. Ed. by ——. Toronto, U. of Toronto Press, 1952. xvii + 278p

**Wiles, Roy McKeen, 1903–**

SERIAL PUBLICATION IN ENGLAND BEFORE 1750. Cambridge, Eng., U. Press, 1957. xv + 391p

**Williams, Cecil**

THE FOUNDATIONS OF INTELLIGENCE. New York, Comet Press Books, 1953. 126p

**Wilson, Daniel, 1816–1892**

CALIBAN, THE MISSING LINK. London, Macmillan, 1873. 274p [BM BVaU LC NSHD OTP QMM

CHATTERTON. A Biographical Study. London, Macmillan, 1869. 328p [BM LC OTU QMM

THE LOST ATLANTIS, AND OTHER ETHNOGRAPHIC STUDIES. Edinburgh, Douglas, 1892. 411p [BM BVaU LC OTU

MEMORIALS OF EDINBURGH IN THE OLDEN TIME. Edinburgh, 1848. 2v [Several later editions.] [BM LC OTU

OLIVER CROMWELL AND THE PROTECTORATE. London, Nelson, 1848. 304p [BM OLU

REMINISCENCES OF OLD EDINBURGH. Edinburgh, Douglas, 1898. [Same as MEMORIALS OF EDINBURGH ... ?] [BVaU

**Wilson, Harold Sowerby, 1904–**

ON THE DESIGN OF SHAKESPEARIAN TRAGEDY. Toronto, U. of Toronto Press, 1957. 256p

**Wilson, Harry Langford, 1867–1913**

THE METAPHOR IN THE EPIC POEMS OF PUBLIUS PAPINIUS STATIUS. Baltimore, Murphy, 1898. 30p [BM LC QMM

**Wilson, Milton Thomas, 1923–**

SHELLEY'S LATER POETRY. A Study of his Prophetic Imagination. New York, Columbia U. Press, 1959. 332p

**Wilson, Neil Leslie, 1922–**

THE CONCEPT OF LANGUAGE. Toronto, U. of Toronto Press, 1959. 153p

**Wilson, Richard Albert, 1874–1949**

THE MIRACULOUS BIRTH OF LANGUAGE. Preface by George Bernard Shaw. London, Dent, 1946. 196p [First pub. in 1937 under title: THE BIRTH OF LANGUAGE.] [BM BVaU OTP QMM

**Winspear, Alban Dewes, 1899–**

THE GENESIS OF PLATO'S THOUGHT. [2nd ed., rev.] New York, S.A. Russell, 1956. 390p [First pub., New York, Dryden Press, 1940.]

**Wood, Louis Aubrey Lorne, 1883–1955**

THE FORM AND ORIGIN OF MILTON'S ANTITRINITARIAN CONCEPTION. Inaugural Dissertation. London, Ont., Advertiser, 1911. 96p [BM NSHD OTP QMM

**Woodcock, George, 1912–**

THE ANARCHIST PRINCE. A Biographical Study of Peter Kropotkin. By George Woodcock and Ivan Avakumovic. New York, Boardman, 1950. 463p [BVaU LC NSHD OTU

BRITISH POETRY TO-DAY. An Address. ... Vancouver, U. of British Columbia, 1950. 15p [BVaU LC NBFU OTU

THE INCOMPARABLE APHRA. London, Boardman, 1948. 248p [Biography of Aphra Behn.] [BM BVaU LC OTU

LETTERS OF CHARLES LAMB. Selected, with intro. and notes by ——. London, Grey Walls Press, 1950. 227p [OTU

THE PARADOX OF OSCAR WILDE. New York, Macmillan, 1949. 250p [BM BVaU LC NSHD OTU

PIERRE-JOSEPH PROUDHON. A Biography. New York, Macmillan, 1956. 291p

WILLIAM GODWIN. A Biographical Study. London, Porcupine, 1946. 266p [BM BVaU LC NSHD OTU

**Woodhouse, Arthur Sutherland Pigott, 1895–1964**

MILTON THE POET. Vancouver, U. of British Columbia, Dent, 1955. 30p

PURITANISM AND LIBERTY. Being the Army Debates (1647–9) ... with Supplementary Documents. Selected and ed. with an intro. by ——. London, Dent, 1938. 100 + 506p [2nd ed.: Chicago, U. of Chicago Press, 1951.] [BM BVaU NBFU OTP QMM

**Woodhouse, Hugh Frederick**

THE DOCTRINE OF THE CHURCH IN ANGLICAN THEOLOGY, 1547–1603. New York, Macmillan, 1954. 223p

**Woodworth, Hugh MacCallum, 1906–**

THE NATURE AND TECHNIQUE OF UNDERSTANDING. Some Fundamentals of Semantics. Victoria, Author, 1949. 142p [BVaU OTU

**Yarrill, Eric Herbert, 1914–**

BROWNING'S "ROMAN MURDER STORY" AS RECORDED IN A HITHERTO UNKNOWN ITALIAN CONTEMPORARY MS. Trans. by ——. With intro. by W.O. Raymond. Waco, Texas, Baylor U., 1939. 47p [BVaU OTU

**Young, George Renny, 1802–1853**

ON COLONIAL LITERATURE, SCIENCE AND EDUCATION. Written with a View of Improving the Literary, Educational, and Public Institutions of British North America. In Three Volumes. Halifax, Crosskill, 1842. 363p [Apparently only v. 1 ever appeared, although the publication of v. 2 was promised "in June next," and its table of contents was included in v. 1 as an addendum.] [NBFU NSHD OLU OTP

# TRAVEL AND DESCRIPTION

Emigrant handbooks, early descriptions of Canada both general and local, travel journals, reports by Canadians of experiences and travel in Canada

**Abbott, Rev. Joseph, 1789–1863**

MEMORANDA OF A SETTLER IN LOWER CANADA; or, The Emigrant to North America. Being a Compendium of Useful Practical Hints. ... By an Emigrant Farmer [pseud]. Montreal, Lovell, 1842. 80p [2nd and 3rd eds. pub. under title: THE EMIGRANT TO NORTH AMERICA, from Memoranda of a Settler. ... Montreal, Lovell, 1843. 116p; Edinburgh, Blackwood, 1844. 120p] [BM LC NSWA OTP

**Alexander, James Edward, 1803–1885**

L'ACADIE; or, Seven Years' Explorations in British America. London, Colburn, 1849. 2v [BM BVaU NSHD OTP

TRANSATLANTIC SKETCHES ... in North and South America, and the West Indies. London, Bentley, 1833. 2v [BM BVaU LC NSHD OTP

**Anderson, Alexander Caulfield, 1814–1884**

THE DOMINION AT THE WEST. A Brief Description of ... British Columbia, its Climate and Resources. The Government Prize Essay, 1872. Victoria, Wolfenden, 1872. 112p [BVaU LC NSWA

NOTES ON NORTH-WESTERN AMERICA. Montreal, Mitchell & Wilson, 1876. 22p [BM BVaU LC OTP

**Anderson, Rev. David, 1814–1885**

THE NET IN THE BAY; or, Journal of a Visit to Moose and Albany. By the Bishop of Rupert's Land. London, Hatchard, 1854. 276p [BM BVaU LC NSWA OTP

**Anderson, William James, 1813?–1873**

THE VALLEY OF THE CHAUDIERE. Its Scenery and Gold Fields. Quebec, Morning Chronicle, 1872. 38p [OOA

**Anonymous**

THE FACE OF CANADA. Toronto, Clarke Irwin, 1959. x + 229p

LETTERS FROM CANADA WITH NUMEROUS ILLUSTRATIONS. Quebec, Morning Chronicle, 1862. 56p [Same title: London, Algar, 1863. 83p] [BVaU NSHP OTU QMSS

LETTERS FROM NOVA SCOTIA AND NEW BRUNSWICK ILLUSTRATIVE OF THEIR MORAL, RELIGIOUS, AND PHYSICAL CIRCUMSTANCES DURING THE YEARS 1826, 1827, AND 1828. Edinburgh, Waugh & Innes, 1829. 201p [LC NSHD OTU

NOTES OF OUR TRIP ACROSS BRITISH COLUMBIA. Hamilton, Spectator Print., 1889. 34p [OTU

**Armstrong, Nevill Alexander Drummond, 1878?–**

AFTER BIG GAME IN THE UPPER YUKON. London, Long, 1937. 287p [BM BVaU LC OLU

**Atkinson, Rev. William Christopher**

THE EMIGRANT'S GUIDE TO NEW BRUNSWICK. Berwick-upon-Tweed, Warder's Office, 1842. 124p [Title change: A HISTORICAL AND STATISTICAL ACCOUNT OF NEW BRUNSWICK. Edinburgh, Anderson and Bryce, 1844. 3rd ed. improved and corrected. 284p] [BVaU QMM

**Bailey, Joseph Whitman, 1865–1932**

THE ST. JOHN RIVER IN MAINE, QUEBEC, AND NEW BRUNSWICK. Cambridge, Riverside Press, 1894. 178p [LC NSWA OTU

**Baillie, Thomas, 1797?–1863**

AN ACCOUNT OF THE PROVINCE OF NEW BRUNSWICK ... with Advice to Emigrants. London, Rivington, 1832. 134p [BM BVaU NSWA OTP

**Baker, Everett**

TRAILS AND TRACES OF RUPERT'S LAND AND THE NORTH-WEST TERRITORIES AS SEEN FROM 1940–1955. Shaunavon, Sask., 1955. 40p

**Barbeau, Charles Marius, 1883–1969**

I HAVE SEEN QUEBEC. Toronto, Macmillan, 1957. 1v [unpaged]

PATHFINDERS IN THE NORTH PACIFIC. Toronto, Ryerson, 1958. 235p

**Barclay, Isabel**

WORLDS WITHOUT END. Explorations from 2000 Years B.C. to To-day. New York, Doubleday, 1956. 352p [Later pub. in three separate vols.: V.1: THE EARLY EXPLORERS. London, Dobson, 1957. 154p; V.2: THE GREAT AGE OF DISCOVERY. London, Dobson, 1958. 168p; V.3: FILLING IN THE MAP. London, Dobson, [1959. 191p]

**Barker, Bertram**

NORTH OF '53. London, Methuen, 1934. 242p [BM BViPA LC OTU

**Barnes, H.H.**

JOURNAL OF A TRIP TO MANITOBA AND BACK, JUNE AND JULY 1878. Halifax, Doley, 1879. 22p [NSHP

**Bartlett, Robert Abram, 1875–1946**

THE LAST VOYAGE OF THE KARLUK. Flagship of Vilhjalmar Stefansson's Canadian Arctic Expedition of 1913–16. As Related by her Master, Robert A. Bartlett, and here set down by Ralph T. Hale. Boston, Small Maynard, 1916. 329p [Title changed to: NORTHWARD HO! THE LAST VOYAGE OF THE KARLUK. Boston, Small Maynard, 1919. 329p] [BM BVaU LC NBFU OTU QMM

SAILS OVER ICE. New York, Scribner, 1934. 301p [BM BVa LC

**Baskine, Mrs. Gertrude**
HITCH-HIKING THE ALASKA HIGHWAY. Toronto, Macmillan, 1944. 317p [BM LC OTU QMM

**Beaven, Rev. James, 1801–1875**
RECREATIONS OF A LONG VACATION; or, A Visit to Indian Missions in Upper Canada. Toronto, Rowsell, 1846. 196p [BM BVaU LC NSWA OKQ QMM

**Bedford-Jones, Henry James O'Brien, 1887–1949**
THE MYTH WAWATAM; or, Alex. Henry Refuted [and] ... Remarks upon ... Fort Michillimackinac, All of Which is Herein Written & Publish'd from the Notes of Henry McConnell, Gent. Santa Barbara, Author, 1917. 21p [LC

**Belaney, George Stansfeld, 1888–1938**
THE MEN OF THE LAST FRONTIER. By Grey Owl [pseud]. Toronto, Macmillan, 1932. 253p [BM BVaU LC NBFU OKQ

**Bell, Charles Napier, 1854–1936**
THE JOURNAL OF HENRY KELSEY (1691–1692), the First White Man to Reach the Saskatchewan River from Hudson Bay. ... Winnipeg, Dawson Richardson, 1928. 43p [BVaU LC NSHD OLU
TANGWEERA, LIFE AND ADVENTURES AMONG GENTLE SAVAGES. London, Arnold, 1899. 318p [BM OTP

**Bell, Rev. William, 1780–1857**
HINTS TO EMIGRANTS. In a Series of Letters from Upper Canada. Edinburgh, Waugh & Innes, 1824. 236p [BVaU LC NSWA OTP

**Bennett, Rev. James, 1817–1901**
DOWN EAST: WHERE TO GO; WHAT TO DO; HOW TO DO IT. Saint John, Chubb, 1872. 114p [NBB

**Bernier, Joseph Elzéar, 1852–1934**
REPORT ON THE DOMINION OF CANADA GOVERNMENT EXPEDITION TO THE ARCTIC ISLANDS AND HUDSON STRAIT ON BOARD THE D.G.S. "ARCTIC," 1906–1907. Ottawa, Gov't. Print. Bureau, 1910. 529p [BM BVaU NSWA OTU QMM

**Berton, Pierre Francis de Marigny, 1920–**
THE MYSTERIOUS NORTH. New York, Knopf, 1956. 345 + xivp

**Bickersteth, John Burgon, 1888–**
THE LAND OF OPEN DOORS. Being Letters from Western Canada. London, Gardner & Darton, 1914. xxiv + 265p [BM BVaU LC NBFU OTU

**Bigsby, John Jeremiah, 1792–1881**
THE SHOE AND CANOE; or, Pictures of Travel in the Canadas. ... London, Chapman & Hall, 1850. 2v [BM BVaU LC NSWA OTU QMM

**Binnie-Clark, Georgina**

A SUMMER ON THE CANADIAN PRAIRIE. London, Arnold, 1910. 311p [BM BVaU LC OLU

**Bird, William Richard, 1891–**

OFF-TRAIL IN NOVA SCOTIA. Toronto, Ryerson, 1956. xiv + 314p

THESE ARE THE MARITIMES. Toronto, Ryerson, 1959. 333p

THIS IS NOVA SCOTIA. Toronto, Ryerson, 1950. 299p [BVaU LC NBFU OTP QMM

**Blakeny, Charles Hanford, 1888–1961**

"BITS AND PIECES." Rambling through Britain, France, Italy and Switzerland. [Moncton?], Author, 1954. 115p

"FRAGMENTS." Impressions of Holland, Belgium, Germany, Austria, Luxembourg, France, Italy, Scotland and England. [Moncton?], Author, 1956. 121p

**Bonnycastle, Richard Henry, 1791–1847**

CANADA AND THE CANADIANS IN 1846. London, Colburn, 1846. 2v [BM BVaU LC NSWA OTP

CANADA, AS IT WAS, IS, AND MAY BE. London, Colburn, 1852. 2v [A continuation of THE CANADAS IN 1841 and CANADA AND THE CANADIANS IN 1846.] [BM BVaU LC NSWA OTP QMM

THE CANADAS IN 1841. London, Colburn, 1841. 2v [Also pub. under title: THE CANADAS IN 1851 (!)] [BM BVaU LC NBFU OTP QMM

NEWFOUNDLAND, IN 1842. ... London, Colburn, 1842. 2v [BM BVaU NSWA OTU QMM

**Borthwick, Rev. John Douglas, 1832–1912**

... THE TOURIST'S PLEASURE BOOK; or, The Water Falls of Canada, its Lakes and Rivers. Montreal, Lovell, 1874. 28p [LC QMSS

**Boulton, D'Arcy, 1759–1834**

SKETCH OF ... UPPER CANADA. London, Rickaby, 1805. 99p [Also: Toronto, Baxter Pub. Co., 1961. 11 + 91p] [BM BVaU LC NSWA OTP QMM

**Boulton, Henry John, 1790–1870**

A SHORT SKETCH OF ... UPPER CANADA. ... London, Murray, 1826. 60p [BM OTP

**Bramble, Charles A.**

KLONDIKE. A Manual for Goldseekers. New York, Fenno, 1897. 313p [BVaU LC

LAND OF THE LOBSTICK. The Log of a Canoe Journey in The Pas District of Northern Manitoba. Winnipeg, Manitoba Publicity Commissioner, 1920. 20p [BVaU MWP OTU

**Brown, James, 1790–1870**

... NEW BRUNSWICK, AS A HOME FOR EMIGRANTS. ... Saint John, Barnes, 1860. 21p [BM NSWA OTP

**Brown, James Bryce**

VIEWS OF CANADA AND THE COLONISTS. ... By a Four Years' Resident [pseud]. Edinburgh, Black, 1844. 266p [2nd ed., enlarged: Edinburgh, Black, 1851. xxxii + 468p] [BM BVaU LC NSWA OTU QMM

**Bryce, Rev. George, 1844–1931**

HOLIDAY RAMBLES BETWEEN WINNIPEG AND VICTORIA. Winnipeg, 1888. 87p [MWU NSWA OLU

**Brydone, James Marr**

NARRATIVE OF A VOYAGE with a Party of Emigrants from Sussex, in 1834 ... to Montreal, thence up the river Ottawa and through the Rideau Canal, to Toronto, Upper Canada, and afterwards to Hamilton. London, Wilson, 1834. 66p [LC OOP

**Buchanan, Alexander Carlisle, 1786–1840**

EMIGRATION PRACTICALLY CONSIDERED. London, Colburn, 1828. 148p [BM OTP

**Buchanan, Alexander Carlisle, 1808–1868**

CANADA, 1863, FOR THE INFORMATION OF IMMIGRANTS. Quebec, Duquet, 1863. 49p [OTP

CANADA, FOR THE INFORMATION OF INTENDING EMIGRANTS. Quebec, Blackburn, 1864. 74p [OTP

**Burpee, Lawrence Johnstone, 1873–1946**

AMONG THE CANADIAN ALPS. New York, Lane, 1914. 239p [BM BVaU LC NSHD OTU QMM

JUNGLING IN JASPER. Ottawa, Graphic, 1929. 200p [BM BVaU LC NSHD OTU QMM

ON THE OLD ATHABASKA TRAIL. Toronto, Ryerson, [Pref., 1926]. 259p [BM BVaU LC NSWA OTU QMM

THE SEARCH FOR THE WESTERN SEA. The Story of the Exploration of North-Western America. New and rev. ed. Toronto, Macmillan, 1935. 2v [Earlier ed.: Toronto, Musson, 1908. 651p] [BM BVaU NSHD OKQ QMM

SCOUTS OF EMPIRE. The Story of the Discovery of the Great North-West. Toronto, Musson, 1912. 104p [BVaU QMM

**Burrows, Charles Acton, 1853–1948**

NORTH WESTERN CANADA. A Practical Guide to the Illimitable Fertile Regions of Manitoba and the North West Territories. Winnipeg, Donaldson, 1880. 87p [NSHP OTU

**Burtis, William Richard M., 1818–1882**

NEW BRUNSWICK, AS A HOME FOR EMIGRANTS. Saint John, Barnes, 1860. 50p [NSWA OTP

**Butler, William Francis, 1838–1910**

FAR OUT. Rovings Re-told. London, Isbister, 1880. xx + 386p [BVaU OOU MWP

THE GREAT LONE LAND. A Narrative of Travel and Adventure in the North-West. London, Sampson Low, 1872. 388p [BM BVaU NSWA OTU QMM

THE WILD NORTH LAND. Being the Story of a Winter Journey, with Dogs, Across Northern North America. London, Sampson, 1873. 358p [Numerous other editions.] [BM BVaU LC NSWA OTU QMM

**Call, Frank Oliver, 1878–1956**

THE SPELL OF ACADIA. Boston, Page, 1930. 427p [BM BVaU LC NSHD OTU

THE SPELL OF FRENCH CANADA. Boston, Page, 1926. 372p [BM BVaU LC NSWA OTU QMM

**Cameron, Agnes Deans, 1863–1912**

THE NEW NORTH. A Woman's Journey through Canada to the Arctic. New York, Appleton, 1910. 398p [BM BVaU LC NSHD OTU QMM

**Cameron, Alexander Alfred, 1912–**

PRAIRIE PROGRESS. By Alex. A. Cameron and Leo Thordarson. Toronto, Dent, 1954. ix + 241p

**Campbell, Mrs. Isabella, 1830–1887**

MRS. CAMPBELL AND HER FRIEND AT THE FAIR. Montreal, 1901. [Dionne

ROUGH AND SMOOTH; or, Ho! for an Australian Gold Field. By Mrs. A. Campbell. Quebec, Hunter Rose, 1865. 138p [NSWA OTP QMSS

**Campbell, Marjorie Elliott (Wilkins), 1901–**

ONTARIO. Toronto, Ryerson, 1953. 219p

**Campbell, Wilfred, 1858–1918**

THE BEAUTY, HISTORY, ROMANCE AND MYSTERY OF THE CANADIAN LAKE REGION. Toronto, Musson, 1910. 191p [New and enl. ed.: Toronto, Musson, 1914. 215p Also various other editions.] [BM BVaU LC NBFU OTU

CANADA. Painted by T. Mower Martin. Described by Wilfred Campbell. London, Black, 1907. 272p [BM BVaU LC NSWA OKQ

**Carmichael, Rev. James, 1835–1908**

A HOLIDAY TRIP, MONTREAL TO VICTORIA AND RETURN, VIA THE CANADIAN PACIFIC RAILWAY, MIDSUMMER, 1888. [Anon] [Montreal? 1888?] 32p [OTP

**Carnegie, Robert Kenneth, 1884–1951**

AND THE PEOPLE CHEERED. Ottawa, Legionary Library, 1940. 176p [BM BViP NBFU OTP

**Carrel, Frank, 1870–1940**

CANADA'S WEST AND FARTHER WEST. Toronto, Musson, 1911. 258p [BM BVaU LC NSWA OKQ

THREE WEEKS OUT WEST. Quebec, Telegraph Print., 1919. 40p [QMBM

**Carter, James, 1831–1925**

IN THE WAKE OF THE SETTING SUN. London, Hurst & Blackett, 1908. [NfSG OKQ QMU

SIX MONTHS IN EUROPE AND THE ORIENT. Descriptive Letters. ... Montreal, Witness Press, 1906. 502p [AEU OTP NfSG

**Cartwright, George, 1739–1819**

A JOURNAL OF ... SIXTEEN YEARS ON THE COAST OF LABRADOR. ... Newark, Allin & Ridge, 1792. 3v [BM BVaU LC NSWA OTP

**Cash, Gwen (Goldsmid), 1891–**

I LIKE BRITISH COLUMBIA. Toronto, Macmillan, 1938. 192p [BM BVaU LC OTU

**Cassap, Rev. William Henry, 1874–1949**

WINNIPEG TO LONDON VIA HUDSON BAY. London, S.P.C.K., 1936. 48p [BVaU OLU

**Chambers, Edward Thomas Davies, 1852–1931**

THE ANGLER'S GUIDE TO EASTERN CANADA. Quebec, "Morning Chronicle," 1898. 114p [BM OTP

THE GUIDE TO QUEBEC. Quebec, Morning Chronicle, 1895. 129p [BM LC OTP

QUEBEC, LAKE ST. JOHN AND THE SAGUENAY. N.p., n.pub., 1902. 62p [NSWA

**Chambers, Ernest John, 1862–1925**

THE BOOK OF MONTREAL. A Souvenir of Canada's Commercial Metropolis. Montreal, Book of Montreal Co., 1903. 257p [BM OTP QMM

**Champion, Helen Jean, 1910–1968**

OVER ON THE ISLAND [Prince Edward Island]. Toronto, Ryerson, 1939. 262p [BVaU LC NSHD OTP

**Champlain, Samuel de, 1567?–1635**

VOYAGES OF SAMUEL DE CHAMPLAIN. Trans. by Charles Pomeroy Otis. Memoir by the Rev. Edmund F. Slafter. Boston, Prince Society, 1878–82. 3v [BM BVaU LC NSHD OTP

THE WORKS OF SAMUEL DE CHAMPLAIN. ... Ed. by H.P. Biggar. Toronto, Champlain Society, 1922–36. 6v [Translation.] [BM BVaU LC NSHD OTP

**Charland, Gustave-Marquis**

FACTS AND FANCIES. By Gustave-Marquis Charland and Dorothy Lovell Charland. Sherbrooke, Tribune, 1943. 404p [Bk.I (Travels) ... by G.M.C.; Bk.II (Poetry and Prose) by D.L.C.] [BVaU LC OTU QMM

**Christie, Alexander James, 1787–1843**

THE EMIGRANT'S ASSISTANT; or, Remarks on the Agricultural Interest of the Canadas. ... Montreal, Mower, 1821. 2v [NSHD OTP QMBM

**Clarke, George Frederick, 1883–**

SIX SALMON RIVERS AND ANOTHER. London, Jenkins; Fredericton, Brunswick Press, 1960. 190p

**Coccola, Rev. Raymond de, 1912–**

AYORAMA. By Raymond de Coccola and Paul King. Toronto, Oxford U. Press, 1955. 316p [Eskimo life as seen by a missionary.]

**Cochrane, John Crawford, 1878–**

TRAILS AND TALES OF THE NORTH LAND. Toronto, Committee on Young People's Missionary Education, 1934. 162p [BVaU NBFU OTU

**Coleman, Kathleen Blake (Watkins), 1864–1915**

TO LONDON FOR THE JUBILEE. By Kit [pseud]. Toronto, Morang, 1897. 154p [BM BVaU OTP

**Colmer, Joseph Grose, 1856–1937**

ACROSS THE CANADIAN PRAIRIES. A Two Months' Holiday in the Dominion. London, European Mail, 1896. 85p [BM OLU SSU

**Comeau, Napoleon Alexander, 1848–1923**

LIFE AND SPORT ON THE NORTH SHORE OF THE LOWER ST. LAWRENCE AND GULF. ... Quebec, Telegraph, 1909. 440p [2nd ed., 1923; 3rd ed., 1954.] [BM BVaU LC NBFU OTU

**Cormack, William Epps, 1796–1868**

NARRATIVE OF A JOURNEY ACROSS THE ISLAND OF NEWFOUNDLAND. ... St. John's, Morning Chronicle, 1873. 99p [Earlier ed., 1856; also London, Longmans, 1928.] [BM BVaU NSWA OTU

**Craig, Gerald Marquis, 1916–**

EARLY TRAVELLERS IN THE CANADAS, 1791–1867. Ed. by ——. Toronto, Macmillan, 1955. xxxvi + 300p

**Croskill, John H., 1810–1855**

COMPREHENSIVE OUTLINE OF THE GEOGRAPHY AND HISTORY OF NOVA SCOTIA. By John Crosskill [*sic*]. Halifax, Author, 1838. 76p [Another ed., Halifax, Crosskill & Co., 1842. 96p] [NSWA

**Cross, Austin Fletcher, 1898–**

CROSS ROADS. Montreal, Southam Press, 1936. 301p [BM BVaU LC OTU

SNOBS AND SPIRES. Toronto, Ryerson, 1937. 342p [BVaU QMM OTU

**Crosskill, Herbert**

NOVA SCOTIA. Its Climate, Resources, and Advantages. ... 2nd ed. Halifax, Annand, 1874. 92p [BM LC OTU

**Cumming, Robert Dalziel, 1871–**

SAILING ON TO ICELAND; and ACROSS CANADA BY RAIL. Ashcroft, B.C., Ashcroft Journal, 1937. 130p (Two works bound together.) [Also: London, Mitre Press, 1938. 79p] [BM BVaU OKQ

**Cuppage, Edith M. (Reade)**

HERE AND THERE ON VANCOUVER ISLAND. Victoria, Buckle, n.d. 28p [BViPA OKQ

ISLAND TRAILS. Highways and Byways on Vancouver Island. Victoria, Buckle, 1945. 36p [BViPA

**Daly, Thomas Mayne, 1852–1911**

DESCRIPTION OF THE PROVINCE OF MANITOBA. Ottawa, King's Printer, 1893. 365p [OTL

**Davenport, Mrs. N.**

JOURNAL OF A FOURTEEN DAYS' RIDE THROUGH THE BUSH FROM QUEBEC TO LAKE ST. JOHN. Quebec, Daily Mercury, 1872. 35p [BM BVaU OOP

**Davies, Blodwen, 1897–1966**

THE CHARM OF OTTAWA. Toronto, McClelland, 1932. 250p [BVaU OTP

GASPE, LAND OF HISTORY AND ROMANCE. New York, Greenberg, 1949. 233p [BVaU LC OTU QMM

QUEBEC. Portrait of a Province. Toronto, Heinemann, 1951. 258p

ROMANTIC QUEBEC. New York, Dodd Mead, 1932. 213p [BVaU LC NBFU OKQ

SAGUENAY "SAGINAWA," THE RIVER OF DEEP WATERS. Toronto, McClelland, 1930. 204p [BVaU LC OTU QMM

**Davin, Nicholas Flood, 1843–1901**

HOMES FOR THE MILLIONS. The Great Canadian North-West. Its Resources Fully Described. Ottawa, Queen's Printer, 1891. 108p [OOA

**Dawson, Rev. Aeneas MacDonell, 1810–1894**

THE NORTH-WEST TERRITORIES AND BRITISH COLUMBIA. Ottawa, Mitchell, 1881. 232p [BM BVaU LC NSWA OLU

**Dawson, Carl Addington, 1887–**

THE NEW NORTHWEST. Ed. by ——. Toronto, U. of Toronto Press, 1947. 341p [BM BVaU LC NSHD OTU

**Dawson, Samuel Edward, 1833–1916**

DISCOVERY OF AMERICA BY JOHN CABOT IN 1497 ... and the Voyages of the Cabots. ... Ottawa, Hope, 1896. 30p [BVaU NSHD OTU

HANDBOOK FOR THE DOMINION OF CANADA. ... Montreal, Dawson, 1884. 335p [BM BVaU NSHD NBFU OTU QMM

**Day, James Wentworth, 1899–**

NEWFOUNDLAND, THE FORTRESS ISLE. Fredericton, pub. for the Govt. of Newfoundland by Brunswick Press, 1960. 65p

**De La Roche, Mazo, 1879–1961**

QUEBEC. Historic Seaport. Garden City, Doubleday, 1944. 212p [BM BVaU NBFU OKQ QMM

**Delaute, Joseph François, 1909–**

THE VOYAGEURS. Canoe Trip Diary, Hayes River, 1956. Ottawa, Author, 1957. 48p

**Denis, Keith, 1909–**

CANOE TRAILS THROUGH QUETICO. Toronto, Quetico Foundation, 1959. ix + 84p

**Denison, Grace Elizabeth (Sandys), –1914**

A HAPPY HOLIDAY. Toronto, 1890. 229p [AEU OLU

**Denison, Merrill, 1893–**

KLONDIKE MIKE. An Alaskan Odyssey. New York, Morrow, 1943. 393p [BM BVaU LC NBFU OTU QMM

**Dennis, Clara**

CAPE BRETON OVER. Toronto, Ryerson, 1942. 342p [BVaU LC NSHD OTU QMM

DOWN IN NOVA SCOTIA, MY OWN, MY NATIVE LAND. Toronto, Ryerson, 1934. 410p [BM BVaU LC NSHD OTU QMM

MORE ABOUT NOVA SCOTIA, MY OWN, MY NATIVE LAND. Toronto, Ryerson, 1937. 412p [BM BVaU LC NSWA OTU

**Devine, Rev. Edward James, 1860–1927**

ACROSS WIDEST AMERICA: NEWFOUNDLAND TO ALASKA. ... Montreal, Canadian Messenger, 1905. 307p [BVaU NBFU OTU QMM

**Doane, Frank Augustus, 1862–1950**

NOVA SCOTIA SKETCHES. Truro, Truro Pub. Co., 1949. 121p [BVaU NSHD OTUV

**Douglas, David, 1798–1834**

JOURNAL KEPT BY DAVID DOUGLAS DURING HIS TRAVELS IN NORTH AMERICA 1823–1827. ... London, Wesley, 1914. 364p [BM BVaU LC NSHD OTP

**Douglas, George Mellis**

LANDS FORLORN. A Story of an Expedition to Hearne's Coppermine River. ... New York, Putnam, 1914. 285p [BM BVaU LC NBFU OTU

**Duncan, Dorothy, 1903–1957**

BLUENOSE. A Portrait of Nova Scotia. New York, Harper, 1942. 273p [BVaU LC NSHD OTU QMSS

HERE'S TO CANADA! New York, Harper, 1941. 334p [BM BVaU LC NSHD OTU QMM

**Duncan, John Morison, 1795?–1825**

TRAVELS THROUGH PART OF THE UNITED STATES AND CANADA IN 1818 AND 1819. Glasgow [etc.], U. Press [etc.], 1823. 2v [BM BVaU LC NSWA OTP QMM

**Duncan, Norman, 1871–1916**

AUSTRALIAN BYWAYS. The Narrative of a Sentimental Traveller. New York, Harper, 1915. 293p [BM BVaU LC NBFU

GOING DOWN FROM JERUSALEM. The Narrative of a Sentimental Traveller. New York, Harper, 1909. 210p [BM BVaU LC OLU

**Duncan, Sara Jeannette (Mrs. Everard Cotes), 1861–1922**

A SOCIAL DEPARTURE. How Orthodocia and I Went round the World by Ourselves. London, Chatto & Windus, 1890. 417p [BM BVaU LC NSHD OTMC

**Dunlop, William, 1792–1848**

STATISTICAL SKETCHES OF UPPER CANADA, for the Use of Emigrants. By a Backwoodsman [pseud]. London, Murray, 1832. 120p [BM BVaU LC OTP

**Edgar, James**

NEW BRUNSWICK, AS A HOME FOR EMIGRANTS. ... Prize Essay. Saint John, Barnes, 1860. 37p [BM BVaU NSWA OTP

**Edwards, Ralph, 1877?–**

TRAIL TO THE CHARMED LAND. [Banff and the Rockies.] Saskatoon, H.R. Larson, 1950. 135p [OONL

**Ellis, John Valentine, 1835–1913**

NEW BRUNSWICK, AS A HOME FOR EMIGRANTS. ... First Prize Essay. ... Saint John, Barnes, 1860. 60p [BVaU NBFU OTP

**Emberson, Alfred J.**

ALL ABOUT VICTORIA. Victoria, Victoria Pub. Co., 1916. 104p [BM BVaU OTU

**Emmerson, John**

BRITISH COLUMBIA AND VANCOUVER ISLAND. Voyages, Travels & Adventures. Durham, Eng., Ainsley, 1865. 154p [BViPA LC OOP

**Englebert, Reginald, 1911–**

THIS IS OTTAWA. Toronto, Garden City Press Co-op., 1950. 64p [OONL

THIS IS TORONTO. Toronto, Garden City Press Co-op., 1950. 88p [OONL

THIS IS VANCOUVER ISLAND. Victoria, Diggon-Hibben, 1948. 88p [BVaU

**Evans, Francis A., –1832**

THE EMIGRANT'S DIRECTORY AND GUIDE to Obtain Lands and Effect a Settlement in the Canadas. Dublin [etc.], Curry [etc.], 1833. 180p [BM BVaU LC NSWA OTP QMM

**Fairchild, George Moore, 1854–1912**

ROD AND CANOE, RIFLE AND SNOWSHOE IN QUEBEC'S ADIRONDACKS. Quebec, Carrel, 1896. 207p [BM BVaU NSWA LC OTU QMM

**Finnie, Richard, 1906–**

CANADA MOVES NORTH. New York, Macmillan, 1942. 227p [Rev. ed.: Toronto, Macmillan, 1948. 239p] [BM BVaU LC NSHD OTU QMM

LURE OF THE NORTH. Philadelphia, McKay, 1940. 227p [BVaU LC OTU QMM

**Fisher, John Wiggins, 1913–**

CANADA. As Seen by the Camera of Yousuf Karsh and described in Words by John Fisher. Toronto, Allen, 1960. 165p

**Fitzgibbon, Mary Agnes, 1851–1915**

A TRIP TO MANITOBA; or, Roughing it on the Line. Toronto, Rose-Belford, 1880. 267p [BM BVaU LC NSWA OKQ SSU

**Fleming, Sandford, 1827–1915**

ENGLAND AND CANADA. A Summer Tour between Old and New Westminster. ... London, Low Marston, 1884. 449p [BM BVaU NSWA OTU QMM

**Footner, Hulbert, 1879–1944**

NEW RIVERS OF THE NORTH. A Yarn of Two Amateur Explorers of the Head Waters of the Fraser, Peace River, the Hay River, Alexandra Falls. New York, Doran, 1912. 281p [BM BVaU LC OTU QMM

**Forster, Victor Wadham, 1909–**

VANCOUVER THROUGH THE EYES OF A HOBO. By V.W.F. Vancouver, McCormick Press, 1934. 63p [OTP

**Fraser, William, 1808–1892**

THE EMIGRANT'S GUIDE; or, Sketches of Canada. ... By a Scotch Minister [pseud]. Thirty-six Years Resident in Canada, from 1831–1867. Glasgow, Porteous Bros., 1867. 72p [OTP

**Futcher, Winnifred M. (Hall)**

THE GREAT NORTH ROAD TO THE CARIBOO. Ed. by ——. Vancouver, Wrigley, 1938. 113p [BVaU LC NBFU OTU QMM

**Galbraith, J.F.**

A SKETCH OF BOTH SIDES OF MANITOBA. By Jeff Gee [pseud]. Nelsonville, Man., Manitoba Mountaineer Book & Job Print., 1881. 143p [OTU

**Galloway, Christian F.J.**

THE CALL OF THE WEST. Letters from British Columbia. New York, Stokes, 1916. 328p [BM BVaU LC NBFU OTP

**Gesner, Abraham, 1797–1864**

NEW BRUNSWICK. With Notes for Emigrants. London, Simmonds, 1847. 388p [BM BVaU LC NSWA OTP QMSS

**Gilbert, Alexander Glen, 1840–1913**

FROM MONTREAL TO THE MARITIME PROVINCES AND BACK. Montreal, Montreal Print. & Pub. Co., 1867. 63p [Also a facsimile ed., with an intro. by Douglas Lochhead. Toronto, Bibliographical Society of Canada, 1967.] [NSHL OOP QMBM

**Gislason, Ingvar**

PRAIRIE PANORAMA. A Brief Study of the Prairie Provinces. Calgary, Western Canada Institute, 1948. 196p [BVa LC OTU

**Glass, Chester, –1921**

THE WORLD: ROUND IT AND OVER IT. Being Letters. ... Toronto, Rose Belford, 1881. 528p [BM LC OTU QMM

**Godsell, Philip Henry, 1889–1961**

ARCTIC TRADER. The Account of Twenty Years with the Hudson's Bay Company. New York, Putnam, 1934. 329p [BM BVaU LC NBFU OTU QMM

RED HUNTERS OF THE SNOWS. An Account of Thirty Years' Experience with the Primitive Indian and Eskimo Tribes of the Canadian North-West and Arctic Coast. ... Toronto, Ryerson, 1938. 324p [BM BVaU LC OTU

THE ROMANCE OF THE ALASKA HIGHWAY. Toronto, Ryerson, 1944. 235p [BVaU LC OTU QMM

**Goldie, John, 1793–1886**

DIARY OF A JOURNEY THROUGH UPPER CANADA AND SOME OF THE NEW ENGLAND STATES, 1819. Toronto, Tyrrell, 1897. 56p [BVaU OKQ

**Gomery, Percy, 1881–1960**

HOT AND COLD LAID ON. Burrowing in Britain. By Percy and Bernadette Gomery. Toronto, Ryerson, 1946. 288p [BVaU LC OTU QMM

A MOTOR SCAMPER 'CROSS CANADA. ... Toronto, Ryerson, 1922. 208p [BM BVaU NBFU OTU QMM

**Gordon, Rev. Daniel Miner, 1845–1925**

MOUNTAIN AND PRAIRIE. A Journey from Victoria to Winnipeg, via Peace River Pass. Montreal, Dawson, 1880. 310p [BM BVaU LC NSWA OTU

**Gourlay, Robert Fleming, 1778–1863**

STATISTICAL ACCOUNT OF UPPER CANADA. ... London, Simpkin & Marshall, 1822. 2v [BM BVaU LC NBFU OTP

**Gowland, John Stafford, 1898–**

RETURN TO CANADA. London, Laurie, 1957. 199p

SIKANASKA TRAIL. London, Laurie, 1956. 207p

**Grant, Rev. George Monro, 1835–1902**

ARTISTIC QUEBEC DESCRIBED BY PEN AND PENCIL. Ed. by ——. Toronto, Belden, 1888. 141p [OKQ

OCEAN TO OCEAN. Sandford Fleming's Expedition through Canada in 1872. ... Toronto, Campbell, 1873. 371p [Various later editions, enl. and rev. Imprint varies.] [BM BVaU LC NSWA OTU QMM

OUR PICTURESQUE NORTHERN NEIGHBOUR. Ed. by ——. Chicago, Belford, 1899. 280p [BVaU NSWA OTP QMBM

PICTURESQUE CANADA. The Country as it was and is. Ed. by ——. Toronto, Belden, 1882. 2v [BM BVaU NSWA OTU QMM

PICTURESQUE SPOTS OF THE NORTH. Ed. by ——. Chicago, Belford, 1899. 205p [OLU

**Gray, Hugh**

LETTERS FROM CANADA, WRITTEN ... IN ... 1806, 1807, AND 1808, SHEWING THE PRESENT STATE OF CANADA ... THE COMMERCIAL IMPORTANCE OF NOVA-SCOTIA, NEW BRUNSWICK, AND CAPE BRETON. ... London, Longmans, 1809. 406p [BM BVaU NBS OTP QMG

**Greenhill, Ralph Ackland, 1924–**

THE FACE OF TORONTO. Toronto, Oxford U. Press, 1960. 22 + 58p

**Grenfell, Wilfred Thomason, 1865–1940**

ADRIFT ON AN ICE-PAN. New York, Houghton, 1909. 68p [BM BVaU LC NSHD OTU

LABRADOR LOOKS AT THE ORIENT. Notes of Travel in the Near and the Far East. Boston, Houghton, 1923. 297p [BM BVaU OTU QMM

LABRADOR, THE COUNTRY AND THE PEOPLE. By Wilfred T. Grenfell ... and Others. New York, Macmillan, 1909. 497p [BVaU LC NSHD OTU QMM

LABRADOR'S FIGHT FOR ECONOMIC FREEDOM. London, Benn, 1929. 36p [BM OTU

THE ROMANCE OF LABRADOR. New York, Macmillan, 1934. 329p [BM BVaU LC NSHD OTU QMM

VIKINGS OF TO-DAY; or, Life and Medical Work among the Fishermen of Labrador. London, Marshall, 1895. 240p [BM BVaU LC MWU NSWA OLU

A VOYAGE ON A PAN OF ICE. Boston, Ellis, 1908. 14p [LC OTU

**Hadfield, Joseph, 1759–1851**

AN ENGLISHMAN IN AMERICA, 1785. Being the Diary of ——. Ed. by Douglas S. Robertson. Toronto, Hunter Rose, 1933. 232p [BM BVaU LC NBFU OTP

**Haight, Canniff, 1825–1901**

HERE AND THERE IN THE HOME LAND. England, Scotland and Ireland, as seen by a Canadian. Toronto, Briggs, 1895. 616p [Later pub. as: A UNITED EMPIRE LOYALIST IN GREAT BRITAIN: Here & There in the Home Land. ... With a Biographical Introduction. ... Toronto, Briggs, 1904. 616p] [BM BVaU LC NBFU OTP

A UNITED EMPIRE LOYALIST IN GREAT BRITAIN. [See under HERE AND THERE IN THE HOME LAND.]

**Haliburton, Thomas Chandler, 1796–1865**

THE AMERICANS AT HOME; or, Byeways, Backwoods, and Prairies. Ed. by the Author of "Sam Slick". ... London, Hurst & Blackett, 1854. 3v [BM BVaU LC NSHD OTU QMM

A GENERAL DESCRIPTION OF NOVA SCOTIA. ... [Anon] Halifax, Royal Acadian School, 1823. 200p [Also: Halifax, Belcher, 1825. Occasionally this work is attributed to Clement Belcher or Walter Bromley.] [BM BVaU LC NSWA OTP

**Hambleton, John O. ("Jack"), 1901–1961**

HUNTER'S HOLIDAYS. Toronto, Longmans, 1947. 207p [BVaU LC OTP

**Hamilton, James Cleland, 1836–1907**

THE GEORGIAN BAY. An Account of its Position, Inhabitants, Mineral Interests, Fish, Timber and other Resources. Toronto, Carswell, 1893. 170p [BM BVaU LC NSWA OTU

THE PRAIRIE PROVINCE. Sketches of Travel from Lake Ontario to Lake Winnipeg, and an Account of the Geographical Position, Climate, Civil Institutions, Inhabitants, Productions and Resources of the Red River Valley. ... Toronto, Belford, 1876. 259p [BM BVaU LC NSWA OTU

**Hamilton, John R.**

NEW BRUNSWICK AND ITS SCENERY. A Tourists' and Anglers' Guide to the Province. ... Saint John, M'Millan, 1874. 157p [BVaU NSHD OTP QMBM

OUR ROYAL GUESTS. A Souvenir of the Visits of the Duke and Duchess of Cornwall and York and other members of the Royal Family to St. John and the Province of New Brunswick, Canada. Saint John, Hamilton, [1902]. 100p [LC NSWA

ST. JOHN AND THE PROVINCE OF NEW BRUNSWICK. A Handbook. 3rd ed. Saint John, Hamilton, 1884. 120p [BM BVaU LC NSHD OTP

**Hamilton, Pierce Stevens, 1826–1893**

NOVA-SCOTIA CONSIDERED AS A FIELD FOR EMIGRATION. London, Weale, 1858. 91p [BM LC NSWA OTU QMM

**Hammond, Melvin Ormond, 1876–1934**

CANADIAN FOOTPRINTS. A Study in Foregrounds and Backgrounds. Toronto, Macmillan, 1926. 305p [BM BVaU LC NSWA OLU

**Hardy, Campbell, 1831–1919**

FOREST LIFE IN ACADIE. Sketches of Sport and Natural History in the Lower Provinces of the Canadian Dominion. London, Chapman & Hall, 1869. 371p [BM BVaU LC NSWA OTU

SPORTING ADVENTURES IN THE NEW WORLD; or, Days and Nights of Moose-Hunting in the Pine Forests of Acadia. London, Hurst & Blackett, 1855. 2v [BM BVaU LC NSHD OTU

**Harmon, Daniel Williams, 1778–1845**

A JOURNAL OF VOYAGES AND TRAVELS IN THE INTERIOUR OF NORTH AMERICA ... from Montreal nearly to the Pacific Ocean. ... Andover, Flagg & Gould, 1820. xxiv + 432p [Also: Toronto, Morang, 1904. 382p; and: Toronto, Courier, 1911. 382p] [BM BVaU NSWA OTU QMSS

SIXTEEN YEARS IN THE INDIAN COUNTRY. The Journal of Daniel Williams Harmon, 1800–1816. Ed. with an intro. by W. Kaye Lamb. Toronto, Macmillan, 1957. xxviii + 277p

**Harrington, Evelyn (Davis), 1911–**

MANITOBA ROUNDABOUT. Toronto, Ryerson, 1951. xii + 237p

**Harrington, Michael Francis, 1916–**

SEA STORIES FROM NEWFOUNDLAND. Toronto, Ryerson, 1958. xi + 172p

**Harrington, Richard Walter, 1911–**

BRITISH COLUMBIA IN PICTURES. Text by Lyn Harrington. Toronto, Nelson, 1958. 1v [unpaged]

THE FACE OF THE ARCTIC. A Cameraman's Story in Words and Pictures of Five Journeys into the Far North. New York, Schuman, 1952. xii + 369p

NORTHERN EXPOSURES. Canada's Backwoods and Barrens Pictured in Monochrome and Color. Text and arrangement by Clifford Wilson. New York, Schuman; Toronto, Nelson, 1953. 119p

**Hart-McHarg, William F.R., 1869–1915**

FROM QUEBEC TO PRETORIA, with the Royal Canadian Regiment. Toronto, Briggs, 1902. 276p [BVaU NBFU OKQ

**Harvey, Daniel Cobb, 1886–**

JOURNEYS TO THE ISLAND OF ST. JOHN OR PRINCE EDWARD ISLAND, 1775–1832. Ed. by ——. Toronto, Macmillan, 1955. 213p

**Harvey, Rev. Moses, 1820–1901**

ACROSS NEWFOUNDLAND WITH THE GOVERNOR. A Visit to our Mining Region; and This Newfoundland of Ours. Being a Series of Papers on the Natural Resources and Future Prospects of the Colony. St. John's, "Morning Chronicle," 1879. 122p [LC NSWA OOA

NEWFOUNDLAND AS IT IS IN 1894. A Hand-Book and Tourist's Guide. St. John's, Withers, 1894. 298p [BVaU LC NSHD OTP QMU

**Hearne, Samuel, 1745–1792**

JOURNALS OF SAMUEL HEARNE AND PHILIP TURNOR. Ed. with intro. by J.B. Tyrrell. Toronto, Champlain Society, 1934. xviii + 611 + xiip [BM BVaU LC NSHD OTP QMM

A JOURNEY FROM PRINCE OF WALES' FORT IN HUDSON'S BAY, TO THE NORTHERN OCEAN ... IN THE YEARS 1769, 1770, 1771, & 1772. London, Strahan & Cadell, 1795. xliv + 458p [New ed., with intro. and notes by J.B. Tyrrell: Toronto, Champlain Society, 1911. xv + 437 + viip. Also ed. with intro. by Richard Glover. Toronto, Macmillan, 1958. 1xxii + 301p] [BM BVaU LC NSWA OKQ

**Heming, Arthur Henry Howard, 1870–1940**

THE DRAMA OF THE FORESTS. Romance and Adventure. Garden City, Doubleday, 1921. 324p [BVaU LC NBFU OKQ

**Henry, Alexander, 1739–1824**

TRAVELS AND ADVENTURES IN CANADA and the Indian Territories, between the Years 1760 and 1776. ... New York, Riley, 1809. 330p [New ed. with notes by James Bain: Toronto, Morang, 1901. xxxv + 41 + 347p] [BM BVaU LC NSWA OTP

**Henry, Alexander, –1814**

HENRY'S JOURNAL, Covering Adventures and Experiences in the Fur Trade on the Red River, 1799–1801. Ed. by Charles N. Bell. Winnipeg, Manitoba Free Press, 1888–89. 2v [BVaU LC OTP

NEW LIGHT ON THE EARLY HISTORY OF THE GREATER NORTHWEST. THE MANUSCRIPT JOURNALS OF ALEXANDER HENRY ... AND OF DAVID THOMPSON ... 1799–1814. Ed. by Elliott Coues. New York, Harper, 1897. 3v [Edited and condensed from the MS copy in the Library of Parliament, Ottawa, made by George Coventry, Montreal, 1824.] [BM BVaU LC NBFU OTP QMM

**Henry, George**

THE EMIGRANT'S GUIDE, OR CANADA AS IT IS. ... Quebec, Gray, [1834?]. xxiv + 173p [NSWA OTU

**Heriot, George, 1766–1844**

TRAVELS THROUGH THE CANADAS. ... London, Phillips, 1807. 602p [BM BVaU LC NSWA OTU

**Herring, Frances Elizabeth (Clarke), 1851–1916**

AMONG THE PEOPLE OF BRITISH COLUMBIA, Red, White, Yellow and Brown. London, Unwin, 1903. 299p [BM BVaU LC NBFU OOA

CANADIAN CAMP LIFE. London, Unwin, 1900. 247p [BM BVaU LC NSHD

IN THE PATHLESS WEST WITH SOLDIERS, PIONEERS, MINERS AND SAVAGES. London, Unwin, 1904. 240p [BM BVaU LC NBFU OTP

**Hill, S.S.**

THE EMIGRANT'S INTRODUCTION TO AN ACQUAINTANCE WITH THE BRITISH

AMERICAN COLONIES, AND THE PRESENT CONDITION AND PROSPECTS OF THE COLONISTS. London, Parbury, 1837. 324p [BM OTP

A SHORT ACCOUNT OF PRINCE EDWARD ISLAND. ... By the Author of "The Emigrant's Introduction. ..." [pseud]. London, Madden, 1839. 90p [BVaU LC NSWA OTP QMM

**Hind, Ella Cora, 1861–1942**

MY TRAVELS AND FINDINGS. Toronto, Macmillan, 1939. 185p [OTU QMBM

**Hind, Henry Youle, 1823–1908**

THE CANOE ROUTE BETWEEN FORT WILLIAM, LAKE SUPERIOR, AND FORT GARRY, RED RIVER. ... 1857. Toronto, Derbishire & Desbarats, 1858. 16p [BM OTP SSU

EXPLORATIONS IN THE INTERIOR OF THE LABRADOR PENINSULA. London, Longmans, 1863. 2v [BM BVaU LC NSWA OLU

LAKE SUPERIOR AND THE RED RIVER SETTLEMENT. Presented to ... Parliament by Command of Her Majesty. London, Eyre & Spottiswoode, 1859. 163p [BM OTP

NARRATIVE OF THE CANADIAN RED RIVER EXPLORING EXPEDITION OF 1857, and of the Assinniboine [*sic*] and Saskatchewan Exploring Expedition of 1858. London, Longmans, 1860. 2v [BM BVaU LC NSWA OLU

NORTH-WEST TERRITORY. ... Assiniboine and Saskatchewan Exploring Expedition. ... Toronto, Lovell, 1859. 201p [With supplementary volume: PHOTOGRAPHS ACCOMPANYING A REPORT ON THE ASSINIBOINE AND SASKATCHEWAN EXPLORING EXPEDITION. N.p., n.d.] [BM BVaU LC NSWA OTP QMM

A SKETCH OF AN OVERLAND ROUTE TO BRITISH COLUMBIA. Toronto, Chewett, 1862. 129p [BVaU NSWA OLU

**Hinton, Arthur Cherry**

THE YUKON. By A. Cherry Hinton in Collaboration with Philip H. Godsell. Toronto, Ryerson, 1954. xiv + 184p

**Hodgins, Samuel Raymond Norris, 1895–**

SO THIS IS QUEBEC! By Norris Hodgins. St. Anne de Bellevue, Author, 1926. 29p [BVaU QMSS

**Hollingsworth, S.**

THE PRESENT STATE OF NOVA SCOTIA. ... [Anon] 2nd ed., enl. Edinburgh, Creech, 1787. 221p [1st ed. in 1786. 157p] [BM BVaU NSWA OKQ QMM

**Hooper, John, 1791–1869**

THE ADVANTAGES OF EMIGRATING TO THE BRITISH COLONIES OF NEW BRUNSWICK, NOVA SCOTIA, ETC. By a Resident of St. John [pseud]. London, Wilson, 1832. 71p [BM EngCat NBB

**Horetsky, Charles G., 1840–1900**

CANADA ON THE PACIFIC. Being an Account of a Journey from Edmonton to the Pacific by the Peace River Valley; and of a Winter Voyage Along the Western

Coast of the Dominion. ... Montreal, Dawson, 1874. 244p [BVaU LC NSWA OTU QMM

**Howard, Hilda (Glynn), 1887–**

THE GLAMOUR OF BRITISH COLUMBIA. By H. Glynn-Ward [pseud]. Toronto, Macmillan, 1926. 238p [BVaU LC NBFU OTU

**Howard, W.H.**

GLIMPSES IN AND ABOUT HALIFAX. ... [Halifax], W.H. Howard, [1897?]. 80p [NSHD

**Howay, Frederic William, 1867–1943**

VOYAGES OF THE "COLUMBIA" TO THE NORTHWEST COAST 1787–1790 AND 1790–1793. Ed. by ——. Boston, Massachusetts Historical Society, 1941. 518p [BM BVaU LC NBFU OTP

**Hunter, George, 1921–**

CANADA IN COLOUR. By George Hunter and Leslie Roberts. Toronto, Clarke Irwin, 1959. 88p

**Hunter, William S.**

EASTERN TOWNSHIPS SCENERY. Stanstead, Hunter, 1860. 35p [BM BVaU NSWA OTL

HUNTER'S PANORAMIC GUIDE FROM NIAGARA FALLS TO QUEBEC. Montreal, Dawson; Boston, Jewitt, 1857. 66p [Later ed., Montreal, Hunter & Pickup, 1860. 66p] [BM BVaU LC OLU

OTTAWA SCENERY. Ottawa, Hunter, 1855. 16p [BVaU LC NSWA OTU

**Hutchison, Bruce, 1901–**

THE UNKNOWN COUNTRY. Canada and her People. New York, Coward McCann, 1942. 386p [Toronto, Longmans, 1943. 326p] [BM BVaU LC NSHD OKQ QMM

**Innis, Mary E. (Quayle), 1899–1972**

TRAVELLERS WEST. Toronto, Clarke Irwin, 1956. ix + 339p

**Jackson, Alexander Young, 1882–**

THE FAR NORTH. A Book of Drawings ... with an Intro. by Dr. F.G. Banting, and Descriptive Notes by the Artist. Toronto, Rous & Mann, [1928?]. 8p 17 plates. [BVaU NSHD OKQ

**Jacobs, Rev. Peter, 1808–1858**

JOURNAL OF THE REVEREND PETER JACOBS. ... From Rice Lake to the Hudson's Bay Territory ... 1852. ... Toronto, Green, 1853. 32p [2nd ed.: Boston, Rand,

1853. 55p; 3rd ed.: New York, Author, 1858. 96p] [BM BViPA LC NSWA OTP

**Jarvis, Thomas Stinson, 1854–1926**

LETTERS FROM EAST LONGITUDES. Sketches of Travel in Egypt, the Holy Land, Greece, and Cities of the Levant. Toronto, James Capmbell, 1875. 267p [AEU OTP

**Johnston, Lukin**

BEYOND THE ROCKIES. Three Thousand Miles by Trail and Canoe through Little-known British Columbia. Toronto, Dent, 1929. 212p [BM BVaU LC OLU

**Johnstone, Walter**

LETTERS, DESCRIPTIVE OF PRINCE EDWARD ISLAND. Dumfries, Swan, 1822. 72p [BM OTP

TRAVELS IN PRINCE EDWARD ISLAND ... in ... 1820–21. Edinburgh [etc.], Brown [etc.], 1823. 132p [BM BVaU LC NSWA OTP

**Judson, William Lee, 1842–1928**

A TOUR OF THE THAMES. Written and Illustrated with A. Faber's B.B. By Professor Blot [pseud]. London, Ont., Advertiser, 1881. 140p [Cover title: KUHLEBORN.] [OLU

**Kane, Paul, 1810–1871**

WANDERINGS OF AN ARTIST AMONG THE INDIANS OF NORTH AMERICA. From Canada to Vancouver's Island and Oregon, through the Hudson's Bay Company's Territory and Back Again. London, Longman, Brown, etc., 1859. 455p [Also: Toronto, Radisson Society, 1925. 329p] [BM BVaU LC NSWA OTU SSU

**Kavanagh, Martin, 1895–**

ASSINIBOINE BASIN. A Social Study of the Discovery, Exploration, and Settlement of Manitoba. Winnipeg, Public Press, 1946. 282p [BVaU LC NSHD OTU QMBM

**Kelsey, Henry, 1670?–1724?**

THE KELSEY PAPERS. With an intro. by Arthur G. Doughty ... & Chester Martin. ... Ottawa, Acland, 1929. lxxxiii + 128p [BVaU LC NBFU OTP QMBM

**Kennedy, Ida Mara**

TOURING QUEBEC AND THE MARITIMES. Toronto, Armac Press, 1929. 112p [OTU

**Kingsford, William, 1819–1898**

IMPRESSIONS OF THE WEST AND SOUTH DURING A SIX WEEKS' HOLIDAY. [Anon] Toronto, Armour, 1858. 83p ["These letters first appeared in a Toronto newspaper" –Preface.] [BM LC NSWA OTU

**Kitto, Franklin Hugo, 1880–**

MAXWELLTON DISTRICT, NOVA SCOTIA. A new Area for Settlement in an old settled Province. Ottawa, Dept. of the Interior, 1924. 44p [NSHP OONL QMSS

**Knott, Leonard Lewis, 1905–**

HIGHWAYS OF HISTORY. Montreal, Northern Electric Co., 1954. 28p

**Kristjansson, Adalsteinn**

IN THE WEST. Santa Barbara, Schauer Print., 1935. 3v [BVa LC

**Ladue, Joseph**

KLONDYKE FACTS. Being a Complete Guide Book to the Gold Regions of the Great Canadian Northwest Territories and Alaska. Montreal, Lovell, 1897. 205p [BM BVaU LC NSWA OTU

KLONDYKE NUGGETS. Being a Brief Description of the Famous Gold Regions of the Great Canadian Northwest and Alaska. Montreal, Lovell, 1897. 92p [BM BVaU OTU

**Landon, Fred, 1880–1969**

LAKE HURON. ... Indianapolis, Bobbs-Merrill, 1944. 398p [BM BVaU LC OKQ QMM

**Lanphier, Rev. Charles B.**

OUR TRIP TO ROME. Toronto, Catholic Truth Society of Canada, 1953. 207p

**Large, Richard Geddes, 1901–**

PRINCE RUPERT, A GATEWAY TO ALASKA. Vancouver, Mitchell Press, 1960. 210p

**Lauder, Mrs. Maria Elise Turner**

EVERGREEN LEAVES. Being Notes from my Travel Book. By Toofie [pseud]. Toronto, Belford, 1877. 384p [Same as following title.] [OTU

EVERGREEN LEAVES; or, "Toofie" in Europe. Toronto, Rose, 1884. 384p [NBFU OTP

**Laut, Agnes Christina, 1871–1936**

THE CONQUEST OF OUR WESTERN EMPIRE. New York, McBride, 1927. 363p [BVaU LC OTU

PATHFINDERS OF THE WEST. Being the Thrilling Story of the Adventures of the Men who Discovered the great Northwest. New York, Macmillan, 1904. 380p [BVaU LC NSWA OTU

VIKINGS OF THE PACIFIC. The Adventures of the Explorers who came from the West, Eastward. Toronto, Macmillan, 1905. 349p [BVaU OTU

**Lawson, Jessie Isabel, 1879–1961**

THIS IS NEW BRUNSWICK. By Jessie I. Lawson and Jean MacCallum Sweet. Toronto, Ryerson, 1951. 202p

**Lawson, John**

LETTERS ON PRINCE EDWARD ISLAND. Charlottetown, Haszard, 1851. 76p [NSHP

**Leacock, Stephen Butler, 1869–1944**

ADVENTURERS OF THE FAR NORTH. A Chronicle of the Frozen Seas. Toronto, Glasgow Brook, 1914. 152p [BM BVaU LC NSWA OTU QMM

THE DAWN OF CANADIAN HISTORY. A Chronicle of Aboriginal Canada and the Coming of the White Man. Toronto, Glasgow Brook, 1914. 112p [BM BVaU LC NSWA OTU

THE MARINER OF ST. MALO. A Chronicle of the Voyages of Jacques Cartier. Toronto, Glasgow Brook, 1914. 125p [BM BVaU LC NSHD OTU

MONTREAL: SEAPORT AND CITY. Garden City, Doubleday, 1942. 340p [BM BVaU LC NSHD OTU QMM

**Lebourdais, Donat Marc, 1887–**

NORTHWARD ON THE NEW FRONTIER. Ottawa, Graphic, 1931. 311p [BM BVaU LC OTU

**Leechman, John Douglas, 1890–**

ESKIMO SUMMER. Toronto, Ryerson, 1945. 247p [BM BVaU LC NBFU OTP

INDIAN SUMMER. Toronto, Ryerson, 1949. 182p [BVaU LC NBFU OTU QMM

**LeMoine, James MacPherson, 1825–1912**

HISTORICAL AND SPORTING NOTES ON QUEBEC AND ITS ENVIRONS. ... Quebec, Demers, 1889. 133p [1st ed.: Montreal, Burland, 1879. 30p] [BM BVaU OTU QMM

PICTURESQUE QUEBEC. A Sequel to QUEBEC PAST AND PRESENT. [See above p.701]. Montreal, Dawson, 1882. 535p [BM BVaU NSHD OKQ QMM

THE TOURIST'S NOTE-BOOK. By Cosmopolite [pseud]. 2nd ed. Quebec, Garant, 1876. 64p [BVaU NSHP OOA QMSS

**Liddell, Kenneth Eric, 1912–**

ALBERTA REVISITED. Toronto, Ryerson, 1960. xiv + 234p

THIS IS ALBERTA. Toronto, Ryerson, 1952. 190p

THIS IS BRITISH COLUMBIA. Toronto, Ryerson, 1958. xiv + 250p

**Lighthall, William Douw, 1857–1954**

MONTREAL AFTER 250 YEARS. Montreal, Grafton, 1892. 149p [Also pub. under title: SIGHTS AND SHRINES OF MONTREAL. Montreal, Grafton, 1907. 180p] [BM BVaU LC NSWA OTU QMBM

**Lillie, Rev. Adam, 1803–1869**

CANADA. Physical, Economic and Social. Toronto, Maclear, 1855. 294p [BM BVaU LC NSHD OLU

**Littlehales, Edward Baker, –1825**

JOURNAL ... of an Exploratory Tour ... Niagara to Detroit, made in ... 1793 by ... Lieut.-Gov. Simcoe. With intro. and notes by Henry Scadding. Toronto, Copp Clark, 1889. 23p [OTP

**Livesay, John Frederick Bligh, 1875–1944**

PEGGY'S COVE. Toronto, Ryerson, 1944. 100p [BVaU LC NBFU OTP

**Lofthouse, Rev. Joseph, 1855–1933**

A THOUSAND MILES FROM A POST OFFICE; or, Twenty Years' Life and Travel in the Hudson's Bay Regions. Toronto, Macmillan, 1922. 183p [BM BVaU LC OTP

**Long, John, fl. 1768–1791**

VOYAGES AND TRAVELS OF AN INDIAN INTERPRETER AND TRADER. London, Author, 1791. 295p [BM BVaU LC NSWA OTP

**Low, Albert Peter, 1861–1942**

REPORT ON EXPLORATIONS IN THE LABRADOR PENINSULA ... IN 1892–93–94–95. Ottawa, Queen's Printer, 1896. 387p [BM BVaU LC NBSM OKQ

**Lucas, Rev. Daniel Vannorman, 1834–1911**

ALL ABOUT CANADA. Montreal, Witness, 1883. 72p [BViPA OTP

CANAAN AND CANADA. Toronto, Briggs, 1904. 247p [BVaU LC OTP

**Lugrin, Charles Henry, 1846–1917**

NEW BRUNSWICK (CANADA): its Resources, Progress and Advantages. Fredericton, Gov't. of New Brunswick, 1886. 191p [BM BVaU LC NBFU OTU

YUKON GOLD FIELDS. ... Victoria, Colonist, 1897. 32p [BVaU LC QMM

**Lugrin, Nellie de Bertrand, 1874–**

A HANDBOOK OF VANCOUVER ISLAND. Victoria, Buckle, [19—?]. 51p [BM BViP OTP

**Lyons, Chester Peter, 1915–**

MILESTONES ON THE MIGHTY FRASER. Toronto, Dent, 1950. xxxvi + 157p [Also: Vancouver, Evergreen Press, 1957. xv + 215p] [OONL

**McAlpine, Thomas H.**

McALPINE'S ILLUSTRATED TOURISTS' AND TRAVELLERS' GUIDE. ... NOVA SCOTIA, NEW BRUNSWICK AND PRINCE EDWARD ISLAND. Saint John, Sun Print., 1897. 692p [BM OTP

**Macaulay, R.H.H.**

TRADING INTO HUDSON'S BAY. A Narrative of the Visit of Patrick Ashley Cooper. ... Winnipeg, Hudson's Bay Co., 1934. 108p [BM BVaU LC OTU

**Macbeth, Madge Hamilton (Lyons), 1878–1965**
OVER THE GANGPLANK TO SPAIN. Ottawa, Graphic, 1931. 359p [BVaU OTUV QQL

**McCormick, James Hanna**
LLOYDMINSTER; or, 5000 Miles with the Barr Colonists. London, Drane's, [1924?]. 254p [BM BVaU OTP SSU

**McDiarmid, Margaret Agnes (Galloway)**
I LIVED IN PARADISE. Winnipeg, Bulman, 1943. 257p [OTP

**MacDonald, Rev. Alexander, 1858–1941**
STRAY LEAVES; or, Traces of Travel. New York, Christian Press Assoc., 1914. 171p [BViPA OOU

**McDonald, Archibald, 1790–1853**
PEACE RIVER: A CANOE VOYAGE FROM HUDSON'S BAY TO THE PACIFIC BY THE LATE SIR GEORGE SIMPSON ... IN 1828; Journal of the Late Chief Factor, Archibald McDonald ... who Accompanied him. Ed. with Notes by Malcolm McLeod. Ottawa, Durie, 1872. 119p [BVaU LC NSWA OTP QMM

**Macdonald, Rev. James Alexander, 1862–1923**
WHAT A NEWSPAPERMAN SAW IN BRITAIN. Toronto, the Globe, 1909. 30p [NBFU OTU

**Macdonald, Rev. Peter McLaren**
LETTERS FROM THE CANADIAN WEST. Truro, N.S., Chronicle, 1903. 55p [BVaU NSWA OKQ SSU

**MacDonald, Wilson Pugsley, 1880–1967**
ON MY OWN IN MOSCOW. Toronto, Northern Book House, 1958. 37p

**MacDougall, James Brown, 1871–1950**
TWO THOUSAND MILES OF GOLD. From Val d'Or to Yellowknife. Toronto, McClelland, 1946. 234p [BVa OTU

**McDougall, Margaret (Dixon), 1826–1898**
THE LETTERS OF "NORAH" [pseud] ON HER TOUR THROUGH IRELAND. Being a series of Letters to the Montreal "Witness" as Special Correspondent to Ireland. Montreal, Pub. by Public Subscription, 1882. 303p [OTP QMSS

**McEachren, Duncan McNab, 1841–1924**
A TRIP TO BOW RIVER. Montreal, n.pub., [1888?]. 23p [NSWA

**McEvoy, Bernard, 1842–1932**
FROM THE GREAT LAKES TO THE WIDE WEST. Impressions of a Tour between Toronto and the Pacific. Toronto, Briggs, 1902. 288p [BM BVaU LC OTP QMBM

**MacEwan, Grant, 1902–**

BETWEEN THE RED AND THE ROCKIES. Toronto, U. of Toronto Press, 1952. 300p

**McGrath, Patrick Thomas, 1868–1929**

NEWFOUNDLAND IN 1911. ... London, Whitehead, Morris & Co., 1911. 271p [BM BVaU NSHD OTU QMM

**Mackay, Robert Walter Stuart, 1809?–1854**

THE STRANGER'S GUIDE TO ... CANADA. ... Montreal, Bryson, 1854. 168p [OTP QMM

THE STRANGER'S GUIDE TO THE ISLAND AND CITY OF MONTREAL. Montreal, Lovell & Gibson, 1848. 46p [OOC QMBM

**McKenna, James Andrew Joseph, 1862–1919**

THE HUDSON BAY ROUTE. A Compilation of Facts with Conclusions. Ottawa, Dept. of Interior, 1907. 54p [BVaU OLU QMBM SSU

**Mackenzie, Alexander, 1764–1820**

VOYAGES FROM MONTREAL ... through the Continent of North America, to the Frozen and Pacific Oceans; in the Years 1789 and 1793. With a Preliminary Account of ... the Fur Trade. ... London, Cadell, etc., 1801. cxxxii + 412p [Many later editions.] [BM BVaU LC NSWA OTP QMM

**Mackenzie, John, 1895–**

ONTARIO IN YOUR CAR. By John and Marjorie Mackenzie. Toronto, Clarke Irwin, 1950. xvii + 291p [OONL

QUEBEC IN YOUR CAR. By John and Marjorie Mackenzie. Toronto, Clarke Irwin, 1952. xii + 302p

**MacKinnon, John [of P.E.I.]**

TRAVELS IN BRITAIN, FRANCE, PRUSSIA, SWITZERLAND, ITALY, BELGIUM AND HOLLAND. ... Summerside, P.E.I., Schurman & Taylor, [189–?]. [NSHD

**Maclean's Magazine**

CANADA. Portrait of a Country. Sel. and ed. by Leslie F. Hannon. Toronto, McClelland, 1960. 248p

**MacLennan, Kenneth John, 1878–**

NOVA SCOTIA. Her Rivers, Lakes, and History. New York, Vantage Press, 1956. 88p

**McNaughton, Margaret (Peebles)**

OVERLAND TO CARIBOO. An Eventful Journey of Canadian Pioneers to the Gold-Fields of British Columbia in 1862. ... Toronto, Briggs, 1896. 176p [BM BVaU LC NBFU OTU QMM

**Macoun, John, 1831–1920**

MANITOBA AND THE GREAT NORTH WEST. An Encyclopaedia of Information in

Regard to the Great North West. ... Guelph, World Pub. Co., 1882. 687p [BM BVaU NSWA OTP QMM

**MacVicar, Nell**

TALES AND TRAILS OF WESTERN CANADA. By —— and Irene Craig. Regina, School Aids & Text Book Pub. Co., 1947. 144p [BVaU SSU

**McVicar, Robert**

LETTERS ON EMIGRATION from the British Isles, and the Settlement of the Waste Lands in the Province of Canada. Hamilton, Hewson, 1853. 118p [BVaU LC OTP QMBM

**MacWhirter, Margaret Grant, –1940**

TREASURE TROVE IN GASPE AND THE BAIE DES CHALEURS. 3rd ed. Quebec, Telegraph Print., 1919. 217p [BM BVaU NBFU OTP QMBM

**Magrath, Thomas William, 1769–1851**

AUTHENTIC LETTERS FROM UPPER CANADA. With an Account of Canadian Field Sports. Ed. by the Rev. T. Radcliff. Dublin [etc.], Curry [etc.], 1833. 334p [Reprinted: Toronto, Macmillan, 1953. xxiv + 207p] [BVaU LC NSWA OTP QMM

**Mair, Charles, 1838–1927**

THROUGH THE MACKENZIE BASIN. A Narrative of the Athabasca and Peace River Treaty Expedition of 1899. Toronto, Briggs, 1908. 494p [BM BVaU LC NBFU OTP QMBM

**Manitoba. Travel and Publicity Bureau**

MANITOBA GUIDE BOOK. Winnipeg, King's Printer, 1951. 207p

**Manning, Ella Wallace (Jackson), 1910–**

IGLOO FOR THE NIGHT. By Mrs. Tom Manning. London, Hodder, 1943. 232p [Canadian ed.: Toronto, U. of Toronto Press, 1946. 234p] [BM BVaU NSHD OTP QMM

A SUMMER ON HUDSON BAY. London, Hodder, 1949. 223p [BM BVa LC NBFU OTP QMM

**Marsden, Rev. Joshua, 1777–1837**

THE NARRATIVE OF A MISSION TO NOVA SCOTIA, NEW BRUNSWICK, AND THE SOMERS ISLANDS; with a Tour to Lake Ontario. To which is added, THE MISSION, An Original Poem. ... Plymouth-Dock, Johns, 1816. 289p [2nd ed., 1827.] [BM BVaU LC NSWA OTP QMSS

**Maxwell, Lilian Mary (Beckwith), 1877–1956**

'ROUND NEW BRUNSWICK ROADS. Toronto, Ryerson, 1951. 191p

**Menzies, George, 1796?–1847**

ALBUM OF THE TABLE ROCK, NIAGARA FALLS. ... Ed. by ——. Niagara, Chronicle Office, 1846. 79p [LC

**Middleton, Jesse Edgar, 1872–1960**

CANADIAN LANDSCAPE. As Pictured by F.H. Brigden. ... Biographical Notes by J.E. Middleton. Toronto, Ryerson, 1944. 111p [BM BVaU LC OTP QMM

THE ROMANCE OF ONTARIO. Toronto, Gage, 1931. 267p [BM BVaU LC OLU

**Mitchell, Peter, 1824–1899**

THE WEST AND NORTHWEST. Notes of a Holiday Trip. Reliable Information for Immigrants. Montreal, 1880. 63p [BM OTP QMM SSU

**Montague, Sydney Robert**

I LIVED WITH THE ESKIMOS. New York, McBride, 1939. 222p [BM BVaU LC

NORTH TO ADVENTURE. New York, McBride, 1939. 284p [BM BVaU LC OTU QMM

**Moodie, John Wedderburn Dunbar, 1797–1869**

TEN YEARS IN SOUTH AFRICA. London, Bentley, 1835. 2v [BM LC

**Moon, Robert James, 1925–**

I FOUND CANADA ABROAD. Toronto, Ryerson, 1957. xx + 156p

THIS IS SASKATCHEWAN. Toronto, Ryerson, 1953. 242p

**Moore, Philip Hooper, 1879–1961**

WITH GUN AND ROD IN CANADA. London, Cape, 1922. 260p [BM BVaU LC NSHD OKQ

**Moorsom, William Scarth, 1804–1863**

LETTERS FROM NOVA SCOTIA. Comprising Sketches of a Young Country. London, Colburn & Bentley, 1830. 371p [BM BVaU LC NSWA OTP QMM

**Morgan, Henry James, 1842–1913**

THE TOUR OF H.R.H. THE PRINCE OF WALES THROUGH BRITISH AMERICA AND THE UNITED STATES. By A British Canadian [pseud]. Montreal, Lovell, 1860. 271p [BM BVaU LC NBFU OLU

**Morris, Alexander, 1826–1889**

THE HUDSON'S BAY AND PACIFIC TERRITORIES. A Lecture. ... Montreal, Lovell, 1859. 57p [BM BVaU NSWA OTP QMSS

**Morton, Arthur Silver, 1870–1945**

UNDER WESTERN SKIES. Being a Series of Pen-Pictures of the Canadian West in Early Fur Trade Times. Toronto, Nelson, 1937. 232p [BM BVaU LC NBFU OTP QMM

**Mountain, Rev. George Jehoshaphat, 1789–1863**

JOURNAL OF THE BISHOP OF MONTREAL DURING A VISIT TO THE CHURCH MISSIONARY SOCIETY'S N.W. AMERICA MISSION. London, Seeley, 1845. 236p [2nd ed.: London, Seeley, 1849. lxxxix + 166p] [BM BVaU LC NSWA OTP QMM

VISIT TO THE GASPE COAST, 1824. Quebec, King's Printer, 1941–42. 44p [NSHD OOA QMSS

**Mowat, Farley McGill, 1921–**

THE DESPERATE PEOPLE. Boston, Little Brown, 1959. xii + 305p [Refers to the Ihalmiut Eskimos: Sequel to PEOPLE OF THE DEER.]

ORDEAL BY ICE. Ed. by ——. Toronto, McClelland, 1960. 364p

PEOPLE OF THE DEER. London, Joseph, 1952. 316p [Also: Boston, Little Brown, 1952. 344p; reprinted, 1958. 320p] [Account of two years spent with the Ihalmiut, an almost extinct Eskimo tribe of the Keewatin District.]

**Mullock, Rev. John Thomas, 1807–1869**

LECTURES ON NEWFOUNDLAND. St. John's, Patriot Office, 1860. 37p [LC

TWO LECTURES ON NEWFOUNDLAND. New York, Mullaly, 1860. 60p [BM QMSS

**Munn, Henry Toke**

PRAIRIE TRAILS AND ARCTIC BY-WAYS. London, Hurst & Blackett, 1932. 288p [BM BVaU LC NBFU OTP QMM

TALES OF THE ESKIMO. Being Impressions of a ... People. London, Chambers, 1925. 196p [BM BVaU LC NBFU OLU QMM

**Munro, William F.**

THE BACKWOODS OF ONTARIO, AND THE PRAIRIES OF THE NORTH WEST. London, Simpkin Marshall, 1881. 127p [BM OTP

EMIGRATION MADE EASY; or, How to Settle on the Prairie. ... Glasgow, Macrone, 1883. 10p [BViPA NSWA

**Murphy, Emily Gowan (Ferguson), 1868–1933**

THE IMPRESSIONS OF JANEY CANUCK ABROAD. Toronto, 1902. 186p [BM OTP

JANEY CANUCK IN THE WEST. London, Cassell, 1910. 305p [Also: London, Dent, 1919. 223p] [BM BVaU OKQ

OPEN TRAILS. By "Janey Canuck" [pseud]. London, Cassell, 1912. 291p [BM BVaU LC NBFU OTP

SEEDS OF PINE. By Janey Canuck [pseud]. London, Hodder, 1914. 307p [Also: Toronto, Musson, 1922. 301p] [BM BVaU LC NBFU OTP

**Neilson, Joseph, 1813–1888**

OBSERVATIONS UPON EMIGRATION TO UPPER CANADA. [Prize Essay.] Kingston, Chronicle & Gazette, 1837. 74p [OTP

**Newcombe, Charles Frederic, 1851–**

THE FIRST CIRCUMNAVIGATION OF VANCOUVER'S ISLAND. Victoria, Cullin, 1914. 69p [BM BVaU LC OTU

**Niven, Frederick John, 1878–1944**

CANADA WEST. London, Dent, 1929. 188p [BM BVaU LC NSHD OONL

COLOUR IN THE CANADIAN ROCKIES. By Walter J. Phillips and Frederick Niven. Toronto, Nelson, 1937. 125p [BM BVaU NSHPL SRL

GO NORTH, WHERE THE WORLD IS YOUNG. Alaska ... Atlin, Land of Reflections and Moods. ... N.p., n.d. 38p [BVaU QMBM

**O'Brien, Godfrey S.**

THE TOURIST'S GUIDE TO QUEBEC. Quebec, Hunter Rose, 1864. 70p [OTP

**Ogilvie, William, 1846–1912**

THE KLONDIKE OFFICIAL GUIDE. Toronto, Hunter Rose, 1898. 152p [BVaU LC NSWA OTP

LECTURE ON THE KLONDIKE MINING DISTRICT. Victoria, Wolfenden, 1897. 14p [BVaU OTU

LECTURE ON THE YUKON GOLD FIELDS (CANADA) DELIVERED AT VICTORIA, B.C. Rev., amplified, and authorized by the Lecturer. Victoria, Colonist Press, 1897. 32p [OTU QMM

THE YUKON TERRITORY. The Narrative of W.H. Dall ... 1866–1868. The Narrative of an Exploration made in 1887 ... by George M. Dawson. Extracts from the Report of an Exploration made in 1896–1897 by Wm. Ogilvie. London, Downey, 1898. 438p [OTU QMSS

**O'Gorman, P.T.**

MAGNIFICENT ONTARIO. Ilfracombe, Devon, Stockwell, 1952. 175p

**Onraet, Anthony (Tony)**

SIXTY BELOW. With an intro. by Dr. Thomas Wood. Toronto, Cape, 1944. 192p [Also pub. as: DOWN NORTH. London, Cape, 1944. 157p] [BM BVa LC NBFU OTP QMBM

**Oppenheimer, David, 1834–1897**

VANCOUVER CITY. Its Progress and Industries, With Practical Hints for Capitalists and Intending Settlers. Vancouver, 1889. 64p [NSWA OOA

**Orford, Mrs. Mena**

JOURNEY NORTH. Toronto, McClelland, 1957. 190p [Experiences among the Eskimos of Baffin Island.]

**Ottawa Publicity Department**

INDUSTRIAL AND PICTURESQUE OTTAWA, THE CAPITAL OF THE DOMINION OF CANADA. Ottawa, Crain, 1905. 40p [LC

OTTAWA, CANADA, THE GREAT CHEAP POWER CITY. ... Ottawa, Esdale, 1912. 48p [LC OTU

OTTAWA, CANADA'S CAPITAL. Ottawa, City Council, [1904?]. 49p [LC

**Outram, James, 1864–1925**

IN THE HEART OF THE CANADIAN ROCKIES. London, Macmillan, 1905. 466p [BVaU LC NSHD OTU

**Outram, Joseph, 1803–1885**

A HANDBOOK OF INFORMATION FOR THE EMIGRANTS TO NOVA SCOTIA. Halifax, 1864. 36p [BM

NOVA SCOTIA. Its Condition and Resources. Edinburgh, Blackwood, 1850. 35p [BM

**Page, Mrs. Elizabeth Merwin, 1889–**

WAGONS WEST. A Story of the Oregon Trail. New York, Farrar, 1930. 361p [Narrative based on letters of Henry Page.] [BViPA LC

WILD HORSES AND GOLD. From Wyoming to the Yukon. New York, Farrar, 1932. 362p [Narrative based on a diary kept by "Kansas Gilbert."] [BM BVaU LC OTU

**Palliser, John, 1807–1887**

EXPLORATION. ... The Journals ... Relative to the Exploration, by Captain Palliser ... between the Western Shore of Lake Superior and the Pacific Ocean during the Years 1857, 1858, 1859, and 1860. London, Eyre & Spottiswoode, 1863. 325p [BVaU NSWA OTP

THE SOLITARY HUNTER; or, Sporting Adventures in the Prairies. London, Routledge, 1856. 234p [BM BViPA LC OOC

SOLITARY RAMBLES AND ADVENTURES OF A HUNTER IN THE PRAIRIES. London, Murray, 1853. 326p [BM BVaU LC MWU OTP QMM

**Panton, James Hoyes, 1847–1898**

RAMBLES IN THE NORTH-WEST, ACROSS THE PRAIRIES, AND IN THE PASSES OF THE ROCKY MOUNTAINS. Guelph, Mercury Steam Print., 1885. 20p [BVa NSWA OTP

**Parker, Gilbert, 1862–1932**

ROUND THE COMPASS IN AUSTRALIA. London, Hutchinson, 1892. 447p [Another ed. pub. in Melbourne.] [BM BVaU OTP

**Parkin, George Robert, 1846–1922**

THE GREAT DOMINION. Studies of Canada. London, Macmillan, 1895. 251p [BM BVaU NBFU OTP QMM

**Peat, Louisa (Watson)**

CANADA, NEW WORLD POWER. Toronto, McLeod, 1945. 293p [BVaU LC OTP QMM

**Percival, Walter Pilling, 1885–1966**

THE LURE OF MONTREAL. Toronto, Ryerson, 1945. 240p [BVaU LC OTU QMM

THE LURE OF QUEBEC. Toronto, Ryerson, 1941. 216p [Also later eds.] [BM BVaU LC OTP QMM

**Phillipps-Wolley, Clive Oldnall, 1854–1918**

SAVAGE SWANETIA. London, Bentley, 1883. 2v [BM BViP OTU

A SPORTSMAN'S EDEN. London, Bentley, 1888. 261p [BM BVaU OTU QMBM

TROTTINGS OF A TENDERFOOT; or, A Visit to the Columbian Fiords and Spitzbergen. London, Bentley, 1884. 252p [BM BVaU NSWA OTP

**Phillips, Walter J.**

COLOUR IN THE CANADIAN ROCKIES. By Walter J. Phillips and Frederick Niven. Toronto, Nelson, 1937. 125p [BM BVaU NSHPL SRL

**Pike, Warburton Mayer, 1861–1915**

THE BARREN GROUND OF NORTHERN CANADA. New York, Macmillan, 1892. 300p [Also: New York, Dutton, 1917. 334p] [BM BVaU LC NSWA OTP QMM

THROUGH THE SUBARCTIC FOREST. New York, Arnold, 1896. 295p [BM BVaU LC OTU QMM

**Pinkerton, Kathrene Sutherland (Gedney), 1887–**

FARTHER NORTH. New York, Harcourt, 1944. 181p [BM BVaU LC

FOX ISLAND. New York, Harcourt, 1942. 195p [BM BVaU LC OOP

THREE'S A CREW. New York, Carrick & Evans, 1940. 316p [BM BVa LC NSHD OTU QMM

WILDERNESS WIFE. New York, Carrick & Evans, 1939. 327p [BM BVaU LC NSHD QMM

**Pocock, Roger, 1865–1941**

TALES OF WESTERN LIFE, LAKE SUPERIOR, AND THE CANADIAN PRAIRIE. Ottawa, Mitchell, 1888. 164p [BM BViPA OTU

**Porter, Jane**

A SIX WEEKS' TOUR IN WESTERN CANADA. By a Lady [pseud]. Montreal, Lovell, 1865. 40p [OTP

**Potvin, Damase, 1881–**

THE SAGUENAY TRIP. Montreal, Canada Steamship Lines, [195–?]. 124 + xiip

**Price, Bertha Maud (Weston), 1872–1955**

THE TRAIL OF THE BROAD HIGHWAY. [With] Pen and Ink Sketches by Maude Gage Pellerin. Sherbrooke, Que., Authors, 1929. 121p [OONL QMBM

**Prowse, Daniel Woodley, 1834–1914**

THE NEWFOUNDLAND GUIDE-BOOK, 1905. Ed. by ——. London, Bradbury & Agnew, 1905. 182p [BM LC NBFU OTU QMM

**Pyke, Magnus, 1909–**

GO WEST, YOUNG MAN, GO WEST. Ottawa, Graphic, 1930. 303p [BVaU NBFU OOP

**Reid, Edgar Cameron, 1902–**

FAST FLOWS THE FRASER. New York, Comet Press, 1958. 45p

**Reid, J.H. Stewart, 1909–1963**

MOUNTAINS, MEN AND RIVERS. British Columbia in Legend and Story. Toronto, Ryerson, 1954. x + 229p

**Reynolds, Helen Mary Greenwood (Campbell) Dickson, 1884–**

UP CANADA WAY. By Helen Dickson [pseud]. Boston, Heath, 1942. 64p [LC

**Reynolds, William Kilby, 1848–1902**

PLEASANT PLACES BY THE SHORE AND IN THE FORESTS OF QUEBEC AND THE MARITIME PROVINCES. ... [Anon] Toronto, Dixon, [1882?]. 65p [NBFU OTP QMSS

**Rickard, Thomas Arthur, 1864–1953**

JOURNEYS OF OBSERVATION. San Francisco, Dewey, 1907. 130p [LC

THROUGH THE YUKON AND ALASKA. San Francisco, Mining and Scientific Press, 1909. 392p [BVaU LC OTP

**Roberts, Charles George Douglas, 1860–1943**

THE CANADIAN GUIDE-BOOK. The Tourist's and Sportsman's Guide to Eastern Canada and Newfoundland. ... New York, Appleton, 1891. 270p [Several later eds. with slight change in sub-title.] [BM BVaU NSWA OTU QMM

DISCOVERIES AND EXPLORATIONS IN THE CENTURY. ... (Nineteenth Century Series). Philadelphia, Linscott, 1904. 529p [BM BVaU LC NSHD

THE LAND OF EVANGELINE AND THE GATEWAYS THITHER. ... With Many Illustrations and Appendices for Sportsman and Tourist. Kentville, Dominion Atlantic Railway Co., [1894?]. 92p [BM BVaU NSWA OKQ QMBM

**Roberts, Leslie, 1896–**

HOME FROM THE COLD WARS. Boston, Beacon Press, 1948. 224p [BVaU LC OTP

SO THIS IS OTTAWA. Toronto, Macmillan, 1933. 222p [BM BVaU OTP QMM

**Robertson, Douglas Sinclair, 1877–**

TO THE ARCTIC WITH THE MOUNTIES. Toronto, Macmillan, 1934. 309p [BVaU NBFU OTU QMM

**Robinson, Frank Alfred, 1874–**

FRIENDLY LETTERS FROM F.A.R. AWAY. Toronto, Mundy-Goodfellow, 1937. 172p [OTU

GUEST ROOMS ENJOYED AND ENDURED IN THE KING'S SERVICE. Toronto, Missions of Biblical Education, 1933. 256p [BViPA NBSaM OLU

**Robinson, Judith**

AS WE CAME BY. Toronto, Dent, 1951. 160p

**Roger, Charles, 1819–1878**

GLIMPSES OF LONDON, AND ATLANTIC EXPERIENCES ... IN THE WINTER OF 1872–73. Ottawa, Robertson Roger, 1873. 47p [BM QMSS

**Rogers, Robert, 1731–1795**

A CONCISE ACCOUNT OF NORTH AMERICA. London, Millan, 1765. 264p [Also: Dublin, Milliken, 1769. 264p] [BM BVaU LC NSWA OTP QMM

**Roper, Edward**

BY TRACK AND TRAIL. A Journey through Canada. With Numerous Original Sketches by the Author. London, Allen, 1891. 455p [BM BVaU LC NBFU OTU

**Rose, Rev. A.W.H.**

THE EMIGRANT CHURCHMAN IN CANADA; or, Canada in 1849. Pictures of Canadian Life by a Pioneer of the Wilderness. Ed. by the Rev. Henry Christmas. London, Bentley, 1849. 2v [Also issued as CANADA IN 1849.] [BVaU NBFU OTP QMSS

**Ross, Alexander, 1783–1856**

ADVENTURES OF THE FIRST SETTLERS ON THE OREGON OR COLUMBIA RIVER. Being a Narrative of the Expedition Fitted out by John Jacob Astor. ... London, Smith Elder, 1849. 352p [Also: Cleveland, Ohio, Clark, 1904. 332p] [BM BVaU NBFU OTP QMM

THE FUR HUNTERS OF THE FAR WEST. ... London, Smith Elder, 1855. 2v [Also: Chicago, Donnelly, 1924, and Norman, U. of Oklahoma Press, 1956.] [BM BVaU LC NSHD OTP QMM

**Ross, Rev. William Wilson, 1838–1884**

10,000 MILES BY LAND AND SEA. Toronto, Campbell, 1876. 284p [BM BVaU LC OTP

**Rowlands, John James, 1892–**

CACHE LAKE COUNTRY. Life in the North Woods. New York, Norton, 1947. 272p [BM BVaU LC OTP QMM

**Ryerson, Rev. John, 1800–1878**

HUDSON'S BAY; or, A Missionary Tour. ... Toronto, Sanderson, 1855. xxiv + 190p [BM BVaU NSWA OTP QMM

**St. John, Frederick Edward Molyneux, 1838–1904**

THE SEA OF MOUNTAINS. An Account of Lord Dufferin's Tour through British Columbia in 1876. London, Hurst & Blackett, 1877. 2v [BM BVaU OTP

**Schaffer, Mary Townsend (Sharples), 1861–1939**

OLD INDIAN TRAILS OF THE CANADIAN ROCKIES. Incidents of Camp and Trail Life. Toronto, Briggs, 1911. 364p [BM BVaU NBFU OTU

**Schrag, Alexander Andrew, 1907–**

CRATER COUNTRY. By Lex Schrag. Toronto, Ryerson, 1958 [i.e., 1959]. ix + 169p

**Scott, H.G.**

FROM STORM TO STORM. Vancouver, Sun Pub. Co., 1947. 242p [BVaU OLU QMBM

**Scott, H. Percy, 1856–1937**

SEEING CANADA AND THE SOUTH. Toronto, Briggs, 1911. 137p [BM BVaU NSWA OTU QMBM

**Secretan, James Henry Edward, 1852–1926**

TO THE KLONDYKE AND BACK. A Journey down the Yukon from its Source to its Mouth. ... With Hints to Intending Prospectors. London, Hurst & Blackett, 1898. 260p [BM BVaU OTP QMM

**Seton, Ernest Thompson, 1860–1946**

THE ARCTIC PRAIRIES. A Canoe Journey of 2,000 Miles in Search of the Caribou. Being the Account of a Voyage to the Region north of Aylmer Lake. ... New York, Scribner, 1911. 415p [BM BVaU LC NBFU OKQ QMM

**Sharcott, Margaret (Brampton), 1928–**

TROLLER'S HOLIDAY. London, Davies, 1957. 221p [Account of a voyage around Vancouver Island.]

**Sibbald, Thomas, 1810–1890**

A FEW DAYS IN THE UNITED STATES AND CANADA, With Some Hints to Settlers. [Anon] London, 1846. 48p [BM

**Silver, Arthur Peters, 1851–1908**

FARM-COTTAGE, CAMP AND CANOE IN MARITIME CANADA; or, The Call of Nova Scotia to the Emigrant and Sportsman. Toronto, Musson, 1908. 249p [BM BVaU LC NSWA OKQ QMM

THROUGH MIRAMICHI WITH ROD AND RIFLE; or, A Birch-bark Canoe Trip in Northern New Brunswick. Halifax, Holloway, 1890. 30p [OOP

**Sime, Jessie Georgina, 1880–**

IN A CANADIAN SHACK. London, Dickson, 1937. 241p [BM BVaU LC NSHD OTP QMM

**Simpson, George, 1787–1860**

CALIFORNIA. ... From Sir George Simpson's OVERLAND JOURNEY ROUND THE WORLD. ... By John T. Hughes. Cincinnati, James, 1848. 105p [LC

FUR TRADE AND EMPIRE. George Simpson's Journal. Ed. by Frederick Merk. Cambridge, Harvard U. Press, 1931. xxxvi + 370p [BM BVaU LC NSHD OTP QMM

JOURNAL OF OCCURRENCES IN THE ATHABASCA DEPARTMENT ... 1820 AND 1821, AND REPORT. Ed. by E.E. Rich, with a foreword by Lord Tweedsmuir and an intro. by Chester Martin. Toronto, Champlain Soc., 1938. lix + 498p [BM BVaU LC NBFU OTP

NARRATIVE OF A JOURNEY ROUND THE WORLD, DURING THE YEARS 1841 AND 1842. London, Colburn, 1847. 2v [BM BVaU LC NBFU OTP QMM

NARRATIVE OF A VOYAGE TO CALIFORNIA PORTS IN 1841–42. ... From the NARRATIVE OF A VOYAGE ROUND THE WORLD. ... San Francisco, Russell, 1930. 232p [BViPA LC

AN OVERLAND JOURNEY ROUND THE WORLD, DURING THE YEARS 1841 AND 1842. Philadelphia, Lee & Blanchard, 1847. 272p [BViPA LC OTP QMM

PART OF DISPATCH FROM GEORGE SIMPSON, ESQR., GOVERNOR OF RUPERTS LAND, TO THE GOVERNOR AND COMMITTEE OF THE HUDSON'S BAY COMPANY ... 1829. Ed. by E.E. Rich, with an intro. by W.S. Wallace. Toronto, Champlain Society, 1947. 277p [BM BVaU LC NBFU OTP QMM

**Sinclair, Gordon Allan, 1900–**

BRIGHT PATHS TO ADVENTURE. Toronto, McClelland, 1945. 280p [BVaU NBFU OTP

FOOT-LOOSE IN INDIA. New York, Farrar, 1933. 312p [BM BVaU LC OTU QMM

CANNIBAL QUEST. Toronto, Doubleday, 1933. 300p [BM BVaU LC NBFU OTU

KHYBER CARAVAN. Toronto, Oxford U. Press, 1936. 316p [BM LC OTU

LOOSE AMONG THE DEVILS. A Voyage from Devil's Island. Toronto, Doubleday, 1935. 276p [BM BVa LC NBFU OTU

SIGNPOSTS TO ADVENTURE. Toronto, McClelland, 1947. 369p [BVa OOP

**Sleigh, Burrows Willcocks Arthur, 1821–1869**

PINE FORESTS AND HACMATACK CLEARINGS; or, Travel, Life and Adventure in the British North American Provinces. London, Bentley, 1853. 408p [BM BVaU LC NBFU OTP QMM

**Smallwood, Joseph Roberts, 1900–**

THE BOOK OF NEWFOUNDLAND. Ed. by ——. St. John's, Newfoundland Book Pub., 1937. 2v [BM BVaU LC NSHD OTP QMM

THE NEW NEWFOUNDLAND. An Account of the Revolutionary Developments which are Transforming Britain's Oldest Colony from "The Cinderella of the Empire" into one of the Great Small Nations of the World. New York, Macmillan, 1931. 277p [BM BVaU LC NBFU OTU QMM

**Smith, Goldwin, 1823–1910**

A TRIP TO ENGLAND. Toronto, Robinson, 1888. 61p [Same title: New York, Macmillan, 1892. 136p] [BM BVaU LC NBFU OKQ QMM

**Smith, Thomas Barlow, 1839–1933**

LITTLE MAYFLOWER LAND. Halifax, Bowes, 1900. 80p [LC NSHD OTP QMM

**Smith, William Henry, fl. 1846–1873**

CANADA. ... A Historical, Geographical, Geological and Statistical Account of Canada West. Toronto, Maclear, 1851. 2v [BM BVaU LC NSWA OTP QMM

SMITH'S CANADIAN GAZETTEER. Comprising Statistical and General Information ... of ... Canada West. Toronto, Rowsell, 1846. 285p [BM BVaU LC NSWA OTP QMM

**Somerville, Alexander, 1811–1885**

CANADA, A BATTLE FIELD. (TRAVELS IN CANADA AND THE FRONTIER UNITED STATES). Hamilton, 1862. 64p [BM OTP QMM

THE WHISTLER AT THE PLOUGH. Manchester, Ainsworth, 1852. 632p [BM LC OTP

**Spedon, Andrew Learmont, 1831–1884**

RAMBLES AMONG THE BLUE-NOSES; or, Reminiscences of a Tour through New Brunswick and Nova Scotia ... 1862. Montreal, Lovell, 1863. 229p [BVaU LC NBFU OTP QMM

SKETCHES OF A TOUR FROM CANADA TO PARIS, by way of the British Isles, during the Summer of 1867. Montreal, Lovell, 1868. 238p [BM BVaU NSWA OLU

**Spragge, Ellen Elizabeth (Cameron), 1854–1932**

FROM ONTARIO TO THE PACIFIC BY THE C.P.R. By Mrs. Arthur Spragge. Toronto, Robinson, 1887. 188p [BM BVaU LC NSWA OTU QMSS

**Springer, John S.**

FOREST LIFE AND FOREST TREES. Winter Camp-life among the Loggers, and Wild-wood Adventure. New York, Harper, 1851. 259p [BM BVaU LC OTP

**Sproat, Gilbert Malcolm, 1832–1913**

DESCRIPTION OF KOOTENAY DISTRICT. Victoria, Wolfenden, 1884. 30p [LC

SCENES AND STUDIES OF SAVAGE LIFE. London, Smith Elder, 1868. 317p [BM BVaU LC OTP

**Steele, Harwood Elmes Robert, 1897–**

POLICING THE ARCTIC. ... Toronto, Ryerson, 1936. 390p [BM BVaU LC OTP QMM

**Stefansson, Vilhjalmur, 1879–1962**

THE ADVENTURE OF WRANGEL ISLAND. New York, Macmillan, 1925. 424p [BM BVaU LC NSHD OTP QMM

THE ARCTIC IN FACT AND FABLE. New York, Foreign Policy Assoc., 1945. 96p [BVaU LC OTP

THE FRIENDLY ARCTIC. Five Years in Polar Regions. New York, Macmillan, 1921. xxxi + 784p [BM BVaU LC NBFU OTP QMM

GREAT ADVENTURES AND EXPLORATIONS. Ed. by ——. New York, Dial Press, 1947. 788p [BVaU LC NBFU OTP QMM

GREENLAND. Garden City, Doubleday, 1942. 338p [BM BVaU LC NSHD OTP QMM

HUNTERS OF THE GREAT NORTH. New York, Harcourt, 1922. 301p [BM BVaU LC OKQ QMM

ICELAND: FIRST AMERICAN REPUBLIC. New York, Doubleday, 1939. 275p [BM BVaU OTU

MY LIFE WITH THE ESKIMO. New York, Macmillan, 1913. 538p [New and abridged ed.: New York, Macmillan, 1927.] [BM BVaU LC NSHD OTP QMM

THE NORTHWARD COURSE OF EMPIRE. New York, Harcourt, 1922. 274p [BM BVaU LC NSHD OTU

NORTHWEST TO FORTUNE. The Search of Western Man for a Commercially Practical Route to the Far East. New York, Duell Sloan, 1958. xix + 356p

NOT BY BREAD ALONE. New York, Macmillan, 1946. 339p [BVaU OTU QMM

THE SHAMAN'S REVENGE. By Violet Irwin, based on the Arctic Diaries of Vilhjalmur Stefansson. New York, Macmillan, 1925. 286p [LC OTMC

THREE VOYAGES OF MARTIN FROBISHER. In Search of a Passage to Cathay and India by the North-West, A.D. 1576–8. London, Argonaut Press, 1938. 2v [NBFU OTU

ULTIMA THULE. Further Mysteries of the Arctic. New York, Macmillan, 1940. 383p [BM BVaU LC NSHD OTP QMM

UNSOLVED MYSTERIES OF THE ARCTIC. ... With an intro. by Stephen Leacock telling how this Book Came to be Written. New York, Macmillan, 1939. 381p [BM LC OTU

**Stewart, Rev. Charles James, 1775–1837**

THE EASTERN TOWNSHIPS IN THE PROVINCE OF LOWER CANADA. Montreal, Mower, 1815. 18p [BVaU NSWA OTP

REPORT OF A MISSIONARY JOURNEY ... THROUGH UPPER CANADA IN 1820. Ed. by James J. Talman. London, Ont., University of Western Ontario, 1942. 18p [BVaU LC OTP OTU QMM

A SHORT VIEW OF THE PRESENT STATE OF THE EASTERN TOWNSHIPS IN THE PROVINCE OF LOWER CANADA. Montreal, Hatchard, 1815. 20p [BM BVaU NSWA QMM

**Stewart, Elihu, 1844–1935**

DOWN THE MACKENZIE AND UP THE YUKON IN 1906. New York, Lane, 1913. 270p [BM BVaU LC NBFU OTP QMM

**Stewart, John, 1758?–1834**

AN ACCOUNT OF PRINCE EDWARD ISLAND. London, Winchester, 1806. 304p [BM BVaU NSHD OTP QMM

**Strachan, Rev. John, 1778–1867**

A JOURNAL OF VISITATION TO THE WESTERN PORTION OF HIS DIOCESE ... 1842. 3rd ed. London, Soc. for the Propagation of the Gospel, 1846. 64p [LC OTP QMM

REMARKS ON EMIGRATION FROM THE UNITED KINGDOM. London, Murray, 1827. 96p [BM OTP

**Stuart, Charles, 1783–1865**

THE EMIGRANT'S GUIDE TO UPPER CANADA; or, Sketches of the Present State of that Province. London, Longmans, 1820. 335p [BM BVaU NSHD OTP QMBM

**Stuck, Rev. Hudson, 1863–1920**

TEN THOUSAND MILES WITH A DOG SLED. A Narrative of Winter Travel in Interior Alaska. New York, Scribner, 1914. 420p [BM BVaU LC OTP QMM

VOYAGES ON THE YUKON AND ITS TRIBUTARIES. New York, Scribner, 1917. 397p [BM BVaU LC OTP QMM

A WINTER CIRCUIT OF OUR ARCTIC COAST. A Narrative of a Journey with Dog-Sleds around the entire Arctic Coast of Alaska. New York, Scribner, 1920. 360p [BM BVaU LC OTP

**Sullivan, Alan, 1868–1947**

THE CYCLE OF THE NORTH. London, Dent, 1938. 180p [BM QMM

**Sutherland, Rev. Alexander, 1833–1910**

A SUMMER IN PRAIRIE LAND. Notes of a Tour through the North-West Territory. Toronto, Methodist Pub. House, 1881. 198p [BVaU LC NSWA OTU

**Sutherland, John Campbell, 1860–1936**

THE PROVINCE OF QUEBEC. Geographical and Social Studies. Montreal, Renouf, 1922. 157p [2nd rev. ed.: Toronto, Nelson, 1931. 126p] [BM BVaU LC NSWA OTP QMM

THE ROMANCE OF QUEBEC. Toronto, Gage, 1934. 246p [BM OLU

**Talbot, Edward Allen, 1801–1839**

FIVE YEARS' RESIDENCE IN THE CANADAS. ... London, Longmans, 1824. 2v [BM BVaU LC NSHD OTP QMM

**Talbot, Thomas, fl. 1844–1882**

NEWFOUNDLAND; or, a Letter Addressed to a Friend in Ireland ... with an Especial View to Emigration. London, Sampson, 1882. 67p [NSHP

**Taylor, Henry, fl. 1819–1860**

JOURNAL OF A TOUR FROM MONTREAL ... to the Eastern Townships. Quebec, Cowan, 1840. 84p [OTP

**Thompson, David, 1770–1857**

DAVID THOMPSON'S NARRATIVE OF HIS EXPLORATIONS IN WESTERN AMERICA 1784–1812. Ed. by J.B. Tyrrell. Toronto, Champlain Society, 1916. xcviii + 582p [BM BVaU LC NSHD OTU QMM

JOURNALS RELATING TO MONTANA AND ADJACENT REGIONS, 1808–1812. Ed. by M. Catherine White. Missoula, Montana U. Press, 1950. 345p [BVaU OTU

NEW LIGHT ON THE EARLY HISTORY OF THE GREATER NORTHWEST. The Manuscript Journals of Alexander Henry ... and of David Thompson ... 1799–1814. Ed. by Elliott Coues. New York, Harper, 1897. 3v [BM BVaU NBFU OTU QMM

**Till, William, –1860**

NEW BRUNSWICK, AS A HOME FOR EMIGRANTS. ... Saint John, Barnes, 1860. 25p [OTP

**Tobe, John H., 1907–**

HUNZA. Adventures in a Land of Paradise. Toronto, McLeod, 1960. 646p

**Tocque, Rev. Philip, 1814–1899**

NEWFOUNDLAND: AS IT WAS, AND AS IT IS IN 1877. Toronto, Magurn, 1878. 511p [BM BVaU LC NSHD OTP QMM

A PEEP AT UNCLE SAM'S FARM, WORKSHOP, FISHERIES, &c. Boston, Pierce, 1851. 229p [LC NSWA OKQ

WANDERING THOUGHTS; or, Solitary hours. London, Richardson, 1846. 387p [BVaU NSHP OTP

**Todd, Henry Cook, –1862**

NOTES UPON CANADA AND THE UNITED STATES, from 1832 to 1840. ... By a Traveller [pseud]. Toronto, Rogers & Thompson, 1840. 184p [Same main title: ... in the year 1835. By a Traveller. Toronto, Coates, 1835. 95p —BVaU] [BM LC OOA QMM

**Tolboom, Wanda (Neill)**

PEOPLE OF THE SNOW. Eskimos of Arctic Canada. New York, Coward-McCann, 1956. 96p

**Tolfrey, Frederic**

THE SPORTSMAN IN CANADA. London, Newby, 1845. 2v [BM LC NSWA OTU

**Traill, Catharine Parr (Strickland), 1802–1899**

THE BACKWOODS OF CANADA. Being Letters from the Wife of an Emigrant Officer. Illustrative of the Domestic Economy of British America. London, Knight, 1836. 352p [Various editions. Editions of 1846 and 1849 precede above title with CANADA AND THE OREGON, and add to subtitle: "To which is Appended an Account of the Country of the Oregon."] [BM BVaU LC NSWA OTP QMM

CANADA AND THE OREGON. ... [See preceding title.]

THE CANADIAN EMIGRANT HOUSEKEEPER'S GUIDE. Toronto, Lovell & Gibson, 1862. 150p [Much the same as THE FEMALE EMIGRANT'S GUIDE.] [NSHD OTP

THE CANADIAN SETTLER'S GUIDE. Toronto, Old Countryman Office, 1855. 13 + 218 + 40p [Numerous editions. Also pub. under title: THE FEMALE EMIGRANT'S GUIDE.] [BM BVaU LC NSWA OTP QMM

THE FEMALE EMIGRANT'S GUIDE, and Hints on Canadian Housekeeping. Toronto, Maclear, 1854. xi + 218 + 40p [Later editions pub. as: THE CANADIAN SETTLER'S GUIDE.] [BM BVaU OTU

**Tranter, Mrs. Gladdis Joy, 1902–**

LINK TO THE NORTH. London, Hodder, 1946. 255p [BM BVaU LC OTP QMM

PLOWING THE ARCTIC. Being an Account of the Voyage of the R.C.M.P. "St. Roch." Toronto, Longmans, 1945. 316p [BM BVaU LC NSHD OTP QMM

**Trow, James, 1825–1892**

MANITOBA AND NORTH WEST TERRITORIES. Letters. ... Ottawa, Dept. of Agriculture, 1878. 100p [BM BViPA LC OTP

A TRIP TO MANITOBA. Quebec, Marcotte, 1875. 86p [BVaU LC OTP

**Tyre, Robert, 1908–**

ALONG THE HIGHWAY. [Travel Tales ... from the Log of Galloping Gus, a Roving Reporter in Saskatchewan.] Regina, School Aids and Text Book Pub. Co., 1950. 124p [OONL

**Tyrrell, James Williams, 1863–1945**

ACROSS THE SUB-ARCTICS OF CANADA. Toronto, Briggs, 1897. 280p [BM BVaU LC NSWA OOA

**Umfreville, Edward, fl. 1771–1790**

NIPIGON TO WINNIPEG. Canoe Voyage ... in 1784. Ed. by R. Douglas. With Extracts from the Writings of other Early Travellers through the Region. Ottawa, Douglas, 1929. 65p [BM BVaU OTU

THE PRESENT STATE OF HUDSON'S BAY. ... London, Stalker, 1790. 226p [Also ed. with intro. and notes by W. Stewart Wallace. Toronto, Ryerson, 1954. xv + 122p] [BM BVaU LC NSWA OTP QMM

**Vancouver, George, 1757–1798**

A VOYAGE OF DISCOVERY TO THE NORTH PACIFIC OCEAN, AND ROUND THE WORLD. ... London, Robinson, 1798. 3v [BM BVaU NSWA OTP QMM

**Waddington, Alfred Penderill, 1801–1872**

OVERLAND ROUTE THROUGH BRITISH NORTH AMERICA. London, Longmans, 1868. 48p [BM BViPA LC OOA QMM

**Wade, Mark Sweeten, 1858–1929**

THE OVERLANDERS OF '62. Ed. by John Hosie. Victoria, Banfield, 1931. 174p [BM BVaU LC NSHD OTP QMM

**Walker, Gertrude E.**

ROMANTIC WINNIPEG. Winnipeg, Farmer's Advocate Press, 1937. 48p [2nd ed.: 1938. 68p] [OTU

**Wallace, Frederick William, 1886–1958**

UNDER SAIL IN THE LAST OF THE CLIPPERS. Glasgow, Brown, 1936. 251p [BM OTU

**Wallace, William Stewart, 1884–1970**

BY STAR AND COMPASS. Tales of the Explorers of Canada. Toronto, Oxford U. Press, 1922. 190p [BM BVaU LC NSHD OTU QMM

**Walsh, William Emmett, 1868–**

THE SOUTH OF FRANCE. Boston, Four Seas, 1928. 175p [LC QMM

**Warman, Cy, 1855–1914**

AT THE RAINBOW'S TIP. N.p., [1908?]. 15p [Issued by the General Passenger Department, Grand Trunk Railway. A description of the Prince Rupert area, B.C.] [NSHD

**Warnock, Amelia Beers, 1878–1956**

CANADIAN CITIES OF ROMANCE. By Katherine Hale [pseud]. Enl. ed. Toronto, McClelland, 1933. 240p [BM BVaU NSHD OTP

CANADIAN HOUSES OF ROMANCE. By Katherine Hale [pseud]. Toronto, Macmillan, 1926. 213p [BM BVaU NSHD OKQ

HISTORIC HOUSES OF CANADA. By Katherine Hale [pseud]. Toronto, Ryerson, 1952. 152p [An enl. and completely rev. ed. of the author's CANADIAN HOUSES OF ROMANCE, *q.v.*]

THE ROMANCE OF CANADIAN CITIES. Toronto, McClelland, 1922. 191p [Subsequently enl. and re-titled CANADIAN CITIES OF ROMANCE, *q.v.*] [OTU

THIS IS ONTARIO! By Katherine Hale [pseud]. Toronto, Ryerson, 1937. 241p [Rev. ed.: 1946. 246p] [BVaU OTU

**Watkin, Edward William, 1819–1901**

A TRIP TO THE UNITED STATES AND CANADA. In a Series of Letters. London, Smith, 1852. 149p [BM NSWA OTP

**Watt, Gertrude Balmer (Hogg), 1879–1963**

TOWN AND TRAIL. Edmonton, New Pub. Co., 1908. 85p [AEU BVaU LC OTU

A WOMAN IN THE WEST. Edmonton, News Pub. Co., 1907. 52p [MWP OTU

**Watt, Madge Robertson**

THE SOUTHMOST DISTRICTS, VANCOUVER ISLAND. Colwood, Metchosin, Sooke. Victoria, Colonist, 1910. 64p [BVaU

**Weir, Arthur, 1864–1902**

A CANUCK DOWN SOUTH. Montreal, Lovell, 1898. 182p [BVaU LC OTU

**Wells, Kenneth McNeill, 1905–**

CRUISING THE NORTH CHANNEL. Toronto, Kingswood House, 1960. xv + 232p [Guide to the channel north of Manitoulin Island.]

CRUISING THE TRENT-SEVERN WATERWAY. Toronto, Kingswood House, 1959. 120p

THE HERITAGE OF CANADA IN COLOUR. London, Batsford, 1960. 64p

**Westbury, George H.**

MISADVENTURES OF A WORKING HOBO IN CANADA. London, Routledge, 1930. 172p [BM BVaU LC NBFU OTU

**Wetherell, James Elgin, 1851–1940**

FIELDS OF FAME IN ENGLAND AND SCOTLAND. Toronto, Macmillan, 1915. 171p [BM NSHD OTU QMM

OVER THE SEA. A Summer Trip to Britain. Strathroy, Ont., Evans, 1892. 120p [NSWA OTU

STRANGE CORNERS OF THE WORLD. New York, Nelson, 1927. 244p [LC OTU QMM

**Whishaw, Lorna (Hall)**

AS FAR AS YOU'LL TAKE ME. New York, Dodd Mead, 1958. 216p [Account of a hitchhiking trip from Edmonton to Alaska.]

**Wife of a British Officer ... , The**

HENRY; or, The Juvenile Traveller. ... By the Wife of a British Officer, Resident in Canada [pseud]. London, Simpkin Marshall, 1836. 136p [BM OOA

**Wilcox, Elmer Naman, 1908–**

GRAND MANAN, NEW BRUNSWICK, CANADA. Ed. by E.N. Wilcox and L.K. Ingersoll. 3rd ed. Grand Manan, Board of Trade, 1959. 40p

**Willison, Marjory (MacMurchy), –1938**

VICTORIA, B.C., CITY OF ENCHANTMENT IN CANADA'S EVERGREEN PLAYGROUND. Victoria, Empress Hotel, 1933. 31p [BVaU OTU

**Wilson, Clifford Parnell, 1902–**

THE NEW NORTH IN PICTURES. Ed. by ——. Toronto, Ryerson, 1947. 223p [BViPA LC OTP QMM

NORTH OF 55°. Canada from the 55th Parallel to the Pole. Ed. by ——. Toronto, Ryerson, 1954. 190p

PAGEANT OF THE NORTH. A Photographic Adventure into Canada's Northland. Ed. by ——. Toronto, Ryerson, 1957. 175p

**Withrow, Rev. William Henry, 1839–1908**

A CANADIAN IN EUROPE. Being Sketches of Travel in France, Switzerland, Germany, Holland, and Belgium, Great Britain, and Ireland. Toronto, Briggs, 1881. 376p [BVaU NBFU OTU QMM

CHINA AND ITS PEOPLE. Toronto, Briggs, 1894. 304p [OTP

OUR OWN COUNTRY. Canada, Scenic and Descriptive. Toronto, Briggs, 1889. 608p [BM BVaU LC MWU NSWA OTU

**Wix, Rev. Edward, 1802–1866**

SIX MONTHS OF A NEWFOUNDLAND MISSIONARY'S JOURNAL. London, Smith Elder, 1836. 264p [BM BVaU LC NSWA OTU QMM

**Woodcock, George, 1912–**

RAVENS AND PROPHETS. An Account of Journeys in British Columbia, Alberta, and Southern Alaska. London, Wingate, 1952. 244p

TO THE CITY OF THE DEAD. An Account of Travels in Mexico. London, Faber & Faber, 1957. 271p

**Work, John, 1792–1861**

FUR BRIGADE TO THE BONAVENTURA. John Work's California Expedition, 1832–1833, for the Hudson's Bay Company. Ed. by Alice Bay Maloney. ... San Francisco, California Historical Soc., 1945. xxii + 112p [BVaU NBFU LC

THE JOURNAL OF JOHN WORK ... during his Expedition from Vancouver to the Flatheads and Blackfeet of the Pacific Northwest. Ed., and with an Account of the Fur Trade in the Northwest, and Life of Work by William S. Lewis and Paul C. Phillips. Cleveland, Ohio, Clark, 1923. 209p [BM BVaU LC NBFU OKQ

THE JOURNAL OF JOHN WORK, January to October, 1835. ... Ed. by Henry Drummond Dee. Victoria, Banfield, 1945. 98p [BVaU LC OOA

**Wright, Esther Isabell (Clark), 1895–**

FUNDY PARK 1950. N.p., Author, 1950. 8p [OONL

**Yeigh, Frank, 1861–1935**

THROUGH THE HEART OF CANADA. Toronto, Frowde, 1910. 319p [BM BVaU LC NSWA OTU

**Young, Rev. Egerton Ryerson, 1840–1909**

BY CANOE AND DOG TRAIN AMONG THE CREE AND SALTEAUX INDIANS. Toronto, Briggs, 1890. 267p [BM BVaU LC NSWA OTU QMM

INDIAN LIFE IN THE GREAT NORTHWEST. London, Partridge, 1901. 126p [BM BVaU LC OTU QMSS

MY DOGS IN THE NORTHLAND. New York, Revell, 1902. 285p [BM BVaU LC NSHD OTU

ON THE INDIAN TRAIL. Stories of Missionary Work among the Cree and Salteaux Indians. New York, Revell, 1897. 214p [BM BVaU LC NSHD OTU QMBM

# INDEXES

# INDEX OF ANONYMOUS TITLES

(The dates in parentheses are dates of publication. Cross-references are to the General Index which follows.)

# GENERAL INDEX OF NAMES, INITIALS AND PSEUDONYMS

Dickson, Gordon Rupert (1923– ) 275

www.ingramcontent.com/pod-product-compliance
Lightning Source LLC
Chambersburg PA
CBHW060603100726
47907CB00006B/1492

* 9 7 8 1 4 8 7 5 7 3 0 7 2 *